W9-BWG-920

# International Encyclopedia of the
# SOCIAL
# SCIENCES

## Associate Editors

Heinz Eulau, *Political Science*
Lloyd A. Fallers, *Anthropology*
William H. Kruskal, *Statistics*
Gardner Lindzey, *Psychology*
Albert Rees, *Economics*
Albert J. Reiss, Jr., *Sociology*
Edward Shils, *Social Thought*

## Special Editors

Elinor G. Barber, *Biographies*
John G. Darley, *Applied Psychology*
Bert F. Hoselitz, *Economic Development*
Clifford T. Morgan, *Experimental Psychology*
Robert H. Strotz, *Econometrics*

## Editorial Staff

Marjorie A. Bassett, *Economics*
P. G. Bock, *Political Science*
Robert M. Coen, *Econometrics*
J. M. B. Edwards, *Sociology*
David S. Gochman, *Psychology*
George Lowy, *Bibliographies*
Judith M. Tanur, *Statistics*
Judith M. Treistman, *Anthropology*

## Alvin Johnson

HONORARY EDITOR

## W. Allen Wallis

CHAIRMAN, EDITORIAL ADVISORY BOARD

# International Encyclopedia of the SOCIAL SCIENCES

DAVID L. SILLS EDITOR

VOLUME 6

The Macmillan Company & The Free Press

Copyright © 1968 by Crowell Collier and Macmillan, Inc.

ALL RIGHTS RESERVED. NO PART OF THIS BOOK MAY BE REPRODUCED OR
TRANSMITTED IN ANY FORM OR BY ANY MEANS, ELECTRONIC OR
MECHANICAL, INCLUDING PHOTOCOPYING, RECORDING,
OR BY ANY INFORMATION STORAGE AND RETRIEVAL
SYSTEM, WITHOUT PERMISSION IN WRITING FROM
CROWELL COLLIER AND MACMILLAN, INC.

LIBRARY OF CONGRESS CATALOG NUMBER 68–10023

MANUFACTURED IN THE UNITED STATES OF AMERICA

# International Encyclopedia of the SOCIAL SCIENCES

[CONTINUED]

## FREUD, SIGMUND

Sigmund Freud was born May 6, 1856, in Freiberg, Moravia (now Czechoslovakia), and died September 23, 1939, in exile in London. When the boy was three, his father, a small wool merchant, was forced by economic reverses to move for a year to Leipzig and thence to Vienna, where Freud spent the rest of his life—1860 to 1938—except for his last year. His biographers agree that the unusual structure of the family into which he was born was partly responsible for his interest in intimate human relationships: Freud's father had two sons by his first wife; when he remarried after her death, it was to a woman of their age. Sigmund, her first child, often played with his year-older nephew. A brother who was born when Sigmund was not yet a year old died after eight months; then came four sisters and another brother.

A dedicated student, Freud graduated *summa cum laude* from the Gymnasium at age 17 and entered the University of Vienna medical school. After three years Freud became deeply involved in research, which delayed his M.D. until 1881; research was to remain his main interest. In 1882 he met and became engaged to Martha Bernays, and he began clinical training in order to be able to earn a living from the practice of medicine. He continued research and publishing, was made *Dozent*, and received a grant in 1885 to study for several months with Charcot in Paris. The next year he married and began practicing neurology; three sons and three daughters were born between 1887 and 1895.

Since existing therapies were not effective for his patients, most of whom were neurotic, he turned to hypnotic suggestion and in 1889 briefly visited Bernheim and Liébeault to perfect his technique. He learned a more helpful method, however, from a close friend, Josef Breuer, whose patient "Anna O." (Bertha Pappenheim) had managed to overcome some hysterical symptoms by talking freely about the circumstances of their first occurrence. Freud's successful experiences with and modifications of this "cathartic" treatment were reported in the book he wrote jointly with Breuer, *Studies on Hysteria* (1893–1895). For the next five years, he continued to develop this psychotherapeutic method into psychoanalysis, gradually withdrawing from neurology, although by then he had an international reputation in that field. [See HYSTERIA; PSYCHOSOMATIC ILLNESS.]

The way his own self-analysis contributed to the growth of his ideas during this period may be seen in the letters and drafts of papers sent to a Berlin colleague, Wilhelm Fliess, who became a close friend and confidant (see 1887–1902; 1895). The first major statement of his theories was *The Interpretation of Dreams* (1900). In 1902 he was made professor extraordinarius at the University of Vienna, and about that time his publications and lectures began to attract a group of followers, which became in 1908 the Vienna Psychoanalytical Society.

The principal focus of Freud's life thereafter was the growth of psychoanalysis—as a theory, a form of treatment, and a movement. The movement did not remain monolithic: dissident followers who withdrew and formed their own schools included Adler (in 1911), Stekel (in 1912), Jung (in 1913), and Rank (in 1926). As Freud's ideas began to

*1*

become more widely known, they attracted respect and scientific interest, but also met with a great deal of hostility as well as extreme rejection. A truly objective weighing of these two kinds of reactions at various periods of Freud's career has yet to be done, but in any event Freud seems to have been more keenly aware of the negative than of the positive reception. An especially welcome early sign of recognition was the award of an honorary degree by Clark University in 1909, on which occasion he visited America with Jung, Ferenczi, and Jones and delivered a series of lectures.

In 1923 he had the first of many operations for cancer of the upper jaw, which finally proved fatal. During his last 16 years, Freud suffered almost constant pain and difficulty in speaking because of an awkward prosthesis, but he continued psychoanalyzing and writing into his final year. Only after the Nazi *Anschluss* could he be persuaded to leave Vienna, though he often had declared his detestation for the city. Long before the end, he had achieved world-wide acclaim and recognition as one of the decisive shapers of the twentieth century.

## The development of Freud's ideas

Freud's first scientific contribution was published in 1877; his last was written only a few months before his death. Only the most superficial sketch of the development of his thought in the six hundred-odd papers and books he produced over these 63 years can be given here. There were four major and overlapping phases of that development.

(1) His prepsychoanalytic work, which lasted about twenty years, may be subdivided into an initial ten years of primarily histological–anatomical research and a partly overlapping 14 years of clinical neurology, with increasing attention to psychopathology, beginning in 1886 when he returned from Paris.

(2) The first theory of neurosis dates from the decade of the 1890s, when Freud used hypnosis and Breuer's cathartic method of psychotherapy, gradually developing the psychoanalytic methods of free association, dream interpretation, and the analysis of transference. The first dozen truly psychoanalytic papers appeared during this time, expounding the view that neurosis is a defense against intolerable memories of a traumatic experience— infantile seduction at the hands of a close relative. With the discovery of his own Oedipus complex, however, Freud came to see that such reports by his patients were fantasies, which led him to turn his interest away from traumatic events in external reality and toward subjective psychic reality. A notable but only recently discovered event in the

development of Freud's thought occurred in 1895 after the publication of the book he wrote with Breuer: he wrote but did not publish a "Psychology for Neurologists" (or "Project for a Scientific Psychology"; see Freud 1895), presenting a comprehensive anatomical–physiological model of the nervous system and its functioning in normal behavior, thought, and dreams, as well as in hysteria. He sent it to Fliess in high excitement, then quickly became discouraged by the difficulties of creating a thoroughgoing mechanistic and reductionistic psychology, tinkered with the model for a couple of years in letters to Fliess, and finally gave it up.

The turn of the century marked many basic changes in Freud's life and work: he severed his close and dependent friendships with colleagues (first Breuer, then Fliess) and his contacts with the Viennese medical society; his father died; his last child was born; he psychoanalyzed himself; he gave up neurological practice, research, and conceptual models; and he created his own new profession, research method, and theory, in terms of which he worked thereafter.

(3) Freud's topographic model was the foundation of two decades of work, during which he published his major clinical discoveries, notably, *The Interpretation of Dreams* (1900) and *Three Essays on the Theory of Sexuality* (1905); his papers on the technique used in psychoanalytic treatment; his five major case histories, the central works of metapsychology; and a series of important surveys and popularizations of his ideas, in addition to his principal applications of his theories to jokes, literature and art, biography, and anthropology. A complete or metapsychological explanation, Freud wrote in 1915, requires "describing a psychical process in its dynamic, topographical and economic aspects"—that is, in terms of a theoretical model in which the central concepts are psychological forces, structures, and quantities of energy (Rapaport & Gill 1959). Hence, we speak of three metapsychological points of view. The topographic model, which was first set forth in Chapter 7 of *The Interpretation of Dreams* and was further elaborated in the metapsychological papers (1915), conceptualizes thought and behavior in terms of processes in three psychological systems: the conscious, preconscious, and unconscious (none of which has an explicit locus in the brain).

(4) In the final period, extending between the two world wars, Freud made four main types of contributions: the final form of his theory of instinctual drives (*Beyond the Pleasure Principle*, 1920); a group of major modifications of both general and clinical theory—most notably, the struc-

tural model of the psychic apparatus (*The Ego and the Id*, 1923) and the theory of anxiety and defense (*Inhibitions, Symptoms and Anxiety*, 1926); applications of psychoanalysis to larger social problems; and a group of books reviewing and reformulating his theories.

To grasp the structure of Freud's work, it is useful not only to adopt such a developmental approach but also to view his theories from the perspective of the following threefold classification:

First and best known is the clinical theory of psychoanalysis, with its psychopathology, its accounts of psychosexual development and character formation, and the like. The subject matter of this type of theorizing consists of major events (both real and fantasied) in the life histories of persons, events occurring over spans of time ranging from days to decades. This theory is the stock in trade of the clinician—not just the psychoanalyst, but the vast majority of psychiatrists, clinical psychologists, and psychiatric social workers. Loosely referred to as "psychodynamics," it has even penetrated into general academic psychology via textbooks on personality.

Second, there is what Rapaport (1959) has called the general theory of psychoanalysis, also called metapsychology. Its subject matter—processes in a hypothetical psychic apparatus or, at times, in the brain—is more abstract and impersonal; and the periods of time involved are much shorter—from fractions of a second up to a few hours. The processes dealt with are mostly those occurring in dreams, thinking, affect, and defense; Freud's reasoning in working out this theory is much closer, and he made more use of theoretical models of the psychic apparatus. The main works are the "Project for a Scientific Psychology," Chapter 7 of *The Interpretation of Dreams*, and the metapsychological papers.

Third is what might be called Freud's phylogenetic theory. The subject matter is man as a species or in groups, and the periods of time involved range from generations to eons. Here are Freud's grand speculations, largely evolutionary and teleological in character; they contain no explicit models of a psychic apparatus, employing instead many literary, metaphorical concepts. The principal works of this type are *Totem and Taboo* (1913), *Beyond the Pleasure Principle* (1920), *Group Psychology and the Analysis of the Ego* (1921), *The Future of an Illusion* (1927), *Civilization and Its Discontents* (1930), and *Moses and Monotheism* (1934–1938).

His clinical contributions are among the earliest of Freud's papers that are still being read, and he

continued to write in this vein all of his life. As far as the other two types of theory are concerned, however, they overlap fewer developmental periods: the major metapsychological works came early, the main phylogenetic ones late. As Freud's concepts became more metaphorical and dealt with such remote issues as man's ultimate origins and the meaning of life and death, he became less concerned with describing or systematically accounting for the course and fate of an impulse or thought.

The rest of this article will concentrate on hypotheses and observations about two groups of Freud's ideas: what now appear to have been his major, lasting contributions, those that have been most influential on and most assimilated into the behavioral sciences (not to mention literature, art, and other aspects of contemporary Western culture); and his major errors, those concepts that have been most cogently criticized by psychoanalysts and other scientists. Finally, it will discuss historical antecedents of his ideas and influences upon them. The literature on these topics is already large and growing rapidly, so this survey must be highly selective.

## Major contributions and weaknesses

**Contributions.**    Freud may be said to have made five major contributions.

(1) He based his work on the assumption of *psychic determinism*: the lawfulness of all psychological phenomena, even the most trivial, including dreams, fantasies, and slips of the tongue.

(2) The lastingly valued aspects of Freud's complex doctrine of the unconscious include the general proposition that cognitive and other psychological events can go on outside of awareness; the influence of unconscious motivation on behavior; and the special qualitative characteristics of unconscious processes—the primary process and symbolism. The primary process is the kind of primitive functioning of the "psychic apparatus" that characterizes the unconscious id; indeed, it is the principal property by means of which the latter is defined. Processes characterized by magical rather than rational logic and by wishfulness—a seeking for immediate gratification of crude sexual or aggressive impulses—are called primary. Freud emphasized the concepts of displacement and condensation of psychic energy in his conceptualization of the primary process and noted that it often makes use of symbols, which differ from other types of displacement substitutes in having been shared by many persons for generations. These were the main theoretical resources Freud called upon to explain dreams, neurotic symptoms, psy-

chotic thought and language, normal character traits, myths, creative thought, art, and humor.

(3) Of the many contributions Freud made to our understanding of *sexuality*, the following seem to enjoy the most acceptance: his stress on its great importance in human life generally; his broad definition, which includes oral, anal, and other bodily pleasures and links them to the phallic–genital; his conception of its plasticity—it can be delayed, transformed, or fixated, and interest can be shifted from one "component drive" or "partial instinct" to another; his discovery that it appears early in human life (infants and young children masturbate, have sexual curiosity, etc.) and follows a typical developmental sequence; his insistence that bisexuality and "polymorphous perversity" are universal endowments or potentialities; his explanation of sexual perversions as pathological developments, not (or not wholly) as constitutional givens and not as sins; and his elaborations of many aspects of the Oedipus complex—the fact of inevitable but tabooed incestuous attraction in families, the associated phenomena of anxiety about castration (or, more generally, mutilation), and of intrafamilial jealousy, hatred, and envy, much of it unconscious.

(4) Three of Freud's concepts—*conflict, anxiety,* and *defense*—are so interrelated that we may look on them as constituting one major contribution. He saw the pervasive importance of conflict (not merely the traditional opposition of reason and passion, or ego versus id, but also ego versus superego and superego versus id) in both normal and abnormal behavior. One of his earliest insights was that defenses—structuralized means of controlling impulse and preventing the outbreak of anxiety, thus being in effect resolutions of conflict—are major factors in the formation of symptoms and character traits and are shaping influences on the organization of thought. He also described the specific mechanisms of defense, such as repression, projection, reaction formation, isolation, and mastery via the turning of passivity into activity. [*See* ANXIETY; CONFLICT, *article on* PSYCHOLOGICAL ASPECTS; DEFENSE MECHANISMS.]

(5) A number of Freud's lasting discoveries and insights make up the *genetic point of view*. He showed the necessity of knowing facts of development in order to understand personality; the importance of the events of early life for the main features of character, including the specific syndromes of the oral and anal character types as outgrowths of events at the corresponding psychosexual stages; the role of identification as a principle of learning and development; the importance

of drive delay and control in development; and the nature of psychopathology as regression along a developmental path.

As Shakow and Rapaport (1964) have pointed out, in each instance it is the general conception and the observations that have been accepted, not the specific concepts and the explanatory theory in which they are embedded. But this is to be expected: theories necessarily age, and any theory in the behavioral sciences formed as long ago as Freud's is bound to contain many anachronisms, obsolete assumptions, and unfortunate turns of thought.

**Flaws.**    Three weaknesses in Freud's work seem to have had the most extensive negative effects upon theory, research, and practice (see Holt 1965*a*; 1966). However necessary they may have been to his positive contributions, they are logically separable from them.

(1) His basic operating model (at first, of the central nervous system; later, of the psychic apparatus) was a passive reflex apparatus with no energies of its own, operating only to rid itself of inputs from the body (instinctual drive) and from the environment (reality), these inputs being conceptualized as quantities of energy (subjectively experienced as tension), and the regulative rule formulated as the principle of constancy. Consequently, the fundamental principle of motivation and affect is tension reduction.

Even in Freud's fourth period, when he said little directly about it, the passive reflex model seems to have operated as a silent pressure in the following directions:

(*a*) Freud tended to overemphasize quantitative as against qualitative aspects of behavior and thought, though only the latter were observable. The quantitative emphasis would have been more defensible if it had actually led to measurement, which is needed, but it did not. The result was a relative neglect of the phenomenology of affects in favor of a primary emphasis on pleasure and unpleasure, including anxiety (Kardiner et al. 1959), and a relative neglect of the phenomenology of the primary process, such as the various specific forms taken by condensation and displacement, in favor of an elaborate theory about unmeasurable energies of various qualitatively and directionally specific types.

(*b*) Similarly, Freud tended to reduce motivation to the somatically based; for example, he assumed that love and affection are derivative forms of a seeking after sensuous pleasure.

(*c*) There was a relative neglect of motives that do not easily fit the tension-reduction conception, such as curiosity and positive interest in stimuli and the seeking of challenges to master (White 1963).

(*d*) The passive reflex model suggests a simple theory of pleasure and unpleasure as perceived concomitants of rises and falls in energic tension. Yet from the beginning, Freud was aware of conflicting data, and he was never able either to abandon the original theory entirely or to account for the anomalous observations in a way that was consonant with the model.

(*e*) There were other shortcomings in the metapsychological economic point of view—the notion of a fixed and limited amount of energy which has to be withdrawn from one locus if used at another: for example, a scarcity economics of love, according to which the more one loves others the less self-esteem is possible—and in the quasi-vitalistic, unmeasurable, and overelaborated concept of psychic energy (Holt 1966).

(*f*) The model was hospitable to the death instinct and nirvana principle as ultimate extensions of tension reduction. But outwardly directed aggression was difficult to fit into the model and was relatively neglected for years.

(2) The second fundamental flaw was Freud's originally physicalistic conception of reality: basically, as "masses in motion and nothing else" ([1895] 1954, p. 369); more generally, as a welter of dangerous energies in which may be found some tension-reducing objects. In this conception, reality lacks significant organization on a large scale, as in the social structures or value systems (especially the latent ones) postulated by modern sociology and anthropology. To be sure, Freud did not consistently hold to such reductionism; he always dealt with meanings as such. Nevertheless, a physicalistic notion of reality lingered in his mind as an implicit conceptual ideal, with several consequences:

(*a*) Without a way to conceptualize an enduring structure of society and culture, Freud needed to assume individual genetic transmission of stable but latent cultural themes by way of a Lamarckian inheritance of acquired characteristics and to assume also that much of what he observed was inherited and universal, not culturally specific (for example, the Oedipus complex, or the inferior status of women as determined by anatomical differences).

(*b*) Freud tended to neglect the problems of adaptation and the relations to reality studied more recently in ego psychology.

(*c*) There were problems in the theory of object relations: for example, the "primary hate of objects," which the model requires, conflicts with the

facts of infant observation; the theory also had difficulty in accounting for sustained interest and affection in a sexually consummated relationship, and psychoanalysts were led to a relative neglect of the natural history of subtleties in human relations.

(3) Freud's third basic error was his unclear and ambivalent handling of the mind–body problem, alternating between psychophysical parallelism and interactionism. The consequences began to show up as soon as he gave up the neurological model of 1895: he carried over its basic assumptions (the passive reflex model and the implicitly physicalistic concept of reality) in his later, ostensibly psychological, theories. There were several consequences of Freud's failure to take a consistent position on the mind–body problem.

(*a*) The status of the basic model remained undeveloped, unclear with regard to the existential status both of psychic energies and forces and of psychic structure.

(*b*) Since the basic model was not made fully explicit, there followed a relative neglect of structural considerations in favor of a "motivational reductionism" (Gill 1959), the explanation of the control and restraint of impulses (especially aggressive ones) in terms of instinctual *fusion and defusion* instead of in structural terms, and the neglect of adaptive and health-maintaining capacities in favor of an emphasis on pathology.

(*c*) A further consequence was Freud's tendency to reify functions as structures and to personify theoretical entities of uncertain existential status.

(*d*) Psychoanalysis became isolated from progress in medical and physiological sciences because of the difficulty in assimilating their findings.

It should be emphasized that none of these shortcomings was as crippling as it might have been if the underlying assumptions had been applied rigidly and consistently. As a group, they did steer Freud's thinking to a demonstrable extent, but thanks to the creative looseness of his cognitive style (Holt 1965*b*) he was able to observe much and to develop many specific theories that were logically incompatible with them.

## Historical background

Before examining the antecedents of those ideas of Freud's that have been outlined above, it will be helpful to sketch in some of the grand trends of intellectual history in the nineteenth century.

**"Naturphilosophie" and its rejection.**    The way for the romantic revolt that broadly characterized all aspects of intellectual life in the early 1800s had been prepared by *Naturphilosophie*, a mystical and often rhapsodic view of Nature as perfused with spirit and with conflicting unconscious forces and as evolving according to an inner, purposive design. Not a tightly knit school, its constituent thinkers included (in chronological order) Kant, Lamarck, Goethe, Hegel, Schelling (perhaps the central figure), Oken, and Fechner. With the exception of Fechner, who lived from 1801 to 1887, they all lived athwart the eighteenth and nineteenth centuries. *Naturphilosophie* encouraged the recrudescence of vitalism in biology, championed by the great physiologist Johannes Müller, and stimulated a humanistic school of romantic medicine (Galdston 1956). In psychiatry, the early part of the century was dominated by the reforms of Pinel, Esquirol, and their followers, who introduced an era of "moral treatment": firm kindness in place of restraints, therapeutic optimism based on etiological theories of a more psychological than organic cast, and an attempt to involve inmates of asylums in constructive activities.

The tough-minded reaction to this tender-minded era was greatly aided by the strides being made in physics and chemistry. Three of Müller's students, Brücke, du Bois-Reymond, and Helmholtz, met Carl Ludwig in 1847 and formed a club (which became the Berlin Physical Society) to "constitute physiology on a chemico–physical foundation, and give it equal scientific rank with Physics" (Ludwig, quoted by Cranefield 1957, p. 407). They did not succeed in their frankly reductionist aim but did attain their other objectives: to promote the use of scientific observation and experiment in physiology and to combat vitalism. Among themselves, they held to the following program:

No other forces than the common physical–chemical ones are active within the organism. In those cases which cannot at the time be explained by these forces one has either to find the specific way or form of their action by means of the physical–mathematical method, or to assume new forces equal in dignity to the chemical–physical forces inherent in matter, reducible to the force of attraction and repulsion. (du Bois-Reymond, quoted by Bernfeld 1944, p. 348)

In Germany especially, this materialistic ferment of physicalistic physiology, mechanism, and reductionism became the mode, gradually putting romantic medicine and other aspects of *Naturphilosophie* to rout. Where earlier there had been Psychic, Psycho-somatic, and Somatic schools in German psychiatry (Earle 1854, see in Hunter & Macalpine 1963, pp. 1015–1018), the Somatic gradually won out; Meynert, for example, conceived mental disorders to be diseases of the forebrain. Despite its therapeutic successes, moral treatment was banished along with its psychogenic (often sexual) theories as "old wives' psychiatry," in favor of strictly organic–hereditarian views and very little by way of therapy (Bry & Rifkin 1962).

The University of Vienna medical school was an outpost of the new hyperscientific biology, with one of its promulgators, Brücke, holding a major chair and directing the physiological institute (Bernfeld 1944). Ironically, Freud tells us that his decision to enter medical school was determined by hearing the "Fragment on Nature" attributed to Goethe read aloud at a public lecture. This short prose poem is an epitome of *Naturphilosophie*, and it must have swayed Freud because of his long-standing admiration for Goethe and perhaps because of a "longing for philosophical knowledge," which had dominated his early years, as he said later in a letter to Fliess. Evolution had been a major tenet of *Naturphilosophie*; so it is not surprising that this 1780 dithyramb could be part of a lecture on comparative anatomy, the discipline that furnished much of the crucial evidence for Darwin's *Origin of Species* (1859).

**Energy and evolution.** Perhaps the two most exciting concepts of the nineteenth century were energy and evolution; both of these strongly influenced Freud's teachers at the medical school. Helmholtz had read to the 1847 group his fundamental paper on the conservation of energy—presented as a contribution to physiology. Thirty years later, Brücke's lectures were full of the closely related (and still poorly differentiated) concepts of energy and force. To use these dynamic concepts was the very hallmark of the scientific approach; Brücke taught that the "real causes are symbolized in science by the word 'force'" (Bernfeld 1944, p. 349). It seems obvious that the first of Freud's three metapsychological points of view, the dynamic (explanation in terms of psychological forces), had its origins in this exciting attempt to raise the scientific level of physiology by the diligent application of mechanics and especially of dynamics, that branch of mechanics dealing with forces and the laws of motion. The heavily quantitative emphasis of the school of Helmholtz and its stress on energy are clearly the main determinants of metapsychology seen from the economic point of view (explanations in terms of quantities of energy). The fact that, among authors Freud respected most, such disparate figures as Fechner and Hughlings Jackson held to dynamic and economic viewpoints no doubt strengthened Freud's unquestioning conviction that these viewpoints are absolutely necessary elements of an explanatory theory.

Despite its physicalistic program, the actual

work of Brücke's institute was largely classical physiology and histology. Freud had had his Darwinian scientific baptism under Claus in a microscopic search for the missing testes of the eel, and his several attempts at physiological and chemical experiments under other auspices were fruitless. He was happy, therefore, to stay at the microscope where Brücke assigned him neurohistological studies, inspired by and contributing to evolutionary theory. When he worked with Meynert, it was again in a structural discipline with a genetic method—the study of brain anatomy using a series of fetal brains to trace the medullar pathways by following their development. His subsequent clinical practice was in neurology, a discipline which, as Bernfeld (1951) has noted, was "merely a diagnostic application of anatomy." Moreover, Freud's first full-scale theoretical model, the "Project" of 1895, is foremost a theory about the structural organization of the brain, both gross and fine. His early training thus demonstrably convinced him that a scientific theory has to have a structural (or topographic) base.

Of Freud's enduring contributions listed above, the two that are most plausibly traced to the intellectual climate of physicalistic physiology and to specific teachings of Brücke and Meynert are psychic determinism and the genetic point of view. The evolutionary surge of *Naturphilosophie*, given a modern, scientific, and nonteleological form in Darwinism, inspired all the biological sciences of the late nineteenth century with a conviction that phenomena of life cannot be understood without the elucidation of how the organism develops—out of its own parental germ plasm and out of a phylogenetic series. This point of view pervaded all of Freud's work in this first period; it would have been surprising if he had not carried it over and extended it when he turned to psychopathology, as Spencer was doing in academic sociology and psychology.

The assumption of exceptionless determinism was so fundamental a principle of mechanistic science as hardly to need discussion. Freud was exposed to it on all sides in the university and in much of his reading, then and later. Doubtless, this conviction that all phenomena are lawful and are thus legitimate subjects of scientific interest helped Freud to pay attention to the trivia of mental life and underlay his conviction that even if a patient relaxed the controls of conscious purpose in favor of free association, the material he produced would not be random but would betray an inner organization, a deeper and more meaningful set of psychological laws.

**The unconscious.** But the existence of psychological forces determining a meaningful inner organization required the assumption of a dynamic unconscious realm of the mind, besides consciousness. Many writers have shown how much a part of the thought of the time one part of this assumption was: "the general conception of unconscious mental processes was *conceivable* . . . around 1700, *topical* around 1800, and *fashionable* around 1870–1880" (Whyte 1960, pp. 168–169). Among the scientists known to have been familiar to Freud during his formative years (before 1900)—Charcot, Bernheim, Breuer, Lipps, H. Jackson, Galton, Fechner, and Helmholtz—all had one or another concept of the unconscious; other such concepts are to be found in writings known to have influenced Freud: those of the philosophers Plato, Kant, and Spinoza (Aron 1963–1964), the Bible, and the works of his favorite writers of fiction, Goethe, Shakespeare, Cervantes, and Dostoevski. Moreover, the Herbartian psychology taught in all Austrian secondary schools when Freud was in the Gymnasium was presented "not as one of several schools of psychology but as a well-established semi-official psychology" (Andersson 1962); together with associationism, it was adopted by Meynert and translated into neurological terms. It was a theory of the dynamic interaction of ideas, some of which may *repress* others below the threshold of consciousness, whence they may be hindered from rising by the *resistance* of the more or less integrated *masses of ideas*. This is, not surprisingly, precisely the terminology used by Breuer and Freud in 1893 ([1893–1895] 1955, chapter 1) in their first attempt at a psychological explanation of hysteria.

It is possible to find some predecessor who expressed one or another of most components of Freud's conception of the unconscious (though it is not established that any of them were known to Freud before he formed his own hypotheses)—for example, symbolism in dreams (von Schubert, Scherner), the role of dream symbols in myths (Carus, von Schubert), dreams as wish fulfillments (Plato, Maass), and the unconscious as the source of powerful motives (Herder, Richter) and of artistic creativity (Goethe, Schiller). Nevertheless, these were mostly isolated *aperçus*; even von Hartmann, whose *Philosophy of the Unconscious* touches on all of them, was not able to integrate these fragmentary insights into a coherent theory, like the psychoanalytic theory of the primary process. Furthermore, Freud differed from all his "anticipators" in that they remained outside the cave and made remarks—often profound ones—on what they glimpsed inside, but Freud went boldly in and devoted himself for decades to its painstaking (and painful) empirical exploration. Although the idea of unconscious processes had been around for centuries, Freud forced us to see the true power and pervasiveness of these processes in man's thought, feeling, and behavior.

**Sexuality.** The enormous importance of sexuality as a basic human motive had long been explored by poets and dramatists, and there had been many times when it was freely discussed in science and medicine as well as in everyday conversation. The prevailing belief today is that the second half of the nineteenth century, when Freud grew to maturity, was an era of unusually strong shame about sexuality and of moralistic attempts to suppress even its scientific study in the name of Christian morality; this climate of opinion influenced Freud's own personality and behavior, so characterized by propriety, self-control, and conventional monogamy. Yet our stereotype of Victorian prudery is probably oversimple; in any case, by the end of the nineteenth century the tide had begun to turn; Bry and Rifkin (1962) and Rieff (1959, chapter 10) have documented many social, literary, artistic, and scientific countermovements. In addition, it might be mentioned that sexology was already an established (if minor) science when Freud's contributions first appeared. Though Freud and Fliess felt like lonely pioneers, Magnus Hirschfeld and Krafft-Ebing had preceded both of them, and Havelock Ellis and G. Stanley Hall were their contemporaries. We know little about how a *Zeitgeist* of slowly liberalizing attitudes about sex may have been transmitted to Freud. We do know that there were contemporary moves to broaden the concept of sexuality and extend it backward in the life span, such as the observations of diffuse sexuality in children by Bell (1902), the relation of sucking and masturbation in the first year by Roehmer (1891), and the plasticity of the sexual drive in children (Barnes 1892).

Again, diligent historical scholarship can uncover predecessors for many, perhaps most, of Freud's lastingly valid formulations about sex. For example, Shakow and Rapaport (1964) have pointed to James's (1890) recognition of the potentiality for perversion in all of us; and many authors have discussed the similarities between Freud's and Plato's broad concept of eros. Freud himself acknowledged that the idea of universal bisexuality had first been suggested to him by Fliess. In the era of moral treatment, various sexual etiologies had been suggested for a number of neurotic conditions, which made Freud's first psychoanalytic papers

seem more reactionary than radical to many of his organically minded psychiatric colleagues.

As with the difference between Freud and earlier writers on the unconscious, so here again it was he alone who really devoted himself to prolonged, focused empirical as well as theoretical work on sexuality. In addition, however, Freud differs from most of the others who have helped to liberalize sexual mores in his mode of presenting his conclusions: he always refused to pull his punches, to make any concessions to prudishness in hopes of gaining a more sympathetic hearing; but at the same time, he had not the slightest tendency to glorify or romanticize sexuality. He presented his facts and theories dryly and as directly as his own distaste allowed him. In the short run, he antagonized the bluestockings and undermined the feminists, while disappointing the libertines and disillusioning the sexual utopians. By overstating the centrality of sexuality and stretching the concept of libido, he laid himself open to misunderstanding as a pansexualist and attained the unwelcome notoriety of a *succès de scandale*. In the long run, however, the net effect was to force the world's attention to the problems of sex, greatly advancing the contemporaneous anti-Victorian movements and, despite vicious opposition and vilification, probably getting his ideas a hearing and ultimate acceptance faster than he could have done in any other way.

**Role of conflict.** Views of man's behavior as the outcome of interior conflicts have been propounded since ancient times. The pervasive human tendency to think in terms of dichotomies is speculatively traceable to anatomical bilateral symmetry and to the diurnal cycle of light and dark. In any case, a probable shaping influence on Freud's conceptual orientations is the centrality of conflict between unconscious purposive forces in the world view of *Naturphilosophie*. More immediately, the Herbartian psychology of Lindner that Freud studied in the Gymnasium treats the life of the mind in terms of conflicting ideas, which could be smoothly absorbed into the paradigm of parallelograms of forces in physicalistic physiology. Hughlings Jackson, whom Freud greatly admired, held to even more proto-Freudian views on the role of conflicting forces (Stengel 1954*a*; 1954*b*).

The substance of the conflicting forces in Freud's final model is clearly related to traditions in Western thought going at least as far back as Empedocles, for whom love alternated with its antithesis, strife, and to religious sources: God versus Satan and the doctrine of conscience as the opponent of the base passions. In the era of moral treatment, there had been no dearth of psychiatrists who saw these inner battles as a cause of neurosis. Carter, writing in 1853, observed the conflict between sexual desire and moral scruple in chaste hysterics of both sexes and even blamed "the modern necessity of [a single woman's] entire concealment" of her sexuality as the social cause of most hysteria (see Hunter & Macalpine 1963, pp. 1002–1003).

**Defense and repression.** Freud's conception of defense, more particularly his ideas about defense against anxiety, seems to be a more original clinical innovation than most other parts of psychoanalytic theory. Perhaps its model was the medical conception of the body's defenses against pathogenic invasion; and the proposition that ideas can be repressed was familiar in Herbartian psychology. Nietzsche described the general outlines of several specific defenses—according to Brandt (1955), repression, isolation, reaction formation, sublimation, and projection—but there is no evidence that Freud knew about it. These conceptions and the closely related signal theory of anxiety are as directly derived from clinical observation as any in psychoanalysis and are among Freud's most original contributions.

**Regression.** The Darwinian origins of the genetic viewpoint in psychoanalysis have been briefly mentioned. An important specific mediator of Darwinism was Hughlings Jackson, from whose view of the evolutionary organization of the brain Freud took the conception of a hierarchic organization of psychic structures (Rapaport 1959), and from whose correlated theory of neurological diseases as "reversals of evolution," Freud derived the concept of regression as an explanation of psychopathogenesis (Stengel 1954a; 1954b). The genetic discipline of embryology had been given an enormous impetus by Darwin; Freud's use of fetal materials in his medullar researches must have caused him to study this discipline with particular care and to become familiar with the epigenetic principle that is implicit in his doctrine of psychosexual development. The phenomenon of identification and its role in interpersonal and social relations of all kinds, as well as its outstanding importance in development, appears to be largely the outgrowth of clinical observation; Rieff's (1959) hint that it may owe something to the "sympathy" of earlier social theorists (for example, Adam Smith) remains unexplored. By contrast, it is easy to find plenty of antecedent recognition of the importance of impulse control in the growth of character.

**Passive reflex model.** Freud put his personal stamp upon all the conceptions he drew—directly or indirectly—from his broad intellectual heritage. His reworking of the ideas of others often brought to the forefront their latent potentialities for advancing the understanding of the central problems—the innermost longings and agonies—of real persons. At times, however, the usefulness of Freud's ideas was marred by his need to fit them into his set of basic working assumptions, the passive reflex model of the nervous system.

This model was synthesized by Freud from the physicalistic physiology of his teachers and was more clearly enunciated in the "Project" than in any of the works of Brücke, Meynert, Breuer, or Exner, in which its elements may be clearly discerned (Amacher 1965). Anticipations of the dynamic, economic, and topographic points of view are plainly to be seen in books that Freud cited, for example, those by Fechner (Ellenberger 1956) and Jackson (Stengel 1954a; Spehlmann 1953); the economic point of view is also traceable to Darwin (Andersson 1962). It seems safe to conclude, therefore, that this set of principles was concurrently developed by many leading scientists in Germany and Austria in their attempts to apply the physics of Helmholtz and his school to biology and to generalize the reflex arc as a model of all mental processes in order to close the doors to such romantic notions as spontaneity, free will, and vitalism. Although virtually all of the assumptions underlying the passive reflex model are demonstrably untrue, much of the same doctrine underlies the behavioristic schools of psychology and is only now being painfully modified.

When Freud put aside explicit neurological theorizing, he was unable to give up the passive reflex model and the closely related physicalistic concept of reality (Spehlmann 1953; Holt 1965a). Although he explicitly postponed any attempt to relate the terms of metapsychology to processes and loci in the body, he substituted psychological theories that carry the same burden of anachronistic assumptions.

Nevertheless, Freud did not make a clean break from neurology, which fact contributed to his unclear and inconsistent stand on the mind–body problem (Rubinstein 1965; Holt 1965a). Jones (1953–1957, vol. 1) and a number of other authors portray him as a consistent follower of Jackson in a psychophysical parallelism that makes mind an "independent concomitant" of brain. But neither Jackson himself, who at times postulated that physical energy is directly transformed into psychic energy (Spehlmann 1953), nor Freud's teachers held to a consistent position (Amacher 1965); it was common to slip into interactionism, and Freud followed suit (Andersson 1962, p. 107). The concept of hysterical conversion is the most obvious instance of interactionism.

**Speculative elements.** The concept of Freud's most frequently rejected, at least among psychoanalysts, is the death instinct; not surprisingly, many of them have attributed this concept to Freud's own needs and conflicts. While the evidence is impressive that for many years Freud had an unusual and probably pathological preoccupation with death, there are plenty of less tendentious hypotheses about sources for this notion. Freud himself traced it to the ancient Greeks; it has been likened to the Christian concept of original sin; pessimistic, late romantic philosophers like Nietzsche contributed a strain of thought of which Freud could not have been unaware, however little he read them directly. More generally, the works in which he developed the theory of the repetition compulsion (clearly related as it is to the ancient conception of "the eternal return") and the virtually mythic concepts of life- and death-instincts are part of his phylogenetic theory. It is tempting to interpret this last development in Freud's thought as a kind of return of the repressed: that youthful speculative bent and yearning for broad philosophical knowledge which he repeatedly admitted fearing in himself and suppressed for many years (Holt 1963). His exposure to and enthusiasm for *Naturphilosophie* antedated his conversion to physicalistic physiology, which helped him put such unscientific ways of thought out of mind. Even the philosopher with whom he studied, Brentano, strongly opposed *Naturphilosophie* and advocated the scientific method as the only valid source of knowledge.

Yet the old mode of thought remained an undercurrent in his thinking, as it did in that of his friend Fliess (Galdston 1956). Finally, after Freud's change of identity at the turn of the century, after his great discoveries, the establishment of the psychoanalytic movement, and his first international recognition, the old mode of thought may have seemed less threatening. In *Totem and Taboo* (1913), one of his favorites among his own books, he created what he himself called a "scientific myth" (the slaying of the Darwinian primal horde's father). Shortly thereafter, he first read Lamarck, who was strongly identified with *Naturphilosophie*. It is Fechner the *Naturphilosoph*, not the psychophysicist, whom he cited in *Beyond the Pleasure Principle* (1920), and the loose, analogical, teleological, and personifying mode of thought he employed there is in marked contrast to the cognitive style of his metapsychological works (Holt 1965*b*).

Many properties of his concept of psychic energy can be traced to the vitalism that was a prominent feature of *Naturphilosophie* (Holt 1966). Some of the specific fallacies in his phylogenetic works can be traced to sources on the more mechanistic–materialistic side: Haeckel's "biogenetic law" that ontogeny recapitulates phylogeny seemed to provide respectable scientific auspices for the extension of genetic speculations based on individuals to the development of all mankind; Spencer and various post-Darwinians were the source of his linear–evolutionary conception of anthropology; and the inheritance of acquired characters had been a general assumption of the organic–hereditarian psychiatrists of Freud's formative period (Andersson 1962), as well as having been given some currency by Darwin himself (Ritvo 1965). Nevertheless, the major flaws of both manner and matter in Freud's speculative works show the unmistakable earmarks of *Naturphilosophie*.

Freud's stature is too great for his errors to require any whitewashing; it is not an apology for him but a fact that the least tenable aspects of his theories are traceable to influences that shaped his basic outlook when he was still a student, while his enduring achievements seem to owe less to antecedent influences. It appears to be one of the marks of a genius that he finds more sources of ideas in his reading and observation and subjects them to a truer integration and transmutation than does the less gifted man. The great contributor to knowledge (who may or may not be a genius) does not only toss off brilliant sparks of ideas; he lights and tends an enduring fire. Freud had both of these innovative capacities and more: his ideas have the remarkable property of being self-transcending. He taught us how to know more than he could, how to find and use the best in what he left by testing it against reality.

ROBERT R. HOLT

[*For a listing of articles describing Freud's influence upon psychology, psychiatry, and the other social sciences, see the detailed guide under the entry* PSYCHOANALYSIS. *Directly related to Freud's work and influence are the biographies of* ABRAHAM; ADLER; ALEXANDER; CHARCOT; ELLIS; FECHNER; FERENCZI; HELMHOLTZ; HORNEY; JONES; JUNG; KLEIN; MÜLLER, JOHANNES; RANK; RAPAPORT; REICH; RÓHEIM; SULLIVAN.]

WORKS BY FREUD

(1887–1902) 1954 *The Origins of Psychoanalysis: Letters to Wilhelm Fliess, Drafts and Notes: 1887–1902.* New York: Basic Books.

(1893–1895) 1955 BREUER, JOSEF; and FREUD, SIGMUND Studies on Hysteria. Volume 2 of *The Standard Edition of the Complete Psychological Works of Sigmund Freud*. London: Hogarth; New York: Macmillan.

(1895) 1954 Project for a Scientific Psychology. Pages 347–445 in Sigmund Freud, *The Origins of Psychoanalysis*. New York: Basic Books.

(1900) 1953 The Interpretation of Dreams. Volumes 4–5 of *The Standard Edition of the Complete Psychological Works of Sigmund Freud*. London: Hogarth; New York: Macmillan.

(1905) 1953 Three Essays on the Theory of Sexuality. Volume 7, pages 123–245 in *The Standard Edition of the Complete Psychological Works of Sigmund Freud*. London: Hogarth; New York: Macmillan.

(1913) 1959 Totem and Taboo. Volume 13, pages ix–162 in *The Standard Edition of the Complete Psychological Works of Sigmund Freud*. London: Hogarth; New York: Macmillan.

(1915) 1957 Papers on Metapsychology. Volume 14, pages 109–243 in *The Standard Edition of the Complete Psychological Works of Sigmund Freud*. London: Hogarth; New York: Macmillan.

(1920) 1955 Beyond the Pleasure Principle. Volume 18, pages 7–66 in *The Standard Edition of the Complete Psychological Works of Sigmund Freud*. London: Hogarth; New York: Macmillan.

(1921) 1955 Group Psychology and the Analysis of the Ego. Volume 18, pages 69–134 in *The Standard Edition of the Complete Psychological Works of Sigmund Freud*. London: Hogarth; New York: Macmillan.

(1923) 1961 The Ego and the Id. Volume 19, pages 12–63 in *The Standard Edition of the Complete Psychological Works of Sigmund Freud*. London: Hogarth; New York: Macmillan.

(1926) 1959 Inhibitions, Symptoms and Anxiety. Volume 20, pages 77–178 in *The Standard Edition of the Complete Psychological Works of Sigmund Freud*. London: Hogarth; New York: Macmillan.

(1927) 1961 The Future of an Illusion. Volume 21, pages 5–58 in *The Standard Edition of the Complete Psychological Works of Sigmund Freud*. London: Hogarth; New York: Macmillan.

(1930) 1961 Civilization and Its Discontents. Volume 22, pages 64–148 in *The Standard Edition of the Complete Psychological Works of Sigmund Freud*. London: Hogarth; New York: Macmillan.

(1934–1938) 1964 Moses and Monotheism: Three Essays. Volume 23 in *The Standard Edition of the Complete Psychological Works of Sigmund Freud*. London: Hogarth; New York: Macmillan.

*Gesammelte Schriften*. 12 vols. Leipzig, Vienna and Zurich: Internationaler Psychoanalytischer Verlag, 1924–1934.

*Gesammelte Werke*. 18 vols. London: Imago, 1940–1952.

*The Standard Edition of the Complete Psychological Works of Sigmund Freud*. 24 vols. London: Hogarth; New York: Macmillan, 1953–1964.

### SUPPLEMENTARY BIBLIOGRAPHY

AMACHER, PETER 1965 *Freud's Neurological Education and Its Influence on Psychoanalytic Theory*. Psychological Issues, Vol. 4, No. 4; Monograph No. 16. New York: International Universities Press.

ANDERSSON, OLA 1962 *Studies in the Prehistory of Psychoanalysis: The Etiology of Psychoneuroses and Some Related Themes in Sigmund Freud's Scientific Writings and Letters, 1886–1896*. Stockholm: Svenska Bokförlaget Norstedts.

ARON, WILLIAM 1963–1964 Freud and Spinoza. *Harofé haivri* [1963] no. 2:260–242; [1964] no. 1:284–265; [1964] no. 2:260–242.

BARNES, E. 1892 Feelings and Ideas of Sex in Children. *Pedagogical Seminary* 2:199–203. → Now called the *Journal of Genetic Psychology*.

BELL, SANFORD 1902 A Preliminary Study of the Emotion of Love Between the Sexes. *American Journal of Psychology* 13:325–354.

BERNFELD, SIEGFRIED 1944 Freud's Earliest Theories and the School of Helmholtz. *Psychoanalytic Quarterly* 13:341–362.

BERNFELD, SIEGFRIED 1951 Sigmund Freud, M.D.: 1882–1885. *International Journal of Psycho-analysis* 32:204–217.

BRANDT, RUDOLF 1955 Freud and Nietzsche: A Comparison. Ottawa, University of, *Revue* 25:225–234.

BRY, ILSE; and RIFKIN, ALFRED H. 1962 Freud and the History of Ideas: Primary Sources, 1886–1910. Pages 6–36 in Academy of Psychoanalysis, *Science and Psychoanalysis*. Volume 5: Psychoanalytic Education. New York: Grune.

CRANEFIELD, PAUL F. 1957 The Organic Physics of 1847 and the Biophysics of Today. *Journal of the History of Medicine* 12:407–423.

DARWIN, CHARLES (1859) 1964 *On the Origin of Species*. Cambridge, Mass.: Harvard Univ. Press.

ELLENBERGER, HENRI F. 1956 Fechner and Freud. Menninger Clinic, *Bulletin* 20:201–214.

GALDSTON, IAGO 1956 Freud and Romantic Medicine. *Bulletin of the History of Medicine* 30:489–507.

GILL, MERTON M. 1959 The Present State of Psychoanalytic Theory. *Journal of Abnormal and Social Psychology* 58:1–8.

HOLT, ROBERT R. 1963 Two Influences on Freud's Scientific Thought: A Fragment of Intellectual Biography. Pages 364–387 in Robert N. White (editor), *The Study of Lives*. New York: Atherton.

HOLT, ROBERT R. 1965a A Review of Some of Freud's Biological Assumptions and Their Influence on His Theories. Pages 93–124 in Norman S. Greenfield and William C. Lewis (editors), *Psychoanalysis and Current Biological Thought*. Madison: Univ. of Wisconsin Press.

HOLT, ROBERT R. 1965b Freud's Cognitive Style. *American Imago* 22:163–179.

HOLT, ROBERT R. 1966 Beyond Vitalism and Mechanism: Freud's Concept of Psychic Energy. Unpublished manuscript.

HUNTER, RICHARD A.; and MACALPINE, IDA (editors) 1963 *Three Hundred Years of Psychiatry, 1535–1860: A History Presented in Selected English Texts*. Oxford Univ. Press. → See especially pages 1002–1003 and 1015–1018.

JAMES, WILLIAM (1890) 1962 *The Principles of Psychology*. 2 vols. New York: Smith.

JONES, ERNEST 1953–1957 *The Life and Work of Sigmund Freud*. 3 vols. New York: Basic Books. → Volume 1: Formative Years and the Great Discoveries, 1953. Volume 2: Years of Maturity, 1955. Volume 3: Last Phase, 1957.

KARDINER, ABRAM; KARUSH, AARON; and OVESEY, LIONEL 1959 A Methodological Study of Freudian Theory. *Journal of Nervous and Mental Disease* 129:11–19, 133–143, 207–221, 341–356.

PARSONS, TALCOTT (1952) 1953 The Superego and the Theory of Social Systems. Pages 13–29 in Talcott Parsons, Robert F. Bales, and Edward A. Shils, *Work-*

*ing Papers in the Theory of Action.* Glencoe, Ill.: Free Press.

PARSONS, TALCOTT (1958) 1964 Social Structure and the Development of Personality: Freud's Contribution to the Integration of Psychology and Sociology. Pages 78–111 in Talcott Parsons, *Social Structure and Personality.* New York: Free Press.

RAPAPORT, DAVID 1959 The Structure of Psychoanalytic Theory: A Systematizing Attempt. Pages 55–183 in S. Koch (editor), *Psychology: A Study of a Science.* Volume 3: Formulations of the Person and the Social Context. New York: McGraw-Hill.

RAPAPORT, DAVID; and GILL, MERTON 1959 The Points of View and Assumptions of Metapsychology. *International Journal of Psycho-analysis* 40:153–162.

RIEFF, PHILIP 1959 *Freud: The Mind of the Moralist.* New York: Viking.

RITVO, LUCILLE B. 1965 Darwin as the Source of Freud's Neo-Lamarckianism. *Journal of the American Psychoanalytic Association* 13:499–517.

ROEHMER, A. 1891 Ueber psychopatische Minderwertigkeiten des Säuglingsalter. *Medizinisches Korrespondenzblatt für Würtemberg* 61:265–269, 273–279, 281–285, 289–292.

RUBINSTEIN, B. B. 1965 Psychoanalytic Theory and the Mind–Body Problem. Pages 35–56 in Norman S. Greenfield and William C. Lewis (editors), *Psychoanalysis and Current Biological Thought.* Madison: Univ. of Wisconsin Press.

SHAKOW, DAVID; and RAPAPORT, DAVID 1964 *The Influence of Freud on American Psychology.* Psychological Issues, Vol. 4, No. 1. New York: International Universities Press.

SPEHLMANN, RAINER 1953 *Sigmund Freuds neurologische Schriften: Eine Untersuchung zur Vorgeschichte der Psychoanalyse.* Berlin: Springer.

STENGEL, E. 1954a A Re-evaluation of Freud's Book *On Aphasia:* Its Significance for Psychoanalysis. *International Journal of Psycho-analysis* 35:85–89.

STENGEL, E. 1954b The Origins and Status of Dynamic Psychiatry. *British Journal of Medical Psychology* 27:193–200.

WHITE, ROBERT W. 1963 *Ego and Reality in Psychoanalytic Theory: A Proposal Regarding Independent Ego Energies.* Psychological Issues, Vol. 3, No. 3. New York: International Universities Press.

WHYTE, LANCELOT L. 1960 *The Unconscious Before Freud.* New York: Basic Books.

# FRIENDSHIP

Friendship is a voluntary, close, and enduring social relationship. The behavior of friends varies greatly among societies and situations and according to personality variables. Values about friendship vary less and can be summarized as involving closeness, solidarity, absence of ulterior ends, reciprocity, impulsiveness in mutual choice, and, perhaps, independence of social distinctions such as age, sex, and class. Friendship is intimate but less so than love and some family ties. Supplementing sexual and familial ties, friendship is a residual cultural category subsuming close and expectedly enduring ties. Since friendship involves voluntary

commitment, intimacy, and spontaneity, its consequences for the individual and for society, through individual growth and security, are presumably crucial. Possibly for this reason, to be without friends often involves shame.

Most other important social relationships exclude friendship. Even highly compatible and close brothers are brothers rather than friends, and friendship tends to be incompatible with such relationships as those of mother and child, lovers, and employer and employee. This incompatibility is probably due to the fact that the obligations and rights of friends typically are subject to overruling by other ties. The impulsiveness of choice and the reciprocity or symmetry of the friendship relation also rule out various choices. If friends are impulsively chosen, few brothers will be friends. Reciprocity and symmetry imply rough equality in mutual rights and obligations and in qualities and performances, requiring fairly equal status in significant respects between friends. In general, friendship can be logically and culturally expected to occur only when there is a low probability of higher or strongly sanctioned obligations intervening directly between friends.

Like distant kinship terms, "friend" is a relational designation: "friend" and "friendship" refer to a relationship between two or more persons rather than to the characteristics of one or more persons. This is in contrast to close kinship terms, which are simultaneously relational and categorical, and to occupational designations, which are on the whole categorical. Accordingly, while friendship is significant in personal terms, it is no less an interpersonal structure. It follows that variants of friendship structure may well be a characteristic of collective units.

In theoretical terms, friendship is definitely a relational phenomenon: it is impossible to assign meaning to statements such as "He is a friend" without implying to whom "he" is related in this way. However, empirically the matter is less clear, partly because the friendship role is vague. Also, the friendship relationship as a social type is made ambiguous by personal descriptions such as "He is friendly," "He is a great friend," or "He is everybody's friend." The suggestion has been made that a highly differentiated society with a high degree of mobility and an emphasis on specific performance cannot also support enduring and important intimate relationships beyond those of the nuclear family. This may be the structural source of "pseudo *Gemeinschaft*"—that is, appeals, usually commercial, that use a presumption of closeness to transfer modes of behavior from a friendship setting to strangers, with the consequent growth of values of superficial friendship, friendliness, and popularity.

Friendship is a distinct institution. In Western societies (loosely the basis for the above considerations) it is a vague institution, whereas in other societies friendship is often more salient and differentiated. In either case, friendship is a low-order (as well as a crosscutting) institution: it is found everywhere but is not a distinct, comprehensive segment of society. It is comparable to money, language, and love rather than to religion, the family, or the economy. Partly for this reason, friendship is not at present a specialized field of inquiry in sociology. While few studies focus on friendship, many find it, since closeness to others is a pervasive potentiality in man.

### Friendship as an institution

To say that friendship is an institution is to ask the cross-cultural question: What links are there between variations in the structure of friendship and in the structure of society? Two studies have initiated the general cross-cultural study of friendship (Eisenstadt 1956; Cohen 1961). At the least, these studies provide a spectrum of variation in friendship institutions; at their best, they provide hypotheses or findings about the place of friendship in encompassing social structures.

**Variations between societies.** S. N. Eisenstadt's subject is "ritualized personal relations," including blood brotherhood, blood friendship, "best" friends, *compadre* and godparent relations, and cases of contractual servitude. All these relationships are particularistic, personal, voluntary, and fully institutionalized (usually in ritual terms). They are both diffusely affective and instrumental, always in the economic sphere, often more broadly (politics, etc.). Eisenstadt hypothesizes that these kinshiplike but voluntary relations are to be found in predominantly particularistic (that is, kinship-dominated or caste-dominated) societies because they alleviate strains in and between the groups that constitute such societies. In effect, Eisenstadt proposes that ritualized personal relations, similar to friendship in Western terms in that they are voluntary and personal or intimate, are mechanisms of social integration. They are parallel to such institutions as kinship extension, extralineage kinship obligations, various types of associations, hospitality toward strangers, and joking relationships in providing ties cutting across groups and categories. Ritualized personal relations are also mechanisms of social control. [See KINSHIP, *article on* PSEUDO-KINSHIP.]

Yehudi A. Cohen presents a typology of friendship institutions that loosely expresses a dimension of degree of commitment between friends. *Inalienable* friendship is a variant characterized by ritual or ceremonial entry and, ideally, permanence—in the main corresponding to Eisenstadt's ritualized personal relations. Three other somewhat separate categories are *close, casual,* and *expedient* friendships. In a sample of about sixty societies, twenty have the inalienable type of friendship as the dominant form, thirty have close friendship, three have casual friendship, and four have expedient friendship (there are no data for ten societies, and some are counted twice because of structural changes). Activities in the friendship relation commonly include material exchange (and/or economic assistance) and sociopolitical and emotional support; in some cases they include the more specialized activities of go-between in love affairs and marriage arrangements, homosexuality, sponsorship in rites of passage, mourning obligations, and exchange of children. Formalized friendship is far more frequent among men than women and is rare across sex lines. Inalienable friendship carries with it incest taboos in half the cases. It is almost invariably joined with just one partner, who in some cases has to be chosen inside the local solidary group and in other cases outside of it; in a few societies either choice is open.

Cohen predicts covariation between type of friendship and the nature of the significant solidary grouping to which the individual is attached. He expects inalienable friendship to coincide with the *maximally solidary* community (generally, localized descent groups where nuclear families and households are socially, physically, and emotionally close as a societal nucleus sharply distinguished from other groupings). Close friendship is expected to be associated with the *solidary-fissile* community (where solidarity is split between kinship group and community). The *nonnucleated* society (where isolated, solidary nuclear families are tied loosely together) is expected to be associated with casual friendship. Finally, an expedient type of friendship institution is expected to occur in *individuated* social structures (where there is emphasis on individual amassing of wealth and relatively little solidarity even in the nuclear family).

Roughly speaking, Cohen's hypotheses are supported by his data. There is an association between the degree of solidarity in the local community and the degree of commitment in the friendship institution (although the number of cases in extreme types of friendship and solidarity is small). Of 13 societies with maximally solidary communities, 11 have predominantly the inalienable type of friendship; of 35 societies with solidary-fissile communities, 27 have close friendship.

Cohen's interpretation of this finding is in terms of holistic compatibility in culture and personality. A dimension of personal generosity versus withholding seems to be the basic variable that unites community structure with friendship structure. There is a correlation between childhood gratification versus deprivation, on the one hand, and adult food sharing versus individual amassment of food or money on the other. For the present, it remains an open question as to how this holistic pressure can be translated into detailed questions about the operation of social arrangements.

Cohen's study raises formal questions about his variables: To what extent are his four-point variables adequate and reliable in use? Is inalienable friendship a more significant category than formalized friendship? Further, under what conditions, and with what effects, are intragroup and intergroup friendships mandatory or preferred? The most crucial and stimulating question would seem to be this: Is institutionalized friendship (i.e., ideal and/or dominant forms) a more relevant variable than distribution of actual forms of friendship? This question leads to interesting problems in Western societies. What, in various settings, is the distribution of close, casual, and expedient friendships? Is degree of differentiation of societies correlated with dominance of expedient friendships? Is a possible dominance of expedient friendships to be contrasted with some of our values concerning friendship rather than with our past—or has there been a real change in the friendship institution over, say, the last fifty years, concomitant with industrialization and increasing differentiation?

**Variation within one society.** Additional demonstrations of the dependence of norms regulating friendship on an encompassing social structure emerge if we compare separate settings within one society rather than comparing different societies. In a study of the merchant marine in a society where it is a significant element economically and culturally, Aubert and Arner (1959) found that the culture and the social structure of the Norwegian merchant marine include a near taboo on personal friendships. This trait is probably a consequence of (as well as a contribution to) other structural elements: the ship is a "total institution" (Goffman 1958); top positions can only be reached from the bottom; there is an extraordinarily high rate of turnover; work roles dominate (to the extent that terms of address and reference are largely job titles, the alternative being home region); there is a cultural and realistic emphasis on crises requiring discipline; and, finally, there is a peculiar combination of equality and inequality (in a num-

ber of respects the crew are sailors "in the same boat," yet each man and his position is unique through pay and shift arrangements). In outline, the occurrence and forms of friendship among the crew are reinforcing consequences of the nature of the ship as a place of work, in particular through its arrangements for interaction, physical closeness, and recruitment. In a significant contrast, friendship is a standard occurrence among the crew in the Hull distant-water fishing fleet (Tunstall 1962); the distant-water trawler lacks the character of the total institution that is inherent in the Norwegian merchant vessel.

### Friendship as interaction

Perhaps the most penetrating study of friendship yet to appear is W. F. Whyte's *Street Corner Society* (1943), a description and analysis of life in an immigrant slum in the late 1930s. Whyte's topic is the interaction between young men, the significance of this interaction for individuals, and its relationship to career, welfare work, and politics. In the first place, Whyte gives a vivid picture of voluntary association among "Cornerville" young adults. This association is marked by a strong informal structure. Loosely integrated gangs, consisting of small cliques, have a clearly hierarchic structure in terms of influence and prestige. Participation and acceptance in these groups are crucial for the balance of individual personalities. Changing and stable group structure is symbolically expressed in interaction. The typical group ties the individual to his community in many ways; it takes membership in atypical groups to foster career ambitions beyond Cornerville. In the first place, then, Whyte describes the social realities, of which friendship is the predominant one, for young men in Cornerville. Second, he analyzes the interrelations of friendship and the Cornerville culture with racketeering and politics, which are intimate, as well as with traditional welfare work, which cuts itself off from the mainstream of Cornerville life.

The kind of friendship structure that Whyte describes is, in all likelihood, unusual. Friendship groups are rarely as highly structured in a hierarchy as in Whyte's community; friends are rarely as dependent on leadership; they are rarely as significant for each other and so often and so regularly in each other's presence; friends are rarely so sharply segregated from nonfriends; and friends of one person are rarely to such an extent also friends of each other. Whyte described a situation that was unusual, arising as it did from the historical accident of a major depression in a lower-class environment of second-generation immigrants.

Several themes above have been investigated in later, more specific studies of friendship. Elizabeth Bott (1957) has investigated friendship networks, stressing the difference between connected networks, where one's friends are also friends of each other, and open ones, where friends do not make up an interconnected group. Her exploratory study of families and their friends indicates that if a married couple is involved in a close-knit set of friends, the couple tends to have a rigid separation of roles in the household. On the other hand, if the network of friends is loosely connected, separation of roles among husband and wife is at a minimum.

**Adolescent friendship.** In his study of friendship among young men, Whyte related variants of friendship to career ambitions in distinguishing between "corner boys" and "college boys." Friendship among adolescents may be more significant than at earlier and later ages, both in general and specifically for career choice. What is the nature and significance of friendship among adolescents? In a discussion of David Riesman's hypothesized "other-directed" personality type, with its assumed peer dependence among adolescents, Parsons and White (1961) see adolescent friendship as a mechanism for loosening children's dependence on parents and as a channel for the testing of career choice. Relying on findings from studies of friendship choices in high schools, they conclude that the adolescent's dependence on peers is far from a seeking of free-floating approval; relations among peers partially consist of commitments to normative standards. Parsons and White emphasize that there are two kinds of normative culture among high school students: one is rather hedonistic, characterized by much value on popularity and reluctance to accept the achievement orientation in the adult world, and the other, which is somewhat less frequent, includes a strong commitment to mastery of this achievement orientation. The availability of friendship cliques (of either type of culture) is both a sorting mechanism and a testing ground for long-term educational and career commitments.

The finding of two distinct normative cultures among adolescents, one centering on hedonism and the other, nearly as important, on scholastic achievement, is unusual. Coleman (1961) found widely varying social climates in the ten high schools that he studied. In all of them, athletic achievement was the major basis for recruitment to the informal elite of the school; scholastic achievement was always a decidedly minor basis; the strongest position of all was held by the all-

rounder. Gordon (1957), in a case study of a Midwestern high school, found a salient structure of dominant cliques, within which close friendship might occur. Cliques centering on scholastic achievement were quite unimportant, although students showed increasing fulfillment of school expectations for scholastic achievement with each additional year in school. The students' school and social life seemed to be dominated by a fierce competition for prestige that was achieved on the basis of conformity to highly developed normative patterns. Adolescent life in school was dominated by efforts to achieve a differentiated social status —that is, essentially a search for identity. Membership in a group gives the protection of being visibly and actively "somebody," but friendship appears to be largely an instrumental and regulative structure rather than a supportive and permissive one. However, the detailed regulation of behavior implied in the adolescent culture is partly (as in dress) a symbol of autonomy relative to adult society and partly (as in puritan morals) an acceptance of explicit adult values.

In spite of variation in content of adolescent culture and friendship groupings, Parsons and White's main points are valid: adolescent culture, with cliques forming around variant values, affords standards of right and wrong, affects career choice, and enforces a degree of independence from parents. Nevertheless, the central place of popularity in this adolescent culture leaves Riesman's claim of a growing "other-directedness" an open issue.

**Friendship in work groups.** Adolescent friendship approaches being a way of life, although a transitional one, related to love and a future family as well as to work and a future career. Friendship is also important in careers. The influence of friendship on recruitment to and work in a career has been shown in community studies (Warner & Lunt 1941, pp. 188–199; Seeley et al. 1956, p. 135). The importance of friendship in one line of work was shown dramatically by Coleman, Katz, and Menzel (1957): doctors' adoption of new therapeutic drugs depends to a considerable extent on membership in informal friendship cliques.

The theme of friendship in work has been a significant one in social science at least since the Hawthorne studies in the 1930s. In one setting it was found that a differentiated set of friendship relations among male workers supported a broad normative orientation, including a norm limiting productivity (Roethlisberger & Dickson 1939, part 4). In another setting, friendly relations among female workers were suggested as an explanatory variable behind a continuously climbing curve of productivity under varying and controlled external work conditions (*ibid.*, part 1). The concept of an informal social structure in organizations has been with us since these studies. With respect to friendship or friendly human relations, these two findings have been duplicated over and over again, in industrial and bureaucratic settings as well as in research on problem solving in laboratory groups: friendly relations may lead to either increased or decreased productivity. The normative basis of friendship, particularly the definitions of relations to higher authorities, is presumably one decisive differentiating variable.

## Selection of friends

The initial view of friendship given in this article is a romantic one; it is empirical in that it formulates surface values concerning friendship in our culture. However, while it may be true that friends are culturally expected to be chosen impulsively, it is certain that choice follows socially structured paths. Friends tend to share social position. The tendency of friends to be alike is well illustrated by a finding in a study of a political election that compared voters' choices with those of their best friends. A sample of voters was divided into four subgroups according to whether three, two, one, or none of their best friends intended to vote for the Republican party; among those whose friends were all intending to vote Republican, 61 per cent expressed strong intentions of voting Republican, and the percentage dropped to 37, to 23, and to 2 for the other three subgroups, respectively (Berelson et al. 1954, p. 99). Two explanatory principles are needed: friends select each other on the basis of similarity, and they influence each other to become similar. The systematic study of similarity and dissimilarity between friends was opened up by Lazarsfeld and Merton (1954) when they asked how selectivity comes about and how it varies for different kinds of attributes and within different kinds of social structures. While they clarify many issues in their article (for example, by distinguishing between status-homophily and value-homophily), their contribution has remained programmatic.

Similarity in attitude is one basis on which friendships are formed. Longitudinal studies (e.g., Newcomb 1961) indicate that the explanatory principle of selectivity in terms of similarity outweighs the principle of similarity resulting from friendship. The balance of the evidence for the view that friends select each other on the basis of complementarity of needs rather than on the basis of similarities is negative (Secord & Backman 1964). Findings based on sociometric studies of friendship concerning other bases of choice have been summed up as follows:

. . . a person is likely to choose the following individuals: (1) those with whom he has a greater opportunity to interact, (2) those who have characteristics most describable in terms of the norms and values of the group, (3) those who are most similar to him in attitudes, values, and social-background characteristics, and (4) those whom he perceives as choosing him or assigning favorable characteristics to him, (5) those who see him as he sees himself, and (6) those whose company leads to gratification of his needs. (Secord & Backman 1964, p. 247)

Two theoretical formulations with implications for the study of friendship have appeared in recent years (Thibaut & Kelley 1959; Homans 1961). Both are exchange theories of interaction, where basic terms are costs, rewards, outcomes, and comparison levels. This framework allows the analysis of steps in attraction processes (Secord & Backman 1964, chapter 7): friendship is the outcome of sampling and estimation, bargaining, commitment, and, finally, institutionalization.

## Problems for research

Both sociometric findings on friendship and Secord and Backman's exchange analysis of friendship focus on the *initiation* of friendship structures; that is, their central theoretical topic is attraction rather than established friendship relations. Research on friendship needs more concentration on the substantive contents of friendship itself. How, in fact, are rights and obligations in friendship experienced in various social environments? What are the institutional and actual encouragements and limits to friendship in various contexts—politics, business, everyday life? What are the major rewards and strains in friendships? Is the ambiguity of friendship a circumstance that serves to initiate as well as to terminate other kinds of relationships? Under what conditions will friendships end? Is friendship, more often than other types of relationships, a subjectively sustained reality in the face of decreased overt interaction? For partial answers to such questions, and for the generation of other specific and significant questions about friendship, analysis of detailed reports on the behavior and orientations of friends, acquaintances, strangers, and enemies in everyday life is required. It would seem that such studies, which demand more descriptive patience than we now see in social science, can give a rich yield, since friendship, as a kind of cement in personality and social fabrics, is probably more strategically related to other social relationships than research has indicated so far.

ODD RAMSØY

[Other relevant material may be found in LEADERSHIP and SOCIOMETRY.]

### BIBLIOGRAPHY

AUBERT, VILHELM; and ARNER, ODDVAR 1959 On the Social Structure of the Ship. *Acta sociologica* 3:200–219.

BERELSON, BERNARD; LAZARSFELD, PAUL F.; and McPHEE, WILLIAM N. 1954 *Voting: A Study of Opinion Formation in a Presidential Campaign.* Univ. of Chicago Press.

BOTT, ELIZABETH 1957 *Family and Social Network: Roles, Norms, and External Relationships in Ordinary Urban Families.* London: Tavistock.

COHEN, YEHUDI A. 1961 *Social Structure and Personality.* New York: Holt.

COLEMAN, JAMES S. 1961 *The Adolescent Society: The Social Life of the Teenager and Its Impact on Education.* New York: Free Press.

COLEMAN, JAMES S.; KATZ, ELIHU; and MENZEL, HERBERT 1957 The Diffusion of an Innovation Among Physicians. *Sociometry* 20:253–270.

EISENSTADT, SHMUEL N. 1956 Ritualized Personal Relations. *Man* 56:90–95.

GOFFMAN, ERVING 1958 The Characteristics of Total Institutions. Pages 43–84 in *Symposium on Preventive and Social Psychiatry.* A symposium held at the Walter Reed Army Institute of Research in 1957. Washington: Government Printing Office.

GORDON, C. WAYNE 1957 *The Social System of the High School: A Study in the Sociology of Adolescence.* Glencoe, Ill.: Free Press.

HOMANS, GEORGE C. 1961 *Social Behavior: Its Elementary Forms.* New York: Harcourt.

LAZARSFELD, PAUL F.; and MERTON, ROBERT K. 1954 Friendship as a Social Process: A Substantive and Methodological Analysis. Pages 18–66 in Morroe Berger, Theodore Abel, and Charles H. Page (editors), *Freedom and Control in Modern Society.* Princeton, N.J.: Van Nostrand.

NAEGELE, KASPAR D. 1958 Friendship and Acquaintances: An Exploration of Some Social Distinctions. *Harvard Educational Review* 28:232–252.

NEWCOMB, THEODORE M. 1961 *The Acquaintance Process.* New York: Holt.

PARSONS, TALCOTT; and WHITE, WINSTON 1961 The Link Between Character and Society. Pages 89–135 in Seymour Lipset and Leo Lowenthal (editors), *Culture and Social Character: The Work of David Riesman Reviewed.* New York: Free Press.

ROETHLISBERGER, FRITZ J.; and DICKSON, WILLIAM J. (1939) 1961 *Management and the Worker: An Account of a Research Program Conducted by the Western Electric Company, Hawthorne Works, Chicago.* Cambridge, Mass.: Harvard Univ. Press. → A paperback edition was published in 1964 by Wiley.

SECORD, PAUL F.; and BACKMAN, CARL W. 1964 *Social Psychology.* New York: McGraw-Hill.

SEELEY, JOHN R. et al. 1956 *Crestwood Heights: A Study of the Culture of Suburban Life.* New York: Basic Books.

THIBAUT, JOHN W.; and KELLEY, HAROLD H. 1959 *The Social Psychology of Groups.* New York: Wiley.

TUNSTALL, JEREMY 1962 *The Fishermen.* London: MacGibbon & Kee.

WARNER, W. LLOYD; and LUNT, PAUL S. 1941 *The Social Life of a Modern Community.* New Haven: Yale Univ. Press.

WHYTE, WILLIAM F. (1943) 1961 *Street Corner Society: The Social Structure of an Italian Slum.* 2d ed., enl. Univ. of Chicago Press.

## FRINGE BENEFITS
*See under* WAGES.

## FROBENIUS, LEO

Leo Frobenius (1873–1938) was one of the last of the great explorers that the nineteenth century turned out in such profusion; he was also one of the first ethnologists who did not confine himself to an ethnographic description of the facts but elaborated a method for organizing in space and time the confused welter of discrete observations about the world's nonliterate peoples.

Frobenius was born in Berlin. In his early youth, he devoted his time to the ethnology of Africa, at the age of 21 publishing a bulky volume on African secret societies (1894). As a scientist, he was self-taught. And although he combined an intuitive mind with tremendous industry, emotional involvement with his material often led him to lapse into pathos.

His works on cultural morphology grew out of a profound knowledge of primitive cultures. In 1893 he began a collection of photographs and other ethnographic materials that later formed the basis of the Africa Archives. Frobenius made 12 expeditions to Africa from 1904 to 1935, devoting himself to ethnological field work and the photographing of rock pictures. He also made a trip to India. The holdings of the Africa Archives were greatly expanded by his expeditions, and in 1922 the archives became the Forschungsinstitut für Kulturmorphologie. In 1932 he was invited to teach cultural anthropology at the University of Frankfurt am Main as an *Honorarprofessor.* In 1934 he was appointed director of the Municipal Museum of Ethnology in Frankfurt am Main. He died in Biganzolo on Lago Maggiore.

As a historian, Frobenius endeavored through his research to provide historical background for the civilizations that had formerly been regarded as having no history because their past was not illuminated by any written records, and thereby to incorporate them into world history. This work stimulated an expansion of the historical perspective, which at the turn of the twentieth century had been almost exclusively confined to the advanced and literate civilizations of Europe and the Near East. The historical field of vision was expanded not only in spatial–geographical terms, by the inclusion of previously neglected parts of the world, but in ethnological terms as well; many primitive cultures have preserved forms of thought, of behavior, and in general, of cultural patterns that are obviously much older than those of the earliest advanced and literate civilizations of the Near East. In his works on the philosophy of history and civilization, Frobenius sought to comprehend not only a particular culture, but culture as such, and therewith the entire history of the world. He tried to grasp and to explain the forces and motives that lead to the origin of a culture, the laws governing its course, the relationship between man and culture, and the meaning and goal of historical development. The broad scope of his research contributed insights and findings of fundamental importance to historically oriented ethnology.

**"Kulturkreise."** At the close of the nineteenth century, there were two conflicting doctrines in ethnology, represented in the German-speaking world by Adolf Bastian on the one hand, and by Richard Andree and Friedrich Ratzel on the other. Both doctrines proceeded from the same set of facts, i.e., the observation that elements of mental and material culture identical in form and function may be found in regions of the world that are far apart, frequently separated by oceans, and among peoples speaking different languages and often belonging to different races. The doctrine advocated by Bastian in *Der Mensch in der Geschichte: Zur Begründung einer psychologischen Weltanschauung* (1860) explained such occurrences by assuming that the evolution of mankind has always, and in all parts of the world, been subject to the same laws; that this evolution has been a linear one; and that, consequently, upon reaching a certain stage of development, all societies are independently compelled by the rigid law of evolution to create and shape the cultural objects that correspond to the given stage of development.

This evolutionary view was opposed by the doctrine advocated by Andree in *Ethnographische Parallelen und Vergleiche* (1878) and by Ratzel in "Geschichte, Völkerkunde und historische Perspective" (1904), who attributed the occurrence of identical elements of culture in different regions of the world to the migrations either of entire cultures or of individual cultural elements and to direct or indirect cultural contact. Frobenius was always a convinced champion of this latter doctrine, which is known as the diffusion or migration theory.

Building on the ideas of Andree, Ratzel, and his own teacher, H. Schurtz, Frobenius made a giant step through his two pioneering works "Der westafrikanische Kulturkreis" (1897) and "The Origin of African Civilizations" (1898*a*), which cleared the way for a new scientific approach in ethnology. He demonstrated that many elements of material and mental culture are by no means scattered at random over the world but are always densely concentrated in certain areas and always occur in a characteristic combination with other cultural manifestations. Frobenius inferred from the identical geographical distribution of certain elements of culture that these could not be fortuitous combinations, but that there had to be a close relationship among several of the elements. He therefore grouped areas of identical distribution into what he called *Kulturkreise;* these, in turn, he arranged in relative chronological order so as to provide a historical background for nonliterate cultures. The core of this method was cultural comparison, and its technical tool was cartography. As the creator of the theory, Frobenius became the trail-blazer of the historical approach in ethnology, for even today, cultural comparison constitutes an important means to the construction of historical accounts of cultures without written traditions. Later on, the theory of *Kulturkreise* was extended by Fritz Graebner and Bernhard Ankermann, and it finally became part of the theory of the "Vienna school" of Wilhelm Schmidt. However, this school did not develop the concept of *Kulturkreise* as Frobenius understood it but instead allowed it to become static, thus impairing its effectiveness.

Although the concept of *Kulturkreise* continued to play a major role in Frobenius' work, he soon came to realize clearly the methodological shortcomings of his own early works that dealt with it. He sharply attacked the use of statistical methods to establish *Kulturkreise*—methods which amounted only to a summation of isolated and often quite heterogenous elements, often totally unrelated and of different historical significance. What he had described as *Kulturkreise* in his initial works were in fact bloodless, empty constructions, mere accumulations of data. Frobenius demanded a morphological mode of considering cultures—a meaningful combination of individual elements into an organic whole and the comprehension of a culture in its complexity and its historical context. As Frobenius saw it, *Kulturkreise* obtained from a cartographic picture of distribution were not cultures in the real sense of the term, but merely starting points for further research, skeletons that must be fleshed out, or auxiliary constructions that might enable him to penetrate to the core of the problem: the question of the nature of culture. The provisional nature of his *Kulturkreise* becomes especially manifest when they are compared to the *Kulturkreise* of Graebner and the Vienna school, which were by no means intended to have a provisional, skeletal character. The latter were of a definitive nature and of fixed, rigid magnitudes; arranged chronologically and combined, they were even supposed to furnish an outline of the history of mankind.

**Development of culture.** Frobenius' intellectual objective was to understand the essential nature of culture. His first book devoted to this problem was *Die naturwissenschaftliche Kulturlehre* (1899, *Probleme der Kultur*, vol. 1). It foreshadowed the concepts of his subsequent theory of *paideuma* (1921), in which he endeavored to provide an answer to the question of the nature, the morphology, and the development of a culture. Frobenius regarded the several cultures as living organisms in the biological sense that every culture is subject to the laws of the organic world, springing up like seed, growing, and attaining its apogee at maturity, after which it begins to age and finally dies. He used the terms *Ergriffenheit* (emotional involvement), *Ausdruck* (expression), and *Anwendung* (application) to characterize the stages of youth, maturity, and age traversed by a culture, comparing them to a life curve.

Frobenius regarded the *Ergriffenheit* of man as the crucial event in the emergence of a culture. Once man is gripped by the world about him, the particular nature of the things in his world and the existential order within which he lives are revealed to him. In this process, man plays a rather passive role, being object rather than subject, affected by the phenomena that overcome him, move him, and shake him to his innermost being. It would be wrong, however, to exaggerate his passivity: in the last analysis, only alert, active, and creative spirits are open to the phenomena of the world around them; only they are capable of reproducing these phenomena and putting together a comprehensive and valid picture of the reality that surrounds them.

Frobenius attributed decisive importance to the creative qualities of man. In his eyes, *Ergriffenheit* and creative will are the motive forces that give rise to the emergence of a culture. The emergence of culture occurs almost exclusively in the realm of ideas, for the process begins not simply with objects but with the inner nature of the objects and phenomena in man's environment. Therefore the *Ergriffenheit*, the youth stage, of a culture is always characterized by fundamental and magnificent spiritual–religious creations. More simply stated: Religion stands at the beginning of a culture. Because the rise and formation of the spiritual–religious foundations generally take place quietly and without any visible indications, it is very difficult to establish precisely the emergent phase of a culture; in the case of nonliterate peoples, precision is almost impossible. As a rule, the historian can identify and describe only those fully developed cultures that already possess a stamp of their own and have reached the stage of maturity, while the decisive mental processes that form a culture are not accessible to observation; at best they can be reconstructed from its mature state.

If the *Ergriffenheit* of man is the crucial event in the origin of a culture, man's environment must be of decisive importance, for it alone is able to move him. That is why Frobenius regarded environment as a factor of overriding significance and recognized the primary bond between every culture and its location, while the factor of race seemed to him unimportant. He attributed differences between various cultures largely to the differences in environmental conditions. The cartographic method he employed in mapping *Kulturkreise* and the patterns of distribution he obtained greatly aided him in reaching this conclusion. Thus, he believed that the extensive rain forests of the equatorial regions, with their uniformity of scenery and climate, give rise to a different form of *Ergriffenheit* than that of the savanna and steppes, with their pronounced alternations of drought and rainy periods.

The second stage that a culture must pass through is that of *Ausdruck*, maturity, the apex of the life curve. At this point of development, men continue to be affected by things, but they have now assimilated the experience of their environment and mastered it in the philosophical sense. They are able to express the essential nature of things and of the existential order, as well as of their own existence, in religious, artistic, and social constructs. Only when man has risen above the level of things can he make them completely his own and shape them creatively. In the period of the maturity of a culture, ideas take on visible shape; they are manifested in religious rites, in the forms of social order, in artistic creations, as well as in the complexity of daily life and the economy. A culture in the stage of maturity is in a state of harmony and draws on abundant resources.

Frobenius' researches were always aimed at comprehending the spiritual center of a culture, from which its impulses proceed and all actions of the culture are controlled. He called this spiritual center the *paideuma*, the soul of the culture, which permeates man and gives his action a direction and goal. Every movement and every expression of a culture, even the simple implements of daily use, are related to the spiritual center and bear the stamp of the particular *paideuma*. All elements are conceived as intimately interrelated in function, which is not true of the elements of the early conception of *Kulturkreise*; this is why Frobenius refused to regard the early *Kulturkreise* as true cultures in the *paideuma* sense.

The last stage is called by Frobenius *Anwendung* (application) because in this phase he saw the rational aspect of reality and the question of the usefulness and possible applications of a cultural asset coming increasingly to the fore. An implement or a social institution is no longer evaluated solely as the expression of a central spiritual idea but is regarded only from the standpoint of its utility. The rational utilitarian aspect of many cultural assets, especially of the material objects, is no doubt inherent from the very outset, but in the *Anwendung* phase it predominates over ideal values. The bonds linking the individual elements of culture to the spiritual center become ever looser, and their progressive isolation finally results in the disintegration of the entire culture. The *Anwendung* stage of a culture is characterized by overemphasis on technical–civilizing forces. The nonpurposeful striving for knowledge of the *Ergriffenheit* phase recedes, and creative spiritual ideas are "applied" and "turned to account" according to their usefulness. An increasing semantic depletion makes itself felt in the religious field, and symbols and religious rites are dominated by routine. When the creative forces are paralyzed, meaningful content dwindles away, cultural forms become petrified, and the culture gradually dies away.

As Frobenius saw it, the various cultures are closed organisms, subject to the same law that governs all living things in this world. Every culture has a soul of its own, a unique character, and an individuality otherwise found only in animate nature. Frobenius therefore attributed to every culture an autonomous set of laws that determines its development, largely independent of its particular human members. This is an inevitable although often misunderstood conclusion if cultures are regarded as living organisms that are governed by the laws of life. Man cannot stem the natural development of a culture. For example, he cannot

prevent the aging of a culture; all he can do is prolong or shorten the process. When Frobenius ventured the opinion that culture might exist even without human beings, he meant that culture is not a fiction but a reality that "takes hold of" men just as do the phenomena of their environment. This notion is supported by the historical fact that cultures tend to expand beyond the boundaries of their original centers, especially in the stage of maturity, and "seize," as it were, people of alien cultures, putting them under their sway.

Although Frobenius was the target of violent attacks, his thoughts and ideas fell upon fertile soil in the German-speaking world. His scientific work in the field of culture founded cultural morphology in ethnology, which is the special concern of the Frobenius Institute. The work of his disciple Adolf E. Jensen on comparative religion refined and advanced Frobenius' description of the history of culture and increased its depth. All work in the cultural-historical aspects of ethnology has been profoundly influenced by Frobenius' doctrines. For a time, he was closely associated with Oswald Spengler, who advocated similar ideas about the essential nature of culture. Outside of Germany, and especially in the English-speaking world, Frobenius was accepted only with reservations.

HELMUT STRAUBE

[*For the historical context of Frobenius' work, see the biographies of* BASTIAN *and* RATZEL. *For discussion of the subsequent development of Frobenius' ideas, see* CULTURE; CULTURE AREA; HISTORY, *article on* CULTURE HISTORY; *and the biographies of* GRAEBNER; KOPPERS; NORDENSKIÖLD; SCHMIDT.]

WORKS BY FROBENIUS

1894   *Die Geheimbünde Afrikas: Ethnologische Studie.* Hamburg: Actien-Gesellschaft.

1897   Der westafrikanische Kulturkreis. *Petermanns Geographische Mitteilungen* 43:225–236, 262–267.

(1898a) 1899   The Origin of African Civilizations. Smithsonian Institution, *Annual Report* [1899]:637–650. → First published in German.

1898b   *Die Masken und Geheimbünde Afrikas.* Halle: Karras.

1898c   *Der Ursprung der Kultur.* Berlin: Bornträger.

1899–1901   *Probleme der Kultur.* 4 vols. Berlin: Dümmler. → Volume 1: *Die naturwissenschaftliche Kulturlehre,* 1899. Volume 2: *Die Mathematik der Oceanier,* 1900. Volume 3: *Die Schilde der Oceanier,* 1900. Volume 4: *Die Bogen der Oceanier,* 1901.

1907   *Im Schatten des Kongostaates: Bericht über den Verlauf der ersten Reisen der D.I.A.F.E. von 1904–1906.* Deutsche inner-afrikanische Forschungs-Expedition, No. 1. Berlin: Reimer.

1910   *Der schwarze Dekameron: Belege und Aktenstücke über Liebe, Witz und Heldentum in Innerafrika.* Berlin: Vita.

(1912–1913) 1918   *The Voice of Africa: Being an Account of the Travels of the German Inner African Exploration Expedition in the Years 1910–1912.* 2 vols. London: Hutchinson. → First published as *Und Afrika sprach.*

1916   Der kleinafrikanische Grabbau. *Praehistorische Zeitschrift* 8:1–84.

(1921) 1928   *Paideuma: Umrisse einer Kultur- und Seelenlehre.* 3d ed., rev. & enl. Frankfurt am Main: Societäts-Druckerei.

1921–1928   FROBENIUS, LEO (editor) *Atlantis: Volksmärchen und Volksdichtungen Afrikas.* 12 vols. Munich: Veröffentlichungen des Forschungsinstituts für Kulturmorphologie. → Volumes 1–3: *Volksmärchen der Kabylen.* Volume 4: *Märchen aus Kordofan.* Volume 5: *Dichten und Denken im Sudan.* Volume 6: *Spielmannsgeschichten der Sahel.* Volume 7: *Dämonen des Sudan: Allerlei religiöse Verdichtungen.* Volume 8: *Erzählungen aus dem West-Sudan.* Volume 9: *Volkserzählungen und Volksdichtungen aus dem Zentral-Sudan.* Volume 10: *Die atlantische Götterlehre.* Volume 11: *Volksdichtungen aus Oberguinea.* Volume 12: *Dichtkunst der Kassaiden.*

(1921–1931) 1937   FROBENIUS, LEO; and FOX, DOUGLAS C. *African Genesis.* New York: Stackpole. → First published in German.

1922–1933   FROBENIUS, LEO; and WILM, LUDWIG VON (editors) *Atlas Africanus: Belege zur Morphologie der afrikanischen Kulturen.* 8 parts. Munich: Beck.

1923   *Das unbekannte Afrika: Aufhellung der Schicksale eines Erdteils.* Munich: Beck.

1925   FROBENIUS, LEO; and OBERMAIER, HUGO *Hádschra Máktuba: Urzeitliche Felsbilder Kleinafrikas.* Munich: Wolff.

1925–1929   *Erlebte Erdteile.* 7 vols. Frankfurt am Main: Societäts-Druckerei. → Volume 1: *Ausfahrt: Von der Völkerkunde zum Kulturproblem,* 1925. Volume 2: *Erschlossen Räume: Das Problem Ozeanien,* 1925. Volume 3: *Vom Schreibtisch zum Äquator,* 1925. Volume 4: *Paideuma,* 1928. Volume 5: *Das sterbende Afrika,* 1928. Volume 6: *Monumenta africana,* 1929. Volume 7: *Monumenta terrarum,* 1929.

(1929) 1938   Die Waremba: Träger einer fossilen Kultur. *Zeitschrift für Ethnologie* 70:159–175.

1931a   *Erythräa: Länder und Zeiten des heiligen Königsmordes.* Berlin and Zurich: Atlantis.

1931b   *Madsimu Dsangara: Südafrikanische Felsbilderchronik.* 2 vols. Berlin: Atlantis.

1932   *Schicksalskunde im Sinne des Kulturwerdens.* Leipzig: Voigtländer.

1933   *Kulturgeschichte Afrikas: Prolegomena zu einer historischen Gestaltlehre.* Zurich: Phaidon.

1937   *Ekade Ektab: Die Felsbilder Fezzans.* Leipzig: Harrassowitz.

1937   The Story of Rock Picture Research. Pages 13–28 in New York, Museum of Modern Art, *Prehistoric Rock Pictures in Europe and Africa.* New York: The Museum.

### SUPPLEMENTARY BIBLIOGRAPHY

ANDREE, RICHARD   1878   *Ethnographische Parallelen und Vergleiche.* Stuttgart: Maier.

BASTIAN, ADOLF   1860   *Der Mensch in der Geschichte: Zur Begründung einer psychologischen Weltanschauung.* 3 vols. Leipzig: Wigand. → Volume 1: *Die Psychologie als Naturwissenschaft.* Volume 2: *Psychologie und Mythologie.* Volume 3: *Politische Psychologie.*

*Leo Frobenius: Ein Lebenswerk aus der Zeit der Kulturwende, dargestellt von seinen Freunden und Schülern.* 1933   Leipzig: Köhler & Amelang.

HAHN, EDUARD   1926   Leo Frobenius. *Preussische Jahrbücher* 205:205–222.

JENSEN, ADOLF E.   1938   Leo Frobenius: Leben und Werk. *Paideuma* 1:45–58.

LOWIE, ROBERT H.   1913   *Und Afrika sprach . . . A Book Review. Current Anthropological Literature* 2:87–91.

MÜHLMANN, WILHELM   1939   Zum Gedächtnis von Leo Frobenius. *Archiv für Anthropologie* New Series 25:47–51.

NIGGEMEYER, HERMANN   1939   Leo Frobenius. *Ethnologischer Anzeiger* 4:268–272.

RATZEL, FRIEDRICH   1904   Geschichte, Völkerkunde und historische Perspective. *Historische Zeitschrift* 93, no. 1:1–46.

# FRUSTRATION

*See* AGGRESSION, *article on* PSYCHOLOGICAL ASPECTS; STRESS.

# FUNCTIONAL ANALYSIS

I. STRUCTURAL–FUNCTIONAL ANALYSIS       *Marion J. Levy, Jr.*

II. VARIETIES OF FUNCTIONAL ANALYSIS       *Francesca M. Cancian*

## I
### STRUCTURAL–FUNCTIONAL ANALYSIS

Few concepts in modern social science history have generated as much discussion as those of structure and function and the type of analysis associated with them. The main difficulty in speaking of structural–functional analysis in general arises from five sources. One, there is the feeling in many quarters that there is something new and special about structural–functional analysis. Two, in general usage elementary procedures in definition have not been observed. The same term has frequently been used for more than one distinct referent. Three, teleology in the sense of scientific fallacy—in this case structural teleology, functional teleology, or both—has frequently been committed in connection with such analysis. Four, the use of stability assumptions in models generally has been both misunderstood and misconstrued. Five, unintentionally, evaluations have been written into the analysis, thereby raising questions about its objectivity.

Structural–functional analysis is not new in either the social or the natural sciences; it has a pedigree that stretches indefinitely back in both fields. The only new aspect of it is its formidable new name, structural–functional analysis. Discussion of it as something new under the sun is the social scientist's counterpart of M. Jourdain's discovery that he had been speaking prose. The only possible novelty associated with this form of analysis is the attempt in recent years to be carefully explicit in the use of these concepts and to differentiate special subsidiary forms of the analysis, although none of the latter are substantively new either. Shorn of careless uses of definitions and of teleology, structural–functional analysis is simply a synonym for explicit scientific analysis in general. In scientific fields marked by greater theoretical development and associated applications of mathematical forms of expression, the increased verbal explicitness that has recommended the various concepts of structure and function to many in the biological and social sciences is more cumbersome than available alternatives. Corresponding increases in theoretical development in the biological and social sciences will lead to similar alternatives there.

Simply speaking, structural–functional analysis consists of nothing more complicated than phrasing empirical questions in one of the following several forms or some combination of them: (1) What observable uniformities (or patterns) can be discovered or alleged to exist in the phenomena studied? (2) What conditions (empirical states of affairs) resultant from previous operations can be discovered or alleged to exist in the phenomena studied? (3) When process (or action, i.e., changes in the patterns, conditions, or both, depending on one's point of view, are discernible between any two or more points in time) can be discovered (or alleged) to take place in terms of observable uniformities, what resultant conditions can be discovered? The first question asks, "What structures are involved?" The second asks, "What functions have resulted (or have been performed)?" And the third asks, "What functions take place in terms of a given structure(s)?" Many special forms of these three questions are useful and necessary for the analysis of different types of problems; for example, one might ask about the possibility of adjustment in terms of a system, the normative content of a system, the "necessary" features of a system, the degree of planning or consciousness involved, etc. All of these are variants of the three basic questions or some combination of them. In addition to the most general form of the concepts of structure and function, six subsidiary sets of concepts most generally associated with this form of analysis, either explicitly or implicitly, are defined and discussed below in terms of the special purposes generally associated with them.

**Function and structure.** These explicit concepts, ostensibly in their most general form, are fre-

quently encountered in the biological and social sciences. In both fields somewhat similar difficulties have been associated with the use of the concepts. Joseph H. Woodger in biology and Robert K. Merton in the social sciences (Woodger 1924, pp. 326–330; Merton 1949, pp. 21–28) have pointed to the profusion of different referents given to the term "function" even in the scientific sense. These different referents have for the most part been left implicit by both authors although the confusion is noted. Perhaps the major difficulty associated with the general concept of function has been the use of a single term to cover several distinctly different referents. This difficulty is much greater with the concept of function than with the associated concept of structure. Most of the general discussions in the literature have been largely preoccupied with the concept of function. The concept of structure has, more often than not, been left undiscussed. To prevent confusion, the most general form of the concepts "structure" and "function" used for purposes of scientific analysis must be defined in such a way that the other uses of the terms represent specific subcategories. The term "function" may be defined as any condition, any state of affairs, resultant from the operation (including in the term "operation" mere persistence) of a unit of the type under consideration in terms of a structure(s). In the case of the biological sciences that unit is usually an organism or a subsystem of an organism. In the case of the social sciences the unit is usually a system of action involving a set of one or more persons (actors). The term "structure" may be defined as a pattern, i.e., an observable uniformity, in terms of which action (or operation) takes place.

In ordinary usage the term "function" is most generally identified with the term "eufunction" defined below. Similar confusion of the term "structure" with "eustructure" is not common. The concept of structure in this general form explicitly covers a wide range of possibilities from highly stable uniformities to highly fleeting ones. Any event may contain an element indicative of a structure if it is considered with regard to nonunique aspects or parts.

Much of the interest of scientific social analysis is centered on the structure of societies and other social systems (or the structures of social action in general), that is, on the interrelationships among different kinds, aspects, and parts of structures. The relationship between the concepts of function and structure is close. Structure refers to an aspect of empirical phenomena that can be divorced from time. The patterns of action, qua patterns, do not exist as concrete objects in the same sense that sticks and stones do. The patterns of action in this sense are abstractions from concrete empirical phenomena, and they "exist" and are empirically verifiable in the same sense that the squareness of a box exists and is empirically verifiable. What has been said here of patterns qua patterns does not apply to the patterns when they are considered in operation. Structures in operation (i.e., the exemplifications of particular patterns) are empirical in the same sense as sticks and stones. In this sense the term "structure" in social science is no departure from the usage of the natural sciences.

The concepts of structure and function fall into a peculiar set of concepts. Classification of a referent as a function or a structure depends in part on the point of view from which the phenomena concerned are discussed. What is a function from one point of view is a structure from another. The concepts of consumption and production are more familiar examples of this peculiar set. The manufacture of automobiles is production from the point of view of an automobile user and consumption from the point of view of a steelmaker. Thus functions in this sense are themselves structures (i.e., patterns) or have important structured (i.e., patterned) aspects, and all structures are the results of operations in terms of other structures (i.e., they are functions). The politeness of small children may be considered as a structure of their behavior or as a function of operation in terms of the structures (i.e., patterns) of discipline indulged in by their parents.

**Functional and structural requisites.**  The concepts functional and structural requisites are primarily oriented to the development of systems of analysis for any cases of a particular type of unit. A functional requisite may be defined as a generalized condition necessary for the maintenance of the type of unit under consideration, given the level of generalization of the definition and the most general setting of such a unit. In seeking to discover the functional requisites of a unit one asks the question, "What must be done to maintain the system concerned in its setting on the level under consideration?" A given condition is a functional requisite if its removal (or absence) would result in (a) the total dissolution of the unit, or (b) the change of one of the structural elements of the unit on the level under consideration (i.e., one of the structural requisites).

A structural requisite may be defined as a pattern (or observable uniformity) of action (or operation) necessary for the continued existence of the type of unit under consideration, given the level of generalization of the definition and the most general setting of such a unit. In trying to discover the structural requisites of a unit one seeks an answer to the question, "For a given unit, what structures (i.e., patterns) must be present such that operations in terms of these structures will result in the functional requisites of the unit?" Briefly, functional requisites are answers to the question, "What must be done?"; structural requisites are answers to the question "How must what must be done, be done?" Both questions involve the qualifying phrase "if the unit is to persist in its setting on the level of generalization given." Most of the misunderstanding about stability mentioned above has been associated with this question of persistence. One utilizes an assumption of stability to get at a list of requisites, but this does not imply that any unit analyzed must in fact be stable. To make such units stable by definition is to reduce most discussions of this sort to trivia. To use a stability assumption as an element in a model (i.e., paradigm) does not. Structural–functional requisite analysis includes the following steps in any specific case: (1) *define* the unit of phenomena to be studied; (2) *discover* (or hypothesize about) the setting (i.e., those factors determining the limits within which the ranges of variations of the unit concerned take place); (3) *discover* what general conditions must be met (i.e., functional requisites) if the unit is to persist in its setting without change (i.e., alteration of structures) on the level under consideration; (4) *discover* what structures must be present in the system, as a minimum, if action in terms of the system is to result in the persistence of the unit in its setting without any change on the level under consideration (i.e., the structural requisites).

Several things should be kept in mind. One, although the definition of the unit is arbitrary, whether empirical referents of such a unit exist is not. Two, the setting of such a unit is not a matter of definition but of discovery. Three, neither structural requisites nor functional requisites can be alleged to exist "because they are requisites." Such allegations constitute the commission of structural or functional teleology. To assert that requisites exist *because they are requisites* is to imply that the unit must continue to exist for some preordained reason. Scientifically speaking, *nothing* can be alleged to exist "because it is a requisite." The fact that this form of teleology is fallacious is in no way contradicted by the fact that it is frequently a useful element of models of action to assume or allege that the action concerned is oriented to future states of affairs. Four, the determination of the functional requisites of a unit is the determination of the minimum implications of interrelationships between the factors setting the limits of variation of the unit and the unit itself, and in this type of analysis it is never necessary to deal with more than these minimal implications. However, when material is collected in these terms, more than the minimum will always be collected, since such minimal materials never exist neatly separated from all others. Five, there is a systematic test for error in requisite analysis. If a structure is alleged to be a requisite of the unit concerned, and if examination of a particular case of such a unit uncovers no material on this score, one of three or some combination of three things is an explanation of the lack of data. First, the hypothesis that the structure is a requisite of the unit concerned may be an incorrect one. Second, the observer may have misobserved; there may be data he has overlooked. Third, the unit concerned, although it may closely resemble the unit as defined, may in fact not be a case of such a unit.

There is nothing new about requisite analysis. There has never been a time in which people failed completely to ask questions as to whether given conditions or patterns were not in some sense necessary for the continued existence of certain types of units.

**Functional and structural prerequisites.** The requisite concepts are not in and of themselves oriented to questions of change; the concepts of functional and structural prerequisites are. All questions of change implicitly or explicitly involve comparisons between at least two of at least three possible distinctions with regard to the units under consideration. These distinctions are those of an initial, a transitional, and a resultant stage. Systematic knowledge about any two of these stages makes possible systematic derivation (prediction or postdiction) of knowledge about the third. Requisite analysis can be used for examining any two of these three or more stages in terms of a constant frame of reference. Constants and variables are therefore more easily detected.

A functional prerequisite may be defined as a function that must pre-exist if a given unit is to come into being in a particular setting. Correspondingly, a structural prerequisite may be defined as a structure that must pre-exist if a given unit is to come into being in a particular setting. The closer two stages of a given unit under consideration are in point of time the greater is the probability that the requisites and the prerequisites of a given unit will be identical. To illustrate this, one of the commonest mistakes in trying to understand the problems of development in "underdeveloped areas"

is the implicit assumption that requisites and prerequisites must or do coincide. It is neither obvious nor tenable to take the position that all of the structures that must be maintained if the United States is to continue as a highly modernized society are identical with the structures that have to pre-exist if Nigeria is to become a highly modernized society, or even that they are identical with all the structures that had to pre-exist, say, in the beginning of the nineteenth century, if the United States was to become a highly modernized society.

Implicitly or explicitly, some form of requisite analysis always underlies any form of prerequisite analysis. Teleology must be avoided in uses of the concepts of structural and functional prerequisites as well as in uses of the concepts of structural and functional requisites. To assert that some structure must pre-exist because it is a structural prerequisite of a given unit is to fall into teleological dynamics as distinguished from the teleological statics described in the case of requisites.

**Eufunction, dysfunction; eustructure, dysstructure.** These concepts focus attention on questions of adjustment and maladjustment of the units under consideration. Although the term "function" is ordinarily used in several different senses in the social sciences, most often it refers to the concept of eufunction as defined here. With respect to a given unit, "eufunction" may be defined as any function that increases or maintains adaptation or adjustment of the unit to the unit's setting, thus making for the persistence of the unit as defined in its setting. With respect to a given unit, "dysfunction" may be defined as any function that lessens the adaptation or adjustment of the unit to its setting, thus making for lack of persistence (i.e., change or dissolution) of the unit as defined in its setting. The terms "eustructure" and "dysstructure" are similarly defined, *mutatis mutandis*. Alternatively, eustructures may be defined as structures in terms of which operations result in eufunctions, and dysstructures may be defined as structures in terms of which operations result in dysfunctions. Eufunctions or dysfunctions and the corresponding variants of structure may exist, as far as a given unit is concerned, as elements of that unit (i.e., internal to it) or as elements of the setting of the unit concerned. Not all eufunctions *for* a unit are eufunctions *of* the unit, although ordinarily, when one uses the concept of eufunction, attention is focused on functions associated with the unit itself rather than on functions of operation in terms of other units in that setting.

The concept of "nonfunction," in the sense of being neither a eufunction nor a dysfunction, is inutile. Where questions of adjustment are not in-volved, the general concept of function as used here or another of its special forms will serve. Where questions of adjustment are involved, nothing is less probable than a precisely poised function with no implications for adjustment or maladjustment. Indeed, such considerations define precisely what might be called the category of irrelevant functions, i.e., those lacking any implications for the focus of interest at the time. Such functions would also have to lack any interdependencies with the eufunc-tions or dysfunctions *for* or *of* the systems con-cerned.

It is in connection with the terms "eufunction" and "dysfunction" (and the corresponding forms of the concept of structure) that most allegations of building evaluations into structural functional analysis are made. In rough terms, a eufunction is a function that tends to preserve the unit as de-fined and a dysfunction is one that tends to dis-solve it. However, loose usage of these concepts results in the use of eufunctional to refer to con-ditions making for "good adaptations" and dys-functional to refer to conditions making for "bad adaptations." Such judgments are a function of one's evaluation of the unit concerned—if one cares to make such an evaluation. No condition or as-pect of a condition is inherently eufunctional or dysfunctional. Without identification of the unit concerned and its setting, no judgment of the eu-functional or dysfunctional character of the condi-tion can be made. The same condition that is eufunctional from one point of view may be dys-functional from another. For example, conditions that were eufunctional for Meiji Japan were dys-functional for the continuation of Tokugawa Japan and vice versa.

While these concepts are susceptible to the un-critical inclusion of value judgments, they are also a useful vehicle for the explicit consideration of policy-oriented analyses. Either implicitly or explic-itly, in seeking to maximize a given policy goal, one asks the questions, "What conditions make for max-imal adjustment of the system concerned to that state of affairs (i.e., the eufunctions for that sys-tem in that setting)?" and "What conditions should be avoided as interfering with the maintenance of that system in that setting (i.e., are dysfunctional for it)?" Two other points should be carefully kept in mind. First, teleology is to be avoided in this connection too. No function or structure exists *because* it is a eufunction or a eustructure, nor is it tenable to hold that any function or structure that persists must be eufunctional or eustructural. Sec-ond, a given element with important eufunctional or eustructural implications for a given unit in its setting may also contain aspects with dysfunctional or dysstructural implications. A functional requisite of a given unit is certainly at least in part eufunc-tional for that unit, but a given function, even though it is a requisite, may also contain dysfunc-tional implications as well, although presumably in this case they would not be sufficiently pronounced to overcome the requisite nature of the function.

The concepts of eufunction, dysfunction, eu-structure, and dysstructure focus on the question of the maintenance or lack of maintenance of a sys-tem in its setting. The requisite concepts focus on the question of what a system is like if it is main-tained. The prerequisite concepts focus attention on what conditions must pre-exist before a given type of unit can come into being. The requisite con-cepts are useful primarily for static theories, al-though dynamic analysis is involved in discovery of the requisites of a given system in its setting. Like the prerequisite concepts, those of eufunction, dysfunction, eustructure, and dysstructure focus attention on dynamic interrelationships—on the implications of the operation of a particular struc-ture or the presence of a particular function for the state of the system concerned at some future point in time.

**Latent, manifest, UIR, and IUR functions and structures.** This set of terms is adapted from Merton's suggestion many years ago about latent and manifest functions. Usage here is somewhat changed, since Merton did not envisage their use apart from the concepts of eufunction and dysfunc-tion as defined here, nor did he develop the implica-tions of the fact that his defining conditions could vary independently. Following Merton's usage an element will be termed "manifest" if it is intended and recognized by the participants in the system of action concerned. It will be termed "latent" if it is neither intended nor recognized. It will be termed "UIR" if it is unintended but recognized and "IUR" if it is intended but unrecognized. These concepts focus attention on the level of explicitness and sensitivity of the members of a given system to the structures in terms of which they operate. Such distinctions are vital to any discussions in-volving rationality, planning, and so forth. The concept of manifest dysfunction is explicitly in-cluded as a possibility here. Failure to consider it explicitly has built implicit evaluations into a great deal of analysis. Social reformers usually concen-trate all their efforts on being manifestly dysfunc-tional for the system they are trying to reform and manifestly eufunctional for what they consider to be a better world.

The concepts of function and structure in general, the requisites, the prerequisites, and eufunction–dysfunction, eustructure–dysstructure, are concepts generally applicable to social and nonsocial phenomena and to human as well as to nonhuman phenomena. Concepts of latent, manifest, IUR, and UIR specifically focus attention on the point of view of the actor and involve the assumptions that such actors can and do orient their behavior to future states of affairs about which they are capable of explicit thinking and observation, and that the presence or absence of such explicit thinking, observation, or both has, in turn, implications for their subsequent behavior. Although it is conceivable that such concepts be utilized with regard to nonsocial phenomena, it is not likely that they will prove useful in such a field nor have they generally been so employed. It is quite conceivable that they could be employed with regard to some animate but nonhuman phenomena, but by far their greatest applications are to human social phenomena.

**Concrete and analytic structures.** The distinction between concrete and analytic structures is oriented to the type of abstraction involved in certain concepts useful for empirical analysis. Concrete structures may be defined as those structures (i.e., patterns) that define the units that are at least in theory capable of physical separation (in time, space, or both) from other units of the same sort. As the term will be applied for social analysis, it refers more specifically to the structures that define the membership units involved in social action, i.e., units in regard to which any given individual may be classified as included or excluded, or some combination of the two. Society, as that term is generally used, is a concrete structure considered in operation. So are organizational contexts generally, such as families, business firms, and governments. Concrete structures other than societies are the structures of action that define the membership units within a given society or those relating to two or more societies, i.e., they are all other social systems. All concrete structures are social systems; all societies are social systems; and all social systems other than societies are either subsystems of a given society or the results of interdependencies among two or more societies. The family, as that term is often used, is a concrete structure; its structures define a membership unit. So are business firms. A given individual may at one and the same time be a member of both a given business firm and a given family; nevertheless, the social structures characterizing the business firm are not part of the social structures characterizing the family concern, however complex the interrelationships

may be, unless the firm is specifically and completely a family affair. It is at least conceivable that all the members of a given family could be put in one room, that the members of a given business firm could be put into another, and if necessary, those individuals who are members of both could be removed from the two rooms and put into a third.

Analytic structures are defined as structures (i.e., patterns) that define the aspects of units that are not even theoretically capable of concrete separation from other structured aspects. If one defines the economic aspect of action as having to do with the allocation of goods and services and political aspects as having to do with the allocation of power and responsibility, then economic and political structures are analytic structures, since there are no social systems that are totally devoid of either economic or political aspects.

Failure to keep this sort of distinction straight constitutes the fallacy of reification (or misplaced concreteness). Thus the terms "economy" and "polity" as generally used cannot occupy the same position in a system of analysis as the term "family." As these concepts are generally defined, they represent analytic structures, and the concept "family" refers to a concrete one. This distinction, though difficult in the context of social phenomena, is a generally familiar one in the natural sciences. Concepts such as atoms, molecules, cells, organs, and elementary particles are concrete structures. Aspects such as mass, shape, color, temperature, and mitosis are analytic structures.

In actual analysis one always uses some combination of both sorts of concepts. One cannot identify analytic structures without some specification sooner or later of the concrete structures of which they are aspects. Correspondingly, one cannot discuss the nature of concrete structures without sooner or later making reference to aspects that cut across such units. Careful observance of the distinction and the avoidance of the fallacy of reification is the key par excellence to the avoidance of much disciplinary parochialism in the social sciences.

Apart from considerations of methodological elegance there is another reason for being careful about this distinction. One of the most general distinctions between concrete structures or organizations is that between those which are specialized in the predominant orientation of their members to one or another of these analytic structures and those which are not specialized in this way. (Organizations may, of course, be specialized in other ways, e.g., in terms of the product orientations of the members.) Thus, a business firm may be spoken of as a predominantly economically oriented structure (or perhaps more accurately, though more cumbersomely, as a specially economic–analytic-structure-oriented concrete structure). A family unit is not specialized in any one of these aspects in any clear-cut predominance over the others.

**Institutions, tradition, and utopian structures.** The three terms "institution," "tradition," and "utopian structure" refer to different types of structure. The concept "institution" may be defined as any normative pattern, conformity to which is generally expected and failure to conform with which is generally met with moral indignation or some other form of sanction by the individuals who are involved in the same general social system and are aware of the failure. This is the sense of the term employed by Talcott Parsons in his early work. A given structure may be more or less well-institutionalized to the degree to which conformity with the structure is generally to be expected and the degree to which failure to conform to the structure is met by the moral indignation or sanctions of the individuals who are involved in the system and who are aware of the failure. Thus, the two sources of variability with regard to the level of institutionalization may be referred to as conformity aspects and sanction aspects. An institution may be regarded as crucial or more or less strategic. A given institution will be called a crucial institution if it is a structural requisite of the system in which it appears. It may be regarded as a more or less strategic institution to the extent that: (1) it is the institutionalized form of all or a portion of a structural requisite; and (2) the structure concerned may not or may be altered without destroying the structural requisite involved. A completely strategic institution *is* a crucial institution. The first of the two aspects of the strategic quality of an institution will be called its substantive aspect, and the second will be called its critical aspect. The critical aspect is a special form of consideration of the general problem of functional substitutes, equivalents, or alternatives (i.e., the question of the possibility of a given condition being the result of behavior in terms of one or more alternative structures).

A great deal of nonsense is talked and written as a result of misunderstanding the problem of functional substitutability. Many use this nonsense to argue the severe limitation of what can be done in these terms. Much of the confusion results from initially posing a question implicitly on one level of generality and in the course of the discussion proceeding, still implicitly, on a different and less general level. If the argument is correct that role differentiation on the basis of absolute age is a requisite of all societies, there can be no functional

substitutability for that. The fact that the members of one society handle role differentiation in terms of five absolute age distinctions whereas those of another handle it in terms of ten simply indicates the fact that a particular solution to absolute age distinctions is not determinant for all societies. For a particular society, however, either five or ten distinctions may be just as much a requisite as some sort of role differentiation on the basis of absolute age is for all societies. Some discussions of functional substitutability imply that the structures involved can be changed without other changes on the level of generality on which the treatment has been focused. There are, of course, instances in which a given function may result from operation in terms of various alternative structures on specific lower levels of generality without changes on the most general level under scrutiny, but that question is by no means settled by the analyst's simply being able to conceive of another structure from action in terms of which the function in question could result—and so asserting his conclusions.

The term "tradition" may be defined as an institution whose perpetuation is institutionalized—that is to say, as a special form of institution. An institution may be considered more or less traditional, or more or less traditionalized, to the extent that its perpetuation is institutionalized without regard to changes of the functional implications of operations in terms of it—whether these be eufunctional or dysfunctional implications. In this sense, monogamous marriage in the United States would seem to be much more highly traditional and traditionalized than the structure of driving on the right-hand side of the road. A tradition in this sense is a double institutionalization: (1) the structure concerned is an institution; and (2) the perpetuation of the structure is also an institution. Traditions may vary in at least two radically different ways. One, they may, of course, vary with regard to the institution that is traditionalized, although implicit in the concept of any institution in its conformity aspects is some degree of traditionalization. More important, traditions—like other institutions—may vary with regard to their combinations of conformity and sanction aspects. For example, the tradition of driving on the right-hand side of the road in the United States has very high conformity aspects and relatively minor sanction aspects, whereas the tradition of the incest taboo has very high conformity aspects and very high sanction aspects.

Utopian structures may be defined as those particular sets of normative patterns which, though not institutionalized, do require allegiance to them as institutionalized ideals. Allegiance to them as ideals is highly traditionalized in both conformity and sanction aspects. Thus, one does not in fact expect conformity to the principle of "Love they neighbor as thyself," but expression of it as an ideal is certainly institutionalized in some social contexts, and its perpetuation is institutionalized. In the social systems in which they are found, utopian structures often have the function of making it easier to teach the actual institutional structures of the system and of setting the framework in terms of which actual conformity to less extreme expectations is, in fact, expected.

**Ideal and actual structures.** Ideal structures may be defined as those structures that the members of any given system (or systems) feel should be the structures of their behavior or those of others. Actual structures may be defined as the structures (i.e., patterns) in terms of which the members of the system in fact behave as they would be described by an observer with theoretically perfect scientific knowledge. The terms "ideal" and "actual" in these respects may be applied in other connections, but they are most generally applied to the concepts of structure. The following generalizations in terms of them are relevant in almost any analysis. One, there are no peoples who do not make some distinction between ideal and actual structures. Two, ideal and actual patterns of a given system never coincide perfectly. Three, the members of the systems concerned are always to some extent aware of the fact that the ideal and actual structures do not coincide perfectly. Four, some sources of stress and strain in any social system inhere in the fact that the ideal and actual structures do not coincide perfectly. Five, not paradoxical relative to the fourth generalization, some of the possibilities of integration in terms of any social system inhere in the fact that the ideal and actual structures do not coincide perfectly. Six, failure of the ideal and actual structures to coincide perfectly is never explicable solely in terms of hypocrisy. Seven, perfect coincidence of the ideal and actual structures would require both perfect knowledge and perfect motivation on the part of all of the members of the system concerned in all possible situations. This would (*a*) overload any known set of cognitive capacities of individuals; and (*b*) were it possible to have perfect coincidence of the ideal and actual structures, the resultant system would be totally brittle, since any change of setting factors necessitating or causing any change internal to the system would require complete resetting of all of the cognitive capacities of the members of the system.

These concepts can be further elaborated; e.g., there may be ideal ideal structures (i.e., utopian structures) as well as many pseudo or pretended ideal structures (i.e., hypocrisies which are ideal structures which are not actual ideal structures).

Structural–functional analysis in the most general sense, shorn of confusion of terminology, misuses of stability assumptions, teleology, and implicit evaluations, is synonymous with scientific analysis in general. The special forms of structural–functional analysis are not new, although the attempt to be explicit about them in general is recent. Of the various special forms of structural–functional analysis, there is one sense in which requisite analysis underlies the rest. It is oriented to the derivation of a system of analysis for any unit of the sort under discussion, and all of the other forms of structural–functional analysis, whether in terms of prerequisites, manifest, latent, UIR, and IUR elements, eufunction–dysfunction, eustructure–dysstructure, etc., presuppose two or more states of some sort of unit(s) which presumably can be analyzed systematically. Of the various special forms of structural–functional analysis, those having to do with the latent, manifest, UIR, and IUR elements, the concepts of institutions, traditions, and utopian structures, and the ideal and actual structures are the most specifically oriented to the analysis of human social phenomena. The other special forms are much more generally oriented.

MARION J. LEVY, JR.

#### BIBLIOGRAPHY

DAVIS, KINGSLEY 1959 The Myth of Functional Analysis as a Special Method in Sociology and Anthropology. *American Sociological Review* 24:757–772.

FIRTH, RAYMOND 1955 Function. *Yearbook of Anthropology* [1955]: 237–258.

HEMPEL, CARL G. 1959 The Logic of Functional Analysis. Pages 271–307 in Llewellyn Gross (editor), *Symposium on Sociological Theory.* New York: Harper.

LEVY, MARION J. JR. 1952 *The Structure of Society.* Princeton Univ. Press.

LEVY, MARION J. JR. 1954 Comparative Analysis of Societies in Terms of Structural–Functional Requisites. *Civilisations* 4, no. 2:191–197.

MALINOWSKI, BRONISLAW 1944 *A Scientific Theory of Culture and Other Essays.* Chapel Hill: Univ. of North Carolina Press. → A paperback edition was published in 1960 by Oxford Univ. Press.

MALINOWSKI, BRONISLAW 1945 *The Dynamics of Culture Change: An Inquiry Into Race Relations in Africa.* New Haven: Yale Univ. Press. → A paperback edition was published in 1961.

MERTON, ROBERT K. (1949) 1957 *Social Theory and Social Structure: Toward the Codification of Theory and Research.* Rev. ed. Glencoe, Ill.: Free Press.

NADEL, SIEGFRIED F. 1951 *The Foundations of Social Anthropology.* London: Cohen & West: Glencoe, Ill.: Free Press.

NADEL, SIEGFRIED F. 1957 *The Theory of Social Structure.* London: Cohen & West; Glencoe, Ill.: Free Press. → Published posthumously.

NAGEL, ERNEST 1957 *Logic Without Metaphysics, and Other Essays in the Philosophy of Science.* Glencoe, Ill.: Free Press.

NAGEL, ERNEST 1961 *The Structure of Science: Problems in the Logic of Scientific Explanation.* New York: Harcourt.

PARSONS, TALCOTT 1937 *The Structure of Social Action: A Study in Social Theory With Special Reference to a Group of Recent European Writers.* New York: McGraw-Hill.

RADCLIFFE-BROWN, A. R. 1952 *Structure and Function in Primitive Society: Essays and Addresses.* London: Cohen & West; Glencoe, Ill.: Free Press.

WOODGER, JOSEPH H. (1924) 1948 *Biological Principles: A Critical Study.* London: Routledge.

## II

### VARIETIES OF FUNCTIONAL ANALYSIS

For the past few decades functional analysis has been a major approach to understanding the organization of society. But at the same time it has become the target of very serious criticism and has been attacked as illogical, value-laden, and incapable of explaining anything. As one would expect, there is a serious problem of definition.

The term "functional analysis" or "structural-functionalism" has been applied to a great variety of approaches (Merton 1949; Firth 1955) that share only one common element: an interest in relating one part of a society or social system to another part or to some aspect of the whole. Within this variety, three aspects or types of functionalism can be distinguished: the first is based on the concepts and assumptions of sociology; the second, on the theoretical orientation that all major social patterns operate to maintain the integration or adaptation of the larger social system; the third, on a model of self-regulating or equilibrating systems. Most functional analyses contain all three aspects, but a clear description and evaluation of functionalism requires their separate consideration.

**A nondistinctive type.** The first type of functionalism consists in stressing sociological analyses as opposed to psychological or historical analyses. It is based on the assumption that the social traits existing in a society at a given time are interrelated in a systematic way and that ordered relationships can be discovered among "social facts" or social institutions without necessarily bringing in psychological or historical factors. This guiding assumption is accompanied by an implicit consensus on the important elements of social structure and by a developing set of hypotheses on their interrela-

tions. The crucial elements of social structure include: the composition and formation of groups, the organization of economics and religion, and the distribution of authority and prestige. These are the now-traditional concerns of sociology and social anthropology, the elements stressed by the major theorists from Émile Durkheim and Max Weber to A. R. Radcliffe-Brown, Talcott Parsons, and George C. Homans.

This type of functional analysis is most characteristic of the monographs of British social anthropologists and their adherents in the United States, and of the essays of sociologists, especially Kingsley Davis and Talcott Parsons, on some aspect of modern societies. The anthropologists typically present a careful description of a primitive society. The sociologists begin with a more impressionistic account of some institution in their own society. Then both go on to show how the various parts of the society or institution are interrelated, how the whole system "hangs together" despite some strains and inconsistencies. This type of work has led to many valuable hypotheses, such as those relating the isolated nuclear family and the modern economic system, or matrilocal residence and divorce rates.

Careful description and a search for general patterns are obviously necessary to social science, and, as Davis (1959) points out, functionalism has been an effective banner under which to fight for these qualities. In anthropology, functionalism successfully opposed the diffusionists and the empiricists, who tended to ignore general patterns, and the evolutionists and the rigid monocausalists, who tended to ignore the necessity of careful description.

However, as Davis also argues, this type of functionalism is essentially equivalent to sociological analysis, and it is misleading to distinguish it by a special name. The functionalist position that societies should be viewed as systems having definite structure or organization means primarily that the parts of a society are interrelated in some nonrandom way; i.e., that there are regular patterns and relationships, and, therefore, it is reasonable to try to construct a science of society. This position underlies all sociological analysis, although there is considerable disagreement on whether all parts of a society are interrelated or whether there are relatively autonomous subsystems. The elements of society that these functionalists consider are also not distinctive, nor are the kinds of relationships among elements. Functionalists do stress reciprocal relationships, but the typical monograph or essay also includes relationships based on similarity, one-way causation, fulfillment of a psychological or social need, etc. The problems and accomplishments of this kind of functional analysis are the same as the problems and accomplishments of sociology and social anthropology in general. Therefore, the discussion below will concern only the other two types of functionalism, both of which are distinct forms of analysis.

**Two distinctive types.** The first of the two remaining types of functional analysis will be called traditional functional analysis because it is the most widely used type. It is based on the theoretical orientation that all major social patterns operate to maintain the integration or adaptation of the larger system, and it is further distinguished by two crucial attributes, both of which make it very difficult to construct adequate explanations. First, a social pattern is explained by the effects or consequences of the pattern, and, second, these consequences must be beneficial and necessary to the proper functioning of society. The traditional approach includes those functionalists who focus on a few aspects of a society at a time and attempt to link one social pattern with one need and thereby "explain" the pattern. It also includes those who deal with a complex system of many elements and try to show how these elements are interrelated so as to form an adaptive and consistent system.

Traditional functional analysis can be contrasted with the second type: formal functionalism. This approach is concerned with homeostatic, or equilibrating, systems, and so with feedback and self-regulation. It abandons the two distinctive attributes of the traditional approach. The effects of a trait for some part of the system are used to explain that part and not to explain the trait; and there is no restriction on the kinds of consequences to be considered. They may or may not be beneficial or necessary to society. This approach is called "formal" because it does not include a theoretical orientation or a substantive hypothesis about empirical events. It is a model of kinds of relationships between elements, like a mathematical model.

The distinctiveness of traditional functionalism from other forms of analysis can be readily illustrated. For example, a traditional functionalist explanation of adolescent rebellion in the United States might point to the positive effects or functions of rebellion in securing independence from parents, which is crucial in our society. A non-functionalist explanation might focus on causes of rebellion, such as parental ambivalence about the desirability of being stable and mature. Formal functionalism would produce an interpretation different from both of the above, since it is concerned

with equilibrating or feedback systems and not with relationships of one-way effect or cause. It should be noted again that these different types of analysis are usually combined in practice. Thus Parsons' discussion of adolescence (1942) includes both of the arguments in the above example, as well as many more.

Functional analysis clearly is not distinct in some ways. It does not have any necessary monopoly on the empirical problems of analyzing total societies or comparing institutions cross-culturally, even though historically these fields have been dominated by functionalists. It is also not the case that complex, formal models of functional systems include some logically special types of propositions. Any model that can be communicated to social scientists can be reduced to a combination of simple statements such as: "if *a* then *b*," and "$a = (f)b$." Nor does traditional functional analysis involve a distinctive form of explanation; rather, it must be evaluated according to the general standards of adequate scientific explanations.

## Traditional functional analysis

**Scientific explanation.** The criteria of an adequate scientific explanation are extremely difficult to state precisely, and the philosophers of science continue to struggle with the problem. However, Nagel (1961), Hempel (1965), and other philosophers have stated the criteria in a way that seems close to the actual practice of scientists and that is based on the idea that explaining a statement necesarily involves deducing it from some more general statement or statements. This is the view of explanation that will be used here.

A scientific explanation consists of deducing the proposition to be explained (the explicandum) from some true or plausible general assumptions in conjunction with a statement of initial or antecedent conditions. The statement of initial conditions connects the explicandum to the assumptions. For example, if one wanted to explain the existence of witchcraft among the Navajo, using the two assumptions: (1) "if a society is subjected to externally imposed change then there will be a high level of aggression within the society," and (2) "if high aggression then witchcraft"; then the appropriate statement of initial conditions would be "imposed change has occurred among the Navajo."

The minimal requirements for an adequate explanation are (1) all the propositions must be clearly stated, that is, stated clearly enough to enable recognition of a negative case; (2) the assumptions must not be empirically false; (3) the statement of initial conditions must be true; and

(4) the explicandum must be derivable from the assumptions and initial conditions according to the rules of logic. Formulating an explanation is equivalent to constructing a theory, for if the assumptions are general it will be possible to deduce from them many verifiable propositions and not only the explicandum. In other words, the logical structure of explanation is identical with prediction if the prediction is based on a theory. In both cases one demonstrates that the phenomenon in question had to occur, given the assumptions. The only difference is that in prediction one starts with the assumption and proceeds to deduce testable propositions; in explanation one begins with a tested proposition and searches for some appropriate assumptions from which it can be deduced. Explanation, no less than prediction, requires precise propositions with clear empirical implications.

Traditional functional "explanations" usually fail to meet most of the minimal requirements of an adequate explanation. It is, of course, difficult to construct adequate explanations or theories in social science, regardless of the type of analysis that is used. However, the concepts and strategy of traditional functionalism create formidable problems, and the problems are especially tenacious. Many contemporary functional analyses contain the same errors that have been pointed out for decades in numerous papers (for an excellent presentation of the problems of functional analysis, see Durkheim 1895, chapter 5).

**Vacuous functional explanations.**  The problems of functional explanation are illustrated in Kluckhohn's sophisticated and complex interpretation of Navajo witchcraft (1944). He uses the three major types of functional arguments: (1) a vacuous explanation in terms of various unrelated, adaptive effects of witchcraft; (2) a more adequate explanation in terms of a functional prerequisite theory; and (3) an interpretation of witchcraft as part of an equilibrating system, using the model of a functional system.

Kluckhohn first explains Navajo witchcraft patterns simply by demonstrating that they have a variety of beneficial effects. He states that the major question (explicandum) is why witchcraft patterns have survived through a given period of time and that his basic postulate is "that no cultural forms survive unless they constitute responses which are adjustive or adaptive, in some sense, for the members of the society or for the society considered as a perduring unit" (1944, p. 46). This postulate is very similar to Merton's statement of the three basic postulates of functional analysis: "Substantially, these postulates hold first, that

standardized social activities or cultural items are functional for the *entire* social or cultural system; second, that *all* such social and cultural items fulfill sociological functions; and third, that these items are consequently *indispensable*" ([1949] 1957, p. 25). These postulates have been criticized for leading to a static, conservative orientation (Dahrendorf 1958); for if every pattern helps to maintain every other pattern, then the system will not generate conflict or change; and if every social pattern is indispensable, then it is clearly unwarranted and probably dangerous to change any pattern.

The postulates also lead to vacuous explanations like Kluckhohn's. After stating the major question and basic postulate, Kluckhohn proceeds to describe many adjustive and adaptive consequences of witchcraft. They include (1) expressing aggression outside the group, since accused witches are generally outsiders; (2) retarding the accumulation of wealth, since rich people are frequently accused; and (3) preventing adultery, since fear of witches keeps people from leaving their homes at night.

The form of this type of explanation is:

(1)  Social patterns persist if and only if they are adaptive (or functional or fulfill needs);
(2)  Pattern X is adaptive;
    Therefore, pattern X has persisted.

Such explanations are vacuous because the term "adaptive" or "needs" or "functional" is so loosely defined that all social patterns can be viewed as adaptive (or maladaptive). "Adaptive" is used to include anything that is beneficial to some groups or system. With a little imagination, one can show that any social pattern has adaptive consequences for some states of some systems and maladaptive consequences for some states of the same or other systems. Therefore, the presence or absence of any social pattern can be "explained" by this assumption, and any social pattern can be used to confirm or falsify the assumption. For example, one could focus on the maladaptive consequences of witchcraft and argue that since witchcraft has persisted and is maladaptive, the assumption is falsified.

This problem has been pointed out clearly in many critiques of functional analysis (Merton 1949; Nagel 1957); it is usually stated as the necessity for clear system reference or for defining "functional" or "adaptive" relative to specific states of specific systems. Kluckhohn is aware of the problem, and Merton discusses it explicitly and at length in his famous paper "Manifest and Latent Functions" (1949). Nonetheless, Kluckhohn, Merton in his explanation of city bosses (1949), and many less competent functionalists often point to the functions or beneficial effects of the phenomenon being considered and write as if this constituted an explanation of the phenomenon. These interpretations often contain valuable hypotheses about how the phenomenon is related to other parts of the society, but they typically ignore the maladaptive consequences of the phenomenon and hinder the development of theory by implying that the task of explanation has already been partially accomplished.

**The form of functional explanations.** Kluckhohn's second line of argument in explaining Navajo witchcraft is based on the beginnings of a theory of functional prerequisites which limits the relevant consequences of witchcraft to the effective management of anxiety and hostility. The outline of his argument, leaving out many complications, is (1) if a society is to survive as an integrated system, it must provide a relatively nondisruptive way of expressing or dealing with hostility and anxiety; (2) hostility and anxiety can be managed through witchcraft and related scapegoating behavior or through withdrawal, passivity, sublimation, or other functionally equivalent patterns; (3) because of various conditions of Navajo society, the functional equivalents of witchcraft cannot be the main ways of dealing with anxiety and hostility; and finally (4) Navajo society has survived. From these assumptions (1 and 2) and initial conditions (3 and 4), Kluckhohn derives his explicandum: Navajo witchcraft patterns have survived.

The form of the argument is represented in the following scheme:

(1) If a society survives ($A$), then hostility is managed ($B$);
(2) If hostility is managed ($B$), then witchcraft ($C$) or a functional equivalent ($D$) is present;
(3) The functional equivalents of witchcraft ($D$) are not present in Navajo society;
(4) Navajo society has survived ($A$);

Therefore, witchcraft is present in Navajo society ($C$).

Kluckhohn's argument here is one of the most sophisticated and precise attempts to construct a general functional explanation. It also illustrates one form of an adequate functional explanation,

which henceforth will be referred to as the paradigm of functional explanations: (1) if a system survives or is integrated, then a functional prerequisite is fulfilled; (2) if this prerequisite is fulfilled, then pattern X or its equivalent is present in the system; (3) the functional equivalents are not present in system $S$; (4) $S$ has survived or is integrated, and therefore X is present in $S$. There are other forms of explanation that use the basic concepts of functionalism, but this form seems to be implicit in most traditional functional analyses.

Let us first consider the simplest question: the logic of the explanation. Substituting symbols for the phrases in Kluckhohn's argument, it is apparent that the logic is sound: (1) if $A$ then $B$; (2) if $B$ then $C$ or $D$; (3) $D$ is false; (4) $A$ is true, and therefore $C$ is true. Hempel (1959) has argued that in the typical functional explanation the second assumption is usually stated in reverse. Ignoring the functional equivalent term $D$ for purposes of clarity, this means changing assumption (2) to "if $C$ then $B$." The argument is then logically incorrect and contains the fallacy of affirming the consequent: if $A$ then $B$; if $C$ then $B$ and $A$ is true; therefore $C$ is true. However, Hempel has misinterpreted the functionalists, which is easy to do given the discursive-essay style of most functional explanations.

In logic, the statement "if $A$ then $B$" or "$A \supset B$" is identical with the statement "if not–$B$ then not–$A$" (Kemeny, Snell & Thompson 1956). But when a functionalist says, "witchcraft results in the effective management of hostility," he does not mean "if witchcraft, then management of hostility." This would be identical to saying, "if hostility is not managed, then there will not be witchcraft," and most functionalists would not want to say that, since they would hypothesize that managing hostility depends on several factors in addition to witchcraft (and its functional equivalents). What they mean to say is "if witchcraft (or its equivalent) is not present, then hostility is not managed," which is logically identical with assumption (2) in the above paradigm. In other words, a given social pattern and its equivalents are typically interpreted as necessary but not sufficient conditions for fulfilling a functional prerequisite.

The major problems in Kluckhohn's explanation concern the basic concepts of functional theory: adaptation or survival, integration, functional prerequisites, and functional equivalents. An adequate theory or explanation requires clear definition of these concepts and direct or indirect verification of the assumptions in which they are interrelated.

However, this requirement is so difficult that almost all functionalists, including Kluckhohn, fail to meet it. It is so difficult that at this stage of the development of social science it might be advisable to abandon the attempt to construct functional theories or explanations at the total society level.

**System reference.** In Kluckhohn's first assumption, the crucial terms are survival and management of hostility. Neither term is defined precisely enough to allow discrimination between societies that have survived or have managed hostility and those that have not. Some of the problems involved in conceptualizing survival, integration, and functional prerequisites will be discussed in later sections.

The remaining term in the first assumption is "society," and here again we run into difficulties. Any theory must specify its scope—the units to which it applies and under what conditions, and "society" is a unit that is notoriously difficult to define. Kluckhohn himself states that it is questionable whether the Navajo as a whole constitute an integrated society, and a crucial part of his interpretation refers not to Navajo society, but to the consumption unit of several families. Witchcraft accusations are generally made outside the consumption unit but within Navajo society; therefore the statement that witchcraft manages hostility by directing aggression outside the group is true only of the consumption groups. Yet Kluckhohn's first assumption refers to a different unit—society. This shift invalidates his argument. His assumptions here are essentially: if a society survives $(A)$, then hostility is directed outside of the society $(B)$; if hostility is directed outside consumption groups $(C)$, then witchcraft is present $(D)$. It is impossible to deduce anything from these assumptions since $B$ and $C$ are not the same.

**Functional equivalents.** In Kluckhohn's second assumption we come to the most admirable part of his argument, for, unlike most functionalists, Kluckhohn explicitly faces the issue of functional equivalents. His inability to handle it adequately indicates the difficulty of the task.

The concept of functional equivalents is based on the idea that several social patterns can fill the same function or have the same consequence; to put it colloquially, "there's more than one way to skin a cat." The concept has been useful in suggesting the classification of social patterns on the basis of common function. Such classification often reveals important similarities among apparently different social patterns, for example, the similarities between witchcraft and racial prejudice

when both are viewed as ways of focusing aggression outside the group. However, the concept leads to great difficulties in functional explanations of a particular social pattern.

Kluckhohn's second assumption states that witchcraft or its functional equivalent is a necessary condition of managing hostility. The assumption is meaningful (directly or indirectly testable) only if it is possible to distinguish between patterns that are and are not equivalents of witchcraft. This requires listing all functional equivalents, or categorizing them, or stating their distinctive attributes. This must be done in such a way that the assumption is falsifiable—in this instance, so that it is logically possible for a society to manage hostility and not contain witchcraft or any equivalent pattern.

Kluckhohn's approach is to list the functional equivalents of witchcraft, and he states: "Withdrawal, passivity, sublimation, conciliation, flight and other responses" are alternative adjustive responses to hostile feelings (1944, p. 51). One problem with this and all lists is that there is no reason not to add more items, thereby making assumption (2) virtually unfalsifiable. Kluckhohn also attempts to identify the distinctive attributes of all the patterns on this list: they are all adjustive responses to hostility. But this only makes assumption (2) a tautology: if hostility is managed, then there will be witchcraft or some other way of managing hostility.

*The need for theory.* After defining the functional equivalents of a pattern, another task remains. In order to explain why a particular social pattern is present instead of another, functionally equivalent pattern, it is necessary to develop a set of assumptions or a theory that specifies which pattern will occur under which conditions. Kluckhohn implicitly states such theories as he eliminates the functional equivalents on his list on the basis of specific conditions of Navajo society or its environment. For example, he says that withdrawal is of limited effectiveness because Navajo "types of shelter and the needs for co-operation for economic ends sharply limit the privacy of individuals" (1944, p. 52). Kluckhohn is moving in the right direction here, but he is clearly a long way from formulating a clear and explicit theory about the conditions determining the occurrence of a particular social pattern.

It should be noted that if such theories are developed, functional explanations would be expanded to include the cause of origin of social patterns and the cause of their persistence (Bredemeier 1955). Most traditional functional explanations of a social pattern X refer to the causes of X only if there is a reciprocal relationship in which X causes itself, that is, if X has certain effects on Y that in turn cause X. In the paradigm of functional explanations, social pattern X is explained by its effects and not by its causes, "cause" here meaning the necessary or sufficient antecedent conditions for pattern X. But the paradigm can be expanded to include assumptions about the conditions determining the presence of a particular pattern, following Kluckhohn's procedure, and these assumptions would probably take the form of stating the causes of the origin and persistence of pattern X.

Such an expansion has the additional advantage of making it easier to include social change in traditional functional analyses. If one excepts the concept of functional differentiation (Parsons 1964), which has limited applicability, it must be admitted that traditional functional analysis is not very useful in dealing with change. However, with the specification of antecedent conditions determining particular social patterns, it would be possible to predict the change from one social pattern to another, functionally equivalent pattern.

Kluckhohn's explanation of Navajo witchcraft illustrates two major problems in traditional functional explanations: consistent system reference and functional equivalents. Other traditional explanations will be considered in the following discussion of the concepts of functional prerequisites, adaptation, and integration. We will return to Kluckhohn in the discussion of models of functional systems.

**Functional prerequisites.** The remaining problems in traditional functional explanations concern the definition of the concepts in the first assumption of such explanations: if a system survives or is integrated, then a certain functional prerequisite is fulfilled.

The best-known attempt to formulate a list of needs or prerequisites is that of Aberle and his co-workers (1950). They start with a definition of the survival of a society, which includes biological survival of its members and the absence of general apathy, and then state nine functional prerequisites, such as regulating affect and controlling disruptive behavior. The list is presented as a tentative set of cross-cultural categories, an improvement on the standard chapter titles in monographs.

This type of list is not very helpful in constructing functional explanations, because it does not limit the domain of functional prerequisites. The needs are so broad that almost any social process can be seen as contributing to at least one of them, and, being a list, there are few constraints on adding more needs. But a limited set of prerequisites is essential to functional explanation; without it, an imaginative investigator can "explain" any social pattern merely by describing some consequence or effect of the pattern and arguing that this consequence is a functional prerequisite.

There are two main approaches to arriving at a limited set of prerequisites. One is to construct a set of prerequisites and empirically test whether they have been fulfilled in surviving societies, while other conceivable prerequisites have not. The second approach is to devise a theory that includes an assumption specifying social prerequisites. The assumption would not be directly testable. It would have to be combined with other propositions stating the empirical implications of (1) asserting that all societies must meet these prerequisites or (2) classifying social patterns according to the prerequisites they meet.

Parsons (1961) is using the second approach when he asserts that all systems must meet the prerequisites of latent pattern maintenance, integration, goal attainment, and adaptation. He is not making an empirical statement but is proposing that it would be fruitful to categorize and interpret social structures in terms of their contributions to these functions. His system is not directly useful in explaining social patterns because, as yet, he has not developed a clear set of propositions that specify the empirical relevance of placing a structure in one of the four categories as opposed to another. This crucial step was made in Bales's general theory of functional prerequisites (1950). He specifies two basic functions—adaptation and integration—and supplements this nonempirical assertion with a complex set of propositions about the empirical processes that accompany each function. For example, adaptation is associated with increasing division of labor, stratification, and formality, while the opposite characterizes integration. This suggests specific predictions about the attributes of organizations oriented to adaptation, or of task leaders as opposed to expressive leaders, or of small groups in the adaptive phase. Although Bales's theory still awaits precise formulation, it is a rare example of a theory that is both general and functional and that leads to adequate explanations or precise predictions [*see* INTERACTION, *article on* INTERACTION PROCESS ANALYSIS].

**Adaptation and integration.** The difficulty in defining the prerequisites for the adaptation or integration of social systems is based in part on the ambiguity of the concepts "adaptation" (or "survival") and "integration." These concepts are crucial to the first assumption in the paradigm of functional explanations: if a system survives or is integrated, then certain functional prerequisites are fulfilled. The assumption requires a definition that will discriminate between systems that are adapted or integrated and those that are not; and this has proved to be difficult. The concept of adaptation is further complicated by its association with evolutionary theory.

The difficulty in defining adaptation has long been recognized (Radcliffe-Brown 1952). Adaptation may be equated with physical survival, but this runs into the problem that societies, unlike organisms, rarely fail to survive in the sense of keeping enough of their members alive and together. Most recorded cases of the physical death of societies are the direct result of hostile action by overwhelmingly powerful outsiders who are new to the environment, and this is not the kind of situation with which functionalists are usually concerned. Since almost all societies survive, barring sudden catastrophe, it is impossible to test a statement of the form "X is necessary for survival" if X is universal. It is also impossible to test a statement of the form "$X_1$ is necessary for the survival of social system $S_1$," if $X_1$ has always been present in $S_1$.

Adaptation or survival may also be defined as maintenance of the social organization or structural continuity. Survival in this sense is by no means universal; in fact it might be difficult to find a society that has survived over the last century, i.e., one that has not undergone basic change. This leads to new problems, because functional explanations of the persistence of social patterns require the assumption that the system has survived (statement 3 in the paradigm). Precise definitions of "stability" or "structural continuity" would have to be worked out, and such explanations would be limited to societies that fit the definition of "stable." Alternatively, adaptation can be defined as ensuring high reproduction rates following the biologists' revision of Darwin (Simpson 1949). This definition has the advantage of discriminating among societies, being easy to measure, and making it possible to distinguish different degrees of adaptation, as opposed to the all-or-nothing criteria of physical survival. These two later definitions or others probably could be formulated precisely and could be used in specifying the prerequisites of adaptation. If the problem of functional equivalents could be solved, it would then be possible to explain social pat-

terns according to the paradigm of functional explanations.

However, many interpretations in terms of adaptation do not follow the paradigm. They often use the form of argument discussed in the section on vacuous explanations (patterns persist only if they are adaptive; pattern X is adaptive; therefore X persists). This type of argument is not vacuous if "adaptive" is precisely defined, and some investigators seem to be moving toward a fairly precise definition which equates "adaptation" with "maintaining adequate levels of nutrition and health for most members of the society." Harris' interpretation of the sacred cows of India (1965) and other recent papers on economics and ecology in primitive societies (Leeds & Vayda 1965; Suttles 1960) are examples of this kind of argument, in which a social pattern is interpreted by showing how it helps to ensure an adequate food supply. These interpretations are unobjectionable if they are viewed as illustrations of a specific hypothesis, such as Harris' hypothesis that here is a "cross-cultural tendency to maximize production of food" (1959, p. 194). However, the interpretations are often presented as if they were explaining a social pattern in terms of the assumption that "social patterns persist only if they are adaptive." Adequate explanations require plausible assumptions, and the plausibility of this assumption rests on shaky grounds.

First, the assumption is plausible if one accepts the idea that there is a process of selection of the fittest social patterns or societies. But I doubt that many social scientists imagine, for example, that some early societies developed the family and therefore survived, while others did not and therefore died out, or that some Northwest Coast Indians developed the potlatch and survived, while the others became extinct. One alternative and somewhat more plausible notion is that some groups developed distinct methods of socialization, or the potlatch, and these groups reproduced faster than the others and eventually dominated the society. However, I know of no data that clearly demonstrate that either of these assumed processes ever occurred except in the few situations where extinction through disease or military aggression was imminent. Another alternative idea is that adaptive social traits are more widespread than less adaptive traits because the weak tend to imitate the strong (Dore 1961). Social patterns may diffuse to weaker groups from groups with more resources and power, that is, with patterns that are more adaptive.

The assumption that only adaptive traits persist is also plausible if restricted to the manifest functions of social patterns, that is, to the effects of the pattern that are recognized and intended by members of the society (Merton 1949). If the decision makers of a society are aware of the adaptive value of a social pattern, this will probably influence whether they want to maintain the pattern. However, the crucial variables here are the decision makers' beliefs about the adaptive or integrative consequences of the pattern. These events are a subset of the class of goal-oriented behavior; people behave so as to maximize certain goals and values, and one of these goals is usually successful adaptation to the environment. In these cases, it would be better to abandon functional terminology for a more cognitive, actor-oriented approach.

The concept of integration is just as problematic as that of survival. Integration is defined in a wide variety of ways and often masks value judgments or unnecessarily complicates a clear nonfunctional statement. This section will focus on the difficulties in defining integration so that it can be used in traditional functional explanations. Many analyses involving integration or adaptation supplement or replace the traditional approach with the use of models of self-regulating systems, and this aspect of functionalism will be considered later in the discussion of formal functionalism.

There are two major approaches to defining integration. One draws on system theory and defines integration in terms of interdependence and frequent interaction among the members of a bounded unit. Although the approach leads to a relatively precise and manageable definition, it excludes many aspects of the intuitive notion of integration. The second approach draws on the ideas of congruency and fit or the absence of conflict, strain, or anxiety. The notion of fit is extremely vague. The statement that pattern $X$ fits with pattern $Y$ means only that there is *some* relationship between $X$ and $Y$. The type of relationship is often left unspecified.

The typical functionalist approach to the concept of integration is to equate fit with lack of conflict. Four kinds of definitions in terms of absence of conflict can be distinguished. The first defines integration as logical–meaningful consistency among social patterns (Sorokin [1937–1941] 1962, vol. 1, pp. 15, 23). Integration means that similar themes, values, or principles are used in all spheres of social life. One ambiguity in this definition is the meaning of absence of integration. It could mean conflict within the cultural system; however, many functionalists seem to mean conflict within individuals, and they make the dubious assumption

that logical inconsistency among the beliefs will produce psychological conflict. The second definition of integration focuses on the absence of aggression and exploitation of the powerless among members of a social system. An integrated system is marked by cooperation, consensus on mutual rights and duties, and loyalties that crosscut the subgroups within the system. The third definition focuses on the absence of conflicting demands on individuals as to the appropriate behavior or feelings in a specific situation; and the fourth definition concerns the fit between an individual's motivation and the behavior required by the social system.

The obvious general problem in using any of these definitions is that a functional explanation must assume that the society being considered is integrated. This is proposition (3) in the argument: (1) if the system is integrated, then need $N$ is filled; (2) if $N$, then pattern $X$; and (3) the system is integrated; therefore $X$. This limitation is implicitly recognized by functionalists, for they tend to shift to nonfunctional explanations when interpreting social patterns that result in increased conflict. One example of such a shift is Parsons' discussion of the female role in the United States (1942).

It seems very unlikely that any society or large social system is perfectly integrated, regardless of which definition is used. Therefore, integration needs to be defined in a relative way: if a system has $Y$ amount of integration, then $N$ will be fulfilled. This is not an impossible task but a difficult one. It requires extensive theoretical and empirical work on the distribution and implications of different levels of integration, the prerequisites for a given level of integration, and the functionally equivalent social patterns that fulfill each prerequisite. Until some such specification of integration is made, the term cannot be used in explanations [*see* INTEGRATION, *article on* SOCIAL INTEGRATION].

**Alternative approaches.** Traditional functionalism has been defined as those analyses that use certain concepts (adaptation, integration, functional prerequisites, and equivalents) and that explicitly or implicitly use the paradigm of functional explanation in which social patterns are explained by their effects. Because of the many problems discussed above, few functionalists succeed in formulating adequate explanations or theories. If some of the concepts are abandoned and the paradigm is changed, then alternative types of analysis are revealed that have a better prospect of leading to adequate explanations. Although some of these alternatives are frequently used, they are not labeled as "functional analysis" as often as the traditional approach.

One frequently used alternative is to turn functional explanations around, that is, to reverse the explicans and the explicandum in the paradigm of explanation so that phenomena are explained by their causes, not by their effects or functions. Instead of explaining a social pattern by deducing it from the assumption that the society has survived, one explains the survival of the society by the patterns whose effect is to ensure survival. For example, the statement that "witchcraft lessens in-group aggression" is used to explain rates of aggression, not witchcraft. This approach, combined with a focus on systems other than total societies, includes studies of the prerequisites for the survival of marriages, utopias, associations, or other social systems. It also includes studies of the prerequisites for the structural continuity of social systems, that is, of the conditions for maintaining a certain type of social organization in a specified environment. This is the approach described by Levy in his outline of "structural–functional requisite analysis" (1952, pp. 34 ff.).

A second possible change of traditional functionalism, as mentioned above, is to consider smaller systems under specified conditions rather than total societies in general. One great advantage in this procedure is that systems such as therapy groups, unions, or lineages often fail to survive or seem to have low levels of integration; therefore, statements about the prerequisites for survival or integration can be tested. In addition, the possible functional prerequisites and equivalents are probably more limited, and, finally, there would be less difficulty in maintaining consistent system reference because there are fewer subsystems than in a society.

A more radical change is to abandon the focus on adaptation and integration and to consider the prerequisites of any state of a system—such states as high suicide rates, for instance, or high or low levels of in-group aggression. With this revision, we have eliminated the distinguishing attributes of functional analysis: explaining patterns by their beneficial (adaptive or integrative) effects. Functionalism so defined includes all analyses of the prerequisites, conditions, or determinants of any attribute or state of human behavior. Very little information is transmitted by labeling all these analyses as "functional," and very few social scientists use the term in this way.

However, there is a type of functionalism that does not involve explaining patterns by their bene-ficial effects and is a distinct form of analysis. This is formal functionalism, which is distinguished by the use of models of self-regulating or functional systems. Traditional functional analyses contain many examples of such systems: of reciprocal relationships, of one pattern varying so as to maintain another within a given range, and of complex feedbacks and causal chains that involve many parts of a system. But some traditional functional explanations do not utilize this type of model. For example, the explanation of the incest taboo in terms of its function of creating alliances among families, or the explanation of rites of passage by their function of reducing conflict between old and new roles, does not involve reciprocal or self-regulating relationships. Therefore, the theoretical orientation of traditional functionalism and the model of self-regulating or functional systems should be kept distinct.

The assumption that models of functional systems fit society is the basis of some of the concepts and procedures of traditional functional analysis. The stress on latent functions—effects that are unintended and unrecognized—is based in part on the assumption that models of complex, self-regulating systems apply to many social systems. Therefore, a change in one social pattern may affect seemingly unrelated patterns or, because of compensating changes in other social patterns, may have effects that are opposite from those intended —or no effects at all. Another instance is the functionalist postulate that all social patterns "are functional for the *entire* social or cultural system" (Merton [1949] 1957, p. 25). This is another way of saying that the whole social system forms some sort of self-regulating system. These are premature judgments about the extent to which models of functional or self-regulating systems accurately represent the relationships found in social systems. The applicability of the models is an empirical question for which the relevant data have not been collected.

### Formal functionalism

Formal functionalism consists in the attempt to construct models that describe how the units of a system are interrelated so as to maintain each other or some other state of the system. In contrast to traditional functionalism, it contains no theoretical orientation and has no empirical content. The models must be supplemented by theory and research that specify the empirical units or variables that correspond to the abstract elements in the models.

As an illustration of the use of such models,

Kluckhohn's analysis of Navajo witchcraft is useful again. Kluckhohn supplements his structural analysis with an examination of changes over time. He describes the deprivation and anxiety of the Navajo during their confinement at Fort Sumner and several decades later, during a period of lesser stress that was caused by the livestock reduction program. He notes that warfare was impossible for the Navajo after Fort Sumner, that witchcraft accusations and executions were most frequent shortly after Fort Sumner, and that accusations also increased after the inception of the livestock program. In his interpretation, Kluckhohn assumes, first, that deprivation and frustration cause increased hostile feelings, and, second, that these impulses will cause in-group aggression unless the hostility is directed outside the group; warfare and witchcraft are viewed as social patterns that direct aggression to outsiders. Given these assumptions, the changes in frustration, hostility, aggression, and witchcraft can be accurately represented as a self-regulating system directed to maintaining a low level of in-group aggression. When the environment (the United States government) imposes increased frustration, hostile impulses increase, but this is followed by increased witchcraft accusations, given the impossibility of warfare, and this aggression to outsiders reduces hostile impulses back to a level where they no longer threaten the maintenance of low in-group aggression.

**Nagel's model.**    The model used in Kluckhohn's analysis has been precisely described by Nagel (1957). Starting with Merton's article "Manifest and Latent Functions" (1949), Nagel rigorously describes the model that seems to be implicit in functional analysis in the social sciences.

A functional system, according to Nagel's definition, is made up of two types of variables: $G$'s and state coordinates. $G$ is the property of the system that is maintained or is stable. State coordinates determine the presence or absence of $G$ and may include parts of the system's environment. The values of the state coordinates vary to such an extent that the maintenance of $G$ is threatened, but when one exceeds the "safe" limits for $G$, the other(s) compensates and $G$ is maintained. Such a system of $G$ and state coordinates may be called functional with respect to $G$, and the state coordinates may be described as having the function of maintaining $G$.

For example, a small task-oriented group could be treated as a functional system (Bales 1950). Let $G$ be the solution of the group's task or problem. Let the state coordinates be task-oriented ac-

tivity and emotionally supportive activity. If these three variables can be usefully treated as a functional system, then: (1) problem solution is dependent on task-oriented activity and emotionally supportive activity; (2) at certain times, there will be such a preponderance of task-oriented activity that problem solution will be threatened because of decreased motivation or resentment over following others' suggestions—at these times emotionally supportive activity will increase, and problem solution will no longer be threatened; (3) at certain times, there will be such a preponderance of emotionally supportive activity that problem solution will be threatened. At these times task-oriented activity will increase to maintain problem solution or $G$.

By definition, more than one state of the system leads to maintenance of $G$. Thus, in the preceding example, eventual problem solution might result both from initially high task-oriented activity and low supportive activity, followed by increased supportive activity, and from initially low task-oriented activity and high supportive activity, followed by increased task activity. In a functional system there is more than one combination of the values of certain parts of the system which will result in the same trait or will have the same consequences (maintenance of $G$). This is one way of stating the notion of functional equivalents.

The other crucial elements in Nagel's model concern the limitations of the variation of state coordinates. Three kinds of limits are relevant. First, there are the limits dictated by physical reality. For example, the amount of interaction in a given period cannot exceed the maximum number of acts possible in that time period. Second, within the limits of physical reality there are limits determined by the definition of the system under consideration. If a property is used to define a system, one cannot analyze conditions under which this property disappears. The third and most important set of limits are those beyond which compensation is impossible and $G$ ceases to exist. The potential stability of a given $G$ in a specific functional system can be expressed in terms of the discrepancy between two of these sets of limits: the possible variation for each state coordinate and the limits of variation within which compensation by other state coordinates will occur. $G$ becomes less stable as the discrepancy between these two ranges increases.

It should be noted that, contrary to the strategy of traditional functionalism, stability of $G$ is not *assumed*. The traditional approach is to assume the stability of $G$ (integration or survival) and explain state coordinates in terms of their efficiency in maintaining $G$; states of the system are explained by their effects. In Nagel's model, the stability or disappearance of $G$ is explained by the extent to which state coordinates compensate for each other's variation; states of the system are explained by their causes. A rough definition of "cause" is being used here: $A$ causes $B$ if the occurrence of $B$ depends on the previous occurrence of $A$.

Some functionalists have suggested that the notion of cause is not applicable to complex social systems, but this seems to mean only that social patterns are often caused by a complex set of interrelated factors and not by one simple factor. For instance, in the small group example, task solution depends on: (1) a certain amount of task-oriented activity; (2) emotionally supportive activity; (3) mechanisms which cause a switch from one type of activity to the other when one type is dangerously low; and perhaps additionally on (4) some reciprocal relationship whereby group perception of progress in solving the task is necessary to maintain the two types of activity. This is a complex system, but these four factors can be isolated as the determinants or causes of task solution. The unwillingness to use the term "cause" often indicates only that the analysis is incomplete and that it is not yet possible to clearly define the relevant parts of the system and to specify the direction and magnitude of the relationships among these parts.

To summarize Nagel's model, a functional system is one that satisfies the following conditions: (1) the system can be analyzed into a set of interdependent variables or parts; (2) the values of these variables determine whether or not a certain property $G$ will occur in the system; (3) there are limits on the variation of state coordinates such that variation within the limits is followed by compensating variation of other state coordinates, and $G$ is maintained; (4) variation beyond these limits is not compensated for by other state coordinates, and $G$ disappears.

The type of analysis suggested by Nagel's formalization would probably avoid many problems of traditional functional analysis. As in any formal model, this one specifies the entities that must be clearly and consistently defined: the system, goal state, state coordinates, and the limits on their variation. Any state of any system might be viewed as a $G$ state in a functional system; therefore the problematic concepts of survival and integration are not necessary, although they could be used as the $G$ state (see, for example, the series of analyses

in Leeds & Vayda 1965, in which the $G$ state is the survival of the population in the face of variation in the environment). The model also encompasses various kinds of change: (1) goal states that are moving equilibria; (2) compensating changes in state coordinates; (3) compensating changes in subsystems that are treated as state coordinates of a higher level system; and (4) disappearance of $G$ resulting from state coordinates exceeding the limits of compensation (Cancian 1960–1961).

The contribution of formal functionalism to the explanation of social patterns is quite different from that of traditional functionalism, because a formal model lacks substantive propositions and therefore, by itself, cannot explain anything. If the correspondence between the model and the parts of a specific system are demonstrated, this would constitute, at the least, a precise description of the system. The description might also be called a "little theory" (Cancian 1965, chapter 13)—a "theory" because it would explain and predict how variance in one part of the system would affect other parts of the system, and a "little theory" because the propositions would be limited to one specific system. In order to construct a general theory or explanation, it would be necessary to add an assumption stating that the model fit a certain class of systems, of which the specific system was a member.

*Specification of functional equivalents.* The major problem left unresolved in this model is that of functional equivalents. An example illustrates the difficulty. Assume that one is investigating the system of relationships between North American college students and their parents and that one attempts to explain independence from parents ($G$) by the state coordinates of peer-organized rebellion against authority, communication with parents, and other variables. How would one deal with the different types of organized rebellion, such as panty raids, burning draft cards, or picketing for civil rights? The approach suggested by the model would be to consider only the primary function of these activities for the goal state of independence. Panty raids, burning draft cards, etc., would be ranked according to the degree of rebellion involved, and all other differences among the activities would be ignored. The advantage of this method is that it results in a general explanation that includes college students participating in various types of peer-organized rebellion. Note, however, that the idea of functional equivalents then has no special meaning; it merely indicates that a general variable takes various empirical forms. For example, reinforcement can take the form of food or water.

As it is usually used, "functional equivalents" does have a special meaning. There is often an implicit assumption that if one social pattern disappeared, a functionally equivalent pattern would appear or would be more likely to appear. This aspect of functional equivalents can be dealt with by treating the equivalent patterns as a subsystem, with the *G* of fulfilling the function of the patterns. In this subsystem, as one rebellious activity decreases, some other activity increases so as to maintain peer-organized rebellion, *if* the subsystem is a functional system with respect to rebellion. An examination of this subsystem would indicate the conditions (limits of variance) under which a functional equivalent would take the place of a disappearing activity. The problem of predicting whether a specific rebellious activity would be maintained within certain limits could be handled by considering the subsystem in which the *G* state is that activity and the state coordinates are the variables that maintain the activity.

**Alternative models.** Every functional system must contain certain minimal attributes: (1) variable *A* that is regulated or maintained within a range; (2) variable *B* that does the regulating; (3) a mechanism that communicates the variation of *A* to *B*. These minimal requirements are exemplified by the famous system: room temperature–furnace–thermostat, and by various systems in the social science area (Lennard & Bernstein 1960). Note that the existence of feedback, or reciprocal or mutual causation between *A* and *B*, is not enough. The feedback must be of a special kind; it must operate so as to maintain at least one of the variables within a given range. For example, according to many observers, the system of "juvenile crime–reform school" is not a functional system with respect to maintaining low crime rates. There is a reciprocal relationship; reform school does feed back to crime rates, but its effect appears to increase crime.

This minimal functional system can be elaborated in many ways, resulting in alternative functional models. The primary alternative to Nagel's model is based on changing his notion of a *G* state. Nagel's system is hierarchical, that is, it contains several variables that interact so as to maintain some state of the system within a given range (*G*), and the effect of *G* on these variables is not considered. In the alternative, horizontal model, the effects of the variation in *G* on the state coordinates are included in the analysis. Both *G* and the state coordinates vary so as to maintain each other within a certain range; therefore there is no reason to dis-

criminate between the two types of variables. There are many illustrations of such systems in the area of complementary roles or interpersonal relations. Thus, an authoritarian professor and a dependent student or a sadistic–masochistic couple often maintain each other in their respective roles.

Within the general framework of a hierarchical or horizontal model, many specific varieties of functional systems can be constructed. The system may be simple and include only the minimal attributes of a functional system, or it may be very complex and contain many parts and subsystems, like McCleery's description of a prison system (Barton & Anderson 1961) or Parsons' model of the social system (1961).

The system may operate so as to maintain one, or several, or all of its components within a given range. Systems also differ in the amount of variation necessary to set off compensating processes, in the limits beyond which compensation is impossible, and in the time required for compensation. When it does occur, the compensation may be too much or too little or out of phase (Scientific American 1955). Compensation for the variance of one component may take the form of pushing back that component within a range that is less threatening to the system, or it may consist of a proportional change in other components. There are many possible complexities and variations in functional systems, some of which are described in the literature, especially in the fields of economics, cybernetics, and systems engineering.

**Using models.** There are two major procedures for utilizing functional models in constructing theories or general explanations. One approach is to begin with a careful investigation of a single system. After describing the major components of the system and how they are interrelated, the model implicit in the description can be examined. Some previously developed model may fit the description and produce new statements about the system, or it may be necessary to construct a model. The next step is to verify the "fit" by examining the particular system over time, observing variations in the components, and seeing if there is, in fact, compensation that maintains some components within a given range. The final step is to try to generalize this "little theory" to other systems by examining the boundary conditions or parameters of the systems and by restating the components in more general terms. An example of this approach is Sweet's analysis of how bedouin camping units maintain a certain size camel herd by raiding, migration, splitting up the social unit, and other means (1965). Her description could probably be restated as a theory of the bedouin camel complex, that is, as a limited set of propositions about herd size, raiding frequency, etc., and the relations between them. This theory could be tested against the historical record of bedouin behavior. If verified, it might be possible to restate the "little theory" in more general terms, so that, given certain conditions, it applies to camel herders in general, or pastoral peoples, or people dependent on material goods whose availability fluctuates widely.

Another approach is to start with an abstract theory about a general class of phenomena that are interrelated so as to form a functional system. This procedure is exemplified in the research on balance theory in social psychology (Heider 1958). The basic idea in the theory is that individuals will vary their sentiments and evaluations so as to maintain a balanced state. Thus, if two individuals like each other and one of them likes a third person but the other does not, then the individuals will move into a balanced state, that is, they will both come to like or dislike the third person, or they will change their feelings about each other. The relationships among components in this theory correspond to the relationships in mathematical graph theory, and the application of this mathematical model has made the theory more precise and has yielded new propositions (Berger et al. 1962).

These two approaches start with a specific or general empirical system and then examine the model or set of relationships in the system. An alternative would be to start with a model and then search for some empirical systems that fit it. This approach would be much less likely to succeed than the first two because the investigator might not encounter any phenomenon of interest that fits the model, and then the effort of constructing the model would be completely wasted. However, there are some guidelines for locating empirical systems that operate like functional systems.

A primary indicator of the applicability of a functional model is the persistence of a social pattern despite forces that tend to destroy the pattern. For example, the apparent persistence of European gypsies suggests the presence of compensating processes, as does the persistence, despite reform movements, of deviant patterns such as city bosses or prostitution. Of course, it may be that such patterns persist because of some constant, powerful factor or factors, but it would probably be fruitful to try to analyze the persistence in terms of a functional model. Another relevant attribute is the presence of inherently runaway processes that are kept within limits. Some of the social processes that might increase indefinitely, but often do not, are the exploi-

tation of followers by powerful leaders or the rejection of competing loyalties by a sexually attracted couple (Slater 1963). Still another attribute is the presence of reciprocal relationships—that is, of regular sequences of social patterns that return to the point of origin. The most obvious class of phenomena in this category is self–other patterns, or complementary roles, but reciprocal relationships also occur in large social systems, as shown by Leach's analysis of cyclic change between two political systems in Burma (1954). These various attributes provide clues as to the applicability of a functional model, but in every case the appropriateness of a functional model and the fit of different types of models are questions that must be empirically investigated.

The usefulness of models in general cannot be disputed, and the importance of constructing models will surely increase as social scientists attempt to deal with complex systems of variables in a precise manner and as they shift from monocausal theories to the notion of interdependent systems. The usefulness of models of functional systems in particular depends on the extent to which the phenomena investigated by social scientists exhibit equilibrating or self-maintaining processes. Formal functionalism is based on the most valuable part of the research strategy of functional analysis: an attempt to view behavior patterns as mutually reinforcing parts of an equilibrating system. Whether or not this strategy will succeed in yielding general and verified theories is an empirical question that will not be settled until this strategy is given a thorough trial.

FRANCESCA M. CANCIAN

[*Directly related are the entries* INTEGRATION; INTERACTION, *article on* INTERACTION PROCESS ANALYSIS; SYSTEMS ANALYSIS. *Other relevant material may be found in* MODELS, MATHEMATICAL; SIMULATION; SOCIAL STRUCTURE; SOCIOLOGY, *article on* THE DEVELOPMENT OF SOCIOLOGICAL THOUGHT; *and in the biographies of* DURKHEIM; HENDERSON; MALINOWSKI; RADCLIFFE-BROWN; WEBER, MAX.]

BIBLIOGRAPHY

ABERLE, DAVID F. et al. 1950 The Functional Prerequisites of a Society. *Ethics* 60:100–111.

BALES, ROBERT F. 1950 *Interaction Process Analysis: A Method for the Study of Small Groups.* Reading, Mass.: Addison-Wesley.

BARTON, ALLEN H.; and ANDERSON, BO 1961 Change in an Organizational System: Formalization of a Qualitative Study. Pages 400–418 in Amitai Etzioni (editor), *Complex Organizations: A Sociological Reader.* New York: Holt.

BERGER, JOSEPH et al. 1962 *Types of Formalization in Small-group Research.* Boston: Houghton Mifflin.

BLACK, MAX (editor) 1962 *The Social Theories of Talcott Parsons: A Critical Examination.* Englewood Cliffs, N.J.: Prentice-Hall.

BREDEMEIER, HARRY C. 1955 The Methodology of Functionalism. *American Sociological Review* 20:173–180.

BUCKLEY, WALTER 1957 Structural–Functional Analysis in Modern Sociology. Pages 236–259 in Howard Becker and Alvin Boskoff (editors), *Modern Sociological Theory in Continuity and Change.* New York: Dryden.

CANCIAN, FRANCESCA M. 1960–1961 Functional Analysis of Change. *American Sociological Review* 25:818–827; 26:930–931.

CANCIAN, FRANK 1965 *Economics and Prestige in a Maya Community: The Religious Cargo System in Zinacantán.* Stanford Univ. Press.

COLLINS, PAUL W. 1965 Functional Analyses in the Symposium *Man, Culture, and Animals.* Pages 271–282 in Anthony Leeds and Andrew P. Vayda (editors), *Man, Culture, and Animals: The Role of Animals in Human Ecological Adjustments.* Washington: American Association for the Advancement of Science.

DAHRENDORF, RALF 1958 Out of Utopia: Toward a Reorientation of Sociological Analysis. *American Journal of Sociology* 64:115–127.

DAVIS, KINGSLEY 1959 The Myth of Functional Analysis as a Special Method in Sociology and Anthropology. *American Sociological Review* 24:757–772.

DAVIS, KINGSLEY; and MOORE, WILBERT E. 1945 Some Principles of Stratification. *American Sociological Review* 10:242–249.

DORE, RONALD P. 1961 Function and Cause. *American Sociological Review* 26:843–853.

DURKHEIM, ÉMILE (1895) 1958 *The Rules of Sociological Method.* 8th ed. Edited by George E. G. Catlin. Glencoe, Ill.: Free Press. → First published as *Les règles de la méthode sociologique.*

FALLDING, HAROLD 1963 Functional Analysis in Sociology. *American Sociological Review* 28:5–13.

FIRTH, RAYMOND 1955 Function. *Yearbook of Anthropology* [1955]:237–258.

GOLDSCHMIDT, WALTER 1966 *Comparative Functionalism.* Berkeley and Los Angeles: Univ. of California Press.

GOULDNER, ALVIN W. 1960 The Norm of Reciprocity: A Preliminary Statement. *American Sociological Review* 25:161–178.

HARRIS, MARVIN 1959 The Economy Has No Surplus? *American Anthropologist* New Series 61:185–199.

HARRIS, MARVIN 1965 The Myth of the Sacred Cow. Pages 217–228 in Anthony Leeds and Andrew P. Vayda (editors), *Man, Culture, and Animals: The Role of Animals in Human Ecological Adjustments.* Washington: American Association for the Advancement of Science.

HEIDER, FRITZ 1958 *The Psychology of Interpersonal Relations.* New York: Wiley.

HEMPEL, CARL G. 1959 The Logic of Functional Analysis. Pages 271–307 in Llewellyn Gross (editor), *Symposium on Sociological Theory.* Evanston, Ill.: Row, Peterson.

HEMPEL, CARL G. 1965 *Aspects of Scientific Explanation, and Other Essays in the Philosophy of Science.* New York: Free Press.

HOMANS, GEORGE C. 1964 Bringing Men Back In. *American Sociological Review* 29:809–818.

JOHNSON, HARRY M. 1960 *Sociology: A Systematic Introduction.* New York: Harcourt.

KEMENY, JOHN G.; SNELL, J. LAURIE; and THOMPSON, GERALD L. (1957) 1962 *Introduction to Finite Mathematics.* Englewood Cliffs, N.J.: Prentice-Hall.

KLUCKHOHN, CLYDE 1944 *Navaho Witchcraft.* Harvard University, Peabody Museum of American Archaeology and Ethnology, Papers, Vol. 22, No. 2. Cambridge, Mass.: The Museum.

LEACH, EDMUND R. 1954 *Political Systems of Highland Burma: A Study of Kachin Social Structure.* London School of Economics and Political Science; Cambridge, Mass.: Harvard Univ. Press.

LEEDS, ANTHONY; and VAYDA, ANDREW P. (editors) 1965 *Man, Culture, and Animals: The Role of Animals in Human Ecological Adjustments.* Publication No. 78. Washington: American Association for the Advancement of Science.

LENNARD, HENRY L.; and BERNSTEIN, ARNOLD 1960 *The Anatomy of Psychotherapy: Systems of Communication and Expectation.* New York: Columbia Univ. Press.

LEVY, MARION J. 1952 *The Structure of Society.* Princeton Univ. Press.

MALINOWSKI, BRONISLAW 1931 Culture. Volume 4, pages 621–645 in *Encyclopaedia of the Social Sciences.* New York: Macmillan.

MARTINDALE, DON (editor) 1965 *Functionalism in the Social Sciences: The Strength and Limits of Functionalism in Anthropology, Economics, Political Science, and Sociology.* Philadelphia: American Academy of Political and Social Science.

MERTON, ROBERT K. (1949) 1957 Manifest and Latent Functions. Pages 21–84 in Robert K. Merton, *Social Theory and Social Structure.* Rev. & enl. ed. Glencoe, Ill.: Free Press.

MILLS, THEODORE M. 1959 Equilibrium and the Processes of Deviance and Control. *American Sociological Review* 24:671–679.

NAGEL, ERNEST 1957 A Formalization of Functionalism. Pages 247–283 in Ernest Nagel, *Logic Without Metaphysics, and Other Essays in the Philosophy of Science.* Glencoe, Ill.: Free Press.

NAGEL, ERNEST 1961 *The Structure of Science: Problems in the Logic of Scientific Explanation.* New York: Harcourt.

PARSONS, TALCOTT 1942 Age and Sex in the Social Structure of the United States. *American Sociological Review* 7:604–616.

PARSONS, TALCOTT (1961) 1965 An Outline of the Social System. Volume 1, pages 30–79 in Talcott Parsons et al. (editors), *Theories of Society: Foundations of Modern Sociological Theory.* New York: Free Press.

PARSONS, TALCOTT 1964 Evolutionary Universals in Society. *American Sociological Review* 29:339–357.

RADCLIFFE-BROWN, A. R. (1952) 1961 *Structure and Function in Primitive Society: Essays and Addresses.* London: Cohen & West; Glencoe, Ill.: Free Press.

RADCLIFFE-BROWN, A. R. 1957 *A Natural Science of Society.* Glencoe, Ill.: Free Press.

SCIENTIFIC AMERICAN 1955 *Automatic Control.* New York: Simon & Schuster.

SIMPSON, GEORGE G. (1949) 1961 *The Meaning of Evolution: A Study of the History of Life and Its Significance for Man.* New Haven: Yale Univ. Press.

SLATER, PHILIP E. 1963 On Social Regression. *American Sociological Review* 28:339–364.

SOROKIN, PITIRIM A. (1937–1941) 1962 *Social and Cultural Dynamics.* 4 vols. Englewood Cliffs, N.J.: Bedminster Press. → Volume 1: *Fluctuation of Forms of Art.* Volume 2: *Fluctuation of Systems of Truth, Ethics, and Law.* Volume 3: *Fluctuation of Social Relationships, War, and Revolution.* Volume 4: *Basic Problems, Principles, and Methods.*

SUTTLES, WAYNE   1960   Affinal Ties, Subsistence, and Prestige Among the Coast Salish. *American Anthropologist* New Series 62:296–305.

SWEET, LOUISE E.   1965   Camel Pastoralism in North Arabia and the Minimal Camping Unit. Pages 129–152 in Anthony Leeds and Andrew P. Vayda (editors), *Man, Culture, and Animals: The Role of Animals in Human Ecological Adjustments.* Washington: American Association for the Advancement of Science.

TUMIN, MELVIN M.   1953   Some Principles of Stratification: A Critical Analysis. *American Sociological Review* 18:387–394. → See the debate in this issue and in Volume 28, 1963.

VAN DEN BERGHE, PIERRE L.   1963   Dialectic and Functionalism: Toward a Theoretical Synthesis. *American Sociological Review* 28:695–705.

# FUNCTIONAL INTERNATIONAL INTEGRATION

*See* INTERNATIONAL INTEGRATION, *article on* FUNCTIONALISM AND FUNCTIONAL INTEGRATION.

# FUNCTIONAL REPRESENTATION

*See* INTEREST GROUPS.

# FUSTEL DE COULANGES, NUMA DENIS

Numa Denis Fustel de Coulanges (1830–1889) devoted his life entirely to the study of the origin, evolution, and transformation of societies. Fustel was born in Paris. He never knew his father, a retired naval lieutenant, who died a few months after his birth. After secondary studies at the Lycée Charlemagne in Paris, he entered the École Normale Supérieure. The reactionary atmosphere then predominant in France pervaded the school and modified Fustel's previous liberalism. Graduating from that school in 1853, he spent two years at the Ecole Française d'Athènes, where he began the study of ancient Greece. Upon his return, he was appointed professor at the *lycée* at Amiens; he defended his theses for the *doctorat-ès-lettres*, the second of which, in Latin, concerned the cult of Vesta and contained in embryo the substance of *The Ancient City*, his first great historical work, published in 1864.

His tastes and his ability destined him for a university career, and in 1860 he was appointed to the chair of history in the Faculté des Lettres at Strasbourg. His brilliant teaching attracted many students, but despite this success he felt alone.

When a vacancy occurred at the Ecole Normale Supérieure, he applied for the post and for five years taught history there. His reputation as a teacher led Victor Duruy, the minister of public instruction, to entrust him with teaching history to the Empress Eugénie, the wife of Napoléon III, but the lessons were interrupted after only a few months by the outbreak of the war with Prussia.

The war had a profound effect on the patriotism of Fustel de Coulanges; it aroused his resentment against the German nation and helped to change the orientation of his investigations. He now plunged into the study of the political institutions of early medieval France and devoted the major part of his scholarly efforts to them from that time on. In December 1875 he was called to the Sorbonne to take the chair of ancient history, and in December 1878 he was appointed to the chair in medieval history, a position he kept until his death in 1889—except for three years, 1880–1883, during which he served, somewhat against his will because his health was poor, as director of the École Normale.

The first of the two principal works of Fustel de Coulanges was *The Ancient City: A Study on the Religion, Laws, and Institutions of Greece and Rome.* In the introduction the author stated that he hoped to reveal the principles and rules by which the societies of Greece and Rome were governed. Fustel's selection of a subject was not determined exclusively by the search for knowledge: what he wanted as well was to prove that the conception of Greece and Rome that people had had ever since the beginning of the French Revolution was false and that the consequences of this erroneous conception had been unfortunate. "They have deceived themselves," he said, "about the liberty of the ancients, and on this very account liberty among the moderns has been put in peril" ([1864] 1956, p. 11). And he added that such errors could be corrected only by an objective study of the history of the Greco–Roman world that would show that modern political conditions were not comparable to those of ancient societies.

According to Fustel, the formation of these societies was, in fact, based on a belief common to all the Aryan races, namely, that after death the soul continues to live, associated with the body, in the tomb. The earliest religion was ancestor worship, and the family unit that tended the sacred fire in the home became the basic unit of the ancient societies. This primitive social organization expanded by gradual stages: the *gens,* the Greek phratry, and the Roman tribe. The end point of the development was the city, which Fustel defined as "a religious association" open only to its citizens, that is, only to the members of patrician families. Over the centuries these primitive institutions lost their simplicity. The priest-kings who had governed the cities lost their political authority. The *gens* lost its cohesion; the plebs, which had been outside the city, entered into it. Then the Roman conquest transformed the character of the old cities bit by bit, by destroying their traditional municipal regimes. The triumph of Christianity was the final blow to traditional city government.

What Fustel de Coulanges argued with great logic, but perhaps at the expense of considering other relevant factors in social development, was that ancient society was founded on a particular belief and that it persisted insofar as that belief prevailed: it changed gradually as the belief weakened, and it did not survive its disappearance.

The *Histoire des institutions politiques de l'ancienne France* (1875–1889) was Fustel's second great historical work. After 1870 he devoted almost all his scholarly activity to it. The many articles that he published after 1872 in the *Revue des deux mondes*, the proceedings of the Académie des Sciences Morales et Politiques (he was elected to membership in 1865), and a number of other journals dealt chiefly with specific problems related to his major work.

The work focuses on the impact of the Germanic invasions. Fustel demonstrated the way in which the political institutions and social organization of Roman Gaul changed gradually, becoming first those of Frankish Gaul and then those of feudal France. According to the prevailing "Germanistic" conception of the great invasions, they were an avalanche that buried the Roman world. Fustel de Coulange's conception was more sophisticated. He saw the invasions as a phenomenon occurring over a long period, a slow infiltration of the empire by barbarian nations. These peoples, whether Visigoths, Burgundians, Franks, or others, were not hostile to Rome; but their invasion, combined with the effects of internal causes, produced a gradual, imperceptible, and nonrevolutionary transformation in the political and social institutions of Romanized Gaul.

This conception of Fustel's has been accepted by most subsequent historians, although they have tried to make the theory somewhat more flexible; Fustel's logician's temperament had left it too rigid.

Fustel de Coulanges has been reproached for having attached exclusive importance to written documents, in particular to charters, at the expense of other historical sources, such as archeological material. Nonetheless his faculty for interpreting texts enabled him to extract the maximum of their historical significance. As the great medievalist Charles Victor Langlois justly observed, Fustel needed only to apply his critical approach to a hundred words such as *villa, marca, allodis,* to revise radically the interpretation of Merovingian times.

Fustel's analysis of texts and vocabulary produced results of considerable value to sociologists. To take one famous example, his method permitted him to show that agrarian collectivism had never really existed, contrary to the theory of *Markgenossenschaft* that was developed by German economists and legal historians and diffused also in Romance countries. Fustel de Coulanges never doubted that the institutions of the family and of individual property were universal and went back to earliest times.

ROBERT LATOUCHE

[*Other relevant material may be found in* FEUDALISM *and in the biography of* GIERKE.]

WORKS BY FUSTEL DE COULANGES

(1864) 1956  *The Ancient City: A Study on the Religion, Laws, and Institutions of Greece and Rome.* Garden City, N.Y.: Doubleday. → First published in French.
(1875–1889) 1888–1892  *Histoire des institutions politiques de l'ancienne France.* 6 vols. Paris: Hachette.

SUPPLEMENTARY BIBLIOGRAPHY

GUIRAUD, PAUL 1896  *Fustel de Coulanges.* Paris: Hachette.
LATOUCHE, ROBERT (1956) 1961  *The Birth of Western Economy.* London: Methuen; New York: Barnes & Noble. → First published in French.
TOURNEUR-AUMONT, JEAN M. 1931  *Fustel de Coulanges.* Paris: Boivin.

# G

## GALIANI, FERDINANDO

Ferdinando Galiani (1728–1787), Italian economist, was born in Chieti. He received a classical education and took religious orders. Entering government service, he became secretary of the Neapolitan embassy in Paris in 1759 and served there for a decade. During this period he also visited England. The remainder of his life was spent in the service of the kingdom of Naples, where he directed a variety of government offices, for the most part engaging in the formulation and administration of national economic policy.

His published works embrace the humanities as well as the social sciences (a bibliography may be found in Nicolini 1909). He also left a large number of letters that are not only of biographical interest but are also important for the light they cast on the social, economic, and political characteristics of eighteenth-century Europe. Galiani's wide circle of personal contacts—his intellectual correspondents and associates included Voltaire, Diderot, Genovesi, Turgot, Vico, Friedrich M. von Grimm, and others, as well as many highly placed diplomatic colleagues—make his letters invaluable documents.

His ideas as an economist had considerable originality. His economic thinking was influenced by Aristotle as well as by more modern theorists such as Bernardo Davanzati (1529–1606), John Locke (1632–1704), and Geminiano Montanari (1633–1687). He read Vico at an early age, and it was because of Vico's influence that Galiani always placed his economic ideas in a social context. Despite his basic rejection of most of physiocracy, his

ideas were close to those current in France, and for a time he had a close intellectual relationship with Turgot and André Morellet. Like the works of other eighteenth-century economists (for example, Cantillon) Galiani's reveal a body of thought that is thoroughly eclectic. It is systematically related to no particular body of ideas, showing traces of scholasticism, of qualified mercantilism (especially where money and wealth are concerned), as well as of the natural-law ideas of the time. A free-thinking rationalist, Galiani appears nevertheless to have retained from mercantilism a protectionist international trade policy, if only with respect to grain.

The theoretical core of Galiani's work is found in *Della moneta* (1750); his policy prescriptions (clothed, incidentally, in a polished polemical literary style) are in *Dialogues sur le commerce des blés* (1770). His originality lies primarily in the fields of value theory, interest theory, and economic policy.

**Value theory.** Galiani's value theory was based on the dichotomy between utility and scarcity that had been at the core of value theory from the time of Aristotle. This dichotomy was fundamental to the theories of his predecessors, Davanzati and Montanari (Gordon 1964, pp. 115–116), and of his contemporaries, Quesnay and Adam Smith. But Galiani's value theory departed from that of his contemporaries: it foreshadowed the subjective demand theory that was so highly developed in the 1870s by Menger, Jevons, and Walras (Einaudi 1953, pp. 272–273; Kauder 1953, p. 638; Schumpeter 1954, p. 300 and *passim*). Moreover, his concept of relative scarcity foreshadowed the theory of diminishing marginal utility, another advance of economics in the last quarter of the nineteenth century. (The theory had, in fact, been clearly stated by Herman Gossen in 1854 but did not become widely known until its rediscovery by Jevons.)

Galiani understood the quantity of a commodity demanded as varying inversely with price, probably in a schedule sense rather than in the stock sense common in his day. The idea of price elasticity of demand is present in *Della moneta* (Einaudi 1953), although not in the mathematical terms developed by Alfred Marshall in 1890.

He did not discuss cost in general, but only the factor of labor in cost. For although he believed value to be subjectively determined and to vary from individual to individual, he did not believe that its source or its measurement is subjective. Rather, he believed that labor is not only the source of value but part of its objective measurement.

**Interest theory.** In economic writing before the seventeenth century, interest theory is rarely discussed, and when it is, the discussion is largely confined to theories of loan interest. This is also true of Galiani's interest theory. Nevertheless, his is one of the first discussions that considers why interest is paid instead of whether interest payments are legal or moral. Using a probability model, Galiani explained that interest is in principle paid to compensate the lender for the risk entailed in parting with his money (here and now)—money that is to be recovered from the borrower sometime in the future (or from a distant shore). Like his subjective value theory, Galiani's interest theory is based on a psychological assumption: men in general prefer present money over money at a future time or at some distant place. This theory has come to be known as the "time preference theory of interest," and Galiani's formulation of it anticipates that of Böhm-Bawerk by more than a century.

**Economic policy.** In matters of policy, Galiani adopted a position of historicogeographical relativism. Even the best-constructed economic models must be adjusted for circumstances of time and place before being applied to specific problems. This became a basic principle of the German historical school of Friedrich List and Wilhelm Roscher, but unlike that school, Galiani did not reject abstract theory.

It is surely remarkable that Galiani's early ideas in the areas of value and monetary theory anticipated corresponding notions of the neoclassical and Austrian schools, respectively. His later writings clearly foreshadow the views of the German historical school on economic policy.

PETER R. TOSCANO

[*For the historical context of Galiani's work, see* ECONOMIC THOUGHT; *and the biographies of* LOCKE; QUESNAY; SMITH, ADAM. *For discussion of the subsequent development of his ideas, see* UTILITY *and the biographies of* BÖHM-BAWERK; LIST; ROSCHER.]

### WORKS BY GALIANI

(1750) 1915 *Della moneta.* Edited by Fausto Nicolini. Bari: Laterza.

(1770) 1803 *Dialogues sur le commerce des blés.* Scrittori classici italiani di economia politica, Vols. 12–13. Milan: Destefanis.

(1818) 1889–1890 *Correspondance avec Madame d'Épinay* . . . 3d ed. 2 vols. Paris: Lévy. → Especially useful as a source of information on Galiani's social activities in Paris.

1880 *Lettere di Ferdinando Galiani al marchese Bernardo T. Tanucci.* Edited by Augusto Bazzoni. Florence: Vieusseux. → An excellent source for students of eighteenth-century diplomatic history.

### SUPPLEMENTARY BIBLIOGRAPHY

ARIAS, GINO 1922 Ferdinando Galiani et les physiocrates. *Revue des sciences politiques* 45:346–366.

ARIAS, GINO 1925 Il pensiero economico di Ferdinando Galiani. *Politica* 21:193–210.

BÖHM-BAWERK, EUGEN (1884) 1959 *Capital and Interest.* Volume 1: History and Critique of Interest Theories. South Holland, Ill.: Libertarian Press. → First published in German.

EINAUDI, LUIGI (1936) 1953 The Theory of Imaginary Money From Charlemagne to the French Revolution. Pages 229–261 in Frederic C. Lane and Jelle C. Riemersma (editors), *Enterprise and Secular Change: Readings in Economic History.* Homewood, Ill.: Irwin. → First published in Italian in Volume 1 of *Rivista di storia economica.*

EINAUDI, LUIGI 1953 *Saggi bibliografici e storici intorno alle dottrine economiche.* Rome: Edizioni di Storia e Letteratura. → See especially pages 267–305 on "Galiani economista."

GORDON, BARRY J. 1964 Aristotle and the Development of Value Theory. *Quarterly Journal of Economics* 78: 115–128. → A skillful critique of Kauder 1953.

KAUDER, EMIL 1953 Genesis of the Marginal Utility Theory From Aristotle to the End of the Eighteenth Century. *Economic Journal* 63:638–650. → Reprinted in Joseph J. Spengler and William R. Allen (editors), *Essays in Economic Thought: Aristotle to Marshall.*

NICOLINI, FAUSTO 1909 Saggio bibliografico. Pages 405–431 in Ferdinando Galiani, *Il pensiero dell'abate Galiani: Antologia dei suoi scritti editi e inediti.* Bari: Laterza.

NICOLINI, FAUSTO 1918 Giambattista Vico e Ferdinando Galiani: Ricerca storica. *Giornale storico della letteratura italiana* 71:137–207.

NICOLINI, FAUSTO 1931 Ferdinando Galiani. Volume 6, pages 546–547 in *Encyclopaedia of the Social Sciences.* New York: Macmillan.

ROSSI, JOSEPH 1930 *The Abbé Galiani in France.* New York: Institute of French Studies.

SCHUMPETER, JOSEPH A. (1954) 1960 *History of Economic Analysis.* Edited by E. B. Schumpeter. New York: Oxford Univ. Press.

TAGLIACOZZO, GIORGIO (editor) 1937 *Economisti napoletani dei sec. XVII e XVIII.* Bologna: Cappelli. → Contains portions of Galiani 1750 and Galiani 1770, prefaced by the editor's comments.

Vico, Giovanni Battista (1725) 1948 *The New Science*. Translated by Thomas G. Bergin and Max Harold Fisch. Ithaca, N.Y.: Cornell Univ. Press. → First published in Italian. A paperback edition was published in 1961 by Doubleday.

## GALL, FRANZ JOSEPH

Franz Joseph Gall (1758–1828), German anatomist, founder of cranioscopy (later known as phrenology), and physician, was born in the grand duchy of Baden and died at Montrouge near Paris. He was the sixth child of a merchant. After the usual schooling, he studied medicine first at Strassburg and later at Vienna, where he was graduated in 1785.

He began his medical practice in Vienna and at the same time studied the healing powers of nature, the subject of his first book, *Philosophisch-medicinische Untersuchungen über Natur und Kunst im kranken und gesunden Zustande des Menschen* (1791). In it, Gall discussed the relationship between body and soul; the latter was located in the brain and was the seat of ideas. This concept led him to the notion of the cerebral localization of mental faculties, and he devoted the remainder of his life to exploring this idea.

There was at the time great interest in methods of determining character and temperament from external bodily configurations, especially the facial (physiognomy), and Gall gradually evolved a new method called "cranioscopy," combining the concepts of cerebral localization with the analysis of bodily configurations.

He argued that faculties or talents are inborn and dependent upon cerebral structures; therefore the brain is made up of as many "organs," or areas, as there are moral and intellectual qualities. These "organs" are on the cerebral surface, and as their size is reflected accurately by the overlying skull, they are palpable. He selected and located the "organs" by his empirical observations: having observed that a good memory is associated with protruding eyes, he therefore postulated that the memory organ is on the cerebral orbital surface and its hypertrophy pushes out the eyes. Character and intellect are represented by 27 organs, or psychic qualities, sharply delineated on the cranial surface.

About 1796 Gall began lecturing on cranioscopy in Vienna. Although the theory won great popularity, its materialism, manifested by an attempt to relate mind to matter, also incited opposition, so that in 1802 Gall's teaching was banned for religious reasons. Gall was joined in 1804 by Johann Gaspar Spurzheim, who had recently received his medical degree and who helped with the dissections of the nervous system that Gall undertook. Unlike other physiognomists, Gall attempted to create a scientific basis for his theory.

Seeking a more congenial atmosphere, Gall and Spurzheim left Vienna in 1805, and after an extended tour of Germany and neighboring countries, where their lectures excited widespread controversy, they settled in Paris in 1807. As in Vienna, Gall established an extensive medical practice with many famous patients, and he also resumed his lecturing and writing. In 1808 he published his *Discours d'ouverture au cours de physiologie du cerveau* (1808) and in the same year prepared with the help of Spurzheim a neuroanatomical memoir which was assessed by a group of distinguished French scientists. On the whole the judges were favorably impressed, and in the following year the report, with replies to the criticisms made by the assessors, was published (Gall & Spurzheim 1809). In 1810 Gall's most important and comprehensive work on neuroanatomy and cranioscopy began to appear, entitled *Anatomie et physiologie du système nerveux en général . . .* (1810–1819). Spurzheim helped with the first and second volumes only, for in 1813 he left France to popularize "phrenology," as he, but not Gall, came to call cranioscopy. Gall's last publication was a revised edition of *Anatomie et physiologie. . . .* He died of a cerebrovascular accident and was buried in Père-la-Chaise cemetery in Paris: his skull is preserved in the Musée de l'Homme.

Gall had an insatiable desire to learn and claimed that he was not guided by a desire for power, honors, or riches, although some of each came his way. He was perfectly sincere, if somewhat uncritical, in his ideas of brain function and was by no means a quack as is often thought; the stigma earned by phrenology was largely due to its popularizers, who claimed that phrenological examination could be used in career selection, for all kinds of prophecies, in choosing members of parliament and other professional men, etc. Gall's own intellectual abilities, his powers of observation, and his honesty, integrity, and independence in matters of principle were outstanding. As a product of the eighteenth-century Enlightenment, he was a social reformer, and he emphasized the need for medical ethics. He deduced moral rules from his phrenology and called for state educational systems and reform of current methods of handling criminals and lunatics.

Gall's influence was widespread. His anatomical investigations and cranioscopy turned attention to the brain, and he had an important influence on brain dissection and neuroanatomy in general in the nineteenth century. Moreover, phrenology first popularized the modern concept of cerebral localization of function, although it made no specific contribution to the concept. Gall's basic idea was right, but for the wrong reasons. Phrenology was also important in the development of scientific psychology, of anthropological investigations of the skull, and of criminology.

Phrenology retained popularity throughout the nineteenth century, and societies furthering its practice still exist today. Apart from its general effects upon the study of anatomy and physiology at the beginning of the nineteenth century, it has played no further role in science. However, its influence on social reform, political groups, religion, philosophy, and literature has been extensive, especially in the United States and Britain.

EDWIN CLARKE

[See also NERVOUS SYSTEM, article on STRUCTURE AND FUNCTION OF THE BRAIN; and the biographies of BROCA; FLOURENS; LASHLEY.]

WORKS BY GALL

(1791) 1800  Philosophisch-medicinische Untersuchungen über Natur und Kunst im kranken und gesunden Zustande des Menschen. 2d ed. Leipzig: Baumgärtner.
1808  Discours d'ouverture . . . au [cours] sur la physiologie du cerveau. Paris: Didot.
1809  GALL, FRANZ JOSEPH; and SPURZHEIM, J. GASPAR Recherches sur le système nerveux en général, et sur celui du cerveau en particulier. Paris: Schoell.
1810–1819  GALL, FRANZ JOSEPH; and SPURZHEIM, J. GASPAR Anatomie et physiologie du système nerveux en général et du cerveau en particulier, avec des observations sur la possibilité de reconnoître plusieurs dispositions intellectuelles et morales de l'homme et des animaux par la configuration de leurs têtes. 4 vols. and Atlas. Paris: Schoell. → A revised edition was published in 1825 in six volumes as Sur les fonctions du cerveau et sur celles de chacune de ses parties.
(1825) 1835  On the Functions of the Brain and of Each of Its Parts: With Observations on the Possibility of Determining the Instincts, Propensities, and Talents, or the Moral and Intellectual Dispositions of Men and Animals, by the Configuration of the Brain and Head. 6 vols. Boston: Marsh, Capen & Lyon. → A partial translation of Anatomie et physiologie du système nerveux en général, et sur le cerveau en particulier. . . . (Rev. ed.)

SUPPLEMENTARY BIBLIOGRAPHY

ACKERKNECHT, ERWIN H.; and VALLOIS, HENRY V. (1955) 1956  Franz Joseph Gall: Inventor of Phrenology and His Collection. Madison: Univ. of Wisconsin Medical School, Department of History of Medicine. → First published in French.
DAVIES, JOHN D. 1955  Phrenology; Fad and Science: A 19th-century American Crusade. New Haven: Yale Univ. Press.
FOSSATI, JEAN ANTOINE L. 1858  Gall (François Joseph). Volume 19, columns 271–284 in Nouvelle biographie générale. Edited by Jean Hoefer. Paris: Didot.
HOLLANDER, B. 1909  The Unknown Life and Works of Dr. Francis Joseph Gall, the Discoverer of the Anatomy and Physiology of the Brain. London: Gall Society. → Written by an ardent latter-day phrenologist and therefore very biased.
TEMKIN, OWSEI 1947  Gall and the Phrenological Movement. Bulletin of the History of Medicine 21:275–321.

# GALTON, FRANCIS

Francis Galton was born in 1822 and died in 1911. He was educated successively at home, at a dame school, at Boulogne, and at Kenilworth. In 1835, at the age of 13, he entered King Edward's School at Birmingham, where he stayed for two years. He spent two years as a medical student, the first at the General Hospital, Birmingham and the second at King's College, London. In 1840 he entered Trinity College, Cambridge, as a mathematics student, but was content to take a poll degree in 1843, when his health broke down.

Galton's father, Samuel Tertius Galton, was a banker. His mother, Violetta Darwin, was the daughter of Erasmus Darwin by his second wife. One of Erasmus Darwin's grandsons through his first wife was Charles Robert Darwin; there was a certain physical resemblance between the two cousins. His mental development is interesting: he is credibly reported to have read a simple book before he reached the age of three, and his restless ingenuity with regard to machinery dates from his early youth. He did not enjoy school, however, nor did he find the profession of medicine, which was chosen for him, congenial. In spite of his interest in mechanics and mathematics, he was not successful in his Cambridge studies.

When his father died in 1844, Galton immediately forsook any idea of continuing his medical career. He found himself the possessor of a more than adequate income and proceeded to spend his time and energy "hunting with a set chiefly noteworthy for their extravagance and recklessness . . . the strange thing [being] that it [shooting] seemed to absorb his whole nature, and to be done not for the sake of the experience, but in the pure pursuit of occupation" (Pearson 1914–1930, vol. 1, pp. 208–209).

It was after these fallow years, as Pearson called

them, that Galton carried out the explorations for which he was later awarded the gold medal of the Royal Geographical Society in 1853. Even before going to Cambridge, Galton had taken an extended trip down the Danube and on to Smyrna, which had perhaps awakened the young man to the delights of foreign scenes and strange peoples. After his father's death he set off again for Egypt, Khartoum, and Syria, but he "was still touring for the boyish fun of movement and of new scenes. He had not yet thoughts of the language, habits, or archaeology of the people he mingled with" (*ibid.,* p. 205). It was not until after four years of idleness in England that he set out on a trip to tropical Africa, the results of which showed that he had come to terms with life and with himself.

In 1850 Galton set off for the Cape and spent two years upcountry exploring from Walvis Bay to Lake Ngami, territory of which little was known. He composed 15 brief laws for the Hottentot chiefs who governed the Damaras of the plain and compiled a rudimentary dictionary for the English who wished to use the local tongue. He returned to England early in 1852 and read a paper to the Royal Geographical Society, which awarded him its gold medal the following year. This award was followed in 1854 by a silver medal from the French Geographical Society. Early in 1853 he met Louisa Butler and married her in August. After an extended honeymoon tour of Europe, punctuated by visits to England, the Galtons finally settled in London, and in 1855 Galton really began to work.

**Early publications.** As might be anticipated, Galton's first publication was on exploration, and in 1855 *The Art of Travel* was published. There were signs that his scientific curiosity was developing in new directions, since in *Vacation Tourists and Notes of Travel* (1861–1864), which he meant to be an annual magazine, there is a description of the eclipse of the sun in 1860, with a drawing of the curved rays of the corona that he had observed. Galton's first piece of fruitful research was on the weather. He started to plot wind and pressure maps and noted, from very scanty data, that centers of high pressure are associated with clockwise directions of winds around the calm center. He coined the name "anticyclone" for such systems in 1863. Several other papers followed, in which he was clearly feeling his way toward the concepts of correlation and regression.

He tried to determine a linear prediction formula for the velocity of the wind, given the pressure, temperature, and humidity. He did not succeed, possibly because of his failure to realize that the prediction formula for pressure from velocity was not the same as the prediction formula for velocity from pressure. The realization that there are two regression lines was still in the future, as was the concept of correlation. In 1870 he read a paper at the British Association entitled "Barometric Predictions of Weather," in which he was fumbling toward a multiple regression, trying to predict the wind from pressure, temperature, and humidity. He failed in his objective at the time, but he posed the problem for others who were to succeed.

**Intellectual influences.** In assessing the intellectual influences on Galton, continuing uncertainty exists as to the extent of Quetelet's influence. Pearson tended to minimize the significance of Quetelet for Galton; he wrote, "I am very doubtful how far [Galton] owed much to a close reading of the great Belgian statistician" (Pearson 1914–1930, vol. 2, p. 12), and he placed perhaps undue weight on the fact that Galton possessed no copy of Quetelet's *Letters . . . on the Theory of Probabilities* (1846). Pearson further remarked that Galton "was never a great student of other men's writings: he was never an accumulator like his cousin Charles Darwin" (Pearson 1914–1930, vol. 1, p. 209). Now Pearson was closer to Galton's time and actually knew him, so that some weight must be given to his opinions. Nevertheless, Pearson would appear to have underestimated the influence of Quetelet; he himself pointed out that Galton's work seemed to flow naturally out of that of Quetelet. Further, Galton's obsession with the normal curve of error which, to a certain extent, has unduly influenced the development of statistical method, can only have stemmed from Quetelet. One of Quetelet's great achievements was to consider all human experience as ultimately capable of being described numerically, which was fundamentally Galton's attitude also.

The other great influence on Galton during the period in which he was establishing himself as a research worker affected the whole of the scientific world in the second half of the nineteenth century —the publication in 1859 of Charles Darwin's *The Origin of Species.* The effect of this work on Galton was not immediately apparent in his writings, but there can be no doubt that the book was responsible for transforming him from a geographer into an anthropologist and eugenist. He began with the article "Hereditary Talent and Character" in 1865 and proceeded through *Hereditary Genius* (1869); *English Men of Science: Their Nature and Nurture* (1874); *Inquiries Into Human Faculty* (1883); and *Natural Inheritance* (1889), by which time he was 67 years of age. As Pearson said, "We see that his researches in heredity, in anthropometry, in psychometry and statistics, were not independent studies; they were all auxiliary to his main object, the improvement in the race of man."

**Application of statistics.** In *Hereditary Genius*, Galton claimed that his discussion of heredity was the "first to treat the subject in a statistical manner" ([1869] 1952, p. vi). He clearly owed much to Quetelet and paralleled Quetelet's use of the normal curve for anthropometric measurements by using it to grade intellectual ability. He was quite explicit about this: "The law is an exceedingly general one. M. Quetelet, the Astronomer-Royal of Belgium, and the greatest authority on vital and social statistics, has largely used it in his inquiries. He has also constructed numerical tables, by which the necessary calculations can be easily made, whenever it is desired to have recourse to the law" (*ibid.*, p. 23).

Galton supplemented Quetelet's tables by a short table of the abscissas of the unit normal curve corresponding to percentiles of area (1889). He examined the abilities of the kin of persons who had achieved eminence of some kind—judges, generals, scientists, statesmen, painters, poets, and clerics. He was concerned with distinguishing between general ability and special ability and regarded each individual personality as a combination of natural ability and the advantages accruing from early environment, i.e., nature and nurture.

This idea of nature and nurture recurs in his writings. Thus we find in *English Men of Science* (1874), "It is, I believe, owing to the favourable conditions of their early training that an unusually large proportion of the sons of the most gifted men of science become distinguished in the same career. They have been nurtured in an atmosphere of free enquiry. . . ." The thesis is that heredity tends to produce eminence in *some* area and that environment tends to be the deciding factor in specifying *what* this area shall be. Galton tried to go beyond this in *Inquiries Into Human Faculty and Its Development* (1883), the book that possibly holds most interest for students of the history of psychology, in which he discussed preliminary results that he had obtained in the psychometric field.

In 1876, at the exhibition of scientific instruments at South Kensington, Galton exhibited his "Whistles for Determining the Upper Limits of Audible Sounds in Different Persons." Both before and after this time he was active in proposing tests for the measurement of muscular sensitivity by weight discrimination, for the perception of differences of tint, for reaction time, for acuteness of hearing, for keenness of vision and judgment of length by the eye, and for the senses of smell and touch. In an attempt to describe the skewed distributions that often resulted from the application of his tests, Galton hypothesized that in some frequency distributions, such as, for example, judgment of length, the geometric mean, rather than the arithmetic mean, is the best "medium" for the distribution, and he wrote a paper on "The Geometric Mean in Vital and Social Statistics" (1879). As usual the mathematical conceptualization was beyond him, and he took the problem to Sir Donald Macalister, who derived what is now known as the log-normal distribution.

At this stage of his work, he was associated with the American psychologist James McKeen Cattell, who on his return to the University of Pennsylvania (and later at Columbia University), began to teach statistical psychology, giving his first course in 1887. Through Cattell, Galton's ideas and experiments exerted possibly the greatest single influence upon American psychology during the last years of the nineteenth century.

From the statistical point of view, *Natural Inheritance* is probably the most important of Galton's writings. As can be seen from his earlier works, the ideas in it had been fermenting in his mind for some time, but it was their expression in *Natural Inheritance* that excited the interest of those whom today we might call the practitioners of applied mathematics. Again he was influenced by the fact that Quetelet was using the normal curve to describe anthropometric data and by the interest in the problems of inheritance aroused in him by *The Origin of Species*.

He began the book with a summary of those properties of the normal curve that appealed to him. He had previously suggested representing a frequency distribution by using grades or percentiles, and he elaborated on this suggestion here, pointing out that the normal distribution is completely determined from a knowledge of the median and one other quantile. Galton had observed that many measured characteristics can be closely described by a normal curve. He used the "quincunx," first shown in print with the publication of his lecture "Typical Laws of Heredity," delivered at the Royal Institution (1877), to illustrate the build-up of the normal curve: He had noticed that a normal curve is reproduced by lead shot falling vertically through a harrow of pins and he tried to explain the stability of measured characteristics by this mechanical device. In this paper he had almost reached the concepts of both regression and correlation but must have felt the need for further thought, since it was at this time that he began to collect data bearing on inheritance in man. Galton published nothing further on heredity for eight years. The foundation of his ideas on regression and correlation did not perhaps become clear to him until a short time before the publication of *Natural Inheritance*.

The regression line arose naturally out of measurements of the sizes of the seeds of mother and daughter sweet pea plants. The sizes of the seeds of daughter plants appeared to "revert" to the mean (the word "revert" was soon replaced by "regress"). This inspired him to look at a bivariate frequency table of the heights of fathers and sons, in which he found a regression to "mediocrity." The arguments he used became familiar ones with the analysis of variance put forward by R. A. Fisher some forty to fifty years later. Suppose, Galton said, that we want to predict the height of brother A, given the height of brother B. We take, therefore, all the individuals who have heights the same as B and form a collection of the heights of all of their brothers. These brothers as a group Galton called a cofraternity, and he proceeded to discuss the variation in height of all individuals about the grand mean, the variation of the cofraternity means about the grand mean, and the variation of the individuals of the cofraternities about their respective cofraternity means. This splitting up of variation had been done previously by Lexis in Germany and Dormoy in France, but Galton was possibly the first to carry out this type of analysis with the idea of assigning the variation.

While studying the bivariate frequency table of heights of fathers and sons, Galton was struck by the observation that the contours of equal frequency in the table were similar and similarly situated ellipses. He also found the lines that fitted the medians of the arrays (possibly drawing them by eye) and the slopes of these lines eventually became his regression coefficients. This early work, as is inevitable with a pioneering effort, is confused and difficult to evaluate, not least because Galton himself was not explicit. When, however, he had determined that he had what would now be termed linearity of regression and homoscedasticity in the arrays of the table, his mathematical powers were not sufficient to enable him to form a mathematical model for his surface, and he took the problem to Hamilton Dickson, a Cambridge mathematician. Dickson's mathematical formulation was published in an appendix to Galton's paper "Family Likeness in Stature," presented to the Royal Society in 1886. Galton was troubled by the fact that the slope of the regression line depends on the variability of the margins, and this concern led to his search for a unit-free measure of association.

Some time earlier, in 1882, Alphonse Bertillon had put forward a scheme for classifying criminals according to 12 physical measurements that was adopted by the prefecture of police in Paris. Galton became interested in this scheme and pondered for some time over which measurements would be the most descriptive—that is, which would discriminate one man most effectively from his fellows. It was from these considerations that he was led to the realization that some measurements might be so highly correlated with other measurements as to be useless for the prescribed purposes and finally to the necessity for describing how any two measurements are related. The slope of the regression line is not adequate for this, since it depends on both the scales of measurement and the choice of dependent variables. However, the regression line fitted between the variables that Galton used (1888) after dividing the heights (reduced by their median) by a measure of their variability (their semi-interquartile range) and similarly dealing with forearm length provides a unit-free measure of association. Given the problem and 65 years of subsequent statistical development, the correlation coefficient may now appear to have been inevitable. There can be no question, however, that at the time at which Galton wrote, 1888–1889, the production of a measure of association that was independent of location and scale was an immense contribution to statistical methodology.

The Bertillon system of measurement also started Galton wondering about the whole procedure of personal identification. In the paper for the Royal Institution in which he discussed bertillonage, he also drew incidental attention to fingerprints. In his book *Finger Prints* (1892), he referred to the work of Jan Purkinje, Kollman, William Herschel, and Henry Faulds, who had preceded him in this study, but it is clear that at the time he wrote little was known. As he himself said:

It became gradually clear that three facts had to be established before it would be possible to advocate the use of finger prints for criminal or other investigations. First it must be proved, not assumed, that the pattern of a finger print is constant throughout life. Secondly that the variety of patterns is really very great. Thirdly, that they admit of being so classified, or lexiconised, that when a set of them is submitted to an expert, it would be possible for him to tell, by reference to a suitable dictionary or its equivalent, whether a similar set had already been registered. These things I did, but they required much labor.

As a result of Galton's book and his evidence to a committee set up by the Home Office in 1893, a fingerprint department was established, the forerunner of many such throughout the world. Galton himself, as might be expected from his previous work and interest, turned to studying the inheritance of fingerprints, a study which was carried on for many years in the laboratory that he founded and that was named after him.

**Eugenics.** The term "eugenics" was introduced by Galton in his book *Inquiries Into Human Faculty* (1883) and soon won general acceptance. The study of human inheritance and the possibility of improving human stock were undoubtedly linked in his mind, as his public lectures and papers witness. He did more than lecture, however. In 1904 he founded a research fellowship in national eugenics at the University of London which was to develop in a few years into the Galton Laboratory of National Eugenics, with Karl Pearson as its first director. Pearson was succeeded by R. A. Fisher, and the now vast complex of statistical theory and method developed there thus owes its origin to Galton.

It was inevitable that Galton's work should attract the interest of young men able in the mathematical and in the biological fields, and the late 1880s saw Karl Pearson, and W. F. R. Weldon—the one a professor of applied mathematics and the other a professor of zoology and both at University College, London—working in the field of "biometry," i.e., the application of mathematics to problems of biological inheritance. Galton himself said, "The primary object of Biometry is to afford material that shall be exact enough for the discovery of incipient changes in evolution which are too small to be otherwise apparent." Pearson and Weldon met difficulties in their attempts to publish papers relating to biometry in existing journals and determined to start their own. A guarantee was required. Galton, on being asked to help, not only guaranteed the whole amount but followed it up with an additional gift that enabled his admirers to go their way in freedom; the journal *Biometrika*, the first to be devoted to both the theory and practice of statistics, was established on a firm footing. In the last decade of his life, Galton played the part of counselor and adviser to the younger men, but he still worked away at his own problems, as his continued output of letters and papers indicates.

During his last years many honors came his way. He had been elected a fellow of the Royal Society in 1856, receiving a gold medal in 1886, the Darwin medal in 1902, and the much-prized Copley medal in 1910, the year before his death. He was awarded the Huxley medal by the Anthropological Institute in 1901 and the Darwin–Wallace medal by the Linnean Society in 1908. He received honor-ary degrees from both Oxford and Cambridge universities and became an honorary fellow of Trinity College, Cambridge, his old college, in 1902. The citation for the Darwin medal said, in part, "It may safely be declared that no one living has contributed more definitely to the progress of evolutionary study, whether by actual discovery or by the fruitful direction of thought, than Mr. Galton." Mr. Galton's private comment was, typically, "Well, I am very pleased except that I stand in the way of younger men" (quoted in Pearson 1914–1930, vol. 3A, p. 237).

F. N. DAVID

[*For the historical context of Galton's work, see the biographies of* DARWIN *and* QUETELET. *For discussion of the subsequent development of Galton's ideas, see* EUGENICS; LINEAR HYPOTHESIS, *article on* REGRESSION; MULTIVARIATE ANALYSIS, *articles on* CORRELATION; *and the biographies of* CATTELL; FISHER, R. A.; PEARSON.]

### WORKS BY GALTON

(1855) 1856  *The Art of Travel: Or, Shifts and Contrivances Available in Wild Countries.* 2d ed., rev. & enl. London: Murray.

1861–1864  GALTON, FRANCIS (editor)  *Vacation Tourists and Notes of Travel in 1860* [*1861, 1862–1863*]. London: Macmillan.

1863  *Meteorographica: Or, Methods of Mapping the Weather.* London: Macmillan.

1865  Hereditary Talent and Character. *Macmillan's Magazine* 12:157–166, 318–327.

(1869) 1952  *Hereditary Genius: An Inquiry Into Its Laws and Consequences.* New York: Horizon Press. → A paperback edition was published in 1962 by World.

1870  Barometric Predictions of Weather. British Association for the Advancement of Science, *Report* 40 [2]:31–33.

1874  *English Men of Science: Their Nature and Nurture.* London: Macmillan.

1876  Whistles for Determining the Upper Limits of Audible Sounds in Different Persons. Page 61 in South Kensington Museum, London, *Conferences Held in Connection With the Special Loan Collection of Scientific Apparatus, 1876.* Volume 2: Physics and Mechanics. London: Chapman.

(1877) 1879  Typical Laws of Heredity. Royal Institution of Great Britain, *Proceedings* 8:282–301. → First published in Volume 15 of *Nature.*

1879  The Geometric Mean in Vital and Social Statistics. Royal Society of London, *Proceedings* 29:365–367.

(1883) 1952  *Inquiries Into Human Faculty and Its Development.* London: Cassell.

1886  Family Likeness in Stature. Royal Society of London, *Proceedings* 40:42–63. → Supplemented with an appendix by J. D. Hamilton Dickson on pages 63–72.

1888  Co-relations and Their Measurement, Chiefly From Anthropomorphic Data. Royal Society of London, *Proceedings* 45:135–145.

1889  *Natural Inheritance.* London and New York: Macmillan.

1892  *Finger Prints.* London and New York: Macmillan.

1908  *Memories of My Life.* London: Methuen.

SUPPLEMENTARY BIBLIOGRAPHY

BURT, CYRIL 1962 Francis Galton and His Contributions to Psychology. *British Journal of Statistical Psychology* 15:1–49.

DARWIN, GEORGE H. (1912) 1939 Sir Francis Galton. Volume 2, pages 70–73 in *Dictionary of National Biography: Second Supplement*. Oxford Univ. Press.

NEWMAN, JAMES R. 1956 Commentary on Sir Francis Galton. Volume 2, pages 1167–1172 in James R. Newman (editor), *The World of Mathematics: A Small Library of the Literature of Mathematics From A'h-mosé the Scribe to Albert Einstein*. New York: Simon & Schuster.

PEARSON, KARL 1914–1930 *The Life, Letters and Labours of Francis Galton*. 3 vols. Cambridge Univ. Press. → Includes a comprehensive bibliography of Galton's works.

QUETELET, ADOLPHE (1846) 1849 *Letters Addressed to H. R. H. the Grand Duke of Saxe-Coburg and Gotha, on the Theory of Probabilities, as Applied to the Moral and Political Sciences*. London: Layton. → First published in French.

# GAMBLING

Gambling may be defined as a form of activity in which the parties involved, who are known as bettors or players, voluntarily engage to make the transfer of money or something else of value among themselves contingent upon the outcome of some future and uncertain event.

While the origins of gambling are lost to recorded history, it appears probable that games of chance developed out of various magical and religious practices employed by man to cope with problems of uncertainty and fate. In contemporary societies gambling appears most frequently in recreational contexts and in association with various sports and games. Among the major classes of games, gambling is especially common in those in which chance plays a prominent role, but it also appears in connection with games of skill or strategy and with games of physical prowess. In nonrecreational contexts gambling occurs in the form of wagers on the outcome of future events about which the bettors have strong convictions, as in the case of election outcomes. Elements closely parallel to gambling appear in conjunction with economic activities, especially those in which risk and uncertainty are prominent. In effect, speculators on the commodity markets bet against each other about the rise or fall of commodity prices.

In its various aspects gambling is at once a major recreational institution, a minor vice, a large-scale industry, a powerful source of crime and political corruption, a perennial social problem, a fascinating psychological puzzle, and an intriguing pastime. Like prostitution, it is ancient, widespread, and widely disapproved. It flourishes, in spite of ethical taboo and legal sanction, as an institutionalized deviant pattern and as a form of crime in which the victims are willing accomplices.

**Social science perspectives on gambling.** Because of gambling's complex and paradoxical nature, it is not surprising that the responses to it by social scientists and others have been extraordinarily diverse. Philosophers and theologians have struggled with the ethical and teleological implications of gambling, viewing it at times as a profane and frivolous stepchild of religion, to which it bears certain disquieting similarities. Mathematicians have exploited gambling to the hilt in the development of probability theory, some of them becoming gamesters in the process. Economists have turned to gambling to clarify the distinction between the functional and dysfunctional aspects of speculation and, more recently, for some sophisticated reformulations of utility theory. In the "theory of games" they have found in gambling a model for analyzing strategies in competitive situations involving risk and uncertainty.

Experimental psychologists have employed gambling situations in studies of probability learning and probability preferences, of levels of aspiration, and of intermittent reinforcement and conflict–drive motivation. Social psychologists have utilized gambling games to study social competition, aggression, and coalition formation. Psychoanalysts and clinical psychologists have concerned themselves with the unconscious motivations and personality structures of gamblers and with the problems of addiction. Sociologists have been interested in the incidence of gambling, its organization in relation to the underworld and the police, its functions for individuals and society, and its control. Finally, ethnographers and social historians have provided some fascinating descriptions of the cultural patterning of gambling in various times and places.

In these many different approaches that have touched on the subject, the interest in gambling has often been peripheral to some other, central interest, with the result that the coverage is piecemeal and fragmentary. While there are scattered bits of useful knowledge and theory, systematic treatises on gambling are sadly lacking. Moreover, many of the treatments that do exist are speculative, impressionistic, and moralistic, and many are also without adequate data.

## The psychology of gambling

From a psychological viewpoint, gambling is at once an instrumental activity, directed toward a consciously recognized economic end, and an expressive activity, enjoyed as an end in itself. Interpretations of gambling motivations have varied widely, depending upon which of these facets has commanded the central focus of attention.

**Gambling as instrumental behavior.** In making their betting decisions, economically oriented gamblers must take two principal factors into account: the odds and the probabilities. In gambling terminology "odds" designates the ratio between the amount staked and the amount the player stands to win if successful. "Probabilities" refers to expectations regarding the outcome of the event bet upon, expressed as a ratio of favorable to unfavorable outcomes or as the percentage of favorable outcomes out of all possible outcomes. The actuarial value of a gambling risk depends upon the relationship between the odds and the probabilities. In gambling situations generally, there is a tendency for these two ratios to approach an inverted balance: as the probabilities of a favorable outcome become smaller, the odds become longer. For example, in horse racing, long shots fetch better prices than favorites. That this tendency exists at all may be taken as evidence for the operation of an element of economic rationality among gamblers.

It is clear, however, that no general theory of gambling behavior can be constructed from the conventional notions of economic rationality alone. In every gambling situation either the odds and probabilities are exactly balanced or they are not. Assume, first, that they are balanced, as in the case of tossing coins for even money. In the gambling world such risks are known as fair risks because neither side has any clear advantage. While it might appear that the rational gambler would have no particular reason to avoid such risks, there is also no apparent reason for him to accept them. Indeed, according to orthodox economic theory, the prudent gambler would presumably assign some element of disutility or cost to risk assumption and to the activity of gambling itself, regarding it as a form of "work." Moreover, if he assigns some function of diminishing utility to successive increments of money income, as economic theory assumes, the utility of each unit of money he might win in a fair-risk situation would be less than that of the money he might lose. Hence, the economically rational gambler would presumably avoid such risks as in this sense "not fair."

In all other gambling situations the odds and probabilities are not in balance. In situations of this sort, since all gambling transactions are between persons, it follows that whereas one player has backed a good risk, his opponent has by definition accepted a poor one. It is evident, therefore, that at least half of all gamblers have lost their rational economic bearings. In fact, in the gambling world the majority of good risks are monopolized by the professional gamblers who operate the various games and devices, always with a comfortable margin of safety. From the lay player's point of view there are no "good risks" at all in any professionally operated gambling house. Yet the market behavior of such gamblers makes it clear that there is always an easy market for poor gambling risks, especially those in which the odds are intriguingly long but offset by disastrously short probabilities.

*The "utility of money."* Economists and psychologists alike have advanced many arguments and theories designed to show how such apparently nonrational behavior may yet be motivationally intelligible. One line of argument has called for a reappraisal of traditional assumptions about the diminishing utility of money. Thus, Vickrey (1945) reasoned that the behavior of lottery players clearly implies that in this situation the utility of money is an increasing rather than a decreasing function of income. Following this same theme, Friedman and Savage (1948) demonstrated that for the gambler even a small probability of a large reward may have more utility than either a much larger probability of small loss or the certainty, if the risk be rejected, of staying at the same income level. Along similar lines, Mosteller and Nogee (1951) recorded the actual market behavior of experimental subjects in a situation that permitted varying amounts to be won, with varying probabilities of success or failure. Observing that the subjects do not automatically accept the bets with the highest actuarial values, they attempted to construct a series of curves showing the actual utility for their subjects of varying amounts of money (see also Coombs & Komorita 1958).

*The "utility of gambling."* A second line of analysis has challenged the assumption that the activity of gambling should be reckoned on the cost, or disutility, side of the calculus. In effect, the gambler may justify his losses as a fair payment for the pleasure he has obtained from the activity itself. Royden, Suppes, and Walsh (1959) have proposed a carefully reasoned model for the experimental measurement of the "utility of gambling" itself, which they argue must be kept independent of notions about the "utility of money." This line of analysis, however, is not much help in explaining why gamblers find pleasure in this activity, while nongamblers presumably do not.

**Subjective probabilities.** A third line of analysis, focusing on the cognitive aspects of gambling orientations, raises the question whether gambling behavior is a function of simple ignorance or error or whether the "subjective probabilities" upon which the gambler premises his behavior are systematically distorted or biased by various motivational factors.

*Ignorance or error.* Studies of probability learning provide evidence that there is ample scope for error in appraising the probabilities in complex gambling situations. Komorita (1959) has shown that experimental subjects are least accurate in estimating probabilities when the number of events or possible outcomes is large and when the probabilities for unit events depart from .50. Brim and Koenig (1959) found, in a sample of 143 college students, that none knew the correct way to combine the probabilities of independent events. And Cohen and Hansel (1958) found that even highly intelligent subjects tended to interpret multiplicative probabilities as if they were additive. Professional gamblers are less prone to such errors and employ their extra knowledge to design gambling situations in which the true probabilities are subtly concealed.

Faulty reasoning may also serve to distort subjective probability estimates, as, for example, in the widespread belief among gamblers in the "maturity-of-chances" doctrine (Jarvik 1951). Since Dame Fortune must keep her books in balance, reason such gamblers, at roulette, for example, after any unduly long run of black the probabilities of red appearing on the next few plays are greatly increased. In fact, of course, the probabilities on unit events are not affected by preceding sequences. Ironically, perhaps, while the ability to estimate true probabilities generally increases with maturity (Cohen 1957), more sophisticated reasoning errors, such as the maturity-of-chances theory, do not occur among young children and become increasingly common with advancing age (Ross & Levy 1958).

Distorted estimates of the true probabilities also result from erroneous information—a principle much utilized by shrewd professionals. Thus, race tracks abound with false tips and spurious "inside information," much of which is deliberately circulated by touts to mislead the fans and thus to skew the betting odds in some desired direction.

*Motivated bias.* While there is ample scope for simple ignorance or error in gambling situations, there is also abundant evidence that such errors are not random or merely cognitive but reflect consistent patterns of motivated bias. Very simply, the "errors" are almost invariably such as to distort the subjective probabilities in the gambler's favor. It has been observed again and again that gamblers consistently overestimate their own skill or luck, and it has been demonstrated experimentally that subjects consistently overestimate low probabilities (cf. Preston & Baratta 1948; Nogee & Lieberman 1960).

A variety of possible explanations of this phenomenon have been advanced. Atkinson (1957) demonstrated experimentally that the tendency to overestimate chances to win is especially likely to be associated with a high need for achievement. Another recent study of probability learning has shown that positive events are learned more rapidly and extinguished more slowly than negative events (Crandall et al. 1958). This might help to explain the tendency among gamblers to think they are ahead—to remember the exciting winning play and forget the losses that preceded it. But, of course, most gamblers do know in a cognitive sense that they might lose and that they have lost in the past. Leon Festinger and his associates would regard this as an example of dissonant information that must somehow be suppressed if the gambler wishes to continue, which of course he does; indeed, this circumstance may cause the actor to develop some extra attraction to the activity, harnessing various secondary drives to it to justify his behavior and compensate for the dissonant information (Lawrence & Festinger 1962).

In terms of learning theory more generally, gambling represents an ideal–typical situation of "intermittent reinforcement," or partial reward, and the evidence is overwhelming that activities reinforced in this way are peculiarly resistant to extinction. One plausible explanation of this is advanced in the conflict–drive theory developed by J. M. Whiting and his associates. Basically, this theory argues that when the same activity is sometimes rewarded and at other times nonrewarded or punished, conflict between the contradictory expectations of reward and punishment has the effect of adding drive strength to the originally reinforced action (Sears et al. 1953). Very simply, if the gambler always won or always lost, he would presumably lose interest; however, the conflict between fear and hope helps keep him going.

**Gambling as expressive behavior.** In considering the purely psychological rewards of gambling, we are clearly getting away from a concern with cognitive orientations and the interpretation of gambling as an instrumental activity directed toward an economic goal and are moving toward interpretations of gambling as an end in itself. It has been shown that even mathematically sophisticated subjects, possessing full information regarding the odds and the probabilities, opt for poor risks most of the time (Scodel et al. 1959). Curiously, it is also clear that there are some kinds of people who would not even bet on a sure thing. Moreover, there are evidently important differences among gamblers themselves: between those who prefer games of pure chance and those who prefer games involving skill or strategy; between system players and long-shot players; or between petty gamblers and addicts, for example. Such differentials as these yield to analysis only in terms of the differential noneconomic needs and motives of different classes of people.

*Games as expressive models.* Games typically occur in times, places, and contexts that are removed from the workaday utilitarian sectors of social structure and hence from the constraints and disciplines that the reality principle imposes on task-oriented activities. Thus, they tend to become intimately involved with the expressive and social–emotional sectors and to be concerned with problems of tension release and integration. Indeed, because they operate in what Kurt Lewin called a "plane of unreality," games are well suited to function as expressive models, onto which a variety of psychological conflicts and problems can be harmlessly projected. As Menninger noted with respect to games of strategy, they may enable us "to express aggression without reality consequences; one can hurt people without really hurting them; we can even kill them without really killing them" (1942, p. 172). In a similar vein, Phillips (1960) has interpreted certain children's games as exercises in the mastery of anxiety, in which psychological problems can be worked through in a miniature and relatively safe context.

Observing that games are not free and spontaneous expressive activities of individuals but are embedded in culture, Roberts and Sutton-Smith (1962) hypothesize that games will have special relevance for psychological problems that are endemic and widespread in the cultures or subgroups in which they are played. While games provide a buffered learning experience for children, game involvement typically diminishes with maturity as individuals become integrated into the mainstream of their culture. Games among adults are thus presumed to represent unresolved areas of conflict, and addicted players are presumed to be persons in a high state of unresolved inner conflict.

We may go on to inquire, for what kinds of needs or conflicts, for what kinds of persons, in what kinds of groups or societies, are gambling games appropriate expressive models? A number of theories have been proposed, each with at least some evidence in its support.

*Teleological motivations in gambling.* Since games of chance apparently originated out of religious and magical practices of divination, it has frequently been proposed that gambling may still perform an important teleological function in helping people orient themselves to the problems and conflicts invoked by the intrusions of chance, risk, and uncertainty in a world presumed to be causally and morally ordered. In principle, chance is meaningless and unintelligible, both causally and ethically. Yet, because of its capacity to violate legitimate expectations in important ways, many people feel that it must mean something: why do these things happen? why do they happen to me? For people who find these problems salient, gambling may assume a cosmic significance as a device for probing after the ground of things and of one's personal relationships to fate (am I lucky today?). In one of the earliest psychological studies of gambling, France (1902) argued that in an environment of uncertainty a belief in luck is functional in encouraging a necessary element of risk assumption but that too much reliance on luck would obviate action and lead to a lack of effort. Relevant empirical evidence is provided in a recent cross-cultural study (Roberts et al. 1959) which demonstrates that games of chance are especially likely to be found in preliterate societies in which the deities are regarded as benevolent and nonaggressive and readily subject to compulsion by humans. In contemporary, rationally oriented societies, gambling appeals particularly to superstitous persons, and it is one of the few areas in which permissive attitudes toward superstition are tolerated.

*Economic conflicts and gambling.* Because of gambling's quasi-instrumental, economic character, it is also peculiarly suitable for the working out of conflicts engendered by the discipline, frustrations, and constraints of the capitalist economic system. Since its rewards are distributed on the basis of chance, gambling would appear to make a mockery of the legitimate economy, with its stress on rationality, discipline, and hard work and its assumed correlations of effort, merit, and reward. Evidence that conflicts in this area are relevant to gambling motivation is provided in another cross-cultural study, which demonstrated that games of chance are most frequently found in preliterate societies in which child-training practices place special stress on responsibility training and arouse high anxiety about achievement performance (Roberts & Sutton-Smith 1962). The authors of this latter study have also demonstrated that in the United States games of chance tend to be preferred by women and low-status economic groups—categories especially involved with positions of frustrating drudgery and with routine responsibilities (Sutton-Smith et al. 1963). A similar hypothesis is tested by Tec (1964) in her study of gambling in Sweden, in which she demonstrated that habitual gambling is especially common in groups that find conventional channels of social advancement blocked (see also Devereux 1949; Caillois 1958).

*Competition and aggression.* Where gambling occurs in conjunction with games of strategy, as in poker (see Riddle 1925), motivations of personal competition and aggression may also play a prominent role. In a classic analysis of this theme, W. I. Thomas (1901) viewed gambling as a form of sublimated combat and suggested that such games may help to keep this vital "instinct" alive in our civilized, bureaucratic world. Among preliterate societies it has been shown that games of strategy tend to occur most frequently in the relatively complex societies with developed systems of stratification, in which social competition becomes problematic and a source of conflict (Roberts et al. 1959). In the contemporary United States a preference for games of strategy and also games of physical prowess is more common among higher-status persons (Sutton-Smith et al. 1963).

*Anxiety and guilt in gambling.* Finally, there are theories that have focused upon thrill-seeking motivations in gambling behavior and their relationship to anxiety. There is broad consensus among students of habitual gamblers that, for all their apparent external calm, gamblers are in fact highly anxious persons. The psychological literature on levels of aspiration provides abundant evidence that persons known to be high in anxiety are particularly prone to set goals for themselves that are grossly unrealistic on the basis of past performance, being either much too high or much too low (cf. Lewin et al. 1944). It has also been demonstrated that unrealistic aspirations are more likely to be set in gaming situations, perhaps because of their miniature and fictitious character, than in real life situations (Frank 1935). Addressing himself to such findings, Atkinson (1957) argues that unrealistic aspirations in fact serve the function of minimizing anxiety about failure, for if one did not really expect to succeed, failure has very little sting. In his studies of probability preferences, he was able to demonstrate that persons high in "need achievement" and presumably high in success drives typically prefer risks at intermediate probability levels, in which success or failure are equally probable and, hence, which generate a maximum of tension and anxiety. Subjects low in "need achievement" and presumably more con-

cerned with fear of failure typically preferred risks at extreme probability levels (either sure things or long shots), in which the success–failure tension is greatly reduced. Persons with high success need would presumably prefer games of skill or strategy, while persons with high fear of failure would prefer games of pure chance, in which failure is peculiarly noninvidious [see ACHIEVEMENT MOTIVATION].

Why do people who are high in anxiety and in fear of failure elect to gamble at all? Edmund Bergler, the only psychoanalyst who has dealt extensively with the problem of addicted gamblers, has argued that such gamblers are genuine neurotics, driven by unconscious aggression and latent rebellion "against logic, cleverness, moderation, morals and renunciation. That latent rebellion, based on the inwardly never-relinquished 'pleasure principle,' scoffs ironically at all the rules of education. Heavy inner retaliation is the result . . . rebellion activates a deep unconscious feeling of guilt" (1943, pp. 385–386). This guilt, Bergler argues, becomes in turn a source of anxiety and creates a need for self-punishment. These unconscious feelings are then neatly displaced into the segregated, miniature, and toylike setting of gambling, where they may be more or less harmlessly worked out. The gambler persuades himself that the real source of his guilt and anxiety is the tension of the game itself, and he achieves the needed self-punishment by keeping going until he loses. Thus, unconsciously, the neurotic gambler wants to lose, and he needs to lose in order to keep his psychological books in balance (see also Bergler 1957; Olmsted 1962).

Because gambling provides such a neat, ready-made, institutionalized, and culturally sanctioned mechanism for the handling of neurotic problems of this sort, the neurotic gambler does not feel neurotic and rarely appears voluntarily for treatment. Hence, to date there has been very little empirical research on gambling addiction, and academic psychologists have largely ignored the problem. There is, however, at least some empirical evidence that gambling may also serve somewhat parallel conflict-resolving functions for nonaddicted petty gamblers, along the lines indicated earlier in this article.

## The sociology of gambling

From a sociological point of view gambling is of interest primarily as an institutionalized deviant pattern. Although it is widely disapproved of, gambling is nevertheless also widely practiced, and it has given rise to an extensive *sub rosa* organization that is elaborately articulated with the underworld, on the one hand, and with the legitimate world of its clientele, on the other.

**Attitudes toward gambling.** The disapproval of gambling is ancient and extremely widespread, although varying greatly in intensity, content, and rationale. At different times and places gambling has been treated as a capital offense or merely as a misdemeanor. Legal restrictions have ranged from total prohibition to selective permissiveness, in which certain types of gambling activities have been permitted or even encouraged while others were forbidden or in which the rules against gaming were lifted during stated holidays or holy days. The laws have often made a distinction between games of pure chance and games of skill or between professional gamblers and their clients. Similarly, the grounds for the disapproval of gambling have varied widely, ranging from views that hold that gambling is fundamentally wrong in principle to views that hold that gambling is wrong only if it produces manifestly evil consequences. Essentially the same conclusions, moreover, have been derived at times from theological and ethical arguments and at other times from rationalistic, scientific, and pragmatic grounds.

In Western society attitudes toward gambling have varied significantly among different religious groups. While the Bible is silent on the subject of gambling, there are numerous references to the use of lots for serious purposes, as when Moses was instructed to allocate the lands of Canaan among the Israelites by lot (Numbers 26.55). Since chance events were considered "acts of God," the use of the lot, with appropriate ritual and respect, was regarded as justified for discerning the divine will in serious matters. However, the use of the lot for frivolous purposes, as in gaming, was regarded as a sacrilege and profanation. While formal opposition to gambling has persisted among Jewish moralists, prevailing attitudes have softened considerably, and they now view gaming as essentially a useless waste of time. Moreover, since the Middle Ages gambling has been widespread within the Jewish community. Roman Catholics have also come to take a liberal attitude toward gambling, holding that there is nothing wrong in principle with gambling, providing only that certain conditions be met: that the game be honest, that the stakes be moderate and within the means of the players, and that the money staked be one's own, for example.

*Gambling and the Protestant ethic.* In Western society fundamental opposition to gambling, as a matter of basic ethical principle, is centered squarely in Protestantism and in the cultures where these denominations prevail. These are also, as

Weber (1904–1905) observed, the same cultures in which modern bourgeois capitalism has achieved its greatest development. This fact suggests the hypothesis that gambling is somehow peculiarly antithetical, in principle at least, to the core of values embraced in this dominant economic system and in its supporting Protestant ethic.

On the surface, at any rate, the antithesis would seem to be clear enough. Among the core values of bourgeois capitalism are its special emphasis on rationality, disciplined work habits, prudence, thrift, methodical adherence to routine, and the assumed correlation of effort, ethical merit, and reward. The values symbolically embodied in gambling are diametrically opposed to these core virtues. Since its rewards are based on chance, gambling is explicitly and spitefully nonethical and makes a mockery of the required correlation of merit and reward. Thus, it tends to undermine disciplined work habits, prudence, and thrift; and in place of the needed rational–empirical orientations, it tends to foster superstitious beliefs and magical practices. If the values fostered by gambling were to become general in the population, the whole system of ethical sentiments that functions to sustain this dominant economic system would simply wither away. So argue the Protestant moralists.

In fact, of course, even in the dominant economic system the alternative values of initiative, daring, boldness, shrewdness, aggressive competitiveness, and willingness to assume risks also play a prominent role, and sheer luck is not always irrelevant. Because these values do not fit so neatly with those of the ethically sanctioned core, they have been the focus of considerable cultural ambivalence and guilt. The American public is uncomfortably aware, for example, of certain disquieting similarities between gambling and transactions on the stock markets; but open discussion of these similarities is strongly tabooed, and standard economic texts make a frantic effort to focus on the differences. In effect, gambling becomes a whipping boy to serve the precarious distinction between forms of speculation that are functionally useful and hence "legitimate" and those that are functionless or dysfunctional. Thus, when speculation gets out of hand, the obviously dysfunctional consequences for the economy are blamed, not on legitimate businessmen and still less on the stock market system, but on "gamblers," who have somehow invaded the market and should be driven from it. More generally, it is quite possible that the disapproval of gambling, in addition to reinforcing certain functionally appropriate values and attitudes, functions as a mechanism through which society seeks to allay its fears and misgivings about the ethical integrity of the dominant system—a fact that may account for the persistence and intensity of this disapproval in Protestant societies (Devereux 1949, chapter 18).

**Functions of gambling for society.** The fact that gambling persists in spite of the powerful legal and ethical taboos against it may be taken as evidence that it serves important psychological functions for the gamblers; the preceding discussion of the psychology of gambling has called attention to at least some of these. But what about functions or dysfunctions of gambling for society? This, of course, is an empirical question that cannot be answered on the basis of a priori principle. The fact that the *disapproval* of gambling is functional for society does not in itself establish that the *practice* of gambling is therefore dysfunctional, for the questions of scale, contexts, and side effects must also be considered. Most observers would probably agree that the addicted gambler, like the alcoholic, is a waste for society. Moreover, it is probably true, as the moralists have argued, that if gambling became a major preoccupation for the whole population and if the attitudes and practices of gambling were to permeate the sphere of the dominant economic system, the consequences for society would be seriously dysfunctional.

However, there is no evidence that petty gambling is in any way damaging to character or that petty gamblers differ in significant ways from nongamblers (Tec 1964). On the contrary, petty gambling may function as a kind of institutionalized "solution" for many of the specific psychological problems generated by the conflicts, strains, and ambivalences embedded in the economic system. It may serve to revitalize certain relevant patterns of motivation that are given little scope in routine economic pursuits, such as motives relating to themes of daring, combat, faith, and willingness to take chances. It has also been argued that the existence of institutionalized petty gambling is functional for society in providing a channel into which potentially disruptive speculative tendencies may be safely deflected from the legitimate market place. To these should be added the positive (and perhaps somewhat perverse) value-reinforcing and scapegoating societal function of the disapproval of gambling, for which institutionalized gambling provides a convenient target.

## The legalization issue

If recreational petty gambling is harmless enough and may even perform useful functions for personality and society, the question naturally arises, should gambling be legalized? In fact, several forms of gambling have already been legalized during the present century. Gambling casinos flourish in many European countries and in Latin America; many nations, including even the Soviet Union and China, have adopted state lotteries; and legalized football betting pools have captured enormous followings in England and Sweden.

**Gambling and law in the United States.** In the United States pari-mutuel betting at racetracks has been legalized in approximately half the states. Several states allow the playing of bingo for charitable purposes; two states (New Hampshire and New York) operate a lottery, and only one state (Nevada) permits all forms of gambling. Although there is unmistakable evidence that moral resistance to legalized gambling is weakening rapidly in the United States, until November 1966, with the above exceptions, proposals to legalize any other form of gambling in the United States had been soundly defeated.

Although legal sanctions may have some dampening effect on the amount of gambling that occurs, they have never been able to stop gambling altogether. Sample polls in the United States have indicated over and over again that a majority of American adults do in fact gamble at least occasionally, in spite of moral taboos and legal restrictions. In 1951 the Kefauver committee estimated the volume of illegal betting in the United States at $20,000 million per year (Kefauver 1951), but that estimate is almost certainly too low. In 1963 an officially recorded $2,700 million was wagered legally on horse races alone, through the pari-mutuel machines, and experts are generally agreed that at least ten times as much was wagered illegally with bookmakers. Scarne (1961, p. 1) places the probable total volume of betting, for all types of gambling in the United States, at closer to $500,000 million a year. While this estimate is probably too large, there is ample evidence that the volume of illegal betting in the United States is sufficient to support a major industry. Indeed, since the legalization of the liquor industry in 1933, gambling has become the major source of support of the organized underworld in the United States.

The antigambling laws are unenforced and unenforceable in the United States for two principal reasons. First, the enormous financial resources controlled by the professional gamblers have enabled them to buy protection from excessive police or political harassment. Indeed, gambling has become one of the principal sources of political corruption and graft in America, especially at municipal levels (Devereux 1949; Kefauver 1951). Second, the general public, although sufficiently ambivalent to insist that antigambling statutes remain on the books, does not really want the gambling laws enforced and hence provides grossly insufficient support to reform-administration and routine enforcement efforts. As noted above, gambling is a peculiar form of crime, which is carried on with the willing consent of its victims; even when the victims have been clearly duped or cheated, they are usually loath to complain to the police, because of feelings of embarrassment and shame.

*Arguments for legalization.*    The proponents of legalization argue that gambling—at least regulated petty gambling—is probably harmless, possibly beneficial, and in any case ineradicable. Antigambling statutes can never be effectively enforced. By keeping them on the books, we throw the entire operation into the hands of the underworld, create thereby an enormous source of revenue and power for organized crime, and keep alive a major source of political graft and corruption in America. Moreover, we place an unnecessary burden of guilt and hypocrisy upon the lay public, which must patronize these illegal and frequently dishonest establishments to indulge their gambling propensities. Partial legalization, as it currently exists in the United States, is doubly unsatisfactory, the argument continues, for it is discriminatory, hypocritical, and sabotages the moral convictions needed for effective law enforcement. Legalization will effectively end this sort of hypocrisy, get gambling into the open where it can be suitably regulated and controlled, dry up a major source of underworld income and power, eliminate the occasion and resource for police graft and political corruption, and make available to the state a highly lucrative source of additional revenue, achieved through the most painless known form of taxation. These arguments were ably stated some thirty years ago by a leading American sociologist, E. W. Burgess (1935), and have been repeated ever since. Until now they have not prevailed, even though recent public opinion polls show unmistakable trends in this direction.

*Arguments against legalization.*    The opposition to legalization stems from several sources and draws on a variety of arguments. The core of resistance in the United States is still firmly rooted in the residual Puritan culture, which regards gambling as inherently sinful and placates its restive conscience by keeping the official façade of culture officially against it. Whatever the merits of the moralists' theological or ethical grounds, their arguments tend to be sociologically naive; in the empirical world one drink does not necessarily make an alcoholic or one lottery ticket an addicted gambler. While conceding that a generalized gambling mania might have disastrous consequences for society, it is an empirical question whether

legalization would have this consequence. However, the moralists undoubtedly score a strong empirical point in their argument that selective legalization weakens the public will to enforce the statutes which remain.

Arguments from other sources have attempted to grapple more directly with empirical consequences. Would legalization in fact rid gambling of gangster influence? No, answers Virgil Peterson (1945), who was for many years chairman of the Chicago Crime Commission, citing the continued influence of the underworld in the liquor business even after the repeal of prohibition laws, and the unsavory history of graft and corruption which accompanied the later days of legalized lotteries in nineteenth-century America. In rebuttal proponents point out that most European state lotteries have operated successfully for years without major scandal. But perhaps the United States is different.

Would legalization set off a wholesale gambling mania, create a population of gambling addicts, and sabotage work disciplines and the ethical attitudes which maintain them? Undoubtedly the incidence of gambling would increase, perhaps quite substantially, if the taboos were lifted and the facilities made more visible, guilt-free, and accessible, but nobody knows for sure how much it would increase. So far, the legalization of football pools and off-track betting shops in England has not produced any runaway mania. But again, perhaps the United States is different. There is at least some evidence that by the 1820s American lotteries had reached such craze proportions that they had seriously disruptive consequences for some communities (Spofford 1892) and some evidence that during the racing season at local tracks many local businesses suffer, absenteeism increases, installment payments fall off, and petty crimes increase (New Jersey State Chamber of Commerce 1939). Regarding the possible long-run effects of wholesale legalization upon the ethical attitudes and beliefs which underpin the system of bourgeois capitalism, there is no relevant empirical evidence. Opponents of legalization point to Latin America, where permissive attitudes to gambling and generally more fatalistic value systems prevail and where bourgeois capitalism has been slow to develop. Who can say whether gambling is cause or consequence in this relationship? Recalling the functions attributed above to the disapproval of gambling, could the United States afford an attitude of moral indifference?

The solution, of course, does not have to be of an either–or nature. Although few are willing to admit it and still fewer to recommend it, since it violates all the principles of logic and common sense, the United States has again and again shown by its behavior that it still covertly prefers the present type of compromise solution, in which a formal façade of disapprobation and legal taboo is combined with halfhearted enforcement and widespread practice. Through this arrangement it does achieve at least some measure of regulation and constraint, keeps the public conscience appeased, and yet provides generous opportunities for those who would gamble to do so (for a carefully reasoned defense of this arrangement, see Dos Passos 1904). But these gains, if they be that, are not achieved without serious cost; and in any event, in this age of increasing secularization it is highly probable that the proponents of further legalization will have won their battle in the United States before another edition of this encyclopedia appears.

EDWARD C. DEVEREUX, JR.

[*See also* GAME THEORY; LEISURE; SOCIAL CONTROL; SPECULATION, HEDGING, AND ARBITRAGE; UTILITY.]

BIBLIOGRAPHY

ATKINSON, JOHN W. (1957) 1958 Motivational Determinants of Risk-taking Behavior. Pages 322–339 in John W. Atkinson (editor), *Motives in Fantasy, Action, and Society: A Method of Assessment and Study.* Princeton, N.J.: Van Nostrand. → First published in Volume 64 of the *Psychological Review.*

BERGLER, EDMUND 1943 The Gambler: The Misunderstood Neurotic. *Journal of Criminal Psychopathology* 4:379–393.

BERGLER, EDMUND 1957 *The Psychology of Gambling.* New York: Hill & Wang.

BLOCK, HERBERT A. 1962 The Gambling Business: An American Paradox. *Crime & Delinquency* 8:355–364.

BRIM, O. G. JR.; and KOENIG, F. W. 1959 Two Aspects of Subjective Probability Among College Students. *Journal of Communication* 9:19–26.

BURGESS, ERNEST W. 1935 *The Next Step in the War on Crime—Legalize Gambling: A Report to Governor Harry M. Horner.* Chicago: Adair.

CAILLOIS, ROGER (1958) 1961 *Man, Play and Games.* New York: Free Press. → First published as *Les jeux et les hommes.*

COHEN, JOHN 1957 Subjective Probability. *Scientific American* 197:128–138.

COHEN, JOHN; and HANSEL, C. E. M. 1956 *Risk and Gambling: The Study of Subjective Probability.* New York: Philosophical Library.

COHEN, JOHN; and HANSEL, C. E. M. 1958 The Nature of Decisions in Gambling. *Acta psychologica* 13:357–370.

COOMBS, C. H.; and KOMORITA, S. S. 1958 Measuring Utility of Money Through Decisions. *American Journal of Psychology* 71:383–389.

CRANDALL, V. J.; SOLOMON, D.; and KELLAWAY, R. 1958 The Value of Anticipated Events as a Determinant of Probability Learning and Motivation. *Journal of Genetic Psychology* 58:3–10.

DEVEREUX, EDWARD C. 1949 Gambling and the Social Structure: A Sociological Study of Lotteries and Horse Racing in Contemporary America. Ph.D. dissertation, Harvard Univ.

DOS PASSOS, JOHN R. 1904 Gambling and Cognate Vices. *Yale Law Journal* 14:9–17.

FRANCE, CLEMENS J. 1902 The Gaming Impulse. *American Journal of Psychology* 13:364–407.

FRANK, J. D. 1935 Some Psychological Determinants of Level of Aspiration. *American Journal of Psychology* 47:285–293.

FRIEDMAN, MILTON; and SAVAGE, L. J. 1948 The Utility Analysis of Choices Involving Risk. *Journal of Political Economy* 56:279–304.

GALDSTON, IAGO 1951 Psychodynamics of the Triad, Alcoholism, Gambling and Superstition. *Mental Hygiene* 35:589–598.

GREENSON, RALPH R. 1947 On Gambling. *American Imago* 4:61–77.

JARVIK, MURRAY E. 1951 Probability Learning and a Negative Recency Effect in the Serial Anticipation of Alternative Symbols. *Journal of Experimental Psychology* 41:291–297.

KEFAUVER, ESTES 1951 *Crime in America.* Garden City, N.Y.: Doubleday.

KOMORITA, S. S. 1959 Factors Which Influence Subjective Probability. *Journal of Experimental Psychology* 58:386–389.

LAWRENCE, DOUGLAS H.; and FESTINGER, LEON 1962 *Deterrents and Reinforcement: The Psychology of Insufficient Reward.* Stanford Univ. Press.

LEWIN, KURT et al. 1944 Level of Aspiration. Volume 1, pages 333–378 in Joseph McV. Hunt (editor), *Personality and the Behavior Disorders.* New York: Ronald Press.

MENNINGER, KARL 1942 *Love Against Hate.* New York: Harcourt. → A paperback edition was published in 1959.

MOSTELLER, FREDERICK; and NOGEE, PHILIP 1951 An Experimental Measurement of Utility. *Journal of Political Economy* 59:371–404.

NEW JERSEY STATE CHAMBER OF COMMERCE, RESEARCH DEPARTMENT 1939 *The Economic Effects of Parimutuel Horse Racing, as Measured by the Experiences of Other States.* Orange, N.J.: The Department.

NOGEE, PHILIP; and LIEBERMAN, BERNHARDT 1960 The Auction Value of Certain Risky Situations. *Journal of Psychology* 49:167–179.

OLMSTED, CHARLOTTE 1962 *Heads I Win—Tails You Lose.* New York: Macmillan.

PETERSON, VIRGIL W. (1945) 1949 Gambling—Should It Be Legalized? *Journal of Criminal Law and Criminology* 40:259–329. → First published by the Chicago Crime Commission.

PHILLIPS, R. H. 1960 The Nature and Function of Children's Formal Games. *Psychoanalytical Quarterly* 29:200–207.

PRESTON, MALCOLM G.; and BARATTA, PHILIP 1948 An Experimental Study of the Auction Value of an Uncertain Outcome. *American Journal of Psychology* 61:183–193.

RIDDLE, E. M. 1925 Aggressive Behavior in a Small Group. *Archives of Psychology* No. 78.

ROBERTS, JOHN M.; ARTH, MALCOLM S.; and BUSH, ROBERT R. 1959 Games in Culture. *American Anthropologist* New Series 61:597–605.

ROBERTS, JOHN M.; and SUTTON-SMITH, BRIAN 1962 Child Training and Game Involvement. *Ethnology* 1:166–185.

ROSS, B. M.; and LEVY, N. 1958 Patterned Predictions of Chance Events by Children and Adults. *Psychological Reports* 4:87–124.

ROYDEN, HALSEY L.; SUPPES, PATRICK; and WALSH, KAROL 1959 A Model for the Experimental Measurement of the Utility of Gambling. *Behavioral Science* 4:11–18.

SCARNE, JOHN 1961 *Scarne's Complete Guide to Gambling.* New York: Simon & Schuster.

SCODEL, A.; RATOOSH, P.; and MINAS, J. S. 1959 Some Personality Correlates of Decision Making Under Conditions of Risk. *Behavioral Science* 4:19–28.

SEARS, R. R. et al. 1953 Some Child Rearing Antecedents of Aggression and Dependency in Young Children. *Genetic Psychology Monographs* 47:135–236.

SPOFFORD, A. R. 1892 Lotteries in American History. American Historical Association, *Annual Report* [1892]:173–195.

SUTTON-SMITH, B.; ROBERTS, J. M.; and KOZELKA, R. M. 1963 Game Involvement in Adults. *Journal of Social Psychology* 60:15–30.

TEC, NECHAMA 1964 *Gambling in Sweden.* Totowa, N.J.: Bedminster.

THOMAS, W. I. 1901 The Gaming Instinct. *American Journal of Sociology* 6:750–763.

THORNER, ISIDOR 1956 Ascetic Protestantism, Gambling, and the One-price System. *American Journal of Economics and Sociology* 15:161–172.

VICKREY, WILLIAM 1945 Measuring Marginal Utility by Reactions to Risk. *Econometrica* 13:319–333.

WEBER, MAX (1904–1905) 1930 *The Protestant Ethic and the Spirit of Capitalism.* Translated by Talcott Parsons, with a foreword by R. H. Tawney. London: Allen & Unwin; New York: Scribner. → First published in German. The 1930 edition has been reprinted frequently. See especially pages 35–92.

# GAME THEORY

I. THEORETICAL ASPECTS          *Oskar Morgenstern*
II. ECONOMIC APPLICATIONS          *Martin Shubik*

## I
### THEORETICAL ASPECTS

The theory of games is a mathematical discipline designed to treat rigorously the question of optimal behavior of participants in games of strategy and to determine the resulting equilibria. In such games each participant is striving for his greatest advantage in situations where the outcome depends not only on his actions alone, nor solely on those of nature, but also on those of other participants whose interests are sometimes opposed, sometimes parallel, to his own. Thus, in games of strategy there is conflict of interest as well as possible cooperation among the participants. There may be uncertainty for each participant because the actions of others may not be known with certainty. Such situations, often of extreme complexity, are found not only in games but also in business, politics, war, and other social activities. Therefore, the theory serves to interpret both games themselves and social phenomena with which certain games are strictly identical. The theory is normative in that it aims at giving advice to each player about his optimal behavior; it is descriptive when viewed as a model for analyzing empirically given occurrences. In analyzing games the theory does not assume rational behavior; rather, it attempts to determine what "rational" can mean when an individual is confronted with the problem of optimal behavior in games and equivalent situations.

The results of the interlocking individual actions are expressed by numbers, such as money or a numerically defined utility for each player transferable among all. Games of strategy include games of chance as a subcase; in games of chance the problem for the player is merely to determine and evaluate the probability of each possible outcome. In games of strategy the outcome for a player cannot be determined by mere probability calculations. Specifically, no player can make mere statistical assumptions about the behavior of the other players in order to decide on his own optimal strategy.

But nature, when interfering in a game through chance events, is assumed to be indifferent with regard to the player or players affected by chance events. Since the study of games of chance has given rise to the theory of probability, without which modern natural science could not exist, the expectation is that the understanding of the far more complicated games of strategy may gradually produce similar consequences for the social sciences.

**History.** In 1710 the German mathematician–philosopher Leibniz foresaw the need and possibility of a theory of games of strategy, and the notion of a minimax strategy (see section on "Two-person, zero-sum games," below) was first formulated two years later by James Waldegrave. (See the letter from Waldegrave in the 1713 edition of Montmort 1708; see also Baumol & Goldfeld 1967.) The similarity between games of strategy and economic processes was occasionally mentioned, for example, by Edgeworth in his *Mathematical Psychics* (1881). Specialized theorems, such as Ernst Zermelo's on chess, were stated for some games; and Émile Borel developed a limited minimax strategy, but he denied the possibility of a general theorem. It was not until John von Neumann (1928) proved the fundamental theorem that a true theory of games emerged (see section on "Two-person, zero-sum games," below). In their *Theory of Games and Economic Behavior*, von Neumann and Morgenstern (1944) extended the theory, especially to games involving more than two players, and gave applications of the theory in economics. Since then, throughout the world a vast literature has arisen in which the main tenets of the theory have been widened and deepened and many new concepts and ideas introduced. The four-volume *Contributions to the Theory of Games* (Kuhn & Tucker 1950–1959) and *Advances in Game Theory* (Dresher, Shapley, & Tucker 1964) give evidence of this continuing movement. These works contain extensive bibliographies, but see especially Volume 4 of *Contributions to the Theory of Games*.

**Game theory concepts**

Games are described by specifying possible behavior within the rules of the game. The rules are in each case unambiguous; for example, certain moves are allowed for specific pieces in chess but are forbidden for others. The rules are also inviolate. When a social situation is viewed as a game, the rules are given by the physical and legal environment within which an individual's actions may take place. (For example, in a market individuals are permitted to bargain, to threaten with boycotts, etc., but they are not permitted to use physical force to acquire an article or to attempt to change its price.) The concrete occasion of a game is called a play, which is described by specifying, out of all possible, allowable moves, the sequence of choices actually made by the players or participants. After the final move, the umpire determines the payments to each player. The players may act singly, or, if the rules of the game permit it and if it is advantageous, they may form coalitions. When a coalition forms, the distribution of the payments to the coalition among its members has to be established. All payments are stated in terms of money or a numerically defined utility that is transferable from one player to another. The payment function is generally assumed to be known to the players, although modifications of this assumption have been introduced, as have other modifications—for example, about the character of the utilities and even about the transferability of payments.

The "extensive" form of a game, given in terms of successive moves and countermoves, can be represented mathematically by a game tree, which describes the unfolding of the moves, the state of information of the players at the moment of each choice, and the alternatives for choices available to each player at each occasion. This description can, in a strict mathematical sense, be given equivalently in a "normalized" form: each player, uninformed about the choices made by any other player, chooses a single number that identifies a "strategy" from his given finite or infinite set of strategies. When all personal choices and a possible random choice are made (simultaneously), the umpire determines the payments. Each strategy is a complete plan of playing, allowing for all contingencies as represented by the choices and moves of all other players and of nature. The payoff for each player is then represented by his mathematical expectation of the outcome for himself. The final description of the game therefore involves only the players' strategies and no further chance elements.

The theory explicitly assumes that each player, besides being completely informed about the alternative payoffs due to all moves made or strategies chosen, can perform all necessary computations needed to determine his optimal behavior. (This assumption of complete information is also commonplace in current economic theory, although seldom stated explicitly.)

The payments made by all players may add up to zero, as in games played for entertainment. In this case the gains of some are exactly balanced by the losses of others. Such games are called zero-sum games. In other instances the sum of all payments may be a constant (different from zero) or may be a variable; in these cases all players may gain or lose. Applications of game theory to economic or political problems require the study of these games, since in a purchase, for example, both sides gain. An economy is normally productive so that the gains outweigh any losses, whereas in a war both sides may lose.

If a player chooses a particular strategy as identified by its number, he selects a *pure* strategy; if he allows a chance mechanism, specified by himself, to make this selection for him, he chooses a *mixed* or *statistical* strategy. The number of pure strategies for a player normally is finite, partly because the rules of games bring the play to an end after a finite number of moves, partly because the player is confronted with only a finite number of alternatives. However, it is possible to treat cases with infinitely many strategies as well as to consider even the borderline case of games with infinitely many players. These serve essentially to study pathological examples or to explore certain mathematical characteristics.

Game theory uses essentially combinatorial and set-theoretical concepts and tools, since no specific calculus has as yet evolved—as happened when differential and integral calculus were invented simultaneously with the establishment of classical mechanics. Differential calculus is designed to determine maxima and minima, but in games, as well as in politics, these are not defined, because the outcome of a player's actions does not depend on his actions alone (plus nature). This applies to all players simultaneously. A maximum (or minimum) of a function can be achieved only when all variables on which the maximum (minimum) depends are under the complete control of the would-be maximizer. *This is never the case in games of strategy.* Therefore, in the equivalent business, political, or military operations there obtains no maximum (minimum) problem, whether with or without side conditions, as assumed in the classical literature of these fields; rather one is confronted there with an entirely different conceptual structure, which the theory of games analyzes.

### Two-person, zero-sum games

The simplest game of strategy is a two-person, zero-sum game, in which players A and B each have a finite number of strategies and make their choices unknown to each other. Let $P$ be the payoff to the first player, and let $-P$ be the payoff to the second player. Then $P$ is greater than, equal to, or less than 0, depending on whether A wins, draws, or loses. Let $A_1, A_2, \cdots, A_n$ be the strategies available to player A and $B_1, B_2, \cdots, B_m$ be the strategies available to player B. In the resulting $n \times m$ array of numbers, each row represents a pure strategy of A, each column a pure strategy of B. The intersections of the rows and columns show the payoffs to player A from player B. The first player wishes to maximize this payoff, while the second wishes to minimize it. This array of numbers is called the payoff matrix, an example of which is presented in Table 1, where payments go from B to A. Player A's most desirable payoff is 8; B's is $-10$. Should player A pick strategy $A_1$, either of these two events may happen depending on B's action. But if A picks $A_1$, B in his own interest would want to pick $B_3$, which would mean that A would have to pay 10 units to B instead of receiving 8. The row minima represent the worst that could happen to A for each of his strategies, and it is natural that he would want to make as great as possible the least gain he can expect from each; that is, he seeks the maximum of the row minima, or the *maximin*, which in Table 1 is $-1$ (strategy $A_3$). Conversely, B will wish to minimize the column maxima—that is, seek the

*minimax*—which is also $-1$ (strategy $B_2$). We would say that each player is using a minimax strategy—that is, each player selects the strategy that minimizes his maximum loss. Any deviation from the optimal strategies $A_3$ and $B_2$ is fraught with danger for the deviating player, so that each will choose the strategy that contains the so-called *saddle point of the payoff function.* The saddle point is defined as the point at which the maximin equals the minimax. At this point the least that A can secure for himself is equal to the most that B may have to part with. (In the above example A has to pay one unit to B.) If there is more than one saddle point in the payoff matrix, then they are all equal to each other. Games possessing saddle points in pure strategies are called *specially strictly determined.* In these games it is immaterial whether the choice of the pure strategy by either player is made openly before the other makes his choice. Games of *perfect* information—that is, games in which each player at each move is always informed about the entire previous history of the play, so that what is preliminary to his choice is also anterior to it—are always specially strictly determined. Chess belongs in this class; bridge does not, since each of the two players (one "player" being the north–south team, the other the east–west team) is not even completely informed about himself—for example, north does not know precisely what cards south holds.

Most games will have no saddle points in pure strategies; they are then said to be not strictly determined. The simplest case is matching pennies. The payoff matrix for this game is presented in Table 2. Here, if one player has to choose openly before the other does, he is sure to lose. Each player will therefore strive to prevent information about his choice from flowing to the other. This is accomplished by the player's choice of a chance mechanism, which selects from among the available pure strategies with probabilities determined by the player. In matching pennies, the chance mechanism should select "heads" with probability $\frac{1}{2}$ and "tails" with probability $\frac{1}{2}$. This randomization may be achieved by tossing the coin before showing it. If there is a premium, say on matching heads over matching tails, the payoff matrix would reflect this, and the probabilities with which the two sides of the coin have to be played in order to prevent disclosure of a pattern of playing to the benefit of the opponent would no longer be $\frac{1}{2}$ for heads and $\frac{1}{2}$ for tails. Thus, when there is no saddle point in pure strategies a randomization by a chance mechanism is called for. The players are then said to be using mixed, or statistical, strategies. This does *not* trans-

**Table 1 — Payoff matrix for a two-person, zero-sum game**

| A's strategy | B's strategy B₁ | B₂ | B₃ | Row minima |
|---|---|---|---|---|
| $A_1$ | 8 | $-3$ | $-10$ | $-10$ |
| $A_2$ | 0 | $-2$ | 6 | $-2$ |
| $A_3$ | 4 | $-1$ | 5 | $-1$ |
| Column maxima | 8 | $-1$ | 6 | |

*Table 2 — Payoff matrix for matching pennies*

| A's penny \ B's penny | Heads | Tails | Row minima |
|---|---|---|---|
| Heads | 1 | −1 | −1 |
| Tails | −1 | 1 | −1 |
| Column maxima | 1 | 1 | |

form a game of strategy into a game of chance: the strategic decision is the specification of the randomization device and the assignment of the proper probabilities to each available pure strategy. Whether pure or mixed strategies are needed to assure a saddle point, the theory at no point requires that the players make assumptions about each other's intelligence, guesses, and the like. The choice of the optimal strategy is independent of all such considerations. Strategies selected in this way are perfect from the defensive point of view. A theory of true offensive strategies requires new ideas and has not yet been developed.

Von Neumann proved that each matrix game can be made strictly determined by introducing mixed strategies. This is the *fundamental theorem* of game theory. It shows that each zero-sum, two-person game has a saddle point in mixed strategies and that optimal mixed strategies exist for each of the two players. The original proof of this theorem made use of rather complex properties of set theory, functional calculus, and combinatorics. Since the original proof was given, a number of alternative, simplified versions have been given by various authors. The numerical solution of a matrix game with $m$ columns and $n$ rows demands the solution of a system of linear inequalities of $m + n + 1$ unknowns, the $m + n$ probabilities for the strategies of players A and B and the minimax value. There exist many techniques for solving such systems; notably, an equivalence with solving dual linear programs has proved to be of great importance [*see* PROGRAMMING]. High-speed computers are needed to cope with the rapid rise of the required arithmetical operations. A more modest view of mixed strategies is the notion of behavioral strategies, which are the probability distributions over each player's information sets in the extensive form of the game. For games such as chess, even the optimal pure strategy cannot be computed, although the existence of a saddle point in pure strategies can be proved and either white or black has a winning pure strategy no matter what the other does (or both have pure strategies that enforce a

draw). The problems of finding further computational techniques are actively being investigated.

### *n*-Person, zero-sum games

When the number of players increases to $n \geqslant 3$, new phenomena arise even when the zero-sum restriction remains. It is now possible that cooperation will benefit the players. If this is not the case, the game is called inessential. In an essential game the players will try to form *coalition*s and act through these in order to secure their advantage. Different coalitions may have different strength. A winning coalition will have to divide its proceeds among its members, and each member must be satisfied with the division in order that a stable solution obtains [*see* COALITIONS].

Any possible division of payments among all players is called an *imputation*, but only some of all possible imputations will be contained in a *solution*. An inessential game has precisely one imputation that is better than any other, that is, one that *dominates* all others. This unique imputation forms the solution, but this uniqueness is trivial and applies only to inessential games. There is no cooperation in inessential games.

A solution of an essential game is characteristically a nonempty set of several imputations with the following properties: (1) No imputation in the set is dominated by another imputation in the set. (2) All imputations not in the set are dominated by an imputation contained in the set. There may be an infinite number of imputations in a solution set, and there may be several solution sets, each of which has the above properties. Furthermore, it should be noted that every imputation in a solution set is dominated by some imputation not in that set, but property (2) assures that such a dominating imputation is, in turn, dominated by an imputation in the solution set.

To be considered as a member of a coalition, a player may have to offer *compensations* or side payments to other prospective members. A compensation or side payment may even take the form of giving up privileges that the rules of the game may attribute to a player. A player may be admitted to a coalition under terms less favorable than those obtained by the players who form the initial core of a coalition (this happens first when $n = 4$). Also, coalitions of different strength can be distinguished. *Discrimination* may occur; for example, some players may consider others "taboo"—that is, unworthy as coalition partners. This leads to the types of discriminatory solutions that already occur when $n = 3$. Yet discrimination is not necessarily as bad for the affected player as defeat is for a nondiscriminated player, because cooperation against the discriminated player may not be perfect. A player who by joining a coalition does not contribute more to it than what he can get by playing for himself merely has the role of a dummy.

The fundamental fact of cooperation is that the players in a coalition can each obtain more than they could obtain by playing alone. This expresses the nonadditivity—specifically, the superadditivity—of value, the explanation of which has long been recognized as a basic problem in economics and sociology. In spite of many efforts, no solution was found, but it is now adequately described by the characteristic function $v(S)$, a numerical set function that states for any cooperative $n$-person game the proceeds of the coalition $S$, and an imputation that describes the distribution of all payments among all players (von Neumann & Morgenstern 1944, chapter 6).

Since there may be many solutions to a cooperative (essential) $n$-person game, the question arises as to which of them will in fact prevail. Each solution may correspond to a specific mode of behavior of the players or a specific form of social organization. This expresses the fact that in the same physical setting different types of social organization can be established, each one consistent in itself but in contradiction with other organizations. For example, we observe that the same technology allows the maintenance of varying economic systems, income distributions, and so on. If a *stable standard of behavior* exists (a mode of behavior accepted by society), then it can be argued that the only relevant solution is the one corresponding to this standard.

The choice of an imputation *not* in the solution set, while advantageous to each of those in the particular coalition that is able to enforce this imputation, cannot be maintained because another coalition can enforce another imputation, belonging to the solution set, that dominates the first one. Hence, a standard is set and proposals for imputations that are not in the solution will be rejected. The theory cannot state which imputation of all those belonging to the standard of behavior actually will be chosen—that is, which coalition will form. Work has been done to introduce new assumptions under which this may become feasible. No imputation contained in the solution set guarantees stability by itself, since each is necessarily dominated from the outside. But in turn each imputation is always protected against threats by another one *within* the solution set that dominates the imputation *not* in the solution set.

Since an imputation is a division of proceeds among the players, these conditions define a certain fairness, such that the classical problems of fair division (for example, cutting a cake) become amenable to game-theoretic analysis.

This conceptual structure is more complicated than the conventional view that society could be organized according to some simple principle of maximization. The conventional view would be valid only if there were inessentiality—that is, if there were no advantage in cooperation, or if cooperation were forbidden, or, finally, if a supreme authority were to do away with the entire imputation problem by simply assigning shares of income to the members of the society. Inessentiality would be the case for a strictly communistic society, which is formally equivalent to a Robinson Crusoe economy. This, in turn, is the only formal setup under which the classical notion of marginal utility is logically valid. Whether cooperation through formation of coalitions is advantageous to participants in a society, whether such cooperation, although advantageous, is forbidden, or whether compensations or side payments are ruled out by some authority although coalitions may be entered—these are clearly empirical questions. The theory should take care of all eventualities, and current investigations explore the different avenues. In economic life, mergers, labor unions, trade associations, cartels, etc., express the powerful tendencies toward cooperation. The cooperative case with side payments is the most comprehensive, and the theory was originally designed to deal with this case. Important results have been obtained for cooperative games without side payments (Aumann & Peleg 1961), and the fruitful idea of "bargaining sets" has been introduced (Aumann & Maschler 1964).

All indications point overwhelmingly to the benefits of cooperation of various forms and hence to the empirical irrelevance of those noncooperative, inessential games with uniquely determined solutions consisting only of one single imputation dominating all others (as described in the Lausanne school's general economic equilibrium).

Cooperation may depend on a particular flow of information among the players. Since the required level may not in fact be attainable, noncooperative solutions become important. Economic markets in which players act independently and have no incentive to deviate from a given state have been studied (Nash 1950). *Equilibrium points* can be determined as those points for which unilateral changes in strategy are unprofitable to everyone. As Nash has shown, every finite game, or the domain of mixed strategies, has at least one equilibrium point. If there is more than one equilibrium point, an intermixture of strategy choices need not give another equilibrium point, nor is the payoff to players the same if the points differ from each other.

There is no proof, as yet, that every cooperative *n*-person, zero-sum game for any *n* > 4 has a solution of the specified kind. However, every individual game investigated, even with arbitrarily large *n*, has been found to possess a solution. The indications are that the proof for the general case will eventually be given. Other definitions of solutions—still differing from that of the Lausanne–Robinson Crusoe convention—are possible and somewhat narrow the field of choices. They are inevitably based on further assumptions about the behavior of the participants in the game, which have to be justified from case to case.

## Simple games

In certain *n*-person games the sole purpose is to form a *majority* coalition. These games are the "simple" games in which voting takes place. Ties in voting may occur, and weights may differ from one player to another; for example, the chairman of a committee may have more than one vote. A player's presence may therefore mean the difference between victory or defeat. Games of this nature can be identified with classical cases of production, where the players represent factors of production. It has been proven that even in relatively simple cases, although complete substitutability among players may exist, substitution rates may be undetermined and values are attributed to the players (factors) only by virtue of their *relation* to each other and not by virtue of their individual contribution. Thus, contrary to current economic doctrine, substitutability does not necessarily guarantee equality as far as value is concerned.

Simple games are suited for interpretation of many political situations in that they allow the determination of the weights, or power, of participants in decision processes. A particular power index has been proposed by Shapley. It is based on the notion of the average contribution a player can make to the coalitions to which he may belong, even considering, where necessary, the order in which he joins them. The weight of a senator, a congressman, and the president in the legislative process has been calculated for the United States. The procedure is applicable to other political systems—for example, the Security Council of the United Nations (Shapley 1953).

## Composition of games

Every increase in the number of players brings new phenomena: with the increase from two to three players, coalitions become possible, from three to four, ties may occur among coalitions, etc.

There is no guarantee that for very large *n* an asymptotic convergence of solutions will occur, since coalition formation always reduces large numbers of individual players to small numbers of coalitions acting upon each other. Thus, the increase in the number of players does not necessarily lead to a simplification, as in the case of an enlargement of the numbers of bodies in a physical system, which then allows the introduction of classical methods of statistical averages as a simplification. (When the game is inessential, the number of participants is irrelevant in any case.)

An effective extension of the theory by the enlargement of numbers can be achieved by viewing games played separately as one composite game and by introducing contributions to, or withdrawals from, the proceeds of a given game by a group of players outside the game under consideration. These more complicated notions involve constant-sum games and demonstrate, among other things, how the coalition formation, the degree of cooperation among players, and consequently the distribution of the proceeds among them are affected by the availability of amounts in excess of those due to their own strategies alone. Strategy is clearly greatly influenced by the availability of greater payments than those that can be made by only the other players. Thus, coalitions—namely, social structures—cannot be maintained if outside contributions become larger than specified amounts, such that as a consequence no coalition can exhaust the amounts offered. It can also be shown that the outside source, making contributions or withdrawals, can never be less than a group of three players.

These concepts and results are obviously of a rather complicated nature; they are not always directly accessible to intuition, as corresponds to a truly mathematical theory. When that level is reached, confidence in the mathematical results must override intuition, as the experience in the natural sciences shows. The fact that solutions of *n*-person games are not single numbers or single sets of numbers—but that the above-mentioned, more complicated structures emerge—is not an imperfection of the theory: it is a fundamental property of social organization that can be described only by game-theoretic methods.

## Nonzero-sum games

Nonzero-sum games can be reduced to zero-sum games—which makes that entire theory applicable—by the introduction of a fictitious player, so that an *n*-person, nonzero-sum game becomes equivalent to an (*n* + 1)-person, zero-sum game. The fictitious player is either winning or losing, but since he is fictitious he can never become a member of a coalition. Yet he can be construed as proposing alternative imputations, thereby influencing the players' strategies and thus the course of the play. He will lose according to the degree of cooperation among the players. If the players cooperate perfectly, the maximum social benefit will be attained. In these games there is an increased role of threats, and their costs to the threatening player, although threats already occur in the zero-sum case.

The discriminatory solutions, first encountered for the three-person, zero-sum game, serve as instruments to approach these problems. Most applications to economics involve gains by the community—an economy being productive and there being no voluntary exchange unless both sides profit—while many other social phenomena fall under the domain of zero-sum games. The non-zero-sum theory is so far the part of game theory least developed in detail, although its foundations seem to be firmly established by the above procedure.

## Applications

Game theory is applicable to the study of those social phenomena in which there are agents striving for their own advantage but not in control of all the variables on which the outcome depends. The wide range of situations of which this is true is obvious: they are economic, political, military, and strictly social in nature. Applications have been made in varying degree to all areas; some have led to experiments that have yielded important new insights into the theory itself and into special processes such as bargaining. Finally, the possibility of viewing the basic problem of statistics as a game against nature has given rise to modern statistical decision theory (Wald 1950). The influence of game theory is also evident in philosophy, information theory, cybernetics, and even biology.

OSKAR MORGENSTERN

[*See also the biography of* VON NEUMANN.]

### BIBLIOGRAPHY

AUMANN, R. J.; and PELEG, B. 1961 Von Neumann–Morgenstern Solutions to Cooperative Games Without Side Payments. American Mathematical Society, *Bulletin* 66:173–179.

AUMANN, R. J.; and MASCHLER, M. 1964 The Bargaining Set for Cooperative Games. Pages 443–476 in M. Dresher, L. S. Shapley, and A. W. Tucker (editors), *Advances in Game Theory.* Princeton Univ. Press.

BAUMOL, WILLIAM J.; and GOLDFELD, STEPHEN M. (editors) 1967 *Precursors in Mathematical Economics.* Unpublished manuscript. → To be published in 1967 or 1968 by the London School of Economics and Political Science. Contains the letter from Waldegrave to Rémond de Montmort, first published in the second (1713) edition of Montmort (1708), describing his formulation, and a discussion by Harold W. Kuhn of the identity of Waldegrave.

BERGE, CLAUDE 1957 *Théorie générale des jeux à n personnes.* Paris: Gauthier-Villars.

BLACKWELL, DAVID; and GIRSHICK, M. A. 1954 *Theory of Games and Statistical Decisions.* New York: Wiley.

BRAITHWAITE, RICHARD B. 1955 *Theory of Games as a Tool for the Moral Philosopher.* Cambridge Univ. Press.

BURGER, EWALD (1959) 1963 *Introduction to the Theory of Games.* Englewood Cliffs, N.J.: Prentice-Hall. → First published in German.

DRESHER, MELVIN 1961 *Games of Strategy: Theory and Applications.* Englewood Cliffs, N.J.: Prentice-Hall.

DRESHER, MELVIN; SHAPLEY, L. S.; and TUCKER, A. W. (editors) 1964 *Advances in Game Theory.* Annals of Mathematic Studies, Vol. 32. Princeton Univ. Press.

EDGEWORTH, FRANCIS Y. (1881) 1953 *Mathematical Psychics: An Essay on the Application of Mathematics to the Moral Sciences.* New York: Kelley.

FRÉCHET, MAURICE; and VON NEUMANN, JOHN 1953 Commentary on the Three Notes of Émile Borel. *Econometrica* 21, no. 1:118–127.

KARLIN, SAMUEL 1959 *Mathematical Methods and Theory in Games, Programming and Economics.* 2 vols. Reading, Mass.: Addison-Wesley.

KUHN, HAROLD W.; and TUCKER, A. W. (editors) 1950–1959 *Contributions to the Theory of Games.* 4 vols. Princeton Univ. Press.

LUCE, R. DUNCAN; and RAIFFA, HOWARD 1957 *Games and Decisions: Introduction and Critical Survey.* A Study of the Behavioral Models Project, Bureau of Applied Social Research, Columbia University. New York. → First published in 1954 as *A Survey of the Theory of Games,* Columbia University, Bureau of Applied Social Research, Technical Report No. 5.

MCKINSEY, JOHN C. C. 1952 *Introduction to the Theory of Games.* New York: McGraw-Hill.

[MONTMORT, PIERRE RÉMOND DE] (1708) 1713 *Essay d'analyse sur les jeux de hazard.* 2d ed. Paris: Quillau. → Published anonymously.

MORGENSTERN, OSKAR 1963 *Spieltheorie und Wirtschaftswissenschaft.* Vienna: Oldenbourg.

NASH, JOHN F. JR. 1950 Equilibrium in *n*-Person Games. National Academy of Sciences, *Proceedings* 36:48–49.

PRINCETON UNIVERSITY CONFERENCE 1962 *Recent Advances in Game Theory.* Princeton, N.J.: The Conference.

SHAPLEY, L. S. 1953 A Value for *n*-Person Games. Volume 2, pages 307–317 in Harold W. Kuhn and A. W. Tucker (editors), *Contributions to the Theory of Games.* Princeton Univ. Press.

SHAPLEY, L. S.; and SHUBIK, MARTIN 1954 A Method for Evaluating the Distribution of Power in a Committee System. *American Political Science Review* 48:787–792.

SHUBIK, MARTIN (editor) 1964 *Game Theory and Related Approaches to Social Behavior: Selections.* New York: Wiley.

SUZUKI, MITSUO 1959 *Gemu no riron.* Tokyo: Keisho Shobo.

VILLE, JEAN 1938 Sur la théorie générale des jeux ou intervient l'habilité des joueurs. Pages 105–113 in Émile Borel (editor), *Traité du calcul des probabilités et de ses applications.* Volume 4: Applications diverses et conclusion. Paris: Gauthier-Villars.

VOGELSANG, RUDOLF 1963 *Die mathematische Theorie der Spiele.* Bonn: Dümmler.

VON NEUMANN, JOHN (1928) 1959 On the Theory of Games of Strategy. Volume 4, pages 13–42 in Harold W. Kuhn and A. W. Tucker (editors), *Contributions to the Theory of Games.* Princeton Univ. Press. → First published in German in Volume 100 of the *Mathematische Annalen.*

VON NEUMANN, JOHN; and MORGENSTERN, OSKAR (1944) 1964 *Theory of Games and Economic Behavior.* 3d ed. New York: Wiley.

VOROB'EV, N. N. (editor) 1961 *Matrichnye igry.* Moscow: Gosudarstvennoe Izdatel'stvo Fiziko–Matematicheskoi Literatury. → A collection of translations into Russian from foreign-language publications.

WALD, ABRAHAM (1950) 1964 *Statistical Decision Functions.* New York: Wiley.

WILLIAMS, JOHN D. 1954 *The Compleat Strategyst: Being a Primer in the Theory of Games and Strategy.* New York: McGraw-Hill.

## II
### ECONOMIC APPLICATIONS

The major economic applications of game theory have been in oligopoly theory, bargaining theory, and general equilibrium theory. Several distinct branches of game theory exist and need to be identified before our attention is limited to economic behavior. John von Neumann and Oskar Morgenstern, who first explored in depth the role of game theory in economic analysis (1944), presented three aspects of game theory which are so fundamentally independent of one another that with a small amount of editing their opus could have been published as three independent books.

The first topic was the description of a game, or interdependent decision process, in extensive form. This provided a phraseology ("choice," "decision tree," "move," "information," "strategy," and "payoff") for the precise definition of terms, which has served as a basis for studying artificial intelligence, for developing the behavioral theory of the firm (Cyert & March 1963), and for considering statistical decision making [see DECISION THEORY]. The definition of "payoff" has been closely associated with developments in utility theory [see UTILITY].

The second topic was the description of the two-person, zero-sum game and the development of the mathematical theory based upon the concept of the minimax solution. This theory has formal mathematical connections with linear programming and has been applied successfully to the analysis of problems of pure conflict; however, its application to the social sciences has been limited because pure conflict of interests is the exception rather than the rule in social situations [see PROGRAMMING].

The third subject to which von Neumann and Morgenstern directed their attention was the development of a static theory for the *n*-person ($n \geqslant 3$), constant-sum game. They suggested a set of stability and domination conditions which should hold for a cooperative solution to an *n*-person game. It must be noted that the implications of this solution concept were developed on the assumption of the existence of a transferable, interpersonally comparable linear utility which provides a mechanism for side payments. Since the original work of von Neumann and Morgenstern, twenty to thirty alternative solution concepts for the *n*-person, non-constant-sum game have been suggested. Some have been of purely mathematical interest, but most have been based on considerations of bargaining, fair division, social stability, and other aspects of human affairs. Many of the solution concepts do not use the assumption of transferable utility.

### Oligopoly and bargaining

Markets in which there are only a few sellers (oligopoly), two sellers (duopoly, a special case of oligopoly), one seller and one buyer (bilateral monopoly), and so on, lend themselves to game-theoretic analyses because the fate of each participant depends on the actions taken by the other participant or participants. The theory of games has provided a unifying basis for the mathematical and semimathematical works dealing with such situations and has also provided some new results. The methodology of game theory requires explicit and detailed definition of the strategies available to the players and of the payoffs associated with the strategies. This methodology has helped to clarify the different aspects of intent, behavior, and market structure in oligopolistic markets (Shubik 1957). So-called conjectural variations and lengthy statements regarding an oligopolist's (or duopolist's or bargainer's) moves and countermoves can be investigated in a unified way when expressed in terms of strategies.

**Oligopoly.** Perhaps the most pervasive concept underlying the writings on oligopoly is that of a non-cooperative equilibrium. A group of individuals is in a state of noncooperative equilibrium if, in the individual pursuit of his own self-interest, no one in the group is motivated to change his strategy. This concept is basic in the works of Cournot, Bertrand, Edgeworth, Chamberlin, von Stackelberg, and many others. Nash (1951) has presented a general theory of noncooperative games, based on the equilibrium-point solution. This theory is directly related to Chamberlin's theory of monopolistic competition, among others.

The outcome given by a solution is called Pareto optimal if no participant can be made better off without some other participant's being made worse off. Noncooperative solutions, whose outcomes need not be Pareto optimal, have been distinguished from cooperative solutions, whose outcomes must be Pareto optimal. Also, equilibrium points are distinguished on the basis of whether the oligopoly model studied is static or dynamic. In much of the literature on oligopoly, quasi-cooperative solutions have been advanced and quasi-dynamic models have been suggested. Thus, while the Chamberlin large-group equilibrium can be interpreted as the outcome of a static noncooperative game, the small-group equilibrium and the market resolution suggested by Fellner (1949) are cast in a quasi-dynamic, quasi-cooperative framework. A limited amount of development of games of survival (Milnor & Shapley 1957) and games of economic survival (Shubik & Thompson 1959) has provided a basis for the study of multiperiod situations and for an extension of the noncooperative equilibrium concept to include quasi-cooperative outcomes.

*New results.* The recasting of oligopoly situations into a game-theory context has produced some new results in oligopoly theory (see, for example, Mayberry, Nash, & Shubik 1953; Shubik 1959*a*). Nash (1953) and Shubik (1959*a*) have developed the definition of "optimum threat" in economic warfare. The kinky oligopoly demand curve and the more general problem of oligopolistic demand have been re-examined and interpreted. Other results concern stability and the Edgeworth cycle in price-variation oligopoly; duopoly with both price and quantity as independent variables; and the development of diverse concepts applicable to cartel behavior, such as blocking coalitions (Scarf 1965), discriminatory solutions, and decomposable games.

Selten (1965) has been concerned with the problem of calculating the noncooperative equilibria for various classes of oligopolistic markets. His work has focused on both the explicit calculation and the uniqueness of equilibrium points. Vickrey (1961), Griesmer and Shubik (1963), and others have studied a class of game models applicable to bidding and auction markets. Working from the viewpoint of marketing and operations research, Mills (1961) and others have constructed several noncooperative game-theoretic models of competition through advertising. Jacot (1963) has considered problems involving location and spatial competition.

*Behavioristic findings.* Game theory can be given both a normative and a behavioristic interpretation. The meaning of "rational behavior" in situations involving elements of conflict and cooperation is not well defined. No single set of normative criteria

has been generally accepted, and no universal behavior has been validated. Closely related to and partially inspired by the developments in game theory, there has been a growth in experimental gaming, some of which has been in the context of economic bargaining (Siegel & Fouraker 1960) or in the simulated environment of an oligopolistic market (Hoggatt 1959). Where there is no verbal or face-to-face communication, there appears, under the appropriate circumstances, to be some evidence in favor of the noncooperative equilibrium.

**Bargaining.**    The theory of bargaining has been of special interest to economists in the context of bilateral monopoly, which can involve two firms, a labor union and a firm, or two individuals engaged in barter in the market place or trying to settle a joint estate. Any two-person, nonconstant-sum situation, be it haggling in the market or international negotiations, can be formally described in the same game-theoretic framework. However, there are several substantive problems which limit application of this framework and which have resulted in the development of different approaches. In nonconstant-sum games communication between the players is of considerable importance, yet its role is exceedingly hard to define. In games such as chess and even in many oligopolistic markets, a move is a well-defined physical act—moving a pawn in a definite manner or changing a price or deciding upon a production rate; in bargaining it may be necessary to interpret a statement as a move. The problem of interpreting words as moves in negotiation is critical to the description and understanding of bargaining and negotiation processes. This "coding" problem has to be considered from the viewpoint of many other disciplines, as well as that of game theory.

A desirable property of a theoretical solution to a bargaining problem is that it predicts a unique outcome. In the context of economics this would be a unique distribution of resources (and unique prices, if prices exist at all). Unfortunately, there are few concepts of solution pertaining to economic affairs which have this property. The price system and distribution resulting from a competitive market may in general not be unique; Edgeworth's solution to the bargaining problem was the contract curve, which merely predicts that the outcome will be some point among an infinite set of possibilities.

The contract curve has the property that any point on it is jointly optimal (both bargainers cannot improve their position simultaneously from a point on this curve) and individually rational (no point gives an individual less than he could obtain without trading). The Pareto-optimal surface is larger than the contract curve, for it is restricted only by the joint optimality condition. If it is assumed that a transferable comparable utility exists, then the Pareto-optimal surface (described in the space of the traders' utilities) is flat; if not, it will generally be curved. Any point on the Pareto-optimal surface that is individually rational is called an imputation. In the two-person bargain the Edgeworth contract curve coincides with two game-theoretic solutions, the *core* and the *stable set*. The core consists of all undominated imputations (it may be empty). A stable set is a set of imputations which do not dominate each other but which together dominate all other imputations. An imputation, $\alpha$, is said to *dominate* another imputation, $\beta$, if (1) there exists a coalition of players who, acting jointly but independently of the others, could guarantee for themselves at least the amounts they would receive if they accepted $\alpha$, and (2) each player obtains more in $\alpha$ than in $\beta$. The core and stable-set solutions can be defined with or without the assumption of transferable utilities. Neither of these solution concepts predicts a unique outcome.

One approach to bilateral monopoly has been to regard it as a "fair-division" problem, and several solution concepts, each one embodying a formalization of concepts of symmetry, justice, and equity, have been suggested (Nash 1953; Shapley 1953; Harsanyi 1956). These are generally known as *value* solutions, since they specify the amount that each participant should obtain. For the two-person case, some of the fair-division or arbitration schemes do predict unique outcomes. The Nash fair-division scheme assumes that utilities of the players are measurable, but it does not need assumptions of either comparability or transferability of utilities (Shubik 1966). Shapley's scheme does utilize the last two assumptions. Other schemes have been suggested by Raiffa (1953), Braithwaite (1955), Kuhn (in Shubik 1967), and others.

Another approach to bargaining is to treat it in the extensive form, describing each move explicitly and showing the time path taken to the settlement point. This involves attempting to parametrize qualities such as "toughness," "flexibility," etc. Most of the attempts to apply game theory in this manner belong to studies in social psychology, political science, and experimental gaming. However, it has been shown (Harsanyi 1956) that the dynamic process suggested by Zeuthen (1930) is equivalent to the Nash fair-division scheme.

## General equilibrium

Game theory methods have provided several new insights in general equilibrium economics. Under the appropriate conditions on preferences and production, it has been proved that a price system that clears the market will exist, provided that each individual acts as an independent maximizer. This result holds true independently of the number of participants in the market; hence, it cannot be interpreted as a limiting phenomenon as the number of participants increases. Yet, in verbal discussions contrasting the competitive market with bilateral monopoly, the difference generally stressed is that between the market with many participants, each with little if any control over price, and the market with few participants, where the interactions of each with all the others are of maximum importance.

The competitive equilibrium best reflects the spirit of "the invisible hand" and of decentralization. The use of the word "competitive" is counter to both game-theoretic and common-language implications. It refers to the case in which, if each individual considers himself an isolated maximizer operating in an environment over which he has no control, the results will be jointly optimal.

**Game-theoretic solutions.** The power and appeal of the concept of competitive equilibrium appears to be far greater than that of mere decentralization. This is reflected in the finding that under the appropriate conditions the competitive equilibrium may be regarded as the limit solution for several conceptually extremely different game-theoretic solutions.

*Convergence of the core.* It has been noted that for bilateral monopoly the Edgeworth contract curve is the core. Edgeworth had suggested and presented an argument to show that if the number of traders is increased on both sides of the market, the contract curve would shrink (interpreted appropriately, given the change in dimensions). Shubik (1959*b*) observed the connection between the work of Edgeworth and the core; he proved the convergence of the core to the competitive equilibrium in the special case of the two-sided market with transferable utility and conjectured that the result would be generally true for any number of markets without transferable utility. This result was proved by Scarf (the proof, although achieved earlier, is described in Scarf 1965); Debreu and Scarf improved upon it (1963). Using the concept of a continuum of players (rather than considering a limit by replicating the finite number of players in each category, as was done by Shubik, Scarf, and Debreu), Aumann (1966) proved the convergence of the core under somewhat different conditions. When transferable utility is assumed, the core converges to a single point and the competitive equilibrium is unique. Otherwise it may split and converge to the set of competitive equilibria.

The convergence of the core establishes the existence of a price system as a result of a theory which makes no mention of prices. The theory's prime concern is with the power of coalitions. It may be looked upon as a formalization of countervailing power, inasmuch as it rules out imputations which can be dominated by any group in the society.

Shapley and Shubik (1966) have shown the convergence of the value in the two-sided market with transferable utility. In unpublished work Shapley has proved a more general result for any number of markets, and Shapley and Aumann have worked on the convergence of a nontransferable utility value recently defined by Shapley. Harsanyi (1959) was able to define a value that generalized the Nash two-person fair-division scheme to situations involving many individuals whose utilities are not transferable. This preceded and is related to the new value of Shapley, and its convergence has not been proved.

There are several other value concepts (Selten 1964), all of which make use of symmetry axioms and are based upon some type of averaging of the contributions of an individual to all coalitions.

If one is willing to accept the value as reflecting certain concepts of symmetry and fairness, then in an economy with many individuals in all walks of life, and with the conditions which are required for the existence of a competitive equilibrium satisfied, the competitive equilibria will also satisfy these symmetry and fairness criteria.

*Noncooperative equilibrium.* One of the important open problems has been the reconciliation of the various noncooperative theories of oligopolistic competition with general equilibrium theory. The major difficulty is that the oligopoly models are open in the sense that the customers are usually not considered as players with strategic freedom, while the general equilibrium model considers every individual in the same manner, regardless of his position in the economy. Since the firms are players in the oligopoly models, it is necessary to specify the domain of the strategies they control and their payoffs under all circumstances. In a general equilibrium model no individual is considered a player; all are regarded as individual maximizers. Walras' law is assumed to hold, and supply is assumed to equal demand.

When an attempt is made to consider a closed economic model as a noncooperative game, considerable difficulties are encountered in describing the strategies of the players. This can be seen immediately by considering the bilateral monopoly problem; each individual does not really know what he is in a position to buy until he finds out what he can sell. In order to model this type of situation as a game, it may be necessary to consider strategies which do not clear the market and which may cause a player to become bankrupt—i.e., unable to meet his commitments. Shapley and Shubik (in Shubik 1967) have successfully modeled the closed two-sided two-commodity market without side payments and have shown that the noncooperative equilibrium point converges from below the Pareto-optimal surface to the competitive equilibrium point. They also have considered more goods and markets on the assumption of the existence of a transferable (but not necessarily comparable) utility.

When there are more than two commodities and one market, the existence of a unique competitive equilibrium point appears to be indispensable in defining the strategies and payoffs of players in a noncooperative game. No one has succeeded in constructing a satisfactory general market model as a noncooperative game without using a side-payment mechanism. The important role played by the side-payment commodity is that of a strategy decoupler. It means that a player with a supply of this type of "money" can decide what to buy even though he does not know what he will sell.

In summary, it appears that, in the limit, at least three considerably different game-theoretic solutions are coincidental with the competitive equilibrium solution. This means that by considering different solutions we may interpret the competitive market in terms of decentralization, fair division, the power of groups, and the attenuation of power of the individual.

The stable-set solution of von Neumann and Morgenstern, the bargaining set of Aumann and Maschler (1964), the "self-policing" properties of certain imputation sets of Vickrey (1959), and several other related cooperative solutions appear to be more applicable to sociology, and possibly anthropology, than to economics. There has been no indication of a limiting behavior for these solutions as numbers grow; on the contrary, it is conjectured that in general the solutions proliferate. When, however, numbers are few, as in cartel arrangements and in international trade, these other solutions provide insights, as Nyblén has shown in his work dealing with stable sets (1951).

**Nonexistence of competitive equilibrium.** When conditions other than those needed for the existence of a competitive equilibrium hold, such as external economies or diseconomies, joint ownership, increasing returns to scale, and interlinked tastes, then the different solutions in general do not converge. There may be no competitive equilibrium; the core may be empty; and the definition of a noncooperative game when joint property is at stake will call for a statement of the laws concerning damages and threats. (Similarly, even though the conditions for the existence of a competitive equilibrium are satisfied, the various solutions will be different if there are few participants.) When the competitive equilibrium does not exist, we must seek another criterion to solve the problem of distribution or, if possible, change the laws to reintroduce the competitive equilibrium. The other solutions provide different criteria. However, if a society desires, for example, to have its distribution system satisfy conditions of decentralization and fair division, or of fair division and limits on power of groups, it may be logically impossible to do so.

Davis and Whinston (1962), Scarf (1964), and Shapley and Shubik (1964) have investigated applications of game theory to external economies, to increasing returns to scale, and to joint ownership. In the case of joint ownership the relation between economics and politics as mechanisms for the distribution of the proceeds from jointly owned resources is evident.

It must be noted that the "many solutions" approach to distribution is in contrast to the type of welfare economics that considers a community welfare function or social preferences, which are not necessarily constructed from individual preferences.

## Other applications

Leaving aside questions of transferable utility, there is a considerable difference between an economy in which there is only barter or a passive shadow price system and one in which the government, and possibly others, have important monetary strategies. Faxen (1957) has considered financial policy from a game-theoretic viewpoint.

There have been some diverse applications of game theory to budgeting and to management science, as can be seen in the articles by Bennion (1956) and Shubik (1955).

Nyblén (1951) has attempted to apply the von Neumann and Morgenstern concept of stable set to problems of macroeconomics. He notes that the Walrasian system bypasses the problem of individual power by assuming it away. He observes that in game theory certain simple aggregation procedures do not hold; thus, the solutions to a four-person game obtained by aggregating two players in a five-person game may have little in common

with the solutions to the original five-person game. He outlines an institutional theory of the rate of interest based upon a standard of behavior and (primarily at a descriptive level) links the concepts of discriminatory solution and excess to inflation and international trade.

MARTIN SHUBIK

[*The reader who is not familiar with oligopoly theory and general equilibrium theory should consult* ECONOMIC EQUILIBRIUM; OLIGOPOLY; WELFARE ECONOMICS.]

BIBLIOGRAPHY

AUMANN, ROBERT J. 1966 Existence of Competitive Equilibria in Markets With a Continuum of Traders. *Econometrica* 34:1–17.
AUMANN, R. J.; and MASCHLER, M. 1964 The Bargaining Set for Cooperative Games. Pages 443–476 in M. Dresher, Lloyd S. Shapley, and A. W. Tucker (editors), *Advances in Game Theory.* Princeton Univ. Press.
BENNION, E. G. 1956 Capital Budgeting and Game Theory. *Harvard Business Review* 34:115–123.
BRAITHWAITE, RICHARD B. 1955 *Theory of Games as a Tool for the Moral Philosopher.* Cambridge Univ. Press.
CYERT, RICHARD M.; and MARCH, JAMES G. 1963 *A Behavioral Theory of the Firm.* Englewood Cliffs, N.J.: Prentice-Hall.
DAVIS, OTTO A.; and WHINSTON, A. 1962 Externalities, Welfare, and the Theory of Games. *Journal of Political Economy* 70:241–262.
DEBREU, GERARD; and SCARF, HERBERT 1963 A Limit Theorem on the Core of an Economy. *International Economic Review* 4:235–246.
FAXEN, KARL O. 1957 *Monetary and Fiscal Policy Under Uncertainty.* Stockholm: Almqvist & Wiksell.
FELLNER, WILLIAM J. 1949 *Competition Among the Few: Oligopoly and Similar Market Structures.* New York: Knopf.
GRIESMER, JAMES H.; and SHUBIK, MARTIN 1963 Towards a Study of Bidding Processes. *Naval Research Logistics Quarterly* 10:11–21, 151–173, 199–217.
HARSANYI, JOHN C. 1956 Approaches to the Bargaining Problem Before and After the Theory of Games. *Econometrica* 24:144–157.
HARSANYI, JOHN C. 1959 A Bargaining Model for the Cooperative *n*-Person Game. Volume 4, pages 325–356 in Harold W. Kuhn and A. W. Tucker (editors), *Contributions to the Theory of Games.* Princeton Univ. Press. → Volume 4 was edited by A. W. Tucker and R. Duncan Luce.
HOGGATT, A. C. 1959 An Experimental Business Game. *Behavioral Science* 4:192–203.
JACOT, SIMON-PIERRE 1963 *Stratégie et concurrence de l'application de la théorie des jeux à l'analyse de la concurrence spatiale.* Paris: SEDES.
MAYBERRY, J. P.; NASH, J. F.; and SHUBIK, MARTIN 1953 A Comparison of Treatments of a Duopoly Situation. *Econometrica* 21:141–154.
MILLS, H. D. 1961 A Study in Promotional Competition. Pages 245–301 in Frank M. Bass et al. (editors), *Mathematical Models and Methods in Marketing.* Homewood, Ill.: Irwin.

MILNOR, JOHN W.; and SHAPLEY, LLOYD S. 1957 On Games of Survival. Volume 3, pages 15–45 in Harold W. Kuhn and A. W. Tucker (editors), *Contributions to the Theory of Games*. Princeton Univ. Press. → Volume 3 was edited by M. Dresher, A. W. Tucker, and P. Wolfe.

NASH, JOHN F. JR. 1951 Non-cooperative Games. *Annals of Mathematics* 54:286–295.

NASH, JOHN F. JR. 1953 Two-person Cooperative Games. *Econometrica* 21:128–140.

NYBLÉN, GÖREN 1951 *The Problem of Summation in Economic Sciences*. Lund (Sweden): Gleerup.

RAIFFA, HOWARD 1953 Arbitration Schemes for Generalized Two-person Games. Volume 2, pages 361–387 in Harold W. Kuhn and A. W. Tucker (editors), *Contributions to the Theory of Games*. Princeton Univ. Press.

SCARF, H. 1964 Notes on the Core of a Productive Economy. Unpublished manuscript, Yale Univ., Cowles Foundation for Research in Economics.

SCARF, H. 1965 The Core of an *n*-Person Game. Unpublished manuscript, Yale Univ., Cowles Foundation for Research in Economics.

SELTEN, REINHARD 1964 Valuation of *n*-Person Games. Pages 577–626 in M. Dresher, Lloyd S. Shapley, and A. W. Tucker (editors), *Advances in Game Theory*. Princeton Univ. Press.

SELTEN, REINHARD 1965 Value of the *n*-Person Game. → Paper presented at the First International Game Theory Workshop, Hebrew University of Jerusalem.

SHAPLEY, LLOYD S. 1953 A Value for *n*-Person Games. Volume 2, pages 307–317 in Harold W. Kuhn and A. W. Tucker (editors), *Contributions to the Theory of Games*. Princeton Univ. Press.

SHAPLEY, LLOYD S.; and SHUBIK, MARTIN 1964 *Ownership and the Production Function*. RAND Corporation Research Memorandum, RM-4053-PR. Santa Monica, Calif.: The Corporation.

SHAPLEY, LLOYD S.; and SHUBIK, MARTIN 1966 *Pure Competition, Coalition Power and Fair Division*. RAND Corporation Research Memorandum, RM-4917. Santa Monica, Calif.: The Corporation.

SHUBIK, MARTIN 1955 The Uses of Game Theory in Management Science. *Management Science* 2:40–54.

SHUBIK, MARTIN 1957 Market Form, Intent of the Firm and Market Behavior. *Zeitschrift für Nationalökonomie* 17:186–196.

SHUBIK, MARTIN 1959a *Strategy and Market Structure: Competition, Oligopoly, and the Theory of Games*. New York: Wiley.

SHUBIK, MARTIN 1959b Edgeworth Market Games. Volume 4, pages 267–278 in Harold W. Kuhn and A. W. Tucker (editors), *Contributions to the Theory of Games*. Princeton Univ. Press. → Volume 4 was edited by A. W. Tucker and R. Duncan Luce.

SHUBIK, MARTIN 1966 Measureable, Transferable, Comparable Utility and Money. Unpublished manuscript, Yale Univ., Cowles Foundation for Research in Economics.

SHUBIK, MARTIN (editor) 1967 *Essays in Mathematical Economics in Honor of Oskar Morgenstern*. Princeton Univ. Press. → See especially Harold W. Kuhn, "On Games of Fair Division"; and Lloyd S. Shapley and Martin Shubik, "Concept and Theories of Pure Competition."

SHUBIK, MARTIN; and THOMPSON, GERALD L. 1959 Games of Economic Survival. *Naval Research Logistics Quarterly* 6:111–123.

SIEGEL, S.; and FOURAKER, L. E. 1960 *Bargaining and Group Decision Making: Experiments in Bilateral Monopoly*. New York: McGraw-Hill.

VICKREY, WILLIAM 1959 Self-policing Properties of Certain Imputation Sets. Volume 4, pages 213–246 in Harold W. Kuhn and A. W. Tucker (editors), *Contributions to the Theory of Games*. Princeton Univ. Press. → Volume 4 was edited by A. W. Tucker and R. Duncan Luce.

VICKREY, WILLIAM 1961 Counterspeculation, Auctions and Competitive Sealed Tenders. *Journal of Finance* 16:8–37.

VON NEUMANN, JOHN; and MORGENSTERN, OSKAR (1944) 1964 *Theory of Games and Economic Behavior*. 3d ed. New York: Wiley.

ZEUTHEN, F. 1930 *Problems of Monopoly and Economic Warfare*. London: Routledge.

## GAMING

*See* SIMULATION.

## GANGS

*See under* DELINQUENCY.

# GAUSS, CARL FRIEDRICH

Carl Friedrich Gauss (1777–1855), greatest of German mathematicians, was born in Brunswick on April 30, 1777. (He was baptized Johann Friedrich Carl, but he later dropped his first name and reversed the second and third.) Ranked with Archimedes and Newton as one of the three greatest mathematicians of all time, he combined in a most unusual way a pure mathematician's interest in abstract ideas and logical rigor, a theoretical physicist's interest in the creation of mathematical models of the physical world, an astronomer's talent for keen observation, and an experimentalist's skill in the application and invention of methods of measurement. He was blessed with a stupendous faculty for mental calculation, which enabled him to explore numerical relationships experimentally and to carry out extensive or involved routine computations quickly and accurately; he also had a gift for learning ancient and modern languages, which became his hobby. He contributed mightily to every branch of pure and applied mathematics that existed in his day, some of which he had founded, and he made major contributions in astronomy, geodesy, physics, and metrology. Each of his many interests had its principal, but not exclusive, season: before 1800, philology and number theory; 1800–1820, astronomy; 1820–1830, geodesy, differential geometry, and conformal mapping; 1830–1840, geomagnetism, electromagnetism, and general theory of inverse-square forces; 1840–1855, topology and the geometry of functions of a complex variable. He died in Göttingen on February 23, 1855. Of his many contributions, those used most widely in the physical, biological, and social sciences today relate to the method of least squares, his first formulation of which dates from 1795 to 1798 and his second from 1821 to 1823.

Gauss was the only child of Gebhard Dietrich Gauss, a bricklayer and gardener, by his second wife, née Dorothea Benze, daughter of a stonemason. Gebhard Gauss, being skilled in writing and calculating, kept accounts for a local insurance company; he was esteemed by the townspeople, but at home he was harsh and uncouth, which repelled his brilliant son. Gauss's mother had no special schooling, could not write, and could barely read, but she was cheerful, intelligent, and of strong character. She had a genial and extraordinarily intelligent younger brother, Johann Friedrich, a skilled weaver of artistic damasks, who quickly spotted his nephew's unusual talents and capacities and enjoyed sharpening his wits on those of his sister's young genius. Gauss, as a small boy, thought highly of his uncle and later, lamenting his untimely death in 1809, often declared that a born genius had been lost in him.

Gauss's precocity is unequaled in the history of mathematics. Before he was three, while watching his father's payroll calculations he detected an error and announced the correct result. He was admitted at age ten to the beginners' class in arithmetic at St. Katherine's Volksschule in Brunswick, where the speed and accuracy of his mental calculations so astonished the schoolmaster that he purchased for the boy the best obtainable textbook on arithmetic, which Gauss quickly mastered, convincing the schoolmaster that Gauss had gone beyond him. Luckily the schoolmaster had an assistant who was interested in mathematics. He and Gauss studied algebra and the rudiments of calculus together in the evenings, helping each other over difficulties and amplifying the textbook proofs. Thus in his eleventh year Gauss became acquainted with the binomial theorem and, finding the textbook "proof" unsatisfactory when the exponent $n$ is not a positive integer, devised his own proof of the convergence of the infinite series involved, which established him as one of the first of the "rigorists" and served as an inspiration for some of his greatest later work.

Early in 1791 Gauss's amazing powers came to the attention of Carl Wilhelm Ferdinand, duke of Brunswick, who became Gauss's patron, paid the expenses of his education at Caroline College from 1792 to 1795 and at the University of Göttingen

from 1795 to 1798, and until his death in 1806 gave Gauss considerable additional financial support. At Caroline College, Gauss devoted himself with equal success to classical literature, philosophy, and advanced mathematics. He studied carefully the original works of Newton, Euler, and Lagrange. In March 1795 (Dunnington 1955, p. 391) he rediscovered that invaluable principle of number theory, the law of quadratic reciprocity, which Legendre had published in 1785, and of which Gauss was to publish the first rigorous proof in 1801. Yet, on entering the University of Göttingen in October 1795, he was still undecided whether to make mathematics or philology his career.

Mathematics won on March 30, 1796, the day Gauss discovered that a regular polygon of 17 sides is amenable to straightedge-and-compass construction; such a construction had eluded mathematicians for two thousand years. By June 1, 1796, he had discovered much more: a regular polygon with an odd number of sides is amenable to such construction if and only if the number of its sides is a prime Fermat number, $F_n = 2^{2^n} + 1$, or a product of different prime Fermat numbers (five of which are known today). In 1796 he also developed the first rigorous proof of the fundamental theorem of algebra (i.e., that every nonconstant polynomial has a root), which became the subject of the doctoral dissertation for which he was awarded a PH.D. in absentia by the University of Helmstedt in 1799. In the autumn of 1798 Gauss polished the final draft of his greatest masterpiece, Disquisitiones arithmeticae, the printing of which began in 1799 but was not completed until September 1801, owing to the sale of the original print shop. Gauss brought together in this work his own original contributions to the theory of integral numbers and rational fractions and all of the principal related, but somewhat disconnected, results of his predecessors, so enriching the latter by rigorous reformulation and blending into a unified whole that this great book is regarded as marking the beginning of the theory of numbers as a separate, systematic branch of mathematics.

Among Gauss's early achievements was his reduction of the ecclesiastical calendar's extremely complicated computational procedure for finding the date of Easter (see Encyclopaedia Britannica, 11th ed., vol. 4, pp. 991–999) to a set of simple formulas from which the answer for any given year can be found in a few minutes. His motivation stemmed from his mother's inability to recall the exact date of his birth—only that it was a Wednesday, eight days before Ascension Day. As first published (1800), his procedure gave an incorrect date for Easter in 1734 and would have been incorrect again in 1886. Gauss supplied the necessary correction in 1807 and later provided an additional correction needed from 4200 on. (A semipopular exposition of Gauss's procedure, with a worked example, has been provided by H. Herbert Howe [1954].)

Gauss's first formulation of the method of least squares dates from his student days. In the autumn of 1794 he read (Galle 1924, p. 5) Lambert's discussion (1765, pp. 428–488) of the determination of the coefficients of a linear relationship $y = \alpha + \beta x$ from a set of $n$ ($> 2$) observational points ($Y_i, x_i$) by the method of averages. In 1795 Gauss conceived the simpler and more objective procedure of taking for $\alpha$ and $\beta$ the values $a$ and $b$ that minimize the sum of squared residuals, $\sum_i (Y_i - a - bx_i)^2$, and worked out the computational details, except for the weighting of observations of unequal precision (Galle 1924, p. 7). In 1797 he attempted to justify his minimum-sum-of-squared-residuals (mssr) technique by means of the theory of probability but "found out soon that determination of the most probable value of an unknown quantity is impossible unless the probability distribution of errors of observation is known explicitly" ([1821a] 1880, p. 98). Therefore, "it seemed to him most natural to proceed the other way around" and to seek the probability distribution of errors that "in the simplest case would result in the rule, generally accepted as good, that the arithmetic mean of several values for the same unknown quantity obtained from equally reliable observations shall be considered the most probable value" ([1821a] 1880, p. 98).

The concept of a probability distribution, or "law," of errors originated with Thomas Simpson (1755): he studied the sampling distribution of the arithmetic mean of $n$ independent and identically distributed errors subject to a discrete rectangular or a discrete triangular law of error, and concluded that "the more observations or experiments are made, the less will the conclusion be subject to err, provided they admit of being made under the same circumstances" (p. 93). In 1757 he extended his analysis to samples of $n$ from a continuous triangular distribution. Studies of other continuous laws of error followed: rectangular, by Lagrange, published in 1774; double-exponential ($Ce^{-m|x|}, -\infty < x < +\infty$), by Laplace in 1774; semicircular ($C\sqrt{r^2 - x^2}, -r \leqslant x \leqslant +r$), by Daniel Bernoulli in 1778; and double-logarithmic ($C \log a/|x|, -a \leqslant x \leqslant +a$), by Laplace in 1781 (for further details, see Eisenhart 1964; Todhunter 1865; Merriman 1877).

Using inverse probability, Gauss found $f(v) = (h/\sqrt{\pi}) \exp(-h^2v^2)$ to be the required probability distribution of errors (1809, art. 175–177). He noted that $h$ ($= 1/(\sigma\sqrt{2})$ in modern notation, where $\sigma$ is the *root-mean-square error*, or *standard deviation*, of the distribution) "can be considered as the measure of precision of the observations" (art. 178). Although De Moivre in 1733 had adduced the *function* $e^{-t^2}$ to approximate sums of successive terms of the binomial expansion of $(a + b)^n$ when $n$ is large (for what he actually wrote, see Smith [1929] 1959, pp. 566–575), and Laplace, in a series of papers published during the period 1774–1786, had explored in great detail the use of this function and its derivatives to approximate various probability distributions arising in games of chance, notably the binomial and hypergeometric distributions and the corresponding incomplete beta-function forms obtained through application of Bayes' theorem, and had suggested tabulation of its integral for use in such problems (see Todhunter [1865] 1949, art. 890–911) neither De Moivre nor Laplace seems to have considered $C \exp(-h^2x^2)$, or an equivalent expression, as a *law of error* or as a *probability distribution* in its own right.

Gauss then went on to deduce his mssr technique from $f(v)$, by what we would today call the method of maximum likelihood, finding that when the respective observations, $Y_i, i = 1, 2, \cdots, n$, are of unequal precision, each residual should be multiplied by the corresponding measure of precision, $h_i, i = 1, 2, \cdots, n$, before squaring (art. 179); derived the formula for the precision, $h(\overline{\overline{Y}})$, of any weighted arithmetic mean, $\overline{\overline{Y}}$, of $n$ independent observations (art. 181), finding that the precision, $h(\overline{Y})$, of the unweighted arithmetic mean, $\overline{Y}$, of $n$ equally precise independent observations is proportional to $\sqrt{n}$ (art. 173); derived for the case of observations on linear functions of several unknown quantities $\alpha, \beta, \cdots$ the rule of formation of (what we call) the *normal equations* that jointly determine optimal estimators $A, B, \cdots$ (art. 180); outlined (art. 182) his famous method of elimination for solving the normal equations—most widely known today through a modification published by M. H. Doolittle (1878)—that provides as a by-product an easily evaluated expression (art. 182, sec. 5) for the corresponding minimum sum of squared residuals in terms of quantities found in the course of their solution; and gave similar expressions (art. 183) for evaluating the precisions $h_A, h_B, \cdots$ of $A, B, \cdots$ as determinations of $\alpha, \beta, \cdots$.

An entry in Gauss's diary (see *Werke*, vol. 10, p. 533) indicates that he completed the foregoing development of the method of least squares on June 17, 1798. A fragment of his first application of these procedures in the spring of 1799 has been found (see *Werke*, vol. 12, pp. 64–68), and a short note ([1799] 1900, p. 136) dated August 24, 1799, on another application was published in October 1799.

In 1801 Gauss became deeply involved in the development and application of new astronomical methods which, in conjunction with his least squares techniques, resulted in amazingly accurate predictions, despite the scanty data available, of the orbits of some newly discovered planets; the success of his new methods brought about Gauss's immediate recognition as a first-rank astronomer (Bell 1937; Dunnington 1955, pp. 49–57). In 1805 Gauss began preparation (in German) of his second masterpiece, *Theoria motus corporum coelestium . . .* (1809), in which he was to give a complete system of formulas and procedures for computing the motion of a body whose orbit is a conic section, and a general method for determining the orbit of a comet or a planet from only three observed positions. The third section (art. 172–189) he devoted to a detailed exposition of the theory and application of his least squares methods. The German text was completed in 1806 (Galle 1924, p. 10). When the work was offered for publication in 1807, the publisher accepted it only on condition that Gauss translate it into Latin, because of the very unsettled political situation in Germany following the disastrous defeat of the Prussian army (under the leadership of Gauss's patron, the duke of Brunswick) by the Napoleonic forces at the battle of Auerstedt in October 1806. Consequently, full details of Gauss's first formulation of the method of least squares were not published until the Latin translation appeared in 1809. In the meantime, Legendre's independent formulation of his methods of least squares had appeared in print (1805); this went little beyond what Gauss had developed in 1795—no probability considerations are involved, and there is no discussion of precision or weighting of observations. A controversy followed, bitter on Legendre's part, in which many persons became involved, and which, as Bell explains, "was most unfortunate for the future development of mathematics" ([1937] 1956, p. 331).

In his 1809 presentation, Gauss regarded the measures of precision $h_1$, $h_2$, $\cdots$ of the respective observations involved as known quantities and said nothing about how to determine their values in practice. F. W. Bessel took the first step in this direction: in 1815 he introduced the *probable error*

as a measure of imprecision (1815, p. 234), which he later defined (1816, p. 142) as the magnitude, $r$, that an error has an equal chance of exceeding (or being less than) in absolute value; and from 48 determinations of the right ascension of the polestar he obtained a value for the probable error of such determinations (1815, p. 234) by means of the formula $R = 0.8453 \sum_i |Y_i - \bar{Y}|/n$, where $\bar{Y} = \sum_i Y_i / n$. (The numerical result given conforms to this formula [cf. Gauss 1816, art. 8], which is not stated.) The following year, Bessel (1816, pp. 141–142) showed that the probable error for Gauss's error distribution, $f(v)$, is given by $r = 0.476936h^{-1} = 0.8453\epsilon = 0.6745\sigma$. In this formulation $\epsilon = 1/(h\sqrt{\pi})$ represents the mean absolute error of the distribution and $\sigma = 1/(h\sqrt{2})$ is the root-mean-square error of the distribution, respectively. Gauss immediately pointed out (1816, art. 3) that given $m$ independent errors $V_1$, $V_2$, $\cdots$, $V_m$ distributed according to his error function, $f(v)$, then for "$m$ large or small" the "most probable values" (or, in modern terminology, the *maximum likelihood estimators*) of $h$ and $r$ are $\hat{H} = \sqrt{m/2\sum_i V_i^2}$ and $\hat{R} = 0.6744897\sqrt{\sum_i V_i^2/m}$, respectively. He showed (art. 4) that for large $m$, $\hat{H} - h$ and $\hat{R} - r$ are distributed approximately as $f(v)$, with $h_H = \sqrt{m}/h$ and $h_R = \sqrt{m}/r$, and gave (*loc. cit.*) explicit expressions, in terms of $\hat{H}$ and $\hat{R}$, for the "probable limits" of (in modern terminology, *50 per cent confidence limits* for) "the true values of $h$ and $r$." Next he considered (art. 5) the estimation of $r$ by $R_p = C_p \sqrt[p]{\sum_i |V_i|^p/m}$, with $C_p = C_p(m,h)$ chosen so that $r$ is the mean of the large-sample distribution of $R_p$, and found $R_2$ to be the most precise, noting (art. 6) that $R_2$ for $m = 100$ is as precise a measure of $r$ as is $R_1$ for $m = 114$, $R_3$ for $m = 109$, $R_4$ for $m = 133$, $R_5$ for $m = 178$, and $R_6$ for $m = 251$. Finally, he considered (art. 7) the estimation of $r$ by the "middlemost" (i.e., the *median*) of the absolute errors $|V_i|$ when $m$ is odd and found that this procedure requires $m = 249$ in order to achieve precision comparable to $R_2$ for $m = 100$. Gauss then evaluated (art. 8) $R_1$, $R_2$, $R_3$, and $R_4$ for the 48 determinations considered by Bessel (1815), taking the residuals, $Y_i - \bar{Y}$, as measures of the corresponding errors, $V_i$, and concluded that Bessel had used the formula $R_1$.

On February 15, 1821, Gauss presented to the Royal Academy of Sciences in Göttingen a completely new formulation of the method of least squares that was entirely free from dependence on any particular probability distribution of errors. Entitled "Theoria combinationis observationum erroribus minimis obnoxiae. Pars prior" (1821a), it stemmed from the earlier work of Laplace: Three years before Gauss's birth, Laplace ([1774] 1891, pp. 41–48) had said that to estimate a parameter $\theta$ one ought to use that function $T = T(Y_1, Y_2, \cdots)$ of the observations, $Y_1, Y_2, \cdots$, for which the mean (or expected) absolute error of estimation, $E\{|T - \theta|\}$, is a *minimum* for the given probability distribution of errors, and, for the case of independent identically distributed observations, Laplace gave an explicit procedure for finding such a function for estimating the location parameter of their common distribution, $f(y - \tau)$, when this is completely specified except for the value of $\tau$. Finally, Laplace showed that in the case of independent observations of equal (or unequal) precision, Gauss's technique of minimizing the sum of squared residuals leads to the same estimators as Laplace's own procedure for minimizing the mean absolute error of estimation when and only when (Laplace [1812] 1820, book 2, chapter 4, sec. 23) the errors $X_i = Y_i - \tau$ of the respective observations are distributed in accordance with Gauss's law of error,

$$\frac{h_i}{\sqrt{\pi}} \exp\left(-h_i^2 x_i^2\right), \qquad\qquad i = 1, 2, \cdots.$$

Gauss ([1821a] 1880, art. 6–7) proposed using instead the mean *square* error of an observation, $E\{(Y - \eta)^2\}$, or of an estimator $E\{(T - \theta)^2\}$, as a better measure of "uncertainty" ("incertitudo") and derived (art. 9) his remarkable inequalities (see Savage 1961, eq. 9) for the probability that a random variable Z with a continuous unimodal probability distribution will differ (positively or negatively) from its modal value $z_0$ by more than $\lambda$ times its root-mean-square error measured from $z_0$. Then he showed (art. 18–23) that when the mean values $E\{Y_i\} = \eta_i$ of a set of $n$ independent observations $Y_1, Y_2, \cdots, Y_n$ are linear functions of $k\ (< n)$ unknown parameters $\theta_j\ (j = 1, 2, \cdots, k)$ and (in modern terminology) the *variances* $E\{(Y_i - \eta_i)^2\} = \sigma_i^2$ of the $Y_i$ are all finite, then the mssr technique yields estimators $T_j$ of the $\theta_j$ having minimum mean-square error $(j = 1, 2, \cdots, k)$, whatever the distribution(s) of errors of the observations. In a second memoir (1823), he extended the preceding result to estimators $L_r$ of linear functions $\Lambda_r(\theta_1, \theta_2, \cdots, \theta_k)$ of the $\theta$'s $(r = 1, 2, \cdots, m; \ m \leqslant k)$ and showed (art. 37–40) that the resultant minimum sum of squared residuals is strictly equivalent to the sum of $n - m$ independent errors (i.e., has $n - m$ degrees of freedom). These results, at one time attributed erroneously to A. A. Markov (for explanation, see Neyman ([1938] 1952, p. 228), are derived and discussed by various recent authors (e.g., Graybill 1961; Scheffé 1959;

Zelen 1962) as the "Gauss–Markov theorem," and the method of least squares is thereby endorsed as a procedure for obtaining *minimum variance linear unbiased estimators*.

Gauss definitely preferred his 1821 formulation of the method of least squares above all others (for his statement to this effect on February 26, 1821, see [1821b] 1880, p. 99). In a letter to F. W. Bessel (Gauss & Bessel 1880) dated February 28, 1839 (an excerpt from which is given in his *Werke*, vol. 8, pp. 146–147), he remarked that he had never made a public statement of his reasons for abandoning the metaphysical approach of his first formulation but that a decisive reason was his belief that maximizing the probability of a zero error is less important than minimizing the probability of committing large errors.

In his later years, Gauss took special pride in his contributions to the development of the method of least squares and, despite a lifelong aversion to teaching, gave a course on this subject at the University of Göttingen each year from 1835 until his death. During his lifetime, the method of least squares became a basic tool in astronomy and geodesy throughout the world and has remained one to this day. And when Karl Pearson and G. Udny Yule began to develop the mathematical theory of correlation in the 1890s, they found that much of the mathematical machinery that Gauss devised for finding "best values" for the parameters of empirical formulas by the method of least squares was immediately applicable in correlation analysis, in spite of the fact that the aims of correlation analysis are the very antithesis of those of the theory of errors. As Galton remarked in his *Memories of My Life* (1908, p. 305), "The primary objects of the Gaussian Law of Error were exactly opposed, in one sense, to those to which I applied them. They were to get rid of, or to provide a just allowance for errors. But these errors or deviations were the very things I wanted to preserve and to know about." In consequence, Gauss's contributions to the method of least squares embody mathematics essential to statistical theory and its applications in almost every field of science today.

Gauss was visited in 1829 by the Belgian astronomer–physicist–statistician Adolphe Quetelet, who was engaged in making geomagnetic measurements in Holland, Germany, Italy, and Switzerland. Gauss had been interested in geomagnetism from around the turn of the century and had remarked, in a letter to Heinrich Olbers dated March 1, 1803, "I believe that this offers a greater field for the application of mathematics than has yet been supposed" (Olbers & Gauss, *Briefwechsel* . . .); his intense activity in other fields had thus far prevented his undertaking research in geomagnetism, despite the strenuous efforts of Alexander von Humboldt, in 1804 and again in 1828, to persuade him to do so. When Quetelet arrived, he found Gauss studying Russian for relaxation: "I have been very fatigued," he said, "from occupying myself with astronomy, geodesy, and other subjects that I know fairly well; I wanted to turn my attention to a language that I did not know at all, and now I am reading Russian" (Quetelet 1866, p. 646). Measurement of the intensity of the earth's magnetism was new to Gauss, and he was eager to know how such measurements were made and the precision that could be achieved (p. 645). Quetelet set up his apparatus in Gauss's yard, and together they conducted a series of experiments, taking observations simultaneously but in slightly different manners. The agreement of the results obtained astonished Gauss, who exclaimed: "But these observations conform to the precision of astronomical observations" (p. 646).

From January 1831 on, geomagnetic measurements were made regularly at Göttingen. By February 1832, Gauss was deeply involved in research on geomagnetism and had found that he could express the intensity of geomagnetism in what he called "absolute units," that is, in terms of units of the three fundamental physical quantities: length, mass, and time. On December 15, 1832, he presented his findings to the Royal Academy of Sciences in Göttingen in a paper entitled "Intensitas vis magneticae terrestris ad mensuram absolutam revocata" (1832), which was promptly recognized as one of the most important papers of the century.

Gauss made electromagnetic measurements for the first time in October 1832. By Easter 1833, he and his young physicist colleague Wilhelm Weber had put into operation an electromagnetic telegraph between Gauss's observatory and Weber's physics laboratory (Dunnington 1955, pp. 147–148, 395). They sent only individual words at first, and later complete sentences. Plans were drawn up in 1835–1836 for its use on the Leipzig–Dresden railroad but were dropped when the railroad authorities declared that the wires would have to be put underground. A monument showing Gauss and Weber discussing their telegraph was erected on the campus of the University of Göttingen.

In 1832 Gauss had begun preparation of his "Allgemeine Theorie des Erdmagnetismus" ("General Theory of Terrestrial Magnetism"); completion was delayed by lack of experimental material. At Gauss's suggestion a magnetic observatory (of nonmagnetic construction) was erected at the University of Göttingen in 1833. By 1836 Göttingen had become the principal European center for research on geomagnetism; and an association of magnetic observatories, known as the Göttingen Magnetic Union, was formed to coordinate simultaneous measurement of geomagnetic phenomena throughout Europe. In 1837 Gauss and Weber collaborated in the invention of a galvanometerlike device, the bifilar magnetometer, for measuring magnetic field intensities; and with it, Gauss verified the inverse-square law of magnetic attraction to which he had already been led by theory. His "Allgemeine Theorie . . ." appeared in 1839 and was followed in 1840 by his (with Weber) "Atlas des Erdmagnetismus" (1840) and his great treatise "Allgemeine Lehrsätze in Beziehung auf die im verkehrten Verhältnisse . . ." (1840)—i.e., what today we call "potential theory"—which marked the peak of his work in physics and the close of his work on magnetism. Near the end of his life, Gauss, like Laplace, Fourier, and Poisson, turned his attention to the social sciences and to the help that they might derive from the physical sciences. In particular, he took an active interest in application of the theory of probability to social laws. Thus, in 1847, he corresponded with the Danish astronomer Heinrich Christian Schumacher on the laws of mortality and on the construction of mortality tables (Quetelet 1866, pp. 653–655).

Called "the prince of mathematicians" even in his lifetime, Gauss received a steady stream of honors (listed chronologically in Dunnington 1955, appendix B), beginning with his election in 1802 as a corresponding member of the Imperial Academy of Arts and Sciences in St. Petersburg. He was elected a fellow of the Royal Society of London in 1804 and received the Copley Medal in 1838; he became a full member of the Royal Academy of Sciences in Berlin in 1810, a fellow of the American Academy of Arts and Sciences in Boston, Massachusetts, in 1822, and a member of the American Philosophical Society in Philadelphia in 1853. In 1842 the highest order conferred by the kingdom of Prussia, *Pour le mérite*, was awarded to him. On July 16, 1849, exactly 50 years after receipt of his doctorate, a Gauss jubilee was held in Göttingen at which honors were showered upon him, including honorary citizenship of Brunswick and Göttingen, which he prized above all the rest.

CHURCHILL EISENHART

[*For the historical context of Gauss's work, see the biographies of* LAPLACE; MOIVRE; *for discussion of the subsequent development of his ideas, see* ESTIMATION; LINEAR HYPOTHESES, *article on* REGRESSION;

MULTIVARIATE ANALYSIS, *articles on* CORRELATION; *and the biographies of* PEARSON; QUETELET; YULE.]

### A BIBLIOGRAPHY OF GAUSS

WORKS BY GAUSS

(1799) 1900  Zur Geschichte der Entdeckung der Methode der kleinsten Quadrate. Volume 8, pages 136–141 in *Carl Friedrich Gauss Werke.* Göttingen: Dieterichsche Universitäts-Druckerei.

(1800) 1874  Berechnung des Osterfestes. Volume 6, pages 73–79 in *Carl Friedrich Gauss Werke.* Göttingen: Dieterichsche Universitäts-Druckerei.

(1801) 1966  *Disquisitiones arithmeticae.* English translation by Arthur A. Clarke. New Haven: Yale Univ. Press.

(1807) 1874  Noch etwas über die Bestimmung des Osterfestes. Volume 6, pages 82–86 in *Carl Friedrich Gauss Werke.* Göttingen: Dieterichsche Universitäts-Druckerei.

(1809) 1963  *Theory of Motion of the Heavenly Bodies Moving About the Sun in Conic Sections.* New York: Dover. → First published as *Theoria motus corporum coelestium.* . . .

(1816) 1880  Bestimmung der Genauigkeit der Beobachtungen. Volume 4, pages 109–117 in *Carl Friedrich Gauss Werke.* Göttingen: Dieterichsche Universitäts-Druckerei. → An English translation appears in *Gauss's Work (1803–1826).* See also section 3 of Whittaker and Robinson 1924.

(1821a) 1880  Theoria combinationis observationum erroribus minimis obnoxiae. Pars prior. Volume 4, pages 1–26 in *Carl Friedrich Gauss Werke.* Göttingen: Dieterichsche Universitäts-Druckerei. → An English translation appears in *Gauss's Work (1803–1826).*

(1821b) 1880  Anzeigen: Theoria combinationis observationum erroribus minimis obnoxiae. Pars prior. Volume 4, pages 95–100 in *Carl Friedrich Gauss Werke.* Göttingen: Dieterichsche Universitäts-Druckerei.

(1823) 1880  Theoria combinationis observationum erroribus minimis obnoxiae. Pars posterior. Volume 4, pages 27–53 in *Carl Friedrich Gauss Werke.* Göttingen: Dieterichsche Universitäts-Druckerei. → An English translation is in *Gauss's Work (1803–1826).*

(1825–1827) 1965  *General Investigations of Curved Surfaces.* Hewlett, N.Y.: Raven Press. → Translations of Gauss's 1827 paper "Disquisitiones generales circa superficies curvas," his abstract of it, and his 1825 fragment "Neue allgemeine Untersuchungen über die krummen Flächen."

(1832) 1877  Intensitas vis magneticae terrestris ad mensuram absolutam revocata. Volume 5, pages 79–118 in *Carl Friedrich Gauss Werke.* Göttingen: Dieterichsche Universitäts-Druckerei. → Magie 1935 contains English excerpts.

(1839) 1966  General Theory of Terrestrial Magnetism. Volume 2, pages 184–251 in Richard Taylor (editor), *Scientific Memoirs, Selected From the Transactions of Foreign Academies of Science, and Learned Societies, and From Foreign Journals.* New York: Johnson. → First published in German.

(1840) 1966  General Propositions Relating to Attractive and Repulsive Forces Acting in the Inverse Ratio of the Square of the Distance. Volume 3, pages 153–196 in Richard Taylor (editor), *Scientific Memoirs, Selected From the Transactions of Foreign Academies of Science, and Learned Societies, and From Foreign Journals.* New York: Johnson. → First published in German.

(1840) 1929  GAUSS, CARL FRIEDRICH; and WEBER, WILHELM Atlas des Erdmagnetismus nach den Elementen der Theorie entworfen: Supplement zu den Resultaten aus den Beobachtungen des magnetischen Vereins unter Mitwirkung von C. W. B. Goldschmidt. Volume 12, pages 335–408 in *Carl Friedrich Gauss Werke.* Göttingen: Dieterichsche Universitäts-Druckerei. → Charts following page 408.

COLLECTIONS OF GAUSS'S WORKS

1855  *Méthode des moindres carrés: Mémoires sur la combinaison des observations.* Translated by J. Bertrand, and published with the authorization of the author. Paris: Mallet-Bachelier.

*Abhandlungen zur Methode der kleinsten Quadrate.* Thesaurus mathematicae, Vol. 5. Würzburg: Physica-Verlag, 1964.

*Carl Friedrich Gauss Werke.* 12 vols. Göttingen: Dieterichsche Universitäts-Druckerei, 1870–1933.

*Gauss's Work (1803–1826) on the Theory of Least Squares.* Translated by Hale F. Trotter. Statistical Techniques Research Group, Technical Report, No. 5. Princeton, N.J. Princeton Univ., 1957. → Prepared from Gauss 1855.

WORKS CONTAINING EXTRACTS BY GAUSS

MAGIE, WILLIAM F. (1935) 1963  *A Source Book in Physics.* Cambridge, Mass.: Harvard Univ. Press. → See especially extracts from Gauss 1832.

MIDONICK, HENRIETTA O. (editor) 1965  *The Treasury of Mathematics: A Collection of Source Material in Mathematics.* New York: Philosophical Library.

SMITH, DAVID EUGENE (1929) 1959  *A Source Book in Mathematics.* 2 vols. New York: Dover.

TAYLOR, RICHARD (editor) 1966  *Scientific Memoirs, Selected From the Transactions of Foreign Academies of Science, and Learned Societies, and From Foreign Journals.* 7 vols. New York: Johnson.

CORRESPONDENCE

*Briefe von C. F. Gauss an B. Nicolai.* Karlsruhe: Braun, 1877.

GAUSS, CARL FRIEDRICH; and BESSEL, FRIEDRICH W. *Briefwechsel zwischen Gauss und Bessel.* Leipzig: Engelmann, 1880.

GAUSS, CARL FRIEDRICH; and BOLYAI, WOLFGANG *Briefwechsel zwischen Carl Friedrich Gauss und Wolfgang Bolyai.* Leipzig: Teubner, 1899.

GAUSS, CARL FRIEDRICH; and GERLING, CHRISTIAN L. *Briefwechsel zwischen Carl Friedrich Gauss und Christian Ludwig Gerling.* Berlin: Elsner, 1927.

GAUSS, CARL FRIEDRICH; and SCHUMACHER, HEINRICH C. *Briefwechsel zwischen C. F. Gauss und H. C. Schumacher.* 6 vols. Altona: Esch, 1860–1865.

HUMBOLDT, ALEXANDER VON; and GAUSS, CARL F. *Briefe zwischen A. v. Humboldt und Gauss.* Leipzig: Engelmann, 1877.

OLBERS, WILHELM; and GAUSS, CARL F. *Briefwechsel zwischen Olbers und Gauss.* 2 parts. Berlin: Springer, 1900–1909. → Published as Volume 2 of Wilhelm Olbers, *Sein Leben und seine Werke.*

SUPPLEMENTARY BIBLIOGRAPHY

BELL, ERIC T. (1937) 1956  Gauss: The Prince of Mathematicians. Volume 1, pages 295–299 in James R. Newman (editor), *The World of Mathematics: A Small Library of the Literature of Mathematics From A'h-mosé the Scribe to Albert Einstein.* New York: Simon & Schuster. → A paperback edition was published in 1960.

BESSEL, FRIEDRICH W. 1815 Ueber den Ort des Polarsterns. *Astronomisches Jahrbuch* [1818]:233–241.

BESSEL, FRIEDRICH W. 1816 Untersuchungen über die Bahn des Olbersschen Kometen. Akademie der Wissenschaften, Berlin, Mathematische Klasse, *Abhandlungen* [1812–1813]:119–160.

DOOLITTLE, M. H. 1878 [Method Employed in This Office in the Solution of Normal Equations and in the Adjustment of a Triangulation.] U.S. Coast and Geodetic Survey, *Report of the Superintendent* [1878], Appendix 8, Paper 3:115–120.

DUNNINGTON, G. WALDO 1955 *Carl Friedrich Gauss, Titan of Science: A Study of His Life and Work.* New York: Hafner. → Contains a comprehensive bibliography of works by and about Gauss.

EISENHART, CHURCHILL 1964 The Meaning of "Least" in Least Squares. *Journal of the Washington Academy of Sciences* 54:24–33.

*Festschrift zur Feier der Enthüllung des Gauss–Weber-Denkmals in Göttingen.* 2 vols. 1899 Leipzig: Teubner.

GALLE, A. 1924 Über die geodätischen Arbeiten von Gauss. Volume 11, part 2, pages 1–165 in *Carl Friedrich Gauss Werke.* Göttingen: Dieterichsche Universitäts-Druckerei.

GALTON, FRANCIS 1908 *Memories of My Life.* London: Methuen.

GRAYBILL, FRANKLIN A. 1961 *An Introduction to Linear Statistical Models.* Vol. 1. New York: McGraw-Hill.

HÄNSELMANN, LUDWIG 1878 *Karl Friedrich Gauss: Zwölf Kapitel aus seinem Leben.* Leipzig: Duncker & Humblot.

HOWE, H. HERBERT 1954 How to Find the Date of Easter. *Sky and Telescope* 13:196.

KLEIN, FELIX et al. 1911–1920 *Materialien für eine wissenschaftliche Biographie von Gauss.* 8 vols. Leipzig: Teubner.

LAMBERT, JOHANN HEINRICH 1765 *Beyträge zum Gebrauche der Mathematik und deren Anwendung.* Vol. 1. Berlin: Buchladen der Realschule.

LAPLACE, PIERRE SIMON DE (1774) 1891 Mémoire sur la probabilité des causes par les événements. Volume 8, pages 27–65 in *Oeuvres complètes de Laplace.* Paris: Gauthier-Villars. → See especially "Problème III: Déterminer le milieu que l'on doit prendre entre trois observations données d'un même phénomène" on pages 41–48.

LAPLACE, PIERRE SIMON DE (1812) 1820 *Théorie analytique des probabilités.* 3d ed., rev. Paris: Courcier. → Smith 1929 contains English extracts from Book 2.

LAPLACE, PIERRE SIMON DE *Oeuvres complètes de Laplace.* 14 vols. Paris: Gauthier-Villars, 1878–1912.

LEGENDRE, ADRIEN M. (1805) 1959 On the Method of Least Squares. Volume 2, pages 576–579 in David Eugene Smith, *A Source Book in Mathematics.* New York: Dover. → First published as "Sur la méthode des moindres quarrés" in Legendre's *Nouvelles méthodes pour la détermination des orbites des comètes.*

MACK, HEINRICH (editor) 1927 *Carl Friedrich Gauss und die Seinen: Festschrift zu seinem 150. Geburtstage.* Brunswick: Appelhans.

MERRIMAN, MANSFIELD 1877 A List of Writings Relating to the Method of Least Squares, With Historical and Critical Notes. Connecticut Academy of Arts and Sciences, *Transactions* 4:151–232.

MOIVRE, ABRAHAM DE (1733) 1959 A Method of Approximating the Sum of the Terms of the Binomial $\overline{a+b}\diagdown^n$ Expanded Into a Series, From Whence Are Deduced Some Practical Rules to Estimate the Degree of Assent Which Is to Be Given to Experiments. Volume 2, pages 566–575 in David Eugene Smith, *A Source Book in Mathematics.* New York: Dover. → First published as "Approximatio ad summam terminorum binomii $\overline{a+b}\diagdown^n$ in seriem expansi."

NEYMAN, JERZY (1938) 1952 *Lectures and Conferences on Mathematical Statistics and Probability.* 2d ed. Washington: U.S. Department of Agriculture. → See especially Chapter 4, "Statistical Estimation," in the second edition.

QUETELET, ADOLPHE 1866 Charles-Frédéric Gauss. Pages 643–655 in Adolphe Quetelet, *Sciences mathématiques et physiques chez les Belges au commencement du XIX$^e$ siècle.* Brussels: Van Buggenhoudt.

SARTORIUS VON WALTERSHAUSEN, WOLFGANG 1856 *Gauss zum Gedächtniss.* Leipzig: Hirzel.

SAVAGE, I. RICHARD 1961 Probability Inequalities of the Tchebycheff Type. U.S. National Bureau of Standards, *Journal of Research, B. Mathematics and Mathematical Physics* 65 B:211–222.

SCHEFFÉ, HENRY 1959 *The Analysis of Variance.* New York: Wiley.

SCHERING, ERNST (1877) 1909 Carl Friedrich Gauss' Geburtstag nach hundertjähriger Wiederkehr. Pages 176–213 in Ernst Schering, *Gesammelte mathematische Werke.* Berlin: Mayer & Müller.

SIMPSON, THOMAS 1755 A Letter to the Right Honourable George Earl of Macclesfield, President of the Royal Society, on the Advantage of Taking the Mean of a Number of Observations, in Practical Astronomy. Royal Society of London, *Philosophical Transactions* 49, part 1:82–93.

SIMPSON, THOMAS 1757 An Attempt to Show the Advantage Arising by Taking the Mean of a Number of Observations in Practical Astronomy. Pages 64–75 in Thomas Simpson, *Miscellaneous Tracts on Some Curious and Very Interesting Subjects in Mechanics, Physical-astronomy, and Speculative Mathematics.* London: Nourse.

TODHUNTER, ISAAC (1865) 1949 *A History of the Mathematical Theory of Probability From the Time of Pascal to That of Laplace.* New York: Chelsea.

WHITTAKER, E. T.; and ROBINSON, G. (1924) 1944 *The Calculus of Observations: A Treatise on Numerical Mathematics.* 4th ed. Princeton, N.J.: Van Nostrand. → Section 103 provides a digest of Gauss 1816.

WINNECKE, F. A. T. 1877 *Gauss: Ein Umriss seines Lebens und Wirkens.* Brunswick: Vieweg.

WITTSTEIN, THEODOR 1877 *Gedächtnissrede auf Carl Friedrich Gauss zur Feier des 30. April 1877.* Hanover: Hahn.

ZELEN, MARVIN 1962 Linear Estimation and Related Topics. Pages 558–584 in John Todd (editor), *Survey of Numerical Analysis.* New York: McGraw-Hill.

# GEDDES, PATRICK

Patrick Geddes (1854–1932), British biologist, sociologist, and town planner, was born in Ballater, Scotland, and died in Montpellier, France. His childhood was spent in Perth. Because he was small and frail, Geddes did not go to school until he was eight; but through working in the cottage garden with his father, a retired professional soldier, he acquired his lifelong interest in plants and gardens. When he was 15, his father took him on a walking trip of more than two hundred miles through a series of river valleys. This tour suggested to young Geddes the practice he was to introduce later into both British education and town planning—the city and regional survey. After his graduation when he was barely 16 from the Perth Academy, where he had been a prize-winning student, his father gave him a free year to spend both reading and working with a local craftsman. During that year, Geddes' interests turned toward the biological sciences; and the reading of Thomas Huxley's *Lay Sermons* led to his beginning his career in the study of biology, at first under Huxley himself.

While pursuing zoological studies in Paris, Geddes came under the influence of Edmond Demolins of the *science sociale* group, who introduced him to Frédéric Le Play's detailed occupational and regional studies of *famille, travail, lieu*. These categories, like organism, function, and environment in biology, constituted the basic triad that Geddes used in his later analyses of society; *famille* was replaced by "folk" or "people."

In 1879, on a British Association for the Advancement of Science grant, Geddes went to Mexico. There his health broke down and he suffered a two-month period of blindness. This misfortune had a decisive effect on his intellectual life. To overcome his handicap, he invented a system of graphic notations by means of paper folded into nine squares. It was the first of his "thinking machines" and one of the earliest applications of graphic methods to nonmathematical problems. By the elaboration of these graphs, using as many as 36 squares, Geddes sought to demonstrate the constant interplay of ideas, forces, functions, groups, and institutions, all of which are usually treated by the specialized sciences as if they were independent and isolated. His basic graph, in which the central figure of the triad represents an activity or a function, and the surrounding squares modes of interaction, was an early systematization of field theory; and the holistic view it presented was much later developed independently by J. L. Moreno.

No longer able to use the microscope, Geddes nevertheless produced a steady stream of scientific papers and encyclopedia articles during the 1880s; he even opened up a new area in biology with his lifelong collaborator, J. Arthur Thomson, in their pioneer volume on the evolution of sex (1889) [*see* ECOLOGY, *article on* HUMAN ECOLOGY]. In that year a special chair in botany was established for him at University College, Dundee, a post he occupied for three months annually until 1919. Meanwhile, his widening social, aesthetic, and historical explorations turned him toward social problems. As early as 1882, Geddes introduced the new concept of energetics, later developed by Wilhelm Ostwald, into the analysis of census statistics; in 1884 he applied functional biological criteria to the more conventional economic analyses of the division of labor.

After his marriage in 1886, Geddes settled in Edinburgh and engaged in a series of activities that laid the basis for his later career as a town planner and as the leading British exponent of regionalism. Among these were the founding of four badly needed university residence halls, run by students; the rehabilitation of sundry sordid tenements of the Old Town; and the transformation by voluntary labor of neglected patches of land into gardens and play spaces. In the 1890s he converted the Outlook Tower atop Castle Hill into what Charles Zueblin described as "the world's first sociological laboratory"—actually a sociological museum, library, and meeting place. In 1891 he instituted a series of 14 collegiate summer meetings at the tower, with scholars like P'etr Kropotkin and Élisée Reclus as lecturers. In the 1890s Geddes gathered round him a group of artists and writers who formed the center of the short-lived Celtic renascence. Among them was the writer of Celtic romances, William Sharp, who called himself Fiona Macleod.

In 1903 Geddes embarked more formally on his career as sociologist and planner by assisting his colleague Victor Branford in the founding of the Sociological Society in London and by entering a planning competition held by the Carnegie Trust for the civic improvement of Dunfermline. Although his ambitious designs for Dunfermline were rejected, Geddes' comprehensive report, *City Development* (1904), remains a landmark in city planning, for it demonstrates his method of "conservative surgery," that is, preserving the complex historic tissue of a city while boldly introducing desirable innovations (see Geddes 1947).

Geddes' own survey of Edinburgh, modest in scale, established the civic survey as an essential first step in town planning, while in a series of city exhibitions and sociological lectures, including numerous extension courses at the University of London, he opened up the neglected study of the city itself. This rediscovery of the city was his outstanding contribution to sociology. Geddes' leadership helped pave the way for the British Housing and Town Planning Act of 1909 and brought him an invitation to put his ideas to work in India. There, between 1914 and 1924, he surveyed and planned some fifty cities; and from 1919 to 1924 he served as professor of civics and sociology at the University of Bombay. His unpublished plans for the Hebrew University of Jerusalem and for Tel Aviv and his remarkable two-volume report on Indore (1918) were also completed between 1914 and 1925. The report on Indore contains his exhaustive critical appraisal of the failings and potentialities of the modern university.

Although Geddes considered his thought a union of the traditions of Comte and Le Play, in his effort at synthesis he was a continuator of Herbert Spencer and more remotely of Aristotle. He treated sociology as a unifying discipline whose main components are geography, economics, and anthropology, all taken in their widest human context. His aim as a systematic thinker was to break down the sterile isolation and impoverished abstraction of specialized knowledge, so as to be able to move and act freely over the entire range of human experience, even that which lay beyond rigorously scientific description. He was as fertile as Bentham in coining neologisms, and many of his new terms, such as "geotechnics," "biotechnics," and "conurbation," have already entered the dictionary, while his characterization of specialism—"knowing more and more about less and less"—has become classic.

The best presentation of Geddes' method, along with his general sociological conspectus, appears in Volume 2 of *Life* (1931, chapters 11–13). These pages reveal the detailed wealth of his scholarship and first-hand experience, which offsets the sometimes arbitrary explications of his graphs. Since he was essentially an oral teacher, like G. H. Mead, his direct influence is best shown in the work of his students and colleagues, such as P. Abercrombie (town planning), V. Branford (sociology), H. J. Fleure (geography), and J. Arthur Thomson (biology). But more important, the influence of his ideas is being felt throughout the world, even in cases where their origin has been forgotten.

Lewis Mumford

[*For the historical context of Geddes' work, see* City, *article on* forms and functions; *and the biographies of* Comte; Le Play; Spencer. *For discussion of the subsequent development of his ideas, see* Housing, *article on* social aspects; Region; *and the biography of* Fleure.]

### WORKS BY GEDDES

1882    On the Classification of Statistics and Its Results. Royal Society of Edinburgh, *Proceedings* 11:295–322.

1884    An Analysis of the Principles of Economics. Royal Society of Edinburgh, *Proceedings* 12:943–980.

(1889) 1914    Geddes, Patrick; and Thomson, John A. *The Evolution of Sex.* 2d ed., rev. London: Walter Scott.

1904    *City Development; A Study of Parks, Gardens, and Culture-institutes: A Report to the Carnegie Dunfermline Trust.* Edinburgh: Geddes.

1905–1906    Civics, as Applied Sociology. Sociological Society, London, *Sociological Papers* 1:103–118; 2:57–119.

1907    A Suggested Plan for a Civic Museum (or Civic Exhibition) and Its Associated Studies. Sociological Society, London, *Sociological Papers* 3:197–240.

(1912) 1923    *Dramatisation of History: A Pageant of Education From Primitive to Celtic Times.* 5th ed. Bombay: Modern Publishing Co. → First published as *The Masque of Ancient Learning and Its Many Meanings.*

(1915) 1950    *Cities in Evolution.* New ed., rev. Oxford Univ. Press.

(1917) 1919    Branford, Victor V.; and Geddes, Patrick *The Coming Polity.* New & enl. ed. London: Williams.

1917    Geddes, Patrick; and Slater, Gilbert. *Ideas at War.* London: Williams & Norgate.

1918    *Town Planning Towards City Development: A Report to the Durbar of Indore.* 2 vols. Indore (India): Holkar State Press.

1931    Thomson, J. Arthur; and Geddes, Patrick *Life: Outlines of General Biology.* 2 vols. London: Williams & Norgate.

1947    *Patrick Geddes in India.* Edited by Jacqueline Tyrwhitt, with an introduction by Lewis Mumford. London: Humphries. → Published posthumously.

### SUPPLEMENTARY BIBLIOGRAPHY

Boardman, Philip L. 1936 *Esquisse de l'oeuvre éducatrice de Patrick Geddes, suivie de trois listes bibliographiques.* Montpellier (France): Imprimerie de la Charité. → Contains a bibliography of Geddes' works.

Boardman, Philip L. 1944 *Patrick Geddes: Maker of the Future.* With an introduction by Lewis Mumford. Chapel Hill: Univ. of North Carolina Press.

Defries, Amelia 1927 *The Interpreter Geddes: The Man and His Gospel.* London: Routledge.

Mairet, Philip 1957 *Pioneer of Sociology: The Life and Letters of Patrick Geddes.* London: Lund Humphries.

*Sociological Review.* → Published since 1908. Most of Patrick Geddes' papers were published in this journal between 1908 and 1931.

# GEIGER, THEODOR

Theodor Geiger (1891–1952) was a German-born sociologist whose chief interests were the fields of general social theory, methodology, social stratification and mobility, the sociology of law, and ideology. Even in Germany, Geiger's work is not widely known, although his writings on social stratification and mobility and on the sociology of law possess current significance. There is practically no secondary literature on Geiger. It was not until some years after his death that his influence was felt at all beyond the confines of Germany and Scandinavia.

Geiger's life mirrors German history in the twentieth century. His numerous publications—a bibliography of his works contains some 160 titles—constitute a courageous and nonideological discussion of the social and methodological problems of his time. He is noteworthy as an early critic of Nazism.

Geiger was the son of a teacher in a Munich Gymnasium; he studied law at the University of Munich and at Würzburg—where he received his doctorate in law—and volunteered for military service in World War I. After the war, until 1932, he was a member of the German Social Democratic party. During this time he began work on some problems relevant to the sociology of law. For some years he was active as a tutor, translator, and writer. He was fluent in the Scandinavian languages and also in Finnish. From 1920 on, he lived in Berlin, collaborating in the publication of the periodical *Die Fremde Presse* and working intensively in the field of adult education. He taught at the Volkshochschule Gross-Berlin and had become the principal of that school by the time he left, in 1928, to occupy the chair of sociology at the Brunswick Institute of Technology. While he was in Berlin he also worked at the National Statistical Bureau.

In 1933 Geiger emigrated to Denmark. For some time his studies in Copenhagen were supported by the Rockefeller Foundation. In 1938 he became professor of sociology at Aarhus. With the German occupation of Denmark, it became desirable for Geiger to leave, and in 1943 he escaped to Sweden. There he was stimulated by contact with the jurists and social scientists of the "Uppsala school." In 1945 he returned to Aarhus and founded the first institute of sociological research in Scandinavia. In collaboration with T. T. Segerstedt (of Uppsala), V. Verkko (of Helsinki), and J. Vogt (of Oslo), Geiger founded a series of publications, *Nordiske studier i sociologi*, Volume 1 of which was published in Copenhagen in 1948. He was also busy with several large-scale empirical studies on stratification and mobility and with developing his ideas on the sociology of law and the critique of ideology —ideas dating back to the stimulation he had received in Sweden. He was one of the founders of the International Sociological Association (ISA) and, together with D. Glass, was a leading spirit in the First International Working Conference on Social Stratification and Social Mobility. In 1951 he went to the University of Toronto as visiting professor; on the return voyage he died suddenly on shipboard.

**General social theory.** Geiger made important theoretical contributions to the study of social groups and to the refinement of Tönnies' categories of *Gemeinschaft* and *Gesellschaft*. He was also concerned with the role of secondary groups in modern society, notably in two articles, one, "Die Gruppe und die Kategorien Gemeinschaft und Gesellschaft," published in 1927 and the other, "Die Legende von der Massengesellschaft," pub-

lished in 1951. After briefly outlining a sociological theory (which he later partly retracted) in *Die Gestalten der Gesellung* (1928), in the 1930s he wrote his powerful introductory text *Sociologi* (1939), at the time a unique work in Scandinavia and for several decades an important textbook. Subsequently, he shifted entirely from the construction of general theory to the study of specific problems.

**Methodology.** In the 1920s Geiger was one of the few European sociologists doing empirical research. One of his first studies was an evaluation of illegitimacy statistics (1920). His book *Die soziale Schichtung des deutschen Volkes* (1932) and several articles—on employees (1933*a*), on the self-employed (1933*b*), and on problems of adult education—also have an empirical foundation. After these early works Geiger, influenced by Scandinavian thought and by American sociology, sought to refine the methods of empirical social research. He developed his own methods of inquiry and presentation, notably in his studies of Danish intellectuals and of changes in social stratification in Aarhus. His theoretical considerations of methodology (e.g., several articles written in 1948 and 1949: see *Arbeiten zur Soziologie*) also raised problems of the philosophy of science and of knowledge.

**Stratification and mobility.** In his studies of social stratification, Geiger initially accepted the Marxist view that German society had a clear-cut class structure, but he departed increasingly from this conception. Under the influence of American sociology and of his own empirical data, he wrote, while he was in Sweden, *Klassesamfundet i støbegryden* ("Class Society in the Melting Pot," 1948). By means of large-scale research he developed a dynamic analysis of social mobility and a typology of social fluctuation, together with a multidimensional model of stratification. A brief article by Geiger on his theory of social stratification was published in the *Wörterbuch der Soziologie*, edited by W. Bernsdorf and F. Bülow (1955).

**Sociology of law and ideology.** Geiger was early concerned with the sociology of law, and his association with the Uppsala school intensified this interest (1946*a*; 1946*b*; 1947). In several publications he took issue with the views of S. Ranulf, A. Ross, and K. Illum. Geiger linked the sociology of law with the analysis of ideology, discussing juristic concepts—norms, sources of law, consciousness of law, etc.—as phenomena of social reality. He examined the general nature of civil order and broke it down into such partial orders as habit, custom, usage, and law. Although this analysis is based on Continental legal conceptions, it constitutes a theory of social control that has bearing, also, on non-European social structures. Indeed, the *Vorstudien* (1947) are, with the fundamental works of G. Gurvitch and N. S. Timasheff, among the most important contributions to the sociology of law.

Geiger's conception of ideology has frequently been misinterpreted. Ideology, to him, is a concept in the theory of knowledge: *Ideologie ist theoretisch gemeintes A-Theoretisches* ("Ideology is the atheoretical taken theoretically"). He was led to this approach by the Uppsala school, especially by the work of A. Hägerström, although he criticized Hägerström and by the same token departed from the view of Karl Mannheim. Geiger's "value nihilism" must be understood in terms of a theory of knowledge: his value nihilism permits primary value judgments, but not their conversion into theories. In his last work, *Demokratie ohne Dogma* (1960), he made a plea for "intellectual humanism," the "enlightenment of the masses," the "democratization of reason," the "asceticism of emotion," and "abstinence from value judgment." Yet he was a pragmatist: he considered his last work to be his political testament and hoped that his ideas would be put into practice.

PAUL TRAPPE

[*See also* COMMUNITY–SOCIETY CONTINUA; IDEOLOGY; ILLEGITIMACY; LAW; SOCIAL CONTROL; SOCIAL MOBILITY; STRATIFICATION, SOCIAL; *and the biographies of* MANNHEIM *and* TÖNNIES.]

### WORKS BY GEIGER

1919 *Die Schutzaufsicht.* Breslau (then Germany): Schletter.

1920 *Das uneheliche Kind und seine Mutter im Recht des neuen Staates: Ein Versuch auf der Basis kritischer Rechtsvergleichung.* Munich: Schweitzer.

1926 *Die Masse und ihre Aktion: Ein Beitrag zur Soziologie der Revolutionen.* Stuttgart (Germany): Enke.

1927 *Die Gruppe und die Kategorien Gemeinschaft und Gesellschaft. Archiv für Sozialwissenschaft und Sozialpolitik* 58:338–374.

1928 *Die Gestalten der Gesellung.* Karlsruhe (Germany): Braun.

(1931a) 1959 Führung. Pages 136–141 in *Handwörterbuch der Soziologie.* New ed. Stuttgart (Germany): Enke.

(1931b) 1959 Gemeinschaft. Pages 173–180 in *Handwörterbuch der Soziologie.* New ed. Stuttgart (Germany): Enke.

(1931c) 1959 Gesellschaft. Pages 201–211 in *Handwörterbuch der Soziologie.* New ed. Stuttgart (Germany): Enke.

(1931d) 1959 Revolution. Pages 511–518 in *Handwörterbuch der Soziologie.* New ed. Stuttgart (Germany): Enke.

(1931e) 1959 Soziologie. Pages 568–578 in *Handwörterbuch der Soziologie.* New ed. Stuttgart (Germany): Enke.

1932 *Die soziale Schichtung des deutschen Volkes: Soziographischer Versuch auf statistischer Grundlage.* Stuttgart (Germany): Enke.

1933a Soziale Gliederung der deutschen Arbeitnehmer. *Archiv für Sozialwissenschaft und Sozialpolitik* 68: 151–188.

1933b Statistische Analyse der wirtschaftlich Selbständigen. *Archiv für Sozialwissenschaft und Sozialpolitik* 69:407–439.

1934 *Erbpflege: Grundlagen, Planung, Grenzen.* Stuttgart (Germany): Enke.

1935 *Samfund og arvelighed: En sociologisk undersøgelse.* Copenhagen: Martin.

1939 *Sociologi: Grundrids og hovedproblemer.* Copenhagen: Nyt Nordisk Forlag.

1941 *Konkurrence: En sociologisk analyse.* Aarhus, Universitet, Acta jutlandica, Aarsskrift, Vol. 13, no. 2. Aarhus (Denmark): Universitets Forlaget.

1943 *Kritik af reklamen.* Copenhagen: Nyt Nordisk Forlag.

(1944) 1949 *Aufgaben und Stellung der Intelligenz in der Gesellschaft.* Stuttgart (Germany): Enke. → First published as *Intelligensen.*

1946a *Debat med Uppsala om moral og ret.* Copenhagen: Munksgaard.

1946b *Ranulf contra Geiger: Et angreb og et offensivt forsvar.* Copenhagen: Nyt Nordisk Forlag.

(1947) 1964 *Vorstudien zu einer Soziologie des Rechts.* Aarhus, Universitet, Acta jutlandica, Aarsskrift, Vol. 19, no. 1. Neuwied (Germany): Luchterhand.

(1948) 1949 *Die Klassengesellschaft in Schmelztiegel.* Cologne (Germany): Kiepenheuer. → First published in Danish.

1949 *Den Danske intelligens fra reformationen til nutiden: En studie i empirisk kultursociologi.* Aarhus, Universitet, Acta jutlandica, Aarsskrift, Vol. 21, no. 1. Aarhus (Denmark): Universitets Forlaget.

1951a Die Legende von der Massengesellschaft. *Archiv für Rechts- und Sozialphilosophie* 39:305–323.

1951b *Soziale Umschichtungen in einer dänischen Mittelstadt.* Aarhus, Universitet, Acta jutlandica, Aarsskrift, Vol. 23, no. 1. Aarhus (Denmark): Universitets Forlaget.

1952 *Fortidens moral og fremtidens.* Copenhagen: Reitzel.

1953 *Ideologie und Wahrheit: Eine soziologische Kritik des Denkens.* Stuttgart (Germany) and Vienna: Humboldt. → Published posthumously.

1954a Intelligenz. Volume 5, pages 302–304 in *Handwörterbuch der Sozialwissenschaften.* Stuttgart (Germany): Fischer. → Published posthumously.

1954b Ideologie. Volume 5, pages 179–184 in *Handwörterbuch der Sozialwissenschaften.* Stuttgart (Germany): Fischer. → Published posthumously.

(1955) 1962 Theorie der sozialen Schichtung. Pages 186–205 in Theodor Geiger, *Arbeiten zur Soziologie: Methode, moderne Grossgesellschaft, Rechtssoziologie, Ideologiekritik.* Neuwied (Germany): Luchterhand. → Published posthumously. Originally appeared in the *Wörterbuch der Soziologie,* edited by W. Bernsdorf and F. Bülow.

(1960) 1963 *Demokratie ohne Dogma: Die Gesellschaft zwischen Pathos und Nüchternheit.* Munich: Szczesny. → First published posthumously as *Die Gesellschaft zwischen Pathos und Nüchternheit.*

*Arbeiten zur Soziologie: Methode, moderne Grossgesellschaft, Rechtssoziologie, Ideologiekritik.* Neuwied (Germany): Luchterhand, 1962.

# GEMEINSCHAFT–GESELLSCHAFT

*See* COMMUNITY–SOCIETY CONTINUA *and the biography of* TÖNNIES.

## GENERAL SYSTEMS THEORY
*See under* SYSTEMS ANALYSIS.

## GENERAL WILL

The concept of the general will involves the moral values and the political aspirations that are shared by the members of a community and to which the policies of its government must broadly conform if that government is to be considered legitimate. The term was used in this minimal sense by Jean Jacques Rousseau, its originator, who also used it, more importantly, to describe the will to justice that would characterize his ideal democracy and achieve its authoritative expression in legislative decisions [*see* ROUSSEAU].

Since Rousseau, different and precise meanings, depending upon the political theory in which they are embedded, have been attached to the term; these have had as their primary and common aim its adaptation to the analysis of politics and national character. Typically, some theory of the general will has been used to explain, to justify, and to prescribe for the institutions of constitutional and liberal democracy, especially by thinkers within or influenced by the British idealist school of political thought. Often, existence of a general will is made the cardinal criterion of community and is seen as the essential prerequisite to political stability and self-government.

For Rousseau, the "general will" was the concept by means of which he summarized his theory of political obligation and displayed its logical dependence upon the psychological, ethical, and institutional components of his political philosophy. In Rousseau's ideal society, as presented in *The Social Contract*, the natural right to moral freedom, to live in accordance with the dictates of one's own conscience and sense of morality, is psychologically and institutionally reconciled with the social necessity for political authority, because there law is the reflection of the individual's desire for justice. Laws that express the general will are acceptable both to reason and to conscience and thus are held not so much to restrict freedom as to enlarge and to sustain it.

Rousseau's general will implies that neither a society that lacks a general will nor a government that disregards it can have rightful authority over the individual. Failure to establish the institutions essential to the creation of the general will inevitably means moral distortion of human personality and frustration of man's capacity for natural goodness. According to Rousseau's view of human

dynamics and moral development, only in a small and equalitarian society can man become an ethical being for whom the realization of justice and its integration with the claim to moral freedom are paramount and compelling objectives—and then only if men participate directly and steadily in the making of the laws to which they will owe obedience.

The social and institutional requisites of the general will as conceived of by Rousseau would appear to preclude its use for the purpose of legitimating constitutional democracy on the scale of the national state. The fundamentally moral and synthetic nature of the concept, however, opens the way for its modification, inspired by the hope of adapting it to the justification of representative government. This process of reinterpretation began with Kant, who derived from Rousseau's general will his conception of the categorical imperative, which served for him as the supreme criterion of both morality and legality. In contrast to Kant's primarily ethical elucidation of the concept, Hegel's political interpretation of it takes the form of his metaphysical and historical conception of reason. The Hegelian conception of rationality as cumulative may be regarded as a historicizing of the general will. The result is that the reconciliation of the right to moral freedom with the demands of social justice is obtained not in acts of legislation but, rather, in reflective acceptance of and willing adherence to the social and political arrangements that have emerged historically in the shape of the national and constitutional state.

The British idealist T. H. Green spoke of a general will with reference to the hopes and aspirations of a people, on which government depends and to which it should be both responsive and facilitative (1882). The most elaborate effort to employ the idea of a general will in the rationale of liberal constitutionalism was made by Bernard Bosanquet (1899). He conceived of the state as a concrete universal, a dynamic and rationally articulated totality, the fulfillment of whose requirements may be understood in terms of "will," which is the moving system of interlocking attitudes and functions that constitutes a politically organized and sovereign society. Here the general will becomes more an attribute of the polity than a moral characteristic of individuality and, as such, gives both direction and significance to the activities of individuals, who are self-governing insofar as they sense and respond appropriately to the intimations of their society [*see* BOSANQUET *and* GREEN].

Less like Hegel and more like Rousseau in tone is the theory of the "neighborhood group" advocated by Mary Parker Follett (1918). She saw the neighborhood as the necessary source of what Rousseau would have recognized as the general will, and she urged the recasting of democratic institutions so as to make this social unit an integrating force of moral and political importance. Her ideas have found effective application in administration and urban planning [see FOLLETT].

Still other interpretations of the general will seek to locate it in the nature of man in society, in the psychological and social foundations of political authority, rather than directly in political agreement and legislative performance. These include W. Ernest Hocking's "will to power" (1926), which requires the state as its vehicle, and Robert MacIver's redesignation of the general will as the "will for the state" (1926), which derives social unity and political authority from a common root in individual and group freedoms. In the field of jurisprudence, Hugo Krabbe's assertion of the "sense of right" of a community as the criterion of the validity of law (1915) is an attempt to convert the general will into a dynamic type of natural law.

More complex reformulations of the general will, which are more directly in the spirit if not the letter of Rousseau's political theory, are presented in the works of Lindsay (1943) and Barker (1951). Both regard discussion as the process distinctive to democratic society and government by which, fittingly differentiated and articulated, the general will may be generated and expressed. In this perspective, the general will is the formative conception in the theory of the deliberative state as set forth in Frederick Watkins' analysis of liberalism (1948) and in J. Roland Pennock's exposition of the principles of liberal democracy (1950). In a deliberative state, political participation not only is essential to social unity but should also be active and substantive, without excessive dependence upon either leadership or disciplined and programmatic parties. Deliberative democracy is the type of democracy most closely in accord with Rousseau's ideal.

Viewed in the light of its origin and development, the general will does not have any single meaning or accepted role in political theory. There is, however, an agreed *core* of meaning and implication. (1) As a legitimating idea the concept directs attention to the criterion of popular consent, expressed through the methods of representative and responsible government; to the desirability of a diversity of forms of participation and access; and to justice and freedom as the proper ends of the state. (2) As an analytic concept the general

will suggests consideration of those conditions of social unity and common purpose sufficiently strong to permit the establishment, acceptance, and control of political authority. (3) From a diagnostic standpoint the concept indicates that a society lacking in moral and political unity is unlikely to be capable of self-government and is liable, therefore, to an imposition of coherence and direction by authoritarian techniques and ideologies. (4) Prescriptively, the general will continues to influence the construction of democratic theory in a liberal, as opposed to a majoritarian, mode and to guide the design of political, urban, and administrative democratic institutions in ways consistent with the meaning Rousseau gave it.

Owing to its fundamentally moral nature, the concept continues to inspire investigation and explication of the ethical purposes of political society and political activity. But in keeping with its composite nature, future research may be conducted in a number of directions: historical investigation of the development of political culture; psychological investigation of the formation of moral and political attitudes, especially those basic to personal independence and resilience; specification and interpretation of the principles of justice; and explanation of the social and political processes integral to liberal constitutionalism in both more mature and less mature industrializing societies. Above all, the concept of the general will invites attention to the interdependence of psychological processes, moral character, and political institutions.

JOHN W. CHAPMAN

[See also AUTHORITY; DEMOCRACY; LEGITIMACY; LIBERALISM; PUBLIC INTEREST; REPRESENTATION; SOCIAL CONTRACT; STATE.]

BIBLIOGRAPHY

BARKER, ERNEST 1951 *Principles of Social and Political Theory.* New York: Oxford Univ. Press.
BOSANQUET, BERNARD (1899) 1951 *The Philosophical Theory of the State.* 4th ed. London: Macmillan. → The 1951 publication is a reprint of the fourth edition, which was first published in 1923.
CHAPMAN, JOHN W. 1956 *Rousseau: Totalitarian or Liberal?* New York: Columbia Univ. Press.
CHAPMAN, JOHN W. 1960 Metropolitan Citizenship: Promises and Limitations. In Carl J. Friedrich (editor), *Responsibility.* Nomos 3. New York: Liberal Arts.
CHAPMAN, JOHN W. 1963 Justice and Fairness. In Carl J. Friedrich and John W. Chapman (editors), *Justice.* Nomos 6. New York: Atherton.
DERATHÉ, ROBERT 1948 *Le rationalisme de J.-J. Rousseau.* Paris: Presses Universitaires de France.
FOLLETT, MARY P. 1918 *The New State: Group Organization, the Solution of Popular Government.* New York: Longmans.

Green, Thomas Hill (1882) 1960 *Lectures on the Principles of Political Obligation*. London: Longmans. → Reprinted from Volume 2 of the three-volume collected *Works of Thomas Hill Green*, edited by R. L. Nettleship and published posthumously in 1885–1888. First published as a separate book in 1895.

Hegel, Georg W. F. (1821) 1942 *Philosophy of Right*. Oxford: Clarendon. → First published in German.

Hocking, William Ernest 1926 *Man and the State*. New Haven: Yale Univ. Press.

Journées d'Étude sur le "Contrat social," Dijon, 1962 1964 *Études sur le* Contrat social *de Jean-Jacques Rousseau: Actes des journées d'étude organisées à Dijon pour la commémoration du 200e anniversaire du* Contrat social. Dijon, Université, Publications, New Series, No. 30. Paris: Belles Lettres. → See especially pages 143–164, "Le sens de l'égalité et de l'inégalité chez J.-J. Rousseau," by Raymond Polin.

Krabbe, Hugo (1915) 1927 *The Modern Idea of the State*. New York and London: Appleton. → Translated from the Dutch.

Lindsay, A. D. (1943) 1947 *The Modern Democratic State*. Published under the auspices of the Royal Institute of International Affairs. Oxford Univ. Press.

MacIver, Robert M. 1926 *The Modern State*. Oxford Univ. Press.

Pennock, J. Roland 1950 *Liberal Democracy: Its Merits and Prospects*. New York: Rinehart.

Pennock, J. Roland 1952 Responsiveness, Responsibility, and Majority Rule. *American Political Science Review* 46:790–807.

Plamenatz, John P. 1963 *Man and Society: Political and Social Theory*. 2 vols. New York: McGraw-Hill.

*Rousseau et la philosophie politique*. Annales de philosophie politique, No. 5. 1965 Paris: Presses Universitaires de France.

*Jean-Jacques Rousseau et son oeuvre: Problèmes et recherches*. 1964 Paris: Klincksieck. → See especially pages 231–247, "La fonction du législateur chez J.-J. Rousseau," by Raymond Polin.

Sabine, George H. 1952 The Two Democratic Traditions. *Philosophical Review* 61:451–474.

Watkins, Frederick 1948 *The Political Tradition of the West: A Study in the Development of Modern Liberalism*. Cambridge, Mass.: Harvard Univ. Press.

# GENERATIONS

## I
### THE CONCEPT

Ever since antiquity, the concept of *generation* has been held in a biological, and consequently in a genealogical, sense of regular descent of a group of organisms from a progenitor. But since the early nineteenth century there has been developed a social and historical concept of generations as comprising the structure not only of societies but also of history itself. Nevertheless, attempts to formulate a sociological theory of generations in the biological sense of kinship descent have been unproductive because the temporal continuity of births makes impossible any determination of *social* generations so long as "generation" is understood in a purely biological sense. It is therefore necessary to arrive at a strictly social and historical interpretation of the generation concept in order for it to acquire relevance in the field of the social sciences.

**History of the generation concept.** Auguste Comte, the founder of modern sociology, considered the duration of human life a decisive element in determining the velocity of human evolution and therefore the passing of one generation to another, the term of full activity for man being thirty years (1830–1842, pp. 635–639 in part 4 of the 1839 edition). Comte did not deal with the phenomena of individual or simply familial life but with social life based on "the unanimous adhesion to certain fundamental notions" (1851–1854, part 4, p. 679).

John Stuart Mill obtained the concept of social generations from Comte and added further refinements of considerable interest. He argued that in each successive age the "principal phenomena" of society are different, and that the interval which marks these changes most clearly is the generation —that is, the period of time in which a "new set" of individuals reaches maturity and takes possession of society. He believed that each social state is generated not only by the preceding one but also by the whole previous history of humanity; one of the key concepts in understanding this process is that of the generation. "History accordingly does, when judiciously examined, afford Empirical Laws of Society" (Mill [1843] 1961, p. 598).

After this philosophical beginning of the theory of generations, the theory received further development at the hands of statisticians and historians. Antoine Augustin Cournot, the French economist and mathematician, first explicated the fact that epochs succeed themselves in continuity and only historical events give evidence of the articulation of generations: "Through education, each generation transmits to the one immediately following, a certain groundwork of ideas; and while this act of education or transmission is in operation, the *educating generation* is still present; unexpected, moreover, is the influence of the survivors of a preceding generation who have not ceased taking a notable part in the government of the society, on the movement of ideas and affairs" (1872, vol. 1, chapter 8).

Giuseppe Ferrari, Italian historian, politician, and editor of Vico, limited himself to the examination of political history, in which he believed he had discovered that the scene changes every thirty years and that the generation is the decisive element. Starting from this basic premise, he formulated laws of political succession: "Generations behave according to these principles, and are in turn preparatory, revolutionary, reactionary, and conciliatory" (1874, p. 182).

The German historian Wilhelm Dilthey also found the idea of generation useful for studying the culture of an epoch, and he applied it in many of his writings. In 1875 Dilthey arrived at the notion that the generation is at once a space of time, an internal metrical concept of human life of about thirty years' duration, and a contemporary relation of individuals to each other.

> The relationship between individuals denoted by the term *generation* is therefore one of simultaneity. We say that certain people belong to "the same generation" when they have, in a certain sense, grown up together, passed through childhood and youth at about the same time, and enjoyed their period of maturity during more or less the same years. It follows, then, that such people are bound together in another, deeper relationship: they also constitute "the same generation" because, in their impressionable years, they have been subject to the same leading influences.   ([1875], 1924, vol. 5, p. 37)

The historian Leopold von Ranke and, to a much greater extent, his disciple Ottokar Lorenz put the theme of generations into a historical context from the point of view of periodization. Ranke took the concept of generation in the usual sense of the word. Lorenz took his point of departure from Ranke and from the French psychologist T. A. Ribot, whose studies of heredity were just beginning to appear; he put forward the conception of a scientific history founded on the study of heredity and genealogy. Lorenz was especially interested in the century as a method of dividing history into periods; thus, he defined a generation as the sum of all those who were employed within a given cultural area during one-third of a century.

In the twentieth century an attempt was begun to study history in terms of generations; thus, new refinements were gradually added to the theory. The principal studies are those of François Mentré (1920), Karl Mannheim (1928), Engelbert Drerup (1933), Pedro Laín Entralgo (1945), and Julián Marías (1949a; 1955). Attempts were also made to apply the doctrine of generations to particular themes: for example, art (Pinder 1926) and literature (Petersen 1930; Peyre 1948). But the most extensive general contribution, based on a philosophical theory of social life, was made by José Ortega y Gasset. His student Julián Marías has continued to write in this tradition.

### The reality of generations

In varying degrees, the studies of generations have left in obscurity the questions of what generations are, why they exist, how long they last, what their scope is, and how they are determined. Some attempts have clarified *some* of these aspects, but in general without sufficient justification. Ortega y Gasset's theory of human life and, more concretely, of historical and social life has the merit of dealing with all of these questions. According to Ortega, all purely biological (and therefore genealogical) consideration of human life is insufficient, since human life does not consist in its psychophysical structures alone, but in what man does with them. Human life is a drama with character, plot, and scenery—the world; and this world is primarily a mass of social interpretations of reality: beliefs, ideas, customs, estimations, etc. These have a life independent of our individual wills; like laws, they stand *in force*, and we cannot avoid meeting them and having to deal with them. Ortega called them *vigencias* (states of being in force), giving social value to a juridical term. The world thus is a system of *vigencias*, or reigning norms, that both permits and compels man to orient himself and live his life (Ferrater Mora [1957] 1963, pp. 46–65; Marías 1949b).

The world system at all times presents the aspect of a *determined historical* level in which historical–social generations appear:

> The changes in vital sensibility which are decisive in history, appear under the form of the generation. A generation is not a handful of outstanding men, nor simply a mass of men; it resembles a new integration of the social body, with its select minority and its gross multitude, launched upon the orbit of existence with a pre-established vital trajectory. The generation is a dynamic compromise between mass and individual, and is the most important conception in history. It is, so to speak, the pivot responsible for the movements of historical evolution.   (Ortega [1923] 1961, pp. 14–15)

Thus, a generation is a human variation; every generation manifests a certain vital attitude. Generations are born one after the other, each encountering the forms of the previous one. There are *cumulative* epochs and others that are *eliminatory* and polemic.

A distinction must also be made between the *contemporary* (those who live in the same time) and the *coeval* (those who are the same age and are, by turns, young, mature, and old together) who constitute a generation (Ortega [1933] 1962, pp. 42–43). Ortega was, of course, well aware of the criticism that, since men are born every day, and since only those born on the same day are of the same age, the concept of generation is an illusion. But he rejected this kind of mathematical exactitude in dealing with the stuff of human life: "Within the human trajectory of life, age is a certain way of living. . . . Age, then, is not a date, but a 'zone of dates'; and it is not only those born in the same year who are the same age in life and in history, but those who are born within a zone of dates" (*ibid.*, p. 47).

Having defined the concept of generation, Ortega went on to consider the problem of applying it to history. Here he made use of the traditional division of human life into five "ages"—childhood, youth, "initiation" (or early manhood), "dominance" (or maturity), and old age. If the complete life-span is set at 75 years, the "ages" or generations of the life-span can be regarded as equal periods of 15 years each. Ortega pointed out that, since history is made largely by men between the ages of 30 and 60, it is the third and fourth generations that are of crucial interest to historians at any one time. But, from the point of view of individual development, these two generations are very different in character: "from thirty to forty-five is the period of gestation, or creation and conflict; from forty-five to sixty, the stage of dominance and command" (*ibid.*, p. 59). Because of their very great difference in outlook, there is always potential or actual conflict between these two generations, and herein Ortega detected the locus of historical change.

There remains the problem of finding a starting point for the generational series: why should any one division of history into 15-year periods be more valid than another? Ortega thought he had solved this problem by introducing the notion of the "decisive generation"; he argued that since it was already clear, from independent historical considerations, which were the crucial years in which a new era came into being, one had only to seek out the individuals who were the most decisive innovators of that period and note when they entered early manhood. Thus, if we take the Middle Ages as lasting until about 1350, and the modern age as beginning at some time between 1600 and 1650, the late fourteenth and all of the fifteenth and sixteenth centuries being a period of transition, the problem, as Ortega saw it, was to find the individual who most decisively represented the emergence of the modern age. In the present case, Ortega decided that that individual was Descartes, who ended his thirtieth year in 1626; thus the key date of the previous generation was 1611, and that of the generation following Descartes was 1641. Not that these dates were hard-and-fast divisions; Ortega intended them only as major reference points: "the center of the zone of dates which corresponds to the decisive generation" (Ortega [1933] 1962, p. 63). Nor did all generations have their great men, although there was a strong presumption that what Ortega called the "tone" of history changed more or less decisively every 15 years.

Ortega did not pretend to have solved the problem of generations in any final sense; what he offered the historian was a series of challenges, of demands to rethink his conception of the past in the light of the generational approach. Indeed, Ortega was not engaged in the writing of history as such; his main interest, so far as history was concerned, was in isolating and defining those periods of crisis and decisive social change which redefine the entire meaning of human existence. Like Wilhelm Dilthey, he continually stressed the importance of studying the meaning of historical events for those who took part in them. His generational schema was thus an indispensable means of detecting regularities in the seemingly endless variation of human experience.

## Dynamics of generations

Most of Ortega's writings were issued as public lectures or newspaper articles, in which forms he excelled. This gives his work great cogency of style but sometimes deters the specialist. A certain amount of systematic elaboration and clarification of his ideas is therefore necessary in order to demonstrate their usefulness to social science and to provide further developments of his method.

The macrostructure of history—epochs—cannot be determined a priori or cyclically, because it is dependent not on any constant structural factor of human life, but on its empirical contents. The microstructure—generations—is based on the mechanism of ages that is constant within certain extensive historical limits. Generations are, by turns, the "actors" and the "acts" of the historical drama, the "who" and the "what" of history whose movement is not continual but gradual. The generation is the elemental historical present, the term of relative stability of a world figure, and the rhythm of historical variation. The empirical determination of generations within a society is difficult and requires investigations that are rigorous and extremely cautious. Only the reigning norms of a society and their variation can be analyzed in detail. If a certain number of representative figures are taken whose origins fall within the same 15-year period (though the boundaries of the generations in question are not known, nor are the generations to which these figures belong), we can at least take each individual as representative of his own generation and study its characteristics in him. If other persons born in subsequent 15-year periods are added to the series, we can continue to assume that each group belongs to the same generation. But if, at a certain moment, a change in the whole series is observed, a "boundary" between two generations is indicated, and an entire generational series can then be established, at least in a provisional manner. This hypothetical series can be applied like a framework to historical reality, which will then confirm or correct it. Thus the proposed scale of generations serves as a provisional "working hypothesis"; its value is methodological.

Generations are not small groups of illustrious men; the latter are only the *representative* men of a generation that comprises innumerable anonymous men born within a certain "zone of dates." If a society is studied from the point of view of generations, it appears to be joined in groups or strata of coevals, each of whom occupies a definite position by virtue of his experiences, his pretensions, and, finally, his social level, since stratification is universal. The generational perspective introduces discontinuity and articulation in place of an amorphous and confused whole. From a historical point of view—inseparable from sociology because society is intrinsically historical—a date "unfolds" itself in several dates that correspond to the different generations. In each date there are four major human strata or generations, coexistents in interaction, with precise and unsubstitutable functions: (*a*) the "survivors" of a previous epoch who indicate the origins of the present situation, that is, the men "of another time" who nevertheless remain in this one; (*b*) those in power in all areas, whose pretensions generally coincide with the actual state of the world; (*c*) the "opposition" or active generation that has not yet triumphed and fights with the previous generation for the transfer of power and the realization of its own innovations; and (*d*) the young, who have new pretensions and look forward to a "putsch" or downfall of the *status quo*. A historical epoch is therefore defined by a principle or form of life that differentiates it from the previous one and affects the totality of a society. It is a process by which an innovation that begins by being individual goes on to permeate a minority and finally becomes dominant throughout the entire society, so that it is the form that individuals encounter as the prevailing way of life. Such a process requires the intervention of at least four successive generations, or about sixty years.

Empirical determination of generational series requires considerable work that has not as yet been accomplished anywhere. It is advisable to take a clearly defined society (a nation, for example) and a not too large space of time, since the normal concatenation of generations can be disturbed by serious historical upheavals. Between two different societies there normally is a time lag in the dates of generations. But the fact that different societies often have certain key dates in common is an indication that the same customs, manners, ideas, beliefs, etc. dominate over a certain historical area; in other words, that this constitutes *one* society, at least on a certain level. For example, it is very probable that the generations of western Europe coincide since the eighteenth century—in our time, perhaps throughout the West. It is certain, on the other hand, that the key dates in the United States are different from those in India or China.

The method of generations would permit a "social cartography" to be arrived at, the difficulties of which would be great but no greater than the requirements for any other empirical investigation of social phenomena. It should be noticed that historical–social generations affect *all* the men of a society in all the dimensions of their life; properly speaking, there is no such thing as (for example) a purely "literary" or "political" generation.

Particular fields can, of course, be investigated to obtain a greater facility of comparison or to pursue a particular interest; it must be borne in mind, however, that the results obtained cannot be extended to the whole society but must be related to a general theory of generations.

Julián Marías

[*Directly related is the entry* Cohort analysis. *Other relevant material may be found in* History, *article on* the philosophy of history; Periodization; *and in the biographies of* Comte; Cournot; Dilthey; Mannheim; Mill; Ortega y Gasset; Ranke; Vico.]

## BIBLIOGRAPHY

Benloew, Louis 1881 *Les lois de l'histoire.* Paris: Germer-Baillière.

Comte, Auguste (1830–1842) 1896 *The Positive Philosophy of Auguste Comte.* Freely translated and condensed by Harriet Martineau, with an introduction by Frederic Harrison. 3 vols. London: Bell. → First published as *Cours de philosophie positive.*

Comte, Auguste (1851–1854) 1875–1877 *System of Positive Polity.* 4 vols. London: Longmans. → First published in French. The translation of the extract in the text was made by the encyclopedia's editorial staff from the 1851–1854 French edition.

Cournot, Antoine A. (1872) 1934 *Considérations sur la marche des idées et des évènements dans les temps modernes.* 2 vols. Paris: Boivin.

Croce, Benedetto (1917) 1960 *History: Its Theory and Practice.* New York: Russell. → First published as *Teoria e storia della storiografia.*

Dilthey, Wilhelm (1875) 1924 Über das Studium der Geschichte der Wissenschaften vom Menschen, der Gesellschaft und dem Staat. Pages 31–73 in Wilhelm Dilthey, *Gesammelte Schriften.* Volume 5: Die geistige Welt. Leipzig and Berlin: Teubner.

Drerup, Engelbert 1933 *Das Generationsproblem in der griechischen und griechisch-römischen Kultur.* Paderborn (Germany): Schöningh.

Dromel, Justin 1862 *La loi des révolutions: Les générations, les nationalités, les dynasties, les religions.* Paris: Didier.

EISENSTADT, SHMUEL N.   1956   *From Generation to Generation: Age Groups and Social Structure.* Glencoe, Ill.: Free Press; London: Routledge.

FERRARI, GIUSEPPE   1874   *Teoria dei periodi politici.* Milan (Italy): Hoepli.

FERRATER MORA, JOSÉ   (1957) 1963   *Ortega y Gasset: An Outline of His Philosophy.* New rev. ed. New Haven: Yale Univ. Press.

JESCHKE, HANS   1934   *Die Generation von 1898 in Spanien.* Halle (Germany): Niemeyer.

LAFUENTE FERRARI, ENRIQUE   1951   *La fundamentación y los problemas de la historia del arte.* Madrid: Tecnos.

LAÍN ENTRALGO, PEDRO   1945   *Las generaciones en la historia.* Madrid: Instituto de Estudios Políticos.

LORENZ, OTTOKAR   1886   *Die Geschichtswissenschaft in Hauptrichtungen und Aufgaben kritisch erörtert.* Berlin: Hertz.

LORENZ, OTTOKAR   1891   *Leopold von Ranke, die Generationslehre und der Geschichtsunterricht.* Berlin: Hertz.

MANNHEIM, KARL   (1928) 1952   The Problem of Generations. Pages 276–320 in Karl Mannheim, *Essays on the Sociology of Knowledge.* New York: Oxford Univ. Press. → First published in German.

MARÍAS, JULIÁN   (1949a) 1961   *El método histórico de las generaciones.* 3d ed. Madrid: Revista de Occidente.

MARÍAS, JULIÁN   1949b   Ortega and the Idea of Vital Reason. *Dublin Review* 222, no. 445:56–79; no. 446:36–54.

MARÍAS, JULIÁN   (1955) 1964   *La estructura social: Teoría y método.* 4th ed. Madrid: Sociedad de Estudios y Publicaciones.

[MARTÍNEZ RUIZ, JOSÉ]   1913   *Clásicos y modernos,* by Azorin [pseud.]. Madrid: Renacimiento.

MENTRÉ, FRANÇOIS   1920   *Les générations sociales.* Paris: Bossard.

MILL, JOHN STUART   (1843) 1961   *A System of Logic, Ratiocinative and Inductive.* London: Longmans.

ORTEGA Y GASSET, JOSÉ   (1923) 1933   *The Modern Theme.* New York: Norton. → First published as *El tema de nuestro tiempo.* A paperback edition was published in 1961 by Harper.

ORTEGA Y GASSET, JOSÉ   (1933) 1962   *Man and Crisis.* New York: Norton. → First published as *En torno á Galileo.*

PETERSEN, JULIUS   1930   Die literarischen Generationen. Pages 130–187 in Emil Ermatinger (editor), *Philosophie der Literaturwissenschaft.* Berlin: Junker & Dünnhaupt.

PEYRE, HENRI   1948   *Les générations littéraires.* Paris: Boivin.

PINDER, WILHELM   (1926) 1928   *Das Problem der Generation in der Kunstgeschichte Europas.* 2d ed. Berlin: Frankfurter Verlags-Anstalt.

RANKE, LEOPOLD VON   (1888) 1954   Über die Epochen der neueren Geschichte. Part 9, section 2 in Leopold von Ranke, *Weltgeschichte.* Leipzig: Duncker & Humblot.

RÜMELIN, GUSTAV   1875   Über den Begriff und die Dauer einer Generation. Volume 1, pages 285–304 in Gustav Rümelin, *Reden und Aufsätze.* Freiburg im Breisgau (Germany): Mohr.

SALINAS, PEDRO   1935   El concepto de generación literaria aplicado á la del 98. *Revista de occidente* 50:249–259.

SCHLEGEL, FRIEDRICH   (1812) 1889   *Lectures on the History of Literature, Ancient and Modern.* London: Bell. → First published as *Geschichte der alten und neuen Literatur.*

SOULAVIE, JEAN-L. G.   1809   *Pièces inédites sur les règnes de Louis XIV, Louis XV et Louis XVI.* Paris: Colin.

WECHSSLER, E.   1929   Davoser Hochschulvorträge und das Problem der Generationen in der Geistesgeschichte. *Zeitschrift für französischen und englischen Unterricht* 28:435–438.

## II
### POLITICAL GENERATIONS

Group consciousness is universally recognized as one of the fundamental elements of political motivation. Individual human beings in every political system seek the security provided by membership in groups. Group consciousness is created by certain basic similarities, and this consciousness in turn creates more homogeneity within the group, a conformity which often leads to common action. Individuals think of themselves as members of a group and therefore act as members of that group. Since the interests of different groups are not always mutually compatible, there is social conflict. Since all individuals have allegiances to more than one group, there is conflict within the individual, who must decide which group is most important to him in given circumstances. In European politics, for instance, there has often been a conflict between national consciousness and class consciousness, which has generally been resolved in favor of the former.

Although political scientists have studied intensively both national consciousness and class consciousness, they have not explored to any considerable extent another kind of group consciousness, that of belonging to a distinct generation. This omission is surprising, for novelists, cultural and political historians, and sociologists have all used the concept of generation with considerable success. Although Turgenev's *Fathers and Sons* is the outstanding example of a literary work in which different generations cannot communicate effectively with each other, generational conflict is one of the major themes running through most of world literature. This fact is perhaps responsible for the emphasis which cultural historians have given to the study of different literary, artistic, and musical generations. Sometimes, indeed, cultural historians have seen only the successive alternation of "romantic" and "classical" generations. Historians, among them Ranke, have speculated about the significance of a generations approach to political history. Sociologists, especially Karl Mannheim (1928) and Rudolf Heberle (1951), have emphasized the importance of generational differences in social movements and social change. Political scientists, however, have used political generation as a conceptual tool only in the study of modern totalitarianism. Sigmund Neumann (1939; 1942) convincingly stressed the generational consciousness of National Socialist leaders and followers. Students of Soviet politics have found basic differences, not attributable merely to life cycle differences, between the responses of younger and older generations to the enforcement of conformity within the Soviet Union.

It could be argued that the concept of political generation can be of major assistance in understanding the motivation of leaders and followers in all political systems, not merely those which are totalitarian. Much of the hesitance of political scientists in applying this concept undoubtedly has arisen from uncertainty as to the precise meaning of a generation in politics. A political generation is not to be equated with a biological generation. Political generations do not suddenly "change" every 30 or 35 years. The process of social change is continuous, and it cannot wait until political power is handed on from father to son. There is undoubtedly much personal conflict between fathers and sons, but most of this conflict has no direct political significance. The history of politics is not primarily that of conflict, or even of consensus, between fathers and sons—although such conflict may take place, as it did between James and John Stuart Mill, with important political consequences. There are always—assuming a minimal rate of social change—more than two generations in politics at any one time. The idea of a "young" generation and an "old" generation as the sole participants in the political process is as oversimplified as Karl Marx's assumption that there are only two classes in modern industrial society. The idea of two generations in politics is frequently linked with the erroneous assumption that the "young" generation is always liberal and the "old" generation is always conservative.

Implicit in a generations approach to politics is the assumption that an individual's political attitudes do not undergo substantial change during the course of his adult lifetime. Once a set of political beliefs has been embraced, it is regarded as unlikely that the individual will abandon his beliefs. Rather than altering his previous outlook on the basis of new facts, the individual either rejects or accepts these new facts depending on whether or not they are consistent with his previous outlook. In this sense, a "liberal" generation will remain "liberal" in terms of the formative years throughout the physical lifetime of its members. Whether this same political attitude will appear liberal under radically changed circumstances is another matter. Much of the confusion in the political vocabulary of any nation may be due to the different meanings given to the same term by members of different generations. In thus explaining the tenacity of "outmoded" policies, generations theory removes these policies from the realm of free choice, from the realm of moral judgments. In this respect, a generations approach has the same fundamental weaknesses and strengths as any other determinist approach.

Especially in times of rapid social change, it is important to know precisely at what period of life political attitudes are formed. It is interesting that no serious advocate of a generations approach has argued that political attitudes are formed during childhood. Rather, it is argued that late adolescence and early adulthood are the formative years during which a distinctive personal outlook on politics emerges, which remains essentially unchanged through old age. The crucial years are regarded as approximately 17 to 25. If these years are in fact formative, neither the years preceding nor the years following them are decisive in the formation of political attitudes. It is during the formative years that the youth discovers his own identity. When he defines who he is in terms of society, he defines his political outlook as well. A political generation is seen as a group of individuals who have undergone the same basic historical experiences during their formative years. Such a generation would find political communication with earlier and later generations difficult, if not impossible.

**The size of a political generation.** Not all historical events are experienced to the same degree by the same number of individuals in their formative years, and political generations therefore vary widely in size. The 1825 Decembrist conspiracy, for instance, decisively influenced a much smaller number of young Russians than did the Russian Revolution of 1917. Assuming that the total degree of political participation is stable, it is the temporal and spatial "limits" of a given historic event that define the size of the resulting political generation, just as the degree of uniqueness of that event determines the degree of difficulty that generation will have in communicating with earlier and later generations. In this sense, for instance, the political generation created by World War I was a general European phenomenon. It was neither world-wide nor confined to one or a few European nations. The enormous transformation of European society which the war involved meant that a new political generation was created throughout Europe. But the limited nature of the war experience outside Europe meant that the war had far less impact on, say, American or Japanese youth. Those Europeans whose formative years, in whole or in part, occurred during 1914–1918, especially those who actually fought in the war, were not all influenced in the same way; but they were nevertheless all decisively influenced by it. Their reactions to the war were often very different, depending upon their national, class, and, especially, personality differences. In a real sense, the fact that they were all involved in the war in their formative years determined their attitude toward politics for the rest of their lives. Some never recovered from the war and retreated from politics, which had, they felt, led directly to such suffering. Others entered politics after 1918 determined above all to prevent a recurrence of war. Still others never spiritually left the battlefield and as a result engaged in politics as the continuation of war by other means. These three alternatives formed what Karl Mannheim termed "generation units," which together constituted a generation precisely because they were oriented toward one another, if only to fight one another. Politics involves more than knowledge of friend and foe, but many of the personal friendships and enmities which in fact later influence political behavior originate during the formative years. Each generation speaks out with more than one voice—there is conflict within each generation as well as among generations.

**The time span of a political generation.** If a political generation is not the same as a biological generation, it becomes all the more important to define the specific time span within which all who experience their formative years can be said to be molded into one distinct political generation. Without such a definition, it is impossible to classify individuals as members of one or another political generation with any precision, especially since few significant historic events "begin" and "end" with as much definiteness as World War I. Such classification cannot be done on an *ad hoc* basis. If the *ad hoc* method is attempted, it may properly be suspected that generational differences are being used as a *deus ex machina* in much the same way that differences in national character are sometimes invoked when there seems to be no other explanation of some political phenomenon. On the other hand, since the concept of political generation is closely related to the process of social change, any arbitrary choice of time span is likely to violate the complexity of reality. The actual time span involved in a generation will differ substantially in periods in which the process of social change is more rapid or less rapid. Karl Mannheim (1928) suggested that whether a new generation

appears every year, every thirty years, or every hundred years, or whether it emerges rhythmically at all, depends entirely on the specific social context. This variability, of course, is merely one aspect of the general problem of applying ideal types to concrete situations. All concepts of comparative analysis must be defined in time and space if they are to be of any use in clarifying reality. This is especially true of the concept of political generation, since membership in the same generation involves common location in time and space. In twentieth-century Western society, in which social change is not only rapid but cataclysmic, the time span of a political generation is considerably shorter than in more stable societies. The most reasonable estimate for the time span of a political generation in twentieth-century Western society is probably ten to fifteen years. In twentieth-century non-Western societies experiencing revolutionary social, economic, and political changes, this time span may be even shorter.

**The spatial span of a political generation.** Although the spatial span of a political generation is difficult to define with precision, it is clear that many coevals in the human race are not members of the same generation. Those whose formative experiences are fundamentally different cannot be members of the same generation, even though they may coexist in time. There was, for instance, as Mannheim pointed out, no community of experience between youths in China and Germany about 1800. It could be argued that there is considerable community of experience between youths in East Germany and Communist China today, since their formative years are spent in similar totalitarian political environments. Indeed, such phenomena as the spread of nationalism and of industrialization indicate that the spatial barriers between generations may be breaking down, at the same time that more rapid social change is increasing the importance of the temporal barriers between generations. The effect of the latter development is to make communication between different political generations more difficult, while the effect of the former development is to increase the world-wide significance of this decline in ability to communicate. The implications of these long-range developments for meaningful communication within and among political systems are not entirely encouraging.

**Significance of the concept.** Generational consciousness is undoubtedly less significant as a source of political motivation than either national or class consciousness. National consciousness finds its organizational expression in national states, and class consciousness finds its organizational expression in class-based private associations and parties. There is no analogous organizational structure created by generational consciousness, except for occasional loosely knit groups such as "Young Turks," "Young England," or "Young Conservatives." There are many powerful men recognized as primarily national or class leaders, but there are relatively few such men recognized as primarily generational leaders. Political personages nevertheless write, as did one Canadian leader, autobiographies with such titles as *My Generation of Politics and Politicians* (Preston 1927). Indeed, perhaps the most impressive evidence for the existence of generational consciousness in politics is the frequency with which it is articulated in the autobiographical writings of political leaders. These writings often demonstrate that, as Léon Blum put it, "a man remains essentially what his youth has made him" and that there is a special kind of communication, in politics as in other aspects of life, between members of the same generation. This should not be surprising, for the latter are simultaneously experiencing the problems and the promise of the life cycle itself.

**Problems for further research.** Clearly generational consciousness is not the single key to understanding political motivation, but equally clearly there is enough evidence of its importance to justify further research efforts. An exact evaluation of this importance waits upon full answers to several questions, some of which have their implications for the social sciences in general:

(1) When do an individual's politically formative years begin and end? To what extent is this period different in different societies?

(2) How substantial is the continuity between political attitudes accepted during the formative years and political attitudes in later years? (Care should be taken not to concentrate exclusively in this research on any one single element of political action, such as voting behavior, for the same fundamental attitudes might cause a voter to shift party allegiance in a changing party constellation. In the United States, for instance, an individual who became a Wilsonian liberal in his formative years might consider himself consistent in voting for Republican candidates in elections after the Democratic party was transformed under Franklin Roosevelt. A supporter of the Congress party at the achievement of Indian independence might in later decades feel that his continuing personal beliefs were best articulated by some other—or by no—party.)

(3) How long is the time span necessary to form a distinct political generation? What is the relationship between the rate of social change—and changes in the rate of social change—and the length of this time span?

(4) What is a generation unit? To what extent do generation units see the totality of politics in terms of each other?

Marvin Rintala

[*See also* Identification, political. *Other relevant material may be found in* Cohort analysis; Socialization; *and in the biography of* Mannheim.]

### BIBLIOGRAPHY

Alexander, Edgar (1956) 1957  The Dilemma: The Generations' Problem. Pages 33–42 in Edgar Alexander, *Adenauer and the New Germany: The Chancellor of the Vanquished*. Preface by Alvin Johnson. New York: Farrar, Straus. → First published in German.

Bauer, Raymond A.; Inkeles, Alex; and Kluckhohn, Clyde 1956  Generational Differences. Pages 190–198 in Raymond A. Bauer et al., *How the Soviet System Works: Cultural, Psychological and Social Themes*. Cambridge, Mass.: Harvard Univ. Press. → A paperback edition was published in 1961 by Vintage.

Eisenstadt, Shmuel N. 1956  *From Generation to Generation: Age Groups and Social Structure*. Glencoe, Ill.: Free Press; London: Routledge.

Evan, William M. 1959  Cohort Analysis of Survey Data: A Procedure for Studying Long-term Opinion Change. *Public Opinion Quarterly* 23:63–72.

Gusfield, Joseph R. 1957  The Problem of Generations in an Organizational Structure. *Social Forces* 35:323–330.

Halpern, Ben 1961  *The Idea of the Jewish State*. Cambridge, Mass.: Harvard Univ. Press.

Heberle, Rudolf 1951  *Social Movements: An Introduction to Political Sociology*. New York: Appleton. → See especially pages 118–127 on "The Problem of Political Generations."

Mannheim, Karl (1928) 1952  The Problem of Generations. Pages 276–320 in Karl Mannheim, *Essays on the Sociology of Knowledge*. New York: Oxford Univ. Press. → First published in German.

Neumann, Sigmund 1939  The Conflict of Generations in Contemporary Europe: From Versailles to Munich. *Vital Speeches of the Day* 5:623–628.

Neumann, Sigmund (1942) 1965  *Permanent Revolution: Totalitarianism in the Age of International Civil War*. 2d ed. New York: Praeger. → First published as *Permanent Revolution: The Total State in a World at War*.

Ortega y Gasset, José (1923) 1933  *The Modern Theme*. New York: Norton. → First published as *El tema de nuestro tiempo*. A paperback edition was published in 1961 by Harper.

Pinder, Wilhelm 1926  *Kunstgeschichte nach Generationen*. Leipzig: Pfeiffer.

Preston, William T. R. 1927  *My Generation of Politics and Politicians*. Toronto: Rose.

Rintala, Marvin 1958  The Problem of Generations in Finnish Communism. *American Slavic and East European Review* 17:190–202.

Rintala, Marvin 1962  *Three Generations: The Extreme Right Wing in Finnish Politics*. Bloomington: Indiana Univ. Press.

Rintala, Marvin 1963 A Generation in Politics: A Definition. *Review of Politics* 25:509–522.

Zeitlin, Maurice 1966 Political Generations in the Cuban Working Class. *American Journal of Sociology* 71:493–508.

# GENETICS

## I
### GENETICS AND BEHAVIOR

Behavior genetics is a relatively new cross-disciplinary specialization between genetics and psychology. It is so new that it hardly knows what to call itself. The term "behavior genetics" is gaining currency in the United States; but in some quarters there, and certainly elsewhere, the term "psychogenetics" is favored. Logically, the best name would be genetical psychology, since the emphasis is on the use of the techniques of genetics in the analysis of behavior rather than vice versa; but the inevitable ambiguity of that term is apparent. Psychologists generally use the terms "genetic" or "genetical" in two senses: in the first and older sense of developmental, or ontogenetic; and in the second, more recent usage relating to the analysis of inheritance. The psychologist G. Stanley Hall coined the term "genetic" before the turn of the century to denote developmental studies (witness the *Journal of Genetic Psychology*), and Alfred Binet even used the term "psychogenetic" in this sense. But with the rapid rise of the discipline now known as genetics after the rediscovery of the Mendelian laws in 1900, William Bateson, one of the founders of this new science, pre-empted the term "genetic" in naming it, thereby investing "genetic" with the double meaning that causes the current confusion. Psychological genetics, with its obvious abbreviation, psychogenetics, is probably the best escape from the dilemma.

**Importance of genetics in behavior.** The importance of psychogenetics lies in the fundamental nature of the biological processes in our understanding of human social behavior. The social sciences, and psychology in particular, have long concentrated on environmental determinants of behavior and neglected hereditary ones. But it is clear that in many psychological functions a substantial portion of the observed variation, roughly of the order of 50 per cent for many traits, can be ascribed to hereditary causation. To ignore this hereditary contribution is to impede both action and thought in this area.

This manifold contribution to behavioral variation is not a static affair. Heredity and environment interact, and behavior is the product, rather than the sum, of their respective contributions. The number of sources of variability in both heredity and environment is large, and the consequent number of such possible products even larger. Nevertheless, these outcomes are not incalculable, and experimental and other analyses of their limits are of immense potential interest to the behavioral scientist. The chief theoretical interest lies in the analysis of the evolution of behavior; and the chief practical significance, so far as can be envisaged at present, lies in the possibilities psychogenetics has for the optimization of genetic potential by manipulation of the environmental expression of it.

**Major current approaches.** The major approaches to the study of psychogenetics can be characterized as the direct, or experimental, and the indirect, or observational. The former derive principally from the genetical parent of this hybrid discipline and involve the manipulation of the heredity of experimental subjects, usually by restricting the choice of mates in some specially defined way. Since such techniques are not possible with human subjects a second major approach exists, the indirect or observational, with its techniques derived largely from psychology and sociology. The two approaches are largely complementary in the case of "natural" genetic experiments in human populations, such as twinning or cousin marriages. Thus, the distinction between the two is based on the practicability of controlling in some way the essentially immutable genetic endowment—in a word, the genotype—of the individuals subject to investigation. With typical experimental animals (rats, mice, etc.) and other organisms used by the geneticist, such as the fruit fly and many microorganisms, the genotype can often be specified in advance and populations constructed by the hybridization of suitable strains to meet this specification with a high degree of accuracy. Not so with humans, where the genotype must remain as given, and indeed where its details can rarely be specified with any degree of accuracy except for certain physical characteristics, such as blood groups. Observational, demographic, and similar techniques are therefore all that are available here. The human field has another disadvantage in rigorous psychogenetic work: the impossibility of radically manipulating the environment—for example, by rearing humans in experimental environments from birth in the way that can easily be done with animals in the laboratory. Since in psychogenetics, as in all branches of genetics, one deals with a phenotype—in this case, behavior—and since the phenotype is the end product of the action, or better still, *interaction* of genotype and environment, human psychogenetics is fraught with double difficulty. Analytical techniques to be mentioned later can assist in resolving some of these difficulties.

**Definition.** To define psychogenetics as the study of the inheritance of behavior is to adopt a misleadingly narrow definition of the area of study, and one which is unduly restrictive in its emphasis on the hereditarian point of view. Just as the parent discipline of genetics is the analysis not only of the similarities between individuals but also of the differences between them, so psychogenetics seeks to understand the basis of individual differences in behavior. Any psychogenetic analysis must therefore be concerned with the environmental determinants of behavior (conventionally implicated in the genesis of differences) in addition to the hereditary ones (the classic source of resemblances). But manifestly this dichotomy does not always operate, so that for this reason alone the analysis of environmental effects must go hand in hand with the search for genetic causation. This is true even if the intention is merely to exclude the influence of the one the better to study the other; but the approach advocated here is to study the two in tandem, as it were, and to determine the extent to which the one interacts with the other. *Psychogenetics is best viewed as that specialization which concerns itself with the interaction of heredity and environment, insofar as they affect behavior.* To attempt greater precision is to become involved in subtle semantic problems about the meanings of terms.

At first sight many would tend to restrict environmental effects to those operating after the birth of the organism, but to do so would be to exclude prenatal environmental effects that have been shown to be influential in later behavior. On the other hand, to broaden the concept of environment to include all influences after fertilization—the point in time at which the genotype is fixed—permits consideration of the reciprocal influence of parts of the genotype upon each other. Can environment include the rest of the genotype, other than that part which is more or less directly concerned with the phenotype under consideration? This point assumes some importance since there are characteristics, not behavioral—at least, none that are behavioral have so far been reported—whose expression depends on the nature of the

other genes present in the organism. In the absence of some of them, or rather certain alleles of the gene pairs, the value phenotypically observed would be different from what it would be if they were present. That is, different components of the genotype, in interplay with one another, modify phenotypic expression of the characteristic they influence. Can such indirect action, which recalls that of a chemical catalyst, best be considered as environmental or innate? It would be preferable to many to regard this mechanism as a genetic effect rather than an environmental one in the usually accepted sense. Hence, the definition of the area of study as one involving the interaction of heredity and environment, while apparently adding complexity, in fact serves to reduce confusion.

It must be conceded that this view has not as yet gained general acceptance. In some of the work reviewed in the necessarily brief survey of the major findings in this area, attempts have been made to retain a rather rigid dichotomy between heredity and environment—nature versus nurture—in fact, an "either/or" proposition that the facts do not warrant. The excesses of both sides in the controversies of the 1920s—for example, the famous debate between Watson and McDougall over the relative importance of learned (environmental) and instinctive (genetic) determinants of behavior—show the fallacies that extreme protagonists on either side can entertain if the importance of the interaction effect is ignored.

**Gene action.** The nature of gene action as such is essentially conducive to interaction with the environment, since the behavioral phenotype we observe is the end product of a long chain of action, principally biochemical, originating in the chromosome within the individual cell. A chromosome has a complex structure, involving DNA (deoxyribonucleic acid) and the connections of DNA with various proteins, and may be influenced in turn by another nucleic acid, RNA (ribonucleic acid), also within the cell but external to the nucleus. There are complex structures and sequences of processes, anatomical, physiological, and hormonal, which underlie normal development and differentiation of structure and function in the growth, development, and maturation of the organism. Much of this influence is determined genetically in the sense that the genotype of the organism, fixed at conception, determines how it proceeds under normal environmental circumstances. But it would be a mistake to regard any such sequence as rigid or immutable, as we shall see.

The state of affairs that arises when a number of genetically determined biochemical abnormalities affect behavior is illustrative of the argument. Many of these biochemical deficiencies or inborn errors of metabolism in humans are the outcome of a chain of causation starting with genic structures, some of them having known chromosomal locations. Their effects on the total personality—that is, the sum total of behavorial variation that makes the individual unique—can range from the trivial to the intense. The facility with which people can taste a solution of phenylthiocarbamide (PTC), a synthetic substance not found in nature, varies in a relatively simple genetical way: people are either "tasters" or "nontasters" in certain rather well-defined proportions, with a pattern of inheritance determined probably by one gene of major effect. But being "taste blind" or not is a relatively unimportant piece of behavior, since one is never likely to encounter it outside a genetical experiment. (It should perhaps be added that there is some evidence that the ability to taste PTC may be linked with other characteristics of some importance, such as susceptibility to thyroid disease.) Nevertheless, this example is insignificant compared with the psychological effect of the absence of a biochemical link in patients suffering from phenylketonuria. They are unable to metabolize phenylalanine to tyrosine in the liver, with the result that the phenylalanine accumulates and the patient suffers multiple defects, among which is usually gross intellectual defect, with an IQ typically on the order of 30. This gross biochemical failure is mediated by a single recessive gene that may be passed on in a family unnoticed in heterozygous—single dose—form but becomes painfully apparent in the unfortunate individual who happens to receive a double dose and consequently is homozygous for the defect.

Alternatively, a normal dominant gene may mutate to the recessive form and so give rise to the trouble. While mutation is a relatively rare event individually, the number of genes in each individual—probably on the order of ten thousand —and the number of individuals in a population make it statistically a factor to be reckoned with. One of the best documented cases of a deleterious mutation of this kind giving rise to a major defect relates to the hemophilia transmitted, with certain important political consequences, to some of the descendants of Queen Victoria of England. The dependence of the last tsarina of Russia on the monk Rasputin was said to be based in part on the beneficial therapeutic effect of his hypnotic techniques on the uncontrollable bleeding of the Tsarevitch Alexis. Victoria was almost certainly heterozygous for hemophilia and, in view of the absence of any previous record of the defect in the Hanoverian dynasty, it seems likely that the origin of the trouble was a mutation in one of the germ cells in a testicle of Victoria's father, the duke of Kent, before Victoria was conceived in August 1818.

But however it comes about, a defect such as phenylketonuria can be crippling. Fortunately, its presence can be diagnosed in very early life by a simple urine test for phenyl derivatives. The dependence of the expression of the genetic defect on the environmental circumstances is such that its effect can be mitigated by feeding the afflicted infant with a specially composed diet low in the phenylalanine with which the patient's biochemical make-up cannot cope. Here again, therefore, one sees the interaction of genotype and environment —in this case the type of food eaten. Many of the human biochemical defects that have been brought to light in recent years are rather simply determined genetically, in contrast with the prevailing beliefs about the bases of many behavioral characteristics including intelligence, personality, and most psychotic and neurotic disorders. This is also true of several chromosomal aberrations that have been much studied recently and that are now known to be implicated in various conditions of profound behavioral importance. Prominent among these is Down's syndrome (mongolism) with, again, effects including impairment of cognitive power. [See INTELLIGENCE AND INTELLIGENCE TESTING; MENTAL DISORDERS, *articles on* BIOLOGICAL ASPECTS *and* GENETIC ASPECTS.]

**Sex as a genetic characteristic.** The sex difference is perhaps the most striking genetically determined difference in behavior and the one that is most often ignored in this connection. Primary sex is completely determined genetically at the moment of fertilization of the ovum; in mammals sex depends on whether the spermatozoon effecting fertilization bears an X or a Y chromosome to combine with the X chromosome inevitably contributed by the ovum. The resulting gamete then has the form of an XX (female) or an XY (male) individual. This difference penetrates every cell of every tissue of the resulting individual and in turn is responsible for the observable gross differences in morphology. These, in turn, subserve differences of physiological function, metabolism, and endocrine function which profoundly influence not only those aspects of behavior relating to sexual behavior and reproductive function in the two sexes but many other aspects as well. But behavior is also influenced by social and cultural pressures, so that the resulting sex differences in behavior as observed by the psychologist are especially good examples of a phenotype that must be the end product of both genetic and environmental forces. There is a large literature on sex differences in human behavior and a sizable one on such differences in animal behavior, but there has been little attempt to assess this pervasive variation in terms of the relative contribution of genetic and environmental determinants. This is partly because of the technical difficulties of the problem, in the sense that all subjects must be of either one sex or the other—crossing males with females will always result in the same groups as those one started with, either males or females—there being, in general, no genetically intermediate sex against which to evaluate either and identical twins being inevitably of like sex. It is also partly because the potential of genetic analyses that do not involve direct experimentation has not been realized. This is especially so since the causal routes whereby genetic determinants of sex influence many of the behavioral phenotypes observed are often better understood than in other cases where the genetic determinants underlying individual differences manifest in a population are not so clear-cut. [See INDIVIDUAL DIFFERENCES, *article on* SEX DIFFERENCES.]

*Sex linkage.* There is one exception to the general lack of interest in the biometrical analysis of sex differences having behavioral connotations: sex-linked conditions. That is to say, it is demonstrated or postulated that the gene or genes responsible for the behavior—often a defect, as in the case of color blindness, which has a significantly greater incidence in males than in females—are linked with the sex difference by virtue of their location on the sex chromosome determining genetic sex. Thus it is that sex can be thought of as a chromosomal difference of regular occurrence, as opposed to aberrations of the sort which give rise to pathological conditions, such as Down's syndrome. Indeed there are also various anomalies of genetic sex that give rise to problems of sexual identity, in which the psychological and overt behavioral consequences can be of major importance for the individual. While the evidence in such cases of environmental modification of the causative genetic conditions is less dramatic than in phenylketonuria, interaction undoubtedly exists, since these chromosomal defects of sex differentiation can in some cases be alleviated by appropriate surgical and hormonal treatment. [See SEXUAL BEHAVIOR, *article on* SEXUAL DEVIATION: PSYCHOLOGICAL ASPECTS; *and* VISION, *article on* COLOR VISION AND COLOR BLINDNESS.]

**Human psychogenetics.** It is abundantly clear that most of the phenotypes the behavioral scientist is interested in are multidetermined, both environmentally and genetically. The previous examples, however, are the exception rather than the rule, and their prominence bears witness that our understanding of genetics and behavior is as yet so little advanced that the simpler modes of genetic expression have been the first to be explored. In genetics itself, the striking differences in seed configuration used by Mendel in his classic crosses of sweet peas are determined by major genes with full dominance acting simply. But such clear-cut expression, especially of dominance, is unusual in human psychogenetics, and more complex statistical techniques are necessary to evaluate multiple genetic and environmental effects acting to produce the observed phenotype.

Whatever the analysis applied to the data gathered in other fields, in human psychogenetics the method employed cannot be the straightforward Mendelian one of crossbreeding which, in various elaborations, remains the basic tool of the geneticist today. Neither can it be the method of selection —artificial, as opposed to natural—that is otherwise known as selective breeding. Indeed, none of the experimental techniques that can be applied to any other organism, whatever the phenotype being measured, is applicable to man, since experimental mating is effectively ruled out as a permissible technique in current cultures. It may be remarked in passing that such has not always been the case. The experiment of the Mogul emperor, Akbar, who reared children in isolation to determine their "natural religion" (and merely produced mutes) and the eugenics program of J. H. Noyes at the Oneida Community in New York State in the nineteenth century are cases in point. The apparent inbreeding of brother with sister among the rulers of ancient Egypt in the eighteenth dynasty (sixteenth to fourteenth century B.C.), which is often quoted as an example of the absence in humans of the deleterious effects of inbreeding ("inbreeding depression"), may not be all it seems. It is likely that the definition of "sister" and "brother" in this context did not necessarily have the same biological relevance that it has today but was rather a cultural role that could be defined, at least in this case, at will.

*Twin study.* In the absence of the possibility of an experimental approach, contemporary research in human psychogenetics must rely on natural genetic experiments. Of these, the one most widely used and most industriously studied is the phenomenon of human twinning. Credit for the recognition of the value of observations on twins can be given to the nineteenth-century English scientist Francis Galton, who pioneered many fields of inquiry. He may be justly regarded as the father of psychogenetics for the practical methods he introduced into this field, such as the method of twin study, as well as for his influence which extended, although indirectly, even to the American experimenters in psychogenetics during the early decades of the present century.

Twin births are relatively rare in humans and vary in frequency with the ethnic group. However, the extent to which such ethnic groups differ among themselves behaviorally as a result of the undoubted genetic differences, of which incidence of multiple births is but one example, is controversial. As is well known, there are two types of twins: the monozygotic or so-called identical twins, derived from a single fertilized ovum that has split into two at an early stage in development, and the dizygotic or so-called fraternal twins, developed from two separate ova fertilized by different spermatozoa. These two physical types are not always easy to differentiate, although this difficulty is relatively minor in twin study. Nonetheless, they have led to two kinds of investigation. The first relates to differences in monozygotic twins who have identical hereditary make-up but who have been reared apart and thus subjected to different environmental influences during childhood; and the second relates to the comparison of the two types of twins— usually restricted to like-sex pairs, since fraternal twins can differ in sex. The latter method supposes all differences between monozygotic pairs to be due to environmental origin, whereas the (greater) difference between dizygotic pairs is of environmental plus genetic origin. Thus, the relative contribution of the two sources of variation can be evaluated.

Findings obtained from either method have not been especially clear-cut, both because of intractable problems regarding the relative weight to be placed upon differences in the environment in which the twins have been reared and because of the sampling difficulties, which are likely to be formidable in any twin study. Nevertheless, interesting inferences can be drawn from twin study. The investigation of separated monozygotic twins has shown that while even with their identical heredity they can differ quite widely, there exists a significant resemblance in basic aspects of personality including intelligence, introversion, and neurotic tendencies, and that these resemblances can persist despite widely different environments in which the members of a pair are reared. Such findings emphasize the need to consider the contribution of genotype and environment in an interactive sense—clearly some genotypes represented

in the personality of monozygotic twin pairs are sensitive to environmentally induced variation, whereas others are resistant to it.

Comparisons between monozygotic and dizygotic twins reared together suggest that monozygotic twins more closely resemble each other in many aspects of personality, especially those defining psychological factors such as neuroticism and introversion–extroversion. The increase in the differences between the two types of twins when factor measures are used—as opposed to simple test scores—suggests that a more basic biological stratum is tapped by factor techniques, since the genetic determination seems greater than where individual tests are employed. Here again, the degree to which any phenotype is shown to be hereditary in origin is valid only for the environment in which it developed and is measured; different environments may well yield different results. The problems of environmental control in human samples are so intractable that some students of the subject have questioned whether the effort and undoubted skill devoted to twin study have been well invested, in view of the inherent and persisting equivocality of the outcome.

*Multivariate methods.* Methods of twin study, introduced largely to improve upon the earlier methods of familial correlation (parents with offspring, sib with sib, etc.), have been combined with them. Familial correlation methods themselves have not been dealt with here, since within-family environments are bound to be even greater contaminants in determining the observed behavior than environments in twin study methods. Nevertheless, used on a large scale and in conjunction with twin study and with control subjects selected at random from a population, multivariate methods show promise for defining the limits of environmental and genotypic interaction. So far, the solutions to the problems of biometrical analysis posed by this type of investigation have been only partial, and the sheer weight of effort involved in locating and testing the requisite numbers of subjects standing in the required relationships has deterred all but a few pioneers. Despite the undoubtedly useful part such investigations have played in defining the problems involved, the absence of the possibility of experimental breeding has proved a drawback in the provision of socially useful data.

**Animal psychogenetics.** Recourse has often been had to nonhuman subjects. The additional problem thereby incurred of the relevance of comparative data to human behavior is probably balanced by the double refinements of the control of both the heredity and the environment of the experimental subjects. Two major methods of genetics have been employed, both intended to produce subjects of pre-determined genotype: the crossbreeding of strains of animals of known genotype; and phenotypic selection, the mating of like with like to increase a given characteristic in a population.

*Selection.* Behavioral phenotypes of interest have been studied by the above methods, often using laboratory rodents. For example, attributes such as intelligence, activity, speed of conditioning, and emotionality have been selectively bred in rats.

Selection for emotional behavior in the rat will serve as an example of the techniques used and the results achieved. Rats, in common with many other mammalian species, defecate when afraid. A technique of measuring individual differences in emotional arousal is based on this propensity. The animal under test is exposed to mildly stressful noise and light stimulation in an open field or arena. The number of fecal pellets deposited serves as an index of disturbance, and in this way the extremes among a large group of rats can be characterized as high or low in emotional responsiveness. Continued selection from within the "high" and "low" groups will in time produce two distinct strains. Control of environmental variables is achieved by a rigid standardization of the conditions under which the animals are reared before being subjected to the test as adults. Careful checks on maternal effects, both prenatal and postnatal, reveal these effects to be minimal.

Such an experiment does little beyond establishing the importance of the genetic effect on the given strains in the given environment. While there are techniques for assessing the relative importance of the genetic and environmental contributions to the variation observed under selection, they are better suited to the analysis of the outcome of experiments using the alternative major genetical method, that of crossbreeding of inbred strains.

*Crossbreeding.* Strains used in crossbreeding experiments have usually been inbred for a phenotypic character of interest, although not usually a behavioral one. However, this does not preclude the use of these inbred strains for behavioral studies, since linkage relationships among genes ensure that selection for factors multidetermined genetically often involves multiple changes in characteristics other than those selected for, and behavior is no exception to this rule. Moreover, the existence of such inbred strains constitutes perhaps the most important single advantage of animals as subjects, since it enables simplifying assumptions

regarding the homozygosity or genetic uniformity of such strains to be made in analysis of the outcome of crosses. Members of inbred strains are theoretically as alike as monozygotic twin pairs, so that genetic relationships—which in human populations can be investigated only after widespread efforts to find them—can be multiplied at will in laboratory animals.

This approach allows a more sensitive analysis of the determinants, both environmental and genetic, of the behavioral phenotype under observation. In addition, the nature of the genetic forces can be further differentiated into considerations of the average dominance effects of the genes involved, the extent to which they tend to increase or decrease the metrical expression of the behavioral phenotype, and the extent to which the different strains involved possess such increasers or decreasers. Finally, rough estimates of the number of these genes can be given. But the analysis depends upon meeting requirements regarding the scaling of the metric upon which the behavior is measured and is essentially a statistical one. That is, only average effects of cumulative action of the relatively large number of genes postulated as involved can be detected. Gone are the elegantly simple statistics derived from the classical Mendelian analyses of genes of major effect, often displaying dominance, like those encountered in certain human inborn errors of metabolism. There is little evidence of the existence of comparable genes of major effect mediating behavior in laboratory animals, although some have been studied in insects, especially the fruit fly.

A typical investigation of a behavioral phenotype might take the form of identifying two inbred strains known to differ in a behavioral trait, measuring individuals from these strains, and then systematically crossing them and measuring all offspring. When this was done for the runway performance of mice, an attribute related to their temperamental wildness, the results, analyzed by the techniques of biometrical genetics, showed that the behavior was controlled by at least three groups of genes (a probable underestimate). The contributions of these groups were additive to each other and independent of the environment when measured on a logarithmic scale but interacted with each other and with the environment on a linear scale. These genes showed a significant average dominance effect, and there was a preponderance of dominant genes in the direction of greater wildness. The heritability ratio of the contributions of "nature" and "nurture" was around seven to three.

The use of inbred lines may be restricted to first

filial crosses if a number of such crosses are made from several different lines. This increases precision of analysis in addition to allowing a proportionate decrease in the amount of laboratory work. One investigation examined the exploratory behavior of six different strains of rats in an open field of the kind used for the selection mentioned above. On a linear scale there were no untoward environmental effects, including specifically prenatal maternal ones. The heritability ratio was high, around nine to one; and while there was a significant average dominance component among the genes determining exploration, there was no preponderance of dominants or recessively acting genes among increasers or decreasers. The relative standing in this respect of the parental strains could be established with some precision.

**Limitations.** While the methods described above have allowed the emergence of results that ultimately may assist our understanding of the mechanisms of behavioral inheritance, it cannot be said that much substantial progress has yet been made. Until experiments explore the effect of a range of different genotypes interacting with a range of environments of psychological interest and consequence, little more can be expected. Manipulating heredity in a single standard environment or manipulating the environment of a single standard genotype can only provide conclusions so limited to both the genotypes and conditions employed that they have little usefulness in a wider context. When better experiments are performed, as seems likely in the next few decades, then problems of some sociological importance and interest will arise in the application of these experiments to the tasks of maximizing genetic potential and perfecting environmental control for the purpose of so doing. A new eugenics may well develop, but grappling with the problems of its impact on contemporary society had best be left to future generations.

P. L. BROADHURST

[*Directly related are the entries* EUGENICS; EVOLUTION; MENTAL DISORDERS, *article on* GENETIC ASPECTS. *Other relevant material may be found in* INDIVIDUAL DIFFERENCES, *article on* SEX DIFFERENCES; INSTINCT; INTELLIGENCE AND INTELLIGENCE TESTING; MENTAL RETARDATION; PSYCHOLOGY, *article on* CONSTITUTIONAL PSYCHOLOGY.]

### BIBLIOGRAPHY

BROADHURST, P. L. 1960 Experiments in Psychogenetics: Applications of Biometrical Genetics to the Inheritance of Behavior. Pages 1–102 in Hans J. Eysenck (editor), *Experiments in Personality.* Volume 1: Psychogenetics and Psychopharmacology. London: Routledge. → Selection and crossbreeding methods applied to laboratory rats.

CATTELL, RAYMOND B.; STICE, GLEN F.; and KRISTY, NORTON F. 1957 A First Approximation to Nature–Nurture Ratios for Eleven Primary Personality Factors in Objective Tests. *Journal of Abnormal and Social Psychology* 54:143–159. → Pioneer multivariate analysis combining twin study and familial correlations.

FULLER, JOHN L.; and THOMPSON, W. ROBERT 1960 *Behavior Genetics.* New York: Wiley. → A comprehensive review of the field.

MATHER, KENNETH 1949 *Biometrical Genetics: The Study of Continuous Variation.* New York: Dover. → The classic work on the analysis of quantitative characteristics.

SHIELDS, JAMES 1962 *Monozygotic Twins Brought Up Apart and Brought Up Together: An Investigation Into the Genetic and Environmental Causes of Variation in Personality.* Oxford Univ. Press.

## II
## DEMOGRAPHY AND POPULATION GENETICS

The best available definition of population genetics is doubtless that of Malécot: "It is the totality of mathematical models that can be constructed to represent the evolution of the structure of a population classified according to the distribution of its Mendelian genes" (1955, p. 240). This definition, by a probabilist mathematician, gives a correct idea of the "constructed" and abstract side of this branch of genetics; it also makes intelligible the rapid development of population genetics since the advent of Mendelism.

In its formal aspect this branch of genetics might even seem to be a science that is almost played out. Indeed, it is not unthinkable that mathematicians have exhausted all the structural possibilities for building models, both within the context of general genetics and within that of the hypotheses—more or less complex and abstract—that enable us to characterize the state of a population.

Two major categories of models can be distinguished: *determinist* models are those "in which variations in population composition over time are rigorously determined by (*a*) a known initial state of the population; (*b*) a known number of forces or 'pressures' operating, in the course of generations, in an unambiguously defined fashion" (Malécot 1955, p. 240). These pressures involve mutation, selection, and preferential marriages (by consanguinity, for instance). Determinist models, based on ratios that have been exactly ascertained from preceding phenomena, can be expressed only in terms of populations that are infinite in the mathematical sense. In fact, it is only in this type of population that statistical regularities can emerge (Malécot 1955). In these models the composition of each generation is perfectly defined by the composition of the preceding generation.

*Stochastic* models, in contrast to determinist ones, involve only finite populations, in which the gametes that, beginning with the first generation, are actually going to give birth to the new generation represent only a finite number among all possible gametes. The result is that among these active, or "useful," gametes (Malécot 1959), male or female, the actual frequency of a gene will differ from the probability that each gamete had of carrying it at the outset.

The effect of chance will play a prime role, and the frequencies of the genes will be able to drift from one generation to the other. The effects of random drift and of genetic drift become, under these conditions, the focal points for research.

The body of research completed on these assumptions does indeed form a coherent whole, but these results, in spite of their brilliance, are marked by a very noticeable formalism. In reality, the models, although of great importance at the conceptual level, are often too far removed from the facts. In the study of man, particularly, the problems posed are often too complex for the solutions taken directly from the models to describe concrete reality.

Not all these models, however, are the result of purely abstract speculation; construction of some of them has been facilitated by experimental data. To illustrate this definition of population genetics and the problems that it raises, this article will limit itself to explaining one determinist model, both because it is one of the oldest and simplest to understand and because it is one of those most often verified by observation.

**A determinist model.**    Let us take the case of a particular human population: the inhabitants of an island cut off from outside contacts. It is obvious that great variability exists among the genes carried by the different inhabitants of this island. The genotypes differ materially from one another; in other words, there is a certain polymorphism in the population—polymorphism that we can define in genetic terms with the help of a simple example.

Let us take the case of autosome ("not connected with sex") gene *a*, transmitting itself in a monohybrid diallely. In relation to it individuals can be classified in three categories: *homozygotes* whose two alleles are *a* ($a/a$); heterozygotes, carriers of *a* and its allele *a'* ($a/a'$); and the homozygotes who are *noncarriers* of *a* ($a'/a'$). At any given moment or during any given generation, these three categories of individuals exist within the population in certain proportions relative to each other.

Now, according to Mendel's second law (the law of segregation), the population born out of a cross between an individual who is homozygote for *a* ($a/a$) and an individual who is homozygote for *a'* ($a'/a'$) will include individuals $a/a$, $a/a'$, and $a'/a'$ in the following proportions: one-fourth $a/a$,

one-half $a/a'$, and one-fourth $a'/a'$. In this population the alleles *a* and *a'* have the same frequency, one-half, and each sex produces half *a* and half *a'*. If these individuals are mated randomly, a simple algebraic calculation quickly demonstrates that individuals of the generation following will be quantitatively distributed in the same fashion: one-fourth $a/a$, one-half $a/a'$, and one-fourth $a'/a'$. It will be the same for succeeding generations.

It can therefore be stated that *the genetic structure of such a population does not vary from one generation to the other*. If we designate by *p* the initial proportion of $a/a$ individuals and by *q* that of $a'/a'$ individuals, we get $p + q = 1$, or the totality of the population. Applying this system of symbols to the preceding facts, it can be easily shown that the proportion of individuals of all three categories in the first generation born from $a/a$ and $a'/a'$ equals $p^2$, $2pq$, $q^2$. In the second and third generation the frequency of individuals will always be similar: $p^2$, $2pq$, $q^2$.

Until this point, we have remained at the individual level. If we proceed to that of the gametes carrying *a* or *a'* and to that of genes *a* and *a'*, we observe that their frequencies intermingle. In the type of population discussed above, the formula $p^2$, $2pq$, $q^2$ still applies perfectly, therefore, to the gametes and genes. This model, which can be regarded as a formalization of the Hardy–Weinberg law, has other properties, but our study of it will stop here. (For a discussion of the study of isolated populations, see Sutter & Tabah 1951.)

**Model construction and demographic reality.** The Hardy–Weinberg law has been verified by numerous studies, involving both vegetable and animal species. The findings in the field of human blood groups have also been studied for a long time from a viewpoint derived implicitly from this law, especially in connection with their geographic distribution. Under the system of reproduction by sexes, a generation renews itself as a result of the encounter of the sexual cells (gametes) produced by individuals of both sexes belonging to the living generation. In the human species it can be said that this encounter takes place at random. One can imagine the advantage that formal population genetics can take of this circumstance, which can be compared to drawing marked balls by lot from two different urns. Model construction, already favored by these circumstances, is favored even further if the characteristics of the population utilized are artificially defined with the help of a certain number of hypotheses, of which the following is a summary description:

(1) Fertility is identical for all couples; there is no differential fertility.

(2) The population is closed; it cannot, therefore, be the locus of migrations (whether immigration or emigration).

(3) Marriages take place at random; there is no assortative mating.

(4) There are no systematic preferential marriages (for instance, because of consanguinity).

(5) Possible mutations are not taken into consideration.

(6) The size of the population is clearly defined.

On the basis of these working hypotheses, the whole of which constitutes panmixia, it was possible, not long after the rediscovery of Mendel's laws, to construct the first mathematical models. Thus, population genetics took its first steps forward, one of which was undoubtedly the Hardy–Weinberg law.

Mere inspection of the preceding hypotheses will enable the reader to judge how, taken one by one, they conflict with reality. In fact, no human population can be panmictic in the way the models are.

The following evidence can be cited in favor of this conclusion:

(1) Fertility is never the same with all couples. In fact, differential fertility is the rule in human populations. There is always a far from negligible sterility rate of about 18 per cent among the large populations of Western civilization. On the other hand, the part played by large families in keeping up the numbers of these populations is extremely important; we can therefore generalize by emphasizing that for one or another reason individuals carrying a certain assortment of genes reproduce themselves more or less than the average number of couples. That is what makes for the fact that in each population there is always a certain degree of *selection*. Hypothesis (1) above, essential to the construction of models, is therefore very far removed from reality.

(2) Closed populations are extremely rare. Even among the most primitive peoples there is always a minimum of emigration or immigration. The only cases where one could hope to see this condition fulfilled at the present time would be those of island populations that have remained extremely primitive.

(3) With assortative mating we touch on a point that is still obscure; but even if these phenomena remain poorly understood, it can nevertheless be said that they appear to be crucial in determining the genetic composition of populations. This choice can be *positive*: the carriers of a given characteristic marry among each other more often than chance would warrant. The fact was demonstrated in England by Pearson and Lee (1903): very tall individuals have a tendency to marry each

other, and so do very short ones. Willoughby (1933) has reported on this question with respect to a great number of somatic characteristics other than height—for example, coloring of hair, eyes and skin, intelligence quotient, and so forth. Inversely, *negative* choice makes individuals with the same characteristics avoid marrying one another. This mechanism is much less well known than the above. The example of persons of violent nature (Dahlberg 1943) and of red-headed individuals has been cited many times, although it has not been possible to establish valid statistics to support it.

(4) The case of preferential marriages is not at all negligible. There are still numerous areas where marriages between relatives (consanguineous marriages) occur much more frequently than they would as the result of simple random encounters. In addition, recent studies on the structures of kinship have shown that numerous populations that do not do so today used to practice preferential marriage—most often in a matrilinear sense. These social phenomena have a wide repercussion on the genetic structure of populations and are capable of modifying them considerably from one generation to the other.

(5) Although we do not know exactly what the real rates of mutation are, it can be admitted that their frequency is not negligible. If one or several genes mutate at a given moment in one or several individuals, the nature of the gene or genes is in this way modified; its stability in the population undergoes a disturbance that can considerably transform the composition of that population.

(6) The size of the population and its limits have to be taken into account. We have seen that this is one of the essential characteristics important in differentiating two large categories of models.

## Demography and population genetics

The above examination brings us into contact with the realities of population: fertility, fecundity, nuptiality, mortality, migration, and size are the elements that are the concern of demography and are studied not only by this science but also very often as part of administrative routine. Leaving aside the influence of size, which by definition is of prime importance in the technique of the models, there remain five factors to be examined from the demographic point of view. Mutation can be ruled out of consideration, because, although its importance is great, it is felt only after the passage of a certain number of generations. It can therefore be admitted that it is not of immediate interest.

We can also set aside choice of a mate, because the importance of this factor in practice is still unknown. Accordingly, there remain three factors of prime importance: fertility, migration, and preferential marriage. Over the last decade the progressive disappearance of consanguineous marriage has been noted everywhere but in Asia. In many civilized countries marriage between cousins has practically disappeared. It can be stated, therefore, that this factor has in recent years become considerably less important.

Migrations remain very important on the genetic level, but, unfortunately, precise demographic data about them are rare, and most of the data are of doubtful validity. For instance, it is hard to judge how their influence on a population of Western culture could be estimated.

The only remaining factor, fertility (which to geneticists seems essential), has fortunately been studied in satisfactory fashion by demographers. To show the importance of differential fertility in human populations, let us recall a well-known calculation made by Karl Pearson in connection with Denmark. In 1830, 50 per cent of the children in that country were born of 25 per cent of the parents. If that fertility had been maintained at the same rate, 73 per cent of the second-generation Danes and 97 per cent of the third generation would have been descended from the first 25 per cent. Similarly, before World War I, Charles B. Davenport calculated, on the basis of differential fertility, that 1,000 Harvard graduates would have only 50 descendants after two centuries, while 1,000 Rumanian emigrants living in Boston would have become 100,000.

**Measurement of fertility.** Human reproduction involves both *fecundity* (capacity for reproduction) and *fertility* (actual reproductive performance). These can be estimated for males, females, and married couples treated as a reproductive unit. Let us rapidly review the measurements that demography provides for geneticists in this domain.

*Crude birth rate.* The number of living births in a calendar year per thousand of the average population in the same year is known as the *crude birth rate*. The rate does not seem a very useful one for geneticists: there are too many different groups of childbearing age; marriage rates are too variable from one population to another; birth control is not uniformly diffused, and so forth.

*General fertility rate.* The ratio of the number of live births in one year to the average number of women capable of bearing children (usually defined as those women aged 15 to 49) is known as the *general fertility rate*. Its genetic usefulness is no greater than that of the preceding figure. Moreover, experience shows that this figure is not very different from the crude birth rate.

*Age-specific fertility rates.* Fertility rates according to the age reached by the mother during the year under consideration are known as *age-specific fertility rates*. Demographic experience shows that great differences are observed here, depending on whether or not the populations are Malthusian—in other words, whether they practice birth control or not. In the case of a population where the fertility is natural, knowledge of the mother's age is sufficient. In cases where the population is Malthusian, the figure becomes interesting when it is calculated both by age and by age group of the mothers at time of marriage, thus combining the mother's age at the birth of her child and her age at marriage. This is generally known as the *age-specific marital fertility rate*. If we are dealing with a Malthusian population, it is preferable, in choosing the sample to be studied, to take into consideration the age at marriage rather than the age at the child's birth. Thus, while the age at birth is sufficient for natural populations, these techniques cannot be applied indiscriminately to all populations.

*Family histories.* Fertility rates can also be calculated on the basis of family histories, which can be reconstructed from such sources as parish registries (Fleury & Henry 1965) or, in some countries, from systematic family registrations (for instance, the Japanese *koseki* or *honseki*). The method for computing the fertility rate for, say, the 25–29-year-old age group from this kind of data is first to determine the number of legitimate births in the group. It is then necessary to make a rigorous count of the number of years lived in wedlock between their 25th and 30th birthdays by all the women in the group; this quantity is known as the group's total "woman-years." The number of births is then divided by the number of "woman-years" to obtain the group's fertility rate. This method is very useful in the study of historical problems in genetics, since it is often the only one that can be applied to the available data.

**Measurement of reproduction.** Let us leave fertility rates in order to examine rates of *reproduction*. Here we return to more purely genetic considerations, since we are looking for the mechanism whereby one generation is replaced by the one that follows it. Starting with a series of fertility rates by age groups, a *gross reproduction rate* can be calculated that gives the average number of female progeny that would be born to an age cohort of women, all of whom live through their entire reproductive period and continue to give birth at the rates prevalent when they themselves were born. The gross reproduction rate obtaining for a population at any one time can be derived by combining the rates for the different age cohorts.

A gross reproduction rate for a real generation can also be determined by calculating the average number of live female children ever born to women of fifty or over. As explained above, this rate is higher for non-Malthusian than for Malthusian populations and can be refined by taking into consideration the length of marriage.

We have seen that in order to be correct, it is necessary for the description of fertility in Malthusian populations to be closely related to the date of marriage. Actually, when a family reaches the size that the parents prefer, fertility tends to approach zero. The preferred size is evidently related to length of marriage in such a manner that fertility is more closely linked with length of marriage than with age at marriage. In recent years great progress has been made in the demographic analysis of fertility, based on this kind of data. This should enable geneticists to be more circumspect in their choice of sections of the population to be studied.

**Cohort analysis.** Americans talk of *cohort analysis*, the French of analysis by *promotion* (a term meaning "year" or "class," as we might speak of the "class of 1955"). A cohort, or *promotion*, includes all women born within a 12-month period; to estimate fertility or mortality, it is supposed that these women are all born at the same moment on the first of January of that year. Thus, women born between January 1, 1900, and January 1, 1901, are considered to be exactly 15 years old on January 1, 1915; exactly 47 years old on January 1, 1947; and so forth.

The research done along these lines has issued in the construction of tables that are extremely useful in estimating fertility in a human population. As we have seen, it is more useful to draw up cohorts based on age at marriage than on age at birth. A fertility table set up in this way gives for each cohort the *cumulative* birth rate, by order of birth and single age of mother, for every woman surviving at each age, from 15 to 49. The progress that population genetics could make in knowing *real* genic frequencies can be imagined, if it could concentrate its research on any particular cohort and its descendants.

## Demography of genic frequencies

This rapid examination of the facts that demography can now provide in connection with fertility clearly reveals the variables that population genetics can use to make its models coincide with reality. The models retain their validity for genetics because they are still derived from basic genetic concepts; their application to actual problems, however, should be based on the kind of data mentioned above. We have voluntarily limited ourselves to the problem of fertility, since it is the most important factor in genetics research.

The close relationship between demography and population genetics that now appears can be illustrated by the field of research into blood groups. Although researchers concede that blood groups are independent of both age and sex, they do not explore the full consequences of this, since their measures are applied to samples of the population that are "representative" only in a demographic sense. We must deplore the fact that this method has spread to the other branches of genetics, since it is open to criticism not only from the demographic but from the genetic point of view. By proceeding in this way, a most important factor is overlooked—that of *genic frequencies*.

**Sample structure.** Let us admit that the choice of a blood group to be studied is of little importance when the characteristic is widely distributed throughout the population—for instance, if each individual is the carrier of a gene taken into account in the system being studied (e.g., a system made up of groups A, B, and O). But this is no longer the case if the gene is carried only by a few individuals—in other words, if its frequency attains 0.1 per cent or less. In this case (and cases like this are common in human genetics) the structure of the sample examined begins to take on prime importance.

A brief example must serve to illustrate this cardinal point. We have seen that in the case of rare recessive genes the importance of consanguineous marriages is considerable. The scarcer that carriers of recessive genes become in the population as a whole, the greater the proportion of such carriers produced by consanguineous marriages. Thus if as many as 25 per cent of all individuals in a population are carriers of recessive genes, and if one per cent of all marriages in that population are marriages between first cousins, then this one per cent of consanguineous unions will produce 1.12 times as many carriers of recessive genes as will be produced by all the unions of persons not so related. But if recessive genes are carried by only one per cent of the total population, then the same proportion of marriages between first cousins will produce 2.13 times as many carriers as will be produced by all other marriages. This production ratio increases to 4.9 if the total frequency of carriers is .01 per cent, to 20.2 if it is .005 per cent, and to 226 if it is .0001 per cent. Under these conditions, one can see the importance of the sampling method used to estimate the frequency within a population, not only of the individuals who are carriers but of the gametes and genes themselves.

*Genealogical method.* It should be emphasized that genetic studies based on genealogies remain the least controversial. Studying a population where the degrees of relationship connecting individuals are known presents an obvious interest. Knowing one or several characteristics of certain parents, we can follow what becomes of these in the descendants. Their evolution can also be considered from the point of view of such properties of genes as dominance, recessiveness, expressivity, and penetrance. But above all, we can follow the evolution of these characteristics in the population over time and thus observe the effects of differential fertility. Until now the genealogical method was applicable only to a numerically sparse population, but progress in electronic methods of data processing permits us to anticipate its application to much larger populations (Sutter & Tabah 1956).

*Dynamic studies.* In very large modern populations it would appear that internal analysis of cohorts and their descendants will bring in the future a large measure of certainty to research in population genetics. In any case, it is a sure way to a dynamic genetics based on demographic reality. For instance, it has been recommended that blood groups should be studied according to age groups; but if we proceed to do so without regard for demographic factors, we cannot make our observations dynamic. Thus, a study that limits itself to, let us say, the fifty- to sixty-year-old age group will have to deal with a universe that includes certain genetically "dead" elements, such as unmarried and sterile persons, which have no meaning from the dynamic point of view. But if a study is made of this same fifty- to sixty-year-old age group and then of the twenty- to thirty-year-old age group, and if in the older group only those individuals are considered who have descendants in the younger group, the dynamic potential of the data is maximized. It is quite possible to subject demographic cohorts to this sort of interpretation, because in many countries demographic statistics supply series of individuals classified according to the mothers' age at their birth.

**Other demographic factors.** This discussion would not be complete if we did not stress another aspect of the genetic importance of certain demographic factors, revealed by modern techniques, which have truly created a demographic biology. Particularly worthy of note are the mother's age, order of birth, spacing between births, and size of family.

The mother's age is a great influence on fecundity. A certain number of couples become incapable of having a second child after the birth of the first child; a third child after the second; a fourth after the third; and so forth. This sterility increases with the length of a marriage and especially after the age of 35. It is very important to realize this when, for instance, natural selection and its effects are being studied.

The mother's age also strongly influences the frequency of twin births (monozygotic or dizygotic), spontaneous abortions, stillborn or abnormal births, and so on. Many examples can also be given of the influence of the order of birth, the interval between births, and the size of the family to illustrate their effect on such things as fertility, mortality, morbidity, and malformations.

It has been demonstrated above how seriously demographic factors must be taken into consideration when we wish to study the influence of the genetic structure of populations. We will leave aside the possible environmental influences, such as social class and marital status, since they have previously been codified by Osborn (1956/1957) and Larsson (1956–1957), among others. At the practical level, however, the continuing efforts to utilize vital statistics for genetic purposes should be pointed out. In this connection, the research of H. B. Newcombe and his colleagues (1965), who are attempting to organize Canadian national statistics for use in genetics, cannot be too highly praised. The United Nations itself posed the problem on the world level at a seminar organized in Geneva in 1960. The question of the relation between demography and genetics is therefore being posed in an acute form.

These problems also impinge in an important way on more general philosophical issues, as has been demonstrated by Haldane (1932), Fisher (1930), and Wright (1951). It must be recognized, however, that their form of Neo-Darwinism, although it is based on Mendelian genetics, too often neglects demographic considerations. In the future these seminal developments should be renewed in full confrontation with demographic reality.

JEAN SUTTER

[*Directly related are the entries* COHORT ANALYSIS; FERTILITY; FERTILITY CONTROL. *Other relevant material may be found in* NUPTIALITY; RACE; SOCIAL BEHAVIOR, ANIMAL, *article on* THE REGULATION OF ANIMAL POPULATIONS.]

BIBLIOGRAPHY

BARCLAY, GEORGE W. 1958 *Techniques of Population Analysis.* New York: Wiley.

DAHLBERG, GUNNAR (1943) 1948 *Mathematical Methods for Population Genetics.* New York and London: Interscience. → First published in German.

DUNN, LESLIE C. (editor) 1951 *Genetics in the Twen-*

*tieth Century: Essays on the Progress of Genetics During Its First Fifty Years.* New York: Macmillan.

FISHER, R. A. (1930) 1958 *The Genetical Theory of Natural Selection.* 2d ed., rev. New York: Dover.

FLEURY, M.; and HENRY, L. 1965 *Nouveau manuel de dépouillement et d'exploitation de l'état civil ancien.* Paris: Institut National d'Études Démographiques.

GEPPERT, HARALD; and KOLLER, SIEGFRIED 1938 *Erbmathematik.* Leipzig: Quelle & Meyer.

HALDANE, J. B. S. 1932 *The Causes of Evolution.* London and New York: Harper.

HENRY, LOUIS 1953 *Fécondité des mariages: Nouvelle méthode de mesure.* Institut National d'Études Démographiques, Travaux et Documents, Cahier No. 16. Paris: The Institute.

LARSSON, TAGE 1956–1957 The Interaction of Population Changes and Heredity. *Acta genetica et statistica medica* 6:333–348.

L'HÉRITIER, PHILIPPE 1954 *Traité de génétique.* Volume 2: *La génétique des populations.* Paris: Presses Universitaires de France.

LI, CHING CHÛN (1948) 1955 *Population Genetics.* 2d ed. Univ. of Chicago Press.

MALÉCOT, GUSTAVE 1948 *Les mathématiques et l'hérédité.* Paris: Masson.

MALÉCOT, GUSTAVE 1955 La génétique de population: Principes et applications. *Population* 10:239–262.

MALÉCOT, GUSTAVE 1959 *Les modèles stochastiques en génétique de population.* Paris, Université, Institut de Statistique, *Publications* 8:173–210.

NEWCOMBE, H. B.; SMITH, M. E.; and SCHWARTZ, R. R. 1965 *Computer Methods for Extracting Kinship Data From Family Groupings of Records.* Chalk River (Ontario): Atomic Energy of Canada Limited.

OSBORN, F. 1956/1957 Changing Demographic Trends of Interest to Population Genetics. *Acta genetica et statistica medica* 6:354–362.

PEARSON, KARL; and LEE, ALICE 1903 On the Laws of Inheritance in Man. *Biometrika* 2:257–462.

PRESSAT, ROLAND 1961 *L'analyse démographique: Méthodes, résultats, applications.* Paris: Presses Universitaires de France.

SUTTER, JEAN; and TABAH, LÉON 1951 Les notions d'isolat et de population minimum. *Population* 6:481–498.

SUTTER, JEAN; and TABAH, LÉON 1956 Méthode mécanographique pour établir la généalogie d'une population: Application à l'étude des esquimaux polaires. *Population* 11:507–530.

UNITED NATIONS 1961 *The Use of Vital and Health Statistics for Genetic and Radiation Studies.* New York: United Nations.

WHELPTON, PASCAL K. 1954 *Cohort Fertility: Native White Women in the United States.* Princeton Univ. Press.

WILLOUGHBY, RAYMOND R. 1933 Somatic Homogamy in Man. *Human Biology* 5:690–705.

WORLD POPULATION CONFERENCE 1965 *Proceedings.* New York: United Nations. → See especially "Recent Advances in the Theory of Population Genetics" by M. Kimura.

WRIGHT, SEWALL 1951 The Genetical Structure of Populations. *Annals of Human Genetics* 15:323–354.

## III

### RACE AND GENETICS

Since 1900, the study of genetics has made two major contributions to the theoretical understanding of the biology of race. First is the replacement of earlier theories of racial heredity based on the blending of characteristics by the newer, genetical notion of a breeding population incorporating gene frequencies based on the particulate, or Mendelian, theory of heredity. Because of the use of a misleading theory of heredity, nearly all of the writing on subspecific taxonomy of the human species before 1900, and unfortunately much written since then, is incorrect.

The second contribution of genetics has been to place race in the perspective of a general theory of organic evolution. This interpretation of racial biology derives from those parts of population genetics initially developed by Wright (1931; 1951) and Haldane (1932) and interpreted variously by Dobzhansky (1962), Mayr (1963), Simpson (1961), and Morton and Yasuda (1963). We cannot adequately understand the evolutionary history of mankind either in terms of individuals or in terms of the species as a whole because individuals do not evolve and the details of the evolutionary process are not necessarily uniform for all subdivisions of the species. This is why it is of theoretical importance to recognize subspecies in evolutionary biology, whether or not they are given taxonomic recognition.

**Race and subspecies.** A "race" is a category logically more inclusive than the notion of "individual" and less inclusive than the notion of "species." Most contemporary authorities equate the anthropological concept of race with the zoological concept of subspecies.

Subspecies and races are two or more genetically distinguishable populations of a species that have separate distributions but which can, and do, interbreed freely in overlap zones or when brought into contact. The frequency of gene exchange between races is highest in the contact zone and decreases away from it.

Since the geographical change in gene frequency is gradual, any attempt to separate sharply local populations into races having different gene frequencies is arbitrary. Often groups defined by one set of genetically determined characteristics show a clear geographical distribution. The distribution of a group defined by another set of alleles may be mapped with equal certainty; usually the geographical boundaries of two such classifications will not coincide very closely.

**Knowledge of race.** Statements about race involve two distinct kinds of knowledge, one about *attributes*, the other about *relationships*. Usually our knowledge of the phenotypes used to define races is direct and observational; in principle there may be full agreement among experts regarding the attributes which characterize a given group of people. Our knowledge about the biological relationships among individuals often is indirect, being based on interviews or inferred from geographical, societal, or cultural circumstances. Two individuals are biological relatives when one developed from a zygote formed by a gamete from the other or both developed from zygotes formed by gametes from a common ancestor. Each individual is connected by gametes to his parents, to the members of one or more races, and, ultimately, to the species. In practice it is rare to know directly all relevant parent–child links connecting the members of a race. Genetics makes rules for predicting the distribution of phenotypes–genotypes among individuals of known relationship. In the study of race such rules are used to infer relationships of populations of individuals whose phenotypes–genotypes are known.

**Particulate versus blending heredity.** The molecular, particulate nature of the genetic material and the facts of gene segregation and recombination have great theoretical significance for the biology of race.

If the hereditary materials were blended (as nineteenth-century biologists assumed) like solutes in solvents, every member of a breeding population would soon reach hereditary uniformity and, barring mutation and hybridization, a "pure" race would be established in each locality. The genetic material would become unique to each local breeding population, and genotypes of offspring would necessarily be a midway blend of those of their parents. But, in fact, segregation and recombination do produce novel genic variation within the local breeding population. Genes in body cells occur in pairs ($AA$, $Aa$, $aa$). When gametes are formed, the members of each pair segregate so that each gamete has only one gene from each pair ($A$ or $a$) and each child receives only one member of a pair from each parent (i.e., two parents of genotype $Aa$ may produce a child who is $AA$, $Aa$, or $aa$). Also, each pair of genes at other loci (nonalleles) is capable of undergoing segregation separately, so that two pairs of genes which are together in one parent (say $AAbb$ or $aaBB$) may be recombined in the child ($AaBb$), the recombination rate being slower for linked than for independent nonalleles.

Before the effective start of genetics in 1900, it was believed that hereditary material was a homogeneous substance which could be mixed or diluted but was identical in all members of a "pure" race. If two individuals were alike in one hereditary aspect, they would be alike in all others. Within a "pure" race all variation was due to environmental effects. Genetics now shows that hereditary material is a heterogeneous collection of separate particles which need not be the same even in close relatives. Two closely related individuals may have many genes in common but may differ in others. Likewise, because of parallel mutation, unrelated people may have some genes of the same function even though these genes are not derived from a common ancestor.

Before genetics, it was believed that the hereditary material differed in kind between races of the same species, just as two elements differ. The pregenetic view of race involved what Aristotle called the "essence" of material bodies. Just as atoms of copper and tin are of different construction, so two races were thought to have hereditary material different in essence; the difference was, accordingly, not in degree but in kind. As atoms of copper can join those of tin to make bronze, so it was thought "pure" races come together to form a mixed race. It was possible to think of individuals of mixed races as being "mostly Alpine" or "mostly Nordic," in the same way that it was possible to think of alloys with varying fractions of different metals. Using an analogy from ceramics, certain anthropologists even as late as the 1940s spoke of race X having a "wash" of race Y. As is shown below, such beliefs are refuted by the identification of homologous genes in different races.

**Kinds of gene differences between races.** It is clear we should not speak of racial characteristics, only of racial differences. Differences between any two races express differently occurring frequencies of autosomal genes. These may be written as follows:

Population 1:
$$(pA + qa)^2(p'B + q'b)^2 \cdots (p''N + q''n)^2 = 1,$$
Population 2:
$$(rA' + sa')^2(r'B' + s'b')^2 \cdots (r''N' + s''n')^2 = 1.$$

Here $A, a, \cdots, N', n'$ represent sets of alleles with frequencies $p + q = 1$, $r + s = 1$, where $0 \leqslant p, r \leqslant 1$. (The arrays of possible genotypes can be derived as the products of the squares of the above binomials. If there are $k$ alleles at a locus, the binomial is replaced by a $k$-nomial. For sex-chromosomal loci, the array of genotypes in the heterogametic sex is given by the first power of the $k$-nomial.) By identifying and comparing the frequencies of genes between populations, we may distinguish four kinds of differences:

(1) If the same kinds and frequencies are present in both, the two populations are identical.

(2) If gene frequencies equal zero or unity in one population but are not fixed ($0 < p, r < 1$) in the other, or if some but not all frequencies are unity in one and zero in the other, the two popula-

tions are qualitatively different in gene frequency at one or more but not at all loci; they show a *specific* difference in kind.

(3) If the allele at all loci is zero in one population and unity in the other, there is a *general* difference in kind.

(4) If none of the frequencies equal zero or unity, the populations differ in degree not in kind.

Prior to the twentieth century, most anthropologists and biologists assumed the differences between local populations within the same race were of sort (1) and those between races were of sort (3). The early students assumed the genetic material of (pure) races was homogeneous within, and qualitatively different between, races.

Today we have frequency information on nearly fifty genes in which some of the alleles at each locus are common enough in one or more human populations to be of anthropological interest. Several hundred rare major genes are known to medical genetics. The knowledge gained from both human and general genetics demonstrates that "pure" races in the sense of homogeneous breeding populations differing in the kind of genes present at all loci do not exist in the human species or in any known sexual species of animals or plants.

For at least eight known human chromosomal loci, specific differences in kind of sort (2) are known to hold between some pairs of human races. For instance, the gene associated with blood group A of the ABO series is present in all known European populations, as is the gene for B, but gene *A* is absent in some, and gene *B* is absent in many American Indian populations. The genes for the Diego, Henshaw, Hunter, Kell, Lutheran, Rhesus, and hemoglobin ACS loci show detectable differences in kind between two or more human races.

Differences of sort (4), i.e., cases where the same kinds of genes are present in different frequency, constitute the most common kind of genetic divergence observed between local and geographical races of man for both normal and nearly all of the identified deleterious major genes. (See Dobzhansky 1962 or recent textbooks of human genetics for further data on the major genes mentioned above.)

**Typology and race.** The pregenetic typological approach to racial anthropology used at least three different concepts of "types." All are unacceptable to modern genetics, each for a different reason.

(*a*) The *average type* of a population is defined by a set of traits used to identify members of the ("pure") race. Thus Nordics in Sweden and elsewhere are characterized by tall stature, long heads, blond hair, and blue eyes. From the genetic point of view there are two basic difficulties in this approach: Only a small fraction of the members of any local breeding population exhibit the full set of traits used to define the type, and the vast amount of genetic variability known to be present in all sexually reproduced populations is not recognized. Retzius and Fürst found only 10.07 per cent of a large sample of Swedish conscripts had all four of the above diagnostic traits for Nordics (Dahlberg 1942). Since a breeding population has no average genotype, it cannot have an average phenotype; thus, it is misleading to pick out a typical (average) member of any race.

(*b*) *Morphological types*, which occur in groups of two to about ten in a given population, are also defined by a cluster of traits. The racial history of a population is explained by the supposed coming together and intermixture of individuals belonging to the several types, all wrongly assumed to be stable over time and to represent ancestral stocks (see, e.g., Hooton 1926; 1931).

An example of misinterpreted history comes from western Europe, where most people in the north are tall, blond, and blue-eyed; most in the south are short, brunet, and brown-eyed; and those in the midland are assorted in stature and pigmentation, with short blonds, tall brunets, brown-eyed blonds, etc. Those who use morphological types to explain racial history assume the people of the midland are a mixture of migrants from the north and south. But this is not necessarily what happened in history; the "mixed" group may be the actual common ancestor of the two "pure" groups concentrated by natural selection in the two extremes of the geographical range. The rather scanty information with historical depth suggests this latter explanation is the correct one for the origin of the "morphological races" of western Europe.

The processes of gene segregation and recombination, together with those of parallel and recurrent mutation, negate the possibility of sorting the members of an interbreeding population into morphological types representing ancestral stocks. A simple hypothetical example will illustrate this. The initial generation includes two "races" (Table 1). Genes *A* and *a* are autosomal and lack dominance. Since the *A* allele is fixed in one and the *a* allele in the other, each "race" is genotypically invariant for the traits. Now if north and south send migrants to

**Table 1**

| | RACE | |
|---|---|---|
| | North | South |
| Phenotype | X | Y |
| Genotype | AA | aa |

midland and there hybridize, the $F_1$ hybrids will all have genotype $Aa$ and phenotype XY. Intercrossing of the $F_1$'s will produce all three genotypes in subsequent generations of the new midland "race." But in this mixed "race," individuals of type XY are more closely related (a distance of one parent–child step) to their homozygous parents of type X or Y than are individuals of type X or Y who turn up in subsequent generations (distant by two or more parent–child steps). It may also happen that, through mutation rather than descent, members of the population may come to possess genes identical to those of the founding generation.

Sameness of phenotype represents neither degree of closeness nor the fact of relationship in a mixed population. Further, sameness of some specific phenotype does not guarantee that a given individual in a mixed population will inherit other desirable or undesirable traits from an ancestor of the same specific phenotype. (See Dahlberg 1943 for extension of this argument to other kinds of major genes and to polygenes.)

(c) The *individual types* of the Czekanowski group of Polish anthropologists are "racial elements" defined by a cluster of traits assumed to be controlled by one, or several closely linked, pleiotropic gene(s). These genes simultaneously affect the set of type-defining traits in whatever population they are found. This typology is compatible with population genetics if the frequencies of the "racial elements" have the empirical properties of the frequencies of pleiotropic genes, a possibility, however, not supported by family studies or by the fit of observed population frequencies of "racial elements" to those expected for genotypes in equilibrium Mendelian populations (Bielicki, 1965).

**Modes of change in gene frequency.** The theory of population genetics builds upon a population model in which gene frequencies are in equilibrium. The relative frequencies of genes and of genotypes remain steady in a randomly mated breeding population if mutation does not preferentially add or subtract genes, if genes flowing into the population from the outside differ neither in kind nor in frequency from those native to the local population, if there is no differential fertility or mortality between genes and genotypes, and if the breeding population is large enough in numbers that genetic drift does not occur. If these equilibrium conditions do not hold, gene and/or genotype frequencies will change until a new steady state is attained.

Inbreeding and assortative mating, the two most important departures from random mating, do not by themselves change gene frequencies but only the relative frequencies of genotypes; such changes are usually in the direction of increased homozygosity.

*Mutation.* Mutation is the primary source of all gene variation. The molecular basis of mutation is change in the sequence of nucleotides in DNA. Estimated spontaneous mutation rates in man vary from about one to one hundred mutations per million gametes. The rates are specific for loci and alleles but may vary somewhat according to the mutagenic nature of the environment. Probably the mutation rates for the more common human genes are sufficiently small compared with the rates for other modes of change that mutation is not a major determinant of observable local and regional differences in gene frequencies. However, it should be emphasized that mutation is repetitive; within a species, a mutation is not likely to occur only once, nor to occur in one major race and not in another.

*Gene flow.* Gene flow refers to introduction of genes from outside the local breeding population. The process is general for loci, haploid sets of genes being introduced on each occasion. In terms of the change in frequency, the most important type of gene flow involves recurrent, more or less regular introduction of gametes from neighboring groups which are partially isolated reproductively. When the parental populations are sufficiently dissimilar in gene frequencies, gene flow is called race mixture. Mixture may result in very rapid changes in gene frequencies. When clines are reflections of gene flow, the gene frequencies of several loci should show similar cline distribution when the incoming and native populations differ in those frequencies.

Recurrent gene flow has been an important factor preventing the splitting of mankind into allopatric species. Before the development of extrasomatic modes of transportation, the vast majority of gene flow involved neighboring populations. With the development of more rapid transportation, the rate and distance of gene flow increased. Since A.D. 1600 mixture has been the most significant factor in population differentiation.

*Selection.* Selection is the main guiding force in race formation. Genes or genotypes which, on the average, increase genetic fitness will become more frequent in later generations. Genetic fitness is defined solely in terms of differential fertility and/or mortality. For a given environment, genes may be harmful, neutral, or beneficial. The population frequencies of harmful genes are determined by the balance between their rate of entry by mutation and their rate of removal by selection. Neutral genes must be very rare, their spread very slow, and their replacement by more successfully adaptive genes very rapid. An important class of genes are those with increased fitness in heterozygotes; such genes spread rapidly through local populations and, given gene flow, through those sections of the species population with similar environmental conditions. These genes with a selective advantage of the heterozygote may have stable equilibrium frequencies largely determined by selection coefficients and nearly independent of initial gene frequencies and mutation rates. If polygenes are additive, selection acts on each locus independently of the others. Linkage between polygenes, unless very strong, is unimportant for selection rates.

*Genetic drift.* The two genes at each autosomal locus in an individual are a sample, one from each parent, of the four genes at that locus in the parents. With small population numbers, random fluctuation in this sampling process may change gene frequencies, leading to concentration or fixation of some alleles and loss of others in local populations. The resulting irregular and patchy gene-frequency distributions may be nonadaptive.

**The origin of races.** The formation of races is not characteristic of all sexual species. Race formation requires partial reproductive isolation. Change in gene frequency is the fundamental event in the formation of races. Race formation, i.e., adaptation to local conditions, must occur in all successful, widespread species with partially isolated local populations. Given the raw materials of gene diversity, the genetic subdivision of a species depends largely on local selection pressures, on the one hand, and gene flow, on the other. If there is much gene flow, local races cannot form; if there is less gene flow, clines may develop; if there is little gene flow, local races will differentiate. If any of the local populations are small in number, say under one hundred, there may be considerable loss and fixation of genes by random genetic drift.

**Race differences in behavior.** Human races differ in languages and culture as well as in genes. One of the most significant contributions of the social sciences to the general knowledge of the twentieth century is the demonstration that a large fraction of functionally important differences between human groups in learned behavior is largely independent of race, or as we put it, independent of genic differences distinguishing races.

Differences in the frequency of major genes between local populations as well as major geographical races are well established for some behavioral traits, e.g., the ability to taste phenylthiocarbamide and the four kinds of X-linked partial color blindness, although these behavioral variations are of limited functional significance in human societies.

One sort of theoretical model in population genetics suggests we should observe statistical differences in the frequencies of polygenes making up the genetical components of intellectual abilities and temperament (e.g., Hogben 1932, p. 169; Sturtevant 1954). Equally valid theoretical models support the opposite conclusion by suggesting that the genotypes making up the capacity underlying cultural learning are a species characteristic maintained in equilibrium in all human populations (e.g., Dobzhansky 1962, p. 320). Since the genetic basis of intelligence is polygenic and since we cannot identify polygenes in man, precise information about racial, i.e., inherited, differences in general intelligence is simply not available. But it seems clear that if differences between major races exist in general intellectual abilities, these differences are small in magnitude compared with the range of genetic variation within all major races (Spuhler & Lindzey 1967).

J. N. SPUHLER

[See also EVOLUTION, *article on* HUMAN EVOLUTION; RACE.]

### BIBLIOGRAPHY

BIELICKI, TADEUSZ 1965 Population Genetics and the Race Process; Typologists Versus Populationists and Genetic Theory; Intensity of Feedbacks Between Physical and Cultural Evolution. *International Social Science Journal* 17, no. 1:91–99.

DAHLBERG, GUNNAR 1942 An Analysis of the Conception of Race and a New Method of Distinguishing Races. *Human Biology* 14:372–385.

DAHLBERG, GUNNAR (1943) 1948 *Mathematical Methods for Population Genetics.* New York and London: Interscience. → First published in German.

DOBZHANSKY, THEODOSIUS 1962 *Mankind Evolving: The Evolution of the Human Species.* New Haven: Yale Univ. Press.

HALDANE, J. B. S. 1932 *The Causes of Evolution.* London and New York: Harper.

HOGBEN, LANCELOT 1932 *Genetic Principles in Medicine and Social Science.* New York: Knopf.

HOOTON, EARNEST A. 1926 Methods of Racial Analysis. *Science* 63:75–81.

HOOTON, EARNEST A. (1931) 1947 *Up From the Ape.* Rev. ed. New York: Macmillan.

MAYR, ERNST 1963 *Animal Species and Evolution.* Cambridge, Mass: Belknap Press.

MORTON, N. E.; and YASUDA, N. 1963 The Genetical Structure of Human Populations. Pages 185–203 in Centre International d'Étude des Problèmes Humains, *Les déplacements humains: Aspects méthodologiques de leur mesure.* Edited by Jean Sutter. Entretiens de Monaco en sciences humaines, Première session, 1962 (24–29 mai). Paris: Hachette.

SIMPSON, GEORGE G. 1961 *Principles of Animal Taxonomy.* Columbia Biological Series, No. 20. New York: Columbia Univ. Press.

Spuhler, J. N.; and Lindzey, Gardner 1967 Racial Differences in Behavior. Chapter 19 in Jerry Hirsch (editor), *Behavior–Genetic Analysis*. New York: McGraw-Hill.
Sturtevant, A. H. 1954 Social Implications of the Genetics of Man. *Science* 120:405–407.
Wright, Sewall 1931 Evolution in Mendelian Populations. *Genetics* 16:97–159.
Wright, Sewall 1951 The Genetical Structure of Populations. *Annals of Eugenics* 15:323–354.

## GENIUS

*See* Creativity, *especially the article on* genius and ability; Intelligence and intelligence testing; *and the biography of* Terman.

## GENNEP, ARNOLD VAN

Charles-Arnold Kurr van Gennep (1873–1957), ethnographer and folklorist, who is best known for his work on rites of passage, was born in Württemberg, Germany, of a Dutch father and a French mother. At his father's death van Gennep was adopted by a French doctor, and thus his already strong ties with France were further strengthened. He received most of his education in France.

His career was not primarily an academic one. He served the French government for two periods, from 1903 to 1910 and again from 1919 to 1921, and worked for such cultural organizations as the Alliance Française and the International Congress of Popular Art. For relatively brief periods he held university appointments at Neuchâtel, Oxford, and Cambridge.

In *The Rites of Passage* (1909), van Gennep systematically compared those ceremonies which celebrate an individual's transition from one status to another within a given society; he concluded that most such ritual observances have a tripartite sequence. The major phases of this sequence are separation (*séparation*), transition (*marge*), and incorporation (*agrégation*). Van Gennep went beyond this analysis of rites of passage to an interpretation of their significance for the explanation of the continuing nature of life. He believed that rites of passage, with their symbolic representation of death and rebirth, illustrate the principles of the regenerative renewal required by any society.

Although van Gennep followed the prevailing system of classification of beliefs and rites associated with magic, when he analyzed rites of passage he introduced a new approach. Instead of utilizing a priori categories as the units of his taxonomy, he abstracted these units from the structure of the ceremonies themselves. This procedure led him to differentiate the rites-of-passage phases: separa-

tion, transition, and incorporation. His inductive procedure included consideration of the variables of time and space. Over a quarter of a century later Julian Huxley was to label this method of classification, in biology, as the "new systematics."

Van Gennep was obviously impressed with the importance of the transitional, or liminal, phase that he had noted within a ceremony. One aspect of its importance is related to his concept of social regeneration. When individuals or groups are in a state of suspension (limen), separated from their previous condition and not yet incorporated into a new one, they constitute a threat to themselves and to the entire group. In this state they are outside the sphere of normal control and must be reintegrated in order to avoid becoming disruptive. The liminal period also has its own internal structure, and it is possible to observe stages of entry into the period, the period itself, and departure from the period of transition.

Some other contributions by van Gennep deserve brief mention. He established, for example, that the time of so-called puberty, or initiation, rites does not coincide with physiological puberty; rather, they are scheduled according to societal definitions. He also emphasized the importance of ritual exchange and thus anticipated Malinowski's analysis of reciprocity. Finally, he noted the similarity between the structure of individual and group rites when either kind is in a state of change. The subsequent designation of group ceremonies as "rites of intensification" by Chapple and Coon (1942) is a welcome conceptual extension.

Van Gennep was highly regarded for his work in the field of European folklore. He did much to change its orientation from its historical and antiquarian origins by introducing the methods and perspective of ethnography. European scholars of his time tended to view the customs of rural peoples as quaint reminders of the past and to treat them as elements of history. Van Gennep saw folk literature and practices as aspects of living culture, to be examined within the context of changes among individuals in their relations with each other. His concern with changes in traditional culture led him to study the disappearance of some of its elements in the urban centers of France and the spread of cosmopolitan culture.

Van Gennep was enormously energetic in the accumulation of folklore materials and in their publication. His writings include several score articles, numerous monographs, and the monumental *Manuel de folklore français contemporain* (1937–1958). Van Gennep's editorial activity in this field also was prodigious: for over thirty years, from

1906 to 1939, he edited the section "Ethnographie-Folklore-Religions-Préhistoire" in the *Mercure de France*, and he founded and directed several French journals of ethnography and folklore.

Van Gennep's adherence to the comparative method in ethnography helps us to understand his theoretical formulations. He based his interpretations on the assumption that man is a part of nature and is therefore subject to the great natural laws of stability, variability, and change. He considered his goal to be the formulation of general syntheses. On this basis he challenged the adequacy of the principles of individual psychology and apriorism. He thought regeneration a necessity of social and individual existence, noting similarities between the cyclical shift of seasons and the passage of the individual through the stages of life. In the ceremonies which celebrate both transitions, he noted the recurring theme of death and rebirth. For him, neither the individual nor the rites can be divorced from the social context, nor from time and space. He insisted that ceremonial patterns should be examined as wholes and that comparison should be based upon similarities in structure rather than upon content.

There are resemblances between van Gennep's concerns and those of his contemporaries, but his approach was so radically different from theirs that the resemblances are largely of a superficial kind. For example, the interest in religion, magic, and myth, which he shared with Lang, Frazer, Marett, and others, proceeded from entirely different conceptual assumptions. Their rational, a priori approach was rooted in a historical perspective which sought to isolate stages of development such as fetishism, animism, animatism, or totemism and to provide definitions for each. Frazer in particular sought to ground his conclusions in universal psychological characteristics—the principle of association and the law of sympathy. In contrast, van Gennep was more interested in the dynamics of change than in the statics of classification and definition. For him, impersonal and personal power (dynamism and animism) unite to constitute religion, while magic consists of the techniques of control. In this he differed from Frazer, in whose view magic preceded religion and was in conflict with it. Van Gennep also differed from Hubert and Mauss, who defined religion as official doctrine and magic as socially prohibited (a view incorporated by Durkheim in his polarization of the sacred and the profane).

Thus, van Gennep saw the tradition, methods, and goals of ethnography as different from those of both the French sociologists and the British school of anthropology. The full exposition of these differences awaits future scholarship. A recently renewed interest in the study of rites of passage is evidenced by the writings of Whiting and Child (1953), Young (1965), and Turner (1964). This resurgence may extend to further study of van Gennep's ethnographic method and of his theoretical formulations.

SOLON T. KIMBALL

[*For the historical context of van Gennep's work, see the biographies of* FRAZER; MARETT; MAUSS; *for discussion of the subsequent development of his ideas, see* LIFE CYCLE; MYTH AND SYMBOL; RITUAL; THEOLOGY, PRIMITIVE.]

#### WORKS BY VAN GENNEP

1908–1914 *Religions, moeurs, et légendes: Essais d'ethnographie et de linguistique.* 5th series. Paris: Mercure de France.
(1909) 1960 *The Rites of Passage.* London: Routledge; Univ. of Chicago Press. → First published in French.
1937–1958 *Manuel de folklore français contemporain.* Volumes 1, 3–4 in 9 parts. Paris: Picard. → Volume 2 will not be published.

#### SUPPLEMENTARY BIBLIOGRAPHY

CHAPPLE, ELIOT D.; and COON, CARLETON S. 1942 *Principles of Anthropology.* New York: Holt.
LECOTTÉ, ROGER 1958 Arnold van Gennep: 1873–1957. *Fabula* 2:178–180.
TURNER, VICTOR W. 1964 Betwixt and Between: The Liminal Period in *Rites de passage.* American Ethnological Society, *Proceedings* [1964]:4–20.
WHITING, JOHN W.; and CHILD, IRVIN L. 1953 *Child Training and Personality: A Cross-cultural Study.* New Haven: Yale Univ. Press. → A paperback edition was published in 1962.
YOUNG, FRANK W. 1965 *Initiation Ceremonies: A Cross-cultural Study of Status Dramatization.* Indianapolis, Ind.: Bobbs-Merrill.

## GENOCIDE
*See* INTERNATIONAL CRIMES.

## GEOGRAPHY

*The articles under this heading describe the main fields of contemporary geography and the field of statistical geography, which is an approach to geography rather than a discrete field. Other material of direct or related interest to geography may be found under* AREA; CARTOGRAPHY; CENTRAL PLACE; CITY; CONSERVATION; CULTURE AREA; DIFFUSION, *article on* THE DIFFUSION OF INNOVATIONS; ECOLOGY; ENCLAVES AND EXCLAVES; ENVIRONMENT; ENVIRONMENTALISM; INDUSTRIAL CONCENTRATION; LAND; LANDSCAPE; LOCATION THEORY; PLANNING, SOCIAL; POPULATION; RANK–SIZE RELATIONS; REGION; REGIONAL SCIENCE; WATER RE-

SOURCES. *Biographical articles of relevance to geography include* BOWMAN; BROWN; FLEURE; HETTNER; HUMBOLDT; HUNTINGTON; KJELLÉN; MACKINDER; MARSH; RATZEL; RITTER; SAUER; TELEKI; VIDAL DE LA BLACHE.

# I

## THE FIELD

Geography is neither a purely natural nor a purely social science. From its early development as an organized field of knowledge in classical Greece, geography has included animate as well as inanimate things, man and his works as well as nature. This was of little concern as long as man was regarded as an integral part of nature. But geography, although a very old subject, did not become established as a university discipline with an organized academic profession until after the natural and social sciences had become divided into separate faculties. Regular university departments of geography were first established in German-speaking countries in the 1870s and 1880s; in France a little later; and in Great Britain and the United States generally in the present century. In each country the first generation of professors of geography had been trained in other fields, in most cases the natural sciences. Self-taught in geography, few of them outside Germany were familiar with its past development.

One consequence was that geography tended to separate into two parts: one natural, more commonly called physical geography, and one human or social, sometimes called economic geography. (In different countries and in different institutions in the same country practice varies as to whether the subject is part of the natural science faculty, part of the social science faculty, or split between the two.) For many students, on the other hand, it was the connections between the two parts, the man–land relationships, that constituted the distinctive subject matter of geography. During the period of its initial establishment as a university subject in the English-speaking countries, geography was commonly defined as the study of the relationships, in whichever direction, between the natural environment and man. This "environmentalist" concept of the field seems to have been first formulated in Germany, and then in France, late in the nineteenth century, but it was very soon dis-carded, both in theory and practice by German geographers and, to a large degree, in practice by those of France; in both countries geography returned to its historic focus of interest in the study of the distinctive character of the areas of the earth. This concept and its historical background were made familiar to American and British geographers only in the 1920s and 1930s. And although today few geographers would assert the environmentalist concept, many of its aspects, notably the emphasis on a man–nature dichotomy, still color much of their writing. [*See* ENVIRONMENTALISM.]

Modern geography, like the geography of past centuries, studies the earth as the space in which man lives—his habitat, milieu, or environment. This includes not just part of the environment, the physical or natural part, but the total environment; in any inhabited area the environment of today has been in part produced by man, and the existing population constitutes a living factor in the present environment. Geography, of course, is not alone in studying man's environment. Many fields in the natural and social sciences study a particular category of phenomena, not excluding its distribution and variations over the earth. What geography, and geography alone, studies is the areal character of the earth in which man lives—the form, the content, and the function of each areal part, region, or place and the pattern of and interconnections between the areal parts.

If the total diversity of places and their interrelations were simply the sum of areal variations and connections of physical, biological, and social phenomena, the subject could readily be divided into distinct fields: physical geography, biogeography, and human, or social, geography; or possibly two parts, the geography of nature and the geography of man. In reality, however, the phenomena of these several abstract categories are in many cases very closely interrelated in their areal variations and connections from place to place. Indeed, what the geographer observes as individual features—i.e., a soil, river water, a farm, a transport route—are element complexes in which factors of physical, animate, and social origin are so intricately interwoven as to require study within a single field.

Places or areas, large or small, may be studied either specifically or generically. Human interest in individual places is indicated by the practice from earliest times of giving each area a proper name—"Hudson River," "Pennsylvania," or "the South." Geography, like history, is ultimately concerned with attaining maximum comprehension of individual cases. An essential step in the description as well as the understanding of the individual area is the determination of its generic characteristics. When we speak of places as "deserts," "canyons," "cities," "farms," or "culture areas," we limit the criteria in each case to a few closely interrelated features, overlooking aspects in which places of the same type may be radically different. Comparative study of the characteristics of places by kind may reveal indications of significant correspondence, leading to hypotheses of generic relationships. [*The use of modern statistical methods to discover and determine such correlations is discussed below in* GEOGRAPHY, *article on* STATISTICAL GEOGRAPHY.]

Among the social sciences geography, like history, overlaps the fields which study a particular category—economic, political, or sociological. In geography, as in history, it is the integrated combinations of diverse elements, in their complex interrelationships, that form the direct subjects of study. While the ultimate objective in geography is comprehension of the full integration of areas, analysis requires focusing successively on partial integrations. Comparative study of areas, to establish generic concepts and relationships, must be limited to partial integrations over many areas or over the whole world. Such studies may be confined to a very narrow topic, such as the relation of crop yield to rainfall, or may cover the whole group of features which form the economy of areas. [*Divisions of human geography based on common groupings of social features are treated in the articles that follow.*]

RICHARD HARTSHORNE

#### BIBLIOGRAPHY

*An excellent introduction by a professional geographer is Broek 1965. A much more exhaustive treatment, with lengthy bibliographies, may be found in Hartshorne 1939; 1959; two collections of essays, James & Jones 1954 and Taylor 1951, should also be consulted. The classic work in German geography is Hettner 1927. The French literature is reviewed in Claval 1964. The bibliographies of the articles that follow should also be consulted.*

BROEK, JAN O. M. 1965 *Geography: Its Scope and Spirit.* Columbus, Ohio: Merrill.

CLAVAL, PAUL 1964 *Essai sur l'évolution de la géographie humaine.* Cahiers de géographie de Besançon, No. 12. Paris: Les Belles-Lettres.

CRONE, GERALD R. 1951 *Modern Geographers: An Outline of Progress in Geography Since 1800 A.D.* London: Royal Geographical Society.

FREEMAN, THOMAS W. (1961) 1963 *A Hundred Years of Geography.* Chicago: Aldine.

HARTSHORNE, RICHARD (1939) 1964 *The Nature of Geography: A Critical Survey of Current Thought in the Light of the Past.* Lancaster, Pa.: Association of American Geographers.

HARTSHORNE, RICHARD 1959 *Perspective on the Nature of Geography.* Association of American Geographers, Monograph Series, No. 1. Chicago: Rand McNally.

→ A restatement and, in part, an extensive revision of Hartshorne (1939).

HETTNER, ALFRED 1927 *Die Geographie: Ihre Geschichte, ihr Wesen und ihre Methoden.* Breslau (then Germany): Hirt.

JAMES, PRESTON E.; and JONES, CLARENCE F. (editors) (1954) 1964 *American Geography: Inventory and Prospect.* Syracuse Univ. Press.

NATIONAL COUNCIL FOR THE SOCIAL STUDIES 1959 *Yearbook, 29th: New Viewpoints in Geography.* Edited by James E. Preston. Washington: The Council.

TAYLOR, THOMAS GRIFFITH (editor) (1951) 1958 *Geography in the Twentieth Century: A Study of Growth, Fields, Techniques, Aims and Trends.* 3d ed., enl. New York: Philosophical Library.

## II
### POLITICAL GEOGRAPHY

Political geography may be defined from the disciplinary perspective of either geography or political science. From the former perspective, political geography appears as "the study of political phenomena in their areal context" (Jackson 1964, p. 1). This is amplified in the statement political geography is "the study of areal differences and similarities in political character as an interrelated part of the total complex of areal differences and similarities" (Hartshorne et al. 1954, p. 178). Attention to areal dimensions and patterns—suggested by such terms as location, distance, space, distribution, configuration—is also evident in research under the rubric of political science; the same holds for research in political history and politically oriented research in sociology and other disciplines.

### Concepts and techniques

Classical writings on political subjects contain many speculations regarding man's relations to the earth (Thomas 1925). Several contemporary political scientists have given special attention to areal aspects of political institutions, processes, relationships, and policies (e.g., Spykman 1938; 1942; 1944; Spykman & Rollins 1939; Deutsch 1953; Smuckler 1953; Herz 1957; Sprout 1931; 1963; Sprout & Sprout 1946; 1960; 1962; 1965). But with very few exceptions (e.g., Van Dyke 1960, p. 128), commentaries on the political science discipline deal with the areal focus trivially or not at all.

Geographers have given more attention to areal aspects of political phenomena. Although its antecedents go back to the nineteenth century and earlier (Hartshorne 1935), the modern field of political geography dates in America from World War I (e.g., Bowman 1921) and in Europe from somewhat earlier (Ratzel 1897; George 1901; Mackinder 1902; 1904; 1911–1923; Fairgrieve

1915; and others). The American college catalogues of 1930 announced few courses in political geography. Thirty years later the number exceeded 300, a growth accompanied by proliferation of teaching materials and buttressed by theoretical and substantive research. Contributors to theory include Whittlesey (1939), Hartshorne (1935; 1950), Gottmann (1952), and Jones (1954*a*; 1954*b*).

In the idiom of modern geography, geographic quality attaches to any phenomena, human as well as nonhuman, intangible as well as tangible, exhibiting areal dimensions and associations that "give character to particular places" (James & Jones 1954, p. 4). To anticipate a point that will be stressed later, areal patterns of behavior and other intangible human phenomena are becoming increasingly central to research in political geography.

Similarly, the "political" in political science refers to more than the formal apparatus of government; political quality attaches to any aspect of power and influence in society. A community organized on the basis of power is by definition a political community. Every political community (though not every political organization) has a territorial base. Country, often used as a synonym for state, denotes the territorial aspect of a state. Province, city, village, school district, port authority, and other subdivisions of a state all carry territorial connotations. The same holds for empire, political bloc, coalition, and other terms that identify units and combinations of units in imperial and international relationships.

**Political areas.**   In the idiom of geography, any section of the earth's surface delineated by reference to political criteria is a political area. These criteria include *de jure* jurisdiction and authoritative decision making. Political areas so delineated include nation-states, their formally constituted subdivisions, and empires. These are unquestionably significant political areas, and a great deal of political geography has been written in terms of them. As geographers have emphasized (e.g., Whittlesey 1935), the "impress" of political authority changes both the physical and social aspects of landscapes: it affects, for example, inspection stations and other boundary structures; transportation grids that conform to political requirements (e.g., Wolfe 1963); movements of goods and people within a frame of migration and commercial laws; and linguistic and other cultural homogeneities imposed by political authority.

But delineating political areas by reference only to political authority and legal jurisdiction leaves many phenomena uncovered: for example, it does not account for frontier zones that exhibit political homogeneities of personal behavior at variance with *de jure* jurisdiction (Hartshorne 1950), and areal patterns of behavior that are within a recognized territorial jurisdiction but not coterminous with its boundaries, such as the region of "isolation" in the United States (Smuckler 1953) or the Washington–Boston "megalopolis" (Gottmann 1961).

The criteria of jurisdiction and authority completely fail to delineate areas that exhibit patterns of political interaction but no overarching organization of authority. These are the characteristic patterns of international politics, whether of the society of nations as a global whole or of less-than-global areas such as the communist "realm," the so-called free world, the Atlantic "community," and many others.

Geographers have traditionally emphasized the more tangible aspects of political areas. This emphasis is evident in Sauer's morphological conception of political geography as "the study of political landscapes"—i.e., "the administrative centers, the boundaries, and the defensive lines and positions" (1927, p. 208). With reference to political boundaries, Fischer (1949) noted that geographers have usually stressed the stabilizing influence of physiographic factors, often to the neglect of historical and other cultural processes. Stephen B. Jones (1959) reviewed the geographical literature on boundaries, analyzing the ways in which these have been conceived in different places and periods.

Geographers have given increasing attention to intangible factors and to processes of social change. This trend is evident in the writings noted above. In a plea for more "functional" political geography, Hartshorne (1950) emphasized the importance of "centripetal" and "centrifugal" ideas and social movements in the evolution of state areas. Gottmann (1951) introduced the concepts of *circulation* (a French term for which the nearest English equivalent is probably "movement") and *iconographie* (symbols that foster loyalty, solidarity, and conformity) as organizing ideas for the analysis of change and resistance to change in political areas. Jones (1954*a*) brought these and other ideas together in a "unified field theory."

**Political potential.**   In a period of history, the results of political interaction, whether within a single national community or upon the broader stage of international politics, exhibit areal patterns of coercion–submission and influence–deference. Within nation-states and empires, these patterns evolve under processes of authoritative decision making, no matter how primitive or obscure these processes may be. The patterns of international politics, however, have evolved in the absence of legitimized overriding authority. In consequence, these patterns are derived in the main from less sharply delineated images of the distribution of power and influence among the interacting national communities.

There is no standard term to denote the aggregate pressure, pull, attraction, or simply effect that one nation or coalition exerts on the behavior of others. The term "power," with its strong military connotations, is too restrictive, since relations of influence–deference are derived from a much broader spectrum of behavior than coercion–submission—i.e., brute force and the threat of it. The term "political potential" has been suggested to denote this broader spectrum (Sprout & Sprout 1962, p. 158).

The concept of political potential has definite areal connotations. It expresses areal variations in the intensity and efficacy of a government's demands on other nations, i.e., when and how it gets what where. In addition, political potential expresses the total, or aggregative, effect of a nation's statecraft plus effects deriving from that nation's sheer presence on the international landscape, which are evident in the behavior of other nations. Common sense, confirmed by observation, indicates that location, distance, space, the configuration of lands and seas, and the distributions of population, raw materials, technology, institutions, ideologies, and other phenomena may all have some bearing on the political potential of every nation and on the resulting patterns of political interaction and relationship [see MILITARY POWER POTENTIAL].

Maps of the international potentials of both particular states and the major regions and the society of nations as a whole might somewhat resemble a topographic contour map. Such maps, however, do not exist; perhaps the available data are too amorphous and ambiguous to render trustworthy mapping possible in the present state of knowledge. But studies of political potential from a geographic perspective, utilizing geographic methods, should help to clarify the areal concepts implicit in the vocabulary of international politics—e.g., bipolarity, polycentricity, balance of power, sphere of influence, political orbit, and many others in common use [see INTERNATIONAL POLITICS].

**Geographic areas and political systems.** Although geographers and political scientists share an interest in political phenomena, their disciplinary frameworks are recognizably different. Political scientists exhibit interest in areal dimensions and patterns

*only* to the extent that these seem to contribute to an understanding of institutions, processes, relationships, and issues of public concern. In consequence, political analysts tend to view geographic dimensions and patterns from a predominantly ecological perspective, i.e., relations between "political actors" and their milieux. The ways in which students of politics generally frame problems tend to focus attention especially on the psychological linkages between actor and milieu (Sprout & Sprout 1965).

For most geographers (but there are many exceptions) interest in ecological relationships, although generally active, tends to be subsidiary to areal patterns per se. However, this contrast in perspective should not be exaggerated. When one considers the increasing attention that geographers are giving to intangible social patterns and their evolution through time and to the values and motivations that underlie such patterns, it may be more nearly correct to say that "area" is simply the frame of reference within which geographers study political behavior and its results.

In political theory the concept of system has come to occupy a position somewhat analogous to the concept of area in geography [see SYSTEMS ANALYSIS]. These organizing ideas are interestingly relatable. What appears from the geographic perspective to be a political area—city, province, state, empire, major political region, etc.—may appear from the viewpoint of political science to be a system, i.e., a constellation of political units (individuals, groups, or organized communities) that interact and relate in describable patterns. Hartshorne and others have emphasized the complementarity of these perspectives (James & Jones 1954, p. 174).

This complementarity comes through strongly in Jones's "unified field theory of political geography" (1954a). Jones's model consists of five interconnecting categories—"political idea–decision–movement–field–political area." These are likened to a "chain of lakes or basins . . . at one level, so that whatever enters one will spread to all the others." There are close counterparts to Jones's "basins" in other vocabularies. His term "political idea" approximates the concepts of image and goal-orientation in behavioral theory. "Decision" is just what it is elsewhere. "Movement" and "field" seem to be more or less analogous to a course of action that changes, even as it is changed by, the encompassing milieu. Finally, "political area" includes "any political organized area" that has "recognized limits, though not necessarily linear or permanent." Thus, the communist international system, the

Atlantic alliance, the British Commonwealth, or any other international system constitutes (with suitable change in perspective and terminology) a political area, just as does a state, a subdivision thereof, or any other areally expressible system of political interaction.

Flow from idea to area, in Jones's model, is the process by which people control and alter their milieu. The idea of man as a geographic agent, refashioning the landscape along with the physical processes of nature, is an important concept of modern geography. It was given arresting expression in the mid-nineteenth century (see Glacken 1956, pp. 70 ff.) and, more recently, by Sauer (1925) and others. The increasing capacity in technically advanced societies to alter the milieu has immense political implications.

The concept of flow from idea to area, in Jones's model—i.e., from image and purpose to operational result in the behavioral idiom—rests (more often implicitly than explicitly) on the general man–milieu hypothesis of "possibilism." This is the proposition that the capacities of the actor and the properties of his milieu set limits to his accomplishment with reference to any *given* course of action and that these limitations may be operative irrespective of whether or how he perceives and takes them into account. One corollary is the hypothesis that the higher the level of technology, the greater becomes human capacity to control and modify nonhuman components of the milieu. Another corollary is that an operator's ability to affect the behavior of human components of his milieu depends on his capabilities in relation to theirs *at the place* where their relative capabilities are tested.

The reverse flow, from area to idea, in Jones's model, is the process by which the milieu is said to condition human behavior. This conditioning process has been a focus of controversy, largely because of the teleological imagery to which many writers (though not Jones) are addicted. The influences ascribed to nature or to other aspects of the milieu can be expressed, free from teleological overtones, by such psychological concepts as perception, cognition, recognition, stimulus, response, feedback, etc. (Sprout & Sprout 1965). Expressing the conditioning process in such terms emphasizes the complementarity of geography and behavioral science. With certain exceptions, usually unimportant in political contexts, the phenomena of psychological stimulus and response provide the only demonstrated path of influence from milieu to actor, from environment to environed organism, from "area" to "ideas." The psychological nature of environmental conditioning of behavior (from which many areal patterns are derived) has long been understood, although not always clearly delineated (e.g., Mackinder 1919, p. 28; Febvre 1922, p. 171; James & Jones 1954, p. 13). At least one contemporary geographer has explicitly restated this process in the idiom of psychological theory (Kirk 1952).

**Geographic techniques.** A major contribution which geographers have made to the study of political phenomena is the development of graphic techniques. Most political areas are too large to be directly perceived *in toto*. The eye may not differentiate and relate various categories of phenomena distributed over the area, even when they are directly perceivable; hence the value of graphic modes of research, analysis, and presentation, by means of model globes, maps, cartograms, photographs, etc. (Bowman 1934, chapter 4; Boggs 1948). Maps delineating selected features of an area can be compared and superposed (e.g., Bowman [1921] 1928, pp. 146, 460). Large segments of the earth's surface can be examined from different perspectives (Harrison 1944; Boggs 1945). High-altitude and low-altitude photographs and oblique-angle pictures add new dimensions and textures to the perception of smaller areas (e.g., Gutkind 1956, pp. 1 ff.). Maps and cartograms can deceive as well as inform and hence are powerful instruments of political propaganda (Boggs 1946). Maps and other graphic tools not only carry preconceived messages but, when studied, may also evoke new insights and hypotheses [*see* CARTOGRAPHY].

## Research in political geography

The substantive literature divides roughly into two categories: (1) works that focus on political areas as such; and (2) works that utilize areal concepts and patterns to explain or to predict political events. This cleavage more or less follows disciplinary lines, but by no means consistently. Some of the more important theoretical works have been cited, and a few teaching books are included in the bibliography, along with works cited in this text. A more comprehensive bibliography is appended to the long essay on political geography in James and Jones (see Hartshorne et al. 1954).

With respect to research on particular political areas, one should distinguish between works that deal primarily with political phenomena in an areal context and those that merely utilize political boundaries as a frame of reference for a wider range of phenomena—e.g., works on areal distributions of agriculture, industry, communication grids, etc.

Works that are politically oriented in the stricter

sense cluster around various focuses. One of these is the formation, expansion, and disintegration of political areas (e.g., Bowman 1921; Whittlesey 1939; Hartshorne 1950; Deutsch 1953). The following are of particular interest: Herz's analysis of the formation of modern "large-area" states and of the advances in technology that are making these states progressively vulnerable to economic, psychological, and military penetration (1957); Vevier's essay on geographical ideas in the territorial expansion of the United States (1960); and Hart's hypotheses regarding the logistical requisites of political areas (1949). There are many studies of functioning political areas which reflect the varied research perspectives and methods of several disciplines. The Searchlight Series, edited by G. W. Hoffman and G. E. Pearcy, offers a continually growing list of short books of this type.

A second focus is on the analysis of political areas in the light of population growth, spreading communication grids, industrialization, and urban sprawl (e.g., Gottmann 1961; Wolfe 1963). Worthy of special mention is Mumford's historical study of cities (1961).

A third focus is on areal patterns delineated not by political authority but by civic attitudes and preferences. This involves studies of integrative and disintegrative ideas and movements within state areas (e.g., Hartshorne 1950); attitudes toward the "national space" (e.g., Herman's study of communist China, 1959); regional variations in civic postures toward public problems such as military defense and foreign policy (e.g., Beard 1934; Sprout & Sprout 1939; Smuckler 1953).

A fourth focus is on the role of political authority in the development, use, depletion, conservation, and renewal of resources. These questions are approached from different angles in International Symposium on Man's Role . . . (1956) and also in Udall (1963) and Herber (1962). The effects of resource use and of regulations governing use constitute important exhibits of the "impress" of political authority upon the earth.

A fifth research focus is on political regions larger than nation-state areas. These include ancient and modern empires (e.g., Fawcett 1951; Fisher 1950) and international regions delineated in various ways (Jones 1955a). Boggs's essay on the Western Hemisphere (1945) focused attention on the need for precise criteria for delineating major political regions. This need is exemplified in some textbooks, in which political regions are variously delineated by physiographic, historical, broadly cultural, or other criteria, sometimes without clear demonstration of political relevance.

The geographic dimensions and patterns of international politics have been analyzed from various perspectives. Virtually every textbook on international politics gives attention to the uneven distribution of people and things among nations. Areal variations are recognized to be strategic in the estimation of state capabilities (e.g., Sprout & Sprout 1962; Jones 1954b). Such variations form the basis of hypotheses invented to explain or to predict patterns of interaction in the society of nations (Jones 1955a; 1955b; Sprout 1963). Such hypotheses represent attempts to identify factors whose uneven distribution in space provides a plausible explanation of international patterns.

## Geopolitics

Most attention has been given to hypotheses derived from the global and regional configuration of lands and seas. These include Mahan's sea-power interpretation of history (1900; Sprout & Sprout 1962); Mackinder's hypothesis of trend toward a world empire based in the "heartland" of Eurasia (1904; 1919), later modified considerably (see especially 1911–1923, vol. 2; 1943); and variants and critiques of Mahan's and Mackinder's theories too numerous to list here [see MACKINDER; MAHAN; see also, e.g., Fairgrieve 1915; Dorpalen 1942; Spykman 1944; East & Moodie 1956, chapter 18].

Climatic variations have inspired another set of geopolitical hypotheses and critiques (e.g., Huntington 1915; Wheeler 1946; Mills 1949; Missenard 1954). International political patterns have also been linked with the uneven distribution of the various raw-material requisites of modern industry. There is some disposition to regard areal differentials in technology as the critical variable (e.g., Brown 1956), a hypothesis that has been linked with demographic distribution to produce a prediction that international political patterns will ultimately be determined by the latter. The prediction is based on the premise that technological primacy will vary with relative numbers of superior scientists and other gifted individuals, the incidence of such individuals varying, in the long run, with the size of population (Blount 1957; critique by Sprout 1963).

The adjective "geopolitical" requires some explanation. Political geography in general, and international political geography in particular, is often confused with geopolitics. This word entered the English language as a loose translation of *Geopolitik*, which came, in the interwar period, 1919–1939, to denote mobilization of areal knowledge for purposes of state—in short, geo-*policy*. Geopolitics was associated in particular with the

Institut für Geopolitik in Munich, directed by Karl Haushofer, a general turned geographer and propagandist, who is widely believed (perhaps mistakenly) to have contributed significantly to Hitler's strategy of conquest (e.g., Dorpalen 1942; Fifield 1945).

Because certain Germans exploited the concept of *Lebensraum* and other geopolitical ideas for aggressive purposes, many in America and elsewhere illogically concluded that any mixing of geography and politics must be tainted with war and conquest. Geographers insisted that geopolitics was a part of political science. Political scientists tossed the pariah subject back to the geographers. Time has blurred the odious policy connotations of geopolitics, perhaps more so in America than in Europe. The term has even acquired some respectability, especially in the context of military-defense analysis.

The adjective "geopolitical," never as value-laden as the noun "geopolitics," was employed sparingly in the 1930s (e.g., Whittlesey 1939), and increasingly in more recent years, to denote the *areal aspect of any political pattern* and, in particular, hypotheses that purport to explain or to predict areal distributions and patterns of political potential in the society of nations. All such hypotheses represent assessments of opportunities and limitations implicit in the properties of the interacting political communities and of the milieu in which they operate. Such assessments (in the idiom of ecological theory) are essentially possibilistic, even though they may be expressed in deterministic or near-deterministic rhetoric (Sprout & Sprout 1965).

HAROLD SPROUT

[*See also* ECOLOGY; INTERNATIONAL POLITICS. *Other relevant material may be found under* ENCLAVES AND EXCLAVES; INTERNATIONAL RELATIONS.]

### BIBLIOGRAPHY

ALEXANDER, LEWIS M. (1957) 1963 *World Political Patterns.* 2d ed. Chicago: Rand McNally. → A college text organized regionally.

BEARD, CHARLES A. 1934 *The Idea of National Interest: An Analytical Study in American Foreign Policy.* New York: Macmillan.

BLOUNT, B. K. 1957 Science Will Change the Balance of Power. *New Scientist* 2, no. 32:8–9.

BOGGS, S. W. 1945 This Hemisphere. U.S. Department of State, *Bulletin* 12:845–850.

BOGGS, S. W. 1946 Cartohypnosis. U.S. Department of State, *Bulletin* 15:1119–1125.

BOGGS, S. W. 1948 Geographic and Other Scientific Techniques for Political Science. *American Political Science Review* 42:223–248.

BOWMAN, ISAIAH (1921) 1928 *The New World: Problems in Political Geography.* 4th ed. New York: World. → The first edition is important as an early compre-hensive American work on political geography; the later editions, considerably revised, have more enduring value.

BOWMAN, ISAIAH 1934 *Geography in Relation to the Social Sciences.* New York: Scribner.

BROWN, HARRISON 1956 Technological Denudation. Pages 1023–1032 in International Symposium on Man's Role in Changing the Face of the Earth, Princeton, N.J., 1955, *Man's Role in Changing the Face of the Earth.* Edited by William L. Thomas et al. Univ. of Chicago Press.

DASMANN, RAYMOND F. 1963 *The Last Horizon.* New York: Macmillan.

DEUTSCH, KARL W. 1953 The Growth of Nations: Some Recurrent Patterns of Political and Social Integration. *World Politics* 5:168–195.

DORPALEN, ANDREAS 1942 *The World of General Haushofer.* New York: Farrar.

EAST, WILLIAM G.; and MOODIE, A. E. (editors) 1956 *The Changing World: Studies in Political Geography.* New York: World. → A symposium textbook in the tradition of Isaiah Bowman's *The New World.*

FAIRGRIEVE, JAMES (1915) 1941 *Geography and World Power.* 8th ed., rev. New York: Dutton. → After 1915 a new Chapter 18 was included that considerably altered the main thesis of the book.

FAWCETT, CHARLES B. (1951) 1957 Geography and Empire. Pages 418–432 in Thomas Griffith Taylor (editor), *Geography in the Twentieth Century.* 2d ed., rev. New York: Philosophical Library.

FEBVRE, LUCIEN (1922) 1925 *A Geographical Introduction to History.* New York: Knopf. → First published as *La terre et l'évolution humaine.*

FIFIELD, RUSSELL H. 1945 Geopolitics at Munich. U.S. Department of State, *Bulletin* 12:1152–1162.

FISCHER, ERIC 1949 On Boundaries. *World Politics* 1:196–222.

FISHER, CHARLES A. 1950 The Expansion of Japan: A Study in Oriental Geopolitics. *Geographical Journal* 115:1–19, 179–193.

FISHER, CHARLES A. 1964 *Southeast Asia: A Social, Economic, and Political Geography.* New York: Dutton.

GEORGE, HEREFORD B. (1901) 1924 *The Relations of Geography and History.* 5th ed., rev. & enl. Oxford: Clarendon.

GLACKEN, CLARENCE J. 1956 Changing Ideas of the Habitable World. Pages 70–92 in International Symposium on Man's Role in Changing the Face of the Earth, Princeton, N.J., 1955, *Man's Role in Changing the Face of the Earth.* Edited by William L. Thomas et al. Univ. of Chicago Press.

GOBLET, YANN M. 1955 *Political Geography and the World Map.* New York: Praeger.

GOTTMANN, JEAN 1951 Geography and International Relations. *World Politics* 3:153–173.

GOTTMANN, JEAN 1952 *La politique des états et leur géographie.* Paris: Colin.

GOTTMANN, JEAN (1961) 1964 *Megalopolis: The Urbanized Northeastern Seaboard of the United States.* Cambridge, Mass.: M.I.T. Press. → An urban-economic evaluation of the nature of a continuously urbanized section of the eastern United States.

GUTKIND, E. A. 1956 Our World From the Air: Conflict and Adaptation. Pages 1–44 in International Symposium on Man's Role in Changing the Face of the Earth, Princeton, N.J., 1955, *Man's Role in Changing the Face of the Earth.* Edited by William L. Thomas et al. Univ. of Chicago Press.

HARRISON, RICHARD E. 1944 *Look at the World: The Fortune Atlas for World Strategy.* New York: Knopf.

HART, HORNELL 1949 Technology and the Growth of Political Areas. Pages 28–57 in William F. Ogburn (editor), *Technology and International Relations.* Univ. of Chicago Press.

HARTSHORNE, RICHARD 1935 Recent Developments in Political Geography. *American Political Science Review* 29:785–804, 943–966.

HARTSHORNE, RICHARD 1950 The Functional Approach in Political Geography. Association of American Geographers, *Annals* 40:95–130.

HARTSHORNE, RICHARD 1959 *Perspective on the Nature of Geography.* Association of American Geographers, Monograph Series, No. 1. Chicago: Rand McNally. → A restatement and, in part, an extensive revision of "The Nature of Geography: A Critical Survey of Current Thought in the Light of the Past," published in 1939.

HARTSHORNE, RICHARD et al. 1954 Political Geography. Pages 167–225 in Preston E. James and Clarence F. Jones (editors), *American Geography: Inventory and Prospect.* Syracuse Univ. Press. → An excellent bibliography appears on pages 222–225.

HERBER, LEWIS 1962 *Our Synthetic Environment.* New York: Knopf.

HERMAN, THEODORE 1959 Group Values Toward the National Space: The Case of China. *Geographical Review* 49:164–182.

HERZ, JOHN H. 1957 Rise and Demise of the Territorial State. *World Politics* 9:473–493.

HUNTINGTON, ELLSWORTH (1915) 1924 *Civilization and Climate.* 3d ed., rev. New Haven: Yale Univ. Press.

INTERNATIONAL SYMPOSIUM ON MAN'S ROLE IN CHANGING THE FACE OF THE EARTH, PRINCETON, N.J., 1955 1956 *Man's Role in Changing the Face of the Earth.* Edited by William L. Thomas et al. Univ. of Chicago Press.

JACKSON, W. A. DOUGLAS 1958 Whither Political Geography? Association of American Geographers, *Annals* 48:178–183.

JACKSON, W. A. DOUGLAS (editor) 1964 *Politics and Geographic Relationships.* Englewood Cliffs, N.J.: Prentice-Hall. → A well-chosen collection of teaching materials drawn from several disciplines.

JAMES, PRESTON E.; and JONES, CLARENCE F. (editors) 1954 *American Geography: Inventory and Prospect.* Univ. of Syracuse Press.

JONES, STEPHEN B. (1954a) 1964 A Unified Field Theory of Political Geography. Pages 101–109 in W. A. Douglas Jackson (editor), *Politics and Geographic Relationships.* Englewood Cliffs, N.J.: Prentice-Hall.

JONES, STEPHEN B. (1954b) 1964 The Power Inventory and National Strategy. Pages 318–338 in W. A. Douglas Jackson (editor), *Politics and Geographic Relationships.* Englewood Cliffs, N.J.: Prentice-Hall.

JONES, STEPHEN B. 1955a Views of the Political World. *Geographical Review* 45:309–326.

JONES, STEPHEN B. 1955b Global Strategic Views. *Geographical Review* 45:492–508.

JONES, STEPHEN B. 1959 Boundary Concepts in the Setting of Place and Time. Association of American Geographers, *Annals* 49:241–255.

KIRK, WILLIAM 1952 Historical Geography and the Concept of the Behavioural Environment. *Indian Geographical Journal* [1952]:152–160.

MACKINDER, HALFORD (1902) 1930 *Britain and the British Seas.* 2d ed. Oxford: Clarendon.

MACKINDER, HALFORD 1904 The Geographical Pivot of History. *Geographical Journal* 23:421–444.

MACKINDER, HALFORD 1911–1923 *Nations of the Modern World.* 2 vols. London: Philip.

MACKINDER, HALFORD (1919) 1942 *Democratic Ideals and Reality: A Study in the Politics of Reconstruction.* London: Constable; New York: Holt.

MACKINDER, HALFORD 1943 The Round World and the Winning of the Peace. *Foreign Affairs* 21:595–605.

MAHAN, ALFRED THAYER (1900) 1905 *The Problem of Asia and Its Effect Upon International Policies.* Boston: Little.

MAULL, OTTO (1925) 1956 *Politische Geographie.* Berlin: Safari Verlag.

MILLS, CLARENCE A. 1949 Temperature Dominance Over Human Life. *Science* 110:267–271.

MISSENARD, ANDRÉ 1954 *À la recherche de l'homme.* Paris: Librairie Istra. → See especially Part 3, "Climat et milieu physique."

MUMFORD, LEWIS 1961 *The City in History: Its Origins, Its Transformations, and Its Prospects.* New York: Harcourt.

PEARCY, GEORGE E. et al. (1948) 1957 *World Political Geography.* New York: Crowell. → A regionally organized symposium textbook.

POUNDS, NORMAN J. G. 1963 *Political Geography.* New York: McGraw-Hill. → A book designed for college teaching.

RATZEL, FRIEDRICH (1897) 1923 *Politische Geographie* 3d ed. Edited by Eugen Oberhummer. Munich and Berlin: Oldenbourg.

SAUER, CARL O. (1925) 1963 The Morphology of Landscape. Pages 315–350 in Carl O. Sauer, *Land and Life: A Selection From the Writings of Carl Ortwin Sauer.* Berkeley: Univ. of California Press.

SAUER, CARL O. 1927 Recent Developments in Cultural Geography. Pages 154–212 in E. C. Hayes (editor), *Recent Developments in the Social Sciences.* Philadelphia: Lippincott.

SCHÖLLER, PETER 1958 Das Ende einer politischen Geographie ohne sozialgeographische Bindung. *Erdkunde: Archiv für wissenschaftliche Geographie* 12:313–316.

SMUCKLER, RALPH H. 1953 The Region of Isolationism. *American Political Science Review* 47:386–401.

SPROUT, HAROLD 1931 Political Geography as a Political Science Field. *American Political Science Review* 25:439–442.

SPROUT, HAROLD 1963 Geopolitical Hypotheses in Technological Perspective. *World Politics* 15:187–212.

SPROUT, HAROLD; and SPROUT, MARGARET 1939 *The Rise of American Naval Power.* Princeton Univ. Press.

SPROUT, HAROLD; and SPROUT, MARGARET (1946) 1960 Atlantic, Command of. Volume 2, pages 628–632 in *Encyclopaedia Britannica.* 14th ed. Chicago: Benton.

SPROUT, HAROLD; and SPROUT, MARGARET (1960) 1964 Geography and International Politics in an Era of Revolutionary Change. Pages 34–51 in W. A. Douglas Jackson (editor), *Politics and Geographic Relationships.* Englewood Cliffs, N.J.: Prentice-Hall.

SPROUT, HAROLD; and SPROUT, MARGARET 1962 *Foundations of International Politics.* Princeton, N.J.: Van Nostrand.

SPROUT, HAROLD; and SPROUT, MARGARET 1965 *The Ecological Perspective on Human Affairs, With Special Reference to International Politics.* Princeton Univ. Press.

SPYKMAN, NICHOLAS J. 1938 Geography and Foreign Policy. *American Political Science Review* 32:28–50, 213–236.

SPYKMAN, NICHOLAS J. 1942 *America's Strategy in World Politics.* New York: Harcourt.

SPYKMAN, NICHOLAS J. 1944 *The Geography of the Peace.* New York: Harcourt.

SPYKMAN, NICHOLAS J.; and ROLLINS, ABBIE A. 1939 Geographical Objectives in Foreign Policy. *American Political Science Review* 33:391–412, 591–614.

TAYLOR, THOMAS G. (editor) (1951) 1957 *Geography in the Twentieth Century.* 3d ed. New York: Philosophical Library.

THOMAS, FRANKLIN 1925 *The Environmental Basis of Society.* New York: Century.

UDALL, STEWART L. 1963 *The Quiet Crisis.* New York: Holt.

VAN DYKE, VERNON 1960 *Political Science: A Philosophical Analysis.* Stanford Univ. Press.

VAN VALKENBURG, SAMUEL; and STOTZ, CARL L. (1954) 1955 *Elements of Political Geography.* Englewood Cliffs, N.J.: Prentice-Hall. → Topically organized text.

VEVIER, CHARLES 1960 American Continentalism: An Idea of Expansion, 1845–1910. *American Historical Review* 65:323–335.

WAGNER, PHILIP 1960 *The Human Use of the Earth.* Glencoe, Ill.: Free Press.

WEIGERT, HANS W.; and STEFANSSON, VILHJALMUR (editors) 1944 *Compass of the World.* New York: Macmillan.

WEIGERT, HANS W.; and STEFANSSON, VILHJALMUR (editors) 1949 *New Compass of the World.* New York: Macmillan.

WEIGERT, HANS W. et al. 1957 *Principles of Political Geography.* New York: Appleton. → Wide-ranging text by several authors, with strong emphasis on economic, demographic, and broadly cultural factors.

WHEELER, RAYMOND H. 1946 Climate and Human Behavior. Pages 78–87 in Philip Harriman (editor), *Encyclopedia of Psychology.* New York: Philosophical Library.

WHITTLESEY, DERWENT 1935 The Impress of Effective Central Authority Upon the Landscape. Association of American Geographers, *Annals* 25:85–97.

WHITTLESEY, DERWENT (1939) 1944 *The Earth and the State.* New York: Holt.

WOLFE, ROY I. 1963 *Transportation and Politics.* Princeton, N.J.: Van Nostrand.

WOLFE, ROY I. 1964 Perspective on Outdoor Recreation: A Bibliographical Survey. *Geographical Review* 54:203–238.

### III
### ECONOMIC GEOGRAPHY

The subject matter of economic geography is related substantively and historically to both disciplines from which the field receives its name. It obtains from geography an emphasis upon similarities and differences from area to area, large and small, on the earth's surface, and upon linkages or circulations between areas. It acquires from economics an interest in the production, distribution, exchange, and consumption of goods and services. Economic geography therefore may be defined as an inquiry into similarities, differences, and linkages within and between areas in the production, exchange, transfer, and consumption of goods and services. Particular attention is given to the location of economic activity, considered both in theo-retical and practical terms [see SPATIAL ECONOMICS].

**Relationship to geography and economics.** Economic geography is so intimately a part of the whole of geography that separating it from the general field is difficult. Because gaining a livelihood not only is essential to human existence but also involves a wide range of cultural and natural (physical and biological) features and interrelationships between those features, most matters of concern within economic geography are of concern within the over-all discipline, and vice versa. This is especially true if natural and noneconomic cultural features are considered in terms of their positive and negative implications for human use of earth space in gaining a livelihood. However, the emphasis upon livelihood in economic geography does mean a corresponding reduction of attention to those cultural or natural conditions which may be only loosely related to spatial aspects of livelihood. Thus, for example, neither the cultural origin of a religious belief nor the process of landform development is of direct interest to the economic geographer unless applicable in some way—as an advantage or constraint—to the location and interrelationships of economic activities.

As in the whole of geography, the spectrum of the totality of interrelationships in economic geography may be horizontal (involving different areas or different points within a given area), vertical (involving a morphological column of cultural and natural features at a specific point on the earth's surface), or both horizontal and vertical. Horizontal relationships are stressed in most work now being carried on.

We may consider economic geography, therefore, as emphasizing the livelihood aspects of the whole of geography, rather than as a compartment of the parent discipline. The field has a direct tie to economics and, by way of the whole of geography, indirect ties to other disciplines in the social and natural sciences. So considered, the field by definition is sufficiently broad in scope to anticipate any methodological changes from time to time and place to place, although specific approaches, concepts, points of view and emphasis, immediate objectives, and methods have ranged rather widely with change of either time or place.

**Trends.** However, among economic geographers there is lack of agreement as to specific direction, particularly in the United States and Canada. For a time after its emergence as a separate field in the United States, during the early years of the twentieth century, economic geography relied primarily upon the inductive approach, with individual scholars aggregating ideas and data from field and library work into descriptions, classifications, and qualitative interpretations, utilizing numerical evidence when possible. Partially because of limitations on the amount of information obtainable in these ways, emphasis was placed on the unique or at least the distinctive features and interrelationships in both systematic and regional work; generalizations were made when possible. Although this approach continues to be utilized profitably by many economic geographers, the past decade has marked the emergence of a new school of thought, with immediate roots going as far back as the 1930s and indirect roots into the early portion of the nineteenth century. This school has chosen an explicitly theoretical approach, emphasizing nomothetic research and depending appreciably upon mathematical abstraction. In the early 1960s the suggestion was made that geography basically is concerned with systems analysis (Ackerman 1963) and that the overriding problem of geography is understanding the man–land system of the earth. This giant system in turn is considered by Ackerman to comprise a large number of hierarchically arranged subsystems and processes. Such a concept places economic geography in the position of searching for laws involving livelihood within a context of systems analysis applied to earth space. The degree to which the concept has been generally accepted is not yet certain.

**Two basic rationales.** Like the over-all discipline, economic geography in the United States and Canada can be visualized in terms of two fundamental rationales—the topical, or systematic (not to be confused with system in systems analysis), and the regional. In economic geography both rationales focus on primary activities (here, as generally in economics, considered to be agriculture, grazing, forest-products industries, mining, fishing, and hunting), secondary activities (manufacturing and construction), and tertiary activities (all other occupations). The two rationales differ especially as to initial starting position. The topical, or systematic, rationale begins with structural aspects and works toward their earth-space expression and relationships, whereas the regional begins with space and works toward structure. The respective starting positions are usually reflected in various emphases in the completed works. Both rationales can be divided into subjects which themselves have become research interests for certain economic geographers. In practice these subjects are usually called systematic or topical specialties. Agricultural geography, manufacturing geography, and marketing geography have been of long-standing interest. Transportation geography and theoretical approaches to certain tertiary activities and domes-

tic trading patterns have been developed actively within the past decade [*see* CENTRAL PLACE]. In addition, increasing attention is being given to recreation geography and to aspects of tertiary activities not yet accorded full consideration, to geographical aspects of international trade, and to the economic geography of primary activities other than agriculture. Work has begun on the geography of consumption and the geography of price.

Because economic activities are earth based and may be clustered, as to location and/or function, into patterns of differing kinds and intensity, regions are important to economic geography. As in the whole of geography, regions in economic geography may be either homogeneous or nodal. The homogeneous region, sometimes called the formal region, is more or less an inventory of static features and relationships within an area that has been delimited on the basis of prevailing homogeneity of at least one feature. Both cultural and natural features and relationships may be so classified: the spring wheat belt, the manufacturing belt between Chicago and New York, and the Appalachian Mountains are three examples in North America of this classification. Each example has been delimited on the basis of a single criterion, but multiple-criterion regions are possible at higher levels of generalization.

The nodal, or functional, region classifies human organization of earth space. This region has a point of focus (such as a city or town), an organized area of mutual interdependence with respect to that point and associated territory (such as the trading area of a city or town), and connecting lines to the territory (such as transportation and communication routes) providing the linkage (such as commuter and freight traffic and communications flows) between the point and the area.

Both the homogeneous and the nodal regions are here envisaged as means of classification and not as objective entities to be discovered in a scientific sense. Either type of region can be considered at various levels of observation and detail. When several levels are superimposed, a pyramidlike framework with hierarchical tendencies may be recognizable.

**Realms of interdisciplinary contact.** Besides its subfields, economic geography extends into realms of interest shared with other disciplines. The utilization and conservation of natural and human resources is of long-standing interest to some economic geographers. More recently, the development of regional science is of definite interest to some economic geographers, many of whom participated in that development. Especially in the 1960s some economic geographers have become very interested in regional inequalities of economic development, whether within a country or at a continental or global level of observation.

**Theoretical and practical implications.** The theoretical importance and practical significance of economic geography are inextricably intertwined. Theories seek optimum circumstances and efficiency in human utilization of earth space: what are the most desirable size, spacing, and intermix of specific economic units of production, exchange, transfer, and consumption within selected typologies of cultural and natural conditions? On the other hand, evaluations of historical and current practices indicate the degree to which theoretical models are actually applicable, especially in view of the cultural institutions, personalities and wills of key individuals, and specific natural conditions of a given area. Such evaluations also provide a degree and type of qualitative insight not obtainable through hypothesis alone.

Once a satisfactory relationship between theory and practice has been established, a logical step is application to planning procedures. In economic geography the value of both theoretical and pragmatic study to planning is clear, whether the viewpoint of the planner is the broad outlook of the regional analyst, concerned with an intermix of varied economic activities and resources, or the more restricted and highly specialized view of the expert in finding locations for individual units of economic activity.

**Methods of study.** Inasmuch as developments and trends in the United States from 1904 to 1954, the first 50 years of geography's existence as a university discipline, have been evaluated elsewhere (James & Jones 1954), the events of succeeding years will be emphasized here. A survey of the literature indicates that research since 1954 can be divided into three categories, on the basis of approach and method: qualitative interpretation, usually with substantial numerical evidence and sometimes making use of the case-study technique; quantitative classification, in a more or less descriptive sense, with qualitative elaboration and explanation and involving a specific procedure applicable to different areas and time periods; and formulation and testing of specific hypotheses and models. These approaches have been applied, with varying degrees of intensity, to most facets of economic geography, but they will be discussed here with respect to agriculture, manufacturing, trade, and transportation.

*Agricultural geography.* All three approaches are utilized in agricultural geography, which is still a subject of keen interest. Books and articles involving qualitative interpretation are diverse as to

specific subject matter, but most can be classified under certain broad headings. Approximately one-third of the articles on agriculture appearing in four professional journals of the United States and Canada—*Annals* (Association of American Geographers), *Canadian Geographer, Economic Geography, Geographical Review*—treated a specific agricultural activity in a definite area, evaluating such aspects as type and size of enterprises, natural environmental advantages or constraints, combinations of selected crops and livestock with other crops and livestock, allocation of land, general farming practices, and trends. One-fourth emphasized over-all use of agricultural land in a specified area, considering other aspects of agricultural geography in a subsidiary way. Nearly one-fifth were concerned primarily with reclamation of agricultural land—irrigation, drainage, erosion control, etc. A final one-fourth involved miscellaneous interests, such as land redistribution in a given area, agricultural colonies of a minority group in a given area, land tenure in a specified place, the economic development of a country that is heavily dependent on agriculture, and the historical geography of agricultural change in a selected location, etc. These four categories of qualitative interpretation, which cover the most numerous writings on agricultural geography in literature published in the United States and Canada, provide valuable insight into conditions evaluated by each author but have almost no common denominator.

Descriptive and analytic interpretation of a quantitative nature involves a classification based on numerical information, preferably official data continually available. The classification reveals pattern when plotted on a map and hence may be used to construct generic regions (typologies of regions) based on quantitative criteria. Once the criteria become standardized on a world-wide basis, the classifications will become standardized and applicable to all parts of the world. In principle both the homogeneous and the functional region may be so constructed, but in practice the homogeneous region has received the most attention to date in agricultural work. Prior to 1954 most studies were based on inadequate quantitative evidence, rather highly generalized, and presented at continental or even global levels of observation. Weaver (1954, especially pp. 175–184) applied a greater measure of objectivity to an area of intermediate size, aggregating data from county units to compute, for the Middle West of the United States, areal differences in crop combinations on the basis of degree of variance from a theoretical curve of optimal combinations. Subsequent work by other geographers includes a quantitative sampling approach to agricultural regionalization, the application of multiple correlation and regression analysis to rural farm population densities in the Great Plains, and the statistical association of cash grain farming in the Middle West with landforms.

The application of hypotheses to agricultural geography has been based on a rediscovery of implications of Thünen's pioneer work treating the effect of transport cost and market price on crop and livestock combinations (1826–1863). Current research suggests that, while the influence of distance to market on agricultural land use does not result today in patterns so simple as those set down by Thünen, the influence of market price and transport cost does exist and can be analyzed mathematically [see RENT].

*Manufacturing geography.* Qualitative interpretation of manufacturing geography, as indicated in publications of the United States and Canada, has been applied especially to areas other than Anglo–America, usually where numerical information is not fully available. Such an article or monograph may be an appraisal of a specific industry or group of industries or may involve a general examination of all manufacturing. The method of the historical geographer, providing the time dimension, may or may not be utilized. The case study is seldom used. Work involving only qualitative interpretation constitutes a relatively small percentage of all studies in manufacturing geography, largely because numerical data are available to a greater degree than, for example, in agriculture.

Quantitative classifications are numerous in manufacturing geography. Labor force and value added are usually the criteria of measurement, although the list of possibilities is long and includes value of product, wages paid, amount of energy consumed, area of ground space, area of floor space, and land value. One such classification, with labor force used as the measuring criterion, has revealed structural and spatial changes in the manufacturing of the United States. Another has been based on magnitude (number of employees, wages paid, and value added) and intensity (ratios of labor force and value added to selected national totals), the classification being applied, with allowance for kind and amount of data available, to the United States, Japan, and the Soviet Union. In still another classification based on labor force and value added, the author developed a technique for showing change over time on a single map and applied his technique not only to conditions within specific regions but also to differential rates of regional growth, as measured by national totals. Another study classified cities by labor force on

the basis of prevailing industries, after first removing from consideration the city-serving functions of the industries. Several indices of industrial diversification also have been developed, with labor force the prime criterion of measurement. A typology of manufacturing flows relies, on the one hand, upon the orientation of manufacturing to raw materials or agglomerations of input factors and, on the other, upon access to both national and regional markets.

Increased attention is also being accorded theoretical approaches to manufacturing geography. Here, especially, work is being shared—by economic geography and regional science [see REGIONAL SCIENCE]. Among initial geographical models was a construction by Harris (1954) showing the importance of market potential to industrial localization. Other geographers have used models to measure association tendencies in manufacturing, concluding that agglomeration is a very important force. Models have been used to examine tendencies of high-value-added manufacturing to concentrate in certain areas, and they have also been used to associate circular and cumulative causation with the growth of manufacturing and associated urbanization. [See ECONOMIES OF SCALE *and* EXTERNAL ECONOMIES AND DISECONOMIES.]

*Geography of trade.* Attention to trade in economic geography has focused especially on domestic trade. Theoretical work is being pursued vigorously under the stimulus of central-place theory. Pragmatic work, whether qualitative interpretation or quantitative classification, also has been of keen interest. This pragmatic work is usually called marketing geography, although some studies in domestic commodity flow would not necessarily be included under such a heading. Early research of this kind was associated especially with urban geography, which developed as a field in the first half of the twentieth century and is becoming increasingly important. This early research has been a valuable antecedent to both central-place theory and marketing geography. From numerous studies of individual urban units and, subsequently, from use of census information three significant contributions were made: the idea of the city-region, a functional region of interdependent units, including an urban unit; the classification of all cities in a country by relatively dominant functions, as measured by nationwide norms; and the concept of an economic base comprised, on the one hand, of trading and related activities or portions of activities which provide financial support for a specified area and, on the other, of activities or portions of activities which merely provide local interaction and have no influence outside that area (James & Jones

[1954] 1964, pp. 142–166, 245–251). Subsequently, Murphy and Vance (1954) developed a technique for delimiting the central business district (CBD), based on land use involving the retailing of goods and services and the provision of office space. Ullman (1957) developed a series of maps interpreting commodity flow within the United States, emphasizing principles of complementarity, transferability, and intervening opportunity. Other writers have been interested in the most appropriate location for shopping centers, especially with respect to market areas shared by competing firms. Questions have been raised as to the necessity of formal theories in marketing geography, but as yet no definite answers have emerged. Meanwhile, in a related area efforts are being made to map and evaluate the spatial distribution of finance as an economic activity and to associate this distribution with trading areas of cities.

Most geographical work in international trade has been pragmatic. One study has associated broad regional patterns (countries or groups of countries) and degree of dependence upon categories of exports and imports, and another has classified countries by degree of dependence upon exports. Still another has examined the free port, concluding that it may have outlived its usefulness in technically advanced, highly industrialized countries. Thoman and Conkling (1967) appraised national and bloc trends in international trade between 1938 and 1963, dependence of individual economies upon exports and export specialties, and logistics and mechanics of such trade.

*Transportation geography.* Although transportation long has been treated in the literature of economic geography, its full significance is only coming to be realized as the functional region, which depends for interpretation largely upon the flow of commodities and people to and from central places, comes to the forefront of attention. This is especially true of linkage studies involving transportation *and* trade—the carrier and route, plus shipping costs, plus direction and composition of commodity and passenger movement, plus alternative opportunities for such movement. Such linkage studies reveal the dynamic aspects of an area, whether for a specified time or with change over time. Again, all three categories of approach are to be seen, with qualitative interpretation utilized particularly to present an unusual idea or to appraise general conditions over a wide area where adequate numerical information is lacking. Some geographers, however, have produced excellent qualitative interpretations concerning areas, small or large, that are covered rather fully by census and comparable data. In addition, historical geographers have provided insight into the development of somewhat analogous transportation routes that have evolved at different times and for different purposes.

Classifications by density of route and by general direction and function of route, again usually at continental or global levels of observation, are not new in transportation geography; but these have been augmented, usually at national or regional levels, by more-detailed and more-meaningful studies. Models have also been used to indicate the impact of highways on geographic change, to anticipate the development of transportation networks, and to explain differential rates of growth in passenger traffic between leading airports.

**Regional economic geography.** Several recent books and monographs have applied regional approaches to economic geography. Gottmann (1961) evaluated the urban-economic aspects of Megalopolis, an urbanized section of the Atlantic seaboard of the United States stretching from Boston southward beyond Washington, D.C. Hance (1964) presented a regional examination of Africa, based on many years of study there. Camu and his associates (1964) produced a regional–systematic survey of the economic geography of Canada, introducing a multiple-criterion regional construct and several new ideas in regionalization, including the areal distribution of the total amount and types of capital investment. These and similar works have carried forward the continuing aspects of traditional economic geography as expressed regionally. In addition, as has been shown, many economic geographers have contributed to regional science and to regional economic development.

**Other viewpoints.** Economic geography is widely accepted outside the United States and Canada and generally is defined in terms already stated. The field is especially comprehensive in the Soviet Union, by definition virtually replacing human geography (Geograficheskoe Obshchestvo SSSR [1961] 1962, especially pp. 31–44). Under the stimuli of dialectical materialism and national development, economic and physical geographers of the Soviet Union have devoted close attention to pragmatic aspects of their respective subdivisions of the over-all discipline. A keen interest also exists in the Soviet Union in planning, particularly in the roles of theory and measurement. An emerging school of thought there holds that geography should not be compartmentalized but be considered as a unit—a view somewhat similar to Ackerman's concept of the discipline as a man–land system.

Europe and the United Kingdom have continued a long-standing interest in economic geography. German geographers have built on the work of

Thünen and Alfred Weber, fusing these studies with evaluations of management practices, enterprises, and land use to produce a well-founded inductive–deductive concept of the field (Otremba 1953). The term "applied geography" has come into use, particularly in France but also in other parts of Europe and, recently, in the International Geographical Union (Phlipponneau 1960). Although not limited to economic geography, applied geography stresses maximum efficiency in man's use of earth space. In the United Kingdom economic geographers have bridged the gap rather smoothly between the deductive and inductive approaches, providing valuable and well-written reviews that take cognizance of historical development (Estall & Buchanan 1961; Chisholm 1962). Planning is of long-standing interest to British economic geographers, and recent work evinces growth of theoretical work (Haggett 1965). In Scandinavia, notably Sweden, theoretical approaches have been utilized actively for a long time, although pragmatic work continues.

There are many examples in other countries of application of the approaches already mentioned. Qualitative interpretation frequently is a detailed inventory of available resources under specified conditions and cutoff limits. Classifications are becoming more numerous, and there is some experimentation with hypotheses.

No one of the three approaches in economic geography necessarily is superior to the others, and more work is urgently needed in all. As additional data become available and increasingly standardized internationally, classifications and theories probably will become more numerous and will be produced mainly by committee or team efforts. Qualitative interpretations by individuals, however, always will be necessary—not only to provide unusual stimuli and insights but also to bring together cogently the threads of complex ideas, a result that cannot be expected from anthologies.

RICHARD S. THOMAN

[See also CENTRAL PLACE; CONSERVATION; REGIONAL SCIENCE; TRANSPORTATION.]

### BIBLIOGRAPHY

ACKERMAN, EDWARD A. 1963 Where Is a Research Frontier? Association of American Geographers, *Annals* 53:429–440. → A logical argument for the process–system concept of geography as a nomothetic science.

ALEXANDERSSON, GUNNAR; and NÖRSTRÖM, GÖRAN 1963 *World Shipping: An Economic Geography of Ports and Seaborne Trade.* New York: Wiley. → A thorough assessment of ocean commerce and ports on a worldwide and regional basis.

CAMU, PIERRE; WEEKS, E. P.; and SAMETZ, Z. W. 1964 *Economic Geography of Canada.* Toronto: Macmillan. → An intriguing systematic and regional survey, using a 68-region classification developed over a ten-year period.

CHATTERJEE, SHIBA PRASAD 1964 *Fifty Years of Science in India: Progress of Geography.* Calcutta: Indian Science Congress Association. → Contains a detailed bibliography.

CHISHOLM, MICHAEL 1962 *Rural Settlement and Land Use: An Essay in Location.* London: Hutchinson's University Library. → An able presentation of theoretical approaches to agricultural geography, viewed at different levels of observation and in cognizance of technical change.

ESTALL, R. C.; and BUCHANAN, R. O. 1961 *Industrial Activity and Economic Geography.* London: Hutchinson's University Library. → An excellent survey of selected theoretical and pragmatic considerations, including government policy, in the location of industry.

GARRISON, WILLIAM L. 1959–1960 Spatial Structure of the Economy. Association of American Geographers, *Annals* 49:232–239, 471–482; 50:357–373. → An excellent review of trends and methods in theoretical economic geography.

GEOGRAFICHESKOE OBSHCHESTVO SSSR (1961) 1962 *Soviet Geography: Accomplishments and Tasks.* New York: American Geographical Society. → First published in Russian. A methodological statement by 56 leading Soviet geographers.

GINSBURG, NORTON S. (editor) 1961 *Atlas of Economic Development.* Univ. of Chicago Press. A careful interdisciplinary effort to map economies by specified criteria and, through factor analysis, by combinations of those indices.

GOTTMANN, JEAN (1961) 1964 *Megalopolis: The Urbanized Northeastern Seaboard of the United States.* Cambridge, Mass.: M.I.T. Press → An urban-economic evaluation of the nature of a continuous urbanized section of the eastern United States.

GRÖTEWALD, A. 1959 Von Thünen in Retrospect. *English Geography* 35:346–355.

HAGGETT, PETER (1965) 1966 *Locational Analysis in Human Geography.* New York: St. Martins.

HANCE, WILLIAM 1964 *The Geography of Modern Africa.* New York: Columbia Univ. Press.

HARRIS, CHAUNCY D. 1954 The Market as a Factor in the Localization of Industry in the United States. Association of American Geographers, *Annals* 44:315–348. → An evaluation of the role of market potential in industrial location, especially as expressed in numbers of people and associated sales less shipping charges from specified central places.

JAMES, PRESTON E.; and JONES, CLARENCE F. (editors) (1954 )1964 *American Geography: Inventory and Prospect.* Syracuse Univ. Press. → A survey of trends in geography during its first 50 years in the United States and of the status of geography at mid-century. See especially pages 3–68, 142–166, 240–332 and references in bibliographies to monographs by Richard Hartshorne.

JOHNSON, HILDEGARD B. 1962 A Note on Thünen's Circles. Association of American Geographers, *Annals* 52:213–220.

MURPHY, RAYMOND E.; and VANCE, J. E. JR. 1954 Delimiting the CBD. *Economic Geography* 30:189–222.

OTREMBA, ERICH 1953 *Allgemeine Agrar- und Indu-striegeographie.* Stuttgart (Germany): Franckh'sche Verlagshandlung. → Provides a thorough review of the development and mid-1950 status of economic geography in Germany, especially the German Federal Republic.

OTREMBA, ERICH 1957 *Allgemeine Geographie des Welt-handels und des Weltverkehrs.* Stuttgart (Germany): Franckh'sche Verlagshandlung.

PHLIPPONNEAU, MICHEL 1960 *Géographie et action: In-troduction à la géographie appliquée.* Paris: Colin. → Emphasis on the need for study of the functional region, with attention to planning.

TAAFFE, EDWARD J. 1962 The Urban Hierarchy: An Air Passenger Definition. *Economic Geography* 38:1–14. → An experiment in the use of a model to predict trends in air passenger traffic between major cities of the United States.

THOMAN, RICHARD S.; and CONKLING, EDGAR C. 1967 *Geography of International Trade.* Englewood Cliffs, N.J.: Prentice-Hall. → A survey of characteristics and trends in world trade by global, regional, and national patterns, and of the logistics and mechanics involved in such trade.

THÜNEN, JOHANN H. VON (1826–1863) 1930 *Der iso-lierte Staat in Beziehung auf Landwirtschaft und Nationalökonomie.* 3 vols. Jena (Germany): Fischer.

ULLMAN, EDWARD L. 1957 *American Commodity Flow: A Geographical Interpretation of Rail and Water Traffic Based on Principles of Spatial Interchange.* Seattle: Univ. of Washington Press.

WEAVER, JOHN C. 1954 Crop-combination Regions in the Middle West. *Geographical Review* 44:175–200. → A pioneer experiment in close measurement of crop combinations in terms of relative percentages of harvested land.

## IV
### CULTURAL GEOGRAPHY

Cultural geography as treated here is peculiar to American geography and can be understood as a complement to certain of the trends in American geography in the early part of this century. Cultural geography in a broader sense deals with any part of man's culture in the same way that plant geography deals with the distribution of plant species and vegetation or that economic geography is concerned with the production and distribution of goods and services. Cultural geography in the narrower sense used here is also characterized by certain cultural topics with which it deals, although its unifying thread is its manner of using the anthropological idea of culture to give meaning to its material. The tracing of continuity in space and time can help account for cultures and culture traits whose presence may not seem satisfactorily explained by their function in meeting overt ends. The subject matter of cultural geography has been winnowed by its need of such probing into origins. Cultural geography is not a self-sufficient field of study that produces all its own data and examines them as part of a closed system; it is rather an exchange in which data and interpretations from many sources are examined from one general point of view.

**Development.** Physiography was emphasized in the formative period of American geography, which occurred around the turn of the century. The first human geography then admitted inquiry into selected relationships between man and his physical environment. Later, concern with the productive capacities of the land came to be coupled with the growth of an economic geography that concentrated on production and trade. Economic geographers either assumed or looked for a functionalism or an adherence to economic laws that assured efficiency.

Carl Sauer (1925; 1931) outlined a new cultural geography dealing with those elements of material culture that give character to area through being "inscribed into the earth's surface." The focus was to be on those works of man rather than on man himself. The study was to be empirical and historical, without preference for environmental or any other selected class of explanation. The elements studied were to be broadly economic as well as material, although Sauer (1941) was later to expand their scope.

Sauer's proposals produced, first, a general change in the direction of American geography and, later, the more special cultural geography, whose early growth was chiefly through his own students. This cultural geography has increasingly occupied the territory its name and rationale have staked out; its content has been limited chiefly by what other fields have previously claimed.

European geography contributes a great portion of the material of cultural geography, especially in dealing with Europe's own rich heritage, but mostly under the heading of a general human geography or a less inclusive social geography. The models for Sauer's program were heavily German, especially Friedrich Ratzel's work on culture spread, Eduard Hahn's work on agricultural development, and regional studies focused on settlement history. *Kulturgeographie* continues as a broad division of geography in Germany, where the modern idea of culture developed, but it does not parallel the American cultural geography as a specific hub for the swapping of ideas (National Research Council . . . 1965). The absence of a recognized cultural geography in Britain and France is hardly surprising, for the culture concept is less used in those countries (the *genre de vie* of Vidal de la Blache is similar in use but much less inclusive).

**Content.** Most studies in cultural geography develop one or more of the following subjects:

*The growth of man's exploitation of his habitat.*
The study of man's use of his environment includes such topics as the early use of tools and implements, domestication of plants and animals, and the various economies of food production. Human development and human invention both have geographic dimensions in that they are composed of specific events occurring in specific places. The geographer's concern with both the spatial arrangement and the qualities of habitats qualifies him for taking part in the reconstruction of man's past as well as in the understanding of the present. The cultural geographer's interest in the past begins with the beginning of man and follows his wanderings with ever more cultural equipment into new surroundings (Sauer 1952).

Archeology, history, physical geography, and field observation provide much of the raw material for work in this field. Archeology and history, each limited by its sources of data, must remain incomplete records. Cultural geography often asks questions they are least likely to have answered. Thus, many early chapters in man's growth can at best be speculative theories that may remain unverified.

*Physical change induced on the surface of the earth by man.*   Man's material advance leaves its mark on the earth he works. Physical change may be an inadvertent product of man's use of the land: soil erosion induced by cultivation, soil enrichment around human habitations, and vegetation change induced by grazing or burning. It may be a deliberate change, such as the clearing of woods or terracing of hillsides for farming (Spencer & Hale 1961). The actions of man and nature have been of such duration and of such intermixture as to be often no longer separable.

American concern with man's part in the processes of physical geography dates from George P. Marsh's writing, in 1864, of *Man and Nature.* A more recent study, *Man's Role in Changing the Face of the Earth* (International Symposium . . . 1956), explores the earth as the imprint of man's way of life, as a record of his past, and as a material resource for the present and future. The processes that explain the past may serve as guides for the future.

*Settlement forms—rural and urban.*   Settlement forms make up a large part of the features of the man-made landscape. Study of rural settlement has dealt mostly with house types, the arrangement of houses and other structures in relation to each other and to road networks, and the arrangement of fields. Although the settlement of the United States is recent, the history of its house forms is already partly lost, and tracing them is difficult

(Kniffen 1965). The settlement patterns, more easily reconstructed, have converged on variations of the isolated farmstead. For most of Anglo–America the field pattern had to fit the rectangular survey; older areas show the confusion of metes and bounds, but traditional patterns survive, particularly in the old French riverine settlements. Reconstruction of the history of American settlement forms has not proceeded nearly so far as the inventorylike studies of rural patterns in Germany or of rural houses in Italy. Even where inventories are thorough, the forms have resisted satisfactory explanatory generalization.

American geographers have done relatively little with urban settlement forms. Enticing opportunities for study may be found in regionally dominant town and city plans, the pattern of street and lot layout, and cross-city comparison of house types, building materials, and architectural styles.

*Nonmaterial culture, such as language and religion.*   Languages are considered the most reliable ethnic tracers, since the arbitrary choosing of words from a very large pool makes accidental repetition most improbable. Further, language, as a means and a mark of intercommunication, is a maker and a product of group cohesion and, hence, of cultures. Analysis of languages and their distributions has usually been the work of the specialist, but the results are widely used in geography. Toponyms are components of language that are very close to geography because of their fixture on the land and their frequent reference to its qualities.

Religion, also a conservative marker of peoples, is a social institution with significant spatial structure and a molder of the cultural landscape. Geography deals with religion in ways that range from the distribution of specific religions to the expression of a primal sense of order in the landscape—for example, orientation of streets or property lines with the compass (Isaac 1965).

*Origin and spread of cultures and civilizations.*
The spread of culture is most simply studied through particular culture traits, but often an entire complex of culture traits may be welded together by a powerful or influential people and spread over a wide area in relatively uniform fashion. A way of living or a civilization may be traced from its inception to its expansion into a greater territorial base, until finally it reaches its limits and is absorbed or replaced by another expanding culture. The growth of potamic civilizations from their home in Mesopotamia, the growth of the Chinese nation from its culture hearth in the Wei Valley, or the grafting of the Marxist politico–economic complex onto a variety of cul-

tural trunks in the past fifty years would be suitable subjects for such analysis.

Geographers have treated cultures in a variety of ways, such as dividing the world into major culture regions (Russell & Kniffen 1951), examining the development of cultures and subcultures, mapping the core and fringe areas of cultures (Meinig 1965), and studying culture islands.

*Cultural evaluation of the environment.* The favorite theories of geography are often themselves generalized evaluations of environment. Their change with the passage of time is evidence that they too, however reasoned, are part and parcel of changing culture. What man does with his natural resources depends on his technology, on his perception of his natural resources and of his place among them, and on a complex of values concerning the present and future. Clarence Glacken (1956) has studied man's place in nature from the viewpoint of changes in Western ideas about the habitable world. Non-Western conceptions, as shaped by cosmologies, modified by experience, and revealed in language, are also essential to interpretation of living patterns (Lowenthal 1961).

The environment may be graded in aesthetic terms. Modification of the landscape, including the productive portion of the landscape, may then be guided by aesthetic senses and axioms. Yet the perception of the environment and the responses to environmental stimuli are probably not purely cultural. Sonnenfeld (1965) has asserted the need for isolating the noncultural parts of the behavior that relate to the environment and effect the shaping of the landscape. To do so would better sort the variables with which the cultural geographer deals and would clarify his ideas of causality.

**Purposes.**    Many studies are undertaken to provide factual answers to specific questions. Some studies are primarily in the geographical tradition of exploration; these include many of the regional inquiries in cultural geography (e.g., Wagner 1958) as well as more specific data-collecting trips (e.g., Zelinsky 1958). Other studies seek links in the solution of specified larger problems, be they geographic in nature or otherwise. A major theme of Kniffen's work has been the use of a particular culture trait as an index to migration and diffusion and the culture regions they shape.

H. C. Brookfield (1964), in a thoughtful critique of American cultural geography, noted its frequent reluctance to compare, generalize, or explain, especially if doing so meant going into social organization or social attitudes. American cultural geographers have often preferred to focus their immediate interest on filling selected gaps in knowledge

rather than on using the material gained primarily as a means to further the abstract concepts of the field. There are advantages in developing a reliable body of elaborated description relatively free of the data selection that would be suitable for testing prechosen abstractions. However, cultural geography should also work ahead with generalization as fast as the data and advance of theory permit. Some division of labor may optimize the exchange between description and abstraction.

Purposes of scholarly study are often indeterminate. Idle curiosity may impel the investigator, even while specific hope of practical application accounts for his financial support. Many of the world's problems are not abstract generalizations but are stresses that arise from unique local conditions. A geography that views every place as *sui generis* is a likely source of help. The theme of man's use of his environment, enmeshed in most of cultural geography, gives geography its widest views and most likely application on a world scale. Certainly the cultural geographer is not much drawn to his study by the hope of immediate application, even though it is with past and present application that he constantly deals. Rather he is lured on by the prospect of a better articulated view of man's work and works in their terrestrial frame.

**Methods.**    Studies of small areas are most likely to depend for their data on field observation. Those on a world-wide scale necessarily depend on secondary sources. Spatial and chronological analysis of the data often form the logical core of the study. The former seeks simplification through the demonstration of spatial order or pattern; the latter emphasizes change in historical depth or the more detailed sequence of change known as process.

Spatial arrangement of data is an essential characteristic of geography. The map is the visual means of arranging the data in its spatial order. (*To spread out* or *to unfold* in this manner approximates the literal meanings of *explanare* and *explicare*, bases for the verb *explain* in English and the modern Latin languages). Mapping the distribution of a culture trait or complex does not constitute an explanation, but it leads to hypotheses as to how the culture trait developed. One common method of map interpretation is to seek correlative distributions that may also be causal associations. A second method is to treat the distribution as a changing product of diffusion and extinction and to seek the conditions that have governed the changes (Zelinsky 1958; Spencer & Hale 1961). An isochronic map is useful in combining both temporal and spatial analysis.

Chronological arrangement of data is essential

to the study of culture. The conservative nature of culture, which follows earlier models even in the process of change, encourages one to study it by tracing its continuity. If a device is not demonstrably functional in every aspect of its design, it may be explained genetically by tracing its origins and movements. John Leighly emphasized this type of cultural explanation in his proposal for a study of the tangible works of man in the landscape in the terms of art history, stressing "the essential time-bond of culture rather than its looser place-bond" (1937, p. 135). The culture concept provides a means of giving intelligibility to what, at least to people removed from the particular cultural context, seems irrational.

Plumbing the basic reasons for cultural choices may provide a functional explanation of what was once considered irrational. Cultural geography would become less dependent on genetic explanation as its mainstay to the extent that culture change—or lack of it—could be explained in terms of human satisfactions. Predictions of the direction of culture change will lead to more application of the findings of cultural geography. Any theory of culture change could have a corresponding theory of cultural geography as the spatial expression of the change. Uses of the culture concept in regional study by geographers and anthropologists have been considered by Thomas (1957).

A battery of general methods is summed up by Wagner and Mikesell (1962, p. 24): "Who? Where? What? When? and How? The themes of culture, culture area, cultural landscape, culture history, and cultural ecology respond to these queries." The themes imply cross sections of investigation, most of them with conceptual dimensions rather than geometrical ones as in the case of the map. Since cultural geography deals with such a great range of phenomena, its methods must also be varied.

**Persistent questions.** The objects of study in cultural geography may be seen as forms—abstract or concrete, single or complex. Many of the general questions of cultural geography hinge on the derivation of these forms, which is variously sought in environment, function, ideology, technology, ornamentation, previous forms, and the chances of invention and accident. The derivation of one form does not necessarily serve as a model for the derivation of others.

*The role of the physical environment.* Cultural geography can deal with man's relations with his physical environment at any depth of understanding of this environment. Sauer's work with early man leaned heavily on assessments of environmental change and of environmental opportunity to supply gaps in the a posteriori record. On the other

hand, the continuity of culture can be traced over the earth without attention to the physical environments through which the culture spread, although to do so is to ignore a part of the possible explanation.

The reaction against environmental determinism (the doctrine that the physical environment determines the way in which man lives in an area) has united with a culturally oriented geography to produce a new geographic etiology that stresses cultural determinism (a doctrine that emphasizes the role of culture as opposed to that of the environment). One statement of cultural determinism is that culture determines what the environment means to man. An even stronger position holds that man's perception of the environment is all that matters about the physical environment; since perception is culturally controlled, explanation of human behavior is then deemed to be cultural. Cultural determinism presents useful views of the continuity of culture growth, but is less successful as an analysis of cause (a precursor without which the result would have been different). One must remember, first, that perception, by its definition, is not merely hallucination (i.e., independent of external stimulus) and, second, that the environment may not respond to man's management in just the way his perception of it orders.

The difficulties of the man–nature and culture–environment dichotomies are sometimes dissolved in union. Man is often conveniently viewed as a part of nature. Man, culture, and environment in a land have been treated as one in sketches of regional "personality."

*Form versus function.* What part does function play in cultural design and what part do previous forms play? How fast do forms change to conform to changing needs? Are forms also molded by aesthetic considerations? A barn is built for certain purposes, and a given design is likely to be retained only so long as it fulfills its function reasonably well. But the differences between two barns performing the same functions must be explained on some other basis. Even if the differing features mirror cultural traditions, they may still have originated in functions of other times and other places. Purely decorative features, too, sometimes originate in function. Relic forms may continue to be built or may survive in structures that have outlived their original functions. Whether function or form is stressed in any particular comparison may depend on whether the similarities or the differences are sought.

*Form and ideals.* A simple feature in the landscape, say a post, serves its function and reflects some particular post-making tradition. It probably has no particular relation to the ethos or set of ideals of the people who use it. A more complicated form with a more complicated function, say the physical form of the village or community built to facilitate a way of living, is more likely to reflect the distinctiveness of that way of living or of the ideals that lie behind it. An ascetic people, not given to social intercourse, probably would not provide their town with plazas and esplanades or decorate it in bright colors. The few geographic studies that deal specifically with form in relation to ideology suggest that rather different peoples may adopt the same readily available forms for the same overt purposes. An account of a Dutch Reformed settlement in Michigan (Bjorklund 1964) tells how immigrants largely gave up their old forms in favor of the common American forms, but it also shows how the American forms still conformed to the old ideology. If identical forms conform to different ideologies, we must assume that the differing peoples see the forms as fulfilling different inner functions and gain different satisfactions from them. In another study Philip Wagner concludes: "Nicoya suggests that thoroughgoing transformations in the social sphere may sometimes produce only moderate variations in technology and landscape, and thus that two or more very dissimilar societies may differ little in the way they conceive and utilize a given habitat" (1958, p. 248). Conversely, peoples with similar ideologies are likely to evolve different community forms for their living. Inquiry into the regulation of form by ideals should be carried further.

*Forms of distributions.* The forms of distributions are also subject to systematization. The significance of continuous and discontinuous distributions, the relation of area of origin to area of greatest intensity, or the persistence of the core area of a culture region are all aspects of the structure or form of culture areas.

**Relation to other fields.** Historical geography is the division of geography most closely related to cultural geography. The two complement each other in a cultural–historical geography, in which history provides the explanation of culture and culture provides the organizing concept for the subjects of most geographic interest in history. Historical geography can stand alone, however, for it is often not organized around the culture concept. On the other hand, culture is always dependent on the past for its explanation.

Economic geography and cultural geography could go separate ways as long as one depended primarily on economic laws for its explanation while the other depended on the patterns of the past. But an entire system of economic laws may

be found to be a culture complex that has evolved somewhat accidentally and not in an inescapable mesh of cosmic law. Even in our market economy the prices bid for goods may be but expressions of cultural preference (for example, the American preference for corn-fed ham versus the European for barley-fed). And within a changing economy new institutions, products, and types of enterprise originate and diffuse in a fashion suggestive of the culture traits that they are. On the other hand, the relevant economic laws are also necessary parts of the cultural explanation. Thus, economic and cultural geography join in any broad view of the two fields.

Political geography, like economic geography, is supported by an independent discipline that has its own laws (although less precise), and its systems fulfill stated functions. A nation represents an idea that had an origin and has been spread with some show of power to the borders of the land. The generic idea of nation is again a cultural concept that had an origin and a diffusion that just now seems about to complete the circuit of the earth. Each nation depends on a community of interests, often including such culture traits as a national language and religion. The behavior of its voters, too, reflects persistent patterns in its regional culture.

Cities have both economic and political dimensions, although the economic has loomed larger in urban geographical studies. City planning and urban sociology are cognate disciplines that help provide the rationale for an independent urban geography. At the same time, cities are concentrations of culture that are very sensitive to cultural differences. Internally, the distribution of subcultures within a complex city and the city landscape are equally concerns of cultural geography. Externally, urban functions and rural–urban attitudes vary from culture to culture.

The mathematical formulations now popular in economic and urban studies will be most successful if they can describe the regularities and implications of cultural behavior. Swedish studies have originated quantitative analysis of culture transmission and have attempted to simulate both its rational and random qualities.

The idea of culture provides a frame into which man-made functional systems fit. The narrower cultural geography and the fields that deal with the functional systems that are also a part of culture can fuse into a broader cultural geography in which the culture concept constantly insists on a proper relativity in time and space. Grasp of the concepts of culture and cultures is perhaps the quickest route to a viewpoint not entirely bound by one's own culture and from which one can even see one's own culture in some perspective. Culture is a fit mediator in a study whose point of departure is the comparison of different peoples and lands.

EDWARD T. PRICE

[*Other relevant material may be found in* CARTOGRAPHY; CULTURE; ENVIRONMENTALISM; LANDSCAPE; *and in the biographies of* MARSH; RATZEL; SAUER; VIDAL DE LA BLACHE.]

### BIBLIOGRAPHY

BJORKLUND, ELAINE M. 1964 Ideology and Culture Exemplified in Southwestern Michigan. Association of American Geographers, *Annals* 54:227–241.

BROOKFIELD, H. C. 1964 Questions on the Human Frontiers of Geography. *Economic Geography* 40:283–303.

GLACKEN, CLARENCE J. 1956 Changing Ideas of the Habitable World. Pages 70–92 in International Symposium on Man's Role in Changing the Face of the Earth, Princeton, N.J., 1955, *Man's Role in Changing the Face of the Earth.* Edited by William L. Thomas et al. Univ. of Chicago Press.

INTERNATIONAL SYMPOSIUM ON MAN'S ROLE IN CHANGING THE FACE OF THE EARTH, PRINCETON, N.J., *1955* 1956 *Man's Role in Changing the Face of the Earth.* Edited by William L. Thomas et al. Univ. of Chicago Press.

ISAAC, ERICH 1965 Religious Geography and the Geography of Religion. Pages 1–14 in *Man and Earth.* Series in Earth Sciences, No. 3. Boulder: Univ. of Colorado.

KNIFFEN, FRED 1965 Folk Housing: Key to Diffusion. Association of American Geographers, *Annals* 55: 549–577.

LEIGHLY, JOHN B. 1937 Some Comments on Contemporary Geographic Method. Association of American Geographers, *Annals* 27:125–141.

LOWENTHAL, DAVID 1961 Geography, Experience, and Imagination: Towards a Geographical Epistemology. Association of American Geographers, *Annals* 51:241–260.

MARSH, GEORGE P. (1864) 1965 *Man and Nature: Or, Physical Geography as Modified by Human Action.* Edited by David Lowenthal. Cambridge, Mass.: Harvard Univ. Press.

MEINIG, D. W. 1965 The Mormon Culture Region: Strategies and Patterns in the Geography of the American West, 1847–1964. Association of American Geographers, *Annals* 55:191–220.

NATIONAL RESEARCH COUNCIL, AD HOC COMMITTEE ON GEOGRAPHY 1965 *The Science of Geography: Report.* National Research Council Publication No. 1277. Washington: National Academy of Sciences–National Research Council.

RUSSELL, RICHARD; and KNIFFEN, FRED B. 1951 *Culture Worlds.* New York: Macmillan.

SAUER, CARL O. (1915–1962) 1963 *Land and Life: A Selection From the Writings of Carl Ortwin Sauer.* Edited by John Leighly. Berkeley: Univ. of California Press.

SAUER, CARL O. (1925) 1963 The Morphology of Landscape. Pages 315–350 in Carl O. Sauer, *Land and Life: A Selection From the Writings of Carl Ortwin Sauer.* Berkeley: Univ. of California Press.

SAUER, CARL O. (1931) 1962 Cultural Geography. Pages 30–34 in Philip L. Wagner and Marvin W. Mikesell (editors), *Readings in Cultural Geography.* Univ. of Chicago Press. → First published in Volume 6 of the *Encyclopaedia of the Social Sciences.*

SAUER, CARL O. (1941) 1963 Foreword to Historical Geography. Pages 351–379 in Carl O. Sauer, *Land and Life: A Selection From the Writings of Carl Ortwin Sauer.* Berkeley: Univ. of California Press. → First published in Volume 31 of the Association of American Geographers, *Annals.*

SAUER, CARL O. 1952 *Agricultural Origins and Dispersals.* New York: American Geographical Society.

SONNENFELD, JOSEPH 1965 A Behavioral Approach to Cultural Geography. Pages 10–18 in Discussion Papers in Cultural Geography. Unpublished manuscript. → Prepared for the 61st annual meeting of the Association of American Geographers, Columbus, Ohio.

SPENCER, J. E.; and HALE, G. A. 1961 The Origin, Nature, and Distribution of Agricultural Terracing. *Pacific Viewpoint* 2:1–40.

THOMAS, WILLIAM L. JR. 1957 *Land, Man and Culture in Mainland Southeast Asia.* Glen Rock, N.J.: Privately published.

WAGNER, PHILIP L. 1958 *Nicoya: A Cultural Geography.* University of California Publications in Geography, Vol. 12. Berkeley: Univ. of California Press.

WAGNER, PHILIP L.; and MIKESELL, MARVIN W. (editors) 1962 *Readings in Cultural Geography.* Univ. of Chicago Press.

ZELINSKY, WILBUR 1958 The New England Connecting Barn. *Geographical Review* 48:540–553.

# V

## SOCIAL GEOGRAPHY

No generally accepted definition of social geography exists. The variety of literature which has appeared under the title of social geography is astounding; even within particular schools there are wide disparities of approach and definition. With some notable exceptions, for example, in Sweden and Holland, social geography can be considered a field created and cultivated by a number of individual scholars rather than an academic tradition built up within particular schools. Furthermore, for many people the term "social geography" itself is in disfavor because of its past association with various forms of determinism that postulated a causal connection between society and the geographical environment.

Perhaps, therefore, the best way to examine social geography is to establish a general theoretical outline of the field and, on this basis, to review the existing literature. Naturally, many of the works relevant to what is here called social geography will have been written as contributions to some other discipline.

The argument that social geography is a necessary discipline can be made in at least two ways. One is by analogy with other, better established branches of geography. A widely accepted definition of "human geography" is that it deals with mankind in the context of his total geographical milieu. For the purposes of analysis this milieu has been subdivided into separate categories corresponding to various orders of human activity, for example, the economic, the political, and the cultural. Therefore, one could postulate that social geography is the subdivision of geography that deals specifically with the social order, or that it is the systematic study of the social dimension in areal differentiation.

An alternative way is to begin with the definition of geography as the study of similarities and contrasts between places on the face of the earth. Society, that is, social organization and values, patterns of social movement and interaction, and social dynamics and change, plays such an important role in producing similarities and contrasts between places on the earth that it justifies systematic consideration within the discipline.

The question immediately arises as to how to isolate this social dimension for independent study. In fact, since human activities characteristically are group activities, how can human geography be anything else but social? The virtually interchangeable use of the terms "human" and "social" by several geographers in the British and Dutch schools serves to emphasize the logical (and etymological) basis for this question. Yet, although in the evolution of human geography emphasis has been placed in varying degrees on purely social elements—and although languages, races, and religions have rarely been excluded from consideration—the function of these social elements in the total conceptual framework has not been very clear. In fact, the idea that such social elements could be systematized into a general framework for geographical analysis has been only recently proposed (Bobek 1959; van Paassen 1965).

There are two primary questions social geography must answer: How do mankind's social characteristics vary through space? How do these characteristics affect (or reflect) man's adaptation to and adaptation of his total geographical milieu? Since such questions touch every aspect of human geography, it is difficult to conceive of social geography as a separate field. Its distinctive feature would thus appear to lie more in its focus and objectives than in any clearly delineated subject matter. In practical terms, the traditional twofold method of geography can be applied to these central questions in the following way: by the examination of spatial variations in the distribution and interaction of social groups within their total geographical milieus and by the examination of dif-

ferential patterns of society's use of the earth, as indicated in settlement forms, livelihoods, circulation networks, and land use patterns. While the first method implies a morphological or formal study of world social patterns, the second method implies a functional interpretation of such patterns in terms of their underlying social processes.

Having thus outlined, in broad terms, the place and function of social geography, let us now see how these fundamental questions have been studied in the past. From such a general and necessarily eclectic survey we may discern some of the major conceptual and technical ingredients from which a definition of social geography can be formulated.

## The development of social geography

Studies explicitly or implicitly directed toward the exploration of social geography can be considered under two broad headings: first, the historical precedents, which fall roughly into three major stages, each one characterized by a different approach; and second, the works of twentieth-century geographers.

**Historical precedents.** Descriptive reports written by explorers and men of letters during classical times, for example, the writings of Herodotus, Thucydides, Strabo, and others, provide the first written recognition of world social differences. Such encyclopedic descriptions continued to appear intermittently in the Occident up to the seventeenth century, for example, the accounts of Marco Polo and the *lettres édifiantes* of Jesuit missionaries. The twofold implication of these works was that social life takes various forms in different parts of the world and that these differences are caused by, or at least are associated with, differences in the physical—particularly climatic—environment.

A second phase consisted of the various philosophical reflections on these and later geographical discoveries. On the one hand, speculative thinkers sought normative principles for an ideal social order from natural law, and, on the other hand, the positivists insisted that such principles should be sought in the existing and empirically observable conditions of society. The essential message of this second phase was that there is a rational order in world society and that this order can be discovered deductively (speculative approach) or inductively (positivistic approach).

A third and far more significant phase began in the nineteenth century, accompanied in France by the emergence of the idea of democracy, in Germany by the rise of national consciousness, and elsewhere by the slow yet effective permeation of a "scientific" approach to knowledge. Ethnographers and historians were among the first to study world social variations in a systematic way. As early as 1725 Giambattista Vico suggested that human development followed an identical series of stages and that the actual variations in world society at any particular time were due to their differential positions within that series. Later in the eighteenth century, Johann Gottfried Herder in Germany and Condorcet in France expressed similar ideas. The geographer Johann Georg Kohl examined the social function and significance of various settlement types; later, his colleague E. Hahn (1896) studied the evolution of livelihoods and demonstrated the religious and social origins of some economic practices. Yet this "scientific" approach to the study of mankind's social differences was also associated with exaggerated single-factor explanations, for example, the biological interpretation first expounded by A. Schäffle (1875–1878) and the psychological interpretation, which found its fullest expression in the Durkheimian school in France. Friedrich Ratzel's *Anthropogeographie* (1882–1891) incorporated both these elements: the ecological view of society within its natural environment and the role of human intelligence (the "idea") in enabling man to overcome physical barriers (1901). Unfortunately, the latter perspective did not emerge too clearly in his monumental work—on which the whole tradition of anthropogeography has been patterned—and so his name has been linked with the idea of society being determined by the physical environment. His *Politische Geographie* (1897) and some articles (1876; 1901) in fact contained hypotheses that were far more relevant to social geography than the *Anthropogeographie*.

One of the most significant precedents to social geography in the nineteenth century was the work of Frédéric Le Play. Disdainful of the various a priori explanations of society prevalent in his day, he set out to study the actual social conditions of worker families in France. His famous monograph technique produced an encyclopedic inventory of social facts, and from a great number of studies he deduced certain basic types, which then served as bases for comparison. Traces of Le Play's analytical formula *lieu–travail–famille*, later adapted by Geddes (1915) into the formula "place–work–folk," can be found in the writings of such early British geographers as H. J. Fleure (1918). French geographers inherited important elements from Le Play, for example, the monograph technique in empirical field studies, but the most important legacy of *lieu–travail–famille* was the social survey movement, which flourished in Britain and America during the early part of the century.

Many geographers, such as Ritter, von Humboldt, Hassinger, Ruhl, and Hettner in Germany, Reclus in France, George Perkins Marsh in America, and H. J. Mackinder in Britain, deserve recognition as pioneers of social geography. However, the three major channels of thought that contained the most useful concepts were those initiated by Le Play (the social survey movement), Ratzel (anthropogeography), and Durkheim (social morphology).

**Twentieth-century social geographers.** The mutual relations of society and environment was a subject that aroused great speculation and interest at the turn of the century. Yet there was no discipline equipped to embrace the entire question. Ratzel had made an abortive attempt to do so, and his environmentalist disciples exaggerated rather than corrected the deterministic premise of anthropogeography. Many scholars, particularly the Durkheimian sociologists, remained unconvinced that geography had any right to entertain such a monumental task.

At this juncture came one of geography's greatest entrepreneurs, Paul Vidal de la Blache. Society for Vidal (1896; 1902) and his school could not be explained entirely in terms of biological, psychological, or environmental interpretations. It was rather an intricate network of ideas and bonds that provided stability and orientation to human life within particular geographical milieus. In his classical studies of the Mediterranean world and of monsoon Asia (1917–1918), Vidal demonstrated the complex, yet harmoniously balanced, interplay between human institutions and particular natural settings. *Genres de vie* (literally, patterns of living) were the concrete expressions of a society's ongoing contact with nature: sets of techniques, cemented through tradition, whereby human groups secured the material necessities of life within a functional social order (Vidal 1911; Sorre 1948). Repeated experiences in meeting life's common problems within a particular geographical milieu occasioned the development of community consciousness, which made a *genre de vie* truly an ecological system. Variations of this basic concept appear in the literature of other disciplines, for example, social anthropology (Kroeber & Kluckhohn 1952; Redfield 1955), American human ecology (McKenzie 1934) and urban sociology (Park & Burgess 1921). By means of *genre de vie* and other concepts, the French school of human geography replaced the exaggerated Ratzelian notions of environmental determinism by the more elastic concepts of possibilism and dismissed the charges made in the *Année sociologique* between 1890 and 1910 more by substantive works than by theoretical arguments. "La géographie humaine," thus formulated, was a social geography in the broad, integral sense: all other dimensions of the human milieu were studied from the vantage point of society. Many British and American human geographers followed almost identical lines, while the Dutch "sociale geografie" was the direct equivalent of the French "géographie humaine." The kernel of this orientation, namely, society as the source and framework for all human activity, reappears in the work of Hans Bobek (1959) in Vienna. Lucien Febvre's famous apologia (1922) articulated the philosophical and historical *raison d'être* of such a discipline.

To Vidal's essentially ecological approach, his disciple Jean Brunhes added the important dimension of group psychology, asking, for example, why similar environments were used in entirely different ways at different periods in history. He defined social geography as the third level of complexity in human geography's fourfold structure. The fourfold structure included the primary groups of family, kin, and culture; the secondary groupings of livelihood and special interest; the various forms of spatial interaction within and among these groups; and, finally, the legal systems which institutionalize a society's subdivision and access to land and property ([1910] 1924, pp. 36–46). This definition, admirably suited to the study of European—particularly French—rural society of the early twentieth century, remained the basic framework for social geography among British, French, and Dutch scholars up to World War II. Most of the early studies in social geography were regional in character, and their excellence consisted more in their artistic cohesion and integrative descriptions than in their analytical or theoretical expertise. The empirical conditions which favored the use of the regional framework by French scholars did not exist to the same extent elsewhere; this partly explains the divergence of orientation and method which developed among the various schools of human geography.

During the 1930s, British social geographers were involved in methodological controversy. Does social geography consist in merely mapping mankind's social characteristics, or must it also analyze the processes involved in relating a society to its geographical environment? What is the relation between social geography and human ecology? Why not replace the term "human" by "social" as the generic term to signify all the nonphysical aspects of geography?

The fundamental dichotomy between a formal and functional approach expressed in this British debate reiterated the duality that had developed in Holland since the 1920s. While at Utrecht the study of social groups within their territorial framework (de Vooys 1950) was being pursued along the lines of the French school, at Amsterdam Steinmetz' "sociography" was used to study the entire social content of space as a system in itself —aside from any considerations of a group's relation to its natural environment. The birth of sociology in Holland—particularly rural sociology as a separate discipline—has no doubt modified the original disciplinary orientations of these two schools (van Paassen 1965).

Prior to World War II little attempt was made to systematize the elements of social geography. In general, the important associations evident in the spatial organization of society—particularly in the United States—appeared in the literature of human ecology (Theodorson 1961) and urban sociology (Park & Burgess 1921). One major exception, of course, was the work of the environmentalists in examining connections between human behavior and the geographical environment (Thomas 1925).

Pierre George and Maximilien Sorre (1943–1953) were the first great systematizers of social geography. In George's works a close link is maintained between social and economic aspects of human behavior, the social being one facet of the economic (1946, p. 1). For Sorre (1948, pp. 13–16, 66–122) society represented a system of techniques—family and kinship systems, livelihoods (*genres de vie*), languages, and religions, each one having a specific influence on the spatial organization of mankind and his work. Sorre's schema does not make clear, however, whether social geography consists of a series of systematic subfields based on these various kinds of techniques, or whether a distinction is to be made between the "social" and "political" techniques. In his work all forms of organization from family and kin groups to giant political blocs form a continuum (1961, pp. 211–264). Gourou's more comprehensive concept of *civilisation* (1964) comprises both material techniques (modes of production) and spiritual techniques (ideas, values). These three approaches at generalization are important because they try to maintain the integral and holistic character of social geography at the same time that they establish some order and a basis for comparative work. Bobek has made a similar attempt to construct a spatiotemporal framework for world society (1959). His work is a fertile synthesis of French and German traditions: his systematic framework is based on a holistic approach involving types of societies defined in terms of their actual use of their geographical environment (1961).

Several other attempts to formulate the problem of society in geography in terms of a particular systematic framework have appeared: for example, those of Wagner (1960), Ackerman (1963), and van Paassen (1965). Yet more characteristic of postwar work is the development of individual systematic lines of enquiry, for example, geography of rural and urban life, population studies, and geography of religions and political behavior. Associated with this is a more lively *va-et-vient* between geographers and scholars in other disciplines, particularly concerning questions of rural and urban life (Friedmann 1953) and regional planning (Phlipponneau 1960). Studies are still being made within a regional framework, but the focus has changed. Juillard in Alsace (1953) studied particular social problems from a regional perspective, while Rochefort in Sicily (1961) studied regional life from the perspective of the social processes at work. Such reorientations have, of course, raised new methodological problems and prospects. Chatelain (1947; 1953), for example, postulates a duality between the geography of social classes (a kind of social morphology) and the geography of social life (a sociological geography). Claval (1964) envisions the latter as the most feasible future direction for the discipline, citing the work of W. Hartke at Munich as an example. It is difficult, however, to see how these two aspects of the field can be separated.

To label the research being done at Munich as sociological geography may be misleading. Certainly the perspective is social: social-geographic differentiation (*sozialgeographische Differenzierung*) implies that social values—as expressed in the occupational structure—are the primary agents of landscape differentiation. Thus, maps of socioprofessional structure (*Sozialkartierung*) for a series of periods are collated with a corresponding series of land-use patterns (*Nutzflächenkartierung*), and significant associations are sought. This basic formula has been applied successfully both in rural and urban contexts. Geipel's study (1952) of one German region, for example, demonstrated that the sources of regional unity—which varied at different periods—are found essentially in the collective decision-making mechanism of the regional community. This is quite a contrast to the sources of regional unity commonly sought in the natural (physiographic) or economic (agricultural) landscape. Hartke (1956) demonstrated that regions where this phenomenon existed had similar geographic (regional) characteristics. Associations found in urban studies are even more interesting. Hartke's intraurban corridors (*Passagen*) suggest some qualifications to the traditional concentric zone and sector theories of urban structure, while his study of urban expansion

patterns provides new bases for the classification of cities (1961).

In marked contrast to the inductive, empirical, and microscopic approach of the Munich social geographers is the more highly developed theoretical and deductive approach found in Sweden. Torsten Hägerstrand (1952) and Sven Godlund (1956) have applied refined mathematical techniques to the study of migration, rural–urban interaction, circulation, and other dynamic aspects of the field. One of the most interesting developments has been the use of simulation models for the analysis and prediction of spatial movement.

This approach has been adopted and modified in the postwar period by a number of American geographers. At Iowa spatial models have been used to study the distribution patterns of schools, churches, and settlements, often with a view to spatial planning. Morrill's study of Swedish towns (1963) exemplifies this approach. Yet, in general, social geography in the United States is not a unified field: on the one hand there are holistic regional studies, for example, Platt's Saarland study (1961) and Broek's southeast Asian study (1944), and, on the other hand, there are a growing number of systematic studies in racial, linguistic, religious, and other spheres. Some interesting associations have been elaborated, for example, between religion, land use, and livelihood (Isaac 1959), between cultural pluralism and political integration (Lowenthal 1961), and between migration and political behavior within ethnic groups (Lewis 1965). However, the exciting developments in the actual social geography of America have been treated mainly by foreigners (Gottmann 1961) or by scholars in other disciplines.

**Résumé of contemporary social geography.** In general, the empirical record would seem to characterize social geography as a multifaceted perspective on the spatial organization of mankind. The implication is that some important sources of areal differentiation emanate from society, thus reversing the premises of anthropogeography and other deterministic explanations of social differentiation. Analysis of this social dimension in human geography has involved two basic approaches: the examination of the formal distributions of social phenomena as indices of areal differentiation and the interpretation of these distributions in the light of their underlying social processes. A recent development, particularly in northwestern Europe, is the involvement of social geographers in interdisciplinary research and regional planning.

Nevertheless, the social dimension is one of the least studied aspects of human geography. Social geography lacks definite boundaries and has neither a central unifying concept nor even an agreed content. Instead, there are scattered individual efforts to analyze the changing social patterns of the modern world. Generalizations regarding the nature and potential function of the field, therefore, can only be proffered as suggestions, based on the substantive research directions and ideas of contemporary experts in the field and on the current trends and technical possibilities in other social science disciplines.

## The future of social geography

**The challenge.** Social geography faces a set of challenges that are unprecedented. Revolutionary changes in world social patterns have rendered past analytical techniques obsolete, while philosophical and cultural currents within modern social life tend to increase the propensity to change of both reality itself and its social-psychological significance. Thus, while technological, economic, and commercial evolution tends to produce a certain degree of standardization in society's spatial order, there is a universal tendency to emphasize social, that is, ethnic, religious, or linguistic, differentiation. The philosophical problems of intersubjectivity and coexistence are ubiquitously discussed. "The home of contemporary man," wrote Plattel ([1960] 1965, pp. 1–2) "does not lie primarily in a localized environment, but in his fellow-man." The traditional methods and objectives of social science are being fundamentally challenged. Analysis must somehow be broadened so as to arrive at a more holistic vision of social reality: the classical Cartesian premises underlying accepted research methodology led to the discovery of systems, but mechanics and structures of systems constitute only a partial view of reality. Today both subjective (internal) aspects of reality and objective (external) aspects of reality must be analyzed. Modern psychology and sociology have endeavored to meet this challenge by forging new analytical techniques, and many other social science disciplines have adopted a decidedly behavioristic approach in recent years.

In the light of these developments, the spatial patterns of world society assume a new significance; the immediate challenge for social geographers would seem to be the collaboration with other scholars in the monumental task of describing world society within its geographical setting. For such an endeavor, social geography needs a unifying theme, a conceptual framework that will enable it to contribute toward and benefit from the research efforts of scholars in related social science disciplines. Such a unified framework seems to be

emerging from the work of some contemporary social geographers. Some of its characteristics are described below.

**Social space as central theme.** Claval's critique of contemporary social geography concludes that "to understand the geography of a place means to understand the social organization of those who inhabit it, their mentality, their beliefs, their 'representations' " (1964, p. 123). Watson's study of Hamilton demonstrates how "The spatial pattern is, in the last analysis, a reflection of the moral order" ([1951] 1965, p. 476). In this article I have postulated that the *raison d'être* of social geography rests on the fact that the social order is distinct from (even if closely interrelated with) the other orders of human activity in space. In order to describe adequately this social dimension or order, contemporary thought would seem to demand the use of both internal and external perspectives. Is this possible?

Sociologists, for example, Chombart de Lauwe (1956) and Gaston Bardet (1951), and human ecologists, for example, Firey (1960), have demonstrated the technical possibility of exploring a society's perception of its geographical milieu. Geographers, for example, Rochefort (1961), Burton and Kates (1964), and Pataki (1965), have also shown that space has different meanings for different societies, and thus distance and spatial movement can no longer be considered in traditional geodesic terms but must be considered in terms of those dimensions perceived by their human occupants. For example, groups of Italians, Poles, Pakistanis, and Negroes may live side by side in one section of a city. Yet each group, because of economic, historical, cultural, or other reasons, may possess an entirely different conception of space. Some groups may have a social horizon that scarcely transcends the block in which they live or the set of stores in which they work or shop, while others may have social contacts with relatives thousands of miles away. Whether contact with distant relatives is frequent or rare does not influence the fact that a bond is perceived which ignores the barriers of space and time. The social geography of urban neighborhoods cannot ignore these differential attitudes toward space.

This illustration, which challenges traditional notions of space, may lead to the impression that only the social-psychological conception of space matters. Rochefort (1963), in discussing this problem, strongly emphasized that the real dimensions of geographic space must always be kept in mind. Therefore, the central conceptual problem in social geography is to define space in such a way that both subjective and objective dimensions are included.

Sorre's response (1957) to this challenge was the concept of social space: the synthesis of real and perceived dimensions of space. The subjective component of social space in his view is embodied in the distribution of fundamental social groups, while the objective component consists of their concrete geographic setting.

Bobek's concept of social landscape already expressed the main idea that a unit of social space is a region or place in which one or several groups live and have a common set of ideas of their environment (1943; 1948). The fundamental merit of this concept, as a central theme for social geography, is that it incorporates the traditional elements of groups and environment, while redefining them in terms which are relevant to the examination of modern society. Let us see how the methodology of contemporary social geography could be organized around such a central theme.

*Subjective component—social groups.* Sociology has shown how the dimensions and meaning of space are colored by the beliefs and group affiliations of its human occupants. Sociologists speak of ethnic space, religious space, and other spaces, and social morphology maps the distribution of groups on the premise that their formal spatial configurations imply the values held by the group (Halbwachs 1938). Social geography must go further: these groups, the subjective component of social space, must be studied not only as morphological patterns on the earth but also as formative influences in molding a society's perception of its environment. The relevant groups include those which determine or condition the spatial distribution and interaction of people, for example, language and ethnic groups; those which influence a society's use of space, for example, religious and kin groups; and, most significantly, those which develop as a result of society's mode of material subsistence, namely, the *genres de vie* or livelihood groups. The bonds and values engendered by participation in these groups are not directly observable on the earth's surface, but they are essential to the understanding of the spatial movements and distribution of people on the earth. Classical French geography used such formal categories of relevant groups, but profound transformations in social structure have occurred since the analytical framework of Brunhes, or even Sorre, was first formulated. Even though the choice of relevant grouping will demand close cooperation with sociologists and others, the social geographer does not have to abandon entirely the analytical techniques of his predecessors. Rather, such traditional concepts should be re-examined in the light of the new analytical possibilities which appear in many social science disciplines. One example which might merit re-examination, for example, is the Vidalian notion of *genre de vie*. Settlements forms, land use, social interaction, and even political integration have been explained by geographers in terms of *genres de vie*. Many feel that the concept has lost its applicability to modern social life (George 1951; Le Lannou 1949), but others argue that it can be reformulated (Sorre 1948; Varagnac 1948). By discounting the various modifications which have accrued through the years and by re-examining the original notion in the light of contemporary developments both in world society and in social science, guidelines for a reformulation may become apparent. A *genre de vie*, in Vidal's opinion (1911), implies more than a means of material subsistence; its geographical significance stems in large part from its spiritual component, the *structures mentales* which persist even after the external modalities of livelihood change. The important point is that both material and spiritual elements are harmoniously integrated in the *genre de vie* community within a particular milieu. Such a conception closely resembles the notion of "community" in rural sociology (Hillery 1950).

Without changing the concept at all, there are some applications in the modern world. Witness the adaptation problems of immigrants from rural to urban areas, the psychological problems involved in the retraining of unemployed miners, the social consequences of colonialism and economic restructuring within the "third world." In the urban industrial world, however, livelihood is a less compelling basis for community consciousness than other similarities, for example, a common racial, professional, or linguistic background or similar consumption habits (Fourastié 1963). But whatever the source, if a recognizable consistency in a group's perception and consequent use of its environment are associated with a common *structure mentale*, why not consider this pattern as a *genre de vie*, for example, that of travel agents, of salesmen, of truck drivers, of commuting students, of social scientists? Chombart de Lauwe (Chombart de Lauwe et al. 1952, p. 243) showed how a deep social rift could prevail in a small dormitory village because the inhabitants belonged to two different *genres de vie*. The same could be said of immigrant ethnic groups in some urban centers (Taeuber & Taeuber 1965). Ideally, within either an urban or a rural region, one could thus identify the component *genres de vie* and see if there is a hierarchy of importance among them, the dominant one giving a character to the place, as in pilgrimage, market, or university towns. Many other possibilities exist, but much more substantive work, preferably in conjunction with other disciplines, is needed before any formal categories of modern *genres de vie* can be made. Until this is done, the existing formal groupings of language, religion, race, etc., may serve to constitute the subjective component of social space; however, if these sociological categories can somehow be integrated into the more geographical concept of *genre de vie*, the result would be an ideal subjective ingredient for social geography.

*Objective component—the social environment.* The term "social environment" is used here to connote all the socially significant aspects of the total geographic milieu. Traditionally, geographers have tended to exaggerate the distinction between the natural (physical–biotic) environment and the artificial network of human establishments created by society. This dualistic conception tends to ignore the fact that mankind's environment-creating apparatus has by no means entirely destroyed the natural framework and that the interplay of natural and artificial assumes very different forms throughout the world. The social environment, as objective component of social space, includes more than these two levels. It includes, for example, the relation of social attitudes and traditions to nature, resource use, and the ethics of group relations.

Social geographers are far from a satisfactory definition of the social environment; they lack substantive studies which would provide the raw material for such a definition. What is the social significance, for example, of purely physical elements, such as humidity, temperature, or altitude? Geographers have added very little to the "findings" of the Huntingtonian environmentalists. Yet the behavioral sciences are interested in knowing the connections, real or perceived, between society and its natural environment. The research challenges proposed in Sorre's *Géographie psychologique* (1954) remain virtually untouched. In addition, little is known about the "synthetic environment" (Herber 1962): the various consequences of atmospheric and oceanic pollution, or the consumption of medicated foods, stimulants, and sedatives. What are the physiological and pathological consequences of changes in the environment, for example, housing, communication, and diet?

Recently some geographers have viewed the environment as an amalgam of systems (Wagner & Mikesell 1962; Ackerman 1963; van Paassen

1965). This approach is satisfactory from the theoretical and technical points of view, but does it admit of nonsystematic (dysfunctional) elements which often play such an important part in social life? The social geographer must be sensitive to the local exceptions which give special character to individual places, such as Rochefort (1961) demonstrated in her study of Sicilian social environment.

**Approaches to the study of social space.** We have seen that the study of social groups within their territorial (environmental) framework has constituted the basic traditional methodology of the Dutch, British, and some French social geographers. In theory, this has involved a combination of a morphological approach (mapping of social groups) and an ecological approach (relations of groups to environment). Today, however, the latter (vertical) dimension is perhaps less significant than the horizontal one, namely, the spatial patterns of interaction between social groups, such as Lowenthal's Caribbean study illustrated (Lowenthal 1961). A psychological approach to group attitudes, such as one finds in the *Revue de psychologie des peuples*, may provide clues to the origins of some spatial discontinuities in social interaction.

In terms of the notions of group and environment, as redefined above, let us see what analytical methods can be used in the study of social space. Two of the many possible approaches are (1) to consider social space as a mosaic of social areas defined in terms of the occupant groups, for example, *genres de vie* or ethnic groups; and (2) to view social space as nodally organized, that is, as a network of spatial relations radiating around certain centers (Sorre's *points privilégiés*) and permeated by the arteries of circulation.

*Formal approach—social areas.* Initially, the formal approach examines the spatial patterns and characteristics of social groups in virtually the same fashion as that used by the disciples of Steinmetz in Amsterdam. On the basis of these distributions a series of regions, homogeneous in terms of individual characteristics, can be compared and associations can be sought. Such associations, however, must then be examined in terms of the social environment in which these social characteristics occur, that is, an ecological approach must supplement the more formal "sociographical" stage of analysis. In addition to these two steps, the geographer must endeavor to see how all these elements combine to form the social whole within a particular region and must seek explanations for the variations through space in the incidence and functional character of these social wholes. Jones sees "social regions" within the city of Belfast (1960), for example, as a product of historical and religious forces, while the "social area analysis" tradition in American human ecology (Theodorson 1961) has demonstrated the use of various other indices in the establishment of intraurban social regions.

*Functional approach.* A more dynamic and increasingly popular approach is to consider social space in terms of its nodal organization. The orbit of group activities and the related horizons of social consciousness can be examined (cartographically) in terms of their use of these nodes, for example, markets, cinemas, and schools (Chombart de Lauwe et al. 1952). The hinterland of each of these nodes varies in scale and significance, and these variations provide crucial insights into the social character of particular places. The study of nodal regions and of circulation are two examples of a functional approach to the study of social space.

Sorre (1961) suggests that settlement units— towns, cities, metropolises—provide a primary set of nodes on a world scale. Within each of these nodes is an internal system of centers (schools, churches, cinemas) whose social significance can also be examined cartographically. Here again the social geographer can collaborate with and utilize some of the existing principles of central place theorists and perhaps somewhat qualify definitions of centrality currently based on commercial and industrial criteria. Edgar Kant's *Umland* studies (Kant et al. 1951), J. Labasse's circulation studies (1955), and Pierre George's studies of the urban fringe (1962) provide orientation for this kind of study. As world society becomes more urbanized, social geographers will concern themselves more with the urban field, and, here, collaboration with other scholars will be imperative.

The essential clue to the internal dynamism of social space can be found in its circulation system. Circulation here includes all kinds of movement of goods, services, people, and ideas—any kind of spatial movement which occasions social communication. As the Paris study (Chombart de Lauwe et al. 1952) demonstrated, the actual and potential use of a circulation system indicates the concrete social horizons of the group it serves; changes within it may indicate or produce changes in the relation between groups and between a group and its social environment.

A vast number of research questions emanate from this dimension of social space, particularly now that the processes of social differentiation and cultural standardization are so closely tied with large-scale, mass-produced goods and services. Interregional traffic, the currents of the tourist world, pilgrimages, daily and seasonal commuting —these are only a few samples of the many activities the student of circulation could investigate.

To summarize, social geography can be defined as the study of the areal (spatial) patterns and functional relations of social groups in the context of their social environment; the internal structure and external relations of the nodes of social activity; and the articulation of various channels of social communication.

Although the discussion has distinguished between various elements and approaches to social geography, it must be emphasized that one of the fundamental characteristics of the field has been, and must remain, its integral, holistic character. Like social history, it must endeavor to maintain the holistic view, that is, to show how the individual parts and their functional connections integrate to give a specific character to the social whole. French geographers have supplied ample precedent for this kind of holism; so, indeed, have the social anthropologists of the Anglo–American world. The more the field becomes theoretically systematized, the greater will the challenge of integration become.

For social geography to fulfill its potential, the various approaches to the field need to be coordinated into a systematic conceptual framework. Sorre's concept of social space could provide a central theme for such a framework. Its ingredient elements could be considered as bases for systematic subdivisions, for example, geography of language, of religions, and of diet, each of which contributes a valuable perspective on society's spatial order. The definition given here seems to incorporate the various elements which have belonged to the field of social geography and which, given the trends in contemporary social science, could constitute fruitful future directions for the discipline.

ANNE BUTTIMER

#### BIBLIOGRAPHY

ACKERMAN, EDWARD A. 1963 Where Is a Research Frontier? Association of American Geographers, *Annals* 53:429–440.

BARDET, GASTON 1951 Social Topography: An Analytico–Synthetic Understanding of the Urban Texture. *Town Planning Review* 22:237–260.

BOBEK, HANS 1943 Der Orient als Soziallandschaft. Unpublished manuscript.

BOBEK, HANS 1948 Stellung und Bedeutung der Sozialgeographie. *Erdkunde* 2, no. 1/3:118–125.

BOBEK, HANS 1959 Die Hauptstufen der Gesellschafts- und Wirtschaftsentfaltung in geographischer Sicht.

*Die Erde: Zeitschrift der Gesellschaft für Erdkunde zu Berlin* 90:259–298.

BOBEK, HANS 1961 Sozialgeographie: Neue Wege der Kultur- und Bevölkerungsgeographie. Deutsche Gesellschaft für Bevölkerungswissenschaft, *Mitteilungen* 3:62–67.

BROEK, JAN O. M. 1932 *The Santa Clara Valley, California: A Study in Landscape Changes.* Utrecht (Netherlands): Oosthoek.

BROEK, JAN O. M. 1944 Diversity and Unity in Southeast Asia. *Geographical Review* 34:175–195.

BROOKFIELD, H. C. 1961 The Highland Peoples of New Guinea: A Study of Distribution and Localization. *Geographical Journal* 127:436–448.

BRUNHES, JEAN (1910) 1924 *Human Geography.* London: Harrap. → First published in French. A fourth French edition was published in 1934 by Alcan.

BURTON, IAN; and KATES, ROBERT W. 1964 The Perception of Natural Hazards in Resource Management. *Natural Resources Journal* 3:412–441.

CHATELAIN, M. ABEL 1947 Les fondements d'une géographie sociale de la bourgeoisie française. *Annales de géographie* 56:455–462.

CHATELAIN, M. ABEL 1953 Horizons de la géographie sociologique. *Revue de géographie de Lyon* 28:225–228.

CHOMBART DE LAUWE, PAUL H. 1956 *La vie quotidienne des familles ouvrières.* Paris: Centre National de la Recherche Scientifique.

CHOMBART DE LAUWE, PAUL H. et al. 1952 *Paris et l'agglomération parisienne.* Volume 1: L'espace social dans une grande cité. Paris: Presses Universitaires de France.

CLAVAL, PAUL 1964 *Essai sur l'évolution de la géographie humaine.* Cahiers de géographie de Besançon No. 12. Paris: Les Belles-Lettres. → Translation of extract in text provided by Anne Buttimer.

DICKINSON, ROBERT E. (1947) 1956 *City Region and Regionalism: A Geographical Contribution to Human Ecology.* London: Routledge.

DURKHEIM, ÉMILE (1893) 1960 *The Division of Labor in Society.* Glencoe, Ill.: Free Press. → First published as *De la division du travail social.*

DURKHEIM, ÉMILE (1895) 1958 *The Rules of Sociological Method.* 8th ed. Edited by George E. G. Catlin. Glencoe, Ill.: Free Press. → First published as *Les règles de la méthode sociologique.*

EVANS, EMYR E. 1942 *Irish Heritage: The Landscape, the People and Their Work.* Dundalk (Ireland): Tempest.

EVANS, EMYR E. 1957 *Irish Folk Ways.* New York: Devin-Adair.

FEBVRE, LUCIEN (1922) 1925 *A Geographical Introduction to History.* New York: Knopf. → First published as *La terre et l'évolution humaine.*

FIREY, WALTER I. 1960 *Man, Mind and Land: A Theory of Resource Use.* Glencoe, Ill.: Free Press.

FLEURE, HERBERT J. 1918 *Human Geography in Western Europe: A Study in Appreciation.* London: Williams & Norgate.

FLEURE, HERBERT J. 1947 *Some Problems of Society and Environment.* London: Institute of British Geographers.

FORDE, DARYLL (1934) 1963 *Habitat, Economy and Society: A Geographical Introduction to Ethnology.* 5th ed. London: Methuen.

FOURASTIÉ, JEAN 1963 *Le grand espoir du XXᵉ siècle.* Paris: Gallimard.

FRIEDMANN, GEORGES (editor) 1953 *Villes et campagnes: Civilisation urbaine et civilisation rurale en France.* Paris: Colin.

GEDDES, PATRICK (1915) 1950 *Cities in Evolution.* New ed., rev. Oxford Univ. Press.

GEIPEL, ROBERT 1952 *Soziale Struktur und Einheitsbewusstein als Grundlagen geographischer Gliederung.* Rhein-Mainische Forschungen, No. 38. Frankfurt am Main (Germany): Kramer.

GEORGE, PIERRE (1946) 1956 *Géographie sociale du monde.* 4th ed. Paris: Presses Universitaires de France.

GEORGE, PIERRE 1951 *Introduction à l'étude géographique de la population du monde.* France, Institut National d'Études Démographiques, Travaux et Documents, Cahier No. 14. Paris: Presses Universitaires de France.

GEORGE, PIERRE 1956 *La campagne: Le fait rural à travers le monde.* Paris: Presses Universitaires de France.

GEORGE, PIERRE 1962 *Précis de géographie urbaine.* Paris: Presses Universitaires de France.

GODLUND, SVEN 1956 The Function and Growth of Bus Traffic Within the Sphere of Urban Influence. *Lund Studies in Geography* Series B, No. 18.

GOTTMANN, JEAN (1961) 1964 *Megalopolis: The Urbanized Northeastern Seaboard of the United States.* Cambridge, Mass.: M.I.T. Press.

GOUROU, PIERRE 1964 Changes in Civilisation and Their Influence on Landscapes. *Impact of Science on Society* 14:57–71.

GROENMAN, S. JOERD (1950) 1953 *Methoden der sociografie: Een inleiding tot de practijk van het sociale onderzoek in Nederland.* Assen (Netherlands): Van Gorcum.

HÄGERSTRAND, TORSTEN 1952 The Propagation of Innovation Waves. *Lund Studies in Geography* Series B, No. 4.

HAHN, EDUARD 1896 *Die Haustiere und ihre Beziehungen zur Wirtschaft des Menschen.* Leipzig: Duncker & Humblot.

HALBWACHS, MAURICE (1938) 1960 *Population and Society: Introduction to Social Morphology.* Glencoe, Ill.: Free Press. → First published as *Morphologie sociale.*

HARTKE, WOLFGANG 1956 *Die Hütekinder im Hohen Vogelsberg: Der geographische Charakter eines Sozialproblems.* Münchner Geographische Hefte, No. 11. Regensburg (Germany): Lassleben.

HARTKE, WOLFGANG 1959 Gedanken über die Bestimmung von Räumen gleichen sozialgeographischen Verhaltens. *Erdkunde* 13:426–436.

HARTKE, WOLFGANG 1961 Die sozialgeographische Differenzierung der Gemarkungen ländlicher Kleinstädte. *Geografiska annaler* 43:105–113.

HARTKE, WOLFGANG 1963 Der Weg zur Sozialgeographie: Der wissenschaftliche Lebensweg von Professor Dr. Hans Bobek. Österreichische Geographische Gesellschaft, *Mitteilungen* 105:5–22.

HARTMANN, F. 1958 Volkach am Main: Kulturgeographische Studien über eine unterfränkische Kleinstadt. Unpublished manuscript.

HARTSHORNE, RICHARD (1939) 1964 *The Nature of Geography: A Critical Survey of Current Thought in the Light of the Past.* Lancaster, Pa.: Association of American Geographers.

HARTSHORNE, RICHARD 1950 The Functional Approach in Political Geography. Association of American Geographers, *Annals* 40:95–130.

HERBER, LEWIS 1962 *Our Synthetic Environment.* New York: Knopf.

HILLERY, GEORGE A. JR. 1950 Definitions of Community: Areas of Agreement. *Rural Sociology* 20:111–123.

INTERNATIONAL SYMPOSIUM ON MAN'S ROLE IN CHANGING THE FACE OF THE EARTH, PRINCETON, N.J., 1955 1956 *Man's Role in Changing the Face of the Earth.* Edited by William L. Thomas et al. Univ. of Chicago Press.

ISAAC, ERICH 1959 Influence of Religion on the Spread of Citrus. *Science* 129:179–186.

JONES, EMRYS A. 1960 *A Social Geography of Belfast.* Oxford Univ. Press.

JUILLARD, ÉTIENNE 1953 *La vie rurale dans la plaine de Basse-Alsace: Essai de géographie sociale.* Strasbourg, Université, Institut des Hautes Études Alsaciennes, Vol. 9. Strasbourg: Le Roux.

KANT, EDGAR et al. 1951 Studies in Rural–Urban Interaction. *Lund Studies in Geography* Series B, No. 4.

KROEBER, A. L.; and KLUCKHOHN, CLYDE 1952 *Culture: A Critical Review of Concepts and Definitions.* Harvard University, Peabody Museum of American Archaeology and Ethnology Papers, Vol. 47, No. 1. Cambridge, Mass.: The Museum. → A paperback edition was published in 1963 by Vintage Books.

LABASSE, JEAN 1955 *Les capitaux et la région, étude géographique: Essai sur le commerce et la circulation des capitaux dans la région lyonnaise.* Paris: Colin.

LE LANNOU, MAURICE 1949 *La géographie humaine.* Paris: Flammarion.

LE PLAY, FRÉDÉRIC (1855) 1877–1879 *Les ouvriers européens,* 2d ed. 6 vols. Tours (France): Mame.

LE PLAY, FRÉDÉRIC (1871) 1907 *L'organisation de la famille: Selon le vrai modèle signalé par l'histoire de toutes les races et de tous les temps.* 5th ed. Tours (France): Mame.

LEWIS, PEIRCE F. 1965 Impact of Negro Migration on the Electoral Geography of Flint, Michigan, 1932–1962: A Cartographic Analysis. Association of American Geographers, *Annals* 55:1–25.

LOWENTHAL, DAVID 1961 *The West Indies Federation: Perspectives on a New Nation.* American Geographical Society, Research Series, No. 23. New York: Columbia Univ. Press.

MCKENZIE, R. D. 1931 Ecology, Human. Volume 5, pages 314–315 in *Encyclopaedia of the Social Sciences.* New York: Macmillan.

MCKENZIE, R. D. 1934 The Field and Problems of Demography, Human Geography and Human Ecology. Pages 52–66 in Luther L. Bernard (editor), *The Fields and Methods of Sociology.* New York: Farrar.

MACKINDER, HALFORD (1919) 1942 *Democratic Ideals and Reality: A Study in the Politics of Reconstruction.* London: Constable; New York: Holt.

MORRILL, RICHARD L. 1963 The Development of Spatial Distributions of Towns in Sweden: A Historical–Predictive Approach. Association of American Geographers, *Annals* 53:1–14.

PAASSEN, C. VAN 1965 *Over vormverandering in de sociale geografie.* Gröningen (Netherlands): Wolters.

PARK, ROBERT E.; and BURGESS, ERNEST W. (1921) 1929 *Introduction to the Science of Sociology.* 2d ed. Univ. of Chicago Press.

PATAKI, K. J. 1965 Shifting Population and Environment Among the Auyuna: Some Considerations on Phenomena and Schema. M.A. thesis, Univ. of Washington.

PELLETIER, JEAN 1959 *Alger; 1955: Essai d'une géographie sociale.* Cahiers de géographie de Besançon, No. 6. Paris: Belles Lettres.

PHLIPPONNEAU, MICHEL 1960 *Géographie et action: Introduction à la géographie appliquée.* Paris: Colin.

PLANHOL, XAVIER DE 1957 *Le monde islamique: Essai de géographie religieuse.* Paris: Presses Universitaires de France.

PLATT, ROBERT S. 1961 The Saarland; an International Borderland: Social Geography From Field Study of Nine Border Villages. *Erdkunde* 15:54–68.

PLATTEL, MARTIN G. (1960) 1965 *Social Philosophy.* Duquesne Studies, Philosophical Series, No. 18. Pittsburgh, Pa.: Duquesne Univ. Press. → First published in Dutch.

RATZEL, FRIEDRICH 1876 *Städte und Culturbilder aus Nordamerika.* Leipzig: Brockhaus.

RATZEL, FRIEDRICH (1882–1891) 1921–1922 *Anthropogeographie.* 2 vols. Stuttgart (Germany): Engelhorn. → Volume 1: *Grundzüge der Anwendung der Erdkunde auf die Geschichte,* 4th ed. Volume 2: *Die geographische Verbreitung des Menschen,* 3d ed.

RATZEL, FRIEDRICH (1897) 1923 *Politische Geographie.* 3d ed. Edited by Eugen Oberhummer. Munich and Berlin: Oldenbourg.

RATZEL, FRIEDRICH (1901) 1902 Man as a Life Phenomenon on the Earth. Volume 1, pages 61–106 in Hans F. Helmolt (editor), *The History of the World: A Survey of Man's Record.* New York: Dodd. → First published in German.

REDFIELD, ROBERT 1953 *The Primitive World and Its Transformations.* Ithaca, N.Y.: Cornell Univ. Press. → A paperback edition was published in 1957.

REDFIELD, ROBERT 1955 *The Little Community: Viewpoints for the Study of a Human Whole.* Univ. of Chicago Press. → A paperback edition, bound together with *Peasant Society and Culture,* was published in 1961 by Cambridge Univ. Press.

REDFIELD, ROBERT; and VILLA ROJAS, ALFONSO (1934) 1962 *Chan Kom: A Maya Village.* Carnegie Institution of Washington, Publication No. 448. Univ. of Chicago Press.

*Recherches sociographiques.* → Published since 1960 by Laval University, Faculty of Social Sciences, Quebec.

*Revue de psychologie des peuples.* → Published since 1946 by the Institute Havrais de Sociologie Économique et de Psychologie des Peuples, Le Havre, France.

ROCHEFORT, RENÉE 1961 *Le travail en Sicile: Étude de géographie sociale.* Paris: Presses Universitaires de France.

ROCHEFORT, RENÉE 1963 Géographie sociale et sciences humaines. Association de Géographes Français, *Bulletin* No. 314–315:18–32.

RUPPERT, KARL 1958 *Spalt: Ein methodischer Beitrag zum Studium der Agrarlandschaft mit Hilfe der kleinräumlichen Nutzflächen und Sozialkartierung und zur Geographie des Hopfenbaus.* Münchner Geographische Hefte, No. 14. Regensburg (Germany): Lassleben.

SAUER, C. O. 1931 Geography, Cultural. Volume 6, pages 621–624 in *Encyclopaedia of the Social Sciences.* New York: Macmillan.

SCHÄFFLE, ALLEN (1875–1878) 1896 *Bau und Leben des sozialen Körpers.* 2d ed. 4 vols. Tübingen (Germany): Laupp.

SCHNORE, LEO F. 1961 Geography and Human Ecology. *Economic Geography* 37:207–217.

SORRE, MAXIMILIEN 1943–1953 *Les fondements de la géographie humaine.* 3 vols. Paris: Colin.

SORRE, MAXIMILIEN 1948 La notion de genre de vie et sa valeur actuelle. *Annales de géographie* 57:97–108, 193–204.

SORRE, MAXIMILIEN 1954 *La géographie psychologique: L'adaptation au milieu climatique et biosocial.* Traité de psychologie appliquée, Vol. 3, part 3. Paris: Presses Universitaires de France.

SORRE, MAXIMILIEN 1957 *Rencontres de la géographie et de la sociologie.* Paris: Rivière.

SORRE, MAXIMILIEN 1961 *L'homme sur la terre.* Paris: Hachette.

STEWARD, JULIAN H. 1950 *Area Research: Theory and Practice.* Bulletin No. 63. New York: Social Science Research Council.

TAEUBER, K. E.; and TAEUBER, A. F. 1965 *Negroes in Cities: Residential Segregation and Neighborhood Change.* Chicago: Aldine.

THEODORSON, G. A. (editor) 1961 *Studies in Human Ecology.* Evanston, Ill.: Row, Peterson.

THOMAS, FRANKLIN 1925 *The Environmental Basis of Society: A Study in the History of Sociological Theory.* New York: Century.

*Tijdschrift voor economische en sociale geografie.* → Published since 1910 by the Nederlandse Vereniging voor Economische en Sociale Geografie.

VARAGNAC, ANDRÉ 1948 *Civilisation traditionnelle et genres de vie.* Paris: Michel.

VIDAL DE LA BLACHE, PAUL 1896 Le principe de la géographie générale. *Annales de géographie* 5:129–142.

VIDAL DE LA BLACHE, PAUL 1902 Les conditions géographiques des faits sociaux. *Annales de géographie* 11:13–23.

VIDAL DE LA BLACHE, PAUL 1911 Les genres de vie dans la géographie humaine. *Annales de géographie* 20:193–212, 289–304.

VIDAL DE LA BLACHE, PAUL 1917–1918 Les grandes agglomérations humaines. *Annales de géographie* 26:401–422; 27:92–101, 174–187.

VOOYS, ADRIAAN C. DE 1950 *De ontwikkeling van de sociale geografie in Nederland.* Inaugural lecture at the University of Utrecht. Groningen (Netherlands): No publisher given.

WAGNER, PHILIP 1960 *The Human Use of the Earth.* Glencoe, Ill.: Free Press.

WAGNER, PHILIP L.; and MIKESELL, MARVIN W. (editors) 1962 *Readings in Cultural Geography.* Univ. of Chicago Press.

WATSON, JAMES W. (1951) 1965 The Sociological Aspects of Geography. Pages 463–499 in Thomas Griffith Taylor (editor), *Geography in the Twentieth Century: A Study of Growth, Fields, Techniques, Aims and Trends.* New York: Philosophical Library.

# VI
## STATISTICAL GEOGRAPHY

Statistical geography is to geography what econometrics is to economics, sociometrics to sociology, psychometrics to psychology, or even jurimetrics to jurisprudence—an approach to the field rather than a subdivision of that field. Like these other approaches, it is of recent development—the manifestation within geography of the trend to a more quantitative approach that has characterized all the social sciences since the end of World War II. As is also the case with these other approaches, many of the pioneering contributions to statistical geography have come from workers in other fields. The parallel term "geometrics" is not used to describe the work of the statistical geographer, however, not so much because it provides an inappropriate picture of the statistical geographer's attempts to identify and measure regularities observable in spatial distributions as because the branch of mathematics that originated in Greek attempts to measure the earth has a two-thousand-year priority in its right to the name. In addition, mathematical geography, concerned as it is with map projections, is the branch of geography that today relies most heavily and directly upon geometry.

The syndrome that characterizes statistical geography today includes a more formal theoretical orientation than was true of geography in the past, a reliance upon statistical inference and numerical analysis in empirical research, the use of mathematical programming and simulation procedures in applied research, a basic concern with model construction, and an involvement with high-speed computers, mass-data banks, and automated mapping devices.

Yet this assemblage of interests is not monolithic. There are differences in emphasis, corresponding to each of the four main traditions of geographic research: spatial, area studies, man–land, and earth science (Pattison 1964; National Research Council 1965). Statistical geography originated within the spatial tradition, with its emphasis upon analysis of spatial distributions and associations, and initially relied heavily upon exercises in distribution fitting and upon regression and correlation analysis. It spread to area studies when the spatial tradition began using multivariate analysis, then to the man–land tradition via behavioral studies of environmental perception and individual decision making, and to the earth-science tradition as spatial studies and related systematic sciences began using systems analysis. To understand these several facets of statistical geography, with their differences in use of theory, choices, and timing of applications of statistical methods, and their contacts with the rest of science, therefore requires some understanding of the four research traditions. These, in turn, can best be viewed within a formal overview of approaches to regional analysis (Berry 1964a).

## Approaches to regional analysis

Virtually any sort of regional analysis may be considered as starting from information about one or more *places*. For each place, one or more *properties*, or characteristics, may be measured, and the measurements may be made at one or more points in *time*. It is often convenient to think in terms of a three-dimensional array **X** of order $v \times p \times t$. Cell $x_{ijk}$ of this array (or matrix) records the value of variable $i$ at place $j$ in time $k$. Rows of the array—vectors of array values for fixed $i$, $k$—record the distribution of variables over places at some point in time. Column vectors inventory the properties of places at time $t$. Time vectors report on the $t$ states of variable $i$ at place $j$.

Operational specification of variables, places, and times varies with the interests of the particular analyst, but a matrix such as **X** is (albeit usually implicitly) the object of all forms of geographic study. A row vector of **X** is a spatial distribution that can be mapped. A column vector is a locational inventory. Such row and column vectors are the bases of systematic (topical) and regional geography, respectively. Time vectors report changes in spatial distributions and at locations and are basic to historical geography.

*The data.* Cell $x_{ijk}$ may contain a variety of different records, depending upon specification of $i$, $j$, and $k$. Columns, for example, may be defined as places with area, such as countries, states, counties, census tracts, or quarter-mile-square cells of a half-mile grid. Alternatively, they may be dimensionless points; three such examples are triangulation points used for measuring altitude, weather stations, and soil-sample-core locations (Kao 1963). Rows may be defined as properties of the places (scalar quantities, such as population residing in each of a set of census tracts or altitude at each of a set of triangulation points), or they may refer to connections between places (vector quantities, such as flow of coal from southern Illinois to each of the Midwestern counties). Rows also might be airline traffic flow between cities; in this case columns would represent *pairs* of cities. In addition, any level of measurement may appear, whether nominal, ordinal, interval, or ratio [*see* STATISTICS, DESCRIPTIVE, *article on* LOCATION AND DISPERSION, *for a discussion of levels of measurement*].

**Spatial tradition.** Geography's spatial tradition is founded upon cartographic portrayal and subsequent study of spatial distributions, thus having as its base row-wise analysis. A few examples of the kinds of spatial distributions studied follow:

(1) A land-use map—scalar, nominal, of areas, an areal distribution.

(2) A map showing the location of major cities by dots—scalar, nominal, at points, a point distribution.

(3) An airline-route map—vector, nominal, joining points.

(4) A map of soil quality—scalar, ordinal, of areas.

(5) A map showing average annual temperature —scalar, interval. If the map shows averages by states or districts, it is also discontinuous and areal (a choropleth map, if different shadings are applied to the units), but if it shows the temperature varying over the country as a surface, it is a continuous generalization. The generalization is of point observations (usually isopleth, since the surface will be depicted by contours) if, for example, weather-station data are used, or of areal data if interpolations were made, for example, with respect to the district averages treated as points central to each of the districts.

(6) A highway map, with routes classified by quality—vector, ordinal, joining points.

(7) A map of city-to-city air-passenger movements—vector, ratio, joining points.

Two dominant themes emerge in spatial analysis of such maps: evaluation of the *pattern* of scalar distributions and of similarities in pattern over a number of such distributions and evaluation of the *connectivity* evidenced by vector distributions and of similarities in the connectivity of several such distributions. Apparently, the fundamental properties of pattern include absolute location (position), relative location (geometry), and scale, with a family of interesting derived properties, including density and density gradients, spacing, directional orientation, and the like. Similarly, accessibility is central to the study of connectivity, and from it are derived such properties as centrality itself, relative dominance, degree of interdependence, etc. The two themes merge in *spatial-systems* analysis, where pattern and connectivity are examined in their association. For example, urban land values decline with increasing distance from the city center, and type of farming varies with distance from market. Such examples are readily generalized to the dynamic, that is, time-dependent, case.

**Area-studies (chorographic) tradition.** Just as row-wise analysis is the basis of the spatial tradition, so columnwise analysis provides the base for geography's area-studies tradition. The essential problems of this tradition are those of regional intelligence: the characterization of place in terms of the associations between characteristics localized in that place. This approach is often restricted to those features of place that are directly observable as landscape but, especially among the French school of human geographers, is also extended to an evaluation of both tangible and intangible aspects of "regional character" and of the differentiation of places (the study of "areal differentiation") [see LANDSCAPE].

An appetite for information, a penchant for the peculiar, emphasis upon field work, attachment to the people and language of a particular part of the world, a strong literary bent, a companionship with history and great reliance upon historical modes of explanation (in contrast to the functional, deterministic, and probabilistic modes of the other geographic traditions)—all these serve to identify the work of the student in the area-studies tradition, whatever the areas examined: countries or continents, regions or culture areas.

**Man–land tradition.** In the tradition of medieval philosophy, classical geographers distinguished between two major sets of variables: the physical (inorganic plus biotic) and the cultural. The associated methodological argument was that these provided the bases of the two major segments of the field: physical geography and cultural geography. Finer groupings of variables within these categories led to the variety of systematic branches of the subject, such as the geographies of landforms, of plants, of industry, of cities, or of language (the many topical fields and subfields might thus be identified as nested subsets of rows of the matrix **X**).

The classical modes of thought, however, also led to a particular tradition in geography, the man–land tradition, in which the relationships between physical variables and human characteristics and activities were examined. In combination with the social Darwinism of the late nineteenth century, simple one-way studies were made of the effects of environment on man. These were later complemented by studies of the effects of man on environment, from which emerged much of the original thinking in the field of conservation. More recently the ancient dichotomy has been relaxed with, for example, studies of the effects of environmental perception on resource evaluation and decision making in resources management (Kates 1962) and with the adoption of a systems-analysis frame (Ackerman 1963).

**Earth-science tradition.** During the eighteenth century, geography was an integral and substantial part of natural philosophy. At that time geographical study embraced all aspects of the earth, air, and waters. Since then, however, most aspects of these studies have branched off as separate systematic sciences, and geography's earth-science tradition has been left with such concerns as the study of landforms and their evolution (geomorphology), descriptive climatology, and certain aspects of the geographies of soils, plants, and animals, together with the attempt to achieve some spatial synthesis of these in order to identify "natural environmental complexes." It is to this latter end that systems-analysis procedures have recently been employed in this research tradition (Chorley 1962).

## Antecedents and stimuli

Prior to World War II few papers of a statistical nature had been published by geographers. Perhaps the only contributions worthy of note were Matui's (1932) fitting of the Poisson distribution to quadrat counts of settlements in a portion of Japan and Wright's (1937) discussion of Lorenz measures of concentration in the spatial case. However, two general antecedents can be distinguished, in addition to the pioneering contributions of workers in other fields: centrography and social physics. From the former came the idea of developing a special family of descriptive statistics for spatial distributions, and from the latter the recognition of certain classes of regularities in such distributions.

**Centrography.** During the early part of the twentieth century there was a lively debate among statisticians concerning such measures as the center of population. Part of the debate stemmed from publication by the U.S. Bureau of the Census of a piece entitled *Center of Population and Median Lines . . .* (U.S. Bureau of the Census 1923). Many articles were published, notably in the *Journal of the American Statistical Association* and in *Metron*, concerning the relative advantages of alternative centers, the center of gravity, the spatial median, and the center of minimum aggregate travel. (The U.S. Census Bureau's geography branch still reports on the center of gravity of the United States' population after each census.) This debate gradually subsided in the United States, but in the Soviet Union centrography flourished during the 1920s and 1930s. A centrographic laboratory was founded at Leningrad, under the auspices of the Russian Geographic Society, in 1925, and its director, E. E. Sviatlovsky, pursued studies of the "actual" and "proper" centers and the distributions of all manner of phenomena. However, the set of "proper" centers of economic activities prepared for the Gosplan of 1929 was at odds with the second Five-Year Plan, and as a result, the laboratory was finally disbanded. Porter (1963) provides a fairly complete bibliography of the relevant literature on centrography. Recently, the Israeli statistician Bachi (1963) has attempted to revive centrography, with the development of a variety of measures of dispersion and association of spatial distributions. Current interest within geography is slight, however, except as embraced by the social physicists (Stewart & Warntz 1958).

**Social physics.** The attempt to describe human phenomena in terms of physical laws has a long history in every social science [*see* RANK–SIZE RELATIONS].

In geographical studies this has been expressed in two major ways: (1) by use of "gravity models" to describe spatial interaction; and (2) by use of "potential models" as general summaries of interdependency between all places in large areas. Such models are said by their advocates to summarize a wide variety of social and economic distributions in economically advanced societies. Gravity models were first used in a relatively formal way by E. G. Ravenstein, in his seminal study "The Laws of Migration" (1885; 1889). Thereafter, these models found wide application, for example, in marketing geography—Reilly's "law of retail gravitation" (1931)—and in urban transportation studies describing interzonal travel. Carrothers (1956) reviews this work and the basic postulate that interactions or movements between places are proportional to the product of the masses and inversely proportional to some exponent of distance: that is, $I_{ij} \propto M_i \cdot M_j / d_{ij}^x$. Such gravity analogs were generalized by the astronomer J. Q. Stewart (1947) to the case of the potential surface, which simultaneously describes the interactions of each place and every other. Thus, the potential at any point $i$ is given by

$$P_i = \sum_{j=1}^{j=n} (P_j / d_{ij}^x).$$

The surface is interpolated from such measures for a sample set of points. There is still considerable interest within geography in social physics (Stewart & Warntz 1958), and new applications are continually being developed. Mackay (1959), for example, used gravity models to translate the depressing effects upon telephone communications of the French–English language boundary in Canada and of the United States–Canadian political boundary into their physical-distance equivalents, thus showing how social space can be transformed into the metric of physical space. Similar applications are to be found in all branches of cultural geography today.

**Pioneering contributions from elsewhere.** Workers in other fields provided several significant examples of the application of statistical methods to geographic problems, identified the major statistical problems of regional analysis, and prepared the first text on statistical geography, thereby doing much to set the pace and tone of statistical geography today. A statistician, M. G. Kendall (1939), for example, showed how principal-components analysis could be used to develop a multivariate index that would portray the geographical distribution of crop productivity in England. M. D. Hagood (1943), an agricultural statistician, used multiple-factor analysis to define multivariable uniform regions. An economist, C. Clark (1951), showed that the negative exponential distribution fitted population density patterns within cities. G. K. Zipf (1949), a philologist, developed the rank–size distribution of cities. A mathematical social scientist, H. A. Simon (1955), showed the bases of this distribution in simple stochastic processes, and sociologists found that a repetitive three-factor structure characterized the social geography of cities (Berry 1964b; 1965). G. U. Yule and M. G. Kendall ([1911] 1939) identified the problem of *modifiable units*: if data are of areas rather than at points, results of any analysis will be in part dependent upon the nature of the areal units of observation utilized. W. S. Robinson (1950) provided the relevant relationship between individual and ecological (areal, set-type) correlations, subsequently extended by Goodman (1959) in the context of ecological regression. A second problem, that of *contiguity*, or spatial autocorrelation, has been examined by Moran (1948) in the nominal case and by Geary (1954) more generally. Geary also applied his measures of contiguity to evaluating lack of independence of residuals from regression in studies of spatial association. These studies are reviewed in *Statistical Geography* (Duncan et al. 1961), the first general book in the field, written by sociologists. Further examination of autocorrelation in spatial series is to be found in "Spatial Variation" (Matérn 1960), a major contribution to areal sampling by a mathematician. Spatial analysis remains basic to quantitative plant ecology and to epidemiology, and from these fields have come many of the ideas used today in the study of pattern in point distributions and of spatial diffusion processes.

## Statistical geography—1950 to 1965

Centrography, social physics, and external stimuli, facilitated by developments in computer technology that for the first time enabled the mass data of geographic problems to be handled conveniently, combined to stimulate workers in geography's spatial tradition to work quantitatively. The older forms of cartographic analysis provided firm bases for this development, and many of the early studies were simply quantitative extensions of analyses cartographically conceived and executed. Arthur H. Robinson (1962), a cartographer, for example, utilized correlation and regression analysis to improve the ways by which he could map spatial associations. McCarty and his associates (1956) used similar procedures to replace older cartographic means of comparison. Thomas (1960) showed the various ways in which residuals from regression could be treated cartographically so as to draw upon traditional geographical means of map analysis in model reformulation and refinement. King (1962) applied the "nearest-neighbor" methods of the quantitative plant ecologist to the study of pattern in point distributions, with, like the 1932 Matui study, expectations derived from the Poisson distribution. These represent but a few examples of the spatial studies concerned with distribution fitting as a means of studying spatial pattern or with uses of correlation and regression in studies of spatial association. Many other examples are to be found in uses of regression to fit gravity models and obtain the distance exponents for different phenomena (Carrothers 1956) or to fit negative exponential distributions to urban population densities and the like (Berry 1965).

These kinds of studies represent the beginnings, from which statistical geography has grown rapidly. Dacey and Tung (1962) have made major advances in point-pattern analysis, for example, by transforming the distribution-fitting exercise into an explicit hypothesis-testing frame, with relevant expectations derived from settlement theory. Curry (1964) views many urban phenomena as the outcome of known-probability mechanisms. The Swedish geographer Hägerstrand (1953) was the first to show that many spatial patterns might be considered as the outcome of diffusion processes that could be simulated, using Monte Carlo methods, and his work led to a burst of similar simulation studies in the United States (Morrill 1963).

New approaches to spatial analysis have also been developed. Most of the examples outlined above use scalar data. Garrison (1960) showed that the mathematical theory of graphs provided an excellent base from which to examine vector distributions, and Nystuen and Dacey (1961) extended his argument to the case of organizational regions, using graph-theoretic measures of accessibility of places to communications networks to define relatively independent subsets of relatively interdependent places. Tobler (1963) showed how

a generalization of map projections, traditionally studied by the mathematical geographer, could be used as the basis for mapping social, economic, cultural, or political space into physical space, as a further means for merging geographical applications of various statistical and mathematical methods with the more traditional means of geographical analysis. Finally, in addition to developments of the descriptive kind, statistical geography has extended its work to embrace investigations of a prescriptive nature. Garrison and Morrill (1960), for example, applied the techniques of spatial price-equilibrium analysis to determining what should be the patterns of interregional trade in wheat and flour in the United States. Other research workers are now much concerned with the procedures of spatial programming. Haggett (1965) has provided an excellent review of the substance of the first decade of quantitative work in the spatial tradition.

With the use of multivariate analysis, statistical geography has spread from the spatial tradition to that of area studies. A traditional geographic problem in this latter tradition is that of regionalization —the attempt to derive areas relatively uniform in terms of a complex of associated characteristics and also relatively different from other areas in terms of that complex. Such problems, involving mass-data analysis, were traditionally handled by overlaying maps. This earlier procedure has been replaced, however, by the use of the modern computer, applying such multivariate procedures as factor analysis to reduce many variables to a few factors representing "complexes" of associated characteristics, and the application of numerical taxonomy to get optimal classification (minimizing within-group variance) of observations into regions on the basis of the distances between observations in the factor space (Berry & Ray 1966). Output from the entire procedure of data analysis and reduction includes the complexes of characteristics that define "regional character," measures of the similarity of the observations, and the regions [*see* CLUSTERING].

Statistical work also characterizes the man–land tradition, largely by virtue of either simple correlation and regression studies that include physical variables, on one side, and cultural variables, on the other (for example, correlations of annual precipitation and population densities in the high plains), or through uses of probability theory. It is the latter, indeterministic type of study that represents new departures. Curry (1962a), for example, shows how livestock management in the intensive grassland-farming areas of New Zealand is related to probabilities of fodder availability, which in turn are derived from probabilities of requisite climatic conditions. Much of the basic research goes into establishment of the relevant probabilities, in this case, of the probabilities of repetitive events that play a central role in farm management. Kates (1962), on the other hand, examined relations of management of flood-plain property to flood hazards, rare events. He found management practices to be conditioned, not by reasonably precise evaluations of the situation, as in the case of the New Zealand farmers, but by a widely varying set of preconceptions, at variance with the actual probability mechanisms.

Work in the earth-science tradition of geography has, also, become statistical and ranges from the attempt to reformulate the geography of landforms generated by fluvial mechanisms in the framework of general-systems theory (Chorley 1962) through studies of climatic change as a random series (Curry 1962b) to the analysis of precipitation climatology using harmonic methods (Sabbagh & Bryson 1962) or to the development of linear models predictive of some characteristic through prior multivariate analysis, so as to satisfy the assumptions of the model ultimately to be produced (Wong 1963). There is today perhaps more work of a statistical kind in the earth-science tradition than in either the area-studies or man–land tradition.

Statistical geography—analysis of both the statistical and the mathematical kind—is to be found in all branches of geography today. However, in the methods utilized, certain differences between geography's four main research traditions are to be noted. In the spatial tradition, distribution fitting, correlation and regression analysis, uses of such methods as the mathematical theory of graphs, and prescriptive uses of spatial programming dominate, along with uses of probability mechanisms to study diffusion processes. The area-studies tradition relies upon multivariate analysis, particularly factor analysis, and upon numerical taxonomy, to facilitate mass-data analysis. In the man–land tradition, a neat contrast is to be noted between those of traditional deterministic outlook, who use regression methods, and those concerned with decision making in resources management, who focus upon probabilities of the a priori and a posteriori kinds. Finally, in the earth-science tradition those procedures that facilitate systems analysis have been those most rapidly adopted and used. At the end of World War II geography was nonquantitative. Statistical geography has played an integral, even critical, part in the transformation of geography into a modern social science in the postwar years.

BRIAN J. L. BERRY

[See also CARTOGRAPHY; CENTRAL PLACE; REGIONAL SCIENCE. *Other relevant material may be found in* CLUSTERING; FACTOR ANALYSIS; MULTIVARIATE ANALYSIS.]

## BIBLIOGRAPHY

ACKERMAN, EDWARD A. 1963 Where Is a Research Frontier? Association of American Geographers, *Annals* 53:429–440.

BACHI, ROBERTO 1963 Standard Distance Measures and Related Methods for Spatial Analysis. Regional Science Association, *Papers* 10:83–132.

BERRY, BRIAN J. L. 1964a Approaches to Regional Analysis: A Synthesis. Association of American Geographers, *Annals* 54:2–11.

BERRY, BRIAN J. L. 1964b Cities as Systems Within Systems of Cities. Pages 116–137 in John Friedmann and William Alonso (editors), *Regional Development and Planning: A Reader.* Cambridge, Mass.: M.I.T. Press.

BERRY, BRIAN J. L. 1965 Research Frontiers in Urban Geography. Pages 403–430 in Philip M. Hauser and L. F. Schnore (editors), *The Study of Urbanization.* New York: Wiley.

BERRY, BRIAN J. L.; and RAY, MICHAEL 1966 Multivariate Socio-economic Regionalization: A Pilot Study in Central Canada. Unpublished manuscript.

CARROTHERS, GERALD A. P. 1956 An Historical Review of the Gravity and Potential Concepts of Human Interaction. *Journal of the American Institute of Planners* 22:94–102.

CHORLEY, RICHARD J. 1962 Geomorphology and General Systems Theory. U.S. Geological Survey, *Professional Paper* 500B.

CHORLEY, RICHARD J. 1963 Geography and Analogue Theory. Association of American Geographers, *Annals* 54:127–137.

CLARK, COLIN 1951 Urban Population Densities. *Journal of the Royal Statistical Society* Series A 114:490–496.

CURRY, LESLIE 1962a The Climatic Resources of Intensive Grassland Farming: The Waikato, New Zealand. *Geographical Review* 52:174–194.

CURRY, LESLIE 1962b Climatic Change as a Random Series. Association of American Geographers, *Annals* 52:21–31.

CURRY, LESLIE 1964 The Random Spatial Economy: An Exploration in Settlement Theory. Association of American Geographers, *Annals* 54:138–146.

DACEY, MICHAEL F.; and TUNG, TSE-HSIUNG 1962 The Identification of Randomness in Point Patterns. *Journal of Regional Science* 4:83–96.

DUNCAN, OTIS DUDLEY; CUZZORT, RAY P.; and DUNCAN, BEVERLY 1961 *Statistical Geography: Problems in Analyzing Areal Data.* New York: Free Press.

GARRISON, WILLIAM L. 1960 Connectivity of the Interstate Highway System. Regional Science Association, *Papers* 6:121–137.

GARRISON, WILLIAM L.; and MORRILL, RICHARD L. 1960 Projections of Interregional Patterns of Trade in Wheat and Flour. *Economic Geography* 36:116–126.

GEARY, R. C. 1954 The Contiguity Ratio and Statistical Mapping. *Incorporated Statistician* 5:115–145. → Includes four pages of discussion.

GOODMAN, LEO A. 1959 Some Alternatives to Ecological Correlation. *American Journal of Sociology* 64:610–625.

HÄGERSTRAND, TORSTEN 1953 *Innovationsförloppet ur korologisk synpunkt.* Lund (Sweden): Gleerupska Universitetsbokhandeln.

Haggett, Peter (1965) 1966 *Locational Analysis in Human Geography.* New York: St. Martins.

Hagood, Margaret D. 1943 Statistical Methods for Delineation of Regions Applied to Data on Agriculture and Population. *Social Forces* 21:287–297.

Kao, Richard C. 1963 The Use of Computers in the Processing and Analysis of Geographic Information. *Geographical Review* 53:530–547.

Kates, Robert W. 1962 *Hazard and Choice Perception in Flood Plain Management.* Department of Geography Research Paper No. 78. Univ. of Chicago Press.

Kendall, M. G. 1939 The Geographical Distribution of Crop Productivity in England. *Journal of the Royal Statistical Society* Series A 102:21–62.

King, Leslie J. 1962 A Quantitative Expression of Patterns of Urban Settlements in Selected Areas of the United States. *Tijdschrift voor economische en sociale geografie* 53:1–7.

McCarty, Harold H.; Hook, J. C.; and Knos, D. S. 1956 *The Measurement of Association in Industrial Geography.* Iowa City: State Univ. of Iowa, Department of Geography.

Mackay, J. Ross 1959 The Interactance Hypothesis and Political Boundaries in Canada: A Preliminary Study. *Canadian Geographer* 11:1–8.

Matérn, Bertil 1960 Spatial Variation: Stochastic Models and Their Applications to Some Problems in Forest Surveys and Other Sampling Investigations. Sweden, Statens Skogsforskningsinstitut, *Meddelanden* 49, no. 5.

Matui, Isamu 1932 Statistical Study of the Distribution of Scattered Villages in Two Regions of the Tonami Plain, Toyama Prefecture. *Japanese Journal of Geology and Geography* 9:251–256.

Moran, P. A. P. 1948 The Interpretation of Statistical Maps. *Journal of the Royal Statistical Society* Series B 10:245–251.

Morrill, Richard L. 1963 The Development of Spatial Distributions of Towns in Sweden: A Historical–Predictive Approach. Association of American Geographers, *Annals* 53:1–14.

Moser, Claus A.; and Scott, Wolf 1961 *British Towns: A Statistical Study of Their Economic and Social Differences.* Edinburgh: Oliver.

National Research Council, Ad Hoc Committee on Geography 1965 *The Science of Geography: Report.* National Research Council Publication No. 1277. Washington: National Academy of Sciences–National Research Council.

Nystuen, John D.; and Dacey, Michael F. 1961 A Graph Theory Interpretation of Nodal Regions. Regional Science Association, *Papers* 7:29–42.

Pattison, William D. 1964 The Four Traditions of Geography. *Journal of Geography* 63:211–216.

Porter, P. W. 1963 What Is the Point of Minimum Aggregate Travel? Association of American Geographers, *Annals* 53:224–232.

Ravenstein, E. G. 1885 The Laws of Migration. *Journal of the Royal Statistical Society* Series A 48:167–235. → Includes seven pages of discussion.

Ravenstein, E. G. 1889 The Laws of Migration: Second Paper. *Journal of the Royal Statistical Society* Series A 52:241–305. → Includes three pages of discussion.

Reilly, William J. 1931 *The Law of Retail Gravitation.* New York: Putnam.

Robinson, Arthur H. 1962 Mapping the Correspondence of Isarithmic Maps. Association of American Geographers, *Annals* 52:414–429.

Robinson, W. S. 1950 Ecological Correlations and the Behavior of Individuals. *American Sociological Review* 15:351–357.

Sabbagh, Michael A.; and Bryson, Reid A. 1962 Aspects of the Precipitation Climatology of Canada Investigated by the Method of Harmonic Analysis. Association of American Geographers, *Annals* 52:426–440.

Simon, Herbert A. 1955 On a Class of Skew Distribution Functions. *Biometrika* 42:425–440.

Stewart, John Q. 1947 Empirical Mathematical Rules Concerning the Distribution and Equilibrium of Population. *Geographical Review* 37:461–485.

Stewart, John Q.; and Warntz, William 1958 Physics of Population Distribution. *Journal of Regional Science* 1:99–123.

Thomas, Edwin N. 1960 *Maps of Residuals From Regression: Their Characteristics and Uses in Geographic Research.* Iowa City: State Univ. of Iowa, Department of Geography.

Tobler, Waldo R. 1963 Geographical Area and Map Projections. *Geographical Review* 53:59–78.

U.S. Bureau of the Census 1923 *Fourteenth Census of the United States; 1920: Center of Population and Median Lines and Centers of Area, Agriculture, Manufactures, and Cotton.* Washington: Government Printing Office.

Wong, Shue Tuck 1963 A Multivariate Statistical Model for Predicting Mean Annual Flood in New England. Association of American Geographers, *Annals* 53:298–311.

Wright, John K. 1937 Some Measures of Distributions. Association of American Geographers, *Annals* 27:177–211.

Yule, G. Udny; and Kendall, M. G. (1911) 1958 *An Introduction to the Theory of Statistics.* 14th ed., rev. & enl. London: Griffin. → M. G. Kendall has been joint author since the eleventh edition (1937) and revised the 1958 edition. See especially pages 310–325 on "Correlation and Regression: Some Practical Problems."

Zipf, George K. 1949 *Human Behavior and the Principle of Least Effort: An Introduction to Human Ecology.* Reading, Mass.: Addison-Wesley.

## GEOPOLITICS

See Geography, article on political geography, *and the biographies of* Kjellén; Mackinder.

## GEORGE, HENRY

Henry George (1839–1897) grew up in Philadelphia. As the author of *Progress and Poverty* he became one of the most telling speakers for social protest anywhere in the world. His father was the son of an English immigrant who had succeeded as a shipper; his mother's family had settled in the city before the Revolution. His father, a Democrat, was a customhouse clerk and for some years a publisher of Episcopalian sunday-school books; he sought to cultivate in his family both Democratic and low-church loyalties. Politically, young Henry George differed from his parents in that he was strongly opposed to slavery and voted Republican during the Civil War and the early Reconstruction period. However, he never abandoned his Episcopalian sympathies: his lifelong belief in the triumph of justice secularized the millennial hope that he had learned as a youngster.

George's family had little money to spare, and he left school when he was only 13. However, the deprivations he suffered were no worse than those of any child in a large family on a white-collar income. He learned how hard life could be for workingmen when, at age 15, shipping to India as a cabin boy, he witnessed a sailors' mutiny. For George himself the trip was pure adventure. His next long voyage, in 1857, which took him to California, was also inspired by restlessness rather than financial need. It was not until he had been in California for about seven years and was responsible for supporting a wife and two children that his inability to find steady work as a printer made him directly aware of the desperation of poverty.

George's journalistic career began with a job on the San Francisco *Alta California* in 1865; subsequently he worked on several other San Francisco papers, the *Times*, the *Chronicle*, and the *Herald*. In the late 1860s he returned to the Democratic party and became an adviser to Henry H. Haight, the state's governor who was crusading against monopoly. Haight put George in charge of the Sacramento *Reporter*, a party organ, but in 1871 George returned to San Francisco as founder, proprietor, and editor of the independent Democratic *Daily Evening Post*. As a business venture (George's only one), the paper failed, but it was a journalistic success. It provided George with the first platform from which he was able to develop fully his critical and reformist ideas.

George's experience with journalists and journalism made him familiar with some of the problems of California's spectacular and troubled economy, but it was several years before he found the "solution" to these problems. When he was still a printer in Sacramento, James McClatchy, the famous editor of the Sacramento *Bee*, acquainted him with the nation's homestead policy and the frustrations of that policy. On the San Francisco *Times*, George fought against private domination of land ownership, arguing that as a legal entity the city of San Francisco had the true ownership of the land it occupied, by devolution of title from the king of Spain through the *pueblo* of San Francisco. This claim was put forward with some success to reduce the claims of land-grabbers and speculators.

While working for the *Herald*, George came face to face with a more general problem, that of tech-

nological monopoly. The paper sent him to New York to obtain contracts for telegraphing the news from the Associated Press by way of Western Union. The failure of the negotiations appeared to George to jeopardize the freedom of the press. Deeply disturbed, he experienced "a thought, a vision, a call," and dedicated himself to combat the evil and want he had observed in New York. A few months later he had a second "vision." Riding in the foothills above Oakland, he looked down on the flatland near San Francisco Bay, which the transcontinental railroad had fantastically increased in value. "Like a flash it came upon me that there was the reason of advancing poverty with advancing wealth. With the growth of population, land grows in value, and the men who work it must pay for the privilege" (quoted in *The Life of Henry George*, by Henry George, Jr. [1871–1900] 1906–1911, vols. 9–10, p. 210).

As early as 1870, when he attributed to every man a "natural right" to a parcel of the earth's surface, George had begun to convert his reformist convictions into economic formulas. In 1871 his pamphlet *Our Land and Land Policy* (1871–1900, vol. 8) appeared, which was sizable enough to be considered his first book. It is a classic of economic criticism. George denounced both the prodigality of the national government in giving away the arable domain and that of the California state government, which permitted speculators to acquire much of the best land. He reasoned that in spite of past errors the homestead policy could yet be made to succeed if oversize holdings already granted were reduced by land taxes or inheritance taxes. Although he still accepted private property in land as a useful institution, George began to insist that "in nature" there is "no such thing as fee simple in land." The following year, in the *Daily Evening Post*, he carried this crucial limitation on land ownership a step further: "The land of a country rightfully belongs to all the people of that country; . . . there is no justification for private property in land except the general convenience and benefit; . . . private rights in land should always be held subordinate to the general good" (Barker 1955, pp. 176–177).

Gradually George systematized his economic ideas. Some time in the 1860s in Sacramento he had attended a meeting on the protective tariff, a policy in which he had long believed, and he had made an impromptu speech *against* the tariff. Free trade thus became his first publicly announced economic doctrine, and one from which he never departed; in the *Post* he was to advocate it repeatedly and dogmatically.

He opposed land monopoly because it denied free and just access to the bounties of earth; concerning the new natural monopolies which had been created by technology he felt differently. He demanded in the *Post* that the latter be transferred from private to public ownership—railroads and telegraphs to be owned by the national government and gas and water systems by the cities. His goal was to turn from private to public advantage the benefits of all monopolies that were not artificial and deserving of destruction. His editorials favored trade unions, a policy of high wage levels (other California papers were deflationist), and a policy of reserving the arable domain to actual homesteaders. Although in many of these ideas he was stimulated by socialists, he rejected the general doctrine of socialism.

When *Progress and Poverty* (1871–1900, vol. 1) first appeared in 1879, in San Francisco, the academic profession of economics was inchoate in the eastern United States and had no existence whatever in California. Economic thought in the east followed mainly the British classical school; the American nationalist school, of which H. C. Carey had been the principal figure, was a minority movement among economists, but its influence on Republican and national policy gave it disproportionate importance. The new analytical and institutional economics, then rising in Germany, Austria, and England, was little known at the time in America, and known not at all to George. Therefore, when George used and adapted the terms and logic of Smith, Ricardo, and John Stuart Mill, he was moving in an accepted tradition, and when he rejected the wages fund doctrine and the iron law of wages, he was merely revising the tradition, much as Francis A. Walker in the United States, and Mill himself had done.

The central four-fifths of *Progress and Poverty* is essentially a syllogism. The first premise appears in Book III, "The Laws of Distribution." There George stated his proposition that economic rent, being a product of monopoly—usable land is by nature monopolistic, not something replaceable—always reduces wages and interest. The second premise occurs in Book IV; on the basis of observation, George asserted that modern industrialism increases rent and that, as resource sites and urban sites rise in value, rent flowing into private hands creates social inequity, depression, and poverty. From these two premises—the first, that the landowner inevitably takes from the laborer and the capitalist and the second, that with private land ownership rent increases exacerbate social injustice—George reasoned to his synthesis, "The Rem-

edy," presented in Book VI. It is the historic proposal to do away with private property in land, or at least with the private privileges of tenure. In the following three books, George spelled out the procedures involved in his "Remedy": either land might be nationalized, or there might be taxation that would transfer economic rent from the landholder to the community (the latter alternative eventually became the "single tax"). The rent so placed at the disposal of the state could be distributed or invested, according to public interest.

The remaining one-fifth of the book contains the 15 pages of introduction and the 90 pages of conclusion, which may be called George's moral and religious sequence. There the author restated his paradox—that modern material "progress" actually widens the gap between the economically privileged and the unprivileged—and he stated his belief that a socially just civilization can be based only on a Christian and democratic conscience: "Association in equality is the law of progress."

It was in Europe that *Progress and Poverty* was first received with understanding, if not always with praise. Émile de Laveleye, the Belgian "socialist of the chair," discussed it with critical appreciation in the *Revue scientifique de la France et de l'étranger* (1880); Adolf Wagner of the University of Berlin was unfavorable; but Gustav Schmoller found freshness in the work, although he also found much to criticize. George wanted attention in the United States so much that even a highly critical review by William Graham Sumner in *Scribner's* pleased him.

George's early international reputation increased, however, not so much by reason of his writings as because of his involvement in public affairs abroad. By 1881 he had moved from California to New York, and the *Irish World* of that city sent him as correspondent to Ireland. Conditions in Ireland had not yet been improved by Gladstone's land reform, and George hoped to affect the situation as well as to report it. He distributed *Progress and Poverty* in Ireland, as well as a pamphlet on *The Land Question* ([1881] 1906–1911, vol. 3). He also went to London, where he established an uneasy relationship with H. M. Hyndman, the wealthy Marxist; made friends with Helen Taylor, the literary executor of John Stuart Mill, who said that Mill would have accepted George's ideas as an extension of his own; and became acquainted with Alfred Russel Wallace, the theorist of evolution who was also interested in land nationalization, and with other prominent men like John Morley and Joseph Chamberlain. George made the speech which George Bernard Shaw says converted him to social reform. George proudly assessed the long, semifavorable review of *Progress and Poverty* in the London *Times* as evidence that he was being taken seriously in high places.

The first visit to Europe led to four subsequent ones. The last one, in 1890, rounded out a trip that included a triumphant speaking tour in Australia. As far as the influence of George's ideas in the United Kingdom is concerned, the visits of 1883–1884 and 1884–1885 were the heyday. All the major British journals reviewed *Progress and Poverty*, and distinguished academic economists reacted to the book, albeit often negatively. Sir Henry Fawcett of Cambridge objected to George's opposition to compensating the landlords whose property rights he would destroy; Alfred Marshall, while admitting "freshness and earnestness" in George, concentrated a barrage of statistics on weaknesses in his findings about wages; Philip H. Wicksteed, a Unitarian minister and distinguished economist, acknowledged a major debt to George; and Arnold Toynbee, the young pro-labor Oxford economist, tried just before his untimely death to refute George in public lectures in London. In Scotland, George discovered many admirers: the Land Restoration League there shared his preference for land taxation as the best means of reform. Keir Hardie became the political link between George's impact on Britain in the 1880s and the modern British Labour party. During an Oxford visit, the students treated George outrageously; at Cambridge, things went better. As J. A. Hobson observed in 1897: ". . . Henry George may be considered to have exercised a more directly powerful formative and educative influence over English radicalism of the last fifteen years than any other man" (p. 844).

After his return from Ireland, George's activities in America took several directions. He wrote a series of articles for *Frank Leslie's Illustrated Newspaper* which was polemically directed against a previous series of articles on current problems written by Sumner for *Harper's Weekly*. In book form Sumner's articles became *What Social Classes Owe to Each Other*, the recognized classic of social Darwinist thought. George's articles, gathered and published as *Social Problems* (1871–1900, vol. 2), initially were better received than *Progress and Poverty*.

George also became active on the political scene. In 1886 a major New York City labor union persuaded him to be the Labor party candidate for mayor. He drew considerable support from early social gospelers, the labor unions, and recent immigrant voters. At the polls he came in second, close enough to the winning candidate to give credence to the charge that he would have won if votes had not been stolen. He did succeed in drawing maximum attention to his ideas and in consolidating his followers.

George's next venture was the single-tax reform. Although the phrase "single tax" does not appear in *Progress and Poverty*, the reform idea does. It was George's lasting conviction that land-value taxation could and should be used to transfer the whole product of economic rent from private owners to the community. A transfer of this kind would be politically easier to achieve in America than land nationalization and would have the same economic effect. George began using the term "single tax" during the mid-1880s, but it was a convert to his ideas, Thomas G. Shearman, a New York lawyer, who transformed the term into a slogan and the name of a reform movement. By 1888 single-tax meetings were being held in the principal cities on the eastern seaboard, in the Middle West, and in California. The long-term leaders of the movement —Louis F. Post, Tom Loftin Johnson, Warren Worth Bailey, William Lloyd Garrison II, Jackson S. Ralston, and Lawson Purdy—were already active, and before 1890, 130 single-tax organizations had appeared. The early movement was strained by an inner struggle between "single-tax, limited" men, like Shearman, who wanted only as much rent appropriated as was necessary for ordinary public services, and "single-tax, unlimited" men, like George, who wanted all the rent taken. After George's death, the proponents of "single-tax, limited" predominated. The movement narrowed, but it endured. During the early 1900s its program was incorporated into municipal reform programs and enactments, conspicuously in Ohio; and during the 1910s it influenced Wilsonian, Democratic progressivism. From 1887 to the present, through organizations which have varied from clubs to schools to endowments, the movement has continuously promoted land-value taxation and free trade.

During the 1890s, Henry George left the advocacy of the single tax largely in the hands of others, as he had earlier abandoned labor politics. With the exception of his round-the-world trip and the final campaign for the New York mayoralty in 1897, he gave his time to writing three books, which were essentially testaments. In *The Condition of Labor* ([1891] 1906–1911, vol. 3) he challenged Pope Leo XIII to permit Catholics to enter his movement; in *A Perplexed Philosopher* ([1892] 1906–1911, vol. 5) he fully dissociated himself from the materialism of Spencerian and like-minded belief in progress and repeated his program for land-value taxation; in *The Science of Political Economy* ([1897] 1906–1911, vols. 6–7), which he never completed, he tried, with new elaboration but without mastery of current modes of economic thought, to persuade readers that his economic theories were scientifically sound. These codicils never had the impact of his earlier books, although they too revealed George's passion for justice and freedom and his intellectual boldness and gift for persuasion. The final statements rounded out a dedicated and prophetic life.

CHARLES A. BARKER

[*See also* RENT; TAXATION, *article on* PROPERTY TAXES; *and the biographies of* MILL; SUMNER; TOYNBEE; WALKER; WICKSTEED.]

### BIBLIOGRAPHY

BARKER, CHARLES A. 1955 *Henry George*. New York: Oxford Univ. Press.

CORD, STEVEN B. 1965 *Henry George: Dreamer or Realist?* Philadelphia: Univ. of Pennsylvania Press.

DE MILLE, ANNA A. [GEORGE] 1950 *Henry George: Citizen of the World*. Chapel Hill: Univ. of North Carolina Press.

GEIGER, GEORGE R. 1933 *The Philosophy of Henry George*. New York: Macmillan.

GEORGE, HENRY (1871–1900) 1906–1911 *The Writings of Henry George*. 10 vols. Garden City, N.Y.: Doubleday. → Volume 1: *Progress and Poverty*. Volume 2: *Social Problems*. Volume 3: *The Land Question; Property in Land; The Condition of Labor*. Volume 4: *Protection or Free Trade*. Volume 5: *A Perplexed Philosopher*. Volumes 6–7: *The Science of Political Economy; Moses: A Lecture*. Volume 8: *Our Land and Land Policy; Speeches, Lectures, and Miscellaneous Writings*. Volumes 9–10: *The Life of Henry George*, by Henry George, Jr.

HOBSON, J. A. 1897 Influence of Henry George in England. *Fortnightly Review* 68:835–844.

LAVELEYE, ÉMILE DE 1880 La propriété terrienne et le paupérisme. *Revue scientifique de la France et de l'étranger* 2nd Series 18:708–710. → A review of *Progress and Poverty*.

LAWRENCE, ELWOOD P. 1957 *Henry George in the British Isles*. East Lansing: Michigan State Univ. Press.

NEW YORK, PUBLIC LIBRARY 1926 *Henry George and the Single Tax: A Catalogue of the Collection in the New York Public Library*, by Rollin A. Sawyer. The Library.

NOCK, ALBERT J. 1939 *Henry George: An Essay*. New York: Morrow.

YOUNG, ARTHUR N. 1916 *The Single Tax Movement in the United States*. Princeton Univ. Press.

# GERSON, JEAN DE

Jean Charlier de Gerson (1363–1429) was born at Gerson-les-Barbey in Champagne. He began his studies at the University of Paris in 1377, becoming a bachelor of arts in 1381 and a doctor of theology in 1392. For much of his life Gerson was a leading academic theologian of his university; he was made chancellor in 1395, succeeding his friend Pierre d'Ailly, with whom he was later to share the intellectual leadership of the conciliar movement.

Gerson was prominent in support of the attempt of the Council of Pisa, 1409, to end the great schism in the papacy by appealing to the allegedly superior authority of the General Council in church government. Later he was a member of the French delegation to the Council of Constance, 1414–1418, where he formulated his mature conciliarist theories. He had strongly alienated the Burgundian faction in French court politics by his strong condemnation of their use of the doctrine of tyrannicide to justify the murder of the anti-Burgundian Duke Charles of Orleans in 1408, and their hostility prevented him from returning to Paris; his surviving years were spent in Vienna and Lyons.

Although he wrote a number of academic theological treatises, in the scholastic manner, Gerson was primarily concerned with the active implementation of the demands of the Christian life. His considerable pastoral experience was gained in Paris and in Bruges, where he was for a time dean of the Church of St. Donatien. A large number of his sermons and pastoral and spiritual treatises, including influential writings on mysticism, survive. His preoccupation with the problem of how best to end the scandal of the papal schism grew out of his pastoral responsibilities.

**Theories of church government.** Gerson's ideas on church authority in general, and on the position of the General Council within the government of the church in particular, are among the most original and permanently influential parts of his works. He arrived at a full-blown conciliar position only after a slow process of disillusionment with the executive power of the papacy. It was as late as 1409, on the eve of the Council of Pisa, that Gerson first put forward the idea that in case of grave necessity the ordinary canon law of the church could be set aside. Gerson was here dealing with the problem of how a council to end the schism could be summoned without papal approval, hitherto considered essential by the canonists. He solved the difficulty by appealing to the principle of epikeia, or equity, which set aside the letter of the law in order to preserve its spirit (a concept going back via Aquinas and other Scholastics to Aristotle).

Gerson's mature conciliar theory is set forth in *De potestate ecclesiastica*, written in 1416–1417, during the Council of Constance. Gerson argued that the General Council, representing the totality of the faithful, was superior to any other institution in the church, including the papacy, even though, as the executive head of the church, the papacy had the prerogative to oversee its day-to-day governance. The theory of conciliar supremacy was not new; it had been discussed freely in the fourteenth century, but Gerson gave it its most comprehensive expression. His application of the theory of representation to the church, the most articulated social organism of the Middle Ages, is his enduring contribution to political science.

There has been some controversy about Gerson's position in the medieval philosophical and theological spectrum. He certainly had close affinities with the Ockhamist school, sharing with them a dislike of the excessive intrusion of man-made intellectual concepts into the data of revelation, a practice characteristic of the Scotists. But he referred freely also to the authority of pre-Ockhamist writers of the realist tradition, such as St. Bonaventure, St. Thomas Aquinas, and St. Albert the Great, as well as to the authority of patristic sources. The truth may be that Gerson's system was an eclectic one, evolved with a constant eye on the needs of practical Christian teaching.

JOHN B. MORRALL

[*Other relevant material may be found in the biographies of* AQUINAS; MARSILIUS OF PADUA; OCKHAM.]

#### WORKS BY GERSON

(1417) 1965  De potestate ecclesiastica. Volume 6, pages 210–250 in Jean de Gerson, *Oeuvres complètes*. Paris: Desclée.

*Oeuvres complètes*. 12 vols. Paris: Desclée, 1960—. → To be published in 12 volumes. Volumes 1–6 have been completed.

*Opera omnia*. 5 vols. in 4. Antwerp (Belgium): Sumptibus Societatis, 1706.

#### SUPPLEMENTARY BIBLIOGRAPHY

ARIÈS, PHILIPPE (1960) 1962  *Centuries of Childhood: A Social History of Family Life*. New York: Knopf. → First published as *L'enfant et la vie familiale sous l'ancien régime*. Contains a discussion of Gerson's pedagogical ideas.

COMBES, ANDRÉ 1940  *Jean Gerson: Commentateur dionysien*. Études de philosophie médiévale, Vol. 30. Paris: Vrin.

COMBES, ANDRÉ 1942  *Jean de Montreuil et le chancelier Gerson: Contribution à l'histoire des rapports de l'humanisme et de la théologie en France au début du XVᵉ siècle*. Études de philosophie médiévale, Vol. 32. Paris: Vrin.

COMBES, ANDRÉ 1945–1959  *Essai sur la critique de Ruysbroeck par Gerson*. 3 vols. Paris: Vrin.

COMBES, ANDRÉ; MOURIN, LOUIS; and SIMONE, FRANCO 1951  Jean Gerson. Volume 6, pages 185–191 in *Enciclopedia cattolica*. Vatican City: The Encyclopedia.

CONNOLLY, JAMES L. 1928  *John Gerson: Reformer and Mystic*. Louvain, Université Catholique, Recueil de travaux d'histoire et de philologie, 2d Series, fasc. 12. Louvain (Belgium): Librairie Universitaire.

MORRALL, JOHN B. 1960  *Gerson and the Great Schism*. Manchester Univ. Press.

MOURIN, LOUIS 1952  *Jean Gerson: Prédicateur français*. Bruges (Belgium): De Tempel.

SCHWAB, JOHANN B. 1858  *Johannes Gerson; Professor der Theologie und Kanzler der Universität Paris: Eine Monographie*. Würzburg (Germany): Stahel.

## GERVAISE, ISAAC

Isaac Gervaise, merchant and writer on economics, was a French Huguenot born in Paris after the mid-seventeenth century. He became a naturalized British citizen. In 1691 his father helped to finance the Royal Lustring Company of England (manufacturers of a fine black silk), and shortly thereafter both father and son became officers of the company.

Gervaise is known for only one work, *The System or Theory of the Trade of the World*, which was published in 1720 but in effect rediscovered by Jacob Viner only in 1935 (see Foreword to Gervaise [1720] 1954). It is a remarkable essay, formulating the first general equilibrium treatment of the international mechanism of adjustment. Gervaise's presentation marks a pioneer application of the "income" or "macroeconomic" approach to problems of international equilibrium and disequilibrium. It analyzes the process that produces disequilibrium and shows under what conditions adjustment is restored or maladjustment persists. Gervaise drew a distinction between disturbances which may arise from fluctuations in trade per se and those which may arise from comparative stability in prices. His formulation embraces domestic and international equilibrium; credit, inflation, and their effects on trade; the role of exchange rates; monopoly, tariffs, and the determinants of free trade.

Although Gervaise's work deserves more attention for its masterly theorizing than for its policy recommendations, it is nevertheless notable as one of the very few unambiguous expressions of a free-trade position in the English economic literature before Adam Smith. Gervaise argued in uncompromising terms that monetary instability and monopoly must be held in strict control. In an age when most writings on economics consisted of special pleading, Gervaise's scientifically objective work was a most unusual achievement. It is the more remarkable since Gervaise was an officer in a company that operated with special monopolistic privileges, and the public policy he advocated was in sharp conflict with his private interests. To be sure, it may have been easier and less noble for him to take an antimercantilist position in 1720, for in that year the Royal Lustring Company had lost its charter. Gervaise wrote in his preface: ". . . this System . . . hath the ill Fate to appear at a time, when I myself could wish it false" ([1720] 1954, p. 3). The statement seems to imply that while repeal was in the public interest it was injurious to his private interests.

Gervaise had not only the advantage of practical experience but also the capacity for general inquiry. A man of his experience and training was in a singularly fortunate position to examine the then existing international mechanism of adjustment, and he examined it with realistic detail and penetrating insight. Every sentence reveals incisive first-hand knowledge of the phenomena he described. The economy of words, the deep insight into the motivations of men and nations, and the vigor of his analysis all contribute to making Gervaise's book a profound study, the wisdom of which appears to grow with each reading.

JOHN M. LETICHE

[*See also* INTERNATIONAL MONETARY ECONOMICS; INTERNATIONAL TRADE.]

BIBLIOGRAPHY
GERVAISE, ISAAC (1720) 1954 *The System or Theory of the Trade of the World.* With a Foreword by Jacob Viner and an Introduction by John M. Letiche. Baltimore: Johns Hopkins Press.
LETICHE, JOHN M. 1952 Isaac Gervaise on the International Mechanism of Adjustment. *Journal of Political Economy* 60:34–43.
LETICHE, JOHN M. 1959 *Balance of Payments and Economic Growth.* New York: Harper.
MAINTRIEU, JEHAN 1909 *Le traité d'Utrecht et les polémiques du commerce anglais.* Paris: Pichon & Durand-Auzias.
VINER, JACOB 1937 *Studies in the Theory of International Trade.* New York: Harper.

# GESELL, ARNOLD L.

Whatever else Arnold Gesell (1880–1961) may have accomplished, he made his name a household word in the United States: his books and articles on child development are legion, and some of the books were best sellers. For example, by 1943 *Infant and Child in the Culture of Today* had gone through 15 printings. At least one generation of American infants and preschoolers was reared according to the manuals provided by Gesell and his colleagues.

Gesell was born in Alma, Wisconsin; by the time

he graduated from the local high school he was already deeply committed to science and the profession of teaching. At Clark University, where he earned his PH.D. degree in 1906, he came under the influence of G. Stanley Hall, one of the earliest psychologists to study child development. Gesell's early dedication to teaching, combined with his contact with Hall, probably pointed him in the direction that led to his fame as the "father of scientific child study."

After graduate study at Clark, Gesell spent several years as a teacher and principal in a public school, as a settlement worker, and as a normal-school and university professor. Finally, he found his niche at Yale, where he founded the Clinic of Child Development in 1911 and remained its director until his formal retirement in 1948. Gesell had already gained substantial professional status when he decided that medicine would give him greater depth as a research worker; accordingly, he studied medicine at Yale at the same time that he was an assistant professor, and he received his M.D. degree in 1915. Retirement 33 years later was only a formality for Gesell—he continued his clinical work and research for the Harvard Pediatric Study and at the Gesell Institute of Child Development.

Gesell's power to attract able, almost fanatically devoted disciples is well known to both scientists and laymen. Most of these followers bear his stamp indelibly, have reflected credit on his name and on their apprenticeship to him, and are themselves well known in the field of child development. Not until the 1940s did a group of Young Turks in the fields of child and clinical psychology come to consider Gesell only as a recorder of norms, neatly labeled and classified but without the explanatory power that is psychology's central interest.

Gesell did a basically respectable, and even a notable, job of combining clinical work with scientific observation of children. His photographic and one-way mirror studies of infants brought a new exactitude to the study of the young child. But his data about older children seem to have been less rigorously gathered. His coauthored books, e.g., *The First Five Years of Life* (1940) and *The Child From Five to Ten* (1946), tend to lose the individual child and to specify rather dogmatically an invariance and a genetic or constitutional universality of child development. These works simply assert the cyclical character of child development and underestimate the influence of the complex culture in which the child develops and learns. Development emerges as something mechanical: invariant, unchangeable, almost fatelike. The question may well be asked whether Gesell, with his rigid norms, his lack of individual variation, his strong emphasis on the constitutional, and his neglect of the cultural, has not hindered parents in their rearing of children more than he has helped them.

The Gesell Development Schedules were perhaps not intended as measures of infant intelligence, but they were widely so used and were long considered nearly infallible. In fact, however, they have failed, for the most part, to predict later intellectual development of children, individually or in groups. The harm that has been done by the trusting employment of the schedules is incalculable: many children have been denied adoption and condemned to prolonged and blighting custody in infant-care institutions because their Developmental Quotients were low (and, predictably, became lower the longer the children stayed in the institutions).

Gesell wrote with a bland, almost Olympian certainty about how children develop, and unless his writings are examined carefully they carry the implication that his conclusions are based on the careful study, over an extended period, of untold hundreds of infants and children. Even the fine print does not reveal precisely the actual number of subjects who were studied at different ages. A sympathetic biographer has referred to "follow-up examinations on about 175 cases, with referrals from different agencies and persons of 600 to 700, mostly of preschool age, and 1,000 or more guidance and observational contacts centering on nursery children" (Miles 1964, p. 55). The considerably less sympathetic Milton J. E. Senn, Gesell's successor at Yale, has pointed out that the sample for Gesell's basic 1925 survey was all white and numbered only 107 middle-class children from a single city in New England, while studies of older children were based on even smaller samples— for example, for six-year-olds, only eleven girls and seven boys (1955).

This is slight evidence, indeed, for statements describing the six-year-old as follows: "He tends to go to extremes . . ." (Gesell & Ilg 1946, p. 90), or "An outstanding characteristic of the 6-year-old is his meager capacity to modulate" (p. 92), or "He does not only smile,—he fairly dances with joy. He cries copiously when unhappy, kicks and shakes with his grief. Even during sleep he pitches his whole organism into his dreams. Hence the gross arousals of his nightmares, which come to a peak at the age of six" (p. 94). And so on and on, for 42 pages.

In sum, Gesell no longer appears the superman of child development that he was considered in his heyday, in the 1930s and 1940s. Serious questions must be raised about the quality of his social influence and the advice to parents by his disciples— for example, the flat statement by Louise Ames that the time of first tooth eruption is perhaps the best predictor of later reading success. Yet none can deny him a measure of greatness: he *was* the most scientific of the early students of infant behavior. He did give great impetus to moving "child study" toward "a *science* of child behavior." He fathered and fostered one of the great centers for child study. He trained some of the best workers in the field of child behavior and development and influenced (and still influences) them all. These are no mean achievements.

BOYD R. McCANDLESS

[*For the historical context of Gesell's work, see the biography of* HALL; *for discussion of the subsequent development of Gesell's ideas, see* ADOLESCENCE; DEVELOPMENTAL PSYCHOLOGY; INFANCY; MORAL DEVELOPMENT; SENSORY AND MOTOR DEVELOPMENT; SOCIALIZATION.]

### WORKS BY GESELL

1940    YALE UNIVERSITY, CLINIC OF CHILD DEVELOPMENT *The First Five Years of Life: A Guide to the Study of the Preschool Child.* New York: Harper. → Contains "Early Mental Growth" by Arnold Gesell and "The Study of the Individual Child" by Arnold Gesell and Catherine S. Amatruda.

(1943) 1949    GESELL, ARNOLD; and ILG, FRANCES L. *Child Development: An Introduction to the Study of Human Growth.* Part 1: Infant and Child in the Culture of Today. New York: Harper.

(1946) 1949    GESELL, ARNOLD; and ILG, FRANCES L. *Child Development: An Introduction to the Study of Human Growth.* Part 2: The Child From Five to Ten. New York: Harper.

1952    Autobiography. Volume 4, pages 123–142 in *A History of Psychology in Autobiography.* Worcester, Mass.: Clark Univ. Press.

### SUPPLEMENTARY BIBLIOGRAPHY

MILES, WALTER R. 1964 Arnold Lucius Gesell, 1880– 1961: A Biographical Memoir. National Academy of Sciences, *Biographical Memoirs* 37:55–96.

SENN, MILTON J. E. 1955 The Epoch Approach to Child Development. *Woman's Home Companion* 82, Nov.: 40–42, 60–62.

# GESTALT THEORY

The problem that gestalt theory confronts is that of an extended event, whether an experience or an action, that cannot be adequately described as a sum of smaller, independent events. Such an event is called a gestalt; this term can be translated as "form," "configuration," or "structure." Facts of this character were largely ignored in the atomistic psychology of the nineteenth and early twentieth centuries, although a few thinkers had begun to question this neglect.

The gestalt movement introduced a new approach to the treatment of psychological facts. It arose in Germany in the second decade of the twentieth century as a reaction against atomistic psychology. Its founders and pioneers were Max Wertheimer, Wolfgang Köhler, and Kurt Koffka. The first 25 years of its existence were a period of rapid development of ideas and of intensive investigation. Beginning with the 1920s it commanded wide attention in the psychological world. With the rise of Nazism the leading gestalt psychologists left Germany for the United States, and the subsequent course of the movement became, in a measure, part of the history of American psychology. [*See the biographies of* Koffka; Köhler; Wertheimer.]

The gestalt movement advanced a searching examination of the presuppositions of atomism; more important, it introduced an alternative conception that became the basis of many investigations and theoretical proposals. The earliest contributions of gestalt psychology were concerned mainly with problems of perception. Subsequently, its investigations extended to the areas of thinking, memory, and learning, and, more recently, to social psychology and the psychology of art; it also made contact with certain aspects of logic and ethics. As its investigations came to include new areas, gestalt theory stood revealed as a systematic orientation within psychology.

The source of the gestalt movement can be traced to one paramount concern. As a rule the events of mental life possess form, sense, and value; these are its striking characteristics. Yet, the prevailing scientific psychology contained virtually no reference to these attributes, and its accounts appeared correspondingly limited and barren. The customary reply to this stricture was that scientific procedure requires analysis into elements and therefore permits no other outcome. Accepting this reasoning, some thinkers concluded that important human phenomena and problems necessarily fall outside the reach of science. Others, among them the vitalists, appealed to higher and undefined agencies as sources of form and sense. Gestalt psychologists rejected such a solution on the ground that it adopted a questionable postulate about the demands of scientific investigation. An approach that fails to do justice to the most obvious facts of experience cannot, they held, be scientifically correct. They saw in this situation a challenge to re-examine the starting point of psychology.

## Perceptual organization

The formulations of gestalt theory were first tested in perception. This was the most advanced part of systematic psychology and the area in which atomism was most strongly entrenched. In the psychology of the early twentieth century the elements of perception were simple and irreducible sensations, each having its unique quality and a constant relationship to a particular excitation of the sense organs. To explain the combinations of these isolated sensations (and their images), this psychology invoked the mechanism of association by contiguity, which, it held, brought order into the initial chaos of sensations. The goals of this psychology were to identify the elements of experience and the corresponding stimulus energies and to describe the manner in which the elements become associated, all based on the method of analytic introspection.

The issue was brought to a head when Wertheimer took the radical step of denying the reality of sensory elements as parts of perceptual experience. His study of apparent movement ([1912–1920] 1925, pp. 1–105), which marks the formal beginning of gestalt theory, provides a specific illustration of this thesis. The experience of motion was traditionally described as a sum of successive sensations of position, each corresponding to successive local excitations. Apparent movement results when two stationary objects in distinct positions— for example, two lines—are exposed in succession with a suitably small time interval between them; the observer sees one line moving from one to the other position in a manner indistinguishable from real motion. This phenomenon, which is at the basis of cinematography, was well known. Wertheimer pointed out that apparent movement is not a series of sensations but an effect of two stimulus events cooperating to produce a new, unitary outcome; perceived movement cannot be split up into successive stationary sensations. The static character of the external situation is not represented in experience, while the movement perceived has no counterpart in the objective situation. From the assumption that experience consists of having one sensation followed by another, one cannot account for the experience of change inherent in motion, a conclusion that applies equally to the perception of real motion.

A further and more important step in this development was the gestalt account of grouping, or unit formation, in perception. Visual experience consists of things that may, in turn, form groups; certain parts of the visual field appear to cohere and to form units that separate themselves from the surrounding space and from other units. The units of perception are trees, houses, persons—not innumerable sensory elements. It was the contribution of gestalt theory to show that the formation and segregation of units cannot be taken as self-evident, as it seems to common sense, but constitutes a central problem for the psychology of perception. The physical energies that are reflected from the points of an external object are entirely discrete; each hits the eye independently of the others, with no indication of whether each comes from the same object. They form a mere mosaic of stimuli that may be grouped in numerous ways and that provide no basis for the veridical organization of the percept. Unity of the physical object does not account for unity of the percept. How then do units emerge from discrete stimulation? Wertheimer described certain fundamental principles of grouping, or unit formation, in perception, among them those of proximity, similarity, closure, common fate, and good continuation (Wertheimer 1925). Working with discontinuous points or lines, he demonstrated that they tend to fall into groups, in accordance with relative spatial proximity and qualitative similarity; grouping also occurs in accordance with closure and good continuation. Wertheimer considered one principle, that of *Prägnanz*, fundamental and inclusive of the others. The principle of *Prägnanz* maintains that grouping tends toward maximal simplicity and balance, or toward the formation of "good form."

The facts of grouping establish, first, that sets of stimuli produce effects not derivable from the effects of the single stimuli. These effects, observable only in extended wholes, are dependent upon strictly objective conditions—namely, specific geometrical relations between stimuli. Second, the stimulus relations logically permit other groupings that do not in fact occur. Thus, the facts of grouping give evidence of selective principles according to which sensory data are organized, and the units of perception must therefore be considered products of organization or specific effects of processes resulting from certain relationships. Third, the same sensory conditions of grouping that usually give rise to veridical perception sometimes produce non-veridical perception. As the facts of camouflage show, physically real units are not necessarily perceived, and perceptual units sometimes arise in the absence of corresponding physical units. Fourth, Wertheimer concluded that he had identified primary principles of grouping in perception. He explicitly included past experience as one determinant of grouping but maintained that it cannot account for the other grouping tendencies that are themselves necessary conditions of learning. Last, the principles of grouping have a broad range of application; foremost is their capacity to explain object and form perception in general.

The treatment of part–whole relations, which is central to the gestalt position, may best be illustrated with the contribution of von Ehrenfels, who in 1890 described perceptual facts that are not a sum of independent local components. A property of a visual entity, such as roundness or symmetry, does not reside in its separate parts or in their sum; the same is true of the character of a temporal unit, such as a melody. Such properties are also transposable; a melody is recognized in a new key, although it shares no tones with that heard originally, and a square is recognizable as such when it is enlarged or reduced or when it appears in a new part of the field. There are innumerable facts of this order that refer to qualities in wholes only, among them those we call straight, closed, hard, smooth, translucent.

These form qualities, or *Gestaltqualitäten*, posed a problem for a psychology that took sensations as the sole contents of experience. Reversing the traditional formulation, Wertheimer proposed not only that a coherent whole has properties and tendencies not discoverable in its isolated parts but also that a part has properties which it does not possess when it stands alone or when it belongs to another unit. The character of a whole often determines whether one of its parts will be perceptible or not and what its properties will be. Given three dots in a linear array, one is perceived as middle, the others as ends; these properties are relationally determined and do not exist for the isolated components. This thesis of part–whole determination asserts that a part is a dependent property of its whole and thus draws a basic distinction between "part" and "element."

Furthermore, a host of discoveries demonstrated that the identical stimulation, at different points in time, of a given region can produce markedly different effects, depending upon the stimulation occurring in neighboring regions. The perceptual constancies and the so-called illusions revealed striking discrepancies between what is in fact observed and what should be observed if local sensations alone were the content of experience. The shapes and sizes of objects remain within limits approximately constant as their orientation and distance are varied, and the colors of objects tend to look the same when the conditions of illumination change widely. The same proximal stimulation may cause perception of bright or dark, of upright or tilted, of large or small, of motion or rest, of motion at a high or at a low velocity, depending upon other stimulus conditions. In an effort to bolster the classical position the interpretation advanced was that the sensations in question were in fact unchanged but were corrected by judgments or "unconscious inferences" formed in the course of past experience. A clearer and more consistent explanation of these and other facts could be given using the assumption that they were effects of perceptual organization initiated by specific stimulus relations. [See PERCEPTION, *articles on* PERCEPTUAL CONSTANCY *and* ILLUSIONS AND AFTEREFFECTS.]

Important support for the gestalt treatment of perception came from the demonstration by Rubin (1915) of the distinction between "figure" and "ground," between the thing-character of the former and the formlessness of the latter. A step in the same direction was the subsequent discovery by Michotte (1946) that particular conditions of successive stimulation produce the experience of causality. When figural units are perceived to move in relation to each other at certain rates, they are experienced as functionally connected; the observer refers to the motion of one object as the cause, while the motion of another object is perceived as the effect. Still other patterns of movements, which can also be clearly specified, produce the impression of animated movement. In the light of these and related findings atomism in perception ceased to be a viable position.

**Physical and physiological gestalten.** The concept of gestalt received a fundamental elaboration in the work of Köhler (1920; 1940). As a first step Köhler called attention to a striking similarity between certain aspects of field physics and facts of perceptual organization. He pointed to certain instances of functional wholes in physics that cannot be compounded from the action of their separate parts. There are macroscopic physical states that tend to develop toward an equilibrium and in the direction of maximum regularity. One can describe the local conditions in such functional wholes with any desired degree of precision, but they do not function as independent parts. Systems of this character, of which there are numerous instances, are physical gestalten. They meet the criteria of von Ehrenfels (1890) for a gestalt quality.

Following the lead of the phenomenal data, Köhler proposed that there are macroscopic field processes in the brain, involving interactions which account for the effects of grouping and segregation and for the operation of the *Prägnanz* principle. Traditionally, cortical action was described in terms of separate excitations conducted along insulated fibers to circumscribed areas. The relational determination of experiences implies that the neural processes corresponding to separate stimulations must influence each other across distances in a manner that depends on their relative properties.

Köhler proposed a fundamental change in the conception of cortical functioning. A region such as the optic sector may be considered an electrolyte; the processes within it occur according to physical laws of self-distribution rather than according to the microanatomy of neural networks. Local states of excitation are surrounded by fields that represent these states in their environment and interact with other local states similarly represented. On this basis Köhler put forward the hypothesis that there are physiological processes which are special instances of physicochemical gestalten and that these are the correlates of phenomenal gestalten.

Implicit in the preceding examination is the assumption of psychophysical isomorphism, or the proposition that brain processes include some structural features that are identical with those of organized experience. Isomorphism refers not to metrical but to topological correspondences; brain processes are assumed to preserve the functional relations of symmetry, closedness, and adjacency, not the exact sizes and angles of patterns projected on the retina. This formulation diverges from the widely accepted view that phenomenal and physiological events are lawfully correlated but have no further likeness between them. The postulate of isomorphism is intended as a heuristic guide to investigation. In this manner Köhler sought a unified explanation for facts in neurophysiology and psychology among certain facts of physics. [See NERVOUS SYSTEM, *article on* STRUCTURE AND FUNCTION OF THE BRAIN.]

### Memory and association

There is a natural transition from the gestalt study of perception to memory. When a form has been perceived it may be subsequently recognized and recalled; thus, the products of perceptual organization are among the contents of memory. The persistence of past experiences requires a concept of memory traces; further, the resemblance between memories and original experiences implies that memory traces preserve the organized character of earlier processes. Gestalt studies of memory start from this assumption; a first effort to elaborate a theory of memory-trace action will be found in Koffka (1935).

The preceding formulations lead directly to one of the problems of memory—recognition. The facts of transposition to which von Ehrenfels first called attention imply the recognition of wholes or gestalten and, further, that recognition occurs on the basis of gestalt similarity and in the absence of identical elements in past and present situations. Since recognition depends upon the activation of specific memory traces and is highly selective, the gestalt proposal is that such memory-trace contact occurs on the basis of distinctive similarity, analogous to grouping by similarity in immediate experience. This formulation further implies that if the process corresponding to a present experience is to contact a corresponding memory trace, it must have its effect beyond its immediate locus and that neural conduction along insulated nerve fibers alone does not suffice to explain recognition. Thus, according to this account recognition depends upon an interaction that is relationally determined.

With respect to the concept of association two points are of main consequence. First, the gestalt account of perceptual organization was intended as a direct alternative to the interpretation that perceptual units are made up of associations between elements. Second, association theories have in practice all but abandoned the phenomena of perception; they tend to take the presence of perceptual units for granted and concentrate instead on connections formed between one unit and another. In treating these facts, one principle, that of association by contiguity, was increasingly singled out as basic. According to this principle, temporal contiguity is the crucial condition of association. In this account an association has the character of a bond that does not alter the terms it connects.

From the standpoint of gestalt theory the concept of an association as a mere bond is not a satisfactory basis of explanation. Processes in nature are as a rule relationally determined. In this connection Köhler (1929; 1941) proposed that an association is not a new process, but an aftereffect of organization and that it is dependent upon the relative properties of the respective terms. When two items are connected they form a unit and leave a corresponding unitary trace; subsequent excitation of a part of this trace will spread to the entire trace. Given this starting point there is no reason to single out the relation of contiguity, to the exclusion of others; all relations, such as those of similarity and good continuation, should bind events to each other. More generally, conditions favorable to organization should be conditions of association. Accordingly, the formation of associations and perceptual organization receive a unified interpretation. There remain unresolved issues in this area, but the available evidence supports the conclusion that relations other than contiguity exert pronounced effects on the formation of associations (Asch 1960). [*See* FORGETTING.]

## Thinking

Two themes have been most prominent in the gestalt treatment of thinking: one concerns the occurrence of understanding or insight; the other, the occurrence of processes of discovery. Of these, understanding is the more general phenomenon; it occurs often in the absence of the discovery of solutions and provides a basis for them. To understand is to have an awareness of a required relation between immediately given facts. When such understanding is present the relation is experienced as "following from" the given facts—that is, the nexus between them is itself understandable. Given two premises and a conclusion the latter either develops out of the former or contradicts it. Such relations, which have the character of "if *A*, then *B* and only *B*," contrast most strongly with the association between heterogeneous facts; the terms and their relation form a unit all parts of which are dependent upon one another. An understandable relation between two terms is not a third term added to them; given any two of the parts the third is demanded. The relation in question is thus a dependent part-property of a whole. The first point of the gestalt account of thinking is that understanding or insight in the sense here described pervades human experience and that no thinking is possible in its absence. Understandable relations have the character of requiredness, or "oughtness." This is the outstanding trait of facts of aesthetics and ethics as well as of logic; in each of these realms requiredness is relationally determined, being a property of an interdependent situation. Thus, the concept of value becomes related to that of organization. One observes an important aspect of requiredness when a situation is incomplete; in such cases the gap has particular properties that produce tendencies toward completion in accordance with the character of what is given. Gestalt theorists have sought to explore the conditions of requiredness out of a concern for establishing whether there are ethical invariants; these invariants would provide an alternative to a relativistic foundation for ethics.

Connections between concrete empirical events are not, however, understandable in the same way as logical connections. That heavy bodies fall when dropped cannot be automatically deduced; the underlying functional connections are hidden, and conclusions concerning them must be based on induction. Accordingly, the prevailing tendency of psychology since David Hume has been to stress the role of purely factual regularities in our knowledge of causal action. Gestalt psychology proposes that empirical events too are often related in ways that are structurally simple and that these relations facilitate the learning of the causal interplay. Duncker (1935) has pointed out that there are far-reaching correspondences between the phenomenal properties of causes and of their effects. They are often coincident in space and time and thus stand out against a background of more indifferent events. A sound is heard where an object is seen to strike; a sheet of paper acquires a crease where it is folded; fire burns shortly after a match is applied to an object. There are also pronounced similarities of content and form between cause and effect. The shape of a footprint corresponds to that of a shoe; a hot object transmits heat to its surroundings; a wet object moistens things in contact with it. Further, variations of cause often produce parallel variations of effect. The accelerated rhythm of the motions of knocking parallels the changing rhythm of the sounds produced; the stronger the push one applies to an object, the faster and farther it moves. These relations make possible a systematic ordering of empirical facts, although the relations are not fully intelligible.

Gestalt psychology treats productive thinking as the development of new structures or organizations. The discovery of a solution begins with a situation and a goal that cannot be directly reached; what requires explanation is how the gap is bridged. The principal point of the gestalt account is that the operations of thinking do not occur piecemeal but are effects of organization and reorganization. First, thinking is a directed process based on an initial view of a coherent but incomplete situation. The direction arises from the problem itself—more accurately, from the gap between the view of the given conditions and the goal. The urge to overcome the difficulty creates the tensions and vectors that lead to a re-examination of the materials and of the problem. This formulation asserts a distinction between an aggregate of independent facts and a structure; there can scarcely be productive thinking when the possibility of grasping a principle is excluded. Further, under the stress of the initially incomplete view the material is reorganized; parts and relations previously unnoted or in the background emerge, often abruptly, analogously to the reversal of perceptual forms, and parts previously separated become united. These changes in the meaning of parts, including changes of relation and direction, produce the transition to a new view that has greater coherence. From the outset the steps are guided by the main lines of the problem and

are taken with reference to each other. The operations of centering and recentering, of separating fundamental from peripheral features, spring from the whole character of the situation or from a structural view of the gap and its stresses. These formulations account for the fact that the organization of the problem situation often changes before the more detailed steps can be elaborated.

The preceding account represents only some first steps toward a theory discovery. There is at this time no satisfactory explanation of the occurrence of sudden reorganization that favors the emergence of a solution. Reference to understanding or insight does not constitute an explanation, since these are descriptive terms that do not clarify the underlying operations.

The treatment of thinking in gestalt psychology was formulated in explicit opposition to the associationism of the early decades of the twentieth century, which excluded reference to understandable relations and, indeed, to relations generally. Associationism postulated that connections between psychological events are neutral and devoid of meaning—that is, given events A and B, nothing in the character of A points to B rather than to any other event. Associationism also excluded reference to operations of organization and reorganization. Accordingly, it described the emergence of changed views and of new solutions in terms of the reshuffling of associative chains, the components of which remain constant. This approach defined knowledge as a repertoire or inventory of specific data and of connections between them. From the standpoint of gestalt theory the striking powers of thinking seem to disappear under the associationistic treatment. Thinking involves functions different from association, although it draws some of its materials from associations. No purely contingent associations, however strong, can provide understanding.

Another point at issue is the role of past experience in the process of solution. Associative accounts treat thinking mainly as a product of past experience. Gestalt theory does not question the contribution of past experience but asserts that thinking involves more than recall. Since innumerable associations lead out from a given problem situation, a solution cannot arise on the basis of associative reproduction alone. Some selection must take place. Further, it is questionable whether the products of past experience enter into thinking in unaltered form; they may have to be reorganized in order to meet the demands of the problem. Nor may one neglect the fact that recalled material is itself often the product of understanding that has occurred in the past; reference to past experience does not exclude understanding. Finally, the solution of a problem may not even require recall of added facts; this is the case when the appropriate facts are given as part of the problem. Conversely, one may fail to solve a problem under these conditions.

In recent decades a revised associationism has attempted to encompass the organized character of thinking operations within the framework of a stimulus–response analysis. Realizing the inadequacy of the earlier one-stage associative paradigm, it has postulated the presence of intervening mediational processes, which would bridge the gap between apparently noncontiguous events (e.g., Osgood 1953). The inferred mediating events in question are assigned the same properties as overt stimulus–response connections. Their function is to introduce further associative links between overtly observable connections and, thus, to provide a replacement for cognitive operations. This elaboration admits no organizing principle other than that of association; it continues to adhere to a linear model of thinking operations, treating them as chains of stimulus–response connections. It is too early to evaluate this effort; at this time it is not clear how it can accommodate the presence of rules or principles, the seeing of given materials in a new way, or the achieving of a view in terms of which one can understand a mass of detail.

The psychology of thinking touches upon questions of education, of teaching and learning, since there is no sharp separation between discovering a solution and understanding it when it is explained. This aspect has been treated most extensively by Wertheimer in *Productive Thinking* (1945). In this connection he has contrasted learning by drill and by understanding. A pupil may memorize the steps of a solution and reproduce them without error, but if he has failed to understand, he will become helpless or make senseless errors when the details of the problem are changed. If he has understood the relation of the steps to the goal, he will be able to adapt the solution to a new set of conditions that retains the essential structural relations. Indeed the ability to produce the necessary transpositions constitutes an operational test of understanding (see, e.g., Katona 1940). In teaching and learning, as in the discovery of a solution, to leave out the relation of a given fact to the whole is to take away the essentials of thinking. Educational practices that stress piecemeal preoccupation with details, exactness of repetition, and instantaneous response tend to be inimical to thinking. [See LEARNING; PROBLEM SOLVING; THINKING.]

## Social psychology

Gestalt theory has in recent decades provided the starting point for a number of systematic efforts in social psychology, among them those of Lewin and Heider. The following are some selected examples of problems studied from this point of view.

(1) Social action in man depends upon the capacity of the participants to perceive and understand one another. These operations involve reference to the mental processes of others; in everyday life one makes sense of the actions of persons by referring to their feelings, perceptions, intentions, and ideas. Yet, it is widely accepted that there is no access to these internal events in others, that one can only observe their actions, and that these actions need not be expressive of internal events. How, then, is one to explain the conviction that another is in pain or is angry or that his voice is charged with sorrow? According to one account such conclusions can only be reached indirectly, on the basis of association and inference by analogy with one's own experiences. A more behavioristic account disregards reference either to the experience of the observer or of the observed; the actions in question are said to acquire significance on the basis of association with other actions and environmental conditions. Each of these formulations treats the perceived actions of others as initially neutral. Gestalt theory proposes a fundamentally different conception of the relation between action observed in others and their experience, holding that these are structurally closely similar. Fearfulness, joy, hesitation, boldness are expressed in action as much as in the dynamics of experience. The outward form of an action is an expression of underlying forces. If so, understanding the mental life of another person is not primarily a question of generalizing from the physical to something unrelated to it.

Perception and understanding of other persons depend to a marked degree on the observation of their expressive, or physiognomic, characteristics. For gestalt theory physiognomic facts are a crucial part of perception (Arnheim 1954; Koffka 1940). Percepts, including those that are inanimate and static, are rarely neutral. One perceives in visual and auditory patterns the dynamic characteristics of tension, balance, rhythm; these are indeed the primary contents of everyday perception. Expressive qualities depend upon the pattern of an entire situation; they tend to be lost when one concentrates on separate parts. They are often more immediately and more vividly observable than shape and color; the clouds that hang in the sky are ominous as well as dark, a face is alert as well as elongated. Expressive qualities are functionally important, since they determine approach and withdrawal. Gestalt theory assumes that certain patterns and movements are initially perceived as inviting or repelling, cheerful or somber; further, the perception of identity of expressions across different media and modalities depends upon similarity of form qualities. Gestalt theory therefore opposes theories that try to derive the expressive character of a whole from those of its separate components. Illustrative of this is the effort to arrive at the expressive characteristics of a face from an analysis of its individual parts or to read character from handwriting based on a list of isolated characteristics. [*See* Expressive behavior.]

(2) The proposition that each individual acts in accordance with his wishes and needs has received a particular interpretation in contemporary psychology—namely, that human relations are without exception based on self-interest. So incontrovertible has this assumption appeared that it has dictated that membership in groups and even concern for others and action in behalf of others be treated as derivatives of self-interest. Gestalt psychology calls attention to the far-reaching ambiguity and vagueness in this position. It begins with the observation that the phenomenal self is only one part of the phenomenal field. The world that is represented in the experience of each person and that spurs him to action includes far more than the self; in fact, the self constitutes a small portion of it. The question then arises of specifying the kinds of relations that obtain under different conditions between the phenomenal field and that part of it we call the self; this is a special case of part–whole relations. Seen in this light it becomes evident that the customary formulation confuses the phenomenal self with the entire psychological field. In consequence the correct—and tautological—proposition that motivational vectors have their source in the individual is equated with the quite different proposition that the vectors arise from the self. The latter proposition too is often correct, but its universal validity is no longer self-evident. In perception one finds that under certain circumstances the coordinates of the surroundings become the coordinates for the self—that is, that the self is perceived and localized with respect to the surroundings, and not conversely. Thus, there are conditions that induce a person to perceive himself in motion when he is stationary or tilted when he is upright.

By analogy it becomes necessary to ask whether there are not also motivational conditions in which the individual feels and is moved to act as part of the social field, subject to its demands. In the light of this analysis it is dogmatic to presuppose that acting in accordance with the needs of others or with the demands of a situation must be interpreted as a version of self-centeredness. There may rather be circumstances when self-centered action is unnatural. Actions called right and wrong are particularly instructive in this connection. They cannot be simply equated with preferences since they often go against personal inclination, nor are they always in accord with convention or social approval. The issue as restated becomes a factual one: under what conditions does action become self-centered, and under what conditions is it in accordance with needs and requirements that are located outside the self and to which the self is responsive? No propositions of gestalt psychology prescribe an answer to this question; rather, the example illustrates the role of phenomenological analysis and of a concern with part–whole relations in the formulations of a psychological problem. [*See* Sympathy and empathy.]

(3) Forming an impression of a person has a place of obvious importance in social psychology. Is it adequate to say, in accordance with an atomistic interpretation, that to have an impression is to possess a number of facts about a person, to know that he has these and these characteristics? Certain initial observations stand in the way of such a conclusion. An impression of a person appears in some sense unitary; also, certain aspects are felt to be more fundamental than others. To this one must add that a change in one characteristic may alter the character of the entire impression. Thus, the discovery of one new fact about a person may have drastic repercussions upon one's entire view of him; one may be compelled to reorganize one's view and to conclude that one had not really known him. Furthermore, even when one "knows" a man, at some point one may realize, without the benefit of new information, that his characteristics are really organized quite differently than one had originally supposed and that one had missed the main point about him.

These observations form the basis of a gestalt theory of impression formation that emphasizes the interrelations among observed characteristics and the manner in which these characteristics modify each other (Asch 1952). An impression has the characteristics of a structure the parts of which cooperate to produce a particular organization. From these initial assumptions the following, more specific propositions emerge from investigation: (*a*) The items of knowledge about a person do not remain isolated but interact and mutually alter each other. (*b*) The interactions depend upon the properties of the items in their relation to one another. (*c*) In the course of interaction the characteristics group themselves into a structure in which some become central and others dependent. (*d*) The resulting interdependence creates a unitary impression which tends to be subjectively completed in the direction of becoming more consistent and coherent. (*e*) It follows that a given item of information or a characteristic functions as a dependent part, not as an element. (*f*) If so, the "same" trait in two persons is not necessarily the same. The issue under discussion is not limited to persons; the same questions arise when one considers the knowledge of any extended and interrelated situation, whether it concerns the perceived character of a group or the structure of an attitude. [*See* PERCEPTION, *article on* PERSON PERCEPTION.]

(4) Acts and utterances of persons and groups are constantly judged and evaluated; how these judgments are made is a problem that has attracted attention. One general observation has been the starting point of considerable investigation: a given act or assertion is often differently evaluated depending upon its source. Thus, one may accept an opinion from one person or group but reject it when it comes from another. The customary explanation of this effect has been in terms of prestige suggestion; a judgment or opinion is said to be changed by the attachment to it of positive or negative prestige. Of theoretical consequence is the assumption that an object of judgment is one thing, its evaluation another, and that these separate factors can be connected at will to produce an arbitrarily desired outcome. An alternative interpretation assumes that actions and evaluations are relationally determined (Asch 1952). Specifically, an act or assertion does not retain a fixed character when it is related to two different sources but functions as a dependent part of its context, altering in content and significance as it is referred to different sources. If so, the datum that is accepted is not psychologically the same as that which is rejected, and the effect in question does not concern primarily a change in the evaluation of an object but of the object being evaluated, not a change of response to a fixed condition but a change in the condition to which one is responding. This interpretation diverges importantly from the usual one for both critical and uncritical judgments. [*See* PERCEPTION, *article on* SOCIAL PERCEPTION.]

(5) A formally similar problem arises at a more comprehensive level in the psychological interpretation of culturally determined values. Thinking must guard against two opposed dangers: taking profound cultural differences too lightly and accepting their incommensurability too readily. Behavioristic learning psychology derives cultural values from the operations of conditioning and reward. The most striking application is to ethical judgments, which are said to be learned by the application of reward and punishment. From this standpoint it follows that the same act evaluated as morally right by one society may well be regarded with indifference or as wrong by another. Gestalt theory introduces several considerations that this approach ignores. First, ethical tendencies may be considered vectors or requirements that follow directly from observation of specific conditions. Second, the relation between conditions having a specific character and the ethical judgment they generate is invariant. This postulate would suffer disproof if it were shown that a situation possesses the same cognitive character for those who judge it differently. However, much evidence in support of ethical relativism fails to consider the definition of the situation, which often varies considerably as a function of differences in knowledge and factual assumptions. Indeed, on the assumption that there are invariant principles of right and wrong, differences of situational meaning must produce differences of evaluation. There is no reason to expect that two people would value identically what they see and hear if they do not see and hear identically, even though they are facing the same objective conditions. A limited conclusion from the available evidence is that the range of cultural relativism is substantially narrowed when one takes the situational context into account. From this examination emerges the following reformulation of the problem of ethical relativism: can one attach different or opposed evaluations to a situation that has a constant cognitive content? Without prejudging a full answer to this difficult question, it appears that such an outcome is far from certain. [*See* CULTURE, *article on* CULTURAL RELATIVISM; ETHICS.]

## Major issues

An examination of the main themes of gestalt theory may clarify their mutual relevance and their relations to other directions within psychology and may point to issues that remain unsolved.

**Parts and wholes.** The most general goal of scientific inquiry is to describe and explain the interdependence of observed events. This has been the aim of both atomistic and gestalt theories in psychology; they are essentially formulations about operations or modes of dependence. Given the atomistic assumption of discrete elements, the connections formed between them are neutral or independent of the terms they join. It follows from this starting point that ordered events, whether simultaneous or successive, are summations of components. This beginning has the appeal of simplicity; it reduces the operations underlying the coherence of phenomena to a bare minimum—namely, to traditional associations. The gestalt treatment of dependence takes as its starting point the evidence of experienced wholes. The observation that a change at one point of a coherent whole creates systematic changes at other points suggests that there is mutual determination of parts within a whole and that there are processes of interaction which depend upon relations between the parts. The recognizability of transposed wholes provides strong support for this formulation. Further, since parts of wholes often have a hierarchical character, their structure is not adequately described in terms of a sum of relations.

The following examples illustrate the point at issue. A child who places a solid geometrical form in a form board appears to be guided by similarity of shape between the object and the area to which he fits it. A gestalt account of this performance would begin with the primary role of perceived similarity in steering the action. An associationistic account finds no place for the direct effect of such an intrinsic relationship; instead it begins with operations based on contiguity and derives the effects of similarity from them. The following quite different illustration bears upon the same point. How can one characterize the relation between an emotional experience and the apprehension of the conditions that produce it? It is customary to suppose that the provoking conditions function as a spark or trigger that releases the emotional effect. In this formulation the connection between the antecedent and consequent conditions is again neutral; nothing in the properties of the former accounts for the properties of the latter. The alternative gestalt account proposes that an intrinsic relation connects the respective events: we flee from the horrible and laugh at what is amusing. More generally, a clarification of interdependence among events may involve more than the statement that A is followed by B; it requires an explanation of how one event grows out of another, how the character of one determines the character of the other.

Despite its pivotal position, the notion of part–whole determination has not been fully clarified. Some students have objected to the gestalt claim that parts do not enter into wholes with a fixed character, on the ground that a whole can alter a part only if the latter has definite properties of its own. This formulation raises no logical difficulties but it does point toward problems that await investigation. Gestalt psychologists have concentrated on two extreme types of conditions: those that give rise to highly coherent units and, in contrast to these, conditions that approximate to a mere aggregate of data. There is doubtless a multiplicity of intermediate instances deserving of study that would clarify the kinds of part–whole relations that occur. Thus, under certain conditions the parts of a unit are clearly perceived and are available in a relatively independent way; the omission of a part may have quite distinct effects depending upon the kind of unit in question.

A difficulty has also arisen over the formulation that an additive analysis is not adequate to account for facts of organization. One generally attempts in investigation to relate a given effect to a number of conditions. The customary procedure in psychology is to trace the total effect to effects produced by pairs of variables—A and B, A and C, B and C, etc.—and to derive the final outcome from an accumulation of these separate effects. This mode of analysis slights the fact that once interaction has occurred between A and B, neither of these is any longer present in its original form when one considers their interactions with C, etc. Given an organized context, the effect cannot be decomposed into independent strands; explanation requires a law of the mutually interacting forces taken as a whole.

Certain misconceptions concerning wholes and parts are probably less widespread at present than in the past. First, it had not been sufficiently understood earlier that experienced gestalten are not related to any possible gestalt characteristics of the objective conditions. These last, when considered as conditions of stimulation, are never gestalten; the consequences of organization on perceptual experience always transcend the conditions of stimulation. Second, emphasis upon wholes does not imply an indiscriminate dependence of facts upon each other or the assumption that there are no facts independent of each other. Wholes are self-limiting, since segregation is the counterpart of unit formation. Third, gestalt psychology is not opposed to analysis. The position it has taken is that analysis is fruitful provided it deals with the units and natural parts actually found in experience. Fourth, the most general implication of whole–part determination is that crucial characteristics of local facts are ignored unless one takes into account their place within a wider scheme. In the early days of gestalt psychology there was a tendency to neglect the converse point, later investigated by Köhler (1958), that a larger organization may suppress the individuality of its parts by obscuring its suborganizations. Last, whether a given experience or action is a sum of components or a product of organization is a wholly empirical question. Thus, the issue of "relational," as against "absolute," choosing in discrimination learning is to be resolved by evidence, as is the question whether an impression one forms of a person consists of a sum of data or of their transformation into organized form. The contribution of gestalt psychology to these problems has been to formulate the alternatives more sharply and, where possible, to devise procedures for testing them.

**The principle of "Prägnanz."** No proposition is more characteristic of gestalt thinking than the principle of *Prägnanz:* experienced perceptual wholes tend toward the greatest regularity, simplicity, and clarity possible under the given conditions. This principle also applies to certain physical systems, and Köhler in particular has applied it to the cortical correlates of perception. Two opposed outcomes derive from the tendency of experienced gestalten to turn into particularly simple and clear structures: depending upon given conditions a gestalt will have either a maximum articulation of its parts, or it will be highly simplified. It is also implicit in these formulations that ambiguous conditions, which do not fully prescribe the perceptual outcome, produce a special direction toward the completion of gaps and the resolving of contradictions, so that all parts are determined by the structure of the whole.

Although intended to have a general application, the principle of *Prägnanz* was oriented mainly toward facts of perception. Thus, Wertheimer subsumed the laws of grouping under it. Some thinkers, while accepting good continuation and closure as clear illustrations of *Prägnanz*, have wondered in what sense the latter describes grouping by proximity or similarity. However, in gestalt theory the tendency toward *Prägnanz* is not one process among others, but is inherent in all processes and products. Accordingly, one would say that grouping per se introduces regularity and simplicity and that to group in accordance with proximity and similarity is to have a radically simpler phenomenal field than absence of grouping would yield. This formulation admittedly renders concrete investigation difficult; accordingly, investigators have sought empirical tests to compare actually obtained "good form" with other alternatives that are logically possible under the same stimulus conditions. While it has not been possible to establish unambiguous criteria for good form, a great deal of selectivity has been demonstrated: where stimulation is compatible with a nearly infinite number of different experienced events, only a limited number—often only one or two—will actually be realized.

There is, however, a set of phenomena that argues convincingly for a principle of maximum simplicity in perceptual experience: where a given stimulus array can be organized in alternate ways, that organization is realized which yields a constant, rather than an ever-changing, perceptual object. A black circle moving across a homogeneous white ground is perceived as such, while the alternative organization, namely, a succession of black areas, each emerging from and returning to the white ground, is not realized. Phenomenal identity as studied by Ternus (1926) and Wertheimer also demonstrates a powerful preference to maintain a constant organization when one views a moving form. Another important instance of this tendency is the kinetic depth effect that Wallach and his associates have described (Wallach & O'Connell 1953). When an observer follows the deforming shadow of a slowly rotating object on a screen, he organizes the successive views so as to see a rigid shape moving in the third dimension; he does not see changing two-dimensional shapes. Wallach (1940) has also shown that in sound localization with head movement, one tends to perceive the sound as coming from a stationary source rather than from a moving source. The perceptual constancies may also be considered instances of the same tendency. [See PERCEPTION, *article on* PERCEPTUAL CONSTANCY.]

In areas other than perception the principle of *Prägnanz* has in general resisted conclusive investigation or clear definition. An early hypothesis of Wulf (1922) that memory traces undergo changes in the direction of greater regularity and simplicity has not been supported. In thinking, the discovery of a solution often marks a transition to a simpler structure, but this formulation lacks explanatory power. Equally rudimentary is our present understanding of tendencies in action toward the completion of situations that contain a gap, in accordance with the demands of the given structure. In social psychology the prevalence of extremely simplified views of groups and of public issues is a striking fact, but investigation has not advanced sufficiently to be theoretically relevant. A somewhat nearer approach is the study initiated by Heider (1958) of preferences for balanced configurations of interpersonal relations, and of the tendency to convert unbalanced configurations into a preferred form. Despite the difficulties, interest in the principle of *Prägnanz* persists and continues to be a concern of investigation.

**Nativism.** Gestalt theory holds that organization in accordance with general principles of physical dynamics is present from the start in psychological functioning. This position leaves wide scope for unlearned processes. At the same time, the widespread view that gestalt theory underestimates the effects of past experience is oversimplified. It is more important to note that the concept of organization determines the treatment of both unlearned and learned functions. Gestalt theory refers unlearned operations mainly to relationally determined physicochemical processes rather than to the action of specific anatomical structures. Similarly, it holds that the effects of past experience are also products of organization, or determined by structural requirements.

The treatment of form perception brings this position into sharp relief. From the standpoint of gestalt theory, unlearned organizing principles determine the perception of form, and past experience cannot exert an influence until the sensory processes are organized. It thus takes issue with the assumption of the empiricists that visual perception consists originally of a mosaic of sensations and that learning transforms them into shaped visual objects. There is in fact substantial evidence that some form perception is unlearned. Figure–ground articulation is governed by an unlearned function, as is articulation in accordance with good form. The selective principles according to which sensory data are organized in perceptual grouping, in perception of visual motion, or in the perception of identity are similarly independent of specific learning. Other perceptual functions also appear to be unlearned, among them stroboscopic motion, brightness contrast, and distance perception in lower organisms. Particularly instructive are observations of perceptually ambiguous situations; the fact that observers markedly agree in favoring one outcome over another indicates that the processes which order perception into coherent entities are not products of specific learning. There is also evidence that spontaneous organization of form often takes effect before an influence of past experience can occur.

The assumption of unlearned organizing principles does not, however, imply neglect of the history of past stimulation. To a degree this becomes evident in the treatment of temporal organization in perception. Gestalt psychology has from the start considered perceptual organization of temporally extended events equal in importance with that of simultaneously given data. The role of successive stimulation in apparent motion was the first phenomenon that Wertheimer formally investigated, and he illustrated the principles of grouping with melodies as well as with static visual forms. Further, he identified one principle of grouping, that of objective set (*objektive Einstellung*), which directly concerns the effect of membership in a temporal sequence upon the phenomenal characteristics of a given structure. In these cases, as in the work of Michotte on phenomenal causality, perceptual organization depends directly on prior stimulation. [*See* Time, *article on* psychological aspects.]

In addition, recent advances in investigation have brought about a further development in gestalt thinking, as in psychology generally, pointing to the conclusion that a history of prior stimulation is a necessary condition of adequate perceptual functioning. Thus the investigation of figural aftereffects by Köhler and Wallach (1944) demonstrates that all perceptual experiences at a given moment are in some important respects a function of what a person has experienced in the past. The import of this conclusion is that the perceptual system requires not only an adequate amount of previous stimulation but particular kinds and distributions of stimulation. [*See* Perception, *article on* illusions and aftereffects.]

The work of Helson (1964) on the organization of data across time illustrates the continuity of current investigation with gestalt contributions. The "adaptation level" demonstrates that temporally separated stimulations interact, so that the phenomenal intensity of a given stimulation is lawfully determined by preceding stimulation. In addition to establishing that perception depends upon the articulation of a stimulus array in the temporal dimension, it also demonstrates that the same datum may be obtained from different structures, each of which determines its subjective values. This line of inquiry brings to the fore the importance of sensitivity to successive arrays of stimulation.

Furthermore, gestalt psychology does not question the more customary effects of past experience upon perception. Indeed, it finds a definite place for them and has formulated the rudiments of a memory-trace theory to account for them (Koffka 1935). Gestalt psychologists have opposed unexamined and *ad hoc* assumptions about the effects of past experience that were introduced to bolster the atomistic position. Such claims, they maintained, require proof and an account of the operations by which past experience exerts its effects. More specifically, they have combated an elementaristic concept of past experience and insisted that unorganized experience cannot organize perception. Accordingly, they have proposed that the organization of form in past experience can reorganize a percept by means of memory-trace contact. The demonstration of a memory effect of three-dimensional form perception by Wallach (Wallach et al. 1953) provides a clear illustration. A pattern which has previously been experienced as three-dimensional on the basis of appropriate depth cues will subsequently be seen as three-dimensional in the absence of these cues; in this case the outcome is dependent upon past organization. [*See* PERCEPTION, *article on* DEPTH PERCEPTION.]

Gestalt psychology leaves vast room for past experience and education in its treatment of thinking and learning. At the same time, it places emphasis in these areas on processes that have not previously occurred. These draw upon materials of the past, but the organizations that occur are not exclusively products of past experience. A chimpanzee needs relevant past experience with the functional properties of sticks, bars, and food in order to solve problems, but the organization of these experiences is a new step. Similarly, a child's understanding of a relation such as that of transitivity requires knowledge of the terms in question. The latter example raises a new question—namely, whether simple logical operations are learned. The implication of the gestalt position is that once the facts are given, the mental operations of creating a structure from them and of reading them off ensue directly. Such relations are mental products; they are not given as facts about the environment. These formulations are consistent with observations, such as those of Piaget, that a given level of maturation is necessary before a child can grasp a relation such as transitivity, that he must pass through earlier intellectual stages before he is capable of handling it. Other developmental studies of the recent period raise a different problem. Harlow has shown that infrahuman primates require prolonged experience before they can handle relations such as those of oddity and reversal. Do these findings demonstrate that the relations in question are "learned"? An alternative that must be considered is that past experience is necessary in order to find out what relation is important, but that the relation per se is not learned. [*See* DEVELOPMENTAL PSYCHOLOGY, *article on* A THEORY OF DEVELOPMENT; INTELLECTUAL DEVELOPMENT.]

**Phenomenological method.** Gestalt theory is phenomenologically oriented. It assigns a place of crucial importance in psychological inquiry to the data of immediate experience. They are part of its subject matter and therefore require explanation; in addition, they are indispensable as a basis for the construction of theory. This position has a general affinity with the phenomenological tradition represented in the modern period by Husserl and is in sharp contrast to the direction of behaviorism. [*See* PHENOMENOLOGY *and the biography of* HUSSERL.]

There is an obvious relation between the character of phenomenal events and the initial formulations of gestalt psychology. In the area of perception the primary concern has been to explain why things look, sound, and feel as they do; the phenomenal facts are in this case the facts requiring explanation. More specifically, the observation that wholes and whole qualities are given in immediate perceptual experience was the basis for the rejection of elementarism and for the adoption of the concept of part–whole determination. Similarly, in thinking, the presence of understandable relations and of reorganization serve as primary observations and as first steps toward an eventual theory. This is equally the case in social psychology, where a clarification of the ways in which persons comprehend a given situation often provides crucial information about the phenomena to be studied and a basis for further exploration. The work of Heider (1958) is an example of the possibilities of a phenomenological procedure in the study of interpersonal relations. Finally, it is hard to conceive of a psychology of aesthetics that ignores direct experience [*see* AESTHETICS].

Although the explanatory concepts that gestalt psychology seeks are not themselves phenomenal facts, it assumes an intimate relation between them. It holds, first, that behavior cannot be adequately explained without reference to central processes and that these may be represented in immediate experience. Second, the postulate of psychophysical isomorphism suggests that an examination of what is phenomenally given can be both a source of hypotheses about neural events and a testing ground for them. From this perspective psychology possesses, in contrast to the natural sciences, a unique access to central processes. As Albert Einstein is reported to have once remarked in connection with this issue: "If atoms could talk about their internal processes I would not believe everything they say, but I would certainly listen."

The main requirement of phenomenological observation is to render an unprejudiced report of immediate experience under specified conditions. This general rule at once differentiates phenomenology from analytic introspection, which was dominated by a prior theory about the character of the events to be described. The phenomenological observer must be open to his experiences as they appear to him, independently of prior beliefs or assumptions about them and should not exclude what is strange or contrary to preconceptions. When viewing a visual contour, he will not allow his knowledge to deter him from noting that it appears in front of the ground, while the ground itself appears unbroken in the area that the figure occupies, or that the contour delineates the figure and not the ground. In turn the investigator will consider the explanation of these facts necessary to a theory of figure–ground organization. Although this mode of observation is not quite naive and requires cultivation, its aim is natural observation. The import of phenomenology as a psychological procedure is that it restores everyday experience, with its qualitative diversities, to psychology.

Phenomenal facts would be of reduced import if they were unconnected with action. In fact, the connection is close; persons act in a situation in accordance with the ways they perceive, feel, and think about it. If a person misperceives a situation, he acts in accordance with his misperception, not on the basis of conditions as they are. It is, consequently, of the utmost importance to relate action to the cognitive apprehension of given conditions. However, in the absence of a coherent rationale the relation between direct experience and action reduces essentially to a correlation between incommensurable data. From the standpoint of gestalt psychology the phenomenal facts are, as stated earlier, the most direct, although partial, expressions of those mediating processes that steer action. These processes are organized representations of external and internal conditions. Interposed between stimulation and action, they have the status of cognitive representations, comprising relations and systems of relations between facts, between means and ends, and between grounds and consequents. Since they steer action, they have the status of causes and are necessary to the prediction of action. Phenomenal facts—percepts, ideas, hypotheses, inferences—are more closely related to these central processes than to any other events, and therefore, they throw light on the events that issue in action. The cognitive analysis that gestalt psychology has pursued in different areas of human psychology and that has opened new paths for investigation derives from these assumptions.

At the same time gestalt theory does not favor a purely phenomenological psychology. Central processes are more inclusive and continuous than phenomenal events; therefore, the latter alone cannot provide the basis for a coherent science. In all areas of psychology, including those of perception and thinking, there are functional relations that are inaccessible to phenomenology. Other areas are at best poorly represented at the phenomenal level; habits and attitudes are formed unawares; the formation of associations and the operations of retention are not open to inspection; and there are always factors outside the phenomenal field that determine action. These considerations point to the need for inductive procedures in psychology; they do not, however, justify the neglect of direct experience when it is accessible.

The importance that gestalt theory attaches to immediate experience rests on a far-reaching examination that cuts across generally accepted categories. It distinguishes sharply between phenomenal and functional facts, the latter referring to events that are outside immediate experience and that are the object of scientific inquiry. Direct experience includes both objective facts, such as rocks and animals, and subjective facts, such as wishes and pains; indeed, the distinction between objective and subjective is one that occurs within the phenomenal domain. Thus, secondary and tertiary qualities are often phenomenally highly objective, since they appear located in specific objects in outside space.

Consequently, direct experience is a condition of all scientific inquiry. Observation consists in the first instance of phenomenal facts; it begins with what is seen, heard, touched. At no point do the procedures of science eliminate these phenomenal components. The most refined observations, such as those represented by pointer readings, are perceptual situations that depend upon the identification of units, the perception of motion, and the discrimination of positions. Moreover, the theoretical constructions erected to explain observations, including the rules of logic and mathematics—in general, the structures of inference and proof necessary to scientific activity—are also strictly phenomenal events. There is thus a necessary continuity of direct experience with the concepts and procedures that science fashions; ultimately all concepts have a phenomenal base. The scientist's picture of the world is based on the achievements of perception and thinking; his choice of units of observation is based on his perception of form, and his inferences must obey logical demands and the cognition of causal relations. Although the investigator who concentrates on a particular problem must take this background for granted, it cannot be ignored in a systematic account of the character of scientific investigation.

These considerations throw a new light on the distrust of phenomenal data in behavioristic psychology. Early behaviorism rejected direct experience in favor of objective data on the ground that the former is private and inaccessible to public check and, therefore, cannot form part of the body of scientific knowledge. Since one cannot place experiences side by side and compare them, behaviorists concluded that one can observe only the behavior of another, not his experiences. However, the assumption that objective data are free of phenomenal components was based on a naive realism that failed to consider the role of the observer. The behaviorist as investigator reports his observations and inferences—that is, the contents of his phenomenal field. It is therefore hardly consistent on his part to rule out the reports of other observers simply because these observers happen to be his subjects. More recently, behaviorists have accepted that the data of science are based on phenomenal reports but have proposed to include only those observations which command agreement among independent observers. It is generally accepted that observations on which qualified observers can agree have a special standing in science. However, the implication that phenomenally subjective events are generally untrustworthy and *ipso facto* fail to command agreement cannot be sustained. [*See* Observation.]

There are, to be sure, sources of error to be guarded against and difficulties to be resolved when one includes the reports of observers in a system of functional concepts. No doubt it may be more difficult to find the appropriate referents to the report "I am feeling dizzy and confused" than to the report "The rat depressed the bar five times." Nevertheless, the methodological purism of the behavioristic position has in important respects had negative effects. The proposals to reduce perception to overt discriminative responses and to treat the reports of persons as "verbal behavior" have not been fruitful. In fact, they marked an abandonment of interest in phenomena and problems that are most specifically and significantly human. They also discouraged, because they failed to realize, the constructive contribution of free observation and description in the discovery of new phenomena. Consequently, they underestimated the creative phases of scientific activity that precede proof and that set the goals for proof. These attitudes have had a profoundly restrictive effect on human psychology.

The more serious reason for the behavioristic distrust of phenomenal data has been the belief that they are epiphenomena, with no place in a causal–explanatory scheme. Gestalt theory reserves judgment on the mind–body problem, while seeking a bridge between direct experience and the concepts of natural science; it sees in the clarification of this relation a challenge to psychology and to science generally. The distrust, bordering on aversion, of direct experience that behaviorism has demonstrated is also motivated by the attempt to imitate the natural sciences in their progressive elimination of phenomenal data. From the standpoint of gestalt theory human experience is an important part of nature and too significant to be discarded. An account of human functioning that omits reference to direct experiences is as incomplete as would be the description of a musical instrument that included all details of its materials, construction, and functioning but made no mention of the music it produces.

**Relation to behaviorism.** Certain other divergences between behaviorism and gestalt psychology have to do with the respective problems they have considered. Gestalt psychology grows out of studies in human perception and thinking, while behaviorism takes its start from the study of infrahuman organisms. There are also diverse tendencies within behaviorism itself, some of which are closely connected with gestalt positions. Thus, a concern with the organization of central processes unites gestalt theory with investigators such as Lashley, and the work of Tolman exemplifies an approximation to a gestalt behaviorism in animal psychology [*see the biographies of* Lashley *and* Tolman].

However, the "stimulus–response" psychologies constitute one variety of behaviorism, highly influential on the American scene, that is strongly opposed to gestalt psychology. Stimulus–response accounts of behavior are atomistic; although their units are molar, they treat behavior as composed of chains of stimulus–response units and changes of behavior as the addition and elimination of such units.

From the perspective of gestalt psychology, action is characterized by organization, and coordination of complex movements poses problems analogous to organization in perception. Accordingly it questions the adequacy of accounts of action that employ isolated stimulus–response units. Further, it holds that organized cognitive representations steer intelligent action in animals and man; sequences of chained units do not do justice to the operations of organizing and reorganizing that external conditions initiate. Also, the "stimulus" of stimulus–response psychologies implicitly refers to perceptual configurations, which are not, however, treated as such.

These problems are magnified when one turns to human psychology. It is a significant feature of the stimulus–response programs that they aspire to base a psychology of man on concepts and methods derived exclusively from the study of infrahuman organisms. This aim presupposes that no problems or processes will be discovered that are unique to human functioning. Instead of freely examining human achievements and asking how one can account for them, they attempt to fit observations to concepts derived from another area. The question arises whether concepts pertaining to one range of facts retain their meaning or relevance when extrapolated to a new area or whether they become mere labels for phenomena that have not been examined in their own right.

## Conclusion

Gestalt theory was the first attempt within psychology to give a fundamental treatment to problems of wholes and part–whole relations. It was productive of new discoveries and concepts; it generated new questions and proved relevant to basic issues of psychology. Its contributions laid the foundations for the modern study of perception; it broke new ground in the investigation of thinking, memory, and learning; it initiated new steps in social psychology. These achievements deeply affected the outlook of psychology, not least so when they provoked opposition. They spurred a sharpening of issues and the revision of alternative positions; there is little work of consequence in psychology that has been wholly untouched by gestalt ideas.

It is nevertheless questionable to conclude, as some students have, that the contributions of this movement have been fully absorbed and that it has died of success. It is more likely that its natural development was blocked when it was uprooted from its milieu in Europe following the Nazi catastrophe. To this one must add that there were barriers to a full comprehension of its perspective and of its conception of science in the profoundly different intellectual environment that prevailed in the United States. It is therefore more appropriate to stress that gestalt theory is not a completed system, that many of the issues it raised await resolution, and that it might be best described as a program of investigation or a region of problems. Thus, there is as yet little understanding of the physiological foundations that gestalt theory sought for psychology, and the postulate of isomorphism remains a heuristic principle. Further, gestalt psychologists were selective with respect to the problems they studied; in general they preferred those that lent themselves to exact investigation and clear theoretical decisions. Consequently, there are

large areas to which it has not notably contributed, among them developmental and abnormal psychology and the psychologies of personality, of language, and of action. Neither has it contributed directly to the psychology of motivation, with the exception of Lewin and his group, whose concepts are related to those of gestalt theory. At the same time, the formulations of gestalt theory contain important implications for these areas. [*See* ACHIEVEMENT MOTIVATION; FIELD THEORY; *and the biography of* LEWIN.]

Although there are no procedures peculiar to gestalt investigators, a distinctive style is evident in their formulations of problems and in their manner of studying them that reflects an implicit attitude toward the tasks of science. Perhaps first in order of importance is a sensitivity to the danger of distorting the subject matter by obeying prior prescriptions about the demands of scientific procedure. It is a natural consequence of the phenomenological orientation of gestalt psychology to think it presumptuous to expect phenomena to conform to rules that precede observation. Connected with this starting point is the belief that faithful observation is an essential step to explanation. Consequently, gestalt psychology accords a place of importance to qualitative observation and, while welcoming exact experimentation, rejects the view that measurement is the sole source of valid evidence. Indeed, some of its own most significant discoveries were essentially systematic demonstrations. One consequence of the more customary assumption is that a phenomenon is not considered important if it cannot be studied experimentally; it is, however, more correct to say that experimentation is only one kind of observation. Indeed, there is danger in stressing experimentation before essential questions have been clarified—the danger of aimless experimentation.

An equally prominent theme of gestalt theory is that clarification of fundamentals requires attention to fairly large areas of phenomena. This becomes evident in gestalt investigations of particular questions, as well as in its broad conception of psychology. It specifically included facts of logic, ethics, and aesthetics as part of the subject matter of psychology at the same time that it sought to establish contact with the concepts of natural science. This approach questions whether the study of ever more detailed problems in special fields will yield knowledge of psychology as a whole. Psychology still has to discover its fundamentals; exclusive attention to those questions that can be studied in exact ways may ignore important phases of the subject and may even lose sight of the realization that the discovery of fundamentals is urgently needed. Indeed, facts in a limited area may be seriously misinterpreted, however carefully they are studied, if their reference to a wider scheme remains obscure.

A sense of the human and philosophical import of psychology pervades gestalt writings. Their critique of arbitrary dissection, of focusing on narrow facts, was based on technical considerations; they also expressed a concern about the destructive implications of such procedures for a conception of man. Science is a way to clarify major issues of mankind. If psychology eliminates or distorts essential facts and if these are represented as the main evidence about his nature, man himself will appear of little account. Gestalt theory questioned the assumption that certain convictions prevalent in psychology were scientifically derived. The denial of understanding, the view that actions and judgments are in principle subjectively determined, the treatment of value in terms of neutral facts, and the consequent rejection of valid value did not, it claimed, necessarily follow from scientific thinking. There is also a quality of moral optimism in gestalt psychology, which some may consider extrascientific if not antiscientific. This charge cannot be easily leveled against a movement that strictly opposed the approach of vitalism to facts of life and that sought to find a basis for psychology in natural science. The charge itself may be an expression of moral pessimism.

SOLOMON E. ASCH

[*Directly related are the entries* FIELD THEORY *and* THINKING, *article on* COGNITIVE ORGANIZATION AND PROCESSES. *Contrasting approaches to behavioral phenomena are discussed in* FORGETTING; LEARNING, *especially the articles on* CLASSICAL CONDITIONING, INSTRUMENTAL LEARNING, REINFORCEMENT, *and* DISCRIMINATION LEARNING; PSYCHOANALYSIS. *Other relevant material may be found in* AESTHETICS; ATTITUDES; GROUPS; PERCEPTION; PHENOMENOLOGY; PROBLEM SOLVING; SOCIAL PSYCHOLOGY; SYSTEMS ANALYSIS, *article on* PSYCHOLOGICAL SYSTEMS; THINKING; *and in the biographies of* HUSSERL; KATZ; KOFFKA; KÖHLER; KÜLPE; WERTHEIMER.]

### BIBLIOGRAPHY

PRIMARY SOURCES

ARNHEIM, RUDOLF 1954 *Art and Visual Perception.* Berkeley: Univ. of California Press.

ASCH, SOLOMON E. (1952) 1959 *Social Psychology.* Englewood Cliffs, N.J.: Prentice-Hall.

ASCH, SOLOMON E. 1960 Perceptual Conditions of Association. *Psychological Monographs* 74, no. 3.

DUNCKER, KARL (1935) 1945 On Problem-solving. *Psychological Monographs* 58, no. 5. → First published as *Zur psychologie des produktiven Denkens.*

EHRENFELS, CHRISTIAN VON 1890 Über "Gestaltquali-

täten." *Vierteljahrsschrift für wissenschaftliche Philosophie und Soziologie* 14:249–292.

ELLIS, WILLIS D. (1938) 1950 *A Source Book of Gestalt Psychology.* London: Routledge. → Contains excerpts from the technical contributions of gestalt psychology which were first published in *Psychologische Forschung* between 1921 and 1938.

HEIDER, FRITZ 1958 *The Psychology of Interpersonal Relations.* New York: Wiley.

HELSON, HARRY 1964 *Adaptation-level Theory: An Experimental and Systematic Approach to Behavior.* New York: Harper.

HENLE, MARY (editor) 1961 *Documents of Gestalt Psychology.* Berkeley: Univ. of California Press.

HENLE, MARY 1965 On Gestalt Psychology. Pages 276–292 in Benjamin B. Wolman and Ernest Nagel (editors), *Scientific Psychology.* New York: Basic Books.

KATONA, GEORGE (1940) 1949 *Organizing and Memorizing: Studies in the Psychology of Learning and Teaching.* New York: Columbia Univ. Press.

KATZ, DAVID (1911) 1935 *The World of Colour.* London: Routledge. → First published in German as *Die Erscheinungsweisen der Farben und ihre Beeinflüssung durch die individuelle Erfahrung.* A revised and enlarged edition was published in 1930 as *Der Aufbau der Farbwelt.*

KOFFKA, KURT (1921) 1928 *The Growth of the Mind: An Introduction to Child-psychology.* 2d ed., rev. New York: Harcourt: → First published as *Die Grundlagen der psychischen Entwicklung: Eine Einführung in die Kinderpsychologie.* The first treatment of questions of learning and education from the perspective of gestalt psychology.

KOFFKA, KURT 1922 Perception: An Introduction to the *Gestalt-theorie. Psychological Bulletin* 19:531–585.

KOFFKA, KURT 1935 *Principles of Gestalt Psychology.* New York: Harcourt. → The only comprehensive treatment of gestalt psychology; by one of its leading figures.

KOFFKA, KURT 1940 Problems in the Psychology of Art. Pages 180–273 in *Art: A Bryn Mawr Symposium,* by Richard Bernheimer et al. Bryn Mawr Notes and Monographs, Vol. 9. Bryn Mawr (Pa.) College.

KÖHLER, WOLFGANG (1917) 1956 *The Mentality of Apes.* 2d ed., rev. London: Routledge. → First published in German. A paperback edition was published in 1959 by Random House. A renowned study of intelligence in apes and of the concept of insight.

KÖHLER, WOLFGANG (1920) 1924 *Die physischen Gestalten in Ruhe und im stationären Zustand.* Erlangen (Germany): Philosophische Akademie.

KÖHLER, WOLFGANG (1929) 1947 *Gestalt Psychology.* Rev. ed. New York: Liveright. → A paperback edition was published in 1947 by New American Library. The first general exposition of the movement; a classic in the literature of psychology.

KÖHLER, WOLFGANG 1938 *The Place of Value in a World of Facts.* New York: Liveright.

KÖHLER, WOLFGANG 1940 *Dynamics in Psychology.* New York: Liveright. → A field theory in perception and memory. A work that develops earlier ideas and foreshadows subsequent directions of investigation.

KÖHLER, WOLFGANG 1941 On the Nature of Associations. American Philosophical Society, *Proceedings* 84:489–502.

KÖHLER, WOLFGANG 1951 Relational Determination in Perception. Pages 200–230 in Lloyd A. Jeffress (editor), *Cerebral Mechanisms in Behavior.* New York: Wiley.

KÖHLER, WOLFGANG 1958 Perceptual Organization and Learning. *American Journal of Psychology* 71:311–315.

KÖHLER, WOLFGANG; and WALLACH, HANS 1944 Figural After-effects: An Investigation of Visual Processes. American Philosophical Society, *Proceedings* 88:269–357.

LEWIN, KURT (1926–1933) 1935 *A Dynamic Theory of Personality: Selected Papers.* New York: McGraw-Hill. → Papers first published in German.

LEWIN, KURT (1939–1947) 1963 *Field Theory in Social Science: Selected Theoretical Papers.* Edited by Dorwin Cartwright. London: Tavistock.

MICHOTTE, A. (1946) 1963 *The Perception of Causality.* London: Methuen. → First published in French.

OSGOOD, CHARLES E. (1953) 1959 *Method and Theory in Experimental Psychology.* New York: Oxford Univ. Press.

RUBIN, EDGAR (1915) 1921 *Visuell wahrgenommene Figuren: Studien in psychologischer Analyse.* Copenhagen: Gylendal. → First published in Danish.

TERNUS, JOSEF 1926 Experimentelle Untersuchungen über phänomenale Identität. *Psychologische Forschung* 7:81–136.

WALLACH, H. 1940 The Role of Head Movements and Vestibular and Visual Cues in Sound Localization. *Journal of Experimental Psychology* 27:339–368.

WALLACH, H.; and O'CONNELL, D. N. 1953 Kinetic Depth Effect. *Journal of Experimental Psychology* 45:205–217.

WALLACH, H.; O'CONNELL, D. N.; and NEISSER, U. 1953 The Memory Effect of Visual Perception of Three-dimensional Form. *Journal of Experimental Psychology* 45:360–368.

WERTHEIMER, MAX (1912–1920) 1925 *Drei Abhandlungen zur Gestalttheorie.* Erlangen (Germany): Philosophische Akademie. → Contains three early contributions: "Über das Denken der Naturfölker" first published in Volume 70 in the *Zeitschrift für Psychologie;* "Experimentelle Studien über das Sehen von Bewegung" published in Volume 61; and *Über Schlafsprozesse im produktiven Denken.*

WERTHEIMER, MAX (1925) 1944 Gestalt Theory. *Social Research* 11:78–99. → First published in German.

WERTHEIMER, MAX 1934 On Truth. *Social Research* 1:135–146.

WERTHEIMER, MAX 1935 Some Problems in the Theory of Ethics. *Social Research* 2:353–367.

WERTHEIMER, MAX 1937 On the Concept of Democracy. Pages 271–285 in Max Ascoli and Fritz Lehmann (editors), *Political and Economic Democracy.* New York: Norton.

WERTHEIMER, MAX (1945) 1961 *Productive Thinking.* Enl. ed., edited by Michael Wertheimer. London: Tavistock. → Published posthumously; the product of a lifelong concern with problems of thinking, logic, and education.

WULF, FRIEDRICH 1922 Über die Veränderung von Vorstellungen. *Psychologische Forschung* 1:333–373.

SECONDARY SOURCES

ALLPORT, FLOYD H. 1955 *Theories of Perception and the Concept of Structure.* New York: Wiley.

BORING, EDWIN G. (1929) 1950 *A History of Experimental Psychology.* 2d ed. New York: Appleton.

GUILLAUME, P. 1937 *La psychologie de la forme.* Paris: Flammarion.

HEIDBREDER, EDNA 1933 *Seven Psychologies.* New York: Appleton.

HENLE, MARY 1965 *On Gestalt Psychology.* Pages 276–292 in Benjamin B. Wolman and Ernest Nagel (editors), *Scientific Psychology.* New York: Basic Books.

METZGER, WOLFGANG (1940) 1954 *Psychologie.* 2d ed. Darmstadt (Germany): Steinkopff.

PETERMANN, BRUNO (1929) 1932 *The Gestalt Theory and the Problem of Configuration.* New York: Harcourt. → First published as *Gestalttheorie und das Gestaltproblem.*

PRENTICE, W. C. H. 1959 The Systematic Psychology of Wolfgang Köhler. Volume 1, pages 427–455 in Sigmund Koch (editor), *Psychology: The Study of Science.* New York: McGraw-Hill.

SCHEERER, MARTIN 1931 *Die Lehre von der Gestalt.* Berlin: Gruyter.

WOODWORTH, ROBERT S. (1931) 1964 *Contemporary Schools of Psychology.* 3d ed. New York: Ronald. → See especially pages 214–250 on "Gestalt Psychology."

## GIDDINGS, FRANKLIN H.

Franklin Henry Giddings (1855–1931), a founder of American sociological theory and research, was born in Sherman, Connecticut, of strict Puritan ancestry on both sides. His father was a Congregational minister. Giddings' intellectual precocity is shown by the fact that before entering college he had read extensively in the then highly controversial writings of Darwin, T. H. Huxley, John Tyndall, and Spencer. These authors, together with Adam Smith, Comte, and J. S. Mill, provided the foundation of his devotion to individualism—his basic philosophical position—and his primary sociological concepts. Graduating from Union College in 1877, Giddings spent the next decade in newspaper work, mainly on the then famous *Springfield Republican* and *Springfield Union.* He lectured on political science and sociology at Bryn Mawr College from 1888 to 1894 and at Columbia University from 1891 to 1894. In 1894 he was appointed professor of sociology at Columbia; he was the first full-time professor of sociology in the United States.

Among the founders of American sociology he occupies a strategic position as the most influential link in the transition of sociology from moral philosophy and the philosophy of history to inductive research. In this he was influenced by his close association with Richmond Mayo-Smith and by the concurrent rapid spread of statistical studies into related fields. Although he made no historically significant contributions to statistical research, he gave a powerful stimulus to quantitative studies of all aspects of community life through his lectures and books and his influence on hundreds of students, including over fifty PH.D. candidates.

Giddings' basic philosophy was a combination of Comtean positivism and Spencerian evolutionism. He saw social evolution as part of cosmic evolution, as basically an equilibration of energy among individuals and groups that results in differentiation, integration, segregation, and assimilation. He thus viewed every social order as always in a state of moving equilibrium, such equilibrium in power and status being essential for internal justice and order and, on a wider scale, for international peace. He considered sociology both a natural science and the basic elemental social science, giving an account of the origin, growth, structure, and activities of human association through the operation of physical, biological, and psychological forces. At times he thought sociology might become a quantitatively exact science.

In his view, "social process," or social life, results from the interaction of "primary causes," the natural resources and accessibility of a given habitat, and the "secondary causes," the human motives arising within society itself. Since all social energy is physical energy transmuted by means of economic activities, the "social composition," or the number, density, and genetic heterogeneity of a given population, is determined by these primary causes. At the same time, harnessing these resources of food and power increases social dynamics and, hence, the processes of differentiation and integration, thus adding complexity to the "social constitution," that is, the functional and purposive groupings, ranging from social clubs to sovereign states. Giddings thus found the task of sociology to be the integration of subjective with objective processes and concepts in terms of mental activity, organic adjustment, natural selection, and conservation of energy.

This basic position is generally sound if rich and accessible natural resources are considered primary only in the sense of being antecedent in time, or as essential, but culturally viewed, static preconditions for the development of a dense population and a highly dynamic social order, or if it is acknowledged that both the manner and extent of their utilization is dependent on the state of cultural advancement. Giddings would probably agree, since he saw all forms of association as "essentially phenomena of thought and feeling," so that his analyses of the stages of society's evolution from zoogenic to demotic forms, as well as his analyses of the social constitution and the social mind, were all couched in psychosocial terms.

In *The Principles of Sociology* (1896) he declared that the original and elementary subjective fact of society is the "consciousness of kind," or Adam Smith's "sympathy," plus a conscious recognition of likeness. In answer to critics who viewed consciousness of kind as merely another name for gregariousness, he c

peatedly, but not convincingly, to show that gregariousness is a purely hereditary "biophysical habit" to which man alone adds the purely psychic activity of conscious recognition of likeness and difference of kind. This raises the question of just where in the evolution of neural structures such recognition emerged, but in the light of studies in animal psychology there can be little doubt that it preceded primitive man. Giddings himself declared consciousness of kind to be dependent on in-group communication and to result in mutual aid, both of which traits were well developed among the higher apes.

Although Giddings continued to argue this issue, in the outline of his "system" in *Studies in the Theory of Human Society* (1922, p. 292), he made "pluralistic behavior," or like response of two or more persons to a given stimulus, antecedent to, and the basis of, consciousness of kind. He declared "interstimulation and response" among individuals to be the causal basis of all collective behavior. Social phenomena thus result from two variables: the psychosocial situation and the pluralistic response to it. Hence he offered a new definition: "Pluralistic behavior is the subject-matter of the psychology of society, otherwise called sociology" (1922, p. 252).

Thereafter, he held that "like" response to an idea, symbol, or group value ensures group solidarity, social control, and concerted volition. Moreover, since "unlike" response to an ideal or purpose leads to segregation, competition, rivalry, and conflict among social groups, the internal solidarity and concerted volition of every group rests upon an awareness of likeness in mental attitude. Differences in the speed, intensity, and duration of response give rise to processes of differentiation and integration, to leadership and followers, the emergence of a guiding "protocracy" of more able members, the division of labor, and to social status. Differences in the intensity of consciousness of kind result in wide variation in the permanence of association and the scope of cooperative activities: the range extends from family to political party. Like and unlike responses result in an endless variety of social groupings, serving varied human purposes, from bridge clubs to nations and international alliances, each of which by the same process develops its own folkways, mores, and institutions. It seems safe to say that no elementary subjective sociological facts have been found that supersede in       ss and universality Giddings' plural           se and consciousness of kind.

           opted Lester Ward's distinction be-
         genesis and social telesis. Like Spencer
        he saw a teleological beneficence in the

evolutionary processes, aided by increasing scientific knowledge. However, his utopianism was restrained. In the matured views of *The Scientific Study of Human Society* (1924) he argued that the only *means* available for "societal engineering" are the same as those now used by religious, educational, economic, and political agencies in current social adjustments, so that the *processes* of societal engineering are the same as those of social genesis. Indeed, the envisaged ends of telic action are the results of the efficient causes operating in social genesis, so that telesis is "a conditioned and projected genesis." Consequently, the fruits of telic efforts are more or less the same as the inevitable consequences of the genetic processes. Nevertheless, he envisaged the ends of these processes to be the development of more able, more tolerant, and more cooperative members of society, as well as an enhancement of social welfare.

These are obviously logical conclusions from his basic philosophy. Moreover, while the language is different, the meaning harmonizes, in general, with that of such cultural determinists as A. L. Kroeber and L. A. White. Giddings saw society caught up in cosmic evolutionary processes; Kroeber and White see it caught up in a self-determining cultural stream. Giddings, however, manifested a latent utopianism in assuming that the realization of his own ideals was the assured end of cosmic forces.

His lectures, articles, and books abound in shrewd insights into human nature and social problems and processes. As a whole, they represent a pivotal point in the development of American sociology. While his own terms did not win wide usage, they contained the essence of the "social distance," the "social interaction," and the "social situation" of later works.

At the same time, his somewhat questionable distinction between "social" psychology as defining individual reactions and "societal" psychology as defining group reactions led to his ignoring almost entirely the then current advances in dynamic and social psychology. Far more enigmatic is his neglect of the concurrent development of cultural concepts and theories in anthropology. Spencer, his master, had added the "superorganic" as the third distinctive realm of phenomena; Giddings had declared in his *Descriptive and Historical Sociology* (1906, pp. 176, 183) that the past products of interstimulation and response become "the most immediate and most important stimuli in modern social life," but he did not develop the implication of this principle in cultural terms.

FRANK H. HANKINS

[For the historical context of Giddings' work, see the biographies of COMTE; DARWIN; MILL; SPENCER; WARD, LESTER F.]

WORKS BY GIDDINGS

1888    CLARK, JOHN B.; and GIDDINGS, FRANKLIN H. *The Modern Distributive Process.* Boston: Ginn.
(1896) 1911    *The Principles of Sociology: An Analysis of the Phenomena of Association and of Social Organization.* New York: Macmillan. → Translated into seven languages. Giddings' most important work.
(1898) 1916    *The Elements of Sociology: A Textbook for Colleges and Schools.* New York: Macmillan. → The most advanced of the early American textbooks.
(1900) 1901    *Democracy and Empire, With Studies of Their Psychologic, Economic and Moral Foundations.* New York: Macmillan. → Views on various public issues; a work of enduring value.
1901    *Inductive Sociology: A Syllabus of Analyses and Classifications and Provisionally Formulated Laws.* New York: Macmillan. → Designed as a basis for statistical studies.
(1906) 1923    *Readings in Descriptive and Historical Sociology.* New York: Macmillan. → Restatement and illustration from literature and history of the concepts outlined in Giddings' *Inductive Sociology.*
1918    *The Responsible State.* Boston: Houghton Mifflin. → Problems of political morality; strong reaction against German militarism.
(1922) 1926    *Studies in the Theory of Human Society.* New York: Macmillan. → Revision and amplification of concepts and analyses; Giddings' second most important work.
1924    *The Scientific Study of Human Society.* Chapel Hill: Univ. of North Carolina Press. → Replaced *Inductive Sociology,* with increased emphasis on statistical researches.
1929    *The Mighty Medicine: Superstition and Its Antidote.* New York: Macmillan. → An exposure of occultism and a plea for enlightened education.
1932    *Civilization and Society: An Account of the Development and Behavior of Human Society.* New York: Holt. → An informal text composed of Giddings' lectures as edited by Howard W. Odum.

SUPPLEMENTARY BIBLIOGRAPHY

ABEL, THEODORE 1930    The Significance of the Concept of Consciousness of Kind. *Social Forces* 9:1–10.
COLUMBIA UNIVERSITY, FACULTY OF POLITICAL SCIENCE 1931    *The Bibliography of the Faculty of Political Science: 1880–1930.* New York: Columbia Univ. Press. → See especially pages 63–76, which list 14 books and at least 200 articles by Giddings.
NORTHCOTT, CHARLES H. 1948    The Sociological Theories of Franklin Henry Giddings: Consciousness of Kind, Pluralistic Behavior, and Statistical Method. Pages 744–765 in Harry E. Barnes (editor), *An Introduction to the History of Sociology.* Univ. of Chicago Press.
ODUM, HOWARD W. 1951    *American Sociology.* New York: Longmans.

# GIERKE, OTTO VON

The German jurist Otto von Gierke (1841–1921) was born in Stettin, the son of a Prussian official. He was reared in a highly respectable, patriotic, and Prussian atmosphere. As a student at the University of Berlin, he was influenced by Georg Beseler, a jurist of the Germanist school, who had already sketched and was teaching the idea of a purely German theory of associations (*Genossenschaftstheorie*). After professorships at Breslau (1872–1884) and Heidelberg (1884–1887) Gierke succeeded to Beseler's chair at Berlin, which he occupied until his death.

At the beginning of Gierke's career, German legal scholarship was dominated by the Romanist school of Savigny; but Gierke began and remained a staunch Germanist. The Germanists, like the Romanists, were historically minded; their research, however, did not take them back to the Roman Empire, Justinian's Code, and the Reception, but followed the path marked out by Jacob Grimm to the law of the ancient German *Mark* and the *Gemeinde* (local community), to feudal records, town charters, and the rules of guilds, in search of "truly German" legal principles. The first volume of Gierke's *Das deutsche Genossenschaftsrecht* (1868–1913), dedicated to Beseler, was the first product of his self-imposed task of broadening the foundation for a German theory of associations by a detailed study of successive types of organizations in German history. This task, diligently pursued through much of his life, was not quite completed when, in 1913, he published the fourth and last volume of his most famous work.

He temporarily abandoned historical research for more immediate problems in 1888, when the first draft of the new civil law code disappointed and challenged the Germanists. Gierke wrote a series of critical articles and, when he and his fellow Germanists failed to obtain substantial modifications of the code, settled down to his second major task. Convinced that the materials of a common German law existed and that legal progress could come only through developing deep-rooted German traditions and weeding out Romanist imports, he felt a solemn obligation "to penetrate the new code with a Germanistic spirit; to develop its Germanic content upon an historical basis; to foster the growth of its Germanism in the future" (1868–1913, vol. 4, p. xii). The first volume of his *Deutsches Privatrecht* ("German Private Law," 1895–1917), on *Personenrecht* ("Law of Persons," 1895), was followed by a second on *Sachenrecht* ("Law of Things," 1905) and a third on *Schuldrecht* ("Law of Obligatory Relations," 1917). Their important impact on German civil law is generally acknowledged.

Gierke's influence on legal and political theory derived from his historical and systematic analyses of associations. The four volumes of *Das deutsche Genossenschaftsrecht* trace the changing forms of groups through four periods of history. In the earliest period of German law the free association (*freie Genossenschaft*) was predominant; it was based on natural coherence; all rights remained with the members collectively and no corporate existence of the *Genossenschaft* was postulated. In the second period (800–1200) the lordly union (*herrschaftlicher Verband*) was predominant; in this, rights attached to a single individual (e.g., a king or feudal lord) who represented the legal unity of the group. In the third period (1200–1525), which interested Gierke most, a new type of association, the free union (*freie Vereinigung* or *Einung*), became predominant. Growing out of the free will of its associates, the free union nevertheless resembled the old Germanic association in that the law, rights, and duties of the association were attributed to the collective membership. The guild was the purest example of this type, but it also appeared in towns, leagues of towns, and many other associations of varying importance, permanence, and respectability. The principle of free union, plus that of the federal organization of associations into larger unions, as illustrated by the Hanse, at one time gave promise, Gierke thought, that the feudalized Empire would be reconstituted as a federation. But rural areas continued to be dominated by feudal relationships; once-free associations became privileged corporations; finally, a new authoritarian principle triumphed, exemplified in the sovereign state, conceived as separate from and above the people and as the exclusive embodiment of the common interest. By the end of the fourth period (1525–1806), the absorption or dissolution of privileged corporations by the state and the establishment of individual liberty and equality before the law had opened the way for a rich development of free associations with all the varied and complex characteristics that modern associations have.

The old German association, Gierke explained, had had no clearly defined theory; Germanic conceptions implicit in the legal characteristics of the manifold associations of the thirteenth, fourteenth, and fifteenth centuries failed to reach explicit formulation. The competition, in legal theory, of German and Romanist ideas was paralleled by the competition, in publicistic thought, of "truly medieval" and "antique–modern" tendencies. In the development of medieval association law, Gierke discerned manifestations of a German tendency to construe each group as a purposive entity that acted as a whole and, as a whole, was the subject of rights and obligations. This tendency, however, never reached its logical conclusion, a concept of the group as a real person. As association law was finally formulated by canonists and postglossators, German views were submerged by Romanist influences: the association was construed as an institution (*Anstalt*), whose legal existence derived from a grant of powers by superior authority and whose *Rechtssubjektivität* was located in an artificial personality (*persona ficta*) constructed by positive law. Similarly, "truly medieval" political thought, which conceived society as a complex structure of mutually articulated group-entities, each with its own purpose, group-law, and organic unity, was defeated by "antique–modern" tendencies which, progressively eroding the autonomous claims of intermediate groups, issued in an irreconcilable dichotomy between theories of the all-embracing sovereignty of an organic state and unsatisfactory attempts to explain the state itself as contractually constructed by the human atoms who alone had natural existence and natural rights.

Gierke's historical and systematic theses meet in his assertion of the Germanic doctrine that should be applied to modern associations. Attacking the prevailing doctrine of Savigny, which construed them as creations of positive law on the ground that "originally and from a naturalistic point of view" (1868–1913, vol. 2, p. 25) true legal personality belongs only to individual men, he propounded a doctrine which seemed to him not only more German, but also superior in scientific realism and philosophical validity. When law treats groups as persons, he insisted, it does not distort reality. Joint-stock companies, churches, trade unions are—like the state itself—real collective persons. They exist whether the state recognizes them or not; the role of the state is declaratory, not creative. The *Genossenschaft* is an organic unity, composed of individuals or other associations, with its own original purpose; it organizes itself through its own system of "social law"; it is autonomously capable of willing and acting; it has thus a real personality, which is the proper subject of rights and obligations. Appreciation of the actual nature of associations opens the way to the only sort of legal theory that corresponds with fact and the only sort of social organization that can be ethically satisfactory, one that resolves the conflicts inherent in human strivings toward unity and liberty.

Gierke repeatedly emphasized that his position lay between that of the extreme individualists, who would reduce human relationships to contracts among sovereign individuals, and that of the organicists, who would absorb the individual and all society into the state. A man is born "as a member of a family, a race, a community, in short, as a member of a whole" (1868–1913, vol. 2, p. 47) and "what man is, he owes to the association of man with man" (1868–1913, vol. 1, p. 1). The system of human associations, natural and voluntary, presents a complex pattern of rich and fluid variety. To primitive natural associations based upon "purely physical" ties are added a complex and fluid variety of associations more deliberately created—some highly specialized in purpose and membership, others more generalized and comprehensive. The process of differentiation and specialization is balanced by a process of generalization. But, as an expression of man's social nature, the lowliest and narrowest association has some of the same dignity and value as the highest and most comprehensive one.

The state is the product of the same sort of process as that which produces all other associations. But it is distinguished from other associations in that it is the highest and most comprehensive; thus its purposes include the forceful carrying out of "the general will" and the coercive conciliation of the wills of all individual and collective persons. Accordingly, although it is "not generically different," the state differs qualitatively as well as quantitatively from other associations. Moreover, its function requires both *Genossenschaft* and *Herrschaft*. The history of the German state, Gierke believed, had culminated in an integration of *Genossenschaft* and *Herrschaft*, organically uniting the state's associational basis with the inherent authority of the monarchy at its apex.

Gierke's theory of law corresponded to his theory of associations. In "Die Grundbegriffe des Staatsrechts" (1874) he attacked the formalist conception of law as a creation of the state. "The final source of all law" is "the social consciousness of any social institution whatever" (Gierke in Lewis 1935, p. 176); the declaration that transforms social convictions of right into law is made by other associations besides the state. In the terminology he used in *Das Wesen der menschlichen Verbände* ("The Nature of Human Associations," 1902), the two basic categories of law are not private and public law, but "individual law," through which the state regulates the external relations of individual and collective persons, and the various bodies of "social law," which treat individuals only as members of groups. Social law is the law produced by the collective persons themselves to regulate their internal life, the relations of the whole with its parts, and the integration of narrower into more inclusive entities. The public law that organizes the structure of the state, and those of narrower associations (e.g., local communities, provinces) insofar as they are a part of the state structure, is simply one among many systems of autonomously developed "social law," differing from other systems only in the specific characteristics appropriate to the specific nature and purpose of the state. Gierke's concept of "social law" enables him to construe the internal rules of churches, trade unions, business corporations, etc., as independent of state determination and to put such bodies on an equal basis with human persons in claiming areas of freedom into which the state cannot intrude.

Gierke's conception of the nature of associations could suggest a highly decentralized federal political structure, which might include as constituent members both functional and territorial units. Morris R. Cohen once referred to Gierke as "a sort of patron saint of political pluralists." But Gierke himself was not a political pluralist, nor did he develop the ideal of a functional federalism. The pluralistic elements of his theory were always carefully balanced by the organic and authoritarian, and by the dominant role he assigned to the state and to its law. His devotion to Prussia and the monarchy and his concern for the assured unity of the German people tipped the balance steadily toward authority. He became increasingly convinced that the constitution of the Bismarckian *Reich* achieved an almost perfect harmony of associational and authoritarian principles. Earlier in his career he had demanded decentralizing reforms, but in 1919 his fear of the disruption that would follow the abolition of the monarchy made him a vigorous critic of the Weimar constitution.

Gierke's theory of social law influenced such writers as Léon Duguit and Hugo Krabbe; his insistence on the autonomous origins of associations influenced, directly or indirectly, the thought of S. G. Hobson, G. D. H. Cole, Harold J. Laski, and others. His influence on English pluralism owed much to Frederic William Maitland, who introduced Gierke to English-speaking academic circles in 1900. With a lawyer's interest in the legal interpretation of corporations and other groups, Maitland emphasized Gierke's legal doctrine of the real personality of associations but paid less attention to his view of their organic nature and to the very special role he attributed to the state. J. N. Figgis contributed to Gierke's reputation as a pluralist when in *Churches in the Modern State* he drew heavily from Gierke in vindicating the "real life and personality" of churches and other associations against the "Leviathan state" and the Aus-

tinian concept of sovereignty. In Germany, Gierke's student and follower Hugo Preuss argued in his early writings for a transformation of the authoritarian, Prussia-dominated *Reich* into a decentralized democratic state whose articulation would be unhampered by the outworn dogma of sovereignty; but Preuss did not minimize his divergence from Gierke. In the Weimar period he moved to an uncompromising assertion of the sovereignty of the united German state.

Gierke's historical interpretations have been criticized as generalizing beyond the evidence, as tending to transform social movements into ideological or spiritual movements, as reading his own categories into past thought. But *Das deutsche Genossenschaftsrecht*, with its massive erudition and often perceptive statement, remains a classic which no historian of its topics can ignore. Gierke's systematic theses have also been criticized, even by generally sympathetic writers, for example, in the penetrating analysis by Ernest Barker (1934). Interest in Gierke's theory has declined with the decline of the pluralist school. The normative and juristic conclusions that he drew from recognition of the spontaneous self-assertion of groups have little in common with more recent descriptive analyses of group action in politics.

JOHN D. LEWIS

[*For the historical context and subsequent development of Gierke's ideas, see* NATURAL LAW; PLURALISM; POLITICAL GROUP ANALYSIS; VOLUNTARY ASSOCIATIONS; *and the biographies of* DUGUIT; FIGGIS; LASKI; MAITLAND.]

### WORKS BY GIERKE

1868–1913 *Das deutsche Genossenschaftsrecht.* 4 vols. Berlin: Weidmann. → Volume 1: *Rechtsgeschichte der deutschen Genossenschaft,* 1868. Volume 2: *Geschichte des deutschen Körperschaftsbegriffs,* 1873. Volume 3: *Die Staats- und Korporationslehre des Altertums und des Mittelalters und ihre Aufnahme in Deutschland,* 1881. Volume 4: *Die Staats- und Korporationslehre der Neuzeit,* 1913. Reprinted in 1954 by Akademische Druck- und Verlagsanstalt, Graz (Austria). Translations of extracts provided by J. D. Lewis.

(1874) 1915 *Die Grundbegriffe des Staatsrechts und die neuesten Staatsrechtstheorien.* Tübingen (Germany): Mohr. → First published in Volume 30 of *Zeitschrift für die gesamte Staatswissenschaft.*

(1880) 1939 *The Development of Political Theory.* Translated by Bernard Freyd. New York: Norton. → First published in 1880 as *Johannes Althusius und die Entwicklung der naturrechtlichen Staatstheorien* by Koebner, Breslau.

(1881) 1958 *Political Theories of the Middle Age.* Cambridge Univ. Press. → A translation of "Die publicistischen Lehren des Mittelalters," a section of Volume 3 of Gierke's *Das deutsche Genossenschaftsrecht.* Translated with a famous introduction by Frederic William Maitland.

1883   *Labands Staatsrecht und die deutsche Rechtswissenschaft. Schmollers Jahrbuch für Gesetzgebung, Verwaltung und Volkswirtschaft im Deutschen Reich* 7: 1097–1195.

1887   *Die Genossenschaftstheorie und die deutsche Rechtsprechung.* Berlin: Weidmann.

1895–1917   *Deutsches Privatrecht.* 3 vols. Munich and Leipzig: Duncker & Humblot. → Volume 1: *Allgemeiner Teil und Personenrecht,* 1895. Volume 2: *Sachenrecht,* 1905. Volume 3: *Schuldrecht,* 1917.

1902 (1954)   *Das Wesen der menschlichen Verbände.* Darmstadt (Germany): Wissenschaftliche Buchgemeinschaft. → Extracts from this work have been translated as "The Nature of Human Associations" and published on pages 139–157 of Lewis 1935.

(1913) 1934   *Natural Law and the Theory of Society, 1500 to 1800.* 2 vols. Translated with an introduction by Ernest Barker. Cambridge Univ. Press. → A 1934 translation of five subsections of Volume 4 of Gierke's *Das deutsche Genossenschaftsrecht.* A paperback edition was published in 1957 by Beacon Press.

#### SUPPLEMENTARY BIBLIOGRAPHY

BARKER, ERNEST   (1934) 1950   Translator's Introduction. Pages ix–xci in Otto von Gierke, *Natural Law and the Theory of Society, 1500 to 1800.* Cambridge Univ. Press. → An important work about Gierke.

EMERSON, RUPERT   1928   *State and Sovereignty in Modern Germany.* New Haven: Yale Univ. Press. → See Chapter 4, pages 126–154 on "The School of the Genossenschaft."

GURVITCH, GEORGES   1922   Otto von Gierke als Rechtsphilosoph. *Logos: Internationale Zeitschrift für Philosophie der Kultur* 11:86–132.

LEWIS, JOHN D.   1935   *The Genossenschaft-theory of Otto von Gierke: A Study in Political Thought.* Madison: Univ. of Wisconsin. → An appendix contains translated extracts from Gierke's *Das deutsche Genossenschaftsrecht; Johannes Althusius . . . ; Das Wesen der menschlichen Verbände; and Die Grundbegriffe des Staatsrechts.*

MAITLAND, FREDERIC WILLIAM   (1900) 1958   Introduction. In Otto von Gierke, *Political Theories of the Middle Age.* Cambridge Univ. Press.

PREUSS, HUGO   1910   Die Lehre Gierkes und das Problem der preussischen Verwaltungsreform. Volume 1, pages 245–304 in Berlin Universität, Juristische Fakultät, *Festgabe der Berliner juristischen Fakultät für Otto Gierke zum Doktor-Jubiläum 21 august 1910.* Breslau (then Germany): Marcus.

SCHULTZE, ALFRED   1923   Otto von Gierke als Dogmatiker des bürgerlichen Rechts. *Jherings Jahrbücher für die Dogmatik des bürgerlichen Rechts* 73:i–xlvi.

STUTZ, ULRICH   1922   Zur Erinnerung an Otto von Gierke. *Zeitschrift der Savigny-Stiftung für Rechtsgeschichte* (Germanistische Abteilung) 43:vii–lxiii. → Contains a bibliography.

TIERNEY, BRIAN   1955   *Foundations of the Conciliar Theory: The Contribution of the Medieval Canonists From Gratian to the Great Schism.* Cambridge Univ. Press. → Pages 98–105 discuss, with references, some criticism of Gierke's interpretations of medieval political theory and canon law.

# GIFFEN, ROBERT

Sir Robert Giffen (1837–1910) was a British statistician, economist, and writer on finance. He was born in the Scottish town of Strathaven and was educated at the local village school. He showed an early aptitude for journalism, he and his brother contributing anonymous poems and articles to the local newspaper. At the age of 13 he entered the office of a Glasgow solicitor in a very minor position but made use of his seven years' stay in that city by attending lectures at the university. Journalism, however, attracted Giffen more than the law, and in 1860 he became reporter and subeditor of the *Stirling Journal.* Like many another Scot before him, he was lured south of the border, and he became connected with the *Globe,* then more or less the official organ of Lord Palmerston's administration. After a short time on the *Fortnightly Review,* in 1868 he became subeditor of the *Economist,* then under the editorship of Walter Bagehot.

The time that Giffen spent in the city of London was to serve him well in his future career. His contact with Bagehot was especially profitable, for he acquired from Bagehot both his style and his methodology. His later connection with the city office of the *Daily News* provided an invaluable acquaintance with the London stock exchange and the ways of the London financial community.

In 1871, when the Report on Local Taxation was published, George Goschen, president of the Poor Law Board and main author of the report, acknowledged Giffen's assistance. The reputation so earned led to Giffen's appointment as chief of the statistical section and controller of corn returns at the Board of Trade. An attempt in 1876 to reorganize this body and transfer some of its functions to the Foreign Office proved unsatisfactory; the old Statistical Department was revived and reorganized with Giffen at its head as assistant secretary. In 1892 he became controller-general of the Commercial, Labour, and Statistical departments, a position he retained until his retirement in 1897, having received the K.C.B. in 1895 in recognition of his service.

When Giffen accepted his position in the civil service he obtained permission to publish his views on matters of economic interest. Indeed, he was very active in the affairs of the Royal Statistical Society and the Royal Economic Society; he was influential in the founding of the latter body in 1890 and president of the former from 1882 to 1884. A frequent, almost prolific, contributor to the journals of both bodies, he was also editor of the

*Journal of the Royal Statistical Society* from 1876 to 1891 and provided the "city notes" in the *Economic Journal* until he died.

Giffen's reputation rests mainly on his work in "official statistics," a field which had been pioneered by G. R. Porter, who was the first to organize the crude, incomplete mass of statistics relating to revenue and commerce. Richard Valpy made further improvements, instituting the system of statistical abstracts. Giffen was largely responsible for the first attempts to collect figures relating to the wages of manual laborers and for setting up the Bureau of Labour Statistics. Although Giffen appeared to have little knowledge of the mathematical theory of statistics, he had a remarkable intuitive grasp of the significance of facts and figures, a gift that allowed him to clear the way through the most complicated problems by the use of bold estimates. He was always inclined to caution, but his imaginative approach caused him to tackle such problems as the measurement of national income, which had formerly been considered too difficult a task by many an able statistician. In addition, his journalistic flair did much to popularize the use of statistics, and his wide acquaintance and knowledge of the world of finance and business led government departments and official bodies to seek his advice. In fact, some of his most important work is to be found in official reports.

While at the height of his career, Giffen's opinion was respected in the fields both of applied and theoretical economics; today he is chiefly remembered for his "Paradox," mentioned in Book 3 of Marshall's *Principles* ([1890] 1961, p. 132). This exception to the general law of demand was held to operate in a community heavily dependent upon one commodity for its staple diet. If the price of this commodity falls, the real income of the community is increased so that it can afford to buy superior foodstuffs and thereby cut down its consumption of the "Giffen good." The opposite will occur in the case of a price rise, producing the unusual effect of quantity demanded increasing as prices rise and falling as prices fall.

Giffen was among the earliest to analyze the workings of the quantity theory of money, and the role played by the rate of interest, within an economy possessing a banking system. His ideas seem to have had a great deal of influence on Alfred Marshall, over and beyond the "Paradox." Giffen was very much concerned with the way in which the volume of "bank money" affects the level of currency. In *Stock Exchange Securities* (1877) and two essays, "The Effects on Trade of the Supply of

Coinage" (in [1879–1885] 1886, pp. 89–104) and "Gold Supply: The Rate of Discount and Prices" (*ibid.*, pp. 37–88), he very clearly indicated the relationship that exists between a banker's cash reserves and the level of deposits, and the part played by the discount rate in bringing about an equilibrium between the supply of gold and the level of prices.

His "dispensation" from refraining to participate in current controversy allowed him to become a leading protagonist in many of the debates of the latter part of the nineteenth century. A staunch laissez-faire economist, he was an avid opponent of the protectionist and socialist schools, both at home and abroad; but he was willing to concede that protection could have political advantages, especially when it concerned colonial produce, and was willing to tolerate it in a mild degree if it was the only alternative to socialism. As might be expected, he was also opposed to much of Gladstone's financial policy and was a foremost antagonist of the bimetallist school.

K. J. PENNEY

[*For the historical context of Giffen's work, see the biography of* BAGEHOT; *for discussion of the subsequent development of his ideas, see the biography of* MARSHALL.]

### WORKS BY GIFFEN

(1869–1879) 1890   *Essays in Finance.* First series. 5th ed. London: Bell.

(1869–1902) 1904   *Economic Inquiries and Studies.* 2 vols. London: Bell.

1877   *Stock Exchange Securities: An Essay on the General Causes of Fluctuations in Their Price.* London: Bell.

(1879–1885) 1886   *Essays in Finance.* Second series. New York: Putnam.

1889   *The Growth of Capital.* London: Bell.

1913   *Statistics . . . Written About the Years 1898–1900.* Edited with an introduction by Henry Higgs, and with the assistance of G. Udny Yule. London: Macmillan. → Published posthumously.

### SUPPLEMENTARY BIBLIOGRAPHY

ANONYMOUS 1910   Sir Robert Giffen. *Economic Journal* 20:318–321.

BATEMAN, A. E. 1910   Sir Robert Giffen. *Journal of the Royal Statistical Society* Series A 73:529–533.

BROWN, ERNEST H. P.; and BROWNE, M. H. 1963   Carroll D. Wright and the Development of British Labour Statistics. *Economica* New Series 30:277–286.

ESHAG, EPRIME 1963   *From Marshall to Keynes: An Essay on the Monetary Theory of the Cambridge School.* Oxford: Blackwell.

MARSHALL, ALFRED (1890) 1961   *Principles of Economics.* 9th ed. New York and London: Macmillan. → See especially Book 3, page 132.

STIGLER, GEORGE 1947   Notes on the History of the Giffen Paradox. *Journal of Political Economy* 55:152–156.

# GIFFORD, EDWARD W.

Edward Winslow Gifford (1887–1959), American anthropologist, was born in Oakland, California. His formal schooling ended with a high school diploma. From 1904 to 1912 he was assistant curator of ornithology in the California Academy of Sciences and a member of academy expeditions to the Revillagigedo Islands in 1903 and to the Galapagos Islands in 1905–1906. He was appointed assistant curator of the Museum of Anthropology at the University of California in 1912 and became, successively, associate curator, curator, and director of the museum. In 1920 he was appointed lecturer in the department of anthropology, in 1938 associate professor, and in 1945 full professor.

In addition to his early interests in natural history (particularly ornithology and conchology), Gifford's range of anthropological interests and competence was very broad, including archeology, folklore, kinship, social organization, material culture, religion, and physical anthropology. In each of these fields he made both substantive and theoretical contributions.

Gifford's major effort was directed toward the ethnology of California Indians. He wrote a number of monographs on tribal groups in California and a number of articles on special aspects of the culture of Californian aboriginal societies. With the exception of those of A. L. Kroeber, Gifford's contributions to California ethnography are quantitatively larger than those of any other worker.

Archeology was a secondary interest, but in 1948, toward the end of his career, he began an investigation of Oceanian archeology that resulted in major excavations in Fiji, New Caledonia, and Yap. The archeology of northwestern Mexico attracted his interest in 1945 and 1946, and he made several important contributions to that field.

Gifford's ethnographies are filled with detail. Informants who contributed information beyond that pertaining to the direct question were apparently allowed to continue, and these bits of volunteered data were usually noted and included. The result of this leniency with informants is that Gifford's ethnographic accounts contain a multitude of data that does not occur in the published ethnographies of any other worker, and these data often provide some fact or allow some insight that cannot be obtained when only those data are reported that relate to generalizations.

Gifford was unusual in sensing the importance of recording individual experiences of aboriginal informants at a time long before this kind of information was considered important. Thus, his study of Clear Lake Pomo society stands as a pioneer attempt to determine the actual composition of local groups by the genealogical method (1922). His monograph on the Northfork Mono includes an extraordinarily detailed history of one informant, recorded in 1918, who could list no fewer than 23 settlements where she had lived in the course of her life, all of which were located within an area of approximately 150 square miles (1922). Such vignettes provide us with a means of viewing life in aboriginal California in terms of individual experience as well as impersonal customs and institutions.

Gifford did not hesitate to take on projects of synthesizing immense bodies of fact. Two of his largest works remain the main sources of primary data on two aspects of the California Indians: their physical characteristics (1926a) and their kinship terminologies (1922).

Beyond being a patient collector of facts, Gifford was competent at seeing and solving theoretical or terminological problems. In a paper on Euro-American culture contact in Tonga published in 1929, he became the first American anthropologist to use the term "acculturation" in the modern sense. The same is true of his use of the term "lineage," which he proposed, in a broad survey of political organization (1926b), as the basic unit of aboriginal California societies.

In archeology he was the first to devise a method, which has since become important, for segregating the components of refuse deposits, identifying them, and deriving from the proportions of each component economic interpretations, indications of dietary change over time, and reflections of the relations of the occupants to local environment. Gifford was among the first to employ the weight, rather than the count, of potsherds from archeological excavations to assess chronological changes in the ceramic complex.

In addition to his field investigations, Gifford guided the Museum of Anthropology at Berkeley for 44 years and directed its development of one of the major anthropological collections in the United States. The importance of the Berkeley collections rests not so much upon their size as upon the fact that an unusually large proportion of the materials was collected in the field by scholars, including Gifford himself, and is accompanied by information on cultural context. Gifford organized the collections to make the context of the objects as explicit as possible and constructed a card index for cross reference. Consequently, it is possible that no other major research collection in anthropology is more accessible to scholars.

ROBERT F. HEIZER

[*For the historical context of Gifford's work, see the biographies of* KROEBER *and* LOWIE.]

### WORKS BY GIFFORD

1916 *Composition of California Shellmounds.* University of California Publications in American Archaeology and Ethnology, Vol. 12, No. 1. Berkeley: Univ. of California Press.

1922 *California Kinship Terminologies.* University of California Publications in American Archaeology and Ethnology, Vol. 18. Berkeley: Univ. of California Press.

1926a *Californian Anthropometry.* University of California Publications in American Archaeology and Ethnology, Vol. 22, No. 2. Berkeley: Univ. of California Press.

1926b *Miwok Lineages and the Political Unit in Aboriginal California.* American Anthropologist New Series 28:389–401.

1929 *Tongan Society.* Bernice P. Bishop Museum, Bulletin No. 61. Honolulu, Hawaii: The Museum.

1939 The Coast Yuki. Anthropos 34:292–375.

1949 KROEBER, ALFRED L.; and GIFFORD, EDWARD W. *World Renewal: A Cult System of Native Northwest California.* University of California Anthropological Records, No. 13. Berkeley: Univ. of California Press.

1951 *Archaeological Excavations in Fiji.* University of California Anthropological Records, Vol. 13, No. 3. Berkeley: Univ. of California Press.

### SUPPLEMENTARY BIBLIOGRAPHY

FOSTER, GEORGE M. 1960 Edward Winslow Gifford, 1887–1959. American Anthropologist New Series 62: 327–329.

HARVARD UNIVERSITY, PEABODY MUSEUM OF ARCHAEOLOGY AND ETHNOLOGY, LIBRARY 1963 Edward Winslow Gifford. Volume 9, pages 243–247 in *Catalogue, Part 1, Authors.* Boston: Hall.

## GIFT TAXES

*See under* TAXATION.

## GIFTS

*See* EXCHANGE AND DISPLAY *and the biography of* MAUSS.

## GILDS

Gild studies form one of the more obvious links between history and the social sciences. Originating in nineteenth-century romantic interest in early Germanic institutions and the theme of liberty, they have played into three lines of speculation about the role of voluntary associations in societal development. The first began with controversy over the respective influence of "Germanist" theory based on the right to associate freely and of the Romanist theory that the right to associate is a concession from the prince. [*See the biographies of* GIERKE *and* SAVIGNY *for discussion of these theories and the controversy.*] This general dialectic is still being reformulated as a fundamental theoretical element in studies of ecclesiastical influence on the philosophy of law and in studies of the development of representative institutions. Research on this last subject is now, under the direction of an international commission, strongly comparative. But it focuses on the wider political communities of medieval and early modern Europe rather than on the smaller associations, which, to social anthropology, would be of at least equal significance. From the start, however, a second line of thought linked these with the elementary bonds of kinship, seeing them at first as an effort to transcend kinship loyalties and later as partially reverting to them. Research on this problem has lagged, although there are signs of its revival in France and Italy. A third line of thought, prominent in much of the better social history written in the third quarter of the nineteenth century and now revived by the influence of twentieth-century sociology, is concerned with nonpolitical aspects of the social controls that small associations may have exercised.

The tendency now is to interpret the term "gild" —the variant spelling "guild" is from the seventeenth century—as applying only to occupational associations. This was not the original sense of the word. It was specific only in signifying that members were under the obligation to "geld," that is, to make payments for purposes agreed upon. Throughout the Middle Ages, it was also synonymous with *fraternitas*—definable as a pseudo-kinship group of a character in principle congenial to Christianity. Since contemporary terminology varied from one period and one area to another, historians writing in English have found it convenient to adopt "gild" as a generic term for all of the smaller associations with a fraternal aspect; French and Italian usage distinguishes the occupational types (*corporations, corporazioni*) from the purely fraternal (*confréries, confraternite*). Within Europe, historians can compare their findings on the basis of a common awareness of the political and social context in which any type of association ran its course. But now that ethnologists and historians of other civilizations are singling out occupational gilds for description and comment, comparative study will call for analyses going beyond the tradition of European political theory.

West European studies can, however, be a source of hypotheses, typologies, and, especially, of developmental models useful in all comparative work. The evidence on which they rest has undergone a great deal of critical examination; in the North it covers a thousand years and in Italy almost two thousand, running back into republican Rome. West European experience was, of course, affected by peculiarities of political and religious organization and by historical contingencies that varied from one country to another. It will be compressed here into a scheme of five phases, in each of which the relationship between small voluntary associations and public authority changed. The functions and the organization of the main types of gild characteristic of each phase will then be discussed, but space will not permit even a catalogue of the accompanying types of local power structures or any discussion of the highly influential examples of differentiated corporate bodies within the church (for which see *Histoire de l'église . . . 1964*).

**The course of development.**    The five phases of development may be described briefly as follows:

(1) In the northern "barbarian" kingdoms of the early Middle Ages, associations contributing to order pass unchallenged by weak monarchies.

(2) Monarchy asserts itself as the source of legitimacy of association. The papacy does the same in regard to religious orders but permits free fraternal association among the laity. This phase culminates in chartered concessions to town governments, which become more or less autonomous organs of public authority.

(3) Town governments, after some lag, permit the differentiation of citizen communities into occupational gilds, which serve both public and private ends.

(4) Gilds are enmeshed in a system of state-regulated privilege. Noneconomic associations in Protestant states survive only through sectarian organization.

(5) Either voluntarily or in consequence of revolution, the state abandons the system of special privilege; economic gilds either atrophy or are abolished.

*Phase 1.*    In the societies to which phase 1 is applicable, customary law prevailed, and feud rather than royal authority was the chief sanction in the enforcement of law against crimes of violence. In other words, kinship was the traditional source of power in local communities. It is uncertain at what point gilds arose to offer supplementary protection (which was available also from lordship). The earliest known example is from the rules of the gild of thanes at Cambridge, written at some time in the late Anglo-Saxon period. This gild combined five functions: protection of members' property, discouragement of violence, mutual aid in sickness, common worship, and responsibility

for decent burial. An oath bound members, and banquets brought them together. They were men of upper middle rank. Their protective plan, if one of them were robbed, was to track down the thief and compel him to raise the large sum of 8 pounds as compensation. Their way of discouraging violence was simply to add to the normal pecuniary penalties: the rules allow for the possibility of the murder of one "brother" by another and demand only that the murderer pay 8 pounds to the gild in addition to the wergild due to the kindred of his victim. A group strong enough to intimidate thieves and to fine its own members heavily was obviously a formidable power in any local community. Even fraternities professing no purpose but group worship, conviviality, and the support of a loan and burial fund could mobilize power to maintain order.

*Phase 2.*    The second phase was inaugurated in Frankish territory by Charlemagne's fear that sworn gilds might disrupt the feeble unity of his realm. Gild power, he realized, depended on the oath; the words "to live or die together" could be added to it secretly to create a group as solidary as a kindred, but also expansible and potentially defiant of all law but its own. Charlemagne banned sworn gilds but was unable to suppress them. His edicts, however, bestowed a kind of legitimacy on unsworn gilds for mutual aid. There were probably already merchant gilds among them; they grew as trade grew and by the eleventh century had a more elaborate organization than the earlier protective gilds. The cloth merchants of Valenciennes, for example, had a salaried secretary elected for life, a treasurer, an almoner, a dean, their own priests, an elected judicial board of 12, and, as chief officer, a mayor.

The specific legitimation of gilds by charter came about slowly as part of that piecemeal granting of judicial or fiscal privileges to successive groups of town residents which preceded the full development of town governments. In early twelfth-century London, two artisan gilds received charters authorizing them to hold private courts, and other unchartered gilds of unspecified nature were made to pay for the privilege of existing. The older freedom of association survived only under the shelter of the church, in the form of parish gilds supporting the cult of chosen saints.

*Phase 3.*    The differentiation of the citizen body into occupational gilds, which characterized the third phase, was a political process. It helped to redefine the line, which rapid immigration had tended to blur, between citizens and noncitizens resident in a town. It domesticated the primitive gild oath, making it a sanction of civic obedience. It turned gild officers into quasi-public officials and used gilds in the assignment of military and night-policing duties. Finally, it fostered political consciousness. Artisan gilds gave the towns whatever drive toward "democratic" reform they had; the new mercantile gilds mobilized resistance to this drive.

In the matter of social controls over economic conduct, the role of the gilds was mainly to introduce collective decisions about how to meet new and difficult situations. The move toward formal organization among artisans did not spread until the late thirteenth century, when, after two centuries of expanding trade, the towns were beginning to face more competitive conditions. The basic values of an ambitious but hard-pressed working population had long been rooted in the master artisan families. The need for hard work, frugality, and calculation had been beaten into many generations of sons and apprentices. Market officials had set checks on dishonesty in selling, and in the export industries merchants and their agents had done the same for manufacturing practices. Neighborhood opinion condemned open quarreling. Above all, Christian doctrine had set a moral and religious value on work and approved of honest gain. In their character as fraternities, both occupational and parish gilds had sharpened sanctions by grudging any grant from their loan or relief funds to members who failed in business through laziness, intemperance, or "folly." The last notion covered bad judgment in not following the regular mercantile practice of dividing capital among separate ventures to reduce risk. Enterprising artisans had undertaken local trade in the materials of their craft as an avenue of upward mobility; in twelfth-century Genoa they had even made small investments in the port's booming overseas trade. The Genoese of that age had already adopted Ben Franklin's maxim that "Time is money," their trade and loan contracts being dated by the hour of the day.

The new formal organizations tried to keep up the reputation of their members' wares for high quality, to lower costs by reducing wages, and to cover up disputes over technical innovations that would lower costs. In all such matters both mercantile and artisan gilds acted to some extent as secret societies. Although gilds had to submit a code of rules to the city authorities in order to be recognized as legitimate, there was no regular check on the interpretation of the rules or their amendment. Disagreement over competitive practices was sometimes so bitter as to lead to the realignment of dissident groups into new gilds.

As is well known, the fund-raising power of the gilds was drawn on to support not only the cult of patron saints but also the major festivals through which the spiritual values of the entire community were reaffirmed. The persistence with which gilds cultivated pleasant manners within their own circles is less well appreciated; at a gild meeting, all overt aggression, whether by word or deed, was relentlessly penalized. This is worth remark in an age when, despite centuries of Christian teaching, overt aggression was still common among the aristocracy, the peasantry, and the floating lower level of the urban population. The gilds may further be credited with inventing the bourgeois pattern of periodic, respectable festivity among married couples.

The Italian gild movement of this period was the first to draw the secular professions into its pattern of organization, and in Tuscany lay "Round Table" clubs imitated the gild practice of employing notaries to draft their "statutes." Neither universities nor military organizations can be dealt with here, but it should be noted that the fraternity form was permitted to alien groups of artisans and that in the Low Countries it was used, at the instigation of lords, to keep archers in training. In illicit, sworn forms it persisted among Frisian pirates, in French resistance to English occupation, and among unfree peasants raising funds to sue for or buy freedom. Heretic groups, on the other hand, preferred hierarchic forms of organization under charismatic leadership.

*Phase 4.* The fourth phase, especially in provincial towns in the sixteenth and seventeenth centuries, saw the social and economic activity of industrial gilds at its height, but political and economic circumstances were changing. State power standing above town administrations was readier than ever to grant enlarged powers to harass local competitors, gild offices fell more than ever into the hands of mercantile entrepreneurs, and subordinate fraternities of wage workers were suppressed.

*Phase 5.* The fifth phase, during which gild organization of trade and industry died out, dragged on from the seventeenth into the nineteenth century, according as new industrial development and reaction against the old system of privilege were precocious or late. There had always been skepticism as to whether gilds stood, as they claimed, for the public interest. North of the Alps the spectacle of rural industry, based either on handicrafts or on new mechanization, progressing without benefit of gilds, fanned this skepticism long before it found theoretical exposition in new economic thought and propaganda. Then, too, as "fraternity" flamed up as a national, and international, slogan, the old local fraternal forms of association became obsolete. True, the question of continuity between the old forms and the new craft unions, burial clubs, etc., intrigues historians, but the story remains incomplete.

Comparisons with developmental models that might be constructed for other civilizations, including the rapidly moving kaleidoscope of present-day Africa, would rest, in the first instance, on the place of universalist principles in the legitimation of association. In all their phases European gilds were in part particularistic in spirit, but it was their contributions to order and religion that, from the first, were the basis of their legitimation. In Europe it was through the medieval gilds that universalist principles of policy protecting the consumer against fraud and dangers to health (e.g., from soiled second-hand mattress stuffing, diseased meat, and impure drugs) were first explicitly formulated. After the demise of the gilds, such functions had ultimately to be taken over by the state, and they have been the essential justification for the revival of professional and trade associations. [*See* LICENSING, OCCUPATIONAL.] In Islam, artisan gilds, whose appearance must now be dated no earlier than the thirteenth century (Goitein 1964), were the bearers of a universalist fraternal philosophy. Particularist aspects of Western gilds have been exaggerated by an uncritical acceptance of the notion that a son necessarily followed his father's trade. Comparative study on this point has to be quantitative and has to take account of general demographic trends and the channeling of migration to towns. Far from being a worked-out field, the study of voluntary associations can still illuminate many aspects of society. [*See* VOLUNTARY ASSOCIATIONS.]

SYLVIA L. THRUPP

BIBLIOGRAPHY

ARNAKIS, GEORGE G. 1953 Futuwwa Traditions in the Ottoman Empire: Akhis, Bektashi Dervishes, and Craftsmen. *Journal of Near Eastern Studies* 12:232–247.

BAZANT, JAN 1964 Evolution of the Textile Industry of Puebla: 1544–1845. *Comparative Studies in Society and History* 7:56–69.

DAVIS, NATALIE Z. 1965 Strikes and Salvation at Lyons. *Archiv für Reformationsgeschichte* 56:48–64.

DE ROOVER, RAYMOND 1962 La doctrine scolastique en matière de monopole et son application à la politique économique des communes italiennes. Pages 149–179 in *Studi in onore di Amintore Fanfani.* Volume 1: Antichità e alto medievo. Milan (Italy): Giuffrè.

ESPINAS, GEORGES 1943 Le droit d'association dans les villes de l'Artois et de la Flandre française depuis les origines jusqu'au début du XVIe siècle. Volume 3, pages 179–230 in *L'organisation corporative du moyen âge à la fin de l'ancien régime.* Louvain, Université Catholique, Recueil de travaux d'histoire et de philo-

logie, 3d Series, fasc. 18. Louvain (Belgium): Bibliothèque de l'Université, Bureau du Recueil.

GOITEIN, S. D. 1964 Artisans en Méditerranée orientale au haut moyen âge. *Annales: Économies, sociétés, civilisations* 19:847–868.

*Histoire de l'église depuis les origines jusqu'à nos jours.* Volume 12, Part 1, Books ii–vi: Institutions ecclésiastiques de la Chrétienté médiévale, by Gabriel Le Bras. 1964 Paris: Bloud & Gay. → Contains a bibliography on Christian fraternities in the footnotes on pages 414–417.

KAHL, WILLIAM F. 1962 A Checklist of Books, Pamphlets, and Broadsides on the London Livery Companies. *Guildhall Miscellany* 2:99–126.

KELLENBENZ, HERMANN 1963 Les industries rurales en occident de la fin du moyen âge au XVIIIe siècle. *Annales: Économies, sociétés, civilisations* 18:833–882.

KELLETT, J. R. 1958 The Breakdown of Gild and Corporation Control Over the Handicraft and Retail Trade in London. *Economic History Review* 2d Series 10:381–394.

LEDOUX, R. 1912 *La suppression du régime corporatif dans les Pays-Bas autrichiens en 1784. Un projet d'édit.* Académie Royale de Belgique, Classe des Lettres et des Sciences Morales . . . , Mémoires, Collection in-8°, 2d Series, Vol. 10, fasc. 1. Brussels: Hayez.

LE TOURNEAU, ROGER 1957 *Les villes musulmanes de l'Afrique du Nord.* Algiers: La Maison des Livres.

LEWIS, BERNARD 1937 The Islamic Guilds. *Economic History Review* 8:20–37.

LITTLE, KENNETH 1957 The Role of Voluntary Associations in West African Urbanization. *American Anthropologist* New Series 59:579–596.

MORSE, HOSEA B. (1909) 1932 *The Gilds of China, With an Account of the Gild Merchant or Co-hong of Canton.* 2d ed. London: Longmans.

SOCIÉTÉ JEAN BODIN POUR L'HISTOIRE COMPARATIVE DES INSTITUTIONS 1954–1955 *La ville.* 2 parts. Recueils, Vols. 6–7. Brussels: Librairie Encyclopédique. → Part 1: *Institutions administratives et judiciaires.* Part 2: *Institutions économiques et sociales.*

THRUPP, SYLVIA L. 1963 The Gilds. Pages 230–280 in *The Cambridge Economic History of Europe From the Decline of the Roman Empire.* Volume 3: Economic Organization and Policies in the Middle Ages. Cambridge Univ. Press. → A bibliography appears on pages 624–634.

WAGNER, DONALD O. 1937 The Common Law and Free Enterprise: An Early Case of Monopoly. *Economic History Review* 7:217–220.

WALTZING, JEAN PIERRE 1895–1900 *Étude historique sur les corporations professionelles chez les Romains depuis les origines jusqu'à la chute de l'empire d'occident.* 4 vol. Louvain (Belgium): Peeters.

# GINI, CORRADO

The work of Corrado Gini (1884–1965) has had a profound impact on many fields within the social sciences. The son of a manufacturer, Gini was born in Motta di Livenza, Treviso Province. He studied law at the University of Bologna, where he also took courses in mathematics. The broad scope of his scholarly contributions is reflected in the variety of subjects he taught, successively, at the universities of Cagliari, Padua, and Rome: statistics, political economy, demography, biometrics, constitutional law, and sociology.

Gini also furthered the development of social science in other than academic capacities. From 1926 to 1932 he was chairman of the Central Institute of Statistics. He directed several scientific expeditions to study the demographic, anthropometric, and medical characteristics of particular ethnic groups in Fezzan, Palestine, Mexico, Poland and Lithuania, Calabria, and Sardinia, as well as the processes of assimilation of immigrant groups generally. He was the founder and editor of the international journal of statistics *Metron*, in 1920, and of the journal *Genus*, the organ of the Italian Committee for the Study of Population Problems.

In recognition of his achievements he was awarded honorary doctorates, one in economic science—from the Catholic University in Milan, in 1932—and another in sociology—from the University of Geneva, in 1934; and he was awarded an honorary doctor of science degree by Harvard at the 1936 tercentenary celebration of that university.

The main currents of thought in Italian culture at the time that Gini began his scientific activity were positivism and idealism. Gini's commitment to positivism was limited. His works manifest a remarkable eclecticism, arising from his systematic study of a variety of disciplines: law, economics, statistics, mathematics, and biology. He always placed the phenomena he was studying in a more general context, bringing essential social, economic, and demographic elements to bear on the topic of his immediate concern.

Gini thoroughly understood the importance of descriptive statistics, as is shown by his particular admiration for Luigi Bodio among Italian statisticians, but at the same time he deeply felt the need to study the procedures of inferential statistics and to find suitable criteria for evaluating those procedures. To this end he studied the works of Bernoulli, Lexis, and Czuber, as well as those of the Italians Angelo Messedaglia and Rodolfo Benini.

**Contributions to statistical method.** Gini's first scientific works deal with the statistical regularity of rare events. To the same period—1908 to 1911 —belongs his initial work on the concept and measurement of probability, with special attention and application to the human sex ratio at birth. His findings were contained in a book (1908) in which he presented analyses of extensive empirical materials on sex ratios from different countries. In the same work, he developed a theory of dispersion,

that is, of the quantitative structure of the scatter or variability among measured quantities of the same kind. He later returned to the topic of dispersion (1940; 1941).

Gini made a lengthy critique of the principles of statistics in order to reinforce the logical basis of statistics and to rid it of naïve empiricism. He wished to raise statistics to the level of an independent science, one of whose tasks would be the systematic investigation of the advantages and limitations of various indexes, or descriptive statistics, under differing structures of error.

In an address entitled "I pericoli della statistica" (1939; "The Dangers of Statistics"), inaugurating the first meeting of the Società Italiana di Statistica, Gini warned statisticians about the faulty logical foundations of some statistical methods and stressed the importance of estimating meaningful parameters. He published further papers on this general subject (1943; 1947). In the latter paper, "Statistical Relations and Their Inversions," he pointed out that poor statistical notation may lead to misunderstanding and error. For example, if one writes $y = 3 + 7x$, as a mathematical relationship between the real variables $x$ and $y$, one may just as well write $x = -\frac{3}{7} + \frac{1}{7}y$; this is called invertibility. On the other hand, in a statistical context of regression, one may loosely write $y = 3 + 7x$, meaning that the expectation (or average) of a random variable $Y$ is thus linearly related to possible values of another random variable $X$. For clarity, one should use a more complete notation like the now conventional

$$E(Y|X = x) = 3 + 7x,$$

and, in general, $E(X|Y = y) \neq -\frac{3}{7} + \frac{1}{7}y$. On the other hand, taking complete averages, $EY = 3 + 7EX$; this situation is called one of subinvertibility.

In a paper written in collaboration with Luigi Galvani, "Di talune estensioni dei concetti di media ai caratteri qualitativi" (1929; "Extension of Mean Value Theory to Qualitative Characteristics"), Gini made an original contribution in another area. The problem here was to find a meaningful analogue of the usual arithmetic mean for a purely qualitative or nominal distribution. By defining a measure of deviation between any two classes of the qualitative classification and by a minimization argument, Gini showed how to choose one of the classes of the classification as a kind of mean.

The theory of generalized means was of continuing interest to Gini, and he was particularly concerned with its very general expression and with a wide variety of mean values (1938). In another article, again with Galvani, he discussed extensively the topic of location parameters for bivariate distributions, noting especially geographical problems (see Gini et al. 1933).

Next to generalized means, measures of variability are of great importance, and Gini discussed these at length, giving special attention to descriptive statistics not intrinsically tied to the normal distribution (1912). He introduced a new measure of variability, the *mean difference*, which is essentially the expected absolute value of $X_1 - X_2$, where $X_1$ and $X_2$ are independent random variables with the same distribution of interest. (Gini thought primarily in terms of the sample version of the mean difference.)

Gini also worked on measures of variability for qualitative or nominal distributions and on measures of variability that are tied to the concentration curve and are considered important in the economic analysis of income and wealth (1921).

**Nontypicality of typical census areas.** Gini set himself the task of selecting a sample of typical census areas in Italy. To this end, he showed that it is not adequate simply to select the sample in such a way that the averages of various characteristics calculated for the sample are equal to those calculated for the entire territory of Italy. Even when the examination is confined to only the characteristics used in selecting the sample, the sample proves to be unrepresentative with respect to the variability and concentration of those characteristics and to the relations existing between them. Accordingly, Gini included in the criteria of representativeness these last two aspects of the distributions of characteristics, and he examined the conditions to which each of the proposed criteria subjects the other criteria.

**Theory of price indexes.** To the theory of price indexes, which is of great importance in economic statistics, Gini contributed a classic paper, "Quelques considérations au sujet des nombres indices des prix et des questions analogues" (1924), in which he solved some logical and technical problems connected with elimination methods.

Distinguishing between simple and complex indices, Gini showed how, in general, the methods for obtaining complex indexes can be considered as particular cases of the method of elimination (which consists in separating the different circumstances affecting a phenomenon in order to make comparisons *ceteris paribus* with similar phenomena at different times or places). The problem was to keep the phenomenon of "price variation" distinct from the phenomenon of "quantity variation."

Operating with the general method of the "typical population" organized into four special methods, Gini obtained various formulas for index numbers, at the same time providing criteria for choosing that one of the formulas best suited to the aims of particular problems. (Another of his papers on the same topic is "Methods of Eliminating the Influence of Several Groups of Factors," 1937).

**Theory of distributions.** Gini made substantial contributions to the study of relationships between two probability distributions and between two random variables with a joint distribution. Particularly important are the following:

(*a*) *Transvariation.* Suppose that one considers two probability distributions, represented for convenience by (independent) random variables $X$, $Y$. Suppose further that $EX < EY$; it may still be quite probable that $X > Y$, that is, the difference between the observations $X$ and $Y$ may show a different sign than the corresponding difference between expected values. Gini proposed a specific measure for this phenomenon, which he called transvariation (1953; 1959*a*; see also Kruskal 1957).

(*b*) *Distance between two distributions.* Gini was one of the first to consider the problem of measuring meaningfully how much two probability distributions differ in gross (1914*a*). He proposed a measure of distance, based on the two cumulative distribution functions, that was in fact a metric in the technical mathematical sense (see Fréchet 1947).

(*c*) *Association between two random variables with a joint distribution.* Gini made the basic distinction between *connection* (any kind of statistical dependence) and *concordance* (dependence in which it makes sense to speak of one variable tending to increase—or decrease—along with the other). The correlation ratio, for example, is a measure of connection, while the coefficient of correlation is a measure of concordance. Gini analyzed previously suggested measures of association and proposed new ones both for the case of numerical variates and for that of qualitative variates (see Goodman & Kruskal 1959, which contains relevant references to Gini, Weida, and Pietra).

**Demography and biometrics.** Gini pioneered in studies that relate demographic phenomena to social and biological phenomena. Thus, he studied the sources of differential fertility (1949), and he related the phenomenon of migration to broader social and demographic considerations (1946*b*).

Gini also proposed a unified research program for analyzing the eugenic and dysgenic effects of war, with special emphasis on the measurement of the effects of war on mortality (1915–1920). Also related to demographic phenomena are Gini's studies of various populations in phases of expansion, regression, and extinction (1934).

**Economic and sociological research.** From the earliest years of his career, Gini tackled the difficult problem of estimating national wealth. He made a constructive criticism of the method of the interval of devolution and the first calculation by a direct method of the private wealth of Italy (1914b). He followed a methodological organization of the data with a comparative study of the qualitative composition of wealth, clarifying the conditions that make nations wealthy (1959b).

Gini originated the idea of including the value of human capital in the calculation of wealth [see CAPITAL, HUMAN]. This makes it possible to indicate the preponderant cause for the incommensurability in time and territory of the wealth and economic well-being of various collectivities (1956a). The value-as-property of the man who labors becomes a factor in estimating wealth, just as the share derived from human labor is included in income (1914a). This conception clearly links economic considerations with sociological and demographic ones.

Related to Gini's conception of human capital is his cyclical theory of population. Observing the differential rates of reproduction of social classes, Gini formulated a theory of social metabolism that is based on an analogy to organic metabolism: the upper classes, having low rates of reproduction, will tend to extinction unless they get new members from the lower classes, which have higher rates of reproduction (1927). Gini intended this theory to replace Pareto's concept of the circulation of elites.

Gini also developed a theory of phases of population growth, these being related to social and economic phenomena (1923). According to his theory, a particular population grows rapidly in the first phase of its development, then has a diminishing rate of growth until it is approximately stationary, and finally begins a decline that may even lead to total extinction. In the first phase, capital is very scarce and there is little differentiation between social classes; later, as capital is accumulated, classes become increasingly differentiated, and there is a concomitant differentiation of reproductive behavior. As birth control spreads, a deterioration in the quality of the population can be avoided only by the influence of external factors, such as the immigration of young people from populations in the phase of demographic expansion.

Gini's neo-organicist approach makes it possible to distinguish normal economic processes from pathological ones—those in which the state of a society is unbalanced—and to initiate economic processes of restoration. In general, he believed that states of imbalance could be remedied by the regulatory activities of political agencies and of economic organizations.

In Gini's view, an important aspect of the development of society is the transition from forced to free labor and then to spontaneous labor (1956b). This last represents the final stage in a psychological process that raises labor from a primordial means of obtaining a living to a free and autonomous activity that enriches the human personality.

Gini's pre-eminent place in the development of Italian statistics is based on a dual contribution: his work in scientific statistics, which included important teaching and editorial activities; and his efforts toward the development of official statistics, notably, the consolidation in a single institute of all the various agencies for the collection of data and the extension of the number of items about which data are collected.

TOMMASO SALVEMINI

[*Directly related are the entries* SAMPLE SURVEYS; STATISTICS, DESCRIPTIVE; VARIANCES, STATISTICAL STUDY OF. *Other relevant material may be found in* CENSUS; GENETICS; INCOME DISTRIBUTION, *article on* SIZE; INDEX NUMBERS; MIGRATION; POPULATION; *and in the biographies of* BENINI; BERNOULLI FAMILY; LEXIS; PARETO.]

### WORKS BY GINI

1908 *Il sesso dal punto di vista statistico: Le leggi della produzione dei sessi.* Milan: Sandron.

(1912) 1955 *Memorie di metodologia statistica.* Volume 1: *Variabilità e concentrazione.* 2d ed. Rome: Veschi.

1914a *Di una misura della dissomiglianza fra due gruppi di quantità e delle sue applicazioni allo studio delle relazioni statistiche.* Venice: Ferrari.

(1914b) 1962 *L'ammontare e la composizione della ricchezza della nazioni.* 2d ed. Turin: Bocca.

(1915–1920) 1921 *Problemi sociologici della guerra.* Bologna: Zanichelli. → A collection of previously published articles.

1921 *Measurement of Inequality of Incomes. Economic Journal* 31:124–126.

(1923) 1952 *Patologia economica.* 5th ed., rev. & enl. Turin: Unione Tipografico–Editrice Torinese.

1924 *Quelques considérations au sujet de la construction des nombres indices des prix et des questions analogues. Metron* 4:3–162.

1927 *Il neo-organicismo: Prolusione al corso di sociologia.* Catania: Studio Editoriale Moderno.

1929 GINI, CORRADO; and GALVANI, LUIGI *Di talune estensioni dei concetti di media ai caratteri qualitativi. Metron* 8, no. 1/2:3–209.

1933 GINI, CORRADO; BERARDINIS, L. DE; and GALVANI, L. Sulla selettività delle cause di morte durante l'infanzia. *Metron* 11, no. 1:163–183.

1934 Ricerche sulla popolazione. *Scientia* 55:357–373.

1937 Methods of Eliminating the Influence of Several Groups of Factors. *Econometrica* 5:56–73.

1938 Di una formula comprensiva delle medie. *Metron* 13:3–22.

1939 I pericoli della statistica. *Rivista di politica economica* 29:901–924.

1940 Sur la théorie de la dispersion et sur la vérification et l'utilisation des schémas théoriques. *Metron* 14:3–29.

1941 Alle basi del metodo statistico: Il principio della compensazione degli errori accidentali e la legge dei grandi numeri. *Metron* 14:173–240.

1943 I testi di significatività. Società Italiana di Statistica, *Atti* [1943]:241–279.

1946a Actualidades demográficas. *Revista internacional de sociología* 4:147–169.

1946b Los efectos demográficos de las migraciones internacionales. *Revista internacional de sociología* 4:351–388.

1947 Statistical Relations and Their Inversions. International Statistical Institute, *Revue de l'Institut International de Statistique* 15:24–42.

1948 Evoluzione della psicologia del lavoro e della accumulazione. Banca Nazionale del Lavoro, *Moneta e credito* Whole No. 2.

1949 Vecchie e nuove osservazioni sulle cause della natalità differenziale e sulla misura della fecondità naturale delle coniugate. *Metron* 15:207–358.

1950 Metodologia statistica: La misura dei fenomeni collettivi. Volume 3, part 2, pages 245–321 in *Enciclopedia delle matematiche elementari*. Milan: Hoepli.

1951 Caractère des plus récents développements de la méthodologie statistique. *Statistica* 11:3–11.

1952 On Some Symbols That May Be Usefully Employed in Statistics. International Statistical Institute, *Bulletin* 33, no. 2:249–282.

1953 The Measurement of the Differences Between Two Quantity Groups and in Particular Between the Characteristics of Two Populations. *Acta genetica et statistica medica* 4:175–191.

1955 Sur quelques questions fondamentales de statistique. Paris, Université, Institut Henri Poincaré, *Annales* 14:245–364.

1956a Valutazione del lavoro e del capitale nell' *Economia lavorista*. *Rivista bancaria* New Series 12:522–530.

1956b *Economia lavorista: Problemi del lavoro.* Turin: Tipografia Sociale Torinese.

(1956c) 1966 *Statistical Methods.* Rome: Biblioteca del Metron. → Lectures delivered at the International Center for Training in Agricultural Economics and Statistics, Rome.

1958 Logic in Statistics. *Metron* 19, no. 1/2:1–77.

1959a *Transvariazione.* Rome: Libreria Goliardica.

1959b *Ricchezza e reddito.* Turin: Unione Tipografico-Editrice Torinese.

1959c Mathematics in Statistics. *Metron* 19, no. 3/4:1–9.

### SUPPLEMENTARY BIBLIOGRAPHY

CASTELLANO, VITTORIO 1965 Corrado Gini: A Memoir With the Complete Bibliography of His Works. *Metron* 24; no. 1–4.

FRÉCHET, MAURICE 1947 Anciens et nouveaux indices de corrélation: Leur application au calcul des retards économiques. *Econometrica* 15:1–30, 374–375.

FRÉCHET, MAURICE 1947–1948 Le coefficient de connexion statistique de Gini–Salvemini. *Mathematica* 23:46–51.

FRÉCHET, MAURICE 1957 Sur la distance de deux lois de probabilité. Paris, Université, Institut de Statistique, *Publications* 6:183–198.

GALVANI, LUIGI 1947 À propos de la communication de M. Thionet: "L'école moderne de statisticiens italiens." Société de Statistique de Paris, *Journal* 88:196–203. → A bitter attack on the 1945–1946 article by Pierre Thionet. See pages 203–208 for Thionet's reply to Galvani.

GOODMAN, LEO A.; and KRUSKAL, WILLIAM H. 1959 Measures of Association for Cross-classifications: II. Further Discussion and References. *Journal of the American Statistical Association* 54:123–163.

KRUSKAL, WILLIAM H. 1957 Historical Notes on the Wilcoxon Unpaired Two-sample Test. *Journal of the American Statistical Association* 52:356–360.

NEYMAN, JERZY (1938) 1952 *Lectures and Conferences on Mathematical Statistics and Probability.* 2d ed., rev. & enl. Washington: U.S. Department of Agriculture, Graduate School.

SALVEMINI, TOMMASO 1943 La revisione critica di Gini ai fondamenti della metodologia statistica. *Statistica* 3:46–59.

THIONET, PIERRE 1945–1946 L'école moderne de statisticiens italiens. Société de Statistique de Paris, *Journal* 86:245–255; 87:16–34.

## GIRSHICK, MEYER A.

Meyer Abraham Girshick (1908–1955), American statistician, was born in Russia and immigrated to the United States in 1922. After graduating from Columbia College in 1932, he did graduate work in statistics under Harold Hotelling at Columbia University from 1934 until 1937. (Several years later he received a doctorate from Columbia.) In 1937–1939 he was a statistician with the Bureau of Home Economics, U.S. Department of Agriculture, where he participated in a pioneer study of body measurements of 147,000 American children that helped manufacturers to develop improved sizing of garments. At the same time, he gave evening courses in statistics at the U.S. Department of Agriculture Graduate School, courses that had a profound influence on the dissemination of sound statistical methods in government work and encouraged many new research workers. In 1939–1944 and again in 1945–1946 he was principal statistician for the Bureau of Agricultural Economics. For one year during World War II he participated in the work of the Statistical Research Group at Columbia University, a panel composed of statisticians and designed to develop statistical methods appropriate to wartime problems. Working with others on the panel, particularly Abraham Wald, had a decisive influence on Girshick's subsequent career. After a brief stay at the Bureau of the Census, he became a research statistician and mathematician at the RAND Corporation in Santa Monica, California (a research organization primarily devoted to work for the U.S. Air Force). From 1948 until his untimely death in 1955 he was professor of statistics at Stanford University. He was elected president of the Institute of Mathematical Statistics (one of the principal learned societies for theoretical statistics) in 1951.

His early papers, written between 1936 and 1944, were primarily concerned with problems of multivariate statistical analysis. His major achievement was to find the distribution of the roots and characteristic vectors associated with certain determinantal equations that are used in testing the null hypothesis that two sets of variates are independent (1939). [See MULTIVARIATE ANALYSIS.]

Subsequently he also found the distribution of these roots when the null hypothesis is not true. From this the power function of certain tests can in principle be obtained (1941).

His interest in multivariate analysis and his substantive work at the Bureau of Agricultural Economics combined to turn his attention to newly developing methods of estimation of simultaneous equations in economics. These methods were originated by Trygve Haavelmo and continued by Tjalling Koopmans, T. W. Anderson, and Herman Rubin. In collaboration with Haavelmo, Girshick conducted one of the first major empirical studies on an econometric model for the agricultural sector of the United States economy (1947), and through unpublished work he contributed importantly to the development of the limited-information approach to simultaneous equation estimation. [See SIMULTANEOUS EQUATION ESTIMATION.]

During the period that Girshick was associated with the Statistical Research Group, Wald was originating two major concepts of statistics: sequential analysis and statistical decision theory [see DECISION THEORY; SEQUENTIAL ANALYSIS; *and the biography of* WALD]. Girshick's subsequent work was almost exclusively confined to these two areas (see Blackwell & Girshick 1954).

His earliest work in sequential analysis concerned the testing of composite hypotheses in which the mean of one process is less than, or equal to, the mean of another, the alternative being that it is greater. He showed that the power functions of such tests were constant on certain curves in the parameter space, and he was able to use this information to derive approximate sequential tests for the parameters of the exponential family of

distributions (1946a). He also found exact relations for tests when the variables take on only a finite set of values. As a by-product of his interest in sequential analysis he found, in collaboration with Frederick Mosteller and L. J. Savage, a method of getting unbiased estimates of a parameter from data that have been generated by a sequential, or similar, sampling scheme (Girshick et al. 1946b). He and David Blackwell found a lower bound for the variance of such estimates (Blackwell & Girshick 1947).

His work in decision theory was developed in a series of papers, most of them coauthored with Blackwell, Rubin, Savage, or Arrow. The major results of these studies were systematically presented in *Theory of Games and Statistical Decisions* (1954), written jointly with Blackwell. This book today represents a major study of statistical method using the concepts of the theory of games from the decision-theory point of view. The theory of games, which is closely allied to decision theory, is also given prominence in the book. [See GAME THEORY.] Among its most noteworthy accomplishments are a study of the interrelations of various criteria for complete classes of solutions and related concepts and a systematic treatment of Bayesian and related procedures in statistical contexts. Other special features include rigorous analysis of the concepts of sufficiency and of invariance, a clear exposition and characterization of sequential probability-ratio tests and their optimal properties, a study of Bayesian estimation procedures with special loss functions, particularly the quadratic and the absolute value, and the theory of comparison of experiments.

Girshick's influence on the development of statistical theory occurred as much through his direct personal relations, his enthusiasm and intelligent guidance, as through his published work, important as the latter is.

KENNETH J. ARROW

### WORKS BY GIRSHICK

1939 On the Sampling Theory of Determinantal Equations. *Annals of Mathematical Statistics* 10:203–224.

1941 The Distribution of the Ellipticity Statistic $L_e$ When the Hypothesis Is False. *Terrestrial Magnetism and Atmospheric Electricity* 46:455–457.

1946a Contributions to the Theory of Sequential Analysis. *Annals of Mathematical Statistics* 17:123–143, 282–298.

1946b GIRSHICK, MEYER A.; MOSTELLER, FREDERICK; and SAVAGE, L. J. Unbiased Estimates for Certain Binomial Sampling Problems With Applications. *Annals of Mathematical Statistics* 17:13–23.

1947 GIRSHICK, MEYER A.; and HAAVELMO, TRYGVE Statistical Analysis of the Demand for Food: Examples of Simultaneous Estimation of Structural Equations. *Econometrica* 15:79–110.

1947    BLACKWELL, DAVID; and GIRSHICK, MEYER A. A Lower Bound for the Variance of Some Unbiased Sequential Estimates. *Annals of Mathematical Statistics* 18:277–280.

1954    BLACKWELL, DAVID; and GIRSHICK, MEYER A. *Theory of Games and Statistical Decisions.* New York: Wiley.

SUPPLEMENTARY BIBLIOGRAPHY

BLACKWELL, DAVID; and BOWKER, ALBERT H.    1955    Meyer Abraham Girshick: 1908–1955. *Annals of Mathematical Statistics* 26:365–367.

## GLOTTOCHRONOLOGY

*See* LINGUISTICS.

## GOALS

*See* ACHIEVEMENT MOTIVATION; DRIVES; MOTIVATION; ORGANIZATIONS, *article on* ORGANIZATIONAL GOALS; VOLUNTARY ASSOCIATIONS.

## GOBINEAU, JOSEPH ARTHUR DE

Joseph Arthur de Gobineau (1816–1882) is best known as the author of the *Essai sur l'inégalité des races humaines* (1853–1855), which made race the principal explanatory factor in history and had an important influence on the development of the concept of race in the nineteenth century. Although during his lifetime Gobineau received little recognition in his native France, after his death his racial theories aroused considerable interest, especially in Germany.

The mystique of elitism and race in Gobineau's thought had its roots in certain circumstances of his life. His family was noble, but the origins of its nobility were obscure. His father, Louis de Gobineau, was a captain in the royal guard, and his mother, Anne-Louise Magdeleine de Gercy, was the daughter (if we believe Gobineau) of an illegitimate son of Louis XV. Gobineau's adolescence was tormented by the marital conflict between his parents, and he began very early to question whether "all kinds of blood and all origins are alike."

Gobineau went to Paris in 1835 and became a member of its literary, artistic, and scientific circles. He attended the salons of Madame de Serre, of Rémusat, and of Tocqueville. Initially he seemed to lean toward a sort of liberalism in politics, but the revolution of 1848 instilled in him a permanent abhorrence of democracy. When Tocqueville served as minister of foreign affairs of the republic in 1849, Gobineau became his private secretary, and upon Tocqueville's fall, Gobineau entered the diplomatic service. The books he wrote about the countries in which he lived—Germany, Persia, Greece, Brazil, and Sweden—were all pervaded by his theories of race.

Aristocratic by temperament himself, Gobineau sought passionately all his life to justify elitism both scientifically and philosophically. From the outset, he defined the elite in ethnic terms, identifying it with a superior race, a "race of masters." He asserted that the white race is superior to the yellow and black races by virtue of its intelligence, its capacity for reflection, its love of order and liberty, its sense of honor, and its pre-emption of all civilized values, and he claimed superiority among the whites for the pure Aryan. Unhappily, however, as he saw it, this ethnic hierarchy has no permanence, for races are constantly mixing; indeed, there are no more pure races. This mixing is disastrous, for it lowers the superior elements to the level of the less gifted and leads eventually to degeneration and to the extinction of civilization. On the political level, the mixing of races finds its expression in democracy, which Gobineau considered the worst form of state. In a draft foreword written in 1877 for a second edition of the *Essai*, he admitted that his race theory was "a natural consequence of [his] horror and disgust at democracy." The *Essai* reveals Gobineau's profound pessimism, ending as it does with an apocalyptic vision of the world in the final stage of decay—an era of uniformity, mediocrity, and passivity on the part of individuals.

Gobineau's pessimism about the fate of civilization came to be reinforced by the justified conviction that he was not being appreciated. His travels to Greece, Persia, and Brazil only served to confirm his idea that the mixture of races causes degeneration. Full of hatred and contempt for the "mixed breeds," he returned from Brazil to France in 1870 to experience the Franco–Prussian War, defeat, the Commune, and the installation of the republic. These events convinced him that the downfall of his country was inevitable, led as it was by the "Gallo–Roman rabble," the "bourgeoisie."

His last ministry was in Stockholm, from 1872 to 1876, and he did much writing there. He finished his novel *Les pléiades* (1874), in which he presented the idea that, as a consequence of racial degeneration, an elite must be sought among individuals—individuals who stand out by virtue of their love of liberty, their sense of honor, and their energy—and he went back to work on his poem *Amadis* (1887), into which he poured his feudal ideas, his hatreds, and his apocalyptic vision of a degenerate world. There too he worked on *Ottar Jarl* (1879), the story of a Norwegian pirate, the imaginary founder of his own family of which he claimed to be the last offshoot; the work is a rather pathetic attempt to prove that he was an elite being. In Stockholm, too, he embraced the pagan spirit, leaving behind not only the Catholicism of his family but also many other forms of religious and philosophical thought that he had accepted successively since childhood.

His growing hostility toward a society that failed to appreciate him led to his being retired prematurely in 1876. He lived out his last years in Italy, full of bitterness and pessimism, separated from his wife, and in financial stringency.

R. THENEN

[*For the historical context of Gobineau's work, see* RACE.]

### WORKS BY GOBINEAU

(1847) 1961 *Mademoiselle Irnois, suivi de Adélaïde.* Paris: Gallimard.

(1853–1855) 1933 *Essai sur l'inégalité des races humaines.* 6th ed. 2 vols. Paris: Firmin-Didot. → Partially translated into English in 1915 as *The Inequality of Human Races.*

(1854–1876) 1933 *Correspondance entre le comte de Gobineau et le comte de Prokesh Osten (1854–1876).* Paris: Plon.

(1856–1863) 1959 *Les dépêches diplomatiques du comte de Gobineau en Perse.* Études d'histoire économique, politique et sociale, No. 30. Geneva: Droz.

(1859) 1923 *Trois ans en Asie (de 1855 à 1858).* Paris: Grasset.

1861 *Voyage à Terre-Neuve.* Paris: Hachette.

(1865) 1933 *Les religions et les philosophies dans l'Asie centrale.* Paris: Gallimard.

(1868–1881) 1936 *Lettres à deux athéniennes (1868–1881).* Athens: Castalie.

1869a *Histoire des perses d'après les auteurs orientaux, grecs et latins.* 2 vols. Paris: Nourrit.

1869b *L'Aphroessa.* Paris: Maillet.

(1870–1882) 1938 GOBINEAU, JOSEPH ARTHUR DE; and PEDRO II, EMPEROR OF BRAZIL D. *Pedro IIe o conde de Gobineau (correspondencias ineditas).* São Paulo: Companhia Editora Nacional. → Letters written between 1870 and 1882. See pages 373–619 for the French originals.

1872 *Souvenirs de voyage (Céphalonie, Naxie et Terre-Neuve).* Paris: Plon-Nourrit.

(1872–1882) 1958 *Correspondance, 1872–1882: Comte de Gobineau et Mère Benedicte de Gobineau.* 2 vols. Paris: Mercure de France.

(1874) 1928 *The Pleiads.* New York: Knopf. → First published in French.

(1876) 1965 *Nouvelles asiatiques.* Paris: Garnier.

(1877) 1927 *The Renaissance: Savonarola, Cesare Borgia, Julius II, Leo X, Michaelangelo.* New York: Putnam. → First published in French.

1879 *Histoire d'Ottar Jarl, pirate norvégien, conquérant du pays de Bray en Normandie, et de sa descendance.* Paris: Didier.

1887 *Amadis, poème.* Paris: Plon. → Published posthumously.

1907 *La Troisième République française et ce qu'elle vaut.* Strasbourg: Trübner. → Published posthumously.

(1923) 1924 *The Golden Flower.* New York: Putnam. → Five historical essays published posthumously in French. Written originally as prefaces to the five parts of Gobineau's play *La renaissance*, 1877.

### SUPPLEMENTARY BIBLIOGRAPHY

DREYFUS, ROBERT 1905 *La vie et les prophéties du comte de Gobineau.* Paris: Lévy.

*Études gobiniennes.* 1966 Paris: Klincksieck.

GAULMIER, JEAN 1965 *Spectre de Gobineau.* Paris: Pauvert.

*Gobineau et le gobinisme.* 1934 *Nouvelle revue française* 49. → The entire issue is devoted to Gobineau.

LANGE, MAURICE 1924 *Le comte Arthur de Gobineau: Étude biographique et critique.* Strasbourg: Librairie Istra.

[Numéro spécial consacré à Gobineau.] 1923 *Europe* No. 9.

[Numéro spécial consacré à Gobineau.] 1923 *Nouveau mercure*, 10.

ROWBOTHAM, ARNOLD 1929 *The Literary Works of Count de Gobineau.* Paris: Champion.

SCHEMANN, LUDWIG 1913–1916 *Gobineau: Eine Biographie.* 2 vols. Strasbourg: Trübner.

SCHEMANN, LUDWIG 1914–1923 *Quellen und Untersuchungen zum Leben Gobineau.* 2 vols. Strasbourg: Trübner.

SEILLÈRE, ERNEST 1903 *La philosophie de l'impérialisme.* Volume 1: Le comte de Gobineau et l'aryanisme historique. Paris: Plon-Nourrit.

SPRING, GERALD M. 1932 *The Vitalism of Count de Gobineau.* New York: Institute of French Studies.

TOCQUEVILLE, ALEXIS DE (1843–1859) 1959 *Oeuvres, papiers et correspondances.* Volume 9: Correspondance d'Alexis de Tocqueville et d'Arthur de Gobineau. Paris: Gallimard.

# GÖKALP, ZIYA

Ziya Gökalp (1876–1924) was primarily responsible for introducing the study of sociology into Turkey, and he drew from sociology the intellectual basis for his ardent Turkish nationalism.

Born in Diyarbakir, the son of a civil servant who edited the official local newspaper, Mehmed Ziya (later Gökalp) attended secular schools there and also learned traditional Islamic lore from his uncle, a Muslim lawyer. At 18 he attempted suicide. By the following year, however, he was able to go to Istanbul and enroll at the Veterinary College.

He had already been influenced by the ideas of the Young Turks, and in 1895 he became a member of the secret society of Union and Progress in Istanbul. In 1898 he was arrested; after a year's imprisonment he was banished to his native town, where he devoted all his time to study. In those years the Young Turks who were in exile in Paris were strongly influenced by French sociology. One of them, Prince Sabaheddin, a follower of Le Play, went so far as to declare that only through sociological studies could the Ottomans introduce social change and thus find a way to achieve harmony among the various elements in the empire, a view later supported by Gökalp (in the first issue of his newspaper, *Peyman*, August 28, 1909).

In 1908, after the Young Turk revolution, Gökalp became the representative of the Union and Progress party in Diyarbakir. The next year he was elected a member of the central council of the party at Salonica and given the task of expounding its doctrine and attracting young people to its ranks. In 1910 he received an appointment to teach sociology in Salonica, the first such appointment in Turkey, and five years later he became the first professor of sociology at the University of Istanbul. He taught in the faculty of letters until 1919, making it a center for studies of Turkey as a nation. Exiled to Malta after World War I, he returned to Diyarbakir in 1921 as a wholehearted supporter of Atatürk and edited the *Küçük mecmua* ("Little Review"), in which he wrote a series of sociological essays designed to instruct the national leaders. In 1922 he was appointed director of Cultural Publications in Ankara, a department of the Ministry of Public Education, and there published his famous *Türkçülüğün essaslari* (1923; "Foundations of Turkism").

Gökalp believed that the political revolution of the Young Turks needed to be completed by a social revolution that would create a "new life" in such areas as economics, the family, fine arts, morality, and law. A new Turkish civilization could be created only by gaining knowledge of Turkey's genuine national values. As late as 1911 he had believed that values are nothing but *idées-forces* based on philosophical considerations, but after 1912 he accepted the Durkheimian interpretation of values as collective representations. (He considered Durkheim to be the most penetrating sociologist and the founder of scientific sociology.) According to Gökalp, collective representations are realizations in the "collective consciousness," which, when they become fully articulated, are called ideals. "The only source of values is society itself and the experience of collective sentiments by individuals constitutes collective conscience" ([1911–1923] 1959, pp. 62–64).

After her defeat in the Balkan War, a critical period began for Turkey. Discussions of reforms were accompanied by conflicts between the Islamists, Westernists, and Turkists. Gökalp, who had come to Istanbul in 1912, felt that these conflicts had to be reconciled in a broader outlook. He argued that humanity was composed of culture groups, each with its own value system, and of civilization groups, with rules and techniques capable of inter-

cultural diffusion and universal acceptance ([1911–1923] 1959, pp. 97–101). It was sociologically valid that Turks belonged at the same time to the Turkish nation, to the Muslim religious community, and to European civilization (Gökalp [1911–1923] 1959, pp. 71–76; Heyd 1950, pp. 149–151). Increasingly Gökalp stressed nationalism as the most powerful ideal of the modern age and nations as the most highly developed species on the scale of culture groups. In the nation he thought it was possible to integrate Turkish culture, Islam, and Western techniques. He later came to identify collective representations with national mores and asserted that "the . . . [discipline] which studies how the culture of a nation is distinguished from the civilization to which it belongs is called *cultural sociology*" ([1911–1923] 1959, pp. 172–173).

Following his belief that the task of the sociologist is to discover the elements of national culture, he embarked on a series of studies on the evolution of the Turkish family and on the pre-Islamic Turkish religion and state. His idea of a modernized Islam was predicated on the theory that the part of the religious law of Islam that is based on consensus is of social rather than divine origin and may therefore change in accordance with secular change ([1911–1923] 1959, pp. 193–196). He was convinced that a national state must be a secular one, and he strongly advocated a national system of education and economy. His programs for secularizing both education and the judiciary and for introducing equal rights for women were partly put into effect in 1917–1918.

Opinion on Gökalp is divided. He himself thought that what was original about his work was his testing of Durkheim's sociological method by applying it to Turkish civilization. His supporters agree that his conceptualizations of the nature of culture and nation are original and that his work represents scientific sociology in the Durkheim tradition; his critics stress that he had a dogmatic and deductive mind with strong collectivist ideas. Above all, he was an impassioned nationalist, and there is no doubt that his teachings provided an intellectual foundation for the modernization of Turkey.

HALIL İNALCIK

[*For the historical context of Gökalp's work, see* ISLAM; NATIONALISM; PAN MOVEMENTS; *and the biographies of* DURKHEIM; LE PLAY.]

WORKS BY GÖKALP

(1911–1923) 1959  *Turkish Nationalism and Western Civilization: Selected Essays.* Translated and edited with an introduction by Niyazi Berkes. New York: Columbia Univ. Press.

(1923) 1940 *Türkçülüğün essaslari* ("Foundations of Turkism"). Istanbul: Arkadas Matbaasĭ.

*Külliyat.* 2 vols. Ankara: Türk Tarih Kurumu Basĭmevi, 1952–1965. → Volume 1: *Siirler ve halk masallari.* Volume 2: *Ziya Gökalp'ın mektupları.*

*Ziya Gökalp'in ilk yazı hayatı, 1894–1909: Doğumu'nun 80. yıldönümü münasebetiyle.* Istanbul: Diyarbakırı Tanıtma Dernegi, 1956.

SUPPLEMENTARY BIBLIOGRAPHY

HEYD, URIEL 1950 *Foundations of Turkish Nationalism: The Life and Teachings of Ziya Gökalp.* London: Luzac.

TÜTENGIL, CAVIT O. 1949 *Ziya Gökalp Rakkĭnda bir bibliyografya denemesi.* Istanbul: Berksoy Matbaasĭ.

ÜLKEN, HILMI ZIYA *Ziya Gökalp.* Istanbul: Kanaat Kitavebi. → Date of publication not ascertained.

ZIYĀ AL-DĪN, FAKHRĪ 1935 *Ziya Gökalp, sa vie et sa sociologie: Essai sur l'influence de la sociologie française en Turquie.* Nancy (France): Berger–Levrault.

## GOLD STANDARD

*See* INTERNATIONAL MONETARY ECONOMICS *and* MONEY.

## GOLDENWEISER, ALEXANDER A.

Alexander Alexandrovich Goldenweiser (1880–1940), American anthropologist, was born in Kiev, Russia, the son of a lawyer with broad intellectual interests. He was educated in Kiev and at Harvard and Columbia, where he earned his PH.D. in 1910. A cosmopolitan figure, he achieved few of the rewards his ability might have earned him. He never held a full-time, permanent academic position, but he taught at many schools, including Columbia, the New School for Social Research, Portland Extension Center, Reed College, and the University of Wisconsin. His appointments were in anthropology, psychology, and sociology, and once he was even professor of thought and culture. He was an exciting teacher; although few of his students went on to become anthropologists, few forgot his lectures. He was also one of the first supporters of, and a contributor to, the *Encyclopaedia of the Social Sciences.*

An early student of Franz Boas, Goldenweiser was one of the most gifted American anthropologists of his generation. Yet his works are now often neglected. One reason for this may be that Boas and his students devoted so much of their time to critical attacks on the then prevalent theoretical positions: early in the twentieth century a simplistic, unilinear evolutionism was dominant; geographic determinism and, to a lesser extent, even racialism and other naïvely biological interpretations of behavior were also respectable posi-

tions. Armchair theorists were writing speculative works, many dealing with the "origins" of institutions. All of this was attacked by Boas and his group. Furthermore, although the group was primarily historical in outlook, it also opposed the extreme position of some historical anthropologists who were active particularly in Germany, Austria, and England and who argued against evolutionism on the grounds that cultural change results from migration or diffusion from one or a few original centers.

Theoretical polemics aside, Goldenweiser's writings might be more widely read had he published the kinds of field reports produced in such quantity by Alfred L. Kroeber, Robert H. Lowie, and others. Although he was popular with his Iroquois informants, he evidently did not enjoy field research and engaged in this activity for only a relatively few months. He preferred to concern himself with anthropological theory and with the broader problems of "social theory." He once told a friend that he would rather read bad theory than none at all. Moreover, he knew a number of languages well and did not limit his reading to anthropology.

Goldenweiser made theoretical contributions in more than one area. His article "The Principle of Limited Possibilities in the Development of Culture" (1913) is concerned with the issue of diffusion versus independent invention; it suggests that objects and acts can take only a limited number of forms and that this can lead to convergences among the traits of disparate cultures. Other early writings centered on totemism—for example, his 1910 article "Totemism: An Analytical Study." Ironically, his discussion of totemism contributed to a decreased interest in it among his colleagues, since it led them to conclude that there is no single, definable category of totemic practices but only diverse, if partially similar, phenomena that may be grouped under this term.

In his writings Goldenweiser made extensive use of the concept of culture. On some occasions he took culture for granted, but on others he advanced cultural, as against alternative, interpretations of behavior, as well as exploring particular cultural concepts, such as "patterning" (1936). This concept served him in his consistent attempts to see mankind in the round.

He may have overestimated the extent to which his own analyses and those of his colleagues could properly be characterized as psychological. Despite the fact that he had read a great deal of Wundt, some Freud, and the works of certain social psychologists, it is doubtful whether he made any attempt to keep abreast of developments in the main stream of psychology. He was particularly interested in the relationship between individuals and their culture, but he was not really one of the architects of the "culture and personality" movement. He was curious about the conceptual worlds of nonliterate peoples—what was then frequently called the primitive mind—and he did not think these conceptual worlds differed fundamentally from that of modern men. He was also curious about philosophy, the arts, and culture history, including various aspects of the history of European civilization.

Goldenweiser was not at home in the world as he knew it. Sometimes he was irresponsible in his relations with publishers or with academic systems. He appears to have lacked a substantial theoretical basis for studying the regularities of human life; the writings of his contemporaries did not readily offer such a basis, and even had it been there, his personal anarchistic predilections might have militated against his finding it. While he made few lasting contributions to theory, he did think well and write well on the questions of concern to him.

DAVID H. FRENCH

[*For the historical context of Goldenweiser's work, see the biographies of* BOAS *and* KROEBER.]

### WORKS BY GOLDENWEISER

1910   Totemism: An Analytical Study. *Journal of American Folk-lore* 23:179–293.
1913   The Principle of Limited Possibilities in the Development of Culture. *Journal of American Folk-lore* 26:259–290.
1922   *Early Civilization: An Introduction to Anthropology.* New York: Knopf.
1931   *Robots or Gods: An Essay on Craft and Mind.* New York: Knopf.
1933   *History, Psychology, and Culture.* New York: Knopf.
1936   Loose Ends of Theory on the Individual, Pattern, and Involution in Primitive Society. Pages 99–104 in *Essays in Anthropology Presented to A. L. Kroeber in Celebration of His Sixtieth Birthday, June 11, 1936.* Berkeley: Univ. of California Press.
1937   *Anthropology: An Introduction to Primitive Culture.* New York: Crofts.

### SUPPLEMENTARY BIBLIOGRAPHY

BUNZEL, RUTH L.   1960   Alexander Goldenweiser (1880–1940). Page 508 in Margaret Mead and Ruth L. Bunzel (editors), *The Golden Age of Anthropology.* New York: Braziller.
WALLIS, WILSON D.   1941   Alexander A. Goldenweiser. *American Anthropologist* New Series 43:250–255.
WHITE, LESLIE A.   1958   Alexander Alexandrovich Goldenweiser. Volume 22, pages 244–245 in *Dictionary of American Biography: Supplement Two.* New York: Scribner.

# GOLDSTEIN, KURT

Kurt Goldstein, American neurologist, psychiatrist, and psychologist, was born in 1878 in Kattowitz, Germany, and died in 1965 in New York City.

Goldstein entered medicine with the intention of devoting his life to the treatment of patients with mental diseases. In 1903 he received his medical degree at Breslau, Germany. He studied psychiatry with Karl Wernicke and neuroanatomy with Ludwig Edinger. His first ten papers, all published between 1903 and 1904, are studies of the anatomy of spinal pathways, of the embryology of the brain, and of comparative neuroanatomy. Clinical papers soon followed: one, in 1906, on memory problems and deficits created by neurological and psychiatric disturbances, foreshadowed important distinctions that underlie present-day differential diagnostic testing. In 1906 he joined the staff of the psychiatric clinic at the University of Königsberg, where he found his high expectations thwarted: mental patients were relegated to custodial care without any attempt at treatment. Nor did the prevailing Kraepelinian nosology indicate any conceivable direction for therapy. Goldstein used the opportunity for careful examination and observation of patients and published papers on neurological and psychiatric topics—motor disturbances, sensory disturbances, the nature of hallucinations, alcoholism, manic–depressive states, schizophrenia—and comparisons of clinical symptoms with post-mortem findings.

In 1919 he was appointed professor of neurology and director of the Neurological Institute at the University of Frankfurt. There he established the Institut zur Erforschung der Folgeerscheinungen von Hirnverletzungen, where, under his aegis and in collaboration with the psychologist Adhémar Gelb and many students, a large number of brain-injured soldiers were studied intensively and for long periods of time. These studies led to entirely novel conceptions of such problems as aphasia, agnosia, and tonus disturbances and generally to systematic descriptions of behavioral changes wrought by brain injury. In 1930 Goldstein became professor of neurology at the University of Berlin and director of the Neurological Hospital Moabit, a post he held until Hitler's advent in 1933. After a year's writing in Amsterdam he came to New York City in 1935; until 1940 he was clinical professor of neurology at Columbia University and head physician at Montefiore Hospital. In 1939 Harvard invited him to deliver the William James lectures, which were published under the title

*Human Nature in the Light of Psychopathology* (1940). From 1940 to 1945 he continued research and teaching as professor of neurology at Tufts Medical School, Boston. He then returned to New York, where he practiced privately and taught at the College of the City of New York, Columbia University, and the New School for Social Research. For many years he was also a guest professor at Brandeis University.

Goldstein's experimental papers and monographs provoked lively discussions among neurologists and psychologists; yet his greatest impact came with the publication of *The Organism: A Holistic Approach to Biology Derived From Pathological Data in Man* (1934), written during his year's exile in Amsterdam. Goldstein viewed behavior as the unified activity of the whole organism, whose basic "motive" is optimum self-actualization in a given environment. Reflexes, clinical symptoms, or functions subjected to laboratory investigation are part processes, and failure to consider that their isolation is artificial results in erroneous interpretation. Study of brain-injured patients reveals the general change underlying specific symptoms and manifestations, namely, an impairment of the patients' "abstract attitude" and a preponderance of "concrete" modes of behavior, affecting all performance fields. The "abstract attitude" is defined, basically, as man's capacity to reason deliberately, to plan and account for his actions, to view particular objects or events as instances of a class. Upon loss of these capacities the individual is at the mercy of the immediate, concrete sensory or mnemonic stimulus situation and is unable to transcend it. The aphasic patient cannot name an object, that is, supply the class symbol, yet he may spontaneously produce the word within a sentence or an action. Thus, aphasia is not a loss of words or word images. Rather, it is a dedifferentiation of language, a loss of concepts and their symbols; in other words, it is the manifestation in language of impaired abstraction. This view has important implications for the problem of cerebral localization. Functions cannot be localized, although defects can be, if we keep in mind the problem of isolated part processes and integrated organismic activity.

Impairment of abstraction is not limited to brain-injured patients. It manifests itself also in psychotic processes. Whatever its cause, impaired abstraction restricts the patient's opportunities for self-realization. Consequently, his conduct becomes rigid; he is vulnerable to anxiety, to the "catastrophic reaction," that is, to the threat of being unable to actualize himself, and to the danger of "losing existence."

Goldstein was only peripherally associated with the gestalt psychologists Wertheimer, Köhler, and Koffka; however, he was an editor of *Psychologische Forschung*, the house organ of gestalt psychology. While he never established a school, his views on aphasia profoundly influenced the English neurologist Sir Henry Head, as well as philosophers concerned with problems of normal language, particularly Goldstein's cousin Ernst Cassirer and the followers of Edmund Husserl. Generally critical of psychoanalytic theory, Goldstein acknowledged the importance of some of Freud's views, especially his broad emphasis on motivation and his discussion of the nature of symptoms. Existential psychology has claimed Goldstein somewhat unsuccessfully. Although phenomenological observation and analysis were fundamental to his work, he did not share the metaphysics of existential psychology and psychiatry.

MARIANNE L. SIMMEL

[*For the historical context of Goldstein's work, see* GESTALT THEORY *and the biographies of* KOFFKA; KÖHLER; WERTHEIMER. *For discussion of subsequent development of his ideas, see* LANGUAGE, *article on* SPEECH PATHOLOGY; MENTAL DISORDERS, *article on* ORGANIC ASPECTS; NERVOUS SYSTEM; SYSTEMS ANALYSIS, *article on* PSYCHOLOGICAL SYSTEMS; *and the biographies of* CASSIRER *and* HUSSERL.]

### WORKS BY GOLDSTEIN

1927 Die Lokalisation in der Grosshirnrinde. Pages 600–842 in *Handbuch der normalen und pathologischen Physiologie, mit Berücksichtigung der experimentellen Pharmakologie.* Volume 10: Spezielle Physiologie des Zentralnervensystems der Wirbeltiere. Berlin: Springer.

(1934) 1939 *The Organism: A Holistic Approach to Biology Derived From Pathological Data in Man.* New York: American Book. → First published as *Der Aufbau des Organismus.*

1940 *Human Nature in the Light of Psychopathology.* Cambridge, Mass.: Harvard Univ. Press.

1941 GOLDSTEIN, KURT; and SCHEERER, MARTIN. Abstract and Concrete Behavior: An Experimental Study With Special Tests. *Psychological Monographs* 53, no. 2, serial no. 239.

1942 *Aftereffects of Brain Injuries in War, Their Evaluation and Treatment: The Application of Psychologic Methods in the Clinic.* New York: Grune.

1948 *Language and Language Disturbances: Aphasic Symptom Complexes and Their Significance for Medicine and Theory of Language.* New York: Grune.

1959 Notes on the Development of My Concepts. *Journal of Individual Psychology* 15:5–14.

### SUPPLEMENTARY BIBLIOGRAPHY

Goldstein Anniversary Number. 1949 *Confinia neurologica* 9:1–272.

HEAD, HENRY 1926 *Aphasia and Kindred Disorders of Speech.* 2 vols. Cambridge Univ. Press.

MEIERS, JOSEPH I. 1958 *Kurt Goldstein Bibliography, 1903–1958.* Document No. 5816. Washington: American Documentation Institute, Photoduplication Service.

MOURGUE, RAOUL 1937 La conception de la neurologie dans l'oeuvre de Kurt Goldstein. *Encéphale* 32, part 1:32–56.

Papers in Honor of Kurt Goldstein. 1959 *Journal of Individual Psychology* 15:1–99.

RIESE, WALTHER 1948 Kurt Goldsteins Stellung in der Geschichte der Neurologie: Versuch einer Würdigung aus Anlass seines 70. Geburtstages, 6 November 1948. *Schweizer Archiv für Neurologie und Psychiatrie* 62: 2–10.

## GOODNESS OF FIT

A goodness of fit procedure is a statistical test of a hypothesis that the sampled population is distributed in a specific way, for example, normally with mean 100 and standard deviation 15. Corresponding confidence procedures for a population distribution also fall under this topic. Related tests are for broader hypotheses, for example, that the sampled population is normal (without further specification). Others test hypotheses that two or more population distributions are the same.

Populations arise because of variability, of which various sources (sometimes acting together) can be distinguished. First, there is inherent variability among experimental units, for example, the heights, IQ's, or ages of the students in a class each vary among themselves. Then there is measurement error, a more abstract or conceptual notion. The age of a student may have negligible measurement error, but his IQ does not; it depends on a host of accidental factors: how the student slept, the particular questions chosen for the test, and so on. There are also other conceptual populations, not properly thought of in terms of measurement error—the population of subject responses, for example, in the learning experiment below.

The distribution of a numerical population trait is often portrayed by a histogram, a density function, or some other device that shows the proportion of cases for which a particular value of the numerical trait is achieved (or the proportion within a small interval around a particular value). The shape of the histogram or density function is important; it may or may not be symmetrical. If it is not, it is said to be *skew*. If it is symmetrical, it may have a special kind of shape called *normal*. For example, populations of scores on intelligence tests are often assumed normally distributed by psychologists. Indeed, the construction of the test may aim at normality, at least for some group of individuals. Again, lifetimes of machines may be assumed to have negative exponential distributions,

meaning that expected remaining life does not vary with age. [*See* DISTRIBUTIONS, STATISTICAL, *article on* SPECIAL CONTINUOUS DISTRIBUTIONS; PROBABILITY; STATISTICS, DESCRIPTIVE.]

It is technically often convenient, especially in connection with goodness of fit tests, to deal with the *cumulative distribution function* (c.d.f.) rather than with the density function. The c.d.f. evaluated at $x$ is the proportion of cases with numerical values less than or equal to $x$; thus, if $f(x)$ is a density function, the corresponding c.d.f. is

$$F(x) = \int_{-\infty}^{x} f(t)\, dt.$$

For explicitness, a subscript will be added to $F$, indicating the population, distribution, or random variable to which it applies. It is a matter of convention that cumulation is from the left and that it is based on "less than or equal to" rather than just "less than."

The *sample c.d.f.* is the steplike function whose value at $x$ is the proportion of observations less than or equal to $x$. Many goodness of fit procedures are based on geometrically suggested measures of discrepancy between sample and hypothetical population c.d.f.'s. Some informal procedures use "probability" graph paper, especially normal paper (on which a normal c.d.f. becomes a straight line).

For nominal populations (for example, proportions of people expressing allegiance to different religions or to none) there is no concept corresponding to the c.d.f. The main emphasis of this article is on numerical populations.

Although goodness of fit procedures address themselves principally to the shape of population c.d.f.'s, the term "goodness of fit" is sometimes applied more generally than in this article. In particular, some authors write of goodness of fit of observed regressions to hypothetical forms, for example, to a straight line. [*This topic is dealt with in* LINEAR HYPOTHESES, *article on* REGRESSION.]

**Hypotheses—simple, composite, approximate.** A test of goodness of fit, based on a sample from a population, assesses the plausibility that the population distribution has specified form; in brief, *tests* the hypothesis that $F_X$ has shape $F_0$. The specification may be complete, that is, the population distribution may be specified completely, in which case the hypothesis is called *simple*. Alternatively, the form may be specified only up to certain unknown parameters, which often are the parameters of location and scale. In this case the hypothesis is called *composite*. Still another type of hypothesis is an *approximate* one, which is composite in a certain sense. Here one specifies first what one would consider a material departure from a hypothesized shape (Hodges & Lehmann 1954). For example, in the case of a *simple approximate* hypothesis, one might agree that $F_x$ departs materially from $F_0$ if the maximum vertical deviation between the actual and hypothesized cumulative distribution functions exceeds .07. The approximate hypothesis then states that the actual and hypothesized distributions do not differ materially in this sense.

Approximate hypotheses specialize to the others, so that a complete theory of testing for the former would be desirable. This is especially true since, as has been pointed out by Karl Pearson (1900) and Joseph Berkson (1938), tests of "exact" hypotheses, being as a rule *consistent*, have problematical logical status: unless the exact hypothesis is exactly correct and all of the sampling assumptions are exactly met, rejection of the hypothesis is assured (for fixed significance level) when sample size is large. Unfortunately, such a complete theory does not now exist, but the strong early interest in "exact" hypotheses was not misspent: The testing and "acceptance" of "exact" hypotheses concerning $F_x$ seems to have much the same status as the provisional adoption of physical or other "laws." If the latter has helped the advancement of science, so has no doubt the former; this is true notwithstanding that old hypotheses or theories will almost surely be discarded as additional data become available. This point has been made by Cochran (1952) and Chapman (1958). Cochran also suggests that the tests of "exact" hypotheses are "invertible" into confidence sets, in the usual manner, thus providing statistical procedures somewhat similar in intent to tests of approximate hypotheses [see ESTIMATION, *article on* CONFIDENCE INTERVALS AND REGIONS].

**Conducting a test of goodness of fit.** Many tests of goodness of fit have been developed; as with statistical tests generally, a test of goodness of fit is conveniently conducted by computing from the sample a *statistic* and its *sample significance level* [see HYPOTHESIS TESTING]. In the case of a test of goodness of fit, the statistic will measure the discrepancy between what the sample in fact *is* and what a sample from a population of hypothesized form *ought to be*. The sample significance level of an observed measure of discrepancy, $d_0$, is, at least for all the standard goodness of fit procedures, the probability, $Pr\{d \geqslant d_0\}$, that $d$ exceeds $d_0$ under random sampling from a population of hypothesized form. In other words, it is the proportion of like discrepancy measures, $d$, exceeding $d_0$, computed on the basis of many successive hypothetical

random samples of the same size from a population of hypothesized form. For many tests of goodness of fit, there exist tables (for extensive bibliography see Greenwood & Hartley 1962) that give those values of $d_0$ corresponding to given significance level and sample size ($n$). Many of these standard tests are *nonparametric*, which means that $Pr\{d \geqslant d_0\}$ is the same for a very large class of hypotheses $F_0$, so that only one such tabulation is required [see NONPARAMETRIC STATISTICS].

If, as is usual, the relevant alternative population distributions (more generally, alternative probabilistic models for the generation of the sample at hand) tend to encourage large values of $d_0$, the hypothesized population distribution will be judged implausible if the sample significance level is small (conventionally .05 or less). If the sample significance level is not small, it means that the statistic has a value unsurprising under the null hypothesis, so that the test gives no reason to reject the null hypothesis. If, however, the sample significance level is very large, say .95 or more, one may construe this as a warning of possible trouble, say, that an overzealous proponent of the hypothesis has slanted the data or that the sampling was not random. Note here an awkward usage prevalent in statistics generally: an observed measure of discrepancy $d_0$ with *low probability* $Pr\{d \geqslant d_0\}$ usually is described as *highly significant*.

**Choosing a test of goodness of fit.** Choosing a test of goodness of fit amounts to deciding in what sense the discrepancy between the hypothesized population distribution and the sample is to be measured: The sample c.d.f. may be compared directly with the hypothesized population c.d.f., as is done in the case of tests of the Kolmogorov–Smirnov type. For example, the original Kolmogorov–Smirnov test itself, as described below, summarizes the discrepancy by the maximum absolute deviation between the hypothesized population c.d.f., $F_0$, and the sample c.d.f. Alternatively, one may compare uncumulated frequencies, as for the $\chi^2$ test. Again, a standard shape parameter, such as skewness, may be computed for the sample and for the hypothesized population and the two compared.

Any reasonable measure of discrepancy will of course tend to be small if the population yielding the sample conforms to the null hypothesis. A good measure of discrepancy will, in addition, tend to be large under the likely alternative forms of the population distribution, a property designated technically by the term *power*. For example, the sample skewness coefficient might have good power if the hypothesized population distribution were normal (zero population skewness coefficient) and the relevant alternative distributional forms were appreciably skew.

**Two general considerations.** Two general considerations should be kept in mind. First it is important that the particular goodness of fit test used be selected without consideration of the sample at hand, at least if the calculated significance level is to be meaningful. This is because a measure of discrepancy chosen in the light of an observed sample anomaly will tend to be inordinately large. Receiving license plate 437918 hardly warrants the inference that, this year, the first and second digits add to the third, and the fifth and sixth to the fourth. It may of course be true, in special instances, that some adjustment of the test procedure in the light of the data does not affect the significance computations appreciably—as, for example, when choosing category intervals, based on the sample mean and variance, for the $\chi^2$ test (Watson 1957).

Second, a goodness of fit test, like any other statistical test, leads to an inference from a *sample* to the *population sampled*. Indeed, the usual hypothesis under test is that the sample is in fact a *random sample* from an *infinite population* of hypothesized form, and the tabulated probabilities, $Pr\{d \geqslant d_0\}$, almost always presuppose this. (In principle, one could obtain goodness of fit tests for more complex kinds of probability samples than random ones, but little seems to be known about such possibilities.) It is therefore essential that the sample to which a standard test is applied can be thought of as a random sample. If it cannot, then one must be prepared either to do one's own nonstandard significance probability computations or to defend the adequacy of the approximation involved in using the standard tabulations. Consider, for example, starting with a random sample involving considerable repetition, say the sample of response words obtained from a panel of subjects taking a psychological word association test or the sample of nationalities obtained from a survey of the United Nations. Suppose now that one tallies the number of items in the sample (response words, nationalities) appearing exactly once, exactly twice, etc. There results a new set of data, consisting of a certain number of one's, a certain number of two's, etc. This collection of integers has the outward appearance of a random sample, and the literature contains instances of the application of the standard tests of goodness of fit to such observed frequencies. Yet the probability mechanism that generates these integers has no resemblance whatever to random sampling, and the

standard probability tabulations cannot be assumed to apply. Other examples arise when the data are generated by time series; for some of these the requisite nonstandard probability computations have been done (Patankar 1954), while, in other cases, special devices have made the standard computations apply. For example, in the case of the learning experiment by Suppes and his associates (1964), the sample consists of the time series of a subject's responses to successive stimuli. Certain theories of learning predict a particular bimodal long-run response population distribution; but the goodness of fit test of this hypothesized shape, on the basis of a series of subject responses, is hampered by the statistical dependence of neighboring responses. However, theory suggests, and a test of randomness confirms, that the subsample consisting of every fifth response is effectively random, enabling a standard $\chi^2$ test of goodness of fit to be carried out on the basis of this subsample. Whether four-fifths of the sample is a reasonable price to pay for validly carrying out a standard procedure is of course a matter of debate.

## Tests of simple hypotheses

**The $\chi^2$ test.** The $\chi^2$ test was first proposed in 1900 by Karl Pearson. To apply the test, one first divides the possible range of numbers (number pairs in the bivariate case) into $k$ regions. For example, if only nonnegative numbers are possible, one might use the categories 0 to .2, .2 to .5, .5 to .7, and .7 and beyond. Next, one computes the probabilities, $p_i$, associated with each of these regions (intervals in the example just given) under the hypothesized $F_0$. This is often done by subtracting values of $F_0$ from each other: for example, when $F_0$ is the exponential cumulative distribution function $1 - e^{-x}$,

$$
\begin{aligned}
p_1 &= F_0(.2) - F_0(0) = F_0(.2) = 1 - e^{-.2} = .18 \\
p_2 &= F_0(.5) - F_0(.2) &= e^{-.2} - e^{-.5} = .21 \\
p_3 &= F_0(.7) - F_0(.5) &= e^{-.5} - e^{-.7} = .11 \\
p_4 &= F_0(\infty) - F_0(.7) &= e^{-.7} = .50
\end{aligned}
$$

The expected numbers $E_i$ of observations in each category are (under the null hypothesis) $E_i = np_i$, where $n$ is the size of the random sample.

After the sample has been collected, there also will be observed numbers, $O_i$, of sample members in each category. The chi-square measure of discrepancy $d_{\chi^2}$ is then computed by summing squared differences of class frequencies, weighted in such a way as to bring to bear standard distribution theory,

$$
d_{\chi^2,0} = \sum_{i=1}^{k} (O_i - E_i)^2 / E_i,
$$

where the subscript 0 indicates the specific sample value of $d_{x^2}$. (Often "$X^2$" or "$\chi^2$" is used to denote this statistic.)

As is shown, for example, by Cochran (1952), the probability distribution of $d_{x^2}$, when $F_x = F_0$, can be approximated by the chi-square distribution with $k - 1$ degrees of freedom, $\chi^2_{k-1}$. This fact, to which the test owes its name, was first demonstrated by Karl Pearson. The larger the expectations $E_i$, the better is the approximation; this has been pointed out, for example, by Mann and Wald (1942). Hence, the significance, $Pr\{d_{x^2} \geqslant d_{x^2,0}\}$, is evaluated to a good approximation by consulting a tabulation of the $\chi^2_{k-1}$ distribution. For example, if $k$, as above, equals 4, and $d_{x^2,0}$ had happened to be 4.6, then $Pr\{d_{x^2} \geqslant d_{x^2,0}\} \cong .20$. With a sample significance level of .20, most statisticians would not question the plausibility of $F_0$. However, were $d_{x^2,0}$ larger, and the corresponding significance equal to .05 or less, the consensus would be reversed.

At what point is the distributional approximation endangered by small $E_i$? An early study of this problem, performed by Cochran in 1942 (referred to in Cochran 1952), shows that a few $E_i$ near 1 among several large ones do not materially affect the approximation. Recent studies, by Kempthorne (1966) and by Slakter (1965), show that this is true as well when *all* $E_i$ are near 1.

These and other studies indicate that, although some care must be taken to avoid very small $E_i$, much latitude remains for choosing categories. How is this to be done? To begin with, in keeping with the spirit of remarks by Birnbaum (1953), if the relevant alternatives $F^*$ to $F_0$ are such that

$$d_{x^2}(F^*, F_0) = \sum_{i=1}^{k} (E_i^* - E_i)^2 / E_i$$

is large for a certain choice of $k$ categories, it is these categories that should be selected. Among various sets of $k$ categories, those yielding large $d_{x^2}(F^*, F_0)$ are preferred.

In the absence of detailed knowledge of the alternatives, the usual recommendation, at least in the one-dimensional case, is to use intervals of equal $E_i$. There remains the question of how many such intervals there should be. The typical statistical criterion for this is power, that is, the likelihood that the value of $d_{x^2}$ will be large enough to warrant rejection of the hypothesis $F_0$ when the population is in fact a relevant alternative one. If large power is desired for *all* alternative population c.d.f.'s departing from $F_0$ at some $x$ by at least a given fixed amount, Mann and Wald (1942) recommend a

number of categories of the order of $4n^{2/5}$. Williams (1950) has shown that this figure can easily be halved.

The $\chi^2$ test is versatile; it is readily adapted to problems involving nominal rather than numerical populations [*see* COUNTED DATA]. It can also be adapted to bivariate and multivariate problems, as, for example, by Keats and Lord (1962), where the joint distribution of two types of mental test scores is considered. As opposed to many of its competitors, the $\chi^2$ test is not biased, in the sense that there are no alternatives $F^*$ to $F_0$ under which acceptance of $F_0$ is more likely than it is under $F_0$ itself. It is readily adapted to composite and approximate testing problems. Also, it seems to be true that the $\chi^2$ test is in the best position among its competitors with regard to the practical computation of power. As is pointed out by Cochran (1952), such computations are performed by means of the *noncentral* chi-square distribution with $k - 1$ degrees of freedom.

**Modifications of the $\chi^2$ test.** Important modifications of the $\chi^2$ test, intended to increase its power against specific families $\mathscr{G}$ of distributions alternative to $F_0$, are given by Neyman (1949) and by Fix, Hodges, and Lehmann (1954). Here $\mathscr{G}$ is assumed to include $F_0$ and to allow differentiable parametric representation of the category expectations $E_i$. Note that the inclusion of $F_0$ in $\mathscr{G}$ differs from the point of view adopted, for example, by Mann and Wald (1942). These modifications are essentially *likelihood ratio* tests of $F_0$ versus $\mathscr{G}$ and are similar to procedures used to test composite and approximate hypotheses.

Another modification, capable of orientation against specific "smooth" alternatives, Neyman's $\psi^2$ test, was introduced in 1937. Other important modifications are described in detail in Cochran (1954).

**Other procedures.** When $(X_1, \cdots, X_n)$ is a random sample from a population distributed according to a *continuous* c.d.f. $F_0$, then $(U_1, \cdots, U_n) = (F_0(X_1), \cdots, F_0(X_n))$ has all the probabilistic properties of a random sample from a population distributed uniformly over the numbers between zero and one. (If the population has a density function, the c.d.f. is continuous.) No matter what the hypothesized $F_0$, the initial application of this *probability integral* transformation thus reduces all probability computations to the case of this *uniform* population distribution and gives a *nonparametric* character to any procedure based on the transformed sample $(U_1, \cdots, U_n)$. Most goodness of fit tests of simple hypotheses are nonparametric in this sense, including the $\chi^2$ test itself, when categories are chosen so as to assign specified values, for example, the constant value $1/k$, to the category probabilities $p_i$.

Another common test making use of the transformation $U = F_0(X)$ is the Kolmogorov–Smirnov test, first suggested by Kolmogorov (1933) and explained in detail by Goodman (1954) and Massey (1951). The test bears Smirnov's name, as well as Kolmogorov's, presumably because Smirnov (as Doob and Donsker did later) gave an alternate derivation of its asymptotic null distribution, tabulated this distribution, and also extended the test to the two-sample case discussed below (1939a). Denote by $F_n(x)$ the *sample c.d.f.*, that is, $F_n(x)$ is the proportion of sample values less than or equal to $x$. The test is based on the maximum absolute vertical deviation between $F_n(x)$ and $F_0(x)$,

$$d_K = d_K(F_n, F_0) = \sqrt{n}\,(\max_{-\infty < x < +\infty} |F_n(x) - F_0(x)|),$$

the dependence of $d_K$ on the quantities $U_i = F_0(X_i)$ being best brought out by the alternate formula

$$d_K = \sqrt{n}\max\left[\max_i\left(\frac{i}{n} - u_i\right), \max_i\left(u_i - \frac{i-1}{n}\right)\right],$$

where $u_1$ is the smallest $U_i$, $u_2$ is the next to smallest, etc.; the equivalence of the two formulas is made clear by a sketch. As Kolmogorov noted in his original paper, the probabilities tabulated for $d_K$ are *conservative* when $F_0$ is not continuous, in the sense that, for discontinuous $F_0$, actual probabilities of $d_K \geqslant d_{K,0}$ will tend to be less than those obtained from the tabulations, leading to occasional unwarranted acceptance of $F_0$.

Computations (Shapiro & Wilk 1965) suggest that this test has low power against alternatives with mean and variance equal to those of the hypothesized distribution. It has, however, been argued, for example, by Birnbaum (1953) and Kac, Kiefer, and Wolfowitz (1955), that the test yields good minimum power over classes of alternatives $F^*$ satisfying $d_K(F^*, F_0) \geqslant \delta$; these, as the reader will note, are precisely the classes of alternatives envisaged by Mann and Wald (1942) in optimizing the number of categories used in the $\chi^2$ test. A detrimental feature of the Kolmogorov–Smirnov test is its bias, pointed out in Massey (1951).

An important feature of the test is that it can be "inverted" in keeping with the usual method to provide a confidence band for $F_0(x)$ centered on $F_n(x)$, which, except for the narrowing caused by the restriction $0 \leqslant F_0(x) \leqslant 1$, has constant width [see ESTIMATION, *article on* CONFIDENCE INTER-

VALS AND REGIONS]. The construction of such a band has been suggested by Wald and Wolfowitz and is described by Goodman (1954). Attaching a significance probability to an observed $d_{K,0}$ amounts to ascertaining the band width required in order just to include wholly the hypothesized $F_0$ in the confidence band.

The Kolmogorov–Smirnov test has been modified in several ways; the first of these converts the test into a "one-sided" procedure based on the discrepancy

$$d_{K^+} = \sqrt{n}[\max_{-\infty < x < +\infty} (F_n(x) - F_0(x))]$$
$$= \sqrt{n}\left[\max_i\left(\frac{i}{n} - u_i\right)\right].$$

A useful feature of this modification is the simplicity of the large sample computation of significance probabilities associated with observed discrepancies $d_{K^+,0}$; abbreviating the latter to $d$, one has $Pr\{d_{K^+} \geqslant d\} \cong e^{-2d^2}$. It is verified by Chapman (1958) that $d_{K^+}$ yields good minimum power over those classes of alternatives $F^*$ that satisfy $d_{K^+}(F^*, F_0) = \sqrt{n}\max_x (F^*(x) - F_0(x)) \geqslant \delta$.

Other, more complex modifications provide greater power against special alternatives, as in the weight function modifications (Darling 1957), which provide greater power against discrepancies from $F_0$ in the tails. Another sort of modification, introduced and tabulated by Kuiper in 1960, calls for a measure of discrepancy $d_V$ that is especially suited to testing goodness of fit to hypothesized *circular* distributions, being invariant under arbitrary choices of the angular origin. This property could be important, for example, in psychological studies involving responses to the color wheel, or in the learning experiment mentioned above. The measure $d_V$ also has been singled out by E. S. Pearson (1963) as the generally most attractive in competition with $d_K$ and the discrepancy measures $d_{\omega^2}$ and $d_U$ mentioned below.

A second general class of procedures also making use of the transformation $U = F_0(x)$ springs from the discrepancy measure

$$d_{\omega^2} = n \int_{-\infty}^{+\infty} [F_n(x) - F_0(x)]^2 dF_0(x)$$
$$= \frac{1}{12n} + \sum_{i=1}^{n}\left(\frac{2i-1}{2n} - u_i\right)^2,$$

first proposed by Cramér in 1928 and also by Von Mises in 1931 (see Darling 1957). Marshall (1958) has verified a startling agreement between the asymptotic and small sample distributions of $d_{\omega^2}$ for sample sizes $n$ as low as 3. Power considerations for $d_{\omega^2}$ are similar to those expressed for $d_K$, and are discussed also in the sources cited by Marshall; the test based on $d_{\omega^2}$ can be expected to have good minimum power over classes of alternatives $F^*$ satisfying the conditions $d_{\omega^2}(F^*, F_0) = n \int_{-\infty}^{+\infty} [F^*(x) - F_0(x)]^2 \, dF_0(x) \geqslant \delta$. However, the test is biased (as is that based on $d_K$).

As in the case of $d_K$, $d_{\omega^2}$ has weight function modifications for greater power selectivity, and also a modification $d_U$, analogous to the modification $d_V$ of $d_K$ and introduced by Watson (1961), which does not depend on the choice of angular origin and is thus also suited for testing the goodness of fit to hypothesized circular distributions.

Other procedures include those based on the Fisher–Pearson measures $d_{FP}^{(1)} = -2 \sum_{i=1}^{n} \ln u_i$ and $d_{FP}^{(2)} = -2 \sum_{i=1}^{n} \ln (1 - u_i)$, apparently first suggested in connection with goodness of fit in 1938 by E. S. Pearson. As pointed out by Chapman (1958), the tests based on $d^{(1)}$ and $d^{(2)}$ are uniformly most powerful against polynomial alternatives to $F_U(x) = x$ of form $x^k$ and $(1 - x)^k$, $k > 1$, and hence are "smooth" in the sense of Neyman's $\psi^2$ test. Computations by Chapman suggest that, dually to $d_K$, $d^{(2)}$ has good maximum power over classes of alternatives $F^*$ satisfying $d_K(F^*, F_0) \leqslant \delta$.

Another set of procedures, discussed and defended by Pyke (1965) and extensively studied by Weiss (1958), are based on functions of the spacings, $u_{i+1} - u_i$ or $u_i - (i + 1)^{-1}$, of the $u$'s, from each other or from their expected locations under $F_0$. Still another criterion (Smirnov 1939b) examines the number of crossings of $F_n(x)$ and $F_0(x)$.

An important modification, applicable to all of the procedures in this section, is suggested in Durbin (1961). This modification is intended to increase the power of any procedure based on the transforms $U_i$, against a certain class of alternatives described in that paper.

Since there are multivariate probability integral transformations, applying an initial "uniformizing" transformation is possible in the multivariate case as well. However, one of several possible transformations must now be chosen, and, related to this nonuniqueness, the direct analogues of the univariate discrepancy measures are no longer functions of uniformly distributed transforms and do not lead to nonparametric tests (Rosenblatt 1952).

## Tests of composite hypotheses

**The $\chi^2$ test.** In the composite case, the null hypothesis specifies only that $F_X(x)$ is a member of a certain parametric class $\{F_\theta(x)\}$. Typically, but not necessarily, $\theta$ is the pair $(\mu, \sigma)$, $\mu$ a parameter of location, and $\sigma$ a parameter of scale, in which case $F_\theta(x)$ may be written $F_0[(x - \mu)/\sigma]$. In any event, there arises the question of modifying the measure $d_{\chi^2}$ of discrepancy between the sample and a particular cumulative distribution function into a measure $D_{\chi^2}$ of discrepancy between the sample and the *class* $\{F_\theta(x)\}$. A natural approach is to set

$$D_{\chi^2} = \min_{\theta} d_{\chi^2}.$$

If $\theta$ is composed of $m$ parameters, it can be shown that, under quite general conditions, $D_{\chi^2}$ is approximately distributed according to the $\chi_{k-1-m}^2$ distribution when $F_X(x)$ equals any one of the $F_\theta(x)$. Hence significance probability computations can once again be referred to tabulations of the $\chi_\nu^2$ distribution. The requisite minimization with respect to $\theta$ can be cumbersome, and several modifications have been proposed, for example, the following by Neyman (1949):

Suppose that one defines $d_{\chi^2}(\theta)$ as the discrepancy $d_{\chi^2}$ between the observed sample and the particular distribution $F_\theta(x)$. Then $D$ is defined also by

$$D_{\chi^2} = d_{\chi^2}(\tilde{\theta}),$$

with the estimator $\tilde{\theta}$ computed from

$$d_{\chi^2}(\tilde{\theta}) = \min_{\theta} d_{\chi^2}(\theta),$$

that is, with $\tilde{\theta}$ the *minimum chi-square estimator* of $\theta$. The suggested modifications involve using estimators of $\theta$ alternate to $\tilde{\theta}$ in this last definition of $D_{\chi^2}$, that is, estimators that "essentially" minimize $d_{\chi^2}(\theta)$; among these are the so-called grouped-data or partial-information maximum likelihood estimators.

Frequently used but *not equivalent* estimators are the ordinary "full-information" maximum likelihood estimators $\hat{\theta}$ of $\theta$, for example, $(\bar{x}, s)$ for $(\mu, \sigma)$ in the normal case. These do *not* "essentially" minimize $d_{\chi^2}$ and consequently tend to inflate $D_{\chi^2}$ beyond values predicted by the $\chi_{k-1-m}^2$ distribution, leading to some unwarranted rejections of the composite hypothesis. However, it is indicated by Chernoff and Lehmann (1954), and also by Watson (1957), that no serious distortion will result if the number of categories is ten or more.

**Composite analogues of other tests.** Adaptation of the tests based on the probability integral transformation to the composite case proceeds much as in the case of $\chi^2$. With definitions of $d_{\omega^2}(\theta)$ and $d_K(\theta)$ analogous to that of $d_{\chi^2}(\theta)$, Darling (1955) has investigated the large sample probability distribution of $D_{\omega^2} = d_{\omega^2}(\hat{\theta})$ and of $D_K = d_K(\hat{\theta})$ for efficient estimators $\hat{\theta}$ of $\theta$ analogous to the estimators $\tilde{\theta}$ for $\chi^2$. Note that in the absence of any $\chi^2$-like categories, the ordinary full-information maximum likelihood estimators now *do* qualify as estimators $\hat{\theta}$.

A major problem now is, however, that the modified procedures are no longer nonparametric. Thus a special investigation is required for every composite hypothesis. This is done by Kac, Kiefer, and Wolfowitz (1955) for the normal scale-location family, and the resulting large sample distribution is partly tabulated.

**Tests based on special characteristics.** The alternatives of concern sometimes differ from a composite null hypothesis in a manner easily described by a standard shape parameter. Special tests have been proposed for such cases. For example, the sample skewness coefficient has been suggested (Geary 1947) for testing normality against skew alternatives. Again, for testing Poissonness against alternatives with variance unequal to mean, R. A. Fisher has recommended the variance-to-mean ratio $\sum_{i=1}^{n}(X_i - \bar{X})^2/\bar{X}$ (see Cochran 1954). This measure is approximately distributed as $\chi^2_{n-1}$ when Poissonness in fact obtains, for $\lambda > 1$ and $n > 15$ (Sukhatme 1938), which follows from the fact that the denominator is then a high-precision estimate of $\lambda$, and the numerator is approximately distributed as $\lambda \chi^2_{n-1}$. Analogous recommendations apply to testing binomiality. Essentially the same point of view underlies tests of normality based on the ratio of mean deviation, or of the range, to the standard deviation.

**Transforming into simple hypotheses.** Another interesting approach to the composite problem, advocated by Hogg and also by Sarkadi (1960), is to transform certain composite hypotheses into equivalent simple ones.

Specifically, there are location-scale parametric families $\{F_0[(x - \mu)/\sigma]\}$ with the following property: A random sample from any particular $F_0[(x - \mu)/\sigma]$ is reducible by a transformation $T$ to a new set of random variables, $Y = T(X)$, constituting in effect a random sample from a distribution $G(y)$ involving no unknown parameters at all. Moreover, *only* random samples from distributions $F_0[(x - \mu)/\sigma]$ lead to $G(y)$ when operated on by $T$.

It then follows that testing the composite hypothesis $H$ that $(X_1, \cdots, X_n)$ is a random sample from a distribution $F_0[(x - \mu)/\sigma]$ with some $\mu$ and some $\sigma$ is equivalent to testing the hypothesis $H'$ that $(Y_1, \cdots, Y_m)$ is a random sample from the distribution $G(y)$. Any of the tests for simple hypotheses is then available for testing $H'$. An example is provided by a negative exponential $F_0$ and uniform $G$, in which case the ordered exponential random sample $(X_{(1)}, \cdots, X_{(n)})$ is transformed

into an ordered uniform random sample $(Y_{(1)}, \cdots, Y_{(n-2)})$ by the transformation

$$Y_{(i)} = \frac{(X_{(n)} - X_{(n-1)}) + \cdots + i(X_{(n-i+1)} - X_{(n-i)})}{(X_{(n)} - X_{(n-1)}) + \cdots + (n-1)(X_{(2)} - X_{(1)})}.$$

**Conditioning.** Another way of neatly doing away with the unknown parameter is to consider the conditional distribution of the sample, given a sufficient estimate of it. This method is advocated, at least for testing Poissonness, in Fisher (1950).

**Tests related to probability plots.** S. S. Shapiro and M. B. Wilk have quantified in various ways the departure from linearity of the sorts of probability plots mentioned above, in particular of the plot of the ordered sample values against the expected values of the standardized order statistics [*see* NONPARAMETRIC STATISTICS, *article on* ORDER STATISTICS]. This new approach bears some similarity to one given in Darling (1955), which is based on the measure $d_\omega^2$ modified for the composite case. Both approaches, in a sense, compare adjusted observed order statistics with standardized order statistic expectations. But the approach of Shapiro and Wilk is tailored more explicitly to particular scale-location families, by using their particular order statistic variances and covariances. It is no wonder that preliminary evaluations of this sort of approach (for example, by Shapiro & Wilk 1965) have shown exceptional promise. As an added bonus, the procedure is *similar* over the entire scale-location family; that is, its probability distribution is independent of location and scale.

## Approximate hypotheses

The first, and seemingly most practically developed, attempt to provide the requisite tests of approximate hypotheses is found in Hodges and Lehmann (1954). Hodges and Lehmann assume the $k$ typical categories of the $\chi^2$ test and formulate the approximate *simple* hypothesis in terms of the discrepancy $d(p, p_0)$ between the category probabilities $p_i$ under $F_x$ and the category probabilities $p_{0,i}$ under a *simple* hypothesis $F_0$. A very tractable discrepancy measure of this type is ordinary distance, for which the approximate hypothesis takes the form

$$d(p, p_0) = \sum_{i=1}^{k}(p_i - p_{0,i})^2 \leq \delta.$$

Denoting $O_i/n$ by $o_i$, the suggested test reduces, essentially, to the *one-sided* test of the hypothesis $d(p, p_0) = \delta$ based on the approximately normal statistic $[d(o, p_0) - \delta]/\hat{\sigma}$, where $\hat{\sigma}$ is the standard deviation, estimated from the sample $o_i$, of $d(o, p_0)$. For example, when $F_0$ specifies $k$ categories with

$p_{0,i} = 1/k$, one treats as unit normal (under the null hypothesis) the statistic

$$S = \frac{\sqrt{n}\,[d(o, p_0) - \delta]}{2\sqrt{\sum o_i^3 - (\sum o_i^2)^2}}$$

and uses an upper-tail test. Thus a value of $S$ of 1.645 leads to a sample significance level of .05. This approach lends itself easily to the computation of power and is extended as well by Hodges and Lehmann to the testing of approximate *composite* hypotheses.

Extension of other tests for simple hypotheses to the testing of approximate hypotheses has been considered by J. Rosenblatt (1962) and by Kac, Kiefer, and Wolfowitz (1955).

## Further topics

That the sample is random may itself be in doubt, and tests have been designed to have power against specific sorts of departure from randomness. For example, tests of the hypothesis of randomness against the alternative hypothesis that the data are subject to a Markov structure are given by Billingsley (1961) and Goodman (1959); the latter work also covers testing that the data have Markov structure of a given order against the alternative that the data have Markov structure of higher order, and the testing of hypothesized values of transition probabilities when a Markov structure of given order is assumed [*see* MARKOV CHAINS].

Many of the tests described in this article can be extended to *several-sample* procedures for testing the hypothesis that several populations are in fact distributed identically; thus, as first suggested in Smirnov (1939a), if $G_m(x)$ denotes the proportion of values less than or equal to $x$, in an independent random sample $(Y_1, \cdots, Y_m)$ from a second population, $d_K(F_n, G_m)$ provides a natural test of the hypothesis that the two continuous population distribution functions $F_X$ and $G_Y$ coincide. Many of these extensions are functions only of the *relative ranks* of the two samples and, as such, are nonparametric, that is, their null probability distributions do not depend on the common functional form of $F_X$ and $G_Y$. [*Several-sample nonparametric procedures are discussed in* NONPARAMETRIC STATISTICS.]

Another topic is that of tests of goodness of fit as preliminary tests of significance, in a sense discussed, for example, by Bancroft (1964). That tests of goodness of fit are typically applied in this sense is recognized by Chapman (1958), and the probabilistic properties of certain "nested" sequences of tests beginning with a test of goodness of fit have been considered by Hogg (1965). The Bayes

and information theory approaches to $\chi^2$ tests of goodness of fit are also important (see Lindley 1965; Kullback 1959).

H. T. DAVID

[*Directly related are the entries* HYPOTHESIS TESTING; SIGNIFICANCE, TESTS OF. *Other relevant material may be found in* COUNTED DATA; ESTIMATION; NONPARAMETRIC STATISTICS.]

### BIBLIOGRAPHY

BANCROFT, T. A. 1964 Analysis and Inference for Incompletely Specified Models Involving the Use of Preliminary Test(s) of Significance. *Biometrics* 20:427–442.

BERKSON, JOSEPH 1938 Some Difficulties of Interpretation Encountered in the Chi-square Test. *Journal of the American Statistical Association* 33:526–536.

BILLINGSLEY, PATRICK 1961 Statistical Methods in Markov Chains. *Annals of Mathematical Statistics* 32:12–40.

BIRNBAUM, Z. W. 1953 Distribution-free Tests of Fit for Continuous Distribution Functions. *Annals of Mathematical Statistics* 24:1–8.

CHAPMAN, DOUGLAS G. 1958 A Comparative Study of Several One-sided Goodness-of-fit Tests. *Annals of Mathematical Statistics* 29:655–674.

CHERNOFF, HERMAN; and LEHMANN, E. L. 1954 The Use of Maximum Likelihood Estimates in $\chi^2$ Tests for Goodness of Fit. *Annals of Mathematical Statistics* 25:579–586.

COCHRAN, WILLIAM G. 1952 The $\chi^2$ Test of Goodness of Fit. *Annals of Mathematical Statistics* 23:315–345.

COCHRAN, WILLIAM G. 1954 Some Methods for Strengthening the Common $\chi^2$ Tests. *Biometrics* 10:417–451.

DARLING, D. A. 1955 The Cramér–Smirnov Test in the Parametric Case. *Annals of Mathematical Statistics* 26:1–20.

DARLING, D. A. 1957 The Kolmogorov–Smirnov, Cramér–Von Mises Tests. *Annals of Mathematical Statistics* 28:823–838.

DURBIN, J. 1961 Some Methods of Constructing Exact Tests. *Biometrika* 48:41–55.

FISHER, R. A. 1924 The Conditions Under Which $\chi^2$ Measures the Discrepancy Between Observation and Hypothesis. *Journal of the Royal Statistical Society* 87:442–450.

FISHER, R. A. 1950 The Significance of Deviations From Expectation in a Poisson Series. *Biometrics* 6:17–24.

FIX, EVELYN; HODGES, J. L. JR.; and LEHMANN, E. L. 1954 The Restricted Chi-square Test. Pages 92–107 in Ulf Grenander (editor), *Probability and Statistics*. New York: Wiley.

GEARY, R. C. 1947 Testing for Normality. *Biometrika* 34:209–242.

GOODMAN, LEO A. 1954 Kolmogorov–Smirnov Tests for Psychological Research. *Psychological Bulletin* 51:160–168.

GOODMAN, LEO A. 1959 On Some Statistical Tests for *m*th Order Markov Chains. *Annals of Mathematical Statistics* 30:154–164.

GREENWOOD, JOSEPH A.; and HARTLEY, H. O. 1962 *Guide to Tables in Mathematical Statistics*. Princeton Univ. Press. → A sequel to the guides to mathematical tables produced by and for the Committee on Mathematical Tables and Aids to Computation of the

National Academy of Sciences–National Research Council of the United States.

HODGES, J. L. JR.; and LEHMANN, E. L. 1954 Testing the Approximate Validity of Statistical Hypotheses. *Journal of the Royal Statistical Society* Series B 16: 261–268.

HOGG, ROBERT V. 1965 On Models and Hypotheses With Restricted Alternatives. *Journal of the American Statistical Association* 60:1153–1162.

KAC, M.; KIEFER, J.; and WOLFOWITZ, J. 1955 On Tests of Normality and Other Tests of Goodness of Fit Based on Distance Methods. *Annals of Mathematical Statistics* 26:189–211.

KEATS, J. A.; and LORD, FREDERIC M. 1962 A Theoretical Distribution for Mental Test Scores. *Psychometrika* 27:59–72.

KEMPTHORNE, O. 1966 The Classical Problem of Inference: Goodness of Fit. Unpublished manuscript. → Paper presented at the Berkeley Symposium on Mathematical Statistics and Probability, Fifth, *Proceedings* to be published.

KOLMOGOROV, A. N. 1933 Sulla determinazione empirica di une legge di distribuzione. Istituto Italiano degli Attuari, *Giornale* 4:83–99.

KUIPER, NICOLAAS H. 1960 Tests Concerning Random Points on a Circle. Akademie van Wetenschappen, Amsterdam, *Proceedings* Series A 63:38–47.

KULLBACK, S. 1959 *Information Theory and Statistics.* New York: Wiley.

LINDLEY, D. V. 1965 *Introduction to Probability and Statistics From a Bayesian Viewpoint.* Volume 2: Inference. Cambridge Univ. Press.

MANN, H. B.; and WALD, A. 1942 On the Choice of the Number of Class Intervals in the Application of the Chi Square Test. *Annals of Mathematical Statistics* 13:306–317.

MARSHALL, A. W. 1958 The Small Sample Distribution of $n\omega_n^2$. *Annals of Mathematical Statistics* 29:307–309.

MASSEY, FRANK J. JR. 1951 The Kolmogorov–Smirnov Test for Goodness of Fit. *Journal of the American Statistical Association* 46:68–78.

NEYMAN, JERZY 1937 "Smooth Test" for Goodness of Fit. *Skandinavisk aktuarietidskrift* 20:149–199.

NEYMAN, JERZY 1949 Contribution to the Theory of the $\chi^2$ Test. Pages 239–273 in Berkeley Symposium on Mathematical Statistics and Probability, First, *Proceedings.* Berkeley: Univ. of California Press.

PATANKAR, V. N. 1954 The Goodness of Fit of Frequency Distributions Obtained From Stochastic Processes. *Biometrika* 41:450–462.

PEARSON, E. S. 1938 The Probability Integral Transformation for Testing Goodness of Fit and Combining Independent Tests of Significance. *Biometrika* 30: 134–148.

PEARSON, E. S. 1963 Comparison of Tests for Randomness of Points on a Line. *Biometrika* 50:315–325.

PEARSON, KARL 1900 On the Criterion That a Given System of Deviations From the Probable in the Case of a Correlated System of Variables Is Such That It Can Be Reasonably Supposed to Have Arisen From Random Sampling. *Philosophical Magazine* 5th Series 50:157–175.

PYKE, RONALD 1965 Spacings. *Journal of the Royal Statistical Society* Series B 27:395–449.

ROSENBLATT, JUDAH 1962 Testing Approximate Hypotheses in the Composite Case. *Annals of Mathematical Statistics* 33:1356–1364.

ROSENBLATT, MURRAY 1952 Remarks on a Multivariate Transformation. *Annals of Mathematical Statistics* 23: 470–472.

SARKADI, KÁROLY 1960 On Testing for Normality. Magyar Tudományos Akadémia, Matematikai Kutató Intézet, *Közlemények* Series A 5:269–274.

SHAPIRO, S. S.; and WILK, M. B. 1965 An Analysis of Variance Test for Normality (Complete Samples). *Biometrika* 52:591–611.

SLAKTER, MALCOLM J. 1965 A Comparison of the Pearson Chi-square and Kolmogorov Goodness-of-fit Tests With Respect to Validity. *Journal of the American Statistical Association* 60:854–858.

SMIRNOV, N. V. 1939a On the Estimation of the Discrepancy Between Empirical Curves of Distribution for Two Independent Samples. Moscow, Universitet, *Bulletin mathématique* Série Internationale 2, no. 2: 3–26.

SMIRNOV, N. V. 1939b Ob ukloneniiakh empiricheskoi krivoi raspredeleniia (On the Deviations of the Empirical Distribution Curve). *Matematicheskii sbornik* New Series 6, no. 1:1–26. → Includes a French résumé.

SUKHATME, P. V. 1938 On the Distribution of $\chi^2$ in Samples of the Poisson Series. *Journal of the Royal Statistical Society* 5 (Supplement):75–79.

SUPPES, PATRICK et al. 1964 Empirical Comparison of Models for a Continuum of Responses With Non-contingent Bimodal Reinforcement. Pages 358–379 in R. C. Atkinson (editor), *Studies in Mathematical Psychology.* Stanford Univ. Press.

WATSON, G. S. 1957 The $\chi^2$ Goodness-of-fit Test for Normal Distributions. *Biometrika* 336–348.

WATSON, G. S. 1961 Goodness-of-fit Tests on a Circle. *Biometrika* 48:109–114.

WEISS, LIONEL 1958 Limiting Distributions of Homogeneous Functions of Sample Spacings. *Annals of Mathematical Statistics* 29:310–312.

WILLIAMS, C. ARTHUR JR. 1950 On the Choice of the Number and Width of Classes for the Chi-square Test of Goodness of Fit. *Journal of the American Statistical Association* 45:77–86.

# GOODNOW, FRANK J.

The impact of Frank J. Goodnow (1859–1939) upon the study of public administration in the United States has been quite durable. Goodnow's classic treatise *Politics and Administration* (1900) was the intellectual point of departure, along with Woodrow Wilson's "Study of Public Administration" (1887), for much of the work in the field up to World War II. It is a book still frequently cited today, although not always praised.

Goodnow began teaching administrative law at Columbia in 1883 and remained there throughout his professorial career. In 1914 he resigned from the Columbia faculty to become president of Johns Hopkins University, a position he held until his retirement in 1929. Goodnow was one of the principal founders of the American Political Science Association and became its first president in 1903. He helped to redraft the New York City charter in 1900, served on President Taft's commission on economy and efficiency in 1911–1912, and in 1913 went to China as legal adviser to its president.

Much of Goodnow's scholarly work was in the field of municipal government. Although his approach to the study of municipal institutions was primarily legal in character, his works also reveal a keen awareness of the realities of city politics around the beginning of the twentieth century. They remain quite useful to students of urban political development in the United States, since current trends and problems in urban government and politics are still structured by the cleavage between bossism and reformism, which was so prominent an issue in Goodnow's day.

A focal point of controversy in political science has been the distinction Goodnow delineated in *Politics and Administration* between politics, as the sphere in which the will of the state is articulated, and administration, as the range of methods and techniques through which the state's purposes are carried out. This functional separation of powers had a great deal of practical utility in the early movement to reform the organization and operation of public administration in the United States, since it justified the introduction into the public service of practices and values—e.g., efficiency, hierarchy, and discipline—altogether alien to the egalitarian ethos of American politics itself. The distinction also helped carve out a sphere of autonomy for public agencies at a time when these administrative units were hard pressed to maintain professional standards in the face of pressures from spoils-oriented and sometimes corrupt party organizations. When it was first formulated, the separation between politics and administration was to a large extent an effort to free administrators from political harassment.

Intellectually, however, the separating of these two segments of governmental activity has not fared very well at the hands of recent critics. Since World War II the study of public administration has been largely "politicized"—in the sense at least that the role of bureaucracy in modern government has increasingly been studied from the point of view of the tactics that agencies follow in securing resources upon which their survival depends, including appropriations, constituency support, and statutory authority, or with a focus on the involvement of administrators in the framing of public policy. The modern tendency has been to point up and to some extent justify the role of administrators in the political process.

However, although Goodnow's distinction be-

tween politics and administration was to serve more often as a target for criticism than as a model, the issues he first raised in a systematic way are still very much at the center of scholarly concern. Dwight Waldo, for example, has noted that the dichotomy between facts and values in the work of Herbert Simon, since World War II one of the central figures in the study of public administration, is closely analogous to Goodnow's own distinction between administration and politics (Waldo 1963, pp. 187–188). The entire effort to create a "science" of administration in modern times does in fact ultimately turn upon the possibility of singling out a sphere of managerial expertise which is distinct from and independent of political preferences and policy goals. Thus, Goodnow's work retains its intellectual relevance today, even though it no longer has the authority it once commanded.

From the point of view of governmental structure, there can be no disputing the fact that the distinction has been an important force in the development of American institutions. Merit systems and a variety of other devices have been established at all levels of government to provide administrative agencies with some degree of legal protection against the grosser forms of political interference. At the same time, there has been a continued effort to limit the political role of executive agencies, for example, by statutes designed to prevent them from engaging in "propaganda" or lobbying activity. Public policy in the United States has thus sought to separate politics and administration, however much the two spheres may overlap in the actual day-to-day work of government.

FRANCIS E. ROURKE

[*See also* ADMINISTRATIVE LAW; CIVIL SERVICE; COMMISSIONS, GOVERNMENT; POLITICAL PROCESS; PUBLIC ADMINISTRATION; PUBLIC LAW.]

### WORKS BY GOODNOW

(1893) 1903   *Comparative Administrative Law: An Analysis of the Administrative Systems, National and Local, of the United States, England, France and Germany.* 2 vols. New York: Putnam.

(1895) 1897   *Municipal Home Rule: A Study in Administration.* New York and London: Macmillan.

1897   *Municipal Problems.* New York and London: Macmillan.

(1900) 1914   *Politics and Administration: A Study in Government.* New York: Macmillan.

(1904) 1910   *City Government in the United States.* New York: Century.

1905   *The Principles of the Administrative Law of the United States.* New York and London: Putnam.

(1909) 1919   *Municipal Government.* 2d ed. New York: Century.

1911   *Social Reform and the Constitution.* New York: Macmillan.

1916a *The American Conception of Liberty and Government.* Providence, R.I.: Standard Printing.
1916b *Principles of Constitutional Government.* New York and London: Harper.
1926 *China: An Analysis.* Baltimore: Johns Hopkins Press.

SUPPLEMENTARY BIBLIOGRAPHY

HAINES, CHARLES G.; and DIMOCK, MARSHALL E. (editors) 1935 *Essays on the Law and Practice of Governmental Administration: A Volume in Honor of Frank J. Goodnow.* Baltimore: Johns Hopkins Press. → See especially pages v–xv for a biographical sketch.
MACMAHON, ARTHUR W. 1958 Frank Johnson Goodnow. Volume 22, pages 250–251 in *Dictionary of American Biography.* New York: Scribner.
WALDO, DWIGHT 1948 *The Administrative State: A Study of the Political Theory of American Public Administration.* New York: Ronald Press. → See especially pages 106–109.
WALDO, DWIGHT 1963 Comparative Public Administration: Prologue, Performance, Problems and Promise. *Indian Journal of Political Science* 24:177–216.
WILSON, WOODROW (1887) 1953 The Study of Public Administration. Pages 65–75 in Dwight Waldo (editor), *Ideas and Issues in Public Administration: A Book of Readings.* New York: McGraw-Hill.

# GOSSEN, HERMANN HEINRICH

Hermann Heinrich Gossen, German writer on economics, was born at Düren in the Rhineland in 1810 and died at Cologne in 1858. His claim to fame is based on a single publication: in 1854 he published a book that develops, with the help of mathematics, a comprehensive theory of the hedonistic calculus. In this work Gossen postulated the principle of diminishing marginal utility and from this derived the following theorem: to maximize utility, a given quantity of a good must be divided among different uses in such a manner that the marginal utilities are equal in all uses. In the Continental literature the postulate is usually referred to as Gossen's First Law and the theorem as his Second Law.

Gossen pioneered in the development of the subjective theory of value on the basis of the marginal principle, but his work was neglected during his life, and he died a disappointed man, having withdrawn the unsold copies of his book from the publisher. His work was briefly mentioned in a history of economic thought published the year of his death and, more appreciatively, in 1870 in the second edition of a book on the labor problem by F. A. Lange, the famed historian of materialism. Gossen's importance in the development of economic thought was first recognized in the late 1870s, when Jevons, Menger, and Walras had already published their own versions of the new theory of value. Gossen's book was brought to the attention of Jevons by a colleague in August 1878, causing him to complain: "I am, therefore, in the unfortunate position that the greater number of people think the theory nonsense, and do not understand it, and the rest discover that it is not new" (Jevons 1886, pp. 387–388). Jevons found comfort, however, in the thought that "the theory in question has in fact been independently discovered three or four times over, and must be true" (*ibid.,* p. 389).

The next month Jevons advised Walras of Gossen's anticipation. Both men publicly recognized Gossen's priority and did much to save his work from oblivion, Jevons in the preface to the second edition of his *Theory of Political Economy* in 1879 and Walras in an article in the *Journal des économistes* (1885). Walras even prepared a French translation of Gossen's book, but this was never published. Much later, in 1950, an Italian translation was brought out.

An estranged Catholic, Gossen offered his work with the messianic fervor of the founder of a new religion: the laws of science were the dogma, the hedonistic calculus was the moral principle, instruction in the laws of science was the cult, experiments the sacraments, and scientists the priests. Some of Gossen's thoughts echo ideas of Bentham, Saint-Simon, and Comte, but since Gossen did not cite authorities, it is uncertain whether, or to what extent, he was indebted to these writers. German translations of two of Bentham's juridical works had appeared in the 1830s, and one of these had been published in Cologne, where Gossen spent many years of his life. He may have come under the influence of Bentham's hedonistic philosophy, but the mathematical treatment was his own work, as probably was his statement of the principle of diminishing marginal utility. There had been other economists who developed the subjective theory of value and the marginal principle, but none of them carried either idea as far as Gossen did.

In matters of economic policy, Gossen's pronounced individualism led him to a modified laissez-faire point of view. All that exists, he held, must by itself create the means to further existence; otherwise it does not deserve to continue to exist. On this basis he rejected government support of religion, art, and science. Public relief of the poor was to be given in the form of loans. A general system of government loans would be established to enable everyone to make the most of his opportunities. Private property was to be protected and freed from restrictions that hamper individual initiative, but land was to be nationalized (purchased by the government) and then auctioned off to the highest bidder in the form of a lifetime lease to facilitate its most productive use.

The reasons for the almost complete neglect of Gossen's work for a quarter of a century are not difficult to trace. His book was the work of a lone outsider, unknown in academic circles. Obedient to his father's wishes, but with great reluctance, Gossen had studied law to prepare himself for a career in the Prussian civil service. After a few years he had relinquished government service and started an unsuccessful venture in the insurance business. When he published his book, with high hopes of recognition, he gave it a forbiddingly pretentious title, which in English translation reads "Development of the Laws of Human Relations, and of the Rules of Human Action Derived Therefrom" (1854). The presentation and style of the work are bizarre and cumbersome. The book is not divided into parts or chapters, and simple dash lines, rather than headings, separate the various topics. Gossen was presumptuous enough to make a favorable comparison, on the first page, of his own study of society with Copernicus' study of the cosmos, and on the penultimate page to claim in enlarged print that the adoption of his system of thought would turn the earth into a paradise. Such claims were bound to appear preposterous to the followers of the historical school, who were beginning to fill the chairs of economics in Germany in Gossen's time, and as late as 1929 Sombart referred to Gossen as a "brilliant idiot." Moreover, Gossen's book abounds with diagrams, formulas, and lengthy arithmetical illustrations. Half a century after its publication, Marshall, under much more favorable circumstances, still deemed it wise to take infinite care to make the mathematical treatment of economics palatable to his readers. Gossen's book might have found some favor because of its polemics against communists and socialists and because the subjective theory of value could be used as a critique of the foundations of socialist economics. The German historical economists, however, had their own ways of coping with the threat of socialism, and several decades after the publication of Gossen's book they were still inclined to deprecate rather than to make use of the ideological weapons available in the armory of the Austrian branch of the new theory of value. The Austrians themselves began to pay attention to Gossen only in 1889.

It is significant also that when Gossen was born, the Rhineland was part of the France of the Emperor Napoleon, in whose revenue service Gossen's father was employed. Gossen's thought was fundamentally un-German, and his fellow countrymen responded as little to his hedonism and utilitarianism as to the idea of natural law. It is thus no accident that recognition eventually came from foreigners.

HENRY W. SPIEGEL

[For discussion of the subsequent development of Gossen's ideas, see UTILITY and biographies of JEVONS; MENGER; WALRAS.]

### WORK BY GOSSEN

(1854) 1927  *Entwicklung der Gesetze des menschlichen Verkehrs und der daraus fliessenden Regeln für menschliches Handeln.* 3d ed. Introduction by Friedrich A. Hayek. Berlin: Prager.

### SUPPLEMENTARY BIBLIOGRAPHY

BAGIOTTI, TULLIO  1955  Nel centenale del libro di Gossen. *Giornale degli economisti e annali di economia* 14:236–253.

BAGIOTTI, TULLIO  1957  Reminiszenzen anlässlich des hundertsten Jahrestages des Erscheinens des Buches von Gossen. *Zeitschrift für Nationalökonomie* 17:39–54.

BEHRENS, FRITZ  1949  *Hermann Heinrich Gossen.* Leipzig: Bibliographisches Institut. → A Marxist interpretation of Gossen as the first scientific apologist of capitalism.

BOUSQUET, G. H.  1958  Un centenaire: L'oeuvre de H. H. Gossen et sa véritable structure. *Revue d'économie politique* 68:499–523.

BRAEUER, WALTER  1952  *Handbuch zur Geschichte der Volkswirtschaftslehre.* Frankfurt am Main (Germany): Klostermann.

EDGEWORTH, F. Y.  1896  H. H. Gossen. Volume 2, pages 231–233 in Robert H. Palgrave, *Dictionary of Political Economy.* London: Macmillan. → A good source on Gossen's technical economics.

HAYEK, FRIEDRICH A.  1932  Herman Heinrich Gossen. Volume 7, page 3 in *Encyclopaedia of the Social Sciences.* New York: Macmillan.

JEVONS, WILLIAM S.  (1871) 1879  *The Theory of Political Economy.* 2d ed. London: Macmillan.

JEVONS, WILLIAM S.  1886  *Letters and Journal.* London: Macmillan.

LANGE, FRIEDRICH ALBERT  (1865) 1870  *Die Arbeiterfrage.* 2d ed. Winterthur (Switzerland): Bleuler.

PANTALEONI, MAFFEO  (1889) 1957  *Pure Economics.* New York: Kelley & Millman. → See pages 28 ff. for the best source in English of Gossen's technical economics.

RIEDLE, HERMANN  1953  *Hermann Heinrich Gossen 1810–1858: Ein Wegbereiter der modernen ökonomischen Theorie.* Winterthur (Switzerland): Keller.

STARK, WERNER  1943  *The Ideal Foundations of Economic Thought.* London: Routledge. → See pages 149 ff. for the best source in English of Gossen's economic philosophy and policy proposals.

WALRAS, LÉON  (1885) 1952  Walras on Gossen. Pages 470–488 in Henry W. Spiegel (editor), *The Development of Economic Thought.* New York: Wiley. → Originally published in *Journal des économistes.*

## GOSSET, WILLIAM SEALY

The impact of W. S. Gosset (1876–1937) on the social sciences was entirely indirect. He was, however, one of the pioneers in the development of modern statistical method and its application to the design and analysis of experiments. He is far better known to the scientific world under the pseudonym of "Student" than under his own name. Indeed all his papers except one appeared under the pseudonym.

He was the son of Colonel Frederic Gosset of the Royal Engineers, the descendant of an old Huguenot family that left France after the revocation of the Edict of Nantes. Gosset was a scholar of Winchester—that is, a boy who was awarded a prize on the basis of a competitive examination to pay for part or all of his education—which shows that his exceptional mental powers had developed early. From Winchester he went, again as a scholar, to New College, Oxford, where he obtained first class degrees in mathematics and natural science.

On leaving Oxford in the autumn of 1899 he joined the famous brewing firm of Guinness in Dublin. He remained with Guinness all his life, ultimately becoming, in 1935, chief brewer at Park Royal, the firm's newly established brewery in London.

At that time scientific methods and laboratory determinations were beginning to be seriously applied to brewing, and this naturally led Gosset to study error functions and to see the need for adequate methods to deal with small samples in examining the relations between the quality of the raw materials of beer, such as barley and hops, the conditions of production, and the finished article. The importance of controlling the quality of barley ultimately led him to study the design of agricultural field trials.

In 1904 he drew up for the directors the first report on "The Application of the Law of Error." This emphasized the importance of the theory of probability in setting "an exact value on the results of our experiments; many of which lead to results which are probable but not certain." He used only the classical theory of errors, such as is found in G. B. Airy's *On the Algebraical, and Numerical Theory of Errors of Observation* (1861) and M. Merriman's *A Text-book on the Method of Least Squares* (1884). But he observed that if $X$ and $Y$ are both measured from their mean, there are often considerable differences between $\sum (X + Y)^2$ and $\sum (X - Y)^2$; in other words, he was feeling his way toward the notion of correlation, although he had not yet heard of the correlation coefficient.

His first meeting with Karl Pearson took place in 1905, and in 1906/1907 he was sent for a year's specialized study in London, where he worked at, or in close contact with, the biometric laboratory at University College.

**Mathematical statistics.** Gosset was once described by Sir Ronald Fisher as the "Faraday of statistics." The comparison is apt, for he was not a profound mathematician but had a superb intuitive faculty that enabled him to grasp general principles and see their relevance to practical ends.

His first mathematical paper was "On the Error of Counting With a Haemacytometer" ([1907] 1943, pp. 1–10); here he derived afresh the Poisson distribution as a limiting form of the binomial and fitted it to four series of counts of yeast cells. The derivation presented no particular difficulty (it had in fact been obtained before by several investigators), but it was characteristic of him to see immediately the correct method of dealing with a practical problem. One of these series has become world famous owing to its inclusion as an example in Fisher's *Statistical Methods for Research Workers* (1925).

His next paper, "The Probable Error of a Mean" ([1908] 1943, pp. 11–34), brought him more fame, in the course of time, than any other work that he did, for it provided the basis of Student's *t*-test.

In his work at the brewery he had been struck by the importance of knowing the accuracy of the mean of a small sample. The usual procedure at the time was to compute the sample average and standard deviation, $\bar{x}$ and $s$, and to proceed as if $\bar{x}$ were normally distributed with the same mean as that of the population and with standard deviation $s/\sqrt{n}$, where $n$ is sample size. The difficulty here is that $s$ is a fallible estimate of the true population standard deviation. Gosset's intuition told him that the usual procedure, based on large sample considerations, would, for small samples, give a spuriously high impression of how accurately the population mean is estimated.

By a combination of exceptional clearheadedness and simple algebra, he obtained the first four moments of the distribution of $s^2$. He then proceeded to fit the Pearson curve that has these moments. His results showed that the curve has to be of Type III (essentially the gamma or $\chi^2$ distribution), and he found the distribution of $s^2$ to be $C(s^2/\sigma^2)^{(n-3)/2} \exp [(- ns^2/2\sigma^2)]d(s^2/\sigma^2)$. He then showed that the correlation coefficient between $\bar{x}^2$ and $s^2$ was zero, and assuming absolute independence (which does not necessarily follow but was true in this case), he deduced the probability distribution of $z = (\bar{x} - \mu)/s$, where $\mu$ is the true mean. With a mere change of notation this is the $t$-distribution. Here $s$ is defined to be $(1/n)\sum(x - \bar{x})^2$ so that

$$t = (\bar{x} - \mu) \Big/ \sqrt{\frac{\sum(x - \bar{x})^2}{n(n-1)}} = \frac{\bar{x} - \mu}{s} \sqrt{(n-1)}.$$

He then checked the adequacy of this distribution by drawing 750 samples of 4 from W. R. Macdonell's data on the height and middle-finger length of 3,000 criminals and by working out the standard deviations of both variates in each sample (see Macdonell 1902). This he did by shuffling 3,000 pieces of cardboard on which the results had been written, possibly the earliest work in statistical research that led to the development of the Monte Carlo method.

Later in his paper on "Probable Error of a Correlation Coefficient" ([1908] 1943, pp. 35–42), Gosset used the 750 correlation coefficients of the two variables. Here his remarkable intuition again led him to a correct answer. By correlating the height measurements of one sample with the middle-finger lengths of the next, he was able to obtain 750 values of $r$, the sample correlation coefficient, for which $\rho$, the true population correlation coefficient, was presumably zero. He noticed that the observed distribution of $r$ was approximately rectangular. If it were a Pearson curve it would have to be Type II, that is, $C(1 - r^2)^\lambda$, and his result from the 750 samples suggested $\lambda = k(n - 4)$. He guessed that $k = \frac{1}{2}$ and confirmed the result by taking 750 samples of 8 to which $C(1 - r^2)^2$ gave an excellent fit. Six years later Fisher proved that all these brilliant conjectures for the distribution of $s^2$, $t$, and $r$ when $\rho = 0$ were indeed correct.

The correlation coefficient between the two measurements in the 3,000 criminals was 0.66. Gosset also examined two sets of 750 samples of sizes 4 and 8 and one set of 100 samples of 30, for which the true value must have been close to 0.66. He could see from his results that the standard deviation given by $(1 - \rho^2)/\sqrt{n}$ was too small and that the distribution could not be of Pearson type except when $\rho = 0$. He succeeded in obtaining the exact repartition of $r$ for any $\rho$ in samples of 2, but the general solution for $\rho \neq 0$ had to await the publication of Fisher's famous paper in 1915.

Gosset's fourth paper ([1909] 1943, pp. 43–48) dealt with the distribution of the means of samples not drawn at random. His brewing experience had repeatedly drawn his attention to the fact that successive observations were not uncorrelated. Here he supposed a sample of $n$ values to be drawn in such a way that the correlation between every pair of observations is the same (say $\rho$), so that $\rho$ is effectively an intraclass correlation. He used the algebraical methods of his second paper to determine the first four moments of the mean, in this case employing as an illustration some data published by Greenwood and White (1909) in which 2,000 phagocytic counts had been grouped in samples of 25. Both the original counts and the distribution of means could be fitted by Pearson Type I (Beta) curves. However, the observed values of $\beta_1$ and $(\beta_2 - 3)$ for the distribution of means were bigger than would have been anticipated if the usual theory for independent observations had been valid. The modified theory produced much better agreement.

Gosset published five more mathematical papers between 1909 and 1921 ([1913; 1914; 1917; 1919; 1921] 1943, pp. 53–89). With the possible exception of the first of these, they are still of interest. The 1921 paper gave for the first time the correction for ties in calculating Spearman's rank correlation coefficient.

**Agricultural and other biometric studies.** It was natural, owing to the high importance of barley quality in brewing, that Gosset should have become interested in agricultural problems. His active interest seems to have started in 1905 when he was first asked for advice by E. S. Beaven, a maltster who had started experimental work in the 1890s. From then onward there was a constant interchange of correspondence and ideas between them, in which the mathematical insight of the younger man supplemented the experimental experience of the older.

Gosset's first meeting with Fisher was at Rothamsted in August 1922; each had the greatest admiration for the other's work and doubtless each had considerable influence on the development of the other's ideas on experimental design. Toward the end of Gosset's life they had a difference of opinion about the relative methods of random and systematic arrangements, but this did not affect the high regard that they always had for one another.

In 1911 Gosset examined the results of some uniformity trials carried out by Mercer and Hall at Rothamsted ([1911] 1943, pp. 49–52). In the most important of these, an acre of wheat had been harvested in 1/500-acre plots. Gosset showed from the results how advantage could be taken of the correlation between the yields of adjacent plots to increase the accuracy of varietal comparisons, and he showed that for a given acreage greater accuracy could be obtained with smaller plots rather than with larger plots.

As early as 1912 and 1913 Beaven had invented the "chessboard" design, and experiments had been laid down, each with eight varieties of barley on yard-square plots, in three centers. These were essentially "block designs," with each variety occurring once in each block; but within the block, the arrangement was balanced rather than random. At this time Gosset discovered the correct estimate of error per plot for the varietal comparisons, precisely the same result as would be obtained from an analysis of variance. He compared every possible pair of varieties and calculated for each pair $\sum(d - \bar{d})^2$, $d$ being the difference in one block. He added these results together for all $n$ varieties and divided by $\frac{1}{2}n(n-1)(m-1)$, where $m$ is the number of blocks. These experiments were discontinued during World War I, but in 1923 Gosset and Fisher discovered, independently, the analysis of variance method of obtaining the result. In a letter to Gosset, Fisher proved the algebraical equivalence of Gosset's original method and the new one.

These chessboard designs were small-scale work. For field trials, Gosset and Beaven favored the "half-drill strip method," in which two varieties were compared on an area of about an acre. In this method, the two varieties are sown in long strips— *CAACCAAC*, etc.—there being an integral number of "sandwiches" (such as *CAAC*).

The error of the varietal comparison was obtained from the variances of the differences $(C - A)$ either in individual strips or in sandwiches. In one such experiment, described by Gosset, on something more than an acre, the standard error of a varietal mean was found to be about 0.6 per cent. Gosset was later criticized by Fisher for preferring this method to randomized strips or randomized sandwiches. Gosset welcomed the advances in the science of agricultural experimentation that came from Fisher and his school. His own attitude was a very practical one, based on his extensive experience in Ireland experimenting with barley.

A good account of much of this kind of work is given in Gosset's most important paper on agricultural experimentation, "On Testing Varieties of Cereals" ([1923] 1943, pp. 90–114). The paper also describes some large-scale work carried out by the department of agriculture in Ireland during 1901–1906 to find the best variety of barley to grow in that country. Here two varieties, Archer and Goldthorpe, were carried right through the whole period and each tested on two-acre plots in a large number of centers. With 50 pairs of plots of this size, the standard error of the comparison was still

about 10 per cent to 15 per cent. However, the result was based on wide experience. In the half-drill strip experiment the corresponding standard error was only 1 per cent, but the result applied only to an acre, in one place, under very particular conditions of soil and season.

While it was important to plan yield trials in such a way as to reduce experimental error and to obtain an accurate estimate of it, it was only by comparison and analysis of the results from a number of soils, seasons, and climates that one could judge the relative value of different varieties or different treatments. Further, products must also be subjected to tests of quality. *Conclusions drawn in one center could in any case be applicable only to the particular conditions under which the trials were carried out.* While he insisted that "experiments must be capable of being considered to be a *random* sample of the population to which the conclusions are to be applied," in an individual center he often preferred balanced (that is, systematic) arrangements to randomized ones. He liked the Latin square, because of its combination of balance (to eliminate soil heterogeneity) with a random element, thus conforming to all the principles of allowed witchcraft ([1926] 1943, pp. 199–215). He was less happy about randomized blocks because he felt that a balanced arrangement within the blocks often gave a greater accuracy than did a random one. Further, he was unwilling to accept the result of the toss of a coin, or its equivalent, if the arrangement so obtained was biased in relation to already available knowledge of the fertility gradients of the experimental area. In his last paper, "Comparison Between Balanced and Random Arrangements of Field Plots" ([1938] 1943, pp. 193–215), he wrote:

It is of course perfectly true that *in the long run*, taking all possible arrangements, exactly as many misleading conclusions will be drawn as are allowed for in the tables, and anyone prepared to spend a blameless life in repeating an experiment would doubtless confirm this; nevertheless it would be pedantic to continue with an arrangement of plots known beforehand to be likely to lead to a misleading conclusion. (p. 202)

He thought that an experimenter with a knowledge of his job could arrange the treatments within a block so that *real error*, that is, the variance of the different treatment means that would be obtained with dummy treatments in a uniformity trial, would be less than if the treatments had been randomized. This statement was no doubt often true in the domain in which he worked, but its general validity has often been questioned. He distinguished between the *real error* as here defined and the *calculated error*, that is, the error variance of the treatment mean, that would be obtained from usual analysis of variance procedures. He maintained, perfectly correctly, that if the real error were reduced by balancing, the calculated error would be too high. In his last paper, he showed, in addition, that in this situation experiments that have a real error less than the calculated one fail to give as many "significant" results as those that have a greater error, if the real treatment differences are small. When, however, the real treatment differences are large, the reverse is the case. Therefore, if balanced arrangements have a small real error, they will less often miss large real differences and more often miss small ones. He regarded this as a positive advantage; where real differences in a particular center were small, he was satisfied to have an upper limit to his error because he thought that only by collating results from different centers could he arrive at the truth. Where real differences were small, even if statistically significant, the results at different centers were likely to be conflicting.

This last paper was written in reply to one by Barbacki and Fisher (1936), which purported to show that the half-drill strip method is less accurate than the corresponding randomized arrangement. Gosset was right in maintaining that these authors were in error, for they had not compared like with like in the actual data they had examined —a uniformity trial carried out by Wiebe (1935). However the data were not very good for deciding the question, for as subsequently shown by Yates (1939), owing to defective drilling they contained a periodic fluctuation, two drill-widths wide. Gosset would almost certainly have welcomed the combination of balance and randomization achieved by some of the designs invented since his day, which are likely to give a gain in accuracy similar to that obtained by his systematic designs over randomized blocks and at the same time are free from difficulties in error estimation.

In an article on Gosset, Sir Ronald Fisher praised "Student's" work on genetical evolutionary theory (see Gosset [1907–1938] 1943, pp. 181–191). He concluded: "In spite of his many activities it is the 'Student' of 'Student's' *test of significance* who has won, and deserved to win, a unique place in the history of scientific method" (Fisher 1939, p. 8).

J. O. IRWIN

[*For the historical context of Gosset's work, see* DISTRIBUTIONS, STATISTICAL; STATISTICS, *article on* THE HISTORY OF STATISTICAL METHOD; *and the*

biographies of FISHER, R. A.; and PEARSON. *For discussion of the subsequent development of his ideas, see* ESTIMATION; EXPERIMENTAL DESIGN; HYPOTHESIS TESTING.]

WORKS BY GOSSET
(1907–1938) 1943 *"Student's" Collected Papers.* Edited by E. S. Pearson and John Wishart. London: University College, Biometrika Office. → William S. Gosset wrote under the pseudonym "Student." The 1943 edition contains all the articles cited in the text.

SUPPLEMENTARY BIBLIOGRAPHY
AIRY, GEORGE B. (1861) 1879 *On the Algebraical and Numerical Theory of Errors of Observations and the Combination of Observations.* 3d ed. London: Macmillan.
BARBACKI, S.; and FISHER, R. A. 1936 A Test of the Supposed Precision of Systematic Arrangements. *Annals of Eugenics* 7:189–193.
FISHER, R. A. 1915 Frequency Distribution of the Values of the Correlation Coefficient in Samples From an Indefinitely Large Population. *Biometrika* 10:507–521.
FISHER, R. A. (1925) 1958 *Statistical Methods for Research Workers.* 13th ed. New York: Hafner. → Previous editions were published by Oliver & Boyd.
FISHER, R. A. 1939 "Student." *Annals of Eugenics* 9: 1–9.
GREENWOOD, M. JR.; and WHITE, J. D. C. 1909 On the Frequency Distribution of Phagocytic Counts. *Biometrika* 6:376–401.
MACDONELL, W. R. 1902 On Criminal Anthropometry and the Identification of Criminals. *Biometrika* 1: 177–227.
MERRIMAN, MANSFIELD (1884) 1911 *A Text-book on the Method of Least Squares.* 8th ed. New York: Wiley.
WIEBE, G. A. 1935 Variation and Correlation in Grain Yield Among 1,500 Wheat Nursery Plots. *Journal of Agricultural Research* 50:331–357.
YATES, F. 1939 The Comparative Advantages of Systematic and Randomized Arrangements in the Design of Agricultural and Biological Experiments. *Biometrika* 30:440–466.

# GOVERNMENT

The study of government has followed several main lines of inquiry. These include both an examination of the source and distribution of authority and the classification of types of government (such as presidential systems and monarchies), as well as analysis of levels of government (including such units as national societies, clubs, churches, and trade unions). Although a thorough review is impossible here, we can examine the main themes which unite these various approaches and evaluate their theoretical status.

At the most general level, government consists of a group of individuals sharing a defined responsibility for exercising power. At this level the definition applies to cases where government is sovereign, as well as to cases where it is not. Sovereign government, the most important type, consists of a group of individuals sharing a defined responsibility for the maintenance and adaptation of a national autonomous community, on behalf of which it exercises a practical monopoly of coercive powers. If by "a defined responsibility" we mean its legitimacy (the sanctified right to exercise power on behalf of others by means of decision making), then the characteristics of sovereign government are as follows: a government is a group of individuals exercising legitimate authority, and protecting and adapting the community by making and carrying out decisions. [See SOVEREIGNTY *and* STATE.]

These characteristics impose certain limits of variation upon government. One limit is efficacy, i.e., the capacity of a government to cater to community needs. A second refers to the internal structure of a given type of government, i.e., its form. Changes in form which occur when one type of government is transformed into another are ordinarily related to the efficacy, or performance, of a particular government. Hence, the limit upon government is observable when for any reason (inability to make decisions, failures to comply with widely distributed but central values) it can no longer function. If this is not merely a matter which can be remedied by changing the incumbents of political office, i.e., if the political roles and supporting offices are no longer acceptable, then the withdrawal of legitimacy denotes that the system of government is no longer regarded as appropriate by the public; its limits have been breached. At that point, change from one type of government to another is likely.

The most common distinctions that have been made between types of governments include the following: is the government competitive or monopolistic? democratic or totalitarian? pluralistic or monistic? presidential or monarchical? Of course, these well-known categories overlap considerably. For example, it is possible to have a totalitarian presidential system. As is the case with all dichotomous variables, these distinctions force the observer to put a particular government in one category or the other, even when it demonstrates characteristics of both. Such distinctions are based on two criteria: the organization of government and the degree of control it exercises over the community. These criteria combine the moral, or normative, dimension of politics with the dimensions relating to governmental structure and political behavior. These three analytically distinct elements, i.e., the normative, structural, and behavioral aspects of government, will now be separately examined.

Normative aspects of government deal with such abstract questions as justice, equity, equality. Through these, men define their lasting values, their ideas of right and wrong. Normative theory represents, therefore, certain speculations about those aims and activities of government which embody the central values and ultimate ends of a political community; it defines political legitimacy.

In contrast, structural principles are those which deal with the arrangements and instruments involved in governmental decision making. Of course, they are related to normative issues insofar as the form of a government is seen as a means of attaining the ends of society. Preoccupation with the structural dimension leads directly to the analysis of alternative forms of government, with normative considerations employed in order to evaluate those most suitable for realizing the goals of the community by means of governmental decision making. In the past, structural analysis has been mainly concerned with the distribution of political power, describing various types of government in terms of how widely power is shared by the members of a political community.

Classical writers were particularly interested in normative issues and structuralists have been preoccupied with governmental forms. Both groups, to the extent that they considered it at all, assumed behavior to be a condition of conflict. For both, a propensity to conflict is regarded as the normal political expression of human nature, much as economists assumed that man has a natural propensity "to truck, barter, and exchange." Hobbes, for example, put this assumption very sharply as "the war of all against all." Such assumptions led both Plato and Hobbes to seek authoritarian governments as the best means of regulating the condition of conflict. Other theorists have seen a division of powers as the best method to control conflict.

Certain combinations of normative and structural approaches have been called institutionalist theories. Institutionalists, such as Carl Friedrich (1937), Harold Laski (1925; 1935), and Herman Finer (1932), concerned themselves with the normative and structural relations between law, constitutional forms, and governmental procedures in wide historical, religious, and economic contexts. Their considerations included an interest in practical reform as well as theory, and they consciously built on the formulations of Ostrogorskii (1902), Bryce (1921), Graham Wallas (1908), and others.

Emphasis on the behavioral dimension originated largely in the 1930s, with the "Chicago school" and, in particular, with Harold Lasswell, who sought to introduce behavioral explanations into political affairs. This is most explicit in his pioneering work *Psychopathology and Politics* (1930). However, until recently, few theorists followed this lead. It is, therefore, not surprising that the study of socialization processes, motivation, and political culture has been handled mainly by political sociologists. [*See* POLITICAL SOCIOLOGY.]

Analysis today is characterized by the refinement of structural theories of government into a system, i.e., a set of interrelated elements which can be integrated with behavioral theories. The resulting analysis has taken many different forms and has made some advances, but it is particularly weak in its treatment of normative theory. [*See* POLITICAL SCIENCE *and* POLITICAL THEORY.]

### Theories of government

Historically, most theories of government have fallen into one or the other of two main analytical sets: mechanistic and organic.

**Mechanistic theories.** The first set reflects the view that society is composed of competing and interacting interests (both individual and group), that these generate conflict, and that it is the job of government to ameliorate or resolve such conflict. Government is thus a device for finding ways to relax tension in the political system. These theories, relying heavily on the free exchange of information, see government as a point in a flow of activity which is initiated by the political community. Since government has a decision-making apparatus, which responds to tension points in the system, the appropriate actions will be forthcoming. Behavioral tensions represent "inputs," or stimuli affecting political leaders, who by responding to them generate decisions, or "outputs" (see Figure 1).

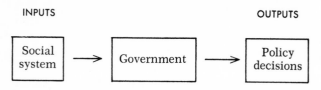

*Figure 1 — Government as a dependent variable*

In Figure 1, assume that the social system is a national society. Government responds to a variety of societally generated inputs, including customs and beliefs (normative characteristics), classes and interests (structural characteristics), and preferences and perceptions (behavioral characteristics). Democratic theories of government are based on this model. This is why they have been particularly concerned with the establishment of a useful set of intervening structural variables between the

social system and government itself. Hence the preoccupation with the analysis of political parties, electoral systems, and the like, which are seen as devices for improving the relationship between the social system and government in order to raise the quality and appropriateness of policy decisions and increase the efficacy of government.

It is the liberal democratic approach which accepts this view, with government cast in the role of mediator and judge in conflicts between contending parties. The principles of structural organization are embodied in law, which serves as a framework for all other forms of organization. Normative consensus centers around the maintenance of the legal framework itself. Government strengthens consensus by ensuring the widest realization of norms already held. Such liberal theories are contained in the ideas of Diderot and d'Alembert, Holbach and Helvétius, Condillac and Locke, Rousseau and Hume. It is a tradition which includes Voltaire's innocent rationalism and Bentham's equitable utilitarianism. What these thinkers had in common was an emphasis on individual knowledge and shared reason, a position which elevates the individual to the center of the political stage. Rationality is a norm, and it requires a framework in which free ideas and competitive views can be put forward.

The Western democratic governments reflect variants of this model, but it was also accepted, at least in principle, in other areas. For example, the constitutions of many of the new Afro–Asian nations were drawn with this general approach in mind, even where the actual practice of government is wholly different from its normative and structural theory.

To sum up, the normative assumption underlying the model is that a social system is composed of individuals or groups with an equal right to be represented. Structurally, it is assumed that a government must reflect proper representation; the behavioral assumption is that competitive conflict between the members of the social system renders representative forms necessary. The model therefore displays the following characteristics: the unit of which the social system is composed is the individual; the ends of the individual are maximized; the structure of government is organized in such a way that a plurality of ends is maximized; the decisions of government, by maximizing a plurality of ends, maintain balance or harmony in the social system; and the principle of legitimacy is equity. The concern of political theorists following this tradition is with the improvement of devices that government can use to maximize a plurality of ends. Certain structural procedures have, therefore, become endowed with the quality of norms. Moreover, underlying this view is an assumption, rather mechanistic, that government is a contrivance. It does not grow organically. It must be established, with each structural principle becoming endowed with a predictable consequence. Government is, first, a kind of social physics, with particular devices having predictable results.

**Organic theories.**   The classical view is different (as are many contemporary ones). For example, both Plato and Aristotle related government to the evolution of human society from lower to higher forms. Therefore, government was essentially an educational body, embodying a set of ideals and perfecting rationality, thereby directing the state toward a new golden age. Moreover, this conception of government has had as durable a tradition as the liberal democratic one. Although such views were widely accepted in medieval Europe (Gierke 1881), it was Hegel who gave the conception its most powerful rationale and Marx who brought it into popular currency. Marx accepted nineteenth-century notions of progress but saw in the evolution of man's higher purposes a relationship between change in the material world and the unfolding human consciousness. Government is an instrument of this relationship. As such, it has its own cycle. It becomes an instrument of revolutionary action, of insurrection, which, if successful, represents the most dynamic class. It comes to power as the instrument which must transform revolutionary impetus into practical accomplishment. Having accomplished this, it will in turn be rendered anachronistic and vulnerable until the final stage, when government is itself no longer necessary.

Nor was Marx alone in accepting an organismic conception of government. More liberal-minded proponents include Thomas Hill Green, who saw government as an instrument of morality. Herder, a philosophical romantic, also shared the view that government was a transitional phenomenon by means of which an "aristo–democracy" would educate the public and develop a sufficient level of political consciousness to render government superfluous. "The ultimate aim of aristo–democracy, Herder saw in the disappearance of the State as an administrative 'machine' of government, and its replacement by an 'organic' way of ordering social life, in which active cooperation would render all forms of subordination obsolete and superfluous" (Barnard 1965, p. 77). Similar views were expressed by Fichte, Schelling, and Bosanquet. Today this approach is particularly attractive in develop-

ing areas, where government is seen as the instrument of an evolutionary ideal.

The organic evolutionary concept remains an alternative to the liberal democratic one. It implies a role for government, which directs society toward higher ends. Evolutionary in conception, this tradition is often enriched by ecclesiastic and theocratic ideals. It stresses the role of the community over and against the role of the individual. Although modern organic conceptions elevate man to a central position, they emphasize that the community is the instrument of his perfection; such views are endemic in revolutionary governments, which see themselves as the instruments of social transformation. Where the role of government is so central, we can say that it becomes the independent variable (Figure 2).

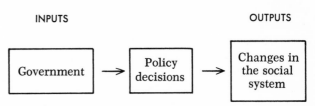

*Figure 2 — Government as an independent variable*

Government is the instrument by means of which change is produced in the social system. The purposes and objects of such change (normative characteristics) are defined by government. The organization of government (structural characteristics) will depend on the best means to accomplish these purposes. The activities of government will include whatever symbolic manipulation through education, communications media, etc., is necessary to affect both the content and manner of policy decision making pursuant to changes in the social system.

In the first model (Figure 1) government is the dependent variable and social system or community is the independent variable. Power is seen to inhere in the public, which creates the inputs of stimuli to which government must cater (Easton 1957; 1965). In the second model (Figure 2) government is the independent variable and social system the dependent one. Such systems tend to be centralized in the form of their authority. They tend to elevate the goals of the government into norms and make them sacred and ethical precepts, through which legitimacy is defined. Governments resembling the first model tend to be competitive, pluralistic, and democratic; those resembling the second tend to be monopolistic, monistic, and totalitarian. Normatively, the first are more secular than the second. Structurally, they are less hierarchically organized. Behaviorally, they rely heavily on internalized norms and self-control, rather than on external authority. As opposing paradigms, these two generalized types, in their various concrete formulations, are perpetually vulnerable to each other. Indeed, one can see over time that they form a permanent dialogue of conflict. They represent two fundamentally different approaches to government.

### Political norms and forms of authority

We can now begin to explore some of the implications of that dialogue of conflict. One way of describing it is in terms of the difference between sacred and secular norms. This difference is important because it draws our attention to the normative basis of a government and, therefore, to its legitimacy. Normative conflict generally takes place between sacred and secular beliefs. [See LEGITIMACY.]

**Sacred political norms.** Governments based on sacred norms cover a wide range of cases, ancient and modern, including ancient China and many of the early Semitic kingdoms. Consider the following description: "The Egyptian of historic times did not have our doubts and difficulties. To him the kingship was not merely part, but the kernel of the static order of the world, an order that was divine just as much as the kingship was divine. . . . From the earliest historic times, therefore, the dominant element in the Egyptian conception of kingship was that the king was a god—not merely godlike, but very god" (Fairman 1958, p. 75). Or take the case of ancient Greece. There the principles of patrilineal authority and ascribed status were linked to an ancestral and religious source, not only for kings but for every citizen (Hignett 1952, p. 63). Ascribed status applied particularly to priests and to the distinction between nobles and commoners. Hence, political norms represented an explicit validation of the structure authority.

Sacredness does not apply only to theocratic or primitive societies. It applies as well to many modern states. The sacred qualities of Marxism–Leninism in the Soviet Union are today enshrined in an elaborate philosophical system. Many of its sacred attributes were cruelly visible in the various purges and trials of the 1930s. It appears, even today, in the controversies over the political role of literature and the arts. Clearer still is the case of modern China. Mao's prescriptive sayings assume such a sacred characteristic as to define the basis of political legitimacy. Many new nations share this characteristic (although to a lesser degree), particularly in cases where an attempt is made to ritualize the authority of a charismatic or highly personalistic leader by endowing his words and teachings with special insight.

No government is entirely free from sacred qualities, whether these be elaborate and ideological or be token symbols, such as a flag, or a constitutional document. These aspects of government may be merely ceremonial, or what Bagehot called the "dignified part," or they may represent high drama in which the solidarity and unity of a community may be expressed.

It is possible to distinguish three main varieties of sacred attachments, which, even if they overlap, are analytically separable. Ranking them in ascending order of sacredness, they are (1) primordial attachments to or beliefs about race, language, and nationality (a typical expression of primordial attachment is nationalism); (2) philosophical attachments (the most generalized moral and philosophical ideal in which a total synthesis is expressed relating man to his environment and specifying the way of the future is to be found today in socialism); and (3) religious attachments (this refers to religious beliefs in which the origin of the society, moral purpose, and a particular pattern of transcendental beliefs are associated in a universal religious doctrine, such as Christianity).

In practice all three of these may be blended. Modern populist and totalitarian regimes, as in Nazi Germany, mixed primordial attachments of race and theological attachments of religion. In the Soviet Union during World War II, the symbols of government were more and more primordial, i.e., nationalist, and less and less philosophical, i.e., Marxist.

**Secular political norms.** Secular norms rely on a framework of rules rather than on some higher purposes of state. The most common cases of secular systems are those in which the sacred elements have declined through institutionalization. They do not disappear, but they become so completely a part of the accepted pattern of right and wrong that it is not necessary to do more than refer to them on ritual occasions. Thus, ceremony rather than the substance of belief is characteristic of these systems.

By tacit agreement secular systems reserve the "higher" goals to the individual, and these goals inhere in his body of private beliefs. If governments should violate these norms, they run the risk of overstepping their limits of variation and of being eliminated.

We can now cut across the sacred–secular normative distinction with a structural variable, the pattern of centralized or decentralized authority [*see* AUTHORITY]. Once again we must employ a caveat and remind ourselves that it is always difficult to use dichotomous variables to divide concrete cases. What is in theory decentralized may be quite the opposite in practice. Or highly centralized systems may show informal patterns of consultation and accountability to various groups in the community. Indeed, at any given time even the most highly centralized system may act on certain issues in a highly decentralized manner. Moreover, centralized government includes monarchical and bureaucratic systems, represented by ancient empires, that can combine monarchy with decentralized administration [*see* EMPIRES]. This configuration includes different types of government: systems where the hierarchy is based on a king who is a father of his people, with authority deriving from a totemic ancestor, as in many tribal governments, or systems where authority lodges in a patrimonial figure and the relationship between ruler and ruled is that of patron and client [*see* KINGSHIP; *see also* Fallers 1956].

**Centralized authority.** Let us ignore all these variations in form and say boldly that centralized power begins from the top and is applied downward through a specific delegation of authority. A military organization or a bureaucracy represents a clear-cut "command" case, with autocratic and totalitarian governments defined as those which employ this system of hierarchy. Government may then be represented by a single figure, a king or dictator, or by an oligarchy or junta (Friedrich & Brzezinski 1956). Such highly centralized systems show the following characteristics: concentrated power is subject to few checks; power inheres at the top; subordinate authority is derivative; and there is strong reliance on the personality of a particular leader. [*See* AUTOCRACY; OLIGARCHY.]

**Decentralized authority.** Decentralized authority represents an opposite conception of power: power is generated by the public through the aggregation of their political wants, is expressed through various groups, and is regulated by an abstract system of rules. (Its usual normative expressions include the acceptance of the principle of majority rule, protection of rights, and representation.) This is what we mean by a democratic government. It is characterized by checks and balances, parliamentary control over the executive, and some form of election as the method of political recruitment to sensitive positions. Of course, such practices do not exhaust the forms of decentralization. Decentralization may be functional, based on the allocation of the economic power in society among various groupings, such as guilds, protective as-

*Table 1 — The derivation of political typologies*

|  |  | CONCENTRATION OF POWER | |
|---|---|---|---|
|  |  | Centralized | Decentralized |
| PREDOMINANT POLITICAL NORMS | Sacred | A | C |
|  | Secular | B | D |

sociations, professional associations, and other interest groups. [*See* CONSTITUTIONS AND CONSTITUTIONALISM.]

The distinctions between sacred and secular and between centralized and decentralized types of government can form the basis of a more general model by means of which to analyze government. Table 1 pinpoints the four combinations that will be examined in detail. To summarize the possibilities, the highly centralized and sacred system, *A*, represents modern populist totalitarian governments. The centralized and secular system, *B*, represents many autocratic forms of government. The sacred and decentralized system, *C*, includes many early forms of theocratic society, from the feudalism of the High Middle Ages in Europe to religious or theocratic governments in America, such as the Puritan colonies of New England. And modern democratic governments fall into the secular and decentralized category, *D*.

### Sacred and centralized governments

The modern sacred–centralized type of system is likely to be associated with the establishment of a new political system. Government is the independent variable and is associated with a new moral framework. Such conditions commonly apply after a major revolution or in territories that have recently gained independence. [*See* DICTATORSHIP; TOTALITARIANISM.]

**Communist governments.** The distinguishing feature of the sacred–centralized communist government is the high degree of centralization encompassing the total community. The sacred object of government is to transform the material conditions of life and the consciousness of the people at the same time. The evolution of the community becomes a moral goal, to be sought under the leadership of a militant vanguard—the Communist party —serving as the spearhead of government. In the classic, Leninist form of the communist regime, no competitive sources of power can be tolerated. In recent times, however, a slight trend toward secularization and decentralization can be seen in the Soviet Union (Brzezinski 1962).

Historically, the Soviet Union is an interesting

case of external beliefs influencing internal social groups to revolt against a highly autocratic monarchy, a weak parliament (the Duma was only founded in 1905), and a centralized bureaucracy liberally sprinkled with foreign, particularly German, immigrants (Pipes 1954). Not only was the revolutionary instrument based on a small but dynamic working-class movement; Marxism itself was largely restricted to Russian middle-class intellectuals. It was essentially an alien doctrine (transformed by Lenin to meet Russian conditions) leading to a revolutionary organization which later became the centralizing mechanism of state power. When the religious beliefs of the Greek Orthodox church were replaced by the secular ideology of Marxism–Leninism, the goals of political development became sacred and formed the new basis of the legitimacy of government. Of course, a wide discrepancy existed between the theory and practice of government. Power was in fact centralized in the hands of the first secretary of the Politburo of the Central Committee of the Communist party, while constitutionally the Soviet Union was a federal system with an elected "supreme organ of state power," the Supreme Soviet, which had, in theory, the exclusive right of legislation. [See COMMUNISM, article on SOVIET COMMUNISM.]

This system formed the model of state organization for all other communist systems until relatively recently. Since the death of Stalin, however, two interesting features may be noted. The sacred quality of Marxist–Leninist ideology has declined, particularly as younger generations find it less significant as a doctrine than as a ritual; and a trend toward decentralization has begun. A struggle is on between the communist political leaders and the technical specialists, economists, scientists, and the like. Moreover, as "polycentricism" on an international level becomes more accepted, the necessity for a more "liberal" approach to Marxism–Leninism reduces its orthodoxy. Alternative structural experiments are increasingly common, such as those in Hungary, Yugoslovia, and Poland, in which "cultural" decentralization (in the case of Hungary and Poland) and economic decentralization (in the case of Yugoslavia) represent experiments in greater freedom. [See COMMUNISM, article on NATIONAL COMMUNISM; see also Laqueur & Labedz 1962.]

The communist examples are of particular relevance because they have become attractive models to governments of developing areas bent on following the Soviet pattern of rapid industrialization (Ulam 1960).

**Fascist governments.** Fascist governments were more secular in their orientations. The develop-

mental or evolutionary sacred ideology around which communist governments try to organize their societies embodies certain universalized moral aims. In contrast, the sacred attachments of fascist governments showed greater attraction to primordial sentiments, including race and nationality. Although there are structural similarities between communist and fascist governments, particularly with respect to the roles of a powerful totalitarian political leader and a weak set of parliamentary institutions, one important difference should be pointed out. In the communist case, government is monolithic, emphasizing the evolution of the entire community. Fascist governments, in contrast, tolerated certain corporate groupings.

Three fascist governments are of interest here: Germany, Italy, and Spain. All were highly centralized, but they varied considerably with respect to the sacredness and secularity of political norms.

The strongest attachment to sacred primordial political norms was exhibited in Nazi Germany. The supremacy of one race and the liberating effects of war and conflict were embodied in the revived Nordic myths ("Odinism") and blended into a set of nationalist political norms. Structurally, although the government was highly centralized under a personal dictatorship, four main groupings were given exceptional attention: army and secret police, large-scale industrial enterprise, labor organized into fronts and battalions, and military scientists and technicians. The Nazi case also shows that even under a highly centralized form of government, economic control can be kept separate from ownership, with private industry continuing to operate under government regulations. Unlike the situation in communist systems, in Nazi Germany a market system of economic allocation coexisted with government-organized fiscal and credit manipulations. Each corporate group obtained special conditions of privilege. [See NATIONAL SOCIALISM.]

Italian fascism showed less commitment to primordial political norms than Nazism, as well as a somewhat less centralized governmental structure. The norms themselves were composed of ambiguous combinations of primordial sentiments, appeals to historical precedent, and claims to philosophical universality. Primordial claims were mixed with the corporate organization of the state, under the inspiration of the collegia of the late Roman Empire. The "corporation" was thus associated with the great period of Italian imperial and cultural achievement and became the legitimizing basis of the regime.

A second claim to universality, which was of

minor importance during the period of Italian fascism, may yet prove to be highly significant. This is the view that the proper way to organize the state is in corporate groupings functional to development and industrialization. In arguing the case of corporate government, it was pointed out that fascism as a form of government, although totalitarian, emphasized the role of the corporation as both the point of reconciliation between state and individual and the instrument of individual expression (see Barker 1942, pp. 328–366). This possibility remains as an important structural device, midway between highly centralized and decentralized systems. [*See* FASCISM.]

Both the German and Italian systems contained important normative ambiguities, which they attempted to resolve in the apotheosis of violence. This was most apparent in their total repudiation of democratic, decentralized forms of government (which were regarded as catering to human weakness). Italian and German fascism both represented an authentic totalitarian populism (a modern form of tribalism), in which medieval ideas of corporation, organic concepts of the community, and primordial sentiments were intertwined within a highly centralized system of administrative government.

The Spanish case has been less ideological and less centralized. Despite the exceptional power of Generalissimo Franco and the concentration of authority in the national cabinet, the Falange, as a political party, plays a lesser role in government than the National Socialist party did in Germany, or the Fascist party in Italy (Payne 1961). One reason is that within six years of Franco's accession to power, Italy and Germany were defeated. Their systems no longer served as models of successful dictatorship. Even more important is the Catholic tradition, to which the right wing of the Falange and significant proportions of the population generally subscribe. [*See* FALANGISM.]

More decentralized than the others, and therefore more autocratic than totalitarian, the Spanish system remains an extension of an old and established bureaucratic system which traces its roots to the imperial Spanish tradition, the Inquisition, and a centralized monarchy. Even today the Spanish government tries to preserve a vague commitment to monarchy as a traditional form of legitimacy. This allows the government to revive memories of Spanish grandeur, treating communism, secularism, and socialism much as Philip II and Archbishop Carranza of Toledo treated Protestantism, Islam, and Judaism (Davies 1937). This fervor would indicate the presence of sacred political norms, derived from Catholicism and more or less indifferent to the structure of authority. Many of the same norms served equally well in Perón's Argentina, and the more socialist forms of Catholic corporatism are sometimes embodied in modern and decentralized socialist or democratic governments, for example, in Chile. [*See* CAUDILLISMO.]

## Secular and centralized governments

The most pronounced characteristics of a secular–centralized system of government are autonomous power in the hands of a president or monarch (or perhaps a presidential monarch); a single political party, whether in the form of an elite (a communist party) or a populist mass party with an elite center (most nationalist parties); a truncated or largely ritualistic parliament, which does not have a real veto power over the executive; and an elections system which does not allow effective competition between candidates for political office.

Such centralized systems show several characteristic problems common to all forms of centralized government with the exception of institutionalized monarchies. The most important of these are, first, succession to high public office (which is usually accompanied by severe struggles for power) and, second, the institutionalization of disagreement.

The normative content of both the communist and fascist forms of government gives direction and shape to the entire society. Historically, however, there have been many cases where the normative content is relatively low (or largely ceremonial and ritualized), while power remains centralized. These include most nineteenth-century monarchical forms of government. Indeed, precisely because their sacred characteristics were emptied of content (while retained in form) they were unable to survive as types and were either transformed or removed. In France the monarchical form, attempted periodically during the nineteenth century, had been effectively destroyed by the French Revolution. Only Bonapartism had any genuine normative success. In Britain the secularization process began with the transformation of the monarchy or, symbolically, with the beheading of Charles I. The Act of Settlement of 1701, whereby the sovereign occupies the throne under a parliamentary title, established parliamentary supremacy, although it took many generations before the full implications were worked out (Dicey 1885). Real structural changes in the form of decentralization were embodied in the widening of parliamentary control over the executive and in popular representation from 1832 onward (Gash 1953). If the record of historical cases of secular–centralized government is any guide, then one useful proposition can be stated as follows: as sacred political norms become secularized through ritualization, government must decentralize, since its legitimacy disappears. [See MONARCHY.]

Examples of secular–centralized governments include czarist Russia (although there were important theocratic elements incorporated in the role of the czar), and Bismarck's Germany. More recent cases are colonial administrative governments in British and French Africa, south Asia, the Netherlands, the East Indies, and the Belgian Congo.

Many of the new nations have gone from one form of highly centralized system, under colonialism, to another, in the form of one-party government, but with a change in the quality of political norms. The norms often become endowed with intense attachment to primordial loyalties associated with race and nation and, to a lesser degree, with some aspects of socialism and public ownership, all wrapped up in a particular ideological message, such as Nasserism in Egypt, Nkrumahism in Ghana, or "Communocracy" in Guinea.

**Sacred and decentralized governments**

Where new constitutional governments have been most successful, they have evolved a shared set of political norms deriving from a previous period when such norms were explicitly sacred, either in an ecclesiastical form, as in the case of the Puritan commonwealths, or in a more directly political form. This suggests the following proposition: decentralized–secular governments are most stable and effective when they have developed out of an earlier centralized–sacred or decentralized–sacred form, with norms of self-control becoming behaviorally widespread. Modern democratic government emerged when the decentralization of authority and secularization of political norms proceeded more or less simultaneously with a corresponding increase in the standard of individual civic obligation (Almond & Verba 1963).

The origins of Western democratic governments derive from a synthesis of generally agreed religious values, which is associated with a generalized Christian ethic. The theocratic origins of democratic government are not to be taken lightly. Even the American experience assumed a unified set of Christian (mainly variants of deistic and Protestant) theological precepts. Law was based on the prior conception of agreed principles of political propriety. The formation of these principles can be found in many different theologically articulated forms, including the religious wars between Catholics and Protestants and between various Protes-

tant groups as well. Nor was the body of precept within the Catholic church much more unified. Certainly the conflicts over conciliarism and the role of the church councils, not to speak of the nationalization of the church itself within each country, all testify to the explicitly political consequences of religion. These issues were so important to politics that much of the process of secularization can itself be traced to the search for some mutually agreeable and satisfactory common denominator of precept in order to render politics more secular. [See CHRISTIANITY.]

In the United States this was most clearly recognized in the works of Brooks and Henry Adams, both of whom saw the modern economic state, with its emphasis on instrumental values, economic exchange, and corporate finance, as destroying the implicit basis of the original Christian values. Nowhere is this more explicit than in Henry Adams' essay on Mont-Saint-Michel (1904; see also Brooks Adams 1898). Such views, which tended to idealize the classical and medieval civilizations, were romantic expressions of this religious ideal. But in addition to energy, there was doctrine and creed. The church militant was not always composed of simple stuff. Even in Catholic Spain during the "golden century," the conquistadors, who combined the adoration of the Virgin with great greed in plundering the New World and founding an empire, were vastly different in their political aims from the various religious orders, Jesuit, Benedictine, and Dominican, and these in turn had their constitutionalists, such as Juan de Mariana, Francisco Suárez, and Bellarmine (Lewis 1954).

The secularization of political norms can be seen as occurring in three historic steps. The first was nationalization of the church. By this means the political universalism of the church, symbolized in the term "Holy Roman Empire," was restricted, and various national churches arose.

The second step was the extension of that process to government. It was symbolized in the expression "divine right of kings," whereby authority was traced to the Deity through the principle of royal inheritance and kinship. This established the idea of a sovereign government as a legitimate unit with rights to protect itself against external sacerdotal power.

The third step was the growth of Protestantism, associated first with the unfolding of Christian principles through equity and with the radicalization of instrumental values. The transition was particularly significant because Protestantism emerged as a particular religious ideology with a mutually reinforcing synthesis between sacred values and instrumental objects germane to industrialization. In this sense, Protestantism was the mode of transition from the more explicitly religious form of government to a more secular one, which merely reflected religious values. This is why the roots of modern Western constitutional ideas are so deeply embedded in the Protestant ideal of the community. [See PROTESTANT POLITICAL THOUGHT.]

In a sense, the secularization of religion emerged as a result of the utter loneliness of Protestantism, which in Calvin's doctrine excluded even the church from participation in individual salvation. Weber makes the point that this is the singular difference between Catholic and Protestant doctrine, and the result was an emphasis on an individualism held in check by the concept of a calling embodying good works and sobriety. Rationality was reflected in a political community of individuals. Thus, self-control became the founding ethic of representative government, in conjunction with the economic doctrine of capitalism. Catholic doctrine, in sharp contrast, "punishing the heretic but indulgent to the sinner," retained a conception of the organic community that, although not necessarily antagonistic to decentralized government, did not support its basis in individualism and the doctrine of individual representation (Weber 1904–1905; McNeil 1954).

The consequences of Protestantism and Dutch, British, and American capitalism helped to create the conditions of secularization, with a greater degree of emphasis on legal and constitutional political devices. Weber quotes John Wesley: "I fear wherever riches have increased, the essence of religion has decreased in the same proportion" (Weber 1904–1905, p. 175 in the 1958 edition). This view is central to modern secular democratic government, where law has replaced religion as the foundation of the community. Thus, secularization in political terms is important in the West because, as a process containing a constitutional element the object of which is to establish a framework of government responsive to change, it leads to an explicit acceptance of the idea of the sovereignty of the people. Secularization paid particular attention to the accumulation of wealth as a duty, which favored rapid economic growth. The process is its own problem, however. Secular and decentralized government has wrestled with the question of how to retain the idea of obligation and responsibility in the face of continuous radical secularization.

It should not be assumed that there is a linear progression from centralized to decentralized or from sacred to secular systems. The opposite occurred (and in a peaceful manner) in Weimar Germany. Legitimacy was withdrawn from the constitutional government when the voters freely chose the Nazi party. This implies that the norms of a secular and decentralized system were relatively weak and insufficiently institutionalized. It also means that such a system can operate only when self-control and nonpolitical restraints on behavior predominate.

## Secular and decentralized governments

As secularization occurred in Western societies, theological obligations were changed into codes of civic responsibility. Law replaced religion as the basis of political norms. With the rising prosperity of Europe, there developed a general belief that free, democratic governments with maximum political participation for all would provide a beneficial political condition. Indeed, struggles during the nineteenth century were over the speed and thoroughness with which constitutional democracy would incorporate the entire membership of a system rather than over structural principles of government. [See DEMOCRACY.]

A view of government analogous to the approach of classical economics was widely accepted. The community is composed of voters, who are like consumers, and their choice is tantamount to consumer sovereignty. The election system represents the market, in which voters choose their representatives on the basis of stated preferences. Government, consisting of parliament and cabinet as well as administrative cadres, is similar to the productive unit and manufactures decisions, which the public evaluates through the electoral mechanism. The courts are present to ensure that the rules of the system are not violated.

The principles on which the system works include a high level of information, rationality as an attribute of voting and decision making, and equal representation (Downs 1957; Easton 1966). Such principles underlie the American form of presidential government and the utilitarian systems advocated by John Stuart Mill and the Benthamites in England. Advocates of this form emphasize the improvement of information, the uses of education in order to reach rationality (only the informed voter can be rational), and, in particular, the improvement of electoral systems in order to achieve the maximum reproduction of public wants in a representative chamber. Hence, for example, one of the problems considered most important is whether proportional representation is preferable to simple plurality voting or some combination of weighted balloting or lists. [See ELECTIONS, *article* on ELECTORAL SYSTEMS.] Important questions also arise about the role of political parties in government. How do parties, acting as agents by which public desires are transformed into government cognizance, facilitate the political process? In this respect political parties are designed to emphasize certain publicly held priorities and make them explicit, so that as the problems confronting government become more complex and individuals cannot make their views known on all of them, politicians stand for some symposium of priorities and on this basis are accepted or rejected by the voters.

The principle of majority rule implies in effect that the rightness of a doctrine is measured by the degree of support it obtains and that support creates power. Hence, majority rule is a principle of power which credits the rationality of the majority and elevates reason, plus numbers, over abstract morality. It is because of this that instrumentalities begin to take on their own moral proprieties. [See MAJORITY RULE.]

Not all democratic polities accepted this highly individualistic form of government. Two alternative forms, one older and one very modern, have stressed the idea of the organic community rather than the more mechanistic doctrine of individualism. The first of these forms, an extension of medieval doctrine, incorporates Catholic beliefs in the context of a decentralized state. This includes various specific approaches to democratic government, such as Christian socialism and Christian democracy. The second form is democratic socialism, which emphasizes the democratic state as a means of fulfilling conditions of equality and freedom in conjunction with the development of the moral and material basis of the community.

Both of these forms see an inadequacy in democracy, resulting from a contradiction between private ownership of the means of production and the maintenance of civic obligation. How can government be secular and decentralized yet retain authority? If the achievement of democratic government is that it is secular in practice and therefore free of formalized commitments to a higher set of priorities than those desired by a majority, the problem is how to retain that self-control implicit in Calvin's formula. One answer is to study the new roles in government, particularly those which provide a "calling," such as the roles of civil servants, of members of professions, and of scientists, whose sense of responsibility and commitment to the exchange of free ideas is perhaps one of the most important characteristics of democratic government in highly industrial societies. [See BUREAUCRACY and SCIENCE, article on SCIENCE–GOVERNMENT RE-

LATIONS; see also Friedrich 1937; Jouvenel 1963; Sartori 1962.]

Types of democratic governments.    Democratic governments require further differentiation. First, they can be divided into unitary and federal forms. Unitary governments are based on the position that all powers not otherwise reserved belong to a central government. Federal governments take the position that residual powers lie with the component geographical units which make up the federation. [See FEDERALISM.]

Second, they can be classified as presidential and parliamentary forms. In a true presidential system, a president elected by the population is responsible to them, rather than to the legislature. The legislature, in turn, is responsible to the population which elects it, and not to the president. This provides checks and balances, with the public acting as arbiters during periodic elections, held at fixed intervals. [See PRESIDENTIAL GOVERNMENT.] The parliamentary system shows parliament supreme, with a prime minister responsible to it and holding office at its pleasure. Through votes of confidence and changes in parliamentary party membership, a government can fall, in which case a new general election to parliament is necessary; the majority or plurality of seats won by a political party provides a mandate to form a government. Under such a system the president (or monarch) is largely a figurehead. Where the parliamentary government is a constitutional monarchy, the transition from earlier forms of monarchy has generally been smooth, rather than abrupt, and has been achieved by virtue of internal structural changes. Notable cases are Holland, Denmark, Sweden, Norway, and Great Britain.

Much of the present concern of democratic government lies with the problems associated with the growing complexity of modern life and the increasingly broad responsibilities which individuals expect a secular government to take upon itself. Whereas the problem in the first half of the twentieth century was the improvement of electoral and representation methods and of local government and administration, the present emphasis is on the work load of parliaments and congresses. Both federal and unitary systems today accept the principle of one man, one vote, and "popular sovereignty" tends to mean a form of parliamentary representation embodying territorial and demographic bases. How to maintain debate on important issues and get through a heavy legislative work load is therefore a critical matter. In Great Britain, for example, the widening of the franchise was accompanied by the decline of the role of the private-member bill as the work load of the committees increased. Parliament divides according to the lines laid down by the party whips, and a free vote, each member voting according to his conscience, becomes rare (see Wheare 1955; McKenzie 1955). Discipline in parliament has given rise to the term "cabinet dictatorship." [See PARLIAMENTARY GOVERNMENT.]

How well parliamentary or cabinet forms of decentralized representative government work depends a great deal on how political parties carry on the work of government. Different structural rules obviously affect this. Since all decentralized and democratic forms of government have some means to control the executive, this may lead, in multiparty systems, to cabinet instability, as it did in France and does in Italy. The stability of such parliamentary governments, therefore, depends on the stability of coalitions. Where two parliamentary parties are characteristic, instability is rare, partly because of rigorous party discipline. [See PARTIES, POLITICAL, *article on* PARTY SYSTEMS; INTEREST GROUPS; *see also* Laski 1951.]

How to improve decentralized and democratic government has posed serious problems of political theory. It is not surprising, therefore, that highly individualistic conceptions of democracy have been replaced by notions of group representation, block voting, and the responsiveness of government to various groups, such as professional bodies, business lobbies, trade unions, cooperative movements, civic and veterans' organizations, churches, and educational and cultural groups. [See PLURALISM *and* POLITICAL GROUP ANALYSIS; *see also* S. E. Finer 1958.] Indeed, so important have group theories become that interest groups have been called in Britain an "anonymous empire."

All of these questions relate directly to the relations between community and government. More precisely, they are devoted to an examination of intervening variables between community and government, such as political parties and interest groups, and even of subgroups within government itself. (See Figure 3.)

### Government in new nations

Governments formed in new nations—those achieving independence after 1945—present some of the most interesting and challenging material confronting constitutional experts, political theorists, and politicians alike. New governments tend to include characteristics of all the forms we have discussed (Apter 1965). For example, in Africa and parts of Asia there are attachments to primitive governments, which remain in competition with central government for the loyalties of the population. Regional clusters associated with a religious or linguistic affiliation may represent powerful primordial loyalties, denying legitimacy to a central government or countering it with a preference for local primordial attachments. Thus, unity and legitimacy within the context of a nation are urgent problems facing political leaders. Inasmuch as certain aspects of primitive government represent a rightful heritage, it may be that traditional qualities of legitimacy should be applied to modern governmental forms, as has been attempted under such ideological forms as "African socialism" or "communocracy." [See NATION.]

Furthermore, new nations commonly emphasize the positive role of government as the great "engine" of social change, actively intervening in all aspects of life, from family relationships to educational opportunities, from road building to the development of local airways. Government in this respect is seen as an independent variable, much as it is, for example, in the Soviet Union.

At the same time, most constitutional patterns follow the line of Western parliamentary government. With sufficient control over parliament, through the instrumentality of party discipline, it is possible to retain popular government, based on

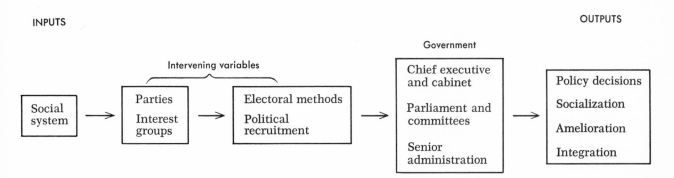

*Figure 3 — Intervening variables relating to democratic government*

parliamentary practice and a cabinet system, with few formal checks on executive authority.

In a very real sense, then, the governments of new nations tend to become amalgams of the other types we have discussed—theocratic, communist, fascist, and democratic. Their roots in primitive government become identified in normative terms, with a mythical past providing a national identity. The communist emphasis on puritanism, public ownership, and discipline is represented in the recruitment of a developmental elite and in its method of exercising power. The representation of corporate functional groups has much in common with fascist governments. And, the populist democratic emphasis and the pattern of parliamentary government represent Western democratic ideals and some of its procedures.

All this is confusing because the various systems of government described appear to be so antithetical that it would seem impossible to blend them into a viable and effective system. This is to a certain extent true; hence, virtually all new governments are in the process of changing into some more stable type. It is not surprising that quite often what holds such a government together is allegiance to a particular political leader, associated with revolution or the development of a mass movement. Indeed, the outstanding common feature of these new governments is their dependence on a personalized leader supported by a dominant political party. This tends to be the case whether or not the system is *formally* a single-party state, as long as there is a dominant party which is capable of controlling large regional areas. In the special case of new governments, therefore, the crucial factors are the relationship between the leader of the government and the leader of the party, and the role of the party. Ordinarily the first two are the same person, and the party operates government.

In terms of the various models employed here, new governments incline in theory to the position that government is an independent variable. In practice, however, government is likely to be an expression of an elite which manipulates a mass party that is itself a reflection of a wide diversity of interests. In other words, government and social system tend to become incorporated into the broad concept of a single party. Party becomes the independent variable, with government the intervening one, and social system the dependent one. (Even where there is more than one party, the situation is not very different. There may be several dominant regional—tribal or linguistic—parties, rather than one party; however, none are deeply committed to a single ideology, and in this they differ sharply from communist or fascist parties.)

The situation illustrated in Figure 4 is found in its clearest form under conditions of radical transformation from dependent to independent status or directly after a revolution. Since the framework within which the parliamentary and cabinet systems operate is not entirely eliminated, it intervenes between government and changes in the social system. In other words, the role of government, derived through the formal decision-making process, is the making of technical decisions, while the main lines of policy are generally laid down by governmental leaders, who are also senior party leaders. Classic examples are Nyerere's Tanzania, Ghana under Nkrumah, Nasser's Egypt, and Algeria under Ben Bella. [See MODERNIZATION.]

INPUTS                                    OUTPUTS

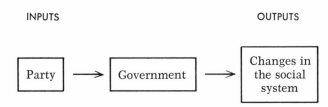

**Figure 4 — Government in the pluralistic single-party state**

How can new governments be evaluated? Normative criteria involve those associated with democratic systems and would include the adequacy of the protection of individual rights, and the degree of pluralism tolerated in government and parliament. On this score governments in new nations show a mixed record. Some, such as Ghana under Nkrumah, have a declaration of fundamental principles to which the president has sworn adherence, but these declarations cannot be enforced in the courts. Nigeria has a bill of rights. Burma emphasizes the social ownership of the means of production. Ghana and India have preventive-detention ordinances. It is safe to say that the protection of civil rights and liberties varies less with governmental form than with the general spirit in which government functions.

Since the legitimacy of new governments tends to be rather weak and is often associated with highly personalistic leaders (a very vulnerable structural condition), another normative criterion is how successfully a government develops primordial loyalties. The quality of such attachments provides a basis for evaluation of new governments and describes the depth of its emerging political culture. [See POLITICAL CULTURE.]

Primordial attachments tend to become linked to problems of economic growth. Planning, technical skills, manpower surveys, and the like, are important areas of governmental decision making.

[*See* ECONOMIC GROWTH.] In addition, they are moral or normative concepts associated with the objectives which commonly take the form of socialism, since socialism explicitly validates a development ideal and is represented, through party and government, in evolutionary ideal terms. Socialism also justifies political demands for personal sacrifice and loyalty. How well socialism (or its variants) can embody new economic rationality and enforce commitment to savings, work, education, and development becomes a third evaluative criterion. [*See* SOCIALISM.]

Behavioral consequences of normative beliefs thus emerge. A combination of political norms, nationalist primordial sentiments, and philosophical ideological expressions of socialism combine to form the motivational system of the society. Structurally these elements are organized less frequently in parliamentary or representative institutions than in functional or corporate bodies within and around a political party. Party wings and various related interest groups are the devices that link individuals to the government.

Despite all the integrative efforts, the most striking feature of new governments is the behavioral weakness in their population vis-à-vis government. Changing allegiances and ritualization of authority, not to speak of the stresses and strains of rapid economic change and industrialization, all require much study of motivation, of the sources of personal identity, and of learning. Indeed, what is now called the identity problem, involving examination of the conditions under which individuals are able to establish a set of personality boundaries compatible with changing normative and structural conditions, is a growing concern. Only a few studies of the relationship between government and identity have been attempted, though many problems of governing derive from the search for identity (Pye 1962; Erikson 1958; Edelman 1964).

## Contemporary research and theory

The author has tried to demonstrate a few of the emphases associated with the study of government and has employed both normative and structural variables to differentiate types of systems. Historically, the most elaborately studied aspect of government has been its normative side, which is still important in trying to determine how governments will evolve because it helps us to relate political means and ends. The structural dimension, almost as well studied in the literature as the normative, has been heavily weighted in favor of the study of the constitution as the foundation of government. Different constitutional systems have been distinguished through enumeration of their characteristics. More recently, work on the structural dimension, developed along the lines of institutionalist analysis and heavily influenced by the work of Max Weber, Karl Mannheim, and others, has related government to art, religion, philosophy, education, and other social institutions. The main concern of these scholars has been to study democracy as a universal system originating in Western civilization and to contrast it with less evolved forms of government, such as monarchy or oligarchy.

This work led to the development of functional analysis in the study of government, with its emphasis on the derivation of more-universalized comparative categories. Such studies have by and large employed one of two forms of systems theory. [*See* SYSTEMS ANALYSIS.] The first tends to follow the organismic analogy. Government is seen in its intimate relationships to society. A good set of functional categories for government will do the following: allow comparison of widely diverse forms and actions in terms of their implications for government as a whole; segregate critical activities from less critical ones; allow one to observe explicit levels of explanatory theory (Almond & Coleman 1960; Apter 1965).

The second emphasis in contemporary systems theory follows a mechanistic tradition. Some of the recent work, based on theories of coalitions, is originally derived from economic theories and attempts to use principles of rational calculation and maximization in order to predict political group behavior [*see* COALITIONS]. Several of the efforts to deal with coalitions begin with the group basis of politics and draw their original inspiration from the writings of A. F. Bentley [*see* POLITICAL GROUP ANALYSIS *and the biography of* BENTLEY]. The most powerful form of systems analysis following this tradition is to be found in cybernetics models and game theory. These represent more-generalized structural models than the ones used for functional analysis. The rules derived for one unit apply to all group behavior. In the game-theory approach these deal primarily with the consequences for action of communications and information. Systems analysis of this type involves analysis of attempts, according to explicit rules, to maximize gains and minimize losses. Formulation of such highly rationalistic models can help us to understand political competition and government actions in priority and other settings. [*See* GAME THEORY; *see also* Downs 1957; Snyder 1961.]

Emphasis on groups has also given rise to an important literature with behavioral, as well as structural, implications. Behavioral and structural aspects of government depend on the analysis of government as a group, with reference to its size, its patterns of communications, and the ways in which motivation and memory are structured within it. Work in this area draws on the theories of psychologists, e.g., Kurt Lewin, R. Lippitt, and Theodore Newcomb, concerning leadership, interaction processes, cohesiveness, control over deviance, internalization of norms, etc., and tends to treat decision making as the main object of analysis. [See DECISION MAKING; see also Cartwright & Zander 1953.] Today such an emphasis can be integrated with informational analysis, group theory, and game theory in certain cybernetics models applied to government. This form of systems theory uses the concept of an information grid, in which a political system represents the flow of messages or of "cues" and government the critical "transformer," i.e., a coding and decision-making instrument. It is concerned with adaptability, and emphasizes the capacity of different systems to learn and adjust, with government performing an essentially creative role. One modern political theory which attempts to bring together these functional and other emphases very systematically is Karl Deutsch's application (1963) of the general cybernetics model, which is an attempt to solve problems of learning, creativity, and adaptation in politics.

To account for these new developments, a more general way of analyzing governments is required. The formulation illustrated in Figure 5 helps to move the analysis of government to a highly generalized level, incorporating the various approaches, new and old, in a single model. In this model political behavior is the independent variable. Political norms and structures can therefore be treated as intervening variables. Their effectiveness is subject to change because political structure is bound and limited by the legitimacy pattern established by the relationships between political behavior and political norms. Political structure can be seen in terms of its consequences for decision making, which in turn is designed to maintain a sustained pattern of political behavior consonant with the maintenance of norms.

It is possible, of course, to enlarge the complexity of this model. More important, it is necessary to rotate these variables for different purposes and to hold each of them independent in turn, in order to estimate their effects. Many of the variations in approach to the study of government derive from holding different of these variables independent without realizing the specific methodological implications of doing so. The selection of variables to be held independent is entirely arbitrary. To estimate the effectiveness of different forms of government, however, it might be useful to treat political structure as the independent variable and see how various types—democratic, totalitarian, centralized, decentralized, monistic, pluralistic, monopolistic, competitive—affect both political norms and political behavior. How does each of these alternative types allow political learning to take place? How does government preserve continuity? How does it affect the course of change? In addition to rotating the variables, it is possible to add new intervening variables. These may be normative ones, such as ideologies, or structural ones, such as political parties, administrative organizations, and the like.

Any general theory of government will require a model which is sufficiently explicit to account for the limits of variation, sufficiently flexible to handle diverse methodological emphasis, and empirical enough to be fully operationalized. We are still far from able to construct such a model, but the foregoing discussion shows that at least the foundations of the model and the theory have been laid. Still needed are improved techniques of gathering data, as well as analytical paradigms by means of which such data can be related to the appropriate theory. These concerns connect the analysis and study of government to the philosophy of science by emphasizing logical and epistemological problems, and also cause us to speculate about the application of highly advanced mathematical and statistical techniques and computer programming to the careful mapping and testing of propositions about government. The concept of government thus remains

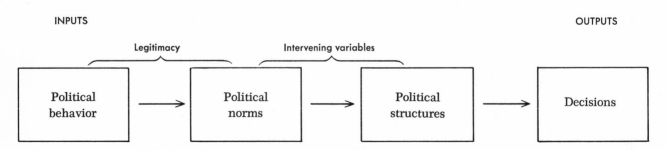

*Figure 5 — A generalized model of government*

a critical point of departure for both the evaluation of the normative issues of political life and the structural and behavioral analysis of politics.

DAVID E. APTER

[Related to the concept of government are the entries ADJUDICATION; ADMINISTRATION; ELECTIONS; LEGISLATION; POLITICAL EXECUTIVE; REPRESENTATION. Guides to other relevant material may be found under LAW; POLITICAL ANTHROPOLOGY; POLITICAL SCIENCE.]

BIBLIOGRAPHY

ADAMS, BROOKS 1898 The Law of Civilization and Decay. New York: Macmillan.
ADAMS, HENRY (1904) 1963 Mont-Saint-Michel and Chartres. New York: Collier.
ALMOND, GABRIEL A.; and COLEMAN, JAMES S. (editors) 1960 The Politics of the Developing Areas. Princeton Univ. Press.
ALMOND, GABRIEL A.; and VERBA, SIDNEY 1963 The Civic Culture: Political Attitudes and Democracy in Five Nations. Princeton Univ. Press.
APTER, DAVID E. 1965 The Politics of Modernization. Univ. of Chicago Press.
BARKER, ERNEST (1942) 1958 Reflections on Government. New York: Oxford Univ. Press.
BARNARD, FREDERICK M. 1965 Herder's Social and Political Thought. Oxford: Clarendon.
BRYCE, JAMES 1921 Modern Democracies. 2 vols. New York: Macmillan.
BRZEZINSKI, ZBIGNIEW K. 1962 Ideology and Power in Soviet Politics. New York: Praeger.
CARTWRIGHT, DORWIN; and ZANDER, ALVIN (editors) (1953) 1960 Group Dynamics: Research and Theory. 2d ed. Evanston, Ill.: Row, Peterson. → A good review of the psychological materials on group behavior.
DAVIES, REGINALD TREVOR 1937 The Golden Century of Spain. London: Macmillan.
DEUTSCH, KARL W. 1963 The Nerves of Government: Models of Political Communication and Control. New York: Free Press.
DICEY, ALBERT V. (1885) 1961 Introduction to the Study of the Law of the Constitution. 10th ed. With an introduction by E. C. S. Wade. London: Macmillan; New York: St. Martins. → First published as Lectures Introductory to the Study of the Law of the Constitution.
DOWNS, ANTHONY 1957 An Economic Theory of Democracy. New York: Harper.
EASTON, DAVID 1957 Political Structures and Processes. World Politics 9:383–400.
EASTON, DAVID 1965 A Systems Analysis of Political Life. New York: Wiley.
EASTON, DAVID (editor) 1966 Varieties of Political Theory. Englewood Cliffs, N.J.: Prentice-Hall. → See especially "An Individualistic Theory of Political Process," by James M. Buchanan.
EDELMAN, JACOB M. 1964 The Symbolic Uses of Politics. Urbana: Univ. of Illinois Press.
ERIKSON, ERIK H. (1958) 1962 Young Man Luther: A Study in Psychoanalysis and History. Austin Riggs Monograph No. 4. New York: Norton.
FAIRMAN, H. W. 1958 The Kingship Rituals of Egypt. Pages 74–104 in Samuel H. Hooke (editor), Myth, Ritual and Kingship: Essays on the Theory and Practice of Kingship in the Ancient Near East and in Israel. Oxford: Clarendon.

FALLERS, LLOYD A. (1956) 1965 Bantu Bureaucracy: A Century of Political Evolution. Univ. of Chicago Press.
FINER, HERMAN (1932) 1949 The Theory and Practice of Modern Government. Rev. ed. New York: Holt.
FINER, SAMUEL E. (1958) 1962 Anonymous Empire: A Study of the Lobby in Great Britain. London: Pall Mall.
FRIEDRICH, CARL J. (1937) 1950 Constitutional Government and Democracy: Theory and Practice in Europe and America. Rev. ed. Boston: Ginn. → First published as Constitutional Government and Politics: Nature and Development.
FRIEDRICH, CARL J.; and BRZEZINSKI, ZBIGNIEW K. (1956) 1965 Totalitarian Dictatorship and Autocracy. 2d ed., rev. Cambridge, Mass.: Harvard Univ. Press.
GASH, NORMAN 1953 Politics in the Age of Peel: A Study in the Technique of Parliamentary Representation, 1830–1850. London and New York: Longmans.
GIERKE, OTTO VON (1881) 1958 Political Theories of the Middle Age. Cambridge Univ. Press. → First published as "Die publicistischen Lehren des Mittelalters," a section of Volume 3 of Gierke's Das deutsche Genossenschaftsrecht. Translated, with a famous introduction, by Frederic William Maitland.
HIGNETT, CHARLES (1952) 1962 A History of the Athenian Constitution to the End of the Fifth Century B.C. Oxford: Clarendon.
JOUVENEL, BERTRAND DE 1963 The Pure Theory of Politics. New Haven: Yale Univ. Press.
LAQUEUR, WALTER; and LABEDZ, LEOPOLD (editors) 1962 Polycentrism: The New Factor in International Communism. New York: Praeger.
LASKI, HAROLD J. (1925) 1957 A Grammar of Politics. 4th ed. London: Allen & Unwin.
LASKI, HAROLD J. (1935) 1956 The State in Theory and Practice. London: Allen & Unwin.
LASKI, HAROLD J. (1951) 1962 Reflections on the Constitution: The House of Commons, the Cabinet [and] the Civil Service. Manchester Univ. Press. → Published posthumously.
LASSWELL, HAROLD D. (1930) 1960 Psychopathology and Politics. New ed., with afterthoughts by the author. New York: Viking.
LEWIS, EWART (editor) 1954 Medieval Political Ideas. 2 vols. New York: Knopf.
McKENZIE, ROBERT T. (1955) 1963 British Political Parties: The Distribution of Power Within the Conservative and Labour Parties. 2d ed. London: Heinemann; New York: St. Martins. → A paperback edition was published in 1964 by Praeger.
McNEIL, JOHN T. 1954 The History and Character of Calvinism. New York: Oxford Univ. Press.
OSTROGORSKII, MOISEI I. (1902) 1964 Democracy and the Organization of Political Parties. 2 vols. Edited and abridged by Seymour M. Lipset. Chicago: Quadrangle. → An abridged edition of a 1902 English translation from the French.
PAYNE, STANLEY G. 1961 Falange: A History of Spanish Fascism. Stanford Studies in History, Economics and Political Science, No. 22. Stanford Univ. Press.
PIPES, RICHARD (1954) 1964 The Formation of the Soviet Union. Rev. ed. Cambridge, Mass.: Harvard Univ. Press.
PYE, LUCIAN W. 1962 Politics, Personality, and Nation Building: Burma's Search for Identity. New Haven: Yale Univ. Press.
RIKER, WILLIAM H. 1962 The Theory of Political Coalitions. New Haven: Yale Univ. Press.

SARTORI, GIOVANNI 1962 *Democratic Theory.* Detroit, Mich.: Wayne State Univ. Press. → A paperback edition was published in 1965 by Praeger.

SNYDER, RICHARD C. 1961 *Game Theory and the Analysis of Political Behavior.* New York: Free Press.

TALMON, JACOB L. (1952) 1965 *The Origins of Totalitarian Democracy.* 2d ed. New York: Praeger.

ULAM, ADAM B. 1960 *The Unfinished Revolution: An Essay on the Sources of Influence of Marxism and Communism.* New York: Random House.

WALLAS, GRAHAM (1908) 1962 *Human Nature in Politics.* 4th ed. Gloucester, Mass.: Smith.

WEBER, MAX (1904–1905) 1930 *The Protestant Ethic and the Spirit of Capitalism.* Translated by Talcott Parsons, with a foreword by R. H. Tawney. London: Allen & Unwin; New York: Scribner. → First published in German. The 1930 edition has been reprinted frequently. A paperback edition was published in 1958 by Scribner.

WHEARE, KENNETH C. 1955 *Government by Committee: An Essay on the British Constitution.* Oxford: Clarendon.

# GOVERNMENT COMMISSIONS

*See* COMMISSIONS, GOVERNMENT; REGULATION OF INDUSTRY.

# GOVERNMENT STATISTICS

*Statistical data generated by government sources are referred to and cited in many articles in this encyclopedia, including* CENSUS; ECONOMIC DATA; FALLACIES, STATISTICAL; INTERNATIONAL TRADE; SAMPLE SURVEYS; VITAL STATISTICS; *and the biographies of* QUETELET *and* WILLCOX. *This article is confined to over-all aspects: the relation of statistics to the establishment of national states; the range of substantive matters on which statistics are collected; the ways in which that collection is organized in different parts of the world; the business and professional environment within which government statisticians work; the problems and difficulties they face in both developed and underdeveloped countries.*

Government statistics in the modern state are an essential part of a wider information system. The first compilers of statistics did not make a sharp distinction between numerical and other facts, and it is still true that numerical data complement other kinds of information in the process by which decisions are made in private and public undertakings. These data are as indispensable in a centralized as in a pluralistic society; as important in the deliberations of government itself as they are in the firms, commissariats, or other groupings concerned with getting out a product. The effectiveness of the market mechanism of a free society depends on the quality of the information on which its entities base their decisions. Western European economic planning consists in large measure in the provision of supplementary information to private enterprise. A tightly controlled, centralized system needs, more than anything else, a feedback—of which the statistics it collects are a pivotal element—if it is not to be the unwitting victim of its own concentration of power.

## Statistics and the state

The history, the present condition, and the problems yet to be solved in government statistics reflect the circumstances of modern national states. A governmental administrative apparatus is a principal user of official statistics, and its existence and efficiency are a main condition for securing them. While sporadic attempts at counting people or goods were known in classical times and in the ancient empires of the Middle East, there is virtually no continuity between these and modern official compilations.

**Modern history.** Like so much else that pertains to the modern state, its statistical system emerged about the time of the French Revolution. One of the early acts of the Constituent Assembly was to see to the publication of a statistical account of the resources of France, prepared by Lavoisier. In 1800 the Bureau de Statistique was created in Paris. The assembly required a census (Articles I and II of the Law of July 22, 1791, according to Faure 1918, p. 277), which was duly taken in 1791. François de Neufchâteau, in a circular dated the 15th of Fructidor of the year VI (presumably September 1, 1799), saw the census—with characteristic revolutionary exaggeration—as "the measure of the strength, the source of the wealth, the political thermometer of the power of states" (Faure 1918, p. 284).

Just as British nationality erupted less violently than did that of France, so its statistical system had a more gradual inception. Early landmarks were the *Domesday Book* of William the Conqueror in 1086; the record of customs dues collected in the Port of London in the time of Edward III; the Tudor counts of men and resources in the face of the danger of war; and the registration of deaths, initiated by Henry VIII in 1532, when there was widespread fear of the plague.

The dependence of statehood on a statistical system has become more and more clear with the passing of time. The mercantilist writers of the epoch of the absolute monarchs were concerned with the power of the state in peace and war; the monarch and his advisers had to have measures of the stock of men and other resources [see ECONOM-IC THOUGHT, *article on* MERCANTILIST THOUGHT]. The British and French colonial administrations in North America, and later the British in India, took censuses, that of the Canadian province of Quebec in 1666 being the first of modern censuses (Linder 1959, p. 330). With democracy there came to be other reasons for statistical compilations. In the first of the major federal constitutions, that of the United States, a means of determining the political weight of the contracting entities was required; their relative populations seemed to provide this, and the first of the regular series of decennial censuses of the United States was taken in 1790, although a printed schedule was not employed until 1830. Confederation in Canada in 1867 was based on a similar provision for representation by population and was followed by a census in 1871; the Australian colonies were united in 1900, and the formation of a statistical office followed in 1905.

Since World War II dynastic, colonial, tribal, and other political forms have been displaced by national organizations throughout the world. Along with attempts to provide themselves with constitutions, elections, and the beginnings of modern industry, new countries have set up statistical systems, both as a precondition for development and as a symbol of nationhood. The new statistical style is far more ambitious than the colonial model that preceded, in proportion as over-all national aims are more extended than colonial aims. An important role in promoting the extension and quality of statistical work was played by the League of Nations, through its Committee of Statistical Experts, and subsequently by the United Nations, through its statistical and population commissions. Under UN auspices a world population census was attempted about 1950 and again in 1960, with a high degree of national cooperation. In the decade of the 1860s censuses were taken in which 17 per cent of the estimated population of the planet was counted; over ten times as many people were counted in censuses around 1960, and these constituted 67 per cent of the population of the globe (*Demographic Yearbook 1962*, p. 1). Results are not uniformly satisfactory; a study of the quality of statistical organization and statistical output of the various countries would undoubtedly show a close relation to the quality of governmental administration in general. Chile is better organized statistically than Burma; Burma than Cambodia.

**Government statistics classified.** A wide range of statistical data has come to be regarded as appropriate for government compilation and publication.

*Classification by source.* One way to classify government statistics is according to source: households for population censuses, family-budget surveys, employment and unemployment counts; business establishments for production and employment data; incorporated and unincorporated firms for profit figures; national-government revenue departments for foreign trade and income tax accounts. The categories are not exclusive; households and commercial establishments often provide complementary data bearing on the same matter.

Where economic statistics are essentially a summary record of transactions, they are in principle available through questions addressed to either of the parties to the transaction; retail prices may be ascertained through surveys of retail stores with respect to goods sold or through household surveys with respect to goods bought. If the business establishment is more often used, this is a matter of the greater availability of records and the larger number of transactions implicitly covered by one report; in underdeveloped countries, where business is less organized, questions addressed to the consumer are relatively more favored. For data on employment and unemployment, the household seems on the whole as satisfactory a source as the business establishment. In North America the contest between rival figures of unemployment has been an important stimulus to improvement not only of the sampling and questioning techniques used in household surveys but also of the administration of unemployment insurance itself, in respects that go far beyond statistics.

*Classification by time of publication.* A grosser form of classification is by the indication of temporal trends that series give. Some are issued promptly and tell the latest news: weekly railway carloadings, department-store sales, stocks of wheat in central elevators, stocks of the several metals. At the other extreme are full censuses of industry and population, taken only at long intervals; their results are released over a period of time, beginning within a few months after enumeration and continuing for some years after the data are collected, and they are valuable for the cross-sectional relations that they reveal. Because of this configuration of prompt summary data and delayed details, the national economic picture of a country with respect to any moment of time is only gradually filled in, over the five or ten years subsequent to that time.

Government statistical activities include analysis and interpretation as well as data collection. Although knowledge of analysis helps in gathering data, and vice versa, the two specializations are different. An example of the division of labor on this basis is that existing between the United States Bureau of the Census and the Department of Labor on statistics of employment and unemployment; the former agency has the responsibility for gathering the material, the latter for the official analysis.

**Expansion in modernization.** A statistical system seems to start with population censuses and foreign trade as the main items; other kinds of data—for example, counts of starts and completions of residential construction—are added as time goes on. As a country develops, the need for statistics mounts with the variety and difficulty of decisions required by an increased division of labor in the economy. A demand for factual justification, in terms of which people can explain their decisions to themselves and to others, seems to have characterized the North American continent from an early date. General Francis A. Walker, speaking before the International Statistical Institute, pointed this out in 1893: "A strong passion for statistics early developed itself in the life of our people, and such statesmen and publicists as Hamilton . . . became working statisticians. . . . No government in the world has ever lavished money and labor . . . more cheerfully and patiently in this respect" (quoted in Cummings 1918, p. 573). But this culture of facts is no longer confined to the United States, to those of English speech, or to Europeans; it is becoming world-wide.

The proposition that the statistics collected by any government are a function of its interests and responsibilities can be exemplified in the process of decolonization. When much of the world was under the hegemony of the states of western Europe, the statistical system centered on foreign trade. What was important for British administrators was the amount of rice exported from Burma, of jute exported from Bengal; the Netherlands wanted to know the amounts of coffee, sugar, and rubber exported from Java in the periods when each of these commodities was at its height. Another phase of colonial development was the land tax; the land tax made it both necessary and possible to have figures on acreages and production of the main crops. A further stage was some rudimentary concern with people, expressed by population censuses. The building of railways in India and Java, for instance, was followed by the collection of transport statistics—data that no one would have collected when oxcarts, proas, and the backs of men were the principal means of shipping commodities. And the evolution that occurred in the colonies in Asia was paralleled in Latin America, where the several governments, although independent, had interests nearly as restricted as those of the colonial powers.

The advent of independence in Asia and of the welfare state everywhere has increased the range of government statistics. Every country concerned with development is trying to expand its educational system, and statistics of schools, teachers, and pupils are nearly universal. In England and Wales educational statistics of a kind date back to the 1820s and 1830s, when public money was first given to the schools (Baines 1918, p. 377). Vital statistics are being gradually improved, a process that requires the inculcation of the habit of recording births and deaths not only on the part of the hierarchy of the civil registration system but also on the part of the medical profession and the public at large; such institutionalization will take at least a generation or two in the new countries. Meanwhile, sample surveys are being introduced, to observe the birth rate and its changes, as well as many other population and economic phenomena. Family-budget surveys, which had been foreshadowed by colonial governments in their moments of welfare-mindedness (a coolie-budget survey was made in the Netherlands Indies in the 1930s), are becoming more frequent; the government of India, through the Indian Statistical Institute in Calcutta, has been particularly active in this and other types of household survey.

## Organization of statistical services

Every government has sooner or later to consider the organizational framework within which its statistics will be collected. When left to themselves, individual departments of the central government tend to collect whatever data their administration generates, and they hardly separate the collection of such information from administrative control of their operations. When the act regulating the collection of duties in the United States was passed in 1789 (Cummings 1918, p. 579), it required the collector of customs to record ships' manifests and other information connected with trade; the series of foreign trade statistics for the United States accordingly dates from 1789. The British Post Office collects and publishes the returns of the postal service; the British Department of Inland Revenues, established in 1849, collects the estate and stamp duties, land taxes, and income taxes. But with increase of scale, such departments come to separate their statistical from their administrative work; the British Board of Trade formed within itself a statistical branch as early as 1833 (Baines 1918, p. 374). Subsequently, labor, local departments of agriculture, and many other departments or boards came to have their own statistical units, not only in the United Kingdom but in the United States, the British dominions, and the countries of western Europe. The Interstate Commerce Commission (ICC) of the United States was from the start insistent on securing data from the railways it regulated, and ICC publications constitute an important series.

Sometimes one of these agencies would be assigned the taking of a decennial census, a periodic task required of the registrar-general in England and Wales, whose continuing work was the civil register and vital statistics. In Canada the decennial census provided for in the British North America Act was the charge of an office established in the Department of Agriculture in 1905. But in all countries, increasing attention to statistics led to proposals for centralization in a specialized agency.

**Degree of centralization.** With the establishment of even small statistical offices within government departments, the work of statistics began to benefit from some degree of separation from the day-to-day exigencies of administration.

*Centralization in national government.* The collection into a single office of all the statistical activities of the national government was considered, in order to secure even more of the gains of specialization. To the argument of efficiency (concentration of specialized personnel and equipment to deal with the large scale of centralized statistical work) was added that of avoidance of duplication, a perennial hazard of government work and one which appeared in statistical work from the earliest days. Separating statistical work from the other work of government lessens the pressure on the statistician to distort his results to protect political or administrative interests—reference is made below to the judicial aspect of the statistician's function. The better coordination of a central system, moreover, ought to permit the recognition of gaps in data. It should also make easier the adoption of uniform classifications; it is highly desirable that production and exports, for instance, be recorded on the same commodity classification, so that comparisons may be possible. But anyone who knows the tendency to autonomy of the divisions of a governmental organization will realize that having the several compilations under a single roof is no automatic guarantee of uniformity; the several sections can pursue different courses. One special danger of a centralized organization is that it will become so self-contained as to be immune to the needs of the users of its data. Centralization offers high returns when the central organization is well coordinated internally and alert to the changing requirements of outside users.

The administrative argument for centralization

was early carried into effect, in one degree or another, in the Netherlands, Canada, Australia, Germany, and Italy. About the middle of the 19th century the Netherlands took important steps in this direction; in 1848 a statistical bureau was established in the Department of Home Affairs whose responsibilities were far wider than the tabulation of data generated in the department. Canada and Australia committed themselves to a statistical system that was centralized in the double sense that statistics were at least as much the affair of the central government as of the states or provinces or of any lower level of government and that among the agencies of the central government there was one with pre-eminence in the collection and tabulation of statistics in a number of different fields. The Canadian system has been in principle entirely centralized since the founding of the Dominion Bureau of Statistics in 1918. A degree of centralization was arranged in Germany with the establishment of the Imperial Statistical Office in 1872, the year after the establishment of the German Empire; in Italy centralization was begun in 1861, the year of the constitution of the monarchy, with a directorate of statistics that was the ancestor of the present Istituto Centrale di Statistica.

In the United States and the United Kingdom practice has evolved closer to the decentralized pole of the centralized–decentralized continuum. The means of coordination in the United Kingdom is an office in the Cabinet Secretariat that operates through a series of understandings with the heads of statistical divisions in the Board of Trade, the Ministry of Food, the Ministry of Agriculture, etc. All the statistical divisions in departments are directed by statistician members of the Professional, Scientific, and Technical Class, one of the five classes of the British civil service; appointments anywhere are open to members of the statistician class irrespective of where they are serving. The Treasury approves the expenditures of statistical departments, and on new expenditures they are advised by the Central Statistical Office.

The American arrangement is more formal; the Office of Statistical Standards of the Bureau of the Budget not only reviews all requests for funds to carry out statistical work within the federal government; its approval is required before any federal government questionnaire can be sent to ten or more respondents. This requirement dates back to the Federal Reports Act of 1942 and was intended to reduce the burden on respondents and to eliminate duplication. Where duplication exists, it not only is wasteful of government funds but also arouses the fiercest resentment of respondents who are required to answer the same questions more than once.

The best coordination does not consist exclusively of the negative injunctions of an enforcement agency. An example of a more positive kind is the collaboration of the U.S. Social Security Administration, essentially an operating agency, and the Bureau of the Census in the creation of a publication showing county business patterns based on Social Security Administration records. The U.S. Bureau of the Census has used tax records to eliminate business-census questionnaires for a million retail establishments without employees. By using Social Security records as a source of lists, the Bureau of the Census is able to take the economic censuses at reduced cost.

Coordination requires fine judgment at a thousand points. Should both the U.S. Bureau of Mines and the Bureau of the Census continue to secure mineral statistics? The Bureau of the Census collects benchmark data on an establishment basis every five years from all establishments within the scope of the census, assigning to the mining industry the output of all those that are classifiable as mining. The Bureau of Mines collects information more frequently, on the output of minerals as well as on engineering and technical matters. These data are thought to be independently valuable and different enough not to seem to constitute duplication.

*Division of responsibility.* Along quite a different dimension is the division of responsibility between the national government and the local governments of states or provinces and cities. In this dimension the United Kingdom is highly centralized, while Germany has problems because of the division of statistical activities among the *Länder*, and even in the Netherlands there is some devolution of statistical activities to organizations in the cities.

Every national statistical system must depend on local sources for its information. At the one extreme is complete central control, as found in the national census of countries such as the United States and Canada, in which the local officers are appointed and instructed by the center through a training ladder that inculcates definitions and procedures that are, at least in principle, fully determined centrally, and which is backed by a central budget from which all participants are paid. More decentralized is the census in countries such as Argentina, where the plans are made by a national statistical office but where the budget does not include the funds for paying enumerators, who are government employees on the payroll of other departments of the center or the provinces (for

example, schoolteachers), co-opted for one or several days' work on the enumeration. Coordination of such an operation requires feats of diplomacy. Further down on the scale of decentralization is the system of vital registration, used in the United States and other countries, in which local registry officials report to a state authority and whatever national uniformity exists is the result of negotiations in which the national office can take leadership more by virtue of its persuasiveness than because of any legal or budgetary power.

**Comparability and change.** The government statistical agency must have both continuity and adaptation of its output to changing needs, a combination of virtues easier to prescribe than to follow. In some instances an agency is very rigid; the disposition to continue collecting the same data in the same fashion year after year is both the strength and the weakness of government agencies. But at other times it changes arbitrarily; A. L. Bowley charged that the United Kingdom census of 1921 was deliberately made noncomparable with anything that went before, a statement challenged by Greenwood et al. (1932, p. 279). Again, judgment is required; the elimination of old series and the initiation of new ones and the modification of definitions that make a given series more useful for the future but lessen its comparability with the past must be discussed on a more specific level than this article can attain.

Practices that are good in one place and time may not be so in a different economy and society. Attempts to transfer categories of statistical compilation from a country in which money economy dominates to one in which households produce for their own use rather than for exchange may not be satisfactory. Some of the greatest difficulties in collecting statistics within the developed countries are in the sector of subsistence agriculture. The relation of statistics to industrial practice is brought home especially strikingly by the present situation in the United States, where the National Bureau of Economic Research and the Bureau of the Census, among other agencies, are trying to find how individual series can be improved or replaced. With the shift of traffic to trucks and airlines, carloadings have become much less useful. Department-store sales mean less when many of the lines of merchandise are also sold by discount houses and drugstores. The inventive spirit that discovered department-store sales and carloadings as key figures in the economy is needed now to go beyond these.

**Interactions with environment.** The government statistical agency is by no means a free agent but depends on the administrative practices of other governmental agencies and of business concerns. Statistics of imports depend on valuations made for customs purposes; comparing the exports of newsprint or metals from Canada to the United States, for instance, with the imports of nominally the same commodities into the United States from Canada will show how substantial is the effect of varying definitions of commodities as well as of sources and destinations. Since definitions are often part of procedures for customs valuation, and these are embedded in laws around which substantial material interests have developed, discrepancies between countries are likely to persist despite many conventions and attempts at accommodation, from that of Brussels in 1910 to those of the United Nations Statistical Commission.

*Effects of accounting practices.*    One important network in which the statistical agency is enmeshed is the accounting practices of industry, themselves in part the consequence of the regulations of the government income tax department. The art of statistical collection includes finding modes of definition of the entities about which inquiry is made that are most in conformity with the accounting practices of business and provide the most useful information to the public. The industrial establishment, as against the firm, is generally taken as the primary element for collection of industrial statistics and is defined in practice as the smallest production unit that maintains more or less complete records. The statistical agency does not always play a purely passive role; it is often in a position to exercise influence and initiative. In Canada the federal agency concerned with financial statistics of the 5,000 municipalities of the country was able to persuade them to adopt a standard accounting procedure, which benefited them as well as national statistics.

*National professional associations.*    The environment within which a statistics-producing office of government has to work includes, besides the operating agencies of the same government and the productive units of the country at large, a host of professional associations, as well as individuals interested in statistics. The American Statistical Association in 1844 petitioned the Congress of the United States to recompile the census of 1840; its policy of protesting poor work and supporting good in the federal statistical field has operated to the present day, although the need for its intervention is not as great as when the government service was staffed almost exclusively by amateurs (Bowman 1964).

*International professional associations.*    To the national associations have now been added important international ones. First among these was the International Statistical Institute, from the nineteenth century on a persistent and wholesome influence in favor of high standards and comparable classifications. The Economic and Social Council of the United Nations, through its statistical and population commissions, has had an effect in stimulating countries to take censuses; to adopt a minimum set of questions in these, for which a serious attempt would be made to attain international comparability; to use modern techniques, in the interest of accuracy and promptness of release of data. Sensitive to the desire of nations to be independent of outside interference in statistics as in other fields, the council has made its chief weapon the argument of international comparability in statistics of production, as well as of population. Also of influence have been the regional agencies of the United Nations for Asia, Europe, Latin America, and now Africa; the Inter-American Statistical Association; the specialized agencies of the United Nations, including the United Nations Educational, Scientific, and Cultural Organization (UNESCO), the Food and Agriculture Organization (FAO), the International Labour Organisation (ILO), etc., in their respective fields. The resolutions and the conventions that these have drawn up often suffer from being stated in highly abstract terms, but they are supplemented by technical assistance services to less developed members, including the sending out of advisers and the providing of training facilities. The publications of international bodies have not only been directly useful to scholars and others but also have been an incentive to members to secure data. FAO conferences of groups of neighboring countries have constituted an effective form of pressure for improvement of agricultural statistics.

*Other influences.*    Series of government statistics have often been initiated from the outside. The Metropolitan Life Insurance Company began collecting statistics of labor turnover in the United States in 1926, and these compilations were later taken over by the United States Department of Labor (Hauser & Leonard 1946, p. 363). In Canada statistics of wage rates collected by the Bell Telephone Company for its own purposes have influenced federal government collections. Statistics of stocks on hand have often been started by associations of manufacturers and then continued by a public statistical agency. In the Netherlands one of the influences that led to the centralized system was the private Union for Statistics, founded in 1856 (Stuart 1918, p. 435), which published many volumes of data, although it did no primary collecting. Later this private union was subsidized by the government, and ultimately all of its activities were taken over. Especially well known is the pressure that Quetelet, the Belgian statistician, exerted through his researches as a private citizen between about 1825 and 1841 (when he became a public official). His avid interest in the regularity of certain social phenomena, e.g., the "budget of the scaffold," finds its monument in the extensive series of criminal statistics produced in Belgium and many other countries (Julin 1918, p. 128). In England the first edition of the essay by Malthus that attracted so much attention to population was followed within three years by the census of 1801 [*see the biographies of* QUETELET *and* MALTHUS].

There are many other examples of the influence of men and ideas—as well as outside organizations—on government statistics. The collection of economic data during the present generation has been altered by the recognition of national accounts as a general framework. The concept was developed by scholars in universities in the United States and Great Britain, following suggestions of J. M. Keynes. The notion of national income makes it possible to arrange a great variety of existing series in the pigeonholes of a national-accounts framework; the output of the statistical systems ceases to appear arbitrary, for each portion measures a contribution to the gross national product; certain gaps become visible—for instance, personal services—and there is pressure to fill them. Furthermore, the examination in this fashion of economic statistics as a whole permits the grand total of the country's economic activities to be calculated in at least three ways—by value added, by income received, and by expenditure—which have important elements of independence as to source of data. The confrontation of calculations of a total derived from more or less independent statistical sources has been an incentive to improve the accuracy of all components.

The current prestige of economic planning has had important effects on government statistical work. Planning may be good or bad, effective or ineffective, but in all instances it requires data. One cannot even go through the motions of planning without statistics. Government planning agencies requiring data are in an especially strong position to see that the necessary resources are allocated to their collection.

**The statistical profession and government.** Underlying recent developments is a rapid professionalization of statistics. Times have changed greatly since Francis A. Walker lamented, in an address before the American Statistical Association in 1896, "I do not know of a single man now holding, or who has ever held, a position in this country as the head of a statistical bureau, or as chief of a statis-

tical service, or as a statistician, who had any elementary training for his work" (quoted in Cummings 1918, p. 574). A recent Bureau of the Census survey of its staff showed 576 employees in professional statistical positions, of whom all but 22 had an academic degree, including 36 PH.D.s and 102 M.A.s (Bowman 1964, p. 14). The change has come about through the extension of the field. Statistical method is applied to acceptance sampling and quality control in industry, to experimental design in agricultural trials, to bio-assay, operations research, and sample surveys of national populations. The interchange among these applications and between each application and a rapidly expanding mathematical statistical theory has had a decisive effect. Backed by a theory based on probability and relatively well-established methods of application of the theory; with a rapidly growing body of literature in books and professional journals; with departments of statistics in a number of universities, and courses in nearly all; there is less and less need for the government statistical agency to depend on the gifted amateur like Quetelet in Belgium, Knibbs in Australia, or Coats in Canada. And yet, present-day expansion and progress can be matched in quality by some of the early work. Florence Nightingale had much effect on the British War Office through her statistics showing deaths from battle and from disease separately. Her data on the army hospitals in India led to important reforms. It is not that the modern professional is better than the old-fashioned gifted amateur, but the former is more certain to be on hand when needed and commands the tools that have now been created.

*Sampling in the new professionalization.* Among the large-scale sample surveys now conducted are those on a monthly basis in the United States and Canada, quarterly in the Federal Republic of Germany and other European countries, and virtually continuously in India. The topics of survey are almost as wide as the topics of statistics itself [*see* SAMPLE SURVEYS].

Like any important change in technique, sampling does not merely attain the earlier objectives at lower cost; it brings a radically new viewpoint on the whole process of data collection. Instead of thinking of himself as charged with passively compiling given data, the statistician orients himself to the purpose of the compilation and the degree of accuracy required if the purpose is to be served; thus, he is led to take account of the nonsampling as well as the sampling error to which his work is subject. He sees himself at his professional best in measuring error, controlling quality, and evaluating results. He comes to measure information, not by the mass of data he can turn out, but rather by the accuracy attained in a single figure. The percentage of the labor force unemployed, for example, may be the occasion for a major decision in regard to the economy. If there is an allotment to improve the figure, he must decide what amount should be spent to improve the accuracy of response and what to increase the sample. In other words, he must decide if there will be more return from applying a given effort to the sampling or to the nonsampling error. The changed attitude toward error—the view that it is both inevitable and to be constantly combated—is seen in the United States Bureau of the Census, where the 1950 and subsequent population censuses have been accompanied by an official estimate of the degree of underenumeration, an estimate in part made by having superior enumerators survey a sample of areas. This practice has been applied in Canada since 1951. It is the mark of the professional statistician that he does not assert that his results are exact; even when he has done the survey by the best means that are available, he is satisfied to consider his one survey as an arbitrary selection from all the surveys that might have been carried out at about the same time and with equally acceptable definitions [see ERRORS, *article on* NONSAMPLING ERRORS].

**Enduring problems of official statistics.** A survey of the statistical agencies of any government, even those of a very advanced country, would show the continuance of some out-of-date practices, the publication of some figures that are not usable because they are based on purely administrative definitions of the entities counted or because the error is not stated by the agency but may be presumed to be large. Besides the valuable statistics they contain, library shelves are weighted with irrelevant, useless, and inaccurate statistics, a situation to be deplored in proportion as good techniques are available.

*Government statistics' judicial function.* Especially pernicious are those inaccuracies intended to serve some political purpose. The strongest argument for statistical centralization relates to what may be called the judicial function of the official statistician. The statistics of foreign trade may show that the government's trade policy is going badly; the statistics of prices may show that its monetary policy is leading to inflation. Protection of the public requires that the agency responsible for the policy not be the one with exclusive control over the statistics; to give it such control is to ask of it superhuman strength to withstand temptation. In a hundred minor decisions of statistical compilation, an operating agency may be swayed by noting

how the result will come out. Presentation also requires impartiality. On issues such as whether a price index ought to be released now, when it has been scheduled to appear, or next week, after a national election has taken place, hangs the virtue of the statistician. Without this virtue and the resulting public confidence in statistics, much of the cost of collecting data is wasted; statistics that are not believed are of no use. In a statistician, as in a judge, ignorance is less dangerous than corruption. The statistician will be most useful to the community when his statistical honor is not in conflict with some nonstatistical responsibility. At a higher administrative level, the political head of the department that includes the statistical office must accept the self-discipline of permitting decisions regarding statistics to be made on statistical considerations, not because such decisions are always correct but because, when they are wrong, they are wrong in a disinterested way. One method that lessens the need for self-discipline is to have a commission entirely outside of politics control the statistical office, as is done in the Netherlands.

Much less subtle than the issues of the preceding paragraph are the distortions as a matter of policy that have been seen in some totalitarian countries. During the Stalin period in the Soviet Union, statistics were not considered to pertain to science but to revolution and to mobilization of the people for national construction. If the statistics do not show progress, the masses will become discouraged and their effort will flag. The same attitude was found in China in the 1950s (Li 1962). The competition between districts to be in the van of socialist production was extended to competition with respect to the figures of production, and this local zeal for declaring high figures reached its peak in 1960, when total production of cereals was announced as 275 million tons, apparently an exaggeration of over 100 per cent. It had been thought democratic to bring the masses into the work of compiling statistics; the consequent socialist rivalry seems to have genuinely deceived the regime, as well as its subjects, with subsequent disastrous consequences. There are clear signs that in the Soviet Union, as in older industrial societies, trustworthy statistics are now recognized as something more than a bourgeois luxury; whether the dependency of good decisions on good statistics is now understood in China is not clear.

### Technical contributions

Extensive contributions have been made to technique in nearly every division of statistics by agencies attempting to implement efficiently their legislative assignment to collect data. One may mention the methods of calculating life tables; the deseasonalization of economic time series; the theory and practice of index-number calculation, as it has been developed in the United States Bureau of Labor Statistics and in the Dominion Bureau of Statistics in Canada; the classification of occupations, industries, and commodities (Coats 1925). Particularly important for the growth of demography were the technical contributions during the nineteenth century by William Farr and other statisticians of the United Kingdom General Register Office [see INDEX NUMBERS; LIFE TABLES; POPULATION; TIME SERIES].

The most striking single example of these contributions is the intimate relation of the U.S. Bureau of the Census to the development of tabulating and computing equipment, from the primitive punch-card devices of the 1890s, built in the Census Bureau itself by Herman Hollerith, to the Univac, built privately with bureau encouragement and financing and technical help from the Bureau of Standards. The Canadian census office also pioneered in this, with some highly original electric and compressed-air tabulators, the result of the ingenuity of Fernand Belisle, a lifelong employee of the Canadian Bureau of Statistics. Both Canadian and United States census offices have in recent years built or stimulated the building of input devices to avoid the keypunching of data, the most tedious part of the processing of large-scale surveys.

Besides having had a part in the development of computers, government statistical agencies have shown great initiative in using them. Such use, whether in an insurance office, an oil refinery, or a government statistical office, requires extensive rethinking of processes that have developed in the course of decades. Several of the more advanced of the world's statistical offices have drastically reorganized their work in order to exploit electronic computation, with consequences of more extensive cross tabulation, better control of error in processing, and economy. In the United States the demand for machine-readable results has increased as users of statistics have acquired their own computers. The Bureau of the Census has an extensive catalogue of results available on punch cards or electronic tape; this mode of publication is sure to become widespread.

## Publication of results

Prompt and full publication is the highest of virtues in government statistics—provided that the data published are accurate as well as relevant. This follows from the place of statistics in a decision-making process: the appropriateness of the decision—for example, to build a factory—will depend on the situation that exists at some future date; and if the statistician is not in a position to count the population of five or 25 years hence, he can at least describe what the situation was up to as recent a moment as possible. On the content of what is published—what cross classifications of distributions, what percentages, what time comparisons, what charts—the judgment of the government statistician becomes better the greater his contact with users of his results. With the multiplicity of governmental and private sources, the need increases for good indexing within any publication, as well as for cross referencing of comparable data in other publications.

Government statistical offices have entered the field of social science in their efforts to interpret their data. This runs from comment on statistical tables that enables the reader to know how the entities counted have been defined, along with measures of sampling and nonsampling error, through calculations distributing not-stated ages and deseasonalizing economic series, to full-scale monographs that have become a regular part of the census, in the United States and Canada going back at least a full generation. India is preparing a set of monographs based on the 1961 census, and Pakistan is planning to do likewise. If one thinks of the continuum, from the collection of raw statistical data to its final use as an ingredient either in scientific investigation or in the making of decisions, then there is room for differences of opinion as to where the role of the government statistical office ends and that of the user begins. The vital minimum is that the government statistician describe all aspects of his collection procedures that can possibly affect the interpretation of the results. It is to be hoped that in some future time no survey will be issued without realistic estimates of the accuracy of its figures, but that time still seems to be far in the future.

Notwithstanding all this, a certain abstemiousness is forced on the official statistician by virtue of his position; he cannot afford to take the sorts of risks in the interpretation of data that newspapermen can take so freely. Public confidence in the accuracy of his figures, and hence their usefulness, would be jeopardized by palpable arbitrariness in judgments expressed in his text. This consideration often drives him to the writing of text that is no more than a gloss on what is obviously revealed in the tables and is perhaps less clear than the figures themselves. On the other hand, the government statistician can argue with justice that interpretation, lively or dull, made without his intimate knowledge of the basis of the figures is likely to be misleading. The answer is that, as a minimum, he give enough detail on his procedures to put the reader in a position to interpret correctly.

**Secrecy.** The matter of secrecy enters into statistical work in two ways, to which exactly opposite principles apply. In the report made by the individual to a government agency, it is generally considered that the most honest reporting will be secured if a guarantee of confidentiality is provided, giving the supplier assurance that his contribution will not be identified outside the statistical office and that only the statistical aggregates of which it is a part will be made public. The government statistician is endowed with the power to enforce reporting on the part of the persons or corporate bodies to which he addresses his questionnaires; the obverse of this power is the obligation to keep individual returns secret (Dobrovits 1947). In the large number of government surveys for which reporting is not mandatory, the degree of voluntary response may be proportional to the public confidence in provisions for maintaining secrecy.

On the other hand, the aggregate results of every survey ought to be given the widest possible publicity. One of the difficulties of government publication is that the government does not have complete access to the distribution channels of the private book trade; sometimes a solution is possible through private publication, as was done for the monographs on the 1950 census of the United States and as is done in the Netherlands and Germany. The principle of equal access of the public to statistics is important; this is safeguarded by preannounced release times, at which statistics are simultaneously made available to all who are interested. In many countries there is much diffusion of government statistical results through nongovernmental intermediate sources, including trade yearbooks and scientific journals; it is customary to allow republishing without specific permission.

A serious problem arises from the desire of government to keep certain statistical results secret. This was a regrettable necessity in the United States and Canada during World War II in respect, for instance, to detailed foreign trade figures, because the information would have been used by the Axis powers in their submarine campaign against Allied shipping. Aside from such exceptional cases, it is fair to say that there are no instances in which the public as a whole benefits from concealment of statistical reports that provide accurate data, although governments and particular departments within them may indeed benefit at the expense of the public. The discussion of the publication of government statistics merges at this point with the wider question of the free flow of information in the society as a whole.

NATHAN KEYFITZ

[*See also* ELECTIONS, *article on* ELECTORAL SYSTEMS.]

BIBLIOGRAPHY

BAINES, ATHELSTANE 1918 The History and Development of Statistics in Great Britain and Ireland. Pages 365–389 in John Koren (editor), *The History of Statistics*. New York: Macmillan.

BOWMAN, RAYMOND T. 1964 The American Statistical Association and Federal Statistics. *Journal of the American Statistical Association* 59:1–17.

COATS, ROBERT H. 1925 The Classification Problem in Statistics. *International Labor Review* 11:509–525.

CUMMINGS, JOHN 1918 Statistical Work of the Federal Government of the United States. Pages 573–689 in John Koren (editor), *The History of Statistics*. New York: Macmillan.

*Demographic Yearbook.* → Issued by the United Nations since 1948.

DOBROVITS, ALEXANDRE 1947 Sur le secret en statistique. Volume 3, pages 769–778 in International Statistical Conference, Washington, D.C., *Proceedings*. Calcutta: Eka.

FAURE, FERNAND 1918 The Development and Progress of Statistics in France. Pages 217–329 in John Koren (editor), *The History of Statistics*. New York: Macmillan.

GODFREY, ERNEST H. 1918 The History and Development of Statistics in Canada. Pages 179–198 in John Koren (editor), *The History of Statistics*. New York: Macmillan.

GREENWOOD, MAJOR et al. 1932 Discussion on the Quantity and Quality of Official Statistical Publications. *Journal of the Royal Statistical Society* 95:279–302.

HAUSER, PHILIP M. 1963 Statistics and Society. *Journal of the American Statistical Association* 58:1–12.

HAUSER, PHILIP M.; and LEONARD, WILLIAM R. (editors) (1946) 1956 *Government Statistics for Business Use.* New York: Wiley.

HOLMES, OLIVER W. 1960 "Public Records"—Who Knows What They Are? *American Archivist* 23:3–26.

JULIN, ARMAND 1918 The History and Development of Statistics in Belgium. Pages 125–175 in John Koren (editor), *The History of Statistics*. New York: Macmillan.

KNIBBS, GEORGE H. 1918 The History and Development of the Statistical System of Australia. Pages 55–81 in John Koren (editor), *The History of Statistics*. New York: Macmillan.

KOREN, JOHN (editor) 1918 *The History of Statistics.* New York: Macmillan.

LEONARD, WILLIAM R. 1958 An Outlook Report. *Journal of the American Statistical Association* 53:1–10.

LI, CHOH-MING 1962 *The Statistical System of Communist China.* Berkeley: Univ. of California Press.

LINDER, FORREST E. 1959 World Demographic Data. Pages 321–360 in Philip M. Hauser and Otis Dudley Duncan (editors), *The Study of Population: An Inventory and Appraisal.* Univ. of Chicago Press.

MEITZEN, AUGUST (1886) 1891 *History, Theory, and Technique of Statistics.* Philadelphia: American Academy of Political and Social Science. → First published in German.

MILLS, FREDERICK C.; and LONG, CLARENCE D. 1949 *The Statistical Agencies of the Federal Government*. Washington: Government Printing Office.

MORGENSTERN, OSKAR (1950) 1963 *On the Accuracy of Economic Observations*. 2d ed. Princeton Univ. Press.

NIXON, JAMES W. 1960 *A History of the International Statistical Institute: 1885–1960*. The Hague: International Statistical Institute.

NORTH, S. N. D. 1918 Seventy-five Years of Progress in Statistics: The Outlook for the Future. Pages 15–49 in John Koren (editor), *The History of Statistics*. New York: Macmillan.

STERN, JOHANNA 1958 [Review of] Th. L. Galland's *Statistik der Beschaeftigten und Arbeitslosen. Journal of the American Statistical Association* 53:1040–1043.

STUART, C. A. V. 1918 The History and Development of Statistics in the Netherlands. Pages 429–444 in John Koren (editor), *The History of Statistics*. New York: Macmillan.

UNITED NATIONS, STATISTICAL OFFICE 1954 *Handbook of Statistical Organization*. Studies in Methods, Series F, No. 6. New York: United Nations.

U.S. BUREAU OF THE BUDGET, OFFICE OF STATISTICAL STANDARDS (1947) 1963 *Statistical Services of the United States Government*. Rev. ed. Washington: Government Printing Office.

WESTERGAARD, HARALD L. 1932 *Contributions to the History of Statistics*. London: King.

WURZBURGER, EUGENE 1918 The History and Development of Official Statistics in the German Empire. Pages 333–362 in John Koren (editor), *The History of Statistics*. New York: Macmillan.

# GRAEBNER, FRITZ

Fritz Graebner (1877–1934), German ethnologist and one of the principal exponents of the culture-historical approach to ethnology, was born in Berlin. The noted botanist Paul Graebner was his brother. Like many German ethnologists at the turn of the century, Graebner started out in another field. He obtained his PH.D. in Berlin in 1901 as a historian, with a dissertation on a topic in medieval history. But as early as 1899, he became a research assistant on the staff of the Royal Museum of Ethnology in Berlin, which was directed by Adolf Bastian. Graebner was assigned to classify the museum's rich holdings of South Seas material in Felix von Luschan's Africa and South Seas department.

Here he worked in close contact with Bernhard Ankermann, the Africanist, and together they developed the method of the Kulturkreis. They collaborated on two lectures that were delivered on November 19, 1904, to the Berlin Gesellschaft für Anthropologie, Ethnologie, und Urgeschichte; these were published in 1905 in the *Zeitschrift für Ethnologie*. The lectures attempted to interpret Oceanian history on the basis of a study of artifacts

and an extensive knowledge of the literature, in terms of the geographical diffusion of clusters of cultural traits. It is of course true that Leo Frobenius had already used a similar approach to Africa in his *Ursprung der afrikanischen Kulturen* (1898), but Ankermann's work and Graebner's research on Kulturkreise in Oceania were considerably more thorough and precise.

Graebner plotted the diffusion of individual culture traits cartographically throughout the South Seas; he recognized the linkages that seemed to occur; and he arranged complexes or clusters of traits into Kulturkreise. He then proposed a chronological sequence for the diffusion of the Kreise: the Tasmanian culture, the Old Australian culture, the western Papuan or totem culture, the eastern Papuan or two-class culture, the Melanesian or bow culture, the Polynesian culture, and a few more recent "cultural movements."

In his article "Die melanesische Bogenkultur und ihre Verwandten" (1909*a*), he tried for the first time to establish in a larger region the Kulturkreise he had worked out locally for parts of the Pacific. This marked the beginning of the trend in European ethnology that was called *Kulturkreislehre*. After World War I, Wilhelm Schmidt of Vienna, who had initially had strong disagreements with Graebner (see, for example, 1909*c*), attempted a world-wide application of Graebner's system. Graebner, in his contribution to the volume on anthropology in Hinneberg's anthology, *Die Kultur der Gegenwart* (1923), himself transferred some of his South Seas Kulturkreise to other regions of the globe, although he did so with much greater moderation than did either Father Schmidt or Father Wilhelm Koppers.

In 1906 Graebner left the Berlin Museum, accepting the invitation of Willi Foy, director of the Rautenstrauch-Joest Museum in Cologne, who became one of his most active supporters. In Cologne he published his *Methode der Ethnologie* (1911), a work that explicitly acknowledged a debt to Ernst Bernheim's *Lehrbuch der historischen Methode und der Geschichtsphilosophie* (1889), and thus reestablished his connection with the discipline of history. By now he had at his command great quantities of ethnological material, and he and Foy considered ethnology as essential to a universal history.

The *Methode der Ethnologie* became the cornerstone for the culture-historical school of ethnology. In this work Graebner's principal concern was to work out methodological guidelines for research into culture affinities, although this work also contained an exemplary chapter on critical study of the original sources and a discussion of the ways of interpreting ethnological sources. The "criteria of cultural links" (1911, pp. 104–125) are still valid. If there are *numerous* homologous elements of culture in a region of the globe that are *not* functionally interdependent (criterion of quantity), and if their *similarity of form* is extensive without being due to identity of purpose and identity of material (criterion of form), it must be presumed that they did not originate independently of one another but came from the same original source or are related by borrowing. If these elements of culture belong to many or all cultural spheres (economy, society, religion, art, etc.), they constitute a Kulturkreis or a "culture complex." If parts of this complex are widely separated geographically, cultural relationship is more likely if certain elements that are, as it were, cultural bridges can be located between them (criterion of continuity). Moreover, if it can be shown that the separated complexes are most alike where their areas of distribution are nearest (criterion of degree of relatedness), cultural relationship and nonindependent origin can be inferred from this situation as well. Zones of "leveling" and "draining" of a Kulturkreis, discontinuity of the area, penetration by groups from another culture complex, and so forth, produce a sequence of Kulturkreise that subsequently may be regarded as culture layers.

Graebner never did any field work. When he did go to Australia at the invitation of the Australian government, the outbreak of World War I prevented him from doing research. He was interned and not released until 1919. Nevertheless he made use of his time there to do much studying, and he produced a comparison of the myths of Indo-European, Mongolian, Polynesian, and Hamito–Semitic peoples, "Thor und Maui" (1919/1920), and a study of Old and New World calendars (1920/1921). These two works were important preliminary studies for *Das Weltbild der Primitiven* (1924). Here Graebner advanced for the first time a broad theory of history, visualizing an archaic "advanced culture" that was diffused throughout the Old World and the New World. Many of his arguments in support of links between the advanced cultures of the Old World and the New are still valid. His theory was wholly independent of the so-called British school of diffusionism led by Grafton Elliott Smith and W. J. Perry.

In 1925 Graebner succeeded Foy as director of the Cologne museum. The following year he was appointed to an honorary professorship at the Uni-

versity of Cologne. A prolonged illness forced him to resign in 1928; he returned to Berlin, where he died in 1934.

HERMANN BAUMANN

[*For the historical context of Graebner's work, see* DIF-FUSION; HISTORY, *article on* CULTURE HISTORY; *and the biographies of* BASTIAN *and* FROBENIUS. *For discussion of the subsequent development of Graebner's ideas, see the biographies of* KOPPERS *and* SCHMIDT.]

### WORKS BY GRAEBNER

1905    Kulturkreise und Kulturschichten in Ozeanien. *Zeitschrift für Ethnologie* 37:28–53.

1906    Wanderung und Entwicklung sozialer Systeme in Australien. *Globus* 90:181–186, 207–210, 220–224, 237–241.

1907    STEPHAN, EMIL; and GRAEBNER, FRITZ. *Neu-Mecklenburg (Bismarck-Archipel)*. Berlin: Reimer.

1908    Die sozialen Systeme in der Südsee. *Zeitschrift für Sozialwissenschaft* 11:663–681, 748–755.

1909*a*    Die melanesische Bogenkultur und ihre Verwandten. *Anthropos* 4:726–780.

1909*b*    Völkerkunde der Santa-Cruz-Inseln. *Ethnologica* 1:71–84.

1909*c*    Zur australischen Religionsgeschichte. *Globus* 96:341–344, 362–366, 373–378.

1910    Handel bei Naturvölkern. Volume 1, pages 149–218 in Karl Andree, *Geographie des Welthandels: Eine wirtschaftsgeographische Schilderung der Erde.* 2d ed. Vienna: Seidel.

1911    *Methode der Ethnologie.* Heidelberg: Winter.

1913    Amerika und die Südseekulturen. *Ethnologica* 2:43–66.

1915/1916    Totemismus als kulturgeschichtliches Problem. *Anthropos* 10/11:248–256.

1919/1920    Thor und Maui. *Anthropos* 14/15:1099–1119.

1920/1921    Alt- und neuweltliche Kalender. *Zeitschrift für Ethnologie* 52/53:6–37.

1923    Ethnologie. Pages 435–587 in *Die Kultur der Gegenwart: Ihre Entwicklung und ihre Ziele.* Edited by Paul Hinneberg. Part 3, section 5: Anthropologie, by Gustav Schwalbe. Leipzig: Teubner.

1924    *Das Weltbild der Primitiven.* Munich: Reinhard.

### SUPPLEMENTARY BIBLIOGRAPHY

BERNHEIM, ERNST (1889) 1960 *Lehrbuch der historischen Methode und der Geschichtsphilosophie.* 2 vols. Burt Franklin Bibliographical and Reference Series, Vol. 21. New York: Franklin.

# GRANET, MARCEL

Marcel Granet (1884–1940), pre-eminent French sociological Sinologist, was born at Luc-en-Diois and died at Sceaux. He was admitted to the École Normale Supérieure in 1904 and received the *agrégation d'histoire* in 1907. He was named *directeur d'études* at the École Pratique des Hautes Études in 1913 and *chargé de cours* at the Sorbonne in 1920, the same year that he received his *doctorat ès lettres.* In 1926 he became the first director of the Institut des Hautes Études Chinoises of the Sorbonne as well as professor at the École des Langues Orientales of Paris. He received the Croix de Guerre for his services in World War I.

It was his teacher Édouard Chavannes who suggested to Granet that his interest in feudalism might well lead to the study of Sinology. Another teacher of Granet's was Émile Durkheim. The historian Marc Bloch was a friend and fellow student of Granet's at the École Normale, as was also Marcel Mauss, the nephew of Durkheim. Granet married Marie Terrien in 1919. While Granet was studying in China, from 1911 to 1913, the Ch'ing dynasty was replaced by the Republic of China. He visited China once more, after World War I, as a member of a mission.

Granet was a special sort of pioneer in the social sciences—he became a Sinologist in pursuit of more general interests in social phenomena. After an initial thorough grounding in the discipline of history, he was exposed to Durkheim's ideas, and these were decisive in developing his more general sociological interests. Granet was also a pioneer figure in stimulating the interest of non-Sinological social scientists in the Far East—most directly in Chinese society, but also, as a consequence of new attention to comparative studies, in Japanese society.

As a Sinologist, Granet freed himself from the dependence on secondary Chinese materials that had hampered earlier social scientists who studied China. He made it clear that difficult language barriers are no excuse for inferior standards of expertise. Moreover, unlike most orthodox Sinologists of his day, he found "inauthentic" texts no less valuable than authentic ones as evidence of social life. Rather than concentrating largely on the question of the "authenticity" of documents, Granet felt social scientists would do well to examine these documents critically in order to distinguish between ideal and actual patterns in Chinese society.

Granet addressed his efforts at broad interpretations of Chinese life, cutting across historical epochs. Mainly, however, he concentrated on feudal China and the transition to imperial China. As was pointed out by Émile Benoît-Smullyan, in a review that introduced Granet's work to many American sociologists (1936), Granet found Durkheim's "sociologistic epistemology" especially relevant to his work, leading him to important empirical elaborations of Durkheim's analysis. Thus, Granet showed the fundamental differences between Chinese and modern European modes of thought and suggested that those differences stemmed from far-reaching differences in social structure.

For scholars with a general interest in the social sciences, as well as for many scholars who are not Sinologists in the strict sense, Granet's most important contributions are to be found in his two volumes *Chinese Civilization* (1929a) and *La pensée chinoise* (1934). Both volumes have excellent introductions by Henri Berr, with carefully chosen titles: "L'originalité de la Chine" and "Mentalité chinoise et psychologie comparée."

Granet's subtitle of *Chinese Civilization* conveys an important distinction: "La vie publique et la vie privée" (the English translation dropped the subtitle). In this book he subdivided his treatment into political history and Chinese society, and these parts in turn contain discussions of traditional history (through the beginning of the imperial era in Han times), the chief data of ancient history, the people of the countryside, the foundation of the chieftainships, the seignioral town, and society at the beginning of the imperial era. Granet used the ancient texts, the legends, dances, and feasts, and what archeological evidence he could find in an attempt to reconstruct the preimperial background and demonstrate its relevance for an understanding of imperial China. Imperial Chinese society represents one of the most elaborate and sophisticated developments in the varied history of mankind: it was perhaps the only society with a large-scale membership, spread over a vast area, which was nevertheless sufficiently stable in its main outlines to endure for some two thousand years. Granet used the available materials to make a careful attempt to reconstruct both the life of the peasants—the vast majority of the people—and the public roles and the domestic lives of the nobles.

The most complex, powerful, and difficult of Granet's contributions is *La pensée chinoise*, and it is this work which still constitutes one of the most important attempts to apply empirically the leads furnished by Durkheim in *Elementary Forms of the Religious Life*. Granet explicitly rejected any interpretation of Chinese thought as mystical or prelogical—any such interpretation, he believed, was "lacking in the humanistic spirit"—and he rested his interpretations of Chinese thought squarely on Durkheim's view that modes of thought are themselves social manifestations and reflect other social facts. Most notably, modes of thought reflect those forms of social organization whose very persistence, Granet held, in some sense proves their value (1934, pp. 27–29). He began his analysis of Chinese thought with an examination of language and writing, and in so doing, he was at once very French and precociously modern. His chapters on the Chinese conceptions of time and space, *yang* and *yin*, numbers, and the Tao are classics, although they are controversial.

Even at the time Granet published his interpretation of China, some scholars felt that his treatment of China as a special instance of social universals led him to overlook or misunderstand many features of Chinese society, and materials discovered since Granet's time necessitate other qualifications of his interpretation. Yet there is general admiration among scholars for the stimulus Granet's work gave to Sinology in particular and to social science more generally. His intellectual descendants do him the honor of challenging his positions within the whole field he opened for them.

MARION J. LEVY, JR.

[*For the historical context of Granet's work, see the biographies of* BLOCH; DURKHEIM; MAUSS. *Also related is the article* CHINESE SOCIETY.]

### WORKS BY GRANET

(1912) 1953  Coutumes matrimoniales de la Chine antique. Pages 63–94 in Marcel Granet, *Études sociologiques sur la Chine*. Paris: Presses Universitaires de France.

(1912–1933) 1953  *Études sociologiques sur la Chine*. Paris: Presses Universitaires de France.

(1919) 1932  *Festivals and Songs of Ancient China*. London: Routledge. → First published as *Fêtes et chansons anciennes de la Chine*.

(1920a) 1953  La polygynie sororale et le sororat dans la Chine féodale: Étude sur les formes anciennes de la polygamie chinoise. Pages 1–62 in Marcel Granet, *Études sociologiques sur la Chine*. Paris: Presses Universitaires de France.

(1920b) 1953  Quelques particularités de la langue et de la pensée chinoises. Pages 95–155 in Marcel Granet, *Études sociologiques sur la Chine*. Paris: Presses Universitaires de France.

(1921) 1953  La vie et la mort: Croyances et doctrines de l'antiquité chinoise. Pages 203–220 in Marcel Granet, *Études sociologiques sur la Chine*. Paris: Presses Universitaires de France.

(1922a) 1953  Le dépôt de l'enfant sur le sol: Rites anciens et ordalies mythiques. Pages 157–202 in Marcel Granet, *Études sociologiques sur la Chine*. Paris: Presses Universitaires de France.

(1922b) 1953  Le langage de la douleur d'après le rituel funéraire de la Chine classique. Pages 221–242 in Marcel Granet, *Études sociologiques sur la Chine*. Paris: Presses Universitaires de France.

(1922c) 1951  *La religion des Chinois*. 2d ed. Paris: Presses Universitaires de France.

(1925) 1953  Remarques sur le taoïsme ancien. Pages 243–249 in Marcel Granet, *Études sociologiques sur la Chine*. Paris: Presses Universitaires de France.

(1926) 1959  *Danses et légendes de la Chine ancienne*. New ed., 2 vols. Paris: Presses Universitaires de France.

1928  L'expression de la pensée en chinois. *Journal de psychologie normale et pathologique* 25:617–656.

(1929a) 1957  *Chinese Civilization*. London: Routledge. → First published in French.

(1929b) 1953  L'esprit de la religion chinoise. Pages 251–260 in Marcel Granet, *Études sociologiques sur la Chine*. Paris: Presses Universitaires de France.

(1933) 1953  La droite et la gauche en Chine. Pages 261–278 in Marcel Granet, *Études sociologiques sur la Chine*. Paris: Presses Universitaires de France.

(1934) 1950  *La pensée chinoise*. Paris: Michel.

1939  *Catégories matrimoniales et relations de proximité dans la Chine ancienne*. Paris: Alcan.

1952  *La féodalité chinoise*. Instituttet for Sammenlignende Kulturforskning, Oslo, Serie A: Forelesninger, 22. Oslo: Aschehoug.

### SUPPLEMENTARY BIBLIOGRAPHY

BENOÎT-SMULLYAN, ÉMILE 1936  [A Book Review of] *La pensée chinoise*, by Marcel Granet. *American Sociological Review* 1:487–492.

# GRAPHIC PRESENTATION

Graphic presentation represents a highly developed body of techniques for elucidating, interpreting, and analyzing numerical facts by means of points, lines, areas, and other geometric forms and symbols. Graphic techniques are especially valuable in presenting quantitative data in a simple, clear, and effective manner, as well as facilitating comparisons of values, trends, and relationships. They have the additional advantages of succinctness and popular appeal; the comprehensive pictures they provide can bring out hidden facts and relationships and contribute to a more balanced understanding of a problem.

The choice of a particular graphic technique to present a given set of data is a difficult one, and no hard and fast rules can be made to cover all circumstances. There are, however, certain general goals that should always be kept in mind. These include completeness, clarity, and honesty; but there is often conflict between the goals. For instance, completeness demands that all data points be included in a chart, but often this can be done only at some sacrifice of clarity. Such problems can be mitigated by the practice (highly desirable on other grounds as well) of indicating the source of the data from which the chart was constructed so that the reader himself can investigate further. Another problem occurs when it is necessary to break an axis in order to fit all the data in a reasonable space; clarity is then served, but honesty demands that attention be strongly called to the break.

A choice among graphic techniques also depends upon the proposed use to which the chart will be put. As Schmid (1954) has pointed out, graphs that are satisfactory in memoranda for private circulation may be inappropriate for a published book or paper.

In classifying charts and graphs, criteria of purpose, of circumstances of use, of type of comparison, and of form have been used. On the basis of form, charts and graphs may be classified as (1) rectilinear coordinate graphs; (2) semilogarithmic charts; (3) bar and column charts; (4) frequency graphs and related charts; (5) maps; (6) miscellaneous charts, including pie diagrams, scattergrams, fan charts, ranking charts, etc.; (7) pictorial charts; and (8) three-dimensional projection charts.

In graphic presentation, three different basic geometrical forms can be utilized for purposes of comparing magnitudes of coordinate items: (1) linear or one-dimensional, (2) areal or two-dimensional, and (3) cubic or three-dimensional. The simplest and most exact comparisons are those made on a linear basis; comparison of relative sizes of areas is more difficult and of volumes most difficult. Accordingly, where possible, the use of areal and cubic forms should be avoided in graphic presentation.

**Rectilinear coordinate graphs.**   Perhaps the best known form of graphic presentation, and certainly one of the most frequently used, is the simple arithmetic line chart, one of several types of the *rectilinear* (or *Cartesian*) coordinate graph.

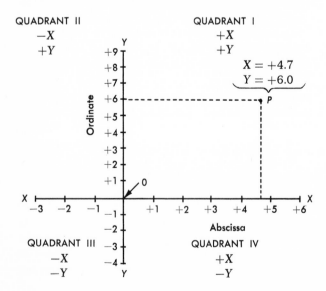

*Figure 1 — Basic structural features of a rectangular coordinate graph*

The basic form of this type of graph is derived by plotting one or more series of figures on a coordinate surface in which the successive plotting points are joined together in the form of a continuous line, customarily referred to as a "curve." A curve on a graph of this kind is not necessarily smooth and regular but instead may be straight and angular. Figure 1 indicates the basic structural characteristics of a rectilinear coordinate system.

Figure 2 portrays the characteristic features and basic standards of the rectilinear coordinate graph. Many of the essential elements and specifications of the rectilinear coordinate graph are also applicable to other graphic forms.

**Semilogarithmic charts.**   The semilogarithmic chart is often superior to the arithmetic chart (as used in Figure 1), for the former can show relative changes clearly; hence it is sometimes referred to as a ratio chart. Sometimes the semilogarithmic chart has the merit of representing as nearly straight lines functions that otherwise would be appreciably curved.

The essential feature of the semilogarithmic chart is that one scale is logarithmic and the other arithmetic, so that the chart effectively is a convenient device for plotting $\log y$ against $x$, or $\log x$ against $y$. There is no zero line on the logarithmic scale, since the logarithm of zero is minus infinity. The logarithmic scale consists of one or more sets of rulings calibrated in terms of logarithmic values; each complete set of rulings is referred to as a "deck," "cycle," "bank," or "tier." The rulings for each deck are the same, but the scale values change from one to the other. For example, if one deck runs from 1 to 10, the adjacent deck above will vary from 10 to 100, the third from 100 to 1,000, and so forth. On the other hand, the adjacent deck below the one from 1 to 10 would vary from 0.1 to 1.0. The logarithmic scale can thus be extended upward or downward indefinitely.

In a semilogarithmic chart, relative rate-of-change comparisons can be made readily between different parts of a single series or between two or more series. The relative rate of change of $y$ with respect to $x$ is the slope of $y$ as a function of $x$, divided by $x$; equivalently it is the slope of $\log y$ except for a constant depending on the logarithmic base. The slope of the logarithmic scale variable is the relative rate of change of the variable. If the slope is steep, the relative rate of change is great. It makes no difference on what part of a semilogarithmic chart a curve is located; the same slope

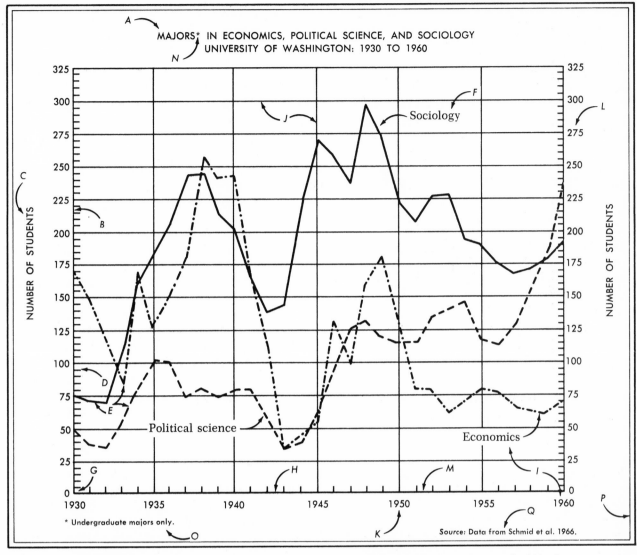

A—title at top
B—axis of ordinates, or Y axis
C—scale legend for Y axis
D—scale points
E—curves differentiated (solid, dashed, and dot-dashed)
F—contiguous legends for curves
G—origin
H—zero lines heavier than other coordinate lines
I—lettering arranged horizontally whenever possible

J—grid, or coordinate lines (no more should be shown
  than are necessary)
K—scale figures for X axis
L—scale figures for Y axis
M—axis of abscissae, or X axis
N—reference symbol
O—explanatory note
P—border (optional)
Q—source

*Figure 2 — Essential characteristics and specifications of a rectilinear coordinate graph*

means the same relative rate of change. This is particularly convenient if the two series being compared have very different ranges of values.

This situation is illustrated in Figure 3, where the same data have been plotted on both arithmetic and semilogarithmic grids, placed in juxtaposition. On the arithmetic grid, the relative rate of growth of the city in comparison to that of the entire state cannot be easily determined; by con-

trast, the curves on the semilogarithmic chart portray relative rate of growth clearly and correctly. Note, however, that this clarity is achieved only at the expense of some distortion; careful labeling is imperative to prevent the reader from mistakenly concluding that the absolute growth of Dallas is greater than that of the state as a whole.

Other special graph papers exist, such as double logarithmic, normal, and hyperbolic.

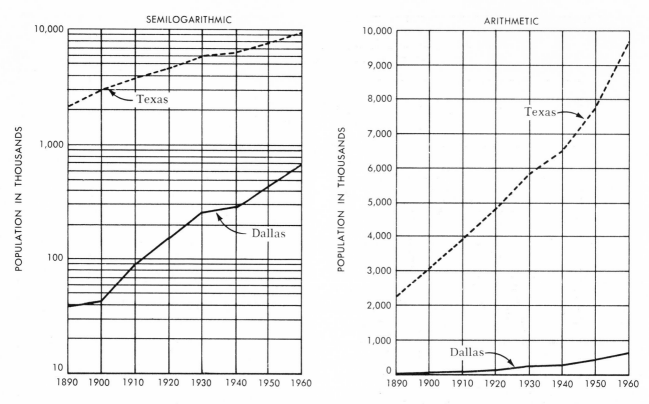

**Figure 3 — Comparison\* of rectangular coordinate and semilogarithmic graphs**

\* Comparison clearly demonstrates the superiority of the semilogarithmic graph in portraying relative rates of change.

Source: Data from U.S. Bureau of the Census 1963, pp. 45-19, 45-22.

**Bar and column charts.** Bar and column charts are simple, flexible, and effective techniques for comparing the size of coordinate values or of parts of a total. The basis of comparison is linear or one-dimensional; the length of each bar or column is proportional to the value portrayed. Bar and column charts are very much alike; they differ mainly in that the bars are arranged horizontally in a bar chart and the columns are arranged vertically in a column chart. In addition, the bar chart is seldom used for depicting time series, whereas the column chart is often used for that purpose.

There are several different kinds of bar and column charts. Four of them are illustrated in Figure 4.

**Frequency graphs and related charts.** The most common graphic forms for portraying simple frequency distributions are the frequency polygon, the histogram, and the smoothed frequency curve. Frequency graphs are usually drawn on rectilinear coordinates, with the $Y$ axis representing frequencies and the $X$ axis representing the class intervals. The $Y$ axis always begins with zero, and under no circumstances is it broken. The horizontal scale does not have to begin with zero unless, of course, the lower limit of the first class interval

is zero. In laying out a frequency polygon the appropriate frequency of each class customarily is located at the midpoint of the interval, and the plotting points are then connected by straight lines. The typical histogram is constructed by erecting vertical lines at the limits of the class intervals and forming a series of contiguous rectangles or columns. The area of each rectangle represents the respective class frequencies. (If the class intervals are unequal, special care must be taken.) Smoothed frequency curves may be constructed by either mathematical or graphic techniques. The main purpose of smoothing a frequency graph is to remove accidental irregularities resulting mainly from sampling errors; the data from which the smoothed curve was obtained should always be presented as should some indication of the method of smoothing employed.

For some purposes, the cumulative-frequency curve, or ogive, is more useful than the simple frequency graph. In a cumulative-frequency distribution, the frequencies of the successive class intervals are accumulated, beginning at one end of the distribution. If the cumulation process is from the lesser to the greater, it is referred to as a "less than" type of distribution; if from the greater to the lesser, it is known as a "more than" type of distribution. In constructing an ogive, the cumulative frequencies are represented by the vertical axis and the class intervals by the horizontal axis. The cumulated frequencies are plotted either at the lower or upper end of the respective class intervals, depending on whether the cumulation is of the "less than" or "more than" type. A common configuration of the cumulative-frequency curve is that of an elongated S.

*Concentration curves.* A special kind of graph, related to cumulative frequency graphs, is known as a concentration curve or a Lorenz curve. Such a graph is used to portray the nature of non-uniformity in the distributions of inherently positive quantities like wealth, income, amount of retail sales, etc. The graph shows the proportions of total wealth (to be definite) held by various proportions of the relevant population; one reads from the graph that the least wealthy 10 per cent of the population holds, say, 1 per cent of total wealth, that the most wealthy 5 per cent of the population holds, say, 30 per cent of total wealth, etc. Thus the graph is a curve running through points given

parametrically by cumulative relative frequencies and cumulative relative totals; it is usually presented in square form, with both axes taking values from 0 to 1 (for proportions) or 0 to 100 (for per cents). If wealth, or whatever, is uniformly (equally) distributed in the population, the concentration curve is a straight line, the diagonal of the square from (0,0) to (1,1). The more the concentration curve deviates from the straight line the greater is inequality.

**Statistical maps.** There are many varieties of maps used in portraying statistical data. They can be grouped under the following basic types: (1) crosshatched or shaded maps; (2) spot or point-symbol maps; (3) isoline maps; (4) maps with one or more types of graphs superimposed, such as the bar, column, line, flow, or pictorial forms (see Figure 7); and (5) a combination of two or more of the preceding types. [*For an overview of map making, see* CARTOGRAPHY.]

*Crosshatched maps.* The crosshatched or shaded map, characteristically, is used to portray rates and ratios that are based on clearly delineated areal units such as regions, nations, states, coun-

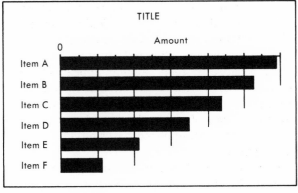

(A) Simple bar chart

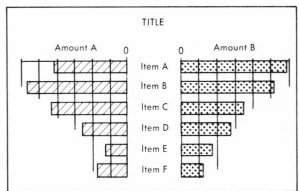

(B) Paired bar chart

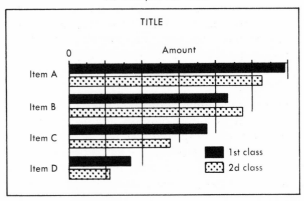

(C) Grouped bar chart

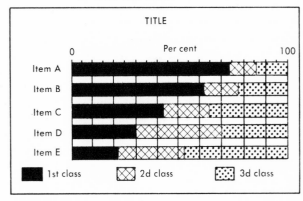

(D) Subdivided 100 per cent bar chart

*Figure 4 — Four types of bar charts*

ties, or census tracts. Value ranges of rates and percentages are represented by a graded series of crosshatchings. Figure 5 is an illustration of a crosshatched map. Since this figure is for illustration only, the medians were computed by the simplest formula, with no attempt made to correct for the fact that most school dropouts occur at the end of a school year.

*Spot maps.* In spot or point-symbol maps emphasis is placed on frequencies or absolute amounts rather than on rates or proportions as in the crosshatched map. Although there may be some overlapping, spot maps may be differentiated into five types on the basis of the symbols used. Symbols may stress (1) size, (2) number, (3) density, (4) shading, or (5) form. In the first type of map the size of each symbol is proportional to the frequency or magnitude of the phenomena represented. Symbols may be either two-dimensional or three-dimensional and are normally in the form of circles or spheres rather than rectangles, cubes, or irregular forms. In the second type of spot map the basic criterion is not size but number or frequency of spots or point symbols. The spots are uniform in size, each representing a specific value. The spots are designed and arranged to make them as readily countable as possible. The third type of map is also a multiple-spot variety; but instead of emphasizing countable frequencies, comparative density and distribution are emphasized. Figure 6 is an example of the third type of spot map, in which over-all density patterns are stressed. In the fourth type of spot map the criterion is shading. The size of the symbols is uniform, but the amount of shading is indicative of the magnitude or value represented. The form of the symbol in the fifth type of map represents certain qualities or attributes rather than quantities, as in the previous types. For example, if the dichotomy male–female is to be portrayed on a map, one type of symbol would represent male and another symbol would represent female.

*Isoline maps.* There are two fundamental types of isoline (from the Greek *isos*, meaning equal) maps: the isometric map, in which the lines are drawn through points of equal value or intensity, and the isopleth map, in which the lines connect equal rates or ratios for specific areas. The isopleth map is particularly valuable in the social sciences.

**Miscellaneous graphic forms.** Although not as basic or as widely used as the graphs and charts discussed in the preceding sections, there are certain other graphic forms that possess advantages for certain problems.

*Pie charts.* The pie or sector chart is widely used to portray proportions of an aggregate or total. Given the several proportions of the total, a pie chart is made by dividing a circle into pieces, one for each separate proportion, by boundary radii. Each proportion corresponds to a single slice, or sector, thus formed; and the central angles (equivalently, the circumference arcs, or again the sector areas) are proportional to the magnitudes of the proportions. Frequently, shading or coloring is used to help distinguish the sectors, and of course proper labeling is essential. Although a pie chart can be very effective in simple situations, it becomes difficult to use if there are more than four or five sectors or if one wishes to compare corresponding proportions for several pie charts.

*Trilinear charts.* The trilinear chart (or barymetric coordinate system) is used to portray simultaneously three nonnegative variables with a fixed sum. Usually they are percentages and the sum is 100. It is drawn in the form of an equilateral triangle, each side of which is calibrated in equal percentage divisions ranging from 0 to 100.

*Scatter diagrams.* The scatter diagram (scattergram) and other types of correlation charts portray in graphic form the degree and type of relationship or covariation between two series of data. The scatter diagram shows a two-way or bivariate frequency distribution. Customarily, arithmetic scales are used in the construction of scatter diagrams, although semilogarithmic or double-logarithmic scales sometimes may be more appropriate.

**Pictorial charts.** Pictorial graphs are used mainly because of their popular appeal, although they rarely convey more information than do more conventional graphic forms. In general, there are four basic types of charts in which pictorial symbols are used, distinguished by criteria of purpose and emphasis.

The four types of pictorial charts are (1) charts in which the size of the pictorial symbol is proportional to the values portrayed; (2) pictorial unit graphs, in which each symbol represents a definite and uniform value; (3) cartoon and sketch charts, in which the basic graphic form, such as a curve or bar, is portrayed as a picture; and (4) charts with pictorial embellishments ranging from a single pictorial filler to elaborate and detailed pictorial backgrounds.

**Three-dimensional projection charts.** In recent years it has become common practice to portray various kinds of graphs and charts in axonometric, oblique, and perspective projection. Charts in three-dimensional form, with depth and other picturelike qualities, unquestionably possess definite popular appeal.

The design of charts and graphs in three-dimen-

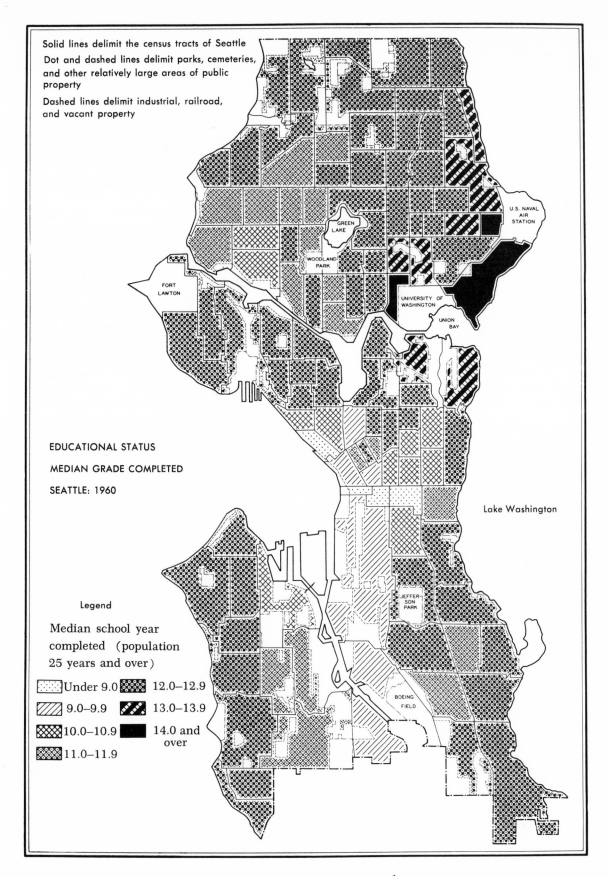

Solid lines delimit the census tracts of Seattle

Dot and dashed lines delimit parks, cemeteries, and other relatively large areas of public property

Dashed lines delimit industrial, railroad, and vacant property

GREEN LAKE

WOODLAND PARK

FORT LAWTON

U.S. NAVAL AIR STATION

UNIVERSITY OF WASHINGTON

UNION BAY

EDUCATIONAL STATUS

MEDIAN GRADE COMPLETED

SEATTLE: 1960

Lake Washington

JEFFER-SON PARK

BOEING FIELD

Legend

Median school year completed (population 25 years and over)

Under 9.0    12.0–12.9

9.0–9.9      13.0–13.9

10.0–10.9    14.0 and over

11.0–11.9

**Figure 5 — Crosshatched map**[*]

* Note hatching gradation from light to dark. Each type of crosshatching represents a value interval in a series of averages.

*Source:* Data from U.S. Bureau of the Census 1962, pp. 15–24.

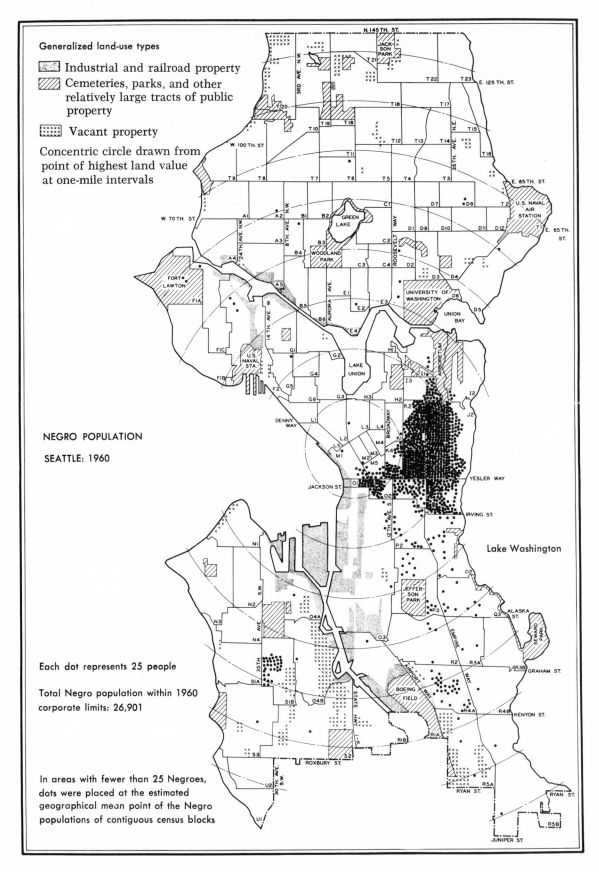

**Generalized land-use types**

- Industrial and railroad property
- Cemeteries, parks, and other relatively large tracts of public property
- Vacant property

Concentric circle drawn from point of highest land value at one-mile intervals

**NEGRO POPULATION**

**SEATTLE: 1960**

Each dot represents 25 people

Total Negro population within 1960 corporate limits: 26,901

In areas with fewer than 25 Negroes, dots were placed at the estimated geographical mean point of the Negro populations of contiguous census blocks

**Figure 6 — Spot map***

* This type of spot map is designed to emphasize comparative density and basic distributional patterns. Note also census tracts, concentric circles, and generalized land-use features on base map.

Source: Schmid & McVey 1964, p. 9.

250

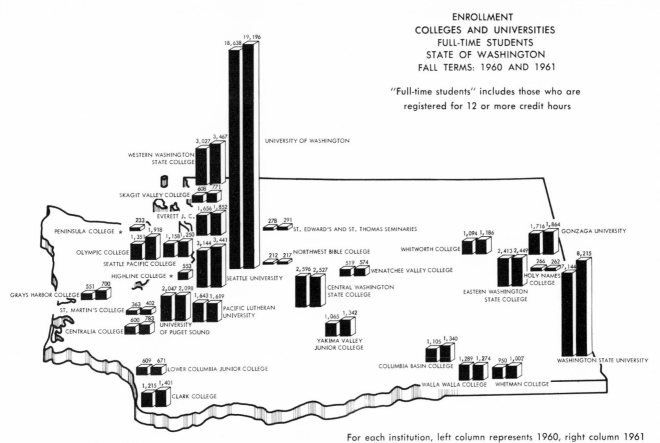

ENROLLMENT
COLLEGES AND UNIVERSITIES
FULL-TIME STUDENTS
STATE OF WASHINGTON
FALL TERMS: 1960 AND 1961

"Full-time students" includes those who are
registered for 12 or more credit hours

For each institution, left column represents 1960, right column 1961

\* Organized after fall term, 1960.

**Figure 7 — Chart in three-dimensional projection**[a]

a. Note especially that columns are drawn in oblique projection.

Source: Schmid et al. 1962, p. 9.

sional form should be based on technically acceptable principles of axonometric, oblique, and perspective projection. Axonometric and oblique projections are the most satisfactory for three-dimensional graphs. Although perspective projection is perhaps the most realistic of the three, it possesses serious limitations as a technique in graphic presentation. Charts constructed in perspective projection are generally distorted; they do not portray exact distance, shape, or size. Figure 7 illustrates a map in three-dimensional form.

CALVIN F. SCHMID

[See also TABULAR PRESENTATION.]

### BIBLIOGRAPHY

REFERENCES ON GRAPHIC PRESENTATION

BRINTON, WILLARD C. 1939 *Graphic Presentation.* New York: Brinton.

FUNKHOUSER, H. G. 1937 Historical Development of the Graphical Representation of Statistical Data. *Osiris* 3:269–404.

HUFF, DARREL; and GEIS, IRVING 1954 *How to Lie With Statistics.* New York: Norton. → Contains a discussion of graphical fallacies. Also published in paperback.

JENKS, G. F.; and BROWN, D. A. 1966 Three-dimensional Map Construction. *Science* 154:857–864.

MODLEY, RUDOLF; and LOWENSTEIN, DYNO 1952 *Pictographs and Graphs: How to Make and Use Them.* New York: Harper.

PÈPE, PAUL 1959 *Présentation des statistiques.* Paris: Dunod.

ROYSTON, ERICA 1956 Studies in the History of Probability and Statistics. III. A Note on the History of the Graphical Representation of Data. *Biometrika* 43:241–247.

SCHMID, CALVIN F. 1954 *Handbook of Graphic Presentation.* New York: Ronald.

SCHMID, CALVIN F. 1956 What Price Pictorial Charts? *Estadistica: Journal of the Inter-American Statistical Institute* 15:12–25.

SCHMID, CALVIN F.; and MACCANNELL, EARLE H. 1955 Basic Problems, Techniques, and Theory of Isopleth Mapping. *Journal of the American Statistical Association* 50:220–239.

SOURCES OF FIGURES AND DATA

SCHMID, CALVIN F.; and McVEY, WAYNE W. JR. 1964 *Growth and Distribution of Minority Races in Seattle, Washington.* Seattle Public Schools.

SCHMID, CALVIN F. et al. 1962 *Enrollment Statistics, Colleges and Universities: State of Washington, Fall Term, 1961.* Seattle: Washington State Census Board.

SCHMID, CALVIN F. et al.   1966   *Studies in Enrollment Trends and Patterns*. Part 1: Regular Academic Year: 1930 to 1964. Seattle: Univ. of Washington.

U.S. BUREAU OF THE CENSUS   1962   *U.S. Censuses of Population and Housing: 1960*. Census Tracts, Final Report PHC (1) 142: Seattle, Wash. Washington: Government Printing Office. → See especially pages 15–34, Table P-1, "General Characteristics of the Population, by Census Tracts: 1960."

U.S. BUREAU OF THE CENSUS   1963   *U.S. Census of Population: 1960*. Vol. 1, Part 45: Texas. Washington: Government Printing Office.

## GRAS, N. S. B.

Norman Scott Brien Gras, pioneer business historian, was born in 1884 in Toronto of German and Irish parentage. His father was an unsuccessful general retailer and moved from place to place in search of a living. As a child, Gras had to work as a mill delivery boy and at other lowly jobs, hard beginnings which help to explain him as an adult. Endowed with extraordinary intellectual capacity, he was able to overcome economic difficulties and complete his undergraduate training at the University of Western Ontario. He went on to obtain his PH.D. in economics at Harvard University. His thesis was written under Edwin F. Gay, America's first economic historian, whom Gras himself considered his "intellectual father." From 1912 to 1917 Gras was an assistant professor at Clark College and in 1917/1918 an associate professor at Clark University. From there he went as a full professor to the University of Minnesota and then in 1927 to the Graduate School of Business Administration, Harvard University, where he remained as Isidor Strauss professor of business history until 1950, when he retired. From 1949 to his death in 1956, he was president of the Business History Foundation, Inc., under whose auspices the history of the Standard Oil Company (New Jersey) was being written.

Gras's career falls into two main periods. In the first he devoted himself chiefly to problems in English social and economic history, and he carried on most of his research in England. English scholars appreciated his work, and he was made a member of the Council of the English Economic History Society and eventually, in 1939, a vice-president.

The second period in Gras's career began with his appointment to the faculty of the Harvard Business School. In the 1920s and early 1930s, which constituted his most creative period, Gras had begun to focus on a new intellectual problem: he began to make business the subject of systematic historical research. Similar ideas were then being broached by leading professors at the Harvard Business School, and when the new field was established at that school, Gras's appointment was eminently suitable.

The result of his endeavors was "business history," a new concept to which Gras gave content and which he initially defined broadly. Because he was the first American teacher in this field, it was incumbent on him to collect source material. Since the Harvard Business School used the case method in its teaching, in 1939 Gras and his lifelong associate, Henrietta M. Larson, brought out a *Casebook in American Business History* for use in his classes. Even earlier he had begun to edit a series of company histories, the Harvard Studies in Business History. He wrote two of them himself, one on the First National Bank of Boston (1937) and another on the Harvard Co-operative Society (1942). In and outside of the school, Gras worked incessantly for the recognition of the new field. It is his merit that the use of business records has become common among economic historians.

Shortly after Gras's arrival at Harvard, the *Journal of Economic and Business History* was founded. It was the first American journal to deal with economic history and the first in the world to aim at combining economic history with the new business history. Gras became its highly efficient managing editor. Unfortunately, he pushed his special interest somewhat too hard and came into conflict with the powerful Edwin F. Gay, the editor of the journal. Gay withdrew in 1931, and Gras succeeded him as editor, but his opportunity to mold the journal was short-lived, since financial reasons compelled the ceasing of publication in 1932. The conflict between Gay and Gras was ultimately to isolate Gras from the rest of the American economic historians, since most of them were Gay's former students; worse yet, it produced a separation between business history and the better-developed older field, economic history.

Gras's attempt to publish a synthesis and generalization of the material on business history he had accumulated for more than 15 years was hardly successful. He failed to distinguish between analytical constructs, such as his stages of capitalist development, and the economic reality which they were designed to explain.

After its auspicious beginnings, the development of business history ran into difficulties in the 1930s. Financial trouble in the wake of the depression made it necessary to abandon the original broad concept of "business history" and to concentrate on company histories. Also, Gras was now faced with that resistance which many innovators are bound to meet. Besides these problems beyond Gras's control, his endeavors did suffer from his alienation from his colleagues. The narrowing down of the field, originally forced on Gras, became after a while a matter of his choice, and he came to identify "business history" with the study of the administration and policies of individual enterprises. His work, moreover, was empiricistic. His attempts to stimulate interest in the new area through an appeal to businessmen and his way of gaining access to business records aroused the suspicion of intellectuals and social scientists, because in this period they tended to be hostile toward business. Finally, although Gras was an inspiring teacher and a friend of students, in his later years he seemed unable to deal with his peers on the basis of intellectual give-and-take. He appeared unwilling to cooperate with other scholars who came to the new field of research on business with more refined tools and with related, yet different, goals. By the time of Gras's death the exponents of business history had returned to the broad and fruitful conception of his earlier years and were developing the field as the social and economic history of business.

FRITZ REDLICH

[For discussion of the subsequent development of Gras's ideas, see HISTORY, article on BUSINESS HISTORY.]

### WORKS BY GRAS

1915  Evolution of the English Corn Market From the Twelfth to the Eighteenth Century. Harvard Economic Studies, Vol. 13. Cambridge, Mass.: Harvard Univ. Press.
1918  The Early English Customs System: A Documentary Study of the Institutional and Economic History of the Customs From the Thirteenth to the Sixteenth Century. Harvard Economic Studies, Vol. 18. Cambridge, Mass.: Harvard Univ. Press.
1922  An Introduction to Economic History. New York: Harper.
(1925) 1940  A History of Agriculture in Europe and America. 2d ed. New York: Crofts.
1930  Industrial Evolution. Cambridge, Mass.: Harvard Univ. Press.
1930  GRAS, NORMAN S. B.; and GRAS, ETHEL C. The Economic and Social History of an English Village (Crawley, Hampshire) A.D. 909–1928. Harvard Economic Studies, Vol. 34. Cambridge, Mass.: Harvard Univ. Press.
1937  The Massachusetts First National Bank of Boston: 1784–1934. Harvard Studies in Business History, No. 4. Cambridge, Mass.: Harvard Univ. Press.
1939  Business and Capitalism: An Introduction to Business History. New York: Crofts.
1939  GRAS, NORMAN S. B.; and LARSON, HENRIETTA M. Casebook in American Business History. New York: Crofts.
1942  Harvard Co-operative Society Past and Present: 1882–1942. Cambridge, Mass.: Harvard Univ. Press.
1962  Development of Business History up to 1950. Edited by Ethel C. Gras. New York: Lincoln Educational Foundation. → Published posthumously.

# GRAUNT, JOHN

John Graunt (1620–1674) is generally regarded as having laid the foundations of demography as a science with the publication of his *Natural and Political Observations Made Upon the Bills of Mortality* (1662a). Graunt began, as many scientists have done, by exercising idle curiosity—"Now having (I know not by what accident) engaged my thoughts upon the *Bills of Mortality* . . ." ([1662a] 1939, p. 3)—and proceeding to "observations, which I happened to make (for I designed them not) . . ." (*ibid.*, p. 5). Characteristically, he did not believe that curiosity should remain idle: "finding some *Truths*, and not commonly-believed Opinions . . . I proceeded further, to consider what benefit the knowledge of the same would bring the World" (*ibid.*, p. 18).

Graunt's application of the statistical method to raw material had two essential elements: (1) *classification* of like with like, so as to break the data down into homogeneous groups, and (2) the *comparison* of those groups in order to recognize significant differentials. Another attribute of Graunt as a statistician was his ability to apply logic to his arithmetic. He never accepted a calculation if it offended his common sense; nor did he accept it without a test, if he had the means of testing it.

As to classification, we may read in Chapter 2 of his *Observations* his very sound remarks about the identification of causes of death, then dependent on the observation of the "ancient matron" searchers (*ibid.*, pp. 27–32). Deaths at advanced ages, he argued, can hardly be safely attributed to one specific cause, and not much worthwhile information can be expected about sudden deaths beyond their suddenness. As to comparison, we find in the same chapter his observation about the stability of proportionate mortality rates for certain causes, and in Chapter 4 (*ibid.*, pp. 45–48) his observation that in plague years, deaths from causes other than plague were inflated to such an extent as to lead to his conclusion that of deaths from plague fully one-fifth were attributed to some other cause (in order to avoid the closure of the plague-infested dwelling and the virtual incarceration of the surviving members of the household). Again in Chapter 3 (*ibid.*, pp. 33–44), we may see how comparison of mortality rates for rickets with mortality rates referring to possible similar names for the same disease led Graunt, after examining the figures, to conclude that rickets was a new disease and not a new name for an old one. (This was probably a wrong conclusion, but Graunt was not a physician and would not have known that medical attention was at that time being drawn to the disease.)

The method of comparison was again employed when Graunt estimated the population of London in Chapter 11 (*ibid.*, pp. 67–70). He used three methods and reconciled them. First, he estimated that a fertile woman had a baby every other year, that fertile women numbered half the married women, and that there were seven other members of a family (husband, 3 children, 3 servants); therefore, the population was 32 times the number of annual births. This gives 384,000. Next he estimated that in certain parishes there were annually three deaths from every 11 families; therefore, the number of deaths (13,000) multiplied by 11/3 yielded 48,000 families, or 384,000 persons. Finally, he observed 54 families per 100 square yards within the walls (12,000 families) and guessed that there were three times as many families outside the walls.

Graunt's most important contribution to demography was his rudimentary life table. Its importance lies not in the table itself, which is indeed defective, but in the novelty of presenting mortality in terms of survivorship. Graunt began with only two observations—the proportion of births surviving to age 6 (.64) and the proportion surviving to age 76 (.01). He then assumed that a constant multiplier is involved in proceeding from the first proportion to the last by decennial intervals of age. He did not make clear how he got his multiplier (or "mean proportion," as he called it), but it was obviously about .6. Michel Ptouka (1938) has put forward the hypothesis that the multiplier was $(64 - 1)/100 = .63$. D. V. Glass has suggested (1950) that Graunt made a second difference interpolation from $l_0 = 100$, $l_6 = 64$, and $l_{76} = 1$. The method and any error in it is not important. (Halley was not to make the correct calculation for another sixty years or so.) So much has been developed from this simple but immensely powerful thought that actuarial criticism would be quite out of place.

Graunt is rarely considered apart from another English scientist of the time, Sir William Petty.

Both were of Hampshire stock; Graunt was born in 1620 and Petty in 1623. They became acquainted in or before 1650. It appears that their relationship was initially that of client and patron (Graunt being Petty's patron; see Greenwood 1941–1943), but the roles were reversed after the fire of London in 1666.

Graunt was the son of a city tradesman and became a haberdasher and a man of substance. Petty, who had sampled the merchant navy, studied mathematics in France, spent a short time in the Royal Navy, returned to the Continent to study anatomy, spent some time in business in London, and went to Oxford in 1649, becoming a doctor of medicine by dispensation. Later he rose to be professor of anatomy and vice-principal of Brasenose. He became a candidate for a Gresham professorship in London and made contact with Graunt. We do not know what interests they shared at that time or whether Graunt (or his father) had any influence in Petty's subsequent appointment as Gresham professor of music. Soon after, Petty (who seems to have had no professional duties) went to Ireland and made a fortune. For many years Graunt remained a prosperous tradesman, but the fire of 1666 destroyed his business. A little later he became a Roman Catholic convert and was apparently not interested in rebuilding his business, for he was soon bankrupt. It was now Petty's turn to be the patron, and Graunt, the client—and apparently not an easy one. Despite Petty's attempts to help him, Graunt's financial troubles were with him until he died in 1674.

Petty's vital statistical work was on a different level from that of Graunt. Petty had inspiration and brilliance, many ideas and a breadth of vision, but he did not pursue his ideas as persistently as Graunt did. It was Petty who proposed a central government statistical office and a system of census taking. He anticipated William Farr in estimating the economic loss due to mortality. Many of his calculations, however, do not stand up to the tests of consistency that Graunt would have applied. It seems to be generally agreed that Graunt made an immeasurably greater contribution to demography.

Essentially, Graunt was a man with an inquiring mind whose ideas laid the foundation of the political arithmetic that we now accept as part of good social organization and government. The Royal Society of London, of which Graunt was elected a fellow, commemorated the tercentenary of the publication of his *Observations* by holding a special series of scientific meetings to which leading demographers in England and other countries contributed papers (Glass 1963). The Institute of Actuaries of England paid its own tribute to Graunt by republishing, in a more modern format but without abridgment or alteration, his original *Observations*.

B. BENJAMIN

[*For the historical context of Graunt's work, see* PUBLIC HEALTH; VITAL STATISTICS; *and the biography of* PETTY. *For discussion of the subsequent development of his ideas, see* LIFE TABLES; MORTALITY; *and the biographies of* KŐRÖSY; LOTKA.]

### WORKS BY GRAUNT

(1662*a*) 1939  *Natural and Political Observations Made Upon the Bills of Mortality*. Edited with an introduction by Walter F. Willcox. Baltimore: Johns Hopkins Press. → See especially Chapter 2, "General Observations Upon the Casualties"; Chapter 3, "Of Particular Casualties"; Chapter 4, "On the Plague"; Chapter 11, "Of the Number of Inhabitants."
(1662*b*) 1964  *Natural and Political Observations Mentioned in a Following Index, and Made Upon the Bills of Mortality: With Reference to the Government, Religion, Trade, Growth, Ayre, Diseases, and Several Changes of the Said City* [London]. *Journal of the Institute of Actuaries* (London) 90:1–61. → Includes a three-page introduction by B. Benjamin.

### SUPPLEMENTARY BIBLIOGRAPHY

GLASS, D. V.  1950  Graunt's Life Table. *Journal of the Institute of Actuaries* (London) 76:60–64.
GLASS, D. V.  1963  John Graunt and His *Natural and Political Observations*. Royal Society of London, *Proceedings* Series B 159:1–38. → Includes six pages of discussion.
GREENWOOD, MAJOR  (1941–1943) 1948  *Medical Statistics From Graunt to Farr*. Cambridge Univ. Press. → First published in *Biometrika*.
NEWMAN, JAMES R.  1956  Commentary on an Ingenious Army Captain and on a Generous and Many-sided Man. Volume 3, pages 1416–1419 in James R. Newman (editor), *The World of Mathematics: A Small Library of the Literature of Mathematics From A'hmosé the Scribe to Albert Einstein*. New York: Simon & Schuster.
PTOUKA, MICHEL  1938  John Graunt, fondateur de la démographie: 1620–1674. Volume 2, pages 61–74 in International Congress for Studies on Population, Paris, 1937, *Congrès international de la population*. Paris: Hermann.
SUTHERLAND, IAN  1963  John Graunt: A Tercentenary Tribute. *Journal of the Royal Statistical Society* Series A 126:537–556.

# GREEN, T. H.

Thomas Hill Green (1836–1882), English philosopher, social theorist, and reformer, was born in Birkin, Yorkshire, where his father was rector. He became a fellow of Balliol College, Oxford, in 1860, and professor of moral philosophy in 1878 but died four years later at the age of 45. Green initiated and inspired the British renaissance of Hegelian idealism, which started in Oxford in the 1870s and dominated academic philosophy in Britain until its retreat before the criticisms of Bertrand Russell and G. E. Moore in the early years of the twentieth century.

Green's aim was to demolish the prevailing system of thought that grafted evolutionary ideas onto the stem of traditional empiricism and to lead his contemporaries away from J. S. Mill and Huxley and toward Kant and Hegel. He began with an attack on received views in metaphysics and theory of knowledge, which appeared in an introduction to the works of David Hume (1874). Knowledge, he held, could not be derived by a merely passive mind from a sequence of discrete sensations. Nature is an unalterable scheme of intelligible relations constructed by the mind; this implies an equally unalterable and objective eternal consciousness of which all finite minds are parts. As the constructer of nature, mind cannot be a part or product of it.

The prevailing system of philosophy, which regarded man as a part of nature governed by deterministic laws, ruled out conduct as much as it ruled out knowledge. Green believed will and choice, the rational determinants of action, must instead be distinguished from passive compliance with the promptings of natural desire. In an act of will, a man identifies himself with his ideal self or character, which is part of the eternal consciousness and not of the mechanical order of nature. The moral end is the full realization of one's potentialities, and these can be realized only in a social community. For Green, as for Rousseau and Hegel before him, genuine human personality was an essentially social phenomenon, and it was inconceivable that isolated natural man should be a moral agent. Green was not entirely hostile to Mill's chastened utilitarianism; he shared its rejection of customary rules but conceived the ideal end of conduct as moral perfection, not individual contentment. (For Green's metaphysics and ethics see Green 1883.)

Green's social theory (1882) follows Rousseau and Hegel to some extent in subordinating the individual to the community. The duty of the citizen is to follow the general will for the common good. But for Green the community is not coterminous with the state; he remained in the liberal tradition in asserting the sovereignty of morals over politics. There is some of Hegel's contempt for the individual conscience in Green's well-known view that there can be no unrecognized rights, but he did not say that all true rights were legal ones. The recognizing authority is not the state but the moral consensus of the community. Positive law can be criticized and improved upon in the light of the state's ideal purpose: the moral perfection of men. Since morality presupposes freedom the state cannot serve this end directly, but it can create favorable conditions for it. Green valued democracy as giving men the kind of responsibility that is conducive to moral improvement. Participation in democracy is a duty, not a right; an opportunity for moral development, not a negative emancipation from authority and constraint.

Green's special combination of moral individualism and collectivism, in particular his idea of the state as an indirect agent of moral improvement, led him to favor the intervention of the state to secure the welfare of its citizens (1881). He was opposed to Mill's libertarianism and Spencer's barbarous version of laissez-faire. In his support of the enlargement of the state's responsibilities he anticipated the doctrines of the British Labour party. He became the first Oxford tutor to serve on the city council, where he actively promoted temperance reform and public secondary education. Realistic in his respect for the force of circumstances and the moral sense of the community, Green was no traditionalist. He admired Cromwell (from whom he claimed descent) and shared his republicanism. He was hostile to class distinction, militarism, and patriotic display. The first important English philosopher since Ralph Cudworth to spend his active life in a university, he supported, by precept and example, the involvement of philosophers in the social and political life of their society. The character of Mr. Grey in Mrs. Humphry Ward's novel *Robert Elsmere* is an admiring portrait of Green's nobly serious personality, in which a determined puritanism was at once strengthened and mitigated by decency and practical good sense.

ANTHONY QUINTON

[*For the historical context of Green's work, see the biographies of* HEGEL; MILL; ROUSSEAU. *For discussion of the development of his ideas, see the biographies of* BOSANQUET; FIGGIS; LINDSAY.]

WORKS BY GREEN

(1874) 1906   Introduction to Hume's *Treatise of Human Nature.* Pages 1–371 in Thomas Hill Green, *Works . . .* Volume 1: *Philosophical Works.* London: Longmans.

(1881) 1906   Lecture on Liberal Legislation and Freedom of Contract. Pages 365–386 in Thomas Hill Green, *Works . . .* Volume 3: *Miscellanies and Memoir.* London: Longmans.

(1882) 1960   *Lectures on the Principles of Political Obligation.* London: Longmans.

(1883) 1929   *Prolegomena to Ethics.* 5th ed. Oxford: Clarendon.

1906   *Works of Thomas Hill Green.* Edited by R. L. Nettleship. 3 vols. London: Longmans. → Volumes 1–2: *Philosophical Works.* Volume 3: *Miscellanies and Memoir.*

SUPPLEMENTARY BIBLIOGRAPHY

FAIRBROTHER, WILLIAM H.   (1896) 1900   *The Philosophy of Thomas Hill Green.* 2d ed. London: Methuen.

MILNE, A. J. M.   1962   *The Social Philosophy of English Idealism.* London: Allen & Unwin.

MUIRHEAD, JOHN HENRY   1908   *The Service of the State: Four Lectures on the Political Teaching of T. H. Green.* London: Murray.

RICHTER, MELVIN   1964   *The Politics of Conscience: T. H. Green and His Age.* Harvard Univ. Press.

RITCHIE, DAVID G.   (1887) 1902   The Political Philosophy of Thomas Hill Green. Pages 125–151 in David G. Ritchie, *The Principles of State Interference: Four Essays on the Political Philosophy of Mr. Herbert Spencer, J. S. Mill, and T. H. Green.* London: Sonnenschein. → First published in *Contemporary Review.*

# GRIEF
*See* DEATH; SYMPATHY AND EMPATHY.

# GROSS NATIONAL PRODUCT
*See* NATIONAL INCOME AND PRODUCT ACCOUNTS.

# GROSS REPRODUCTION RATE
*See* FERTILITY.

# GROTIUS, HUGO

Huig de Groot (1583–1645), better known by the Latinized version of his name, Hugo Grotius, was born at Delft in the province of Holland. He was carefully educated by his father, whose intellectual interests were both broad and profound, and who imbued in him the characteristic civic pride of the Dutch patriciate.

Grotius was extraordinarily young when his exceptional gifts became apparent. From 1594 to 1597 he studied in the faculty of arts of the University of Leiden, the Protestant university that had been opened in 1575. In 1599 he was called to the bar at The Hague; and in 1607 he received his first public office as *advocaat fiscaal* (deputy attorney general) at the highest law court in the province of Holland. Five years later he was appointed pensionary of Rotterdam, a political office that gave him power not only in the city itself but also in the States (the representative assembly) of the province, where he acted as Rotterdam's representative.

Meanwhile, Grotius' publications established him both as an accomplished neo-Latin poet and dramatist and as an ambitious historian and jurist. As a jurist he wrote a short book *The Freedom of the Seas* (1609)—it was, in fact, just one chapter of the manuscript *De jure praedae* (1604), not published until 1868—in which he tried to prove that no authority is entitled to claim sovereignty over the high seas; although it was aimed at Spanish pretensions, the book also aroused the wrath of James I of England.

In the 1610s Grotius became one of the major supporters of the grand pensionary, Johan van Oldenbarnevelt, who was engaged in a bitter struggle with the stadholder, Prince Maurice of Orange, on two issues: Oldenbarnevelt and Grotius supported the cause of the Arminians and of provincial sovereignty, particularly that of Holland. After their defeat in 1618, Oldenbarnevelt was executed and Grotius sentenced to life imprisonment. Thanks to the resourcefulness of his wife, Grotius escaped to France after three years; he was welcomed by Louis XIII, who paid him a pension, albeit irregularly. From 1621 to 1631 he lived in Paris with his family in relatively poor circumstances. He lived by his pen, expecting all the while that the justice of his cause would lead to his eventual rehabilitation in the Netherlands. In 1631 he made an attempt to re-establish himself there but was forced to leave the following year. In 1634 he accepted the offer of Queen Christina of Sweden to become her ambassador to France, and for ten years he worked in that capacity in Paris, a somewhat eccentric scholar of bourgeois origin among titled professional diplomats.

Diplomacy bored Grotius, and he could not afford to wait long years for his salary to be paid, as could his noble colleagues. He tried to compensate for his inadequacy as a diplomat by working for a goal far above the pettiness of routine politics: the restoration of Christian unity. During his last years, this came to be his major preoccupation. In 1645 he went to Sweden to offer his resignation. He went by way of Holland, where at last he was welcomed with the warmth he had been expecting in vain for two decades. On the journey back from Sweden, where Christina had received him with utmost politeness and with equal politeness accepted his resignation, his ship was driven off course, and he went ashore on the Pomeranian coast. He took the road to Lübeck but did not reach that city: forced to rest in Rostock, he died there from exhaustion.

Grotius' intellectual achievement has a paradoxical character. He won great fame as a poet and dramatist, as a historian, a philologist, a theologian, and, of course, a jurist. But learned discussions about the contributions he made to all these different fields have not come to any conclusion about whether he was essentially a con-

servative who put together in magnificent syntheses opinions previously held by others or an innovator boldly treading new ground. The endless variety of his work, the mixture of precision and suppleness in his thought, and the sheer bulk of his learning make it almost impossible to determine with any certainty the degree of originality of his views.

He was very much a man of the baroque age. His motto, *ruit hora* (time flies), the Latin language in which he wrote most of his books, and his profound awareness of life's antinomies indicate how fully he belonged to the civilization of his time. Yet in the deeply pessimistic early seventeenth century his optimism and rationalism were exceptional and so effortless that they may seem shallow in comparison with the views of such philosophers as Descartes. His theological studies were inspired by deep religious feelings, but they brought him into conflict with Protestants of various denominations and gave both Catholics and, later, deists the erroneous impression that he supported their views. His constant endeavors to heal the breaches in the Christian church caused the most confusing misunderstandings and involved him in acrimonious controversy.

During his imprisonment, from 1618 to 1621, Grotius wrote, in rhyme, *The Truth of the Christian Religion*; it was published in Dutch in 1622, and in 1627 Grotius' own Latin version followed. In this simple book, written for seamen who might be impressed by foreign religions, Grotius explained and lauded the main tenets of Christianity. The book was a great success; it was translated not only into all the major European languages but also into Danish, Irish, Hungarian, and Arabic, and there are 110 known editions of it.

Grotius' masterpiece, *The Law of War and Peace* (1625), was also an immediate and widespread success, if not on the same scale as his little book on Christianity: it has gone through at least 75 editions and has been translated 24 times. In this book he presented his famous doctrine of the just war. War, in his view, is justified as a means of obtaining justice in cases where no law court exists to give a ruling upon the matter under dispute. Most of these cases are, of course, international conflicts, such as the revolt of the United Provinces against Spain. A contestant may take up arms in order to defend his property or his rights, to take possession of what is due to him, or to punish criminal offenses. Thus, war is essentially a lawsuit carried out by armed force because there is no court that can deal with it.

Other concepts are also presented in this large book, which is like a warehouse of opinions, quotations, conflicting doctrines, and debates. Especially noteworthy is Grotius' doctrine of natural law, for it exerted considerable influence, even if it was neither coherent nor strikingly original. Since he considered natural law to be basic to all social organization, international or national, Grotius' initially juridical theory developed into a more general one that analyzed and explained not only the conditions of international justice but every aspect of human society. In other words, his work pertains as much to general sociology as to international law.

Grotius defined the law of nature as "a dictate of right reason, showing the moral necessity or moral baseness of any act according to its agreement or disagreement with rational nature, and indicating that such an act is either commanded or forbidden by the author of nature, God" (1625, pp. 20–21 in a 1949 edition). This does not differ essentially from scholastic conceptions, and it is somewhat misleading to claim, as has often been done, that Grotius made an original contribution by secularizing the medieval interpretation of natural law. For Grotius, just as for the medieval thinkers and the sixteenth-century Spanish lawyers whom he quoted, the law of nature is an objective datum, an absolute norm given for all eternity. It is only later in the century, with Hobbes and other theorists, that the law of nature, identified with the instinct of self-preservation, developed into an essentially individualistic, subjective, and secular concept. Grotius, according to Erik Wolf (Wolf 1939) saw God, nature, and reason as only different names for the metaphysical foundation of life, which to human beings becomes manifest in law. Society is a natural and necessary form of concrete law because man is a social being endowed with reason. Thus, human society is also by definition rational.

These premises served Grotius as starting points for determining the rational quality in social and political life. It was not his purpose to draft a political theory. Various political concepts that seemed essential to his contemporaries were rather indifferently treated by him. Sovereignty, for example, did not mean much to a thinker educated in the corporative, patrician Dutch republic that was slowly emerging when he was young. Yet he transcended his origins by regarding all nations, sovereignties, and even churches as mere elements of the largest possible social entity, the human race in general. Therefore, the societies under examination appeared to him as manifestations of a social and ethical order in which each social element has its place, determined by its own existential principle.

But all of them are embraced by the corporative unity which is humanity—primarily, of course, Christian humanity.

The *Law of War and Peace* is more than a philosophical and sociological monograph. To make it useful to the practical statesman, Grotius endeavored to determine the justifiability of particular actions that are often taken prior to war or in war, according to simple principles laid out by him. Although, for example, Gustavus Adolphus is said to have consulted the book frequently while campaigning in Germany, it is obviously impossible to assess the actual impact of its prescriptions on the conduct of war. But this much is certain: the work exercised a profound influence on the development of international law, and even in the present century it is referred to not only by professional lawyers but also by statesmen. The remarkable mixture of idealistic optimism—for in spite of international chaos, Grotius viewed the ethical content of natural law as a principle that automatically asserts itself, since, in the last analysis, rational and natural behavior are identical—and realism, which sprang from a critical study of history, rendered his concepts and advice applicable to many situations and attractive to many different groups.

E. H. KOSSMANN

[See also INTERNATIONAL LAW *and the biography of* VATTEL.]

## WORKS BY GROTIUS

(1597–1628) 1928–1965 *Briefwisseling van Hugo Grotius.* 4 vols. Edited by P. C. Molhuysen and B. L. Meulenbroek. The Hague: Nijhoff. → Additional volumes are projected.

(1604) 1950 *De jure praedae commentarius: Commentary on the Law of Prize and Booty.* 2 vols. Oxford: Clarendon Press. → The manuscript of 1604 was first published in 1868.

(1609) 1916 *The Freedom of the Seas: Or, the Right Which Belongs to the Dutch to Take Part in the East India Trade.* New York: Oxford Univ. Press. → First published as *Mare liberum.*

(1622) 1823 *The Truth of the Christian Religion.* 16th ed. Corrected and illustrated with notes by Le Clerc. Oxford: Baxter. → First published in Dutch.

(1625) 1962 *The Law of War and Peace: De jure belli ac pacis.* Translated by Francis W. Kelsey, with an introduction by James Brown Scott. Indianapolis, Ind.: Bobbs-Merrill. → An edition was published in 1949 by Black.

1687 *Epistolae quotquot reperiri potuerunt: In quibus praeter hactenus editas, plurimae theologici, iuridici, philologici, historici, et politici argumenti occurrunt.* Amsterdam: Blaeu.

## SUPPLEMENTARY BIBLIOGRAPHY

KNIGHT, WILLIAM S. M. 1925 *The Life and Works of Hugo Grotius.* London: Sweet & Maxwell.

MEULEN, JACOB TER; and DIERMANSE, P. J. J.  1950  *Bibliographie des écrits imprimés de Hugo Grotius*. The Hague: Nijhoff.

MEULEN, JACOB TER; and DIERMANSE, P. J. J.  1961  *Bibliographie des écrits sur Hugo Grotius imprimés au XVIIe siècle*. The Hague: Nijhoff.

WOLF, ERIK  (1939) 1963  *Grosse Rechtsdenker der deutschen Geistesgeschichte*. 4th ed., rev. & enl. Tübingen: Mohr. → See especially "Hugo Grotius," pages 253–311.

# GROUP DYNAMICS

*See* FIELD THEORY *and the biography of* LEWIN.

# GROUPED OBSERVATIONS

*See under* STATISTICAL ANALYSIS, SPECIAL PROBLEMS OF.

# GROUPS

## I
### THE STUDY OF GROUPS

In social science the study of groups is often called *small-group research*. A "group" is defined as a number of persons, or members, each of whom, while the group is meeting, interacts with every other, or is able to do so, or can at least take personal cognizance of every other. This requirement, which cannot be met for larger social units, such as armies, justifies calling groups "small." Although no investigator has specified the number of members that would make a group "large" rather than "small," the groups actually studied have seldom had more than fifty members. It is, moreover, often difficult to draw the boundaries between groups, as marginal persons may interact with members of two or more groups.

Investigators working within the field of small groups seldom study the behavior of groups as such. More often they study the characteristics of face-to-face interaction among men, of which the behavior of groups considered as units is only a part. Accordingly, the subject should perhaps be called "elementary social behavior" (Homans 1961) rather than "small groups." A group so small that an investigator can observe the behavior of each of its members in some detail is a good setting for the study of this subject, but the group usually remains the setting rather than the object of investigation.

For this reason the problem of defining a group or demarcating its boundaries is seldom of theoretical importance. When the behavior of a group as such is to be studied, its boundaries, in practice, are apt to be quite clear.

## History of small-group research

The interest in groups has sprung from two main sources, which may be called psychological and sociological after the disciplinary affiliations of the chief investigators. In psychology the interest perhaps began with studies of social facilitation. From the 1930s on, it was stimulated by the experimental and theoretical work of Kurt Lewin on social influence. Lewin trained a group of students, including R. Lippitt, D. Cartwright, A. Bavelas, and L. Festinger (Cartwright & Zander 1953; compare Lewin 1939–1947). Members of the Tavistock Institute in England largely shared their viewpoint. Although many psychologists in the field were not students of Lewin's, few escaped his influence.

In sociology much of the work of Georg Simmel (1902–1917) lay in the field now called small-group research. But his influence was not direct: indeed, later research had the effect of reviving interest in him. The other early name of importance is that of Charles H. Cooley, who pointed out the influence of certain kinds of groups, such as the family and the children's play group, which he called *primary groups*, in forming the attitudes of men (Cooley 1909).

Simmel and Cooley were intuitive observers and theorists. For empirical investigation, Elton Mayo was to sociology what Lewin was to psychology. The researches carried out in the 1920s in the Hawthorne plant of the Western Electric Company by Mayo and his associates of the Harvard Graduate School of Business Administration were conceived as studies of human relations in industry (Roethlisberger & Dickson 1939). But several of the researches put small industrial groups under close scrutiny and suggested the possible fruitfulness of more general work. E. D. Chapple and C. M. Arensberg (1940), who developed operational measures of face-to-face interaction, were indirectly associated with the Western Electric researches; so were sociologists like W. F. Whyte (1943) and G. C. Homans (1950), who have worked in the small-group field, as well as investigators at the Harvard Business School. Yet there is plenty of such work in sociology that does not stem directly from the school of Mayo.

A third, rather specialized, influence in the 1930s was that of J. L. Moreno (1934) and his associate, H. H. Jennings, who worked at the New

York State Training School for Girls. They contributed interesting empirical findings and, more important, the technique they called the *sociometric test*, which in one form or another is now used by most investigators.

Great Britain, France, and the Scandinavian countries have also made important contributions to the field; in France an early theoretical influence was the "microsociology" of G. Gurvitch (1950).

## Methodology

One justification for speaking of psychological and sociological "schools" is that until recently they tended to use somewhat different research designs. True to the traditions of their discipline, the psychologists emphasized experimental and survey methods. They would bring groups, sometimes groups artificially constituted for research purposes, into laboratories where some of the variables affecting the subjects' behavior might be held constant and others experimentally manipulated. They developed quantitative measures of behavior and administered standardized questionnaires; they formulated hypotheses relating the independent, experimentally manipulated variables to the dependent ones; they tested the significance of these hypotheses statistically. They also exploited natural situations that provided some approximation to experimental control—for instance, a set of groups all alike in some respect, such as residents of houses of identical design or groups having identical tasks to perform. The psychologists would correlate statistically the variations along a number of dimensions of behavior occurring naturally in these groups.

Instead of studying several similar groups under more or less controlled conditions, the sociologists were apt to concentrate on single, "real-life" groups. Instead of using systematic quantitative and survey methods, they would use the techniques of anthropological field work and nondirective interviewing, which provided, as they hoped, a richer and more rounded understanding. And instead of testing hypotheses statistically, they would work out a qualitative description of the social structure of the group in question.

It is easy to exaggerate the differences between the psychological and sociological methodologies. Although the Western Electric researches are thought of as belonging to the sociological tradition, the study of the Relay Assembly Test Room employed a more rigorous method of measuring output, gathered a greater body of quantitative data, and made a more elaborate statistical analysis than any other small-group study has ever done

(Whitehead 1938). Today all investigators use in different mixtures much the same battery of techniques. The sociologists are ready to use survey methods in order to provide support for hypotheses first suggested by field work; and the psychologists will admit both that field work is a necessary preliminary to the design of a survey and that it helps the investigator understand what the findings of his survey "mean"—that is, how they are to be explained. Most investigators now think of themselves as social psychologists rather than as either psychologists or sociologists.

Above all, both methodologies lead to the same end. The first business of any science is to state propositions, or hypotheses, about the relations between variables. The psychologists tend to make their propositions explicit and to pretend they were formulated before the data were gathered. The sociologists are more apt to pretend that they studied their groups with open minds, ready for any relationship to appear in the data, and they often leave their propositions implicit in their descriptions of social structure. But their propositions can always be made explicit, and a proposition supported by data remains a finding, whether formulated ex ante facto or ex post facto. Nor is it easy to understand why one should put greater confidence in a proposition tested on a set of groups similar in some controlled respect than in one that can be shown, as many of the findings of field research can be shown, to hold good for a number of otherwise quite dissimilar groups. In any event, no one has ever demonstrated that the findings of, for instance, laboratory research are inconsistent with those of field research, once the very different conditions that obtain for artificial and for "real" groups are taken into account. They are not always taken into sufficient account.

## Some leading problems

Within the field of small groups numerous problems call for investigation, and there have been a number of surveys and anthologies of research (Cartwright & Zander 1953; Hare 1962; Hare et al. 1955; Olmsted 1959). Here only the chief questions to which research has sought answers are mentioned.

What determines whether a man changes his behavior or opinion under the influence of others? In particular, what determines whether or not he conforms to the norms of a group? What gives some men power over others?

Small-group research deals with all these questions within the context of a general concern about interpersonal relations, which may often be regarded as stabilized resultants of processes of in-fluence. Accordingly, the researcher in this area, starting with a broad interest in the relations between the behavior and opinions of men and their attitudes toward one another, may come to ask more specific questions. Here the ideas that have come to be called "balance theory" (Heider 1958) should be specially mentioned. What are the conditions of status congruence and distributive justice, and what are the effects on interpersonal relations of failure to meet these conditions? What determines an attitude of "respect" for another, rather than a more relaxed "liking"? What determines embarrassment or a "joking relationship"?

Interpersonal relations combine to form larger social structures; consideration of this elementary social fact raises a new order of problems. How do coalitions form in the smallest social groups, such as triads? How do differences in status build up among the members of a group? What are the determinants of different forms of status system? What are the relations between status, influence, and conformity, or between status, the channels of communication in a group, and its division of labor? What are the determinants of conflict between groups, and what are its effects on social structure within groups? Finally, there is the question of social control: What are the conditions maintaining stability in a social structure?

Many studies have been devoted to questions arising from collaboration among group members in attaining a common goal. Is a group more effective than an individual in solving problems? What are the results of competition as opposed to collaboration? How do the motivation of its members, their interpersonal relations, patterns of communication, and division of labor render a group more or less effective in attaining a goal? Are there any necessary phases a group goes through in solving its problems and reaching its goals? What are the effects of success or failure upon its internal structure? What are the determinants of individual satisfaction with collaborative work?

There are also a number of special questions related to what English-speaking people call *leadership*. A "leader" may be defined as someone whose orders are in fact obeyed by many other persons, especially by the members of a group to which he belongs. What, if any, are the traits of personality that make a man a leader? What are the relations between the values of members and the behavior of the man who emerges as leader of a group? What is the relation between status and leadership, or between leadership informally won and authority formally assigned to a man by a larger organiza-

tion of which his group is a part? What makes a leader successful in attaining individual goals or goals assigned to, or adopted by, a group? What are the effects of strong leadership on the other behavior of the leader himself and on the behavior of others toward him?

Many of these questions lend themselves to applied research, which is research designed to provide people with knowledge that might allow them to change social behavior for the better from their point of view. The "better" behavior envisaged has ranged all the way from more productive industrial groups to discussion groups better organized to train the leaders of other discussion groups. In this field, research has been none the worse for being "applied" [*see* LEADERSHIP].

## Codification of research findings

The findings, the tested empirical propositions of small-group research, possess the following characteristics. In substance, they are very varied. They are formulated in many different terminologies: almost every investigator makes up one of his own. And they often appear to have no high degree of generality, to be contradictory or to hold good only in special circumstances.

Since, nevertheless, the findings are all concerned with face-to-face social behavior, their chaotic nature in other respects has stimulated a few investigators to the kind of criticism sometimes called *codification* (Homans 1950; 1961; Thibaut & Kelley 1959). When carried out deliberately, which it seldom is, codification goes behind the different names given to the variables entering the findings and asks how these variables were actually measured. When the same or equivalent operations of measurement were used in different investigations, codification gives these variables the same name. By this means it can sometimes show that the same findings have been reached in different investigations and so reduce the number of findings.

When apparently contradictory findings survive such criticism, codification goes on to examine the conditions under which the findings were established, since two findings are not contradictory unless all the circumstances in which each holds good are identical. If one research, for instance, shows that two persons who interact often with each other tend to like each other and another shows that they do not, an examination of the other features of the two researches may reveal that in the latter the two persons were constrained to interact, whereas in the former they were not.

These first steps in codification immediately suggest the next: an effort to reduce the number of independent findings still further by showing that a number of different findings, including contradictory ones, can be derived from the same set of general propositions under specified given conditions. From an assumption, for instance, about the determinants of sociometric choice (expressions of liking), together with the condition, which is approximately true of some groups, that members use the same criteria for choice, it follows both that a few members will receive many more choices than others do—which is an empirical finding—and that highly chosen members will choose one another—which is another empirical finding.

At this point codification begins to organize and unify the findings by explaining them. In any science, what is to be explained is always an empirical proposition of the general form $x$ varies as $y$. Explanation is the process of showing that the proposition follows logically in a deductive system from more general propositions under specified given conditions, themselves stated in the form of propositions. The more general propositions are more general in the sense that they enter into deductive systems by which other empirical propositions are explained; this is their unifying function. The given conditions are not general propositions, nor does the investigator undertake to explain them; he simply accepts them as matters of fact. A characteristic given condition in small-group research is the physical layout of the room in which a group meets.

To explain a phenomenon is to produce a theory of the phenomenon: a theory is nothing if it is not an explanation. Many investigators, especially psychologists, begin their research reports by formulating a theory from which, they assert, the propositions (hypotheses) they tested were derived. Codification begins by disregarding these theories and looking at the empirical findings themselves. But it must come back in the end to asking how they are to be explained. For this purpose it need not come back to the investigators' own theories. A theory may be fruitful in suggesting hypotheses to be tested without in the long run providing the most general way of explaining the hypotheses [see SCIENTIFIC EXPLANATION].

## The uses of theory

The process of codification almost forces the codifier to ask himself what his general theory is. Two main types of general theory have been used, not always explicitly, in small-group research. They may be called sociological and psychological, but here these words refer to the characteristics of

their general propositions and not to the academic affiliations of the men who use them, since a sociologist may perfectly well use a psychological theory, and vice versa.

**Sociological theory.** The sociological type of theory is an offshoot of the "functional" theory with which the name of Talcott Parsons is particularly associated. It is sociological because its general propositions are propositions about social units as such and not about the behavior of individuals. It attempts to state the general conditions under which any social system survives, maintains itself, or remains in equilibrium. From these general conditions it claims to derive the particular features a given social system remaining in equilibrium "must" possess. The empirical findings represent these features.

In small-group research a good example of such a theory is that of R. F. Bales (1950). He argues that if a discussion group is to remain in equilibrium and reach its goal, such as the formulation of a decision, the behavior of the members must collectively display certain characteristics. For instance, the group must pass through certain characteristic phases in discussion, or its members must develop a certain distribution of attitudes of respect and liking for one another. Like other functional theories, Bales's derives the features of individual behavior from the necessities of group equilibrium, and not vice versa [see INTERACTION, *article on* INTERACTION PROCESS ANALYSIS].

The difficulties with functional theories of small groups are those of functional theories in general. No social scientist has ever succeeded in formulating a rigorous statement of the general conditions of social equilibrium. The statements actually used are so vague that nothing definite can be derived from them. Moreover, many social groups do not remain in equilibrium, however it is defined, so that the range of phenomena the theory could explain must at best be limited. Finally, it is not at all clear that another type of theory cannot explain the phenomena, one that lacks the disadvantages of functional theory and possesses the further advantage of explaining findings functional theory cannot cope with. Indeed, functional theorists often find themselves inadvertently using the propositions of the other type of theory.

**Psychological theory.** Most students of small groups use in explanation, not always explicitly, some form of psychological theory. Psychological theories are so called because their most general propositions are propositions about the behavior of individual men, and not about the conditions of equilibrium in groups. They do not in the least deny that the behavior of men is social. What they do, in effect, deny is (for instance) that the general propositions describing the behavior of men when rewarded by the physical environment are different from those describing their behavior when rewarded by other men, although the analysis may be much more complex in the latter case than in the former. Psychological theories also assume there is no characteristic of a group that cannot be explained by the characteristics of the individuals making it up: in this sense the whole is not greater than the sum of its parts. Finally, psychological theories assume that their propositions hold good for all men, that although, for instance, members of different societies learn to behave in concretely different ways because the present circumstances and past histories of these societies have been different, yet the general characteristics of the learning process remain the same for all men.

*Behavioral theory.*    In particular, some of the most prominent codifiers of small-group research have come to find most satisfactory for the explanation of the phenomena one or another of the psychological theories (called "behavioral" or "learning" theories) first developed by experimental psychologists working with animals. These theories need not be incompatible with other psychological theories, such as psychoanalytic ones, although the terminologies employed may be quite dissimilar.

The chief propositions of behavioral theory are of the following sorts: A man whose activity (some item of "voluntary" behavior) has been rewarded (or "reinforced") is apt to repeat that activity. He will repeat it the more often, the more successful it is in obtaining the reward. He is also more apt to repeat it, the more valuable (reinforcing) the reward is to him, and the value of the reward depends on the degree to which he has been deprived of it. Any activity that allows a man to escape or avoid punishment is also by that fact rewarded. A man usually has more than one activity open to him and more than one reward for these activities. The probability of his emitting one of the activities rather than another depends on the relative value of the alternative rewards and the relative probability of the success of the activities in obtaining them. When a particular stimulus situation (some set of cognitive elements) has also attended an occasion in the past when an activity has been rewarded, the presence of some similar stimulus on a new occasion will render it more probable that the activity will again be emitted. Finally, behavioral psychology states various propositions about emotional behavior, such as that when a man's activity has been regularly rewarded under particular circumstances and then suddenly ceases to be so, he is apt to become angry, and in anger he is apt to find aggressive behavior rewarding. This is sometimes called the frustration–aggression hypothesis.

Behavior is social when the activities of each of at least two men reward (or punish) the activities of the other. Accordingly, the propositions of behavioral psychology may be used to explain the characteristics of social behavior, which is the real subject of small-group research. The variables whose relations are explained are the relative frequency with which each person emits alternative activities, the values to each of the rewards provided by the other, and the variations of stimuli along various cognitive dimensions, including the stimuli each person presents to the other. Since the value and frequency of the activities each emits affect the value and frequency of the other's activities, the way is at once opened for the explanation of social influence. As the number of persons in interaction increases the analysis obviously becomes very complex, but it can sometimes be handled with the help of simplifying assumptions that may approximate real conditions. Particularly interesting is the situation in which many members of a group set a high value on a scarce reward (scarce in the sense that only a few of the members are able to supply it). In this situation behavioral psychology is able to explain why there should be differences between the members in status and power. It can also begin to explain how a social structure, a stabilized set of social relations, may develop and maintain itself in a group. Indeed, most of the phenomena investigated by small-group research can be explained, at least in a gross way, by the propositions of behavioral psychology [see LEARNING THEORY].

Since this theory envisages social behavior as an exchange between persons of goods (rewards) in different amounts and of different values, it envisages social behavior as a generalized economy, and the specialized and highly developed economics dealing with prices and markets can be used to sharpen its formulations. Alternatively, behavioral psychology can help to explain the propositions of elementary economics, thus contributing to the intellectual unification of social science.

## The need for explanatory principles

Too high hopes should not be held out for detailed explanation and prediction. The problem is partly one of getting the necessary information. Among the crucial variables, for instance, is the relative value to individuals of different rewards.

Yet many values are not innate in men but acquired by them in the course of their past experience. If the investigator knows that a man grew up in a particular culture, he may infer correctly that the man has shared the experiences, and hence the values, of other members of that culture. In other cases, the man's values may be quite atypical, the precipitate of idiosyncratic experiences. Without detailed knowledge of the man's past, the investigator, even if he commands the best psychology in the world, may be unable to predict the man's social behavior. Behavioral psychology itself explains why this should be so.

It must also be remembered that any small group, even one artificially formed, is part of a larger institutional structure. The behavior of its members cannot be wholly explained without reference to that structure. Thus a jury is certainly a small group, but one required by law to reach a unanimous decision in secret. So far as its members conform to the legal norms, their conformity affects their other relations. This does not mean that conformity to institutional norms, or even the nature of the norms themselves, cannot be explained by psychological principles. It does mean that institutional norms are always among the given conditions to be used in explaining face-to-face social behavior. Differences in cultural and institutional norms may help explain why apparently similar small-group experiments do not always yield the same results in different societies.

Detailed explanation and prediction also presents a problem of a different kind. The fundamental propositions of behavioral psychology are very general and refer to the behavior of individuals. How is the investigator to show what the resultant, or synthetic, implications of a set of propositions would be when many individuals are interacting in complicated and varying circumstances? Here the best hope lies in the increasing use of high-speed computers, whose virtue is precisely that of working out quickly the detailed implications of general propositions under varied parametric conditions.

Although students of elementary social behavior will take their basic explanatory principles from behavioral psychology, they will get little other help from the behavioral psychologists. Psychologists who have experimented with animals tend, when applying their principles to human behavior, to explain the learning processes of individuals or to jump to the gross features of institutions like religion and government in the larger society. Yet it may well be that in the long run a more convincing link between psychology and sociology will be forged by those who study at the same time the detailed behavior of individuals in interaction and the simpler social structures that emerge therefrom. They may indeed establish the first theoretical organization of the social sciences on a sound basis. This is the continuing justification of small-group research.

GEORGE CASPAR HOMANS

[*Directly related are the entries* COHESION, SOCIAL; INDUSTRIAL RELATIONS, *article on* HUMAN RELATIONS; SOCIOMETRY. *Other relevant material may be found in* FUNCTIONAL ANALYSIS; ROLE; SOCIAL PSYCHOLOGY; STATUS, SOCIAL; *and in the biographies of* COOLEY; LEWIN; MAYO; SIMMEL.]

### BIBLIOGRAPHY

BALES, ROBERT F. 1950 *Interaction Process Analysis: A Method for the Study of Small Groups.* Reading, Mass.: Addison-Wesley.

BLAU, PETER (1955) 1963 *The Dynamics of Bureaucracy: A Study of Interpersonal Relations in Two Government Agencies.* Rev. ed. Univ. of Chicago Press.

BLAU, PETER M. 1964 *Exchange and Power in Social Life.* New York: Wiley.

CARTWRIGHT, DORWIN; and ZANDER, ALVIN (editors) (1953) 1960 *Group Dynamics: Research and Theory.* 2d ed. Evanston, Ill.: Row, Peterson.

CHAPPLE, ELIOT D.; and ARENSBERG, CONRAD M. 1940 Measuring Human Relations: An Introduction to the Study of the Interaction of Individuals. *Genetic Psychology Monographs* 22:3–147.

COHEN, ARTHUR R. 1964 *Attitude Change and Social Influence.* New York and London: Basic Books.

COOLEY, CHARLES H. (1909) 1956 *Social Organization: A Study of the Larger Mind.* In Charles H. Cooley, *Two Major Works: Social Organization* and *Human Nature and the Social Order.* Glencoe, Ill.: Free Press. → Each title reprinted with individual title page and pagination. Separate paperback editions were published in 1962 by Schocken.

GOLEMBIEWSKI, ROBERT T. 1962 *The Small Group: An Analysis of Research Concepts and Operations.* Univ. of Chicago Press.

GURVITCH, GEORGES (1950) 1957–1963 *La vocation actuelle de la sociologie.* 2d ed., 2 vols. Paris: Presses Universitaires de France. → Volume 1: *Vers la sociologie différentielle.* Volume 2: *Antécédents et perspectives.*

HARE, A. PAUL 1962 *Handbook of Small Group Research.* New York: Free Press.

HARE, A. PAUL; BORGATTA, E. F.; and BALES, R. F. (1955) 1965 *Small Groups: Studies in Social Interaction.* Rev. ed. New York: Knopf.

HEIDER, FRITZ 1958 *The Psychology of Interpersonal Relations.* New York: Wiley.

HOLLANDER, EDWIN P. 1964 *Leaders, Groups, and Influence.* New York: Oxford Univ. Press.

HOMANS, GEORGE C. 1950 *The Human Group.* New York: Harcourt.

HOMANS, GEORGE C. 1961 *Social Behavior: Its Elementary Forms.* New York: Harcourt.

HOPKINS, TERENCE K. 1964 *The Exercise of Influence in Small Groups.* Totowa, N.J.: Bedminster Press.

JENNINGS, HELEN H. (1943) 1950 *Leadership and Isolation: A Study of Personality in Inter-personal Relations.* 2d ed. New York: Longmans.

KLEIN, JOSEPHINE 1956 *The Study of Groups*. London: Routledge; New York: Humanities.

LEWIN, KURT (1939–1947) 1963 *Field Theory in Social Science: Selected Theoretical Papers*. Edited by Dorwin Cartwright. London: Tavistock.

MORENO, JACOB L. (1934) 1953 *Who Shall Survive? Foundations of Sociometry, Group Psychotherapy and Sociodrama*. Rev. & enl. ed. Beacon, N.Y.: Beacon House.

OLMSTED, MICHAEL S. 1959 *The Small Group*. New York: Random House.

ROETHLISBERGER, FRITZ J.; and DICKSON, WILLIAM J. (1939) 1961 *Management and the Worker: An Account of a Research Program Conducted by the Western Electric Company, Hawthorne Works, Chicago*. Cambridge, Mass.: Harvard Univ. Press. → A paperback edition was published in 1964 by Wiley.

SHEPHERD, CLOVIS R. 1964 *Small Groups: Some Sociological Perspectives*. San Francisco: Chandler.

SIMMEL, GEORG (1902–1917) 1950 *The Sociology of Georg Simmel*. Translated and edited by Kurt H. Wolff. Glencoe, Ill.: Free Press.

THIBAUT, JOHN W.; and KELLEY, HAROLD H. 1959 *The Social Psychology of Groups*. New York: Wiley.

WHITEHEAD, THOMAS N. 1938 *The Industrial Worker: A Statistical Study of Human Relations in a Group of Manual Workers*. 2 vols. Cambridge, Mass.: Harvard Univ. Press.

WHYTE, WILLIAM F. (1943) 1961 *Street Corner Society: The Social Structure of an Italian Slum*. 2d ed., enl. Univ. of Chicago Press.

## II
## GROUP BEHAVIOR

Although William James, Charles H. Cooley, and George H. Mead had, at the beginning of the century, stressed the importance of primary groups in the development of individual personality, it was not until the 1930s that the small group became a serious focus of scientific attention. A most remarkable independent development of research interest in small groups by a number of creative people in different social science disciplines occurred during this period. Elton Mayo and his colleagues at the Harvard Business School conducted their famous studies of industrial work groups at Western Electric; Jacob Moreno and Helen H. Jennings developed sociometric methods for investigating group structure; William F. Whyte employed anthropological techniques in the study that led to *Street Corner Society*; and Kurt Lewin, Ronald Lippitt, and Ralph White initiated the experimental study of democratic and authoritarian group leadership. At the same time, Paul Schilder, Samuel Slavson, and Trigant Burrow were doing pioneer work in group therapy.

These early interests and activities collectively seemed to have reached the "critical mass" by the end of World War II, resulting in an explosive and rapidly mushrooming interest in small groups. By 1960, about 2,200 small-group studies had been published, more than 80 per cent of which appeared in the decade 1950–1960. Since 1960, articles have been appearing at the rate of more than 250 per year.

No attempt will be made in this article to present the detailed findings of this enormous outpouring of research. Hare (1962) and McGrath and Altman (1966) provide useful summaries of the literature. Here I shall attempt to provide a framework within which some of the important findings can be integrated. The framework is oriented to such questions as: what is a group? what are the significant ways in which groups differ from one another? what are the effects of such differences?

**What is a group?** An examination of the different usages of the term "group" suggests that each combines a greater or lesser number of the following distinguishing criteria: two or more persons who (1) have one or more characteristics in common, (2) perceive themselves as forming a distinguishable entity, (3) are aware of the interdependence of some of their goals or interests, and (4) interact with one another in pursuit of their interdependent goals. In addition, some writers, particularly those with sociological backgrounds, indicate that (5) groups endure over a period of time and as a result develop (6) a set of social norms that regulate and guide member interaction and (7) a set of roles, each of which has specific activities, obligations, and rights associated with it. I shall use the term "group" to signify at least the first four of the distinguishing criteria listed above. This usage is consonant with the intuitive notion that a group is an entity that consists of interacting people who are aware of being psychologically bound together in terms of mutually linked interests. A group is thus to be distinguished from an aggregate, class, category, or type, which consist of people who are classified together because of some common characteristic. Also, "group" implies a psychological or perceived bond, not merely an objective linkage, between the members' interests or goals. Moreover, the psychological linkage has some cohesive feature to it—i.e., members of a group see that in some respects they sink or swim together. This latter statement is not meant to deny that divisive and disruptive tendencies may exist within a group; rather, it is meant to indicate that by definition a group does not exist if its cohesive bonds are not strong enough to contain its disunifying influences.

**How groups differ.** There are endless ways in which groups differ. It is useful to have some simplifying outline that highlights the central characteristics of groups and that permits a proliferation of detail as this becomes necessary. It is well to recognize that an outline abstracts variables from their contexts and their interrelationships, and thus presents them in somewhat distorted form. The outline that follows is guided by—but not limited to—the criteria of groups listed in the preceding section.

(1) Group size: the number of members in a group.

(2) Group composition: the individual characteristics of the members, including their distribution and patterning.

(3) Group structure: the patterning of member characteristics as perceived by the group members.

(4) The existential criteria of groups: the criteria for recognizing a group's existence, members, action, property, etc.

(5) Group cohesiveness: the type and strength of the interests binding the members to the group.

(6) Group task and environment: the task confronting the group, and the environment within which the group functions.

(7) Interactional process: the modes and patterns of interaction between members and with the task environment.

(8) Group culture: the norms, standards, role patterns, traditions, and customs operating within the group.

(9) Group effectiveness: the task performance, the viability of the group, the membership satisfaction, and the change within individual members.

It is useful to recognize that any causal arrow connecting an item with any other item in this outline is likely to be bidirectional rather than unidirectional. Consider group size and group composition. It is evident that increasing the number of members in a group will affect the composition of the group—e.g., the more people there are in a randomly composed group, the more likely it is that the group will contain an individual whose intelligence is above or below any specified level. However, the causal arrow also points in the other direction; if a group is composed of a certain kind of members, its size is likely to be affected. Thus, groups of young children are likely to have fewer members than groups of older children. Of course, the causal path in the direction from group composition to group size is longer and more circuitous than the path in the opposite direction: it weaves from group composition to interactional process to group effectiveness (member satisfaction) to group cohesiveness and arrives finally at group size (presumably a size that permits interactions that are satisfying to the children because they are within

their cognitive capabilities, and hence, the children are motivated to continue the group).

## Some findings from the study of groups

I shall employ the outline presented above to organize the discussion of illustrative findings obtained from the study of groups. The studies of groups have been mainly of temporary *ad hoc* laboratory groups, created by the investigator, rather than of ongoing natural groups in their native habitats. Hence, there is no assurance that the research findings are generalizable. However, they do not seem inconsistent with everyday observations. Necessarily, the presentation is oversimplified. It largely ignores the evident fact that the effects of any given variable upon another (e.g., of group size upon interaction patterns) are very much influenced by other factors in the situation (e.g., the nature of the group task).

**Group size.** Hare (1962) and Thomas and Fink (1963) have reviewed the relevant research literature in some detail. The latter have presented a useful framework for viewing the major effects of variations in size. The schema presented here borrows from theirs. It is helpful to make a distinction between the statistical properties of size and the psychological properties of size. The former are those properties of a group that come from taking a given-sized sample of individuals, according to a given procedure, from a population with certain characteristics. The group is considered as an aggregate, and the psychological properties that arise from the compresence and interaction of its members are disregarded.

The statistical properties of size can be appreciated by observing how variations in size affect some common statistical measures: the sum, the mean, intragroup variability, the probability of the occurrence of any characteristic, the probability of concordance of characteristics, the variability of the statistical properties. Consider the resources (perceptual capacity, memory capacity, information, intellectual capacity, physical strength, skills, money, tools, and so forth) available as size increases. Clearly, the *total* resources, such as the total money in the group, will increase as a linear function of size. However, the *usable* resources will be determined by the task and environment. In certain tasks it does not help the group to have any duplication of a resource (e.g., to have more than one person who knows how to type; to have several mimeographing machines). Hence, the usable resources will often increase at a slower rate than the total resources and often will, beyond a certain point, not increase at all. If this is so, as size increases, the average usable resource per member will decrease. This reasoning explains why, for certain kinds of tasks, group performance as measured by production per group member decreases as size increases, even as total production goes up: not all of the total resources are usable.

As the size of a sample increases, the probability that any given characteristic will appear (that someone will have red hair, that someone will favor vegetarianism) increases. The probability that at least one individual of a group has some given characteristic clearly depends on the frequency of the characteristic in the population from which the group was formed, the size of the group, and the manner of group formation. If the members of the group manifest statistical independence regarding the characteristic, and if the probability, $P_I$, that any individual has the characteristic is a constant, then the probability that *at least* one member of the group has the characteristic is $1 - (1 - P_I)^N$, where $N$ is group size. Thus, as $N$ increases, the probability increases toward 1. Even for more realistic assumptions about group formation, it is clear that, as group size increases, so does the probability that the group contains at least one individual having any preassigned characteristic. Thus, the larger the size of a group, the more likely it is to have any or all of the following: a very bright person, a very stupid person, a quiet person, a talkative person, a "right-winger," a "left-winger."

Similarly, the probability that *every* member of the group has the given characteristic generally decreases as group size increases, for most reasonable assumptions about group formation. Under the assumptions of independence and constancy, the probability that all group members have the characteristic is $P_I^N$, which decreases exponentially as $N$ increases. Hence, as the size of a group increases, it is less likely that all individuals will have the same opinion or speak the same language or be equally informed or be equally resourceful. Although heterogeneity is likely to be greater within larger groups, larger groups are less likely to vary from one another in aggregate properties than are smaller groups. (A group of 20 persons is more likely to have the same average IQ as another group the same size than are two groups of three persons.)

**Size** affects not only the statistical properties of the aggregated resources and other characteristics of the group but also the *opportunity* to satisfy individual wants—for example, the larger the group, the more time, space, supplies, and facilities it will

need to enable all individuals in the group to talk and be heard. Thus, if the total amount of time, reward, and space remain constant for a given task environment, the opportunity for individual participation and reward will decrease as the size of the group increases. On the other hand, the number of potential interpersonal relations increases geometrically as size increases. For example, the number of possible dyadic relations in any group increases with size $(N)$ according to the formula: $(N^2 - N)/2$. Since there appears to be a numerical limit to the capacity to establish close associations with others, a smaller proportion of the possible linkages will be formed as size increases.

From our discussion so far, it should be clear that different-sized aggregates of noninteracting individuals should differ predictably. The larger-sized aggregates should have more resources and more handicaps; more good solutions and more bad solutions; more diversity and difference; more demands for the available opportunities; more opportunity for diversified interpersonal contact but less for repeated contact. If the task environment is such that the presence of resources, good solutions, heterogeneity, and so forth, are more important factors than the presence of handicaps, bad solutions, and homogeneity in determining productivity, then larger aggregates should be more productive than smaller aggregates. But groups are not simply aggregates; they are composed of interacting individuals. A group's performance may differ from the performance of a comparable aggregate of individuals because the contributions the individuals make in the group will be affected by the group milieu and because the group will combine or assemble the individual performances in a unique manner.

*Audience effects.* Social influence on individual thinking may reflect either the effect of working before an audience (such as other group members) or the impact of the contributions being made by the other group members. Research results, generally, indicate that there is increased motivation and increased distraction when a person works on intellectual problems before an audience rather than by himself (Kelley & Thibaut 1954). In addition, there tend to be fewer idiosyncratic thoughts, more moderation in judgments, more common associations, more cautiousness, and a general taking into account of the anticipated reactions of the audience. Over a period of time, adaptation to being observed tends to occur (Deutsch 1949), and hence the "audience effects" tend to decrease. Some research evidence (Atkinson 1964) suggests that once motivation to achieve passes beyond a certain moderate level, further increase in motivation tends to result in less effective performance.

*Problem solving and productivity.* The preceding discussion of "audience effects" suggests the possibility that as the size of a group increases, the intellectual functioning of its members will deteriorate: they will be "overmotivated," more distracted, and more conventional. But other members of a group do not merely serve as an audience. They also contribute new information and different perspectives; they invoke more aspects of memory and demand greater attention; they provide more material for the individual to think with and about. That is, the contributions of other members may provide new associational starting points, may help the individual to break out of an ineffective set by suggesting new orientations, may fill in gaps or reveal unnoticed errors in the individual's thinking. On the other hand, the contributions of other members may distract, interrupt a chain of thought, blot out an individual's own associations, or confuse him by providing too much material for him to assimilate at one time. The meager relevant research indicates that the contribution of others may be more distracting than useful when the task confronting the individual is one that requires sustained, directed attention to a complex pattern where the relations between sequentially ordered parts must be kept in mind (e.g., in "reasoning" problems). In such a task, individuals working alone will hit upon different approaches (or will symbolize the same approach differently), and once they have taken a few steps on their respective approaches, understanding each other may be difficult without going back to the initial formulation of the approach or until an obvious solution has been reached. Hence, with such a task, the larger the group, the more likely it is that it will interfere with the individual's thinking. On the other hand, when the task is such that the individual is likely to have an initial set that would lead to a clichéd or superficial solution to the problem and would overlook some of its major dimensions, the contributions of other members (starting from different sets, which may also be superficial) may force the individual to go deeper into the problem [see PROBLEM SOLVING].

A group solution will depend not only upon the abilities of its members to think within the milieu of the group but also upon the readiness and ability of the members to contribute to the group and upon the way in which their contributions are coordinated, assembled, or weighted to produce the resultant group solution. With regard to the readiness and ability of members to contribute, research indicates that the inequality of participation among the various members of a group increases as the size of the group increases (Stephan & Mishler 1952; Bales et al. 1951). These results suggest that individuals who tend to be shy are unlikely to participate actively in larger groups, although they may contribute much in small groups. On the other hand, individuals who tend to be assertive are likely to have a disproportionately large influence in larger groups as compared with smaller groups.

With regard to the coordination, assembling, or weighting of the contributions that individual members make, investigations have found that the difficulty of keeping track of the contributions of the various members, of coordinating and assembling them, will increase as the size of the group increases. For success in resolving this difficulty, larger groups have to devote more of their energy to activities directed toward coordination than do smaller groups. In addition, it is reasonable to hypothesize that such personality factors as self-confidence, assertiveness, and persuasiveness are more likely to play a significant role in determining the individual's impact upon the group solution in larger groups than in smaller groups.

Member satisfaction, also, is affected by the size of the group. Laboratory and field studies both indicate that members of small groups are more likely to feel satisfied with their group, more likely to inhibit expression of disagreement, and less likely to develop cliques and factions. Large groups, on the other hand, are characterized by more absenteeism, more formality, and more internal conflict than are smaller groups.

**Group composition.** How are the individual members of a group characterized? The answers to this question presuppose that one knows what features of the members may influence the way they interact, interrelate, and function together. There is as yet, however, little systematic knowledge of how group composition—the distribution and patterning of member characteristics—affects group behavior. Nevertheless, it is reasonable to think that a group's behavior will be affected by the distribution and patterning of such member characteristics as abilities, knowledge, resources, attitudes, interests, personality dispositions, age, sex, and social status. The combined characteristics of the members may be considered in terms of their influence upon the group's effectiveness in coping with the task confronting it. Or they may be related to the compatibility of the members with one another, the attraction of the group for various members, the likelihood of the formation of cliques, and so forth.

*Effectiveness.* With regard to group effectiveness, considerable research supports the common-sense proposition that groups whose members have high abilities, training, or experience are more effective than groups whose members are lacking in these respects (McGrath & Altman 1966). However, it is not simply the average level of abilities that is important, but rather whether the kinds of abilities necessary to carrying out the role requirements set by the group's task exist among the group members and are appropriately distributed. Group composition must be evaluated in reference to the demands confronting the group rather than in a vacuum. Homogeneity of member characteristics is an asset when the various group members are called upon to fulfill the same task functions, but it is a liability when there are varied functions to perform. For example, it is reasonable to assume that a group composed of both "abstract thinkers" and "concrete thinkers" will be more effective in performing in a task requiring both intellectual analysis and action than a group composed exclusively of one or the other type. Hoffman, Harburg, and Maier (1962) report results indicating that groups composed of individuals with dissimilar personalities are more productive than homogeneous groups. Schutz (1958) has theorized that compatibility is likely to be greater when people with different but complementary personality dispositions are paired together (e.g., people who wish to give affection and people who wish to receive it) than when people of similar dispositions are paired together (e.g., two people who wish to dominate). His research indicates that groups composed of members with compatible interpersonal tendencies are more productive than those composed of members with incompatible tendencies.

*Patterns of interaction.* There is a vast body of research on the effect of the personal and social characteristics of members on the development of attitudes toward the group, interactional patterns within the group, etc. Much of this research is considered in the sociometric literature. In general, research supports the saying, Birds of a feather flock together. People prefer to associate and interact with others who are similar rather than dissimilar to themselves in attitudes, status, background, interests, and so forth. The major exceptions to this generalization occur when similarity enhances competition (e.g., when two suitors are interested in the same girl); personal needs require complementarity rather than similarity (e.g., in heterosexual relations); or task requirements necessitate differentiated functions and statuses.

*Individual behavior.* There has also been much study of the personality characteristics that affect the performance of members in small groups. Mann (1959), reviewing the literature from 1900 through October 1957, focused on seven personality factors: intelligence, adjustment, extroversion–introversion, dominance, masculinity–femininity, conservatism, and interpersonal sensitivity. He summarized the relations between each of the seven personality variables and each of the following measures of an individual's status and behavior in groups: leadership, popularity, total activity rate, task activity, social–emotional activity, and conformity. His survey indicates that the best single predictor of an individual's behavior in the group is his intelligence. Intelligence and also extroversion and adjustment are positively related to total activity rate, leadership, and popularity in the group. In addition, the more intelligent and better-adjusted members are likely to contribute a relatively larger share of their total activity to building up group solidarity and providing emotional support for other members and a relatively smaller share to being critical or rejecting other members. Dominance is related positively to leadership and negatively to conformity; conservatism, on the other hand, is associated negatively with leadership and correlated positively with conformity. Masculinity and interpersonal sensitivity show positive relationships to leadership and popularity. Mann (1959, p. 266) concludes his review with the caution that the magnitude of the median of the correlations between an aspect of personality and performance is in no case higher than .25, and most of the medians of the correlations are nearer .15.

**Group structure.** Popular conceptions of group and organizational structure have been very much influenced by organizational charts, developed in the military and other large bureaucracies, that stress lines of formal authority. This is too limited a view. It is more fruitful to think of structure in terms of the way members actually relate to one another. In a sense the term "group structure" is a misnomer; there may be many different "structures" within a group—the work structure, the communication structure, the friendship structure, the power structure, the prestige structure, and so forth.

There is often a correspondence among the positions an individual holds in the different structures, so that an individual who holds a central position in one structure (e.g., the communication structure) is likely to hold a central position in other structures (power, friendship, and prestige). The research of Galtung (1964) in Norway indicates that this is the case for Norwegian society: people who are more central on social variables (income, education, occupation, residence, age, and sex) are also more central in the communication and power structures. In the status-equilibration hypothesis, Benoît-Smullyan (1944) and, later, Homans (1961) have stressed the forces that operate to make for similarity in the positions of an individual in different structures. However, status equilibrium is not always achieved. Research by Adams (1953) with air crews demonstrated that lack of congruence on such status dimensions as age, military rank, education, reputed ability, popularity, combat time, and position importance was related to poor morale, less friendliness, and lack of mutual confidence. Exline and Ziller (1959), working with experimentally created groups, found that groups constructed so as to have incongruent status hierarchies manifested more interpersonal conflict and less productivity than congruent groups.

In addition to research on status congruency, research on group structures has investigated such topics as (1) the effects of different communication structures (Guetzkow 1953); (2) the effects of different leadership structures, for example, leaderless groups versus groups with leaders, and of leadership style (Fiedler 1964); (3) the effects of different residential and propinquity structures (Festinger et al. 1950); (4) the effects of similarity or dissimilarity on various social and personal characteristics, such as age, sex, religious belief, attitudes; (5) the Kafkaesque effects of complex organizational structures, which are dimly perceived and little understood by members; (6) the determinants of sociometric structure, leadership structure, communication structure, etc.; (7) methods of classifying and identifying roles within groups (Bales 1950); and (8) mathematical procedures for characterizing different types of structures and different positions within a structure (Coleman 1964).

**The existential criteria of groups.** Although a vast body of legal principle and practice has been concerned with the conditions under which a "legal personality," such as a corporation, can come into existence, and with the identifying of those who can act in its name, there has been little social-psychological research that bears upon such related problems as how a group is identified and what determines whether an action of a member

is attributed to the group or to him personally. However, drawing upon studies of perceptual organization, it is possible to indicate some general principles concerning the conditions that are conducive to the perception that a collection of individuals or units are part of a system rather than an unorganized aggregate of elements.

As Koffka (1935) pointed out, abrupt discontinuity produces segregating forces between the parts of a visual field that it separates, as well as unifying forces within the separated parts. Further, he indicated that homogeneity tends to produce unifying forces in the visual field. Homogeneity may be based upon (1) the common fate of the elements perceived (they move together); (2) their qualitative or quantitative similarity (they have the same color or the same luminosity); (3) proximity (they occur in spatial or temporal contiguity); (4) a common boundary; (5) past experience or custom that has led to similar responses to the various elements; and (6) set or the expectation that the elements are to be grouped together [see GESTALT THEORY].

It seems evident that processes analogous to these determine whether an individual will perceive a collection of individuals as a social group and whether he will perceive himself to be part of the group. Thus, if an individual perceives that he and some others are strikingly different in certain respects from the remainder of the people in their surroundings; that he and the others tend to be satisfied or dissatisfied at the same time or under similar circumstances; that he and the others have similar attitudes or similar backgrounds; that he and the others live or work in close proximity; that he and the others are associated together in other people's minds or treated similarly by other people —if he perceives any of these patterns, the individual is likely to perceive himself and the others as cooperatively interdependent. I would stress, as does Campbell (1958), the central role of the perception of common fate in determining the consciousness of being joined with others to form a group.

**Group cohesiveness.** In everyday usage "cohesiveness" refers to the tendency to stick together; its usage in social psychology is much the same. It refers to the linkages that bind the members of a group together. Deutsch (1949; 1962) has stressed that the linkages among members are cohesive, rather than disruptive, when the goals and interests of the members are cooperatively, rather than competitively, interrelated. Various aspects of these linkages have been the focus of research: the nature of the mutually linked goals or interests—such as friendship, work, money; the strength of the mutually linked goals or interests; the degree of linkage, and the availability of other means of obtaining one's goals; the forces operating to restrain members from leaving the group; other interests or memberships that are in opposition to continued membership in the group.

Since group cohesiveness is central to the existence of groups, it is natural that its determinants and also its consequences have been studied extensively (Hare 1962; Collins & Guetzkow 1964; McGrath & Altman 1966). Research findings, over-all, indicate that cohesiveness (as measured by interpersonal congeniality, the desire to remain a member of the group, attitudes toward the group's functioning, or other similar measures) is consistently associated with greater communication between group members, greater readiness of group members to be influenced by the group, more consensus among members on attitudes and beliefs that relate to group functioning, more sense of responsibility toward each other among group members, a greater feeling of personal ease and security within the group by the group members, and so forth. Also, task effectiveness is generally positively correlated with cohesiveness if high accomplishment on the task is valued by the group (some groups restrict performance to achieve their objectives) and if the task is such that its performance is likely to be enhanced by increased group effort. It should be noted that the causal arrow is bidirectional: group cohesiveness not only increases intragroup communication and group success, but group success and intragroup communication increase group cohesiveness [see COHESION, SOCIAL].

**Group task and environment.**   It is self-evident that the task confronting the group and the environment within which the group functions can influence all the other characteristics of a group. Unfortunately, however, the research relating to task and environmental characteristics has been meager, largely because there has not yet been developed any systematic way of characterizing tasks or environments. Nevertheless, certain useful distinctions have been made.

It is possible to characterize many tasks and environments in terms of the type of requirements for success that they impose upon the group. It is apparent that tasks differ in the types and amounts of skills, knowledge, effort, and resources required and in the way these factors have to be interrelated. In other words, the roles within the group, the structure of the group, the size of the group, etc., may vary as a function of the group's task and environment.

Fiedler (1964), for example, has shown that the effectiveness of different types of leaders is very closely related to the structure of the task confronting the group. In both field and laboratory studies, his findings indicate that controlling, authoritarian leaders tend to be most effective either in very favorable or else in relatively unfavorable group-task situations, while the permissive, considerate, democratic leaders are most effective in situations that are intermediate in favorableness. Fiedler indicates that a situation is very favorable when (1) the leader–member relations are positive, (2) the task is clear and well structured, and (3) the leader has well-defined authority and power to reward and punish. Thus, for example, if a leader has good personal relations with his group and the task is routine and his authority well-defined, he is likely to be more effective if he is "directive," rather than democratic and permissive. On the other hand, if the task is novel and unstructured but the situation is otherwise similar, democratic, permissive leadership is likely to be more effective [see LEADERSHIP].

Task structure helps to determine the types and amounts of interaction and communication within a group and also the sequencing and organization of the activities within the group. These, in turn, will often affect the social relations that develop within a group. Much research has supported the proposition (Homans 1950) that people who interact frequently with one another tend to like one another, and vice versa. Thus, tasks that require certain group members to work closely with one another and limit their interaction with other members may, if the task is long-enduring, help to create patterns of friendship that parallel the interactional requirements of the task. Further, the research indicates that if a task places a given individual in a central position because he is able to communicate readily with other members or because he possesses a scarce resource (a skill, specialized information, or a particular tool) that is of critical value to group success, then he is likely to have high status within the group (and high satisfaction with the group).

Tasks differ in the degree to which they permit division of labor and specialization of function. The problem of dividing tasks into subtasks, of sequencing them, and of assigning personnel and resources to them has been of major interest to economists and operations-research analysts, and they have had considerable success in developing rational methods of predicting the effectiveness of different methods of dividing up a task. Here let us note some psychological aspects of the division of labor. Among its possible negative consequences are the loss of one's identification with the over-all group objectives; the loss of a sense of an over-all significance and meaning to one's activities; the development of vested interests in one's specialized activities; the development of specialized languages, values, and modes of thought that interfere with coordination and communication between the various specialized activities. Among the possible positive consequences of specialization is, in addition to increased group productivity and individual economic reward, the greater chance that an individual will be able to find some activity that matches his particular interests and abilities.

Tasks and environments differ not only in their activity and interaction requirements but also in their stressfulness. The term "stress" has been used to refer to a hypothetical state of tension, frustration, or internal conflict induced by such conditions as task difficulty (e.g., a problem without any solution), lack of information about how well the task is being performed, threat of punishment for task failure, danger (e.g., as in combat or survival in the Arctic), intense criticism, time pressure, an unpredictable environment. The results of studies of the effects of such varied conditions are not univocal. The safest generalization seems to be that mild stress often improves group performance and enhances group cohesiveness, while severe stress often has the opposite effects. Optimal stress for a group is presumably higher the more able and cohesive the group is and the more the members see themselves as able and motivated to cope with problems (Deutsch 1959).

Finally, it is relevant to note that environments differ in the probability of reward and the amount of reward they provide for effective group action and also in the manner in which rewards are distributed within a group. Little research has been done on the effects of different "schedules of reinforcement" upon group behavior, yet there is reason to assume that they would influence group performance (Shapiro 1963). On the other hand, a considerable number of research studies (e.g., Deutsch 1949; Raven & Eachus 1963) have demonstrated that whether rewards are distributed cooperatively or competitively within a group may have a striking effect on member behavior. In general, group members who are rewarded cooperatively show more positive response to one another, have greater involvement in the group, are less likely to work at cross-purposes, communicate with one another more effectively, and work more productively together than group members who are rewarded competitively.

**Interactional process.** The observable transactions between members and their observable transactions with their task environments are lumped together under the term "interactional process." It is, in effect, what goes on in groups. There are many different ways of characterizing what goes on. Most of them focus on one or more of the following aspects of a transaction: *who* communicates or does *what* to or with *whom;* with what *intent* or function; *how, when,* or under what conditions; through what *media* or channels; with what *effects* upon *whom,* as perceived by *whom.* Each of the italicized terms could be elaborated in considerable detail. For example, if one specified the characteristics of the potential communicators and communicatees (the *who* and the *whom*)—their statuses, their personality tendencies, their preexisting attitudes toward one another—one could predict, to some degree, *who* will talk to *whom* and *how* they will talk. (The demeanor of a subordinate making a critical remark to a superior will be rather different from that of a superior criticizing a subordinate.) Similarly, knowledge of the *conditions* —e.g., what stage in problem solving the group is at—enables one to predict what kinds of content (the *what*) a transaction is likely to have.

The most widely used system for categorizing interactions is the one developed by Bales (1950). It focuses on the *who*-to-*whom*-and-*what* interaction. His system consists of 12 distinct categories of the content of communication: content that (1) shows solidarity, (2) shows tension release, (3) agrees, (4) gives suggestion, (5) gives opinion, (6) gives orientation, (7) asks for orientation, (8) asks for opinion, (9) asks for suggestion, (10) disagrees, (11) shows tension, and (12) shows antagonism. The categories are grouped in various ways. One major grouping is into task categories (subdivided into questions and attempted answers) and social–emotional categories (classified as positive and negative). More recently Stone and his co-workers (1962) have devised a more generalized system of content analysis called the General Inquirer, which employs a computer to code the actual verbal text of group interaction into 164 categories [*see* INTERACTION, *article on* INTERACTION PROCESS ANALYSIS].

Slater (1955) has shown that members who are ranked high as "idea men" by the other members in problem-solving groups initiate interaction more markedly in "attempted answers," while members who are ranked high in likability participate more heavily in the categories grouped as "positive social–emotional." His research has also indicated that often the task leader, or idea man, and the social–emotional leader are not the same person; this specialization of interaction function is more evident if the group exists over a period of time. In other words, as Barnard (1938) had noted earlier, the two major problems confronting groups —adaptation to their task environment and provision of personal satisfaction to the individual members—do not necessarily lead to the same emphases within a group.

Why do people interact? Few theorists have gone beyond the common-sense viewpoint that they do so because it is instrumental to a given end or because it is gratifying in itself. Festinger and his associates (1950), however, have suggested that one of the major instrumental functions of inter-action is helping to establish "social reality": the validation of opinions, beliefs, abilities, and emotions in terms of a social consensus. That is, one of the functions of communication within a group is to establish uniform views about reality, so as to provide the members with some confidence in their beliefs and to enable them to coordinate their behavior for effective group action. Thus, group members whose views deviate from those held by the rest of the group will be subject, through communication, to pressures to change their views to conform to those of the rest, or they will be rejected or isolated by the group, so as to eliminate a source of disturbance to the group. Festinger hypothesized that these pressures are greater the more cohesive the group is, the more relevant the belief is to the group, the more discrepant the deviant's viewpoint is, etc. A considerable body of research is consistent with these hypotheses. Festinger has also suggested that communication may function as a substitute for social locomotion—people who would like to be in powerful positions direct their communication toward those who hold such positions. The study by Kelley (1951) of communication in experimentally created hierarchies is consistent with this hypothesis. However, Cohen (1958) suggests that upward communication may be more directly motivated by the desire to receive the benefits that a higher-status person can bestow upon someone of lower status.

**Group culture.** The members of any group who have had a prolonged experience of interacting with one another tend to develop shared values, expectations, and rules—a normative consensus that helps to regulate interaction between members and between the group and its task environment and that also serves to define the roles of the various members, including their specialized activities, rights, and responsibilities. A normative consensus, or group norm, sets criteria for evaluating the desirability–undesirability, acceptability–unacceptability, of the group members' activities, beliefs, appearance, etc., and for responding with various sanctions, positive or negative, such as reward–punishment, approval–disapproval, to a member's conformity with or violation of the norm [*see* NORMS].

Norms develop about many things, from the type of pronoun to be used in addressing intimates or strangers to the type of wine one should serve on certain occasions. Yet not everything is regulated. Norms tend to develop mostly in areas that are relevant to the group's functioning, and it seems likely that the more important an area is to the group, the more norms there will be, the more intense will be the sanctions employed to obtain conformity to them, and the smaller will be the range of acceptable behavior. Thus, as Sutherland has shown, the norm of punctuality in appearing at a prearranged time and place is strictly enforced among professional thieves because its violation may endanger an enterprise and lead to arrest (Conwell 1937). Norms are more often developed with regard to overt behavior than private beliefs, not only because the former are usually more important to group functioning but also because beliefs are less controllable, being less observable than behavior. Further, it is apparent that the norms of different types of groups will differ—for example, the norms of a friendship group and those of a work group. It is not uncommon for a person to experience conflict because he belongs to groups that have conflicting norms [*see* CONFORMITY].

There is an extensive research literature on the determinants of conformity and deviation to group norms (for a summary, see Symposium on Conformity . . . 1961). It is not a great oversimplification to sum up the findings as indicating that conformity appears to be a function of such factors as the person's awareness of the norm, the strength of the norm, the strength of the person's attraction to the group, the likelihood that conformity or deviation will be observable by others, the strength of the sanctions expected for conforming or deviating, personality predisposition (such as dependency, acceptance of authority, self-confidence). Whether a person will conform will depend not only on these factors but also on the strength of the tendency to deviate, which is determined by parallel considerations (e.g., is the tendency to deviate from the norms of one group a tendency to conform to the norms of another group to which the person belongs?).

Groups not only develop norms, which specify the "shoulds" and "should nots"; often they also develop styles, traditions, or customs (and these often become the object of norms), which are the habitual ways of dealing with recurring situations. Thus, a group may develop a unique language (almost every profession and trade develops its own "slang," its own peculiar abbreviations); distinctive garb, insignia, or appearance, to permit ready identification; a distinctive locale for meeting and engaging in its activities; a special style of inducing emotional responsiveness and of expressing emotion (e.g., distinctive dances, ceremonies), etc. Case-study material suggests that groups are most likely to develop idiosyncratic traditions if they are relatively isolated, as a result of geographical or social factors (due to superior or inferior status); if they are in conflict with other groups; or if their task environment is unique.

Anthropologists have, of course, studied and described in considerable detail the customs and traditions of many simple societies. A similar kind of analysis could be made of the development of customs and traditions in experimentally created or naturally formed groups, to investigate some of the determinants of particular kinds of traditions and customs. Unfortunately, little research has been conducted, apart from the pioneering studies of Sherif (1936), Merei (1949), and Rose and Felton (1955).

**Group effectiveness.** A group's effectiveness may be characterized in such terms as (1) *task performance*—the quality and quantity of the group's outputs, as measured in terms of external criteria; (2) *group viability*—the group's ability to maintain itself as a functioning group under varying conditions; (3) *member satisfaction*—the desire of the members to maintain their membership and to contribute to the group's viability and the attainment of group goals; and (4) *member change*—the change in knowledge, skills, attitudes, adjustment, or personality of the individual members of the group. Although there may be relations between these different types of group effectiveness over the long run, in the short run, however, it is evident that these different types of outcome may vary independently of one another. For example, high member satisfaction may result from or result in high task accomplishment, but high task accomplishment may also occur at the cost of member satisfaction (as when a demanding leader drives the group members on despite their protests).

The bulk of research on group effectiveness has been concerned with the determinants of task performance. This research highlights the importance of the following types of determinants: (1) the strength of the values associated with effective task performance—e.g., the greater the potential rewards for good performance and the more task-oriented the group norms, the more effort the group will be willing to put into the task; (2) the cohesiveness of the group—e.g., the more the members value the group and one another, the more willing they will be to expend effort in compliance with group norms or to achieve group-defined goals; (3) the perceived difficulty of the task—e.g., a task that is perceived to be very easy or virtually impossible is likely to stimulate less effort than a task that is viewed as difficult but attainable; (4) the amount of task-revelant abilities, information, and experience of the group members; (5) the appropriateness of the group structure to the requirements of the task—e.g., how efficient is the particular kind of division of labor for the task? how do the abilities, knowledge, and interests of the role occupants fit the requirements of their roles?; (6) the central role of the group leader and the appropriateness of his leadership style to the task and to the group.

Although there have been many studies of task performance, research in this area has been plagued by the problem of establishing reliable and valid measures of group achievement. There is little evidence to indicate that one group tends to perform reliably or consistently better than another group on a given task. Nor can one predict with much confidence, from a group's performance on one task, how it will do on another similar task. Research investigators in this area have not yet begun to develop any measures of group achievement that have the usefulness of many of the measures of individual achievement.

The determinants of member satisfaction have been studied as extensively as those of task effectiveness (for summaries, see Collins & Guetzkow 1964; McGrath & Altman 1966). In brief, the relevant research indicates that a member's satisfaction is affected by (1) the status of the group—its successfulness, its task achievements, its prestige; (2) the interpersonal relations within the group—the attractiveness of the other group members, their attitude toward him, their attitude toward belonging to the group; (3) the member's role within the group—its prestige, communication centrality, power, significance, interest; (4) the direct rewards and benefits received from membership; (5) the group atmosphere, as determined by such factors as leadership style, group size, group composition; and (6) the nature and desirability of conflicting memberships or activities.

Little research has been done on the determinants of environmental input and of group viability.

There is, however, an extensive literature on member change. Much of the relevant research has been done under the rubric of conformity and deviation (for summaries, see Symposium on Conformity . . . 1961). Also, the growing literature on group psychotherapy (for representative papers, see Rosenbaum & Berger 1963) contains many insightful case discussions, even though the amount of systematic research is still quite small [see MENTAL DISORDERS, TREATMENT OF, *article on* GROUP PSYCHOTHERAPY].

In addition, there is a rapidly developing list of publications dealing with human-relations training groups that are concerned with helping people learn how to function more effectively in groups. Here, too, the amount of published research is negligible. Nevertheless, since the stimulus to this approach to human-relations training came from the theoretical writings on re-education and re-action research of Kurt Lewin (1935–1946), much of the literature on training groups is imbued with social science concepts and suggests research. The major ideas of Kurt Lewin that underlie the training-group approach are that the re-education process basically involves the equivalent of a change in culture, and that for the individual to accept a new system of values and beliefs, he must come to value his membership in a group that has these new values and beliefs as a central component of its culture.

MORTON DEUTSCH

[*Other relevant material may be found in* SOCIAL PSYCHOLOGY *and in the biography of* LEWIN.]

### BIBLIOGRAPHY

ADAMS, STUART 1953 Status Congruency as a Variable in Small Group Performance. *Social Forces* 32:16–22.

ATKINSON, JOHN W. 1964 *An Introduction to Motivation.* New York: Van Nostrand.

BALES, ROBERT F. 1950 A Set of Categories for the Analysis of Small Group Interaction. *American Sociological Review* 15:257–263.

BALES, ROBERT F. et al. 1951 Channels of Communication in Small Groups. *American Sociological Review* 16:461–468.

BARNARD, CHESTER I. (1938) 1962 *The Functions of the Executive.* Cambridge, Mass.: Harvard Univ. Press.

BENOÎT-SMULLYAN, ÉMILE 1944 Status, Status Types, and Status Interrelations. *American Sociological Review* 9:151–161.

CAMPBELL, DONALD T. 1958 Common Fate, Similarity, and Other Indices of the Status of Aggregates of Persons as Social Entities. *Behavioral Science* 3:14–25.

COHEN, ARTHUR R. 1958 Upward Communication in Experimentally Created Hierarchies. *Human Relations* 11:41–53.

COLEMAN, JAMES S. 1964 *Introduction to Mathematical Sociology.* New York: Free Press.

COLLINS, BARRY E.; and GUETZKOW, HAROLD 1964 *A Social Psychology of Group Processes for Decision-making.* New York: Wiley.

CONWELL, CHIC 1937 *The Professional Thief: By a Professional Thief.* Annotated and interpreted by Edwin H. Sutherland. Univ. of Chicago Press. → A paperback edition was published in 1960.

DEUTSCH, MORTON 1949 An Experimental Study of the Effects of Co-operation and Competition Upon Group Process. *Human Relations* 2:199–231.

DEUTSCH, MORTON 1959 Some Factors Affecting Membership Motivation and Achievement Motivation in a Group. *Human Relations* 12:81–95.

DEUTSCH, MORTON 1962 Cooperation and Trust: Some Theoretical Notes. Volume 10, pages 275–319 in *Nebraska Symposium on Motivation,* edited by Marshall R. Jones. Lincoln: Univ. of Nebraska Press.

EXLINE, RALPH V.; and ZILLER, ROBERT C. 1959 Status Congruency and Interpersonal Conflict in Decision-making Groups. *Human Relations* 12:147–162.

FESTINGER, LEON; SCHACHTER, STANLEY; and BACK, KURT (1950) 1963 *Social Pressures in Informal Groups: A Study of Human Factors in Housing.* Stanford Univ. Press.

FIEDLER, FRED E. 1964 A Contingency Model of Leadership Effectiveness. Volume 1, pages 149–190 in *Advances in Experimental Social Psychology.* New York: Academic Press.

GALTUNG, JOHAN 1964 Foreign Policy Opinion as a Function of Social Position. *Journal of Peace Research* 1:206–231.

GUETZKOW, HAROLD (1953) 1960 Differentiation of Roles in Task-oriented Groups. Pages 683–704 in Dorwin Cartwright and Alvin Zander (editors), *Group Dynamics: Research and Theory.* 2d ed. Evanston, Ill.: Row, Peterson.

HARE, ALEXANDER P. 1962 *Handbook of Small Group Research.* New York: Free Press.

HOFFMAN, L. RICHARD; HARBURG, ERNEST; and MAIER, NORMAN R. F. 1962 Differences and Disagreement as Factors in Creative Group Problem Solving. *Journal of Abnormal and Social Psychology* 64:206–214.

HOMANS, GEORGE C. 1950 *The Human Group.* New York: Harcourt.

HOMANS, GEORGE C. 1961 *Social Behavior: Its Elementary Forms.* New York: Harcourt.

KELLEY, HAROLD H. 1951 Communication in Experimentally Created Hierarchies. *Human Relations* 4:39–56.

KELLEY, HAROLD H.; and THIBAUT, JOHN W. 1954 Experimental Studies of Group Problem Solving and Process. Volume 2, pages 735–785 in Gardner Lindzey (editor), *Handbook of Social Psychology.* Cambridge, Mass.: Addison-Wesley.

KOFFKA, KURT 1935 *Principles of Gestalt Psychology.* New York: Harcourt.

LEWIN, KURT (1935–1946) 1948 *Resolving Social Conflicts: Selected Papers on Group Dynamics.* Edited by Gertrud W. Lewin. A publication of the University of Michigan Research Center for Group Dynamics. New York: Harper.

McGRATH, J. E.; and ALTMAN, I. 1966 *Small Group Research: A Synthesis and Critique.* New York: Holt.

MANN, RICHARD D. 1959 A Review of the Relationships Between Personality and Performance in Small Groups. *Psychological Bulletin* 56:241–270.

MEREI, FERENC 1949 Group Leadership and Institutionalization. *Human Relations* 2:23–39.

RAVEN, BERTRAM H.; and EACHUS, H. TODD 1963 Cooperation and Competition in Means-interdependent

Triads. *Journal of Abnormal and Social Psychology* 67:307–316.

ROSE, EDWARD; and FELTON, WILLIAM 1955 Experimental Histories of Culture. *American Sociological Review* 20:383–392.

ROSENBAUM, MAY; and BERGER, MILTON (editors) 1963 *Group Psychotherapy and Group Function.* New York: Basic Books.

SCHUTZ, WILLIAM C. 1958 *FIRO: A Three-dimensional Theory of Interpersonal Behavior.* New York: Holt.

SHAPIRO, DAVID 1963 The Reinforcement of Disagreement in a Small Group. *Behavior Research and Therapy* 1:267–272.

SHERIF, MUZAFER (1936) 1965 *The Psychology of Social Norms.* New York: Octagon.

SLATER, PHILIP E. 1955 Role Differentiation in Small Groups. *American Sociological Review* 20:300–310.

STEPHAN, FREDERICK F.; and MISHLER, ELLIOT G. 1952 The Distribution of Participation in Small Groups: An Exponential Approximation. *American Sociological Review* 17:598–608.

STONE, PHILIP J. et al. 1962 The General Inquirer: A Computer System for Content Analysis and Retrieval Based on the Sentence as a Unit of Information. *Behavioral Science* 7:484–498.

SYMPOSIUM ON CONFORMITY AND DEVIATION, LOUISIANA STATE UNIVERSITY, *1960* 1961 *Conformity and Deviation.* Edited by Irwin A. Berg and Bernard M. Bass. New York: Harper.

THOMAS, EDWIN J.; and FINK, CLINTON F. 1963 Effects of Group Size. *Psychological Bulletin* 60:371–384.

### III
#### GROUP FORMATION

Groups are composed of individuals. But when and how does a collection of individuals become a group? The phrase "group formation" suggests that something is formed. The task here is to trace the appearance of essential properties or characteristics that distinguish a *human* group.

Both for theory and research, it is instructive to adopt the strategy of tracing the formation of informal groups rather than of those instituted formally through blueprints handed down by outside authority (such as a committee or board). Despite the limitation of considering groups formed through the interaction of the membership, the implications are broad. Many social institutions and formal organizations (including governments) had informal beginnings. Informal groups are almost invariably found within stable formal structures such as industrial, commercial, political, educational, religious, military, and recreational organizations. Finally, informal groups possess the *minimal* characteristics essential to any organized association, whether large or small.

**Background.** The properties characterizing the formation of a group were treated by the nineteenth-century social philosophers for various reasons and with varying emphasis, each using illustrative examples known to him. But the topic was doomed

to controversy until data were collected through scientific methods.

In the 1920s, Robert E. Park at the University of Chicago inspired and directed a series of investigations into human groups and their relationships to their settings (for example, Thrasher 1927; Landesco 1929; Shaw 1929; Zorbaugh 1929). Initiated to deal with the problem of homeless and antisocial children, the work of the Soviet educator Makarenko included concrete data on the formation of group properties, which he gradually came to regard as crucial conditions for the effectiveness of his educational efforts (Makarenko 1933; Bowen 1962).

In the 1930s, under the impetus of Elton Mayo of the Harvard Business School, studies in Western Electric's Hawthorne plant revealed the emergence of groups and their impact on the behavior of workers who had initially been placed together in observation rooms for the purpose of studying the effects of varying illumination and rest periods (Roethlisberger & Dickson 1939). J. L. Moreno (1934) and his co-workers began the systematic sociometric mapping of friendship choices among girls in reformatory cottages and children in classrooms. Using the methods of laboratory psychology, Sherif (1936) tested sociological theories dealing with the formation of social norms in situations of ambiguity and instability, demonstrating the subsequent retention of the norms as personal standards when individuals were alone. Lewin and his students (Lewin et al. 1939) initiated experiments varying the manner of adult supervisors of children's clubs. Meanwhile, the failure of "personality" or "intelligence" tests in selecting military leaders led the military in several countries to sponsor studies of what came to be called "leaderless groups" (Gibb 1954; U.S. Office of Strategic Services 1948).

### Properties

The definition presented here includes only the minimal properties found essential through extensive surveys of empirical and theoretical literature on groups of all kinds (Sherif & Cantril 1947; Sherif & Sherif 1948).

**Definition.** A group is a social unit consisting of a number of individuals who stand in status and role relationships to one another that are stabilized in some degree at a given time and who possess a set of values or norms regulating their behavior, at least in matters of consequence to the group.

By this definition, the "groupness" of a group is a matter of degree. A collection of persons forms into a group proportional to (*a*) the degree of stability of its organization (consisting of roles and status relations) and (*b*) the degree to which its particular set of norms for behavior are shared and binding for the participants. The undefined terms in the definition (role, status, norms) will be specified through research operations with conceptual relationship to the process of group formation.

It should be noted that this definition includes the properties covered in many modern works, while excluding others. Similar specifications are found in Bales (1950), Blau and Scott (1962), Bonner (1959), Cartwright and Zander (1953), Golembiewski (1962), and Hare (1962). The following characteristics, included by some investigators, were omitted here for the reasons specified:

*Interaction* and *communication* are not distinctive to group formation but are essential to any kind of human association of consequence. *Shared sentiments, attitudes,* and *behavior patterns* of group members are implied in the normative property; in fact, the extent of sharing is one of the research measures for the degree of group formation at a given time. Many properties of existing groups (for example, *morale, solidarity* or *cohesiveness,* and *loyalty* of members) are dependent upon the conditions of group formation, especially the degree of stability attained.

The properties essential to group formation will aid the reader in evaluating the large body of experimental research on so-called "small groups" conducted in both the United States and Europe since World War II. In summarizing this literature, Golembiewski (1962, p. 47) found that the great majority of these "groups" consisted of strangers exposed briefly in the laboratory to tasks or instructions creating temporary interdependence. Very few studies have allowed a sufficient time span for group properties to form.

**Generality of group formation.**    Beneath the organized forms and routines of societies, the formation and disintegration of groups occur in all walks of life, frequently with important consequences. Informal group formation is well documented within industrial, military, school, prison, and neighborhood settings (see Hare 1962; Sherif & Sherif 1948). In studying the Near North Side of Chicago, Zorbaugh (1929, p. 192) reported group formations in neighborhoods of all socioeconomic ranks with "an enormously important role in the lives of their members": exclusive clubs on the fashionable Gold Coast, intimate groups of nonconformists in artists studios, mutual benefit societies in foreign colonies, gangs in slum areas, and cults and sects in the rooming house district.

The extensive documentation on the generality of group formation also shows the striking dependence of the process on other groups and on the material and ideational features and facilities of the environment. The process of group formation is not insulated by the bounds of the membership. The formation that results is not a closed system. The circumstances bringing individuals together initially, their motives in continuing to interact, the particular organization and norms that develop, and the degree of their stability are inevitably dependent upon environmental circumstances. Included in the environmental circumstances are other groups whose activities and aims impinge favorably or unfavorably upon those of the group in formation.

### Four essentials of group formation

The essentials of group formation can be traced, starting with the initial conditions for interaction among individuals. The encounter with another person is the most elementary social situation. Even the mere presence of other persons has consequential effects on behavior and task performance. From the time when individuals are merely together to the time when the properties of a group begin to appear, we see that the consequential effects on behavior begin to assume regularities. As time goes on, these regularities reflect patterns that are the organizational and normative properties of the group. Accordingly, the essentials in the process of group formation are the following: (1) A motivational base conducive to repeated interaction; (2) formation of an organization (structure) consisting of roles and statuses; (3) formation of rules, traditions, values, or norms; and (4) differential effects of the group properties on the attitude and behavior of participants over time.

**Motivational base.**    Any human motive, frustration, problem, or desired goal that an individual cannot handle effectively alone is conducive to his interaction with others who are seen as being in the same plight. The prerequisite for group formation is that persons with motives conducive to initial interaction have the opportunity over a span of time to recognize the concerns they share or reciprocate and to attempt to deal with them in concert.

The common motive or motives faced in the initial stages of interaction may be one or several of those found in any society—for example, hunger, sexual desire, desire for recognition or power in some respect, and fear or anxiety in the face of threat. They may be culturally defined—for example, desire for material possessions or prestige through particular activities, or pursuit of political goals. Here only a few points can be considered:

The common problem, motive, or goal conducive to repeated interactions is necessarily dependent on environmental circumstances, both in its occurrence and in attempts to deal with it. Whatever its nature, the motivational base for group formation invariably affects the activities and tasks engaged in by the group's members and the kinds of personal qualities that become prized by them. When a set of norms takes shape, those most binding are typically related to the motives or problems that initially brought the persons together. One reason why the many controversies over problems of conformity–nonconformity are inconclusive is that many theorists pay scant attention to the relationship between the particular norms of a group and the initial motivational base underlying them.

However, to the degree that group formation achieves a degree of stability over time, new sources of motivation and new goals, arising from the existence of the group itself, are generated among the members. These may even take precedence over those that originally brought the members together. Thus, the hungry person may refrain from eating until he can share with his starving fellows; the politician may spurn an advantageous political bargain out of loyalty to his supporters; the member of a group struggling for equal opportunity and freedom from fear may undergo great deprivation and bodily injury to secure recognition of his group.

**Formation of organization or structure.**   As individuals interact over a period of time in activities related to the common problems that brought them together, their behavior and their expectations for one another's behavior assume regularities from which a pattern can be constructed. Here we shall define certain features of these regularities that appear to be crucial in any group formation. Heavy reliance will be placed upon findings from three experiments on group formation and relations between groups, each experiment lasting several weeks (summarized in Sherif & Sherif [1948] 1956, chapters 6 and 9; and Sherif 1966), and from more recent studies of naturally formed groups (Sherif & Sherif 1964). In each case the experiments started with unacquainted persons divided into collections of 10–12 as similar as possible in composition. All of these studies were conducted under naturalistic conditions, and data were collected without constant awareness by the individuals that they were being investigated.

The development of organization has been defined in terms of role and status relationships among a number of individuals. *Role* denotes reciprocities in the treatments and expectations of individuals, each for the others. Unlike well-defined occupational or sex roles, definite prescriptions for behavior are lacking when unacquainted persons first meet. Reciprocities among them must be built on the basis of performance in the activities engaged in, the reactions of others to a person, and his reactions to them. The typical finding at early stages of interaction is that individual contributions to task performance differ from one activity to the next (U.S. Office of Strategic Services 1948; Gibb 1954). Thus, observers rating behavior in the different situations find that the degree of participation and prominence of the individuals differs from one task to the next, according to individual differences in skills, abilities, temperament, or physical resources and tools relative to the activities in question.

The single most salient feature of group formation is that over time the various member roles become differentiated, not merely with regard to task performance or personal qualities but according to the evaluation of the roles by the members themselves. Members are accorded differing degrees of prestige and respect by their fellows. The member roles acquire different degrees of relative *power* to initiate and control activities important to all of the individuals in the group.

A member's position (rank) in a developing power structure is his *status* in the group, defined in terms of the relative effectiveness of his actions in initiating activities, making or approving decisions affecting the group, coordinating interaction, and invoking correctives for deviation.

Power, defined as effective initiative, is not identical with influence, in the limited sense that person A affects the actions of person B. Influence of this kind may occur with little or no relation to the effectiveness of person A's actions in the group. Power is implemented by *sanctions*, while influence is not.

Status (rank in power) is not identical with popularity or degree to which the person is liked. In fact, status and popularity may be poorly correlated (see Hare 1962, p. 115; Sherif & Sherif 1964, chapter 6). Nor should status be confused with the use of force or aggression. As Whyte (1943) showed, even in a street corner group whose members valued masculine toughness, the best potential fighter was not necessarily highest in status. Status was rooted in "mutual obligations" incurred among the group members over time and the reliability with which a member lived up to his obligations.

Since it is defined as effective initiative, status in a group is necessarily hierarchical. The highest status represents the leadership role. Especially in societies or situations where social equality is emphasized, the operational leader, defined by observation of his effectiveness over time, may not be openly chosen "leader" by the group's members.

The accompanying figure is a diagram of the stabilization of statuses, based on experimental findings for six groups. At time $T_i$ (the top) the individuals in two collections have first encountered one another. The circles represent the individuals and indicate that, at that time, independent observers do not agree on regularities in the relationships among them from one situation to the next. Instead, their ratings of effective initiative are different in various activities. (See Figure 1.)

Just below, at time $T_j$, the observers' ratings begin to agree (from one activity to the next and one day to the next) that the highest and lowest

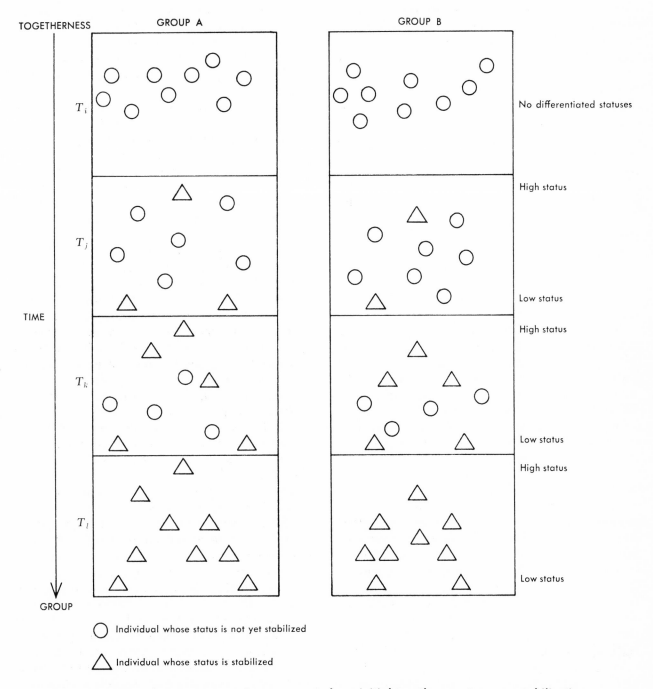

Figure 1 — Formation of status structure in two groups, from initial togetherness to group stabilization

Source: Sherif & Sherif 1964.

positions (represented by triangles) are stabilized. Both in the experiments and in real-life groups, the leader position typically stabilizes earlier than other high positions. This does not imply that group formation consists of the "search for a leader." On the contrary, leadership is subject to change. As Hofstätter correctly pointed out (1957, especially p. 24), tracing group organization over time is necessary to clear up many glib formulas propounded without sufficient evidence.

At time $T_k$ in the figure, observers are able to agree on the positions most members occupy, except in the middle of the diagram. Again, this is a typical finding. In part it reflects attempts by those in the middle to improve their standing or to align themselves with those higher in status. At time $T_l$ in the diagram the status relationships are stabilized, all observers agreeing on the status structure, which is also revealed in members' perceptions of it as manifested by sociometric choices obtained from them.

The diagram is intended to be representative. The different patterns of status in the two groups are intended to suggest that there is no predetermined form to the "steepness" or "flatness" of the hierarchy. Group formation represents an ideal occasion to study factors affecting the organization of groups, but little research has been done on this problem.

The rate of stabilization varies. In the experiments, the groups stabilized within about a week of continuous living together. Other investigators have reported the discernible beginnings of group structure among individuals meeting in the same location with similar activities within three to five meetings of a few hours duration (Merei 1949). Environmental events are as important as internal events in affecting the speed of stabilization. The stability of the pattern is sensitive to the introduction of new members, to changes in location and facilities, and to outside threat or emergency.

In particular, the stabilization of group structure is never independent of relationships with other groups. Prolonged competition between groups for mutually incompatible goals is particularly effective in quickly stabilizing a structure. Important intergroup confrontations, especially those resulting in defeat or humiliation, produce changes in the internal organization of a group (Sherif 1966).

The leader of a group, although most powerful, is still a member subject to loss of status. When the group structure is stabilized in some degree for the time, no person within it is free to ignore its regulation. It defines for members the bounds of "we"

or the in-group, as compared to others who are not members. If sufficiently stabilized, the group can continue after a leader's departure with little disruption (see Toki 1935). This persistence of a group structure and the effects of the group even on the leader are clearer in terms of the normative property of group formation.

**Formation of group norms.** As a group structure takes shape, members come to prefer certain ways of going about their important activities. They may adopt a group name. They set up standards for the ways members should and should not behave among themselves and with outsiders. "Norm" is a general term to refer to such results of interaction which produce regularities among group members.

Unlike the "norm" on an examination or a test, a group norm does not necessarily refer to the average of individual behaviors. It designates what is expected as proper, as moral, or even as ideal. Yet a group norm seldom denotes a single action as the only way to behave. A range for individual variations is permissible in any group. A norm denotes the range of behaviors that members come to deem socially desirable and acceptable (latitude of acceptance) and a range of behaviors condemned as objectionable (latitude of rejection).

A norm implies, therefore, an evaluative scale (measuring rod) defining for individual members a latitude of acceptance and a latitude of rejection, to regulate their behavior in matters of consequence to the group (Sherif et al. 1965). Not all social behavior is regulated by clear-cut norms, particularly when groups are in formation.

How can a group norm be detected? There are at least three objective ways:

(1) By observing similarities and regularities in the behaviors (words and deeds) found among one set of persons but not another set in a similar situation.

(2) By observing correctives (sanctions) for certain behaviors and praise or reward for others. *Reactions to deviations* are among the best evidence of the bounds of acceptable behavior. These may range from disapproval, frowns, and correctives to threats and actual punishment.

(3) By noting the increasing similarity or convergence over time in the behaviors of individuals who initially behaved differently. For example, the entrance of a new member into a group provides an opportunity to detect the existence of its norms.

When groups are in the process of formation, as in the experiments, one of the best indicators of their stability is the degree of consensus among members on the correctness of their norms and the degree to which the latitude of acceptance is binding without direct social pressure or threat of sanctions. Stabilization of the set of norms is indicated when members privately regulate their own behavior within the latitude of acceptance. The person's own conception of how he should behave and how others should act comes to fall within bounds defined by the norms. Especially when the individual has had a part in creating the norms as a group member, they become aspects of his self concept relative to others. He experiences personal guilt or shame if he violates them.

The personal acceptance of group norms during group formation accounts in large measure for the tenacity of tradition once established. Merei (1949) demonstrated this tenacity by permitting play groups to develop procedures and rules and then introducing a new child who was older and had evidenced leadership skills in other situations. In every group the new child quickly found that his superior skills in coordinating play were not effective, for no one paid attention. In every case, the new child was then absorbed into the group, adopting its traditions and rules.

Sherif and Sherif (1964) present evidence that the stringency of norms and resistance to their change varies according to the importance of the norm for the group. Violations in major activities or in dealings with outsiders, exposure of group secrets, or other behavior jeopardizing the maintenance of the group were unerringly responded to by strong sanctions such as expulsion, threat, or physical punishment. Even leaders whose actions exposed the group or its members to humiliation, embarrassment, or danger were chastised.

In less important activities the range of tolerance for individual differences was much wider, particularly for the leader and higher-status members. In matters of daily routine or amusement strictly within the group, leaders were free to innovate and sometimes engaged in behavior that would not have been tolerated in lesser members. In these fairly stable groups, the great bulk of conforming behavior occurred without direct social pressure or threat of sanctions, particularly behavior by members of moderate or high status.

**Differential effects on behavior.**   The formation of a group structure and norms has consequences for the attitudes and behavior of individuals within its fold. These consequences may be referred to as the differential effects of group formation.

Any social situation provides a context for behavior which differs from that in a solitary situation. The context includes the other people present, the activities and tasks undertaken, the physical site and its facilities, and the person's relationship to all of these. Experiments have repeatedly shown the differential effects of various aspects of the social context on behavior as compared to behavior when alone.

The formation of a role system and norms during interaction among persons over time brings about alterations in the relative contribution of the task, activity, setting, and individual reactions. When the persons are at first simply *together*, without stabilized reciprocities, their personal characteristics and skills relative to the tasks and those of other people are important determinants of behavior (Gibb 1954; Hare 1962). As the process of group formation starts taking shape, the developing organizational and normative schemes become more and more binding on members. As a result, over time, the characteristics of the task and location—in short, immediate situational factors—recede in relative importance, and behavior increasingly reflects the person's role in the group, the roles of others, and the emerging norms.

The group formation experiments of Sherif and Sherif ([1948] 1956, chapters 6 and 9) traced the development of a "we-feeling." It was found that sociometric friendship choices became almost exclusively concentrated within the group, even though initial choices before group formation had been given predominantly to persons placed (deliberately) in another group. In one experiment it was shown that estimates made by members of one another's performance became significantly related to the member's status, the relationship being closer when the structure was more stable. Performance by high-status members was overestimated, and that of low-status persons was minimized.

In another experiment the groups formed separately, then competed for a series of mutually exclusive goals. As predicted, norms developed in each group justifying hostility to the other group. The performance by members of the other group in a novel task was estimated to be significantly lower than performance by members of the in-group, revealing the prejudicial norm in the judgments of individual members (Oklahoma, University . . . 1961).

In proportion to the significance a particular group has in a person's life, his membership in it affects his attitude and behavior. As the group formation stabilizes, his sense of identity becomes tied to being a member of that group, proportional to its scope and importance in his daily living. For this reason the socialization of the person is incompletely described by reference only to his acquisition of formal prescriptions from family, school, and other official institutions. From early childhood through adolescence, groups formed among agemates exert compelling impact upon the person's conceptions of what is desirable for him, what is acceptable in others, and what is right and wrong (Campbell 1964; Sherif & Sherif 1964). In other words, they become aspects of the individual's own conscience.

Recognition of the consequences for the self concepts and attitudes of participants has led to attempts in various countries to utilize group formation for corrective and therapeutic purposes. The varied outcomes reveal both gaps in the knowledge of group formation and lack of familiarity with the knowledge available on the part of many practitioners (Rosenbaum & Berger 1963, especially pp. 1–32).

The emphasis earlier in this article on the motivational base of group formation and on the importance of environmental alternatives suggests fruitful lines of inquiry. The significance of the motivational base was revealed in a study of group formation among "emotionally disturbed young adolescents of poor prognosis" by Rafferty (1962, p. 263). They interacted rather freely in a wide range of activities for five hours daily, five days a week for nine months. They lacked motivation toward the institution's aim of changing their behavior, and their personal disturbances hindered any kind of stable interpersonal relationships. However, they did unite with incipient group formation in activities reflecting a motivation genuine to them: defiance of the hospital staff in forbidden activities.

This instructive finding raises the issue of predicting or controlling the character of the structure and norms during group formation. Here the importance of the environmental setting and the behavioral alternatives it encourages or permits becomes evident. In the group experiments referred to frequently here, solidary groups devoted to constructive activities were formed simply by placing unacquainted persons in situations of high appeal to them, with facilities and conditions so arranged that coordination of activity was the only way to secure individual satisfaction. Subsequently, conflict and hostility between the groups were produced, followed by their reduction through cooperative efforts by the groups. These effects were achieved merely by varying the facilities available, the other persons present, and other conditions external to both groups. Future research on group

formation and its applied implications might profitably focus on the effects of varying the environmental alternatives and facilities available to groups, including other groups and persons, upon the character of the organization and norms that develop.

## Conclusions

The material briefly presented above warrants the following conclusions:

Whenever individuals with similar motives, similar frustrations, and similar personal concerns for acceptance, for recognition, and for stabilizing their perception of themselves encounter one another, and when these goal-directed concerns are not effectively dealt with through the established channels of custom and law or the routine of prevailing arrangements of social organization—these individuals then tend to interact among themselves.

Repeated interaction in some common striving is conducive to differentiation of roles or functions to be performed toward the common end. And differentiation of roles and functions among the participating individuals, *over a time span*, is the pattern or formation that can be designated as *the group*. Every such human formation creates its own set of rules or norms to stabilize the regulation of behavior and the attitudes of members within its bounds.

In a natural group, as in any other group, the rules or norms that count and have salience in the eyes of the members are generally the ones that pertain to the existence and perpetuation of the group and to the spheres of activity that are related to the common motivational concerns that were initially conducive to repeated interaction among the individuals in question.

The main properties of the group thus formed are an organization (structure) of roles and statuses and a set of rules or standards (norms) for its activities toward the common ends. The "organization" (which need not be formally recognized) and the set of norms (which need not be formally written in blueprints) define the sense of "we-ness" cherished within the group and upheld by its members in their dealings with outsiders.

In time, the standards or norms shared in the feeling of "we-ness" become personally binding for individual members. The members who are worthy and true make their judgments and justify or condemn events within the sphere related to their "we-ness" in terms of their sense of identification with the group. Proportional to the importance of the group in the lives of its members, the person's self picture, his sense of personal accountability, his loyalty, and the "do's" and "don'ts" of the group become parts of his *conscience*. Hence, group formation has broad implications for the regulation of individual attitude and behavior with and without external sanctions and controls.

MUZAFER SHERIF AND CAROLYN W. SHERIF

[*Directly related are the entries* COHESION, SOCIAL; CONFORMITY; LEADERSHIP. *Other relevant material may be found in* ATTITUDES; FRIENDSHIP; INTERACTION; NORMS; ROLE; SELF CONCEPT; SOCIAL PSYCHOLOGY; SOCIAL STRUCTURE; SOCIALIZATION.]

## BIBLIOGRAPHY

BALES, ROBERT F. 1950 *Interaction Process Analysis: A Method for the Study of Small Groups.* Reading, Mass.: Addison-Wesley.

BLAU, PETER M.; and SCOTT, W. RICHARD 1962 *Formal Organizations: A Comparative Approach.* San Francisco: Chandler. → Contains an extensive bibliography.

BONNER, HUBERT 1959 *Group Dynamics: Principles and Applications.* New York: Ronald Press.

BOWEN, JAMES 1962 *Soviet Education: Anton Makarenko and the Years of Experiment.* Madison: Univ. of Wisconsin Press.

CAMPBELL, JOHN D. 1964 Peer Relations in Childhood. Volume 1, pages 289–322 in Martin L. Hoffman and Lois W. Hoffman (editors), *Review of Child Development Research.* New York: Russell Sage Foundation.

CARTWRIGHT, DORWIN; and ZANDER, ALVIN (editors) (1953) 1960 *Group Dynamics: Research and Theory.* 2d ed. Evanston, Ill.: Row, Peterson.

GIBB, CECIL A. 1954 Leadership. Volume 2, pages 877–920 in Gardner Lindzey (editor), *Handbook of Social Psychology.* Cambridge, Mass.: Addison-Wesley.

GOLEMBIEWSKI, ROBERT T. 1962 *The Small Group: An Analysis of Research Concepts and Operations.* Univ. of Chicago Press.

HARE, ALEXANDER P. 1962 *Handbook of Small Group Research.* New York: Free Press.

HOFSTÄTTER, PETER R. 1957 *Gruppendynamik: Die Kritik der Massenpsychologie.* Hamburg (Germany): Rowohlt.

LANDESCO, JOHN 1929 Organized Crime in Chicago. Pages 823–841 in Illinois Association for Criminal Justice, *The Illinois Crime Survey.* Chicago: The Association.

LEWIN, KURT; LIPPITT, R.; and WHITE, R. K. 1939 Patterns of Aggressive Behavior in Experimentally Created "Social Climates." *Journal of Social Psychology* 10:271–299.

MAKARENKO, ANTON S. (1933) 1951 *The Road to Life: An Epic of Education.* 3 vols. Moscow: Foreign Languages Publishing House. → First published as *Pedagogicheskaia poema.*

MEREI, FERENC 1949 Group Leadership and Institutionalization. *Human Relations* 2:23–39.

MORENO, JACOB L. (1934) 1953 *Who Shall Survive? Foundations of Sociometry, Group Psychotherapy and Sociodrama.* Rev. & enl. ed. Beacon, N.Y.: Beacon House.

OKLAHOMA, UNIVERSITY OF, INSTITUTE OF GROUP RELATIONS 1961 *Intergroup Conflict and Cooperation: The Robbers Cave Experiment,* by Muzafer Sherif et al. Norman, Okla.: University Book Exchange.

RAFFERTY, F. T. 1962 Development of a Social Structure in Treatment Institutions. *Journal of Nervous and Mental Disease* 134:263–267.

ROETHLISBERGER, FRITZ J.; and DICKSON, WILLIAM J. (1939) 1961 *Management and the Worker: An Account of a Research Program Conducted by the Western Electric Company, Hawthorne Works, Chicago.* Cambridge, Mass.: Harvard Univ. Press. → A paperback edition was published in 1964 by Wiley.

ROSENBAUM, MAX; and BERGER, M. (editors) 1963 *Group Psychotherapy and Group Function.* New York: Basic Books.

SHAW, CLIFFORD R. 1929 *Delinquency Areas: A Study of the Geographic Distribution of School Truants, Juvenile Delinquents, and Adult Offenders in Chicago.* Univ. of Chicago Press.

SHERIF, CAROLYN W.; SHERIF, M.; and NEBERGALL, R. E. 1965 *Attitude and Attitude Change: The Social Judgment–Involvement Approach.* Philadelphia: Saunders.

SHERIF, MUZAFER (1936) 1965 *The Psychology of Social Norms.* New York: Octagon. → A paperback edition was published in 1966 by Harper.

SHERIF, MUZAFER 1966 *In Common Predicament: Social Psychology of Intergroup Conflict and Cooperation.* Boston: Houghton Mifflin. → A British edition was published by Routledge as *Group Conflict and Cooperation: Their Social Psychology.*

SHERIF, MUZAFER; and CANTRIL, HADLEY 1947 *The Psychology of Ego-involvements, Social Attitudes and Identifications.* New York: Wiley; London: Chapman & Hall.

SHERIF, MUZAFER; and SHERIF, CAROLYN W. (1948) 1956 *An Outline of Social Psychology.* Rev. ed. New York: Harper.

SHERIF, MUZAFER; and SHERIF, CAROLYN W. 1964 *Reference Groups: Exploration Into Conformity and Deviation of Adolescents.* New York: Harper.

THRASHER, FREDERIC (1927) 1963 *The Gang: A Study of 1,313 Gangs in Chicago.* Abridged and with an introduction by James F. Short. Univ. of Chicago Press.

TOKI, K. 1935 The Leader–Follower Structure in the School Class. *Japanese Journal of Psychology* 10:27–56. → A discussion of Toki's article appears on pages 8–10, 604, 608, 613, and 631–635 in *Fundamentals of Social Psychology,* by Eugene L. and Ruth Hartley.

U.S. OFFICE OF STRATEGIC SERVICES, ASSESSMENT STAFF 1948 *The Assessment of Men.* New York: Rinehart.

WHYTE, WILLIAM F. (1943) 1961 *Street Corner Society: The Social Structure of an Italian Slum.* 2d ed., enl. Univ. of Chicago Press.

ZORBAUGH, HARVEY W. 1929 *The Gold Coast and the Slum.* Univ. of Chicago Press.

## IV
### ROLE STRUCTURE

"Role" refers to a set of "expectations" for interaction between a person who holds one position in a group and another person who holds a reciprocal position. In other words, there can be no "leader" role without a "follower" role. Since the person playing the role has a personality (or self) which he brings to the situation, the behavior of a person in a role will be some combination of the tendencies of his personality and the expectations of his role.

Roles in discussion groups, which are the focus of much of the research on groups, are usually not fixed. Any aspect of an individual's behavior that is initially an expression of his personality can come to be expected by other group members and thus become part of his role. In general, the dimensions of role are the same as the dimensions of interaction and of personality. Roles have a *form* and a *content*, where the form includes the frequency of interaction and the communication network and the content includes task and social–emotional behavior. Within the task area, the expectations refer to problem-solving behavior and within the social–emotional area, according to one recent formulation, to behavior along at least three dimensions: dominance–submission, positive–negative, and joking–serious (Couch 1960; Hare 1962).

**Patterns of role differentiation.**   Natural groups which have been in existence for some time will probably have a greater degree of role differentiation than laboratory groups (Sherwood & Walker 1960), unless the group organization allows only one leader who is expected to perform all functions. Thus, in some industrial and governmental conference groups a "sharing" of leadership is resisted by the members (Berkowitz 1953). Over the life of a group there may be more differentiation in roles when functional problems of the group become more acute, for example, when the group is under stress or the task is complex (Bales 1953). Similarly, members in cooperative groups are more apt to be differentiated in their functions than members who are competing (Homans 1961, p. 135).

The small military unit or industrial work team is perhaps the best example of the simplest form of role differentiation. In each case one or two members may have clearly defined functions with little overlap in their "expectations," while the remainder of the members play undifferentiated roles of "soldier" or "worker." In discussion groups (and especially in laboratory groups) it is not always clear whether a single person plays one role or many roles, or whether these roles are assumed at the same or at different times.

In some research all members are viewed as specializing in some content area, with those with the highest interaction rates identified as the leaders (Heinicke & Bales 1953; Grusky 1957). In other research some individuals may be described as playing a variety of roles and others none (Davis et al. 1961; Cloyd 1964). In either case the authors are not usually concerned with the rights and duties associated with each role. They rather use

the terms "expectations" in the sense that group members can predict or "expect" that a group member will act in a given way on the basis of past performance. There is no sense that the member is "obliged" to act in this way to fulfill a function in the group or that he is entitled to any special privileges for performing this function [*see* ETHICS, *article on* ETHICAL SYSTEMS AND SOCIAL STRUCTURES].

In some research, the evidence that a person is playing a given role is that other members associate a certain set of behavioral characteristics with him; these behavioral characteristics are presented as a cluster without any special rationale concerning their interconnection (Bates & Cloyd 1956; Davis 1961; Cloyd 1964). In other research a person is described as playing a role because he has been nominated as a frequent contributor of some specified type of behavior, for example, giving information or giving opinion (Bales 1958; Borg 1960). An even less functionalist view is taken in research in which some members are described as playing individual or self-oriented roles that presumably are extraneous to the group task (Benne & Sheats 1948). Another variation on the use of the term "role" is for the experimenter to describe someone as playing a role such as "newcomer" (Mills et al. 1957) or "doctor's assistant" (Margolin 1952) without actually assessing the perceptions of the other group members.

Most of the research on small groups has so far not used a definition of role as a set of rights and duties but rather as a description of recurring patterns of behavior. But the former, more limited definition of role still appears to be theoretically useful even though it is not widely used. For instance, in those studies that report the interaction in initially "leaderless" groups, the expectations for the average member are probably most clearly related to the directions given by the experimenter at the beginning of the session. Often, indeed, the experimenter will test to see if the subjects have been as friendly or as competitive as he directed them to be, but he will not refer to these instructions as "role expectations" (Olmsted 1954).

The power of an experimenter's instructions is evident in an experiment in which one member in each of several discussion groups was given more information about the task than the other members. In some of these groups the experimenter announced, "Some of you may have more information than others." In other groups he gave the impression that all members were equally informed. It was observed that group members reacted negatively to the best-informed man unless they had been led to "expect" that he would play a different role (Shaw & Penrod 1962).

Although early research on groups, especially with children, often described "individual" or "self-oriented" roles as if the only role of some individuals was to satisfy their own needs in the group (Benne & Sheats 1948), later formulations by Redl (1942), Bion (1961), and Stock and Thelen (1958) suggest that all roles in the group serve some function. However, some of these roles, particularly the ones that allow members to deal with emotional themes, may not be recognized as part of the "official" group structure. For example, in a training group composed of teachers who were being led by Bion's methods of "interpretive group discussion," the group members persisted, without success, in trying to induce the leader to act as a therapist. Finally six members did not appear at the scheduled group session and a spokesman for the absentees sent in a paper on truancy to be discussed by the remaining members. Thus, by taking the "role" of absent members, some of the group acted out the group's need for flight from the task (Herbert & Trist 1953).

**Task versus social–emotional roles.**   The most common division of roles that has been described in small discussion and work groups, as well as in families viewed as small groups, is specialization in the task and social–emotional areas (Bales & Slater 1955; Bales 1958). This has been shown most clearly in small laboratory groups in which members have a high degree of consensus at the end of a meeting on the relative amount of interaction in each of these areas exhibited by group members. These groups appear to recognize two kinds of role specialists: one an "idea man" who concentrates on the task and plays a more aggressive role; the other a "best-liked" man who concentrates on social–emotional problems of group process and member satisfaction, giving emotional rewards, and playing a more passive role. However, in groups similar to these in which there is less consensus on the status of members, a third type of person appears to be present, one who talks a great deal but who is not well liked or highly rated on his task ability. He has been referred to as a "deviant." In addition, researchers have found a more passive task specialist and a "popular" person (Slater 1955).

The so-called "deviant" who overtalks is probably expressing the group's anxiety about the discussion task. To please the experimenter, the group allows a member to fill the time with "discussion"

even though he may not be the most effective at the task. This tendency to have a high or low interaction rate has often been reported as the first of three factors or dimensions that may be used to describe behavior, the other two being task behavior and sociability (Carter 1954). However, the frequency of interaction should probably be considered an independent dimension because it describes the "form" of interaction and not because it represents a separate area of "content."

In families, the father has been identified as the task specialist, the mother as the social–emotional specialist (Parsons & Bales 1955). A similar dichotomy has been reported among caseworkers in a welfare agency where some colleagues were respected and sought out for consultation on cases and others were attractive because of their sociable companionship (Blau 1962). However, a study of therapy groups reported that the distinction was not evident in this setting, since the "task" of the group was to deal with social–emotional problems (Talland 1957).

When the same individual is required to play the role of both the task and the social–emotional leader, he may find some aspects of the roles incompatible and thus experience "role conflict" (Seeman 1953). Officers in small military units, for example, may be required to consider the personal problems of their men as well as to be task leaders. The second role requires distance, since some assignments must be made without regard to personal feelings, yet the first role requires closeness and intimacy (Hutchins & Fiedler 1960).

**The joker.**   In addition to these two roles, a third role has been identified in some groups which actually has a long history in many cultures. This is the role of the clown or the joker. Just as the English court jester's costume set him apart from the group, so the joker tends to take a somewhat marginal position with regard to the task. He tends to look at things differently, providing both a source of humor and of new ideas. Under the cover of wit he is able to introduce ideas that the group might otherwise find unacceptable.

In its literary form, comedy has been described as "an escape, not from truth but from despair: a narrow escape into faith" (Fry 1960, p. 27). One must be able to grasp the tragic nature of life before one can go on to grasp its comic nature. Thus, the comic person in a play or in a real-life small group is often one who gives special insight into the problem. This is evident from a study of a series of "great-books" discussion groups where the joking role was most highly correlated with the role of providing "fuel" for the discussions in the form of new ideas and opinions (Davis et al. 1961). In a study of laboratory discussion groups the following cluster of behavioral characteristics was identified as composing a role: jokes and makes humorous remarks, is liberal, challenges other's opinions, gets off the subject, is egotistical, is cynical, and interrupts others (Cloyd 1964). Within the dimension of "joking versus task-serious behavior" there may be different styles of wit. Thus, sarcastic wit may be perceived as powerful but unpopular in a group, while clowning wit may be seen as popular but powerless (Goodchilds 1959).

**The member.** The fact that simple membership in a group carries with it a set of rights and duties is evident in the group's concern for the "silent member." Although silence may be functional if it means that more able persons are being allowed to solve problems (Homans 1961, p. 136), group members are usually dissatisfied with a member's performance if he does not participate. This dissatisfaction may be reduced if it is made clear at the outset that certain members will not participate at all (Smith 1957). On the other hand the group will be more concerned if a member appears indifferent and neglectful in his role (Rosenthal & Cofer 1948).

Another type of member role that has received some attention in the literature is that of the "newcomer." Group members will have an easier time assimilating the newcomer if they have been told to expect change (Ziller et al. 1961), provided that the newcomer is not seen as too different from other group members (Ziller et al. 1960) and that group members have already had a pleasant time with each other (Heiss 1963). In any event there will probably be a minimal alteration in the role patterns of the old members at first (Mills et al. 1957).

**Other roles.** Other roles may be found in groups with special tasks. In therapy groups a "doctor's assistant" may fill the group's need to keep the discussion going when the therapist is playing a rather passive role and a "help-rejecting complainer" may give the group case material to discuss (Frank et al. 1952; Margolin 1952). Somewhat similar to the "doctor's assistant" may be the "feeder-to-leaders" identified in a sociometric study of a home for girls (Jennings 1947). These were girls who would have their ideas accepted after they had been endorsed by highly chosen leaders, although they were not highly chosen themselves [see LEADERSHIP].

The classic study of authoritarian and demo-cratic group atmospheres by Lewin, Lippitt, and White does not focus on role differentiation; however, two types of roles are mentioned in addition to the leaders. In the "democratic" groups the authors describe two boys who are allies of the adult leaders, and in the "autocratic" groups they describe a scapegoat who receives the aggression of the group (White & Lippitt 1960, pp. 160–186). Thrasher (1927) in his study of gangs in Chicago gives a longer list of special roles, to which he gives such names as brains of gang, funny boy, sissy, show-off, and goat. Redl (1942) lists ten types of roles of central persons, which may be grouped into three categories: identification objects, objects of drives, and ego supports.

In addition to roles which may arise naturally in groups, some authors have suggested certain roles which should be introduced if a group is to operate with maximum efficiency. For example, Jenkins (1948) suggests that effective discussion requires attention to such mechanics of operation as awareness of direction, goal, and rate of progress. He proposes that groups appoint a "group productivity observer" who will report at the end of each meeting.

Where role differentiation occurs in a group, individuals accustomed to playing the same roles in other groups will probably continue to play them in the new situation (Strodtbeck & Mann 1956; Davis et al. 1961). In addition, differences in age, sex, social class, and occupation between members will result in role differentiation in small discussion groups even when these differences are not related to the task at hand (Maas 1954; Torrance 1954).

**Six roles in discussion groups.** From the review of the literature presented above it is evident that a variety of roles have been identified in discussion groups. The number of roles reported may be small or large depending upon the level of analysis, the task, the group size, and the length of time the members have been together. Although the dichotomy of task versus social–emotional roles is adequate to describe the basic differentiation in some groups, in others there are probably more distinct roles that have been grouped under these two more general headings. A framework for the description of more distinct and independent roles is provided by Couch's (1960) factor analysis of categories of interaction in five-man laboratory discussion groups. He finds that interpersonal behavior can be described by the following independent dimensions: dominance versus submission; positive versus negative; task serious versus joking; influence attempts versus receptivity; and surface acquiescence versus resistance. If we assume that behavior at the extremes of each dimension may identify a role, we find a rather good fit with six role patterns identified by Cloyd (1964) without reference to any particular dimensions and without actually assigning them names.

At the dominance end of Couch's first factor we find a set of behaviors similar to a cluster identified by Cloyd that includes "aggressive, self-confident, and gets things started." This role might be called the "high talker." At the submissive end of Couch's first factor is Cloyd's cluster of traits: "modest, shy, and ill at ease." This role might be called the "silent member."

In a similar way one could match dimensions and clusters of traits to identify a "supporter" who is friendly and objective, a "critic" who is idealistic and argumentative, a "serious worker" who is dependable and constructive, and a "joker" who makes humorous remarks and challenges others' opinions. Cloyd does not provide examples that would fit the last two of Couch's dimensions; however, the last dimension suggests the roles of "conformist" and "nonconformist."

From this example it will be seen how small group experiments, although independently designed by researchers using different concepts, can be said to deal with a recurrent, scientifically identifiable class of phenomena. Indeed, such is the wealth of suggestive findings in this area that the organization of our present knowledge has become both an indispensable and a rewarding preliminary to future progress.

A. PAUL HARE

[*See also* INTERACTION, *article on* INTERACTION PROCESS ANALYSIS; LEADERSHIP; SOCIOMETRY.]

### BIBLIOGRAPHY

*Many of the articles listed below are discussed in more detail in Hare 1962, while 11 of them have been reprinted in whole or in part in Hare, Borgatta & Bales 1964. References to other introductory texts or readers will be found in the bibliographies to* GROUPS, *article on* THE STUDY OF GROUPS; *and* SOCIOMETRY. *For the layman who has no training in statistics but would like to savor some of the interest and importance of the field,* Bion 1961; Homans 1961; *and Mills 1957 should prove rewarding.*

BALES, ROBERT F. 1953 The Equilibrium Problem in Small Groups. Pages 111–161 in Talcott Parsons et al., *Working Papers in the Theory of Action.* Glencoe, Ill.: Free Press.

BALES, ROBERT F. 1958 Task Roles and Social Roles in Problem-solving Groups. Pages 437–447 in Eleanor E. Maccoby, T. M. Newcomb, and E. L. Hartley (edi-

tors), *Readings in Social Psychology.* 3d ed. New York: Holt.

BALES, ROBERT F.; and SLATER, PHILIP 1955 Role Differentiation in Small Decision-making Groups. Pages 259–306 in Talcott Parsons and Robert F. Bales, *Family, Socialization and Interaction Process.* Glencoe, Ill.: Free Press.

BATES, ALAN P.; and CLOYD, JERRY S. 1956 Toward the Development of Operations for Defining Group Norms and Member Roles. *Sociometry* 19:26–39.

BENNE, KENNETH D.; and SHEATS, PAUL 1948 Functional Roles of Group Members. *Journal of Social Issues* 4, no. 2:41–49.

BERKOWITZ, LEONARD 1953 Sharing Leadership in Small Decision-making Groups. *Journal of Abnormal and Social Psychology* 48:231–238.

BION, WILFRED R. 1961 *Experiences in Groups, and Other Papers.* New York: Basic Books. → Seven of these papers were published in *Human Relations* from 1948 to 1951.

BLAU, PETER M. 1962 Patterns of Choice in Interpersonal Relations. *American Sociological Review* 27:41–55.

BORG, WALTER R. 1960 Prediction of Small Group Role Behavior From Personality Variables. *Journal of Abnormal and Social Psychology* 60:112–116.

CARTER, LAUNOR F. 1954 Evaluating the Performance of Individuals as Members of Small Groups. *Personnel Psychology* 7:477–484.

CLOYD, JERRY S. 1964 Patterns of Role Behavior in Informal Interaction. *Sociometry* 27:161–173.

COUCH, A. S. 1960 Psychological Determinants of Interpersonal Behavior. Ph.D. dissertation, Harvard Univ.

DAVIS, JAMES A. 1961 Compositional Effects, Role Systems, and the Survival of Small Discussion Groups. *Public Opinion Quarterly* 25:575–584.

DAVIS, JAMES A. et al. 1961 *Great Books and Small Groups.* New York: Free Press.

FRANK, JEROME D. et al. 1952 Two Behavior Patterns in Therapeutic Groups and Their Apparent Motivation. *Human Relations* 5:289–317.

FRY, CHRISTOPHER 1950 Comedy. *Adelphi* Third Series 27:27–29.

GOODCHILDS, JACQUELINE D. 1959 Effects of Being Witty on Position in the Social Structure of a Small Group. *Sociometry* 22:261–272.

GRUSKY, OSCAR 1957 A Case for the Theory of Familial Role Differentiation in Small Groups. *Social Forces* 35:209–217.

HARE, A. PAUL 1962 *Handbook of Small Group Research.* New York: Free Press.

HARE, A. PAUL; BORGATTA, E. F.; and BALES, R. F. (1955) 1964 *Small Groups: Studies in Social Interaction.* 2d ed. New York: Knopf.

HEINICKE, CHRISTOPHER; and BALES, ROBERT F. (editors) 1953 Developmental Trends in the Structure of Small Groups. *Sociometry* 16:7–38.

HEISS, JEROLD S. 1963 The Dyad Views the Newcomer: A Study of Perception. *Human Relations* 16:241–248.

HERBERT, ELÉONORE L.; and TRIST, E. L. 1953 The Institution of an Absent Leader by a Students' Discussion Group. *Human Relations* 6:215–248.

HOMANS, GEORGE C. 1961 *Social Behavior: Its Elementary Forms.* New York: Harcourt.

HUTCHINS, EDWIN B.; and FIEDLER, FRED E. 1960 Task-oriented and Quasi-therapeutic Role Functions of the

Leader in Small Military Groups. *Sociometry* 23:393–406.

JENKINS, DAVID H. 1948 Feedback and Group Self-evaluation. *Journal of Social Issues* 4, no. 2:50–60.

JENNINGS, HELEN H. 1947 Leadership and Sociometric Choice. *Sociometry* 10:32–49.

MAAS, HENRY S. 1954 The Role of Member in Clubs of Lower-class and Middle-class Adolescents. *Child Development* 25:241–251.

MARGOLIN, JOSEPH B. 1952 The Use of an Interaction Matrix to Validate Patterns of Group Behavior. *Human Relations* 5:407–416.

MILLS, THEODORE M. et al. 1957 Group Structure and the Newcomer: An Experimental Study of Group Expansion. *Studies in Society* No. 1.

OLMSTED, MICHAEL S. 1954 Orientation and Role in the Small Group. *American Sociological Review* 19:741–751.

PARSONS, TALCOTT; and BALES, ROBERT F. 1955 *Family, Socialization and Interaction Process.* Glencoe, Ill.: Free Press; London: Routledge.

REDL, FRITZ 1942 Group Emotion and Leadership. *Psychiatry* 5:573–596.

ROSENTHAL, DAVID; and COFER, CHARLES N. 1948 The Effect on Group Performance of an Indifferent and Neglectful Attitude Shown by One Group Member. *Journal of Experimental Psychology* 38:568–577.

SEEMAN, MELVIN 1953 Role Conflict and Ambivalence in Leadership. *American Sociological Review* 18:373–380.

SHAW, MARVIN E.; and PENROD, WILLIAM E. JR. 1962 Does More Information Available to a Group Always Improve Group Performance? *Sociometry* 25:377–390.

SHERWOOD, CLARENCE E.; and WALKER, W. S. 1960 Role Differentiation in Real Groups: An Extrapolation of a Laboratory Small-group Research Finding. *Sociology and Social Research* 45:14–17.

SLATER, PHILIP E. 1955 Role Differentiation in Small Groups. *American Sociological Review* 20:300–310.

SMITH, EWART E. 1957 The Effects of Clear and Unclear Role Expectations on Group Productivity and Defensiveness. *Journal of Abnormal and Social Psychology* 55:213–217.

STOCK, DOROTHY; and THELEN, H. A. 1958 *Emotional Dynamics and Group Culture: Experimental Studies of Individual and Group Behavior.* New York Univ. Press.

STRODTBECK, FRED L.; and MANN, RICHARD D. 1956 Sex Role Differentiation in Jury Deliberations. *Sociometry* 19:3–11.

TALLAND, GEORGE A. 1957 Role and Status Structure in Therapy Groups. *Journal of Clinical Psychology* 13:27–33.

THRASHER, FREDERIC M. (1927) 1963 *The Gang: A Study of 1,313 Gangs in Chicago.* Abridged and with an introduction by James F. Short. Univ. of Chicago Press.

TORRANCE, E. P. 1954 Some Consequences of Power Differences on Decision-making in Permanent and Temporary Three-man Groups. Washington State University, *Research Studies* 22:130–140.

WHITE, RALPH K.; and LIPPITT, RONALD 1960 *Autocracy and Democracy: An Experimental Inquiry.* New York: Harper.

ZILLER, ROBERT C.; BEHRINGER, RICHARD D.; and GOODCHILDS, JACQUELINE D. 1960 The Minority Newcomer in Open and Closed Groups. *Journal of Psychology* 50:75–84.

ZILLER, ROBERT C.; BEHRINGER, RICHARD D.; and JANSEN, MATHILDA J. 1961 The Newcomer in Open and Closed Groups. *Journal of Applied Psychology* 45:55–58.

## V
## GROUP PERFORMANCE

It was a practical interest in group performance which led to the massive literature dealing with experimental studies of groups. The industrial revolution and the growth of the large factory raised such practical questions as: How can groups of workers become more productive? How might the performance of the individual worker be affected by the presence of others? When is a group more effective than the sum of its individual members? Thus, the typical study of group performance will vary some factor and measure differences in quantity, quality, speed (number of units produced per unit time), or efficiency (number of units produced per man per unit time). Some studies might concentrate on homogeneity or similarity of behavior and production of individuals in the group as compared to that of individuals working alone. The original industrial interest spread to other areas, such as military situations, research laboratories, and classrooms, where the problems were often quite different. Reviews of studies of group performance may be found in Hare (1962), Kelley and Thibaut (1954), and Lorge and his associates (1958).

Studies of group performance have been grouped into four major problem areas: (*a*) *group productivity*—e.g., studies of how many relays can be wired by a group in a given period of time, or how many addition problems can be completed; (*b*) *group problem solving*—e.g., studies of the solution of puzzles, construction of a complex design involving thought and planning, creativity in determining unusual uses for everyday implements; (*c*) *group judgment*—e.g., group estimation of the number of parachutes seen in an air photo of military exercises, estimation of number of beans in a jar, judgment of lengths of lines or movement of lights; and (*d*) *group learning and retention*—e.g., group memorizing of a complex story, learning a maze or series of words, military units learning complex strategy as a unit. Although these categories are convenient, it is obvious that a given task will often involve several of the above problems in combination: the group must form some judgments in learning and retention, learning and retention are involved in problem solving, group productivity may be improved through creative problem solving in the reorganization of group operations, etc.

**Individual versus group performance.** Early observations suggested that workers on production lines would tend to increase their level of activity when working together. Floyd H. Allport (1920) considered such "social facilitation" in terms of classical conditioning. The sounds of tapping from the shoemaker's hammer become conditioned stimuli for the muscular movements which move his hammer. When he works in the presence of others, the tapping sounds from his co-workers serve as additional conditioned stimuli and thus increase further the rate at which the shoemaker pounds his shoes. Allport found, in fact, that subjects given word-association tasks, vowel-cancellation tests, or multiplication tests performed more rapidly when working in the presence of others. This was true even when rivalry was diminished by using instructions and by not permitting knowledge of the scores of others. [*See the biography of* ALLPORT.]

Early studies of problem solving also indicated the superiority of groups over individuals. It was suggested that this resulted from erroneous solutions being rejected in group discussions (Shaw 1932). It would follow that the superiority of the group over individual problem solving would be greater in tasks which permitted a greater variety of responses, with elimination of incorrect solutions being more crucial. Such was, indeed, demonstrated by Thorndike (1938). [*See the biography of* THORNDIKE.]

In one of the few clear-cut experiments on group versus individual learning, subjects were asked to learn lists of nonsense syllables. Some learned cooperatively, in groups of three, and then alone; for others the order was reversed. It appeared that, generally, subjects learned more rapidly in groups and after the group experience could learn better on their own. Some superior subjects, however, did not benefit from the group learning experience (Perlmutter & de Montmollin 1952).

There is evidence that groups can inhibit the behavior of individuals. In an early study most children asked to turn a crank to move a flag to a finish line tended to show "social facilitation" when operating together. However, some operated less effectively when coacting with others. This decrement was attributed to overstimulation (Triplett 1898).

While the studies of individual versus group performance indicated some superiority of group performance, they also suggested limitations on any such conclusions. The problem can be reconsidered in terms of the factors which lead to variations in group performance.

**Size of group.** In an early study by Moede (1927), a man was given a rope to pull as hard as he could, then a second man was added and given the same instructions, then others, until eight men were pulling, with the strength of pull measured. The first man pulled, on the average, 63 kilograms; the two together pulled 118; three, 160; and eight, 248 kilograms. Clearly the total amount of pull increased with each man, but the work per man was reduced with additional members—each new member reduced the work per man by approximately 10 per cent. This early study of group productivity is a prototype of later research on size of group in group performance. The results of later studies seem to be the same. A study of problem solving in the game "Twenty Questions" found four-person groups asking fewer questions than dyads, but the four-person groups were less efficient (Taylor & Faust 1952). Thomas and Fink, summarizing the literature, say that generally "both quality of performance and group productivity were positively correlated with group size under some conditions, and under no conditions were smaller groups superior. In contrast, measures of speed showed no difference or else favored the smaller groups" (1963, p. 373).

**Cohesiveness and morale.** In 1927 the Hawthorne plant of the Western Electric Company initiated a series of experiments to raise productivity and morale. A group of female workers engaged in wiring relays was placed in a separate room and, in the tradition of efficiency experts Frederick W. Taylor and Frank B. Gilbreth, changes in working conditions were introduced which were calculated to improve efficiency—changes to piecework production, increased rest periods, hot meals, earlier quitting times, etc.—and with each change productivity increased. However, when all these improvements were removed, productivity rose still higher. It was pointed out that, clearly, the physical factors were not as crucial for increasing productivity as cohesiveness and morale [*see* COHESION, SOCIAL; INDUSTRIAL RELATIONS; *see also* Roethlisberger & Dickson 1939, p. 86].

Later studies in various types of work groups, including railroad maintenance workers, office staffs, and machinery workers, also indicated that productivity increased with attraction to the work group (Michigan, University of . . . 1954, p. 7). Other research indicated similar relationships in military crews (Berkowitz 1956). In a careful experiment, Van Zelst, working in conjunction with the supervisor and foreman of a large construction project, made up some work groups of carpenters and bricklayers according to their personal choices of co-workers and some of members who were not mutually attracted to one another. The former groups showed greater job satisfaction, lower labor and material cost, and lower turnover rates (1952).

There are, however, limitations to any generalization that cohesiveness increases productivity. Mutual friendliness, when it shows itself in high sociability and horseplay, can decrease productivity (Horsfall & Arensberg 1949). Thus, group goals and group norms must also be considered.

**Interdependence, cooperation, and competition.** Patterns of interdependence can have a great effect on group performance. The individual worker on the production line may be under great pressure to work rapidly either through the "pull" of the man next in line, who is waiting for the next piece, or through the "push" of the preceding worker, whose rapid rate of work leaves work piling up on his successor. In the British coal mines, a change to a "longwall method" of mining led to each shift of workers becoming less aware of other shifts and less aware of the extent to which each was dependent upon the other. Accidents increased because a preceding shift departed without allowing proper safeguards for those that followed. For similar reasons, productivity decreased. A major remedy involved increasing both formal and informal communications between shifts and, through other means, making shifts and workers aware of their interdependence (Trist & Bamforth 1951). Thomas (1957) indicates the importance of considering both interdependence with respect to means and with respect to goals. He found greatest productivity in a group with division of labor where both types of interdependence obtained, though there were signs of greater emotional tension as well.

Early studies indicated that rivalry, or competition, tended to increase rate of performance, though sometimes at the expense of quality (Triplett 1898). However, later studies found more rapid performance among persons who are cooperating.

Part of the answer lies in the extent to which there is also interdependence with respect to means. When each person works on a parallel task, as in the Triplett experiment in which each subject turned his own crank, with speed being the basis of success, then competition will likely be more effective in increasing performance. When each person depends on others for his own movement— for example, three persons raising or lowering corners of a triangular board so as to center carpenter's levels (Raven & Eachus 1963)—then com-

petition will be detrimental. With competition and interdependence of means, each person is concerned about his activity helping others. There is less division of labor, and a person may not wish to give information to a co-worker who might thus be helped to defeat him (Deutsch 1949).

**Division of labor and information.** While division of labor may be beneficial to a cooperative work group, mutual interdependence also imposes additional pressures on the individual, resulting in greater pressures to produce but also greater tension and greater loss of individuality and craftsmanship. This has been observed in industrial settings. It has been demonstrated that such resulting tensions can be alleviated somewhat, with greater group cohesiveness, greater acceptance of influence from co-workers, and less hostility, through clarifying for the individual the nature of the final product and the ways in which the individual worker's task fits in with that of his co-workers (Raven & Reitsema 1957).

The question arises as to how information should be distributed for maximal group retention. If, for example, a complex military tactic must be learned by a squad, giving all the information to each member would increase learning time and lead to an increased rate of forgetting. On the other hand, giving each person a nonoverlapping portion, while reducing redundancy, increases the possibility of a piece of information being permanently lost if only one member forgets it. Zajonc and Smoke (1959) suggest a mathematical model for dealing with this problem, but extensive empirical testing is still lacking.

**Group norms and decisions.** In the Hawthorne study, while it was found that group morale contributed to higher productivity, it was also observed that norms developed which prevented production from either exceeding a given level (such a worker would be considered a "rate-buster") or falling below (being a "slacker"). Similarly, the study by Seashore found that increased cohesiveness did not lead to greater productivity but rather to greater homogeneity of performance in a work group (Michigan, University of . . . 1954). It has been demonstrated in experimental situations that a highly cohesive group will not only be better able to influence a member to increase his production but also to decrease it (Schachter et al. 1951).

Lewin suggested that changing the level of productivity of a work group involves a process of "unfreezing" an old norm, then change, and "refreezing" at a new normative level (1951, p. 228). A reduction in productivity, due to a change in methods of production, may lead to establishment of a lower group norm, which will remain long after necessary relearning has taken place. Members who exceed the norm may be subject to strong group pressure to work more slowly. This suggestion led to studies which indicated that involving the work group in the re-evaluation of the job, with establishment through group discussion of an appropriate group standard of production, will ultimately lead to a higher level of production with less tension and higher morale among the workers (Coch & French 1948).

With respect to group judgments, group norms might also have a deleterious effect. Though a group would be more likely to have the combined skills necessary to make a proper judgment, it may sometimes happen that a majority is wrong. In that case, there will be strong pressures for an individual who might otherwise judge correctly to refrain from uttering the correct answer and, instead, to go along with the group. A properly trained leader can sometimes assist a group in group judgment or problem solving through encouraging the expression of minority opinion and bringing out the useful ideas and contributions of members who are otherwise restrained by conformity pressures (Maier & Solem 1952).

**Communication networks.** An application of principles of topology to group behavior by Alex Bavelas (1950) led to a series of studies of the effects of restriction of communication channels on productivity and morale. In an early study, five-man groups were given a problem of finding which symbols were held in common by all members. The communication possibilities were varied. The most effective group was that in which four members could communicate only with the one "central person," a pattern called a "wheel." A "circle" was least effective, with a "chain" and a "Y" being intermediate. The more involved the person was in the network, the happier he was with the group task. The "circle," while least effective, had the greatest overall morale (Leavitt 1951). The initial findings indicate that restriction of communication leads to greater efficiency. It is suggested that this may be true for the simple problems in which information must be collated to find a correct answer. The restricted pattern of the "wheel" saves the group from spending time on organization for effective problem solving. However, it also lessens flexibility, making for less efficiency when the tasks are changed or become more complex (Guetzkow & Dill 1957). When the problem is complex and involves a number of alternative paths to solution, the less restricted network is more efficient (Shaw 1954). Personality factors undoubtedly play a role.

Workers high in acceptance of authority will be relatively more efficient in a centralized group structure; those low in acceptance of authority will be more effective in a decentralized structure (Shaw 1959). It might also follow that an increase in intelligence and skills would lead to increased efficiency for the decentralized structure relative to the centralized network.

**Leadership and supervision.** Clearly, leadership and supervision play a very important part in group performance, since the leader can often affect and control many of the other critical variables discussed above. The style of leadership has been given particular attention in the literature. In a pioneer experiment with groups of boys, it was found that the greatest productivity and morale occurred with a "democratic" leader, who encouraged participation in decisions, gave a clear picture of the group activities and the reasons for his requests, took an active but not overactive role in the group's activities, etc. A "laissez-faire" leader, who allowed complete freedom and assumed no active role, achieved the least productivity. An "authoritarian" leader, who was very active in issuing commands without giving reasons, was effective in raising productivity only insofar as the group was under his immediate surveillance. Morale was lowest in the last case (White & Lippitt 1960). Other studies in industrial settings confirm that productivity and morale are higher with a participatory leader or supervisor who assumes an active role in the group, gives support to his workers, delegates authority, and maintains an optimal degree of supervision (Kahn & Katz 1953). There is evidence that similar group-oriented roles on the part of the teacher may also lead to improved learning.

Characteristics of the leader have also received some attention in relationship to productivity. For example, Fiedler (1958), in investigations in a large variety of settings, has found that productivity is highest in teams where the leader maintains an optimal distance from his team and where he perceives clear differentiation between his best and worst co-workers [*see* LEADERSHIP].

**Training and group process.** Given a knowledge of factors which contribute toward improved group performance, it should follow that training and education in the application of these principles would be a logical next step. Indeed, there have been many attempts to introduce training for improved group performance—either through training the groups themselves or the leaders and supervisors. It has been demonstrated that a discussion leader who is trained to encourage expression of minority opinions will effect superior problem solving and decision making (Maier 1953; Maier & Solem 1952). It is generally assumed that educators can be taught to improve learning in the classroom.

On the assumption that group ideation can be more productive than individual ideation and that a group may sometimes inhibit the expression of unusual ideas which might be modified so as to be fruitful, Alexander F. Osborn introduced training in what he called "brainstorming." In this problem-solving situation, members are given a problem, such as how to increase the attractiveness of teaching as a profession, and then are asked to give whatever ideas come to mind, no matter how outlandish. Thus, group norms are established to encourage rather than discourage strange suggestions. These are then gradually selected and evaluated, and a unique practical solution may be developed from an initially bizarre suggestion. Though the basis appears sound, one of the few careful evaluative experiments suggests that "brainstorming" inhibits rather than facilitates creative thinking (Taylor et al. 1958). [See CREATIVITY; PROBLEM SOLVING.]

The National Training Laboratories were established at Bethel, Maine, for the purpose of providing summer workshops in interpersonal relations. Educators, military leaders, supervisors in industry, and others participate in programs involving some theory sessions, but largely free interaction in groups, in order to become aware of how they affect others and others affect them. The original program spread widely and may now take place in sessions lasting from a few hours to months. "Sensitivity training" is said to have produced dramatic changes in the effectiveness of organizations. Unfortunately, the problems of evaluating the effectiveness of "sensitivity training" are immense, but the clearest evidence to date of its effectiveness consists of testimonials from members of organizations which have participated and the fact that many such organizations have continued to train their supervisors and employees in this way (Tannenbaum et al. 1961, pp. 233–238).

Another recent approach to training is that developed in the System Development Corporation. In "system training," the working unit (in this case, most work has been done with air defense crews) is considered as a "man–machine system" involving more than the time–motion aspects emphasized in an earlier period and the interpersonal relationships of a later stage. In practice, an air defense crew at its home site is presented with a series of problems which are simulated on the crew's own radar scopes, with detailed flight plans, etc. After the problem, a careful record is available of all relevant

interactions, and the crew holds a debriefing session in which members analyze their faults and attempt to make necessary corrections. One goal is to develop greater flexibility in the crew, allowing for rapid changes in task assignment so as to provide for effective adjustment to all sorts of problem situations. Data indicate that there is, indeed, improvement in ability to deal with the simulated problems. It is assumed that such improvement also applies to future problems which the crew might encounter in real life as well (Gagné 1962).

BERTRAM H. RAVEN

[See also FIELD THEORY.]

BIBLIOGRAPHY

ALLPORT, FLOYD H. 1920 The Influence of the Group Upon Association and Thought. Journal of Experimental Psychology 3:159–182.
BAVELAS, ALEX 1950 Communication Patterns in Task-oriented Groups. Journal of the Acoustical Society of America 22:725–730.
BERKOWITZ, LEONARD 1956 Group Norms Among Bomber Crews: Patterns of Perceived Crew Attitudes, "Actual" Crew Attitudes and Crew Liking Related to Aircrew Effectiveness in Far Eastern Combat. Sociometry 19:141–153.
COCH, LESTER; and FRENCH, JOHN R. P. JR. 1948 Overcoming Resistance to Change. Human Relations 1:512–532.
DEUTSCH, MORTON 1949 An Experimental Study of the Effects of Co-operation and Competition Upon Group Process. Human Relations 2:199–231.
FIEDLER, FRED E. 1958 Leader Attitudes and Group Effectiveness. Urbana: Univ. of Illinois Press.
GAGNÉ, ROBERT M. (editor) 1962 Psychological Principles in System Development. New York: Holt.
GUETZKOW, HAROLD; and DILL, WILLIAM R. 1957 Factors in the Organizational Development of Task-oriented Groups. Sociometry 20:175–204.
HARE, ALEXANDER P. 1962 Handbook of Small Group Research. New York: Free Press.
HORSFALL, ALEXANDER B.; and ARENSBERG, C. M. 1949 Teamwork and Productivity in a Shoe Factory. Human Organization 8, no. 1:13–25.
KAHN, ROBERT L.; and KATZ, DANIEL 1953 Leadership Practices in Relation to Productivity and Morale. Pages 612–628 in Dorwin Cartwright and Alvin F. Zander (editors), Group Dynamics: Research and Theory. Evanston, Ill.: Row, Peterson.
KELLEY, HAROLD H.; and THIBAUT, JOHN W. 1954 Experimental Studies of Group Problem Solving and Process. Volume 2, pages 735–785 in Gardner Lindzey (editor), Handbook of Social Psychology. Cambridge, Mass.: Addison-Wesley.
LEAVITT, HAROLD J. 1951 Some Effects of Certain Communication Patterns on Group Performance. Journal of Abnormal and Social Psychology 46:38–50.
LEWIN, KURT 1951 Field Theory in Social Science: Selected Theoretical Papers. Edited by Dorwin Cartwright. New York: Harper. → A collection of papers first published between 1939 and 1947. A British edition was published in 1963 by Tavistock.

GUMPLOWICZ, LUDWIG    293

LORGE, IRVING et al. 1958 A Survey of Studies Contrasting the Quality of Group Performance and Individual Performance: 1920–1957. *Psychological Bulletin* 55:337–372.

MAIER, NORMAN R. F. 1953 An Experimental Test of the Effect of Training on Discussion Leadership. *Human Relations* 6:161–173.

MAIER, NORMAN R. F.; and SOLEM, ALLEN R. 1952 The Contribution of a Discussion Leader to the Quality of Group Thinking: The Effective Use of Minority Opinions. *Human Relations* 5:277–288.

MICHIGAN, UNIVERSITY OF, SURVEY RESEARCH CENTER 1954 *Group Cohesiveness in the Industrial Work Group*, by Stanley Seashore. Ann Arbor: Univ. of Michigan Press.

MOEDE, W. 1927 Die Richtlinien der Leitungspsychologie. *Industrielle Psychotechnik* 4:193–209.

PERLMUTTER, HOWARD V.; and DE MONTMOLLIN, GERMAINE 1952 Group Learning of Nonsense Syllables. *Journal of Abnormal and Social Psychology* 47:762–769.

RAVEN, BERTRAM H.; and EACHUS, H. TODD 1963 Cooperation and Competition in Means-interdependent Triads. *Journal of Abnormal and Social Psychology* 67:307–316.

RAVEN, BERTRAM H.; and REITSEMA, JAN 1957 The Effects of Varied Clarity of Group Goal and Group Path Upon the Individual and His Relation to His Group. *Human Relations* 10:29–45.

ROETHLISBERGER, FRITZ J.; and DICKSON, WILLIAM J. (1939) 1961 *Management and the Worker: An Account of a Research Program Conducted by the Western Electric Company, Hawthorne Works, Chicago.* Cambridge, Mass.: Harvard Univ. Press. → A paperback edition was published in 1964 by Wiley.

SCHACHTER, STANLEY et al. 1951 An Experimental Study of Cohesiveness and Productivity. *Human Relations* 4:229–238.

SHAW, MARJORIE E. 1932 A Comparison of Individuals and Small Groups in the Rational Solution of Complex Problems. *American Journal of Psychology* 44:491–504.

SHAW, MARVIN E. 1954 Some Effects of Problem Complexity Upon Problem Solution Efficiency in Different Communication Nets. *Journal of Experimental Psychology* 48:211–217.

SHAW, MARVIN E. 1959 Acceptance of Authority, Group Structure and the Effectiveness of Small Groups. *Journal of Personality* 27:196–210.

TANNENBAUM, ROBERT; WESCHLER, IRVING R.; and MASSARIK, FRED 1961 *Leadership and Organization: A Behavioral Science Approach.* New York: McGraw-Hill.

TAYLOR, DONALD W.; BERRY, PAUL C.; and BLOCK, CLIFFORD H. 1958 Does Group Participation When Using Brain-storming Facilitate or Inhibit Creative Thinking? *Administrative Science Quarterly* 3:23–47.

TAYLOR, DONALD W.; and FAUST, WILLIAM L. 1952 Twenty Questions: Efficiency in Problem Solving as a Function of Size of Group. *Journal of Experimental Psychology* 44:360–368.

THOMAS, EDWIN J. 1957 Effects of Facilitative Role Interdependence on Group Functioning. *Human Relations* 10:347–366.

THOMAS, EDWIN J.; and FINK, CLINTON F. 1963 Effects of Group Size. *Psychological Bulletin* 60:371–384.

THORNDIKE, R. L. 1938 On What Type of Task Will a Group Do Well? *Journal of Abnormal and Social Psychology* 33:409–413.

TRIPLETT, NORMAN 1898 The Dynamogenic Factors in Pacemaking and Competition. *American Journal of Psychology* 9:507–533.

TRIST, E. L.; and BAMFORTH, K. W. 1951 Some Social and Psychological Consequences of the Longwall Method of Coal-getting. *Human Relations* 4:3–38.

VAN ZELST, RAYMOND H. 1952 Validation of a Sociometric Regrouping Procedure. *Journal of Abnormal and Social Psychology* 47:299–301.

WHITE, RALPH K.; and LIPPITT, RONALD 1960 *Autocracy and Democracy: An Experimental Inquiry.* New York: Harper.

ZAJONC, ROBERT B.; and SMOKE, WILLIAM H. 1959 Redundancy in Task Assignments and Group Performance. *Psychometrika* 24:361–369.



## GUIDANCE
*See* COUNSELING PSYCHOLOGY; EDUCATIONAL PSYCHOLOGY; VOCATIONAL INTEREST TESTING.

## GUILDS
*See* GILDS.

## GUILT
*See* MORAL DEVELOPMENT; PSYCHIATRY, *article on* FORENSIC PSYCHIATRY; PSYCHOANALYSIS; PUNISHMENT.

## GUMPLOWICZ, LUDWIG

Ludwig Gumplowicz (1838–1909), of Polish-Jewish parentage, was professor of public law at the University of Graz, Austria, from 1875 until his death. He is best known for his pioneer work in establishing sociology as a social science. His contributions to political science and jurisprudence were also important, but they consisted mainly of applications of his sociological generalizations to government and law. A clear and vigorous writer, he was much given to controversy in all three fields.

The sociological system of Gumplowicz was based on a number of fundamental dogmas or principles: (1) social phenomena are governed by universal laws that operate in a completely secular manner, unrelated to religious or moral considerations, and they must be studied by using a thoroughly scientific method; (2) sociology rejects all value judgments; and (3) sociology is the science of the interaction of groups.

Applying these principles to the evolution of society and states, Gumplowicz held that the earliest forms of group life were small, natural, ethnic or blood-kin hordes. These groups were unified by consanguinity and common, rudimentary economic interests; their members lived in sexual promiscuity and relative equality of social position. Solidarity developed in a group through a process of "syngenism," which gradually produces unity in any social group. Out of this earliest form of group life arose, in succession, the matriarchate and the patriarchate, the first types of organized control.

Since the appearance of the matriarchate and the patriarchate, social and political evolution has been a never-ending process of external conflict between groups, in the form of wars, and of internal conflict of interests within groups. The motive in all conquests has been the desire for the material gain that may be obtained by exploiting the labor of the conquered. Material interests, therefore, have furnished the dynamic impulse in social evolution. "So conquest and the satisfaction of needs through the labor of the conquered, essentially the same though differing in form, is the great theme of human history from prehistoric times to the latest plan for a Congo state. . . . It cannot be otherwise since man's material need is the prime motive of his conduct" ([1885] 1963, pp. 203–205).

When the process of conquest and subjugation becomes well developed, the principle of amalgamation supplements syngenism in producing unity in the state, which, as the highest form of social grouping, is the culmination of a long process of conquest and of many adjustments subsequent to conquest. Gumplowicz believed that there is no such thing as indefinite social progress; the historic process is the record of the rise and fall of states and follows an inevitable cyclical course of growth and decline.

In the initial stage of conquest, there were only two social classes, the conquerors and the subjugated. Foreign merchants who moved in produced a third class—the middle class or bourgeoisie. With the development of social and political institutions, the activities of the primary classes of rulers, merchants, and exploited masses created a need for secondary or derived classes, such as priests, professional men, and artisans. These social classes were based on a division of labor which was created and maintained by coercion.

The rise of social classes produced a complex and unending struggle among them to control the policy of the state in order to promote their various special interests. These interests were best advanced through participation in legislation, and social classes found that political parties were the most effective agencies for controlling the legislative process. Whatever form the struggle of classes within the state has taken, it has provided the dynamic core of history ([1877] 1907, pp. 33 ff.).

Paralleling political and economic developments there were various processes of assimilation, such as the adoption of the language, religion, and manners and customs of the conquerors, which tended to produce cultural unity. Finally, through intermarriage, an ethnic unity was achieved. The homogeneous society thus created is the "folk-state" or nation, which is the ultimate outcome of social and political evolution. The tendency throughout history has been for such a folk-state or nation to seek to conquer a neighboring nation, and when it is successful the whole process of subjugation, assimilation, and amalgamation is repeated.

Gumplowicz' sociological system is not simply an application of Darwinian biology to the operation of human society. He was indebted to Darwin for the general idea of a struggle for existence, but he was also indebted to others: to Comte for the determination to analyze social phenomena with scientific rigor, and to Spencer for the idea of universal evolution and the application of the laws of universal evolution to society. His conception of the primordial and ceaseless conflict of races and social groups came from the writings of Count Joseph Arthur de Gobineau and from his own lifelong contact with the intense struggles among races and groups in the Austro–Hungarian Empire. He had participated in the Polish revolt of 1863 and had absorbed much of the socialist and anarchist literature of the first half of the nineteenth century: his dogma that the basis of conflict is always the promotion of material self-interest was based chiefly on the stress laid in this literature on the exploitation and expropriation of the masses by the property owners, and to a lesser extent on Marxist writings.

The outstanding contribution of Gumplowicz to sociology was his naturalistic and secular approach to society and social evolution and his conception of social evolution as a process of conflict. The concept of "social process" appeared in the writings of such European sociologists as Franz Oppenheimer and Gustav Ratzenhofer; in America, the works of Gumplowicz and Ratzenhofer were read and digested by Albion Small, founder of the so-called Chicago school of sociology. Small and his disciples, such as Park and Burgess, and other American sociologists, notably Ross and Cooley, carried further the development of the concept of the "social process."

Gumplowicz' contributions to realistic political science were notable. He assembled and developed in a well-integrated and systematic fashion the previously scattered suggestions relative to the social conditioning of political phenomena: that society is a group held together by material interests; that the state is a society organized and controlled by coercion; and that political legislation is a product and reflection of the social process at any given time ([1877] 1907, pp. 33 ff.; [1892] 1902, pp. 49–66). Gumplowicz' well-documented argument that the state has always been founded through wars and conflict cleared away pietistic, idealistic, and metaphysical misconceptions. His argument has won general acceptance, although some sociologists, notably Jacques Novicow, have charged that he neglected the role of pacific and cooperative factors in the origins of states. Gumplowicz' conception of political parties as interest groups has become, perhaps, the most useful truism of dynamic political science and has been adopted and developed by Durkheim, Duguit, Laski, and A. F. Bentley, among others.

Gumplowicz' fundamental assumptions led him to reject the possibility that man can plan his social future and promote his happiness by such social inventions as the welfare state. He even suggested that the practical value of sociology may be to save mankind from wasting time and energy on futile schemes of utopian reform. There is some evidence, however, that Lester Ward was able to convince Gumplowicz to a certain extent that the social sciences may enable man to plan a better future (1905).

Gumplowicz spent most of his professional life as a professor of law. His legal theories were a direct outgrowth of his sociological doctrines, and he is generally regarded as one of the founders of the sociological school of jurisprudence. He saw laws as invariably growing out of the conflict of classes and interests within the state, as social products rather than divine revelations, or as wise and rational human creations, or as derived in some mysterious manner from nature. He believed that there are no natural laws, except in the sense that laws are a result of the nature of man and of the social processes. This precludes the validity of classifying laws as good or bad: laws are not passed to promote justice in any abstract sense but rather to enable the dominant social class or classes to carry out their exploitation ([1892] 1902, pp. 55 ff.). Justice does not determine political and legal rights; rather, these rights are the product of the conflict of interests among social classes:

The premise of "inalienable human rights" rests upon the most unreasonable self-deification of man and overestimation of the value of human life, and upon complete misconception of the only possible basis of

the existence of the State. . . . Rights are not founded upon justice. On the contrary, justice is created only by the actual rights as they exist in the state. . . . It is the simple abstraction of political rights, and it stands or falls with them.   ([1885], pp. 180–181, 263 in 1899 edition)

HARRY ELMER BARNES

[*For the historical context of Gumplowicz' work, see* LEGAL SYSTEMS; *and the biographies of* COMTE; DARWIN; GOBINEAU; SPENCER. *For discussion of the subsequent development of his ideas, see* CONFLICT; CONSTITUTIONAL LAW, *article on* CIVIL RIGHTS; LAW, *article on* THE LEGAL SYSTEM; *and the biographies of* BENTLEY; DUGUIT; DURKHEIM; LASKI; OPPENHEIMER; RATZENHOFER; SMALL.]

### WORKS BY GUMPLOWICZ

(1877) 1907  *Allgemeines Staatsrecht.* 3d ed. Innsbruck (Austria): Wagner. → First published as *Philosophisches Staatsrecht.*

1881  *Rechtsstaat und Socialismus.* Innsbruck (Austria): Wagner.

1882  *Verwaltungslehre mit besonderer Berücksichtigung des österreichischen Verwaltungsrechts.* Innsbruck (Austria): Wagner.

(1883–1905) 1926–1928  *Ausgewählte Werke.* Edited by F. Oppenheimer, F. Savorgnan, M. Adler, G. Salomon. 4 vols. Innsbruck (Austria): Wagner. → Volume 1: *Geschichte der Staatstheorien,* (1905) 1926. Volume 2: *Grundriss der Soziologie,* (1885) 1926. Volume 3: *Der Rassenkampf,* (1883) 1928. Volume 4: *Soziologische Essays* (1899), *Soziologie und Politik,* (1892) 1928.

(1885) 1963  *The Outlines of Sociology.* Edited with an introduction and notes by Irving L. Horowitz. 2d ed. New York: Paine-Whitman. → First published in German.

1887  *System socyologii.* Warsaw: Orgelbrand.

(1892) 1902  *Die soziologische Staatsidee.* 2d ed. Innsbruck (Austria): Wagner.

1905  An Austrian Appreciation of Lester F. Ward. *American Journal of Sociology* 10:643–653.

1910  *Sozialphilosophie im Umriss.* Innsbruck (Austria): Wagner.

### SUPPLEMENTARY BIBLIOGRAPHY

BARNES, HARRY E. 1919  The Struggle of Races and Social Groups as a Factor in the Development of Political and Social Institutions: An Exposition and Critique of the Sociological System of Ludwig Gumplowicz. *Journal of Race Development* 9:394–419.

BEROLZHEIMER, FRITZ (1905) 1912  *The World's Legal Philosophies.* Boston: Boston Book. → First published as *Die Kulturstufen der Rechts- und Wirtschaftsphilosophie.*

KOCHANOWSKI, I. 1909  Ludwig Gumplowicz. *American Journal of Sociology* 15:405–409.

POSNER, STANISLAW 1911  *Ludwik Gumplowicz 1838–1909: Zarys życia i pracy.* Warsaw: Orgelbrand.

WARD, LESTER F. 1909  Ludwig Gumplowicz. *American Journal of Sociology* 15:410–413.

ZEBROWSKI, BERNHARD 1926  *Ludwig Gumplowicz: Eine Bio-Bibliographie.* Berlin: Prager.

## GUTHRIE, EDWIN R.

American psychologist, educator, and philosopher, Edwin Ray Guthrie (1886–1959) was the oldest of five children. He was born in Lincoln, Nebraska, where he spent his boyhood. His mother, Harriet Pickett Guthrie, the daughter of a newspaperman, was an elementary-school teacher before marriage; his father was the son of a minister and the manager of a piano store.

Guthrie had exhibited vivid intellectual interests even as a child. At the University of Nebraska, which he entered in 1903, he majored in mathematics and minored in philosophy. After receiving his A.B. in 1907 he remained at Nebraska for graduate work, majoring in philosophy and minoring in mathematics and psychology. In 1910 he received his A.M. from Nebraska and was made a Harrison Fellow at the University of Pennsylvania, where he received his PH.D. in 1912 with a thesis resolving various paradoxes of Bertrand Russell (1915a).

**Professional life.** For five years Guthrie taught high-school mathematics, from 1907 to 1910 in Lincoln and from 1912 to 1914 in Philadelphia. He then joined the faculty of the University of Washington, where he remained, except for temporary leaves, for the rest of his life.

At Washington, Guthrie started as instructor in the department of philosophy, then chaired by William Savery. Savery (a student of William James at Harvard) and Guthrie (a student of Edgar A. Singer at Pennsylvania) became lifetime friends. In 1918 Guthrie became assistant professor and in 1919 joined the department of psychology, chaired by Stevenson Smith, who also became Guthrie's close friend. Guthrie was made associate professor in 1925 and professor in 1928.

Guthrie married Helen Macdonald in 1920. With her, he translated Pierre Janet's *Principles of Psychotherapy* (1924) and traveled extensively—especially in France, where Guthrie met Janet, and in England, Italy, and Hungary.

Guthrie was the second winner of the gold medal awarded by the American Psychological Foundation for "outstanding lifetime contributions to psychology." Awarded an honorary LL.D. from the University of Nebraska in 1945, he was elected president of the American Psychological Association in the same year. During World War II, he was chief consultant to the overseas branch of the general staff of the U.S. War Department in 1941 and chief psychologist of the overseas branch of the Office of War Information in 1942. He was dean of the graduate school of the University of Washington from 1943 to 1951 and was honored by a building on the campus being named after him while he was still alive.

### Contributions to science

Guthrie's close association with philosophers and his formal training in philosophy at an advanced level had considerable impact on the problems to which he addressed himself and on his resolutions of some of these.

**Philosophical clarifications.** *The nature of explanation.* Guthrie deemed the question "why" as unprofitable and almost nonsensical—unless by "why" one means "how come," "under what circumstances," or "what next." "Why" in the sense of "for what purpose" carries implicit teleological assumptions perhaps unwarranted and not the most fruitful for understanding.

The most illuminating explanations, Guthrie pointed out, are those which summarize sequences of observable events: Given this set of observable circumstances, what observable subsequent events may be most reasonably expected? Such explanations answer the question "what next" or "how come." An explanation states the general class of which some particular sequence is an instance, nothing more.

*Causation and the nature of theory.* Seeking "causes," as ordinarily conceived, distracts and confuses us. The usual notion of "cause" implies that there is a force within some set of circumstances which somehow pushes events in a certain direction. Building on the work of David Hume, Guthrie abandoned the usual notion of "cause" and thought instead in terms of sequences of events. Certain events precede other events in time. The earlier events need not be assumed to force the later ones; they simply precede them.

Certain events do precede others with great regularity. Our problem as theorists then becomes one of devising general terms to label these classes of events and to describe these more regular sequences. Theory construction, so conceived, is an inductive process and consists in devising general statements (principles) to summarize as many sequences as possible.

*Hedonism.* One of the very ancient Greek philosophies (refined by Aristotle and Plato) held that man by his nature is a pleasure-seeking organism. A variation of this turns up in the popular idea that learning occurs only when some satisfaction or need reduction is involved for the learner [*see* LEARNING, *article on* REINFORCEMENT]. This is a very comforting view. It is heartening to believe that, whenever we learn, at least some of our needs are thereby being met. The view poses difficulties, however, in accounting for the many instances in which learning is followed by distress, and no apparent satisfaction or need reduction. To handle this difficulty, psychologists posited an ever-lengthening list of motives (conscious and unconscious) or drives (primary, secondary, tertiary) or needs, in an attempt to account for seemingly dysfunctional learning.

Guthrie handled the difficulty by abandoning the idea that we learn only what is followed by some need reduction. His approach has economy in the numerosity of presumed "needs" or "drives." It also facilitates understanding of mistakes, learned awkwardnesses, and habitual stupidities—without having to presume a "death instinct," "will to failure," or anything similar—and alerts us to circumstances in which learning may lead to damage or disaster.

*The unity of learning.* There is, Guthrie suggested, one kind of learning only; the same principles which hold for learning in one instance hold also for learning in all other instances. The apparent diversity of learning does not stem from there being different kinds of learning following different principles but arises instead from differences of other sorts: different kinds of situations, different kinds of responses possible to organisms with different musculatures, and different kinds of stimuli that can become cues for differing species with their differing sense organs and differing neural structures. We need not formulate separate principles for each of the differing situations, differing response types, or differing stimulus sensitivities. The same set of principles may hold for all and be illustrated by all.

**New concepts.** *Multiple "causation."* At the time when Guthrie wrote, a prevalent way of thinking about the responding organism was in terms of "a" stimulus or "the" *CS* (conditioned stimulus) for various responses. In contrast, gestalt psychologists (Köhler, Koffka, et al.) were stressing the importance of the totality of the situation. Their emphasis was on the totality as a unit—responses purportedly being evoked by the total situation as a unified, in some ways indivisible, whole.

Guthrie's idea, inspired by both theories, was also different from both. He emphasized multiple stimulation as a more adequate basis for comprehending behavior than either the single stimulus or than the whole situation as merely a unitary totality. He suggested we view any response as a consequence of the interplay and, in a way, the summation of all stimuli impinging on the organism at that moment. He held that the nature of the response made by the responding organism is not a function merely (or even primarily) of the feature most salient to the observer or experimenter—for example, not a function of "the" conditioned stimulus merely. Neither is the response a function of an unanalyzable total situation. Rather, the total situation can be analyzed into component stimulus patterns and their relationships, the organism's response being predictable from these various components simultaneously considered.

*Role of internal stimuli.* Throughout the first half of the twentieth century, psychologists primarily emphasized external stimuli, except for those internal stimuli considered under the heading of "drives." In accord with his view that all stimuli acting on the organism should be considered in predicting behavior, Guthrie called attention to the many internal stimuli besides those thought of as drives. He emphasized that proprioceptive stimuli, kinesthetic stimuli, stimuli from visceral responses, stimuli from endocrine states, fatigue states, and chemicothermal conditions, and other internal stimuli all are present too and should be considered for the best understanding of behavior.

He saw no particular advantage in subdividing internal stimuli into two classes: drive-connected stimuli versus others. It appeared to Guthrie that the various internal stimuli and the various external stimuli all act in substantially the same way and are of equal importance when of equal duration and equal intensity. Our difficulty in understanding behavior stems largely from our failure to note enough of the dimensions of the stimulus situation acting upon the organism rather than from a lack of knowledge about an individual's "motives" or "drives."

*Movement-produced stimuli.* Every time we make any response whatsoever, a wealth of new stimuli is brought into existence: new visual stimuli, new tactual stimuli, new proprioceptive stimuli, sometimes new auditory and olfactory stimuli, and others. This class of stimuli Guthrie called "movement-produced stimuli," emphasizing that our own responses always change the stimulus world we are in.

*Conditioning.* The work of Bekhterev and Pavlov was immensely stimulating to Guthrie, as it was to other American psychologists [*see* LEARNING, *article on* CLASSICAL CONDITIONING]. One result of their influence was Guthrie's suggestion concerning the relationship between conditioning and learning. Instead of thinking of the phenomena found in conditioning experiments as arising primarily from a pairing of the so-called *CS* and *US* (unconditioned stimulus), Guthrie considered them as arising from the pairing of the *CS* and some *response* (the unconditioned response [*UR*] or others)—or more precisely, from the concomitance of various stimuli and some ongoing response. Conditioning so conceived becomes a paradigm of one subclass of the more general class of "learning," and all learning, including that called conditioning, becomes the result of a pairing of new stimuli with ongoing *responses*. In what appears to be Pavlov's only paper published in a United States journal (1932), he restated his original position that it is the pairing of stimuli rather than of stimuli and responses that is critical. Guthrie (1934a) rejected Pavlov's view and the problem remains moot today.

## A theory of learning

Guthrie thus created a highly original, parsimonious theory of learned behavior, presenting much of it in *The Psychology of Learning* (1935). Formulations of the basic principles and concepts are given in a paper by Voeks (1950).

Learning, as Guthrie conceived of it, is the process of establishing new stimuli as cues for some specified response. This process occurs in a single trial and is disrupted only through unlearning.

**Recency versus postremity.** Ebbinghaus, Watson, and others, on the basis of experimental work, stressed that the length of time elapsed since learning is a key dimension in the preservation of learning [see FORGETTING]. Recency was adopted as a crucial factor in the preservation of learning. Sigmund Freud, through his clinical work, came to the conclusion that learning which has occurred early in childhood often is preserved strikingly even when there has been little or no opportunity for further strengthening of that learning. People observing daily life noted that sometimes things recently learned are best preserved, whereas at other times things learned in the distant past seem most intact and reappear after long lapses of time. A hodgepodge of chaotic data accumulated.

Guthrie proposed a new conceptualization and a new principle which reconciles these divergent findings. He suggested that what most other psychologists call a "response" or "behavior" is actually a series of discrete, more-or-less integrated responses. For example, the response labeled "picking up a pencil" involves a large number of separate muscular activities. Similarly, even so simple a "stimulus" as a pencil combines many visual, tactile, and other stimuli. Each component of such a compound stimulus object can be, according to Guthrie, a cue for a separate response and may tend to elicit such a response. The response remaining cued to each component will always be the

response most recently made in the presence of that particular component.

When a series of responses is made to a changing series of situations which—while changing—have some components in common, responses are successively attached and detached from the reappearing stimulus components. Again, the response remaining cued to each stimulus component is the response last made to that particular part. Even when the stimulus component and the response occur early in the stimulus series and at a remote time, nonetheless the response remains cued to that component whenever the component has not turned up subsequently.

The role of recency in this theory differs a great deal from the role it plays in the traditional recency principle. According to the latter, as has been mentioned, a given stimulus–response connection tends to grow weaker with elapsed time. But Guthrie held that the cue properties of stimuli cannot be weakened by time alone. So long as the response is the last-made response to the particular stimulus component, the cue properties remain at full strength; as soon as some other response is made contiguously with the perceived stimulus, the original cue property will cease to exist and a new cue property will be at full strength. This sequential regularity has been formulated in the principle of postremity: the last response an organism makes to each component in a particular situation is the response remaining cued to that component—regardless of how long the time since that stimulus occurred.

Thus, Guthrie would argue, the old principle of recency on occasion tends to operate because the more recent the stimuli and the given bit of behavior, the less time there has been for those stimuli to reappear while any other behavior is occurring; and hence the less likelihood there is that some other response can have become cued to those stimuli. However, certain very early stimulus–response connections will tend to be perpetuated (as Freud reported) because the particular stimulus conditions are highly unusual, thus reducing the possibility of their being present while some other new response is being made; hence it becomes likely no new response will be cued to those sets of stimuli.

**Removal of stimuli established as cues.** The view derived from philosophical hedonism, that we learn only those forms of behavior which are in some way rewarding, was common when Guthrie was writing. Both psychologists and laymen believed that unless a response is reinforced by drive reduction or tension reduction or in some other way satisfies some need, no learning will occur.

Guthrie, however, did not hold that view. He noted that under some circumstances men and animals learn forms of behavior that make matters worse for them, satisfy no need whatsoever, accord with no "motive," and attain no goal. Furthermore, under some circumstances these unwanted habits are preserved.

The necessary and sufficient condition for learning, Guthrie suggested, is the occurrence of a response in the presence of a stimulus not already a cue for that response. Similarly, the necessary and sufficient condition for the preservation of learning is to have the current cues for some response absent whenever incompatible responses occur. By this theory, a "reward" will preserve learning either when it is itself a cue for the new response or when it closely follows the response and removes the stimulus established as a cue for that response. But *any* state of affairs, including "punishment," will likewise preserve learning equally well, so long as the cue is removed from the organism (or the organism is removed from the cue) immediately after the response is made—i.e., before another response can be made in the presence of the same stimulus, thus canceling the original association. Punishment will disrupt learning when it induces the organism to make a response incompatible with the previously learned response while the original stimulus is yet present. Rewards also will disrupt learning under those circumstances. Degree of "removal from a situation" (or partial removal of the situation from the animal) may enable us to predict learning and its preservation or disruption more fully than do "reward" and "punishment."

**One-trial learning.**    For two thousand years, following Aristotle and his basic assumptions, philosophers, laymen, and behavioral scientists alike have put great faith in frequency of association as a mode of strengthening associations. In our century, Pavlov, Thorndike, and Hull all stressed the desirability or even necessity of repetitive trials to inculcate learning. In contradistinction, Guthrie was much impressed by the experimental work of Köhler and others on "insight" behavior.

Guthrie suggested that frequency of trials as ordinarily conceived may well be a misleading way of thinking about learning and an often futile way of addressing oneself to the practical problems of learning. He offered his revolutionary principle of one-trial learning: Whatever stimuli happen to be acting on the behaving organism become full-strength cues for whatever responses the organism is making at that time. A single occasion on which the specified response occurs concomitantly with various stimuli will establish all those stimuli as full-strength cues for the specified response. Additional trials are useful only for establishing additional stimuli as cues for the specified response.

According to this principle, repetition is often futile and under some circumstances actually worse than no trials at all. Repetition is futile to the degree that the stimuli are the same from one trial to another, that the desired response is not being made in each trial, or that the stimuli one wishes to establish as cues for the response are not those actually present.

Repetition is worse than futile whenever the responses actually being made by the organism are incompatible with the desired response; for under those circumstances more and more stimuli become cues for responses incompatible with the desired responses. This has the dual effect of increasing the number of stimuli which are cues for some undesired response (thus increasing the probability of the undesired response being the one to appear on subsequent occasions) and of decreasing the pool of stimuli which could elicit the desired response.

Frequency has value only to the degree that new stimuli are present from trial to trial and then only when the desired response actually is being made on the various trials. Under these circumstances, additional stimuli become cues for the response each time it occurs. Thus, repeatedly practicing a difficult passage on the piano will be profitable only when correct notes actually are being played in a variety of circumstances, the correct notes thus becoming cued to additional combinations of auditory, muscular, and other stimuli accompanying them or immediately preceding them. What happens otherwise is either nothing or the learning of errors.

**Probability of response.**    The likelihood of any specified response occurring at some particular time is directly proportional to the extent to which the stimulating situation is composed of cues for that response. The greater the number of cues present at some particular time for the response desired, the greater the probability that that response will occur (if the total number of stimuli is the same for the various situations being compared). This principle in the hands of William Estes became the basis of what currently is called "modern statistical learning theory" [see MODELS, MATHEMATICAL; see also Estes 1950; 1959].

## Cross-disciplinary implications

**Education.** Dewey emphasized that "we learn by doing." Guthrie extended this to "we learn only what we ourselves do." If in classrooms the student watches a teacher skillfully solve problems or engage in intricate feats of cogent reasoning, the student will become an intent observer of the teacher solving problems—but he will not become better at solving problems himself, unless he himself is doing something other than watching. The responses we wish to cue to various stimuli must be made by the individual himself in the presence of those stimuli.

Guthrie's theory of learning leads one also to place considerably less faith in drill. Making the same response over and over again will not further learning unless the circumstances are changed—and only to the extent that the circumstances are changed. Sitting in the same seat in the same room with the same internal stimuli from the same emotional make-up acting upon one while making the same response would add nothing to what was gained by making the response in the presence of those stimuli once.

A further implication is that the circumstances under which one wishes the desired response to be made in the future should be approximated as closely as possible by the present circumstances. The responses made get cued only to those stimuli actually present.

The theory implies too that teachers commonly are too prominent a part of the schoolroom situation. Whenever a learner is making desired responses, the teacher would be wise to be as small a part of the stimulating situation as possible. When the teacher is a large part of the situation, the learner's responses will, of course, be cued to the sight and sound of the teacher (as well as to other stimuli from the teacher); when these stimuli constitute a major part of the total situation, the desired responses are being cued to relatively little else besides the teacher. Hence, in the teacher's subsequent absence, the desired response is less apt to be made than would be the case had the teacher been less prominent.

Many further implications for formal education are presented in a book by Guthrie and Powers (1950).

**Psychotherapy.** We ask "Why did you do this?" assuming the person acts toward some end. We search for "motives" and speculate on what the person gains by his unwanted behavior. But possibly he gains nothing by it—even in his own eyes.

That could be the crux of his problem: he does not customarily act in accord with his own values or goals. His behavior is largely unaimed.

From Guthrie's theory we should expect that much learned behavior may be unsatisfying even to the person engaged in it. The person does not necessarily direct his behavior toward any goal, conscious or unconscious. He is not necessarily acting in a fashion that meets his basic needs or fulfills his major hopes. He simply is doing what he has been trained to do, making the responses to various stimuli that he last made to those stimuli, responses that in some prior context he had perhaps been forced to make. The responses may meet no need and yet persist.

Instead of assuming that all behavior is goal-directed and meets some need, we should try in psychotherapy to help the person develop more goal-directed behavior and develop behavior consonant with his needs: for example, we should help him to acquire habits of aiming at goals, habits of evaluating his actions, habits of ascertaining *whether* any need is indeed being met by his behavior [see MENTAL DISORDERS, TREATMENT OF, *article on* CLIENT-CENTERED COUNSELING].

Further, in light of Guthrie's theory, instead of concentrating primarily on the circumstances under which the unwanted behavior or feelings occur, we should search also for the circumstances under which the individual currently does make valued responses. The latter offer leads concerning the stimuli which already are cues for valued responses and thereby offer a basis on which to build.

Subsequently, when confronted with unwanted behavior, the appropriate question is not "Why?" but "What are the circumstances eliciting that unwanted response?" and "What stimuli are cues for it?" To get a different response cued to those stimuli, one should not present all at once many of the stimuli that are cues for the unwanted response. (That is, one should not, for example, put the individual back in the original situation.) This would make the unwanted response very likely, according to the probability principle. Rather, we should present only a few of those stimuli that now are cues for the unwanted response while simultaneously presenting many stimuli that are cues for a desired response. When the new response occurs, a few more of the stimuli may be introduced that are cues for the unwanted response. Thus, gradually, we could detach from unwanted behavior more and more of the stimuli formerly cues for unwanted behavior and establish them as new cues for the new response. On this installment plan, unlearning of the old and learning of the new proceeds most efficaciously.

One of the most brilliant and kindly of men, Guthrie has given us a rich heritage through his teaching, articles, and books. He worked with sustained endeavor on an extraordinary array of topics. His writings, remarkably illuminating, thoughtful, and thought-provoking, reflect his high good humor, courage, and great concern for his fellow men.

VIRGINIA VOEKS

[*For the historical context of Guthrie's work, see the biographies of* BEKHTEREV; KÖHLER; PAVLOV.]

## WORKS BY GUTHRIE

1914a   Formal Logic and Logical Form. *Midwest Quarterly* 1:146–155.

1914b   Old Solutions of a New Problem. *Midwest Quarterly* 1:236–241.

1915a   *The Paradoxes of Mr. Russell: With a Brief Account of Their History.* Lancaster, Pa.: New Era Printing.

1915b   Russell's Theory of Types. *Journal of Philosophy, Psychology and Scientific Methods* 12:381–385.

1916   The Field of Logic. *Journal of Philosophy, Psychology and Scientific Methods* 13:152–158.

1921a   SMITH, STEVENSON; and GUTHRIE, EDWIN R. *Chapters in General Psychology.* Seattle: Univ. of Washington Press.

1921b   SMITH, STEVENSON; and GUTHRIE, EDWIN R. *General Psychology in Terms of Behavior.* New York: Appleton.

1922   SMITH, STEVENSON; and GUTHRIE, EDWIN R. Exhibitionism. *Journal of Abnormal and Social Psychology* 17:206–209.

1924   Purpose and Mechanism in Psychology. *Journal of Philosophy* 21:673–682.

1927a   Measuring Student Opinion of Teachers. *School and Society* 25:175–176.

1927b   Measuring Introversion and Extroversion. *Journal of Abnormal and Social Psychology* 22:82–88.

1928a   Psychological Bases of War and Peace. Pages 78–83 in Charles E. Martin and Edith Dobie (editors), *Problems in International Understanding.* Seattle: Univ. of Washington Book Store.

1928b   GUTHRIE, EDWIN R.; and MORRILL, H. The Fusion of Non-musical Intervals. *American Journal of Psychology* 40:624–625.

1930   Conditioning as a Principle of Learning. *Psychological Review* 37:412–428.

1933a   On the Nature of Psychological Explanations. *Psychological Review* 40:124–137.

1933b   Association as a Function of Time Interval. *Psychological Review* 40:355–367.

1934a   Pavlov's Theory of Conditioning. *Psychological Review* 41:199–206.

1934b   Reward and Punishment. *Psychological Review* 41:450–460.

(1935)   1960   *The Psychology of Learning.* Rev. ed. Gloucester, Mass.: Smith.

1936   Thorndike's Concept of "Belonging." *Psychological Bulletin* 33:621 only.

1937a   YACORZINSKI, GEORGE K.; and GUTHRIE, EDWIN R. A Comparative Study of Involuntary and Voluntary Conditioned Responses. *Journal of General Psychology* 16:235–257.

1937b   Tolman on Associative Learning. *Psychological Review* 44:525–528.

(1938)   1962   *The Psychology of Human Conflict: The Clash of Motives Within the Individual.* Gloucester, Mass.: Smith.

1939   The Effect of Outcome on Learning. *Psychological Review* 46:480–485.

1940a   Association and the Law of Effect. *Psychological Review* 47:127–148.

1940b   [A Book Review of] *Organizing and Memorizing: Studies in the Psychology of Learning and Teaching,* (1940) by G. Katona. *Psychological Bulletin* 37:820–823.

1942a   The Principle of Associative Learning. Pages 100–114 in *Philosophical Essays in Honor of Edgar Arthur Singer, Jr.,* edited by F. P. Clark and M. C. Nahm. Philadelphia: Univ. of Pennsylvania Press.

1942b   Conditioning: A Theory of Learning in Terms of Stimulus, Response, and Association. National Society for the Study of Education, *Yearbook* 41, part 2:17–60.

1943   Leadership. Pages 366–384 in National Research Council, *Psychology for the Fighting Man, Prepared for the Fighting Man Himself. . . .* Washington: Infantry Journal. → An unsigned article by Guthrie. A paperback edition was published in the same year by Penguin.

1944   Personality in Terms of Associative Learning. Volume 1, pages 49–68 in Joseph McV. Hunt (editor), *Personality and the Behavior Disorders: A Handbook Based on Experimental and Clinical Research.* New York: Ronald Press.

1945   The Evaluation of Faculty Service. American Association of University Professors, *Bulletin* 31:255–262.

1946a   The Conditioned Response. Pages 100–104 in Philip L. Harriman (editor), *Encyclopedia of Psychology.* New York: Philosophical Library.

1946b   GUTHRIE, EDWIN R.; and HORTON, GEORGE P. *Cats in a Puzzle Box.* New York: Rinehart.

1946c   Psychological Facts and Psychological Theory. *Psychological Bulletin* 43:1–20.

1946d   Recency or Effect? A Reply to V. J. O'Connor. *Harvard Educational Review* 16:286–289.

1949a   The Evaluation of Teaching. *Educational Record* 30:109–115.

1949b   GUTHRIE, EDWIN A.; and EDWARDS, ALLEN L. *Psychology: A First Course in Human Behavior.* New York: Harper.

1950   GUTHRIE, EDWIN R.; and POWERS, FRANCIS F. *Educational Psychology.* New York: Ronald Press.

1959a   *The State University: Its Function and Its Future.* Seattle: Univ. of Washington Press.

1959b   Association by Contiguity. Volume 2, pages 158–195 in Sigmund Koch (editor), *Psychology: A Study of a Science.* New York: McGraw-Hill.

## SUPPLEMENTARY BIBLIOGRAPHY

American Psychological Foundation Gold Medal Award 1958.   1958   *American Psychologist* 13:739–740.

CARTER, L. F.   1936   Maze Learning With a Differential Proprioceptive Cue. *Journal of Experimental Psychology* 19:758–762.

ESTES, WILLIAM K.   1950   Toward a Statistical Theory of Learning. *Psychological Review* 57:94–107.

ESTES, WILLIAM K. 1959 The Statistical Approach to Learning Theory. Volume 2, pages 380–491 in Sigmund Koch (editor), *Psychology: A Study of a Science.* New York: McGraw-Hill.

JANET, PIERRE 1924 *Principles of Psychotherapy.* Translated by H. M. and E. R. Guthrie. New York: Macmillan. → Contains lectures delivered at Harvard University.

KIMBLE, GREGORY A.; and KENDALL, JOHN W. JR. 1953 A Comparison of Two Methods of Producing Experimental Extinction. *Journal of Experimental Psychology* 45:87–90. → An experiment testing Guthrie's theory.

OSGOOD, CHARLES E. (1953) 1958 *Method and Theory in Experimental Psychology.* New York: Oxford Univ. Press. → See especially pages 362–372, "Guthrie: A Contiguity Theory."

PAVLOV, I. P. 1932 The Reply of a Physiologist to Psychologists. *Psychological Review* 39:91–127.

SHEFFIELD, FRED D. 1948 Avoidance Training and the Contiguity Principle. *Journal of Comparative and Physiological Psychology* 41:165–177. → An experimental test of Guthrie's theory.

SHEFFIELD, FRED D. 1949 Hilgard's Critique of Guthrie. *Psychological Review* 56:284–291.

SHEFFIELD, FRED D. 1951 The Contiguity Principle in Learning Theory. *Psychological Review* 58:362–367.

SHEFFIELD, VIRGINIA F. 1950 Resistance to Extinction as a Function of the Distribution of Extinction Trials. *Journal of Experimental Psychology* 40:305–313.

VOEKS, VIRGINIA W. 1945 What Fixes the Correct Response? *Psychological Review* 52:49–51.

VOEKS, VIRGINIA W. 1948 Postremity, Recency and Frequency as Bases for Prediction in the Maze Situation. *Journal of Experimental Psychology* 38:495–510.

VOEKS, VIRGINIA W. 1950 Formalization and Clarification of a Theory of Learning. *Journal of Psychology* 30:341–362.

VOEKS, VIRGINIA W. 1955 Gradual Strengthening of S–R Connections or Increasing Number of S–R Connections? *Journal of Psychology* 39:289–299. → An experiment testing Guthrie's theory.

ZEAMAN, DAVID; and RADNER, LOUIS 1953 A Test of the Mechanisms of Learning Proposed by Hull and Guthrie. *Journal of Experimental Psychology* 45:239–244.

# H

**HABIT**

*See* LEARNING.

## HADDON, ALFRED CORT

Alfred Cort Haddon (1855–1940), "the father of Cambridge anthropology," was the son of strictly Nonconformist parents living on the outskirts of London. His father, John, was more successful as a Baptist deacon and Sunday-school teacher than in business, and the printing works that he had inherited produced dwindling profits. Haddon's mother, Caroline Waterman, eked out their scanty income by writing children's books, mostly religious, but, significantly, her best seller was *Look, Listen and Learn,* an introduction to nature study based on walks with her children. Her son dedicated his *Head-hunters* "to my Mother who first taught me to observe."

After a scrappy schooling Haddon entered the family business, "duty and drudgery," as he called it. There, however unwillingly, he learned some useful lessons: careful and exact lettering and drawing, printing technique, proofreading, and business methods. But his whole heart was devoted to the study of plants and animals, and his spare time was spent in collecting, drawing, dissecting, bottling, and noting in his diary everything he could find, from squashed hedgehogs and unwanted kittens to water fleas and animalcula.

"Duty and drudgery" came to an end in 1875, when his father decided that the young scientist was a bungling failure in the office and that he would lose less money by sending him to the university. Haddon was enrolled at Christ's College,

Cambridge. He won a scholarship and did brilliantly in his tripos. He was nominated to the zoological station at Naples and in 1880 was appointed professor of zoology at Dublin.

Haddon's marriage the following year to Fanny Rose was the climax of a college joke that the participants never regretted. He and his friend Holland Rose had arranged to exchange sisters for the May Week festivities of 1877. Rose married Laura Haddon in 1880, and at their wedding Haddon announced his engagement to Fanny Rose.

Armchair science never satisfied him, and in 1888, "tired of lecturing about things I have never seen," he planned his first visit to the Torres Strait, a turning point in his life and in the history of anthropology. His carefully kept journal shows how his interest in coral reefs was gradually eclipsed by interest in the natives. He realized that corals could wait but native culture was disintegrating so rapidly with the impact of civilization that the saving of vanishing data was an urgent need.

When he left the islands, in 1889, he was already planning the Cambridge Anthropological Expedition to the Torres Strait, a landmark in anthropological research. It took him almost ten years to collect the men and the money. He felt a thorough record of native life needed a team of specialists that included not only those equipped to study physical characters, arts and crafts, music, language, religion, and folklore but also, for the first time, a psychologist who might interpret native thought. In the end there were two psychologists, W. H. R. Rivers, a lecturer in the medical school, and his pupil C. S. Myers, who was a musician as well; from the medical school also came William McDougall and C. G. Seligman. All these names

303

later became famous in the social sciences. The team was completed by S. H. Ray, an elementary-school teacher with an uncanny knowledge of Melanesian languages, and Anthony Wilkin, a capable photographer interested in material culture. Their work is enshrined both in the six volumes of the *Reports* (1901–1935) and, more popularly, in *Head-hunters* (1901).

The expedition was a tremendous success, mainly because of Haddon's foresighted organization and the affectionate welcome he received from the islanders. Its members hoped that on its return it would be crowned by some recognition from the university. But Haddon's only reward was a lectureship in ethnology at £50 a year. He had never been interested in money and was used to a frugal life, but with a wife and three children to support he had to augment his meager income by lecturing all over the country and writing articles and reviews at the same time he was writing and editing the *Reports*.

Americans were more appreciative than "poor blind Cambridge," as Haddon's own university was described. G. A. Dorsey of the Field Columbian Museum invited him to lecture at Chicago and elsewhere in 1900, offering twice as much as Cambridge paid him in a year. And when, later, at the invitation of W. Z. Ripley, Haddon gave the Lowell lectures at Boston, he calculated gleefully that he was getting two dollars a minute. He would return to England from these visits enriched and encouraged, only to be depressed again by the apathy and financial anxieties at home. It was not until 1904 that a readership at £200 a year was established, and Haddon assumed this post and undertook all the lecturing it entailed, pursuing his duties with unflagging energy and enthusiasm until his resignation, in 1925.

When Haddon first came to Cambridge, in 1875, the science of anthropology was nonexistent. When he died, in 1940, it had been raised, mainly by his selfless devotion, to an honored position in the university. His influence was due primarily to his personality. He was not a good lecturer, his thoughts dashing ahead of his hesitant speech. He lacked social graces, retaining to the end of his life something of the gaucherie of a schoolboy. At the same time that his Nonconformist conscience never forsook him, he was intolerant of cramping conventions, ignored creeds and sects, and respected only those aspects of religion, civilized or uncivilized, that were heartfelt and genuine. He made friends with high and low. He was a welcome associate of academic dignitaries (although barely polite to the pompous or pretentious) and was always at his best

with those in the humbler ranks—illiterate Irish peasants, fishermen, and his beloved "savages." His students were among his most devoted admirers, and they have maintained his high standards of honest work in the study of mankind.

A. H. QUIGGIN

[*For discussion of the subsequent development of Haddon's work, see* OCEANIAN SOCIETY *and the biographies of* RADCLIFFE-BROWN; RIVERS; SELIGMAN, C. G.]

### WORKS BY HADDON

(1895) 1914 *Evolution in Art: As Illustrated by the Life-histories of Designs.* New ed. London: Scott.

(1898) 1908 *The Study of Man.* 2d ed. New York: Putnam.

1901 *Head-hunters: Black, White and Brown.* London: Methuen.

1901–1935 *Reports of the Cambridge Anthropological Expedition to Torres Straits.* 6 vols. Cambridge Univ. Press; New York: Macmillan. → Volume 1: *General Ethnography,* 1935. Volume 2: *Physiology and Psychology,* 2 parts, 1901–1903. Volume 3: *Linguistics,* 1907. Volume 4: *Arts and Crafts,* 1912. Volume 5: *Sociology, Magic and Religion of the Western Islanders,* 1904. Volume 6: *Sociology, Magic and Religion of the Eastern Islanders,* 1908.

(1909) 1929 *Races of Man and Their Distribution.* Rev. ed. Cambridge Univ. Press; New York: Macmillan.

(1911) 1927 *Wanderings of Peoples.* 2d ed. Cambridge Univ. Press.

1936 HUXLEY, JULIAN S.; and HADDON, ALFRED CORT *We Europeans: A Survey of "Racial" Problems.* New York and London: Harper.

1936–1938 HADDON, ALFRED CORT; and HORNELL, JAMES *Canoes of Oceania.* 3 vols. Honolulu, Hawaii: Bishop Museum. → Volume 1: *Canoes of Polynesia, Fiji, and Micronesia,* 1936. Volume 2: *Canoes of Melanesia, Queensland, and New Guinea,* 1938. Volume 3: *Definition of Terms and General Survey of Oceanic Canoe,* 1938.

### WORK ABOUT HADDON

QUIGGIN, A. H. 1942 *Haddon the Head-hunter: A Short Sketch of the Life of A. C. Haddon.* Cambridge Univ. Press.

# HALBWACHS, MAURICE

Maurice Halbwachs (1877–1945), a sensitive and humane scholar whose works are among the most important in the sociology of the first half of the twentieth century, was arrested by the Gestapo in Paris in July 1944 and died about eight months later in the Buchenwald concentration camp.

Halbwachs was born in Rheims. For three years one of his teachers at the Lycée Henri IV in Paris was Henri Bergson, who influenced him greatly. He completed his studies at the École Normale Supérieure with a well-written book on Leibniz (1907) and participated in the preparation of the *Catalogue des manuscrits leibniziens.* Soon, however, the social sciences attracted his interest. He worked with Simiand, Lévy-Bruhl, and especially Durkheim and helped edit *L'année sociologique.* His dissertation, *La classe ouvrière et les niveaux de vie* (1913*a*), marked the beginning of his extensive studies in social psychology.

This study is characteristic of Halbwachs' work. It reveals his sense for the concrete and his concern for getting down to reality. Only after immersing himself in concrete data did he develop general ideas, working hypotheses, theories, and laws. Moreover, Halbwachs made specific methodological and theoretical contributions in this study. By discovering what the group accepted as the proper order of importance of expenditures, he established a scale of working-class needs. He revealed the primary importance in these choices of the group's representation and of what is consistent with it. Clearly, Halbwachs was here applying Durkheim's theory of collective representations.

This scientific study of the scale of working-class needs was supported by a theory of the worker's position in modern capitalist societies, a theory that now seems questionable at certain points. According to Halbwachs, these societies assign to the working class the task of mastering matter, and since the members of this class are thereby limited to contact with things, they become isolated from the rest of mankind. In their isolation as a group from other groups in society, the solidarity among the members of the working class becomes enhanced, and it is only by virtue of their class consciousness that they remain attached to the larger society at all.

A later work, *L'évolution des besoins dans les classes ouvrières* (1933), applied the principal conclusions of the 1913 thesis to those social groups in the great industrial nations of the West that occupy positions analogous to that of the older working class.

Georges Gurvitch raised some questions about Halbwachs' criteria of social-class membership, but he gave him credit for having been clearly aware of the great complexity of social class phenomena and for having kept his concepts entirely separate from all philosophy of history and all political positions (Gurvitch 1950).

Halbwachs displayed a distinct tendency to explain needs by relative and subjective factors. He admitted that trends of opinion are important factors in defining needs, but he did not consider the extent to which objective elements also enter into the subjective experience of need. For example, a *real* lack of food or clothing is felt by the workers when they compare their standard of living with that of the middle class, or the bourgeoisie.

Halbwachs' influence as a pioneer in research on the definition of needs, as well as on budgets and consumption patterns, has been stressed by P. Chombart de Lauwe in his book *La vie quotidienne des familles ouvrières* (1956). Chombart de Lauwe also points out that Halbwachs was the first to make a genuinely sociological study of the development of workers' budgets.

Halbwachs' study *Les causes du suicide* (1930) extends and refines Durkheim's classic work on the same subject. For Durkheim, religious factors are most important in determining the extent of an individual's integration into a society (and he related a lack of integration to a high rate of suicide). Halbwachs felt that the nature and importance of the religious factor vary with the social and psychological context and that this context, in turn, varies in different countries.

He was interested in the influence of collective memory and tradition on beliefs, and his essay *La topographie légendaire des évangiles en terre sainte* (1941) was a specific study of this influence. Thus, in various periods of history, the appearance attributed to the holy places has changed according to the needs and hopes of the Christian groups describing these places.

In his recent book on social psychology, Jean Stoetzel (1963) shows how Halbwachs influenced the study of memory by distinguishing between individual memory, i.e., the present knowledge of the past, and collective memory and by seeking the patterns governing this collective, or group, memory. Halbwachs' contributions in this area are only now beginning to be appreciated outside France.

During the last years of his life, Halbwachs became increasingly preoccupied with social morphology and demography. He contributed an important article on demographical statistics to the *Encyclopédie française.* He also developed the concept of social morphology that appears in a rudimentary and rather abstract form in Durkheim's work. Halbwachs was frequently able to discern the social and economic structure behind morphological data, especially the influence of social classes. In his *Psychology of Social Class* (1938), he examined motivation among the peasant classes, the bourgeoisie, industrial workers, and the lower middle classes.

It is possible here only to suggest the importance of the results of Halbwachs' studies and the originality of his methods. He invariably looked at reality from many different perspectives. There is no rigidity or dogmatism in any of his work. He culled important elements from several intellectual traditions: he was inspired by Durkheim's vigorous mind and was concerned to use such new scientific approaches as those of American sociology, but he also incorporated Marxist sociology in certain broad orientations of his work.

GEORGES FRIEDMANN

[*For the historical context of Halbwachs' work, see the biographies of* DURKHEIM; LE PLAY; LÉVY-BRUHL; SIMIAND. *For discussion of the subsequent development of Halbwachs' ideas, see* SUICIDE, *article on* SOCIAL ASPECTS.]

### WORKS BY HALBWACHS

1907    *Leibniz.* Paris: Delaplane.
1913a    *La classe ouvrière et les niveaux de vie: Recherches sur la hiérarchie des besoins dans les sociétés industrielles contemporaines.* Paris: Alcan.
1913b    *La théorie de l'homme moyen: Essai sur Quetelet et la statistique morale.* Paris: Alcan.
1930    *Les causes du suicide.* Paris: Alcan.
1933    *L'évolution des besoins dans les classes ouvrières.* Paris: Alcan.
(1938) 1959    *The Psychology of Social Class.* With an Introduction by Georges Friedmann. Glencoe, Ill.: Free Press; London: Heinemann. → First published as *Analyse des mobiles dominants qui orientent l'activité des individus dans la vie sociale.*
1941    *La topographie légendaire des Évangiles en Terre Sainte: Étude de mémoire collective.* Paris: Presses Universitaires de France.
(1949) 1950    *La mémoire collective.* Edited by Jeanne Alexandre. Paris: Presses Universitaires de France. → Published posthumously.

### SUPPLEMENTARY BIBLIOGRAPHY

ALEXANDRE, JEANNE 1949 Maurice Halbwachs. *Année sociologique* 3d Series [1940–1948] 1:3–10.
CANGUILHEM, GEORGES 1947 Maurice Halbwachs (1877–1945). Volume 103, pages 229–241 in Strasbourg, Université, Faculté des Lettres, *Mémorial des années: 1939–1945.* Paris: Belles Lettres.
CHOMBART DE LAUWE, PAUL H. 1956 *La vie quotidienne des familles ouvrières: Recherches sur les comportements sociaux de consommation.* Paris: Centre National de la Recherche Scientifique.
GURVITCH, GEORGES (1950) 1957–1963 *La vocation actuelle de la sociologie.* 2d ed., 2 vols. Paris: Presses Universitaires de France. → Volume 1: *Vers la sociologie différentielle.* Volume 2: *Antécédents et perspectives.*
STOETZEL, JEAN 1963 *La psychologie sociale.* Paris: Flammarion.

# HALE, HORATIO

Horatio Emmons Hale (1817–1896), American ethnologist, was born at Newport, New Hampshire. His mother was Sarah Josepha Hale, for many years editor of *Godey's Lady's Book.* While Hale was still a student at Harvard, which he entered in 1833, he made a study of the language of an Algonquian-speaking band encamped on the college grounds; he himself set into type and published the results of the study. This early attempt at linguistic research within an ethnological context set the tone for all his later work in the emerging anthropology of the nineteenth century: throughout a long life of periodic, although always enthusiastic, involvement in anthropological research, he continued to stress language as the "true basis of ethnology."

Upon his graduation from Harvard, Hale accepted a position as philologist with a United States expedition to survey and chart areas of the Pacific, under the command of Captain Charles Wilkes. Hale's senior colleague in the scientific corps of this first research expedition sponsored by the United States government was Charles Pickering, who with du Ponceau and Gallatin was a leader among those early nineteenth-century ethnologists who stressed the collection of comparative linguistic data from the human societies recently discovered and constantly threatened by western expansion. When the expedition stopped at the Oregon Territory, toward the end of its four-year voyage in the Pacific, Hale left it to devote more time to the study of the languages of the Indians of the Northwest Territory, after which he returned overland to the East. Hale's contribution to the *Reports of the Expedition* was published in 1846 as Volume 6, *Ethnography and Philology.* Its primary emphasis was upon his collection from the southern Pacific, and although it contained a mass of miscellaneous and often superficial ethnographic observations, Hale's linguistic data, especially those from the Polynesian islands, were carefully recorded and are still useful. It was upon this linguistic evidence that Hale built his theory of Polynesian migrations, which, except for refinements derived from more recent data, is still essentially sound.

After the Wilkes expedition and Gallatin's death in 1849, the linguistic emphasis of American ethnology gave way to the rapid rise of archeological interests. About this time, also, Hale married and moved to Clinton, Ontario, where for the next twenty years he devoted himself to business activities. Yet, he was to resume his ethnological investigations, stimulated by the proximity of the Six Nations Reserve, on the Grand River at Brantford and probably also by a developing friendship with Lewis H. Morgan. Toward the end of the 1860s he began the collection of traditional literature from older informants on the reserve. These form the basis of his most important substantive contributions to the anthropological literature and particularly to that of Iroquoian studies.

His interest in language as the foremost indicator of ethnological status led him to concentrate upon that aspect of Iroquois culture. And it was his continuing concern for language that led Hale in all his work to stress the distinction between race, defined biologically, and language and to stress the superiority of language for establishing the historical (i.e., ethnological) relations of existing groups. More particularly, he defined Tutelo as a Siouan language within the Iroquoian geographical range; he rescued Wyandot Huron from disappearance and demonstrated that it had been the most ancient Iroquoian language; using a technique which anticipated more recent glottochronological methods, he attempted an arrangement of existing Iroquoian languages into a historical sequence; and perhaps most important of all for later ethnological methods, he used the traditional tales of the Iroquois as a source for ethnological data.

In his most significant work, *The Iroquois Book of Rites* (1883a), he summarized much of his work on the Iroquois. Here, using his several approaches, he reconstructed the late prehistory of the Six Nations, with a particular emphasis, drawn from the traditions he had recovered, upon the story of the legendary hero Hiawatha (which he rescued from the romanticism and errors of H. R. Schoolcraft) and the formation of the League of the Iroquois. Hale's published contributions to the ethnological literature are relatively few, but all of them are graced with his intelligence and originality, with his theoretical bent and his humanism.

Hale's greatest contribution to American anthropology, however, lies in his influence upon Franz Boas, much of whose early field work on the Northwest Coast was done under Hale's supervision and direction. Although Boas had spent a productive season among the Northwest Coast Indians in 1886, his subsequent field work in this area during the early 1890s was subsidized by a special committee of the British Association for the Advancement of Science, of which Hale was the driving force. It was Hale who recruited Boas for this work; and although differences of approach to field problems developed, Hale was Boas' constant and enthusiastic supporter. Correspondence between the two men indicates that Hale not only provided Boas with the material support required but was also the source of much in Boas' emerging point of view toward the anthropological enterprise, a point of view which was to form the foundation of American anthropology for half a century. Hale transmitted to Boas the intensity of his feeling for the diversity of culture and language and his distaste for the construction of universal historical systems;

he provided Boas with the technique for the recapture of lost elements of culture through the collection and analysis of myths and legends; he persuaded Boas of the insufficiency of biological criteria for the establishment of a classification of the varieties of man and for the evaluation of his varying capacities; and by his insistence that Boas collect all the data relating to the differences between human groups, Hale laid the foundation in a field approach for the concept of a "general anthropology," which came to be the hallmark of the work of Boas and his followers.

Horatio Hale died in 1896. He was mourned by Boas as "a man who contributed more to our knowledge of the human races than perhaps any other single student." Sufficient praise indeed.

JACOB W. GRUBER

[*For discussion of the subsequent development of Hale's ideas, see* INDIANS, NORTH AMERICAN *and the biography of* BOAS.]

WORKS BY HALE

1846    *Ethnography and Philology: United States Exploring Expedition.* Philadelphia: Lee & Blanchard.
(1883a) 1963    *The Iroquois Book of Rites.* With an introduction by William M. Fenton. Univ. of Toronto Press.
1883b    The Tutelo Tribe and Language. American Philosophical Society, *Proceedings* 21:1–47.
1890    *An International Idiom: A Manual of the Oregon Trade Language, or "Chinook Jargon."* London: Whitaker.
1891    *Language as a Test of the Mental Capacity: Being an Attempt to Demonstrate the True Basis of Anthropology.* Ottawa.
1894    The Fall of Hochelaga: A Study of Popular Tradition. Pages 252–266 in International Congress of Anthropology, Chicago, 1893, *Memoirs.* Chicago: Shulte.

SUPPLEMENTARY BIBLIOGRAPHY

Bibliography of the Royal Society of Canada: Hale, Horatio. 1894    Royal Society of Canada, Ottawa, *Proceedings and Transactions* 12:44–46.
BRINTON, DANIEL G. 1897    Horatio Hale. *American Anthropologist* 10:25–27.
GRUBER, JACOB W. 1967    Horatio Hale and the Development of American Anthropology. American Philosophical Society, *Proceedings* 111:5–37.

# HALÉVY, ÉLIE

Élie Halévy (1870–1937), French historian, produced a monumental history of England and also wrote about socialism and other modern political ideas. He was born into a family known for its contributions to the arts. Its founder, a Bavarian cantor, came to Paris at the end of the eighteenth century. He believed in the possibility of combining the moral principles of Judaism with the political program of the French Revolution, which had emancipated his people from their ancient disabilities. This faith found its way into the title of the review *L'Israélite français*, which he founded during the Bourbon restoration. His two sons were soon assimilated into Parisian intellectual and musical circles. Jacques Fromental became a prominent composer, professor at the Conservatory, the first Jewish member and, ultimately, the secretary of the Academy of Fine Arts. His wife was a member of the Rodrigues family. Like so many other Saint-Simonians, members of this family came to be bankers and entrepreneurs during the Second Empire. Fromental's daughter Geneviève married Bizet. She was a friend of Proust and was among his models for the Duchesse de Guermantes.

Léon Halévy, Fromental's brother, succeeded Comte as Saint-Simon's secretary. Léon himself wrote extensively, but he was most notable for having two sons who were elected to the Académie Française. Lucien Anatole Prévost-Paradol, an illegitimate son, was a brilliant essayist and a critic of the Second Empire. His ideas greatly influenced the authors of the Third Republic's constitution. Léon's other son, Ludovic Halévy, was a prolific and successful author as well as a librettist for Offenbach and Bizet. Although brought up as a Catholic, his mother's faith, Ludovic married Louise Breguet, whose Protestant family of artisan inventors had gone from watchmaking to the position of France's leading constructors of precision instruments. Breguets were among the pioneers of telegraphy and aviation.

Ludovic's sons, Élie and Daniel, were raised as Protestants. Their home was the center of a brilliant set, which included their uncle, Marcellin Berthelot, the great chemist, as well as the painter Degas. Both sons were ardent supporters of Dreyfus and helped organize the famous "Manifesto of the Intellectuals." Daniel, who collaborated with Péguy on the *Cahiers de la quinzaine*, later supported Georges Sorel, contributed to the foundation of *L'Humanité* and the *universités populaires* (what the English call workingmen's colleges). His name was prominent for more than half a century as historian, journalist, and editor.

Élie was more ascetic and brilliant, placing first in the national philosophy examination he took before entering the École Normale Supérieure. There philosophy continued to be his main concern, as it was of such life-long friends as Xavier Léon, Alain [E. Chartier], Celestin Bouglé, Léon Brunschvicg, and Dominique Parodi. Committed to a secular and rationalist individualism, passionately concerned to unite theory and practice, Élie Halévy

helped found the *Revue de métaphysique et de morale* and the Société Française de Philosophie, associations he maintained until his death. Like Max Weber and Durkheim, Halévy gained much from participation in a great journal that brought him into contact with the pivotal works and authors of his time. Even after he turned from philosophy to the history of ideas and thence to general history, his analytical method still marked everything he wrote.

In his first book, *La théorie platonicienne des sciences* (1896), Halévy carefully demonstrated Plato's apparent contradictions before establishing their ultimate congruity. This way of proceeding stemmed from Halévy's belief that if "one has the courage to go to the very end of a 'negative dialectic,' he then perceives that such criticism prepares the way for a 'progressive dialectic.' By distinguishing levels, this positive dialectic leads to the discernment of values in terms of a conception of the world and of life that is at once hierarchical and constructive, that not only *founds* and *justifies* but also fulfils the no less essential function of condemning what does not meet its standards" (Brunschvicg 1937, p. 680). Plato served as an example of a thinker who had made his way from criticism of others to positive construction of his own. His standards were rational and self-conscious; he used them to pass judgment on the institutions of his society.

As a historian of ideas, Halévy made extensive use of "negative dialectic" as a means of penetrating to the real, if often contradictory, values and motives underlying a school of thought. In addition, he sought to chart and explain the discrepant actual effects of a doctrine. In *The Growth of Philosophic Radicalism* (1901–1904), Halévy used his method to order the results of his extraordinarily thorough research on Benthamism. Its political and economic aspects could not, he thought, be logically reconciled. In his political theory, Bentham assumed that only by a legislator can conflicts of interest be reconciled in such a way as to secure the greatest good of the greatest number; in his economic theory, he assumed that individual interests are harmonized naturally by some sort of invisible hand. Thus, utilitarianism could produce either faith in bureaucratic paternalism based on legislative intervention or belief in anarchical individualism and laissez-faire. Both conclusions were in fact drawn by Bentham's disciples; both had important effects upon political theory and public policy.

From this model work in intellectual history, Halévy moved to a study of England that owed much to his teaching responsibilities at the École Libre des Sciences Politiques. The school was established after the defeat of 1871 and the Commune. Its founders sought to discover the sources of France's political instability as well as her failure to develop an elite and institutions such as those of England, the pre-eminent example of a nation that combined national power with liberty. Halévy taught two courses at the "Sciences Po" alternately for over forty years: English history and European socialism. The first was the subject, the second the polemical target, of his life's work, *A History of the English People in the Nineteenth Century* (1912–1932). In the first volume, *England in 1815*, he isolated his dominant theoretical concern: "Why [is] it that of all the countries of Europe England has been the most free from revolutions, violent crises, and sudden changes?" (*ibid.*, vol. 1, p. 424). His answer was a sustained effort to demonstrate the inadequacy of Marxism as a monistic theory of historical explanation. But like Max Weber, Halévy respected Marx enough to accept his formulation of the problem: England, the first country to be dominated by the capitalist mode of production, should have been the first to experience a revolution produced by the internal contradictions of that economic system. It did not. What could explain this? Again like Weber, Halévy did not wish simply to replace Marxism by an idealist hypothesis asserting that ideas and beliefs cause events. Rather, he wished to show that this was an instance, and a crucial one, in which religion had exercised a force independent of the means of production. Weber emphasized the effects of religious movements upon economic activity; Halévy, their political consequences.

The decisive difference between British and French development stemmed from indirect and unanticipated consequences of the Methodist revival. In France religion had been identified with an established church, controlled by the same class that dominated the state. Consequently, radicals were forced to attack both institutions simultaneously. But in England, Wesleyanism, rejected by the Church of England, became associated with the Nonconformist tradition of the free churches and contributed to their reinvigoration. Thus, Nonconformity could act as a social control, disposing radicals to think in terms of piecemeal reforms. Because in every class Methodism had made converts who shared its philanthropic values, channels were created for communicating the grievances of the lower classes. Reforms from above moderated injustices unacknowledged by the Continental bourgeoisie.

Working-class leadership was likewise affected. The sects supplied many causes with men from the working class, who had learned organizational techniques and means of influencing opinion from their chapels and classes. Yet the teaching of these same sects imposed internal restraints upon any tendency to resort to violence. Thus, those members of the working class who led their fellows differed from the middle-class and atheist revolutionary elite on the Continent. Orderly change focused on specific measures, and abuses were attacked as violations of Christian morality. These elements of political style were discovered rather than invented by the Independent Labour party.

In seeking in the sociology of religion the explanation for British stability, Halévy did not perform a speculative leap. Before discounting the significance of explanations based on political institutions on the one hand and economic forces on the other, he subjected the evidence for both to the rigorous "negative dialectic" essential to his method. It was only after this that he passed to his own positive theory based on inquiry into "beliefs, emotions, and opinions, as well as [into] the institutions and sects in which these take a form suitable for scientific inquiry" (*ibid.*, vol. 1, p. 383).

This hypothesis remained at the center of the following volumes in Halévy's *History*, although as he approached his own time, he became more narrative and covered subjects essential to general history. *Imperialism and the Rise of Labour* and *The Rule of Democracy*, which took his account up to 1914, are more remarkable for their thoroughness and objectivity than for the analytical and sociological qualities that characterized *England in 1815*.

As his work progressed, Halévy became one of the intellectual symbols of the *entente cordiale*. Sequestered and indefatigable in France, he was more sociable during his frequent visits to England, where he spent several months every year. Accompanied by his wife, who aided him in his research, he mingled freely with politicians of all parties, as well as with his university friends. The Webbs, Bertrand Russell, H. A. L. Fisher, Sir Ernest Barker, G. P. Gooch, and Graham Wallas were among his oldest and best friends. During World War I he voluntarily served in the medical service. When fighting ended, he was offered an important position in the League of Nations Secretariat. This he refused, as he did the offer of a chair at the Sorbonne, so that he could devote himself to the writing of his life work. Although he never accepted any of the French decorations offered him, he was touched by the honorary D.PHIL. awarded him by Oxford. Halévy played an important part in the commission charged with the publication of official French documents on the origins of World War I.

Two other volumes of Halévy's work were not published until after his death. The *Histoire du socialisme européen* (1948) consists largely of students' notes from his lectures. Halévy had planned to write such a book but died before he could do so. More valuable is the collection called *L'ère des tyrannies* (1938). The title address, given in 1936, summed up his views not only of socialism but also of the regimes of Stalin, Hitler, and Mussolini. Halévy was among the first to assert that communism and fascism, as actually practiced, shared crucial characteristics:

In both cases the country is governed by an armed sect, which claims to rule in the interests of the community, and which is able to impose its will because all of its members are inspired by a common faith. (*Ibid.*, p. 226)

On the one side and the other, the same mixture of a proletarian ideology with militarism. Labor camps. Labor front. Battles for this or that. As for the regime itself, it can be defined only as a permanent state of siege under the control of para-military formations united by a common faith. (*Ibid.*, p. 245)

Because such regimes constitute a durable form of rule rather than a temporary expedient, Halévy called them "tyrannies" in preference to "dictatorships." Despite his use of classical terms, he considered such governments to be unprecedented. Their rulers exercised political and intellectual controls never before available. As for their origin, he attributed such tyrannies less to ideas than to certain means adopted by the belligerents during World War I: central economic planning, nationalization, use of union leaders to eliminate strikes, "organization of enthusiasm" by propaganda, and suppression of all opinions judged by the regime as adverse to the national interest.

In *The World Crisis of 1914–1918* (1930), Halévy examined the concepts of "revolution" and "war" to show their interrelation and cumulative effects during that period. Previously, historians had treated these two subjects in isolation from each other. Halévy found the causes of the war and the Russian Revolution not in decisions consciously taken by statesmen but in collective and anonymous forces, such as the beliefs in national self-determination and the reality of class struggle. As in his *History*, he turned to collective sentiments for explanation. He concluded that the waste of lives and resources in twentieth-century wars and revolutions was due to what men thought and be-

lieved. Only by transforming their ideas and emotions can international peace be attained, only by substituting compromise for fanaticism can there be an end to violence. No one knew better than Halévy how unlikely it was that such advice would be accepted. He died in 1937, believing that war was inevitable and that it would perpetuate tyranny throughout Europe.

MELVIN RICHTER

[*Directly related are the entries* LIBERALISM; RADICALISM; UTILITARIANISM. *Other relevant material may be found in* ANGLO–AMERICAN SOCIETY; DICTATORSHIP; HISTORY, *article on* SOCIAL HISTORY; *and in the biographies of* BENTHAM; DURKHEIM; MARX; WEBER, MAX.]

WORKS BY HALÉVY

1896 *La théorie platonicienne des sciences.* Paris: Alcan.
(1901–1904) 1952 *The Growth of Philosophic Radicalism.* New ed. London: Faber & Faber. → First published in French.
(1912–1932) 1961 *A History of the English People in the Nineteenth Century.* 6 vols. 2d rev. ed. London: Benn. → Volume 1: *England in 1815.* Volume 2: *The Liberal Awakening, 1815–1830.* Volume 3: *The Triumph of Return, 1830–1841.* Volume 4: *Victorian Years, 1841–1895.* Volume 5: *Imperialism and the Rise of Labour, 1895–1905.* Volume 6: *The Rule of Democracy, 1905–1914.* First published in French.
1930 *The World Crisis of 1914–1918: An Interpretation.* Oxford: Clarendon.
1938 *L'ère des tyrannies.* Paris: Gallimard. → The translations of the extracts in the text were provided by Melvin Richter. A paperback edition was published in 1965 by Doubleday as *The Era of Tyrannies: Essays on Socialism and War.*
1948 *Histoire du socialisme européen.* Paris: Gallimard.

SUPPLEMENTARY BIBLIOGRAPHY

BREBNER, J. BARTLET 1948 Halévy: Diagnostician of Modern Britain. *Thought* 23:101–113.
BRUNSCHVICG, LÉON 1937 Élie Halévy. *Revue de métaphysique et de morale* 44:679–691. → The translation of the extract in the text was provided by Melvin Richter.
[CHARTIER, ÉMILE] 1958 *Correspondance avec Élie et Florence Halévy,* by Alain [pseud.]. Paris: Gallimard.
GILLISPIE, CHARLES C. 1950 The Work of Élie Halévy: A Critical Appreciation. *Journal of Modern History* 22:232–249. → The best criticism and appraisal of Halévy.

# HALL, G. STANLEY

G. Stanley Hall (1844–1924), American psychologist and educator, was born in the rural hamlet of Ashfield, Massachusetts. In 1863 he enrolled at Williams College, where he studied with Mark Hopkins. After graduation, although he was without a strong sense of vocation, he enrolled at the Union Theological Seminary in New York City. He spent a year there, more intent on absorbing the various facets of city life than on theological study. He then sought and received from Henry Ward Beecher a loan of $500 for foreign study. He went to Bonn, where he concentrated on philosophy and theology, but afterward, at Berlin, his interests broadened to include physiology, physics, and work in a clinic for mental diseases. He also enjoyed the lighter side of Berlin, its beer gardens and theaters. In 1871, heavily in debt and without a degree, he returned home. Failing to receive an appointment at a midwestern university, he accepted a position as tutor to the children of a New York City banker and remained for more than a year in this post.

A charming, enthusiastic person, Hall had a lively interest in many of the intellectual issues and writers of the day, from associationism to evolutionism, and from John Stuart Mill to Thomas Carlyle. His religious leanings, which had never been strong, disappeared and were replaced by a mild skepticism. University teaching became his professional goal.

He was offered a post at Antioch College, the midwestern outpost of Unitarianism, where for three years he taught English literature, French and German language and literature, and philosophy, as well as serving as librarian, choirmaster, and even occasionally as preacher. He read Wilhelm Wundt's *Principles of Physiological Psychology* when it first appeared and immediately decided to return to Germany to study psychology. But he got only as far as Cambridge, Massachusetts, when an offer of an instructorship in English at Harvard diverted him from his plan. Although the grading of sophomore English themes consumed much of his time, he also carried on research in the Medical School laboratory of Henry P. Bowditch. This physiological research and some study with William James were accepted by the department of philosophy as fulfilling the requirements of a PH.D. degree in psychology. Hall was the first in the United States to receive this degree.

Immediately thereafter he left for Europe. He did work in physiology at Berlin and then went to Leipzig where he was the first of Wundt's many American students. Yet the enthusiasm engendered by his reading of Wundt's work did not survive direct contact: although he attended Wundt's lectures and served as a subject in his psychological experiments, he apparently did not carry on any research of his own.

On returning to Boston he was without a job or even any prospects of one. A providential offer from President Eliot of Harvard to sponsor him in

a series of extension lectures on education saved the day financially and, what is more important, brought him to the attention of Daniel C. Gilman, president of the then recently founded Johns Hopkins University, an institution already celebrated for its pioneer graduate program, organized after the plan of the German universities. In 1882 Hall arrived in Baltimore, and in 1884 he was made professor of psychology and pedagogics.

To further scientific psychology, in 1883 Hall set up a laboratory in a private house adjacent to the campus. The following year he opened the first university psychology laboratory to win formal acceptance in the United States. While at Johns Hopkins he and his students published papers on optical illusions, skin sensitivity, the perception of space, and the time sense. John Dewey completed a dissertation on the psychology of Kant, William Burnham published on memory, and James McKeen Cattell (1890) wrote papers on reaction time and speed of association, as well as his famous "Mental Tests and Measurements," which introduced the term mental test.

Hall had for some time dreamed of the possibility of establishing a journal devoted to psychology. One day a stranger walked into his office and offered him $500 to help found a journal. Although the gift was apparently based on a misunderstanding—the benefactor discontinued his subscription after the second year when he discovered that the journal did not intend to foster psychic research (spiritualism)—it did result in the appearance, in 1887, of the *American Journal of Psychology*, the first psychological journal in this country.

Meanwhile, Hall was preparing to leave for Clark University in Worcester, Massachusetts, to become its first president. The school was being financed by Jonas G. Clark, a wealthy, retired merchant who wished to endow an educational institution in his home town. After what eventually turned out to be too sketchy an understanding with Clark, Hall departed for a tour of European educational centers to inspect possible models for the new university and to find likely prospects for professional appointments (Rush 1948). He had visions of a graduate school modeled on the German universities and perhaps even superior to Johns Hopkins. Research was to be paramount, teaching secondary.

In 1889 Clark University opened its doors with only a few departments staffed and with no pretense at covering all academic fields. Mr. Clark, a reticent man, had different ideas from those of the eager Hall and proved to be secretive about his financial plans for the university. The amount of money he advanced was small, very much smaller than Hall had been led to expect. Hall did not disclose this discrepancy to the faculty, who blamed him for the less than expected equipment, salaries, and assistantships. "Calls" from the University of Chicago, then being founded—and supported by the Rockefeller millions—decimated the Clark faculty. Over the next few years, those who remained made the necessary adjustments, some more money was raised, and toward the end of the century, the bulk of the Clark estate did come to the university. It was divided among the library, the graduate school, and a new undergraduate college. Although Clark's will stipulated that he was to have no connection with the college, Hall continued as president.

Hall, fortunately, had appointed himself professor of psychology and all through these hectic years taught in the graduate school; it was his most brilliant and productive period. From Johns Hopkins he had brought along Edmund C. Sanford to head the laboratory and W. H. Burnham to teach pedagogy, which was interpreted to mean educational psychology and mental hygiene. Adolf Meyer, then with the Worcester State Hospital and destined to become the leading psychiatrist of his day, gave lectures in abnormal psychology.

Hall was an inspiring teacher to a majority of the first generation of American-trained psychologists. By 1893, 11 of 14 and by 1898, 30 of 54 of the PH.D.s granted in psychology were awarded to his students (Harper 1949). Among them were Lewis M. Terman, who developed the Stanford–Binet Scales of Intelligence, Henry H. Goddard, who was a pioneer student of the mentally retarded, and Arnold Gesell, who did so much painstaking research on the mental and physical development of children.

Their work indicated that Hall's own interest had shifted from experimental to developmental psychology, although he continued eloquently to defend laboratory work of all sorts. While at Hopkins he had published a paper entitled "Content of Children's Minds" (1883). With the aid of a questionnaire technique, which he was the first to apply in the United States, he unearthed a variety of information about the thinking of children. He questioned them about such matters as the sense of self, religious experience, fears, and favorite foods. This approach generated great public enthusiasm and before long led to the so-called child study movement. Large numbers of parents and teachers, outside of Hall's personal sway, uncritically and dogmatically used his technique to secure information about children. Hall lost interest in

the technique and not long afterward a reaction, both within psychology and from the public itself, set in and the movement disappeared. It did have the salutary effect of bringing to the public some awareness of the importance of child study and, by its very excesses, created a more critical attitude toward research in child psychology (Bradbury 1937).

Hall had a more sustained interest in adolescence. His monumental and influential work, *Adolescence* (1904), contained the most complete statement of his particular theory of recapitulation in development. The individual child was seen as repeating the life history of the race: when a child played at cowboys and Indians, for example, he was seen as behaving at the level of primitive man. In his old age Hall returned to the problem of development and published a volume entitled *Senescence* (1922).

Along with his research, writing, teaching, and administrative duties, Hall was concerned with psychology on the national scene. In July 1892 he called the meeting which resulted in the founding of the American Psychological Association (Dennis & Boring 1952). Almost as a matter of course he was elected its first president. The scientific purpose of this organization was firmly established under his guidance. He founded and edited still other journals: in 1891 the *Pedagogical Seminary* (now the *Journal of Genetic Psychology*), in 1904 the *Journal of Religious Psychology*, and in 1917 the *Journal of Applied Psychology*.

Hall was one of the first Americans to arrange for a hearing of Freud's views and to teach his theories. Indeed, Freud's only visit to the United States was at Hall's invitation to the twentieth anniversary celebration of Clark University in 1909. In view of the suspicion and dislike that the psychoanalytic movement raised at this time, the invitation showed courage on Hall's part.

Hall's administrative–organizational efforts continue to live on: the American Psychological Association that he founded had 24,000 members by 1966; Johns Hopkins and Clark University departments of psychology each went through a series of unsettling experiences but at present are among the strong graduate departments; the journals he founded, in all but one instance, continue to flourish. He was very modern in his stress on development despite the fact that his way of using Haeckel's discredited biogenetic principle has disappeared without a trace. He has had little direct effect upon current intellectual traditions, but his enthusiasms, his broad convictions, and his emphasis on developmental issues were transmitted to his students, many of whose formulations are very much part of the current scene.

ROBERT I. WATSON

[*Other relevant material may be found in* ADOLESCENCE; AGING, *article on* PSYCHOLOGICAL ASPECTS; DEVELOPMENTAL PSYCHOLOGY; INTELLECTUAL DEVELOPMENT; *and in the biographies of* BALDWIN; CATTELL; GESELL; SEASHORE; TERMAN; WUNDT.]

#### WORKS BY HALL

1883    Content of Children's Minds. *Princeton Review* 11: 249–272.

1904    *Adolescence: Its Psychology and Its Relations to Physiology, Anthropology, Sociology, Sex, Crime, Religion and Education.* New York: Appleton.

1922    *Senescence: The Last Half of Life.* New York: Appleton.

1923    *Life and Confessions of a Psychologist.* New York: Appleton.

*Letters of G. Stanley Hall to Jonas Gilman Clark.* Edited by N. Orwin Rush. Worcester, Mass.: Clark Univ. Library, 1948.

#### SUPPLEMENTARY BIBLIOGRAPHY

BRADBURY, DOROTHY E. 1937    The Contribution of the Child Study Movement to Child Psychology. *Psychological Bulletin* 34:21–38.

CATTELL, JAMES MCKEEN 1890    Mental Tests and Measurements. *Mind* 15:373–381.

CATTELL, JAMES MCKEEN 1943    The Founding of the Association and of the Hopkins & Clark Laboratories. *Psychological Review* 50:61–64.

DENNIS, WAYNE; and BORING, EDWIN G. 1952    The Founding of APA. *American Psychologist* 7:95–97.

HARPER, ROBERT S. 1949    Tables of American Doctorates in Psychology. *American Journal of Psychology* 62: 579–587.

WATSON, ROBERT I. 1963    *The Great Psychologists: From Aristotle to Freud.* Philadelphia: Lippincott.

## HAMILTON, ALEXANDER

Alexander Hamilton (1757?–1804) was born on the West Indian island of Nevis and therefore lacked the attachment to state or region which characterized many eighteenth-century Americans. His experiences during the American Revolution and the decade of government under the Articles of Confederation reinforced his belief that American greatness must be based on a strong and energetic central government.

In 1777, five years after his arrival in the United States, he was appointed aide-de-camp to General George Washington. Viewing the Revolution from the vantage point of Washington's headquarters, he was deeply concerned about the state rivalries, the weakness of the Continental Congress, and the absence of national sentiment that impeded the American war effort. In the years that followed independence, Hamilton worked steadily to breathe life into the moribund Confederation government. As a delegate to the Continental Congress in 1782–1783, he worked closely with such like-minded nationalists as James Madison to invest the Confederation with powers, in his phrase, "adequate to the exigencies of the Union" (*Papers*, vol. 3, p. 689). Despairing of this effort, he became one of the prime promoters of the Constitutional Convention and served as a delegate from the state of New York.

**Political ideas.** Hamilton's proposals for a government modeled closely on the British system were unacceptable to most members of the convention, but he labored industriously to have them "tone their Government as high as possible" (*ibid.*, vol. 4, p. 218). Although ultimately "no man's ideas were more remote from the plan" (*ibid.*, vol. 4, p. 253), Hamilton signed the constitution and was one of its most eloquent and persuasive defenders. At the New York State ratifying convention, which met in June 1788, Hamilton combined the gifts of political theorist and practical politician to lead a reluctant New York into the federal fold.

Hamilton's greatest contribution to American political thought was *The Federalist* (1788), a brilliant defense of the convention's work, which he, John Jay, and James Madison wrote to persuade the people of New York to adopt the proposed constitution. Hamilton wrote more than half of the 85 essays. Some of the issues he discussed at length are no longer important (the dangers of a standing army, for example), but his analysis of a viable federalism as a system in which laws operate directly upon individuals rather than upon states, his exposition of the powers of the presidency, and his arguments for the necessity of judicial review in a federal system remain among the most astute comments on American government.

Hamilton was not an original political thinker of the stature of Hobbes, Locke, Montesquieu, Rousseau, or Hegel. His particular genius lay in the bold and imaginative way in which he adapted and applied the ideas of others to the needs of an infant republic. He had read many of the political philosophers of the eighteenth century, among them Adam Smith, David Hume, and Sir William Blackstone, and he was familiar with the work of such European statesmen as William Pitt and Jacques Necker. But he learned the most from his experience in the American Revolution, the Continental Congress, and the New York legislature, namely, that a strong government is necessary to promote national prosperity and safeguard personal liberty. Like other Federalists, Hamilton believed that liberty must be predicated on order and that a just and enduring government must be one of laws and not of men. Far from subscribing to Thomas Jefferson's dictum that that government is best which governs least, he believed that government to be best which, possessing ample powers, uses them energetically to achieve national goals. In any discussion of the state, his favorite word was "energy." As Clinton Rossiter has remarked, to Hamilton "energy was the essence of good government, impotence the sign of bad: here was one obsessive principle of his political science that set him off sharply from the progressives of his time" (1964, p. 163).

The belief that Hamilton favored a government of the rich, the well-born, and the able, and that he despised democracy, has long been a commonplace of American history. That he wished to win over the wealthy to the support of the Union is indisputable; that the purpose of his policies was to enrich any particular class is debatable. The object of his statecraft, as he said, was ". . . a great Federal Republic, closely linked in the pursuit of a common interest, tranquil and prosperous at home, respectable abroad . . ." (*Papers*, vol. 3, p. 106). That he distrusted democracy is also certain. But by democracy he meant a government that is directly responsive to the peoples' whims or moods, as in ancient Athens or in eighteenth-century New England towns. He was, on the other hand, "affectionately attached to the republican theory" (*Works*, vol. 9, p. 533), by which he meant democracy modified by a system of checks and balances such as those imposed by the U.S. constitution.

**Economic ideas.**  By common consent Hamilton is ranked as the most forceful and influential secretary of the treasury in U.S. history. He was appointed to that post on September 11, 1789, and within the brief span of two and a half years (1790–1792) submitted to Congress a number of reports that are among the greatest state papers in U.S. history. The first and most controversial of these papers was the "First Report on the Public Credit" ([1790], 1934, pp. 1–50), in which he called for the payment in full of the foreign and domestic debt contracted by the Confederation government; for the assumption of the debts incurred by the separate states in the prosecution of the War of Independence; and for a system of finance and taxation adequate to meet these new national obligations. Hamilton's report was based on the assumption that national honor, strength, and prosperity are inseparably connected with the estab-

lishment of sound national credit. After six months of acrimonious debate and a famous compromise in which Hamilton gave his support to a site on the Potomac River as the national capital in exchange for the support of his plan by Thomas Jefferson and James Madison, Hamilton's proposals were adopted in only slightly modified form.

In December 1790, six months after the funding and assumption measures became law, Hamilton submitted to Congress a "Report . . . on a National Bank . . ." ([1790] 1934, pp. 51–95), calling for a great quasi-public institution that would provide a uniform circulating medium for the country, increase its "active wealth," and furnish a safe depository for government funds and a source of government loans in time of national need.

The "Report on Manufactures" ([1791] 1934, pp. 175–276), Hamilton's only major report rejected by Congress, was perhaps his most important state paper and certainly the clearest statement of his economic philosophy. Rejecting the laissez-faire economics of Adam Smith as well as the agrarian philosophy of Thomas Jefferson, he called on the federal government to foster and encourage manufactures. The report was based on Hamilton's interpretation of the stage of economic development which the United States had reached and the measures necessary for further economic growth.

**Administrative activity.**  Hamilton's work as secretary of the treasury was not confined to recommendations for the country's financial and industrial growth. His organization and management of the Treasury Department was a model of efficiency and his administrative theory was, in the words of the leading student of the history of public administration in the United States, "the first systematic exposition of public administration, a contribution which stood alone for generations" (White [1948] 1959, p. 127).

Hamilton's role in the Washington administration was not restricted to fiscal policy. He provided congressional leadership, preparing detailed reports for congressional guidance, drafting legislation, defending his conduct of the treasury, and occasionally preparing speeches for political allies. Nor did he refrain from interfering in the management of other departments. His help was welcomed by his friend Henry Knox, the phlegmatic secretary of war, but resented by his political opponent Thomas Jefferson, the secretary of state. Hamilton, in brief, was the chief policy maker as well as the storm center of the administrations of George Washington.

In the perspective of a century and a half, it may well be that Hamilton's most important contribution to American history was his interpretation of the constitution. To him it was not a mere compact among states but a grant of power to the central government. The powers conferred on the federal government were not to be construed narrowly but interpreted so broadly as to allow the exercise of powers adequate to its needs. That the constitution has been sufficiently flexible to endure for so long is due in no small part to Hamilton's role in making it the charter for a strong national state.

JACOB E. COOKE

[*See also the biographies of* JEFFERSON *and* MADISON.]

WORKS BY HAMILTON

(1788) 1961 HAMILTON, ALEXANDER; MADISON, JAMES; and JAY, JOHN *The Federalist.* Edited with introduction and notes by Jacob E. Cooke. Middletown, Conn.: Wesleyan Univ. Press.

(1790–1792) 1934 *Papers on Public Credit, Commerce and Finance.* Edited by Samuel McKee, with an introduction by Harvey Williams. New York: Columbia Univ. Press. → A paperback edition was published in 1957 by Liberal Arts Press. See especially pages 1–50, "First Report on Public Credit," pages 51–95, "Report on a National Bank," and pages 175–276, "Report on Manufactures."

*The Papers of Alexander Hamilton.* Edited by H. Syrett and Jacob E. Cooke. Vols. 1–11. New York: Columbia Univ. Press, 1961–1966.

*The Works of Alexander Hamilton.* 2d ed., 12 vols. Edited by Henry Cabot Lodge. New York and London: Putnam, 1904. → The standard edition of Hamilton's writings.

SUPPLEMENTARY BIBLIOGRAPHY

HAMILTON, JOHN C. (1857–1864) 1879 *The Life of Alexander Hamilton: A History of the Republic of the United States as Traced in His Writings and Those of His Contemporaries.* 7 vols. Boston: Houghton Mifflin. → Marred by J. C. Hamilton's reverence for his father's memory, but a storehouse of facts relating to Alexander Hamilton's life and times.

MILLER, JOHN C. 1959 *Alexander Hamilton: Portrait in Paradox.* New York: Harper. → The best one-volume work on Hamilton's life. A paperback edition was published in 1964 as *Alexander Hamilton and the Growth of a New Nation.*

MITCHELL, BROADUS 1957–1962 *Alexander Hamilton.* 2 vols. New York: Macmillan. → Volume 1: *Youth to Maturity: 1755–1788.* Volume 2: *The National Adventure: 1788–1804.* The definitive biography.

ROSSITER, CLINTON L. 1964 *Alexander Hamilton and the Constitution.* New York: Harcourt. → An excellent study of Hamilton's political philosophy.

WHITE, LEONARD DUPEE (1948) 1959 *The Federalists: A Study in Administrative History.* New York: Macmillan. → An account of Hamilton's contributions to administrative theory and practice.

# HAMILTON, WALTON H.

Walton Hale Hamilton (1881–1958), economist and lawyer, was born in Madisonville, Tennessee. He was educated at the University of Texas and later taught in the economics department there. He then taught economics at the University of Michigan and the University of Chicago. In 1915 he went to Amherst College and remained at Amherst until 1923. During this period there occurred the celebrated intrafaculty dispute over the resignation of the president of Amherst, Alexander Meiklejohn, who was allegedly compelled to resign because the trustees of Amherst objected to his progressive educational views. Hamilton was the leader of a group among the faculty that protested against what they considered interference by conservative businessmen in the educational policies of the college. Subsequently, the entire group resigned, and Hamilton was immediately appointed to the Brookings School of Economics and Political Science in Washington, D.C. (now the Brookings Institution). He was entirely in sympathy with the liberal economic and political views that prevailed at the Brookings School.

In 1928 Hamilton shifted from teaching economics to teaching law. Although he had no previous legal training, he was selected by Robert Hutchins, then dean of the Yale Law School, as one of a new group of professors who would teach the law as a part of a larger social, political, and economic system. Hamilton remained at Yale for 20 years.

While at Yale, Hamilton also served the federal government. He was one of the brain trusters of Roosevelt's New Deal, and he held important posts in the National Recovery Administration. He worked with the antitrust division of the Department of Justice in connection with the economic problems involved in the administration of the antitrust laws. He served on the staff of the Temporary National Economic Committee, which was appointed by President Roosevelt to study and report on the economic structure of the United States during the depression, especially with regard to the operation of the free competitive market and the sources of its failure to achieve economic equilibrium.

In 1948, Hamilton retired as professor of law at Yale, and at age 67 he began a new career as a practicing lawyer. Joining the newly organized firm of Arnold, Fortas & Porter, he brought to the practice of law and the writing of legal briefs a fresh economic outlook, and he was very successful in actual litigation before courts and administrative bodies.

The dominant theme of Hamilton's academic thought and of his legal arguments was the essential unity of law, economics, political science, and social science. He maintained that all of the social sciences deal with precisely the same problems and that only their points of reference with regard to social phenomena differ. This orientation was most noticeable in Hamilton's contribution to the reform of legal education that was undertaken at Yale.

Hamilton and his colleagues at the Yale Law School, William O. Douglas, Wesley A. Sturges, Charles E. Clark (who succeeded Hutchins as dean), Myres S. McDougal, George H. Dession, Fleming James, Jr., Thurman W. Arnold, and others, criticized the conservative method of legal analysis, epitomized by the Harvard Law School, for its fragmentation of subject matter and its rigid classification and separation of the traditional fields of law—contracts, torts, conflicts of law, etc. Instead, they adopted an entirely new philosophical attitude toward the law, based on the premise that the only laws to have any practical impact on society are the rules of procedure. Procedure, therefore, became the center of the Yale curriculum, and this required a complete reorganization of the so-called substantive law courses.

What was involved here was not a debunking of the law to show that legal principles are simply horses which judges and attorneys ride to get wherever they choose to go; rather, the legal realists at Yale held that reverence for the immutable logic of the substantive law is essential to the maintenance of social institutions. Although the function of this logic is purely symbolic, it has considerable importance in that it is part of the process by which we form images of social institutions. Widely as this approach to the law is accepted today, it was revolutionary when Hamilton and his colleagues first advocated it.

What Hamilton mainly taught at Yale was called "public control of business," which in fact covered a sizable part of public and constitutional law. He had initially tackled law untutored, out of the realization that no one could understand the nation's economy without knowing the legal rules-upon-rules that had made Adam Smith's and Herbert Spencer's theories obsolete, and without an understanding of the ways and workings, the facts and folklore of the U.S. Supreme Court, where so many of the final decisions affecting business, industry, commerce, and agriculture seemed to be made. This concern with the noneconomic factors in economics had as a by-product an important impact on the development of American sociology: Talcott Parsons was a student at Amherst when Hamilton was teaching there; Hamilton's approach aroused his interest in the study of the institutional

bases of economics, which led ultimately to his study of sociology.

Throughout his life Hamilton combined keen observation and commentary on the American political, legal, and economic scene with active participation in the cause of social justice.

THURMAN ARNOLD

[*See also* PUBLIC LAW.]

WORKS BY HAMILTON

(1915) 1925 *Current Economic Problems: A Series of Readings in the Control of Industrial Development.* 3d ed. Univ. of Chicago Press.
1923 HAMILTON, WALTON H.; and MAY, STACY *The Control of Wages.* New York: Doran.
(1925) 1926 HAMILTON, WALTON H.; and WRIGHT, HELEN R. *The Case of Bituminous Coal.* New York: Macmillan.
1932 Institution. Volume 8, pages 84–89 in *Encyclopaedia of the Social Sciences.* New York: Macmillan. → Hamilton contributed 16 other articles to the *Encyclopaedia of the Social Sciences.*
1940 *The Pattern of Competition.* New York: Columbia Univ. Press.
1941 . . . *Patents and Free Enterprise.* U.S. Temporary National Economic Committee, Monograph No. 31. Washington: Government Printing Office.
1957 *The Politics of Industry: Five Lectures Delivered on the William W. Cook Foundation at the University of Michigan, February–March, 1955.* New York: Knopf.

# HAMMOND, J. L. and BARBARA

John Lawrence le Breton Hammond (1872–1949) was the son of a Yorkshire clergyman; Lucy Barbara Bradby (1873–1961), the daughter of the headmaster of Haileybury School. Both took greats at Oxford—Barbara with distinction—and it was by standards derived from Greece and Rome that they passed judgment on later times. When they married in 1901 Hammond was already deeply involved in Liberal journalism; he published a study of the political career of Charles James Fox (1903) and for several years edited the *Speaker,* a weekly journal that later became the *Nation.* But from 1907, when he was appointed secretary to the Civil Service Commission, he gave his spare time to collaboration with Barbara. She had become deeply involved in research in public and private archives; it was his role to transmute her findings into vivid and arresting prose. In 1933 Oxford gave recognition to the parity of their contribution by conferring on each an honorary D.LITT.

Their most widely read books, *The Village Labourer* (1911), *The Town Labourer* (1917), and

*The Skilled Labourer* (1919), treat the period from the accession of George III to the first Reform Act and consist primarily of "a discussion of the lines on which Parliament regulated the lives and fortunes of a class that had no voice in its own destinies" ([1911] 1948, Preface). These were path-breaking works, and, as is usual with such, it is not difficult to point to errors of fact and emphasis. It is now generally agreed that the enclosure of land was carried out less ruthlessly than they thought. Their use of the report of Sadler's Committee of 1832 on the employment of children was uncritical. Their concentration on the records of the Home Office led them to present the abnormal cases brought to the notice of this department as though they were typical. But few historians would deny that the dismal account of class struggles presented in this trilogy is substantially accurate. In 1923 came their sympathetic, though critical, biography of Lord Shaftesbury (1923), to be followed two years later by an admirable background study, *The Rise of Modern Industry* (1925). In *The Age of the Chartists; 1832–1854* (1930), they extended their inquiries to a later generation in which repeal of the Corn Laws, and the Ten Hours Act of 1847, the Public Health Act of 1848, and other measures reflected a growing sensitivity of the wealthier classes to the needs of the poor and the beginnings of what the Hammonds called "common enjoyment." In none of these works did the authors pay much attention to strictly economic or demographic trends. But, at a time when the "depersonalization of history" has gone quite far enough, it is worth-while to turn again to books which are emphatically about people and in which moral judgments are freely and forcefully expressed.

Lawrence Hammond was special correspondent of the *Manchester Guardian* at the Paris Peace Conference in 1919 and the Conference on Ireland in 1921. He continued for the rest of his life to contribute articles, reviews, and occasional editorials to the paper and in World War II became a permanent member of its staff. His later books are all biographical. *James Stansfeld: A Victorian Champion of Sex Equality* (1932) was written jointly with Barbara; but *C. P. Scott of the Manchester Guardian* (1934) and *Gladstone and the Irish Nation* (1938)—the greatest, if least known, of his works—are from his pen alone. They show his liberalism, insight, and command of words.

After his death in 1949, Barbara continued to follow her earlier interests: she lived to the age of 88, leaving an almost completed (but as yet unpublished) book on the enclosure of commons in

the nineteenth century. The Hammonds were modest about their own achievements and generous toward opponents. Their books had wide popular appeal and, apart from quickening interest in the social life of the past, did much to shape contemporary opinion and policy.

T. S. Ashton

WORKS BY THE HAMMONDS

1903    Hammond, J. L. *Charles James Fox: A Political Study.* London: Methuen.
(1911) 1948    *The Village Labourer.* London: Longmans. → First published as *The Village Labourer; 1760–1832: A Study in the Government of England Before the Reform Bill.*
(1917) 1949    *The Town Labourer; 1760–1832: The New Civilisation.* London: Longmans.
(1919) 1927    *The Skilled Labourer: 1760–1832.* 2d ed. London: Longmans.
(1923) 1924    *Lord Shaftesbury.* 2d ed. New York: Harcourt.
(1925) 1947    *The Rise of Modern Industry.* 7th ed. London: Methuen.
(1930) 1962    *The Age of the Chartists; 1832–1854: A Study of Discontent.* Hamden, Conn.: Shoe String Press.
1932    *James Stansfeld: A Victorian Champion of Sex Equality.* London: Longmans.
1934    Hammond, J. L. *C. P. Scott of the Manchester Guardian.* London: Bell.
(1938) 1964    Hammond, J. L. *Gladstone and the Irish Nation.* 2d ed. Hamden, Conn.: Shoe String Press.

SUPPLEMENTARY BIBLIOGRAPHY

Tawney, Richard H.    1960    J. L. Hammond: 1872–1949. British Academy, London, *Proceedings* 46:267–294. → Contains a bibliography of the Hammonds' works on pages 293–294.

# HANKINS, FRANK H.

Frank Hamilton Hankins, an American sociologist, devoted special attention to the role of biological factors in human traits and in social behavior. He was born in Wilshire, Ohio, in 1877 and received his bachelor's degree from Baker University in Baldwin, Kansas, in 1901 and his PH.D. from Columbia University in 1908. In 1964 Clark University awarded him an honorary degree. Most of his academic career was spent at Clark, from 1906 to 1907 and again from 1908 to 1922, and at Smith College, from 1922 until 1946.

Hankins was a philosophical realist, tough-minded, and rigorously scientific. He was most deeply influenced in philosophy and logic by John Stuart Mill; in his general sociological thinking by Herbert Spencer, Lester F. Ward, William Graham Sumner, and Franklin H. Giddings; and in the quantitative approach to social problems by Adolphe

Quetelet, about whom he wrote his doctoral dissertation, Francis Galton, Karl Pearson, and Henry L. Moore, who in turn had studied under Benini in Italy. To be sure, although Hankins himself was a talented statistician, he was caustically skeptical of the assumptions and methods of the extreme quantitative approach of some of his sociological colleagues: he characterized their work as "merely sinking postholes here and there in the vast field of social phenomena."

He was a strict scientific determinist and conceived all phenomena, personal and social, as undergoing endless change and rearrangement in adjustment to environmental conditions. Thus, a particular personality was for Hankins the product of an individual's genetic constitution and his molding experiences. The self so formed has to express itself, and this self-expression is the sociological equivalent of the traditional metaphysical freedom of the will. By his reason and by the acquisition of scientific methods man can discover causal sequences, not only in the physical world but also in the psychosocial and cultural realms, and he can learn to adjust to these sequences and even to modify or direct them. Yet Hankins had no utopian illusions; he doubted that the social sciences could achieve control of change comparable to that of the physical sciences. Whereas the laws of physical science do not vary with time and place, the causes of cultural sequences differ from one era to another, even in the same society. Cultural phenomena emerge in what are often new causal combinations, and predictability is therefore severely limited. Hankins agreed with Spencer that efforts to control political and economic life more often than not produce unexpected results.

In the realm of social institutions, Hankins' determinism was economic: he saw successive political theories as rationalizations of new class or sectional interests and new religious doctrines as sanctions of new economic modes. He believed that cultural change is the cumulative product of slow alterations in the everyday activities of increasing proportions of the populations—changes in daily routine that carry with them modifications of folkways, mores, techniques, and political policies and that eventuate in new values and new ideologies.

Deeply influenced as he was by the work of Galton and Pearson, Hankins was perennially concerned with the effect of such selective processes as war, celibacy, persecution, urbanization, and education on the quantity and quality of the population, and with the consequences of demographic changes on social life. He regarded population pressure as an important factor in group hostilities, and he believed uncontrolled differential fertility of the social classes to be dysgenic: modern medicine and hygiene, combined with humanitarian views, made it possible for people with hereditary deficiencies to bear children and so to imperil racial soundness and human well-being. He believed genetically above-average parents are most likely to produce children who are morally superior and capable of greater success in a competitive social order.

Hankins did of course recognize the moral imperative of a humanitarian perspective and rejected any scheme for the ruthless elimination of the unfit. He did not believe that the speedy adoption of positive eugenic measures was likely and therefore favored the active spreading of information about contraception, of facilities that would give the less favored strata of the population access to contraceptive equipment, and of realistic eugenic instruction for all. He doubted on both historical and genetic grounds the validity of the assumption that the number of potential men of genius is constant in any given population at all times. However, further advances in the science of human genetics may conceivably enable man not only to modify human nature in general but also to increase the number of potential geniuses, to discover them early in life, and to develop their powers.

These concerns naturally led Hankins to consider the role of heredity and inborn ability in relation to social leadership and to question the assumptions of egalitarian democracy. He was highly critical of egalitarian doctrine, holding that for "democratic society . . . to continue in a sound, healthy condition, it must concern itself quite as much, if not more, with the hereditary constitution of its people as with efforts at a further equalization of material conditions" (1923, p. 411). Any realistic approach, he thought, must take the form of effective birth control policies, which will, in a quantitative sense, keep the number of people down to a level where their material needs can be supplied and, in the qualitative realm, assure an increase in the number of the superior types required to deal with the increasingly difficult problems of our era. Thus, in order to survive, democracy must both accept hereditary differentiation in ability and, by education and other means, mitigate and undermine hereditary stratification in society. If the channels between the different strata are kept as wide-open as possible, the basic fact of individual differences may be harmonized with democratic ideology.

Hankins was deeply interested in the problem of race and the impact of racial dogmas on political theories. His chapter "Race as a Factor in Political Theory" (1924) remains the most authoritative exposition and appraisal of the subject. In his book, *The Racial Basis of Civilization* (1926*a*), he took a middle ground between the fervid exponents of racial superiority and racial purity and the followers of Franz Boas and others who contended that there is no real validity in the notion of racial differences and hence, scientifically, no race problem. Hankins believed that all nations and nationalities, although greatly mixed racially through conquest and immigration, ultimately acquire a sense of racial solidarity and pride of both race and culture. He maintained that race crossing is a source of racial soundness and strength and that the historical record shows that periods of high civilization have been preceded by an extensive mingling of racial stocks. While he doubted, in principle, that all racial stocks have the same capacity for cultural achievement, since this would mean that they all had had identical mutational and selective processes, he recognized that actual racial superiority or inferiority cannot be proved or disproved because race mixture is so extensive and cultural environments are so different.

Hankins' place in American sociology is secure. His concern with the problem of population quantity was shared by his professional colleagues, and he stood out among them by stressing the important issue of population quality. His work on the race issue was a sane and valuable contribution. Despite the fact that most of his students were undergraduates, a surprisingly large number of them became professional sociologists as a result of his influence, and some of them, like Howard Odum, Clifford Kirkpatrick, and Franklin Frazier, became well-known in the field. The esteem in which he was held by his fellow sociologists is evident from the fact that he was elected first president of the Eastern Sociological Society in 1930, president of the American Sociological Society in 1938, and president of the Population Association of America in 1945. Hankins' most important editorial contribution in the sociological field was to act, from 1936 to 1937, as the first editor-in-chief of the *American Sociological Review*, the official journal of the American Sociological Society (now Association).

HARRY ELMER BARNES

[*For the historical context of Hankins' work, see* CREATIVITY, *article on* GENIUS AND ABILITY; RACE; *and the biographies of* BENINI; GALTON; GIDDINGS; MILL; MOORE, HENRY L.; PEARSON; SPENCER; SUMNER; WARD, LESTER F.]

WORKS BY HANKINS

1908    *Adolphe Quetelet as Statistician.* New York: Longmans.
1922    Individual Differences and Their Significance for Social Theory. American Sociological Society, *Publications* 17:27–39.
1923    Individual Differences and Democratic Theory. *Political Science Quarterly* 38:388–412.
1924    Race as a Factor in Political Theory. Pages 508–548 in Charles E. Merriam and Harry E. Barnes (editors), *A History of Political Theories: Recent Times.* New York: Macmillan.
1925*a*    Individual Freedom With Some Sociological Implications of Determinism. *Journal of Philosophy* 22:617–634.
1925*b*    Sociology. Pages 255–332 in Harry E. Barnes (editor), *The History and Prospects of the Social Sciences.* New York: Knopf.
1926*a*    *The Racial Basis of Civilization: A Critique of the Nordic Doctrine.* New York: Knopf.
1926*b*    Humanitarianism in the Light of Biology. *American Review* 4:52–60.
(1927) 1931    Society and Its Biological Equipment. Book 2, part 2, pages 307–394 in Jerome Davis and Harry E. Barnes (editors), *An Introduction to Sociology.* Boston: Heath.
1928*a*    Organic Plasticity Versus Organic Responsiveness in the Development of the Personality. American Sociological Society, *Publications* 22:43–51.
(1928*b*) 1935    *An Introduction to the Study of Society.* Rev. ed. New York: Macmillan.
1931*a*    Charles Robert Darwin. Volume 5, pages 4–5 in *Encyclopaedia of the Social Sciences.* New York: Macmillan.
1931*b*    Divorce. Volume 5, pages 177–184 in *Encyclopaedia of the Social Sciences.* New York: Macmillan.
1931*c*    The Prospects of the Social Sciences. Pages 27–53 in Edward M. East (editor), *Biology in Human Affairs.* New York: McGraw-Hill.
1933    Is the Differential Fertility of the Social Classes Selective? *Social Forces* 12:33–39.
1935    Quetelet's Average Man in Modern Scientific Research. Institut de Sociologie Solvay, *Revue* 15:577–586.
1936    Sociology and Social Guidance. *American Sociological Review* 1, no. 1:33–37.
1938    Freedom of Speech and Freedom of Teaching. American Association of University Professors, *Bulletin* 24, no. 6:497–508.
1939    Social Science and Social Action. *American Sociological Review* 4:1–15.
1940    Demographic and Biological Contributions to Sociological Principles. Part 4, pages 279–325 in Harry E. Barnes et al. (editors), *Contemporary Social Theory.* New York: Appleton.
1950    Underdeveloped Areas With Special Reference to Population Problems. *International Social Science Bulletin* 2:307–316.
1956    A Forty-year Perspective. *Sociology and Social Research* 40:391–398.

## HANSEN, ALVIN

Alvin Hansen's place in the history of economic thought and the importance of his role as an economic adviser are undisputed. By propagating and developing the ideas formulated by Keynes, Hansen did more to effect the Keynesian revolution than any other American economist. His books are widely read in the United States and abroad; his *Guide to Keynes* (1953), for example, was translated into Spanish, Japanese, Italian, French, Hindi, and Korean. Most of his other books have also been widely translated.

Born in 1887 in South Dakota of Scandinavian parentage, Hansen achieved academic eminence despite the handicap of having received his education at small, impoverished Yankton College. For some years he worked as a schoolteacher, principal, and school superintendent. Then he went for graduate training to the University of Wisconsin, where he also began teaching. From Wisconsin he moved to Brown and then to the University of Minnesota before going to Harvard in 1937 as the Lucius N. Littauer professor of political economy. He spent almost twenty years as an economist in Cambridge. After retirement he yielded to demands to serve as a visiting professor at various institutions, including the University of Bombay, Yale, Smith, Vassar, Michigan State, Haverford, and Wesleyan.

Hansen excelled as a teacher. A Harvard seminar in fiscal policy, which he shared with John H. Williams, became one of the most famous in the country. Week after week, for almost twenty years, outstanding scholars and public servants attended this seminar. The gifts of Hansen and Williams were dissimilar but complementary. Williams was a cautious theorist and rather critical of many of Keynes's ideas, but open-minded and far from dogmatic either in criticism or advocacy and acute in analyzing issues. Hansen, too, could be critical, but his dominant attitude was one of enthusiasm for the New Economics. The interplay between Williams' skepticism and Hansen's acceptance provided just the right atmosphere for the exploration and examination of the new ideas. Hansen's zest was contagious: he not only inspired his students; there were few visitors who came away from these seminars uninfluenced. The seminars served as a platform for debates among the participants, whether regular members, other Harvard colleagues, or guests. Faculty members who were too sensitive to indulge in public debates with their peers soon learned to stay away. It is a tribute both to Williams and Hansen that their debates never led to personal differences.

Although Hansen's influence is most effectively conveyed by cataloguing his students, it is not possible here to list the hundreds of students he inspired and the numerous doctoral dissertations he supervised. His former students are members of virtually every distinguished department of economics, for example, the departments at the Massachusetts Institute of Technology, Yale, Harvard, the University of California, Stanford, the University of Chicago, Princeton, and Cambridge, England.

There was a reciprocal exchange of ideas between Hansen and his students. His influence is clearly evident in *An Economic Program for American Democracy* (1938), a prescient document signed by R. V. Gilbert and six other young Harvard and Tufts economists. Hansen, in turn, was influenced by the young economists who wrote the book. At age 50, he had a receptivity to new ideas that was quite remarkable.

It is likely that no American economist of the twentieth century has had more influence on economists in the government than Hansen. As early as 1933–1934 he served as director of research and secretary of the important Committee of Inquiry on National Policy in International Economic Relations. In the years when Cordell Hull's reciprocal trade agreements were first being established, Hansen served as an aide to the State Department; this was a time when economists were rare indeed in the department. A few years later, he was the economic adviser to the prairie provinces before the Canadian Royal Commission on Dominion–Provincial Relations. At the same time, 1937–1938, he became a member of the Advisory Council on Social Security. Again, in 1941–1943, he had the privilege of being the chairman of the United States–Canadian Joint Economic Committee. One of his most important assignments was that of special economic adviser to the Federal Reserve Board, a post which he held from 1940 to 1945.

Before 1933 Hansen had been somewhat of a deflationist and a critic of those who questioned Say's law, which assumes that what is produced will be taken off the market. Keynes was the boldest critic of Say's law: he asserted that investment may not equal the gap between what the economy is capable of producing and what people wish to consume. Hence his great emphasis on investment and the means of stimulating it. In fact, Keynes built a theory of income formation on the basis of a relatively stable consumption function and multiplier.

Hansen was always capable of changing his mind, and in a review of Keynes's *General Theory* (1936) he was generally favorable to Keynes's views. But neither Hansen nor, very likely, any other economist in the United States at that time anticipated the tremendous impact the *General Theory* was to have. (In part, its many obscurities concealed the cogency of its argument.) Hansen appreciated Keynes's intellectual adventurousness:

"We are living in a time when economics stands in danger of a sterile orthodoxy. The book under review warns us once again, in a provocative manner, of the danger of reasoning based on assumptions which no longer fit the facts of economic life . . ." (1936, p. 686). But Hansen was clearly at odds with Keynes on some issues. Keynes had urged a reduction of the rate of interest as a means of stimulating investment, since the amount of investment depends upon the relation of the rate of interest and the marginal efficiency of capital, although his stress on manipulation of the interest rate was not nearly so great in the *General Theory* as it had been in his earlier *Treatise on Money*. Hansen was not as enthusiastic as Keynes about interest rate policy, cautioning that efforts at general monetary control had already revealed the weakness of this method.

Both in the *Treatise on Money* and in the *General Theory*, Keynes had shown an awareness of the need for adequate investment and of the dependence of the amount of investment on the opportunity for investment. Hansen was the principal architect of a theory of stagnation, built on this theme of Keynes and concerned with the circumstances of insufficiency of demand. Hansen agreed with Keynes that the business cycle reflects the variations in the marginal efficiency of capital and that the impact of secular trends is more disrupting than that of the cycle. He wrote in 1938 that "not every period can be characterized as a kind of new industrial revolution. . . . Add to this the wholly new fact of a rapidly approaching cessation of population growth. Let the perennial optimist reflect on the enormous masses of capital that found investment outlets during the nineteenth century for no other reason than that the population of England quadrupled, that of Europe trebled, while that of the United States increased fifteen-fold. For these and other reasons we shall do well to ponder deeply the problem of . . . secular stagnation" (1938a, pp. 477–478).

Time and again, and especially in the 1930s, Hansen returned to the theme of the insufficiency of demand and the method of treating it. One of his great contributions was to establish and popularize the idea that compensatory fiscal policy is the most powerful means of maintaining the right level of aggregate demand. One cause of the unsatisfactory conditions of the 1930s, he believed, was the accumulation of reserves in the Old Age Insurance Fund. This meant that purchasing power was being hoarded. The recovery of the 1930s was, according to Hansen's theory, a consumption recovery generated by a $4,000 million expansion in consumer installment credit and by $14,000 million of federal expenditures for recovery and relief; and it vanished when these two stimuli were played out. Hansen was among the earliest to develop a pump-priming policy to deal with recessions.

In the 1930s Hansen's stagnation theory attracted much attention, but in the prosperous 1940s and 1950s its validity was doubted and even ridiculed. Detractors of the theory did not take into account, however, the extent to which World War II created a pent-up and temporarily sustained demand, which Hansen *had* predicted but which he did not expect to be permanent. By the late 1950s Hansen appeared to be vindicated: demand was insufficient to curb the rise of unemployment that resulted from productivity gains and the inflow of new entrants into the labor market. (This influx rises with improved conditions and requires an even larger increase in output—and consequently an increased demand—to prevent rising unemployment.) And it was the expansion of government, which Hansen had advocated and which his critics had considered absurd, that served to prevent the stagnation that Hansen had warned against. Ironically, the same critics who had denied that the slowing of population growth could depress business were predicting booms for the 1960s as the result of the acceleration of population growth.

In the 1930s Hansen anticipated some of the problems that were to confront the United States in the 1960s (see 1938b, pp. 303–318). Unlike Keynes, he was not inclined to assume that if general demand is adequate, most of our problems will be solved. He found that between 1870 and 1930 the rise in the white-collar group was six times as large as that of other classes and that the gains of the managerial and professional classes had also been large. He related this relative growth to the large amount of unemployment among unskilled workers and concluded that these workers needed more education. He was well aware that although adequacy of demand is crucial, there are some pockets of unemployment that must be treated directly, for example, the mining areas and the textile towns.

Keynes's theory was broadly conceived and left much for others to do. He was not concerned about the consequences of a rising national debt, and Hansen was able to show that the elimination of the national debt would raise more problems than it would solve. Interested in the consumption function, Keynes was aware of the relation of consumption to tax structure; but it was Hansen, in his *State and Local Finance in the National Economy* (Hansen & Perloff 1944), who revealed the perversity of modern state and local tax systems and spelled out the required tax and spending policies for periods of boom and depression. In this book Hansen revealed that a basic inadequacy of fiscal policy in the 1930s was the lack of control over state and local government contributions to total spending. In periods of boom these governments, with their slight dependence on income taxes, were unable to achieve the automatic rise of tax receipts that would help contain the boom, while in a period of depression they aggravated the economic situation and discouraged consumption when they compensated for the declining yield of direct taxes by an increasing recourse to consumption taxes.

Today there is wide acceptance of views that were generally rejected before Keynes's *General Theory* was published—witness the 1964 federal tax cut. Among the innovations in economic thinking that owe much to Hansen's influence are the following: an appreciation of the importance of keeping interest rates low enough vis-à-vis the marginal efficiency of capital to assure adequate investment; an awareness that the level of investment depends not only on interest rates and the marginal efficiency of capital but also on the relation of consumption and income, and that without adequate consumption investment outlets will soon dry up; the concept of an equilibrium in modern economies at a point far below full employment, with full employment only a "limiting point of the whole range of possible positions of equilibrium"; a policy of national debt management that does not only strive to keep interest costs at a minimum but also considers the effects on the economy of issuing securities when rates are low and money is being created to stimulate the private economy. Hansen deserves as much credit for these advances as any American economist. He helped clothe the Keynesian skeleton, and his simple, clear presentation, in the classroom and out, won many adherents to the New Economics.

Hansen did not, however, limit his work to the elaboration of Keynesian economics. He had, for example, much to say about international monetary policy, and he contributed to the creation of the International Monetary Fund. Yet even in this area he was influenced by Keynes (1944), asserting that international disequilibrium prevails even if gold or foreign exchange reserves are not being reduced, so long as the domestic restraints which are used to conserve reserves bring about unemployment. Adequacy of demand is crucial. Hence the need to keep international reserves large enough so that temporary imbalance can be treated, thus leaving enough time to deal with structural change.

As an economic analyst, also, Hansen made significant contributions. Here are but a few examples: (1) The familiar diagram with the marginal cost curve cutting up through the unit cost curve at its bottom seems to have been first presented by Hansen in the 1920s. (2) About 1930, when the Anglo-Saxon literature stressed monetary factors in cycles, Hansen (with D. H. Robertson) was one of the few to stress real fluctuations in exogenous investment opportunities, in the fashion of Marx, Tugan-Baranovskii, Spiethoff, Cassel, Schumpeter, and other Continental writers. (3) Hansen pioneered accelerator–multiplier models, and he and Keynes stressed the importance for investment of steady income growth. (4) He and some of his students were among the independent discoverers of the balanced-budget multiplier theorem. Associated with Hansen in this discovery were such economists as William A. Salant, Paul A. Samuelson, Harold Somers, and Henry C. Wallich, and the theorem was also discovered in Denmark by J. Galting and in the United Kingdom by Keynes and N. Kaldor. (5) Independently of J. K. Galbraith, Hansen emphasized the important social utility at the margin of the public sector as against the private sector.

The diversity and the importance of Hansen's contributions to the theory and application of economics place him among the great economists of recent times.

SEYMOUR E. HARRIS

[*For the historical context of Hansen's work, see the biography of* KEYNES, JOHN MAYNARD. *For discussion of the subsequent development of his ideas, see* FISCAL POLICY.]

### WORKS BY HANSEN

1921 *Cycles of Prosperity and Depression in the United States, Great Britain and Germany: A Study of Monthly Data 1902–1908.* University of Wisconsin Studies in the Social Sciences and History, No. 5. Madison: Univ. of Wisconsin Press.

1927 *Business-cycle Theory: Its Development and Present Status.* Boston: Ginn.

1932 *Economic Stabilization in an Unbalanced World.* New York: Harcourt.

1936 Mr. Keynes on Underemployment Equilibrium. *Journal of Political Economy* 44:667–686.

1938a The Consequences of Reducing Expenditures. Academy of Political Science, *Proceedings* 17:466–478.

1938b *Full Recovery or Stagnation?* New York: Norton. → See especially pages 303–318 on "Investment Outlets and Secular Stagnation."

1941 *Fiscal Policy and Business Cycles.* New York: Norton.

1944 A Brief Note on "Fundamental Disequilibrium." *Review of Economics and Statistics* 26:182–184.

1944 HANSEN, ALVIN H.; and PERLOFF, HARVEY S. *State and Local Finance in the National Economy.* New York: Norton.

1945  *America's Role in the World Economy.* New York: Norton.

1947  *Economic Policy and Full Employment.* New York and London: McGraw-Hill.

1947  HANSEN, ALVIN H.; and SAMUELSON, PAUL A. *Economic Analysis of Guaranteed Wages.* U.S. Bureau of Labor Statistics, Bulletin No. 907. Washington: Government Printing Office.

1949  *Monetary Theory and Fiscal Policy.* New York: McGraw-Hill.

(1951) 1964  *Business Cycles and National Income.* Enl. ed. New York: Norton.

1953  *A Guide to Keynes.* New York: McGraw-Hill.

1957  *The American Economy.* New York: McGraw-Hill.

1960  *Economic Issues of the 1960s.* New York: McGraw-Hill.

1965  *The Dollar and the International Monetary System.* New York: McGraw-Hill.

SUPPLEMENTARY BIBLIOGRAPHY

*An Economic Program for American Democracy,* by Seven Harvard and Tufts Economists. 1938  New York: Vanguard.

# HARRINGTON, JAMES

James Harrington (1611–1677), English political theorist, was the oldest son and heir of Sir Sapcotes Harrington, a member of an aristocratic family that had risen to eminence under the Tudors. Orphaned at an early age, he enjoyed throughout his life the means to live as he pleased. After a brief stay in Oxford, where he perfected his knowledge of languages, he traveled extensively on the Continent. There he befriended the exiled elector palatine and professed a militant Protestantism. By the time he returned to England in 1635 he was a firm republican. He was, however, also deeply attached to Charles I and remained with him to the end. Torn by such a conflict between personal friendship and political conviction, he took no direct part in the Civil War. After the execution of the king he devoted himself entirely to his studies. The product of his retirement was *The Commonwealth of Oceana*, a constitutional blueprint. Published in 1656 after some opposition by Cromwell, it remained Harrington's only book. All his other writings are explanations of its main points or answers to its critics. His public life was limited to publishing and debating his proposals for a constitution. After the Restoration he was put in prison, where his health, mental as well as physical, was utterly destroyed. He died without ever recovering his mental health.

It was perhaps Harrington's own social position that made him a decidedly aristocratic republican: no society, he felt, can do without the military and political talents of the nobility. The greatest influence upon his thinking was not personal experience, however, but the works of the "masters of ancient prudence"—Plato's *Laws*, Aristotle's *Politics*, Polybius' *Histories*, and the works of their only heir, Machiavelli. In stark contrast to these sources of wisdom, he saw the "modern prudence" of feudal and absolutist theories as nothing but a series of errors. Among his contemporaries only Hobbes won his grudging approval. For although he despised Hobbes's reasoning "by geometry" and his monarchical ideas, he shared with Hobbes a distaste for religious warfare. Harrington's solution to the problem of religious strife was to establish a state church that would represent "the public conscience" without limiting toleration, leaving theological disputes to the universities.

Political theory, according to Harrington, has to be historical, and he based his own ideas on a theory of historical development. As he saw it, the "Gothick balance," or feudalism, had come to an end. It had never been a stable order, but a tug of war between the nobility and the kings, who had uneasily shared both property and power. In England this order had come to an end when Tudor legislation reduced the nobility and put the balance of property into the hands of the people. This had made the old order impossible and had brought about the Civil War. The same impersonal forces, moreover, were at work in the revolutions in Europe as well, and this linking together of all the upheavals of the age was one of Harrington's most original perceptions.

Government is, in Harrington's view, a superstructure based on property. Ruling requires armies and whoever feeds the soldiers will thereby rule. Hence, if the balance of property is in the hands of the people, stability requires a republican form of government, and stability is the great end of political organization.

Harrington saw his own task as that of revealing to the people of England the necessities of their situation and of suggesting to them the appropriate political institutions. This was "political anatomy," which he considered a science analogous to that of William Harvey. The analogy implies that attention to details, to every artery of the body politic, is necessary, and such was the approach he used. His suggestion for producing the necessary order in England was a bicameral legislature, indirectly elected by all "who lived off their own," by secret ballot, with rotation in office, and a citizen army to defend the new society. Eternal stability was to be ensured by an agrarian law that would permanently limit the amount of property any one person might own. For changes in the balance of ownership of land had always been the source of strife and had caused the decline of ancient and modern republics.

While Harrington's influence upon his contemporaries was limited, he enjoyed a great reputation in eighteenth-century America. Constitution makers have continued to admire him, since he was the very epitome of the constitutional engineer. In recent years his contribution to social history has become the subject of debate. Since Eduard Bernstein, many Marxist historians have regarded Harrington as a precursor of dialectical materialism. They have found evidence in his ideas for the theory that the Civil War in seventeenth-century England was a bourgeois revolution caused by the "rise of the gentry." Against this view, it has been said that the gentry was a declining class, in no sense bourgeois, and that Harrington used his political fantasy to justify its power. All these theories tend to underestimate his passionate classicism. Harrington avowedly looked to the remote past to find guidance for a desirable future. From Polybius he learned that deliberately planned constitutions are more likely to endure than those that develop haphazardly. From him, too, he took the theory of the inevitable cycle of decline that all the "pure," unbalanced forms of government—monarchy, aristocracy, and democracy—must suffer. However, while Polybius thought of these constitutions entirely in terms of divisions of governmental power, Harrington held that they depend upon the distribution, or "balance," of landed property. If stability was his end, no less than Polybius', he did not stop with the latter's theory of a mixed constitution, in which democratic, aristocratic, and monarchical elements are poised in such a way as to prevent any changes in the political order. Instead Harrington proposed his agrarian law as the means of achieving stability: its enactment would permit a "natural" aristocracy to form a deliberative assembly and the people to be represented in a deciding body. This proposal was, indeed, his own contribution to constitutional theory. His ideas of historical change, however, were derivative, as he was perfectly happy to admit—witness his endless tributes to "ancient prudence." The necessity for a return to the classical past both in theory and in practice was not, in his view, a historical inevitability, but the sole means by which England might learn to become stable and powerful.

JUDITH N. SHKLAR

[*For the historical context of Harrington's work, see* CONSTITUTIONS AND CONSTITUTIONALISM; UTOPIANISM; *and the biographies of* ARISTOTLE; HOBBES; MACHIAVELLI; PLATO. *For discussion of the subsequent development of his ideas, see the biography of* BERNSTEIN.]

WORKS BY HARRINGTON

(1656) 1924 *The Commonwealth of Oceana*. Edited by S. B. Liljegren. Heidelberg: Winter.
(1700) 1963 *The Oceana of James Harrington, and His Other Works*. Edited by John Toland. Aalen (Germany): Scientia.
1955 *Political Writings: Representative Selections*. Edited with an introduction by Charles Blitzer. New York: Liberal Arts Press.

SUPPLEMENTARY BIBLIOGRAPHY

BERNSTEIN, EDUARD (1908) 1963 *Cromwell and Communism: Socialism and Democracy in the Great English Revolution*. New York: Kelley. → First published in German.
BLITZER, CHARLES 1960 *An Immortal Commonwealth: The Political Thought of James Harrington*. New Haven: Yale Univ. Press.
DWIGHT, THEODORE W. 1887 James Harrington and His Influence Upon American Political Institutions and Political Thought. *Political Science Quarterly* 2:1–44.
FINK, ZERA S. (1945) 1962 *The Classical Republicans: An Essay in the Recovery of a Pattern of Thought in Seventeenth Century England*. 2d ed. Evanston, Ill.: Northwestern Univ. Press.
GOOCH, GEORGE P.; and LASKI, HAROLD L. (1898) 1954 *English Democratic Ideas in the Seventeenth Century*. Cambridge Univ. Press. → First published as *The History of English Democratic Ideas in the Seventeenth Century*, by George P. Gooch.
GREENLEAF, W. H. 1964 *Order, Empiricism and Politics: Two Traditions of English Political Thought, 1500–1700*. Oxford Univ. Press.
KOEBNER, RICHARD 1927–1928 Die Geschichtslehre James Harringtons. Volume 3, pages 4–21 in *Geist und Gesellschaft: Kurt Breysig zu seinem sechzigsten Geburtstage*. Breslau: Marcus.
MACPHERSON, CRAWFORD B. 1962 *The Political Theory of Possessive Individualism: Hobbes to Locke*. Oxford: Clarendon.
POCOCK, JOHN G. A. 1957 *The Ancient Constitution and the Feudal Law: A Study of English Historical Thought in the Seventeenth Century*. Cambridge Univ. Press.
POLIN, RAYMOND 1952 Économique et politique au XVIIᵉ siècle: L'Oceana de James Harrington. *Revue française de science politique* 2:24–41.
RAAB, FELIX 1964 *The English Face of Machiavelli: A Changing Interpretation, 1500–1700*. With a foreword by Hugh Trevor-Roper. London: Routledge.
RUSSELL SMITH, HUGH F. 1914 *Harrington and His Oceana: A Study of a Seventeenth Century Utopia and Its Influence in America*. Cambridge Univ. Press.
SHKLAR, JUDITH 1959 Ideology Hunting: The Case of James Harrington. *American Political Science Review* 53:662–692.
TAWNEY, RICHARD H. 1941 Harrington's Interpretation of His Age. British Academy, *Proceedings* 27:199–223.
TREVOR-ROPER, H. R. 1953 *The Gentry: 1540–1640*. Economic History Review, Supplement 1. Cambridge Univ. Press.

# HARTLEY, DAVID

David Hartley (1705–1757), called the father of British psychology, was indeed the first to use the word "psychology" in its modern sense. He attempted a comprehensive interpretation of psychological phenomena based on the observation of behavior, bearing in mind its physiological substrate. His *Observations on Man: His Frame, His Duty and His Expectations* (1749) sets out a philosophy of human life in terms of a special theory of association. It is as the first comprehensive "associationist" that Hartley is chiefly remembered in histories of philosophy and psychology. But he also deserves study for his general method and his grasp of the special complexities involved in any attempt to elucidate mental processes by reference to physiological mechanisms.

Hartley's theory of association is derived from Locke's *Essay Concerning Human Understanding* (1690) and John Gay's preface to King's *Essay on the Origin of Evil* (King 1702). Parallel to the formulation in terms of the association of ideas and equally important is his physiological theory. This avowedly hypothetical physiology is based on Newton's suggestion that the sensation of seeing comes from "vibrations, being propagated along the solid Fibres of the optic Nerves into the Brain. . . . For because dense Bodies conserve their heat a long time . . . the Vibrations of their parts are of a lasting nature, and therefore may be propagated along solid Fibres of uniform dense Matter to a great distance, for conveying into the Brain the impressions made upon all the Organs of sense" (Newton [1704] 1952, Query 12, p. 345). Hartley was thus among those who denied the view, then commonly held, that the nerve fibers are hollow and allow the transmission of influence by flow of animal spirits. He thought such vibrations might underlie the transmission of all sensory and motor messages to and from the brain and considered how the resulting cerebral activity might represent the whole variety of human experience. He supposed that all coding and decoding of both sensations and ideas take place within the "medullary substance" of the brain—that is, the white matter —and that "Vibratiuncles"—miniature vibrations that correspond to the incoming vibrations of sensation—are generated and persist there, giving rise, by combination and contiguous association, to memory and ideas. He illustrated and tried to test these suppositions against his own observations of human and animal behavior, ranging from "automatic actions" (that is, reflexes) such as respiration and digestion to such "ideas of intellect" as "theopathy."

For this ambitious and possibly premature undertaking, Hartley had good qualifications. Son of a country clergyman, a scholar of Jesus College, Cambridge, he studied classics, mathematics, and divinity, intending to take holy orders. Doctrinal scruples caused him to turn instead to medicine.

While a fellow of Jesus College, he came across Gay's suggestion of the all-pervasive power of association and elaborated on this theme in a brief pamphlet, *Conjecturae quaedam de sensu, motu, et idearum generatione* (1730). All his further work was devoted to the development of the ideas here outlined, and he determined to try physiological and philosophical theory "to give guidance to the art of ethics and customs." Nineteen years elapsed before the publication of his magnum opus. During this time he was occupied with a medical practice among rich and poor, with family life, and with the cultivation of numerous friends. Among his intimates were Stephen Hales, Sir Hans Sloane, William Cheselden, Bishop Butler, and John Byrom. He was elected fellow of the Royal Society in 1743. Always receptive to other people's ideas, he was courageous, if not always discreet, in trying out new ones, and his contemporaries did not take him quite seriously as a philosopher or scientist.

The *Observations* seems to have made little impression at the time of its publication. Joseph Priestley, however, who found the implied necessitarianism congenial, republished the work in 1775, omitting all the physiological parts, which he regarded as valueless speculation. Hartley's theory of association became the major influence on the English empiricist school of the nineteenth century, notably in the psychological works of the Mills and Alexander Bain (Warren 1921; Ribot 1870).

Although there is little in Hartley's work that directly influenced his immediate successors, it still bears examination for its freshness of outlook and catholicity of interest. Hartley wove into his formal argument a mass of material whose relevance to the science of psychology has progressively increased since his day. Parallel to the analysis of consciousness, from primitive sensations to abstract ideas, runs an account of the evolution of behavioral mechanisms, from the simplest "automatic actions" (reflexes) through the "secondarily automatic actions"—that is, basic muscular skills such as walking, whose character Hartley was the first to define and comment on—to the supposed cerebral concomitants of such "mental" skills as thinking. The reflexes, of course, derive from Descartes (1662). Of particular interest is the analysis of the mechanics of habit, which Hartley evidently gained from some lesser known passages in Malebranche's *De la recherche de la vérité* (1674–1675). In his account of the higher mental functions, Hartley revealed the considerable influence of the work of John Wilkins, bishop of Chester, on language (1668). Thus, his theory of memory relies on the "perpetual recurrency of the same impressions, and clusters of impressions" which come to form "the rudiments or elements of memory" in the same way as letters of the alphabet form the rudiments of language (1749, part 1, pp. 374–375). Similarly, his discussion of conjecture and hypothetical thinking draws on the work of Abraham de Moivre (1718) and other contemporary mathematicians who were concerning themselves with the practical aspects of probability theory.

It was from Thomas Willis (1664; 1672) that Hartley gained the knowledge of the anatomy of the brain which brought him close to a post-Darwinian view of the relation of man and animals. "The brute creatures," he wrote, "prove their near relation to us, not only by the general resemblance of the body but by that of the mind also" (1749, part 1, pp. 413–414). Hartley was led, on the basis of the very meager information available, to a primitive doctrine of the localization of cerebral function. This preoccupation passed out of psychology and neurology and, in the form in which he stated it, only reappeared in late nineteenth-century experimental and clinical studies of brain function. Nor had Hartley neglected that other preoccupation of nineteenth-century medicine, the hysterical disorders.

Hartley's theology, sometimes trite and always constrained by contemporary Biblical interpretations, is nevertheless nodal to his philosophy as a whole. It was his primary concern to provide religion with a natural and scientific basis through a genuinely psychological analysis of religious experience. Hartley regarded the second (and much longer) part of the *Observations*, devoted to man's "Duty and Expectations," as interdependent with the first. He seems to have perceived that his attempt did not wholly succeed, but he pressed the laws of mechanism as far as they would go. "All the evidences for the mechanical nature of body and mind," he wrote, "are so many encouragements to study them faithfully and diligently, since what is mechanical *may* be both understood and remedied" (1749, part 1, p. 267). Later psychologists have increasingly adopted this principle of method, even if some, like Hartley, have remained aware of elements in human consciousness that are resistant to it.

KATHLEEN C. OLDFIELD

[*For the historical context of Hartley's work, see the biography of* LOCKE; *for discussion of the subsequent development of Hartley's ideas, see* NERVOUS SYSTEM, *article on* STRUCTURE AND FUNCTION OF THE BRAIN; STRESS.]

### WORKS BY HARTLEY

(1730) 1837 *Conjecturae quaedam de sensu, motu, et idearum generatione.* Pages 143–185 in Samuel Parr

(editor), *Metaphysical Tracts by English Philosophers of the Eighteenth Century.* London: Lumley.
(1749) 1834 *Observations on Man: His Frame, His Duty and His Expectations.* 6th ed., corr. & rev. London: Tegg.

### SUPPLEMENTARY BIBLIOGRAPHY

DESCARTES, RENÉ 1662 *De homine.* Lugduni Batavorum (now Leiden): Moyardus & Lessen.
KING, WILLIAM (1702) 1732 *An Essay on the Origin of Evil.* Preface by John Gay. 2d ed. London. → First published as *De origine mali.*
LOCKE, JOHN (1690) 1959 *An Essay Concerning Human Understanding.* 2 vols. New York: Dover.
MALEBRANCHE, NICOLAS 1674–1675 *De la recherche de la vérité.* 2 vols. Paris: Pralard.
MOIVRE, ABRAHAM DE (1718) 1756 *The Doctrine of Chances: Or, a Method of Calculating the Probabilities of Events in Play.* 3d ed. London: Millar.
NEWTON, ISAAC (1704) 1952 *Opticks.* New York: Dover.
OLDFIELD, R. C.; and OLDFIELD, KATHLEEN C. 1951 Hartley's *Observations on Man. Annals of Science* 7:371–381.
PRIESTLEY, JOSEPH 1775 *Hartley's Theory of the Human Mind, on the Principle of Association of Ideas.* London: Johnson.
RIBOT, T. (1870) 1873 *English Psychology.* London: King. → First published in French.
WARREN, HOWARD C. 1921 *A History of the Association Psychology.* New York: Scribner.
WILKINS, JOHN 1668 *An Essay Towards a Real Character and a Philosophical Language.* London: Gellibrand.
WILLIS, THOMAS 1664 *De cerebri anatome cui accessit nervorumque descriptio et usus.* London: Roycroft.
WILLIS, THOMAS 1672 *De anima brutorum quae hominis vitalis ac sensitiva est. . . .* Oxford: Shelden.

## HAURIOU, MAURICE

Maurice Hauriou (1856–1929), French legal theorist, was born at Ladiville (Charente). He studied law at Bordeaux and, after taking first place in the 1882 competition for *agrégation*, was appointed professor at Toulouse. He taught there for 46 years, until his death.

Hauriou taught the history of law for several years. He then went on to teach administrative law, and it was in this field that he was to make his most lasting contributions. He became deeply interested in sociology—in 1893 he wrote *Les facultés de droit et la sociologie*—but after his most important work in this area, *La science sociale traditionelle* (1896), aroused considerable opposition, he decided, as he wrote to Georges Renard, to present in juridical dress the ideas that he had at first tried to get accepted in sociological dress (Renard 1931). Indeed, this approach is implicit in the commentaries on decisions that he made for the Sirey collection for 37 years, from 1892 to 1929 (1929), and in his *Précis de droit administratif* (1892), which went through 11 editions during his lifetime. But it is primarily in his *Principes de droit public* (1910), his *Précis de droit constitutionnel* (1923), and in his article "La théorie de l'institution et de la fondation" (1925) that his sociophilosophical views may be found.

Hauriou's thought is marked by liberalism, individualism, and attachment to tradition. He was strongly influenced by Bergson and by the doctrine of the Catholic church; he described himself, in the *Principes de droit public*, as a Comtean positivist turned Catholic positivist, that is, as a positivist who will go so far as to utilize the social, moral, and juridical content of Catholic dogma. As a traditionalist, he saw himself restoring the classic doctrines of French public law and defending natural-law conceptions from the menace of the aggressive objectivism of Hans Kelsen.

However, Hauriou was not simply a conservative content to do battle from old positions. He did not regard the substance of law as purely conceptual but saw it as a concrete reality that embodies objective ideas and is subject to their creative influence. In this way he introduced into juridical thinking the sociological data that the normative (objective) method prescribed. Hauriou did not believe that the sociological study of the law meant merely the observation of social facts; instead, he was concerned with discovering how government *de facto* becomes government *de jure* (1892). As he saw it, this transformation occurs as ideas are incorporated into facts, thus creating what G. Gurvitch has called normative facts.

What has become known as the "Hauriou theory of the institution" focuses on this process of the penetration of social reality by ideas and analyzes the way in which ideas order that reality. An institution, by Hauriou's definition, is an "idea of a project, or enterprise, that becomes a reality and persists juridically in a social milieu" (1925, p. 10). An institution is an objective reality, the product of a particular social equilibrium, and the source of legal rules. With this definition Hauriou eliminated all voluntaristic interpretations of the creation of law. He introduced a dynamic factor into the realm of law, for although institutions give stability to the law, this is not a stability that precludes change. The continuity of an institution depends on its constant adaptation to new conditions of social life (1910, pp. 213, 250).

On these bases Hauriou erected a theory of the state. Rejecting the theory of the social contract, he based the origin of the state on the institution: individuals do not delegate power to a governing minority; they assent, *by custom*, to that institution which is the state. While the subject consents only indirectly to the power of the law, he accepts directly the institution to which that power is linked and in whose behalf it is exercised. Furthermore, Hauriou believed that the state exists only in certain civilizations, that the institution of the state is taken seriously only by certain races, and that with certain others it becomes a mere facade behind which traditions of personal power or the organization of clans and clienteles are perpetuated. As he saw it, there are peoples that are incapable of putting into effect the idea of the commonweal (1929).

The state, therefore, is distinct from the nation. It is subject to law only at its own will, and this is why Hauriou, on the political plane, believed firmly in the merits of democracy and, more particularly, of parliamentary democracy. But taking a wide historical perspective, he considered this type of government to be nothing more than a temporary political form. For all its recognized merits, parliamentary democracy is only a stage in an irreversible development that begins with aristocratic monarchies and ends with administrative empires (1929, p. 142). The successive types of government evolve as governmental institutions become nationwide; within the nation, more and more numerous elites are formed, which enter into the machinery of government and transform its operation by their presence.

So far as the functioning of parliamentary democracy in particular is concerned, Hauriou advocated the dominance of the executive over the legislative power. He believed that the best way to maintain the superiority of the executive over the legislative power is to limit the power of the deputies to initiate legislation. In his view, the conciliation of power and liberty is brought about by virtue of order, that order which follows if the people support actions originated by the executive. This support is almost always spontaneous; force enters into the picture only in exceptional cases, to keep refractory minorities within bounds.

Hauriou stressed that the character of the state is determined to a large extent by what he called its social constitution; that is, its socioeconomic structure, the place of citizens within the state, and the rights and liberties of individuals. He was deeply committed to individual liberty as the prerequisite to law that is based on the juridical person and on subjective right, and he believed that individual initiative is the basis of social order (1929, p. vii). However, he did recognize that human fallibility makes the limitation of individualism necessary: liberty must be conditional on rules of morality and social sanctions. On the socioeconomic level, limitations on individual liberty can be achieved by certain modifications in the structure of power: "Freedom of association, decentralization, corporative representation, here are three essential reforms, all three interdependent, which will assure a harmonious separation between the state and positive society, and permit the development of collective intervention in economic conflicts without a monstrous increase in the power of the state" (1896, pp. 392–393).

In the sphere of administrative law, Hauriou succeeded in erecting an extremely solid body of doctrine that is still suggestive, although it has become outmoded by changes in the extent and modes of action of the state. In general, to be sure, his influence was less in his day than that of Duguit, the other master of French public law at the turn of the century. Yet despite certain obscure points, Hauriou's thinking is still provocative, and his work foreshadowed the orientation of those French political scientists who are studying the nature of political institutions in general and of power in particular.

G. BURDEAU

[*See also* ADMINISTRATIVE LAW; STATE; *and the biographies of* DUGUIT *and* KELSEN.]

### WORKS BY HAURIOU

(1892) 1933 *Précis de droit administratif et de droit public.* 12th ed. Paris: Sirey.

1893 *Les facultés de droit et la sociologie.* Paris: Thorin.

1896 *Cours de science sociale: La science sociale traditionelle.* Paris: Larose.

(1910) 1916 *Principes de droit public à l'usage des étudiants en license (3ᵉ année) et en doctorat ès-sciences politiques.* 2d ed. Paris: Tenin.

(1923) 1929 *Précis de droit constitutionnel.* 2d ed. Paris: Sirey. → The second edition is particularly recommended.

1925 *La théorie de l'institution et de la fondation.* Pages 1–45 in *La cité moderne et les transformations du droit.* Paris: Bloud & Gay.

(1929) 1931 *La jurisprudence administrative de 1892 à 1929.* 3 vols. Paris: Sirey.

### SUPPLEMENTARY BIBLIOGRAPHY

RENARD, GEORGES 1931 *La filosofia politica di Maurice Hauriou.* Volume 2, pages 195–204 in *Scritti di diritto pubblico in onore di Oreste Ranelletti nel XXXV anno d'insegnamento.* Padua (Italy): Milani.

SFEZ, LUCIEN 1966 *Essai sur la contribution du doyen Hauriou au droit administratif français.* Paris: Librairie Générale de Droit et de Jurisprudence.

## HAWTREY, R. G.

Ralph George Hawtrey, English economist, was born in 1879. He was educated at Eton and Trinity College, Cambridge, where he obtained a first-class honors degree in mathematics. After leaving Cambridge he entered the administrative civil serv-

ice and worked at the Treasury from 1904 until his retirement in 1945. He was knighted in 1956.

Throughout his career he held only two academic (or quasi-academic) appointments: in 1928–1929 he was given special leave by the Treasury to lecture in economics at Harvard University; and after his official retirement he was elected Price professor of international economics at the Royal Institute of International Affairs, a post which he held from 1947 to 1952.

Hawtrey is often wrongly regarded as one of the Cambridge academic economists and is grouped with Pigou, Keynes, Robertson, and other pupils of Marshall. But he acquired his knowledge of economics not at Cambridge (he never attended even one of Marshall's lectures) but at the Treasury, where he came under the stimulating influence of Sir John (later Lord) Bradbury, permanent secretary of the Treasury.

The first of Hawtrey's books, *Good and Bad Trade* (1913), contains the germ of many of his later ideas on monetary theory. He subsequently developed these ideas at greater length and with more precision in such major works as *Currrency and Credit* (1919), *The Art of Central Banking* (1932), and *Capital and Employment* (1937).

Hawtrey was one of the outstanding figures among those British economists who led the way in much of the rethinking of monetary theory after World War I, and he had a considerable influence on the early development of Keynes's thought (Harrod 1951, p. 357). The emphasis he laid on the concept of money as something abstract, though capable of numeration—a unit of account, divorced from any necessary link with a metallic or other substance—made a marked impact on the minds of a generation of economists who had grown up with the traditional nineteenth-century attitude toward the gold standard.

He was one of the English pioneers of the "income" approach; thus, he wrote in *Good and Bad Trade*: "The total effective demand for all commodities per unit of time is the aggregate of all money incomes. The total cost of production of all commodities per unit of time is the aggregate of all money incomes" ([1913] 1962, p. 7). He developed this idea further in his *Currency and Credit* by bringing in, for example, the notion of the income velocity of money, which he defined as the ratio of consumers' outlay to the unspent margin: Consumers' outlay (out of income) includes investment, while the unspent margin is the supply of the means of payment—that is, the excess of the purchasing power people and businesses have acquired over what they have spent.

Hawtrey based his monetary explanation primarily on the argument that credit is inherently unstable because of the working of the banking system and its effect on the holders of stocks in particular. Dealers (merchants, wholesalers, and retailers) occupy a key position in the economy: "[They] are the economic leaders. They take the initiative in production, and the activity of the manufacturers depends on the orders they give" ([1919] 1950, p. 427). Since dealers hold stocks largely with borrowed money, they are peculiarly susceptible to changes in the rate of interest they have to pay for the money they borrow. It is chiefly because of the importance which he attached to the role of dealers that Hawtrey, unlike Keynes and many other economists of recent times, always maintained that the operative instrument for credit regulation is the short-term, not the long-term rate of interest.

While Hawtrey agreed that a low short-term rate may be able to do little to assist an economy to recover from a deep depression, he was convinced that a sufficiently high bank rate (possibly even 10 per cent or higher) can damp down and counteract inflationary forces caused by credit expansion, however strongly they may be working. He recently contended that the 7 per cent bank rate, which operated for six months in 1964–1965, was largely ineffective because it was too low at a time when the long-term rate (the yield on consols) was itself 7 per cent.

His views as to the utility of public works underwent a good deal of modification in the course of time. In his earliest work he contended that "the Government by the very fact of borrowing for this expenditure is withdrawing from the investment market savings which would otherwise be applied to the creation of capital" ([1913] 1962, p. 260). Later he said: "It is not the Government expenditure [on capital works] that gives employment, but the Government borrowing. The borrowing would have the same effect if it were to meet a deficit due to a remission of taxation" (1928, pp. 112–113). The shift in his position is even clearer in the following passage: "Now it is quite true that capital outlay undertaken by the Government may conduce under appropriate conditions to an expansion of general demand. It must be *additional*, that is to say, must not by using up the resources of the investment market, prevent or delay an equal amount of privately initiated capital outlay. It need not necessarily be financed by avowedly inflationary methods; if it merely sets in motion money held idle in balances for want of eligible investments, it will enlarge the flow of money" (1944, p. 95). But he went on to say that business ought never to be allowed to lapse into such a state of depression and

stagnation that government expenditure is the appropriate remedy. If this is allowed to happen, it points to a failure on the part of those who control the banking system to exercise their proper function. He consistently preached the doctrine that the best way to stop depression is to stop the preceding boom; and for this purpose credit regulation can be fully effective.

Hawtrey's position in the ranks of modern monetary theorists does not depend so much upon the validity of his views on the causation and control of the trade cycle as upon the deeper and clearer understanding which he made possible of both the operation of the banking system and the role of money in a modern economy.

His name is associated in the minds of most economists with the doctrine that the trade cycle is essentially a monetary phenomenon, and it should not be overlooked that his writings include a careful analysis of the part played by the period of production and by the widening and deepening of capital in different phases of the cycle.

No account of his work, however short, should omit mention of the contribution Hawtrey made at the International Monetary Conference held at Genoa in April 1922. He was one of the representatives of the British Treasury there, and it was largely through his influence that agreement was reached on the desirability of cooperation between the central banks in the regulation of credit in order to prevent undue fluctuations in the purchasing power of gold. However, the Genoa Resolutions were never put into effect.

When Hawtrey was 82 years of age, he published *The Pound at Home and Abroad* (1961), in which, *inter alia*, he upheld with customary vigor the thesis that the primary causes of the recent difficulties of the British economy were, first, the fixed parity of the sterling exchange with a depreciating dollar, and second, the undervaluation of the pound ever since it was devalued in 1949 from $4.03 to $2.80—in this latter contention his has been a lone voice among British economists. This book also contains his memorandum of evidence submitted to the Radcliffe Committee on the Working of the Monetary System and some trenchant criticisms of parts of the report of that body.

Although Hawtrey adhered in general to the same fundamental tenets throughout his career, he modified their expression so as to take account both of historical developments and of the evolution of contemporary economic thought, and it is by his later books and editions that his work should be assessed.

C. W. GUILLEBAUD

[*See also* BANKING, CENTRAL; BUSINESS CYCLES.]

WORKS BY HAWTREY

(1913) 1962 *Good and Bad Trade: An Inquiry Into the Causes of Trade Fluctuations.* New York: Kelley.

(1919) 1950 *Currency and Credit.* 4th ed. New York and London: Longmans.

1921 *The Exchequer and the Control of Expenditure.* New York: Oxford Univ. Press.

(1923) 1926 *Monetary Reconstruction.* 2d ed. London: Longmans.

1926 *The Economic Problem.* London: Longmans.

(1927) 1947 *The Gold Standard in Theory and Practice.* 5th ed. London: Longmans.

1928 *Trade and Credit.* London and New York: Longmans.

(1930) 1952 *Economic Aspects of Sovereignty.* 2d ed. London and New York: Longmans.

(1931) 1933 *Trade Depression and the Way Out.* New ed. London and New York: Longmans.

(1932) 1962 *The Art of Central Banking.* 2d ed. London: Cass.

(1937) 1952 *Capital and Employment.* 2d ed. London and New York: Longmans. → See especially pages 157–219 on "Keynes' *General Theory of Employment, Interest and Money.*"

(1938) 1962 *A Century of Bank Rate.* 2d ed. London: Cass.

1944 *Economic Destiny.* New York and London: Longmans.

1946a *Economic Rebirth.* London and New York: Longmans.

1946b *Bretton Woods for Better or Worse.* London and New York: Longmans.

1949 *Western European Union: Implications for the United Kingdom.* London: Royal Institute of International Affairs.

1950 *The Balance of Payments and the Standard of Living.* London: Royal Institute of International Affairs.

1954 *Towards the Rescue of Sterling.* London and New York: Longmans.

1955 *Cross Purposes in Wage Policy.* London and New York: Longmans.

1961 *The Pound at Home and Abroad.* London: Longmans. → See especially Chapter 2, "Relative Strength of the Pound and the Dollar"; Chapter 12, "The Under-valuation of the Pound"; and Chapter 14, "The Radcliffe Committee: Aims of Monetary Policy."

SUPPLEMENTARY BIBLIOGRAPHY

ARMITAGE-SMITH, GEORGE (1906) 1935 *Principles and Methods of Taxation.* 11th ed. Revised by R. G. Hawtrey. London: Murray.

HARROD, R. F. 1951 *The Life of John Maynard Keynes.* London: Macmillan. → A paperback edition was published in 1963 by St. Martins.

# HEALTH

"Health is a state of complete physical, mental and social well-being and not merely the absence of disease or infirmity," according to the World Health Organization (1946). It will be the purpose of this article to develop some concepts about health and disease, exploring a few implications of the WHO definition in the context of both Western and non-Western medical ideas. First, notions of singular and multiple causation of disease will be contrasted. Second, three types of ideas about health will be defined. Finally, some applications of the health concept to units beyond the human individual will be mentioned.

## Disease and its causes

Illness is a disvalued process that impairs the functioning or appearance of a human person and may ultimately lead to death. The definition of health given by the WHO includes *social* as well as physical and mental well-being. This reflects a concern with the person as a member of human groups—an entity certainly not limited to the body of that person. The components of an individual (e.g., blood, body, soul, spirit, shadow, name, etc.) are defined differently from one culture to the next. The death of the organism, however, is a biological constant which is taken into account conceptually in all cultures, and customs prescribe how the disposition of the corpse is to be arranged. Different components of the individual may be thought to depart from the presence of the living at different times, and these various departures are marked by a series of ceremonies (van Gennep [1909] 1960, pp. 146 ff.). Some components, such as the "soul," may be thought never to cease existing entirely but to remain near the living or in some locality specially set aside for its kind.

Disease, then, may involve a temporary or permanent impairment in the functioning of any single component, or of the relationship between components making up the individual. An impairment of a person, furthermore, need not be restricted to a decrease in his ability to function in his ordinary ways: for example, among the Ashanti of West Africa, a congenital birthmark which leads to no discomfort or danger of death can be considered a sufficiently severe fault to disqualify a man from the office of chief. In many cultures, theories of disease will include explanations of congenital defects or imperfections, and the distinction between these and other illnesses may become relevant for further analysis (Polgar 1963).

Explanations of illness are not only useful to reaffirm the values of a social unit or to make death psychologically more tolerable for the next of kin but serve most immediately to indicate courses of preventive and curative action. To effect prevention or cure one should identify a course of events which presumably has produced the impairment. Herein lies the rationale of *diagnosis*, which is one of the three basic elements of all medical systems (the other two being therapy and prophylaxis).

**Notions of singular causation.** During the last decades of the nineteenth and the early part of the twentieth century, Western medicine was heavily dominated by the notion that most diseases are a result of infection caused by microorganisms. This type of conception—that disease simply results from the entry by a foreign agency into the body of the patient—is paralleled by the ideas found among many tribal people that illness is caused by "object intrusion" or "spirit possession." Walther Riese has drawn attention to this similarity of ideas in stating that "ontologic" etiology (a conception of disease as caused by a monadic "alien-ferment") "in its crudest form . . . identifies these agents, if not the diseases themselves, with demons, in its scientific form, with germs" (Riese 1953, pp. 66–67). He does not imply, of course, that demons and germs are equally valid concepts in an empirical sense.

The emergence of the "doctrine of specific etiology of disease" (Dubos [1959] 1961, p. 90) as the dominant idea in medicine is related to the mechanistic world view prevalent in the late nineteenth century. Far older features of Western thought, such as the grammatical dualism of subject and predicate, the Judeo–Christian and Platonic mind–body dichotomy, and the experimental approach of the alchemists, provided a suitable background for the development of this "doctrine." Of the greatest immediate relevance to it were the discoveries of Pasteur and Koch in the realm of bacteriology. Instead of emphasizing the patient and his total environment, as Western medical traditions had done previously, proponents of this "doctrine" spread the notion that all important infections could be controlled by therapeutic serums and preventive vaccines specific for all microbes (Dubos [1959] 1961, p. 130). Although a number of vaccines and antitoxins had been developed before the turn of the century, it was not until the 1930s that the sulfa drugs were discovered, and it was another decade later that penicillin came to be used. The great decreases in the mortality of children and young adults, which are nowadays often attributed to clinical medicine and the use of specific drugs, actually preceded these discoveries and mostly resulted from better nutrition and the hygienic measures carried out under the leadership of medical reformers, many of whom had even opposed the germ theory of disease (Rosen 1958, pp. 225 ff.; Dubos [1959] 1961, p. 131).

In the contemporary practice of clinical medicine, the inadequate care often received by patients unfortunate enough to suffer from a disability for which no specific etiology can be identified is symptomatic of the legacy of the bacteriological era. Von Mering and Earley (1965) trace the difficulties of such problem patients to, among other factors, the hospital as the main locale for diagnosis and treatment, as well as to the "growth of medicine as a science of tests and measurements rather than an art involving the five senses." These authors find that "the clinic physician and general practitioner share a kind of 'molecular man' orientation which seems to predispose them to be more concerned with the specifics of the presenting complaint, and to look eagerly for major disease in every bed or consulting room" (von Mering & Earley 1965, p. 199; see also Pflanz 1964).

**Multicausal conceptions of disease.** The recent theoretical developments away from the doctrine of specific etiology are spearheaded by advocates of comprehensive medical care and psychosomatic medicine and by some epidemiologists. All three of these segments of the medical community regard illness as an interaction of many factors and, correspondingly, favor treatment of patients once more as total organisms in a complex setting. One of the foremost modern exponents of this view is the epidemiologist John Gordon, who has shown the interplay of the *host*, the *agent*, and the (physical, biological, and social) *environment* in the spread of a good number of both infectious and noninfectious diseases (see, for example, Gordon 1958). The studies of John Cassel, another noted epidemiologist, on the spectrum of health disorders resulting from independently documented sociocultural processes exemplify a further step away from the one cause–one disease manner of thinking (Cassel 1964). Although writers in the psychosomatic tradition of medicine often use concepts like "stress" or "conflict" as if they were specific causes of illness, the emphasis in this school of thought is on the patient's physical *and* mental well-being, and consideration is often given to his social milieu as well (King 1963). Comprehensive medical care is more than a movement to improve the institutional means by which patients and sometimes families are medically supervised. The theory that underlies these arrangements includes rejection of both the dominant disease orientation of modern Western medicine and the organic–functional dichotomy, and it places a strong emphasis on the patient as a person (Steiger et al. 1962).

Multicausal conceptions of disease are neither new in the Western medical tradition nor unique to it. One main theme in the Hippocratic writings is that disease is to be traced to an imbalance between the person and his external environment; much emphasis is also given to the relationships among different environmental factors, such as exercise and diet, and to the connections between disturbances in an organ and the whole body (Sigerist 1951–1961, vol. 2, pp. 317 ff.; Dubos [1959] 1961, pp. 117 ff.). In non-Western societies there are many multicausal ideas about disease. The distinction between conditions that make persons particularly susceptible and events that precipitate the onset of the disease is particularly common: for example, the Maori of New Zealand see "bad acts" by the patient as predisposing to, and external spirits or objects as the immediate cause of, an illness episode (Newell 1957); in the Middle East, a well-formed male child is identified as especially susceptible to attack by the "evil eye" (Shiloh 1958).

Related to this division between predisposing and precipitating factors is the division between the reasons why a particular person becomes ill at a particular time and the explanation of the way in which it happens. These latter two types of causes may be termed *incidence notions* and *etiological notions* (Polgar 1962, pp. 166 ff.); they also bear some similarity to the Aristotelian efficient and material causes (Riese 1953, pp. 66 ff.). In some non-Western medical systems there are categories for "natural" diseases—usually minor ills such as the digestive problems of infants (Nurge 1958)—which do not require an explanation for the occurrence of the disability in the particular instance and hence do not raise questions about who is "responsible." In urbanized as well as nonurban societies, however, the search for the transgression of the patient himself or the malevolent action of another being (human or supernatural) is a major element of the diagnostic process.

In small tribal or peasant communities, the assignment of responsibility for illness to a relative or neighbor (whose departure from prescribed norms of behavior is pinpointed as a breach of taboo, witchcraft, irresponsibility, or sin) helps to bring latent interpersonal conflicts into the open where they are more easily resolved (Paul 1953; Firth 1959, pp. 135 ff.). Similarly in the Judeo–Christian tradition the attribution of illness to sinful behavior served to reinforce the mores of the society. With increasing secularization, this diagnostic category became less satisfactory, and in scientific medicine it was replaced by "naturalistic" explanations. However, residues of this earlier concept of sin still affect attitudes toward disease; for patients and their families, a physician's diagnosis which fails to blame anyone for the occurrence of the illness also fails to deal with the sense of guilt they often have and leaves them vaguely dissatisfied (Sigerist 1951–1961, vol. 1, p. 157).

## Three conceptions of health

If disease is seen as an individual's departure from perfectly well-meshed social or physiological performance, health, by contrast, becomes an *asymptote*—an ideal that can be approached but never attained in actuality. In the WHO definition, the expression "*complete* physical, mental and social well-being" [emphasis added] echoes this type of conception.

**Variants of the asymptotic concept.** Two main variants of the asymptotic notion about health can be identified. One variant, the harmonious working together of disparate elements, is a dominant theme in the Indo–European tradition, antedating Galen's notion of the "four fluids" and manifest today in the influence of Walter B. Cannon's ideas about homeostasis. The yang and yin of Chinese philosophy also indicate a search for balance, the restoration of which is one of the healer's primary goals (Huard & Wong 1959, pp. 105 ff.). Grand designs of physiological, physical, and metaphysical order —each replicating the elements of the other—are typical of classical times.

The second type of asymptotic conception is a backward-looking romanticism, which has been described by Dubos in his chapter "The Gardens of Eden" ([1959] 1961, pp. 1–25). For Rousseau and his followers, the ills that beset Western society are consequences of the departure from a perfect state of harmony with nature that is entailed in the process of becoming civilized. Freud also accepted the myth of a precursor of modern man who was exempt from the latter's neuroses, since this imaginary "savage" did not inhibit the biological drives toward aggression and sexuality (Riese 1953, pp. 14 ff.). Remnants of ideas about "primitive man's" closeness to "nature" remain today in such medical folklore as the myth of easier parturition among American Indians and the "innate" superiority of their sense organs. When this theme is transposed to the life cycle of individuals, children may be seen romantically (for example, by the poet Wordsworth) as endowed with sensitive understanding which they gradually lose by exposure to the eroding influence of the "civilized" ways of adults.

In operational terms, the asymptotic definition of health is mostly negative; it implies the *absence* of manifest disturbance. While this notion has advantages in focusing attention on the nonexistence of a clear break between the presence or absence of disease, by the same token it makes for difficulties in conducting health surveys and planning for medical facilities (Lewis 1953; U.S. Department of Health . . . 1966).

**The elastic concept.** Another set of notions about health centers on the accumulation of resistance to potential danger. This may be termed the *elastic* concept. Examples of health behavior derived from this manner of thinking include restricting the water intake of children to make them hardy, homeopathic medicine, and variolation (of differing empirical value, of course). Adversity is not regarded here as a disruption of some prior or ultimate harmony but rather as an ordinary and expected circumstance for which preparations can and should be made. This manner of regarding health seems to play a substantial part in modern preventive medicine. Another good contemporary example of an application of the elastic view of health is psychoprophylactic training for childbirth, by which women are taught to cope with the hardships of delivery through psychological conditioning together with certain exercises (Bing et al. 1961). Some accumulated resistance potentials can be measured operationally in the scientific laboratory by testing an individual's capacity to produce specific antibodies when challenged by an antigenic substance or his capacity for continued adequate performance of sensory tasks under controlled changes in temperature, humidity, pressure, and other conditions.

**The open-ended concept.** The outstanding difficulty with the asymptotic notion of health (which is circumvented by elastic conceptions) is its unattainability. By turning the argument around, one can start with death as a kind of absolute zero and fix no upper limit for human functioning (Bates 1959, p. 59). This may be termed the *open-ended* conception of health. The outstanding example of this ideology is involved in the attempts to formulate a philosophy of "positive mental health." While some concepts used by the writers in this tradition, such as "self-actualization," would fall in the category of asymptotic notions, the criteria of *growth*, *zest*, and *creativity* clearly belong under the open-ended rubric. The theorists of positive mental health share with the authors of the WHO definition and others mentioned above the desire to construct a manner of looking at health which is based "not merely on the absence of disease or infirmity." However, they go beyond the WHO view

of health, and beyond most of preventive medicine generally, in their search for positive goals which are independent of disease (Jahoda 1958). Health promotion in nutrition, for example, aims to prevent deficiency diseases (a goal which is of the "elastic" type) or persuade people to consume recommended daily norms of nutrients (an asymptotic-type idea). By contrast, "zestful living" does not reach an optimum at certain levels of energy expenditure and could even make people occasionally *more* prone to injury or disease.

### Modern medical practice

In terms of actual health behavior in urban societies, open-ended conceptions are more likely to be put into practice in national parks, beauty parlors, bathrooms, or athletic studios than in the offices of doctors or psychologists. Physicians may recommend vacations, walks in the "fresh air," or other types of exercise, but this is usually prescribed for incipient illness or problems of overweight rather than for promoting health as such. In non-Western societies one may find practices aimed at increasing supernatural power, physical strength, prosperity, wisdom, virility, or femininity, which are conceptually and behaviorally integrated with actions to prevent or cure disease. In industrialized societies, however, increased specialization results in the separation of medical institutions from the religious, esthetic, recreational, and economic spheres. As mentioned above, the focus of Western medicine narrowed as the doctrine of specific etiology of disease became the dominant view. Thus, health promotion through such customs as taking cold showers, swallowing vitamin pills to "pep you up," giving laxatives routinely to children, taking walks, and the like is seldom transmitted as part of the professional medical system but rather is passed on through relatives, friends, or the mass media.

The attempt of the mental hygienists to develop a new and positive content for the concept of health is further limited by concern for the possibility of their encroachment on other institutions. Brewster Smith (1961, p. 301) has commented on the difficult position of the psychologist who is asked to provide notions of mental health as substitutes for weakened religious values; and Freidson (1961/1962, pp. 125 ff.) has warned about the dangers of bringing questions of nonconformity to moral, legal, or political norms under the umbrella of medicine. In spite of these problems, it may be predicted that scientific medicine will gradually adopt a more open-ended conception of health as the technological tasks of health maintenance in a population with increasing proportions of older people are accomplished and as the relationship between people and their environment once again becomes the central arena of medical concern.

## Health beyond the individual

The WHO definition does not specify whether its terms apply only to the health of the individual. In the Greek medical system of the fifth century B.C. and that of some modern Western physicians, as described above, health is seen as an *interaction* between a person and his surroundings. This type of conception is carried even further in the ideas of many non-Western peoples. Margaret Mead (World Federation for Mental Health 1953, pp. 217 ff.) mentions several examples of "continuity" between the well-being of man and of the soil and between the body and "other bodies of the social unit." It is but a short step from a focus on these interrelationships to a consideration of the larger unit itself, without necessarily looking at the individual within it at all times.

As the student in schools of public health is often reminded, his "patient" will usually be a community. Public health is thus not only the name of a medical specialty but also refers to the well-being of various publics (Brockington 1958, pp. 19 ff.). The health of other entities, such as families, societies, the human species, or the entire ecosphere of this planet, has also been discussed.

The resistance potential of a human collectivity to an epidemic of infectious disease cannot be described as the sum or the average of individual immunity: the degree of resistance in different age groups or the spatial dispersion of the population are crucial in estimating the level of "herd immunity" (Gordon 1958). Mental illness is regarded by a number of psychologists and psychiatrists as a pathological state of an entire family. The illness may be discovered through the request for treatment of a single member who acts as the "messenger boy," carrying the information about the trouble to the outside world, although he is neither the only one sick nor necessarily the one most seriously disturbed (Gruenberg 1957). There are also some writers who consider it appropriate to label entire societies (for example, Nazi Germany) as pathological and to wonder if any "healthy adjustment" is possible for individuals living in them (Devereux 1956).

Western medical practitioners almost inevitably put a higher value on prolonging individual life than on the health of the social unit—witness the grotesque situation where catheters, sedatives, exorbitant hospital bills, and oxygen tents prevent a dying man from making a decent and meaningful departure from his relatives. Under different cultural circumstances the reverse evaluation may predominate, as among the Navajo Indians of the southwestern United States, who are more concerned with the well-being of the entire kin group than with the maximum comfort of, say, a congenitally malformed infant (Levy 1962).

For an entire species, health may be regarded as a matter of Darwinian "fitness" for continued survival. Unless a species is approaching death through extinction, however, it may be impossible to diagnose its current degree of fitness. The possibility of using modern medicine to keep alive individuals with genetically inherited diseases and the higher reproductive rate of the impoverished classes have been a focus for alarm by some eugenicists. Whether any real danger of "deterioration" exists for the gene pool of the whole human species is debatable (Medawar 1960); but, of course, conceptions of health which regard the proliferation of a "chosen people" as good and their relative submergence by "heathens" or other out-groups as bad are not a recent development (Haller 1963).

The health of the entire ecological system that exists on the surface of the earth can also be evaluated in terms of the survival potential of "life." Evolution on this planet—inorganic, biological, and social—has in the past moved toward increasing degrees of entropy retardation (Polgar 1961). The catastrophe of nuclear war or the slower but equally irreparable consequences of accelerating population growth are threats to the survival not only of "civilized" man but also of the energy balance of our entire terrestrial ecosystem. According to this view, our future well-being in this world as we know it depends on mankind's acting deliberately to safeguard and to continue accumulating the ordered energy and information that evolution represents.

STEVEN POLGAR

[*See also* ILLNESS; MEDICAL CARE; MENTAL HEALTH; PUBLIC HEALTH. *Other relevant material may be found in the articles on* CREATIVITY; EPIDEMIOLOGY; EUGENICS; PSYCHOSOMATIC ILLNESS; SOCIAL DARWINISM.]

### BIBLIOGRAPHY

BATES, MARSTON 1959 The Ecology of Health. Pages 56–77 in Iago Galdston (editor), *Medicine and Anthropology.* New York: International Universities Press. → The health of human individuals and collectivities seen in relation to the rest of living organisms on the planet. A primary source.

BING, ELIZABETH D.; KARMEL, MARJORIE; and TANZ, ALFRED 1961 *A Practical Training Course for the Psychoprophylactic Method of Childbirth.* New York: American Society for Psycho-prophylaxis in Obstetrics.

BROCKINGTON, C. FRASER 1958 *World Health.* Harmondsworth (England): Penguin. → A compendium on diseases and the organizations involved in public health. An excellent basic volume.

CASSEL, JOHN 1964 Social Science Theory as a Source of Hypotheses in Epidemiological Research. *American Journal of Public Health* 54, no. 9:1482–1488.

DEVEREUX, GEORGE 1956 Normal and Abnormal: The Key Problem in Psychiatric Anthropology. Pages 23–48 in Anthropological Society of Washington, *Some Uses of Anthropology: Theoretical and Applied.* Washington: The Society. → Discusses the usefulness of the culture concept, with particular emphasis on the shaman. A unique and illuminating essay.

DUBOS, RENÉ J. (1959) 1961 *Mirage of Health, Utopias, Progress, and Biological Change.* New York: Harper. → A discourse on health and disease—their history, treatment and characteristics—by an eminent biologist. A primary source.

FIRTH, RAYMOND 1959 Acculturation in Relation to Concepts of Health and Disease. Pages 129–165 in Iago Galdston (editor), *Medicine and Anthropology.* New York: International Universities Press. → A fine essay on the sociocultural context of medical practice. A primary source.

FREIDSON, ELIOT 1961/1962 The Sociology of Medicine: A Trend Report and Bibliography. *Current Sociology* 10/11: 123–192. → The best sociological summary.

GENNEP, ARNOLD VAN (1909) 1960 *The Rites of Passage.* London: Routledge; Univ. of Chicago Press. → First published in French. A classic anthropological essay on birth, puberty, marriage, childbirth, and death.

GORDON, JOHN E. 1958 Medical Ecology and the Public Health. *American Journal of the Medical Sciences* 235:337–359. → A summary of Gordon's views, with examples from numerous investigations.

GRUENBERG, ERNEST M. 1957 Socially Shared Psychopathology. Pages 201–225 in *Explorations in Social Psychiatry.* Edited by A. L. Leighton et al. New York: Basic Books.

HALLER, MARK H. 1963 *Eugenics: Hereditarian Attitudes in American Thought.* New Brunswick, N.J.: Rutgers Univ. Press. → History and evaluation of the eugenics movement in the United States.

HUARD, PIERRE A.; and WONG, MING 1959 *La médecine chinoise au cours des siècles.* Paris: Dacosta. → The best contemporary summary of Chinese medicine in a Western language.

JAHODA, MARIE 1958 *Current Concepts of Positive Mental Health.* New York: Basic Books. → A good synopsis of the field.

KING, STANLEY H. 1963 Social Psychological Factors in Illness. Pages 99–121 in *Handbook of Medical Sociology.* Edited by H. E. Freeman et al. Englewood Cliffs, N.J.: Prentice-Hall. → Psychological aspects of doctor–patient relations, as well as of illness.

LEVY, JERROLD E. 1962 Comment on "Health and Human Behavior" by Steven Polgar. *Current Anthropology* 3:186–187.

LEWIS, AUBREY 1953 Health as a Social Concept. *British Journal of Sociology* 4:109–124. → Separates health from social well-being, delineating operational

criteria for physical and mental illness in the "asymptotic" tradition.

MEDAWAR, PETER B. 1960 *The Future of Man.* New York: Basic Books; London: Methuen. → An essay on human genetics; grapples with many difficult and fundamental value problems.

MERING, OTTO VON; and EARLEY, L. WILLIAM 1965 Major Changes in the Western Medical Environment: Impact of Changes in Care of Undifferentiated Disorders. *Archives of General Psychiatry* 13:195–201.

NEWELL, KENNETH W. 1957 Medical Development Within a Maori Community. *Health Education Journal* 15:83–90.

NURGE, ETHEL 1958 Etiology of Illness in Guinhangdan. *American Anthropologist* New Series 60:1158–1172.

PAUL, BENJAMIN D. 1953 Mental Disorder and Self-regulating Processes in Culture: A Guatemalan Illustration. Pages 51–68 in Milbank Memorial Fund, *Interrelations Between the Social Environment and Psychiatric Disorders.* Proceedings, No. 29. New York: The Fund. → Describes the sequence of events in serving patients and their significance for treating disturbances in social relationships.

PFLANZ, MANFRED 1964 Der unklare Fall. *Münchener medizinische Wochenschrift* 106:1649–1655. → A discussion of the characteristics of patients, physicians, and medical thought, as these bear on the frequency of undifferentiated diagnoses in medical practice.

POLGAR, STEVEN 1961 Evolution and the Thermodynamic Imperative. *Human Biology* 33:99–109. → A development of four principles in organic and social evolution, from which a value position is derived.

POLGAR, STEVEN 1962 Health and Human Behavior: Areas of Interest Common to the Social and Medical Sciences. *Current Anthropology* 3:159–205. → A charting of the field, with an extensive bibliography.

POLGAR, STEVEN 1963 Health Action in Cross-cultural Perspective. Pages 397–419 in *Handbook of Medical Sociology.* Edited by H. E. Freeman et al. Englewood Cliffs, N.J.: Prentice-Hall. → An essay-review on the values and notions relevant to health, on medical practitioners, and on cross-cultural health programs.

RIESE, WALTHER 1953 *The Conception of Disease: Its History, Its Versions and Its Nature.* New York: Philosophical Library. → Fourteen types of disease conceptions, almost exclusively from the Western tradition.

ROSEN, GEORGE 1958 *A History of Public Health.* New York: MD Publications..

SHILOH, A. 1958 Middle East Culture and Health. *Health Education Journal* 16:232–244.

SIGERIST, HENRY 1951–1961 *A History of Medicine.* 2 vols. New York: Oxford Univ. Press. → Volume 1: *Primitive and Archaic Medicine.* Volume 2: *Early Greek, Hindu, and Persian Medicine.* A lucid, scholarly, and thorough history.

SMITH, M. BREWSTER 1961 "Mental Health" Reconsidered: A Special Case of the Problem of Values in Psychology. *American Psychologist* 16:299–306. → An excellent attempt to cut through the conceptual dilemma in order to arrive at operational guidelines for applied psychology.

STEIGER, W. A. et al. 1962 A Definition of Comprehensive Medicine. *Journal of Health and Human Behavior* 1:83–86.

U.S. DEPARTMENT OF HEALTH, EDUCATION, AND WELFARE, DIVISION OF VITAL STATISTICS 1966 *Conceptual*

*Problems in Developing an Index of Health,* by Daniel F. Sullivan. Washington: Government Printing Office.

WORLD FEDERATION FOR MENTAL HEALTH (1953) 1955 *Cultural Patterns and Technical Change.* Edited by Margaret Mead. New York: New American Library. → A very useful overview in the form of a collage of case histories and topical discussions.

WORLD HEALTH ORGANIZATION 1946 *Constitution of the World Health Organization.* Geneva: The Organization.

# HEARING

Hearing is an especially important avenue by which we gain information about the world around us; one reason is that it plays a primary role in speech communication, a uniquely human activity. Clearly, then, our ability to perceive our environment and therefore to interact with it, both in a physical and verbal or abstract sense, is dependent in large measure upon our sense of hearing [*see* LANGUAGE, *article on* SPEECH PATHOLOGY; PERCEPTION, *article on* SPEECH PERCEPTION].

The study of the auditory system is carried on by a variety of disciplines, including psychology, physics, engineering, mathematics, anatomy, physiology, and chemistry. This article deals primarily with work in psychology, although it will be necessary to refer to other areas for a more complete understanding of certain phenomena. The peripheral hearing mechanism is reviewed from the standpoint of anatomy, hydromechanical action, and electrical activity. The basic subjective correlates of auditory stimuli are discussed, together with current research and theory. In all cases, we are concerned with the normal rather than pathological auditory system.

**The peripheral hearing mechanism.** When one speaks of the ear, the image that first comes to mind is the flap of cartilaginous tissue, or the *pinna,* fixed to either side of the head. The presumed function of the pinna is to direct sound energy into the ear canal, or *external auditory meatus.* In some animals, such as the cat, the pinna may be directionally oriented independently of the head. For all practical purposes, however, man does not possess this ability. It has been shown that because of the particular shape of man's pinnae, sound arriving at the head is modified differentially depending on its direction of arrival. This may well provide a cue for the localization of a sound source in space.

*The external meatus and the eardrum.* The external meatus is a tortuous canal about one inch in length, closed at the inner end by the eardrum, or *tympanic membrane.* The meatus forms a passageway through which sound energy may be transmitted to the inner reaches of the ear. The meatus has the general shape of a tube closed at one end; it tends to resonate at a frequency of about 3,000 cycles per second. Because of this resonance the pressure of sound waves at the eardrum, for frequencies in this vicinity, is twenty times greater than that at the pinna. The meatus, therefore, serves as a selective amplification device, and, interestingly enough, it is primarily in this frequency range that our hearing is most sensitive.

*The middle ear.* The eardrum marks the boundary between the outer and middle ear. At this point variations in sound pressure are changed into mechanical motion, and it is a function of the middle ear to transmit this mechanical motion to the inner ear, where it may excite the auditory nerve. This transmission is affected by three small bones, the *auditory ossicles,* which form a bridge across the middle ear. The ossicles are named for their shapes: the *malleus* (hammer), which is attached to the eardrum; the *incus* (anvil), which is fixed to the malleus; and the *stapes* (stirrup), which articulates with the incus and at the same time fits into an oval opening of the inner ear. The ossicles not only provide simple transmission of vibratory energy but in doing so actually furnish a desirable increase in pressure. The ossicles are held in place by ligaments and may be acted upon by two small muscles, the *tensor tympani* and the *stapedius.* The function of these muscles is not clear, but it has been suggested that their contraction, together with changes in mode of ossicular motion, serves at high levels of stimulation to reduce the effective input to the inner ear.

*The inner ear.* The "foot plate" of the stapes marks the end of the middle ear and the beginning of the inner ear. The inner ear actually consists of two portions that, although anatomically related, serve essentially independent functions. Here we are concerned only with the *cochlea,* which contains the sensory end organs of hearing. The cochlea, spiral in shape, is encased in bone and contains three nearly parallel, fluid-filled ducts running longitudinally. The middle of the three ducts has as its bottom a rather stiff membrane known as the *basilar membrane.* On this membrane is the *organ of Corti,* within which are the *hair cells,* or the sensory receptors for hearing. The hairs of the hair cells extend a short distance up into a gelatinous plate known as the *tectorial membrane.* When the basilar membrane is displaced transversely, the hairs are moved to the side in a shearing motion and the hair cells are stimulated. Displacement of the basilar membrane is brought about by fluid movement induced by the pistonlike action of the stapes in the oval window. Since fluid is essentially noncompressible, its displacement is possible because of the existence of a second opening between the cochlea and the middle ear, the *round window*. When the stapes moves inward, a bulge is produced in the basilar membrane and the round window membrane moves outward. The bulge or local displacement of the basilar membrane is not stationary but moves down the membrane away from the windows. If the movement of the stapes is periodic, such as in response to a pure tone, then the basilar membrane is displaced alternately up and down. Thus, when a pure tone is presented to the ear, a wave travels continuously down the basilar membrane. The amplitude of this wave is not uniform but achieves a maximum value at a particular point along the membrane determined by the stimulus frequency. High frequencies yield maxima near the stapes; lower frequencies produce maxima progressively farther down the membrane.

*Electrical potentials.* Many of the mechanical events just described have an electrical counterpart. The *cochlear microphonic*, an electrical potential derived from the cochlea, reflects the displacement of the basilar membrane. The *endocochlear potential* represents static direct current voltages within various portions of the cochlea, whereas the *summating potential* is a slowly changing direct current voltage that occurs in response to a high-intensity stimulus. Also observable is the *action potential*, which is generated by the auditory neurons in the vicinity of the cochlea. Neural potentials reflecting the activity of the hair cells are transmitted by the eighth cranial nerve to the central nervous system.

**Psychoacoustics.** Although it is true that one of the principal functions of man's auditory system is the perception of speech, it does not necessarily follow that the exclusive use of speech stimuli is the best way to gain knowledge of our sense of hearing. In the study of hearing, the use of simple stimuli predominates and the common stimulus is the sine wave, or pure tone.

Traditionally, psychophysics has investigated problems in (1) detection of stimuli, (2) detection of differences between stimuli, and (3) relations among stimuli. Psychoacoustics has followed a similar pattern.

*Threshold effects.* It has been shown that a number of factors are influential in determining the minimum magnitude (often called intensity or amplitude) of an auditory signal that can be detected. Specifically, absolute thresholds are a function primarily of the frequency and duration of the signal. Under optimum conditions, sound magnitudes so faint as to approach the random movement of air molecules, known as Brownian movement, may be heard; the displacement of the basilar membrane in these cases is a thousand times less than the diameter of a hydrogen atom. Masked thresholds, those obtained in the simultaneous presence of a signal and other stimuli that mask its effect, depend on the frequency and relative magnitude of each stimulus.

In addition, previous auditory stimulation will affect subsequent absolute thresholds. Generally the effect is to lower auditory sensitivity, although in some instances sensitivity may be enhanced. Pertinent factors here include the magnitude, frequency, and duration of the "fatiguing" stimulus as well as the interval between the presentation of the fatiguing and test stimuli.

*Differential thresholds.* There are as many studies dealing with the detection of differences between two stimuli as there are ways in which stimuli may be varied. Only a few examples, therefore, will be cited here. With pure tones thresholds for hearing frequency differences become greater as frequency is increased, and smaller as magnitude is increased. Differences as small as one part in a thousand are detectable. Differential thresholds for magnitude depend upon the same parameters, but in a more complex way.

Noise stimuli, those sound waves lacking a periodic structure, may be varied with respect to magnitude, bandwidth, and center frequency, but differential thresholds with noise are generally predictable from the pure tone data.

**Signal detection theory.** Recently, there has come into psychophysics, principally by way of psychoacoustics, a new way of thinking about detection data. This new approach makes use of signal detection theory and offers some novel ideas. First, it offers a way to measure sensory aspects of detection independently of decision processes. That is, under ordinary circumstances, the overt response to the signal depends not only upon the functioning of the receptor but on the utility of the response alternatives. If it is extremely important that a signal be detected, under ordinary circumstances a subject is more likely to give a positive response regardless of the activity of the receptor.

Second, it rejects the notion of a threshold; that is, a threshold in the sense that a mechanism exists which is triggered if some critical stimulus level is exceeded. One basis for such rejection is clear from the previous paragraph.

The theory of signal detectability substitutes for the concept of a threshold, the view that detection of a stimulus is a problem in the testing of statistical hypotheses. For example, the testing situation can be so structured that two stimulus conditions exist: the signal is present and the signal is absent. Clearly, there are four alternatives: (1) the listener can accept the hypothesis that the signal was present when, in fact, it was; (2) he can reject this hypothesis under the same conditions; (3) he can accept the hypothesis that the signal was absent when, in fact, it was; (4) he can reject this hypothesis. By making certain assumptions about the characteristics of the stimulus and proceeding under the ideal condition that the observer makes use of all information in the signal, the probabilities associated with these alternatives may be mapped out. It has been shown that an actual observer behaves as if he were performing in this fashion, and his performance may therefore be compared to that ideally obtainable.

**Suprathreshold phenomena.** With signals that are easily audible, it is generally conceded that there are three primary perceptual dimensions to hearing: pitch, loudness, and quality. Considerable effort has been expended in searching for the stimulus correlates and physiological mechanisms associated with these dimensions.

*Pitch and theories of hearing.* With a simple pure tone, pitch is usually associated with the frequency of vibration of the stimulus. High frequencies tend to give rise to high pitches. Historically, there have been two general types of theories of hearing: "place" theories and "volley" theories (often called frequency theories).

The most commonly suggested mechanism of pitch is based on a place hypothesis, which holds that the pertinent cue for pitch is the particular *locus of activity* within the nervous system. It seems likely that stimulation of specific neurons or groups of neurons is related to the displacement patterns of the basilar membrane. The chief alternative to the place hypothesis is the volley or rate of neural discharge hypothesis, which holds that the *rate* or *frequency* with which neural discharge occurs within the auditory nerve is the determinant of pitch; the higher the frequency, the higher the pitch. The frequency of neural discharge, in turn, is synchronous with the stimulus frequency.

Any results in which pitch is influenced by any parameter other than frequency is not in accord with the neural discharge hypothesis. Such results include changes in pitch brought about by differences in the magnitude of the stimulus, by masking, fatigue, or auditory pathology. On the other hand, the place hypothesis cannot readily explain how a pitch corresponding to a particular frequency is perceived, when, in fact, little or no energy exists in the stimulus at that frequency. Such a situation exists for several pitch phenomena: the residue, periodicity pitch, time separation pitch, and Huggins' effect.

*Loudness.* Loudness is related to the magnitude of the stimulus, but not exclusively so. Frequency and duration of the stimulus are secondary factors in determining loudness. The loudness of a stimulus depends upon prior acoustic stimulation in somewhat the same manner that absolute threshold does. Generally, loudness decreases following adaptation, and the pertinent parameters are the same as those that influence threshold shifts.

*Quality.* Quality, or timbre, is a complex perceptual quantity that appears to be associated with the harmonic structure of the sound wave. The greater the number of audible harmonics, the richer or fuller the sound will appear. The converse also appears to be true. Relatively little work has been done in this area.

**Scaling and harmonics.** Psychophysical scaling, or the assessment of the relation between the magnitude of the stimulus and the magnitude of the sensation, has been of interest for many years. New methods, whose chief virtues are simplicity and relative freedom from bias, have recently stimulated additional research. Auditory dimensions that have been studied include loudness, pitch, duration, volume, density, and noxiousness.

The principal finding is that in nearly all cases the relation between stimulus and sensation is a power function.

*Nonlinear effects.* In simple systems in which response magnitude is a nonlinear function of stimulus input, harmonics are generated when the system input is in the form of a simple sinusoid. When the input is two sinusoids, or pure tones, then in addition to harmonics, components exist whose frequency is equal to the sum and the difference of the input frequencies. Such effects are seen when the auditory system is driven at moderate and high intensities. That is, additional tones called aural harmonics and sum and difference tones are perceived corresponding to the predicted frequencies. This seems to indicate that the auditory system behaves in a nonlinear fashion over the upper part of its dynamic range.

**Binaural hearing.** Under most conditions, stimuli arising from a single sound source are represented somewhat differently at each of the two ears. The auditory system makes use of these subtle differences in such a fashion that we are able to localize the sound in space. The binaural system is especially sensitive to small temporal disparities in the two inputs, being capable of discriminating differences as small as 0.000008 second. Intensity differences at the two ears also play a role in localization.

Although localization effects are the most dramatic event in binaural hearing, other interesting binaural phenomena occur. For example, less energy is required for threshold if both ears, rather than just one ear, are stimulated. Similarly, the same loudness may be achieved binaurally with less energy than it could be monaurally.

Our sense of hearing provides us with information relative to vibratory or acoustic events. This information relates to the magnitude, frequency, duration, complexity, and spatial locus of the event. The peripheral auditory system is an elegantly designed hydromechanical structure. The sensory cells themselves and complexities of their enervation are of considerable importance, but are less well understood. In total, hearing is an extremely versatile sensory process with exquisite sensitivity.

                                        ARNOLD M. SMALL, JR.

[*Other relevant material may be found in* ATTENTION; NERVOUS SYSTEM; PSYCHOPHYSICS; SENSES; *and in the biography of* HELMHOLTZ.]

### BIBLIOGRAPHY

CONFERENCE ON THE NEURAL MECHANISMS OF THE AUDITORY AND VESTIBULAR SYSTEMS, BETHESDA, MD., *1959* 1960 *Neural Mechanisms of the Auditory and Vestibular Systems.* Springfield, Ill.: Thomas. → The first 16 chapters deal with the auditory system.

GELDARD, FRANK A. 1953 *The Human Senses.* New York: Wiley.

HARVARD UNIVERSITY, PSYCHO-ACOUSTIC LABORATORY 1955 *Bibliography on Hearing.* Cambridge, Mass.: Harvard Univ. Press. → Contains more than ten thousand titles.

HELMHOLTZ, HERMANN L. F. VON (1862) 1954 *On the Sensations of Tone as a Physiological Basis for the Theory of Music.* New York: Dover. → First published as *Die Lehre von den Tonempfindungen als physiologische Grundlage für die Theorie der Musik.* A classic which in many ways is as important today as when it was written.

JERGER, JAMES (editor) 1963 *Modern Developments in Audiology.* New York: Academic Press. → Especially valuable for its readable review of signal detection theory and its coverage of the effect of acoustic stimulation on subsequent auditory perception.

VON BÉKÉSY, GEORG (1928–1958) 1960 *Experiments in Hearing.* New York: McGraw-Hill. → A compilation of Georg Von Békésy's writings on cochlear mechanics, psychoacoustics, and the ear's conductive processes.

WEVER, ERNEST G. 1949 *Theory of Hearing.* New York: Wiley. → A review of theories of hearing with a special attempt to show the cogency of a volley theory.

WEVER, ERNEST G.; and LAWRENCE, MERLE 1954 *Physiological Acoustics.* Princeton Univ. Press. → Emphasis on the mechanics of the middle ear.

## HECKSCHER, ELI

Eli F. Heckscher (1879–1952) was from the beginning of his academic studies at the University of Uppsala (Sweden) both an economist and a historian. A distinctive feature of his life work was his insistence on the importance of both economic theory and statistical evidence to economic history. He first stated this position in his dissertation *Till belysning af järnvägarnas betydelse för Sveriges ekonomiska utveckling* (1907; "The Contribution of the Railroads to Swedish Economic Growth") and later expressed it in the acknowledgment of his debts to Alfred Marshall and William Cunningham, one a theorist and the other a historian.

In 1909 Heckscher became the first professor of economics and statistics at the new business school in Stockholm, and twenty years later a personal chair was created for him as the head of the Stockholm Institute for Economic History.

Heckscher's passionate involvement with the central issues of Swedish economic and social policy throughout the first half of the twentieth century produced a steady flow of pamphlets and articles, and even an incomplete bibliography contains 1,148 items (Ekonomisk-historiska Institutet, Stockholm 1950). As a publicist he was independent of political parties and spoke from a position of laissez-faire liberalism. He considered state intervention proper to few areas other than education and basic social legislation, although he did advocate strong government measures to maintain competition. He was orthodox in monetary and fiscal matters; he championed the restoration of the gold standard in the 1920s and objected to deficit finance in the 1930s.

The application of economics to problems of policy and history was more congenial to Heckscher than the development of pure theory. His most important theoretical contribution, an article entitled "The Effect of Foreign Trade on the Distribution of Income" (1919), was, in fact, provoked by Knut Wicksell's review of a collection of his essays on Swedish economic policy. In this article Heckscher stressed the role of factor endowments in giving rise to comparative advantage. His purpose was to establish that free trade, possibly combined with a policy of redistributive taxation, was preferable to protection, which would give rise to economic loss for the country as a whole. Elaborated by Bertil Ohlin, the argument came to be known as the Heckscher–Ohlin theorem about the tendency, on certain assumptions, for the prices of factors of production to move toward equality as the result of trade in commodities.

In his teaching, articles, and essays, Heckscher roamed the entire span of Western economic history, but he made his main scholarly contributions in two specific fields. His active concern with public affairs led him first to the historical study of economic policy. His *Continental System* (1918), written during World War I concurrently with a study of war economics, remains the classic interpretation of Napoleonic policy, although he has been charged with dismissing too lightly the potential danger to the English economy. It was, however, as the author of the monumental study of *Mercantilism* (1931) that Heckscher secured a lasting international reputation. Conceived as a study of the intellectual history of European economic policy between the Middle Ages and the coming of laissez-faire, this extensive analysis of the objectives and the rationale of mercantilism united strands of earlier appraisals. Like Schmoller and Cunningham, Heckscher regarded the pursuit of power and national unification as the mainspring of mercantilist policy; like Adam Smith he found protectionism and erroneous monetary conceptions to be central and objectionable features of the "mercantile system" of commercial policy.

In spite of his exposure of the intellectual crudeness of mercantilist doctrine and despite his own distrust of regulatory policy, the doctrine emerged in Heckscher's treatment as a comprehensive view of economic life rather than a system of random fallacies. Indeed, since he believed that the concept of "mercantilism" explains the general characteristics of European history at that time, he stressed the uniformity rather than the diversity of national economic policies. Later criticism and controversy arose from Heckscher's emphasis on economic ideas, i.e., his refusal to explain economic policy in terms of particular conditions and interests, which he regarded as of secondary importance compared to the prevailing *conception* of economic facts and relationships.

Heckscher's second field of major achievement was his pathbreaking economic history of Sweden. His magnum opus on *Sveriges ekonomiska historia från Gustav Vasa* (1935–1949) was to remain unfinished; but his shorter history of Swedish economic growth (1941a) constitutes the first survey of its kind. The backwardness of the medieval Swedish economy relative to the European continental countries and the lateness and rapidity of Swedish industrialization were the problems that Heckscher attacked, with a rare attention to both details and the grand design. Although his humanism and erudition led him into every branch of historical inquiry, his scholarly credo stressed the importance of quantifiable evidence. The relatively rich material on Swedish demographic conditions since the early eighteenth century provided him with especially valuable material, but he also studied every aspect of the economy by his creative statistical use of archival sources.

Heckscher's view of Swedish economic history has on several points been revised by later research. (See the appendices to the second Swedish edition of *Svenskt arbete och liv* 1941b.) This does not detract from its significance as a point of departure for any interpretation of the growth of the Swedish economy. Some of Heckscher's statistical analyses —for instance, his studies of the role and prevalence of "natural economy" in fiscal administration and of the structure of Swedish foreign trade in the sixteenth century, and his Malthusian analysis of Swedish population movements in the eighteenth century—have, of course, been modified or replaced. However, such revisions are in the spirit of Heckscher's own achievement and are therefore a tribute to it rather than a rejection.

GORAN OHLIN

[*Directly related are the entries* ECONOMIC THOUGHT; *article on* MERCANTILIST THOUGHT; INTERNATIONAL TRADE; *and the biographies of* CUNNINGHAM; MARSHALL; SMITH, ADAM.]

## WORKS BY HECKSCHER

1907 *Till belysning af järnvägarnas betydelse för Sveriges ekonomiska utveckling.* Stockholm: Centraltryckeriet.

(1918) 1922 *The Continental System: An Economic Interpretation.* Edited by Harald Westergaard. Oxford: Clarendon Press; New York: Milford. → First published in Swedish.

(1919) 1949 The Effect of Foreign Trade on the Distribution of Income. Pages 272–300 in American Economic Association, *Readings in the Theory of International Trade.* Philadelphia: Blakiston. → First published in Swedish.

(1929) 1953 A Plea for Theory in Economic History. Pages 421–430 in Frederic C. Lane and Jelle C. Riemersma (editors), *Enterprise and Secular Change: Readings in Economic History.* Homewood, Ill.: Irwin.

(1931) 1955 *Mercantilism.* 2 vols., rev. ed. London: Allen & Unwin; New York: Macmillan. → First published in Swedish.

1935–1949 *Sveriges ekonomiska historia från Gustav Vasa.* 4 vols. Stockholm: Bonnier. → Volumes 1–2: *Före frihetstiden.* Volumes 3–4: *Det moderna Sveriges grundläggning.*

(1941a) 1954 *An Economic History of Sweden.* Translated by Goran Ohlin, with a supplement by Gunnar Heckscher and a preface by Alexander Gerschenkron. Cambridge, Mass.: Harvard Univ. Press. → First published as *Svenskt arbete och liv.*

(1941b) 1957 *Svenskt arbete och liv från medeltiden till nutiden.* 2d ed., rev. & enl. Stockholm. Bonnier. → See especially the appendices to the 1957 edition.

SUPPLEMENTARY BIBLIOGRAPHY

COLEMAN, DONALD C. 1957 Eli Heckscher and the Idea of Mercantilism. *Scandinavian Economic History Review* 5, no. 1:3–25.

EKONOMISK-HISTORISKA INSTITUTET, STOCKHOLM 1950 *Eli F. Heckschers bibliografi: 1897–1949.* Stockholm: The Institute.

GERSCHENKRON, ALEXANDER A. 1954 Preface. In Eli F. Heckscher, *An Economic History of Sweden.* Cambridge, Mass.: Harvard Univ. Press.

# HEDGING

*See* SPECULATION, HEDGING, AND ARBITRAGE.

# HEGEL, GEORG WILHELM FRIEDRICH

Georg Wilhelm Friedrich Hegel (1770–1831), who left his deepest mark upon the philosophy of history, is commonly regarded as the representative philosopher of German idealism in the post-Kantian era. To his contemporaries, however, he appeared rather as the continuator of a mode of thought begun by Kant (1724–1804) and amplified by Fichte, Schelling, and the romantic school, which responded to certain logical and metaphysical problems originally raised by the natural sciences. Born in 1770, the year in which Kant inaugurated his professorship at Königsberg with his dissertation *De mundi sensibilis atque intelligibilis forma et principiis* ("The Form and Principles of the Sensible and Intelligible Worlds"), Hegel grew up in the relatively liberal milieu of refugee Protestantism in the south German Duchy of Württemberg. As a student in Tübingen, 1788–1793, he participated in the then widespread enthusiasm for the French Revolution. He was to spend the next seven years in Bern and Frankfurt, tutoring the children of patrician families. During these years he immersed himself in the philosophy of religion, was influenced by his reading of Spinoza, and wrote (but did not publish) some highly critical studies of Christian theology, which remained unknown for over a century. His appointment to a post at the University of Jena in 1801 set him free for systematic teaching in philosophy; and this phase of his activity was crowned by the publication of his first major work, *The Phenomenology of Mind* (1807), completed during the battle of Jena.

The upheaval that followed the triumph of Napoleon over the Prussian army gave Hegel the personal satisfaction of seeing the emperor—that "world-soul on horseback," as he described him—but it also deprived him of his teaching position. After editing a newspaper in Bamberg (Bavaria) for a year, he was appointed rector of a Gymnasium at Nuremberg, a post he held from 1808 to 1816. During these years (which also witnessed his marriage to Marie von Tucher) he completed his second great work, the *Science of Logic* (1812–1816). Appointed to a chair of philosophy at Heidelberg (1816–1818), he there published his *Encyclopedia of Philosophy* (1817), a work which carried into effect a scheme already propounded by him in 1801: that of a tripartite philosophical system embracing a logic, a philosophy of nature, and a philosophy of spirit. The last mentioned formed the basis of the *Philosophy of Right* (1821), the last major work published during his lifetime, which was written during his early years at the University of Berlin, where he taught from 1818 to 1831. By that time he had become famous, and his courses attracted students from all over Germany. The lectures he gave during those years on history, religion, aesthetics, and the history of philosophy were published after his death and helped to spread his fame to a wider public. During these last years he had become a confidant of the Prussian minister of education and something of a conservative, but he retained his theological rationalism and some of his early enthusiasm for the French Revolution and Napoleon. His death in November 1831, during a cholera epidemic, precipitated the dissolution of his school into conflicting liberal and conservative factions.

The extreme complexity of Hegel's thought, and the all-embracing character of his system, along with a certain ambiguity in his political utterances, made it possible for exponents of very different schools to lay claim to his authority; and throughout the remainder of the century his name was a battle cry for opposing parties in philosophy and politics. Contrary to a widespread misconception, Hegel was never in his lifetime associated with German nationalism; he gave guarded support to the Prussian state but remained firmly committed to the principle of equality before the law. His mature political philosophy has affinities with that of Edmund Burke, and even his notorious utterances on the subject of the Prussian monarchy and the loyalty due to its representatives maintain a balance between Hobbesian authoritarianism and conventional Toryism: they are not in the slightest degree "totalitarian" and bear only an indirect relation to the doctrines of those twentieth-century German and Italian ideologists who invoked his authority.

While the philosophy of history (notably in the form it assumed in nineteenth-century Germany) bears Hegel's mark, the impact of Hegelianism on the social sciences is more difficult to assess. Social thought in Hegel's own day was subsumed under political theory. The study of economics was still in its infancy (although Hegel had become acquainted with it during his Frankfurt years), and social theorizing in general turned upon constitutional problems. These indeed had been the subject of Hegel's first publication, in 1798, a critical study of Swiss constitutional developments. His last major work, the *Philosophy of Right*, develops a political philosophy which holds a precarious balance between rationalism and authoritarianism, somewhat in the manner of Fichte, Kant, and the Enlightenment theorists who preceded them. By the 1840s this book had furnished a target for the first major broadside directed by the youthful Marx against Hegel in his *Kritik des Hegelschen Staatsrechts* (1843). In general the theory of civil society is subsumed by Hegel under the theory of the state; the latter is viewed as the embodiment of rationality, as against the conflicts of material interests that make up the daily life of the civil society. Hegel counterposes the rational universality of the whole to the particular desires and strivings of the individuals in a manner reminiscent of Hobbes and contrary to Rousseau, for whom the "general will" springs from the fusion of individual wills. Such a fusion, and with it the notion of a social contract, is denied by Hegel on the grounds that civil society is too anarchic to generate a true consensus. The "actuality of the ethical Idea" is attained in the state, which is "absolutely rational," "mind objectified," "the actuality of concrete freedom" ([1821] 1942, pp. 155–160). Hegel differs from Hobbes in holding that the state is not to be viewed as the guarantor of civil society, but as an end in itself. It is not simply the guardian of personal freedom and property, for in that case loyalty to the state would be optional, whereas according to Hegel it is only as a member of the political realm that the individual has objective reality and an ethical life (*ibid.*, p. 156). This exaltation of the state appears to have been a fruit of Hegel's youthful enthusiasm for the classical *polis*. It led him into what even his contemporaries regarded as an extravagant glorification of the Prussian monarchy; but since it was coupled with conservative distrust of popular movements and indeed of the people, of that part of the body politic "which does not know

what it wants" (*ibid.*, para. 301), Hegel's doctrine cannot be described as totalitarian even by implication. Its nature is traditionalist rather than romantic and belongs to the eighteenth century rather than to the twentieth.

Hegel did, however, repudiate traditional natural law and—by implication—international law. His influence on European (notably German) thinking thus ran counter to the gradual acceptance of liberal doctrines throughout the nineteenth century. The Hegelian view of interstate relations, which entered the consciousness of the German educated classes by way of the Prussian bureaucracy and the educational system it controlled, is Hobbesian and subversive of much that is regarded as fundamental in Anglo–American jurisprudence. On Hegelian principles, contracts between states are not valid, since sovereignty cannot be abrogated by treaty. The test of sovereignty is war, which discloses the truth that nations are not subordinate to law but operate in a Hobbesian "state of nature." War is necessary and may even be regarded as beneficial, since it is the test of a people's willingness to maintain its freedom and independence. It also makes it possible to achieve a degree of social integration which civil society by itself cannot secure (*ibid.*, para. 324). These doctrines became part of the official credo of Bismarckian Germany and may be said to have deepened the ideological gulf between Germany and the West which was first made manifest in the war of 1914–1918. They clearly run parallel to the critique of natural law doctrine implicit in the "pure theory of law" (*reine Rechtslehre*) associated with H. Kelsen and his followers. This influential school of "legal positivism" maintains that the substantive concept of law as the embodiment of prelegal rules of a moral nature is metaphysical and irrelevant to the actual practice of lawmaking (Kelsen 1955; cf. Kelsen 1945). The displacement of the older doctrine by this positivist doctrine, which implicitly sanctions the abrogation of "so-called fundamental liberties," may be regarded as a belated triumph of Hegelianism, although outside central Europe similar ideas were developed without reference to Hegel's philosophy. So far as the U.S.S.R. is concerned, its legal theory may perhaps be described as Hegelian; but there are elements of natural law doctrine both in classical Marxism and in the Russian Populist tradition, and since the late 1950s there has been a tendency to revive them.

Hegel's ideas also reached the social sciences by a different channel: via the philosophy of history, and in particular through the growing influence of

Marxism. The relationship of Marx to Hegel is, however, more complex than appears from the popular notion that Marx merely inverted the Hegelian system by "standing it on its head," i.e., by substituting a supposed "materialist dialectic" for Hegel's idealist one. Marx took over from Hegel the conception of history as the self-creation of man and the idea (first expounded by Hegel in the *Phenomenology*) that the prime motive force of the historical process is human labor, or the practical activity of men in society. Marx did not, however, subscribe to the notion that this process can be reduced to a logical schematization, and his approach to empirical history is more in tune with French materialism than with German idealism. (This part of his work in some respects anticipates modern sociology.) He also repudiated Hegel's political doctrine. The state appears in the Marxian corpus as an arbitrary external power superimposed upon human society; and it is thus a form of "human self-alienation" [see ALIENATION]. Hegel's authoritarian political philosophy did have some influence on Ferdinand Lassalle (1825–1864), and through him on German socialism, but was antipathetic to Marx.

The relevance of Hegel's general philosophy to what is often called "historicism" is difficult to assess. The notion (which Whitehead restated and applied to the natural sciences) that the peculiarities of reality are only local and temporary concretions of a process stretching beyond them has been popularized by Marxian writers, but it is not held by them alone. Its conservative counterpart is the doctrine that cultures are to be regarded as "organic wholes" rather than as casual accretions of unrelated features. The Hegelian concept of dialectical change can be, and has been, reformulated as a description of processes whereby social organisms create their own environment and are in turn influenced by it. Hence it has been said that "a philosopher–scientist like Whitehead can restate Hegel's theory, not knowing that it is Hegel's" (Collingwood 1946, p. 128). Although originally intended by Hegel to account for natural processes, the idea of a "dialectical" interrelationship between man and his environment is clearly of general application, and it may be that the long-run significance of Hegel's philosophy for the social sciences will be found to lie in this kind of approach. Hegel is unquestionably the chief originator of what is sometimes called "process thought." His philosophy finds room for the efflorescence of the higher forms of culture and for the values we attach to them by postulating a series of "levels of organization," rising from the lower to the higher through historically conditioned transformations which introduce new qualitative changes. This concept has proved fertile in inducing historians and sociologists to look upon history not as a field governed by immutable "laws" but as a process in which something fresh is created at every moment.

GEORGE LICHTHEIM

[*See also* HISTORY, *article on* THE PHILOSOPHY OF HISTORY; MARXISM; POLITICAL THEORY; *and the biographies of* CROCE; DURKHEIM; GREEN; HOBBES; KANT; KELSEN; MARX; STIRNER.]

### WORKS BY HEGEL

(1795–1809) 1961   *On Christianity: Early Theological Writings.* Gloucester, Mass.: Smith. → First published in 1907 as *Hegels theologische Jugendschriften.* Edited by Herman Nohl. A paperback edition was published in 1961 by Harper.

(1799–1831) 1964   *Hegel's Political Writings.* Translated by T. M. Knox, with an introductory essay by Z. A. Pelczynski. Oxford: Clarendon Press. → The first essay, "The German Constitution," was written by Hegel between 1799 and 1802 and left in manuscript until after his death.

(1807) 1961   *The Phenomenology of Mind.* 2d ed., rev. London: Allen & Unwin; New York: Macmillan. → First published as *Phänomenologie des Geistes.*

(1812–1816) 1951   *Hegel's Science of Logic.* 2 vols. London: Allen & Unwin; New York: Macmillan. → First published as *Wissenschaft der Logik.*

(1817) 1959   *Encyclopedia of Philosophy.* New York: Philosophical Library. → First published as *Encyklopädie der philosophischen Wissenschaften im Grundrisse.*

(1821) 1942   *The Philosophy of Right.* Oxford: Clarendon. → First published as *Grundlinien der Philosophie des Rechts.*

(1837) 1956   *The Philosophy of History.* New York: Dover. → First published as *Vorlesungen über die Philosophie der Weltgeschichte.*

*Sämtliche Werke.* 26 vols. Stuttgart (Germany): Frommann, 1927–1940.

### SUPPLEMENTARY BIBLIOGRAPHY

COLLINGWOOD, R. G.   1946   *The Idea of History.* Oxford: Clarendon. → A paperback edition was published in 1956.

FINDLAY, JOHN N.   1958   *Hegel: A Re-examination.* London: Allen & Unwin. → A paperback edition was published in 1962 by Collier.

GURVITCH, GEORGES D.   1962   *Dialectique et sociologie.* Paris: Flammarion.

HABERMAS, JÜRGEN   1963   *Theorie und Praxis.* Neuwied (Germany): Luchterhand.

HYPPOLITE, JEAN   1955   *Études sur Marx et Hegel.* Paris: Rivière.

KELSEN, HANS   (1945) 1961   *General Theory of Law and State.* New York: Russell. → First published in German.

KELSEN, HANS   1955   Foundation of Democracy. *Ethics* 66, part 2:1–101.

KRONER, RICHARD   (1921–1924) 1961   *Von Kant bis Hegel.* 2d ed., 2 vols. Tübingen (Germany): Mohr.

Löwith, Karl (1941) 1964 *From Hegel to Nietzsche: The Revolution in 19th Cent. Thought.* New York: Holt. → First published in German.

Marcuse, Herbert (1941) 1955 *Reason and Revolution: Hegel and the Rise of Social Theory.* 2d ed. New York: Humanities Press. → A paperback edition was published in 1960 by Beacon.

Marx, Karl (1843) 1953 *Kritik des Hegelschen Staatsrechts.* Pages 20–149 in Karl Marx, *Die Frühschriften.* Stuttgart (Germany): Kroner.

Mure, Geoffrey R. G. (1940) 1948 *An Introduction to Hegel.* Oxford: Clarendon Press.

Stace, Walter T. (1924) 1955 *The Philosophy of Hegel: A Systematic Exposition.* New York: Dover.

# HELLER, HERMANN

Hermann Heller (1891–1933), German political scientist, was born at Teschen in Austria. He taught at Kiel, Leipzig, Berlin, and Frankfurt. In 1933, he emigrated and died in Madrid in the same year.

Heller revived political theory in Germany, where it had been emptied of content by both legal positivism and political voluntarism. The central problem of order, Heller taught, is the tension between will and norm, which must not be resolved in favor of either pole. Man's nature is essentially utopian, looking toward what ought to be. What ought to be, however, cannot order human existence without the acts of a public will that in any society makes binding decisions about legal rules and assures their regular enforcement. The modern state is essentially a hierarchically organized unity of will that performs the function of deciding and enforcing positive law within a given territory. In relation to the legal system, the state is sovereign, that is, a supreme will subject to no other will. For the sake of the law, the state must in an emergency maintain itself even against the law. The sovereign will, however, can posit law only within the range of transpositive fundamental principles of law (*Rechtsgrundsätze*), which are either formal (logical) or substantive (ethical) norms.

Heller construed this higher law not as unchanging but as shaped by various historical civilizations. Political theory must explain the state in world-immanent terms but not reduce it to nature. Rather, the state is a part of human culture (defined as facts suffused with meaning). It exists in and through human activities, among which it has reality as a gestalt, a structure retaining its identity in the flow of its changing parts. The proper method of political theory is neither normative nor causal but, rather, sociological. It can never be "value-free" in Max Weber's sense, although it can free itself from bias. An explanation of the state must take into account underlying social entities, for example, historical entities of national culture (*Kultureinheiten*). Human nature, a constant in any political order, must be seen as shaped by history. Man, society, and culture are basic conditions of any state and cannot be artificially produced.

Much of Heller's work dealt with the political crisis of the West. He conceived of it as a collapse of political order stemming from the destruction of political theory by positivism. The antipolitical notion of the automatically self-regulating natural order produced modern legal positivism, which construed the concept of order without the state and apart from any concrete content. As a reaction there arose the twentieth-century cult of sheer force—or the strong man—and the notion of the intrinsic value of a command. Heller blamed this development on the bourgeoisie, which, when it was in power, disavowed its former moral convictions about the necessity of order and embraced positivist legality instead.

Heller was a leading German socialist, although not a follower of Marx, whose materialism and historical messianism he rejected. Socialism was justified, he felt, by the desirability of social homogeneity, of a community of interests and values that alone can form the basis of a democratic state. Class antagonism endangers this community, which can be restored only by including the workers in its economic and cultural benefits. No such community is possible apart from the historically grown unity of common national language, traditions, values, and ways of life. Socialism and the national community are interdependent. Heller's socialism was national although not nationalistic. He favored the unification of Europe as the only way of safeguarding national cultures in an age of superpowers.

Heller's thought was eclectic rather than derived from any one master. Although he rejected the major conclusions of Hegel, Marx, Weber, Dilthey, and Kelsen, he made use of some of the ideas and methods of each to compensate for the biases of the others. The result was not a historical dialectic but a dialectic that synthesized elements which political theorists had often separated. Man consists of both body and soul, society includes physical as well as spiritual meaning, legal order presupposes both norm and will, political theory must use not only causal but also normative analysis, and so forth. It was his ability to hold such tensions in his mind without trying to resolve them for the sake of a unified system that secured Heller's position as one of the strong voices of sanity in an age of political disorder.

GERHART NIEMEYER

[*See also* POLITICAL THEORY; POSITIVISM; STATE; *and the biographies of* AUSTIN; KELSEN.]

WORKS BY HELLER

1921    *Hegel und der nationale Machtstaatsgedanke in Deutschland: Ein Beitrag zur politischen Geistesgeschichte.* Leipzig and Berlin: Teubner.

(1925) 1931    *Sozialismus und Nation.* 2d ed. Berlin: Rowohlt.

1926a    *Die Krisis der Staatslehre. Archiv für Sozialwissenschaft und Sozialpolitik* 55:289–316.

1926b    *Die politischen Ideenkreise der Gegenwart.* Kiel (Germany): Hirt.

1927    *Die Souveränität: Ein Beitrag zur Theorie des Staats- und Völkerrechts.* Leipzig and Berlin: de Gruyter.

(1929) 1931    *Europa und der Fascismus.* 2d ed. Leipzig and Berlin: de Gruyter.

1930    *Rechtsstaat oder Diktatur?* Tübingen (Germany): Mohr.

1934a    Political Science. Volume 12, pages 207–224 in *Encyclopaedia of the Social Sciences.* New York: Macmillan.

1934b    Political Power. Volume 12, pages 300–305 in *Encyclopaedia of the Social Sciences.* New York: Macmillan.

1934c    *Staatslehre.* Leiden (Netherlands): Sijthoff.

# HELMHOLTZ, HERMANN VON

From the perspective of posterity, Hermann Ludwig Ferdinand von Helmholtz (1821–1894) made his most significant contributions to the fields of sensory physiology and psychology. In particular, he laid the foundations for the experimental investigation of the sensory processes in audition and vision. His successes resulted from his unusual mathematical and mechanical abilities and from his skill in assembling, sifting, and logically interrelating large quantities of information.

Helmholtz was born in Potsdam, the eldest of five children. The atmosphere of his home, although not scientific, was intellectual. Helmholtz mentioned that he frequently listened to the philosophical discussions between his father, August, a distinguished teacher of languages and philosophy in the Gymnasium, and his colleagues. August Helmholtz was most important in guiding his son's early education. He taught him Greek and Arabic, encouraged him to study poetry, art, and music, and trained him in the writing of expository essays. Even at an early age, however, Helmholtz was attracted more to physics and mathematics than to the humanities. Speaking of his youth, Helmholtz recalled, in 1891, that while the rest of his class in the Gymnasium read Cicero and Vergil, he himself would work out optical and geometrical problems under his desk.

Helmholtz represented a scientific ideal to his contemporaries. He was a man of remarkable talents, universal interests, and indefatigable energy. He published over 200 papers and books making fundamental contributions to the fields of anatomy, medicine, physics, physiology, and psychology. He invented scientific and medical instruments. A contemplative mind led him to consider the philosophic questions raised by developments in science. A sense of social responsibility led him to deplore the gulf separating those trained in the humanities and those trained in the sciences; this gulf he sought to bridge by delivering popular lectures explaining the developments of science to laymen.

For the social sciences, Helmholtz' views on the methodology of science and the theory of knowledge are of most immediate relevance. The method of studying and interpreting biological and psychological phenomena was a crucial issue for the scientists and philosophers of the nineteenth century. Helmholtz was convinced that the same scientific method is appropriate for the analysis of vital and mental phenomena as for the analysis of physical phenomena. However, he did not advocate a reductive materialism. For him, memory and learning are facts, the laws of which can be investigated by experimental procedures, even if they cannot be reduced to known physiological processes (Koenigsberger [1902–1903] 1906, p. 305). Rather, he emphasized that the basic method of all scientific inquiry is to discover facts through systematic experimentation and to go beyond these facts to general laws by analysis and abstraction. His lecture on Goethe (see Helmholtz [1853–1870] 1962, pp. 1–21) contains an interesting presentation of his views. After acknowledging Goethe's insightful contributions on the morphology of the skull and the plant, Helmholtz brought up the matter of Goethe's obstinate animosity to Newton's analysis of color. The difference between them, Helmholtz suggested, lay in their attitudes toward the acquisition and conception of knowledge. Goethe, the artist, believed that direct confrontation with a phenomenon is sufficient to provide an understanding of it. He was "accustomed to look as it were, right into the subject, and to reproduce his intuition. . . . His success [was] proportionate to the vividness of the intuition" (*ibid.*, p. 16). Helmholtz acknowledged that intuitive insight is the source of the creative idea for both the scientist and the artist but insisted that, for the scientist, careful observation and reflection are an initial step sufficient only to suggest a hypothesis. The establishment of scientific truth depends on experimental verification. Moreover, the artist is satisfied simply to describe and hesitates to abstract. "A step into the region of abstract conceptions which must be necessarily taken if we wish to penetrate into the causes of phenomena, scares the poet away" (*ibid.*, p. 16). Goethe objected to Newton's theory of color because it substitutes quantitative measurements of the color-mixing relationships for direct naturalistic observation of colors. Helmholtz correctly described how observational intuition led Goethe badly astray when he asserted that it is absurd for white light to be the result of a fusion of colored lights. On the other hand, Goethe's appeal to experience did reveal important phenomenological facts (the distinction between warm and cold colors, the existence of a psychologically unique red, yellow, green, and blue, and the coupling of the colors red and green and yellow and blue) whose potential physiological significance Helmholtz apparently overlooked. Helmholtz' intellectual attitude was that of the nineteenth-century physicist: it was the source of his acute and penetrating analyses, although it occasionally led him to miss the point.

**Work in physics.** At the age of 16, Helmholtz announced to his father that he wanted to study physics. His father, however, could not support the cost of an academic course and enrolled him in the Friedrich Wilhelm Medical Institute in Berlin. This institute gave free instruction on the condition that those enrolled later spend some years as surgeons in the Prussian army. In Berlin, Helmholtz came under the influence of Johannes Müller, professor of physiology at the University of Berlin, and Müller's influence is apparent throughout his physiological research. In 1842, at 21, he received his doctorate for a thesis in anatomy confirming Müller's conjecture that the nerve fibers originate in the ganglion cells. Yet Helmholtz was to join Du Bois-Reymond, Brücke, and Virchow, all Müller's students, in a pact to abolish Müller's notion that within the living organism there exists a separate vital force distinct from chemical and physical forces. These men realized that physiology needed to be securely established as a branch of chemistry and physics. Liebig had placed the question of vitalism within the domain of experimental science by transforming the philosophic question into the experimental problem of whether or not the mechanical energy and the heat produced by

an organism result entirely from its own metabolism. Helmholtz realized that this problem is closely connected to the law of the conservation of energy and turned his attention to that law. Joule had already established the equivalence between mechanical work and heat, and Helmholtz sought to extend the principle of the conservation of energy to physiology. He began by investigating the relation between muscular activity and heat. For this purpose he devised the myograph, a device which records the twitching of a muscle, a thermal galvanometer sensitive to temperature changes of .001° centigrade, and a means by which a muscle can be stimulated by electric shocks of short duration. He found that a single muscle contraction can give rise to an increase in temperature of from .001° centigrade to .005° centigrade, showing that the chemical processes in muscle contraction produce heat. Helmholtz then turned to determining the equivalence between the heat produced by an animal and the caloric value of the food taken in. He calculated the amounts of heat given off in various ways and the efficiency of an animal's metabolism and concluded that the total heat given off corresponds to the heat generated by the oxidation of the food consumed. Unknown to Helmholtz, the extension of the law of the conservation of energy from inanimate to animate phenomena had already been suggested by Robert Mayer. Helmholtz next set himself the task of showing the universal application of the conservation of energy principle by theoretically deriving it from more fundamental physical principles. He showed that if all matter consists of particles, and if these interact according to forces acting along the lines joining the particles, and if all forms of energy depend upon the motion and position of the particles, then the conservation of energy must hold. These results he announced in a lecture he gave (at the age of 26) to the Physical Society of Berlin on July 23, 1847.

**Work in physiology.** Helmholtz' scientific ability now became generally recognized, and with the aid of Alexander von Humboldt, president of the Academy of Sciences in Berlin, he was released from further military service. After a year as a lecturer in anatomy at the Academy of Arts in Berlin, Helmholtz became professor of physiology at Königsberg. He remained in Königsberg from 1849 to 1855.

*Nerve impulses.* The first important physiological problem to concern Helmholtz after his move to Königsberg was the rate of nerve transmission. Müller had stated that the speed of the nerve impulse is comparable to the speed of light and unmeasurable. Du Bois-Reymond's theory of the polarization of molecules in nervous tissue suggested to Helmholtz that the nerve impulse, although electrical in nature, is not simply an electric current. Helmholtz stimulated nerves near and far from a muscle and measured the time it takes for the muscle to contract. The difference in time divided by the distance between the two points showed that the rate of the neural impulse in the motor nerve of a frog is about 27 meters per second. Helmholtz also devised the reaction time experiment to measure the speed of nerve transmission in humans. An electric shock was given to a point on the skin and the observer was directed to move his hand as quickly as he could. Although variable, the results showed that the rate of transmission of the impulse is between 50 and 60 meters per second. The novelty of these studies provoked opposition from physiologists. In fact, both Müller and von Humboldt refused at first to believe the results and it was only through the continued arguments of Du Bois-Reymond that they were convinced of the correctness of Helmholtz' work.

*Optics and visual perception.* In 1851 Helmholtz invented the ophthalmoscope, the most celebrated of his inventions. He suggested that the blackness of the pupil results from the fact that the head of an observer looking at the eye of a person blocks the rays of light that would illuminate the retina. The ophthalmoscope is a device that illuminates the retina through the pupil, rendering it visible. In its modern form, constructed by H. Reute in 1852 (M'Kendrick 1899, p. 78), the ophthalmoscope enables one to look at the retina through a small opening in a reflecting plate. In 1852 Helmholtz invented the ophthalmometer, a device for measuring the radii of curvature of the anterior and posterior surfaces of the cornea and the lens. At this time Helmholtz turned to the problem of accommodation. A Dutch physiologist, Cramer, had shown that accommodation consists in an increasing curvature of the lens when the eye changes from a far point to a near point. Helmholtz, unacquainted with the work of Cramer, arrived independently at the same conclusion. Helmholtz' new contribution to the theory of accommodation was his hypothesis about the way in which the curvature of the lens is altered. Using his anatomical knowledge, he suggested that when the fibers of the ciliary muscles contract, the tension of the lens capsule is reduced, and the lens's own elasticity causes the anterior surface of the lens to bulge forward.

From 1851 to 1856 Helmholtz was mainly engaged in research in physiological optics. The result of this work, together with a survey of the germane literature, is presented in his monumental three-volume handbook on physiological optics (Helmholtz 1867). The handbook demonstrates Helmholtz' mastery of the physical, mathematical, and physiological problems involved in vision and visual perception. The worth of the handbook is attested to by its continued scientific pertinence a hundred years later. Volume 1 describes the anatomy and optical properties of the eye. Volume 2 deals with problems of visual sensation. In 1852 Helmholtz undertook to test the laws of color mixture. Newton had failed to distinguish between the mixture of colored lights and of colored pigments. Thomas Young, in his famous paper of 1801, had suggested (in analogy to the mixture of pigments) that red, yellow, and blue are the three primaries from which all colors can be derived by suitable mixtures. But to his surprise, Helmholtz discovered that the combination of yellow and blue lights produces not green, as was supposed, but white. Helmholtz was the first to differentiate clearly between the addition of lights, which produces a color because of the superposition of excitations of different wave lengths stimulating the eye, and the addition of pigments, which produces a color that is a result of the wave lengths reflected by both pigments. Yellow and blue pigments when mixed give green because neither pigment absorbs green light. After clearing up the confusion between light mixtures and pigment mixtures, Helmholtz proceeded to develop a comprehensive theory of color vision. He based his theory on the extension of Müller's law of specific nervous energies to the sense organs and on the assumption that the facts of color matching accurately mirror underlying physiological processes. Just as the difference between the sensations of light and sound depends on the kind of nerve fibers stimulated, so the sensation of color depends on the kind of nerve fiber excited in the eye. The data on color mixture, moreover, indicate that all hues except the most saturated can be obtained by suitable combinations of three primaries: red, green, and violet. Helmholtz made explicit that part of Young's theory which dealt with nerve activity, by postulating that the nerve fibers must respond in varying degrees to all wave lengths. Hue depends on the relative frequencies of the impulses set up in the three types of fibers, brightness on the total excitation of the fibers, and saturation on the amount of white produced by fusion. He also extended the theory to account for color blindness, negative afterimages, and successive contrasts. The Young–Helmholtz theory of color vision is still widely accepted, although certain facts of color blindness and color thresholds pose difficulties for it.

Volume 3 deals with problems of space perception and object perception. Central to Helmholtz' theory of space and object perception is his doctrine of unconscious inference. Helmholtz argued in his inaugural lecture at Königsberg in 1852 that the law of specific nerve energies implies that sensations serve only as the signs of external objects. That is, sensations tell us as much about the real nature of external phenomena as the name of a man tells us about the man. Accordingly, perceptual experience involves a construction on the part of the observer. A problem of great concern for Helmholtz was to determine what in the nature of perceptual experience is innate and what is derived from experience. He asserted that what in the perceptual image can be modified by experience must itself be considered a product of experience ([1867] 1924–1925, vol. 3, p. 13). Applying this criterion, he concluded that the only innate properties are the intensity and the quality of a sensation. Thus, conscious experience consists initially of a mass of sight, sound, taste, and smell sensations, each differentiated only with respect to quality and intensity. How does one come to experience coherent objects ordered in space and time? The answer lies in the distinction between sensation and perception. Perception involves a two-stage process: (1) sensation and (2) unconscious inference. Sensations are the immediate products of stimulating sense organs and associated neural systems. Unconscious inference is a central reasoning-like process which utilizes the information provided by sensation to infer the properties of external objects and events. Thus, perception is not simply an aggregate of sensations. Perception goes beyond the sensations provided by the receptor organs and entails a judgment about the environment. The unconscious judgments in perception are automatic and irresistible. The knowledge gained in perception, based on sensations and the memory of sensations, is a knowledge of acquaintance (*kennen*). In contrast, the conscious judgments in thought are flexible and deliberate, and the knowledge gained, based on concepts, is a knowledge of awareness (*wissen*). For Helmholtz these differences, however, are only superficial. Both the unconscious judgments in perception and the conscious judgments in thought involve the same mental operations and have the same logical status ([1853–1870] 1962, pp. 178–181). The view that perception inherently involves a judgment has played an important role in psychological theory.

*Acoustics.* In 1855 Helmholtz was appointed professor of anatomy and physiology at Bonn, where he remained until 1858, when he became professor of physiology at Heidelberg. While still immersed in the preparation of his *Physiological Optics* Helmholtz had decided to write a similar work on acoustics. In 1856 he reported the discovery of summation tones. These tones, whose frequencies are the sum of two input frequencies, are generated because of the nonlinear response of structures in the external ear. In 1857 Helmholtz formulated his well-known theory of vowel quality. Differences between vowel sounds arise because the mouth cavity when shaped for different vowels serves as an adjustable resonator which differentially strengthens the harmonic components of the fundamental voice tone. Papers quickly followed on sound production, tone quality, harmony, and the musical scales. In 1862 Helmholtz' classic work, *On the Sensations of Tone*, appeared. This book brings together his many experimental and historical studies in acoustics and music theory. The aim of the work is to provide connecting links between the fields of physical acoustics, physiological acoustics, and music. The most famous of Helmholtz' contributions to audition is his theory of pitch perception. Applying the law of specific nerve energies to the ear, Helmholtz suggested that there exist specific fibers in the inner ear that respond by resonance to the different frequencies. Each fiber excites its own nerve so that the neural impulses transmitted to the brain correspond to the component frequencies of a sound wave. Thus, the resonance theory of pitch provides an explanation of Ohm's law which asserts that it is possible to hear the simple harmonic components into which a complex sound may be analyzed. Although such a simple resonance theory is no longer tenable, experiments have demonstrated that a locus of maximum vibration which changes with sound frequency does occur on the basilar membrane in the way Helmholtz suggested. Helmholtz extended his theory of pitch to provide an account of timbre, dissonance, consonance, and melody. Timbre depends upon the relative intensities of the harmonics present, dissonance on the beats generated when two frequencies affect overlapping segments of the basilar membrane, consonance and melody on the identity of harmonics produced by simultaneous tones or a succession of tones. Helmholtz' views on the musical relationships have been much discussed and criticized but are still relevant today.

**Aesthetics.** Since his early student days, Helmholtz had been concerned with problems of aesthetic significance. Although science and art differ in their methods, he believed them to be intimately connected because both seek to acquaint us with reality (Koenigsberger [1902–1903] 1906, p. 172). While the scientist expresses truth by means of abstract concepts, the artist expresses truth by means of images. Since art has a cognitive function, the articulation of meanings that cannot be conveyed by words, it must conform to the laws governing human intelligence. The function of the scientist is not, however, to instruct the artist. This is essentially impossible since neither the artist nor the observer is consciously aware of the laws on whose fulfillment beauty depends ([1862] 1954, p. 366). Rather, the function of the scientist is to provide the artist with the information which may aid him in his artistic invention. The artist can succeed in his work only when he is aware of the subtle relations present within a phenomenon and of their effects upon an observer (Koenigsberger [1902–1903] 1906, p. 106). In a lecture on anatomy and sculpture delivered in 1848, Helmholtz considered the methods and benefits of teaching anatomy to artists (*ibid.*, pp. 51–57), and in a lecture on optics and painting, Helmholtz ([1853–1870] 1962, pp. 250–286) discussed the complex problems faced by the painter who seeks to produce an accurate representation of the forms, sizes, distances, and illuminations of objects in a scene. To cope successfully with these problems, the artist must translate rather than copy nature, taking into careful consideration the operation of the sensory system. For Helmholtz the relations between art and science are particularly clear and striking in music. Musical composition depends more on the immediate sensations than is the case with the other arts, like sculpture, in which the object represented has a much greater importance ([1862] 1954, p. 3). Part 3 of the *Sensations of Tone* deals with the agreeableness of different chords, the formation of scales, and the elementary rules of musical composition. Helmholtz cautioned that the history of music shows that the construction of scales and musical composition is by no means determined by the properties of the ear but depends on artistic invention and aesthetic principles which change with time (*ibid.*, p. 235).

**Epistemology.** Helmholtz' interest in sensory physiology naturally led him to the problems of epistemology. Following the English tradition, he appealed to psychology for an understanding of epistemology. He argued that a knowledge of the sensory mechanisms is necessary for determining the status of objects. In a letter to Carl Ludwig, in 1855, Helmholtz wrote, "I believe that philosophy will only be reinstated when it turns with zeal and energy to the investigation of epistemological processes and of scientific methods. . . . Most essential of all in this critical investigation is the exact knowledge of the processes of sense-perception" (Koenigsberger [1902–1903] 1906, p. 139). Kant had established 12 categories of a priori concepts. These represented the operation of inherent characteristics of the mind, which condition experience and do not arise from experience. Examples of a priori concepts are space and time, the geometrical axioms, and the law of causality. Helmholtz first questioned the correctness of Kant's position concerning the inherent nature of space. He concluded that the experience of an ordered space is not innate but is derived from movements of the eye and body ([1853–1870] 1962, p. 156). Helmholtz' empirical theory of perception led him to an empirical theory of cognition. In 1866 he turned to the epistemology of mathematics. He undertook to show that the geometric axioms are also the products of experience and that they depend upon the notion of congruence, which is based upon mechanical movements and is itself acquired through experience. Thus, the axioms of geometry are not innate but have their origin in an individual's experience with objects and with the space in which he lives. To show that the axioms of Euclidean geometry are not examples of a priori intuitions, Helmholtz independently developed Riemannian non-Euclidean geometry. In 1888 Helmholtz tried to show that the axioms of arithmetic can also be derived from experience. He accepted only the law of causality as a priori and transcendental and asserted that all thought presupposes the law of causation, which is therefore not derivable from experience (Koenigsberger [1902–1903] 1906, p. 142). For example, the law of causation underlies the unconscious inference by which we pass from sensation to perception, since this process assumes the existence of external objects that cause our sensations. Whether the mechanism of unconscious inference is itself innate or is derived from experience, Helmholtz left as an open question (*ibid.*, p. 110).

In 1871 Helmholtz became professor of physics in Berlin. He spent the last years of his life primarily in physical research. He was concerned with experiments in electrodynamics, physical optics, meteorological physics, and the physical significance of the principle of least action. Helmholtz also encouraged Heinrich Hertz, perhaps his most famous student, who verified Maxwell's theory by producing electromagnetic waves. In 1887 the Physical–Technical Institute was founded in Berlin, with Helmholtz as director. In 1893 he visited the Chicago World's Columbian Exposition and toured the United States and Canada. While returning home, he fell down the ship's stairs and suffered a concussion and severe loss of blood. He recovered, but those who saw him reported that he tired easily and found it difficult to work. In July 1894 he suffered a cerebral hemorrhage and died in September of that year.

JACOB BECK

[*See also* HEARING; PERCEPTION, *article on* DEPTH PERCEPTION; PSYCHOPHYSICS; VISION, *especially the article on* COLOR VISION AND COLOR BLINDNESS.]

### WORKS BY HELMHOLTZ
(1853–1870) 1962 *Popular Scientific Lectures.* New York: Dover. → First published in German.
(1862) 1954 *On the Sensations of Tone as a Physiological Basis for the Theory of Music.* New York: Dover. → First published as *Die Lehre von den Tonempfindungen als physiologische Grundlage für die Theorie der Musik.*
(1867) 1924–1925 *Helmholtz's Treatise on Physiological Optics.* Edited by James P. C. Southall. 3 vols. New York: The Optical Society of America. → Translated from the third German edition.

### SUPPLEMENTARY BIBLIOGRAPHY
BORING, EDWIN G. (1929) 1950 *A History of Experimental Psychology.* 2d ed. New York: Appleton.
KOENIGSBERGER, LEO (1902–1903) 1906 *Hermann von Helmholtz.* Oxford: Clarendon. → First published in German.
M'KENDRICK, JOHN G. 1899 *Hermann Ludwig Ferdinand von Helmholtz.* New York: Longmans.

# HENDERSON, L. J.

Lawrence Joseph Henderson (1878–1942), American chemist and sociologist, was born in Lynn, Massachusetts. His father was a ship chandler of Salem, with business interests in the French islands of St. Pierre and Miquelon; and it was there, of all strange places, that Henderson acquired his life-long devotion to the civilization of France.

His regular academic career lay in the field of biological chemistry. He graduated from Harvard College in 1898 and from Harvard Medical School in 1902. There followed two years' work in chemical research at the University of Strasbourg. Henderson then returned to Harvard, rising through the academic ranks to become professor of chem-

istry. In the light of his later interests in social science, it is significant that his early research was devoted to the mechanisms of neutrality regulation in the animal organism and that in 1908 he achieved a precise mathematical formulation of the acid–base equilibrium. There was much interest in research on problems of physiological equilibrium at Harvard at the time. Henderson had some influence on, and was always interested in, the work on homeostasis carried out by his colleague Walter B. Cannon, professor of physiology (Cannon 1932). Henderson's later research turned to similiar problems in the chemistry of blood. Here his investigations were of fundamental importance, leading, through the work of his students, to such applications as the use of blood plasma to save the lives of the wounded in World War II. He was one of the most original and distinguished biological chemists of his time.

Henderson also kept up an irregular interest in the wider problems suggested by his chemical research, problems in the philosophy of science and the methodology of inquiry into systems of variables in complex relations of mutual dependence. For years he took part in seminars in the philosophy department at Harvard, and in 1911 he offered the first course given there on the history of science. He wrote two general books on the relationships between the organism and its environment and between determinism and teleology: *The Fitness of the Environment* (1913) and *The Order of Nature* (1917). His general question might be put thus: How do nature's efficient causes cooperate with her final ones?

Henderson's interest in sociology came late in his life but was a natural development of what had gone before. About 1926 William M. Wheeler of Harvard, whose study of insect societies led him to read widely in human sociology, suggested to Henderson that he read Pareto's *Sociologie générale* (see Pareto 1916). At once Henderson became an enthusiast. He felt that Pareto's treatment of scientific methodology and equilibrium phenomena was excellent and that Pareto's substantive views on human society made explicit conclusions he himself had arrived at more intuitively. In 1932–1933 Henderson conducted a seminar on Pareto's sociology—the first such seminar in an English-speaking country. One of the products of the seminar was *An Introduction to Pareto* (1934) by Homans and Curtis, the first book on the subject in English. Henderson published his own book, *Pareto's General Sociology* (1935), emphasizing such matters as equilibrium, the social system, the mutual dependence of variables, and the problems of induction and abstraction. Through his book, his seminar, and a later course he offered called "Concrete Sociology," he made these ideas part of the thinking of a number of sociologists present at Harvard at the time, including Talcott Parsons and Robert K. Merton. Henderson was also the first chairman of the Society of Fellows at Harvard, established in 1933, whose members, besides receiving scholarships to study whatever they wished, dined together once a week. Among the early members were C. M. Arensberg, B. F. Skinner, W. F. Whyte, and G. C. Homans. They soon became familiar, through their conversations, with Henderson's views.

One final connection of Henderson with social science should be mentioned. In 1926 he became director of the Fatigue Laboratory of the Harvard Graduate School of Business Administration. In the adjoining office was Elton Mayo, then beginning his researches in the Western Electric Company. The plan was that Henderson should study the physiology of work, while Mayo studied its psychology. Henderson had no direct influence on the conduct of the Western Electric researches, but his ideas became part of the intellectual atmosphere in which the research team—Mayo, T. N. Whitehead, and F. J. Roethlisberger—did their work. Through the Harvard Business School Henderson also came into contact with Chester I. Barnard and encouraged him to write *The Functions of the Executive* (1938). In 1939 Henderson was appointed chairman of the Committee on Work in Industry of the National Research Council, and under his leadership the committee surveyed and evaluated much research in this field, both physiological and sociological (National Research Council 1941).

Henderson never carried out any empirical research in social science, nor did he become widely read in its literature, but his ideas about methodology in the broadest sense of the word were deeply influential at a time and place of more than ordinary significance in the development of sociology.

GEORGE CASPAR HOMANS

[*Other relevant material may be found in the biographies of* BARNARD; CANNON; MAYO; PARETO.]

WORKS BY HENDERSON

1913    *The Fitness of the Environment: An Inquiry Into the Biological Significance of the Properties of Matter.* New York: Macmillan. → A paperback edition was published in 1958 by Beacon.
1917    *The Order of Nature: An Essay.* Cambridge, Mass.: Harvard Univ. Press.

1935    *Pareto's General Sociology: A Physiologist's Interpretation.* Cambridge, Mass.: Harvard Univ. Press.

SUPPLEMENTARY BIBLIOGRAPHY

BARNARD, CHESTER I. (1938) 1962 *The Functions of the Executive.* Cambridge, Mass.: Harvard Univ. Press.
CANNON, WALTER B. (1932) 1963 *The Wisdom of the Body.* Rev. & enl. ed. New York: Norton.
CANNON, WALTER B. 1945 Biographical Memoir of Lawrence Joseph Henderson: 1878–1942. Volume 23, pages 31–58 in National Academy of Sciences, *Biographical Memoirs.* Washington: The Academy.
HOMANS, GEORGE C. 1962 *Sentiments and Activities: Essays in Social Science.* New York: Free Press. → See especially pages 1–49, "Autobiographical Introduction."
HOMANS, GEORGE C.; and BAILEY, ORVILLE T. (1948) 1959 The Society of Fellows, Harvard University, 1933–1947. Pages 1–37 in Clarence C. Brinton (editor), *The Society of Fellows.* Cambridge, Mass.: The Society.
HOMANS, GEORGE C.; and CURTIS, CHARLES P. JR. 1934 *An Introduction to Pareto: His Sociology.* New York: Knopf.
NATIONAL RESEARCH COUNCIL, COMMITTEE ON WORK IN INDUSTRY 1941 *Fatigue of Workers: Its Relation to Industrial Production.* New York: Reinhold.
PARETO, VILFREDO (1916) 1963 *The Mind and Society: A Treatise on General Sociology.* 4 vols. New York: Dover. → First published as *Trattato di sociologia generale* and in 1917 as *Sociologie générale.* Volume 1: *Non-logical Conduct.* Volume 2: *Theory of Residues.* Volume 3: *Theory of Derivations.* Volume 4: *The General Form of Society.*

# HERDING

*See* PASTORALISM.

# HEREDITY AND ENVIRONMENT

*See* ENVIRONMENTALISM; EUGENICS; GENETICS, *especially the article on* GENETICS AND BEHAVIOR; IMPRINTING; INSTINCT.

# HERING, EWALD

Ewald Hering (1834–1918) was a sense physiologist who played an important role as a pioneer in the new experimental physiological psychology that got under way as a separate discipline in the 1860s. The founder of this new branch of psychology was, it is said, Wilhelm Wundt, who was Hering's contemporary. Hering's fame was based specifically upon his contributions to the understanding of the phenomena of vision—the psychophysiology both of visual space perception and of color vision. Hering was a nativist; that is to say, he believed that the spatial ordering of points on the retina and the skin is innate, that it is not learned, as the empiricists, led by Hermann von Helmholtz, believed. Hering is, however, best known to posterity for his theory of color vision, a theory that for many years remained the alternative to Helmholtz' theory. Moreover, he designed many beautiful pieces of apparatus to illustrate crucial points in his theories and is more responsible than anyone else for this new psychology's being dubbed "brass-instrument psychology." Indeed, he participated in the new experimental movement in many ways; he was, for instance, one of the first editors of the *Zeitschrift für Psychologie*, the first independent journal of experimental psychology in Germany.

Hering was born in Altgersdorf, a small town south of Berlin. At the age of 19 he went to Leipzig to study medicine; there he was influenced by E. H. Weber, the physiologist who established the law that bears his name, and G. T. Fechner, the founder of psychophysics. The dean of physiologists, Johannes Müller, at Berlin, influenced him from afar, and Hering would have liked to work under him but never did. In 1860 Hering began practicing as a physician and also writing in the field of physiology. He had published the five parts of his treatise on space perception by 1864, a year before Helmholtz published the third volume of a handbook on psychophysiological optics—the part that included what Helmholtz had to say about the perception of space. Thus began a long-continued opposition between Hering and Helmholtz—Hering, the nativist; Helmholtz, the empiricist. Hering was following Johannes Müller, whose thought had been influenced by Kant. Helmholtz, an empiricist, was holding to the tradition of Hermann Lotze and found himself supported by Wundt. Hering's views were taken up presently by Carl Stumpf and later, after the turn of the century, by the gestalt psychologists, who have readily acknowledged their debt to him. There was a bitter and indecorous quarrel between Hering and Helmholtz about the true shape of the visual horopter, the locus of points perceived as single by the two eyes.

Hering's publication on space perception was enough to effect a call to Vienna to succeed the distinguished physiologist Carl Ludwig, who himself went to Leipzig. Five years later Hering was invited to Prague to succeed J. E. Purkinje, another well-known physiologist. At Prague his attention turned to the problems of color. His volume of 1878 presented his theory of color vision and again brought him into conflict with Helmholtz, who held to the three-element theory originally suggested by Thomas Young. Hering argued for three different color substances in the retina, each one capable of two reversible, opposite reactions, giving respec-

tively the colors red or green, yellow or blue, and white or black, and their combinations. Both types of theory were still alive eighty years later. Hering also, in 1879, suggested a theory of the temperature sense that was similar to his color theory, cold and warmth being elicited by a pair of antagonistic reactions in the thermal sense organ.

After 25 years at Prague, Hering was called to Leipzig in 1895, to succeed for a second time the now very famous Ludwig. Here he undertook his more mature work on visual sensation, which came out in four fasciculi from 1905 to 1920, the last published posthumously, for Hering died at Leipzig in 1918, at the close of World War I.

At the turn of the century every undergraduate student of psychology was taught Hering's and Helmholtz' theories of vision. For a while Helmholtz' conception seemed to prevail over Hering's, but subsequently Hering's view of antagonistic biological processes gained plausibility as a result of new research, and both types of theory continued to receive consideration at a sophisticated level. Hering, the nativist, also influenced gestalt psychology and the scientific movement toward phenomenology and existentialism. With respect to phenomenology, Hering himself showed the influence of two of his great predecessors in visual theory—Goethe and Purkinje.

EDWIN G. BORING

[*Directly related are the entries* VISION, *especially the article on* COLOR VISION AND COLOR BLINDNESS; PERCEPTION, *article on* DEPTH PERCEPTION. *Other relevant material may be found in the biographies of* HELMHOLTZ; MÜLLER, JOHANNES; STUMPF.]

WORKS BY HERING

1861–1864 *Beiträge zur Physiologie*. 5 parts. Leipzig: Engelmann.

1868 *Die Lehre vom binocularen Sehen*. Leipzig: Engelmann.

(1872–1875) 1964 *Outlines of a Theory of the Light Sense*. Cambridge, Mass.: Harvard Univ. Press. → First published in German. Contains a biographical note and historical discussion by L. M. Hurvich and D. Jameson, translators.

1879 Der Raumsinn und die Bewegungen des Auges. Part 1, pages 343–601 in Ludimar Hermann (editor), *Handbuch der Physiologie*. Volume 3: Physiologie der Sinnesorgane. Leipzig: Vogel. → For an English translation of this essay, see "Spatial Sense and Movements of the Eye" in the *Manual of Physiology of the Sense Organs*, published by the American Academy of Optometry in 1942.

1880 Der Temperatursinn. Part 2, pages 415–450 in Ludimar Hermann (editor), *Handbuch der Physiologie*. Volume 3: Physiologie der Sinnesorgane. Leipzig: Vogel.

1931 *Wissenschaftliche Abhandlungen*. 2 vols. Edited by M. Gildemeister. Leipzig: Thieme. → Contains a portrait and a complete bibliography.

WORKS ABOUT HERING

BORING, EDWIN G. (1929) 1950 *A History of Experimental Psychology.* 2d ed. New York: Appleton. → See pages 351–356 and 379.

GARTEN, SIEGFRIED 1918 Ewald Hering zum Gedächtnis. *Pfluger's Archiv für die gesamte Physiologie des Menschen und der Tiere* 172:501–522.

## HERSKOVITS, MELVILLE JEAN

Melville Jean Herskovits (1895–1963) was an American anthropologist. Two points are central in understanding his conception of anthropology: first, he was a humanist concerned with the total range of cultural behavior and, second, he believed that the inductive method is the only valid methodology for anthropology. In both he revealed the pervasive influence of Franz Boas, his teacher at Columbia University.

The most complete presentation of Herskovits' views is found in *Man and His Works* (1948), revised and abridged as *Cultural Anthropology* (1955). Culture was the inclusive concept for him, comprehending the behavioral and the ideational, the group and the individual. His humanistic orientation was apparent in his interest in the individual, whom he viewed as an active participant in the shaping of culture. As the individual was important in his view of culture, history was important in his ideas of culture change. Acculturation, reinterpretation, retention, and syncretism are concepts which he helped formulate and each has its historical dimension.

The continuity of past and present was a frequent theme of Herskovits' studies of Africa and of the Negro in the New World. It was his thesis in *The Myth of the Negro Past* (1941) that New World Negroes reveal their west African heritage in motor habits, codes of behavior, social institutions, family organization, religion, language, and art. In opposition, sociologists argued that synchronic factors adequately explain American Negro behavior and that it is unwise to link the Negro so directly to his origins in west Africa [*see the biography of* FRAZIER]. Although the book stimulated interest in Africa among some students of the New World Negro, it did not achieve general attention for almost two decades, when some of the facts about Africa became better understood.

Herskovits' approach to cultural change was theoretical as opposed to practical in its orientation. He was always critical of applied anthropology and, in this as well as in his historical approach, was at variance with much of the work of British anthropology in Africa. His views on these points were summarized in *Acculturation: The Study of Culture Contact* (1938a), which was the subject of a rejoinder by Malinowski (1939) in behalf of functionalism and administration-oriented anthropology that appeared in *Africa*.

Herskovits' opposition to applied anthropology was to a large extent based in cultural relativism. Although he in no sense originated the concept, in *Man and His Works* and in subsequent writing he became one of its most uncompromising spokesmen. He derived relativism from the enculturative experience through which standards of judgment are learned, and from this he concluded that judgmental evaluations of cultures are culture-bound. This, of course, does not abrogate comparison but implies that the bases of comparison are culturally determined and should be made explicit. He insisted that the concept of relativism had relevance to all cultural learning and called attention to the influence of culture on perception. He felt that it was important to distinguish between "absolutes," which vary from culture to culture, and "universals," which are consequences of the human condition; and he concluded, "To say that there is no absolute criterion of value or morals, or even, psychologically, of time or space, does not mean that such criteria, in differing *forms*, do not comprise universals in human culture" (1948, p. 76). Cultural relativism led him to reject the term "primitive," though he had used it extensively, as a pejorative, to indicate a lack of unity of custom, tradition, belief, or institution. He subsequently used "nonliterate," a term which he felt was more neutral and descriptive.

Consistent with his humanistic interests, Herskovits was interested in religion, music, graphic and plastic arts, and folklore, particularly in African cultures. *Dahomean Narrative: A Cross-cultural Analysis* (1958), written with Frances S. Herskovits, who collaborated with him throughout his career, is a detailed group of tales assembled during their first African field trip. It is an important work because it carefully relates the narratives to their cultural matrix and abstracts from them items of comparative theoretical interest. Herskovits was interested in the ways culture influences the arts, as well as the ways the arts validate culture. He used both religious and aesthetic data to document African retentions among New World Negroes.

If Herskovits was often humanistic in his orientation he was not narrowly so, and he did not neglect the social aspects of culture. One of his earliest interests was in the field of economics, and *The Economic Life of Primitive Peoples* (1940) was the first general text in that field. It stressed the importance of the cultural context of economic behavior and the limitations of a conception of economics based exclusively upon experience in Western society. However, he adopted the conventional, "formal" definition of economics, the application of scarce means to given ends, and, in the main, tried to follow the categories of academic economics in ordering his data. This compromise is most apparent in the first chapter of the revised edition, entitled *Economic Anthropology* (1940). While Polanyi and his followers (Polanyi et al. 1957) proposed a more sociological, "substantive" definition of economics, Herskovits, typically, objected that their approach seems to deny the role of individual choice and concluded that "we must not reject Economic Man only to substitute Society as an exclusive formula for understanding economic behavior and as a base-point for analysis" ([1940] 1952, p. 8). Polanyi was even more skeptical than Herskovits about the application of traditional economics to nonliterate behavior. His followers have suggested that the characteristics of markets, money, and surpluses in industrial society are so peculiar that the terms are scarcely applicable in nonliterate societies. While Herskovits saw the difference between the economies of nonliterate and industrial society as being one of degree, followers of Polanyi, like George Dalton, see them as differing in kind. It is worth noting that the field of economic anthropology has developed along the general directions of Herskovits' pioneering efforts. [*See* ECONOMIC ANTHROPOLOGY; EXCHANGE AND DISPLAY; TRADE AND MARKETS; *and the biography of* POLANYI.]

Africa was an early interest of Herskovits; his doctoral thesis was on the cattle complex of east Africa. His culture area mapping (1924; see also Bascom & Herskovits 1959) has been used extensively. Many early American Africanists were trained in the program of African studies that he founded and directed at Northwestern University. As interest in Africa expanded, the African Studies Association was formed with Herskovits as its first president. One of his last books, *The Human Factor in Changing Africa* (1962), is a summary of his encyclopedic knowledge of the continent, his interest in culture change, and his humanistic orientation.

JAMES H. VAUGHAN, JR.

[*For the historical context of Herskovits' work, see the biography of* BOAS; *for discussion of the subsequent development of Herskovits' ideas, see* FOLKLORE; HISTORIOGRAPHY, *article on* AFRICAN HISTORIOGRAPHY; PRIMITIVE ART.]

## WORKS BY HERSKOVITS

1924 A Preliminary Consideration of the Culture Areas of Africa. *American Anthropologist* New Series 26: 50–64.

1928 *The American Negro: A Study in Racial Crossing.* New York: Knopf.

(1937) 1964 *Life in a Haitian Valley.* New York: Octagon Books.

(1938a) 1958 *Acculturation: The Study of Culture Contact.* Gloucester, Mass.: Smith.

1938b *Dahomey: An Ancient West African Kingdom.* 2 vols. New York: Augustin.

(1940) 1952 *Economic Anthropology: A Study in Comparative Economics.* 2d ed., rev. & enl. New York: Knopf. → First published as *The Economic Life of Primitive Peoples.* A paperback edition was published in 1965 by Norton.

1941 *The Myth of the Negro Past.* New York: Harper. → A paperback edition was published in 1958 by Beacon.

1948 *Man and His Works: The Science of Cultural Anthropology.* New York: Knopf.

1955 *Cultural Anthropology.* New York: Knopf. → An abridged revision of *Man and His Works,* 1948.

1958 HERSKOVITS, MELVILLE J.; and HERSKOVITS, FRANCES S. *Dahomean Narrative: A Cross-cultural Analysis.* Northwestern University African Studies, No. 1. Evanston, Ill.: Northwestern Univ. Press.

(1959) 1962 BASCOM, WILLIAM R.; and HERSKOVITS, MELVILLE J. (editors) *Continuity and Change in African Cultures.* Univ. of Chicago Press. → See especially page 37 in the 1959 edition.

1962 *The Human Factor in Changing Africa.* New York: Knopf.

## SUPPLEMENTARY BIBLIOGRAPHY

MALINOWSKI, BRONISLAW 1939 The Present State of Studies in Culture Contact: Some Comments on an American Approach. *Africa* 12:27–47.

MERRIAM, ALAN P. 1964 Melville Jean Herskovits, 1895–1963. *American Anthropologist* New Series 66:83–109. → Includes a bibliography of 479 items by Herskovits, compiled by Anne Moneypenny and Barrie Thorne.

POLANYI, KARL; ARENSBERG, CONRAD M.; and PEARSON, HARRY W. (editors) 1957 *Trade and Market in the Early Empires: Economics in History and Theory.* Glencoe, Ill.: Free Press.

# HETTNER, ALFRED

Alfred Hettner (1859–1941) was an important leader in the development of German geography and was particularly influential in defining for geographers generally the scope and methods of their subject.

He was born in Dresden and grew up there in a large family with intellectual and artistic interests. He became interested in geography while he was in secondary school and declared his intention of specializing in that field as soon as he began his university training. He studied at four different German universities and traveled and did field work for four years in South America. After teaching for ten years in Leipzig, he was appointed in 1897 to the newly established chair of geography at Tübingen and then, less than two years later, to the new chair at Heidelberg, which he held until his retirement in 1928.

Although his training and his early work were principally in geomorphology, Hettner, like Ritter and Ratzel, was more interested in human geography. Moreover, he became increasingly involved in establishing a methodology for geography, an enterprise he had initially regarded as auxiliary to work on other problems but which ultimately became a primary aspect of his life's work (1927, p. iii).

The opportunity to present his methodological position came in 1895, when at the age of 36 he founded the *Geographische Zeitschrift*. The new journal was to be devoted to "the advancement of genuine geographical learning," and Hettner opened his introductory article with the questions, "What is geography? What does it seek to accomplish and what is it able to accomplish?" (1895, p. 1). During the following two decades he presented detailed answers to these questions in a series of essays that came to be regarded as classics in geographic methodology (1927). During his career he also published numerous substantive studies in different aspects of systematic geography, which elaborate or illustrate his methodological principles (see his four-volume work in systematic physical geography, *Vergleichende Länderkunde*, 1933–1935; and his three-volume *Allgemeine Geographie des Menschen*, 1947–1957). Important as these studies were, Hettner's principal influence was exerted through the *Geographische Zeitschrift*, over which he maintained close control for forty years (Schmitthenner 1941, p. 453; "Drei autobiographische Skizzen," pp. 22–26).

The concepts of geography that Hettner promoted were not derived by logical deduction from any a priori philosophical position; they were developed empirically from the study of the history of the development of the field since antiquity (1927, pp. 110 ff.). Among geographers he was influenced particularly by Humboldt, Ritter, Kirchhoff, Marthe, and Richthofen ("Drei autobiographische Skizzen"; Hartshorne 1939). His distinctive function was to justify the conclusions drawn from the historical development of geography in terms of the methodology and philosophy of science. His general philosophical viewpoint was based, he said,

neither on Kant nor on Comte but on Lange's *Geschichte des Materialismus;* and his scientific methodology, on Wundt's *Logik* (Hettner 1926, p. 306). But in explaining the relation of geography to other fields, Hettner formulated a scheme of the division of the sciences which, as he later learned, had been presented a century earlier by Kant and by Humboldt, also, apparently, independently (Hartshorne 1958).

In examining the historical development of geography, Hettner found that major misunderstandings had arisen through the failure to identify correctly the object of study. Geography is not, as its name suggests, the over-all science of the earth but the study of the earth shell, more commonly called earth surface, as it varies in the character or content of its areal parts. The basic approach is chorological: to describe and interpret the varied character of the earth surface. This areal variation is formed by many diverse elements, which vary from place to place, interrelated in any particular place and interconnected between different places.

If geography is basically chorological, Hettner reasoned, it is not dualistic; rather, in any inhabited area the physical and human features are so intricately interlaced as to form a single subject for study. Geography is, therefore, not to be divided between the natural and the social sciences or defined as the study of relations between natural and human features of the earth surface. It is a unitary discipline, and the reality it studies is composed of heterogeneous but interrelated elements.

Two theoretically different approaches are usefully combined in the study of areas: the approach of regional geography, which analyzes the full complex of features in individual areas, and the approach of general (or systematic, or topical) geography, which compares areas in terms of particular kinds of features. While Hettner regarded the former, the analysis of individual regions, as the "crowning" product of geographic study, he considered comparative systematic studies no less essential. Geography, then, is both nomothetic and idiographic (1927, pp. 217–218, 221–224, 398–404).

Hettner's work helped to produce a marked degree of agreement among German geographers in the early decades of the twentieth century; such agreement does not exist in many other countries. Outside of German-speaking countries Hettner's ideas were not widely known until they were expounded at length in English (Hartshorne 1939). They have since become familiar and influential in many countries. In establishing his basic methodological structure, Hettner did not attempt to build something new; rather, he believed that he "had clearly expressed and methodologically established what was actually present in the development" of geography (1934b, p. 382). This may well be the reason why the influence of his work has been so strong and can be expected to endure.

RICHARD HARTSHORNE

[*For the historical context of Hettner's work, see the biographies of* HUMBOLDT; RITTER; WUNDT. *For discussion of the subsequent development of his ideas, see* GEOGRAPHY, *especially the article on* SO-CIAL GEOGRAPHY.]

#### WORKS BY HETTNER

1895   Geographische Forschung und Bildung. *Geographische Zeitschrift* 1:1–19.
1926   [Book Review of] Otto Graf, *Vom Begriff der Geographie. Geographische Zeitschrift* 32:304–306.
1927   *Die Geographie: Ihre Geschichte, ihr Wesen und ihre Methoden.* Breslau: Hirt.
1933–1935   *Vergleichende Länderkunde.* 4 vols. Leipzig: Teubner.
1934a   *Der Begriff der Ganzheit in der Geographie. Geographische Zeitschrift* 40:141–144.
1934b   *Neue Angriffe auf die heutige Geographie. Geographische Zeitschrift* 40:341–343, 380–383.
1947–1957   *Allgemeine Geographie des Menschen.* 3 vols. Edited by Heinrich Schmitthenner and E. Plewe. Stuttgart: Kohlhammer. → Published posthumously.
Drei autobiographische Skizzen. Pages 41–80 in *Alfred Hettner, 6.8.1859: Gedenkschrift zum 100. Geburtstag.* Heidelberg (Germany): Keyser, 1960.

#### SUPPLEMENTARY BIBLIOGRAPHY

*Alfred Hettner, 6.8.1859: Gedenkschrift zum 100. Geburtstag.* 1960 Heidelberg (Germany): Keyser. → A bibliography of Hettner's works compiled by E. Plewe appears on pages 81–88.
HARTSHORNE, RICHARD (1939) 1964 *The Nature of Geography: A Critical Survey of Current Thought in the Light of the Past.* Lancaster, Pa.: Association of American Geographers.
HARTSHORNE, RICHARD 1958 The Concept of Geography as a Science of Space, From Kant and Humboldt to Hettner. Association of American Geographers, *Annals* 48:97–108.
PFEIFER, GOTTFRIED 1959 Alfred Hettner zum 100. Geburtstag. *Kosmos* 55:351–353.
SCHMITTHENNER, HEINRICH 1941 Alfred Hettner. *Geographische Zeitschrift* 47:441–468.

## HILDEBRAND, BRUNO

Bruno Hildebrand (1812–1878), economist and one of the founders of the German historical school, was born in Naumburg (Thuringia), the son of a civil servant. He entered the University of Leipzig as a student of theology but soon shifted to history. He very early joined the liberal–nationalist student movement, and since this affiliation made him the object of police attention, he fled to Breslau to escape harassment; however, he was imprisoned there before being allowed to continue his studies. In 1836 the University of Breslau awarded him his doctorate and shortly afterward the rights of *Dozent.* In 1839 he was promoted to acting professor of history. But Hildebrand's restless and intensely political nature found the scope of historical study too confining; increasingly his interests and his lectures focused on political philosophy and economics.

The most productive decade of Hildebrand's academic career began with his appointment, in 1841, to the chair of *Staatswissenschaften* (government) at the University of Marburg. Here, once again, he clashed with the authorities, especially when as university rector he championed the liberties of students and staff; in 1845 he was relieved of his administrative position, and in 1846 he was charged with *lèse-majesté* and dismissed from his teaching post. Hildebrand was eventually acquitted, but he was not reinstated in his professorship until the 1848 revolution had swept a liberal government into office.

Hildebrand was elected deputy of the Frankfurt National Assembly, where he distinguished himself as an uncompromising protagonist of constitutional government and as an indefatigable member of the parliamentary commission on economic and social affairs. With the triumph of absolutism, however, his cause was doomed. The Diet was abolished, and Hildebrand, as one of the outspoken liberals, was charged with high treason and forced to flee into Switzerland where, in 1851, he was appointed to a chair at the University of Zurich. Hildebrand spent five years in Zurich, active not only as a professor but also as a company director promoting and building a railway. He then moved to the University of Bern and helped establish the first Swiss statistical office at Bern.

In 1861 Hildebrand accepted an invitation extended by the University of Jena and returned to his native Thuringia. In 1863 he started the *Jahrbücher für Nationalökonomie und Statistik.* In the following year he was instrumental in founding the statistical office of the Thuringian states. As its first director, he planned the work of the new bureau in such a way as to link it closely with the research and teaching activities of the university program in economics.

Although Hildebrand was neither a fluent nor an exciting lecturer, good students found him an inspiring teacher, and some of the better economists of the German historical school were products of his "Jena seminar." Because of this impact, Hildebrand's position in the history of German economic thought cannot be assessed in terms of his writings alone.

One of Hildebrand's earliest works, *Die National-ökonomie der Gegenwart und Zukunft* (1848), is also his most important; it is clearly the work of a youthful *homme engagé*. The first chapter is devoted to an evaluation of Adam Smith. Acknowledging the greatness of the Scotsman's contribution, Hildebrand proceeded to criticize the philosophy of natural law and the instinct of self-interest underlying Smith's reasoning. Hildebrand denied the universality that Smith claimed for his theory and asserted that Smith's basic assumptions were ahistorical; inasmuch as they derived from the English scene, they were irrelevant to an understanding of the problems in other eras and other lands. Above all, Hildebrand felt that the premises did not fit the peculiarities of German conditions.

Hildebrand admitted that his view of classical economics had been influenced by Adam Müller. Yet he added that he could accept neither the feudal and medieval notions of the German romantic school nor its reactionary conclusions. Even Friedrich List, though allowed some credit for his insights and for his contributions to the important public debate on international trade policy, was given short shrift by Hildebrand.

Significantly, Hildebrand devoted the largest part of *Die Nationalökonomie der Gegenwart und Zukunft* to a review of socialist literature, in particular to an examination of the recently published *Condition of the Working Class in England* by the then unknown Friedrich Engels. He saw the socialist writers as "up-to-date," with a historical perspective and above all a focus on the predicament of the proletariat in industrial society. At the same time, Hildebrand rejected all socialist values, warning that the socialist society would be the "grave of individualism and civilization," and his stage theory of economic progress was surely intended as a polemic against Marxist socialism. According to Arthur Sommer, Hildebrand's vision of society as advancing from barter to monetary exchange before reaching its highest synthesis in a credit economy was meant as an anticommunist manifesto. In this scheme the fully developed credit economy would give the propertyless wage earner access to capital and thereby resolve one of modern society's most pressing problems without recourse to socialism.

In the last 15 years of his life, Hildebrand turned away from theoretical issues and concentrated on directing statistical studies bearing upon important social problems. He thus anticipated the program of the Verein für Sozialpolitik, which he joined as a charter member in 1873. (He was the only one of the founders of the German historical school to do so.)

Hildebrand failed to develop a coherent system of economics. The source of his failure lies (see Eisermann 1956) in his petty bourgeois parochialism, with all its fears and prejudices regarding the rapidly industrializing world. This was the cause of his fuzzy thinking and of his pathetic efforts to reconcile basically irreconcilable points of view. Fighting, as it were, a two-front battle against the feudal aristocracy on the one hand and the emerging proletariat on the other—while simultaneously concerned about the precariousness of its own economic status—the German middle class was doomed to political impotence. Its intellectual leaders, including Hildebrand, reacted to their conflict by abandoning clarification of the social process in favor of politically innocuous empirical research and social engineering.

HERBERT KISCH

[*For the historical context of Hildebrand's work, see* ECONOMIC THOUGHT, *article on* THE HISTORICAL SCHOOL; *and the biographies of* MÜLLER, ADAM HEINRICH; SMITH, ADAM.]

### WORKS BY HILDEBRAND

(1848) 1922  *Die Nationalökonomie der Gegenwart und Zukunft, und andere gesammelte Schriften.* Jena: Fischer.
1853  *Statistische Mitteilungen über die volkswirtschaftlichen Zustände Kurhessens, nach amtlichen Quellen.* Berlin: Guttentag.
1863  Die gegenwärtige Aufgabe der Wissenschaft der Nationalökonomie. *Jahrbücher für Nationalökonomie und Statistik* 1:5–25; 137–146.
1864  Natural-, Geld- und Kreditwirtschaft. *Jahrbücher für Nationalökonomie und Statistik* 2:1–24.
1866a  Die wissenschaftliche Aufgabe der Statistik. *Jahrbücher für Nationalökonomie und Statistik* 6:1–11.
1866b  Zur Geschichte der deutschen Wollenindustrie. *Jahrbücher für Nationalökonomie und Statistik* 6: 186–254; 7:81–153.
1866–1878  THURINGIAN STATES, STATISTISCHES BÜREAU, *Statistik Thüringens: Mitteilungen des statistichen Büreaus vereinigter thüringischer Staaten.* 2 vols. Edited by Bruno Hildebrand. Jena (Germany): Frommann. → Volume 1: *Das Land; Die Bevölkerung,* 1866–1867. Volume 2: *Agrarstatistik,* 1871–1878.
1869  Vergangenheit und Gegenwart der deutschen Leinenindustrie. *Jahrbücher für Nationalökonomie und Statistik* 13:215–251.
1872  Die Verdienste der Universität Jena um die Fortbildung und das Studium der Staatswissenschaften. *Jahrbücher für Nationalökonomie und Statistik* 18: 1–11.

### SUPPLEMENTARY BIBLIOGRAPHY

CONRAD, JOHANNES 1878  Bruno Hildebrand. *Jahrbücher für Nationalökonomie und Statistik* 30:i–xvi.
EISERMANN, GOTTFRIED 1956  *Die Grundlagen des Historismus in der deutschen Nationalökonomie.* Stutt-

gart (Germany): Enke. → See especially pages 158–188 on Bruno Hildebrand.

FRANZ, GOTTFRIED 1928 *Studien über Bruno Hildebrand.* Kirchhain (Germany): Schroeder.

GRÜNBERG, CARL 1925 Bruno Hildebrand über den kommunistischen Arbeiterbildungsverein in London: Zugleich ein Beitrag zu Hildebrands Biographie. *Archiv für die Geschichte des Sozialismus und der Arbeiterbewegung* 11:445–459.

Hildebrand. 1880 Volume 12, pages 399–402 in *Allgemeine deutsche Biographie.* Leipzig: Duncker & Humblot.

HOSELITZ, BERT F. 1960 Theories of Stages of Economic Growth. Pages 193–238 in Bert F. Hoselitz et al., *Theories of Economic Growth.* Glencoe, Ill.: Free Press.

KALVERAM, GERTRUD 1933 *Die Theorien von den Wirtschaftsstufen.* Leipzig: Buske. → See especially pages 91–97 on "Die Wirtschaftsstufentheorie von Bruno Hildebrand."

SOMMER, ARTHUR 1948 Über Inhalt, Rahmen und Sinn älterer Stufentheorien (List und Hildebrand). Pages 535–565 in *Synopsis: Festgabe für Alfred Weber, 30.VII.1868–30.VII.1948.* Heidelberg (Germany): Schneider.

# HINDUISM

Hindus are found living in many parts of the world, but the vast majority of them (approximately 376.5 million) are concentrated in the Indo–Pakistan subcontinent. Of this population, approximately 366.5 million are in India and ten million in Pakistan. Hindus are also found in the Himalayan states of Nepal (the only contemporary Hindu state), Sikkim, and Bhutan; in Burma, Ceylon, Malaysia, and other countries of southeast Asia; and in east and south Africa, the Caribbean islands, Guyana (British Guiana), Fiji, and the United Kingdom.

## The study of Hinduism

The doctrines of Hinduism, unlike those of Christianity and Islam, are not embodied in any one sacred book, nor does Hinduism have a single historical founder. There are not one but innumerable gods, and it is not essential to believe in the existence of God in order to be a Hindu. Hinduism is rich in contradictions, there being no particular beliefs or institutions that are common to all Hindus. Every belief considered basic to Hinduism has been rejected by one Hindu group or another.

A major problem in the study of Hinduism, as in that of any world religion, is to understand the interaction between the theological and popular levels. There is a vast body of sacred literature in Hinduism, including the Vedas, Brāhmaṇas, Upaniṣads, Vedāṅgas, Dharmaśāstras, Nibandhas, Purāṇas, Itihāsas, Darsanas, Āgamas, and Tantras. These texts contain elaborate and abstract philosophies and theologies, mythologies, manuals for the performance of sacrifices and other sacred rites in temples and homes, and codes of conduct for daily life. Generally speaking, until recently Indian and foreign scholars concentrated on the literature, while the description of actual institutions, rites, and beliefs was left to missionaries, travelers, and administrators. It is only in the last twenty years that bibliocentricism has been replaced by a more rounded view of Hinduism and the relation between the texts and actual behavior.

The social scientist's concern for understanding any religion in its social context is likely to be satisfied more for the modern than for the earlier periods of history. Source materials are almost entirely lacking for the study of the history of popular Hinduism; even in the study of the history of literary Hinduism, data are not available for the reconstruction of the social context. For example, the date, provenance, and authorship of texts are not certain. And finally, the student of contemporary Hinduism is faced with the problem that the systematic reconstruction of Indian history, which began with the coming of the British, has brought to light material that has since become an active part of the Hindu religion. In the reinterpretation of Hinduism that has been occurring since the nineteenth century, the philosophical and literary levels have been emphasized, to the neglect of actual institutions, rites, and beliefs.

## Hinduism and the social order

Hinduism, lacking a centralized church, is so inextricably entangled with Hindu society that it is very difficult to say where one ends and the other begins. This is particularly true of caste, which according to creation beliefs expressed in the Ṛg Veda has a divine origin. The four *varṇas*, or caste orders, emerged from the limbs of primeval man, who is a victim in the divine sacrifice that produced the cosmos. The *brāhmans* emerged from his mouth, *kṣatriyas* from his arms, the *vaiśyas* from his thighs, and the *śūdras* from his feet. (The untouchables are not mentioned in the hymn.) There are in reality not four but innumerable castes, called *jātis*, each of which claims to belong to one of the four *varṇas*. When the Hindu sacred or legal texts discuss caste, it is mostly *varṇa* that they have in view and very rarely *jāti*.

Certain ideas regarding pollution and purity are cardinal in Hinduism, although there are differences among the various castes in the strictness with which rules deriving from these ideas are adhered to and the degree of elaboration found in behavior governed by them. Intercaste relations are generally defined by ideas of pollution. Normally, each caste is endogamous and complete commensality prevails only within it. Thus, there are many kinds of restrictions between castes—on the free acceptance of food and drink, on intermarriage and sex relations, on touching or going near a member of another caste, etc.—and they are expressed in terms of pollution. This means that failure to observe the rules makes the upper-caste person impure, and he has to perform a purificatory rite, simple or elaborate, according to the seriousness of the violation.

While caste is central, it does not entirely determine Hindu religious behavior. There are other aspects of the social structure that embody religious behavior. The village community and the family also function as cult groups. There are deities—usually goddesses—in every village who, if suitably propitiated, keep out epidemics and drought and look after the villagers. There is an elaborate complex of *rites de passage*, including wedding rituals and funeral rites that may take several days to perform. Calendrical festivals and *vratas*, or ritual austerities carried out for specific periods to attain particular ends (e.g., birth of a son), consume a good part of people's energies, time, and money.

It is important to demarcate those aspects of religious behavior that are affected by caste from those that are not. The relation between sect and caste, in particular, offers a fruitful area for research.

## Dominant theological ideas of Hinduism

Hinduism does not have a body of clearly defined dogma, but some theological ideas may be considered basic. And while the many sects and schools have taken different standpoints on theological issues, the issues themselves are common to most. Since the time of the Upaniṣads, which laid the foundations of Hindu philosophical thinking, certain concepts recur again and again. A major issue has been the nature of Brahman (universal soul) and its relation with Ātman (the individual soul). One view is concerned only with this dichotomy, does not posit the existence of God, and considers Brahman as absolute and attributeless. (There was also the Chārvāka school, which was atheistic and hedonistic.) Most other views, however, recognize the existence of God and consider the issue of his relation with Brahman, on the one hand, and Ātman, on the other. The Ātman is considered to be indestructible and passes through an endless migration, or series of incarnations. The character of any incarnation,

human, animal, or superhuman, is influenced by *karma*, the net balance of good and bad deeds in previous births. Goodness or badness is defined by reference to *dharma*. The reward for a saintly life is *mokṣa*, which releases the individual from the chain of births and deaths and brings him into contact with God.

The ideas of *karma*, *dharma*, and *mokṣa* are intimately related to the caste system. The Dharmasūtra states that if a man does good deeds, he will be reborn in a high caste and well endowed, while if he does sinful acts, he will be reborn in a low caste or even as an animal. *Dharma* is thus identified with the duties of one's caste, and birth in a particular caste becomes an index of the soul's progress toward liberation.

The nature of *mokṣa* and how to achieve it are major issues in Hindu theology. The main ways of achieving *mokṣa* are through knowledge, deeds, and love and devotion toward God. Generally, the way of knowledge requires an individual to renounce the world, including caste and family, and lead the life of an ascetic. This way has been followed by only a few. It was the Bhagavad Gītā that first emphasized the way of works and devotion and thus brought liberation within reach of the "man-in-the-world," including women and the lower castes. The most popular form of devotion, however, is the worship of one's chosen god according to tradition. In the last hundred years the Bhagavad Gītā has been reinterpreted by Indian political leaders, including Gandhi and B. G. Tilak, to provide the basis for a life devoted to altruistic action.

Discussion of these issues by theologians has been in Sanskrit and in the context of ideas developed in logic, metaphysics, astronomy, grammar, literature, law, and other branches of traditional learning. The basic theological positions have, however, reached the common people through myths and stories narrated in local languages. How influential these ideas were and the nature of their relation to strictly local or sectional ideas and beliefs are still subjects for research (see, in this connection, Srinivas 1952, p. 227).

**Sanskritic deities.** Those deities whose attributes and modes of worship are described in mythological, liturgical, and other texts may be called Sanskritic. The Vedic pantheon reflects the syncretism that resulted from the conquest by nomadic Indo-European Aryans of the ancient urbanized civilizations of the Indus Valley and a continuing contact with the aboriginal tribal peoples of the subcontinent. Most of the deities, major and minor, are nature gods: Indra, the most prominent of all, is the sky god; Agni, the fire god; Varuṇa, the water god; Sūrya, the sun god; and so on. Viṣṇu, who later became a high god, began as only a minor figure, a mere aspect of the sun god. The Vedic god of thunder, Rudra, was at first associated with Śiva, who eventually became the dominant partner. The chief Vedic gods were gradually transformed into the trinity of Brahmā, the creator; Viṣṇu, the protector; and Śiva, the destroyer. Brahmā does not appear in the Vedas but seems to have developed during the period of the Brāhmaṇas. His importance subsequently declined, and nowadays Viṣṇu and Śiva are the two most important gods.

Every major deity in Hinduism has many forms, and around each form there is a myth. Viṣṇu has a number of incarnations, the chief of which are Rāma (man), Krishna (man), Narasiṃha (man-lion), and Varāha (boar). The idea behind the many forms is that God periodically allows himself to be reborn on earth, to overcome evil and restore righteousness. In addition to incarnations, Viṣṇu has one thousand names, according to the Mahā-bhārata, and many more according to other texts. Rāma and Krishna, originally incarnations of Viṣṇu, became important gods in themselves, each with many forms and names. The idea of incarnation is not associated with Śiva, but he, too, has many names. In addition, each deity or each form of a deity has a wife, who is usually worshiped along with her husband.

Śakti, the personification of the female principle in the creation of the universe, occupies almost as important a place in the Hindu pantheon as Viṣṇu and Śiva. In the Śakti cult a female deity is sometimes worshiped independently of association with a male deity, but when a male deity alone is worshiped, generally he is some form of Śiva rather than of Viṣṇu. Further, Skanda and Ganeśa, the sons of Śiva, and Hanumant, the chief of the monkey army of Rāma, are also popular deities. The birds and animals on which the gods sit are called *vāhanas* ("vehicles") and are worshiped. The sun, moon, stars, fire, mountains, lakes, animals, snakes, trees, and plants continue to be objects of worship. Frequently river deities are anthropomorphized. For example, Ganga, or Ganges, is a form of the goddess Pārvatī, and many smaller rivers are believed to be manifestations of Ganga. The cobra cult in southern India is identified with Skanda. There are also deities symbolizing the synthesis of different deities, such as the three-headed Trimūrti and Dattatreya, representing the unity of Brahmā, Viṣṇu, and Śiva. The union of Śiva and Viṣṇu is expressed in the composite god Harihara; Ardha-

narīśvara represents an attempt to symbolize the unity of Śiva and Pārvatī.

The henotheistic tendency is important in Hindu mythology and ritual: the deity who is being worshiped is praised above all others. Pantheism prevails, but all deities, from Viṣṇu or Śiva to the lowest village deity, are considered to be manifestations of the same god. These ideas have enabled Hinduism to absorb local cults and deities and even accept all other religions as true.

A Hindu temple embodies the henotheistic idea. There is, accordingly, one principal deity, from whom a temple derives its name and whose image occupies a prominent place in the temple, and there are also a few minor deities, represented by smaller images in different parts of the temple. Thus, in a Śiva temple Śiva would be the principal deity, and Pārvatī, Ganeśa, and the bull Nandi would be minor deities; whereas in a Śakti temple, Śakti would be the principal deity and Śiva would be one of the minor deities. Not all Hindu deities are associated with temples, however. Some of the Vedic deities, such as Varuṇa and Agni, are invoked mostly during sacrifices, while Brahmā and Sūrya seem to have had temples in the past but do not have them nowadays. Some deities (e.g., Ganeśa) have temples only in certain regions.

### Sectarianism

Like other religions, Hinduism has given birth to many sects in the course of its history, and it is not always easy to say whether a sect is within the Hindu fold or outside. Buddhism and Jainism had emerged as distinct sects by about the fifth century B.C., and both spread over wide areas, Buddhism, in particular, spreading over almost the entire country. But over the centuries their influence declined, and Buddhism had almost entirely disappeared from the country of its origin by about A.D. 1000. It is only in recent years that large numbers of Untouchables, in particular the Mahar of Maharashtra, became converted to Buddhism in protest against the indignities they were subjected to under the caste system. There is a sizable Jain population in India today, and Jains are very similar to Hindus. Not only are there castes among them, but some trading castes of Gujarāt have Jain and Hindu subdivisions, and marriage occurs across sect lines. Islam has presented a serious challenge to Hinduism. There are about 129.5 million Muslims (nearly 47 million in India and 82.5 million in Pakistan) in the subcontinent. While a small proportion of them came from the Middle East, the majority were converts from among the Hindus. They have a caste system in some ways similar to that of the Hindus, and the converts have retained many Hindu practices —so much so that in the case of some groups it is even now extremely difficult to say whether they are Hindu or Muslim. There are also sects (Kabīrpanthi, Sikhism) and cults that combine both Hindu and Muslim traits. One of them, Sikhism, has claimed to be a distinct religion, but this does not mean that Sikhs do not have anything in common with Hindus. The Sikhs are divided into castes, with even an Untouchable division, and have veneration for Hindu holy places. Until recently, in many families in rural Punjab one son would become a Sikh while the others remained Hindu. Many Hindu castes became Sikhs in an effort to improve their status. The Pirāna sect in Gujarāt and the recent Saibaba cult have both Hindu and Muslim followers. In its later phase the Bhakti movement was influenced by Sufism.

At the present time there are a very large number of sects, a few major and many minor. Each sect has a founder, a cult, a body of doctrine, and a social organization of its own.

In most sects one deity is considered to be supreme and is identified with the supreme Brahman. While Viṣṇu, Śiva, and Śakti are the most important nuclei for the formation of sects, they are not, however, the only nuclei, sects having also arisen around Sūrya, Ganeśa, and Dattatreya. It is wrong to speak of a single, homogeneous sect associated with any of these deities. The many Vaiṣṇavite sects, for example, are distinguished from each other, first, by the particular form of Viṣṇu and his consort that they worship; and second, where the same form and consort are worshiped, by differences in the mode of worship and body of theological doctrine; and finally, by their internal organization. There are elaborate rules regarding the making of idols, and there is a systematized iconography. The Śrī-Vaiṣṇavas worship Viṣṇu and his consort Lakṣmī; the Madhvas worship Krishna but not Rādhā; the Nimbarkas, Vallabhacharis, and Chaitanyaites worship both Krishna and Rādhā but differ in several other respects; and the Rāmanandis worship only Rāma and his associates. Comparable differences exist among Śiva and Śakti sects.

Each sect recognizes several minor deities, including its chief deity's spouse, but they rarely include the entire Hindu pantheon. In each sect the founder and the things associated with him are objects of special veneration. Each sect has an elaborate complex of rituals for temple and domestic worship and for life-cycle ceremonies. It has its own specially emphasized festivals and sacri-

fices and its own identifying word or sentence of great religious potency. A sect mark put on the forehead easily distinguishes a member of one sect from that of another.

The major sects are known for their distinctive philosophical standpoints, as for example, the pure monism of the Smartas, the qualified monism of the Śrī-Vaiṣṇavas, and the dualism of the Madhvas. Minor sects do not have elaborate philosophies, although they do have their own special ideas and beliefs. While the philosophical and ethical position of a sect is important in understanding its religious practices, other elements are influential.

Each sect has not only its own sacred literature, written by its founder and other leaders, but also a selective attitude toward the great texts of Hinduism.

Another major problem in the study of sects is understanding the nature of their relation to asceticism. Sects composed entirely of ascetics represent a bizarre element in Hinduism. The members of these sects go about scantily clothed, smear their bodies with funeral ashes, wear long, matted hair, and perform a number of physical feats. They maintain monasteries (akhādas, literally "gymnasiums"), where they are reputed to carry on occult practices, and they also manage temples, which enable them to keep in touch with the masses and recruit members.

Sects composed entirely of householders and those consisting of both ascetics and householders are the most numerous and popular. The ascetics in the latter sects are grouped into different monasteries, each having its own core of hereditary adherents and its corporate property in temples, land, etc. Many ascetics are found to be involved in intersectarian rivalry and politics. When a sect is composed only of householders, the patrilineal descendants of the founder preside over the sect.

There are many small sects, whose membership is confined to a single linguistic region or to a small area within a linguistic region, but the membership of the major sects cuts across language barriers. In the case of a major sect, it is necessary to distinguish between areas with a high concentration of its members and areas with relatively few members. Thus, while the majority of the Madhvas are found in southern India, there are small groups of them in Gujarāt, Uttar Pradesh, Bihār, and Bengal. While the majority of Vallabhacharis are found in Gujarāt and Rājasthān, there are small groups of them all over northern, western, and eastern India. Another noteworthy feature is that, while the majority of the members, temples, and monasteries of a sect may be found in one part of the country, it may have a temple or a monastery in each of the major pilgrim centers in the country. The founder of every major sect traveled about the country, first in search of knowledge, then to win dialectical battles, and finally, to give discourses and recruit followers. Frequently the founder and his followers came from different regions. There were centers of religious learning in different areas, and there was a convergence of schools of learning at each center; finally the centers were woven into networks. Some of these centers, such as Banāras, Vrindāban, and Śrīrangam, enjoyed high prestige, and a scholar's victory in religious disputation may have taken place at the court of the king or at a religious fair.

Normally, membership in a sect, unlike that in a caste, is not hereditary but comes through initiation. And there is hardly any sect that is composed of only one *jāti*. Even the Lingāyat sect of the Kannada region, which is commonly regarded as a caste, is composed of a number of *jātis*, or endogamous units. And even when a whole caste is included in a single sect, membership in the sect is not automatic but by initiation. Sometimes the members of a caste will be distributed among more than one sect, and some may not belong to any sect at all. Some castes in Gujarāt contain not only members of two or three Hindu sects but also Jains. Sometimes the members of a single family have different sectarian affiliations. The rise and fall of various sects over the centuries indicates that religious positions were not always determined by birth.

No sect recruits members from all castes. Untouchables are very rarely admitted into sects including the high castes; even a sect admitting "touchable" castes would cover only a certain span in the caste hierarchy. Generally speaking, Untouchables have produced their own sects. The older sects recruited *brāhmans* and higher non-*brāhmans* but not lower non-*brāhmans*, and there are sects founded by non-*brāhmans* that do not include *brāhmans*. Even though a sect includes members from more than one caste, caste distinctions are not entirely obliterated.

### Nonsectarian Hinduism

Nonsectarian Hinduism is found both in towns and villages; it is largely Sanskritic in towns and non-Sanskritic in villages.

Non-Sanskritic Hinduism is, however, an ideal type and has the following characteristics: the deities have non-Sanskritic names and oral myths attached to them; they are represented by unhewn stones or crude images; the modes of worship are local and do not follow any liturgy; offerings include meat and liquor, and the priests, or shamans, as well as the devotees, are generally drawn from the lower castes. All these conditions rarely occur simultaneously, and it is more common for the Sanskritic and non-Sanskritic elements to be mixed in varying proportions. Thus, a deity's name may be a corrupt form of a Sanskritic name or a compound of a Sanskritic and a non-Sanskritic name. Usually village goddesses are regarded as manifestations of Pārvatī, and village gods of Śiva. Such identification makes possible the acquisition of Sanskritic characteristics by non-Sanskritic deities, and it is not unknown for a deity with a single name to be worshiped according to non-Sanskritic modes in one village and Sanskritic modes in another. In one village the deity's image may be housed in a fine temple, while in another it is embedded in the earth at the foot of a tree. Frequently, there are institutionalized links between a village deity and the pilgrim center of the Sanskritic deity with which he is identified.

There are also temples to Sanskritic deities, where *brāhmans* are priests, the offerings vegetarian, and the mode of worship Sanskritic. But on certain occasions, such as the deity's festival, the *brāhman* withdraws and animals are sacrificially decapitated by a non-*brāhman*. The *brāhman* priest re-enters the temple only after purifying it. In temples where non-*brāhmans* are priests, *brāhmans* may propitiate such a deity during an epidemic or other disaster. In exceptional situations a *brāhman* might even make an offering of a fowl to a non-Sanskritic deity through a non-*brāhman* friend.

It is important to note that the attitude of *brāhmans* and other high castes toward non-Sanskritic deities is not fixed and unalterable. There are different types of *brāhmans*, high as well as low, and learned as well as ignorant. (Among the Smarta *brāhmans* of Tamilnad, the priests, Kurukkals, are regarded as lower than other *brāhmans*. In Gujarāt, the priestly Tapodhan *brāhmans* are rated very low indeed.) A learned *brāhman* may have to oblige his powerful non-*brāhman* patrons by manufacturing a myth in Sanskrit for one of their deities. Hindu mythology has grown in this manner (see the Appendix on "The Kāvēri Myth" in Srinivas 1952, pp. 241–246).

A temple is sectarian only when it is part of a sectarian organization. In this sense a large majority of Hindu temples, including some of the biggest, are nonsectarian. Many of these are extremely wealthy, having vast land estates, large amounts of jewelry and precious metals, and also a considerable income from offerings by devotees. They employ many people and have an elaborate and complex body of ritual, calendrical festivals, special *pūjās*, etc. Although nonsectarian, these temples are subject to regional sectarian influences. For example, the modes of worship in nonsectarian temples of Krishna in Gujarāt are influenced by the modes of worship prevalent in Krishna temples of the dominant Vallabhachari sect of the area.

In the majority of temples dedicated to Sanskritic deities, the priests are *brāhmans;* only vegetarian and nonalcoholic offerings are made, and the rituals are conducted according to a liturgical text. Even in some Śiva temples, where priests are Lingāyats (southern India) or Gosais (Gujarāt), they perform liturgical rituals and make only vegetarian and nonalcoholic offerings. In many Śakti temples, particularly those influenced by the left-hand Śakti sects, the deity is worshiped according to the Tantric texts and offerings of meat and liquor are made. However, although Sanskritization has had a widespread effect, some temples continue to sacrifice animals and make liquor offerings on certain occasions. In Bengal, Bihār, and Assam blood sacrifice still remains a normal mode of worship.

Nonsectarian Hindus generally worship many deities, although there are some who are devotees of a single deity, sometimes a deity in a particular temple. It is common to see a devout Hindu going on a daily round of the principal temples in a village or in a ward of a city. They observe the festivals of Śiva, Viṣṇu, and others, and they go on pilgrimages to great shrines all over the country.

### Hinduism and the polity

Devout Hindus regarded their king as a representative of God on earth. This belief was common to all, including *brāhmans*, who themselves claimed to be gods on earth. The social order, as represented by the caste system, was also believed to be divinely created. The rules of the social and moral order were subsumed under the ethicoreligious concept of *dharma*. In his role as the guardian of *dharma*, the king had to maintain the caste system. This meant that the idea of inequality expressed in the caste system had the king's support and sanction. Different castes had different rights, duties, and privileges, and punishment had to take into account the caste of the offender and that of the victim. The disabilities traditionally imposed on untouchables also had the king's sanction. His powers included the right to promote or demote individual castes, and he was the final court of

appeal in any matter pertaining to caste. This power was so integral to kingship that it was exercised by the Mughal rulers and also by the British in their very early days in India.

It is important to remember that the king had this power, inasmuch as uncritical reliance on the sacred literature conveys the impression that the *brāhmans* were all-powerful and that kings only carried out their decisions. The privileges enjoyed by *brāhmans* and religious personages were in fact conferred on them by the king, and they could be withdrawn. As recently as 1892, in the princely state of Mysore, the government passed an order that all nominations to the headship of monasteries must have the prior approval of the maharaja, and failure to obtain this approval would involve the retraction of grants of land and money made by the state (Smith 1963, pp. 302–303). A *swāmī*, or head of a monastery, is revered, and the maharaja even performs the ritual of washing the feet of some *swāmīs;* but he also has the power to determine who becomes a *swāmī*.

The Hindu king had the same beliefs and values and took part in the same ceremonies as his people, although the manner of his celebrating a festival or his devotion to a particular deity or temple often set the religious style of the kingdom. Temples favored by royalty (e.g., Tirupati, Tanjore, and Madurai) developed into great pilgrimage centers. They were generously endowed with land and jewelry; famous sculptors were invited to lavish their skill on them; and great musicians sang there on certain occasions. The conversion of a prince to a sect was an important event in its history, and a large number of people followed their king into the new faith. And while there is a tradition of tolerance in Hinduism, discrimination against the members of a rival sect was not unknown.

It is clear that no conceptual separation between the state and the church was possible in the Hindu system of ideas. Nor was the need for such a distinction very necessary. First, Hinduism did not possess a powerful, centralized church, with a single pontiff and a hierarchy of officials, which would constitute a potential threat to kingly supremacy. Second, the castewise division of functions confined *brāhmans* to the religious realm, while the *kṣatriyas* had the political realm to themselves. That a separation between the two did not always obtain should not surprise us. In fact, the development of sacrifice during the late Vedic period marked an increase in *brāhman* power and arrogance, and Buddhism and Jainism both appealed to *kṣatriyas* and *vaiśyas*, partly because of their rejection of *brāhman* pretensions (Ghurye 1932, pp. 65, 69, 70, in 1950 edition). Speaking generally, it was not so much the throne that attracted *brāhmans* as the power behind it.

Hinduism has a tradition of tolerance, and Hindu rulers in general seem to have been hospitable to different sects and religions. Hindu tolerance is, however, related to the caste system in several ways. First, each caste has its own style of life, and from childhood onward people accept diversity as a basis for relationship. Second, caste, along with village and extended kin groups, ensured conformity in practice, and a stable society could afford to give its members intellectual freedom. The other source of such freedom was the institution of the holy man, who ritually renounced the world—his relatives even performed funeral rites for him at his initiation into the order—and who could then preach as he wished. Max Weber has rightly said, "The freedom of thought in ancient India was so considerable as to find no parallel in the West before the most recent age" (quoted in Smith 1963, p. 62).

Hindu tolerance of other religions and its hospitality to new ideas provided a favorable soil for the eventual declaration of India as a secular state. There were, however, other tendencies, and certain nineteenth-century attempts (e.g., the Ārya Samāj) to purge Hinduism of its many evils by advocating a return to the Vedas contained frankly revivalist elements. Moreover, Indian nationalism also expressed itself occasionally in the Hindu idiom, and this had the effect of alienating the Muslims. But during British rule there emerged a highly westernized Hindu elite, which, while rooted in the country and its traditions, was committed to independence, democracy, egalitarianism, and secularism. It is this elite that not only declared India a secular state but also attempted wholeheartedly to establish the principle of the equality of man.

**Hinduism and economic development.** Weber (1921) thought that the Hindu belief in the transmigration of the soul and the related doctrines of *karma* and *dharma*, seen in the context of caste, produced an irrational, otherworldly social ethic that prevented the development of industrial capitalism. Weber's thesis has gained wide popularity, and Hinduism is now believed to be one of the major obstacles in India's economic development. This belief, however, rests on a partial view of Hinduism. Weber himself noted a few elements of a "rational" ethic in Hinduism—the existence of this-worldly asceticism and positive economic motivation among Jains, Liṅgāyats, and Madhvas, and

an occupational ethic among merchants and artisans. There are elements in Hinduism favorable to economic development (Singer et al. 1958; Lambert & Hoselitz 1963). The very ascetics whom Weber considered disseminators of irrational and otherworldly ideas among the masses are often the heads of large and wealthy monasteries and temples, the management of which calls for considerable administrative ability.

**Hindu reform and modernization.** Hinduism has, in the course of its long history, undergone many and radical changes, and several diverse forces have contributed to making Hinduism what it is today. The establishment of the Pax Britannica released many new forces, affecting Hinduism at every point. The disruption by the British of some of the social institutions of Hinduism, such as caste, untouchability, *satī*, human sacrifice, female infanticide, infant marriage, etc., made it clear to the orthodox that the state could use its power to alter their religious institutions. European missionaries who came to India for evangelical purposes sharply criticized Hinduism, and Hindus were made to realize poignantly that some influential outsiders thought that everything was wrong with their religion. Reformist Hindus—many of whom had attended mission schools—could not help remembering missionary criticisms of their religion, and in creating institutions to bring about changes in their society, they naturally emulated the organizations and work of their critics. From a long-term point of view the most important element in the reinterpretation and reformulation of Hinduism was the emergence of a westernized Indian elite, which eventually took over power from the British and which used that power to introduce fundamental changes, such as the abolition of untouchability, the legalization of intercaste marriage, widow marriage, and divorce, and the enforcement of monogamy. It is this elite that after a century and a half of Western influence declared India to be a secular state. Secularism does not mean that evil social institutions will be allowed to flourish, just as the principle of equality has not prevented the state from giving a variety of special privileges to Scheduled Castes and Tribes for a specific period of time, in order to enable them to catch up with the others.

One of the great reforming leaders of the new elite was Rājā Rām Mohan Roy, who founded a religious society, the Brāhma Samāj, in 1828. A daring religious thinker, scholar, and educator, Rām Mohan Roy was influenced by Vedānta and Islam before he studied Christianity; he was a monotheist and opposed to idolatry. He was an able and courageous controversialist and fought the orthodox *pandits* with arguments they could appreciate. For instance, in his efforts to purge Hinduism of the idolatrous accretions it had acquired over the centuries, he advocated a return to Vedic Hinduism: "Like Luther, who appealed to the Bible as an authority against medieval corruptions, he took his stand on the *Vedas*, the earliest Hindu scriptures, in which he found a form of pure Hinduism, of which the basis was a belief in one God, which was not vitiated by idolatry, and which gave no sanction to distinctions of caste or such practices as suttee" (O'Malley 1941, p. 67). (Dayananda Saraswati, who founded the Ārya Samāj, a religious brotherhood, in 1875, was only following Rām Mohan Roy in his efforts to introduce radical changes in Hinduism by championing a revival of Vedic Hinduism.) Rām Mohan Roy was aware that an appeal to the authority of the Vedas would carry weight with the orthodox *pandits*, and he set the style for a debate that went on for nearly a hundred years between reformists and diehards, both of whom quoted the scriptures in support of their views.

Rām Mohan Roy also discovered that a principle of reason lay at the basis of the classical Indian philosophy of Vedanta, as set forth in the Upaniṣads. "Ram Mohan Roy abandoned the traditionally accepted bases of Hindu religion and Brahminic authority in favor of reason. Hinduism could be justified in its essentials on the ground that it provided a reasoned explanation of reality. Everything from the West could be considered in the same light. There could be assimilation and not merely borrowing at random" (Spear 1961, p. 296). He thus laid the foundation for a reinterpretation of Hinduism freeing it not only from social institutions such as caste and untouchability but also from a welter of beliefs, ideas, myths, and ritual. He did not regard these as the "essence" of Hinduism. The essence was selected portions of the Vedānta, the Bhagavad Gītā, and *bhakti* or devotional literature. Subsequent reformers, such as Vivekānanda, Saraswati, Aurobindo Ghose, Tilak, Gandhi, and Rādhākrishnan, carried on the work of reinterpretation. Over the years the reformers, the greatest of whom was Gandhi, built up a body of public opinion in favor of introducing drastic changes in Hinduism. It was this opinion which later enabled the state to take legislative action against certain Hindu practices that were repugnant to the modern outlook.

The second half of the nineteenth century saw the beginnings of the growth of nationalist sentiment among Hindus, and nascent patriotism drew upon Hindu sentiment and traditions. A concern for the people and the country inevitably meant activism, and the Bhagavad Gītā provided a religious source for political activism and altruism. The *karma marga*, or "path of works," received emphasis at the expense of the other two paths.

Two contrary processes have been gaining strength in modern India. The first one is Sanskritization, a process by which the rites, customs, beliefs, and style of life of the higher castes, and in particular the *brāhmans*, are taken over by the lower groups, including the Untouchables and the tribal peoples. But while the lower groups increasingly Sanskritize their style of life, the higher strata become increasingly westernized. Westernization, like Sanskritization, is a multilayered process, including the acceptance of Western technology, Western political, legal, and social institutions, and Western literature, philosophy, and science. The spread of Sanskritization and westernization across the country and to different structural levels is beginning to produce nationwide uniformities in religion and culture. Everywhere village deities traditionally associated with epidemics of diseases such as plague, smallpox, and cholera seem to be losing ground, while the prestigious Sanskritic deities are becoming more popular. Blood sacrifices and offerings of liquor to deities are also becoming less popular. The horizon of the peasant is widening, and the richer peasants now visit pilgrimage centers several hundred miles away from their villages. Films, radio, textbooks, newspapers, journals, and paperback books are strengthening "regional" and "all-India" Hinduism, at the expense of strictly "local" forms. Life-cycle rituals are becoming abbreviated, while the purely social aspects of such rituals get elaborated; this seems to be particularly true of educated Hindus in towns. In fact, the forms Hinduism is taking among the educated urban Hindus is only beginning to be explored by social scientists (see, for example, Singer 1959). The search for a satisfying philosophy leads many members of this class to become devotees of one or another spiritual leader. Some of these leaders are traditional heads of monasteries, while others are modern figures. Hinduism has in the past depended upon caste, village, joint family, Hindu kings, monasteries, and centers of pilgrimage for its perpetuation. Radical changes have occurred in all of them. Moreover, there has been a growth in secularization, egalitarianism, and rationalism. But new organizations such as the Rāmakrishna Mission, the various hermitages of religious leaders, the Bharatiya Vidya Bhavan, and finally, departments of the central government such as the All-India Radio, and in some states departments supervising temple administration, are reinterpreting Hinduism in a modern direction.

M. N. Srinivas and A. M. Shah

[See also Asian society, *article on* south asia; Caste, *especially the article on* the indian caste system; Pollution.]

## BIBLIOGRAPHY

Basham, Arthur L. (1954) 1963 *The Wonder That Was India: A Study of the History and Culture of the Indian Sub-continent Before the Coming of the Muslims.* New ed., rev. New York: Hawthorn.

*Contributions to Indian Sociology* (Paris). → Published since 1957 under the editorship of Louis Dumont and D. Pocock.

Farquhar, John N. 1920 *An Outline of the Religious Literature of India.* Oxford Univ. Press.

Ghurye, Govind S. (1932) 1961 *Caste, Class and Occupation.* 4th ed., rev. Bombay: Popular Book Depot. → First published as *Caste and Race in India.*

Ghurye, Govind S. 1953 *Indian Sadhus.* Bombay: Popular Book Depot.

Ghurye, Govind S. 1962 *Gods and Men.* Bombay: Popular Book Depot.

Hubert, Henri; and Mauss, Marcel (1899) 1964 *Sacrifice: Its Nature and Function.* Univ. of Chicago Press. → First published in French.

Kane, P. V. 1930–1962 *History of Dharmaśāstra: Ancient and Mediaeval Religious and Civil Law in India.* Vols. 1–5. Poona: Bhandarkar Oriental Research Institute.

Lambert, Richard D.; and Hoselitz, Bert F. (editors) 1963 *The Role of Savings and Wealth in Southern Asia and the West.* Paris: UNESCO.

Marriott, McKim (editor) 1955 *Village India: Studies in the Little Community.* Univ. of Chicago Press. → Also published as Memoir No. 83 of the American Anthropological Association, which was issued as *American Anthropologist,* Volume 57, No. 3, Part 2, June 1955.

Morgan, Kenneth W. (editor) 1953 *The Religion of the Hindus.* New York: Ronald Press.

O'Malley, Lewis S. S. (editor) 1941 *Modern India and the West: A Study of the Interaction of Their Civilizations.* Oxford Univ. Press.

Singer, Milton (editor) 1959 *Traditional India: Structure and Change.* Philadelphia: American Folklore Society.

Singer, Milton et al. 1958 India's Cultural Values and Economic Development: A Discussion. *Economic Development and Cultural Change* 7:1–12.

Smith, Donald E. 1963 *India as a Secular State.* Princeton Univ. Press.

Spear, Percival 1961 *India: A Modern History.* Ann Arbor: Univ. of Michigan Press.

Srinivas, M. N. 1952 *Religion and Society Among the Coorgs of South India.* Oxford: Clarendon.

Srinivas, M. N. 1962 *Caste in Modern India, and Other Essays.* New York: Asia Pub. House.

Stevenson, Margaret 1920 *The Rites of the Twiceborn.* London: Milford.

Weber, Max (1921) 1958 *The Religion of India: The Sociology of Hinduism and Buddhism.* Translated and edited by Hans H. Gerth and Don Martindale. Glencoe, Ill.: Free Press. → First published as *Hinduismus und Buddhismus,* Volume 2 of *Gesammelte Aufsätze zur Religionssoziologie.*

# HINTZE, OTTO

Otto Hintze (1861–1940) spent the first twenty years of his life in his native Prussian province of Pomerania. After studying for two years at the University of Greifswald, he transferred in 1880 to the University of Berlin, where as a student of J. G. Droysen he became deeply imbued with the ethical implications and political principles of the Prussian tradition. He early impressed his teachers at the university with his capacity for relating minutiae to generalizations as well as with his independent, critical judgment (Hartung [1941] 1961, pp. 500–501). At a later point in his studies Hintze became associated with Gustav Schmoller, and this association greatly influenced his development as a professional historian, an influence reflected in his publications during the next decades.

Hintze's first major work was a study of the Prussian silk industry in the eighteenth century. It consisted of two volumes of documents and a third volume that analyzed the effects on the industry of the mercantilist policies of Frederick ii. At the completion of this work Hintze, at the age of 34, was given an appointment at the University of Berlin, and thereafter he was rapidly promoted. His position entailed lecturing on constitutional, administrative, and economic history as well as on politics, a rather unusual combination at the time.

As a collaborator of Schmoller's in the publication of the *Acta borussica,* Hintze next turned to the study of Prussian administration from 1740 to 1756. The six volumes of documents published as a result of this work carried an introduction by Hintze (1901) that was a penetrating analysis of this administrative system and of the major political decisions it embodied. Subsequently, Hintze continued to be associated with the *Acta borussica* in a leading capacity, while also becoming editor-in-chief of the *Forschungen zur brandenburgischen und preussischen Geschichte.*

Hintze's writings on Prussian history—a series of essays published at various times between 1896 and 1931 and collected as *Geist und Epochen der preussischen Geschichte* (1896–1931) and his summary volume *Die Hohenzollern und ihr Werk* (1915)—show a high order of critical, scholarly judgment. Although he was an avowed admirer of the Prussian monarchy and an avowed conservative, his approach to Prussian political institutions was objective and comparative. He came to see the Prussian case as a "paradigm for the formations and transformations of the modern state generally" (Hartung [1941] 1961, p. 506). The case of Prussia, as Hintze saw it, illustrates J. R. Seeley's dictum that the degree of internal freedom in a country is inversely proportional to the political and military pressures on its frontiers. More generally, this means that the internal social structure of a country—its class conflicts and constitutional framework—and its international position must be analyzed together. Such an approach shows that Prussia's militarism and monarchical constitution were by-products of her central European location; no attempt to form a nation-state in this area could succeed without the discipline and centralized authority of Prussian institutions (1915, pp. vi–vii). Applying this analysis to other times and places Hintze showed that in the sixteenth and seventeenth centuries the great struggle between France and the Hapsburg empire, together with the impotence of Germany, left countries like Poland in a power vacuum, which greatly facilitated such internal conflicts as those between powerful families and thus militated against the formation of a strong political structure ([1902–1932] 1962, pp. 515–521). Again, in England, early political centralization, together with relative military security, strongly militated against absolutism, bureaucracy, and militarism of the Continental type, so that the modern English state of the eighteenth and nineteenth centuries depended on the ruling agrarian and industrial classes rather than on the crown ([1902–1932] 1962, pp. 362–368).

Hintze's nationalist and monarchist persuasion was severely shaken by Germany's defeat in 1918. That experience brought greater acceptance on his part of democratic tendencies nationally and federative tendencies internationally, although so great a change of view was naturally difficult for a convinced conservative (Oestreich 1964, pp. 21–22). Impaired health forced him to discontinue university teaching, and during the years of the Weimar Republic he was a private scholar and publicist. Hitler's rise to power completely destroyed the world in which he had grown to maturity, and in 1938 Hintze, whose wife was Jewish, resigned from the Prussian Academy of Science. When his collected essays were published shortly after his death in 1940, all his discussions of the work of Jewish authors were excised.

Despite disillusionment and personal adversity, after World War I Hintze turned to a fuller elab-

oration of his projected comparative, constitutional history. There are indications that he completed a major work in this field but that it was lost during World War II. What remains is a series of essays on administrative history, feudalism, the estate-constitutions of Europe, the world-historical conditions of representative institutions in Western European societies, and Polish constitutional history, as well as brief synopses of his views concerning the major phases of European political history. Taken together, these writings do for the study of political institutions what Max Weber's sociology of religion did for the study of religious beliefs. By comparative analysis they reveal the institutional preconditions that shaped the Western system of constitutional states and the major types of constitutions that emerged within this system.

Hintze's work, which is informed with his wide knowledge of history, has a developmental emphasis that is not evolutionist and a conceptual approach that, like Weber's, brings out the singularity of a historical sequence or configuration by means of strategic contrasts with other civilizations. He had no use for biological analogies in social analysis, since he was much concerned with the role of ideas and political decisions in social change. For him as for Weber, functional relations are the end products of human actions that may produce innovations that are no less genuine because they are conditioned. Although it remained fragmentary, Hintze's work is a major contribution to the comparative analysis of social and political institutions.

REINHARD BENDIX

[For the historical context of Hintze's work, see the biographies of SCHMOLLER; WEBER, MAX.]

WORKS BY HINTZE

(1896–1931) 1943 Geist und Epochen der preussischen Geschichte: Gesammelte Abhandlungen. Leipzig: Koehler & Amelang.
(1897–1930) 1964 Soziologie und Geschichte: Gesammelte Abhandlungen zur Soziologie, Politik und Theorie der Geschichte. 2d ed., enl. Göttingen (Germany): Vandenhoeck & Ruprecht. → A collection of essays first published in book form in 1942 as Zur Theorie der Geschichte.
1901 Einleitende Darstellung der Behördenorganisation und allgemeinen Verwaltung in Preussen beim Regierungsantritt Friedrichs II. Volume 6, Part 1 in Acta borussica: Denkmäler der preussischen Staatsverwaltung im 18. Jahrhundert. Berlin: Parey.
(1902–1932) 1962 Staat und Verfassung: Gesammelte Abhandlungen zur allgemeinen Verfassungsgeschichte. 2d ed., enl. Göttingen (Germany): Vandenhoeck & Ruprecht. → Contains a bibliography of Hintze's writings.
1915 Die Hohenzollern und ihr Werk: Fünfhundert Jahre vaterländischer Geschichte. Berlin: Parey.

SUPPLEMENTARY BIBLIOGRAPHY

HARTUNG, FRITZ (1941) 1961 Otto Hintze. Pages 497–520 in Fritz Hartung, *Staatsbildende Kräfte der Neuzeit: Gesammelte Aufsätze*. Berlin: Duncker & Humblot.

OESTREICH, GERHARD 1964 Otto Hintzes Stellung zur Politikwissenschaft und Soziologie. Pages 7–67 in Otto Hintze, *Soziologie und Geschichte: Gesammelte Abhandlungen zur Soziologie, Politik und Theorie der Geschichte*. Göttingen (Germany): Vandenhoeck & Ruprecht.

# HISTORICAL SCHOOL

*See under* ECONOMIC THOUGHT.

# HISTORIOGRAPHY

*The articles under this heading deal with the problems and traditions of history writing. A detailed guide to related articles will be found under* HISTORY. *For discussions of historians who have contributed to the development of historiography, see the biographies of* ACTON; BEARD; BLOCH; BÜCHER; BURCKHARDT; CROCE; DILTHEY; FEBVRE; FUSTEL DE COULANGES; GIERKE; HALÉVY; HECKSCHER; HINTZE; HUIZINGA; IBN KHALDŪN; KOYRÉ; LAMPRECHT; MACAULAY; MAINE; MAITLAND; MARX; McILWAIN; MEINECKE; NAMIER; PIRENNE; RANKE; ROBINSON; SARTON; SOMBART; SPENCER; SPENGLER; TAWNEY; TOCQUEVILLE; TOYNBEE; TREITSCHKE; TROELTSCH; TURNER; VICO; WEBER, MAX.

| | |
|---|---|
| I. THE RHETORIC OF HISTORY | *J. H. Hexter* |
| II. AFRICAN HISTORIOGRAPHY | *K. O. Dike and J. F. A. Ahayi* |
| III. CHINESE HISTORIOGRAPHY | *Arthur F. Wright* |
| IV. ISLAMIC HISTORIOGRAPHY | *Franz Rosenthal* |
| V. JAPANESE HISTORIOGRAPHY | *John Whitney Hall* |
| VI. SOUTH AND SOUTHEAST ASIAN HISTORIOGRAPHY | *Wang Gungwu* |

## I
### THE RHETORIC OF HISTORY

In this article the word "historiography" will be taken to mean the craft of writing history and/or the yield of such writing considered in its rhetorical aspect. The term "history" will be used to describe the study of the past as a systematic discipline. It will not be used to refer to the past as such. Unnecessary ambiguities created by using the term "history" to identify both the past and the systematic study of it have occasionally led to gratuitous confusion. The terms "historiography," "the rhetoric of history," and "history writing" will be used as synonyms. Historiography is different from the collection of historical evidence, the editing of historical sources, the exercise of historical thought and imagination, the criticism of historical writing, and the philosophy of history, but it is related to all of them and overlaps some of them. It is also different from the history of history writing. This distinction must be kept in mind because in recent decades the term "historiography" has increasingly been used to mean the history of history writing—in effect, a branch of intellectual history or a subbranch of the sociology of knowledge. It will not be used in that sense here.

Perhaps the drift of the term "historiography" from its initial moorings of meaning resulted from the neglect of systematic study of the rhetoric of history and from the view, usually implicit rather than explicit, that that rhetoric is not specific to history, or not specific enough to warrant systematic study; for if the rhetoric of history is generic rather than specific, then historiography so defined has no separate identity and merges into general rhetoric. Although many historians have said wise and witty things about the writing of history, none has focused more than intermittent attention on the problems it raises. The casualness with which historians have investigated the structure of historiography, compared with the care and exacting scrutiny to which they subject the nature of data, evidence, and inference in works of history, indicates that in their role as critics they regard the latter as the historians' legitimate central preoccupation and the former as a secondary and independent matter in which excellence, although desirable, is dispensable and without effect on the validity of the finished work.

To test this implied judgment—which is very hard to reconcile with the care and pains which many of the best historians lavish on their own history writing—this article will attempt an analysis of historiography.

The models of history writing that will be dealt with will be those provided in recent times by the better historians in their better moments. "In recent times" because, although the writing of history is old, the *general* professional commitment of historians *always* to write it with the maximum verisimilitude to the past is relatively new—scarcely 150 years old. The focus will be on "the better historians in their better moments" because they should and often do set the standards at which the profession aims. It is the practice of these historians when actually writing history, not their explicit theoretical or quasi-philosophical views, that is of concern here; for it is in their practice of historiography rather than in peripheral excursions into the problems of methodology that they reveal their effective commitments. Although much that follows will apply to all historiography, the article is only incidentally concerned with historical writings intended to codify knowledge of history already available, such as textbooks; primarily it is focused on history writing aimed at extending the bounds of historical knowledge. Since historiography communicates what the historian knows or thinks he knows, a consideration of the historian's way of writing that does not relate it to his way of knowing is doomed to triviality. Finally, as an overarching principle this article will seek to relate the rhetoric of history to the rhetoric of the mathematizing natural sciences, taking physics and chemistry as models, in order to make clear the similarities of historiography to these other ways in which men seek to communicate what they think they know, and its differences from them.

## The language of historians

The most cursory comparison of any professional journal of history with an issue of the *Physical Review* will carry the conviction that the rhetoric of history differs grossly from that of physics. Ideally the vocabulary of physics is exact and denotative, and its syntax is mathematical, expressing quantitative relations between entities defined with the minimum ambiguity possible, given the current state of knowledge of the science. Now a part of the distinctive vocabulary of historiography is also denotative and unambiguous—the terms "pipe roll" or "writ of trespass" no less so, for example, than the term "specific gravity," although most if not all of the vocabulary of history that is at once distinctive and unambiguous is likely to refer to universes more constricted in time and space or less homogeneous and uniform than the ones the vocabulary of physics refers to. Moreover, historians often use quantitative data: grain yields per acre, rates of population growth, average rainfall; and sometimes they employ the syntax of mathematics to determine such matters as median income, ratio of cargo weight to number of sailors, range of probable error in equating number of manors owned with gross income from land. Thus, they occasionally mathematize, they often quantify and enumerate, and part of their vocabulary is wholly denotative. When operating in a sector of history writing where they deem rhetorical devices of this sort alone to be appropriate, they assimilate the form of their vocabulary very closely to that of the natural sciences and exercise a like care to decontaminate it of con-

notative and evocative overtones. Yet very few historians consistently write history this way, and scarcely any of that very few would insist that *all* history ought to aim at the rhetoric of the natural sciences as an ideal goal; they do not seek to make the rhetorical form which they find convenient into a prescriptive rule for the entire profession, as they would be obligated to do if they thought that *only* with such a rhetoric could one come close to an account of things past that approaches maximum verisimilitude.

In this respect historians differ notably from many social scientists. Both historians and social scientists claim, as natural scientists do, that by their method of investigation and formulation appropriately applied, they are able to produce cumulative increments to men's knowledge. Both historians and social scientists acknowledge that the form of their rhetoric is not always coincident with that of the natural sciences. But since most social scientists take the rhetoric of the natural sciences as their goal and ideal, they make a major intellectual effort to assimilate their way of writing to that of the natural sciences. In this matter they regard any nonconformity on their part as a deformity, to be either overcome or lamented. In practice, historians rarely see historiographic problems in this light. Far from always seeking the forms of language which will enable them to make historiography into the closest possible replica of the language of the natural sciences, they choose —often unself-consciously, but sometimes well aware of what they are doing—to write in a way that the rhetoric of the sciences forecloses. They deliberately choose a word or a phrase that is imprecise and may turn out to be ambiguous, because of its rich aura of connotation. Without compunction they sacrifice exactness for evocative force. Since the only common purpose to which historians are bound by their calling to commit themselves is to advance understanding of the past, the only possible justification for such a sacrifice is that it serves to increase knowledge of the past, that sometimes an evocative rhetoric is the best means a historian has for formulating and communicating what he knows. Whether or not the historians who in practice follow this rhetorical strategy are fully aware of it, the implication of this strategy is very radical. It entails the claim that historians can produce cumulative increments of knowledge without consistent resort to the rhetoric which scientists have found indispensable for formulating and communicating what they know. Positively it implies that for communicating what the historian knows, a rhetoric more like that employed in the fictive arts than like that employed in the sciences is not only permissible but on occasion indispensable.

### Knowing and communicating

To analyze historiography, we must first determine its place in the general process of knowing and communicating. In order to identify and comprehend this general process, we will start with a concrete proposition: Willie Mays knows baseball. To deny this proposition is to fly in the face of the unanimous and considered judgment of several million people who have seen Mays play ball. Alternatively, it is to restrict the meaning of the term "know" so drastically as to impede the flow of discourse and snarl up a channel of communication. For a man who can convince some five million observers out of five million, and his employers to the tune of a salary of $125,000 per year, that he knows has come as close to ironclad demonstration as one can get in matters involving human judgment. To generate this conviction, Mays employs the rhetoric of action, the most common and universal method of demonstrating that one knows. (The author realizes that he is rather stretching the common sense of the term "rhetoric" in the present context.) The adequacy of such demonstration is measured by consistent appropriateness of visible (or perceivable) response. Briefly, Willie Mays shows that he knows by what he does. While he demonstrates almost perfectly *that* he knows, for two reasons he would have great difficulty in saying how he knows what he knows. (1) Since much of what he knows lies in the area of action, he probably knows no way of putting it into words. (2) Much of what he knows, he knows from long experience, and although some of what he knows in this way can be rendered accessible in verbal form, and is known by others in that form, that is not in fact how *he* knows it. If we went further and insisted that he so exactly communicate in words what he knows that others could test its validity by replication, we would clearly be asking the impossible, because he does not know what he knows with some abstraction from himself called his discursive intellect but with his whole person; and in every game he plays, he demonstrates its validity, not by verbal or mathematical formulation but by the unique and unreplicable perfection of his response.

In one area of human knowing, investigation in the natural sciences, however, formal convention has established as a minimal evidence of knowing the ability to state the results in a wholly denotative rhetoric of verbal signs; all consistently appropriate responses are required ulti-

mately to assume this form. This convention has been adopted because scientists set a very high value on generalizability of statement, replicability of experiment, and logical entailment as tests of knowing; and the rhetoric they have chosen enforces entailment and makes generalization and replication possible with maximum efficiency and certainty. Scientists have no doubt adopted this particular rhetorical stratagem because they have found it very useful for eliciting and testing answers to the kinds of questions they habitually ask. Correlatively, however, it prevents them, as scientists, from asking questions that are recalcitrant to formulation in the rhetoric they have chosen, and a fortiori from answering such questions. As a result of this set of circumstances, in the sciences it is by definition meaningless to say that one knows or understands a result, a law, or a hypothesis but cannot state or communicate what one thus claims to understand. If I cannot state the binomial theorem, or the law of inverse squares, or the valence rule, I do not know it, and any claim to the contrary is simply nonsense. In effect, the strategy of the sciences in the codification of their results is to reduce to a minimum in practice and to nothing in theory the gap between cognition and written communication.

The range of knowing, then, extends from what Willie Mays knows about baseball, which we would accept as demonstrated whether or not Mays can put together a single coherent sentence on the subject, to what a physicist knows about the results of investigations in physics, which he can demonstrate only with a denotative vocabulary and a mathematical syntax. The common factor is the capacity of each to render a consistently appropriate response; the difference lies in the nature of the response that is deemed appropriate; and the criterion of appropriateness is efficacy in encompassing the purpose of the activity to which the actor has committed himself.

In this general setting of the relation between knowing and communicating, what is the relation between knowing history and its communication in writing, that is, historiography? In the first place, among professional historians there is a rough consensus about the responses appropriate for writers of history when they set out to communicate what they know. This consensus enables one to speak of "the better historians" with a sense that one's judgment is not merely personal, random, or arbitrary. The consensus is approximately registered by the price a particular historian fetches in the current job market. (Only approximately, however, since a number of items other than the profession's estimate of his history writing go to make his price—his age, his reputed aptitude in face-to-face teaching, his personal qualities, the relation of supply to demand in his special field of interest, and so on.) Second, in writing history, as we have seen, some historians consistently use a vocabulary and a syntax similar to those which are standard in the natural sciences and some do not. There is, however, no significant correlation between the list of those who do so and the list of "better historians." This implies that in historiography, historians do not accept the scientists' conception of what constitutes a consistently appropriate response in the public presentation of the results of scientific investigation. An inquiry of no very pressing sort would reveal that in practice they have refused fully to commit themselves to a scientific rhetoric because they concern themselves with questions and answers which are not wholly tractable to the kind of formulation that scientists aim at, and because they assume in practice a relationship between cognition and communication in history different from that which is currently acceptable in the sciences.

Historians acquire their command of the data that they ultimately deploy in writing history through reading and considering what men have written in the past and about the past and by giving attention to remnants and traces of men's handiwork surviving from the past: buildings, tools, pictures, field systems, tombs, pots—archeological data in the broadest sense. The process of learning starts in a haphazard way with the student's earliest interest in history, and for the professional historian becomes more systematic and more sharply focused in the course of his training. In general, the training of a historian aims at the complementary but sometimes conflicting goals of simultaneously extending the range of his knowledge and of bringing it intensively to bear on some limited constellation of past happenings, in writing about which he is expected to make some contribution to the advancement of historical knowledge.

This process of knowing which goes on throughout the historian's active professional life is not identical with the knowing through experience which enables most men to meet most of the contingencies of their days on earth without continual bafflement, frustration, and disaster; but it is similar to it. It is not identical because in some measure the historian chooses what he will confront, while much of what men know through day-to-day experience comes at them haphazardly by no choice of their own.

Second, the layman's kind of knowledge is in large part acquired through face-to-face confronta-tion with persons and situations, while the historian's confrontation with men and situations of the past is mainly (in most cases, wholly) indirect, mediated by the surviving documentary and archeological record. Nevertheless, the difference ought not to be exaggerated, for there is considerable overlap. The printing press and more recent media of communication have vastly extended the role of indirect confrontation in day to-day experiential knowledge. Moreover, in his quest for understanding of the past, the historian relies to a considerable extent on the cautious and qualified analogical application of experiential knowledge which he has accumulated in personal, face-to-face transactions during his own lifetime.

Finally, the difference between face-to-face confrontation and confrontation mediated by the historical record is one of mode but not necessarily of quality, or intensity, or depth, or coherence, or completeness. Any man who reads and meditates on the 12 volumes of the correspondence of Desiderius Erasmus, extending over a span of four decades, plus his massive literary output, may justly argue that in quality, intensity, depth, coherence, and completeness his experiential knowledge of that sixteenth-century intellectual, acquired through mediated confrontation, is more firmly based than the experiential knowledge that any contemporary of Erasmus had of him. Indeed, it is as firmly based as the knowledge available today about any intellectual now living. The similarity between the two kinds of knowledge we have been considering is that for many purposes the consistently appropriate response which indicates their presence is not and need not be verbal, and when verbal, it need not and quite possibly cannot take the form of wholly denotative statement, much less of mathematical formulation. For such purposes it lies closer to the Willie Mays pole of response by effective action than to the scientific pole of response by communicating results in unambiguous statement.

In a large part of his work, the historian has no need at all for such statement or for any coherent verbal statement at all. He is massively engaged in finding out what happened and how it happened. To do these things he must formulate rough hypotheses, often very rough, about what happened and how it happened, and then examine the available record to verify or correct his hypotheses. But at the outset, from an almost limitless range of conceivable hypotheses he must select for investigation the very few that lie somewhere in the target area; he must select only those for which the surviving records hold forth some hope of verification; and he must have a sense of what records among a multitude are likely to provide the evidence he needs. A historian unable to do any of these things would remain an inept novice all his life. Relying on their knowledge of the past, historians successfully do these things day after day, yet most of them would be at a loss to explain their particular choices. They tend to ascribe their general aptitude for making better rather than worse choices to "knowing the ropes" and "having been around a long time in this period." In effect, the knowledge that a historian relies on for a very considerable part of his work is experiential and results from a long and extensive familiarity with the historical record. (There is a legitimate doubt whether much of the foregoing does not apply as readily to the actual work of scientists as to that of historians.) For the historian the link between knowing and communicating is loose and weak; on the basis of his own experience of this looseness, he inclines to give some, if not full, faith and credit to colleagues who claim to know about the past much that they cannot adequately express in writing. Communication through historiography requires historians to put into written words what they know experientially and diffusely about the past, to organize it into coherent and sequential statements in order to make it fully accessible first to themselves and then to others. Their communication with others, the history they end up writing, thus starts four removes from the episodes in the past that concern them. Between the two lie the historical record, the historians' experiential knowledge acquired through their exploration of that record, and their attempts to communicate to themselves what they know.

Through these interposed layers historians, in and by their writing, seek, along with many other things, to enable their readers to follow the movement and to sense the tempo of events; to grasp and do justice to the motives and actions of men; to discern the imperatives that move men to action; and to distinguish those imperatives from the pseudo imperatives that have become mere exercises in pious ejaculation; to recognize the impact on the course of events of an accident, a catastrophe, or a bit of luck; and to be aware of what the participants in a struggle conceived the stakes to be. (This particular set of items which historians sometimes feel called on to communicate through the three layers has purposely been selected because (1) none of them are explanatory in the scientific sense and (2) none can be effectively communicated in a purely scientific rhetoric.) The historian's ability both as an investigator of the past and as a writer of history is measured nega-

tively by the extent to which he lets the layers that intervene between the episode in the past and the reader of his work insulate the reader from the past, positively by the extent to which he is able to make these layers serve as a conductor of knowledge of the past to his readers. Historians give faith and credit to their fellows who protest that they know and yet confess that they cannot communicate what they know, because in some measure every historian is aware how far he has failed in his writing of history to penetrate those layers in his effort to communicate what he knows of the past.

Given this sense of the inadequacy of their use of language to their task, historians would surely welcome as an alternative a wholly denotative universal vocabulary which would narrow to a scarcely discernible crevice the perilous chasm that for them separates cognition from communication and sets them ransacking the whole storehouse of their mother tongue instead of relying on a manageable number of well-designed symbolic structures to overcome it. The fact that no such alternative adequate to communicate what historians know about the past has up to now emerged suggests that the relation between knowing the past and the writing of history is such as to preclude that alternative, that in practice historians believe that the sacrifice of the knowledge of the past which it would entail renders inappropriate the universal imposition in historiography of the denotative rhetoric of scientific discourse.

Of course historians can avoid their rhetorical difficulties (1) by attempting to communicate about the past only that knowledge which can be expressed in a rhetoric nearly like that of the natural sciences or (2) by attempting to know about the past only what can be so communicated. In fact, historians have pursued both these courses. Some historians have taken the first course either because of a special interest in the sorts of historical problems manageable within the confines of a quasi-scientific rhetoric or because their special aptitude for that rhetoric has turned their attention to the sorts of problem with which it can deal. Others have taken the second course either out of allegiance to a conception (or misconception) called scientific history or because by calling their thinking and writing about the past scientific history, they thought they could sanctify their incompetence and dullness.

On the whole, however, historians have not been willing to truncate their knowledge of the past to fit the special aptitudes of a few historians or the misconceptions or painful ineptitude of a number of others. Instead, to make their experiential knowledge of the past accessible to readers who cannot recapitulate the processes by which that knowledge was acquired, they have used almost every device of rhetoric compatible with their commitment to a clear and intelligible presentation of the evidence on which their knowledge is based. That the language they use is frequently evocative and even metaphorical and that much of its vocabulary is not that of scientific demonstration but of the ordinary discourse of educated men, testifies to their conviction—rarely explicit, sometimes not wholly conscious—that these are the appropriate means for bringing their readers into that confrontation with events long past and men long dead which is an indispensable condition of knowing them. To the extent that the historian's rhetoric falls short of communicating what he believes he has discovered about the past, what he thinks he knows does not become generally available and cannot be tested publicly by other historians. To that extent, therefore, there is a loss of potential knowledge of the past. Conversely, to the extent that he succeeds in communicating anything that hitherto he alone has known, there is gain. Therefore, the advancement of historical knowledge depends to a considerable extent on the quality of the historian's rhetoric, on the efficacy of his historiography, and is almost inseparable from it; far from impeding the advancement of historical knowledge, language evocative rather than wholly denotative in intent and character becomes a means and a condition of that advancement.

## Modes of explanation

Historiography is the means for communicating in writing what the historian thinks he knows about the past. Efficient and effective communication requires him, in writing history, to array what he knows according to some principle of coherence. The principle of coherence traditionally and still most generally employed by historians is narrative. Usually, but not always, they communicate what they know by telling a story or stories. Despite its venerable antiquity, narrative has recently come under attack as a means for providing coherence in history. The most general ground for attack seems to be the contention that the coherence it provides is nonexplanatory or inadequately explanatory. In this respect it is compared invidiously with the principle of coherence by subsumption under general laws supposedly standard in the rhetoric of the sciences, which is said to provide adequate explanation. If subsumption under general laws is the principle of coherence standard in the sciences, if by the criteria of the sciences it alone provides adequate explanation, and if the provision of adequate explanation is the sole or prime function of the sciences, then clearly narrative does *not* meet the scientific standard of coherence, nor does it provide adequate scientific explanation. It remains to ask, however, why historians should prefer a principle of coherence and criteria of explanatory adequacy borrowed from the rhetoric of the sciences both to narrative, their own traditional principle of coherence, and to the view of the nature and conditions of historical explanation which their use of narrative implies.

The ascription of adequacy to explanations of the general-law type seems to be based on both aesthetic and practical considerations. (1) Elegance, precision, clarity, internal consistency, and structural tidiness—a place for everything and everything in its place—in the domain of knowing: all these are aesthetically attractive concomitants of general-law explanations and are the generator and the justification of the denotative vocabulary and the mathematical syntax at which scientists aim. (2) In many or most cases, such explanations afford scientists the opportunity to replicate the experiment that was offered as evidence of the applicability of the general law, and thus to test the validity either of the law or of its application. (3) The rhetoric of the sciences facilitates the rapid and efficient identification of new problems and problem areas. (4) The expansion of the range and precision of general-law explanations has roughly coincided on the temporal scale with an extraordinary expansion of man's control of vast tracts of his environment over which hitherto he had exercised no control at all. Although by the general-law canon, or indeed by any canon of explanation that has not been in disrepute since Aristotle, such a coincidence taken alone does *not* adequately explain the expansion of control, still nothing succeeds like success, and the aura of prestige acquired by the natural sciences in the past three centuries has rubbed off on the criteria of adequate explanation ascribed to them, especially in the eyes of intellectually insecure social scientists and historians.

No one has ever made clear why the criteria of adequate explanation acceptable to scientists in their work should also be acceptable to historians in theirs, or why adequacy of explanation should be the *sole* criterion of consistently appropriate response for the historian engaged in the work of communicating his knowledge in writing. Adequacy of explanation is clearly relative to that which is to be explained. A guidebook to a city, for example, explains the location of a "point of interest" by designating what streets it is on and nearest to and by indicating the means of access to it from other points by various means of transportation. A real estate survey explains its location by designating the frontage and length of the lot, the street it faces on, and the distance of the lot from the nearest intersecting street. Both explanations are accurate, exact enough for their respective purposes, and therefore adequate; each communicates the knowledge likely to be sought by one particular sort of seeker and thus provides the appropriate response to his questions; neither invokes any general law, nor need it do so; neither is a scientific explanation, nor need it be so. Moreover, the notion that the sole appropriate response of the historian to his commitment to communicate what he knows is something designated "explanation" is wildly arbitrary. It involves either consigning a large part of that response to the domain of irrelevance or so extending the meaning of "explanation" as to render it unrecognizable by scientists, philosophers, ordinary readers, and historians themselves.

**Historical narrative.** Narrative, which is the rhetorical mode most commonly resorted to by historians, is also their most common mode of explanation. It is not in fact scientific by the criteria just indicated; it cannot be rendered scientific because it is formally not reducible to the general-law type of explanation; and no more than the "explanations where" set forth above need it be scientific in order to be adequate, unless one insists on applying the scientific criteria of adequacy to a nonscientific explanation. Narrative is the most common mode of historical explanation because it is often the kind of explanatory answer solicited by a kind of question that historians very often ask and that is very often asked of them. Two ordinary forms of this question are "How did it come about that . . . ?" and "How did he (or they) happen to . . . ?" For example, "How did it come about that a Labour government took power in England in 1964?" or "How did the New York Giants happen to play in the World Series in 1951?" The following discussion will be organized around a treatment of this second question. The writer has selected it because it leads quickly into so many of the topics of this section and because its evidential base is one on which he is more than ordinarily well informed.

The call for an explanation of how the Giants happened to play in the World Series of 1951 can be so construed as to make it amenable to explanation of the general-law type.

*A. The particular facts*

1. In 1951 the New York Giants were a baseball team in the National League.

2. In 1951, during the official National League baseball season, the New York Giants won more games from the other teams in that league and lost fewer to them than any of the other teams in the league won or lost.

*B. The general law*

Whenever during the official National League season a National League team wins more games and loses fewer than any other team in that league, it plays in the World Series.

The answer perfectly fulfills all the requirements of the general-law type of explanation, including denotative univocal vocabulary and strict deductive entailment. Yet from the point of view of the writer and reader of history, such an answer is patently unsatisfactory. The reason is that in the context of the National League season of 1951, the appropriate response to the question "How did the Giants happen to play in the World Series of 1951?" is the historical *story* of how the Giants came to lead the National League at the end of the official season that year. A general-law explanation cannot tell that story; indeed, it cannot tell any story. It is not built to tell stories. From this very simple instance an important conclusion follows: general law and narrative are not merely alternative but equally valid modes of explanation. In the above instance the general-law explanation does not tell the questioner what he wants to know; for him it is neither a good nor a bad, neither an adequate nor an inadequate, explanation—it is no explanation at all. And conversely, to other questioners asking scientists *and* historians for an "explanation," a response in the form of a story would be quite inappropriate and therefore no explanation at all. The validity of either mode of explanation is determined by the appropriateness and adequacy of its response to a particular question. In effect, the validity of modes of explanation is not something that exists *in vacuo*, but only in relation to what particular inquirers at particular moments seek to know.

In view of the frequent irrelevance of pure general-law explanation to past situations that require the telling of a story, attempts have been made to adapt the general-law type of explanation to narrative. Narrative explanation is usually presented as a series of statements of continuous causal linkages between events such that in the chains of causation (1) each effect is imputed to precedent causes and (2) the imputation implies either the actuality or the possibility of a general law or laws such that, taken with the precedent causes, they entail the effect.

For present purposes it is to our advantage that the official rules of baseball provide us with a vocabulary almost as purely denotative as that of the sciences. In that vocabulary we can produce a narrative explanation of how the New York Giants won the 1951 National League pennant and thus played in the World Series; this explanation conforms to the foregoing model.

National League Standings as of September 30, 1951

|  | Won | Lost |
|---|---|---|
| Brooklyn Dodgers | 96 | 58 |
| New York Giants | 96 | 58 |

Because of the tie at the end of the regular season Brooklyn and New York were required to play additional games, the first team to win two games to be designated as the National League entry in the World Series.

First additional game, Oct. 1, 1951: final score, New York 3, Brooklyn 1; games won, New York 1, Brooklyn 0.

Second additional game, Oct. 2, 1951: final score, Brooklyn 10, New York 0; games won, New York 1, Brooklyn 1.

Third additional game, Oct. 3, 1951: inning-by-inning score to second half of the ninth inning:

| Brooklyn | 1 | 0 | 0 | 0 | 0 | 0 | 0 | 3 | 0 |
| New York | 0 | 0 | 0 | 0 | 0 | 0 | 1 | 0 |

Score to second half of the ninth inning, Brooklyn 4, New York 1. New York at bat.

The first batter singled. The second batter singled. Because the first batter was a reasonably fast runner, he advanced to third base. Because the third batter hit a short fly ball which was caught, he was out. Because the fourth batter doubled, the first batter scored a run, and the second batter advanced to third base, where he was replaced by a substitute runner because he had hurt his leg. The Brooklyn pitcher was replaced because three New York players out of four had made safe hits off his pitching. Because the fifth batter hit a home run the substitute runner, the fourth batter, and the fifth batter scored runs. Because New York scored four runs in the second half of the ninth inning, making the score 5 to 4, they won the game. Because they won two games of the play-off before Brooklyn did, they won more games and lost fewer than any other team in the National League. Because of this they played in the World Series of 1951.

About the preceding narrative explanation a number of highly instructive points are worth noting.

(1) It almost perfectly conforms to the proposed structure of narrative explanation outlined above; that is, it is a series of sentences in which the causal connections between the events mentioned are explicit or clearly implicit, and into which the relevant possible general laws may readily be inserted. Any number of such laws are not merely possible but actually available, e.g., if the two leading teams in the National League have won and lost the same number of games at the end of the regular season, the rules require that they resolve the tie by playing against each other until one of them has won two games.

(2) All the facts as stated are verifiably true and all the causal inferences are valid, and therefore the whole narrative explanation is historically true and accurate in every respect.

(3) Nevertheless, at a number of crucial points it is hard to see how particular effects were strictly entailed by a combination of antecedent causes and general laws. What, for example, is the general law which with the precondition (three hits and one out, among four men at bat) entails the replacement of one pitcher by another? Even if one elaborated further on the boundary conditions— and that can be done—it is difficult to see how general laws can be invoked and a strict entailment made to work here.

(4) It is true that once the substitute Brooklyn pitcher, Ralph Branca, whose mere presence in the game seems not amenable to narrative explanation (see above), released the ball, and once the fifth New York batter, Bobby Thomson, began his swing of the bat, a combination of a few special cases (mainly ballistic) of the general laws of motion with the National League ground rules on home runs suffices strictly to entail that Thomson hit a home run. It is hard, however, to envision the combination of conditions and laws that would strictly entail a decisive precondition of that home run: to wit, that Thomson decided to swing at Branca's pitch in the first place.

(5) Even if these problems of the logic of narrative explanation can be resolved, the account as presented raises a number of difficulties and questions. (a) Why does the explanation begin with the play-off at the end of the regular season? On the face of it, in a regular season that ends in a tie, every game played throughout the season by the tied teams is of equal causal importance and therefore should receive equal treatment. (b) By the same token, why is a fuller account (inning-by-inning score) given of the last game of the official season than of the two previous games, and a still fuller account of the last half of the last inning of the last game?

(6) Most important, the explanation is historio-

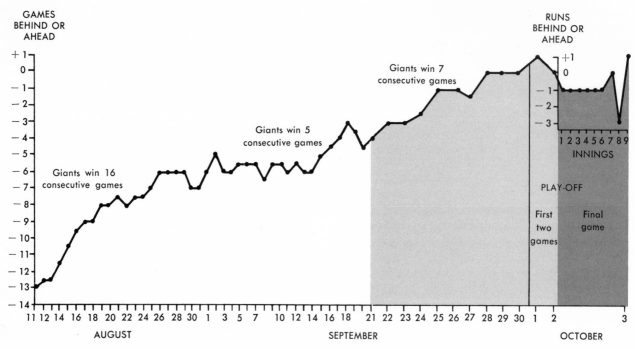

*Figure 1 — The positions of the New York Giants in relation to the Brooklyn Dodgers in the 1951 pennant race, with standings shown at end of play on given date*

graphically pitiful, and the historian who offered it would immediately lose the historian's moral equivalent of a union card.

Given the problem with which we started, these difficulties go to the heart of the trouble. They make it clear that offering an answer in the form of a narrative explanation which is structurally determined solely by the logic of causal ascription is not an appropriate response to the difficulties or an adequate solution to the problem. Within the bounds of the logic of causal ascription there is no solution for them. That logic cannot justify the shifts in the scale of the story. Yet it is reasonable to suspect that one of the few things which most readers would intuitively regard as appropriate about the above dreary but true narrative response to the question about New York being in the World Series in 1951 would be precisely the successive expansions of the scale of the story. The reason for this is that the appropriate response to the question is not a true narrative explanation determined by the logic of causal ascription but the historical story truest to the past, determined by the rules of historical evidence and the rhetorical rules of historical storytelling. Of this larger context a true narrative explanation is a part, but only a part. If this is so, then the true historical story rightly determined by the rules of historical rhetoric will be preferable to a true narrative explanation because it communicates more knowledge and truth about the past

than such an explanation does. But if that is so, then the rhetoric of history writing, not its logic alone, is implicated in providing increments of knowledge and truth about the past.

Let us continue with the example under examination, keeping in mind the problems of where to start the historical story and on what scale to tell it. Figure 1 describes the relative positions of the two contenders in the National League pennant race of 1951.

The first things to note in Figure 1 are the shifts in scale and the considerations which determined them. The over-all consideration is that of telling a historical story in such a way as to maximize the increment of knowledge and truth communicated. That within a framework identical with the one in which the figure is constructed (the 154-game baseball season) it may be desirable to have no change of scale and not to tell a story at all becomes clear on considering the description of the American League season of 1939 in Figure 2.

Figure 2 is constructed on uniform scales for each axis, plotting the games won by the New York Yankees against the games won by the team in the league that was in second place. That this season calls for no narrative explanation is manifested by the nonconvergence of the lines in Figure 2, which shows (1) that by June 1, the Yankees were seven games ahead, (2) that thereafter the minimum gap between them and their nearest rival was six

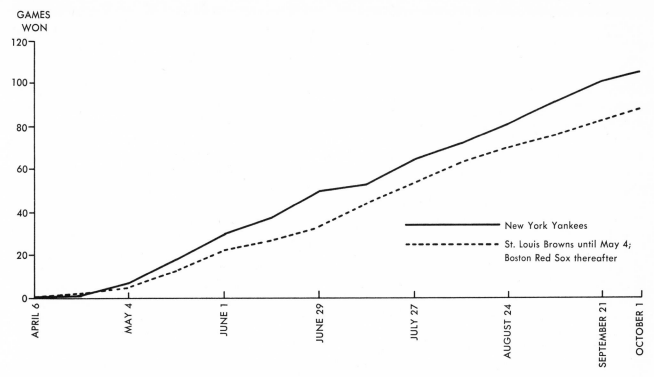

*Figure 2 — The positions of the New York Yankees and the second-place American League team in the 1939 baseball season*

games, (3) that by the end of the season the Yankees led by 17 games. In short, for more than the latter two-thirds of the season there was never a moment when it even looked like a pennant race, so that on the face of the record, to answer the question "How did the Yankees come to be in the World Series?" with a historical story would be a historiographic error: the even-paced, dull, and trivial chronicle which the effort would yield would itself demonstrate the inappropriateness of such a rhetorical response.

By the same token, the climbing line in Figure 1 indicates that the record of the 1951 National League season calls for a historical story, and that to write about its history without telling such a story is to fail to make the appropriate historiographic response. The data in Figure 1 start at the point where the extended historical story should begin: August 11, 1951, at the end of play. At that point New York was at its maximum distance behind Brooklyn, 13 games; and the next day New York began a series of 16 consecutive wins. For the next extension of the narrative and for the expansion of the scale of the graph, the directive of the record is more ambivalent. The options lie between (1) September 14, when, still six games behind, New York began a series of five consecutive wins which by September 18 moved it to within three

games of Brooklyn and (2) **September 21, when,** four games behind, New York won the last seven games of the regular season. It had moved into a tie at the end of play September 28, kept the tie by winning the last two games of the regular season, and was again tied at the end of the second game of the play-off. It is to be noted that (1) although there are two options for starting this expansion, there are *only* two serious options, and (2) they have an identical *terminus ad quem*, the point at which the next expansion of scale begins in the final game of the play-off. Either of the above alternative solutions is historiographically correct; *any other* is incorrect. There may be two or more right answers to some historiographic, as to some mathematical, problems. This does not imply or entail that there are no wrong answers. This simple observation and distinction, evident to any mathematics student who has gotten as far as quadratic equations, seems to have escaped most historians.

The expansions of scale, then, are not arbitrary; each can clearly be justified from the historical record on historiographic grounds, and each expansion coincides with a period in telling about which the historical storyteller would extend the dimensions of his story. Three further points must be made.

(1) On the basis of true narrative explanation

determined by the logic of causal connection, it proved impossible to determine where to begin the historical story of the 1951 pennant race or what dimensions to give to any of its parts. Indeed, since causal connection is subject both to infinite regress and to infinite ramification, and since that historical story and any other must have a beginning and finite dimensions of its parts, it is in principle impossible on the basis of the logic of narrative explanation alone to tell a historical story at all. On the other hand, the rhetoric of historical storytelling provided us with the means of recognizing whether there was a historical story to tell, where the story should start, and roughly what the relative dimensions of its parts should be. If this is so, (*a*) in the telling of a historical story, increments of historical knowledge and truth are unattainable on the basis of the logic of narrative explanation alone, for on that basis alone it is impossible so much as to begin such a story; and (*b*) for achieving such increments, insights into the rhetoric of historical storytelling, whether experiential and implicit or discursive and explicit, are indispensable.

(2) The clock and the calendar provide no guidance to the appropriate dimensions of a historical story. Between those dimensions and mere duration, measured in homogeneous scaled increments, there is no congruence. The historical storyteller's time is not clock-and-calendar time; it is historical tempo. The problems involved in reasonably accurate determination of historical tempo have never been systematically studied, although results of the disaster of not studying them strew the historiographic landscape. But two points are clear. (*a*) Disproportions in historical stories induced by failure correctly to appraise historical tempo result in the telling of distorted stories about the past. To that extent they diminish, and correct perception of tempo increases, available knowledge of the past. (*b*) The logic of narrative explanation has nothing to say on the subject of historical tempo; it is a question that can be dealt with only in the area of the rhetoric of historical storytelling. And so once again the communication of increments of knowledge and truth about the past hinges on the correct solution of problems of historiography. (*c*) Correct determinations of historical tempo and the appropriate correlative expansions and contractions of scale in a historical story depend on the examination *in retrospect* of the historical record. That is to say, when the historian tells a historical story, he must not only know something of the outcomes of the events that concern him; he must use what he knows in telling his story.

In the case of writers of history, Gallie's interesting analogy between historical understanding and following a game or story breaks down (1964, pp. 22–50). It applies to consumers of history, the readers, not to its producers, the writers. The readers need not know the outcome of the story; and it is well if, at least, they do not know the writer's construal of the outcome, since not knowing it whets their curiosity and intensifies their engagement and vicarious participation in the story, thus augmenting their knowledge of the past. But unless the writer has the outcome in mind as he writes the story, he will not know how to adapt the proportions of his story to the actual historical tempo, since that is knowable only to one who knows the outcome. For example, the decisive point for transforming the proportions of the historical story of the 1951 pennant race was entirely unobserved, unpredictable, and unpredicted by any contemporary observer. On August 11, at the point of maximum distance between Brooklyn and New York, no one foresaw or could have foreseen that New York was on the point of beginning a 16-game winning streak that transformed the baseball season into a pennant race in which New York was the ultimate victor. Indeed, the perspective of the historical storyteller throughout should be double —that of a contemporary observer and that of one who knows about Bobby Thomson's home run; but it is from the latter perspective, not the former, that the historian can perceive the historical tempo and thus determine the appropriate proportion of the historical story.

**Historical analysis.** Telling a historical story is not the only way in which a writer of history can increase knowledge of the past, as we have seen in the case of the American League season of 1939. Even to the question "How did it happen that . . .?" it is not always an appropriate response. Yet in the case in point, the response must have a historical character. The structure of Figure 2 suggests that it should take the form of historical analysis; for with its nonconverging lines it indicates that New York was a team so much better than any other in the league that it was beyond effective challenge. Consequently, to increase historical understanding there is nothing to do but analyze that betterness of New York, to seek out its ingredients and render them intelligible to the reader. Here, of course, the abundant surviving statistics of baseball provide a useful historical record to start with—the base-on-balls, strike-out, and earned-run averages of the pitchers; the batting and total base averages, the stolen bases, runs scored, and home runs of the hitters. (Fielding statistics, however, do not provide a satisfactory statistical basis for evaluating defensive performance in baseball.)

If the rhetoric of historical storytelling has received little attention from historians or others, the rhetoric of historical analysis has received none. When considering historical storytelling, the rhetoric of the fictive story offers a useful model; when considering historical analysis, the rhetoric of sciences in which the subject matter is less compatible with universal generalization than in physics might be appropriate. The almost complete lack of any serious concern with the problem may be due to the notion that the sciences have no rhetoric; but if one conceives of rhetoric as the organization of language appropriate to that particular kind of communication which is relevant to a particular activity, then any activity which is committed to verbal communication of its results has a rhetoric.

In recent years, instead of giving serious consideration to the serious problems of historical rhetoric, historians have engaged in considerable, and sometimes somewhat rancorous, discussion of the nonproblem of the relative merits of analysis and narrative in history writing. The discussion is footless because of two false assumptions: (1) that regardless of the character of the historical record, the historian has a wholly free option between analysis and narrative; (2) that these two historiographic modes mutually exclude each other, so that historians in all their work must opt wholly for the one or wholly for the other. With respect to the first assumption, we have seen in the instance of the two baseball seasons that the historical record presents us with constellations of events in which there is no serious option, where in one case to choose analysis, in the other to choose narrative, as the *predominant mode* would be a historiographic error and would prevent the historian from communicating what he knows about the past, and even from knowing it adequately.

In the second place, these modes are not mutually exclusive, and this again is evident with respect to our two "models." Although the mode of writing the history of the 1939 season should be predominantly analytical, still the force of the analysis would be strengthened by the resort to exemplary stories; and this is particularly the case with respect to fielding, in which the New York Yankees indeed excelled but which, because of limitations in the statistical record, lends itself better to anecdotal treatment, that is, to telling short illustrative stories. The case for the use of any analysis at all in the instance of the 1951 season might seem more dubious. The very fact of the tie at the end of the regular season could be taken as fair proof from

**Table 1 — Percentage of games won by the New York Giants and the Brooklyn Dodgers in the 1951 baseball season**

|  | New York Giants | Brooklyn Dodgers |
|---|---|---|
| Beginning of season to August 11* | 54% | 66% |
| August 12 to end of season | 84% | 60% |
| Total season (154 games) | 62% | 62% |

* As of August 11 the Giants had played 110 games and the Dodgers 106.

a large sample of 154 games that overall the two teams were so well matched as to make analysis an exercise in futility. Actually, an examination of the record yields a quite different result.

Table 1 shows the percentage of games won out of games played by each team up to August 11, and from August 12 to the end of the regular season. It clearly poses two analytical questions: (a) how to account for the marked superiority of Brooklyn in the first hundred-odd games of the season; (b) how to explain the overwhelming superiority of New York in the last forty-odd games. For such an undertaking, as we have seen, analysis is the proper historiographic mode. Note that the selection of analysis as the dominant mode for the first seven-tenths of the season does away with the need for telling an inevitably thin story and thus enables the historian to maintain the proportion called for by the demand of historical tempo. One further complication: The analysis would fail to reveal a part of what made the difference, the part, told by Eddie Stanky more than a decade later, about a battered battalion with pulled muscles, bad throwing arms, and cracked bones that still could not lose for winning. And thus, to do the analysis itself justice, the historian would have to afforce it with historical stories about Alvin Dark, Wes Westrum, Sal Maglie, and Stanky's own slides-into-bases that were hard to distinguish from overt assault and battery. Our two examples were themselves carefully selected extreme cases of records that call respectively for analysis and storytelling. In most history writing, the need for a mix of the historiographic modes of storytelling and analysis is even more obvious. The serious historiographic problem is not how to avoid the mix in order to maintain the superiority of one mode over the other, but how to proportion it and how to manage it.

In the foregoing "model" of the pennant race of 1951, the discussion has slipped—the author has intentionally allowed it to slip—insensibly from the problem of narrative explanation to the problems of historical storytelling. In this it has followed the curve, as it were, of historical curiosity itself, both in the reader and in the writer of history. The original question, "How did it come about that . . .?," has become the more amorphous "Tell me (or let me find out) more about. . . ." The demand is no longer merely further *explanation*. A reasonably full explanation is presumably already in hand. That explanation itself has led reader and writer of history alike to shift the ground of their interest. Because of it they have become aware that they have stumbled onto one of the great events in baseball history, the event that culminated in Bobby Thomson's home run—the equivalent (in its sphere) of the defeat of the Armada, the battle of Stalingrad, the Normandy landings. What they want under these circumstances is not more or fuller explanation; what they want is confrontation with the riches of the event itself, a sense of vicarious participation in a great happening, the satisfaction of understanding what those great moments were like for the ordinarily cool Russ Hodges, Giant radio announcer, who, as the ball arched from Thomson's bat into the stands, went berserk and screamed into the microphone, "The Giants win the pennant! *The Giants win the pennant!* THE GIANTS WIN THE PENNANT!" And what those moments were like for those who saw what he saw and for those who heard him. Confrontation and vicarious participation are not historical explanation or explanation of any sort in any ordinary sense of the word. Yet clearly they are sometimes a part, and an indispensable part, of understanding the past as it actually was. Therefore, to argue that they have no place in historiography is at once arbitrary and absurd.

Finally, when the historian needs to bring those who seek to understand the past into confrontation with and vicarious participation in some part of it, he often finds the rhetoric of the sciences wholly inadequate for his purposes. In this sector of historiography it is hard to imagine a response to the proper demand on historians to render an accurate and effective account of the past that would be less appropriate than one couched in scientific rhetoric. In this sector, indeed, to do his work properly, *to tell the truth about the past*, the historian must marshal resources of rhetoric utterly alien to the rhetoric of the sciences in order to render his account forceful, vivid, and lively; to impart to it the emotional and intellectual impact that will render it maximally accessible and maximally intelligible to those who read it.

### The analysis of historiography

The attitude of the historical profession to the writing of history has been ambivalent. Compared with the systematic attention historians have given to the techniques of historical investigation, their attention to the problems of historiography has been casual, and in their public judgments of the work of other historians they have tended to regard the rhetoric of history as at best a peripheral concern. On the other hand, some very able historians take far greater pains with their writing than would be warranted if the rhetoric of history were a mere pleasing embellishment not substantially involved in the advancement of the understanding of the past; and the consensus of the profession has ratified their practice by conferring on the most skillful writers of history rewards in prestige and pay that would be exorbitant if the yield of that skill were judged to be merely an amusing but supererogatory display of verbal pyrotechnics.

If the preceding arguments about the inseparability of the communication, and therefore the advancement, of historical knowledge from the rhetoric of history have any merit, then it would seem that a concerted effort to develop useful methods of analyzing historical rhetoric should stand high on the agenda of historians. In fact, however, their general concerns seem to be directed mainly toward two other areas, indeed, toward two nonproblems: (1) generalization and (2) the application of new knowledge in the social sciences to the study of history. The first is a nonproblem because in fact historians generalize and have generalized fruitfully at many levels for at least a couple of centuries, so that to raise at this late date the question of whether they do so or whether they ought to do so seems a little useless. Second, the application to the historical enterprise of any viable new technique for knowing is always desirable and is conditional only on the mastery of the technique and the identification of historical problems to which it can be usefully applied. In this respect the social sciences do not constitute a special case distinct from other techniques. Some historians have found some of the work of the social sciences useful for their particular purposes; others have not; still others have been preoccupied with other legitimate professional concerns. Their resistance to the demand for immediate and universal application to history of quantitative methods and of psychoanalytic insight does not seem to warrant the concern that it elicits from those who regard it as a chronic and possibly fatal disease of the historical profession as a whole. It does not appear to stand much above the level that reasonable professional prudence, sensible and limited skepticism, and resentment of new encroachments on limited resources of time, energy, and ability ordinarily generate.

Indifference to the problems of analyzing historiography, however, is easy to understand. In the first place, such analysis may well turn out to be a sterile exercise. In the second place, the need for analysis is evident only if one accepts the view that such attributes of historiography as accessibility, force, vividness, and depth are not merely decorative but have true noetic value. Although in unselfconscious practice many historians in fact accept this view, it remains submerged because of the counterthrust of an equally unself-conscious and incoherent assent to the ascription of noetic value only to the rhetoric of the sciences, especially to its denotative vocabulary and to its attributes of precision, simplicity, univocality, and so on.

In order to justify presenting the sketchy program for the analysis of historiography which this section will offer, it may be well to indicate the noetic bearing of at least one of the potential and requisite traits of historiography mentioned above —accessibility. In *On the Origin of Species* Charles Darwin says, "Nothing is easier to admit in words than the truths of the universal struggle for life, or more difficult—at least I have found it so—than constantly *to bear this conclusion in mind*." The rhetorical problem that Darwin here points to is that of accessibility. It is a persistent problem for explanation in the narrative mode. The writer of history needs to be always watchful to see that pertinent previous generalizations, pertinent patterns of action previously identified, and pertinent parts of the story, already told, come to bear for the reader at the places where they are enlightening and revelatory. Even where it is technically accurate, dull history is bad history to the extent to which it is dull. By subjecting all the historian knows to the homogenizing and flattening operations of his own mechanical rhetoric, dull history blurs his findings for himself and for those who read his writing. Those findings then fail to become, or rapidly cease to be part of, the "workable reserve," the readily accessible knowledge, of the writer and reader, which remains concurrently present in their minds as the one composes and the other tries to follow the narrative or analysis. Consequently, in the course of events neither will see a partly ordered and patterned, and therefore partly intelligible, procession of change but a disjointed and arbitrary and therefore unintelligible one—just one damn thing after the other. A reader to whom almost nothing is communicated may reasonably suspect that the writer had almost nothing to communicate; but, as we have seen, because of the gap between knowing and communicating in history, this is not necessarily so. Rather, unintelligible communication is not communication at all; uncommunicated knowing can add no increment to the available body of

knowledge, and frequently the failure to produce such an increment is a failure in historiography, the absence of accessibility.

Accessibility has been treated here as an absolute trait of history writing, and of course it is not so. It is relative not only to the historian's rhetorical capacities but also to the absorptive capacities of the historian's audience, which depend on their prior knowledge. An amount of detail necessary to render what he wishes to communicate accessible to one audience would simply clutter the text for another audience and stultify their imaginations, thus diminishing for that second audience the range of conceptions that the historian wants them to have in mind. The problem that this situation poses for the writer of history is a complex one; it is another of the many places where the rhetoric of the historian intersects and is entwined with the knowledge he communicates and the truth-value of what he has to say. There is not space to treat the matter of accessibility further here, but what is said below on the matter of word lists indicates some of the ramifications of the problem.

The analysis of historiography can conveniently be divided into macroanalysis, microanalysis, and analysis of structure. Macroanalysis is the analysis of an individual piece of history writing as a whole; microanalysis is the analysis of any fragment of historical rhetoric without primary regard to and out of relation to the historiographic whole of which it is a part. Analysis of structure deals with historiographic traits, devices, and practices which are common to all or to a very considerable number of historical works. Hitherto we have keyed our discussion of historiography to the rhetoric of scientific statement and explanation in order to make and keep clear the likenesses and differences between the two. We have suggested, however, that in at least one trait which it requires in order to communicate some of the things the historian knows—its reliance on a connotative and evocative vocabulary—the rhetoric of history is nearer to that of the fictive arts than to that of the natural sciences. So before examining the types of historiographic analysis, it will be appropriate to point out a major difference between historical and fictive rhetoric—the overriding commitment of historians to fidelity to the surviving records of the past

**Fidelity to records.** The difference between historical and fictive rhetoric blurs slightly at the extreme limits, where, on the one hand, a novelist tells a story which he intends to reflect his conception of historical actualities and, on the other, a historian makes a story of a "typical case" that he imaginatively constructs out of his long experience with the historical record. The blurring itself becomes visible in a comparison of Conrad's *Nostromo* and Oscar Handlin's *The Uprooted*, but so does the difference that is blurred. For the worth of *Nostromo* as a novel would not diminish if the patterns of life Conrad ascribes to Costaguana, the imaginary Latin American republic which provides its setting and the substrate of its characters, were shown to be quite remote from extrinsic actuality. On the other hand, unless the record suggested that the immigrants' emotional response to their move to America was something like what *The Uprooted* imputes to them, the historiographic worth of *The Uprooted* would be nil, regardless of any merits that literary critics might ascribe to Handlin's prose style.

The standard of judgment of a fictive work does not depend on its compatibility with external actuality. The work as such depends for its authenticity or validity only on its relevance to the sector of general human experience which its author intends it to explore, describe, and render accessible. It can be true or false only to itself; and the knowledge which it communicates is independent of any particular in the record of man's past (though not, of course, independent of human experience in general). Or as A. J. Liebling put it, in treating the problems of a newspaperman, "To transmit more than half of what you understand is a hard trick, far beyond the task of the so-called creative artist who if he finds a character in his story awkward can simply change its characteristics. (Even to sex, *vide* Proust and Albertine. Let him try it with General de Gaulle.)"

It is precisely with Charles de Gaulle and his sort that reporters like Liebling and historians often have to deal. The standard of judgment of a historical work is ultimately extrinsic. Its authenticity, validity, and truth depend on the effectiveness with which it communicates knowledge (not misunderstanding) of the actual past congruent with the surviving record. The quality of its rhetoric is to be measured solely by its success in communicating such knowledge.

**Macroanalysis.** It follows from what has just been said that the unit of macroanalysis in historiography differs from the unit of macroanalysis in fictive studies. In the latter it is the entire particular work—novel or drama, ode or sonnet—considered as a self-contained unit. The macroanalyst can therefore demand of himself an examination of the whole relevant documentation and can reasonably expect those for whom he is writing to have the core element of that documentation (the work under analysis) before them. Ordinarily the macro-

analyst of historiography cannot demand so much of himself, still less expect so much of his readers. For him the relevant documentation is the work itself plus the historical record of the episodes with which the author concerned himself, not merely the part he used but any important part that through errors of omission he failed to use. It is improbable that in most instances the analyst will command the full range of documentation; it is practically impossible under ordinary circumstances to expect the reader of the analysis to have the documentation in front of him.

Despite these limitations, some experiments in detailed macroanalysis seem desirable because only in such analysis does one deal with the actual unit of historiography—the historical work. Whether that work be a long treatise or a short article, its presentation is the means by which by far the largest part of the increments of historical knowledge is communicated. It is also the place where historians meet their worst failures—from the novices who, having researched their subject, have not a notion how to organize it for effective communication to those senior historians who have so completely surrendered to their own ineptitude as to transform verbosity into a criterion of excellence. By selecting a relatively short piece of historical writing based on a record of manageable dimension and reproducing both the piece and the record, it would be possible to perform the sort of detailed macroanalysis in historiography that is a commonplace in the field of literary criticism.

Until a few such analyses are attempted, it is impossible to estimate what gains, if any, in the understanding of historiography may accrue from them; but it is hard to see why the macroanalysis of a historical study would be less fruitful of knowledge than the analysis of, say, *Waiting for Godot*. It is evident that unless such analysis is attempted, some aspects of the writing of history are bound to remain wrapped in mystery. For example, the present writer is a reasonably competent practitioner of history writing, and he has done a reasonable amount. One of the most effective sentences he has ever written in a historical essay is the following: "It was just the right thing for him to do." To understand why that simple declarative statement composed of flat monosyllables should be effective would depend on a careful macroanalysis of the entire essay of which it is the last sentence.

To the best of the writer's knowledge, up to the present no macroanalysis of any historical work has even been attempted on the scale and in the way above proposed. Only after it has been attempted several times will any estimate of its value be more than an idle guess. In the meantime, the discussion of historical story writing and historical analysis in previous sections of this article points to a very few of the problems—proportion of the story, historical tempo, balance of analysis and narrative—with which macroanalysis would have to concern itself.

**Microanalysis.** Although microanalysis is primarily concerned with single small items of historical rhetoric, the radical severance of it from macroanalysis is not practically possible. Some sense of the whole framework remains essential, because only through that sense can one arrive at a judgment on the ultimate efficacy and appropriateness of a given small item of historical writing which is a part of a historiographic whole. "The Army of the Covenant of the Scots with their God marched across the Tweed to rescue their sore beset English brethren" is historiographically sound, if its general context requires at the point of its introduction a quick communication of the spirit in which the Scots took the field in 1644. If the total context is the logistical problems created by the presence of a considerable military force in the agriculturally unproductive north of England in the mid-seventeenth century, however, a less allusive statement, detailing the number of Scots who entered the northern counties and their daily requirement of food and forage, would be rather more appropriate.

For the examination of any single element of historical rhetoric, macroanalysis (although not necessarily on the scale above suggested) is desirable. Only by means of it can one finally judge whether that element is appropriate, for its appropriateness is a function of the *whole* context of which it is a part. Ostensible grotesquerie—Alexander in full plate armor—may be appropriate enough if we see the whole picture, as Panofsky showed in discussing medieval representations of that hero. Because, however, the single historical statement has a dual context—both the work of history in which it is embedded and the actuality of the past to which it refers—it is possible to clarify some of the specific characteristics of the rhetoric of history by microanalysis considered with minimal reference to the total structure of the historical work of which the fragment under microanalysis is a part. In effect, given a five-page account of the battle of Waterloo embedded in a historical work, by referring the account to the historical record, it is usually possible to say within the limits the historian set for the account whether it is historiographically sound at the level of microanalysis. On examining it in connection with the whole work, however, we might alter our judgment on the grounds that in its

macroanalytic context it is disproportionately long or short, that it is dissonant with the rest of the book, or even that it is wholly irrelevant.

Microanalysis of historiography is therefore provisional in the judgments it yields on the material it deals with, but it does at least yield provisional judgments. Here we have space to treat only one hypothetical example of microanalysis. Let us suppose a historian faced with the problem of dealing in two pages with the character and administration of U.S. President Warren G. Harding. One can conceive of his choosing to do it in the style of the late Ring Lardner and with a rhetoric—a vocabulary and syntax—as close to Lardner's as his own sense of historiographic proprieties and that of his editor would permit. Or one can conceive of a characterization the whole tone of which was heavily heroic in vocabulary and syntax—so long as the undertone made it evident that the verbal heroics were mock heroics. What would be wholly inappropriate to a brief characterization of Harding and his entourage would be a rhetoric of intentional, unrelenting, and unremitting solemnity. On the other hand, briefly to characterize Abraham Lincoln in either of the former rhetorical modes would not only be bad taste, it would be bad historiography; and the historian who employed either would promptly be marked by his peers as inept and incompetent. For Lincoln was a serious man (which did not prevent him from being a very humorous one) and a serious historical figure, and any attempt to present him in a short sketch which failed to reflect this fact would to that extent fail to communicate to the reader something he needed to understand about the realities of a part of the past. It would thereby not only fail to advance but perhaps would even diminish his knowledge and understanding of the past, his grasp of part of its meaning, his store of historical truth.

The implications of this excursus on the use of microanalysis of historiography in connection with characterizing actual persons of the past are worth a little further attention, since one of the persistent problems of history writing, calling for microanalysis, is that of characterization. In effect, in many kinds of historical investigation the historian encounters persons in the record of the past. He can disregard them as persons and transform them into, say, numbers; and a demographic historian quite rightly does just this, simply because that is in fact the aspect under which he encounters them. He is like a man trying to get on a full elevator who encounters the persons already aboard merely as "a full elevator." But that is not always, or even often, the way a historian encounters persons in the record of the past. If he encounters them *as persons*, an attempt to avoid characterizing those implicated in an important way in the account he is rendering is a refusal to deal faithfully with the record of the past.

No one whose judgment is worth serious consideration has ever suggested that historians must never characterize people they encounter in the past; and it is at least arguable that the normal rhetoric of history is such that a historian dealing with extensive data on the deeds and words of a person of the past cannot avoid characterizing him, that the only question is whether he characterizes him well or ill, whether he does him justice or injustice. Nor has anyone ever argued that it is desirable or indeed even possible adequately to characterize a man in the wholly denotative rhetoric that is appropriate to scientific discourse. Indeed, the very phrase "do justice," which is quite appropriate to describe the goal of characterizing a man, is itself so massively connotative, so indispensably imprecise, as to render nugatory any hope of accomplishing with a sterilized denotative vocabulary and syntax a mission so vaguely described and imprecisely delimited. And yet it is possible by microanalysis of historical writing to arrive at judgments not merely of "bad" and "good" but also of "false" and "true" (or at least "truer") with respect to the connotative rhetoric which a historian chooses to employ in fulfilling his commitment to do justice to the character of a man. Nor is there any great mystery about this in the case of men concerning whom the historical record is reasonably ample. Considering the rhetorical possibilities as a very broad spectrum and also as a complete spectrum within the bounds of the rhetorical potentialities of the common language structure, there will be areas of that spectrum into which what is known about a particular man cannot be fit without manifest distortion of the record and areas into which it fairly fits, although in both cases there may be several such areas. This was manifestly the case in the instances of Harding and Lincoln dealt with above. But to distort the record is precisely to communicate ignorance rather than knowledge, misunderstanding rather than understanding, falsehood rather than truth.

The only necessary qualification here is that no historian does, and no sensible historian claims to, communicate the whole truth about a man, since there are many things about any man living or dead which no human being, not even the man himself, knows. The full knowledge on which alone a final judgment is possible exists only in the mind of God. The facts remain that in certain reaches of

historiography the characterization of men is inescapable, that the rhetoric of such characterization is inescapably nonscientific, and that the knowledge, understanding, and truth communicated by the history of which the characterization is a part will in some measure depend on how well or ill the historian deploys the resources of this inevitably nonscientific rhetoric, on the appropriateness of his response to the demands that the historical record makes on his ability to use nonscientific language in delineating a character. The curious problems that this situation implies deserve further examination.

**Analysis of structure.** The general analysis of historiography deals with those traits and devices of historical rhetoric which are unique to the writing of history, or, more frequently, with those traits and devices which historians use in a unique way, a way which differentiates them from their use in the sciences or in the fictive arts. In the following treatment of structural analysis of historiography we will focus attention on three devices of the rhetoric of history: (1) the footnote, (2) the quotation in the text, (3) the word list; and we will concentrate on what differentiates the historian's use of these devices from the use scientists make of their homologues in scientific rhetoric.

*Footnotes.* Historians and scientists both use footnotes, and for one purpose they use them in about the same way: they use them to cite to the "literature" of the subject or problem about which they are writing. Historians, however, also use footnotes in a variety of other ways. One way historians use them and physicists do not is to cite to the historical record, the substrate of evidence on which historians erect their accounts of the past. Citation to that record is the way a historian makes his professional commitment clear in action, as the report on the experiment is the way a physicist makes his commitment clear. In both instances it is a commitment to maximum verisimilitude (which does not mean exact replication in every detail). For the physicist it is maximum verisimilitude to the operations of nature as glimpsed through consideration of the experimental cluster; for the historian, verisimilitude to the happenings of the past as glimpsed through consideration of the surviving record.

The well-nigh universal use of footnotes to the record by historians indicates that they are all still committed to writing about the past, as Ranke put it, *wie es eigentlich gewesen*, as it actually happened. In today's somewhat more sophisticated language, we might say that historians are concerned and committed to offer the best and most likely account of the past that can be sustained by the relevant extrinsic evidence. Let us call this statement about the historian's commitment the "reality" rule.

Historians employ the footnote for a host of residual matters other than citations to the record—lists of names, minor qualifications of assertions made in the text, polemic criticisms of other historians, short statistical tables, suggestions for future historical investigation, and many more. This raises two questions. (1) Amid the apparent chaos of "residual" footnotes, are there any rules at all regulating their use? (2) What is the relation of any rules found to the "reality" rule?

As to the first question, the application of any rule about footnotes requires an act of judgment in each case, and among historians judgment about the uses of residual footnotes differs. It might seem that in matters of judgment, as in those of taste, there is no disputing. But is this so? Let us consider an example.

At Shilbottle, in the case of three separate parcels of meadow, 31, 20 and 14 acres respectively, the first rendered 42s. in 1415–16 and 30s. in 1435–6, the second 28s. in 1420–1 and 23s. in 1435–6, and the third 24s. in 1422–3 and 14s. in 1435–6. At Guyzance 6½ husbandlands each rendered 13s.4d. in 1406–7, but 10s. in 1435–6.

At Chatton and Rennington, on the other hand, the situation was more stable. At Rennington the clear revenues were £17.8s.3d. in 1435–6 and £17 in 1471–2 and at Chatton £40.18s.7d. in 1434–5 and £36.18s.7d in 1472–3. At Chatton the decline was due to a fall in the value of the farm of the park, from £6.13s.4d. to £2.13s.4d. . . .

The above passage is embedded in the *text* of a study of the wealth of a magnate family in the fifteenth and early sixteenth centuries and the effect on that wealth of concurrent changes in the economy, the military apparatus, and the political situation in England. Can anyone suggest that embedding it in the text instead of quarantining it in a footnote was *not* an error of judgment? But to say it was one is to imply a *rule* from which the erroneous judgment was a deviation. Can such a rule, a "law" of historical rhetoric or historiography, be stated? Approximately the rule might go: "Place in footnotes evidence and information which if inserted in the text diminish the impact on the reader of what you, as a historian, aim to convey to him."

So although in the matter of the use of residual footnotes judgment is inescapable, we are not at all confronted with mere arbitrariness but with a reasonably precise rule or law. We may name it the "maximum impact" rule. Inevitably, marginal situations exist in which historians disagree about how to achieve maximum impact or the success of a particular rhetorical presentation. The existence of such marginal situations, however, does not mean that all situations are marginal and that therefore there is no rule, or that any rule is as good as any other. Lawyers have a saying that hard cases make bad law, but they do not feel impelled thereupon to argue that there are no easy cases and no good law. Because there are some matters both substantive and procedural concerning which they are very uncertain, some historians have fallen victim to the notion that everything about the past and about writing about it is infected with a total uncertainty. Yet this is clearly not so in the case of the residual footnote, where there was no difficulty in finding a rule not heavily infected with uncertainty.

What, then, is the relation of the two rules—the "reality" rule and "maximum impact" rule—to each other? In the example of data that, by the second rule, ought to be withdrawn from the text and consigned to a residual footnote, those data are informative and relevant with respect to the substantive historical argument the historian is presenting, and they are as complete, as explicit, and as exact as possible. But the historian is also committed to conveying to the reader with maximum impact his conception and understanding of the past as it actually happened, the "reality" of the first rule. And paradoxically, this implies that in the interest of conveying historical reality to the reader with maximum impact, the rules of historiography may require a historian to subordinate completeness, explicitness, and exactness to other considerations. If this is so, it indeed separates historiography from the rhetoric of the sciences as currently conceived.

*Quotation in the text.* Again, although both may quote in the text, there is a major difference here between the historians and the physicists. If physicists could not quote in the text, they would not feel that much was lost with respect to advancement of knowledge of the natural world. If historians could not quote, they would deem it a disastrous impediment to the communication of knowledge about the past. A luxury for physicists, quotation is a necessity for historians, indispensable to historiography.

The kind of quotation that historians deem indispensable is quotation from the record. Again two questions arise. (1) Is there any rule governing quotation from the record? (2) How does that rule relate to the "reality" rule?

Consider a hypothetical case of inept quotation.

Suppose in writing the history of the Civil Rights Act of 1964, a historian were to quote verbatim from the *Congressional Record* the entire debate on the act in both the House and the Senate. The result would be relevant, exact, and accurate—and not only the judgment but the sanity of the historian would fall under serious question. Again the paradox: maximum completeness, accuracy, and exactness are not always essential or even desirable in the historian's work of trying to tell the reader what really happened. Now consider an adept quotation taken from E. Harris Harbison's *The Christian Scholar in the Age of the Reformation*:

Erasmus had absorbed [Lorenzo] Valla's historical perspective, his sense of the historical discontinuity between pagan antiquity and the Christian era . . . a sensitivity to anachronism. On one occasion he ridiculed the absurdity of the practice . . . of using Ciceronian words to describe an utterly different modern world: "Wherever I turn my eyes I see all things changed, I stand before another stage and I behold a different play, nay, even a different world." The world of Cicero (or of Paul) can be understood and even in a sense relived—but only if we recognize that it had its unique existence, once, in a past now dead. (1956, p. 93)

The function of Harbison's brief but apt quotation from Erasmus is not mere validation or proof of his assertions; he could as well have effected that by citation or quotation in a footnote. By using Erasmus' own words in the text, he sought and won a response not merely of assent but of conviction, not just "Yes," but "Yes, indeed!" Nothing Harbison could have said about Erasmus' sense of history could produce the conviction about it that Erasmus' own assertion of his intense feeling of distance from antiquity produces.

The quotation aims at something in addition to conviction, however. The quotation communicates the historian's own view of what happened in the past by the particular means of confrontation. It says in effect, "In my judgment the most economical way at this point to tell you what I believe Erasmus meant and to convince you that he meant it is to confront you directly with what Erasmus said." This provides us with a third general rule of historiography—an "economy-of-quotation" rule: Quote from the record of the past only when and to the extent that confrontation with that record is the best way to help the reader to an understanding of the past *wie es eigentlich gewesen*. It is evident, however, from the instance of the hypothetical case of the *Congressional Record* that mere confrontation with the *record* of the past is not necessarily the best way to achieve this understand-

ing or even to achieve historical confrontation. Indeed, far from being a clear glass window through which the reader may capture an image of the past, quotation from the record injudiciously used can be a thick opaque wall that cuts him off from it. Granted that confrontation is an appropriate means for a historian to avail himself of in his efforts to convey to the reader an understanding of what actually happened, it then becomes possible to transcend the paradox previously noted. It opens up the possibility that the microscopic means of historiography have to be adapted to its macroscopic ends and that it is part of the task of the writer of history to mediate understanding and confrontation by devices of the rhetoric of history less direct but more compelling, more to the purpose than a simple maximizing of completeness, accuracy, and exactness.

*The word list.* The word list is a device useful both in the rhetoric of history and in the rhetoric of the sciences. (It is a sequence of words, usually nouns, whose relations as members of a set are often made evident by a sequence of commas and/or semicolons, the conjunction "and," or typographical arrangement in a table.) Consider the following lists:

An inert element will not react or enter into chemical combination with any other element. In order of increasing atomic weight the inert elements are helium (4), neon (20), argon (39), krypton (84), xenon (131), and radon (222).

The average incomes of only three of the learned professions fall into the first quartile of all average incomes. In descending order of quartile and rank, the average incomes of members of the learned professions were as follows: surgeons (1,2), physicians (1,4), dentists (1,7), college professors (2,23), high school teachers (3,41), clergymen (3,47), grade school teachers (3,52).

The first list is scientific; the second, historiographic. They are in many respects similar. In intent the words composing them are wholly denotative. They are not supposed to cast any shadow, to connote or evoke anything. Their arrangement (ascending order, descending order) is dictated entirely by considerations of rational utility. They both implicitly relate to an informational framework equally denotative in intention—the periodic table of all chemical elements, the table of average incomes of the total population classified by profession and trade. Both listings aim to achieve a purpose universal in the rhetoric of the sciences, common but not universal in the rhetoric of history. The scientist always wants the state, process, and set of entities he is dealing with so labeled that the labels unambiguously and unequivocally point to that state, process, and set only. For the scientist's purpose when he is formally communicating what he knows, words need to be free of contamination, of connotation, evocation, and emotive force, as sterile as the apparatus in an operating room. Otherwise he may find the wires of communication snarled and, as a consequence, have to rectify avoidable confusion. In this matter the historian's purpose often coincides exactly with that of the scientist. It is only under the conditions and with a vocabulary of the kind above specified that he can to his own satisfaction transmit some of the kinds of information and understanding that he intends to communicate. Yet even the very close approximation to scientific rhetoric exemplified by the foregoing historiographic word list deviates from the scientific standard in ways that help to differentiate both the problems and the purposes of history from those of the sciences. Consider the question "Is not zinc (65) also an inert element?" To answer this question one can pour hydrochloric acid over zinc. Since one of the yields of this operation is zinc chloride (ZnCl), a chemical combination or compound, zinc is not an inert element.

The taxonomic system of chemical elements—the periodic table—is thus free of ambiguity. Suppose, on the other hand, the question were raised whether clergymen and elementary and high school teachers should be included as members of the learned professions when the executives of large corporations are excluded. The question points to doubts about a system of classification that might include store-front preachers and graduates of retrograde teacher-training colleges among members of the learned professions while excluding the products of the better graduate schools of business administration. These doubts thus revolve about the identifying traits of the learned professions and the expediencies involved in the selection of any one set as against alternative sets of traits for classificatory purposes.

In any developed natural science, expediency in the choice of traits for a taxonomic system depends on the "importance" of the traits within the bounds of that science—e.g., in chemistry, valence and atomic weight as against color and taste. And importance is graded by applicability within the framework of generalizations or "scientific laws" that articulate the structure of the science in question and form the basis of its dominant mode of explanation. The dominant mode of historical explanation, narrative, emits no such clear, uniform signal for determining importance, and therefore in historiography the expediencies of alternative

taxonomic systems often remain equivocal and debatable. It is this situation which generates the interminable discussions among historians about whether sixteenth-century monarchies were *really* absolute, whether the Indians in the *encomiendas* in the Spanish colonies were *really* in servitude, whether the owner–operator of a small newsstand is *really* a capitalist. Such discussions seem futile because they purport to deal directly with the actual character of the past, a historical problem, when in fact they are concerned with the relative expediencies of alternative taxonomic devices for communicating knowledge of the past, a historiographic problem. The problem of taxonomy so considered, however, is anything but trivial (1) because classification systems both condition effectiveness of communication and channel the course of historical thinking, and (2) because in the very nature of the rhetoric of history, terms like "capitalist," "absolute," and "learned profession" cannot be rendered wholly denotative to the consumer of history writing. Given the nonscientific values pursued in historiography, a historian using such terms will have to decide, for the purposes of the story or narrative explanation engaging him at the moment, how much time and effort he should expend in separating the connotative values from those terms and how important those connotative values are for advancing the historical understanding of the matter at hand. It is evident, in any case, that the general analysis of historical rhetoric involves a study of problems of taxonomy in history closer than any undertaken up to now.

One further trait of the above historiographic word list needs to be noted: it is either elliptical or meaningless. It acquires meaning only if time and place are specified, whereas no such specification is necessary in the above scientific list. A statement whose formal structure and manifest purpose seem very close to those that characterize the natural sciences illustrates the dominant time–place specificity of the rhetoric of history as against the dominant time–space generality of the rhetoric of the sciences. Thus the analysis of a historical word list reinforces the conclusion that has emerged time and again in the course of this discussion of the rhetoric of history: despite occasional likenesses, historiography is radically unassimilable to the rhetoric of the natural sciences.

This can be even more effectively illustrated by another example of the historiographic use of a list.

The Christian Revival, that intensification of religious sentiment and concern that began long before 1517 and extended long beyond, in its full span had room for Cardinal Ximenes and Girolamo Savonarola; Martin Luther and Ignatius Loyola, the Reformed churches and the Jesuits, John of Leiden and Paul IV, Thomas Cranmer and Edmund Campion and Michael Servetus.

The names constitute a historiographic list, intended to serve a particular purpose of the rhetoric of history. It emits a signal, and what the signal says to all who hear it is: "Draw on the reservoir of your knowledge of the times in which these men lived to give meaning to this list." If that reservoir is altogether empty, then inevitably the list will itself be historiographically empty, meaningless, a mere collection of sounds, just as the sentences about the inert gases are empty of meaning to any who have no notion of what a chemical element or a chemical reaction or atomic weight is. The reason for this similarity is that in the present case both the historiographic rhetoric and the scientific rhetoric presuppose that the reader already possesses a body of precise and exact knowledge of the particular universes to which they refer. The scientific and the second historiographic statement both conform to the "reality" rule; they are meaningless unless there are such elements as helium, neon, and argon; and unless there were such men as Loyola, Cranmer, and Paul IV. Yet the second historiographic list serves a rhetorical function quite different from that served by the scientific list. First, consider the order of the two lists. Given the gases' common trait of inertness, the order of the scientific list indicates the scientist's normal preoccupation with establishing scalable differences of homogeneous traits—in this case, weight. In the historiographical list, on the other hand, no such preoccupation is discernible, yet the arrangement of the names lies at the very heart of the matter.

Note that there are three alternative ways of writing the historiographic list, all of which maintain the essential arrangement, to convey whatever information it contains.

(1) Cardinal Ximenes and Girolamo Savonarola, Martin Luther and Ignatius Loyola, the Reformed churches and the Jesuits, John of Leiden and Paul IV, Thomas Cranmer and Edmund Campion and Michael Servetus.

(2) The pre-Reformation cardinal who reformed the church in Spain, and the pre-Reformation monk who was burned at the stake for his reforming efforts in Florence; the first great figure of the Reformation and the first great figure of the Counter Reformation; the cutting edge of the Protestant attack and the cutting edge of the Catholic counterattack; the most fanatical prophet of the radical Reformation and the most fanatical pope of the era of religious strife; the Protestant martyred by the Catholics, the Catholic martyred by the Protestants, and the martyr who escaped death

at the hands of the Catholics only to receive it at the hands of the Protestants.

(3) Cardinal Ximenes, the pre-Reformation cardinal who reformed the church in Spain, and Girolamo Savonarola, the pre-Reformation monk who was burned at the stake for his reforming efforts in Florence; Luther, the first great figure of the Reformation, and Loyola, the first great figure of the Counter Reformation; the Reformed churches, the cutting edge of the Protestant attack, and the Jesuits, the cutting edge of the Catholic counterattack. . . .

The persons balanced in tension with one another are the same for all three versions of the list, and the arraying is identical in all three. On mathematical principles, a member of any of the lists should be freely substitutable for the corresponding member of either of the other two, but in writing history *this is not so.* Each list must retain its integrity. On what grounds can a historian choose among the three? One might argue that the second list is preferable to the first since it explicates the rationale upon which the persons in the first list were arrayed and that, in point of information about the past, the third is best of all, since it both names the persons and explicates the rationale of their array. Yet a reasonably experienced historian committed to communicating what he understands about the past actually chose the *first* option—the bare list of names with no indication as to his grounds for choosing them or for ordering them as he did. His choice is explicable when related to an earlier observation about the signal emanated by the list: "Draw on the reservoir of your knowledge of the times in which these men lived to give meaning to the list." The writer assumed that most of his readers could and would in fact draw from their particular reservoirs the items of general information in the second and third lists.

The effect of spelling out that information, however, is to emit another kind of rhetorical signal, a stop signal: "Stop drawing on the reservoir of your knowledge. I have already told you how I want you to think about these men." And this stop signal is just what the writer did *not* want the list to emit. The third version of the list is more exact, more overtly informative than the bare names in the first list, and just for that reason it is more empty, less ample. It dams up the informed reader's imagination instead of letting it flow freely, bringing with it the mass of connotation and association that those names have for him. Therefore, to prevent such a blockage the writer chose the first list. In doing so, he made a judgment. He judged (or gambled) that the connotative, evocative list would communicate a fuller meaning than the exact one, that it would more effectively confront the reader with the reality of the Christian revival, and that therefore it was the more appropriate device for advancing the reader's understanding of it. Whether he was correct in his judgment or not is immaterial. In setting forth his findings, a scientist never needs to make such a judgment at all. Scientific rhetoric is purposefully constructed to free him of that need by barring connotative terms and evocative devices. To a scientist the idea that he had to choose between a rhetoric of clarity and precision on the one hand and one of evocative force on the other would be shocking. The idea that the writer of history has to select between mutually exclusive ways of setting forth the same data and that the knowledge of history that he conveys depends in some measure on his judgment in selecting among alternative rhetorical devices is perhaps as disturbing and perplexing. But one is impelled to the latter conclusion by an investigation of the peculiarities of the way writers of history use footnotes, quotations, and word lists.

## Codification of historiographic principles

The whole preceding article may be regarded as a prolegomenon to a codification of principles of historiography. Its aim has not been to produce such a codification but (1) to indicate that it might be possible to produce one and (2) to educe a few of the rules that would have place there. It has been concerned time and again to mark the irreducible differences that separate the rhetoric of history from that of the natural sciences because, given the prestige of those sciences and the striking similarity of some of the objectives of history writing and science writing, there is a danger that an attempt to codify the principles of historiography might take the form of a systematic effort to reduce as far as possible those principles to the ones current in the natural sciences. This indeed has already been the outcome of attempts by analytic philosophers from Carl Hempel to Morton White to codify the rules of historiography. The outcome of such an effort would be catastrophic, not because it would be an utter failure but because it would be a partial success. It would succeed in codifying rules about a great deal of what historians write in a way that would relate it closely to what scientists write. It might then be inferred that only the part of the rhetoric of history which can be articulated with that of the sciences is fit for communicating what in the course of

their researches historians learn about the past, or that only that part is amenable to codification. In the foregoing discussion, however, we have already seen that in the writing of history it is often necessary to employ language in ways that scientists quite properly reject for communicating the results of their investigations. Therefore, instead of extending our knowledge of the past, to limit historiography to those statements about the past which can be formulated in the rhetoric of the sciences would sharply constrict it.

The rational procedure in attempting to elicit general rules of historiography would be, rather, to make a series of analyses of the kinds classified and discussed in the previous section, taking as their subject pieces of historical writing which on the basis of a broad consensus of historians have been extraordinarily successful in transmitting what their writers knew about the past. It is impossible, of course, to predict in substance the outcome of such an analytical effort. Because in the section on general analysis we were able to elicit a few sample rules, it may, however, be possible to hazard a conjecture about its form. On the basis of that small sample one might conjecture that a codification of the rules of historiography would resemble a manual of military strategy more than a handbook of physics. It would consist of a number of maxims generally applicable to the solution of recurrent problems in writing history, leaving the identification of his particular problems and application of the maxims to the experience of the trained historian.

The most important professional use of such codification would be precisely in the training of historians. Historians do not lack the ability to discriminate between historiography which badly and inadequately communicates what a historian knows and historiography which communicates it well. Unfortunately, because that ability is now acquired almost wholly through experience rather than through a combination of experience and systematic knowledge, it is rarely and inefficiently transmitted from teacher to pupil. Indeed, the systematic training of historians is almost solely given over to the transmission of competence in the operations they must perform *before* they engage in the activity that defines their craft—the writing of history. Many historians receive the doctoral degree, which is supposed to certify their competence in their craft, without ever being compelled to rewrite anything they have written after having it subjected to rigorous and systematic criticism. The chronic ineptitude that hosts of historians display in their attempts to communicate what they know is a testimonial to the inadequacy of their training in this respect, or to its complete neglect. This ineptitude may suggest the desirability of an attempt to state coherently at least part of what the better historians know experientially about writing history and demonstrate visibly in the consistent appropriateness of their responses to the problems of historiographic statement.

## Theoretical implications

The examination of historiography in this article has at various points suggested what becomes quite evident in the treatment of narrative explanation as against historical storytelling and in the section on the analysis of the form of a historical work —that the practices of historians in writing history may have some peculiar and serious implications in that wide area of human concern in which men struggle with the difficult problems of the meaning and nature of knowledge, understanding, and truth. The principal relevant points that have emerged may be summarized as follows.

First, historiography is a rule-bound discipline by means of which historians seek to communicate their knowledge of the past.

Second, the relation of writing history, of its rhetoric, to history itself is quite other than it has traditionally been conceived. Rhetoric is ordinarily deemed icing on the cake of history, but our investigation indicates that it is mixed right into the batter. It affects not merely the outward appearance of history, its delightfulness and seemliness, but its inward character, its essential function—its capacity to convey knowledge of the past as it actually was. And if this is indeed the case, historians must subject historiography, the process of writing history, to an investigation far broader and far more intense than any that they have hitherto conducted.

Third, there is an irreducible divergence between the rhetoric of history and the rhetoric of science; the vocabulary and syntax that constitute the appropriate response of the historian to his data are neither identical with nor identifiable with the vocabulary and syntax that constitute the appropriate response of the scientist to his data. But the historian's goal in his response to the data is to render the best account he can of the past as it really was. Therefore, by his resort to the rhetoric of history, regardless of its divergence from that of the sciences, the historian affirms in practice and action his belief that it is more adequate than the latter as a vehicle to convey the kind of knowledge, understanding, truth, and

meaning that historians achieve. Indeed, instances were discovered in which, in order to transmit an increment of knowledge and meaning, the very rules of historiography demand a rhetoric which sacrifices generality, precision, control, and exactness to evocative force and scope—a choice entirely out of bounds according to the rules of scientific statement. And this implies that in the rhetoric of history itself there are embedded assumptions about the nature of knowing, understanding, meaning, and truth and about the means of augmenting them that are not completely congruent with the corresponding assumptions in the sciences, at least insofar as the philosophy of science has succeeded in identifying them.

Historiography has generated a crisis in the currently dominant Anglo–American school of philosophy, the school that has as its main subgroups logical positivism, the philosophy of science, and language analysis. That it has done so is evident from a cursory examination of the index of one of the more recent works on history writing by an analytical philosopher (Danto 1965). Besides the philosophical magnates, living and dead, tangentially involved in the dialogue—Ayer, Bradley, Dewey, Hume, Kant, Lewis, Peirce, Ryle, Russell, Wittgenstein—the index mentions Agassi, Danto, Donegan, Dray, Gallie, Gardiner, Gellner, Hempel, Mandelbaum, Nagel, Passmore, Popper, Scriven, Walsh, and Watkins, all of whom since 1940 have directly confronted the problems that in their view historiography poses for philosophy; and the list is by no means complete. The close attention that this group of philosophers has directed to history writing is especially significant because of their central preoccupation with the way in which language communicates knowledge, understanding, meaning, and truth. In the broadest sense this large collective enterprise has been trying to define the relationship between the practices of writers of history and the nature of knowledge, understanding, meaning, and truth, especially as revealed in the structure of scientific rhetoric.

The preceding prolegomenon to an inquiry into the rules of the rhetoric of history provides a clue to the character of the crisis (symptomatically marked by the profusion of their output on the subject) with which the writing of history has confronted the analytical philosophers. History has posed for them a very difficult puzzle. Most historians in theory, *all* in practice, treat their subject as if through their current methods and their current rhetoric they were achieving and transmitting increments of knowledge about it. That is to say, they declare that if a piece of historical work is well done and properly set down, readers will know more about the past after they have read it than they did before. And for practical purposes very few people have seriously doubted the propriety of this claim (the few that do, appear to have read very little history). And yet historiography—the forms of statement historians adopt, their rhetoric—does not seem to fit into the sign structure suitable for scientific explanation, the classical rhetoric for communicating increments of knowledge, and most historians have been either indifferent or actively hostile to the notion that in the interest of rendering an account of the past as it actually was, they ought to elaborate and consistently employ such a sign structure. It is with this paradox that so many analytical philosophers have tried to deal systematically since 1940.

The course of this large collective effort is far too complex and has had too many ramifications to be dealt with here in detail. Briefly, the initial supposition (Hempel 1942), set forth above, was (1) that the universal valid model of explanation is that of the natural sciences, (2) that this consists in linking an event to general laws in such a way that the event is entailed by the laws through strict deduction, (3) that any activity of a historian that does not achieve this end does not explain anything, (4) that although in some instances historians can perform the necessary operations, they rarely do so, and therefore (5) that by and large in most of their actual operations historians explain nothing. Twenty-five years of intensive discussion by analytical philosophers has taken off from, and resulted in a number of proposals for modifying, this rigorist position. It seems likely that the dis-ease which some of these modifications manifest is in part the consequence of an often unarticulated sense on the part of analytical philosophers who have read history books that the actual procedures of historians, for knowing, understanding, and giving an account of the past as it actually was, do achieve their explicit or implicit purpose. In the course of bringing about a *partial* confrontation of the general-law theory of explanation with historiography, the analytical philosophers discovered a number of facts about the latter which because of their apparent deviation from the general-law or scientific model caused them perplexity. Among these were (1) that for many purposes of "explanation why," historians do not resort to general laws but to truisms; (2) that when historians are confronted with the question "Why?" their frequent, indeed normal, impulse is not to recite or seek relevant general laws, as a scientist would do, but to tell a story,

and that such a story often seems to provide a satisfying answer to the question "Why?" while a general law does not; (3) that the questions historians are often most heavily engaged in answering are not why-questions at all but what-questions (and also, one might add parenthetically, who-, when-, and where-questions); and (4) that a great deal of the activity of historians can be construed as having explanation as its aim only by so far extending the meanings of explanation current in analytical philosophy as to destroy even the appearance of synonymy and to impose well-nigh unbearable strains even on analogy.

In the process of coping with these problems, the analytical philosophers have produced a series of solutions, not always coherent with each other, of considerable interest to themselves but apparently of very little interest to historians as such. The character of most of these answers (and perhaps the explanation of their lack of interest for historians) may properly be described as "assimilationist." The common characteristics of these assimilationist answers are first to seek out all traits of historiography that can reasonably be identified with or assimilated to the model of scientific explanation by means of general laws; then to make epicyclic modifications of the general-law structure of explanation to accommodate some of the more evident deviations of historiography from its pattern, always holding such modifications to the minimum; and finally wholly to prescind from some of the most evident traits of historiography on the ground that they are irrelevant to the quest for knowledge, understanding, and truth. The last procedure, which for present purposes is of the most importance, is illustrated by a passage in Morton White's *Foundations of Historical Knowledge*, a passage of special interest because among the practitioners of analytical philosophy White alone is also a practitioner of historiography at a very high level of excellence.

The historical narrative, the extended story, is so large and rambling by contrast to the single sentence treated by the logician that any effort to treat it as a repeatable and identifiable pattern of language may give an impression of remoteness and distortion well beyond what might be felt by the historian who finds his causal statements cast in a single syntactical mold. On the other hand, the very qualities of narrative which might lead a historian to think that logical analysis distorts it are those that might inhibit a logician from trying to discern its structure. The complexity and variety of narrative, the fact that one story seems so different in structure from another, may give both the romantically minded historian and the classically minded logician pause. Yet the vast differences that human beings exhibit do not prevent us from X-raying them in an effort to discern the skeletal structure that each of them possesses. . . . History is a literary art as well as a discipline aimed at discovering and ordering truth, and if we neglect some of the narrative's literary qualities in order to clarify certain epistemological problems connected with it, our procedure is like that of the sane roentgenologist, who searches for the skull without denying that the skin exists and without denying that the skin may vary enormously in color, texture, and beauty.   (1965, pp. 220–221)

The equation here is at once interesting, dubious, and exemplary of the assimilationist posture above described. Before presenting it, by the addition of a couple of rather large epicycles, White had already assimilated several common traits of historiography as closely as possible to the general-law model of scientific discourse. The quotation announces his intention to do the like with another major trait, the storylike character of much history writing. But he knows this is going to leave him with a very large residue of what historians write still on his hands. This residue consists in part of matters that the analysis of historical rhetoric in this article has called attention to. He disposes of this uncomfortable residue by assigning it to history as "a literary art" rather than history as "a discipline aimed at discovering and ordering truth." In this connection his analogy with roentgenology is not wholly fortunate. For it is at least arguable that the knowledge that history makes accessible is no more fully revealed by the mere skeletal structure of its narrative than the knowledge of the human head is fully exhausted by what an X-ray plate shows about its mere ossature. Just as it may be suggested that while the human head is partly a bony structure and partly (sometimes) a thing of beauty, it is also a number of other things, too, so it is possible to grant that history *is* a literary art while denying that all those aspects of history writing which White consigns to that function and that function alone are actually irrelevant to the function of history as a discipline aimed at discovering and ordering truth. It has been one purpose of the foregoing article to suggest some grounds for such a denial.

The mention of epicycles in the preceding paragraphs provides us with a clue to the dis-ease of analytical philosophy with historiography, a dis-ease so acute that it has become an intellectual disease which may be a prelude to a general and deep intellectual crisis. Epicycles suggest the Ptolemaic system of astronomy, and examination of the ultimate crisis of that system may by analogy help toward an understanding of the current crisis with respect to knowing, understanding, explaining, and truth that the study of historiography has

induced in analytical philosophy. The crisis in the Ptolemaic system came in the sixteenth century, when it was destroyed by the Copernican revolution. For centuries before, it had been normal science. Following the terminology of Thomas Kuhn, it was structured about several paradigms, among which were (1) the earth is at the center of the cosmos; (2) the earth does not move; (3) the orbits of all heavenly bodies are circular; (4) the circular motion of each heavenly body is uniform in rate. These paradigms were invoked to support an area of pre-Copernican science far more extensive than celestial mechanics; and to save this science, the observed deviations of the planets from presumed circular orbits and uniform speeds were dealt with by an ingenious but exceedingly intricate system of epicycles, eccentrics, and equants. The Copernican revolution was initiated by Copernicus' allegation that this system could be greatly simplified by assuming that the earth was not at the center of the cosmos and that it moved around the sun annually and rotated on its own axis daily.

Certain facts about the Copernican revolution are worth noting in the present context. (1) Copernicus' own work by no means provided a wholly satisfactory solution to the difficulties it sought to deal with. (2) Although the third and fourth paradigms of Ptolemaic astronomy—those dealing with the orbit, shape, and speed of the planets—ultimately crumbled under the impact of the revolution Copernicus started, he had no intention of displacing them and in fact held firmly to them. (3) Copernicus' heliocentrism and geomobilism implied the destruction not merely of Ptolemaic celestial mechanics but of other large tracts of the science of his day; what he offered in place of what he destroyed was, however, unsatisfactory. In some matters he offered nothing in place of it, and in others he does not seem to have been aware that he had destroyed it, so that overall for a long time the old normal science provided better explanations of many phenomena than the Copernicans did. (4) For all the above reasons the marginal advantage of the Copernican over the Ptolemaic celestial mechanics was not at all clear, and the conservatism of those who continued to adhere to the older scientific paradigms for a long time is quite intelligible.

Let us now apply this analogy to the crisis that has confronted the analytical philosophers as a result of their explorations of historiography. Until and except for that confrontation, their paradigms—essentially the modes of rhetoric they ascribed to the sciences—provided them with a reasonably satisfactory way of understanding and rendering intelligible the syntactical structure and vocabulary of a language capable of conveying frequent increments of knowledge, meaning, and truth—the language of the natural sciences. From this fact of experience they assumed that all knowing, meaning, and truth can be incorporated into statements in their paradigmatic rhetoric and that nothing that cannot be reduced to that rhetoric can claim a place in the region of knowing, meaning, and truth. During their 25-year confrontation with historiography they have discovered one anomaly after another in the rhetoric of history, place after place where it appears to deviate from the language of the sciences. Their most general response has been to try to save their normal view of the nature of knowing, meaning, understanding, and truth and of the proper rhetoric for communicating them by constructing a complex structure of the logical equivalents of epicycles, eccentrics, and equants in order to assimilate to it as much of the rhetoric of history as possible and thereby save the paradigms which support that structure. This procedure has been less than satisfactory, since it requires them quite arbitrarily and without evidence to assign to many traits of the rhetoric of history an altogether aesthetic rather than a noetic function. This has been especially the case with respect to those aspects of the work of the writer of history which concern themselves with the telling of a historical story and with the disposition and arrangement of his evidence and the choice among alternatives, all connotative rather than purely denotative, for the communication of what he knows. The philosophers have proceeded as they have for the very good reason that to do otherwise would be to raise extremely perplexing questions about the nature of knowing, understanding, meaning, and truth to which, as of now, neither they nor anyone else has any very plausible answers.

One of the aims of this article is to suggest that nevertheless a paradigm shift which would raise such questions may now be desirable and even necessary. The first step would be to assume that the rhetoric of history, including much to which analytical philosophers assign only aesthetic value, constitutes an appropriate response on the part of historians to their commitment to advance the knowledge and understanding of the past as it actually was. There are no better reasons for rejecting this assumption than for making it; logically to reject it or to accept it involves decisions equally arbitrary. It has, however, a certain prima-facie empirical plausibility; it is based on an uninvidious view of the consistent refusal of some of the very best historians dedicated to communi-

cating the truth about the past wholly to adopt the rhetoric of the sciences. To start with this favorable assumption would provide room among the means of knowing for certain rules of historiography concerned with the advancement of knowledge, for which there seems to be no room within the present structure of knowing as the analytical philosophers conceive it.

It would by no means open the way for the sort of intellectual slatternliness that analytical philosophers rightly object to and oppose. On the contrary, it would assist in the introduction of some much-needed conscious intellectual rigor into regions in which rigor has often been sadly lacking or in which its presence has been due to the experience and temperament of particular historians rather than to thoughtfully codified professional standards of performance. But to do all this requires an acknowledgment and acceptance (1) that in some areas of human inquiry the pursuit of truth can be effectively carried on only by means of a rhetoric which diverges from that of the sciences and (2) that this is not wholly due to the peculiarities and perversities of those who pursue the truth in those areas but in part to the very nature of the terrain over which they must pursue it. Once analytical philosophers fully recognize that there may and indeed must be more than one style, one rhetoric, for communicating the things that are both knowable and communicable, and that the problem is not that of reducing all styles to one but of carefully investigating what style is appropriate to the particular problems of communication inherent in a particular kind of knowing, it will be possible to bridge the now ever-widening gaps that separate analytical philosophers, historians, and rhetoricians. They might then join in trying to discover whether a thorough exploration of historiography, the rhetoric of history, can teach them anything worth finding out about knowing, understanding, meaning, and truth.

J. H. HEXTER

[See also SCIENTIFIC EXPLANATION; HISTORY; PERIODIZATION; SCIENCE.]

### BIBLIOGRAPHY

*This bibliography includes selected works on the history of history writing in the Western world. Extensive bibliographies can also be found in Nevins 1932; Gottschalk 1963.*

AGASSI, JOSEPH 1963 *Towards an Historiography of Science.* History and Theory, Beiheft 2. The Hague: Mouton.

ANTONI, CARLO; and MATTIOLI, RAFFAELE (editors) 1950 *Cinquant'anni di vita intellettuale italiana, 1896–1946.* 2 vols. Naples (Italy): Edizioni Scientifiche Italiane.

ARON, RAYMOND (1935) 1957 *German Sociology.* Glencoe, Ill.: Free Press. → First published in French.

BARNES, HARRY ELMER (1937) 1962 *A History of Historical Writing.* 2d rev. ed. New York: Dover.

BELLOT, H. HALE 1952 *American History and American Historians: A Review of Recent Contributions to the Interpretation of the History of the United States.* Norman: Univ. of Oklahoma Press.

BOWMAN, FRANCIS J. 1951 *A Handbook of Historians and History Writing.* Dubuque, Iowa: Brown.

BUTTERFIELD, HERBERT 1955 *Man on His Past: The Study of the History of Historical Scholarship.* Cambridge Univ. Press. → A paperback edition was published by Beacon in 1960.

COLLINGWOOD, R. G. 1946 *The Idea of History.* Oxford Univ. Press. → A paperback edition was published in 1956.

CROCE, BENEDETTO (1921) 1947 *Storia della storiografia italiana nel secolo decimonono.* 3d ed. 2 vols. Bari (Italy): Laterza.

DANTO, ARTHUR C. 1965 *Analytical Philosophy of History.* Cambridge Univ. Press.

DIWALD, HELLMUT 1955 *Das historische Erkennen: Untersuchungen zum Geschichtsrealismus im 19. Jahrhundert.* Leiden (Netherlands): Brill.

*Encyclopédie française.* Volume 20: Le monde en devenir. 1964 Paris: Société de Gestion de l'Encyclopédie Française.

ENGEL-JANOSI, FRIEDRICH 1944 *The Growth of German Historicism.* Baltimore: Johns Hopkins Press.

FERGUSON, WALLACE K. 1948 *The Renaissance in Historical Thought: Five Centuries of Interpretation.* Boston: Houghton Mifflin.

FITZSIMONS, MATTHEW A. et al. (editors) 1954 *The Development of Historiography.* Harrisburg, Pa.: Stackpole.

FUETER, EDUARD (1911) 1914 *Histoire de l'historiographie moderne.* Paris: Alcan. → First published in German.

GALLIE, W. B. 1964 *Philosophy and the Historical Understanding.* London: Chatto & Windus.

GOOCH, GEORGE P. (1913) 1952 *History and Historians in the Nineteenth Century.* 2d ed. New York: Longmans.

GÖRLITZ, WALTER 1949 *Idee und Geschichte: Die Entwicklung des historischen Denkens.* Freiburg (Germany): Badischer Verlag.

GOTTSCHALK, LOUIS R. (editor) 1963 *Generalization in the Writing of History.* Univ. of Chicago Press.

HARBISON, E. HARRIS 1956 *The Christian Scholar in the Age of the Reformation.* New York: Scribner.

HEMPEL, CARL G. 1942 The Function of General Laws in History. *Journal of Philosophy* 39:35–48.

HIGHAM, JOHN; KRIEGER, LEONARD; and GILBERT, FELIX 1965 *History.* Englewood Cliffs, N.J.: Prentice-Hall.

*Histoire et historiens depuis cinquante ans.* 2 vols. 1927–1928 Paris: Alcan.

KESTING, HANNO 1959 *Geschichtsphilosophie und Weltbürgerkrieg: Deutungen der Geschichte von der französischen Revolution bis zum Ost–West Konflikt.* Heidelberg (Germany): Winter.

KRAUS, MICHAEL 1953 *The Writing of American History.* Norman: Univ. of Oklahoma Press.

MAZOUR, ANATOLE (1939) 1958 *Modern Russian Historiography.* 2d ed. Princeton, N.J.: Van Nostrand. → First published as *An Outline of Modern Russian Historiography.*

NEVINS, ALLAN 1932 History and Historiography. Volume 7, pages 357–389 in *Encyclopaedia of the Social Sciences.* New York: Macmillan. → A bibliography appears on pages 389–391.

PASSMORE, JOHN (editor) 1965 *The Historiography of the History of Philosophy.* History and Theory, Beiheft 5. The Hague: Mouton.

POCOCK, J. G. A. 1957 *The Ancient Constitution and the Feudal Law: A Study of English Historical Thought in the Seventeenth Century.* Cambridge Univ. Press.

ROSSI, PIETRO 1956 *Lo storicismo tedesco contemporaneo.* Turin (Italy): Einaudi.

SAMPSON, RONALD V. 1956 *Progress in the Age of Reason: The Seventeenth Century to the Present Day.* Cambridge, Mass.: Harvard Univ. Press.

SANCHEZ ALONSO, BENITO 1941–1950 *Consejo superior de investigaciones científicas: Historia de la historiografía española.* 3 vols. Madrid.

SRBIK, HEINRICH VON 1950–1951 *Geist und Geschichte vom deutschen Humanismus bis zur Gegenwart.* 2 vols. Munich (Germany): Bruckmann.

THOMPSON, JAMES W. 1942 *A History of Historical Writing.* 2 vols. New York: Macmillan.

VAN TASSEL, DAVID 1960 *Recording America's Past: An Interpretation of the Development of Historical Studies in America, 1607–1884.* Univ. of Chicago Press.

WAGNER, FRITZ 1960 *Moderne Geschichtsschreibung: Ausblick auf eine Philosophie der Geschichtswissenschaft.* Berlin: Duncker & Humblot.

WHITE, MORTON G. 1965 *Foundations of Historical Knowledge.* New York: Harper.

WISH, HARVEY 1960 *The American Historian: A Social–Intellectual History of the Writing of the American Past.* New York: Oxford Univ. Press.

ZIFFER, BERNARD 1952 *Poland, History and Historians: Three Bibliographical Essays.* New York: Mid-European Studies Center.

## II

### AFRICAN HISTORIOGRAPHY

A belief in the continuity of life, a life after death, and a community of interest between the living, the dead, and the generations yet unborn is fundamental to all African religious, social, and political life. Thus, although the serious writing of African history has only just begun, a sense of history and tradition has always been part of the African way of life.

The ancient Egyptians were very conscious of the continuity of life and death. They were conscious not only of the overriding importance of an after-life but also of the continuing relevance of the dead to the living. They prepared the burial chambers and preserved the bodies of the dead with great care. The essence of the Horus myth was that the dead, particularly the kings, continued to influence the life of the living by affecting the annual inundations of the Nile and the germination of crops. A good deal of Egyptian religion revolved around the commemoration of the dead. Impressive monuments were erected, and the priests who ministered in those shrines became very knowledgeable about the traditions and folk-lore of the past.

This fundamental belief in the continuity of life is found among all African peoples. It is an essential element in traditional African historiography. Throughout sub-Saharan Africa one finds the continuing relevance of the dead to the life of the present and of future generations. It is expressed in the belief that each community was founded by an ancestor or a group of ancestors, that whatever the status or possessions of the community, they were owed to the ancestors, and that the ancestors had established for all time the basic charter of life, which could be adapted and modified but which could not be completely changed. The ancestors and the tradition they represented were a living reality. Reverence for the ancestors sometimes became worship. The fear of "what the ancestors would say" was an ever-present consideration and one of the most powerful sanctions in African societies.

## Traditions of origins

Each community—family, clan, village, town, or state—however large or small, had an established tradition concerning its origins. The community might split up, migrate, and assimilate new elements, or be conquered by others and absorbed by new immigrants. At each stage of transformation, the tradition was recrystallized to accommodate changed conditions, and a new tradition of origin was formulated by the new community. These traditions became the core of the community's view of history. The very process of tradition-making and acculturation in the community, and of transmitting tradition to succeeding generations, developed a consciousness of history that became widespread in Africa.

These origin traditions did not attempt a historical explanation in the modern European sense of verifiable texts and chronology. They promoted understanding of and a respect for the institutions and practices of the community. They offered explanations of the world as the community conceived of it—the origin of land and sea, man and the other species, the origin of the state, the basis of different laws and customs, the title of the community to the land it held, how and why it differed from its neighbors in the gods it worshipped and the customs it upheld—but the explanations were not so much historical as philosophical, literary, and didactic. Accurate chronology and causation were of little relevance. To a large extent, history was merged with myth and was part of the general philosophy of life. In this way

traditional African historiography resembled that of Europe before the scientific revolution split philosophy into its component parts. The making and transmission of tradition was not the work of historians in the modern sense, but of priests and diviners, elders, and wise men in general. Tradition explained not only the relationship between the ancestors of different communities but also the relationship between the existing community, the ancestors, and the gods. It was expressed not only in narrative but also in sacred poetry, in ritual re-enactments, and other religious manifestations. Tradition was part of the philosophy of the community, part of its own peculiar way of life. Thus there could be no concept of universal history extending beyond the life of the particular community.

The making and the transmission of tradition varied from place to place. It depended on the size, nature, beliefs, and resources of the particular community. In segmented societies where roles were often not differentiated, it was part of the functions of the clan head as he fulfilled specific political and religious roles. In organized states, however, particularly those with centralized monarchies, such as Benin, Ashanti, or Dahomey, where the political and legal implications of tradition were of everyday importance, the making and transmission of tradition became a controlled and well-regulated specialism.

## Oral transmission

The commonest method of transmitting tradition was through stories, fables, and proverbs told by the elders as part of the general education of the young. In those story-telling sessions, after the evening meal in the family compounds or during festivals of the full moon when people stayed up late, traditions telling of the origin of the whole community or of the particular family or clan were related. More recent events that had occurred within remembered history, particularly those of the previous two or three generations, were also talked about.

Traditions were transmitted more formally when there were organized educational institutions such as those connected with puberty rites, initiation into age-grades and secret societies, or during the training or apprenticeship of priests and diviners. The rites by which the king-elect was initiated into the kingship were of particular interest. As the successor to and representative of the ancestors, the king became the custodian of the traditions of the community. One of the most important functions of the rites preceding his coronation, therefore, was to initiate him into the secrets of his ancestors and the traditional lore of his people. More than that, partly as ritual offerings to the ancestors, partly as entertainment and education for the people at large, the traditions of the people were recited publicly: symbolic events from the past were dramatized; the names, genealogies, cognomens, titles, and praise songs of the ancestors were chanted. The new king announced his own title. The title frequently was intended to characterize the expectations of his reign. The praise singers responded, and a new chapter in the people's tradition opened.

Thus the process of transmitting tradition cannot be separated from the process of creating tradition. Tradition was made by those who transmitted it—the village and clan elders, the singers and drummers who assisted at coronations and other public festivals, the officials of age-grades and secret societies who conducted the puberty rites or initiated new members. These persons were appointed sometimes from among eligible members of a single family, sometimes from a wider circle of candidates who had to demonstrate their mastery of past traditions and folklore and their wit at entertaining people and making tradition out of contemporary affairs. In the daily life both of the community and of individuals, tradition was invoked, challenged, modified, and created in the processes of litigation, of settling disputed successions to all types of offices, of recording new events and new situations that resulted when masterful individuals or communities made innovations in the guise of merely fulfilling tradition.

## Factual versus literary traditions

It is necessary to distinguish between different types of tradition, or oral tradition, as it is now generally described (Vansina 1961). The first distinction is between traditions of a factual and historical type and those of a literary and philosophical type. Of the more factual type, it is important to distinguish between events of the recent past that can be recalled from the personal experience of grandfathers and fathers and events of the more distant past. The authenticity of these remote traditions is in large part dependent on the special institutions that may have existed for making and transmitting tradition and on how efficiently these institutions functioned. Such factual traditions include formal lists of kings and other office holders, chronicles of each reign, appellations and praise verses (which often included either direct or implied criticism) of each king or other leading chiefs, genealogies, and certain laws or customs.

But even traditions that appear well preserved and factual may turn out on examination to be symbolic; apparent biographical data may represent summaries of the life of the whole community over one or more generations. References to years, generations, and periods may in fact refer to structural and not chronological time.

The more literary types of tradition include proverbs and sayings, songs and lyrics, of which some are general and others peculiar to particular guilds, age-grades and other associations. The more philosophical traditions are enshrined in the sacred chants of different religious organizations and cults, such as the praise verses of the gods, divination poems, funeral dirges, liturgies, and hymns. Finally, one should distinguish between traditions narrated in the words of the speaker and those with set and formal texts.

## Ethiopian influence

There have been, of course, other historical traditions in Africa whose influence on African historiography is difficult to evaluate at the present state of our knowledge. One important example is the Ethiopian historical tradition, partly African and partly of Judaeo–Christian inspiration. The supremacy of the Solomonid dynasty, the unity of church and state, and the integrity of the monophysite church were the dynamic historical forces. As in other parts of Africa, in the twelfth century Ethiopia developed a legend that linked the ruling dynasty with the Holy Land. But it was a written tradition, enshrined in the *Book of Kings* that became a major feature of coronation rites. The monasteries recorded the annals of each reign and preserved important texts and charters. Yet the primary interest of Ethiopian intellectual life was theological, not historical; there was little attempt until recent times to analyze and interpret the annals and the chronicles to produce history. Of more relevance to African historiography are the traditions of the Berbers. Like other Africans, the Berbers were very conscious of the continued relevance of the past. In their reaction both to Roman Christianity and Arabian Islam they manifested an attitude of mysticism and dissent combined with the veneration of ancestors. It may be said that this attitude produced hagiography and not critical history, but hagiography itself was a method of enshrining and immortalizing the idealized social and religious virtues of the people. It was, in a sense, the literary expression of respect for the norms and virtues of ancestors, similar to the traditions found in other parts of Africa. The tracing of real genealogy, always of great importance to the Arabs, has remained a marked feature of Muslim Africa, but, in addition, the Berbers introduced veneration of ancestors in the form of tracing spiritual genealogies of Muslim leaders. This was expressed in the *tariqa* chains and the handing down of the *wird* among Muslim Brotherhoods. Initiation into the *tariqa* conferred spiritual knowledge and benefits; this paralleled initiation into traditional African associations, guilds, and cults.

## Muslim influence

Muslim influence was important not only in north Africa but also in east Africa, the whole of the Sudan, and even in a few places within the forest areas. In addition to real and spiritual genealogies, Muslim writers produced a number of *tarikhs* and chronicles, especially in the eleventh to the seventeenth centuries. These embodied eye-witness accounts, oral tradition, and evidence from earlier accounts by geographers, travelers and traders. Muslim writers were particularly interested in the spread and influence of Islam and in the religious and the economic life of the main centers of Islam. These factors were singled out of the totality of African life and traditions and given undue emphasis. In important centers of Muslim learning like Timbuktu, Gao, Djenné, Kano, Katsina, and Bornu in the west and central Sudan, or Kilwa, Malindi, and Mombasa in east Africa, traditions of the people were written down, mostly in Arabic but sometimes also in the Arabic transcriptions of the vernacular. The accounts centered on leading personalities of the Muslim community rather than traditional states or clans. Rulers were judged good or bad insofar as they extended or hindered the influence of Islam and the privileges of Muslim scholars.

It is now recognized that the *Prolegomena* of Ibn Khaldūn, the famous Tunisian scholar of the fourteenth century, is one of the world's most important works on historiography. He emphasized the importance of sociology to history. He sought to study the past not only in terms of the actions of individuals but also by an analysis of the laws, customs, and institutions of the different peoples as well as the interaction of state and society. This approach would have provided a basis for synthesizing the many traditions in Africa into a history of the continent, but until recently, his work had little influence. The contemporary medieval world was more interested in the study of theology, law, and rhetoric. Within Africa itself, Islamic scholarship declined and was at its lowest ebb in the eighteenth century. It was in this period that the study of history was revived in Europe, but because

of the abundance of written documentary evidence, European scholars did not adopt the sociological approach of Ibn Khaldūn, but concerned themselves mainly with the decrees, wars, and politics of kings. In the nineteenth century the legal and biographical approach was broadened to take social and economic factors into account, but documentary evidence had become so overwhelmingly important for the European scholar that he tended to equate written documents with history. The absence of documents was thus taken to mean the absence of any events worthy of historical study.

## European influence

In the nineteenth century, when European influence intruded into Africa, it did not build on the existing historical traditions but challenged and supplanted them. The European view of documentary history supported the propaganda of the colonial rulers: Africa had no history worthy of record; therefore the history of European traders, missionaries, explorers, conquerors, and rulers constituted the sum total of African history. European history and the history of European expansion began to displace local history and tradition in the education of the African youth, although some attention was given to Arabic and other sources. European historians of the late nineteenth and early twentieth centuries sought to explain the Atlantic slave trade, the European technological supremacy, and the subjugation of Africa not in terms of any historical study of the continent but in terms of racial and psychological prejudices about the inherent inferiority of people with dark skins. Missionary circles even introduced the religious explanation that Africans were the children of Ham and were under Noah's curse to be hewers of wood and drawers of water for their lighter-skinned brethren. African historiography thus became nothing more than a justification of European imperialism.

Africans who became literate in the European languages at first accepted these theories, but because the traditional African historical consciousness remained alive, they soon began to challenge the absurdities of the European historians. Some of them who did not necessarily question the basic European standpoint began, nevertheless, to record the laws, customs, proverbs, sayings, and historical traditions of their own communities. They recorded also the major events of the nineteenth century, especially in the period just preceding the establishment of European rule. Notable among such writers may be mentioned James Africanus Horton of Sierra Leone, Carl C. Reindorf and John M. Sarbah of Ghana, Otomba Payne and Samuel Johnson of Nigeria, and Apolo Kagwa of Uganda. For a long time the work of these men and the material in missionary and government records on specifically African peoples escaped the attention of historians. It was the anthropologists who discovered them, but they were then not interested in history. With a few notable exceptions like Franz Boas and Emil Torday, their primary concern was to describe the quaintness and the peculiarities of "tribes," to justify as well as to facilitate the imposition of colonial rule. Other literate Africans, more conscious and more resentful of the European standpoint, began to protest. But since they were restricted by the axiom that only documentary history is real history, they could only reply with polemics and counter-theories. Uncritical use of the few written sources available, particularly those of the ancient Greek writers on Africa, the Muslim geographers or travelers, and the European traders on the west and east African coasts, laid the foundation of new myths. An example of such a myth is the so-called "Hamitic hypothesis," the view that all light and civilization in sub-Saharan Africa had come from north Africa and the Middle East and that the civilizations of Africa are thus civilizations of the Hamites; another myth regards the influence of the Atlantic slave trade as so all-pervasive that it can explain all major trends in African history since the fifteenth century.

World War I, the Russian Revolution, the rise of the Indian National Congress, the increasing dissatisfaction with the facile theory of European superiority—all these encouraged a new appraisal of the African past. African works of art, looted from Africa and scattered all over Europe and North America, inspired new art forms in Europe. New masterpieces of sculpture and terracotta were discovered, and their African origin became more difficult to deny. Anthropologists became less tied to the colonial regimes, less ethnocentric, and consequently more appreciative of African culture and historical traditions. The International Institute of African Languages and Cultures in London began to publish *Africa*, and the French established the Institut Français d'Afrique Noire in west Africa. The *Journal of Negro History*, in the United States, primarily concerned with the history of the Negro in America, drew attention to the possibilities of African history. Anthropologists like Melville J. Herskovits began to take African culture and its survivals in the New World seriously and to seek understanding of the African past.

The impulse toward a new African historiography came with the movement toward independence, which gathered pace in Africa during and immediately after World War II. This nationalist movement firmly rejected the European appraisal of the African past and demanded a new orientation and improved educational facilities to produce this reappraisal. With the establishment of new universities in Africa, it was inevitable that the teaching of history and the training of African historians would receive special attention. The old theories were maintained at first: besides European history, there were courses only on "European Activities in Africa" and some postgraduate research on British or French policy toward this or that territory at such and such a period. By the late 1940s, however, African research students were insisting that African history must be the history of Africans and not of Europeans in Africa, that local records and historical traditions must be used to supplement European metropolitan archives —in short, oral tradition must be accepted as valid material for historical research. This new approach produced works like *Trade and Politics in the Niger Delta* (Dike 1956) and *The Egba and Their Neighbours* (Biobaku 1957).

### Research problems and prospects

No doubt the validity of nonwritten sources for historical research had been pointed out before, but it was new for university departments of history to accept it. Even then not everyone was happy about it. Anthropologists replied cautiously that oral tradition, even when seemingly factual, was not history and could only be interpreted in terms of its function in society and within the particular culture. But this did not destroy its validity as material for history; it only argued for a return to the link between history and sociology advocated in the fourteenth century by Ibn Khaldūn. This interdisciplinary approach has been the most fruitful trend in African historiography in the last decade.

There have been three major developments to promote this interdisciplinary approach. The first has been the creation of special centers or institutes of African studies within which historians, anthropologists, linguists, and archeologists can cooperate, both in research and in the training of future historians. The second consists of specific culture-history projects like the Benin and Yoruba schemes, in which teams of people from different disciplines cooperate under the direction of one person to throw light on the culture history of a particular culture. The third is the formation of associations and the convening of periodic conferences or congresses on African history or African studies in general, bringing experts together from many disciplines to review progress in different fields and bring their joint consideration to bear on specific problems of Africa history. This cooperation has extended beyond the social and humanistic studies; the experimental sciences are also applying the benefit of their techniques to resolving problems in African history.

The interdisciplinary approach has been very fruitful in the collection and evaluation of material for African history. Since the end of the war, many African states have founded national archives. This in turn has stimulated the exploitation of government, missionary, commercial, and private archives in Europe. Materials relevant to African history are now being copied and transferred to archival centers and places of learning in Africa, where they are supplemented by local records in European, Arabic, and other African languages. Similarly, more care is now taken of ancient monuments, and museums of art and crafts are being established. The recording of oral tradition has become a major preoccupation. Evidence from all these sources is cross-checked and supplemented by the study of linguistics and African languages, social anthropology, archeology, and other sciences. Gaps in our knowledge are being filled, and a specific chronology is beginning to emerge. Historians can now attempt a synthesis of the history of the whole continent, particular regions, or of the newly independent states. While insisting on the validity of traditional African historical material, the new African historiography has been able to accept the European concept of continental and universal history.

African historians have also adopted rigorous standards and methodology in the collection of data. Indeed, the emphasis in the last decade has been placed so much upon this scientific methodology that it is a question worth raising whether the proper interpretation and synthesis of the material has not tended to lag behind. While the interdisciplinary approach has been very successful in the collection of data, teams or conferences of experts from different disciplines do not write history. The interdisciplinary approach has alerted the historian to the validity of nonwritten sources; it has not superseded him or relieved him of the necessity to sift the diverse evidence, synthesize, and write history. Moreover, it would appear that the new historiography is still so tied to the universities that the proper functions of history in the new

Africa, to educate and entertain society as a whole, have received little attention. We have still to create a new philosophy of African history to replace that of the old palace historians and singers.

K. O. DIKE AND J. F. A. AJAYI

[*See also* AFRICAN SOCIETY; HISTORIOGRAPHY, *article on* ISLAMIC HISTORIOGRAPHY; *and the biographies of* HERSKOVITS *and* IBN KHALDŪN.]

### BIBLIOGRAPHY

ABRAHAM, D. P. 1961 Maramuca: An Exercise in the Combined Use of Portuguese Records and Oral Tradition. *Journal of African History* 2:211–225.

AJAYI, J. F. A. 1961 The Place of African History and Culture in the Process of Nation-building in Africa South of the Sahara. *Journal of Negro Education* 30:206–213.

ANDRZEJEWSKI, BOGUMIL W.; and LEWIS, I. M. 1964 *Somali Poetry: An Introduction.* Oxford: Clarendon.

BIOBAKU, SABURI O. 1957 *The Egba and Their Neighbours: 1842–1872.* Oxford Univ. Press.

BIOBAKU, SABURI O. 1963 African Studies in an African University. *Minerva* 1:285–301.

BRADBURY, R. E. 1959 Chronological Problems in the Study of Benin History. *Journal of the Historical Society of Nigeria* 1:263–287.

CONFERENCE ON AFRICAN HISTORY AND ARCHAEOLOGY, THIRD, LONDON, *1961* 1962 Report. *Journal of African History* 3, no. 2.

DIKE, KENNETH O. 1953 African History and Self-government. *West Africa* 37:177–178, 225–226, 251.

DIKE, KENNETH O. (1956) 1962 *Trade and Politics in the Niger Delta; 1830–1885: An Introduction to the Economic and Political History of Nigeria.* Oxford: Clarendon.

DIKE, KENNETH O. 1964 The Study of African History. Pages 55–67 in International Congress of Africanists, First, Accra, 1962, *Proceedings.* London: Longmans.

EVANS-PRITCHARD, E. E. 1961 *Anthropology and History.* Manchester (England) Univ. Press.

INTERNATIONAL AFRICAN SEMINAR, FOURTH, DAKAR, SENEGAL, *1961* 1964 *The Historian in Tropical Africa.* Oxford Univ. Press.

JONES, G. I. 1963 European and African Tradition on the Rio Real. *Journal of African History* 4:391–402.

JORDAN, A. C. 1957–1960 Towards an African Literature. *Africa South* 1, no. 4:90–98; 2, no. 1:97–105, no. 2:101–104, no. 3:112–115, no. 4:113–118; 3, no. 1:114–117, no. 2:74–79, no. 3:114–117, no. 4:111–115; 4, no. 1:117–121, no. 2:110–113, no. 3:112–116.

LAWRENCE, A. W. 1961 Some Source Books for West African History. *Journal of African History* 2:227–234.

LEWIS, I. M. 1962 Historical Aspects of Genealogies in Northern Somali Social Structure. *Journal of African History* 3:35–48.

McCALL, DANIEL F. 1964 *Africa in Time-perspective: A Discussion of Historical Reconstruction From Unwritten Sources.* Boston Univ. Press.

MORRIS, HENRY F. 1964 *The Heroic Recitations of the Bahima of Ankole.* Oxford: Clarendon.

SMITH, M. G. 1961 Field Histories Among the Hausa. *Journal of African History* 2:87–101.

VANSINA, JAN 1960 *Recording the Oral History of the Bakuba*. *Journal of African History* 1:45–53, 257–270. → Part 1: "Methods." Part 2: "Results."

VANSINA, JAN (1961) 1964 *The Oral Tradition: A Study in Historical Methodology*. Chicago: Aldine. → First published in French. Contains a comprehensive bibliography on and discussion of the nature and significance of oral traditions.

WHITELEY, W. H. (compiler) 1964 *A Selection of African Prose*. 2 vols. Oxford: Clarendon. → Volume 1: *Traditional Oral Texts*. Volume 2: *Written Prose*.

## III

### CHINESE HISTORIOGRAPHY

China can claim the oldest continuous historical tradition on earth. The appointment of court historians has been attributed to the Yellow Emperor, one of the legendary founders of a Chinese order. Modern archeology has shown that the court diviners of the Shang kings (1751–1111 B.C., according to Tung Tso-pin) maintained "archives" of their divinations, inscribed on bone and shell; here at the beginning was an association between magico-religious operations and record keeping that was to have long-term effects on the historiographical tradition.

Fragmentary records from the early part of the Chou dynasty (1111–221 B.C.)—principally certain chapters of the *Shu-ching*, or "Classic of History"—reflect a continuing interest in royal genealogy, ritual operations, and political legitimacy. With the gradual emergence of semi-independent states, from the eighth century B.C. on, traditions of recording and compilation developed in several courts. The Warring States period (481–221 B.C.) was China's first great age of systematic thought. Scholars searched the records of the past for examples and precedents to sustain their arguments; this habit of appealing to history figures importantly in all subsequent Chinese thought. Confucius (551–479 B.C.) and his followers laid great stress on the moral content of history, maintaining that the records of the past, if properly studied, would reveal the operation of moral norms in the affairs of men. The *Ch'un-ch'iu* chronicle of the state of Lu, allegedly edited by Confucius to express his judgments, came to be regarded as the prototype of moralistic–normative history.

The unified empire created in 221 B.C. was to be the model for subsequent Chinese political development. The imperial court continued and elaborated earlier traditions of historian-officials who kept records of the actions of the emperor and of events in the realm. These historians were deeply influenced by Confucian orthodoxy of the Han period, with its interest in the moral and didactic uses of history. In the Former Han dynasty (206 B.C.–A.D. 8) the Grand Historian Ssu-ma Ch'ien, continuing the work of his father, drew on court records, on chronicles and inscriptions from earlier times, and on oral traditions to produce the *Shih-chi*, the first great history of the Chinese ecumene from its shadowy beginnings to about 100 B.C. During the Later Han dynasty (A.D. 25–220) another great court historian, Pan Ku, wrote the first of the "dynastic histories" (*tuan-tai shih*), his *History of the Former Han Dynasty*. These two Han works provided models that were returned to again and again by later historians.

The breakup of the Han empire was followed by a long period of political disunion, from 220 to 589. During much of this period north China, the heartland of Chinese civilization, was under the domination of "barbarian" invaders, while Buddhism gradually became a pervasive force in Chinese thought and life. The early part of this period was the second great age of creative thought— thought that ranged with greater depth and imagination than ever before over the problems of man, society, and the cosmos. This is reflected in historical writings, which became more self-conscious and more critical. Historiography began to achieve its independence. Liu Hsieh (465–522) devoted part of his great treatise on literature to problems of historiography: the need for general principles, criteria for the selection of particulars, standards of credibility, and problems of objectivity and bias. The autonomy of the Chinese historical tradition was strikingly affirmed in this age of Buddhist dominance; Buddhism had slight effects on Chinese historical thinking, and Buddhist historians shaped their works after approved secular models.

The great reunified empire of T'ang (618–906) was notable for its artistic and literary brilliance. History became, for the first time, a standard ingredient of the curriculum for state examinations. The noted T'ang official Tu Yu (735–812) sought to break free of dynastic chronicles and wrote an encyclopedic compilation, the *T'ung-tien*, that may be regarded as the first institutional history of China. In the early T'ang the bureaucratic apparatus for recording events, processing documents, maintaining archives, and writing history was greatly elaborated. At this time imperial commissions replaced individual authors in the compilation of dynastic histories. This marked the inception of a division between official and unofficial historiography that persisted until the end of the imperial order. A severe critic of this change was Liu Chih-chi (661–721), whose "Conspectus of History" (*Shih-t'ung*) is the first major work of historical criticism, signaling the emergence of history as a separate and independent branch of study. In it Liu dealt with such problems as the credibility of evidence, historical style and form, the qualities of historians, the effects of bias and political pressure, and the moral dilemmas of historians.

Toward the end of the T'ang, Confucianism, which had long seemed intellectually anachronistic, began to be revived and modernized. The resulting system of Neo-Confucianism had far-reaching effects on the writing of history. The rationalism of the new system was reflected in lessened attention to supernatural events and interpretations. It fostered, in the centuries that followed, a strong tradition of historical empiricism and critical scholarship. The historical writings of the Neo-Confucianists of the Sung (960–1279) show a new meticulousness in historical inquiry, a disposition to use unofficial sources, a devotion to rational explanation combined with a profound belief in moral dynamics. Perhaps the greatest historian of this age was Ssu-ma Kuang (1019–1086). His *Tzu-chih t'ung-chien* was a history of the Chinese world from 403 B.C. to A.D. 959, arranged in annalistic form. The author drew on an immense variety of works and appended his study of doubtful points (*k'ao-i*) to the completed history. He emphasized in his preface his moral–political purpose: ". . . taking in all that a prince ought to know—everything pertaining to the rise and fall of dynasties and the good and ill fortune of the common people, all good and bad examples that can furnish models and warnings."

The development of printing in the Sung dynasty and the spread of literacy among an enlarged elite meant a great proliferation of private historiography, an expanded reading public, and vastly increased possibilities for preserving historical records. These trends and the dominant Neo-Confucian view of history—most authoritatively expressed by Chu Hsi (1130–1200) in his "epitome" (*kang-mu*) of Ssu-ma Kuang's history—continued through the age of Mongol rule (1279–1368) and the Chinese dynasty of Ming (1368–1644). These centuries are better known for monumental compilations and exhaustive commentaries than for creative historical works. An exception is the second major institutional history of China, the *Wen-hsien t'ung-k'ao*, by Ma Tuan-lin (c. 1250–1325).

The shock of the imposition of Manchu rule in 1644 plus a growing impatience with Neo-Confucian orthodoxy as it devolved into pedantry on the one hand and vapid philosophizing on the other provoked a new critical movement of great importance. A new rational empiricism produced new principles of textual criticism and new work in historical geography, epigraphy, archeology, and other fields. Ku Yen-wu (1613–1682) was one of the pioneers in this movement and began the development of the inductive method of research that had far-reaching effects on historical and philological studies. Chao I (1727–1814) wrote of recurrent patterns and forces in Chinese history with unusual acumen. Chang Hsüeh-ch'eng (1738–1801), ignored in his own time, presented an enlarged view of history, a conception of historical synthesis, and ideas about the qualities of a historian that were new to the Chinese tradition. These men and the other historians of this autumnal flowering never—for all their new ideas and rigorous methods—renounced their allegiance to Confucian morality, to the belief that history should be written to illuminate moral truths and thereby to reform the world. When the imperial order and Confucian orthodoxy had collapsed, the methods and skeptical spirit of these men figured largely in the modernization of Chinese historiography.

## The Chinese view of history

The usual Chinese term for history, *shih*, has several meanings: writings about the past, one who (usually under official appointment) records events, and, in early times, "astrologer" or "astronomer." The term does not have the second meaning of the English word "history," the past as such. The Chinese conception of history was shaped by certain elements in the Chinese world view. One of these was ethnocentrism, derived from the relative isolation of Chinese civilization. History was primarily concerned with the "Central Kingdom" (*chung-kuo*), with the world (*t'ien-hsia*) in which China was "central." Thus peoples peripheral to China were treated as "barbarians," or peoples to be contained, "chastised," or converted to Chinese culture. Since the Chinese had only fragmentary knowledge of other great civilizations, there was no trace of comparative history, such as one finds in Ibn Khaldūn. A second element is holism, the view that human and natural events are interrelated in a coherent whole; symptoms of dislocation in one order are interpreted as signs of malfunction in the other. Especially in histories written before about A.D. 1000, much attention is given to natural catastrophes, portents, and the like. Yet the force for harmony or dislocation originates in the actions of men, and a rational–secular view of historical causation gradually becomes dominant. A third element is a view of history as a devolution from a golden age: the sage-kings of the distant past had presided over an ideal order; in later times men moved further and further from that ideal. Change was considered desirable if it promised a return to ancient ideals. This gives to all Chinese histories—even those of periods of innovation—a pronouncedly archaistic tone. A fourth element is a cyclical conception of political history; polities, like men, have sequences of birth, youth, maturity, senescence, and death. The habit of holistic thinking led historians to see symptoms of the same cyclical stages in all the spheres of culture: literature, the arts, the ethos of the villages, the customs and habits of the elite. The practice of dating all events by dynasty and era name (*nien-hao*) reinforced the conception of political change as the dominant force in cyclical change.

A fifth element is the view that there is a moral dynamic in the affairs of men; the Confucian sages had specified the principles. History, if properly written, would lay bare the working of those principles in a nexus of events or in an individual life. This belief tended to give a moralistic coloration to all cause-and-effect statements and to reduce biography to exemplary or minatory stereotypes.

**Scope and purposes of historiography.** From the earliest times the keeping of records and the writing of history were official functions. Every dynasty had its history office. It was staffed by men who had been educated in the standard curriculum and had passed the state examinations. The common experience of all officials included a great deal of history: study of the style and content of the ancient chronicles, memorization of historical sequences, the use of historical allusion and historical precedent in the most routine official communications, the marshaling of historical cases in policy argument. Thus, history was an integral part of training and of official life. This meant that a high percentage of officials at some point in their careers would be assigned for a period to the history office, where they might work at daily record keeping or at one of the several types of compilation periodically ordered by the throne. From the T'ang dynasty (618–906) on, high-ranking officials were appointed to chair or to serve on the commissions in charge of major historical compilations. All works compiled in the history office were presented to the throne for approval. Private historians were usually members of the official class, were largely dependent for their materials on official records, and often felt it politic to present their works to the throne for approval.

Historians of all kinds were thus deeply involved in official life and shared the general concerns of

the official class: the maintenance of stability and order through governmental operations and the institutions of social control, the preservation of Confucian orthodoxy and the maintenance of Confucian ethical standards in society, the upholding of inherited standards of excellence in literature and the arts, the defense of the privileged position of the literate gentry against threats from autocratic emperors and upstart power groups.

These interests, working together with the world view discussed above, determined the scope of Chinese history writing. The overriding concern with order produced a concentration of attention on political history and the lessons about stability and change that could be drawn from it. Similarly, the history of institutions was viewed from the capital and from the official viewpoint; thus, for example, the "economic" monographs of the dynastic histories are focused on the regulatory function of government, and the "geographical" monographs are concerned with what we would call administrative geography. Biographies deal less with individual character than with the subjects' official posts and social role; they tend to be grouped according to a common social role or according to certain moral standards that the subjects exemplified, for example, "loyal ministers," "literary men," "virtuous women," "harsh officials," "partisans."

Slight attention was given to all the groups that challenged the literate gentry's power: military leaders, merchants, eunuchs, court favorites, and members of the empresses' families. (The last three were treated when their machinations were adduced as prime causes of dynastic weakness or collapse.) Heterodox religions tended to be given little attention. Although Buddhism dominated Chinese culture for five hundred years or more (from 350 to 850) and was a major force in life and thought in later centuries, references to it in official histories are few; only one monograph in one dynastic history is devoted to Buddhism and religious Taoism. References to these and other heterodoxies are usually pejorative and emphasize their socially disruptive effects. Unsuccessful rebels are given scant attention beyond the account of measures taken to suppress them. Common life and popular culture are seldom given detailed treatment, except when natural calamities created problems of relief and rehabilitation or subversive movements appeared among the oppressed peasantry.

The whole picture of life that appears in the standard histories and official compilations tends to minimize tensions, cultural differences between one region and another, clashes of opinion, and other phenomena that in the modern Western view seem most significant in the development of Chinese civilization. Yet these defects are in part counterbalanced by the sheer volume of the record; it would require 45 million English words to translate the 25 dynastic histories. And from the sixth or seventh century on the dynastic histories can be checked and supplemented by an enormous wealth of published official and private sources: diaries, memoirs, collected papers, essays, poems, collections of inscriptions, stories, travelogues, and miscellanies. Surviving manuscripts, notably those discovered at Tun-huang, provide further raw material and additional checks. The *shih-lu*, or "veritable records," of the last two dynasties have been preserved and provide a daily record of court and government from 1368 to 1912. Thus the modern historian can, by using all these varieties of material, reconstruct substantial segments of the Chinese past.

**Historical method.** The methods used by Chinese historians fall into two closely related groups. One consists of the methods of recording contemporary happenings, the other of the methods of compiling a coherent account from such records. Court historians were charged with writing up, day by day, the events at court: audiences, rituals, memorials to the throne, imperial edicts, digests of reports received from outside the capital. Private historians would usually record events they witnessed, journeys they took, or the lives of their relatives and friends. The exercise of the recording function, especially at the official level, was a solemn obligation, for the historian had the moral duty to record accurately, without fear or favor, and this usually in a power situation fraught with tensions. Heroic examples of historians who died rather than distort the record were constantly before them.

The second type of method is compilation. Court historians from time to time edited and digested the daily records into chronological accounts of a dynastic period (*kuo-shih*) or of a single reign (*shih-lu*). These accounts in turn formed the basis for the "annals" (*pen-chi*) section of the dynastic history written by the historians of the succeeding dynasty. The bare chronological accounts in the dynastic histories were supplemented with biographies prepared from both official and nonofficial records and with monographs pieced together from official papers dealing with particular topics, for example, imperial edicts on judicial administration, ceremonies, economic and fiscal affairs, etc. The procedure of compilation was to select integral passages from the records and piece them together

with words or sentences of transition, usually within a chronological framework. Thus, official histories were compiled rather than written afresh, and the same may be said of most private historiography.

In the whole process of recording and compilation, the historian was circumscribed by a variety of attitudes and conventions, many of which had come down from the distant past. The world view and interests of the Chinese elite limited the historian's horizons, and Confucian morality governed his choices. Moreover, the Chinese attitude of respect for the written word meant that he handled documents from the past with care and circumspection. He did not alter them lightly, and when two accounts of an event were in conflict he generally chose the one that showed greater consistency with his other materials and inserted it integrally into his text. The discussion of discrepancies in evidence appeared rather late in the tradition and was then relegated to separate sections of a history or to separate works.

The chronological arrangement of historical particulars derived naturally from the system of court record keeping. It also had an ancient and authoritative prototype in the "Spring and Autumn Annals" (*Ch'un-ch'iu*), allegedly edited by Confucius. This method of compilation (*pien-nien*) was dominant in the tradition, and even the institutional historians who sought to transcend dynastic chronology arranged the materials in their topical chapters chronologically. The devolutionary view of history precluded the full development of ideas of history-as-process. In general, "befores" and "afters" were thought to indicate to the discerning reader the elements of moral causation that were believed to inhere in any sequence of events.

But the historian was enjoined by tradition to make clear the moral lessons of history. There were certain approved means of doing this. Two of these were methods attributed to Confucius: "appropriate concealment," which meant omission or disguise by euphemism of particulars that might impair the image of a worthy individual or group, and the selection of terminology in such a way as to apportion moral praise or blame, for example, "succeed to" or "usurp" the throne. More explicit judgments by the historian were to be found in brief comments appended to a section or chapter of his work; there the moral point was made, the lesson drawn. Furthermore, the historian could express degrees of approval and disapproval by his arrangement of material. For instance, in a collection of biographies the lives were grouped according to certain types. The historian's judgment was reflected in the group to which a given biography was assigned and in the position of the group in the collection: the most worthy were placed first; the least worthy came at the end.

Both recording and compilation were subject to verbal and ritual conventions. Drawing up an imperial edict was a solemn and complex task that involved choosing the right references to the classics and the appropriate allusions to historical precedent, the observance of the official taboos in referring to members of the ruling house, choosing the rhetorical flourishes proper to the matter in hand. When the historian used such an edict in compiling a history, he had to understand what it meant and fit it into his narrative with only those minor verbal changes dictated by the lapse of time. There were proper and improper ways of recording all events: the selection of a crown prince, the death of an emperor or empress dowager, the reception of a tributary envoy. The recorder used these conventions, and the subsequent historian reproduced them in his account. To all these formulas were added standardized literary locutions for describing certain types of events: famine in the provinces, incursions along the frontiers, and so forth. Much of Chinese history, particularly official history, is thus cast in standardized ritualistic or literary formulas.

Biography was also subject to formulas. This had two roots in historiographical tradition. One was the dependence of the biographer on funerary writings of all kinds, which presented individual lives in the conventional formulas of filial piety and the cult of ancestors. The other was the conception of the individual life as having an exemplary or minatory purpose; if history was to teach moral lessons, biographies must serve to illustrate virtue and vice in individual lives. The historian–compiler, as we have noted, grouped his biographies and thus tended to stereotype the lives classified according to any one type. Particulars concerning the life of a man that were at variance with the type to which his biography was assigned were sometimes included in other parts of the same history.

The weight of convention was heaviest upon the compilers of dynastic histories and other official works. In general, the historian who recorded or compiled accounts of nonofficial personages (monks, recluses, certain literary figures) or of events of marginal concern to the court (ethnography of certain peoples, popular festivals) enjoyed greater freedom. It was always in the sector of private historiography that innovation occurred: for example, the invention of a new type of "unofficial biography" (*pieh-chuan*) in the Ch'ing dy-

nasty, the development first of the "life chronicle" (*nien-p'u*) and subsequently of the autobiographical life chronicle, the creation of institutional history (which later atrophied under official sponsorship), and the development of local histories (*fang-chih*) given a fresh impetus by Chang Hsüeh-ch'eng and his successors. But if some of the official conventions were less burdensome in such cases as these, the method of compilation, governed as it was by tradition and the world view of the elite, remained very much the same. One of the effects of this is that the reader seldom—except in certain kinds of prefaces—glimpses the personality or point of view of the historian in the objective, factual flow of the prose. Another effect—especially pronounced after the bureaucratization of history —was that nearly all personal and evocative writing was relegated to "nonhistorical" categories: novels, anecdotes, and the like. This deprived the historiographical tradition of the vividness and color found in the early chronicles.

## The modernization of historiography

The breakup of the millennial traditions of Chinese historiography occurred gradually in phases paralleling the dissolution of the imperial order of which it had been a part: a period of resistance to the intrusive forces from the West, followed, from about 1860 to 1905, by a phase of attempted compromise and accommodation, followed in turn by a period of increasing acceptance of Western ideas and institutions. The abolition of the examination system in 1905, accompanied by sweeping educational reforms after the models of the Japanese modernizers, ushered in revolutionary changes in the organization of learning. The old academies were swept away and replaced by state-supported schools; the long-gowned man of learning who divided his time between official service and scholarly activities gave way—as scholar and teacher— to the new generation of Western-trained and Japanese-trained professors in the newly established universities and research institutes. History was institutionalized in new careers and in new institutions, where it struggled to re-establish itself as one of the new disciplines among the many transplanted from the West.

The universities were the first of the new institutions for the study of history. They grew from small beginnings under the empire to a nationwide system of state, provincial, and accredited private universities under the Nationalist government (1927–1949). Although the scale was small (only about 25,000 students attended accredited universities in 1930–1931), the universities provided positions for historians engaged in teaching and research and the intellectual forums in which they developed their ideas. The principal institution for advanced research was the Institute of History and Philology, one of the branches of the Academia Sinica established by the government in 1928. The institute supported a variety of research activities aimed at the reorganization of the historical heritage and the application of new methods of analysis. This included an approach to validating historical documents through archeological investigation. Its excavations of the late Shang capital at Anyang revolutionized the study of early Chinese history. National libraries in Peking and Nanking and libraries attached to universities grew in size and were organized along Western lines. After a considerable lapse of time, the Nationalist government took over the archives of the defunct dynasty, and the collection and organization of archival materials were gradually modernized; substantial archival collections were published, notably by the Palace Museum in Peking.

The senior historians who worked within this new framework of institutions were scholars trained under the old order. The younger men—those who wrought the modernization of historiography—were, typically, deeply influenced by Western ideas and in many cases by study in Japan, Europe, or the United States.

The movement for a new history, although it had earlier beginnings, may best be seen in the context of the May Fourth Movement of 1919, which was basically a movement in search of a new Chinese culture adapted to the needs of a modern society. In the intellectual ferment of Peking in the 1920s, ideas and programs were vigorously discussed. Western ideas from Diderot to Dewey (and from Plato to Lenin) found their champions and interpreters. Historians, like other intellectuals, argued the great issues: Why had the Chinese order weakened and fallen victim to Western imperialism? What should be the ingredients of a modern Chinese civilization, and how could this develop in the midst of political chaos and continuing foreign pressures? What elements from the Chinese past could be used as explanations of China's present and as guides to its future? And which of these elements might be worked into the fabric of a new Chinese culture?

Although there were last-ditch defenders of the older scholarly traditions, the net effects of these controversies on historiography were revolutionary. The classics ceased to be regarded as sacred and were rigorously re-examined for authenticity and credibility as historical documents; "heterodox"

works—Taoist, Buddhist, and others—were reappraised for their historical and philosophic content; the vast range of popular stories, novels, dramas, and other works disdained by the older literati as "vulgar" were seriously studied for the light they might shed on China's social past; field-work techniques from the West were put to use in the study of village life, popular cults, and folklore, and the findings were used to further understanding of traditional popular culture. The comparative method was introduced, and the age-old habit of regarding everything Chinese as *sui generis* was broken. The moral–political emphasis of traditional history was challenged from every side, and materials were collected, regrouped, and studied for the light they might shed on social and economic history or the history of material culture and the arts. Archeology, although underfinanced, produced rich new finds and new ways of understanding the life of the past from surviving objects; analytical history based on stated hypotheses replaced the time-honored forms of compilation. Exact citations and footnotes began to replace the ancient method of piecing together passages from earlier works.

The publications of the new historians of the 1920s and early 1930s reflect all these changes. Research societies, with their quarterly bulletins and monograph series, were a typical medium of communication, and their publications reflect the effort to reorganize China's past. Thus, for example, there were new journals of economic history and geography, the journal and the monographs of the Society for Research in the History of Chinese Architecture, journals of Buddhist studies, and numerous journals of general historical studies, many of them the organs of new university departments and institutes. Semipopular magazines and newspaper supplements carried the findings of historians to a wider reading public. The great publishing houses of Shanghai (notably Chung-hwa and the Commercial Press) commissioned new works, organized series on the national past, and reprinted large collections of choice editions of the literary and historical works of the past. Punctuated editions and vernacular translations of classical works made the heritage more accessible to the young. Modern reference works, indexes, and concordances of traditional sources were developed. Despite the social and political instability of these years, the vitality of the new historical scholarship promised well for the future.

These prospects were dimmed, first by the Japanese attack of 1931 and then by the Japanese invasion of north China in the summer of 1937. Centers of learning were destroyed, and faculties and students fled to the southwest, where the universities continued valiantly to function, but in dire poverty and without libraries or other facilities for scholarly research. Despite these hardships, important works of scholarship were published in the years 1937–1945. The return of the universities to north China in 1945 was followed by catastrophic inflation and the onset of civil war. The Nationalist government was increasingly intolerant of dissent, and the atmosphere became steadily more tense and oppressive.

In the deepening crisis of the civil war, historians, like other intellectuals, had to make a choice: to remain in China under the Communist party or to flee with the Nationalists to Taiwan. The great majority remained. After 1949 there were two principal centers of historical studies: the People's Republic of China and the Republic of China on Taiwan.

Historical scholarship in the People's Republic is institutionalized in academic posts at the universities and in several of the institutes of the Academy of Sciences (Chung-kuo K'o-hsüeh Yüan). Voluminous publications of many kinds have appeared since 1949. Large documentary collections have been published, for instance, on the peasant revolts of Chinese history, on China's wars with the Western powers, on the beginnings of capitalism, on economic history, on reform movements. Excellent punctuated editions of traditional works and vernacular translations have been published on a large scale, and many of the important historical studies of the period from 1920 to 1949 have been reprinted, often with few changes other than a new preface. As the ground has been cleared for public construction, archeologists have conducted new excavations; publication has lagged behind discovery, but it is clear that the new finds now being assembled and classified in national and provincial museums will permit the rewriting of much of China's history.

Like other intellectuals, historians in the People's Republic have been subjected to "thought reform," so that their thinking and writing would wholly conform to the dominant orthodoxy. They have been constantly exhorted to perfect their theoretical grasp of Marxism, to use Marxist theories to bring forth a new history that will serve the new order. Each article may bring upon the historian the wrath of a party theorist who finds something in it that does not conform to the party's view of the past and future. The historian enjoys less prestige than the scientist and is far more exposed to ideological pressures. The older generation that came to maturity under the Republic have not maintained their earlier creativity, and Peking critics have complained that after ten years of the "New China" the younger historians are poorly trained in language and Chinese and Western history and that there are no satisfactory textbooks or general histories.

Since 1949 the problems and results of historical study have been laid down by the government and the party according to the doctrines of Marxism–Leninism–Stalinism and Maoism. The historian has been ordered to document and validate, not to explore and question. The long period from 770 B.C., or perhaps from 481 B.C., to 1840 has been authoritatively categorized as "feudal"—a necessary stage in the Marxist evolution of society. The only sustained attention given to this long period has been in the study of peasant rebellions, each of which, as Mao Tse-tung has said, "dealt a blow to the existing feudal regime and more or less furthered the development of the social productive forces." Mao Tse-tung has also prescribed the study of the "sprouts of capitalism," for it is his thesis that China would herself have progressed from "feudalism" to her own "capitalism" if it had not been for the intrusion of foreign imperialism. The discussion of this thesis has produced polemics, but it has also led to the publication of important historical documents and a few usable monographs. Modern history from 1840 to 1919 is characterized as semifeudal and semicolonial, and much effort has been expended on documenting imperialist aggressions and on attempting to periodize these years in terms of their "contradictions," changes in the "mode of production," and so on. The concentration on universal Marxist determinants has, by depriving China of a distinctive past, come into conflict with the intense nationalism of the People's Republic. Recently there have been efforts to re-examine the key figures of Chinese history rather than to restrict historical emphasis to peasant rebels and impersonal social forces. This is at least a step toward the re-creation of a distinctive Chinese history. In general, however, dogmatic concerns have made sterile the historical studies since 1949; indeed, one noted Peking historian exclaimed in 1957 that they had brought historiography to "the brink of death."

On Taiwan, the government re-established the Academia Sinica, which now has its old Institute of History and Philology and a new Institute of Modern History. National Taiwan University has a history faculty, as do the smaller colleges on the island. Considerable collections of rare books, archeological materials, government archives, and works of art were brought from the mainland.

There has been a steady output of documentary collections, notably on the history of the nineteenth and the early twentieth centuries. Some of the Academia Sinica's earlier serials have been resumed, and the output of historical monographs has been considerable. Yet the historical community on Taiwan is small and impoverished; historians are sensitive to their insularity and the garrison-state atmosphere around them. It is not surprising that no major works of synthesis and interpretation have appeared on Taiwan.

The present is indeed one of the low points in the long history of Chinese historiography. Meanwhile, scholars in Japan, Europe, and the United States—many of them of Chinese birth—are in a position to push forward in an atmosphere of freedom toward new understandings of the Chinese past.

ARTHUR F. WRIGHT

[*See also* CHINESE SOCIETY *and* CHINESE POLITICAL THOUGHT.]

### BIBLIOGRAPHY

BEASLEY, WILLIAM G.; and PULLEYBLANK, E. G. (editors) 1961 *Historians of China and Japan.* University of London, School of Oriental and African Studies, Historical Writing on the Peoples of Asia, Vol. 3. London and New York: Oxford Univ. Press.

BIELENSTEIN, HANS 1953 Historiography. Pages 9–81 in Hans Bielenstein, *The Restoration of the Han Dynasty; With Prolegomena on the Historiography of the Hou Han Shu.* Stockholm: No publisher given.

GARDNER, CHARLES S. (1938) 1961 *Chinese Traditional Historiography.* Harvard Historical Monograph No. 11. Cambridge, Mass.: Harvard Univ. Press.

NIVISON, DAVID S. 1966 *The Life and Thought of Chang Hsüeh-ch'eng: 1738–1801.* Stanford Studies in the Civilization of Eastern Asia. Stanford (Calif.) Univ. Press.

WATSON, BURTON D. 1958 *Ssu-ma Ch'ien, Grand Historian of China.* New York: Columbia Univ. Press.

WRIGHT, ARTHUR F. 1963 On the Uses of Generalization in the Study of Chinese History. Pages 36–58 in Louis R. Gottschalk (editor). *Generalization in the Writing of History.* A report of the Committee on Historical Analysis of the Social Science Research Council. Univ. of Chicago Press.

## IV
### ISLAMIC HISTORIOGRAPHY

Islamic historiography is the historical literature written by adherents of the various branches of the religion of Islam. Although much of it is written in Arabic, a great deal has appeared in other languages employed by Muslims; Persian (beginning with the tenth century) and Turkish (from the sixteenth century onward) were used intensively for the writing of histories. Various minorities living under Muslim domination, especially the Eastern Christian denominations, produced historical works bearing a close resemblance to their Islamic counterparts, but these will not be considered here. On the other hand, the rapidly growing number of historical works written by Muslims in our time must not be excluded, even if the old forms and techniques have been abandoned, together with most of the values that were characteristic of Islamic historiography from medieval times well into the nineteenth century.

**Origins and early beginnings.** Pre-Islamic Arabs took a keen interest in genealogy and in major events affecting tribal politics, but the memory of the past was transmitted orally. In the Byzantine and Persian territories conquered by the Muslims during the first half of the seventh century, historiographical traditions of long standing were alive, if not exactly flourishing. In these areas, personal contacts between Muslims and learned non-Muslims or converts seem to have set in motion a certain minor impetus toward the creation of Muslim historical writing.

The principal motivation behind the subsequent tremendous development of this historical writing lies in the conception of Islam as a historical religion. The Prophet Muḥammad (ca. 570–632) saw himself as the culmination and fulfillment of a historical process that started with the beginning of the world in time. Through a chain of divinely ordained messengers (principally, the great figures of Judaism and Christianity), of whom he was the last, this process was leading toward a clearly foreseeable end of the world. Moreover, Muḥammad saw himself as a religiosocial reformer fulfilling prophecies and giving directions for the future. Thus, he provided the outline on a vast historical canvas that was left to be filled in and interpreted by the historian. There was another aspect of the awareness of history fostered by the Prophet. Historical precedent, in all its essential manifestations, was very important in the development of Islamic civilization. From the outset, and increasingly so with the passing of time, political, legal, religious, and scholarly institutions, as well as moral ideas and values, were considered as deriving their ultimate authority from the events of early Islam and the actions and behavior of the early Muslims. The historical truth and significance of these events and actions required constant reaffirmation, confirmation, and re-evaluation. This sharpened historical consciousness and was responsible for a great amount of historical research and writing.

Although there is no doubt as to the motivation that made Islamic historiography an inevitability, the mechanisms through which this took place are much harder to trace. The early authorities responsible for the historical information reported in later writings are represented as having transmitted the material orally. This may be true, but it is more likely that there existed a method of oral transmission that was supplemented by unpublished written notes that were the reporters' personal *aide-mémoires*. In fact, there seems to have been no regular procedure for the orderly publication of works written in Arabic until the end of the seventh century. The subsequent introduction of paper, at about 750, or the beginning of the 'Abbâsid dynasty, made possible a literary activity that in the quantity of production was something not seen before in the Mediterranean world. However, it would seem that relatively few works that could be called histories were written, and they almost certainly enjoyed no wide circulation. Earlier Muslim historical works have largely been lost because of the absence of institutions of publication and durable writing materials and also, perhaps, because of the dynastic change that made works written under the Umayyads (660–750) largely unacceptable. 'Urwah b. az-Zubayr (ca. 650–711), a member of the Muslim elite, is credited with the composition of the book *Raids of the Prophets*. In the generation following 'Urwah, al-Zuhrî (ca. 670–740) is said to have written a work on "the genealogy of his people." He also wrote, apparently for his personal use, on the length of the reigns of the caliphs. From the work of a third early authority, Mûsâ b. 'Uqbah (d. 758/ 759), a brief fragment, not entirely historical in character, has come down to us. The earliest large-scale work that is preserved, although only in later recensions, is the biography of the Prophet (*Sîrah*, "Way of Life") by Ibn Isḥâq (ca. 704–767). It deals with the history of pre-Islamic Arabia and with all the details and events of the Prophet's life. The same author is also credited with a history of the caliphs. From the evidence now at our disposal, we may conclude that by around 700 historical research, focused on the life of Muḥammad, began to serve the political and social needs of the new religion. It also seems certain that most of the formal elements of later historical writing were to some degree already present at that time.

**Forms and contents of historical works.** The importance of form in literary presentation is particularly noticeable in Islamic historiography, which has, for better or for worse, always remained in bondage to the forms it first developed. Pre-Islamic Arab tradition had already stressed the concrete "factual" element in history, isolated from

its environment and as much as possible unmodified by human thought processes. Thus, simple statements, isolated events, superficial, if colorful, characterizations, put next to each other and left without any explicit elaboration of their inner or causal connections, came to determine the basic appearance of Muslim history books. Historical truth, like religious truth, was considered ensured by the unimpeachable character of the succession of men through whom a given item of information was transmitted, the so-called chain of transmitters or *isnâd*. Even if the historian did not mention these chains of authorities for all the individual items he reported (and many historians did not), the concept of each historical fact possessing a great, even absolute, degree of autonomy was strengthened. The effects have been felt throughout all Muslim historical writing, which can be characterized as fundamentally episodic, no matter how long and detailed and skillfully narrated the individual episode.

*Annalistic histories.* Larger units for organizing the historical material were soon needed to hold together the constantly growing volume of data. They were readily found in the proven principles of dynastic arrangement according to the reigns of successive rulers and in annalistic arrangement according to the years of the era. The era of the *hijrah* was introduced about the year 638, and Muslim historians were fortunate compared to all their predecessors inasmuch as they were able, from the outset, to rely upon a continuous, unambiguous, and generally accepted chronology. The strictly annalistic arrangement was thought particularly suitable to historical presentation. It was also easily combined with other arrangements, such as that according to reigns; and it fitted in well with the fragmented episodic approach and helped to perpetuate it. Systematically practiced, it was rarely interrupted even to the extent of the consecutive reporting of events that extended over several years. It was especially useful in that it facilitated the continuation of standard histories in the form of supplements often called *dhayl* ("tail") or some variant. Such continuations might be independent works containing only new material, or they might repeat the earlier material, shortening the narrative for the older period and becoming more and more detailed as they approach the actual time of writing. Authors then would systematically date events according to the month and the day and list even trivial news. The oldest preserved, at least in part, annalistic histories in Arabic were written by Khalîfah b. Khayyâṭ in the first half of the ninth century and by Ya'qûb b. Sufyân in the second half of the same century. The multivolume standard work of Muslim annalistic historiography, which decisively influenced its future course, was written by aṭ-Ṭabarî (d. 923).

*Biographies.* Of the areas of study cultivated by the Muslim historians, the most important was biography. This was due not so much to the often expressed fact that history is the record of man and his actions, but rather to the fact that Muslim historiography, in its early beginnings, was concerned with the story of the life of a great individual, the Prophet Muḥammad, and with the circumstances surrounding the activities of the early Muslims. It then became necessary to scrutinize the lives of all those connected in any way with Muslim law and religion and to learn the dates of their birth and their death, their local affiliations, their teachers and disciples, their moral character, and their works and activities. Depending on the importance attached to a given individual, biographies could at times grow into large volumes while still remaining restricted, by and large, to these topics. The majority of biographies were brief and were entered early, in the form of obituaries of notable persons, into annalistic histories. Biographies dealing with representatives of certain scholarly categories were collected in special works, and biographies of religious scholars constituted the main contents of the large, theologically oriented segment of local historiography.

In order to facilitate reference, biographies were grouped in "classes" (ṭabaqah, plural ṭabaqât) comprising those who had died in approximately the same period. This somewhat clumsy arrangement served quite well the need of religious scholars to judge the genuineness and reliability of a chain of transmitters. However, as the number of biographees increased, an alphabetical arrangement was instituted. Beginning with the tenth century, alphabetization thus became the preferred method of arrangement in collections of biographies, although the ṭabaqât system continued to be used. It must be noted that the merchants, military men, government officials who were not at the same time religious scholars, scholars in the nonreligious disciplines, poets, and so on were originally not the object of any systematic biographical research. Factual information was often plentiful but always scattered. Much of it would have been lost if some later Muslim authors had not put together the scattered information and produced excellent biographical collections dealing with some of these groups, such as the littérateurs treated by Yâqût (d. 1229) in his *Irshâd al-arîb*

*ilâ ma'rifat al-adîb*, the physicians collected in the great work on the history of medicine by Ibn Abî Uṣaybi'ah (d. 1270), entitled *'Uyûn al-anbâ' fî ṭabaqât al-aṭibbâ'*, or the fine choice of biographies of illustrious men presented by Ibn Khallikân (d. 1282) in his *Wafayât al-a'yân*.

*General histories.* Political history, restricted to the administrative and military exploits of rulers and statesmen, was the essential raw material for most Muslim historical writing. Monographs on particular events or periods were written in great profusion; in fact, the early ninth-century historians, most of whose works are known to us only by title, wrote copiously on politically significant individual events. Comprehensive world histories, usually traced from the creation of the world or from the coming of Islam to the times of their particular authors, also met with success. They were universal only in the Muslim sense, not admitting more than a rather limited amount of set data from pre-Islamic times and largely insensitive to non-Muslim history, even where it impinged upon Muslim affairs. The assimilation of the Hellenistic heritage, and with it the development of a taste for cultural history, broadened the horizons of historiography. In the late ninth century, political history combined with intellectual history to touch on all the noteworthy and accessible features of the various civilizations then known. This trend produced such outstanding works as the *History* by al-Ya'qûbî and the series of publications by al-Mas'ûdî (d. 945/946), among them the preserved *Murûj adh-dhahab*. It continued to echo weakly in the works of much later periods. Interest in the contemporary or near-contemporary non-Muslim world remained nevertheless subdued. While the scholarly curiosity of historians welcomed "strange" information, they undertook no systematic search for it. Measured against the enormous mass of Muslim historical writing, references to events that took place outside the Muslim world are few indeed. Al-Mas'ûdî, for instance, included a list of the kings of the Franks (see Maqbul Ahmad 1960, pp. 7–10). Embassies from abroad occasionally provided an opening for referring to events on the international scene. Historians of the time of the Crusades were well aware of cultural and political differences, but in their political and military analysis they did not venture beyond the borders of Islam. In central Asia, the singular circumstances created by the Mongol Empire, with its tentacles stretching far outside the old Muslim world, produced the statesman and historian Rashîd-ad-dîn Faḍlallâh (d. 1318). His *General History* (*Jāmi' at-tawārikh*), written in Persian, is probably the first genuine universal history of Islam. The local historiography of cities and regions was also persistently cultivated. It emphasized political and religious history but also included topographical description and antiquarian data. As might be expected, data on social, economic, and financial history are incidental to most historical writing in Islam and, therefore, comparatively scarce. Some annalistic histories give us a rather intimate view of medieval urban life with its crimes, suicides, recurrent inflation, and other social problems.

**Historians.** For a very large and influential part of its production, Islamic historiography is indebted to scholars trained in the religious studies who earned their living by virtue of this training but whose literary activities included the writing of histories. For example, al-Bukhârî (d. 870), the author of the most authoritative collection of Prophetic traditions, wrote several collections of terse biographies of religious authorities. He entitled each of these works *History*, thus establishing himself in Muslim consciousness as a historian. From the eleventh century on, a great many historians were religious scholars who held positions in the judiciary, in the civilian branch of the political administration, and in the madrasahs (mosque schools), all of them depending on the religious establishment for their livelihood.

*Court historians.* In Islamic countries, wherever ambitious and powerful rulers were to be found, history was the "royal science" par excellence, which kings, courtiers, and wazirs, as well as the tutors of princes, were expected to master. Caliphs and sultans often ordered officials to set down the history of their reign or dynasty. It may have happened even more frequently that historical works were written for presentation to the ruler in the hope of a reward or preferment. The professional court historian became an established fixture at certain courts. For example, the courts of the later dynasties in Persia and the Ottoman Empire provided a particularly favorable atmosphere for historical studies. However, it would hardly be correct to speak of a clearly defined Muslim court historiography. Regardless of the position and the motivation of these writers, their works as a rule remained individualistic efforts. The personalities of their authors can be glimpsed even through the curtain of flattery and obsequious verbosity that was often extremely dense.

The term "court historian" would also hardly be the appropriate designation for government officials who, because of their proximity to the seats of power where they were able to witness important events in the making, wrote historical works. Their number was not inconsiderable, and to them we owe some of the best historical works produced in Islam. Late tenth-century historians such as Miskawayh (d. 1030) and Hilâl aṣ-Ṣâbi' (d. 1036) were government officials who not only possessed an inside knowledge of political affairs (the family of aṣ-Ṣâbi' had served in government for generations) but were also accomplished writers and well versed in philosophy and the secular sciences. All of this is reflected in the quality of their works and in their historical insight. The work of 'Imâd-ad-dîn al-Iṣfahânî (d. 1201) is an outstanding example of historical memoirs written by a high official who consulted documents and diaries. In particular, his *Barq ash-Sha'mî* deserves high praise as representing the apogee of diplomatic historiography in Islam.

*Amateur historians.* 'Imâd al-Iṣfahânî and rulers who wrote historical works and memoirs may be called amateur historians. Most of the numerous genealogical works were written privately by men who frequently were members of the only true Muslim nobility, the descendants of 'Alî. In general, quite a few historical works were probably produced as labors of love, out of reverence for the importance of history and in recognition of the need for preserving an adequate historical record.

*Professional historians.* In exceptional cases, it appears that an author might be paid for writing historical works on the basis of copies sold through booksellers; but in any case, we may safely surmise that this was not sufficient to live on. The professional historian, in the modern sense, could hardly have existed in the medieval Muslim environment. History was not included in the curriculum of the madrasahs, although lectures on historical topics were occasionally given by professors employed and paid for teaching other subjects. However, there were men who spent their lives producing historical works and who came to consider themselves, and to be considered by Muslim tradition, as historians, for example, al-Mas'ûdî and, during the Mamlûk period in Egypt, when interest in history ran high, al-Maqrîzî (d. 1442) and many others like him.

**Purpose and methodology of Muslim historiography.** Muslim historians were in the habit of introducing their works with statements concerning the purpose of historical writing (for a number of these statements collected by as-Sakhâwî, see Rosenthal 1952, pp. 219 ff.). The ideas expressed in this connection soon became standardized and did not possess any individual ring. This fact itself is significant in that it shows the general and unquestioned acceptance of their validity. These statements expressed the belief that history is useful; it teaches by both negative and positive examples, that is, it teaches everybody how to handle his own affairs in this fleeting world and, most importantly, it teaches political leaders how to govern properly. Furthermore, history is entertaining; it provides amusing, yet thoughtful, relaxation from more exacting intellectual tasks. And history is instructive and edifying as a handmaiden of religion, proving the truth of Islam and the correctness of the view of the world expounded by it. On the surface, this last point may seem to have been raised merely in order to provide the greatly needed excuse for the waste of time assumed to be involved in any occupation with secular subjects. In reality, it touches on the very meaning of historiography as a part of Muslim civilization. Only as an integral component of the religiously determined structure of the world and society could the study of history be meaningful in Islam.

The idea of history as a powerful weapon in political and ideological struggles does not seem to have been entertained openly or commonly by Muslim historians. On occasion, they were conscious of the fact that their work was used to serve the purpose of exalting an individual or of fortifying the political aspirations of a ruling house. In some instances, minutely detailed modern research has been able to uncover concealed political tendencies or a purposeful manipulation of the evidence in historical writings. However, Muslim historians considered themselves as the custodians and transmitters of facts that could not be altered and neither required nor admitted of interpretation. The historian's proper activities were restricted to reporting, shortening, collecting different recensions of, and, perhaps, retelling the information provided by the available sources.

This view largely determined the method of historical research. The historian's main task was setting down what had actually happened, and his main problem was ascertaining the truth of his information, whether it came to him orally or through written sources. Truth was understood, above all, as verification of the presumption that an item of information was derived from someone in a position to know. All history being in a sense contemporary history, personal observation was the real basis of historical knowledge and the best assurance of historical truth. For the rest, the elaborate system developed by scholars of the science of Prophetic traditions, a system for ascertaining the genuineness of these traditions, came to be considered as applicable also to historical research. Of

necessity, written histories were granted evidential authority. Archival research and the study of inscriptions, coins, and similar historical evidence were only sporadically practiced. A full discussion of the methodology of medieval Muslim historiography is preserved in a work written in Arabic by a Persian scholar, Muḥammad b. Ibrâhîm al-Îjî, who wrote in 1381–1382 and whose work is thus the oldest extensive treatise on the subject known so far. On a less theoretical level, comprehensive works on Islamic historiography, its methods, its problems, and its history were composed in Egypt in the following century by al-Kâfiyajî (d. 1474), who wrote in 1463, and, following him, by as-Sakhâwî (d. 1497), who wrote in 1492.

**Philosophy and sociology of history.**    The Islamic historians' own views regarding the meaning of history are implied in their works and spelled out in the methodological writings just mentioned. They were convinced that history was the chosen instrument of God for the gradual improvement of mankind and for man's preparation for the final reckoning at the inevitable end of the world. The coming of Muḥammad and Islam was viewed as the great turning point of world history, at which, for the first time, the purpose of history revealed itself clearly and history became a comprehensible reality. From then on, control of history's progress was within the reach of human beings, if—and that remained the great question—they followed the comprehensive plan for the good life laid down, for both the individual and society, in the religious injunctions of Islam. While there was no automatic sin-and-retribution mechanism operative in history, the rulers at least were judged by their compliance or noncompliance, according to the historian's sources of information, with Islamic moral norms. There were, however, a few exceptional historians who, while not denying the validity of Islamic theology, tried to understand history as a purely human social phenomenon. This approach ran counter to the major premises of the Muslim world view and was, therefore, always slightly suspect. It was hinted at by Miskawsyh when, in his large history entitled *The Experiences of the Nations*, he denied that events caused by the interference of the supernatural in history, such as the events connected with the life of the Prophet, could provide a useful experience for students of history. Eventually, the northwest African Ibn Khaldūn (d. 1406), writing in 1377, constructed a coherent system of the historical process in purely human terms and devoted to its exposition the famous *Muqaddimah* ("Introduction") of his large universal history, *Kitâb al-'Ibar*. He explained human society as depending on material and psychological forces, which were described by him in detail; and he defined history in terms of a cyclic motion (with a slight, but continuous, forward movement) of growth and decay within the various forms of human associations. [*See the biography of* IBN KHALDŪN.]

**Contemporary Muslim historiography.** The old forms of historical writing have persisted until recent times, especially in the more shielded regions of the Muslim world. At the time of the first true clash of Islam with the modern world, precipitated by Napoleon's Egyptian campaign, it was still possible for an important work of the annalistic type to be produced by a man of genuine historical perception, the Egyptian al-Jabartî (d. 1826?). During the nineteenth century, there were a few Arabic translations of then popular Western historical works. The study of certain aspects of world history not directly affecting the Muslim countries began to attract some limited interest, especially on the educational level. To this day, it can fairly be said that the interest in all non-Islamic history has remained limited, and nothing of first-rate importance appears to have been produced in the field. On the other hand, from the beginning of the twentieth century and increasingly accelerated by the political developments that took place in the wake of World War II, the meaning of history and the practice of historiography as it affects Muslim life has become a major concern everywhere in Muslim countries. Some have contended, for example, that the communal conflict between Muslims and Hindus preceding the partition of India was largely the result of the wrong teaching of history and, therefore, amenable to redirection through the efforts of historians (see S. Nadvi, in Philips 1961, p. 493). Others have held that Muslim history is unable to give any guidance for the solution of present-day problems and remains better forgotten and disregarded.

Popular feeling tends to glorify the study of the great Muslim past as an inexhaustible source for the building of national morale and the strengthening of nationalist aspirations. This use of history is fostered by writers devoting their literary talents to historical themes, writers such as Muḥammad Ḥusayn Haykal and Maḥmûd 'Abbâs al-'Aqqâd. Motion pictures and, to a lesser degree, stage plays effectively exploit historical themes (see Landau 1958, pp. 114 ff., 198 f.). More recently, numerous Muslim historians with Western training in scholarship and methodology have begun to publish, in their various languages, serious and often important historical works as well as biographical, social, and economic studies on past Muslim history.

Archival studies are getting underway—particularly in Turkey, where much of the preserved material is concentrated. The publication of medieval historical texts is being continued at an accelerated pace with the maintenance of, generally speaking, satisfactory standards in editing technique.

The great pre-Islamic past of the Muslim countries inspired different political ideologies and movements based on historical speculation. These had their greatest efflorescence between 1920 and 1945. At present, the excavation, conservation, and study of the archeological remains of the pre-Islamic and the Islamic past are competently cultivated nearly everywhere.

FRANZ ROSENTHAL

[*See also* ISLAM.]

### BIBLIOGRAPHY

*The bibliography is restricted to works written in west European languages. The most convenient sources of information on contemporary Islamic historiography are Lewis & Holt 1962 and Philips 1961; other works on this subject are Ayalon 1960; Chejne 1960 and 1963; Haddad 1961; Hourani 1962; Inalcik 1953; Key 1954; and Von Grunebaum 1962.*

#### GENERAL

ABBOTT, NABIA 1957 *Studies in Arabic Literary Papyri.* Volume 1: Historical Texts. Univ. of Chicago Press.

AYALON, DAVID 1960 The Historian al-Jabartī and His Background. London, University of, School of Oriental and African Studies, *Bulletin* 23:217–249.

BABINGER, FRANZ 1927 *Die Geschichtsschreiber der Osmanen und ihre Werke.* Leipzig: Harrassowitz.

BROCKELMANN, CARL 1937–1949 *Geschichte der arabischen Litteratur.* 5 vols. Leiden (Netherlands): Brill.

CHEJNE, ANWAR G. 1960 The Use of History by Modern Arab Writers. *Middle East Journal* 14:382–396.

CHEJNE, ANWAR G. 1963 Intellectual Revival in the Arab World: An Introduction. *Islamic Studies* (Karachi) 2:413–437.

FISCHEL, WALTER J. 1967 *Ibn Khaldūn in Egypt; His Public Functions and His Historical Research (1382–1406): An Essay in Islamic Historiography.* Berkeley: Univ. of California Press.

GIBB, HAMILTON A. R. 1962 *Studies on the Civilization of Islam.* Boston: Beacon.

HADDAD, GEORGE M. 1961 Modern Arab Historians and World History. *Muslim World* 51:37–43.

HARDY, P. 1960 *Historians of Medieval India: Studies in Indo–Muslim Historical Writing.* London: Luzac.

HOURANI, ALBERT H. 1962 *Arab Thought in the Liberal Age: 1798–1939.* New York: Oxford Univ. Press. → See especially pages 87 and 333 ff.

INALCIK, HALIL 1953 Some Remarks on the Study of History in Islamic Countries. *Middle East Journal* 7:451–455.

KEY, KERIM K. 1954 *An Outline of Modern Turkish Historiography.* Istanbul: Kâğit ve Basım Isleri.

LANDAU, JACOB M. 1958 *Studies in the Arab Theater and Cinema.* Philadelphia: Univ. of Pennsylvania Press.

LEWIS, BERNARD; and HOLT, P. M. (editors) 1962 *Historians of the Middle East.* Oxford Univ. Press.

MAQBUL AHMAD, S. (editor) 1960 *Al-Mas'ûdî Millenary Commemoration Volume.* Algiers: Aligarh Univ., Institute of Islamic Studies. → See especially pages 7–10, written by Bernard Lewis.

PHILIPS, CYRIL H. (editor) 1961 *Historians of India, Pakistan and Ceylon.* University of London, School of Oriental and African Studies, Historical Writing on the Peoples of Asia, Vol. 1. New York: Oxford Univ. Press.

ROSENTHAL, FRANZ 1952 *A History of Muslim Historiography.* Leiden: Brill. → Includes translations of the works of al-Kâfiyajî and as-Sakhâwî.

SAUVAGET, JEAN; and CAHEN, CLAUDE (1943) 1965 *Introduction to the History of the Muslim East.* Berkeley and Los Angeles: Univ. of California Press. → First published in French.

STOREY, CHARLES A. 1935–1953 *Persian Literature: A Bio–Bibliographical Survey.* London: Luzac.

VON GRUNEBAUM, GUSTAVE E. (1962) 1964 *Modern Islam: The Search for Cultural Identity.* New York: Vintage.

TRANSLATIONS OF HISTORICAL WORKS

AL-BALÂDHÛRÎ *Il Califfo Mu'âwiya I.* Translated by Olga Pinto and Giorgio Levi Della Vida. Rome: Bardi, 1938. → A translation of a chapter from al-Balâdhûrî's *Ansâb.*

AL-BALÂDHÛRÎ *The Origins of the Islamic State, Being a Translation From the Arabic, Accompanied With Annotations, Geographic and Historical Notes of the* Kitāb futūḥ al-buldān. 2 vols. in 3. Translated by Philip K. Hitti. New York: Columbia Univ. Press, 1927–1958.

AL-SÛLI *Akhbâr ar-Râdî billâh wa'l-Mutaqqî billâh (Histoire de la dynastie abbaside de 322 à 333/934 à 944).* Translated from the Arabic by Marius Canard. Institut d'Études Orientales de la Faculté des Lettres d'Alger, Publications 10, 12. Algiers: Carbonel, 1946–1950.

AṬ-ṬABARÎ *The Reign of al-Mu'taṣim (833–842).* Translated and annotated by Elma Marin. American Oriental Series, Vol. 35. New Haven: American Oriental Society, 1951.

IBN HISHĀM *The Life of Muhammad.* A translation of Ibn Hishâm's adaptation of Ibn Isḥâq's *Sīrat rasūl Allāh,* with introduction and notes by A. Guillaume. London and New York: Oxford Univ. Press, 1955.

IBN KHALDŪN (1375–1382) 1958 *The Muqaddimah: An Introduction to History.* 3 vols. Translated by Franz Rosenthal. New York: Pantheon Books. → Contains a selected bibliography by Walter J. Fischel.

IBN ṢAṢRĀ *A Chronicle of Damascus 1389–1397.* 2 vols. Translated, edited, and annotated by William M. Brinner. Berkeley and Los Angeles: Univ. of California Press, 1963. → Volume 1 is the English translation; Volume 2 is the original Arabic text.

JOVEYNÎ *The History of the World Conqueror.* 2 vols. Translated from the text of Mirza Muhammad Qazvini by John A. Boyle. Cambridge, Mass.: Harvard Univ. Press, 1958. → A translation of *Tā'rīkh-i-Jahân-gushâ.*

MISKAWSYH *Tajârib al-umam: And Excerpts From Other Historians of His Time.* Edited by H. F. Amedroz. Volumes 1–2 in H. F. Amedroz and David S. Margoliouth, *The Eclipse of the Abbasid Caliphate.* 7 vols. Oxford: Blackwell, 1920–1921. → Volumes 4–5 are the English translation, by D. S. Margoliouth, of Volumes 1–2.

NARSHAKHÎ *The History of Bukhara.* Translated by Richard N. Frye from a Persian abridgment of the Arabic original. Cambridge, Mass.: Mediaeval Academy of America, 1954.

YŪSUF IBN TAGHRĪ-BIRDĪ *History of Egypt: 1382–1469 A.D.* Translated by William Popper. Parts 1–7 and indexes. Berkeley and Los Angeles: Univ. of California Press, 1954–1960. → First published as *an-Nujûm az-zâhirah.*

V

## JAPANESE HISTORIOGRAPHY

The Japanese historiographical genius has extended less to the fashioning of grand systems of interpretation than to the assiduous working out of domestic history. Of all national histories outside the Western world, none has been revealed in such precise and abundant detail or in such a variety of interpretive forms as that of Japan. The work of Japanese historians, particularly in the last century, has been both prolific and comprehensive. And while the events of Japanese history have yet to find a prominent place in the main body of world historiography, the reverse condition, whereby Japanese history is treated in world context, has been carried forward in impressive fashion by the Japanese. Today every segment of Japanese history is served by the professional archivist, the scholarly monographer, and the interpretive synthesizer, alive to modern currents of historical philosophy and methodology.

History is one of the most popular academic fields in Japan today. The standard Japanese *Publisher's Annual* for 1964 lists 1,249 single titles under history. Each of Japan's more than 230 universities has its department of history, often in more than one faculty. A recent handbook of historical research lists 75 libraries and archival repositories worthy of general note. The same handbook lists 56 scholarly serials published by national historical associations and 40 by societies of primarily local importance.

While Japan does not have a central national archives, the Historiographical Institute of Tokyo University serves somewhat in this capacity, and in addition, numerous private and government libraries preserve or collect materials on a large scale. Printed archival collections are abundantly available. The Historiographical Institute alone has published over 350 weighty volumes of sources, while the standard reprinting of premodern Japanese histories runs to more than sixty volumes. The aspiring Japanese historian has at his command the product of four generations of modern historical scholarship and a full reference shelf of encyclopedias and dictionaries on every major subject from bibliography to religion. For stimulus to his thinking he may turn to volumes on the meaning of history by notable Japanese historians or to translations of standard works by Croce, Weber, Marx, Toynbee, Freud, or Parsons.

## Japanese use of history

History is more than a popular field well served by its specialists; history is, and has been, important to the Japanese people in their persistent search for their own identity and for a sense of order in the world about them. Japanese historians have been eclectic in the theories to which they have subscribed but remarkably consistent in the objectives that they have pursued. Since the eighth century, Japanese historians have looked to history to explain the political and moral order. This search has been served by a variety of world views and historiographical traditions just as it has had to respond to the constantly shifting conditions of Japan's domestic politics and world position. The earliest and most original view of history adopted by the Japanese grew out of an age when Japan existed in comparative isolation from China and the dominant culture of the continent. It conceived of a world with Japan at the center, the proud inheritor of an ideal order built around the imperial house and protected by the native (Shinto) deities. This world view was kept alive into modern times as the Japanese clung to various tokens of their imagined cultural or racial superiority. But Japanese ethnocentrism was seldom free of competition from other, more widely based systems, and by the sixth century both Confucianism and Buddhism were challenging the claims of Shinto.

By medieval times, while not openly admitting the moral superiority of China or India, Japanese historians had taken to explaining causation in political affairs by reference to Confucian conceptions of proper or improper conduct or to Buddhist interpretations of retribution for good and evil. Japan's confrontation with Western civilization was historiographically even more traumatic, for it not only presented Japan with a multiplicity of theories of historical explanation, but also imposed upon her a view of the world order that placed the West at the center of the human drama and made the Judaeo–Christian tradition the driving force in human progress.

Japanese historical writing, reacting to these several pressures, has tended to be assimilative in concept and methodology. In strictly technical terms it has demonstrated a growing sophistication in its capacity to deal with basic facts and causal phenomena. And this cumulative quality of Japanese historiography—its constant increase in historical detachment and critical judgment and its steady improvement in basic techniques—is one of its most impressive over-all features. On the other hand, the search for order and status has proved continually illusive. The questions asked by every Japanese—who are we? what distinguishes us as a people and culture? what is our place in the world order?—remain a source of uncertainty even today; and it is this uncertainty that has kept Japanese historiography oscillating between the extremes of nationalism and universalism.

The Japanese have never been ones to accept a secondary position in the world gracefully. Historiography in modern Japan has kept pace with the national desire to achieve world prominence. History and nation, in fact, have been closely linked. For history has been drawn into the service of the state, either to provide the people with a crucial sense of continuity with their traditional values or as a means of justifying the revolutionary changes endorsed by a government intent upon modern reform. Throughout most of the last century, history has seemed inevitably to teach the lesson of Japan's inferiority to the more enlightened peoples of the West. Only once did the Japanese people appear to have it in their power to turn history in their favor so that their private view of the world could be extended into a universal vision. During the era of continental expansion, the march of Japanese armies seemed on the verge of making truth out of the propagandist's claim that the goal of world history was to draw mankind under the benevolent rule of the Japanese emperor. The discrediting of that claim gave back to the Japanese historian the task of finding a realistic position for Japanese history in an objectively conceived world environment. The task has not been easy.

## Early historical writing

Japan's earliest extant histories, the *Kojiki* (A.D. 712; "Record of Ancient Matters") and the *Nihon shoki* (A.D. 720; "Chronicle of Japan"), were both products of the desire of the Japanese ruling house to "clarify the political order" and to produce a national chronicle comparable to those that added luster to the dynasties of China. The *Kojiki* is a narrative of the Japanese people from the "age of the gods" through the establishment of the Yamato hegemony to the end of the reign of Empress Suiko in A.D. 628. The purpose of the work is to display the background of the Yamato house and to document the dependent status of various noble lines. While the sources of the *Kojiki* are obscure, and hence its historiographical conceptions difficult to date, it is safe to assume that it exemplifies the earliest recorded views of the Japanese people regarding themselves and their past. The work is notable for its matter-of-fact treatment of supernatural events, particularly its uncomplicated handling of the relationship between human society and the deities. The *Kojiki* contains no generalized myths of creation and no culture heroes. Nor does it depict the Japanese gods as active agents in the lives of mortals once the world of man was set down upon the Japanese islands. Rather, the story of creation begins with the first male and female deities, proceeds through generations of their offspring, and then by genealogical descent enters the age of man in Japan. In the human political world, power and status derived simply from the circumstances of lineal descent from particular ancestral deities. The imperial family established its claim to sovereignty by virtue of direct descent from Amaterasu, the Sun Goddess.

Because of its limited circulation, the *Kojiki* had little immediate influence on Japanese historians. Not until the eighteenth century, when nationalistic scholars found in its archaic contents the ingredients of an idealized society based on "pure Japanese" values, did it become the revered source of the Japanese view of history. For over a millennium, therefore, it was the *Nihon shoki* that had the reputation of being Japan's first history. The *Nihon shoki* had the advantage of being written in Chinese and being more closely based on Chinese models than was the *Kojiki*; it sought, in other words, to place Japanese history into a world that acknowledged the existence of China as the source of a Confucian world view, although it sought to maintain Japan's independent and competitive position in that world. More historiographically self-conscious than the writers of the *Kojiki*, the *Nihon shoki*'s authors attempted to assign dates to the amorphous events associated with the early generations of the imperial house and thus establish a chronology comparable to that of China. It was from this effort, using the Chinese theory of "great cycles," that the authors arrived at the controversial date 660 B.C. for the ascension of Jimmu, "the first emperor," a date that modern historians more properly place in the third or fourth century A.D.

The *Nihon shoki* and five succeeding official histories that chronicled the events of the imperial court down to 887 are known together as the *Rikkokushi* ("Six National Histories"). Although they constitute an attempt of the Japanese to write history in the Chinese official manner, they differ considerably from their models. The writer of history met in Japan conditions very different from those in China, for the Japanese dynasty had already established itself "in perpetuity," and the historian could have very little to say about its right to rule. As a consequence, the Japanese never fully adopted the premises of the Confucian moral order which made political power contingent on virtue but rather found ways of equating their own highly aristocratic social hierarchy to that of China by the assumption that the moral right to sovereignty followed the line of hereditary succession. In fact, as the Japanese imperial line continued unbroken for century after century, the Japanese began to turn the Confucian order to their advantage and to claim superiority in matters of government over the Chinese, who were constantly rebelling against their emperors.

The writing of official history lost its meaning in Japan once the imperial bureaucracy gave way to the direct rule of aristocratic houses and the emperor was pushed above politics to serve as a sacred legitimizer. By the tenth century the compilation of official annals had given way to the writing of private histories. The *monogatari* (narratives) and *kagami* (mirrors) exemplify a style of history that was as distinctive a product of the aristocratic society of the Heian court as the literary masterpiece, the "Tale of Genji." Written in Japanese, not Chinese, the new histories combined the intimacy of single authorship with the immediacy of narrative writing. The most famous of these, the *Ōkagami* ("Great Mirror"), combined a synthesis of Japanese history up to the eleventh century with an explanation of the rise of the Fujiwara family, which then dominated the court.

### The Middle Ages

By the twelfth century Japanese historical works were showing the influence of Buddhist concepts of karma and salvation. The immensely popular epic history of the war between the Minamoto and Taira, *Heike monogatari*, was written and recited chiefly for its didactic message. The writing of history generally passed into the hands of priests, who relied on Buddhist explanations for the rise and fall of family or individual fortunes. Their works were characteristically suffused with a sense of compassion for human suffering, sadness over the transience of life, and concern over the imminence of the age of decay. Works written from the point of view of the Buddhist establishment, therefore, looked at Japan from a viewpoint that played down worldly political orders in the face of the universality of the human condition. Visible power and circumstance were often depicted only to reveal the inevitability of decline. Yet even among the

Buddhists, a voice was raised which claimed Japan to be the center of the Buddhist world. Nichiren (1222–1282) militantly proclaimed Japan to be the land destined to bring the Buddhist faith to perfection.

In terms of domestic history, the rise of the military aristocracy and the creation of the shogunate (headquarters of the military hegemony) in 1192 added new dimensions to the historians' task of interpretation. Historians now had to explain not only the virtue of the imperial house but also the reason for the decline of the civil aristocracy and the ascendancy of military houses. Two noteworthy products of the Middle Ages in Japan deal with these questions at the same time that they show distinct advances in historiographical technique. *Gukanshō* ("Miscellany of Ignorant Views"), written by the priest Fujiwara Jien (1155–1225), explains the balance between civil and military ministers as dependent on the quality of service they provided and on the requirements of the times. Jien, to some extent, therefore, applied Confucian concepts of rulership to the behavior of "imperial advisors." But the *Gukanshō* is particularly noted for being the first example of "purposeful" historical writing in which the author was able not merely to record but to survey, interpret, and explain while exercising personal detachment.

*Jinnō shōtōki* ("Records of the True Descent of the Divine Emperors") by General Kitabatake Chikafusa (1291–1354) was written to inform the scion of a displaced branch of the imperial family of the true state of political affairs into which he was born. Its great importance to later generations lay in its emotional revival of the theme of Japan's superiority as a nation because of the unique virtue of the unbroken imperial line.

## The Tokugawa period

Japan's great age of historical writing prior to modern times came in the peaceful years of the Tokugawa period (1600–1868). Up to this point the writing of history had been the province of relatively few courtiers and priests. With the cessation of civil war in 1600, the Tokugawa house and the territorial lords (the daimyo) gave official encouragement to the pursuit of learning, and history became a major concern of the entire samurai class. The multicentered political order, which included a regenerated imperial court, a shogun with unmatched powers, and stable daimyo administrations in the provinces, provided incentive for the compilation of numerous official histories, while the cultivation of intellectualism led many a private

scholar into the fields of Japanese history and literature.

At the same time, profound changes were affecting the Japanese climate of opinion. The rigorous pursuit of Confucian philosophy among the samurai, not simply as an esoteric pastime, but for practical use in political affairs and the betterment of education, improved the Japanese scholar's mastery of historical technique. More important, it rejected Buddhist mysticism for a more rationalistic view of history. In addition, a new interest in native Japanese studies (e.g., study of the *Kojiki*), which refocused interest upon the imperial house, gave the Japanese the ingredients of a nationalistic revival in scholarship and the confidence to reject in time even the Confucian values that had so long dominated their thinking.

Chief among the historical works of this age were certain products of official patronage and committee authorship. Heading the list of "house histories" was the voluminous *Tokugawa jikki* ("Veritable Annals of the Tokugawa House"), the first part of which was completed in 516 chapters between 1809 and 1849. The primary effort of the Tokugawa house to write a national history so as to legitimize its rule was the *Honchō tsugan* ("Comprehensive Mirror of Japan"), completed in 1670 by the Hayashi family of shogunal Confucian advisors. The text was in Chinese, and, as the title indicates, the form was modeled after Ssu-ma Kuang's famous *Tzu-chih t'ung-chien* (1084; "Comprehensive Mirror for Government").

Destined to become more influential than the *Honchō tsugan* was the *Dai Nihon shi* ("History of Japan"), compiled under the auspices of the Mito branch of the Tokugawa house. It was the first (and only) successful attempt of the Japanese to write according to the full specifications of the Chinese dynastic history style and required the efforts of a large compilation bureau from 1657 to 1906, when the essays were finally complete. But the annals had been made public in 1720, and from that time the work had acquired a reputation for its sentiments of loyalty to the imperial house.

Historiographically more important than the works of group authorship, however, were the writings of two private historians. Arai Hakuseki (1657–1725), a scholar–statesman in the Confucian sense, was a writer of wide versatility. His *Dokushi yoron* ("Commentaries on History") contained an entirely original system of periodization based on the shifting locus of political power. The *Koshi tsū* ("Survey of Ancient History"), in which he called for philological studies to penetrate the Japanese classics and state that the *kami* (gods) were humans and understandable in rational terms, exemplified both the high moral sense of the Confucianist and the growing rationalism with which many Japanese scholars were able to approach historical causation.

Rai Sanyō (1780–1832), less competent as a historian, exemplified the new interest in national studies. His *Nihon gaishi* ("Unofficial History of Japan") continued in the tradition of Kitabatake's emperor-centered historical narrative. More accessible than the Mito *Dai Nihon shi*, it was widely read and everywhere stirred up sentiments of loyalty toward the emperor and pride in the uniqueness of Japan's national structure.

Such works of compilation and interpretation could hardly have been written had it not been for the diligent labor of a large body of archivists and antiquarians during the Tokugawa period. This labor, in fact, laid the foundations of Japan's modern archival repositories. The contemporary Cabinet Library, for example, is heavily dependent upon collections begun under Tokugawa patronage. The program of the Historiographical Institute today is also a continuation of the remarkable work of the blind bibliographer Hanawa Hokiichi (1746–1821) and his son, who scoured the country collecting and collating historical texts, which they published according to a subject classification under the title *Gunsho ruijū* ("Classified Texts").

These highlights of the historiographical story of the Tokugawa period constitute but a small fraction of the total activity of the age. By the eighteenth century, historical studies were no longer limited to a narrow court circle or to individuals patronized by the central military authorities. Nearly all of the more than 250 daimyo promoted the writing of house histories or the collection of local documents. The spread of learning among diverse groups (even outside the ruling class) encouraged variety and specialization. Antiquarians wrote on ancient usages or court ceremonies, philologists studied the meaning of archaic Japanese words, and bibliographers began the task of examining critically Japan's heritage in the field of letters. Adding impetus to the growth of scholarship and the diffusion of ideas was the remarkable expansion of the printing industry, which put much of the output of Tokugawa writers on the market and into the hands of other scholars. The growth of private and official academies, particularly in the great cities of Edo, Osaka, Kyoto, and Nagasaki, led to a lively interchange of ideas.

By the middle of the nineteenth century, when Japan was abruptly thrust into the company of Western powers and her intellectuals were brought face to face with the latest products of science and scholarship from the West, Japan had at her disposal a mature tradition of historical scholarship, based on sound, though antiquated, principles of Chinese methodology and suffused with a growing national self-consciousness. It required only the touch of Western influence to set in motion a complex historiographical revolution. On the one hand, the Japanese were quick to absorb the methods and philosophies of history offered by the West. On the other hand, they comprehended immediately that the West posed a vital threat to their intellectual security and their historical importance as a nation. In the world views of the West, Japan had no recognized place other than among the "uncivilized" peoples.

### The Meiji period

The basic revolution in historiography took Japan roughly thirty years, the same period of time required to lay the foundation for the modern Japanese state. Japan's first task was the fairly straightforward one of recapturing in modern scientific form the facts of Japan's past. For several years the government dominated this work of basic compilation. Interest in history ranked high among the Meiji leaders, for they sought justification for the new regime as well as knowledge about past laws and administrative practices to serve as a basis for new legislation. In 1869 an Office for Collection of Historical Materials and Compilation of National History was established by government order. Its director, Shigeno Yasutsugu, was immediately caught in the dilemma of objective versus propagandistic compilation. The projected national history was eventually abandoned after attack from Shintoist scholars, who claimed the work gave insufficient support to the emperor. The collection of materials, however, has been continued to the present. Meanwhile most of the new departments of government were busy collecting records and compiling documentary histories. The most ambitious and currently useful of these transitional works is *Koji ruien* ("Encyclopedia of Ancient Matters"), a monumental encyclopedia in the Chinese manner compiled by the Department of Shrines between 1879 and 1913.

The conflict over interpretation that divided the official historiographers of the early Meiji era reflected the deep problems that Japan faced in the realm of historical ideology. Ranged on one side were the successors to the Shinto revivalist school of the Tokugawa period, who wished to use history to stimulate patriotism and to keep alive the memory of a noble past with which they could proudly confront the rest of the world. For them Rai Sanyō's history remained a model, and between 1876 and 1884 five supplements to this work were printed. Yet just as in the political arena, the traditionalists were attacked by the advocates of "progress" and intellectual freedom. Private historians with more flexible and cosmopolitan views were at work absorbing new Western concepts and rethinking Japan's historical circumstances. Many of them, in fact, saw Japan as half-civilized in contrast to the "enlightened" peoples of the West. Soon translations of such contemporary laissez-faire writers as Mill and Spencer began to circulate in Japan, and the broadly interpretative works of men like Henry Thomas Buckle and François Guizot showed the way to the writing of cultural history. Fukuzawa Yukichi's *Bummei ron no gairyaku* (1875; "A Short Account of the Theory of Civilization") and Taguchi Ukichi's *Nihon kaika shōshi* (1877–1882; "Short History of Japanese Civilization"), based on these models, opened a new era of Japanese historiography that would shift the attention of the historian away from the purely political to encompass the intellectual, artistic, and religious dimensions of Japanese culture and would begin the task of finding a place for Japan in a world view made larger by the addition of the West.

These two streams of historiography, official–nationalistic and private–international, carried on into the 1890s, but not until the government had abandoned direct interference in the writing of history behind an avowed insistence on objectivity and the advocates of patriotic history had turned their attention to the more impressionable field of elementary education. In the realm of scholarship it was expected that history would become an objective science. And for this purpose a German scholar, Ludwig Reiss (1861–1928), had been invited to establish a chair of history at Tokyo University. Under Reiss the German *Geschichtswissenschaft* school was accepted as the basis for historical training at Tokyo. In 1895 the government attached its Historical Bureau to Tokyo University with the aim of compiling the *Dai Nippon shiryō* ("Historical Materials of Japan") along the lines of the German *Monumenta germaniae historica*. Thus the combination of the University of Tokyo professorships and the Historiographical Institute became the hard core of Japan's modern historical profession, from which emanated the dominant academic orthodoxy.

## Beginnings of modern historiography

Japanese historiography came of age as a modern discipline during the forty years after 1890. This era was marked by conspicuous success along four main lines: (1) the perfection of a modern historical methodology, (2) the writing of specialized monographic studies on particular institutions and aspects of Japanese civilization, (3) the preparation of general historical surveys, and (4) the publication of reference works and source materials. The outstanding historiographic work of the period was undoubtedly Kuroita Katsumi's *Kokushi no kenkyū* (1908; "Study of Japanese History"). Kuroita, of Tokyo University and schooled in the German historical–scientific tradition, succeeded in formalizing the periodization of Japanese history and in supplying a definitive critique of the standard sources in the field of political history. Simultaneously, Japanese historians began the task of dividing their history both horizontally by periods and vertically by topics into numerous specialties. Monographic studies of political history, foreign relations, legal institutions, economic history, and the history of art, literature, and religion were produced in abundance. By the 1920s the ground had been prepared for the appearance of new and more satisfactory historical surveys, such as *Nihon bunkashi* (1922; "Cultural History of Japan," 12 volumes) and *Sōgō Nihon shi taikei* (1926; "Synthetic Survey of Japanese History," 20 volumes), both works of multiple authorship.

The mid-1920s stand out as a quiet and productive interlude in Japanese historiography, when few fundamental conflicts of interpretation disturbed the academic calm. Although "academic" and "cultural" historians were separated by obvious differences in approach or subject matter, they shared basic premises about the function and aim of history. Both believed essentially in "scientific" methodology, and both were concerned with the task of "discovering" Japan's past in all its political subtleties and cultural richness. They saw Japan as having successfully joined the ranks of the modern powers, so that Japanese history could be viewed as simply another tributary flowing into the mainstream of modern progress. The Japanese were content to study their past descriptively as a subject sufficient to itself and worthy of pride.

But this atmosphere was not to last long. First of all, Japanese historians began of their own accord to look beyond their own history to discover relationships with other histories and to subject their history to new comparative judgments. Nishida Naojirō's brilliant analysis of Japanese culture saw in Japan its "Gothic art," and its "rise of a commercial spirit." Tsuda Sōkichi broke through the taboos that still obscured Japan's early history to reveal Japan's cultural growth as an unfolding of human qualities shared by "all people." Honjō Eijirō, Ono Takeo, and Tsuchiya Takao began the economic interpretation of Japanese history.

The new currents of historical inquiry were sufficiently strong to bring into being a number of new societies dedicated to specific types of history. Up to then the chief association of Japanese historians had been the Shigakkai (Historical Society of Japan), founded at Tokyo University in 1889. Among the new associations, the Keizaishi Kenkyūkai (Society for the Study of Economic History) was organized at Kyoto University in 1929, and the Shakai Keizaishi Gakkai (Social and Economic History Society) was organized in Tokyo in 1931. In 1933 a group of young historians of the Tokyo area, organizing themselves into the Rekishigaku Kenkyūkai (Historical Science Society), began the move toward "progressive" history that was to lead increasingly in the Marxian direction.

By the late 1920s history had again become a pivotal subject for a people who had begun to question the course their country was pursuing both at home and abroad. Social and political problems that followed World War I and were accentuated by the depression now agitated the academic world. Intellectuals saw a growing discrepancy between "government" and "people," between the way things were and the way they ought to be. The fading of the democratic ideal, not only in Japan but in much of Europe, left the Japanese open to the competitive ideals of socialism and national socialism.

During the 1930s, as Japan began her expansion on the continent and drifted toward war in the Pacific, her scholarly world was torn increasingly between the ideas of left and right. Marxist historians rewrote Japanese history as a story of national development from primitive to socialist society. They hotly debated whether or not the Meiji Restoration was a bourgeois revolution and criticized the government of Japan as capitalist and imperialist. Perhaps the most significant contribution of the Marxist school in these years was the series entitled *Nihon shihonshugi hattatsu shi kōza* (1932; "Essays on the History of the Develop-

ment of Capitalism in Japan"). Marxists eventually came under heavy attack. After the middle 1930s open expression of their views declined, although a strong underground commitment to them continued among Japanese intellectuals and much of the Marxist vocabulary passed into common usage.

By the mid-1930s the tempo of nationalistic writing had accelerated. Incited by government and public opinion, historians lent their energies to propagandistic purposes and the rewriting of national history along messianic lines. Although the higher levels of scholarship were able to maintain a precarious objectivity, by the time of the war Japan's youth was uniformly being taught a brand of history that stressed the old myths of uniqueness and invincibility and claimed as the goal of history the ultimate conquest of the world by the Japanese.

## Postwar historiography

After disastrous defeat in war, Japan embarked upon the slow process of economic and spiritual rehabilitation. The very foundations of her history had been challenged: much of her heroic past had been discredited, and the seemingly successful attempt at modernization had ended in failure. Where did Japan now stand in the world? And what of Japan's past was now worthy of remembrance? These questions were put to a generation of scholars strongly disillusioned by their wartime experience. The purging of old-guard scholars brought younger men in large numbers into the universities, while the freedom of expression that the Occupation authorities permitted encouraged a vigorous iconoclasm among all intellectuals. Many of the new scholars were men of strong Marxist conviction whose desire to express themselves had been increased by the long years of silence imposed upon them during the war.

Few subjects were as controversial as history during the first fifteen years after World War II. For history lay both at the heart of the revised system of "education for democracy" and of the Japanese attempt to understand a world divided between two great power blocs and two ideologies. Battles raged over the rewriting of elementary school history textbooks, and lines were drawn between the Marxist-dominated Rekishigaku Kenkyūkai and the still academically oriented Shigakkai.

In the first years after the war, it seemed as though Japanese historians had uniformly and precipitously abandoned the extreme of nationalist history only to take up another extreme of socialist history in which nation and emperor were both totally rejected. The theme of the common man in his struggle against feudalism, absolutism, fascism, and capitalism was played with dramatic eloquence.

Yet by the 1950s, as political and economic conditions began to settle down, historians also began to relax their extreme ideological orientation. In volume of research and publication, historians of the 1950s had begun to surpass their prewar output; new encyclopedias, new survey histories, new works of basic research were published, so that by the end of the decade the entire literature of Japanese history had practically renewed itself. New documentary series that penetrated even more deeply into the details of government or economic activity encouraged research at new levels of refinement and precision. The creation of new universities and research centers served to break up the prewar factions of historians and increase the variety of historical writing.

In the face of such diversity, any simple characterization of the Japanese historiographical scene today is hardly possible. Most of the vast product of the Japanese historian is of a strictly empirical nature and is little affected by problems of bias or interpretation. But there are underlying issues of great consequence. Japanese historians are still troubled by questions of fundamental philosophy. Marxism continues to provide the most widely accepted historical world view. Recent experimentation with various social science methods has offered certain alternatives to Marxism, although nothing like a "complete system." There are followers of Max Weber and of special techniques of statistical data gathering or group research, but these are chiefly techniques, and the Japanese must still grapple with the question of where history is taking them and where Japan fits into the ultimate scheme of things. Increasingly, however, it does appear that the Japanese are gaining the assurance to forgo their ideological preconceptions and engage in a less self-conscious approach to their own history.

JOHN WHITNEY HALL

[Directly related are the entries BUDDHISM and JAPANESE SOCIETY.]

### BIBLIOGRAPHY

BEASLEY, WILLIAM G.; and PULLEYBLANK, E. G. (editors) 1961 Historians of China and Japan. New York and London: Oxford Univ. Press. → Contains five essays on Japanese historiography. The first three provide the most complete analysis of premodern historical writing available in English.

COMITÉ JAPONAIS DES SCIENCES HISTORIQUES 1960 Le Japon au XIe congrès international des sciences historiques à Stockholm: L'état actuel et les tendances des études historiques au Japon. Tokyo: Nippon Gakujutsu Shinkōkai. → Part 1 contains essays by leading Japanese historians on the state of research, latest trends, and major fields of Japanese history. Parts 2 and 3 cover Asian history and European history. Contents are in English; a Japanese language version was also published.

HALL, JOHN W. 1954a Historiography in Japan. Pages 284–304 in Henry S. Hughes (editor), Teachers of History: Essays in Honor of Laurence Bradford Packard. Ithaca, N.Y.: Cornell Univ. Press. → A survey of Japanese historical writing from its origins to the time of writing.

HALL, JOHN W. 1954b Japanese History: A Guide to Japanese Reference and Research Materials. Ann Arbor: Univ. of Michigan Press. → A bibliographical study of the Japanese treatment of Japanese history. Introductory essays cover basic reference works, historical sources, documentary collections, journals, and secondary works in each major field of study. A total of 1,551 works are annotated.

Iwanami kōza Nihon rekishi (Essays on Japanese History). 1963 Tokyo: Iwanami. → Volume 22 is devoted to essays on Japanese historians. This is the latest of many Japanese works surveying Japanese historical writing.

Nihon shi kenkyū nyūmon (Introduction to the Study of Japanese History). 2 vols. Compiled by Tōyama Shigeki and Satō Shin'ichi. 1954–1962 Tokyo Univ. Press. → Practical handbooks for aspiring Japanese historians, these volumes contain essays on the latest trends in major fields, bibliographical lists, and information on research institutions and libraries.

NIHON SHISŌSHI KENKYŪKAI 1961 Nihon ni okeru rekishishisō no tenkai (The Development of Japanese Historical Thought). Tokyo: Shibundō. → A collection of fourteen essays on historiography and historical thought in Japan from early times to the present. Contains a chronology and one of the most complete bibliographies of Japanese historiography available.

1963-nen no rekishi gakkai (Historical Studies in 1963). 1964 Shigaku zasshi [1964] Annual summary. → Begun in the journal Shirin, the series has been kept alive since 1916 and provides an annual summary of the previous year's publication by Japanese historians. The journal Rekishigaku kenkyū has published a similar series since 1933.

## VI

### SOUTH AND SOUTHEAST ASIAN HISTORIOGRAPHY

Historiography in south and southeast Asia, as elsewhere, developed in close relation with the sources of literacy. As literacy came from several sources and at different times, so was history writing similarly varied and differentiated. Most important of such sources before the twentieth century, however, were the many religions which, for at least six centuries, united some parts of the region and divided others. Five of the areas representing different religions and literate experiences may be distinguished for a survey of historiographical traditions.

There has been little in common between popular Hinduism in India and the Theravada Buddhism of Thailand, Cambodia, Burma, and Ceylon. These two areas again have little in common with a third area, the extensive sphere of Islam, with large centers in Pakistan and India and in Muslim societies throughout Malaysia, Indonesia, and the southern Philippines. The fourth and the fifth areas are somewhat peripheral to the rest, that of Vietnam, where a variety of Chinese religion and culture still survives, and that of the largely Christianized society of the Philippines. In each of these areas a different attitude toward the idea of history may be discerned.

## Traditional historiography

**South Asia.** The earliest literate religion introduced to the preliterate animistic communities of the region was that of the Vedas. The religion was restricted primarily to India and produced its earliest annalistic literature in the Purāṇas. The purāṇic tradition was further extended and other dynastic and regional annals were compiled, but they remained "marked by obscurity, exaggeration, paucity of authentic data and neglect of topography and chronology" (Ghoshal 1961, p. 2) down to the Muslim invasions of the twelfth century. The only exception to this Hindu heritage was a work completed in the middle of the twelfth century, the Rājataraṅgiṇī ("Kashmir Chronicle") by Kalhaṇa. Of Kalhaṇa, Majumdar (1961a, p. 21) says that he "held that the first requisite of a true historian was to keep a detached mind, free from bias and prejudices (and), like a judge, must discard love and hatred while recounting the events of the past . . .," but Basham (1961a, p. 61) maintains that Kalhaṇa was more concerned "to teach moral lessons."

The great epics, the Mahābhārata and the Rāmāyaṇa, had considerable influence and were used as sources by an independent historical tradition. While they did not lead to the growth of history writing, they were remarkable repositories of stories which were as real and meaningful to most of the peoples of south and southeast Asia as the Homeric epics were to the peoples of Europe. For centuries, they were the nearest thing to history and may be said to have performed the role of history among the peoples who transmitted the stories.

In addition, the two epics, in conjunction with the stories of the Pañcatantra and the Buddhist Jātaka stories, also provided a strong anecdotal and narrative tradition for the Buddhist genealogies and chronicles of Ceylon and mainland southeast Asia. Such Buddhist stories and chronicles ranged from simple eulogies to types of hagiography and

were used for moral and spiritual education in the monasteries and at the courts. It took several centuries before the chronicles advanced from recounting the philosophical progress of Gautama Buddha and his disciples to the conscious record of contemporary political and religious events. Eventually, in Ceylon, where the *vaṃsa* tradition (notably, the chronicles known as the Dīpavaṃsa, the Mahāvaṃsa, and the Cūlavaṃsa) produced several court-sponsored chronicles compiled by learned monks, a kind of history writing appeared. The works were annalistic and anecdotal and mainly written in verse. They were also restricted to court use. There was no tradition of individual authorship, for each chronicle was largely the continuation of a previous one and incorporated materials from earlier chronicles. The success of any set of chronicles was determined more by its literary quality than by its historical accuracy. If a new compilation achieved high literary standards, it might supersede earlier works altogether (Perera 1961; Godakumbura 1961).

Indian historiography was greatly enriched after the Muslim conquests of northern India at the end of the twelfth century. A well-developed tradition of history writing was introduced, and for more than six centuries a branch of Muslim historiography dominated the south Asian scene. The main features of these Muslim writings are common to those of Muslim historiography in Persia, west Asia, and north Africa. They remained bound to the need for orthodox authority and the desire to serve God and the Muslim community. They were also largely directed to teaching moral and religious lessons through descriptions of prophets, caliphs, sultans, and other great men of both religion and government. Furthermore, they were limited to the accounts of the triumphs and disasters of Muslim rulers and kingdoms and barely touched on the peoples of other faiths in India.

Despite these limitations, the Muslim writings provided a historical picture of India not available among any other community in India until recent times. For this reason, at least two of the greatest Indo–Muslim historians may be singled out to illustrate the range and scope of the tradition. The first is Ziauddin Barani, whose work, the *Tarīkh-i Feroz-shāhī*, was completed in 1357. Here, Barani achieved a new consciousness of the value of history. Not only could history strengthen faith, reason, and judgment, give comfort, teach patience, and distinguish between good and evil, but it was also "the necessary foundation of truth" (Hardy 1960, pp. 22–23). Although his awareness of truth was strictly within the framework of Islam, it remains a vital ingredient in distinguishing the best Muslim histories from the many written.

This was also true of the Moghul historian Abul Fazl (1551–1602), whose history of the reign of the emperor Akbar (1556–1605) is regarded as the height of Indo–Muslim historiographical achievements. This work, the *Akbar Namah*, is not free from conventional eulogy and stylistic flourish, but it represents the result of great steps forward in archival collection, document examination, and close analytical research. To this day the section called *Ain-i-Akbari* is regarded as the classic study of the institutions and workings of an empire at the height of its extent and power.

Although all Indo–Muslim writings were determined by extraneous non-Indian concepts of history, they have become part of the Indian (and now also Pakistani) historical heritage and may be seen now as an integral part of traditional south Asian historiography (Hardy 1961; Rashid 1961; Elliot 1867–1877).

**Southeast Asia.** The Mon–Khmer and Cham peoples of mainland southeast Asia acquired much of the art and architecture of India and left many great historical monuments which are still intact to attest to the richness of the heritage (Coedès [1948] 1964, pp. 35–72). But the earlier Hindu–Buddhist accretions left little impact on the Mon and Cambodian chronicles that came to be written later.

With the spread of Theravada Buddhism after the thirteenth century, the Mons in particular compiled chronicles (Rājāwan, or genealogies of various kinds) which established the tradition of bringing together dynastic information, anecdotes about the kings, and various myths and legends which gave meaning to each reign (Shorto 1961, p. 64). This tradition was strengthened by the Burmese, who brought a keener sense of chronology to the compilations. Although still essentially a derived tradition from Buddhist Ceylon, the later Burmese Yazawin ("Chronicles") of the eighteenth and nineteenth centuries were clearly indigenous writings influenced by local animism and Burmese concepts of kingship and cosmology. As works compiled by learned monks, learned brāhmaṇs, and learned ministers, they provided valuable material for early European works on Burmese history (Htoot 1961; Ohn 1961; Mahā Yāza Win Taw Kyī).

Similarly, the Thai tradition, also developed by learned monks and ministers, was derived from Ceylon, probably through the Mon–Khmer-speaking peoples of the Menam valley. Most of the earlier versions of the Thai chronicles were destroyed when Ayuthia was sacked by the Burmese in 1767.

A notable exception was the *P'ongsawadan*, compiled in 1680, which covered the period 1350–1605. This chronicle form was revived during the late eighteenth century, and many chronicles were written not only for Thailand but also for Burma, Cambodia, and the states of southern Thailand, including the Malay states of Songkhla and Saiburi (Kedah).

The situation was different, however, among the Javanese and Malay peoples. Hindu–Buddhist monuments and inscriptions abound, but there also developed quite independently a native concern with the past and the use of the past as symbol and magic to give power and confirm authority. From the epic poem *Nagara–Kertagama* to the *Pararaton* and the *Babad Tanah Jawi* (fourteenth to seventeenth centuries), the court poets lauded their kings, worked out impressive genealogies, and perfected their verse. These were not works of history, but they were approaching an autonomous tradition in historical awareness. Of particular interest is the framework of Hindu gods, Buddhist identifications, and indigenous beliefs in the first two works and their extension to include Muslim prophets in the *Babad*. The sense of continuity is unmistakable. The desire to link legitimacy and sovereignty to past heroes and their origins is sustained through the centuries. Lacking both an accurate chronology and a secular concern with kings, ministers, subjects, and enemies, the great lists of names of people and places are more like exercises in metrics and incantation than history writing. But as the tradition developed into the nineteenth century, later *Babad* closer to modern histories were produced, notably, the *Babad Dipanagara* and the *Sejarah Banten*. In addition, there were lesser historical writings in south Celebes (Sudjatmoko et al. 1965; Berg 1965; Graaf 1965; Noorduyn 1965; Johns 1964).

Far better developed as histories are the writings in Malay, especially the *Sejarah Melayu* and a number of works concerning the Johore and Riau Lingga empires, as well as "rhymed chronicles" like the *Sha'ir Perang Mengkasar* and similar compositions. Malay writing is richer than the Javanese in anecdote and more vivid in the description of men and places. It still lacks chronology but is more accurate about personal relationships. There is less concern with magic than with moral values like loyalty and sincerity, and, as a whole, Malay histories entertain as well as teach. Three outstanding examples of a nascent social history, the *Misa Melayu*, the *Hikayat Abdullah*, and the *Tuhfat-ul Nafis*, appeared in the eighteenth and nineteenth centuries. It is possible to discover a certain amount of outside influence in these works, but they clearly show their continuity with the *Sejarah Melayu* tradition (Bottoms 1959; Amin 1963, pp. 1–46; Teeuw 1964; Josselin de Jong 1964).

Finally, a brief note on the importation of traditional Chinese historiographical forms in the writing of Annamese (Vietnamese) history. In ruling the Tongking region of north Vietnam for a thousand years, the Chinese determined the nature of its historiography. Such traditional works were still being written throughout the nineteenth century and even during the early years of the twentieth century. But, interestingly, these forms are not traceable in those parts of the Indochinese peninsula which fell under the influence of Theravada Buddhism. Similarly, with the Spanish invasion of the Philippines at the end of the sixteenth century, a kind of traditional Roman Catholic historiography was introduced which matched the Malay chronicles of the Sulu Archipelago. This limited European clerical tradition remained dominant in the Philippines until the latter half of the nineteenth century, and vestiges remain even today.

**Features of traditional historiography.** It has often been noted that the history of south and southeast Asia had little unity of theme until the coming of modern industrial civilization during the last hundred years. The traditional historiography of the region seems to confirm this view. Except for the common lack of chronology in the historical works and the fact that there are so many gaps to be filled in the region's history, there appear to be more major differences than similarities in the types of writings mentioned above. Some of the traditions may have had common origins, but they developed as discrete and autonomous traditions in Ceylon, Burma, Thailand, Java, and the Malay world. Even the Islamic tradition was not homogeneous, and what emerged in northern India was quite different from Muslim historical writings in Acheh, Java, Malacca, Johore, south Celebes, and Sulu. This suggests that there were strong indigenous features in each of the traditions which were peculiar to the different peoples. The subject has now aroused considerable interest, and it is to be expected that more precise analyses of the indigenous cultures will soon appear to help us understand the differences better.

Based on present information, the following list indicates the common features and major differences.

Common features are that (*a*) most of the works are strong in genealogy but weak in chronology and biographical detail; (*b*) the emphasis is on literary style, anecdotal material, and the use of history as moral and religious teaching; (*c*) where they are primarily secular, there is a common central interest in kingship, and the emphasis is placed on orthodox qualities of loyalty and conformity; (*d*) cosmological and astrological considerations tend to exclude causal explanations as well as the idea of progress.

Major differences are that (*a*) religion cut off the Indo–Muslim historians from the Hindu socio-economic background of Indian history; it cut off the Thais and Cambodians from the east Asian historiographical tradition in its Vietnamese form; and it cut off the Malayo–Javanese world from the Thais and Burmese on the one hand and the Filipinos on the other; (*b*) national rivalry influenced, for example, Burmese and Thai historical writing about each other; (*c*) language differences in India before the use of Persian and in mainland southeast Asia after the decline of Pali were complex; most of the works were not intelligible outside of the country's boundaries; (*d*) royal policies about historical writings varied considerably; Muslim and Malay works were in circulation, while Thai, Burmese, and Vietnamese works were kept mainly for official use.

Two further points about the nature of the early traditional chronicles need to be emphasized. First, modern scholarship has begun to show appreciation of such traditional writings and has applied the techniques of Biblical and Homeric criticism to their study. It is now realized that these chronicles are best understood in the context of the total cultural system in which they were compiled. Second, whether these works may be called "histories" or not, their value as historical documents has now been proved. What is required are finer and more sensitive techniques for obtaining from them the data needed to write the history of south and southeast Asia.

## Modern historiography

The growth of modern historiography in Europe coincided with the expansion of European activities in Asia. But as European activities were peripheral to Asian history between the sixteenth and nineteenth centuries and as traditional European attitudes toward the nature and use of history changed very slowly, there was no impact on the historiography of south and southeast Asia during this period. It was only in the latter half of the nineteenth century, when Western science and culture were consciously taught and learned, first in south Asia and then in parts of southeast Asia, that the region became affected by Western historical methods. What was being widely introduced, however, were the traditional techniques of the late eighteenth and early nineteenth centuries, for example, the philological methods of William Jones and the historical writings of James Mill, Mountstuart Elphinstone, and Vincent Smith. There was a time lag in methodological change, and these traditional techniques were still regarded in the early part of the twentieth century as advanced and valid for imitation. The developments toward "scientific" history and the growth of social sciences in Europe and America were hardly noticed until after the end of World War II. Application of Western historiographical techniques to the study of India and Ceylon came first, but the Dutch eventually applied them to Indonesia, and the French, although coming last, were quick to apply them in their thorough study of Indochina.

**South Asia.** Serious Western scholarship in India dates from William Jones's founding of the Asiatic Society at Calcutta in 1784. The activities of this and similar kinds of societies for Oriental research in Bombay, Madras, Mysore, and Ceylon, together with the growth of learned societies in France and Germany and the creation of university chairs in Europe during the nineteenth century, laid the foundations of modern south Asian historiography.

The most important contributions were initially in the field of Sanskrit philology and in the editing of Vedic and Buddhist texts, but the study of Indian antiquities eventually provided a more scientific basis for dealing with the otherwise intractable materials on ancient India. The pre-Muslim period was the most challenging because there were none of the essentials for the historian—no chronology, no reliable genealogies, no clear identifications of people and places. It was here, too, that the most dramatic discoveries and achievements were recorded. Particularly notable was James Tod's *Annals and Antiquities of Rajast'han*, published from 1829 to 1832, and James Prinsep's epigraphical and numismatic studies published in 1858 under the title *Essays on Indian Antiquities*. Their success led to the setting up of an archeological department in 1862 under Alexander Cunningham; this became in 1902 the famous Indian Archaeological Survey under John Marshall (*Ancient India*, 1953).

In comparison, the traditional European historians were far less successful. Mill, Elphinstone, and Smith, as well as French and German historians of India, were either too ready to show the superiority of Western rule or too uncritical of the available Muslim and non-Muslim material. Their impact was initially greater on European audiences

than on Indians. It was not until the establishment of British-type universities in Calcutta, Bombay, Madras (all three in 1857), and elsewhere that formal history teaching introduced the European writings to young Indian scholars. By that time, while historical sciences in Europe had made further progress, Indian scholars like R. G. Bhandarkar were learning the techniques and attitudes of the earlier period well enough to criticize the works of European historians themselves (Philips 1961a; Basham 1961b).

It is only in the twentieth century that south Asian historiography began to respond directly and strongly to Western methodology. It did so in at least two different directions. The first was a more intensive appreciation of Western scientific methods, especially following the brilliant archeological work on the Indus civilization at Mohenjo-daro and Harappa. The second was a nationalistic or anti-imperialistic approach, which in its extreme forms produced obscurantist and revivalist historical writings on the one hand and stimulated Marxist and other forms of radical historiography on the other (Majumdar 1961b).

Modern historiography may be said to have begun with the British publication of the *Cambridge History of India*, published in 6 volumes between 1922 and 1932. This aroused considerable interest in India, even among those who resented the dominance of British contributors. It was recognized, however, that in the fields of archeology, epigraphy, and numismatics, the great collections produced by European scholars were indispensable. So also were the collections of documents and the interpretative works on British activities, the politics of the East India Company, and the extension of British power in India. But this was not the case with works that dealt with Indian religion and culture, the Indian response to British rule (for example, the 1857 mutiny and the nationalist movement), and the social and economic changes in India since the beginning of the nineteenth century. It was in these fields that a new generation of scholars first challenged the results of European scholarship. Notable among this generation were R. C. Majumdar, H. C. Raychaudhuri, K. A. A. Nilakanta Sastri, and K. M. Pannikar. Most of them were products of university departments of history, whether in Britain or in India, and many were professional teachers of history. They continued the tradition of forming learned societies to publish scholarly journals and learned to use and appreciate the great libraries and archival collections organized by the states and the government of India (see Nilakanta Sastri 1956; Datta 1957).

Since independence, the work of history writing has continued. Institutions like the Archaeological Survey, the Historical Records Commission, and the Indian History Congress are particularly active. Among the historical publications of academic standing, two are noteworthy: the *Indian Historical Quarterly* and the *Journal of Indian History*. A major enterprise has been the 11-volume series, *History and Culture of the Indian People*, published by the Bharatiya Vidya Bhavan under the general editorship of R. C. Majumdar. Also significant has been the Indian History Congress conference on Asian history in 1961 and the meeting at Delhi in 1965 of the International Congress of Orientalists. These developments reflect the new Indian historical consciousness, which has revealed a considerable acceptance of modern scientific methods of historiography. The most important measure of modern Indian achievements is that there are today trained historians to cover almost every period and type of problem in Indian history. In addition, several of the younger historians have begun to apply the tools of social science to the study of modern history. In this respect, many have turned to new academic disciplines developed in the United States for their methodological assistance.

Less outstanding has been the development of historiography in Pakistan after 1947. Separation from India deprived the new state of the best developed research facilities and the best library and archival collections in the region. The scholars, therefore, had to work under grave disadvantages. They continued to revive the traditions of Islamic historiography, but the most important achievements are the works of those scholars who first made their reputations before separation from India, for example, A. Yusof Ali, Shafa'at Ahmad Khan, and I. H. Qureshi. Although the majority of the scholars feel greater kinship with the historical traditions of Persia and west Asia, they cannot deny their Indian heritage completely. Their struggles with modern historiography, therefore, are part of the progress of history writing in south Asia.

In Ceylon, modern historical attitudes developed later, but standards are high, as may be seen in the publications of the Ceylon Branch of the Royal Asiatic Society and the recent *Ceylon Journal of Historical and Social Studies*.

Finally, the remarkable fact must be noted that the bulk of historical works of significance in south Asia have been written in English. There have been important works published in Bengali, Urdu, and Hindi from the early years of the twentieth century, but so far none are widely known outside of regional schools and universities. It is important to note they all show the influence of modern historical works. There is no reason to doubt that in time more scholarly studies in the Indian languages will reach the high academic standards achieved by works in English.

**Southeast Asia.** Unlike south Asia, there was no center in southeast Asia where modern scholarship could take root and fan out over the whole region. The manner in which different parts of the region came under European control and the limited resources of the small states prevented a systematic development of modern historiography. For example, the early Portuguese, Spanish, Dutch, and English accounts of the region (sixteenth to eighteenth centuries) had no influence on southeast Asian writings and were really part of the history of European historiography. Even the founding of the famous Bataviaasch Genootschap von Kunsten en Wetenschappen (Batavian Society for the Study of Arts and Sciences) in Jakarta in 1778 and the publication of William Marsden's *History of Sumatra* in 1783 and T. S. Raffles' *History of Java* in 1817 gave little impetus to the study of history. Only in the latter half of the nineteenth century, with the revival of the Bataviaasch Genootschap and with the founding of the Straits Branch of the Royal Asiatic Society in 1878, did serious scholarship begin in Indonesia and Malaysia. In fact, European writings of the nineteenth century were produced while the indigenous traditions of *Babad* and *Sejarah* were still alive, and Western scholars often depended on native chronicles for their material on earlier history. In any case, such European works ran parallel to and were external to the local efforts at historical writing and did not affect the traditional forms and attitudes.

Similarly, among the mainland countries of southeast Asia, the Burmese and the Thais were particularly active at compiling their Yazawin and P'ongsawadan, even as European amateur scholars like Arthur Phayre (*History of Burma*, 1883) and W. A. R. Wood (*A History of Siam*, 1926) were working on their histories and as research journals like the *Journal of the Burma Research Society* and the *Journal of the Siam Society* were being published. Both British scholars, for example, acknowledged their great debt to native scholarship. In Vietnam, traditional Vietnamese historians helped early French scholars attached to the École Française d'Extrême Orient (founded in 1900), whose works were to gain fame for the school's *Bulletin*. Also, the Imperial Archives at Hué preserved their documents in the traditional fashion for some years after the French conquest.

The Philippines was a special case where one stage of Western historical scholarship displaced another. Still, Spanish traditional history continued to be written under American rule (after 1898), while scholars from the United States studied Philippine history from Spanish colonial and missionary records. The most valuable of its kind was E. H. Blair and J. A. Robertson's 55-volume work *The Philippine Islands, 1493–1898*, published between 1903 and 1909.

In the nineteenth and first half of the twentieth centuries, there have been three distinct areas of modern southeast Asian historiography. First, ancient history, of which the native peoples had little or no knowledge, was being recovered by the methods of philology, epigraphy, and archeology. Second, colonial history, involving European trade, wars, treaties, and administration, was the special interest of European historians themselves and aroused little interest among local scholars. And third, the "middle period," varying from four to ten centuries before the nineteenth century, was a period of some indigenous historical writing; modern methods can be used to help rearrange, date more accurately, and even reinterpret the writings of this period (Hall 1961).

In contrast to what they did in south Asia, the British, the Dutch, and the French in southeast Asia made no effort to train local historians until the years just before World War II. Except among the Dutch in the twentieth century, history writing was primarily an amateur affair, a by-product of administration and long residence in the country concerned. There were fine scholarly works, in particular by the professionals, for example, N. J. Krom on early Indonesian history and George Coedès on southeast Asian epigraphy before the coming of Islam. R. O. Winstedt's textual work for Malay history and G. H. Luce's great collections of inscriptions for Burmese history were also outstanding. The best work, however, was done in early history; no historians of the colonial period produced works of comparable stature. Furthermore, such colonial history as was written could better be seen as part of European historiography than of southeast Asian historiography.

There were two countries in the region where developments were different—independent Thailand and the Philippines under United States administration. In Thailand, Thai royal patronage was given to the Siam Society, which published a useful journal; and Chulalongkorn University, founded in 1917, taught both traditional and modern history. In the Philippines, missionary universities like Santo Tomás, founded in 1611,

taught little secular history but began to introduce modern historical methods into the curriculum by the end of the nineteenth century. In addition, the Americans founded in 1908 a secular university, the University of the Philippines, which taught some modern history from the start, although little work was done on southeast Asian history itself.

Since the end of World War II and particularly following the independence of the Philippines, Burma, Indonesia, and Malaya (now Malaysia), there have been new advances in the historiography of the region. A major landmark was the publication in 1955 of D. G. E. Hall's *A History of Southeast Asia*, which has successfully established that the whole span of history for all of southeast Asia is an intelligible historical unit. Also, a searching debate on the nature of European scholarship on southeast Asia has followed the provocative studies on early Asian trade by J. C. van Leur. As a result, southeast Asia was given a separate place in the series of conferences held in London in 1956 on historical writings on the peoples of Asia (Hall 1961). This stimulated another collection of papers on Indonesian historiography, first sparked by the seminar on national history held in Jogjakarta in 1957 (Singhal 1960; Smail 1961; Benda 1962; Sudjatmoko et al. 1965; cf. Seminar Sedjarah 1958).

The region still faces a long debate about whether national history should form the basis of the new southeast Asian historiography. The struggle for national identity in Burma, Indonesia, and Vietnam has reduced historical research to a trickle in those countries. Only in the Philippines, Malaysia, and Singapore has there been sustained interest in modern research, and these countries have supported international conferences on history to keep this interest alive. A joint effort led to the creation of the International Association of Historians of Asia, which meets every three or four years and shows signs of being an organization primarily for southeast Asian historians.

**Features of modern historiography.** In the two regions of south and southeast Asia, modern Indian historiography is clearly the most impressive both in volume and in quantity. Pakistan and Ceylon, however, have much in common with Indonesia, Burma, Malaysia, and the Philippines in terms of stage of growth, present and future resources, and trends of scholarship. There is a chance that Ceylon, the Philippines, Malaysia, and Singapore may develop differently because their traditional historiography does not stand in the way of rapid modernization. What is clear is that modern historiography is being confronted by nationalism and may well be subordinated to national needs. The example of India is before the others. National history takes precedence over scientific history, but as long as the means of teaching and using modern academic tools and methods remain, this situation may soon change. Thailand remains the exception. Active historical research is limited, and some work is still being done within the framework of traditional values, but there is no nationalist flavor in the work. Also, a new generation is using modern methods with increasing skill and confidence.

## Autonomy of historiographic tradition

History has had a relatively small place in south and southeast Asian traditions. Its main functions had been to strengthen the authority of kings, to teach moral and religious lessons, and possibly also to please and amuse. Exact times and places and the lives of great and lesser men had never been important in themselves. They had to serve the purpose of the historian's audience, which often comprised only the kings, priests, and courtiers of the day. Each historiographical tradition had evolved according to the needs of different audiences and had been either strong or weak depending on whether the institutions which produced the audiences were stable or unstable. As long as the institutions had been able to survive, the historical tradition which supported them also survived.

In south Asia and in the Philippines, the impact of colonial rule was felt over a long period, and this had marked consequences on the indigenous historiographical traditions. Hence, apart from some of the traditions of Muslim historiography, no other tradition has survived. In other parts of southeast Asia, however, Western influence has had only a brief history—in most cases, much less than a hundred years, during which colonial scholars and policy makers did not try to destroy the local traditions. Thus, much of the traditions still survive within the new historiography itself. This is particularly true where nationalist movements have effectively revived the historical works of the past.

But historiography is no longer a static discipline even in the West, and it is undergoing radical changes as new social science disciplines are turning to the study of the past. What is important is not that historiography in south and southeast Asia has still not freed itself completely from traditional attitudes and their limitations. It is that lines of communication have been established between Asian and Western academic institutions, important works have become mutually available, and new disciplines have been introduced and understood. The key concepts have already reached south and southeast Asia: that time and place must be accurate, that knowledge about man's past must be secular and humanistic, and that historical fact and interpretation must always be tested by the best scientific methods.

WANG GUNGWU

[See also ASIAN SOCIETY, articles on SOUTH ASIA and SOUTHEAST ASIA. Other relevant material may be found in BUDDHISM and ISLAM.]

### BIBLIOGRAPHY

AMIN, ENTJI' 1963 Sja'ir Perang Mengkasar (The Rhymed Chronicle of the Macassar War). Edited and translated by C. Skinner. Instituut voor Taal-, Land-en Volkenkunde, The Hague, Verhandelingen, Vol. 40. The Hague: Nijhoff.

Ancient India. → Published since 1946. See especially the "Special Jubilee Number," No. 9, 1953.

BASHAM, A. L. 1961a The Kashmir Chronicle. Pages 57–65 in Cyril H. Philips (editor), Historians of India, Pakistan and Ceylon. Oxford Univ. Press.

BASHAM, A. L. 1961b Modern Historians of Ancient India. Pages 260–293 in Cyril H. Philips (editor), Historians of India, Pakistan and Ceylon. Oxford Univ. Press.

BASTIN, JOHN; and ROOLVINK, R. (editors) 1964 Malayan and Indonesian Studies: Essays Presented to Sir Richard Winstedt on His Eighty-fifth Birthday. Oxford: Clarendon.

BENDA, HARRY J. 1962 The Structure of Southeast Asian History: Some Preliminary Observations. Journal of Southeast Asian History 3, no. 1:106–138.

BERG, C. C. 1965 The Javanese Picture of the Past. Pages 87–117 in Sudjatmoko et al. (editors), An Introduction to Indonesian Historiography. Ithaca, N.Y.: Cornell Univ. Press.

BOTTOMS, J. C. (1959) 1965 Some Malay Historical Sources: A Bibliographical Note. Pages 156–193 in Sudjatmoko et al. (editors), An Introduction to Indonesian Historiography. Ithaca, N.Y.: Cornell Univ. Press.

COEDÈS, GEORGE (1948) 1964 Les états hindouisés d'Indochine et d'Indonésie. New ed. Paris: Boccard.

DATTA, KALIKINKAR (1957) 1963 A Survey of Recent Studies on Modern Indian History. 2d ed. Calcutta: Mukhopadhyay.

ELLIOT, HENRY M. (1867–1877) 1964 The History of India, as Told by Its Own Historians: The Muhammadan Period; the Posthumous Papers of the Late Sir H. M. Elliot. Edited and continued by John Dowson. 8 vols. Allahabad (India): Kitab Mahal. → Reprinted with an introduction by Muhammad Habib.

GHOSHAL, U. N. (1944) 1957 Studies in Indian History and Culture. Rev. ed. Calcutta: Orient Longmans. → First published as The Beginnings of Indian Historiography and Other Essays.

GHOSHAL, U. N. 1961 Presidential Address. Part 1, pages 1–20 in Indian History Congress, Proceedings of the Twenty-third Session, Aligarh, 1960. Calcutta.

GODAKUMBURA, C. E.  1961  Historical Writing in Sinhalese. Pages 72–86 in Cyril H. Philips (editor), *Historians of India, Pakistan and Ceylon.* Oxford Univ. Press.

GRAAF, J. J. DE  1965  Later Javanese Sources and Historiography. Pages 119–136 in Sudjatmoko et al. (editors), *An Introduction to Indonesian Historiography.* Ithaca, N.Y.: Cornell Univ. Press.

HALL, DANIEL G. E. (editor)  1961  *Historians of South East Asia.* University of London, School of Oriental and African Studies, Historical Writing on the Peoples of Asia, Vol. 2. Oxford Univ. Press.

HARDY, PETER  1960  *Historians of Medieval India: Studies in Indo–Muslim Historical Writing.* London: Luzac.

HARDY, PETER  1961  Some Studies in Pre-Mughal Muslim Historiography. Pages 115–127 in Cyril H. Philips (editor), *Historians of India, Pakistan and Ceylon.* Oxford Univ. Press.

HTOOT, U TET  1961  The Nature of the Burmese Chronicles. Pages 50–62 in Daniel G. E. Hall (editor), *Historians of South East Asia.* Oxford Univ. Press.

INDIAN HISTORY CONGRESS *Proceedings.* → The first congress was held in 1935.

JOHNS, ANTHONY H.  1964  The Role of Structural Organisation and Myth in Javanese Historiography. *Journal of Asian Studies* 24:91–99.

JOSSELIN DE JONG, P. E. DE  1964  The Character of the *Malay Annals.* Pages 235–241 in John Bastin and R. Roolvink (editors), *Malayan and Indonesian Studies.* Oxford: Clarendon.

MAHĀ YĀZA WIN TAW KYĪ  *The Glass Palace Chronicles of the Kings of Burma.* Translated by Pe Maung Tin and G. H. Luce. Oxford Univ. Press, 1923.

MAJUMDAR, R. C.  1961a  Ideas of History in Sanskrit Literature. Pages 13–28 in Cyril H. Philips (editor), *Historians of India, Pakistan and Ceylon.* Oxford Univ. Press.

MAJUMDAR, R. C.  1961b  Nationalist Historians. Pages 416–428 in Cyril H. Philips (editor), *Historians of India, Pakistan and Ceylon.* Oxford Univ. Press.

NILAKANTA SASTRI, K. A.; and RAMANA, H. S.  1956  *Historical Method in Relation to Indian History.* Madras (India): Viswanathan.

NOORDUYN, J.  1965  Origins of South Celebes Historical Writing. Pages 137–155 in Sudjatmoko et al. (editors), *An Introduction to Indonesian Historiography.* Ithaca, N.Y.: Cornell Univ. Press.

OHN, TIN  1961  Modern Historical Writing in Burmese, 1724–1942. Pages 85–93 in Daniel G. E. Hall (editor), *Historians of South East Asia.* Oxford Univ. Press.

PERERA, L. S.  1961  The Pali Chronicle of Ceylon. Pages 29–43 in Cyril H. Philips (editor), *Historians of India, Pakistan and Ceylon.* Oxford Univ. Press.

PHILIPS, CYRIL H.  1961a  James Mill, Mountstuart Elphinstone, and the History of India. Pages 217–229 in Cyril H. Philips (editor), *Historians of India, Pakistan and Ceylon.* Oxford Univ. Press.

PHILIPS, CYRIL H. (editor)  1961b  *Historians of India, Pakistan and Ceylon.* University of London, School of Oriental and African Studies, Historical Writing on the Peoples of Asia, Vol. 1. Oxford Univ. Press.

RASHID, ABDUR  1961  The Treatment of History by Muslim Historians in Mughal Official and Biographical Works. Pages 139–151 in Cyril H. Philips (editor), *Historians of India, Pakistan and Ceylon.* Oxford Univ. Press.

SEMINAR SEDJARAH, JOGJAKARTA, INDONESIA, 1957  1958  *Laporan lengkap atjara I dan II tentang konsepsi filsafat sedjarah nasional dan periodisasi sedjaraj Indonesia.* Jogjakarata (Indonesia): Universitas Gadjah Mada.

SHORTO, H. L.  1961  A Mon Genealogy of Kings: Observations on *The Nidāna Ārambhakathā.* Pages 63–72 in Daniel G. E. Hall (editor), *Historians of South East Asia.* Oxford Univ. Press.

SINGHAL, D. P.  1960  Some Comments on the Western Element in Modern Southeast Asian History. *Journal of Southeast Asian History* 1, no. 2:118–123.

SMAIL, JOHN R. W.  1961  On the Possibility of an Autonomous History of Modern Southeast Asia. *Journal of Southeast Asian History* 2, no. 2:72–102.

SUDJATMOKO et al. (editors)  1965  *An Introduction to Indonesian Historiography.* Ithaca, N.Y.: Cornell Univ. Press. → The author's name is spelled Soedjatmoko on the title page.

TEEUW, A.  1964  *Hikayat Raja-Raja Pasai* and *Sejarah Melayu.* Pages 222–234 in John Bastin and R. Roolvink (editors), *Malayan and Indonesian Studies.* Oxford: Clarendon.

# HISTORY

*The articles under this heading deal with varying conceptions of the nature of history and its subject matter, as does the article on* THE HISTORY OF SCIENCE, *listed under* SCIENCE. *An analysis of what historians do when they write history and discussions of traditions of history writing in different parts of the world will be found under* HISTORIOGRAPHY. *Major related topics are* ARCHEOLOGY; EVOLUTION; KNOWLEDGE, SOCIOLOGY OF; PERIODIZATION; TIME, *article on* SOCIAL ORGANIZATION. *Other relevant material appears in* ECONOMIC THOUGHT; POLITICAL THEORY; RELIGION; SOCIOLOGY, *article on* THE DEVELOPMENT OF SOCIOLOGICAL THOUGHT.

| | |
|---|---|
| I.   THE PHILOSOPHY OF HISTORY | *Patrick Gardiner* |
| II.  HISTORY AND THE SOCIAL SCIENCES | *Peter Laslett* |
| III. ETHNOHISTORY | *Bernard S. Cohn* |
| IV.  CULTURE HISTORY | *Joseph H. Greenberg* |
| V.   SOCIAL HISTORY | *J. Jean Hecht* |
| VI.  INTELLECTUAL HISTORY | *Crane Brinton* |
| VII. ECONOMIC HISTORY | *Douglass C. North* |
| VIII. BUSINESS HISTORY | *Ralph W. Hidy* |

I

THE PHILOSOPHY OF HISTORY

The expression "philosophy of history" has come to refer to two quite distinct types of inquiry.

Traditionally, it has been used to refer to attempts to provide a comprehensive explanation or interpretation of the entire historical process. "Philosophies of history" in this sense have been characteristically concerned with such questions as: "What is the meaning (significance, purpose) of history?" or "What fundamental laws govern historical development and change?" Among the chief exponents of this type of theory may be numbered Vico, Herder, Hegel, Comte, Marx, Buckle, Spengler, and—in our own time—Arnold Toynbee and Pitirim Sorokin. Men like these have been inspired by the belief that history presents problems beyond those that occupy the attention of ordinary practicing historians, whose activities, being largely confined to the investigation of particular areas or sections of the past, fail to satisfy the demand for an intellectually or morally acceptable conception of the course of history "as a whole." By offering accounts of the human past that exhibit it as conforming to certain principles of universal validity, they have sought to meet this demand; at the same time they have often (though not always) claimed that their interpretations may enable us to make predictions or forecasts concerning the future development of society.

The grounds upon which such interpretations have been based, ranging from empirical considerations to notions that are frankly religious or metaphysical, have been various. Nor have they always taken the same form. Marx, for example, portrayed history as following a unilinear pattern in the direction of a particular foreseeable "goal"; Spengler and Toynbee have presented it as conforming to certain regular and recurrent cycles of change; while others, again, have treated it as somehow combining both these features. Common to all, however, has been the assumption that the historical process is more than an agglomeration of events "senselessly" succeeding one another in time: there is an underlying structure or theme waiting to be discovered, in terms of which this apparently arbitrary sequence can be seen to be ultimately meaningful or intelligible.

Even in the nineteenth century, when such speculation was at its peak, there were philosophers and historians—Schopenhauer and Burckhardt, for instance—who challenged its pretensions; and in the twentieth, it has been exposed to a series of logical and methodological criticisms which in their cumulative impact have proved extremely damaging. In any case, projects of this kind must be sharply distinguished from the type of inquiry that will be chiefly considered here, and which is sometimes referred to as "formal" or "critical" philosophy of history. Philosophy of history in this sense has developed comparatively recently, its rise broadly coinciding with the decline of its speculative counterpart. It has for its subject matter not the course of historical events, but rather the nature of history conceived as a specific discipline

and branch of knowledge. In other words, it may be said to be concerned with such topics as the purposes of historical inquiry, the ways in which historians describe and classify their material, the manner in which they arrive at and substantiate explanations and hypotheses, the assumptions and principles that underlie their procedures, and the relations between history and other forms of investigation. Thus, while the problems with which it deals are not speculative problems of the sort previously mentioned, neither are they problems of the type to which practicing historians typically address themselves in the course of their work: the questions involved arise from reflection upon historical thinking and reasoning and are primarily of an epistemological or conceptual character.

## The autonomy of history

Philosophical concern with the nature of historical understanding originated largely as part of a general protest against the tendency (prevalent among followers of the Enlightenment) to regard the natural sciences as representing the paradigm of all true knowledge. Even to some of the earlier speculative philosophers of history, the view that the categories and modes of interpretation employed so successfully in the investigation of physical nature could be validly extended to human studies appeared far from self-evident; in particular, the writings of both Vico and Hegel can be said to embody an implicit challenge to this opinion. Yet the belief that there are no differences in principle separating history from other disciplines and that the historian should strive as far as possible to apply to his own field the methods established in other areas of inductive inquiry was a persistent one: in the eighteenth century, empiricists like David Hume saw no reason to question it, and in the nineteenth it was to be constantly reaffirmed by a host of positivistically minded theorists. And, insofar as it was maintained, there appeared to be no grounds for supposing that the study of history presented any *special* problems from a philosophical point of view; logically and epistemologically it was on a level with any other form of empirical science.

**Dilthey and Croce.** The close of the last century, however, witnessed the emergence of a number of thinkers to whom this comfortable assumption no longer seemed acceptable and who raised awkward questions: among the more influential of the writers involved in the new trend were Georg Simmel, Heinrich Rickert, and (above all) Wilhelm Dilthey (see Hodges 1944) in Germany, and the philosopher and historian Benedetto Croce

(1917) in Italy. To summarize what they said would be difficult; they were not lucid expositors of their ideas, and they incorporated into their theories metaphysical conceptions that have lost much of their appeal since they wrote. Nevertheless, they succeeded in focusing attention upon features of the historian's activity that had been overlooked and ignored by many of their predecessors. It was pointed out, for instance, that the historian's aims are ostensibly very different from those characteristic of the natural scientist: historians are not concerned with the discovery of universal laws or theories from which predictions can be derived and which can serve as guides to action in practical or technical contexts; on the contrary, their primary purpose is to determine what happened in the past and why. This necessarily involves a concentration upon the concrete particularity of events that are in themselves unique and unrepeatable. The abstract categories of science ("pseudo-concepts," as Croce called them) are, however, adapted to quite different ends; their proper field of application is the sphere of the universal and unchanging, and they can therefore play no role in history as truly conceived. For the historian is not interested in phenomena regarded as "specimens" or as instances of general truths; as Michael Oakeshott (1933, p. 154) has expressed it, "the moment historical facts are regarded as instances of general laws, history is dismissed."

There is, moreover, a further point of fundamental importance that such critics have wished to emphasize. Both Dilthey and Croce underlined the distinction, considered by them to be crucial, between the respective subject matters of science and history. In crude terms, this may be represented by the familiar dichotomy of "spirit" and "nature"; more specifically, it involves the belief that it is impossible to view the activities of historical agents as mere pieces of observable "behavior," reducible to (or explicable in terms of) purely physical items. It follows that the principles of knowledge and understanding that are appropriate here cannot be those presupposed by scientific interpretations of the world. For the historian it is essential that he should be able to reconstruct "from within" the reasons, purposes, and emotions that motivated the persons with whom he is concerned and that found outward expression in their deeds. Various notions, such as "reliving" and *Einfühlung*," or "empathy," were appealed to in order to characterize this process; but, however described, it was posited as a distinctive feature of historical thinking, sufficient in

itself to mark history off from typically scientific modes of inquiry.

**Collingwood.** The basic contention was perhaps most forcefully and clearly formulated by the English philosopher R. G. Collingwood (1946), who was in his own work deeply influenced by Croce. According to Collingwood, the essential task of the historian is to "rethink" or "re-enact" in his mind the deliberations of historical agents, thereby rendering intelligible the events with which he has to deal in a way that finds no parallel in the physical sciences. This led him to claim, among other things, that the term "cause" has its own meaning in the context of historical narrative, not to be confused with any it may bear elsewhere. Thus, to show what caused a given occurrence in history is not a matter of subsuming it beneath scientific laws or empirical generalizations; rather, it is a question of eliciting its "inner side"—that is to say, the thoughts and reasons that, once uncovered, exhibit what happened as the response of a rational being confronted by a situation requiring a practical solution.

### The rise of analytic philosophy

Considerations like the above provided the stimulus to much modern philosophical analysis of history. This has turned very largely on the issue of whether, and if so in what way, historical thought has its own distinctive logic that resists interpretation in scientific terms. In general, controversy has tended to center on two main topics. The first concerns the logical character of the explanations historians give of particular events and developments. The second relates to the epistemological status of historical accounts of the past and to the question of whether they possess an objective validity comparable to that claimed for the results of scientific investigation.

**Historical explanation.** A major difficulty that tends to beset discussions of historical explanation derives from the variety of forms such explanation can assume. It is tempting to imagine that there is a single model to which all explanations in history ultimately conform; to explain an historical occurrence, it may be suggested, is always to exhibit it as being in some sense the consequence of certain other events or conditions. Yet in practice it is far from clear that the narratives historians provide, rich as they are in interpretative devices, invariably follow this neat pattern. For example, we may be told that a particular happening or circumstance was of a certain type (e.g., it is described as representing a "political revolution" or an "imperialist war"); or that it was part of a general trend ("The struggle was a phase of evolving nationalism."); or that it was significant as indicating changes with wider social implications ("The influence of women at court was a symptom of dynastic decline."). These may all constitute valid ways of increasing or illuminating our understanding of what occurred; they do not, however, appear to do so by providing anything obviously analogous to a causal explanation.

Nevertheless, whatever supplementary methods the historian may use to render the past intelligible, it may still be urged that causality remains the fundamental category of historical understanding. The crucial problem, therefore, is one of elucidating the notion of causal connection in history (Gardiner 1952; Dray 1957). Has this notion some special application in historical contexts, as Collingwood claimed? Or is it susceptible to an interpretation which demonstrates that historical explanations do not, after all, diverge in any essential manner from those characteristically employed in the natural sciences?

*The theory of "covering laws."*   The view that no radical differences divide historical from other kinds of explanation has found its chief defenders among philosophers whose general conception of causality largely derives from Hume. Since there are no "necessary connections" between matters of fact, any claim to the effect that a causal relation holds between certain events must contain a covert reference to a natural regularity or law. In other words, to explain an occurrence is to show that it was bound to occur, given the fulfillment of certain antecedent or initial conditions, and given the existence of some law or laws correlating such conditions with events of the type to which the *explicandum* belongs. According to this account, the historian, along with any other inquirer into causes, cannot avoid appealing to general statements asserting empirically verified uniformities; it is the latter that afford the essential backing or warrant that his explanations require. To point out that his direct concern is with the particular, not the general, is to say something that, though true, does not materially affect the issue. There is no incompatibility between the claim that the historian's object is to explain particular events and the claim that, in doing so, he necessarily commits himself to the acceptance of certain general truths. To accept the second of these contentions is not even to deny that there may be an intelligible sense in which each historical event is "unique" (though here it is worth emphasizing that, if such events were unique in the absolute and unrestricted manner sometimes suggested, it would be impossible

to say anything about them at all). For all that is required for explanatory purposes is that the occurrence to be explained should resemble other happenings in *certain* respects or aspects—namely, those that permit the application of relevant generalizations or laws. From this point of view there is no difference in principle between the procedures of the historian and the natural scientist; if a chemist or an astronomer wishes to explain a particular phenomenon falling within his field, a similar abstraction is involved.

On the face of it, this theory seems to have much to commend it, agreeably combining conceptual economy with empirical hardheadedness. A closer look may, however, reveal difficulties. In the first place, the theory appears to assume that all causal explanations in history take the form of showing that, given certain initial conditions, a particular event *had* to occur. But this is far from being universally true: the historian's object in citing causes is frequently the more limited one of explaining how a certain historical occurrence was *possible*, not why it was bound to happen; the causes referred to represent the necessary rather than the sufficient conditions of what happened. In itself, this hardly constitutes a conclusive objection; it might, for instance, be replied that the determination of necessary conditions also involves an implicit reference to laws, and that a more complex formulation of the proposed analysis, capable of accommodating this kind of case, could easily be devised. Where the theory is more clearly vulnerable is in its bland assumption that laws of the type it postulates lie ready to hand and that it is these to which historians refer when they offer their explanations. For when attempts are made to specify general statements connecting "causes" and "effects" in the required fashion, the propositions elicited tend to be so vague and indeterminate as to make it hard to see how they could conceivably perform the explanatory function attributed to them. Nor does historical practice appear to bear out the suggested interpretation. Thus it may be argued that a historian, when confronted by the task of explaining what caused a specific event, such as the French Revolution, does not do so by attempting to subsume it beneath putative laws concerning revolutions in general; on the contrary, he proceeds to an analysis of the particular case, showing through detailed inquiry how various connected sequences of factors combined to give rise to the complex phenomenon under examination.

*The theory of "continuous series."*   Appreciation of such points has led some modern writers to oppose to the previous "covering law" conception of historical explanation one that has been called "the model of the continuous series." In the latter view, the historian traces, step by step, the relations between earlier and later phases of historical change, thereby building up an intelligible narrative whose various components can be seen to stand in "intrinsic" or "natural" connections with one another: it is by such careful and particularized investigation, and not by applying universal laws or generalizations, that explanation in history characteristically proceeds. But this account, though plausible in many ways, still leaves a question unanswered. For it may be inquired how we are to understand the individual connections stated to obtain between the events of which the series is composed. To say that they are "intrinsic" or "natural" is surely, if anything, to appeal to the notion of what generally happens or can normally be expected to occur; but is this not to reintroduce the conception of empirical uniformities? It would appear, in other words, that the essential difference between the two interpretative models consists not in the fact that one relies upon the notion of generalizations whereas the other does not, but rather in an (admittedly important) disagreement concerning the kinds of generalizations that are relevant, and the levels of inquiry at which they are employed or presupposed.

## The historical point of view

It is perhaps hard to see how any theory of historical explanation could wholly dispense with reference to general statements at some stage of its analysis. What is less clear is whether such general statements have the status and role in history which the use of the term "law," with its predominantly scientific associations, implies. There is something eccentric in the idea that the construction of an historical narrative involves a continuous resort to generalizations concerning human behavior, if by "generalizations" is meant a set of inductively established or experimentally confirmed propositions that can be precisely listed and formulated. It is not merely that words like "insight" and "judgment," together with others that are embedded in the vocabulary of ordinary historical criticism, would seem to have little application to history conceived along such rigorous and tidy lines; the picture further suggests an "external" or "spectatorial" approach to the material that appears to obscure a salient feature of much historical writing and understanding. For it is arguable that in order truly to comprehend the policies or decisions of a particular historical figure or the motives or ideals that inspired some large-scale historical

movement (whether political, intellectual, or artistic), it is necessary to be able to share imaginatively the point of view of the participants; and this in turn requires a firsthand acquaintance with what it is, for example, to appreciate a situation and plan accordingly or to entertain certain hopes, desires, or fears. To speak of historical events as being "naturally" related or as forming an "intelligible" sequence may well be to imply that what happened was such as to fulfill our normal expectations; but it is important to recognize that, in human contexts, what we expect is closely tied to what we find understandable in the light of our own experience as rational purposive agents. It was this consideration, above all others, that earlier thinkers like Collingwood wished to stress when criticizing positivist attempts to assimilate history to natural science. Though often expressed in misleading or exaggerated terms, it is a point that still retains considerable force.

**Is objectivity possible?**   The claim that the historian stands in an especially intimate relation to his subject matter has sometimes been regarded as indicating a further significant difference between history and the natural sciences. This is the suggestion that the very nature of the historian's task and situation precludes him from achieving in his descriptions and interpretations the kind of objectivity that characterizes scientific work. It is not merely that, as a matter of fact, historians often offer widely dissimilar accounts of the same historical phenomena, even when basing what they say on broadly identical sources; it may be argued that such striking divergences are necessary and inevitable. Thus, suppose it is held—as it was, for instance, by Croce—that historical knowledge essentially involves the "re-creation" of the past by each historian within his own mind; it then becomes difficult to see how any historical account can fail to be to some extent colored and shaped by the individual interests and personality of its author—a conclusion tacitly accepted by Croce himself when he spoke of all history as "contemporary."

Even if such "idealist" theories of historical knowledge are rejected, further independent factors may be adduced that point in the same general direction. It has been maintained, for example, that the fact that the historian is engaged in discussing human beings and their activities, using everyday language to do so, commits him to introducing considerations which would be manifestly out of place in scientific contexts: there can be no such thing as a purely objective or "value-free" historical account, since language that is adapted to the description of what people feel, think, and do necessarily reflects the element of evaluation and appraisal that pervades the whole texture of human life and experience. Again, attention may be drawn to the manner in which all history is necessarily selective. The historian cannot pack into his account everything he knows about the subject he is studying, nor would he be considered a good historian if he tried to do so; the employment of judgments of relevance, of relative importance or triviality, is fundamental to his undertaking. But such judgments are founded upon assumptions and preconceptions of diverse kinds that are inherently disputable and that vary from person to person, society to society, age to age. What is of significance to an historian belonging to one period or milieu may seem unworthy of mention to another whose time and background are different; religious opinions, political beliefs, moral or social ideals, must all, consciously or unconsciously, influence such things as the historian's presentation of his material, his decisions as to what to include or omit, the weight he assigns to particular factors, and even his critical assessment of evidence and sources.

**Subjectivity and historical evaluation.** A conclusion frequently drawn from all this, both by philosophers and by practicing historians who have reflected on their craft, is that history is infected by some kind of radical and irremediable "subjectivity." Yet the claim in question, together with the arguments used to support it, have tended to be framed in highly general and abstract terms; in consequence, as a number of recent critics have pointed out (see, for instance, Carr 1961), several significant distinctions are in danger of being overlooked. It is a mistake, for instance, to suppose that the selection and presentation of material are always determined by "subjective" convictions and preconceptions of the kind stressed above; they may be, and very often are, dictated in a quite incontestable manner by the particular nature of the problem with which the historian is concerned. Likewise, it is one thing to say that an historian's choice of problem is due to certain personal interests or predilections he may have, and another to argue that these will necessarily affect his manner of solving it; the two have not, however, always been clearly separated. Again, judgments of relative importance may sometimes be made in the light of what has been called the "causal fertility" of events; but the question of whether some specific occurrence was productive of more far-reaching changes than another is an empirical matter, decidable by investigation—it has nothing essen-

tially to do with subjective values or attitudes peculiar to the historian.

Similar possibilities of confusion may arise with regard to the suggestion that the historian's subject matter is such as to render evaluation unavoidable. No doubt it is true that the purposes and doings of historical agents were to a large extent informed by the values and principles (moral or otherwise) to which they subscribed; but this by itself in no way entails that the historian cannot discuss their activities without engaging in such evaluation on his own account. If, on the other hand, it is the historian's use of common language that is held to preclude the possibility of his providing "neutral" descriptions, the precise force of this contention (assuming it to be correct) is open to doubt; what, for example, is to prevent historians from devising a reformed terminology to meet the difficulty?

**Remaining problems.** Taken together, the above and related points may go some way toward reducing the prima facie persuasiveness of the claim that anything akin to objectivity in the scientific sense is unattainable in history. But the issue remains a curiously intractable one, involving various puzzles and ambiguities into whose complexities it is impossible to enter here. Nor does it stand alone in this respect. The rich field of the critical philosophy of history contains a host of similarly disputed problems, with roots extending into many adjoining areas of inquiry (Gardiner 1959; see also Stern 1956; Meyerhoff 1959; New York University ... 1963). From this point of view their further investigation does not only concern the future development of the historical studies: it also has an obvious and important bearing upon some of the fundamental methodological questions that, at the present time, confront the neighboring social sciences.

PATRICK GARDINER

[See also MARXIST SOCIOLOGY; POSITIVISM; SOCIOLOGY, article on THE DEVELOPMENT OF SOCIOLOGICAL THOUGHT; and the biographies of COMTE; CROCE; DILTHEY; HEGEL; HUME; MARX; SIMMEL; SOROKIN; SPENGLER; VICO; WEBER, MAX.]

BIBLIOGRAPHY

ARON, RAYMOND (1938) 1961 Introduction to the Philosophy of History: An Essay on the Limits of Historical Objectivity. Boston: Beacon. → First published in French.
BERLIN, ISAIAH 1955 Historical Inevitability. London and New York: Oxford Univ. Press.
CAIRNS, GRACE E. 1962 Philosophies of History: Meeting of East and West in Cycle-pattern Theories of History. New York: Philosophical Library.
CARR, EDWARD H. (1961) 1962 What Is History? New York: Knopf.

Collingwood, Robin G. 1946 *The Idea of History.* Oxford Univ. Press. → A paperback edition was published in 1956.

Croce, Benedetto (1917) 1960 *History: Its Theory and Practice.* New York: Russell. → First published as *Teoria e storia della storiografia.*

Danto, Arthur C. 1965 *Analytical Philosophy of History.* Cambridge Univ. Press.

Dray, William 1957 *Laws and Explanation in History.* Oxford Univ. Press.

Gallie, W. B. 1964 *Philosophy and the Historical Understanding.* London: Chatto & Windus.

Gardiner, Patrick (1952) 1958 *The Nature of Historical Explanation.* Oxford Univ. Press.

Gardiner, Patrick (editor) 1959 *Theories of History: Readings From Classical and Contemporary Sources.* Glencoe, Ill.: Free Press.

Hodges, Herbert A. 1944 *Wilhelm Dilthey: An Introduction.* London: Routledge. → Contains extracts from some of Dilthey's principal writings.

Kahler, Erich 1964 *Meaning of History.* New York: Braziller.

Löwith, Karl (1949) 1950 *Meaning in History: The Theological Implications of the Philosophy of History.* Cambridge Univ. Press. → A paperback edition was published in 1957 by Phoenix.

Mandelbaum, Maurice H. 1938 *The Problem of Historical Knowledge: An Answer to Relativism.* New York: Liveright.

Meyerhoff, Hans (editor) 1959 *The Philosophy of History in Our Time: An Anthology.* Garden City, N.Y.: Doubleday.

New York University, Institute of Philosophy, 5th, 1962 1963 *Philosophy and History: A Symposium.* Edited by Sidney Hook. New York Univ. Press.

Oakeshott, Michael 1933 *Experience and Its Modes.* Cambridge Univ. Press.

Popper, Karl R. 1957 *The Poverty of Historicism.* Boston: Beacon.

Stern, Fritz R. (editor) 1956 *The Varieties of History: From Voltaire to the Present.* New York: Meridian.

Walsh, William H. (1951) 1958 *An Introduction to Philosophy of History.* London: Hutchinson. → A paperback edition was published in 1960 by Harper as *The Philosophy of History.*

White, Morton G. 1965 *Foundations of Historical Knowledge.* New York: Harper.

Winch, Peter 1958 *The Idea of a Social Science and Its Relation to Philosophy.* London: Routledge; New York: Humanities.

## II

### HISTORY AND THE SOCIAL SCIENCES

To social scientists, all history is social history, whether historians classify it as social history, political history, economic history, religious history, or history of some other kind. It cannot be said, therefore, that there is a distinct category of historical study which is devoted specifically to the past as the social scientist would deal with it. Rather, a new method of studying history of all kinds is emerging which is intended to satisfy the criteria of the social sciences and which provides or will provide evidence to illuminate the task of the sociologist, the anthropologist, the social psy-chologist, and so on. The historian working in this way makes use of the theories, categories, and techniques of the social scientist whose work he is trying to parallel. The social scientist, when he turns to accounts of the past for evidence, attempts to master the outlook and methods of the historian. The purpose of the present article is to examine in a summary way the principles which are beginning to govern these activities of historians and social scientists. It must not be supposed, however, that all history is now to be written or ever will be written with the scientific study of society as the end in view. The writing of history is a much more general activity than the systematic study of social relationships. Accounts of the past seem to have been composed in some form or other in every society. In literate societies with a high degree of cultivation, these accounts are rewritten every century or every generation, in some cases every few years, in conflicting versions.

The writing of history is undertaken for many purposes, which themselves would be a legitimate object of a social scientific investigation. These purposes can only be hinted at here. Reconstructions are worked out and interpretations are built up in order to reconcile a national society (or a group of any kind) with its past and with the way in which its present differs from that past. They are needed to make intelligible to every new generation its ordained place in time. They are needed to justify religious beliefs and practices, to provide political rationalizations, to enrich aesthetic and intellectual experience, and merely to satisfy curiosity. Even the simple keeper of the annals of his people or his church does something in all these directions and also does something to ensure, as d'Alembert said in the great *Encyclopédie*, that the achievements of the past shall not be lost to the men of the future.

The successive authors of the *Anglo-Saxon Chronicle* could not possibly have conceived of a science of society or imagined that the work which they produced could give rise to such an enterprise, let alone that it might provide an alternative to it. But since their time and down to our day, historians have advanced all these propositions about the relationship between history and the social sciences. It has been claimed that there is a distinctive historical method which provides its own account of how society works or, perhaps, its own unique attempt to do all that can be done, in view of the fact that the workings of society can never be more than partially established. According to this view, narration and description are the proper methods to be used (for an argument of this kind, see Collingwood 1946). Since no social situation, no past event, can ever be described in full in all its changing aspects, selection of the typical, after as exhaustive a study as possible, has to govern the undertaking. Some claim that the principles of such selection can be scientific principles, but others deny this, on the grounds that the selection can only be intuitive. Thus, the study of history has been seen as the point of origin of the social sciences; or as the rationale of an alternative type of special explanation; or as all that can be advanced, since social science is a chimera. A very different claim has also been put forward. The domain of the historian has been defined as all the social scientific evidence coming from the past. In this way, the phrases "historical science" and "the historical sciences" have come into being.

All the various claims about the relationship between history and the social sciences raise logical, conceptual, and philosophical issues, some of them of great intricacy [see HISTORY, *article on* THE PHILOSOPHY OF HISTORY]. In the present article recourse will be had to an archaic or even obsolete use of the word "history," as an aid to understanding history's present relationship with the social sciences. History will be conceived of here as bearing the very wide meaning it had in the phrase "natural history." Some biological scientists still call themselves naturalists.

Nowadays "natural history" is a way of referring to biology, botany, zoology, and geology, with a distinct implication of their being pursued rather unsystematically by amateurs, as a diversion. Before and during the scientific revolution, however, "natural history" meant all that could be known about nature simply by description, as contrasted with "natural philosophy," which meant that part of nature which could be understood on principle, scientifically, and which was acquired by the systematic use of certain techniques of observation. If we substitute the word "societal" for "natural," the new phrase "societal history" can be used in contrast with the phrase "social science," in rather the same way "natural history" was used in contrast to "natural philosophy" or "natural science." Such a usage recognizes that history is legitimately pursued for many purposes other than the complementing of the social sciences. It avoids the difficulties, already described, which attach to the phrase "social history." It emphasizes that social information which does not yet belong to the analytically formulated and technically cultivated social sciences (and which may never belong there) can nevertheless be apprehended, if not understood, in the historical, narrative, descriptive, intuitive mode.

Societal history, or the "history" of ordinary usage taken in its very widest sense, stands to the social sciences as natural history stands or once stood to the natural sciences. Once this roundabout definition is laid down, it becomes clear that although every form of historical study necessarily belongs to societal history whether or not it would usually be described as social, no form of historical study necessarily belongs to the social sciences. Particular types of historical inquiry may be said to be part of the social sciences, nevertheless, if certain conditions, discussed later in this article, are satisfied. We shall, in fact, distinguish those historical studies intended to advance the social sciences as a particular area of societal history and give them a collective name, "deliberative societal history."

The limitations usually placed upon the simple word "history" will be disregarded in a further way. Archeological evidence is sometimes excluded from history, but it will be included here as part of societal history, as will the material gained by anthropologists and sociologists in direct observation and oral communication. But although societal history is a descriptive undertaking, dealing with a very wide range of sources and with indefinitely extensible information, it has to satisfy the strictly chronological criterion rather more exactly than does natural history. It can deal only with those facts which belong to past time and which are to be understood in one-way temporal succession. Even this limitation becomes tenuous in the case of evidence assembled for the current situation by social scientists, which must all belong to past time, even if it is only the very recent past. But in practice the very near past, as represented by the most recently available social survey data, and so on, is excluded from societal history.

Since their subjects are related in this way, the social scientist and the societal historian are by no means always distinct individuals, any more than are the natural historian and the natural scientist; each individual is more the one than the other—more the sociologist, for example, than the social-structure historian. Some important sociologists (e.g., Max Weber and T. H. Marshall) wrote specifically historical works, and most technical works of the social sciences contain some discussion of a historical character. This is true even of economic theory (see, for example, John Maynard Keynes 1930), while the studies of anthropologists and sociologists sometimes have to present a considerable amount of descriptive and narrative history of the conventional kind. Only theoretical statistical works are likely to be entirely wanting in historical content. There are, moreover, as is well known, books written as history which are rightly regarded as classics of the social sciences (Tocqueville's works are good examples).

## Types of societal history

It is possible to delineate five types of historical undertakings, together with their particular functions in the study of society. They are listed here in descending order of significance to the social sciences, and, of course, they overlap to a certain extent.

**Social science works.** The first type of historical writing of significance to the social scientist belongs to the literature of the social sciences themselves, since it consists of parts of works written by social scientists. Every such work, as has been said, contains narrative–descriptive components, and these belong to societal history. They are of varying length and importance. There are the short historical descriptions and arguments which are found in such books as Gunnar Myrdal's *An American Dilemma* (1944) and in the very long historical citations and discussions which go to make up most of the text of Wittfogel's *Oriental Despotism* (1957). Neither this latter book nor any other book of the same type belongs wholly with societal history, since its object is to illuminate a particular institution in its significance for all societies at all times.

**Social structural studies.** The second type of historical writing of significance to the social scientist is social structural history. It consists of complete works deliberately undertaken by scholars calling themselves historians, rather than social scientists, that provide comparative historical examples which can be used alongside the comparative geographical examples of anthropologists. Such studies may take various forms: they may be comprehensive surveys of particular societies at certain points in the past, or they may contain records of social change over a particular period. But they will always tend to embrace whole national societies or whole cultural areas, rather than dealing in specified institutions alone. Although they belong with the established tradition of social history, they are undertaken, as far as possible, in conformity with two principles not usually made explicit in traditional works. One is that the evidence shall be assembled and analyzed in accordance with the methods and techniques of all the social sciences. The other is that conclusions shall be presented in a form which can be used in social analysis generally.

An example of an experimental work of this kind, using the method of comparison rather than

of narrative and dealing with the whole social structure rather than with specific institutions, is Laslett's *The World We Have Lost* (1965), which covers English society before and after industrialization and attempts to satisfy the principles just cited. If it is compared with Trevelyan's *English Social History* (1942), the difference between social structural history and traditional social history is brought out. A summary of the principles of this emerging form of historical writing is attempted below.

**Areas of social activity.** The third type of historical writing of significance to the social scientist consists of studies of the past of some isolable area of social activity. The distinctions between these special historical areas consist, to a large extent, simply of their varying subject matter. But a more interesting and important principle of difference is beginning to appear. Part of the definition of a recognized social science is that it should possess its own particular body of theory and technique, although there are differences between various social sciences in this respect. Historical writing within the area of each social science must attempt to make use of its theory and its technique, and in one conspicuous case, that of economic history, it has certainly begun to do so. Only one other isolable historical area shows signs of a similar evolution, and that is demographic history, using the theory and technique of demography. These are the two social sciences which lend themselves most easily to quantification and mathematical analysis; but it need not be supposed that the less effective tools and devices at the disposal of other social scientists are quite without their effect on historical studies. The history of religion and the history of education, for example, can in principle make use of religious and educational psychology and sociology.

The theory and technique of sociology and psychology can in principle be adapted so as to apply to the history of literature and the fine arts, to the history of social and political thinking, and to the history of mathematics and science. All these historical studies may also come to be illuminated by such techniques as content analysis and the other expedients used by sociologists and psychologists to reach an understanding of beliefs, attitudes, opinions, and ideologies in the contemporary world. (For an example of these expedients, see Lane 1962; and for a highly speculative attempt at psychological and intellectual analysis in past time, see Erikson 1958.) A further historical area may soon show signs of independence, making use, where it can, of the theory and techniques of political sociology. This new subject might tentatively be called the history of political systems, communication, and participation. Although such a subject will inevitably have to grow out of voting studies undertaken historically, there are already signs that even in societies without democratic procedures, past and present political behavior can be fruitfully studied (see, e.g., Vincent 1966). The distinction between this nascent subject and political history of the conventional kind will concern us below.

Nevertheless, these studies are difficult to classify, as can be seen from the example of the history of technology, which certainly belongs as much to economic history as it does to the history of mathematics and science and which may well have its part to play in some other areas as well. These studies, by treating their data and presenting their conclusions in a manner appropriate to their subject, will be of direct use to the social scientist, providing him with comparative historical examples in specialized spheres. Social structural history would ideally represent an amalgamation of all possible studies of this kind, as well as a general framework within which each of them might be pursued.

It is unlikely that many books of this type would actually deal with any one specialized area as a whole, although it is possible that works, especially multivolume collaborative studies, will continue to appear with titles such as "A History of Social and Political Thought." Most of the narrower studies can have two distinct objectives. The first objective is the social analysis of certain features of historically distant situations, with the issues of the social sciences generally in view. An example of this kind of study is Smelser's *Social Change in the Industrial Revolution* (1959). Although a historical monograph, applying theory to a particular topic, the Lancashire cotton factories of the early nineteenth century, it is also intended as a contribution to general social theory. The second objective is to illuminate past events and to revise interpretations of them, with only incidental reference to social analysis of present institutions and attitudes. It is noticeable that the studies carried out so far by the econometric economic historians tend to belong to this second type.

**Documentary and preparatory works.** The fourth category of historical writing of significance to the social sciences consists of documentary and preparatory works. Studies of this kind have considerable value, especially in the present, developing stage of many of the subjects already described. For example, the discovery and preparation of data for the description of social structure from listings of inhabitants, including familial structure and

kinship systems, has been of the first importance for social structural history. The editing and printing of records such as licenses to marry issued by episcopal courts, regular series of documents drawn up in connection with poor relief, and parochial registers containing detailed recordings of baptisms, marriages, and burials all come under this heading and are of great value to demographic as well as social structural history (Wrigley 1966).

**Traditional historical studies.** The fifth category of historical writing of significance to the social scientist is the residual one and consists of all other historical works, of whatever kind.

Works of traditional history are less likely to be of direct importance to the social scientist than any of those listed in the first four categories. But this does not mean that works which have been or are now being produced in accordance with traditional historical conventions are irrelevant. According to the definition adopted here, they belong to societal history and could have been mentioned as containing documentary and preparatory material. Many of them are, in fact, of great value in the hands of percipient and conscientious social inquirers. Moreover, the realistic and critical historian is often in a position to illuminate the use made of historical evidence by social scientists in a peculiarly effective way. He may even, on entirely historical criteria, demonstrate the inefficacy of explanations used both by his fellow historians and by social scientists. An example of this is the devastating work recently done by Hexter (1961) on the-rise-of-a-class hypotheses. Even if a historical work is composed without any intention of recording or illuminating social change, it may nevertheless do so or it may be shown to have done so by a later critic.

### Deliberative societal history

There clearly is a distinction between historical works intended by their authors as contributions to social analysis and those written in indifference to such an aim. Works of the first type constitute the category of deliberative societal history, in contrast with traditional historical studies. Although some of the characteristics of deliberative societal history have been sketched above, the criteria which mark historical work of this kind are not yet clear, distinct, or universally recognized. Nevertheless, it is already obvious that most traditional historical studies could not conform to the required conditions.

In the first place, many historians would be unwilling to recognize deliberative societal history as a description of their work. Some would reject the whole project of social and political science. Their methods belong to the category of tacit knowledge, not only in the understanding of past events but also in the selection of what will interest, inform, or even elevate their readers. Analysis of society and of social situations is by no means absent, even from writing of this kind, but the emphasis is upon description and narration, and the task is regarded as being entirely literary, with, perhaps, philosophical overtones. History, after all, as well as being the companion to the social sciences, is one of the traditional arts, with its own individual muse. Historians who insist that any human experience is unique are understandably skeptical of attempts at formulating general rules for the study of society and social change.

But even if and when it is not done in conscious divergence from the social sciences, most traditional historical study is still accomplished in ignorance of them. It is undertaken without knowledge of the relevant theories, concepts, and techniques. This is the second reason so much writing of this character is of problematic value to the social scientist.

The interests of the general public, rather than of the academic world or of the social scientists, give rise to the third reason that the relationship between traditional historical studies and the social sciences is so indirect and arbitrary. The demand that history shall be "interesting," that it shall tell a relevant, informative story with a moral or a message, has effects on the academic historian as well as on the writers of textbooks, the biographers, and the journalists. Tradition has tended to establish in historical studies specific requirements which have been even more limiting. It is expected that a national society will ordinarily be the unit of historical investigation and of historical narrative. The chronological divisions usually have to be those of the conventional political landmarks, and the events, sentiments, and attitudes to be explained have for the most part to be political, chosen for the importance they have for the reader's sense of citizenship.

These influences continue even when the subject matter is no longer of the traditional political character. Hence, many specialized studies still bear titles such as "The History of American Science in the Colonial Period" or "The History of Japanese Education Under the Tokugawa." It is true that the growing importance of the social sciences in recent years is beginning to remove some of these limitations and that the domination of politics, the state, and the values of citizenship is much less than it used to be. It is also true that economic history shows signs of transcending these limitations altogether, although it still seems to select topics as much for their polemical, and often political, interest as for their economic significance. Quite apart from traditional historical studies, then, none of the subjects we have classed as deliberative societal history can as yet be said to be under the controlling influence of the social sciences.

**Quantitative history.** Of all recent developments, it is clear that econometric economic history stands in sharpest contrast to traditional historical pursuits. Its rapid development in recent years makes it necessary to consider the question of the use of quantification in historical studies and its effect on their relationship with the social sciences. Douglass C. North sets out the characteristics of econometric economic history, but even among the economic historians there are some who do not consider it history at all or, at most, call it, in Fritz Redlich's term, quasi history. [See HISTORY, article on ECONOMIC HISTORY.]

The insistence on giving a numerical value to everything in a historical situation which is relevant to the problem in hand is one source of the criticism. This has given the title "cleometrics" to the new pursuit and brings it directly into line with trends in the social sciences. Although this pursuit has been severely criticized, I do not believe that its numerative characteristic makes the subject any the less historical.

Even if the numerical equivalents seem quite unreal to the common-sense observer and introduce a host of uncertainties into the issues which have to be judged, it has to be remembered that all historical judgments are beset with uncertainties of the same logical kind. Attempting to reckon the percentage of the gross national product of the United States made up by the railroads in 1850 is the same kind of undertaking as estimating the amount of influence which the growth of Christianity had on the decline of imperial Rome. Nor does it appear that the counterfactual type of argument used in cleometrics is necessarily a contradiction of the historical outlook and method. Estimating what might have happened if what did happen had not happened is characteristic of much historical argument of a conventional kind, and all that cleometrics does is to argue confessedly in this way, openly estimating the risk of error.

The truly significant point about cleometrics, for traditional historical studies, is that it attempts to do economic analysis on noncontemporaneous subjects. That is why this type of economic history belongs to the social sciences to an extent that no other historical study yet does. It has ceased to be mere societal history and has become social science. Only the recent advances in the theory of economic growth have made such work possible, and it is clear that the more fragmentary the quantifiable evidence, the more sophisticated the necessary theory is likely to be. For most of the other social sciences having equivalents among types of deliberative societal history, no such advanced theory exists or seems likely to be developed, except perhaps in demography. It must be remembered, also, that vast areas of information from the economic past cannot be dealt with by cleometrics and will never become susceptible to such methods.

It seems unlikely, therefore, that the rise of cleometrics is a portent of the future course of the relationship between traditional historical studies and the social sciences. In the foreseeable future only very few historians will be able to call themselves social scientists. Not many more social scientists will, perhaps, be able to apply their theories and practice their techniques on chronologically distant materials. The most important change will come at a more modest level: much more historical writing will surely come under the heading of "deliberative societal history." The elaboration of social structural history will be an important means by which this change will take place.

## Social structural history

Two of the characteristics of social structural history have also been made plain: first, it should assemble its evidence and carry out its analysis in accordance with the methods and techniques of the social sciences, and second, it should present its conclusions in a form which can be used in social analysis generally. It has also been suggested that social structural history may dispense with the narrative method, which has in the past been an almost universal feature of historical writing.

Since social description is to be done in wholes, narrative would in any case be a peculiarly difficult form for history written in this way. But although works of this kind will probably tend to consist of contrasts between a "before" and an "after," the dates selected will represent the median years of particular generations, rather than exact moments. The choice of the generations to be described will itself be a matter of importance and, like everything else, will have to be made with the interests of the social sciences generally in mind, as well as being made in accordance with historical criteria.

The social structural historian should begin his descriptions where the anthropologists and the sociologists do, that is, with the size, structure, and functions of the family in the society in question. Then will come the kinship system, then the other relationships, the geographical, the economic, the religious, the intellectual, that go to make up the community. "Community" here is understood in a plural sense, for the local, the tribal, and the regional associations and finally the national community, if indeed all these existed, are all to be included. Only then, and this is in sharp contrast with the practice of the traditional historian, will he concern himself with political institutions and the state itself.

It is clear that historical writing of this character will be faced with a particularly acute form of the problem which affects all historiography, that of summarizing and abbreviating sufficiently to make its account intelligible. Traditional history has a traditional expedient for this purpose: the choosing of significant instances, which are presented as typical. Since the social structural historian is still writing societal *history*, rather than social *science*, he will of course be at liberty to use the same method. But he must be expected to have a much clearer notion of the social theory or theories which make his chosen instances significant, and he will recognize that total description is a chimera, that all he can ever put on paper is a model of the society he is dealing with. The function of theories and the usefulness of models in pursuits of this kind is to order the data, to select and insist upon the regularities, to simplify drastically by approximation.

In the course of time, then, the social structural historian may find himself having to handle whole sets of theories and several different types of models. By this time the theories and models used by economists and demographers should be familiar to him. But his first concern will be to construct a model of his society in the much simpler sense just referred to; perhaps "miniature" would be a better term. He must, at all points in his descriptions, analyses, and comparisons, have the whole of the society in mind as well as a simplified notion of its over-all workings. He may find it useful to think of two separate models, or miniatures, one static and one dynamic, fitting into each other in the way any theory appropriate to a system in the process of change fits into a theory of that system as it is when at rest. He should at all times be aware of the ways in which his chosen models misrepresent the realities he is striving to deal with, and his duty will be to try to improve them. He should be conscious of the haphazard nature of the theories he has to use and aware of the areas in which, like his companions and predecessors among the traditional historians, he has to rely on intuition and guesswork. He may or may not find general theories of social action, like those of Talcott Parsons, useful to him in his difficult and challenging task. The essential point is that he should recognize that his is a theoretical, as well as an empirically descriptive, undertaking.

Social structural history and the other forms of deliberative societal history which have been defined here are not propounded as alternatives to traditional historical writing which should, and ultimately will, replace it. The writing of history has many functions other than providing social scientists with comparative instances and with a continuum in which they can do their work. History will continue to be written for all the many purposes for which it has always been written, regardless of what the social sciences do and how they may develop. All that has been attempted here is a sketch of the somewhat complex relationship between history as traditionally written and the social sciences as they are now pursued. Let it be stressed again that the historian and the social scientist have often been the same person, and this will probably increasingly be the case in the future. But in the writing of social structural history, the differences between the two roles become especially clear. Complicated and difficult as composing history of this kind may be, it presents a challenge which neither the historian nor the social scientist can any longer afford to ignore.

PETER LASLETT

#### BIBLIOGRAPHY

*The Anglo-Saxon Chronicle.* Translated with an introduction by G. N. Garmonsway. London: Dent, 1953.

CAHNMAN, WERNER J.; and BOSKOFF, ALVIN (editors) 1964 *Sociology and History: Theory and Research.* New York: Free Press.

COLLINGWOOD, R. G. 1946 *The Idea of History.* Oxford Univ. Press. → A paperback edition was published in 1956.

ERIKSON, ERIK H. (1958) 1962 *Young Man Luther: A Study in Psychoanalysis and History.* Austin Riggs Monograph No. 4. New York: Norton.

FÜRER-HAIMENDORF, CHRISTOPH VON 1955 Culture History and Cultural Development. *Yearbook of Anthropology* 1:149–168.

HEXTER, J. H. 1961 *Reappraisals in History: New Views on History and Society in Early Modern Europe.* Evanston, Ill.: Northwestern Univ. Press. → A paperback edition was published in 1963 by Harper.

History and Social Science. 1965 *International Social Science Journal* 17, no. 4 (entire issue).

KEYNES, JOHN MAYNARD (1930) 1958–1960 *A Treatise on Money.* 2 vols. London: Macmillan. → Volume 1: *The Pure Theory of Money.* Volume 2: *The Applied Theory of Money.*

LANE, ROBERT E. 1962 *Political Ideology: Why the American Common Man Believes What He Does.* New York: Free Press.

LASLETT, PETER 1965 *The World We Have Lost.* London: Methuen.

MYRDAL, GUNNAR (1944) 1962 *An American Dilemma: The Negro Problem and Modern Democracy.* New York: Harper. → A paperback edition was published in 1964 by McGraw-Hill.

REDLICH, FRITZ 1965 "New" and Traditional Approaches to Economic History and Their Interdependence. *Journal of Economic History* 25:480–495.

SMELSER, NEIL J. 1959 *Social Change in the Industrial Revolution.* London: Routledge; Univ. of Chicago Press.

TREVELYAN, GEORGE M. (1942) 1947 *English Social History: A Survey of Six Centuries, Chaucer to Queen Victoria.* London: Longmans.

VINCENT, JOHN 1966 *The Formation of the Liberal Party, 1857–1868.* London: Constable.

WITTFOGEL, KARL A. 1957 *Oriental Despotism: A Comparative Study of Total Power.* New Haven: Yale Univ. Press. → A paperback edition was published in 1963.

WRIGLEY, EDWARD A. (editor) 1966 *An Introduction to English Historical Demography.* London: Weidenfeld.

## III

### ETHNOHISTORY

Although it has appeared sporadically since the early twentieth century, the term "ethnohistory" was first used systematically in the 1940s by some North American cultural anthropologists, archeologists, and historians, to describe their writings and research on the history of the aborigines of the New World. In more recent years "ethnohistory" has come to mean the historical study of any non-European peoples. Utilizing documentary, oral, and archeological sources and the conceptual framework and insights of cultural and social anthropology, these studies attempt to reconstruct the history of indigenous peoples before and after European contact.

Ethnohistorians combine their "historical" sources with ethnographic field work among the present-day members of the societies whose past they aim to reconstruct. Their goal is to present "rounded" history, which will take into account the social and cultural systems of indigenous peoples; thus, ethnohistorians of North America have paid particular attention to the location and migration of Indian tribes, changing cultural adaptions to environment, demographic history, the exact nature of the relations of particular tribes with Europeans, and the effects which activities such as the fur trade and warfare have had on American Indians ("Symposium on the Concept of Ethnohistory" 1961).

Ethnohistory has led mainly to studies of particular cultural units, equivalent to the field anthropologists' ethnographic accounts. There has been little effort to build a body of generalizations, either through comparison or through the development of concepts or categories of sequences which would make interregional comparison possible. The characteristic approaches and problems of ethnohistory derive from the nature of the indigenous societies being studied, the period, type, and duration of European domination, the kinds of documentation available, and the theoretical orientation of the anthropologists who have studied the region.

Ethnohistory differs from the work of conventional colonial historians in several respects. The ethnohistorian usually has firsthand field experience in the area; this experience increases his knowledge of the indigenous society and how it actually functions or functioned. Thus, his interpretation of documentary evidence is deepened. The ethnohistorian tends to think in systemic, functional terms rather than in terms only of accident and particulars. He tries to use his general knowledge of social and cultural organization and constructs his units in terms of such concepts as "segmentary lineage-based societies," "peasant societies," and "patrimonial societies." The ethnohistorian tries to perceive historical events from the position of the aborigine rather than that of the European administrator, even when he is using the administrator's documents. He is more interested in the impact of colonial policy and practice than in the genesis of these policies in the metropolitan society.

### History of the approach

One of the major sources of the field of anthropology was a concern with the history of man in general, the comparative study of societies and institutions, and the reconstructions of the history of particular societies. Voltaire, Gustav Klemm, Sir Henry Maine, J. F. McLennan, J. J. Bachofen, N. D. Fustel de Coulanges, L. H. Morgan, and E. B. Tylor drew heavily on historical materials to establish a comparative science of society and culture. These early anthropologists utilized information about classical civilizations, Hindu India, European barbarians, medieval European institutions, and missionary and traveler accounts of primitive societies. In their broad-ranging and speculative reconstructions of the history of man, they discovered and labeled some of the basic features of primitive and peasant societies. [*See the biographies of* BACHOFEN; FUSTEL DE COULANGES; MCLENNAN; MAINE; MORGAN, L. H.; TYLOR; VOLTAIRE.]

Subsequently, the broad schemes of "evolutionary history" put forward by these early anthropolo-

gists were rejected; however, they did illustrate how documentary material, illuminated by comparative theory, may be used to understand particular sequences of social and cultural change.

At the beginning of the twentieth century the diffusionists, e.g., Ratzel and Graebner, and then the distributionists, e.g., Wissler, Kroeber, and Lowie, denied the possibility of the use of direct historical methods to reconstruct the history of aboriginal societies. Kroeber believed that for the study of "poor dateless primitives . . . we do not possess even one document written before our day" ([1901–1951] 1952, p. 65). Lowie, in his attack on Swanton and Dixon's use of oral traditions and travelers' accounts in their history of North American Indian migrations (Swanton & Dixon 1914), utterly denied "that primitive man is endowed with historical sense or perspective" (Lowie [1917] 1960, p. 206). Lowie believed that the anthropologist's "historical problems can be solved only by the objective methods of comparative ethnology, archeology, linguistics and physical anthropology" (*ibid.*, p. 210).

The American distributionist, or "historical," school was based on the attempt to discover items of culture and society from the "memory culture" of surviving elderly members of American Indian tribes. These social and cultural items or traits— items of material culture and linguistic data—were plotted geographically, in attempts to infer historical or chronological relationships between tribes. The distributionists were not concerned in any detailed fashion with the history of particular tribes. Typical of this approach, Sapir's "Time Perspective in Aboriginal American Culture: A Study in Method," published in 1916, devoted only two pages out of 87 to the use of documents and indigenous oral traditions. Dependence on distribution studies of individual traits or complexes (e.g., the Sun Dance, particular tales and myths) and lack of systematic use of documents and oral histories weakened the work of the American historical school, and they tended to produce timeless descriptions of phenomena on an areal basis or descriptive synchronic accounts of particular memory cultures.

In England in the 1920s Malinowski and Radcliffe-Brown also rejected historically oriented research in anthropology. Both argued that documents for the study of primitive society were unavailable. Radcliffe-Brown contended that the nature of social anthropology and history were antithetical: social anthropologists, as distinguished from ethnologists, were to be concerned with the development of generalizations about the structure of society derived from the comparative study of primitive societies, without reference to their history. Synchronic, or cross-sectional, studies of societies were carefully distinguished from diachronic studies, or studies of societies as they changed through time; the latter could lead only to explanations of uniqueness. Until the 1950s most British social anthropologists kept to Radcliffe-Brown's strictures and avoided diachronic studies. [*See the biographies of* MALINOWSKI; RADCLIFFE-BROWN; SAPIR.]

British and American anthropologists continued to study social and cultural change without reference to historical materials, even when, as in the case of Lucy Mair's study of the Baganda (1934) or Monica Hunter Wilson's of the Pondo (1936), documentary sources were readily available. Gluckman's study of the Zulu political system (1940) and Nadel's *Black Byzantium* (1942) did use historical materials to develop a model of political structures before European incursions. However, these studies are not histories but analytical abstractions from historical sources to illuminate structural principles. The one outstanding exception during this period is E. E. Evans-Pritchard's study of the bedouin of Cyrenaica (1949). In this study Evans-Pritchard analyzed the process by which a lineage-based society developed centralized political roles and institutions. The Sanusi, an order of Muslim religious leaders, had moved into Cyrenaica in the early nineteenth century and provided needed religious and trade functions in the society. Geographically and structurally they located their religious centers at boundaries of existing lineage and tribal territories. Largely through the pressure of Turkish and, subsequently, Italian administrators who tried to rule the bedouin, the heads of the religious order, as the only visible leaders, were impelled into society-wide political roles. Evans-Pritchard used available colonial records and reports, published narratives, oral traditions, and the memories of participants in the events which make up the historical narrative. *The Sanusi of Cyrenaica* is based on Evans-Pritchard's understanding of the operation of an acephalous lineage-based political system, and it is this which gives him the structural principles on which he organized his historical narrative and provides a model for the study of the process of internal structural change in such a society under the impact of foreign rule.

In the United States in the period from 1910 to 1930 a few anthropologists, notably John R. Swanton, in his studies of the Indians of the American southeast (1922; 1946), and Frank G. Speck, working on the tribes of the northeastern United States (1928), used direct historical methods to reconstruct the tribal pasts. For this task they drew on their field work among the remnants of the tribes of the areas and made intensive use of a wide range of documentary materials. [*See the biography of* SWANTON.]

Fittingly, the clearest early examples of systematic ethnohistorical work are found in a volume of studies dedicated to Swanton and published by the Smithsonian Institution in 1940. William Fenton used seventeenth-century and eighteenth-century documents to trace location and movement of Iroquois bands (1940); William Duncan Strong demonstrated that documentary materials could be used with archeological data to provide a continuous record from present into the past of particular sites (1940); Julian Steward's study of Great Basin societies combines ecology, history, archeology, and ethnography and yielded insight into structural and cultural processes (1940). These three studies indicated the ethnohistoric approach that was to become formalized in the 1950s. [*See the biography of* STRONG; ECOLOGY, *especially the article on* CULTURAL ECOLOGY.]

The accumulation of ethnographic data made it clear that early assumptions about the stability of cultures and societies before European contact were false. Anthropologists began to recognize that instead of a precontact situation of stagnation in aboriginal societies, changes of three types had occurred. First, there were small-scale cyclical changes, exemplified by the growth and fission of extended families and lineages. There were also larger cycles of political and cultural expansion as lineages within tribes came to dominate similar units; however, many societies could not develop institutions to contain reassertion of independence of such units, so that large-scale tribal organizations would develop for a time under one or another section of a tribe, only to break apart into smaller units again. The third type of change involved large-scale tribal migrations, leading to greatly changed political, social, and ceremonial orders.

In addition to these internal processes of change, ethnohistorians have demonstrated the indirect effects of outsiders—Europeans and Arabs, for example—on indigenous societies and cultures even before the period of European domination. The slave trade in both east and west Africa, the trans-Sahara trade in west Africa, and the ivory trade in east and central Africa led to major political changes in African societies. The fur trade in North America led to major intertribal warfare, the development of ideas of property, and the emergence of a stratified social system based on differential possession of or access to furs. The introduction of the horse to the Great Plains of North America changed the way of life of many tribes who then bordered the region. In each case the culture and society that anthropologists assumed were static and stable and from which one could measure or describe change were in themselves changing because of outside influences (Ewers 1955; Leacock 1954; Jones 1963; Dike 1956).

The passage of the Indian Claims Act in 1946 by Congress led to a marked rise in ethnohistorical research in the United States. Under the provisions of this act Indian tribes could sue the federal government for recompense for lands taken from them after the Indians had signed treaties protecting their rights. Anthropologists were employed as experts by both Indian tribes and the government, to establish location, extent, and nature of aboriginal control over various territories and the exact nature of treaty obligations. This drew the attention of many ethnographers, who previously had paid little heed to the extensive archival resources of the federal government and the various states in their study of the American Indian. *Ethnohistory*, the principal journal in the field, was founded in 1954 partly to provide an outlet for materials and interest developed by the Indian claims cases.

The expansion of field-work opportunities in Latin America and Asia and the emergence of many states from colonial rule has been a tremendous stimulus to ethnohistorical work since the end of World War II. In many of these areas there are long literary traditions and a wealth of documentary material. In Latin America, for example, certain areas have been covered in historical sources for a four-hundred-year period (for a brief review of the literature, see Adams 1962; Armillas 1960; Gibson 1955). In east and southeast Asia there have been important ethnohistorical studies of kinship and clan structure (Freedman 1958; R. J. Smith 1962), land tenure (T. C. Smith 1959), the recruitment and training of indigenous bureaucracies (Ho 1962; Marsh 1961; Silberman 1964), urban social history and mobility (R. J. Smith 1963), immigrant communities (Skinner 1957), and indigenous political systems (Gullick 1958). Ethnohistorical studies of south Asia and the Middle East are beginning to appear (Cohn 1962a; 1962b; Polk 1963).

In European studies there has been a long tradition in the study of classical, medieval, and early modern society, enlightened by sociological and anthropological method and concepts. Most of this work has been carried out by social, economic, and legal historians rather than by anthropologists themselves. The ethnohistorical study of classical society has attracted considerable attention (Kluck-hohn 1961). M. I. Finley, on the basis of the *Odyssey*, has written an essay on the culture and social structure of the Greeks of the heroic era; in this he consciously used the ideas of Malinowski, Mauss, and Radcliffe-Brown (Finley 1954). E. R. Dodds, in his analysis of Greek literature, has drawn on some of the concepts of psychoanalytically oriented anthropology (1951). Marc Bloch's great works on feudal society (1939–1940) and the rural structure of medieval France (1931) illustrate the possibilities of an ethnohistory of medieval Europe.

The writing of British social history from the time of Maitland (1897) and Vinogradoff (1905) has been marked by the conscious and unconscious use of social anthropology. Modern subjects that have received sophisticated ethnohistorical treatment include the blood feud of the Franks (Wallace-Hadrill 1959), Anglo-Saxon kinship (Lancaster 1958), and marriage systems of the early modern period (Stone 1965, pp. 589–671; Habakkuk 1950). Although social anthropologists have done considerable field work in European peasant societies, few examples of systematic and careful ethnohistorical work have appeared. An exception is the work of Lawrence Wylie, a student of French literature and civilization, who on the basis of field work among French peasants has been able to show the usefulness of oral traditions and documents for studying the changing value systems of a peasant village (Wylie 1965).

In areas without long written traditions, careful and important ethnohistorical work has begun. The *Journal of African History*, founded in 1960, demonstrates the utilization of official records, recorded African traditions, and Arabic and Coptic materials. The institutional history of the Maori from the eighteenth century is being written (Vayda 1961; Biggs 1960). The *Journal of Pacific History* was recently established as an outlet for the growing ethnohistorical research on the Pacific area.

### Sources and methods

**Written documents.** In his use of written documents, the ethnohistorian initially has the same problem and uses the same techniques as conventional historians. The ethnohistorian who has been trained as an anthropologist and has carried out field work is often highly frustrated when he has to depend on documents. The research problems of the ethnohistorian usually pertain to local history or "subhistorical" problems. He is not concerned with major, well-documented events, which a political historian deals with; very often he wants to know the minutiae of the past, e.g., the kinship connections of shadowy historical figures in an indigenous society, the movement and location of particular lineages at particular times, the symbolic meanings of a coronation ceremony in an African kingdom, the population of an American Indian group in the seventeenth century.

Often it is difficult to identify adequately the individuals and groups the ethnohistorian is concerned with. As an anthropologist, he expects to build inductively, from disparate bits of information, a picture of a functioning system; but he cannot generate his own data by asking people questions and observing their behavior in the context of living experiences. The documents he deals with are rarely written by the people whose social structure or culture he wants to study but are accounts by observers, naïve and biased, who often only half understood what they were recording. If he uses administrative records, not only must he know, as a good historian, who wrote the minutes or the statements of decisions taken and why they wrote them; he must place the data in a broader context of administrative policy. Certain official records, such as tax records, land surveys, and documents from actual legal proceedings, as distinguished from decisions and policies, frequently yield the best data. These materials are less finely filtered through the cultural screen of the administrators. The ethnohistorian must constantly try to understand the categories of the administrator and outside observer, as well as the indigenous classification systems. The interpretation of official or nonofficial documents, of policy statements and other primary data, requires an understanding of the culture and society of colonial administrators. This in itself is difficult, for the gross features of the metropolitan society may be misleading. The ethnohistorian has to know what particular group in the society the administrator came from, whether his values, education, and social and political philosophy differed from the rest of the society, and if so, how. The ethnohistorian must understand the structure of the colonial administration and know the partisanship of the men responsible for the documents he studies. He must understand the relationships between the decision makers in the metropolitan center, the administrators in the colonial center, and the men in the field. He has to know how administrators collected data and information and whom they dealt with and employed from the indigenous society. He must perceive which notions developed about the indigenous society were mistaken, how they affected decisions and observations, and how decisions which may have been based on such misinformation affected

the indigenous society. The ethnohistorian's task is to use conventional historical methods but to ask different questions and to keep in mind his concern with the indigenous society (Curtin 1964).

There are, for almost every region, extensive published collections of source material; for example, Thwaites's 73-volume series (Jesuits Letters From Missions 1896–1901) for North America, the collections of Theal (1883) and Brásio (1952–1960) for southeast Africa, and parliamentary papers of Great Britain for India and Africa. The main resources, however, are to be found in the national and regional archives and local administrative and record offices of the area being studied.

In areas such as Uganda, the emirates of northern Nigeria, and the Malay States, where Europeans ruled indirectly and tried to maintain the indigenous political system, documents were produced by members of the society themselves. Political and social development can be traced through the eyes of some of the indigenous peoples.

**Oral traditions.** In recent years, particularly in the study of the history of African societies, the ethnohistorian and the anthropologist with a historical interest, have demonstrated convincingly how oral tradition can be recorded, collated, checked, and utilized for historical purposes (Abraham 1961; Vansina 1961; M. G. Smith 1961). Oral traditions cover a wide variety of subject matter and can be found in a variety of forms. Societies with centralized political institutions and conquest states have often produced well-developed oral histories, and frequently there are specialists whose concern it is to memorize and transmit these traditions. In the use of this form of oral tradition, great caution is obviously necessary, since the history reflects as much about present social and political structure as it does about the past and is constantly being changed to account for changing situations (Barnes 1951; Cunnison 1951).

Oral history reflects the social units within the society; villages and lineages will have accounts of their past, which perform the specific function of relating groups to each other and which validate or correct local claims and support relationships. The ethnohistorian is often confronted with an extraordinary multiplicity of conflicting accounts of the past, even from the same village (Cohn 1961). Tribal segments, royal lineages, and courts may have well-preserved histories, which function as charters to justify contemporary social structure.

As Vansina (1961) demonstrates, historical narratives are not the only aspect of oral tradition that can be recorded, collated, and utilized; sacred formulas, names, poetry, genealogies, folk tales, myths, and legal precedents are useful to the ethnohistorian. In the interpretation of oral tradition, stress must first be put on the cultural context in which the tradition is found. Vansina defines oral tradition as "testimonies of the past which are deliberately transmitted from mouth to mouth." As he does in the case of written documents, the researcher must always ask what function the tradition performs in the contemporary society. Even material which is demonstrably false can be of great value, as it might incidentally contain historical facts.

Where outsiders have been recording indigenous oral traditions for a long time (as, for example, among the Maori), the relationship between the oral tradition and contemporary political structure can be used to understand not only the past referred to in the tradition but the actual political situation existing at the time the tradition was recorded.

**Field work.**    Field work is essential to the work of the ethnohistorian. The basic anthropological orientation, which differentiates the ethnohistorian from the conventional colonial historian, is developed through the experience of systematic field observation and the collection of data from living people; the aim of field work is to present a description and analysis of a functioning social system.

Field work, then, is a major part of the ethnohistorian's training; through field work he develops a sensitivity to the structure of a society that is difficult to achieve from study of documentary evidence alone. Ideas relating to historical relationships and processes may actually be tested in the field, where aspects of the society and culture are still in operation. [See FIELD WORK.]

## Ethnohistory and anthropology

Thus far diachronic studies have not yielded theoretical formulations. While synchronic studies are useful in enabling the ethnohistorian to infer social processes from documentary evidence, the contribution that diachronic studies will make to theory building or even to the development of descriptive generalizations regarding society and culture is harder to demonstrate. Even in the most rigid synchronic ethnographic study, the ethnographer must deal with the dimension of time. At the very least, he is dealing with three generations and with individuals whose lives have covered a sixty-year period. Invariably the field ethnographer asks questions about the past; he must confront the question of norms and changing norms, accidental social arrangements, and enduring aspects of the social structure.

Through historical study the anthropologist may identify changes within the system which are the result of flux, accident, or cyclical sequences and those which are due to structural realignments. Nadel and others have argued that to know the direction of social structural change, one needs time depth (Nadel 1957, chapter 6; Lévi-Strauss 1949). Thus, for example, careful statistical study frequently shows that there are in some, if not all, societies degrees of latitude or freedom in an individual's choice of residence, whether it be virilocal or uxorilocal, and these choices may be related to other variables. Synchronic studies may account for these relationships, but if we want to account for change, then historical methods for studying a society—primitive, peasant, or industrial—are the prerequisite for the development of adequate theories (Evans-Pritchard 1961; M. G. Smith 1962; Thomas 1963).

## Historians and anthropologists

The development of nineteenth-century "scientific history"—the study of the past divorced from the values and passions of the historian's times, the idea that historical facts could be determined and, if chronologically ordered, would speak for themselves—has led, with some notable exceptions, to the historian's consciously eschewing concepts and generalizations that might guide and illuminate his description and analysis of the past. In the twentieth century, though, historians have become increasingly aware that they do use and have to use generalizations if they are to do more than edit texts. H. Stuart Hughes (1960, pp. 25–26) has pointed to at least four levels at which historians generalize. First, they generalize semantically; by using words, such as "nation," "revolution," "development," "trend," and "social class," historians implicitly abstract, generalize, and compare. Second, "conclusions" in the form of a grouping of statements about a man, a period, or a movement are generalizations. Third, schematizations, inherent in such ideas as "urbanization" and "industrialization," by which bits and pieces of historical study are organized in terms of process or structure, are generalizations and are close to the kinds of generalizations social scientists make. Finally, there are the broad, all-inclusive systematizations of history or metahistory, associated with the work of men like Spengler and Toynbee. It is at this fourth level, that is, in the conscious use of concepts regarding process and structure in society and culture, that the social scientist and the historian can best interrelate their study. If the characteristic activity of the historian is the study of the past and if his organizing principle is a time sequence, then he must borrow organizing principles from other disciplines, both the humanities and the social sciences. In major subfields of history, this process of borrowing is explicit, for example, in economic history, where the concepts and methods of economics are consciously used to provide the conceptual framework. Intellectual and social history have borrowed from psychology, sociology, and anthropology.

In the last thirty years there have been several efforts to utilize the anthropologist's approach in the study of history; the anthropology which has proven most congenial to historians is cultural anthropology. The concept of culture as an all-embracing idea covering behavior and values of a particular people at a particular time fits well with historians' predilections. Hughes puts it well when he says: ". . . the approach of the cultural anthropologist so closely resembles that of the historian as frequently to seem identical with it. Like the historical scholar, the student of exotic cultures adopts a highly permissive attitude towards his data; he is perfectly happy in the realm of imprecision and of 'intuitive' procedures; and he tries to grapple with what he regards as the central problems of the societies with which he is concerned" (Hughes 1960, p. 34; see also Ware 1940; Social Science Research Council 1954; Gottschalk 1963). Books such as Ruth Benedict's *Patterns of Culture* (1934) and attempts on the part of anthropologists to do national character studies are taken by historians as models (for example, see Potter 1954) because the approach, rather than the techniques, methods, and concepts, of the cultural anthropologist is useful to historians. With notable exceptions, such as Marc Bloch, historians have not been eager to combine field work with historical research to find still extant in societies traces of previous industrial and agricultural techniques or surviving forms of social organization [*see the biography of* BLOCH].

It is, however, in the study of the preindustrial and modernizing societies of today and of the historical societies that characterized the whole world before the beginning of the nineteenth century that the anthropologist and the historian would appear to need each other.

BERNARD S. COHN

[*See also* ARCHEOLOGY; ETHNOLOGY; HISTORIOGRAPHY.]

### BIBLIOGRAPHY

ABRAHAM, D. P. 1961 Maramuca: An Exercise in the Combined Use of Portuguese Records and Oral Tradition. *Journal of African History* 2:211–225.

ADAMS, RICHARD N. 1962 Ethnohistoric Research Methods: Some Latin American Features. *Ethnohistory* 9:179–205.

ARMILLAS, PEDRO 1960 *Program of the History of American Indians.* Part 2: Post Columbian America. Social Science Monographs, No. 8. Washington: Pan American Union, Department of Cultural Affairs, Social Science Section.

BARNES, J. A. (1951) 1961 History in a Changing Society. Pages 318–327 in Simon Ottenberg and Phoebe Ottenberg (editors), *Cultures and Societies of Africa.* New York: Random House.

BELSHAW, CYRIL S. 1957 The Changing Cultures of Oceanic Peoples During the Nineteenth Century. *Journal of World History* 3:647–664.

BENEDICT, RUTH 1934 *Patterns of Culture.* Boston: Houghton Mifflin. → A paperback edition was published in 1961.

BIGGS, BRUCE 1960 *Maori Marriage: An Essay in Reconstruction.* Polynesian Society Maori Monographs, No. 1. Wellington: The Society.

BLOCH, MARC (1931) 1952–1956 *Les caractères originaux de l'histoire rurale française.* 2 vols. New ed. Paris: Colin. → Volume 2, *Supplément établi d'après les travaux de l'auteur (1931–1944),* was written by Robert Dauvergne.

BLOCH, MARC (1939–1940) 1961 *Feudal Society.* Univ. of Chicago Press. → First published as *La société féodale: La formation des liens de dépendance* and *La société féodale: Les classes et le gouvernement des hommes.*

BRÁSIO, ANTÓNIO D. (editor) 1952–1965 *Monumenta missionaria africana: Africa ocidental.* 10 vols. Lisbon: Agência Geral do Ultramar, Divisão de Publicações e Biblioteca.

COHN, BERNARD S. 1961 The Pasts of an Indian Village. *Comparative Studies in Society and History* 3:241–250.

COHN, BERNARD S. 1962a The British in Benares: A Nineteenth Century Colonial Society. *Comparative Studies in Society and History* 4:169–199.

COHN, BERNARD S. 1962b Political Systems in Eighteenth Century India: The Banaras Region. *Journal of the American Oriental Society* 82:312–320.

CUNNISON, IAN 1951 *History of the Luapula: An Essay on the Historical Notions of a Central African Tribe.* Rhodes–Livingstone Papers, No. 21. Oxford Univ. Press.

CURTIN, PHILIP D. 1964 *The Image of Africa: British Ideas and Action, 1780–1850.* Madison: Univ. of Wisconsin Press.

DIKE, KENNETH O. (1956) 1962 *Trade and Politics in the Niger Delta, 1830–1885: An Introduction to the Economic and Political History of Nigeria.* Oxford: Clarendon.

DODDS, ERIC R. (1951) 1963 *The Greeks and the Irrational.* Berkeley: Univ. of California Press.

EGGAN, FRED 1937 Historical Changes in the Choctaw Kinship System. *American Anthropologist* New Series 39:34–52.

EVANS-PRITCHARD, E. E. (1949) 1954 *The Sanusi of Cyrenaica.* Oxford: Clarendon.

EVANS-PRITCHARD, E. E. (1961) 1963 Anthropology and History. Pages 46–65 in E. E. Evans-Pritchard, *Essays in Social Anthropology.* New York: Free Press. → A lecture delivered at the University of Manchester in 1961.

EWERS, JOHN C. 1955 *The Horse in Blackfoot Culture: With Comparative Material From Other Western*

*Tribes.* U.S. Bureau of American Ethnology, Bulletin No. 159. Washington: Smithsonian Institution.

FENTON, WILLIAM N. 1940 Problems Arising From the Historic Northeastern Position of the Iroquois. Pages 159–251 in Smithsonian Institution, *Essays in Historical Anthropology of North America in Honor of John R. Swanton.* Smithsonian Miscellaneous Collections, Vol. 100. Washington: The Institution.

FENTON, WILLIAM N. 1951 Locality as a Basic Factor in the Development of Iroquois Social Structure. Pages 35–54 in *Symposium on Local Diversity in Iroquois Culture.* U.S. Bureau of American Ethnology, Bulletin No. 149. Washington: Government Printing Office.

FENTON, WILLIAM N. 1961 Iroquoian Culture History: A General Evaluation. Pages 253–277 in *Symposium on Cherokee and Iroquois Culture.* U.S. Bureau of American Ethnology, Bulletin No. 180. Washington: Government Printing Office.

FINLEY, MOSES I. (1954) 1956 *The World of Odysseus.* Rev. ed. London: Chatto & Windus.

FREEDMAN, MAURICE (1958) 1965 *Lineage Organization in Southeastern China.* London School of Economics Monographs on Social Anthropology, No. 18. New York: Humanities.

GIBSON, CHARLES 1955 The Transformation of the Indian Community in New Spain. *Journal of World History* 2:581–607.

GIBSON, CHARLES 1964 *The Aztecs Under Spanish Rule: A History of the Indians of the Valley of Mexico, 1519–1810.* Stanford Univ. Press.

GLUCKMAN, MAX 1940 The Kingdom of the Zulu of South Africa. Pages 25–55 in Meyer Fortes and E. E. Evans-Pritchard (editors), *African Political Systems.* Oxford Univ. Press.

GOTTSCHALK, LOUIS R. (editor) 1963 *Generalization in the Writing of History.* Univ. of Chicago Press.

GULLICK, J. M. 1958 *Indigenous Political Systems of Western Malaya.* London School of Economics Monographs on Social Anthropology, No. 17. London: Athlone.

HABAKKUK, H. J. 1950 Marriage Settlements in the Eighteenth Century. Royal Historical Society, *Transactions* Fourth Series 32:15–30.

HO, PING-TI 1962 *The Ladder of Success in Imperial China: Aspects of Social Mobility, 1368–1911.* New York: Columbia Univ. Press.

HOMANS, GEORGE C. (1941) 1960 *English Villagers of the Thirteenth Century.* New York: Russell.

HUGHES, H. STUART 1960 The Historian and the Social Scientist. *American Historical Review* 66:20–46.

JESUITS, LETTERS FROM MISSIONS (NORTH AMERICA) (1896–1901) 1959 *The Jesuit Relations and Allied Documents: Travels and Explorations of the Jesuit Missionaries in New France, 1610–1791. . . .* 73 vols. Edited by Reuben G. Thwaites. New York: Pageant.

JONES, G. I. 1963 *The Trading States of the Oil Rivers: A Study of Political Development in Eastern Nigeria.* Oxford Univ. Press.

KLUCKHOHN, CLYDE 1961 *Anthropology and the Classics.* Providence, R.I.: Brown Univ. Press.

KROEBER, A. L. (1901–1951) 1952 *The Nature of Culture.* Univ. of Chicago Press. → See especially pages 63–65 on "History and Science in Anthropology."

LANCASTER, LORRAINE 1958 Kinship in Anglo-Saxon Society. Parts 1 and 2. *British Journal of Sociology* 9:230–250, 359–377.

LEACOCK, ELEANOR 1954 The Montagnais "Hunting Territory" and the Fur Trade. American Anthropological Association, *Memoir* No. 78.

LÉVI-STRAUSS, CLAUDE (1949) 1963 Introduction: History and Anthropology. Pages 1–27 in Claude Lévi-Strauss, *Structural Anthropology.* New York: Basic Books. → First published in French.

LOWIE, ROBERT H. (1917) 1960 Oral Tradition and History. Pages 202–210 in Robert H. Lowie, *Selected Papers in Anthropology.* Edited by Cora DuBois. Berkeley: Univ. of California Press.

MAIR, LUCY P. (1934) 1965 *An African People in the Twentieth Century.* New York: Russell.

MAITLAND, FREDERIC W. 1897 *Domesday Book and Beyond.* Cambridge Univ. Press.

MARSH, ROBERT M. 1961 *The Mandarins: The Circulation of Elites in China, 1600–1900.* New York: Free Press.

MORGAN, LEWIS HENRY 1871 *Systems of Consanguinity and Affinity of the Human Family.* Smithsonian Contributions to Knowledge, Vol. 17, Publication No. 218. Washington: Smithsonian Institution.

NADEL, SIEGFRIED F. 1942 *A Black Byzantium: The Kingdom of Nupe in Nigeria.* Published for the International Institute of African Languages and Cultures. Oxford Univ. Press.

NADEL, SIEGFRIED F. 1957 *The Theory of Social Structure.* London: Cohen & West; Glencoe, Ill.: Free Press. → Published posthumously.

OLIVER, DOUGLAS L. (1951) 1961 *The Pacific Islands.* Rev. ed. Garden City, N.Y.: Doubleday.

POLK, WILLIAM R. 1963 *The Opening of South Lebanon: 1788–1840.* Cambridge, Mass.: Harvard Univ. Press.

POTTER, DAVID M. (1954) 1963 *People of Plenty: Economic Abundance and the American Character.* Univ. of Chicago Press.

ROWE, JOHN H. (1946) 1963 Inca Culture at the Time of the Spanish Conquest. Pages 183–330 in Julian H. Steward (editor), *Handbook of South American Indians.* Volume 2: *The Andean Civilizations.* U.S. Bureau of American Ethnology, Bulletin No. 143. New York: Cooper Square.

SAPIR, EDWARD (1916) 1949 Time Perspective in Aboriginal American Culture: A Study in Method. Pages 389–462 in Edward Sapir, *Selected Writings . . . in Language, Culture and Personality.* Edited by D. Mandelbaum. Berkeley: Univ. of California Press.

SILBERMAN, BERNARD S. 1964 *Ministers of Modernization: Elite Mobility in the Meiji Restoration, 1868–1873.* Tucson: Univ. of Arizona Press.

SKINNER, GEORGE W. 1957 *Chinese Society in Thailand.* Ithaca, N.Y.: Cornell Univ. Press.

SMITH, MICHAEL G. 1960 *Government in Zazzau: 1800–1950.* Oxford Univ. Press.

SMITH, MICHAEL G. 1961 Field Histories Among the Hausa. *Journal of African History* 2:87–101.

SMITH, MICHAEL G. 1962 History and Social Anthropology. *Journal of the Royal Anthropological Institute of Great Britain and Ireland* 92:73–85.

SMITH, ROBERT J. 1962 Stability in Japanese Kinship Terminology: The Historical Evidence. Pages 25–33 in Pacific Science Congress, Tenth, Honolulu, 1961, *Japanese Culture: Its Development and Characteristics.* Edited by Robert J. Smith and Richard K. Beardsley. Chicago: Aldine.

SMITH, ROBERT J. 1963 Aspects of Mobility in Pre-industrial Japanese Cities. *Comparative Studies in Society and History* 5:416–423.

SMITH, THOMAS C. 1959 *The Agrarian Origins of Modern Japan*. Stanford Univ. Press.

SMITHSONIAN INSTITUTION 1940 *Essays in Historical Anthropology of North America in Honor of John R. Swanton*. Smithsonian Miscellaneous Collections, Vol. 100. Washington: The Institution.

SOCIAL SCIENCE RESEARCH COUNCIL, COMMITTEE ON HISTORIOGRAPHY 1954 *The Social Sciences in Historical Study: A Report*. Social Science Research Council, Bulletin No. 64. New York: The Council.

SPECK, FRANK G. 1928 *Territorial Subdivisions and Boundaries of the Wampanoag, Massachusetts and Nauset Indians*. Indian Notes and Monographs, No. 44. New York: Museum of the American Indian, Heye Foundation.

SPICER, EDWARD H. 1962 *Cycles of Conquest*. Tucson: Univ. of Arizona Press.

STEWARD, JULIAN H. 1940 Native Cultures of the Intermontane (Great Basin) Area. Pages 445–502 in Smithsonian Institution, *Essays in Historical Anthropology of North America in Honor of John R. Swanton*. Smithsonian Miscellaneous Collections, Vol. 100. Washington: The Institution.

STONE, LAWRENCE 1965 *The Crisis of the Aristocracy: 1558–1641*. Oxford: Clarendon.

STRONG, WILLIAM D. 1940 From History to Prehistory in the Northern Great Plains. Pages 353–394 in Smithsonian Institution, *Essays in Historical Anthropology of North America in Honor of John R. Swanton*. Smithsonian Miscellaneous Collections, Vol. 100. Washington: The Institution.

SWANTON, JOHN REED 1922 *Early History of the Creek Indians and Their Neighbors*. Smithsonian Institution, Bureau of American Ethnology, Bulletin No. 73. Washington: Government Printing Office.

SWANTON, JOHN REED 1946 *The Indians of the Southeastern United States*. Smithsonian Institution, Bureau of American Ethnology, Bulletin No. 137. Washington: Government Printing Office.

SWANTON, JOHN REED; and DIXON, ROLAND B. 1914 Primitive American History. *American Anthropologist* New Series 16:376–412.

Symposium on the Concept of Ethnohistory. 1961 *Ethnohistory* 8:12–92.

THEAL, GEORGE McC. (editor) (1883) 1964 *Basutoland Records*. Capetown: Struik.

THOMAS, KEITH 1963 History and Anthropology. *Past and Present* 24:3–24.

VANSINA, JAN (1961) 1964 *The Oral Tradition: A Study in Historical Methodology*. Chicago: Aldine. → First published in French.

VAYDA, ANDREW P. 1961 *Maori Warfare*. Maori Monographs, No. 2. Wellington: Polynesian Society.

VINOGRADOFF, PAUL (1905) 1920 *The Growth of the Manor*. 3d ed. New York: Macmillan.

WALLACE-HADRILL, J. M. 1959 The Bloodfeud of the Franks. John Rylands Library, *Bulletin* 41:459–487.

WARE, CAROLINE F. (editor) (1940) 1965 *The Cultural Approach to History*. Port Washington, N.Y.: Kennikat.

WILSON, MONICA [Hunter] (1936) 1961 *Reaction to Conquest: Effects of Contact With Europeans on the Pondo of South Africa*. 2d ed. Oxford Univ. Press. → The first edition was published under the author's maiden name.

WYLIE, LAURENCE 1965 The Life and Death of a Myth. Pages 164–185 in Melford E. Spiro (editor), *Context and Meaning in Cultural Anthropology*. New York: Free Press.

## IV
## CULTURE HISTORY

Culture history is the subdivision of general history that is concerned with the historical development of nonliterate peoples, present and past. It is almost always practiced by cultural anthropologists, if we include under this designation such specialists as archeologists and anthropological linguists. This definition implies that there is no real difference in principle between the history of the professional historian and the culture historian. Sometimes an attempt is made to distinguish between the two by contrasting the use of written documentary sources as the chief or only kind of evidence admitted by the historian proper with the variety of other, more conjectural methods used by the student of nonliterate cultures. This point of view has occasionally been taken either by historians who wished to resist extension of the field of history through these methods or by "schools" of anthropologists, such as the earlier social functionalists, who admitted the value of "genuine" history based on documentary evidence, while rejecting the "conjectural" culture history of historically minded anthropologists.

It is clear, however, that such a distinction cannot be maintained on principle. As noted in standard handbooks of historiography, the task of historical investigation involves the use of all types of evidence regarding the past. Thus E. Bernheim ([1905] 1926, p. 62) states that all peoples can be subject to historical investigation and that the principles of historical investigation are everywhere the same but that differences in the nature of the evidence require specialized knowledge and training. Thus, ". . . it is in the interest of a scientific division of labor to assign the history of primitives and prehistoric peoples to the ethnologist and archeologist." Besides, even where documentary evidence exists in abundance, as it does from the ancient classical world, nondocumentary techniques, such as archeology and comparative linguistics, have made essential contributions and are used by professional historians. On the other hand, anthropologists have come to realize that they are by no means limited to nondocumentary methods. For many parts of the world there are frequently historical documents that may shed valuable light on cultural changes undergone during the centuries between first contact with the West and professional anthropological field study. In some instances, there may even be indigenous historical records neglected by the historians because the area is outside of the normal purview of their interests. This was the case, for example, with the Islamized peoples of the Sudan.

The aim, then, of culture history, is in no essential respect different from that of conventional history, particularly when the latter is viewed in its most general aspect as not merely political history but as history of all aspects of culture. It may be added that for his primary goal, the understanding of cultural development, the culture historian will need certain noncultural data, such as environmental changes, human racial differentiation as the result of isolating mechanisms paralleling ethnic differentiation, and inferences concerning ancient demographic factors. The differences between culture history and conventional history is then one of degree rather than kind. Since he necessarily relies to a greater extent on nondocumentary sources, the culture historian will be concerned with groups and not individual actors, and the time scale will often be relative rather than absolute. However, with the development of radioactive and other methods of absolute dating, even this latter difference tends to be effaced.

### General methodology

All historical investigations proceed by inferences, often very complex, from evidence existing in the present. The relation between the evidence itself and the fact of which it is a trace is of two main logical types: cause and effect, as when an artifact is taken as evidence for the human activity that produces it, or symbol and referent, as in verbal accounts (whether written or oral) in which the evidence is a description of the fact. Traces differ, as will be seen later, in still other respects. Particularly in culture history, where documentary evidence is usually minimal or lacking, the general strategy of the historical enterprise is based on the circumstance that the same event may leave multiple traces, each of which provides independent evidence for the fact.

For example, if at some time in the past one people has borrowed the cultivation of a food plant from another, it will have taken over the genetic varieties utilized by the donors and the same or similar methods of cultivation. They may have borrowed the word for the plant itself or other terminology connected with its cultivation. These aspects are independent, in that some might have been present in the original event without the others and since their present outcomes are distinct, e.g., the genetic plant varieties now utilized, the observable agricultural methods, and one or more words in the present language. Each of these evidences may be said to belong to a different system, because for its interpretation we must put it into a context of different facts. Thus the data concerning a particular genetic variety of plant are significant in the light of the totality of varieties, their geographical distribution, and the reconstructed genetic history of the species itself in relation to the wild ancestral form. The agricultural methods are part of an ethnologic distribution. The linguistic terminology is part of a language and must be evaluated in terms of appearance or nonappearance in related languages deriving from a linguistic classification itself based on linguistic evidence.

Each of these traces, then, is interpreted in terms of the system to which it belongs. Although the details of method differ for each system, they all have in common the important characteristics of being comparative and involving assumptions regarding diachronic processes.

It has sometimes been felt that certain types of historical inferences involve a comparative method, for example, those based on language or ethnological trait distributions, while archeological artifacts or documents give direct testimony concerning the facts for which they are evidence. There is at best, again, merely a difference of degree of complexity and not of kind. An archeological implement must be compared with other implements with regard to form, function, place, and time before it can be assigned any historical meaning. This is true for written documents, as we are reminded emphatically by the historians Langlois and Seignobos, who state that a document "in respect of which we necessarily are in total ignorance of the author, the place, and the date is good for nothing" ([1898] 1925, p. 87).

Another fundamental set of considerations involved in the construction of such interpretive systems refers to process. By a process is meant a class of similar changes. To draw an example from textual analysis, if the same word appears twice within a few lines of a manuscript that is being copied, a scribe, in looking back through the manuscript, will sometimes mistake the second occurrence for the first and so eliminate the intervening material. Such an error is called haplology and may be called a process. Since manuscripts of all periods, places, and languages are subject to haplological change, like other such processes it may be considered as a class in abstraction from its specific temporal and spatial loci. If two manuscripts share the same haplologies along with other specific changes, one may conclude that they have both been copied from the same version and thus do not furnish independent evidence regarding the original text. By such reasoning, manuscripts may be arranged in a genealogy and their comparative study can lead to the reconstruction of the lost original. In reasoning by means of process, such factors as the frequency with which instances are likely to occur, whether two identical instances will tend to occur independently, and the length of time required for their occurrence are all among the fundamental considerations. For example, another process in manuscript transmission is the interpolation of marginal explanatory glosses into the body of the text. Obviously, it is more likely that a particular haplological error will occur twice independently than that an interpolation involving precisely the same words will occur at all.

Human activities are not the only processes relevant to cultural-historical reconstruction. For example, the patination due to the weathering of artifacts is a process of change and allows us to draw very approximate conclusions regarding age. The point here is that the historical conclusions to which we are led by particular existing evidence is dependent on our assumptions about the processes of change it has undergone since the time it came into existence.

### Specific methods

A number of the independent methods mentioned earlier may now be considered in greater detail.

**Verbal evidence.** All verbal evidence has as its source linguistically formulated descriptions by observers of the original event or events. Whether this primary source is oral or written in its first form makes little or no difference; it is subject to the same possibilities of error through observer bias, inaccuracy, or prevarication. The differences between written and oral sources stem from the mode of subsequent transmission. The advantage of writing is that, because of its semipermanence, it will go through fewer reproductions and will be less changed in the course of such reproductions. Since it will thus be closer to the original report, it will be easier to reconstruct the exact verbal form of the report. The form in which the historian encounters the report is not in itself decisive. Thus, literary sources often contain accounts written down at some time from oral tradition, so that the report has been transmitted orally during the earlier part of its career and in writing later on. The opposite also occurs when literary formulations become the subject of folkloristic transmission.

The critical use of written documents, the chief source of the historian's history, falls under the methodology of history proper and is thus only briefly discussed in the present connection. It is relevant, however, to point out that the culture historian's written documentation is most frequently that of the outside observer, such as the explorer or missionary, rather than the participant. It is therefore subject to errors based rather on the outsider's inability to comprehend the cultural frame of reference of the actors than on bias. Therefore, the inaccuracies are characteristically of a different kind from those of the internally placed participant. Thus, contrary to the latter, the outside observer will not tend to conceal military defeats or the historical illegitimacy of the power exercised by a ruling dynasty.

Anthropologists take as their point of departure the notion of primitive peoples as peoples without written history; but beginning about 1950 it became apparent that the extent and the value of both external and, in certain cases (e.g., west Africa), internal documentary sources had been seriously underestimated. The Indian land claims cases in the United States also led to much documentary research into land occupation and use patterns of the aboriginal period. Such interests led to the development of ethnohistory as a subdiscipline of anthropology [see HISTORY, *article on* ETHNOHISTORY].

The other chief source of verbal reports is oral tradition, which includes not only orally transmitted narrative history but other kinds of spoken material containing historical information, e.g., proverbs and epic poetry. This source is perhaps the most controversial. Thus, G. P. Murdock (1959) discounts it as altogether unreliable, while J. Vansina (1961) makes it the very keystone for his reconstruction of the history of a number of African peoples. As Vansina has pointed out, oral tradition must be used critically, and, indeed, it requires a methodology very similar in principle to that required for the study of documentary sources. More perhaps than any other source, it has been employed uncritically in the past. Oral traditions have been published without indication of the individual, place, or date from which they derive, of facts, if any, regarding the manner of their earlier transmission, and without variant versions. As for manuscripts, it is possible to develop a genealogy of lines of independent transmission and reconstruct the archetype or original version, a method similar in basic respects to that developed by the Finnish school of folklorists for oral literature in general. The time depth and chronological precision of oral traditions are necessarily limited, but within these limitations they can give important and reliable information when treated critically.

**Archeology.** Among the remaining research methods, which have in common the reasoning from trace as effect to historical cause, archeology is to be distinguished from the rest in that it deals with material objects as evidences of cultural activities of the period in which they were produced rather than with existing cultural phenomena viewed as developments from, and hence evidences for, earlier cultural traits. Thus, subsequent modifications of form, if any, are normally the result of natural forces independent of man. The strength of archeology is the reliability and concreteness of its evidence and the definiteness of its spatial attribution. Its necessary limitations stem from the fact that it is confined to material culture and deductions that can be made therefrom. The set of artifacts found at a particular site and stratigraphic level, sometimes called a *component*, is taken as the material expression of the life of a local community. Often very similar assemblages are found over a continuous area with indications that they all date from roughly the same chronological period. Such a unit, often called a *phase*, may be conjectured to represent some sociocultural unit, such as a tribe. The interpretation of archeological evidences regarding a phase has both cultural and social aspects. From settlement patterns, density of remains, the functions of the artifacts themselves, and evidences regarding contemporary climate, fauna, and flora, the attempt is made to reconstruct the basic technologic and demographic patterns with whatever further, usually less certain, inference can be made regarding other aspects of culture, such as social structure or religion. There has also been an attempt to identify and determine the geographic boundaries of ethnic groups. Contemporary evidence shows that such conclusions are subject to a considerable margin of error, since, on occasion, ethnic groups with highly similar material cultures may differ fundamentally in language and other cultural aspects and constitute politically independent groupings.

The second fundamental aim of archeology is to reconstruct the time–space relationships of the sociocultural entities inferred from material remains. The basic problem is, of course, chronological rather than spatial. Relative dating methods include the stratificational (when in the same site more recent material is superimposed on more ancient), estimates of length of occupation from the nature of the deposits, inferences regarding the rough contemporaneity of sites with similar material, cross-dating from traded objects whose date and provenience is known from documentary sources, and geochronology. Where other methods fail, the evolutionary assumption that simpler types precede more developed has been utilized. Such conclusions are most plausible where we are dealing with mechanical inventions that presuppose other less complex devices that enter into them or where a more efficient device requires the development of some specific and recondite skill, e.g., smelting metal as compared with the utilization of stone. In recent years the development of methods of radioactive dating, such as carbon-14, has revolutionized archeology by providing absolute dates.

Beyond the placing of archeological units in space or time, there are inferences regarding the historical relationship of particular cultural traits, complexes, or cultures as a whole. With the prerequisite of space–time continuity established or reasonably to be conjectured, cultural similarities are interpreted as resulting from such historical processes as geographic migration of a people or by diffusion, in which the traits are borrowed through contact with a neighboring people. Such integral spread or adoption of cultural features is often called genetic. Sometimes however the connection is not genetic, although historical. For example, trade objects may be distributed along recognizable trade routes, which indicate cultural connections, although the objects themselves are not actually produced in all of the sites in which they are found. There are of course cultural resemblances that are nonhistorical in origin and are the result of independent parallel developments. What is to be assumed a similarity will, of course, depend on the definitional criteria adopted. Under more general criteria things will be considered similar that are rejected under narrower criteria. The disputed cases are characteristically those that combine generality of criteria with absence of well-proved space–time continuity, e.g., Egyptian and Mayan pyramids.

A further major contribution of archeology has been to furnish materials from the distant past that complement the documentary history of more recent periods and permit speculation about the long-term "evolutionary" trends of cultural development. Thus, archeology provides support for theories regarding the evolution of technology and systems of economic subsistence. [*See* DOMESTICATION; HUNTING AND GATHERING, *article on* NEW WORLD PREHISTORIC SOCIETIES; URBAN REVOLUTION.]

**Trait distribution.** Another basic method for reconstructing history that employs cultural materials is the study of the geographical distribution of cultural traits, which reads historical depth into spatially arranged data. In the broadest sense, comparative linguistics is but one example of this approach, but since it is the least controversial, has the most explicitly developed method, and contributes most largely and reliably of all cultural distributional methods, it will be discussed first.

*Comparative linguistics.* We may consider that every language is a cultural subsystem, that such subsystems are distributed over geographical space, and that each meaningful item in a language is a cultural trait that involves form ("sound") and function ("meaning"). The first step in comparative linguistics is the classification of language into mutually exclusive families, each consisting of related languages. A family of languages is a set of distinct languages presumed to have arisen from a single earlier language (the so-called protolanguage) through a course of differential changes. In the initial period of such changes, when the differences are still small and mutual intelligibility still obtains, localized variants are called dialects. Dialects, as they diverge more and more in the course of time, cease to be mutually intelligible and rank as separate languages. The languages resulting from such an earlier process are said to have a common origin and form a family of related languages. This process may occur a number of times successively and still give recoverable results. Thus, Proto-Indo-European developed dialects that became the ancestral languages of the various branches of Indo-European, e.g., Celtic, Germanic, Slavic, Indo-Aryan, Italic. Italic, like the others, in turn split into separate languages, e.g., Latin, Oscan, Umbrian, Venetic. Of those, only Latin survived, and it in turn has developed into the modern Romance languages.

The comparative method reconstructs this course of events by classifications, such as the one just briefly sketched. Through the observation and evaluation of resemblances involving sound and meaning and, further, through the regularities inherent in processes of linguistic change, most conspicuously phonetic change, the further step is taken of reconstructing as far as possible, and often in considerable detail, the phonetic system, grammar, and vocabulary of the ancestral language. Only exceptionally, as in the case of Latin as ancestral to the Romance languages, is there independent written evidence regarding this language.

Thus every family of languages at whatever level of classification implies an ancestral language that is capable of at least partial reconstruction. Such an ancestral language implies a community of peo-

ple as its users, a degree of cultural homogeneity, such as is normally found among speakers of the same language at the present time and for past documented history, and a placement within geographical and chronological limits. It is clear that the determination of spatial–temporal location of a sociocultural unit speaking a language whose features have been largely reconstructed and historically related to later or contemporary speech communities is in itself an important cultural-historical datum.

*Nonlinguistic inference.* The reconstructed linguistic facts are themselves cultural-historical facts, but what is of wider interest to the culture historian are the nonlinguistic cultural inferences that flow from such linguistic facts, as, for example, words that show the probable acquaintance of the speakers with certain technological items or religious concepts. Such items of protovocabulary are reconstructed word-forms, continued in a sufficient number of later instances to allow us to infer their approximate phonetic shape and meaning and to assign them to the ancestral language. It is a further advantage of the comparative linguistic method that it almost always allows us to distinguish between resemblances among languages that result from continuation of an actual item in modified form (cognates) and resemblances among languages, whether related or not, that result from the borrowing of words from one language by another where the speakers have been in contact. It is also often possible through purely linguistic methods to arrive at conclusions regarding the direction of borrowing.

Accordingly, there are three chief types of inference regarding nonlinguistic cultural phenomena that can be derived from the comparative study of language: those drawn from facts concerning the classification and distribution of languages, those based on protovocabulary, and those based on interlinguistic contacts. From the detailed classification and subclassification of the members of a linguistic family, combined with their present geographical distribution or, where available, from the evidence of documentary history, their past distribution, it is possible to draw probabilistic conclusions regarding the area occupied by the ancestral speech community. From this will also follow certain hypotheses regarding subsequent migrational spread resulting in the distributions found in later historical periods. The fundamental assumption made is that every genetic branch of a linguistic stock, regardless of its present population size or geographical extent, provides, by its location, equal and independent evidence regarding the original center of linguistic distribution. The procedure implicit in this assumption may be called the "center of gravity" method. The best possible guess is the average of positions of each genetic branch. The center of each of these branches that enters into such a calculation may itself require calculation in terms of its subbranches, if any. Thus, if we had no written records to show whether English had originated in the British Isles, North America, South Africa, or Australia, the classification of English as a Germanic language within Indo-European, the fact that its closest relative within Germanic is Frisian, spoken by a small fishing population on the Dutch and German coasts, and the distribution of other subbranches of Germanic in Germany and Scandinavia would point to England as the immediate point of dispersal and to the continent of Europe as the location of ultimate origin. In fact, considering the level of classification represented by dialect variation, since the deepest and most fundamental dialect divisions exist in the British Isles, one can assume that this is the center of dispersal and that the rest of English distribution results from the relatively recent spread of certain older dialects from this center. An important independent check involves an application of the protoword method. Part of the reconstructed vocabulary of the protolanguage may reflect the geographical environment of the original area of settlement but must be interpreted in the light of paleoclimatic and paleontological knowledge. This method requires considerable caution in its application because of the possibility of parallel semantic changes and because it is often necessary to argue from the negative standpoint of the absence of a given terminology. Both points can be illustrated for a hypothetical example of a language family in which it is impossible to reconstruct an original word for "ocean," thus leading to the conclusion that the protocommunity lived inland. It may either be the case that there was such a word but it has independently been replaced by different terms in each linguistic branch or that it survived but transferred its meaning to "lake" several times independently through movements inland, so that the meaning of the term has been incorrectly reconstructed. The possibility of the reconstruction of a whole set of semantically related terms obviously strengthens such a case greatly.

For reconstructing the time as against the place of the ancestral speech community, the only method of absolute chronology that has been proposed is that of glottochronology (see Hymes 1960). The method is based on the assumption that every language has a basic vocabulary that is composed of certain elements, such as pronouns, low numerals, and parts of the body, and that this basic vocabulary has a relatively low and constant rate of replacement by new forms, whether by internal changes or by borrowing. The rate of replacement is estimated from test cases involving historical documentation with a known chronology, e.g., Latin to French. If we assume random and independent loss for related languages at the same rate as for the test cases, then from the proportion of cognates in the list for any pair of languages the date at which the ancestral language began to diverge can be estimated. The estimate in current use is that in one millennium 14 per cent of the 100-word list is lost. This method has been widely applied but has also suffered severe criticism, both regarding the empirical results obtained in the test cases and the mathematical assumptions. It is, however, quite possible that when subjected to necessary revisions, it will give useful results.

The protoword method also permits inference from reconstructed vocabulary regarding the culture of the ancestral speech community. Thus the essentially village, neolithic nature of the Proto-Indo-European culture is shown by the existence of reconstructed terms for a number of domesticated plants and animals, the words for "plow," "village," etc. Other reconstructible parts of the ancestral vocabulary of Indo-European include the kinship terminology and the names of certain divinities.

*Culture contact.* The remaining major source of cultural-historical information based on linguistic data is the study of linguistic-contact phenomena. The most important data are furnished by loan words because they frequently have specific cultural content and because the direction of borrowing can be determined in favorable cases. One type of linguistic-contact study is that which concentrates on the contact of one language with another over an extended period. Such an investigation may be considered the linguistic analogue of acculturation studies. It is often possible to distinguish different periods of contact based on the "stratigraphy" of the changes undergone in the borrowing language. An over-all study of this kind will also show the specific aspects of culture in which borrowings are most numerous and fundamental and thus provide important evidence concerning the nature of the culture contact.

Instead of considering the language communities and the nature of their linguistic contacts as the primary interest, we may focus our attention on a specific cultural item. For example, we may examine the linguistic evidence in its bearing on the details of the spread of tobacco. Since a cultural item may be borrowed without the word being borrowed and because the direction of borrowing cannot in every case be discovered, linguistic evidence will not usually provide a complete history of diffusion, but it will furnish many important detailed hypotheses.

The detection of borrowed words may sometimes show that speech communities not now in contact must have been so in the past. Sometimes the contact must have been with an earlier protocommunity. Thus, Finnish has a number of words borrowed from very early Germanic that approximate reconstructed Proto-Germanic forms.

In addition to borrowings, where languages have been in intimate contact with a large bilingual population over a considerable period, there will be a tendency to convergence in the sound system and grammatical structure. Thus, a number of Balkan languages of diverse branches of Indo-European share such features as a postposed definite article (Rumanian, Albanian, Bulgarian), a future formed from an auxiliary "to wish" (Rumanian, Albanian, Serbo-Croatian, Bulgarian, Greek), and other details. These are not borrowings, since, for example, the verb "to wish" is in each case the indigenous word. Thus, areas of mutual linguistic influences can be determined that parallel the notion of culture area in cultural anthropology.

The independent nonlinguistic methods involve the mapping of the distribution of cultural traits. The main conclusions drawn are that highly detailed traits, e.g., specified art motifs, if found in a restricted geographical area, have a common historic origin. The place of origin and process of spread are difficult to recover on purely distributional evidence. One widely accepted principle of inference is that a trait is older in an area in which it is more elaborated and more integrated in the cultures in which it is found or exists in a greater variety of forms, since such developments require time. Another is known as the age–area hypothesis: other things being equal, a more widely distributed trait is older, since such spread requires time.

*Reconstructing social systems.* One class of methods using nonlinguistic cultural data involves an extension of the comparative linguistic method. The attempt can be made to reconstruct aspects of the culture of the ancestral speech community by a comparison of nonlinguistic traits of the speakers of the languages. This method has met with limited success in the case of comparative Indo-European mythology. Just as the names of divinities may be reconstructed by linguistic comparisons, so the plots of myths involving the divinities may be compared in order to reconstitute their original forms. Such attempts encounter the difficulty that for nonlinguistic aspects of culture, there is no systematic way to differentiate between resemblances resulting from diffusion and those stemming from common origin. The method developed by Murdock (1949) belongs here. Since only certain changes of type are regarded as possible and since social structure is presumed to be, like language, relatively impervious to external diffusional influences, the comparison of social structures of linguistically related peoples leads to the reconstruction of the type of social structure of the ancestral population and its subsequent changes. Unlike language, where there are thousands of independent vocabulary elements, there are relatively few types of social structure; therefore, the same type of social structure is not probative of historical connection between two peoples. Linguistic comparison is thus a method for reconstructing the social structure of peoples known to be related on other grounds and not primarily a method of discovering historical relationships not otherwise known.

*Biological history.* The study of certain noncultural phenomena may be coordinated with that of culture history. Thus the genetic history of human populations is clearly relevant to culture history. The isolating mechanisms that produce partly or fully discrete breeding populations are in general congruent with those producing cultural and linguistic isolation. For example, the linguistic distinction of Eskimo–Aleut from the remaining language groups of the indigenous Americas parallels a physical distinction and is the common result of the same isolating factors. There is thus the possibility of mutual corroboration for historical inferences in both areas. For example, the genetic distinctness of the African and Oceanic Negro, which now seems assured on genetic grounds, is in agreement with the linguistic evidence, which is also negative on the same point.

*Domestication.* A further important noncultural source of cultural-historical conclusions is the study of domesticated plants and animals. Given a genetic classification of species and varieties or races and their relationship to wild forms, the basic principle is one parallel to the center-of-gravity method discussed above in relation to linguistic classification. Thus, the center of origin should be in the same area as the wild forms, and the earlier and more basic genetic differentiations of the domesticated forms should have taken place at earlier centers of cultivation. Here again, the history of plant and animal domestication is in itself important as culture history and provides further independent evidence regarding contacts of people.

The potentialities of the methods outlined here have been only very partially realized. The reasons for this are both theoretical and technical. Since they were applied on a grand scale but based on limited range of evidence and an unsophisticated methodology by the cultural-historical schools of the early twentieth century, in the reaction that followed, interest was focused on structural–functional problems to the relative neglect of culture history. Moreover, practical difficulties are raised by the wide variety of methods required that cannot easily, if at all, be controlled by a single specialist. The most noteworthy attempt thus far is that of Murdock's study of Africa (1959), which utilizes evidence from archeology, linguistic classification, social structure, and plant genetics. But even this study does not take into account many further lines of evidence, such as loan words and the distribution of art styles.

JOSEPH H. GREENBERG

[*Directly related are the entries* ARCHEOLOGY; DIFFUSION; ETHNOLOGY; FOLKLORE; LINGUISTICS, *articles on* HISTORICAL LINGUISTICS *and* THE SPEECH COMMUNITY. *Other relevant material may be found in* HISTORIOGRAPHY, *article on* AFRICAN HISTORIOGRAPHY; *and in the biographies of* GRAEBNER; KOPPERS; NORDENSKIÖLD; RATZEL; SCHMIDT.]

### BIBLIOGRAPHY

BERNHEIM, ERNEST (1905) 1926 *Einleitung in die Geschichtswissenschaft.* 4th ed. Berlin: Gruyter. → Translation in text provided by Joseph Greenberg.
GREENBERG, JOSEPH H. 1953 Historical Linguistics and Unwritten Languages. Pages 265–286 in A. L. Kroeber (editor), *Anthropology Today.* Univ. of Chicago Press.
HYMES, DELL H. 1960 Lexicostatistics So Far. *Current Anthropology* 1:3–44.
LANGLOIS, CHARLES V.; and SEIGNOBOS, CHARLES (1898) 1925 *Introduction to the Study of History.* London: Duckworth. → First published in French.
MURDOCK, GEORGE P. 1949 *Social Structure.* New York: Macmillan. → A paperback edition was published in 1965 by the Free Press.
MURDOCK, GEORGE P. 1959 *Africa: Its Peoples and Their Culture History.* New York: McGraw-Hill.
SAPIR, EDWARD (1916) 1949 Time Perspective in Aboriginal American Culture: A Study in Method. Pages 389–462 in Edward Sapir, *Selected Writings . . . in Language, Culture and Personality.* Edited by David Mandelbaum. Berkeley: Univ. of California Press.
VANSINA, JAN (1961) 1964 *The Oral Tradition: A Study in Historical Methodology.* Chicago: Aldine. → First published in French.
WILLEY, GORDON R.; and PHILLIPS, PHILIP 1958 *Method and Theory in American Archaeology.* Univ. of Chicago Press.

## V
### SOCIAL HISTORY

Ideally considered, social history is the study of the structure and process of human action and interaction as they have occurred in sociocultural contexts in the recorded past. In practice, however, it has seldom been conceived in such analytical terms and has by no means always been envisaged in such comprehensive ones. Its investigators, in fact, have been content for the most part to chronicle, recount, and describe. They have been sharply divided, moreover, as to the proper scope of social history. Some have held that it embraces the whole range of life and culture in societies that have existed in historical time. Others have insisted that its concern is most properly confined to a residuum left by the abstraction of the polity, the economy, and large areas of culture, such as religious beliefs and technology. Still others have restricted it more narrowly to a heterogeneous lot of domestic and communal institutions, customs, attitudes, and artifacts. Numerous minor variations of these basic definitions also have been propounded. This diversity of views as to the scope of social history has engendered much confusion concerning the nature of the discipline.

The sources of social history are virtually omnifarious. They include such diverse materials as official reports, legal documents, newspapers, pamphlets, art objects, graffiti, literary works, and artifacts. One important category of materials is personal papers, such as letters, diaries, and journals, which reveal in depth and detail highly intimate areas of human experience. But there are no materials that social history can claim as peculiarly its own—another cause of confusion regarding its nature.

### Origins

Ever since Herodotus reported the folkways of the Scythians and Tacitus described the institutions of the Germanic tribes, historians have written accounts that are identifiable as social history of one variety or another. Until the eighteenth century such accounts invariably appeared as insignificant fragments embedded in general works. Then, however, as acute concern with the institutions of the past was created by the growing desire to place the study of man and society on a solid empirical basis, social history emerged as a distinctive genre.

Although Justus Möser is traditionally credited with having been the progenitor of the genre and his *Osnabrückische Geschichte* (1768) is often acclaimed as its first intensive treatment of the commonality of a region, Voltaire was really the primary agent of its emergence. In *The Age of Louis XIV* (1751) he treats French society as a totality. Essaying to present a comprehensive view, he examines numerous facets of its life and culture, such as its wars, finances, administration, science, literature, art, customs, and religion. Moreover, he attempts to identify the ethos that animated the whole. Essentially the same approach is employed in his *Essai sur l'histoire générale et sur les moeurs et l'esprit* (1756), a series of disparate and unconnected discourses in which he surveys "the genius, manners, and customs of the principal nations" that flourished between the time of Charlemagne and the era of Louis XIV. Implicit in both works is the assumption that since mankind effected the transition from the "barbarism" of the Middle Ages to the "enlightenment" of the eighteenth century, the historical process advances by stages.

## "Kulturgeschichte" as social history

The pioneer works by Voltaire inaugurated the development of *Kulturgeschichte*, which, although nominally preoccupied with the description and dissection of cultural patterns, is vitally concerned with social types and institutions. Basic among the postulates of *Kulturgeschichte* are the notions that each society, although characterized by multiformity of life and thought, possesses an essential unity, that it is pervaded by a peculiar ethos, and that it inevitably passes, like an organism, through a series of developmental phases. These postulates were strongly supported in the eighteenth century by major ideological currents. One was that congeries of ideas conventionally denominated romanticism, which, as in Johann Gottfried von Herder's *Outlines of a Philosophy of the History of Man* (1784–1791), attributed to each people certain basic psychological peculiarities that, through the operation of a characteristic spirit, produce a unique set of social and cultural forms. Another was the concept of progress, which, as in A. R. J. Turgot's *On the Progress of the Human Mind* (1750) and Condorcet's *Sketch for a Historical Picture of the Progress of the Human Mind* (1795), implied that history is a cumulative process and that each of its stages is a necessary antecedent of the next. These currents of thought were fused in the idealism of Fichte, Schelling, and Hegel, which during the

early nineteenth century provided similar support. As conceived by idealism, history is a plan whose inner logic obliges it to unfold step by step, each step representing a progression, each being an epoch endowed with a distinctive character that penetrates every detail of life.

Buttressed by the influence of this concept, *Kulturgeschichte* developed rapidly. Sometimes it was less dynamic and comprehensive in practice than in theory, epochal and thematic works being no rarity among those that bore its stamp. As a rule, however, it traced societal development over a protracted temporal span. An early, embryonic example of the genre is Henry Hallam's *View of the State of Europe During the Middle Ages* (1818), which includes surveys of social institutions, literature, education, and commerce. More fully endowed with its essential attributes are François Guizot's history of European civilization (1828) and Jules Michelet's universal history (1831), which dilate on ideology and values. With the publication of Jacob Burckhardt's *The Age of Constantine the Great* (1853), a study of the decline of the Roman Empire, the genre reached maturity; with the appearance of his *Civilization of the Renaissance in Italy* (1860), a study of the birth of modernity, it achieved its full fruition.

Burckhardt's treatment of the Italian Renaissance is in many respects an excellent example of the *kulturgeschichtliche* method. Concerned with the development of the cities of northern Italy between the fourteenth and sixteenth centuries, he centers his attention on the cultural configuration that evolved there, tracing the various mutations that it underwent as medieval elements were gradually replaced by modern. Its genesis he attributes to the prevailing illegitimacy of political power. He identifies its ethos as an ineluctable individualism that manifested itself in distinctive patterns of vision, thought, and norms. Closely interwoven with his delineation of these cultural patterns is a detailed survey of the concomitant social order. He explains how the dominant patriciate arose from a fusion of nobility and burghers; he describes the origins, growth, and characteristics of other new groups, such as humanists and artists. His examination of behavioral patterns illuminates a wide variety of interrelated matters, like the frequency of violence, the prevalence of corruption, the liberty accorded women, and the intensity of competition. Similarly enlightening is his depiction of significant social types, such as the despot, the polyhedrous man, and the perfect courtier. In sum, as he charts the phases of a changing society, he effectively portrays its full complexity.

There are other works that, although of lesser stature, are equally representative of *Kulturgeschichte* in its heyday. One of them is Gustav Freytag's enormously popular *Bilder aus der deutschen Vergangenheit* (1859–1867), a detailed and intimate survey of the social and cultural life of the German people from the earliest times to the mid-nineteenth century. Another is Wilhelm Riehl's well-received *Culturstudien aus drei Jahrhunderten* (1859), a miscellany of essays on sociocultural themes. A later example of distinction is Karl Lamprecht's *Deutsche Geschichte* (1891–1909), which traces the course of social and cultural change through a sequence of six periods of German history.

Lamprecht represented a positivistic variety of *Kulturgeschichte*, which, inspired by the progress of natural science, especially the elaboration of the evolutionary hypothesis and the application of the concept of natural selection, rested on the premise that a veritable historical science could be constructed by diligent scholarship, i.e., that the laws governing the historical process could be ascertained. The means of realizing this possibility, it assumed, was the application of the methodology of the social sciences to the whole course of human history. It thus bore a strong affinity to historical sociology, which from Auguste Comte through Herbert Spencer to Franklin Giddings sought to discriminate the principles and successive phases of sociocultural evolution. One of the earliest exponents of this position was Henry T. Buckle, whose *History of Civilization in England* (1857–1861) exerted considerable influence, especially in the United States and Russia. The most important of its later advocates included Lamprecht himself and his disciples Kurt Breysig, who, in *Der Stufen-Bau und die Gesetze der Welt-Geschichte* (1905), presumed to formulate 24 laws of history, and James Harvey Robinson, whose *New History* (1912) pointed the way to the contrivance of similar fabrications. These were the last paladins of *Kulturgeschichte;* the vitality of the genre did not long survive them.

### Unschematic social history

Simultaneously with the development of *Kulturgeschichte*, which had begun with Voltaire, there also evolved an unschematic species of social history. Characterized by a virtual absence of concern with sociocultural morphology and dynamics, its objective is essentially the depiction of life in society. It varies widely as to the range of life that it considers, sometimes presenting a societal conspectus, as in Sir Albert Richardson's survey of England under the Georges (1931) and Sir Arthur Bryant's essays on England during the reign of Charles II (1935), and sometimes confining its inquiry to a narrow sector, as in Warwick Wroth's *London Pleasure Gardens of the Eighteenth Century* (1896) and Robert J. Allen's *Clubs of Augustan London* (1933). Social history likewise varies greatly in seriousness of purpose and therefore in scholarly level, as is evident in the considerable qualitative difference between such works as F. Karl Biedermann's sober and solid study of Germany in the eighteenth century (1854–1880) and Max von Boehn's light and airy sketch of England during the same period (1920). Moreover, it varies markedly in degree and character of interpretation; some studies, like Arthur W. Calhoun's history of the family in the United States (1917–1919), are almost wholly devoid of tendentiousness, others, like Ulrich B. Phillips' classic work on slavery in the American South (1918), argue, or at least suggest, a cogent thesis. Diversity, in short, is one of the principal attributes of social history.

Typical of the genre in essentials is Ludwig Friedländer's *Roman Life and Manners Under the Early Empire* (1862–1871), which treats Roman society from the reign of Augustus to the reign of Commodus. Beginning with a panoramic view of the imperial city, its sights and sounds, Friedländer proceeds to survey the court, the various social classes, the diurnal routine, the position of women, the experiences of the traveler, the means of communication, the spectacles, and the proliferation of luxury. Although he also considers art, religion, and philosophy, his primary objective is the recreation of past life, its vivid and realistic portrayal. Those of its aspects that constitute the cardinal features of his tableau are a rather arbitrary selection. They are dealt with in a succession of virtually independent essays whose order follows no particular principle. The essays are almost entirely descriptive; when here and there Friedländer interjects interpretive comments, they are fragmentary, belletristic, and simple: homiletic judgments, comparisons between Roman and later times, general observations on human progress. Another essential characteristic of the essays is their complete disregard of social change and development; they treat two centuries of history as a static unit.

A number of influences contributed to the rise of this unschematic type of social history. Despite a long historiographical ancestry composed of rudimentary prototypes, such as the account of the plague at Athens given by Thucydides, it received its first really significant impetus when the example of Voltaire sanctioned the historical investigation of every aspect of society. Something of the early effect of that example is apparent in the latitude of Arnold Heeren's *Ideen über die Politik, den Verkehr, und den Handel der alten Welt* (1793–1812), which examines agriculture, trade, finances, and manufactures as well as law, constitutional systems, and politics. This new breadth of scope was soon further extended by the inclusion of the ordinary people of the past among the subjects of historical inquiry. Long before the influence of Marx produced a school that made those strata its primary focus, they were extensively treated in studies like John Wade's *History of the Middle and Working Classes* (1833) and James A. St. John's *History of the Manners and Customs of Ancient Greece* (1842). Their inclusion in the historian's purview had a twofold origin, deriving in part from romanticism, which placed strong emphasis on the folk in all its aspects, in part from the social problems created by industrialization and from the resultant quest for panaceas.

No less important than this expansion of scope were the effects of the influence subsequently exerted by other disciplines. As legal and economic history developed into distinctive fields of inquiry, scholars like Sir Henry Maine, Sir Paul Vinogradoff, Sir Frederic Seebohm, and Gustav Schmoller adopted a new approach. Thoroughly convinced of the sterility of studying legal and economic institutions *in vacuo*, they investigated them in relation to the rest of the social structure. The adoption of this practice gradually produced an intensified awareness of the social aspect of all institutions. Moreover, it created a strong tendency to consider social and economic history as closely conjoined and complementary fields, as in such works as Henri Pirenne's *Medieval Cities: Their Origins and the Revival of Trade* (1925) and Henri Sée's *Esquisse d'une histoire économique et sociale de la France* (1929).

But the two disciplines were not conceived to be of equal consequence. As a result of the protracted and pervasive vogue enjoyed by the concept of economic determinism, which found its fullest expression in Marxian historiography, social history was regarded as ancillary to economic history. Only toward the middle of the present century did the conjunction of social and economic history tend to dissolve, as advances in theory and technique gave the latter a new preoccupation with problems of its own.

### The Bloch–Febvre movement

While the conjunction of social and economic history was at its closest, a movement was launched

that sought to disrupt it. Led by Marc Bloch and Lucien Febvre, the movement represented a convergence of the traditions of *Kulturgeschichte* and unschematic social history. Much of the inspiration that actuated it derived from Émile Durkheim; some may also have come from Max Weber and Ernst Troeltsch, whose practice belied their belief that history and sociology are immiscible (see Troeltsch 1922; McGrew 1958).

The aim of the movement was ambitious. Imbued with the conviction that the comprehension of sociocultural contexts demands they be studied as totalities, it aspired to convert social into societal history. It envisioned such history as a reconstruction of past epochs that would include their entire physical, ideational, and normative milieus and that would be at once more "scientific" and more "human" than the treatment they have usually received, an ideal that bears a strong resemblance to the objective of much recent cultural anthropology. Illustrative of the success with which that ideal could be translated into reality is Marc Bloch's own masterpiece, *Feudal Society* (1939–1940). The principal means that the movement prescribed for the achievement of such success was the creation of a coherent synthesis out of data drawn from sociology, psychology, economics, and geography. But it also ordained that the data to be accorded the most serious consideration were survivals from an earlier time, a variety of evidence whose value was first fully appreciated by Giovanni Battista Vico (1725) and a century later first fully used by Wilhelm Riehl. Assuming that such survivals, whether archeological, cartographical, linguistic, or folkloric, were much more reliable than documentary material, it held that they could provide the basal insight necessary to recreate the past. To give expression to this approach, Bloch and Febvre founded in 1929 the *Annales d'histoire économique et sociale*, which has both perpetuated and diffused the influence of the movement. That influence, which remains strongest in France, where it is at present represented by such scholars as Charles Morazé and Robert Mandrou, has contributed heavily over the decades to the weakening of the traditional position enjoyed by political history.

### The dominance of political history

Almost from the inception of both *Kulturgeschichte* and unschematic social history, their practitioners were obliged to strive against the dominance of political history. The completeness of that dominance in the nineteenth century is strikingly reflected in Edward A. Freeman's terse definition of history in general as "past politics" (1886). Its vestiges in the mid-twentieth century may be seen in Geoffrey R. Elton's insistence (1956) that political history provides the best possible framework for the marshaling of historical data.

As long as this dominance subsisted unimpaired, one of its major manifestations was a strong resistance to any broadening of the scope of historical studies and to any deviation from Leopold von Ranke's prescription of their proper concerns, which he held to be factual accretion, not generalization; narration, not analysis; individuals, not groups; notables, not nonentities. This resistance affected the development of social history in significant ways. Beginning with August Böckh's seminal *Die Staatshaushaltung der Athener* (1817), which treats both state and society with about equal thoroughness, it was not unusual for research undertaken in that discipline to appear as a volume, either monographic or comprehensive. But the amount of space allocated to the fruits of such research in works of general narrative history was extremely small. An outstanding case in point is the celebrated third chapter of Thomas B. Macaulay's *History of England* (1849–1861), which serves as a diminutive *mise-en-scène* for a massive political survey. Similarly, only five of the 21 chapters that comprise William E. H. Lecky's great work on eighteenth-century England (1878–1890) are concerned with nonpolitical institutions. An even smaller proportion, 7 out of 55 chapters, exists in G. M. Trevelyan's history of England during the reign of Queen Anne (1930–1934), although the author is known primarily as a social historian. This engrossment of general narrative history by politics constituted a major impediment that the advocates of social history had to overcome in order to advance their discipline. Not until the early twentieth century did they achieve a substantial measure of success. The essence of that success was a marked expansion of the scope of general history. Very frequently, however, the new breadth amounted to no more than a compartmentalized presentation of diverse aspects of society, with political matters still receiving the largest share of attention. Even much later, when the space allotted to such matters had finally been greatly reduced, there were relatively few attempts to achieve the sort of highly fused synthesis advocated by scholars like Marc Bloch and Henri Berr, whose views may be gleaned from Berr's prefatory article to his *Revue de synthèse historique* ("Sur notre programme" 1900).

Underlying this disparity in the attention accorded political and social history was the difference in the prestige enjoyed by the two disciplines. Political history was highly esteemed. Regarded as edifying as well as informative, it was taken seri-

ously; viewed as a custodian of national tradition as well as an inculcator of patriotism, it was considered valuable. In contrast, social history commanded much less respect. Whether *Kulturgeschichte* or the unschematic variety, it was thought of primarily as entertainment that might invoke nostalgia, gratify curiosity, and generate fantasies. As the new disciplines of sociology and anthropology developed, their insistence that society was more important, more fundamental than the state contributed somewhat to the reduction of this differential in prestige. But it survived for a protracted period. Moreover, it created an antagonism between the two disciplines that erupted most forcibly in the years 1888 to 1891, when Eberhard Gothein engaged in heated controversy with Dietrich Schäfer over whether society or the state ought to be the subject of historical research (Gothein 1889; Goldfriedrich 1902). The antagonism has long been extinct; the difference in prestige, although much diminished, continues.

### Current trends

**Dissatisfaction.** Although at present there is little concern regarding the relative prestige of social history, there is much disquiet at its unsatisfactory state. This disquiet is occasioned by its amorphous, invertebrate character, which derives very largely from the absence of a corpus of theory capable of providing concepts and hypotheses; its indeterminate confines, whose nature arises from the persistent disagreement over scope and from the lack of a peculiar type of source material; its insufficiently rigorous discipline, which, tolerant of impressionistic portrayal, imprecise assessment, and ill-supported assertion, stems from its strong humanistic heritage; and its penchant for description and eschewal of analysis, which proceed from the Rankean prescript.

**The hostility to sociology.** These defects could be remedied to a large extent through an extensive and systematic application of sociological concepts and techniques. But for the most part historians are unwilling to adopt this course, which would effectively transmute social into sociological history. Their unwillingness originates in a deeply rooted hostility to sociology that has existed for a century, except among such deviates as the exponents of positivistic *Kulturgeschichte* and the epigoni of Marc Bloch and Lucien Febvre. That hostility arose out of profound apprehension and prejudice. Historians feared sociology's synoptic pretensions and its putative design to reduce their discipline to the secondary role of fact collection. Moreover, they abhorred its techniques and aspirations as pseudoscientific. Finally, they disdained its achievement as negligible and its subordination of empirical research to the construction of grandiose abstractions as only the philosophy of history in a new guise. The transformation that sociology has undergone since about 1940, when it entered its modern age, has almost entirely dispelled their apprehension and extinguished their disdain; but the strong humanistic bias that inspired their aversion for its concerns, techniques, and objectives continues to foster hostility.

**The hostility of sociologists.** This hostility has had its counterpart among sociologists. Resentful of the ancient heritage, academic respectability, superior prestige, and large-scale pretensions of history, they long entertained a strong animus against it. Two pretensions in particular contributed to this animus, because they seemed to be in serious conflict with the claims of sociology. One was history's pre-emption of all recorded behavior as its proper sphere; the other was the pedagogic role that it assumed as grand interpreter of human experience. But if history was disliked as a rival discipline, it was also looked upon as an inferior one. Sociologists regarded its data as of dubious validity; they considered its concern with discrete facts as obsessive and its refusal to seek uniformities as unscientific. As sociology's claims to intellectual and institutional legitimacy gained greater recognition, all these attitudes tended to soften; but the residues are substantial.

To explain the origins and persistence of such hostility on both sides, historians and sociologists alike have emphasized that a fundamental antithesis exists between their disciplines. Drawing their principal argument from the neoidealism formulated by Wilhelm Dilthey and Heinrich Rickert toward the end of the nineteenth century, both sides have maintained that history is idiographic, hence concerned with the unique, the singular, the individual, which makes descriptive treatment inevitable; whereas sociology is nomothetic, hence concerned with the recurrent, the repetitive, the regular, which makes generalization and abstraction possible. They have likewise contended that history's perspective is diachronic, since it considers data in temporal sequence, while sociology is synchronic, since it considers data without reference to time. Then, too, they have argued that the techniques of historical research are particularly suitable for investigation of the past, whereas the techniques peculiar to sociology are applicable only to contemporary phenomena.

## The rapprochement of history and sociology

On both sides, however, there has long been a spirited minority, which, denying these contentions and repudiating the hostility that underlies them, has resolutely advocated close communion between history and sociology. From time to time during the past half century, its efforts to promote such communion have produced intensive discussion, punctuated by exhortatory and programmatic pronunciamentos. The most recent efforts have received powerful support from the growing sentiment in favor of interdisciplinary exchange in general, which has exalted the mutual advantages to be derived from close cooperation between history and all the social sciences. They have likewise received considerable support from sociologists who have lately become uneasy over the ahistorical orientation of their discipline. That orientation, which was deliberately adopted when sociology was striving for intellectual autonomy and creating a unified system of theory, has been emphatically rejected by the empiricist C. Wright Mills and his followers, who have held a knowledge of the past to be valuable, if not essential, for an understanding of contemporary society and its problems. Much more important is the increasing number of proponents of systematic theory who, captained by scholars like Robert K. Merton and Bernard Barber, have not only strongly recommended the data of history and the course of social change as worthy of investigation but have also energetically encouraged a *rapprochement* between historians and sociologists.

Although such a *rapprochement* remains no more than a possibility, some progress has been made in that direction. As certain relatively simple sociological concepts have gained currency among scholars in general, they have been employed half consciously by historians. Then, too, some scholars in areas like political, intellectual, and religious history have toyed with such concepts, permitting them to serve as stimuli to the imaginative faculty in research as well as in synthesization. Again, still others have adopted them deliberately and applied them directly, albeit in an irregular, immethodical manner. As a result of these practices, recent historiography includes a substantial segment of partially sociologized work. Representative of such work are the writings of Georges Lefebvre, Albert Soboul, and Pierre Goubert.

**Sociological history.** Few social historians have gone further than this piecemeal, *ad hoc* use of sociological theory. Those few, however, who have employed theory both extensively and systematically have produced genuine sociological history. Their work is well exemplified by Elinor G. Barber's *The Bourgeoisie in Eighteenth Century France* (1955), which forcefully demonstrates the full potentialities of the approach. Utilizing concepts drawn from structural–functional theory, this pioneer study skillfully analyzes the changing position of the middle strata of French society during the decades prior to the revolution of 1789. At the outset, it identifies the prevailing stratificational system as a composite in which caste elements were predominant and open class elements were secondary; accordingly, social mobility was given only limited approval. Then, having carefully examined the composition and internal differentiation of the bourgeoisie, it demonstrates the harassing strains experienced by the socially mobile class, which sought to reconcile a partial abandonment of traditional Catholic values with a partial adoption of modern secular ones, and an acceptance of a hierarchical class structure with a determination to rise. These conflicts, it likewise shows, produced in many of the bourgeoisie a strong ambivalence concerning the choice of an appropriate style of life—guilt, uneasiness, and apprehension attaching them to the traditional pattern of their class, ambition driving them to adopt the pattern of the nobility, whose ranks they sought to enter. Finally, after examining the channels whereby they might ascend to noble status, the study analyzes their plight when such mobility became increasingly difficult to achieve, showing how their frustration intensified the strains created by their conflicting values and how in consequence they were impelled to reject the whole class structure. Thus Elinor Barber, by considering familiar data within a new framework, achieves a superbly articulated interpretation of unusual depth and subtlety and provides an entirely fresh perspective.

Some sociologists, animated by their recently found interest in historical data, have likewise undertaken studies of this type. The possibility of their eventually pre-empting the area of social history is raised anew by such works as Robert N. Bellah's *Tokugawa Religion: The Values of Pre-industrial Japan* (1957), Neil J. Smelser's *Social Change in the Industrial Revolution* (1959), Seymour M. Lipset's *The First New Nation: The United States in Historical and Comparative Perspective* (1963), and Charles Tilly's *The Vendée* (1964). It is this challenge from the outside no less than the current defects within that makes it imperative for social historians to put themselves under the tutelage of sociologists in order to transform their discipline.

J. JEAN HECHT

[*Other relevant material may be found in the biographies of* BLOCH; CONDORCET; FEBVRE; LAMPRECHT; MACAULAY; MILLS; PIRENNE; ROBINSON; SÉE; TURGOT; VOLTAIRE.]

EXAMPLES OF SOCIAL HISTORY

ALLEN, ROBERT J. 1933 *The Clubs of Augustan London.* Cambridge, Mass.: Harvard Univ. Press.

BARBER, ELINOR G. 1955 *The Bourgeoisie in Eighteenth Century France.* Princeton Univ. Press.

BELLAH, ROBERT N. 1957 *Tokugawa Religion: The Values of Pre-industrial Japan.* Glencoe, Ill.: Free Press.

BIEDERMANN, F. KARL 1854–1880 *Deutschland im achtzehnten Jahrhundert.* 2 vols. Leipzig: Weber.

BLOCH, MARC (1939–1940) 1961 *Feudal Society.* Univ. of Chicago Press. → First published as *La société féodale: La formation des liens de dépendance* and *La société féodale: Les classes et le gouvernement des hommes.*

BÖCKH, AUGUST (1817) 1886 *Die Staatshaushaltung der Athener.* 3d ed., 2 vols. Berlin: Reimer.

BOEHN, MAX VON 1920 *England im achtzehnten Jahrhundert.* Berlin: Askanischer Verlag.

BREYSIG, KURT 1905 *Der Stufen-Bau und die Gesetze der Welt-Geschichte.* Berlin: Bondi.

BRYANT, ARTHUR 1935 *The England of Charles II.* London and New York: Longmans.

BUCKLE, HENRY T. (1857–1861) 1913 *The History of Civilization in England.* 2d ed., 2 vols. New York: Hearst.

BURCKHARDT, JACOB (1853) 1949 *The Age of Constantine the Great.* London: Routledge. → First published as *Die Zeit Constantin's des Grossen.*

BURCKHARDT, JACOB (1860) 1958 *The Civilization of the Renaissance in Italy.* New York: Harper. → First published as *Die Cultur der Renaissance in Italien.*

CALHOUN, ARTHUR W. (1917–1919) 1945 *A Social History of the American Family From Colonial Times to the Present.* 3 vols. New York: Barnes & Noble. → A paperback edition was published in 1960.

CONDORCET, MARIE JEAN ANTOINE NICOLAS CARITAT (1795) 1955 *Sketch for a Historical Picture of the Progress of the Human Mind.* New York: Noonday. → First published in French.

ELTON, GEOFFREY R. 1956 *England Under the Tudors.* London: Methuen.

FREYTAG, GUSTAV (1859–1867) 1930 *Bilder aus der deutschen Vergangenheit.* New ed., 3 vols. Berlin: Deutsche Buchgemeinschaft.

FRIEDLÄNDER, LUDWIG (1862–1871) 1908–1913 *Roman Life and Manners Under the Early Empire.* 7th ed., rev. & enl., 4 vols. London: Routledge. → First published as *Darstellungen aus der Sittengeschichte Roms.*

GUIZOT, FRANÇOIS P. (1828) 1896 *General History of Civilization in Europe.* Edited, with critical and supplementary notes, by George Wells Knight. New York: Appleton. → First published in French.

HALLAM, HENRY (1818) 1904 *View of the State of Europe During the Middle Ages.* 2 vols. New York: Appleton.

HEEREN, ARNOLD H. L. (1793–1812) 1824–1826 *Ideen über die Politik, den Verkehr, und den Handel der alten Welt.* 4th ed., 3 vols. Göttingen (Germany): No publisher given.

HERDER, JOHANN GOTTFRIED VON (1784–1791) 1800 *Outlines of a Philosophy of the History of Man.* London: Hansard. → First published in German.

LAMPRECHT, KARL G. 1891–1909 *Deutsche Geschichte.* 12 vols. Berlin: Gärtner.

LECKY, WILLIAM EDWARD H. (1878–1890) 1892–1893 *A History of England in the Eighteenth Century.* New ed., 7 vols. New York: Appleton.

LIPSET, SEYMOUR M. 1963 *The First New Nation: The United States in Historical and Comparative Perspective.* New York: Basic Books.

MACAULAY, THOMAS B. (1849–1861) 1953 *History of England From the Accession of James II.* 4 vols. New York: Dutton.

MICHELET, JULES (1831) 1962 *Introduction à l'histoire universelle.* Paris: Colin.

MÖSER, JUSTUS (1768) 1819–1824 *Osnabrückische Geschichte.* 3d ed., 3 vols. Berlin: Nicolai.

PHILLIPS, ULRICH B. 1918 *American Negro Slavery: A Survey of the Supply, Employment and Control of Negro Labor as Determined by the Plantation Régime.* New York: Appleton.

PIRENNE, HENRI (1925) 1956 *Medieval Cities: Their Origins and the Revival of Trade.* Garden City, N.Y.: Doubleday. → First published in French.

RICHARDSON, ALBERT E. 1931 *Georgian England: A Survey of Social Life, Trades, Industries and Art From 1700 to 1820.* New York: Scribner; London: Batsford.

RIEHL, WILHELM H. 1859 *Culturstudien aus drei Jahrhunderten.* Stuttgart (Germany): Cotta.

ROBINSON, JAMES HARVEY (1912) 1958 *The New History: Essays Illustrating the Modern Historical Outlook.* Springfield, Mass.: Walden.

ST. JOHN, JAMES A. 1842 *The History of the Manners and Customs of Ancient Greece.* 3 vols. London: Bentley.

SÉE, HENRI 1929 *Esquisse d'une histoire économique et sociale de la France.* Paris: Alcan.

SMELSER, NEIL J. 1959 *Social Change in the Industrial Revolution.* London: Routledge; Univ. of Chicago Press.

TILLY, CHARLES H. 1964 *The Vendée.* Cambridge, Mass.: Harvard Univ. Press.

TREVELYAN, GEORGE M. 1930–1934 *England Under Queen Anne.* 3 vols. London and New York: Longmans.

TURGOT, ANNE ROBERT J. (1750) 1929 *On the Progress of the Human Mind.* Hanover, N.H.: Sociological Press. → Originally a lecture given in Latin at the Sorbonne.

VICO, GIOVANNI B. (1725) 1948 *The New Science.* Ithaca, N.Y.: Cornell Univ. Press. → First published in Italian. A paperback edition was published in 1961 by Doubleday.

VOLTAIRE, FRANÇOIS M. A. (1751) 1962 *The Age of Louis XIV.* New York: Dutton. → First published in French.

VOLTAIRE, FRANÇOIS M. A. (1756) 1835 *Essai sur l'histoire générale et sur les moeurs et l'esprit.* 4 vols. Paris: Treuttel.

WADE, JOHN (1833) 1835 *History of the Middle and Working Classes, With a Popular Exposition of the Economical and Political Principles Which Have Influenced the Past and Present Condition of the Industrious Orders.* 3d ed. London: Wilson.

WROTH, WARWICK 1896 *The London Pleasure Gardens of the Eighteenth Century.* London and New York: Macmillan.

### WORKS ABOUT SOCIAL HISTORY

BERGER, BENNETT 1957 Sociology and the Intellectuals: An Analysis of a Stereotype. *Antioch Review* 67:275–290.

BRIGGS, ASA 1962 Sociology and History. Pages 91–98 in Alan T. Welford et al. (editors), *Society: Problems and Methods of Study.* New York: Philosophical Library.

CAHNMAN, WERNER J.; and BOSKOFF, ALVIN (editors) 1964 *Sociology and History: Theory and Research.* New York: Free Press.

COBBAN, ALFRED 1961 History and Sociology. *Historical Studies* 3:1–8.

ELIOT, THOMAS D. 1922 The Use of History for Research in Theoretical Sociology. *American Journal of Sociology* 27:628–636.

FREEMAN, EDWARD A. 1886 *The Methods of Historical Study.* London: Macmillan. → See especially Lecture 1.

GINSBERG, MORRIS 1932 *Studies in Sociology.* London: Methuen.

GOLDFRIEDRICH, JOHANN A. 1902 *Die historische Ideenlehre in Deutschland.* Berlin: Gärtner.

GOTHEIN, EBERHARD 1889 *Die Aufgaben der Kulturgeschichte.* Leipzig: Duncker & Humblot.

HERTZLER, JOYCE O. 1925 The Sociological Uses of History. *American Journal of Sociology* 31:173–198.

HOLLOWAY, S. W. F. 1963 Sociology and History. *History* 48:154–184.

McGREW, R. E. 1958 History and the Social Sciences. *Antioch Review* 18:276–289.

McKINNEY, JOHN C. 1957 Methodology, Procedures, and Techniques in Sociology. Pages 186–235 in Howard Becker and Alvin Boskoff (editors), *Modern Sociological Theory in Continuity and Change.* New York: Dryden.

MANTOUX, PAUL 1903 Histoire et sociologie. *Revue de synthèse historique* 7:121–140.

MERTON, ROBERT K. 1961 Social Conflict Over Styles of Sociological Work. Pages 21–44 in World Congress of Sociology, Fourth, Milan and Stresa, 8–15 September 1959, *Transactions.* Volume 3: Abstracts of Papers and Discussions. Louvain (Belgium): International Sociological Association.

PERKIN, HAROLD J. 1953 What Is Social History? John Rylands Library, Manchester, *Bulletin* 36:56–74.

PERKIN, HAROLD J. 1962 Social History. Pages 51–82 in H. P. R. Finberg (editor), *Approaches to History: A Symposium.* London: Routledge.

Sur notre programme [by Henri Berr]. 1900 *Revue de synthèse historique* 1:1–8.

TROELTSCH, ERNST 1922 *Der Historismus und seine Probleme.* Tübingen (Germany): Mohr.

WOLFF, KURT H. 1959 Sociology and History: Theory and Practice. *American Journal of Sociology* 65:32–38.

## VI
### INTELLECTUAL HISTORY

The term "intellectual history" is fairly well established in the United States, though the American Historical Association's *Guide to Historical Literature* (1961) uses it sparingly, preferring such rubrics as "cultural history" or "social ideas." There are in common use in the Western world, however, many other terms: history of ideas, *Geistesgeschichte*, *Ideengeschichte*, *histoire de la pensée*, and various others. In its widest sense, intellectual history may be said to have as its subject matter whatever record is left of the activities of the human mind. Its most important and most available materials are the products of philosophers, artists, writers, scientists, recorded in their works and in the special histories of specific disciplines—philosophy, literature, religion, the sciences, the arts. But intellectual history is not merely a summary or even a synthesis of such materials; it commonly also attempts to trace and understand the dissemination of the work of cultural leaders—their "ideas"—in a given society; and it also seeks to understand the relation between such ideas on one hand and, on the other, "drives," "interests," and nonintellectual factors generally, in individual and in social psychology. At its narrowest, intellectual history attempts to tell who produced what intellectual or cultural achievement when and how; at its broadest, it can come close to being a kind of retrospective sociology of knowledge, even a retrospective general sociology.

Yet intellectual history is not to be understood as a kind of master history. It takes the products of the human intellect as its source materials; it does not in itself exhaust the possible play of the historian's own intellect on all the diverse materials left by the past. All historical writing, of course, requires from the historian at least minimal attention to the record of man thinking. Especially in modern works in such fields as social and economic history, awareness of the role of ideas is increasing. Usually, however, intellectual history can, if only roughly, be delimited by its major concern with the written or spoken word, and even, to use a term still somewhat suspect among historians, with "theory." There remains then the difficulty of clearly distinguishing between intellectual history and, for example, the history of philosophy, the history of literature, the history of science, and of other branches of culture. It is not quite enough to say that intellectual history is the all-inclusive history of all these. Sometimes an intellectual historian, like Preserved Smith in the two volumes of his *History of Modern Culture* (vol. 1, *Origins of Modern Culture, 1543–1687*; vol. 2, *The Enlightenment, 1687–1776* 1930–1934), left unfinished at his death, does attempt such a difficult all-inclusive task, and some of Smith's topical headings—"The Propaganda of the Enlightenment," "Persecution and Tolerance," "Humanitarianism," "Morals and Manners"—show that he did not limit himself to the discussion of clusters of ideas and their affiliation. But generally the historian of philosophy, for instance, is primarily if not exclusively concerned with explaining to philosophers or to students of philosophy the ideas of other philosophers. He may indeed criticize these ideas, that is, evaluate, praise, blame; he may, though he need not, attempt to find some explanation of these ideas in a given philosopher's personal history and in his total environment; but he may also treat ideas as breeding

ideas in a vacuum—or in a "mind." The intellectual historian, concerned, as he very often is, with the same set of philosophical ideas, must also do some of what the historian of philosophy does; but his main concern must be with what happens to these ideas among ordinary educated people and even among ordinary uneducated people.

Perhaps the point can be made more clearly from the history of science. It is possible to write a history of science, and a very scholarly one, in which the aim of the historian is to record discoveries, inventions, theories; place them in chronological sequence; and even explain their dissemination *among scientists.* Such, in fact, was the whole work of the distinguished historian of science George Sarton. An intellectual historian concerned at all with natural science would certainly have to master much of the foregoing; but he would also have to ask himself what happened to these scientific theories when they passed into circulation among the many. You could write a good history of what the work of Darwin has meant to the science of biology in its present state without a word about what is commonly called "social Darwinism"; but you could not write a good intellectual history of the nineteenth century without very serious attention to social Darwinism. The difference between what the work of Freud means to practicing psychoanalysts, and indeed to psychiatrists who are not orthodox Freudians, and what Freud's work has meant to novelists, playwrights, painters, essayists, and the general public is very great indeed. The intellectual historian will have to deal with all these last, even though for the professional psychoanalyst this *Vulgar-Freudismus* is a shocking perversion of the master's true meaning. Much of this is well treated in Erik Erikson's *Insight and Responsibility* (1964).

This difference, then, between concentrating on, placing emphasis on what ideas mean to the expert, the professional in a given field, and what they mean to the many to whom they somehow do filter down is the basic distinction between the historian of a special intellectual discipline and the historian of ideas.

Some component of intellectual history is to be found in historical writing as far back as the Greeks. Herodotus, when he discussed the religious beliefs of the Egyptians, and Thucydides, when he contrasted the national character of the Athenians and the Spartans, were both writing intellectual history. The vein of philosophical history that attempts to discern what Alfred Kroeber called "configurations of culture growth" was never quite pinched out even in the Middle Ages, as witness the sequence Augustine–Orosius–Otto of Freising, and has widened greatly in our own time. Machiavelli's *Discorsi* has as its major theme an attempt to explain the influence of the religious beliefs of the Romans on their political achievements. With the Enlightenment of the eighteenth century, intellectual history, still unnamed, assumed a prominent place in historiography, if only as "philosophy teaching by example."

The actual designation "intellectual history," or history of ideas or of thought, and its general acceptance as a form of historical writing date from the late nineteenth century and the organization of professional academic history. In the United States the term was made popular by James Harvey Robinson, whose *Mind in the Making* (1921) was a best-selling sketch of Western intellectual history based largely on his famous Columbia University course on "the history of the intellectual classes." In Germany Dilthey was in many ways a precursor of modern intellectual historians, and Max Weber, although formally listed as a sociologist, set the mold for much work in the field. Indeed, his *Protestant Ethic and the Spirit of Capitalism* may be taken as a most representative piece of intellectual history. Among the works of professional historians, Friedrich Meinecke's *Die Entstehung des Historismus* and the Austrian Friedrich Heer's monumental *Europäische Geistesgeschichte* are evidence that the field is solidly established in Germany and Austria.

Professional historians in both France and Great Britain have been more reluctant to write intellectual history, at least under that name. In France historians interested in synthesis, such as Henri Berr and Lucien Febvre, have certainly made contributions to the field; and literary scholars like Paul Hazard, whose *European Mind, 1680–1715* is now standard, have written in the mainstream of intellectual history. British historians like J. B. Bury, R. H. Tawney, and Christopher Dawson have paid full attention to the intellectual element in history, but intellectual history has been written primarily by literary men like Leslie Stephen, whose *History of English Thought in the Eighteenth Century* is a classic. The philosophy of history is represented in Great Britain by H. T. Buckle (*History of Civilization in England*), Charles Collingwood (*The Idea of History*), and Arnold J. Toynbee, whose 12-volume *Study of History*, as summarized in two volumes by D. C. Somervell, has had a very wide audience, especially in the United States. Croce set the pattern for a whole generation of historians in Italy. Croce must be

listed first as a philosopher, but almost all his writing as a historian shows the hand of the intellectual historian. Among his many writings in the field, we may note *La Spagna nella vita italiana durante la Rinascenza* and *Storia della età barocca in Italia*.

Among the first few generations of professional historians throughout the Western world, there was considerable resistance to the formal field of intellectual history as not "scientific" enough. As compared with the concreteness of the materials of institutional, economic, and conventional social history, the materials of intellectual history seemed vague and difficult to pin down as part of "real" life. Moreover, what the intellectual historian probably has to call—for want of a better term—the "spirit of the age" or the "climate of opinion" of the late nineteenth century, at least among scholars, tended to minimize, if not to deny, the driving force of "ideas," particularly philosophical ideas or ideals, in human life.

Although traces of this resistance to intellectual history still exist, the subject has now attained academic respectability; indeed, in the United States it has become fashionable. It is proving to be one of the most effective bridges between historians and the practitioners of the social sciences, groups still rather definitely separated by mutual distrust in most Western countries. The problems that the intellectual historian must face, while often essentially philosophical, are increasingly like those confronting the social scientist. The intellectual historian is bound to try to be a thinker rather than a storyteller. Indeed, he hardly has a story to tell. Passage from general sociology and the sociology of knowledge to intellectual history has become both easy and frequent; it is equally easy—some would say too easy—to go from depth psychology to historical writing. It seems likely that many historians for a long time to come will proudly and a bit defensively call themselves humanists and scorn the social sciences; the intellectual historian, however, cannot really practice his craft if he shares this scorn.

## Types of intellectual history

No rigorous classification of the kinds of intellectual history is possible. We shall here attempt a rough classification into three types, with the necessary warning that any given work may display some touches of all three.

First, there is intellectual history that tries to establish the "facts" about who wrote what when, in what form it was published, as well as similar facts about what was produced in cultural media other than words, particularly if these other media served for "propaganda." A good example of this kind of intellectual history is afforded by the work of Charles H. Haskins, notably the articles collected as *The Renaissance of the Twelfth Century* (1927) and *Studies in Medieval Culture* (1929). Haskins was an impeccably trained medievalist of the old school who did much work in institutional history. What interested him in intellectual history was chiefly the ways in which Greco-Roman works —the actual manuscripts—survived, were copied, indeed often came back into Western culture via translations into Arabic and thence into medieval Latin. He was certainly not indifferent to the content of the manuscripts he so carefully studied— in fact his very use of the term "Renaissance" in his title involves another level of historical generalization, another kind of intellectual history. Still, his main task was to establish by research in the original sources a straightforward account in the Rankean tradition of *wie es eigentlich gewesen*.

Spadework of a similar kind is, of course, always essential. For the modern intellectual historian there are even many problems of "fact" that must be cleared up before he can go on to other problems—problems such as who wrote certain pseudonymous or anonymous works, problems of clandestine publication, authenticity of memoirs, and the like. In this classification too belongs the effort to establish the facts (sometimes capable of being put statistically) of the dissemination in specific circumstances of certain works and even of the ideas contained in them. Ancillary to this effort is work close to demography, such as the study of the degree of literacy in a given population. In actual practice many of these investigations can hardly be separated from studies of problems in the sociology of knowledge, from simple literary ones of "influence of A on B" to more sophisticated attempts to analyze the relations between words and deeds. But the establishment of the facts is essential spadework in intellectual as in any other kind of historical writing.

Second, there is the more difficult kind of intellectual history, also concerned rather more with establishing than with evaluating or synthesizing facts, to which American usage in particular tends to apply the term "history of ideas." We are here concerned with what can be called the cartography of ideas or (perhaps) semantics. The school formed around Arthur O. Lovejoy at Johns Hopkins affords a good example of this approach. Lovejoy identified as a "cluster of ideas" such complex and usually

very common terms as "nature," "reason," "romantic." His major task was that of analyzing the constituent elements of these clusters of ideas. His *Great Chain of Being* (1936), for example, traces in Western culture the history of one such cluster of ideas, that of a hierarchy of interrelated living beings from barely sentient ones to the highest and best developed. Although other historians have not always matched the scholarly subtlety of Lovejoy and his colleagues—who have found some sixty shades of meaning for the word "nature"— this sort of analysis is an essential part of intellectual history. It can be applied to the work of a given thinker: what did Hobbes, Locke, Rousseau understand, "really mean," by "social contract," or just what did Nietzsche intend the "superman" to be and do? It can also be applied to distinguish between different uses, different emotional effects, of certain words or phrases in given times and places. For this a very neat example is the difference between the effect of the word "federalist" when used in France and in the United States in 1793—or, indeed, when used in New England and in Virginia at the same time.

Both these first two kinds of intellectual history are essential to the third, which is the central concern of intellectual history in our time. Its task may be put with undue simplicity as the study of the relation between what men say and what they do. "Do" has its obvious complexities; but "say" too is mere shorthand for all that goes on in the cerebral cortex, and unless modern psychology is wholly on the wrong track, in less noble parts of the human central nervous system. A very good if rather worn example of this kind of intellectual history is afforded by the old debate over the influence of the Enlightenment on the French Revolution (see Church 1964). One extreme position in this debate, taken for instance by Felix Rocquain in *L'esprit révolutionnaire avant la révolution*, is that hard, specific grievances were all-important in producing the revolution and that the work of the *philosophes* was of little, if any, importance. Rocquain's position has significance for later intellectual historians as a probable reflection of Marxist ideas and is certainly a reflection of the distrust felt by French political radicals in the 1870s for any form of "idealism." The opposite extreme position is commonly taken by conservatives who dislike the French Revolution and who subscribe to one form or another of the conspiracy theory of history. Freemasons, *philosophes*, Illuminati, Jacobins, are variously singled out as the fanatics of the Enlightenment responsible for everything that happened during the revolution. Taine's famous metaphor in his *Origines de la France contemporaine* is typical: if you see a healthy man take up a full glass, drain it, and then fall down foaming at the mouth in convulsions, you know there was a poison in the glass; the man was the Jacobin, the glass contained the ideas of the *philosophes*. In between these extremes the debate, which is by no means ended, shows many variants of interpretation of the nature and extent of the effect of the Enlightenment on what really happened.

The intellectual historian who attempts to judge the nature of the effects of an idea or cluster of ideas on human events is confronted with the old problem of value judgments. It is all very well to use, as we have used above, the metaphor of intellectual history as the "cartography of ideas." But the map maker does not judge, evaluate, criticize, or even comment on the actual piece of the terrestrial globe he is mapping; only the traveler using the map as guide may indeed feel and say "This is lovely" or "This is ugly" as he looks at the landscape. The historian, strive though he may to be like the map maker, can hardly avoid being like the traveler.

To use once more the field of the Enlightenment as an example, intellectual historians have not only varied greatly in their interpretations of what certain eighteenth-century political thinkers meant, but in whether what they meant was productive of good or bad. Rousseau's *Social Contract* is a good focusing point for this problem. One school, represented by Jacob T. Talmon, in his *Rise of Totalitarian Democracy*, finds that Rousseau himself meant the work to set up a sovereign power whose will was absolute and that the effect of the work on political activists like Robespierre and Babeuf was certainly to justify their arbitrary "democratic totalitarianism." An opposite point of view is represented by the distinguished German philosopher Ernst Cassirer, whose *Question of Jean-Jacques Rousseau*, translated with an illuminating introduction by Peter Gay, holds that Rousseau meant the general will to represent a kind of idealized moral imperative and that its real influence has indeed been to promote the democratic and individualistic freedoms.

### Types of studies

It must be admitted that into whatever subclassifications intellectual history is broken down, it is a sprawling field, with a very great range of subject matter and treatment. It can be concerned with tracing over a long period a recurring theme of man's thinking. Such "thread" accounts are Lovejoy's above-mentioned *Great Chain of Being* or J. B. Bury's *Idea of Progress*. It can adopt the approach of comparative history, which tries to discern common as well as unique elements in ideas and attitudes expressed at different times and in different places. An interesting and highly controversial instance of this approach is the work in American intellectual history of Richard Hofstadter, who finds common elements, such as belief in the "conspiracy theory" of politics, in groups commonly held to be quite unlike—Populists, Progressives, and McCarthyites. At least as controversial, if not of such timely interest, is Carl Becker's *Heavenly City of the Eighteenth-Century Philosophers*, in which, as the title implies, the author finds significant intellectual attitudes common to medieval Augustinians and the *philosophes* of the Enlightenment.

Histories of utopias—both the writings usually so classified in histories of literature and the actual experiments with group living in communities under the influence of utopian thinking—are obviously subjects for the intellectual historian. Although there is an enormous body of historical and literary writing about utopias, the subject has not had a first-rate general treatment in all its phases, a difficult and challenging task. Many wide topics in intellectual history, however, have had such treatment. This is especially true of the history of Christianity and, indeed, of the history of religion generally. While the historian of formal philosophy can always limit himself to the analysis of ideas in and for themselves, a process which is *not* intellectual history, the historian of religion can hardly avoid taking up the relation between religious beliefs and the behavior of human beings, as well as the history of institutions founded on these beliefs. Much in this field that can be classified as intellectual history has been the work of sociologists, particularly in Germany. Although Harnack is commonly listed as a historian, Troeltsch and Weber are listed as sociologists.

An important problem in intellectual history, that of the cultural generation, has been neglected by historians; it has had its best specific treatment in a short article by Karl Mannheim, "The Problem of Generations" (1928). There are interesting reflections on the problem in Ortega y Gasset, *Man and Crisis* (1933, pp. 30–85 in 1959 edition), a translation of his *En torno a Galileo*.

It would be hard to deny an element of intellectual history to all the interpretative "leads," the suggestive "ideas" in the folk sense of that word, that have enriched historical writing. There are recent examples, such as the Pirenne thesis that the real break between late Roman culture and that of the Middle Ages was not caused by the Germanic invasions of the fifth and sixth centuries but by the Arab invasions several centuries later, followed by the Viking incursions; Marc Bloch's interpretation of French agrarian history in *Les caractères originaux de l'histoire rurale française;* the contrasting conceptions advanced by Tawney and Trevor-Roper on the composition and the role of the "gentry" in early modern England (Tawney's *Religion and the Rise of Capitalism* is an English variation of the work of Max Weber); Braudel's use of leads from human geography in his study of the Mediterranean; Meinecke's clear definition of one kind of historicism; the very familiar Turner thesis of the role of the frontier in American history; and so on down to theses involving apparently very minor concrete details, such as that brought out by Lynn White on the wide-reaching effects of the early medieval invention of the horse collar or that advanced by Walter Webb on the changes in the American great plains made possible by the availability of inexpensive barbed wire.

The task of the intellectual historian is difficult. He must try to get source materials for the opinions and attitudes of at least a sampling of those strata in a given society that he thinks are touched by the ideas he discusses. With the invention of printing and especially with the development of the mass media and, in our own day, opinion polling, he gets almost too much material. For earlier periods he has to scrape together what he can, much helped by what several generations of workers have accumulated under such headings as social history, history of morals, *Sittengeschichte,* and the like. The very great body of what is commonly called "literature" from the Egyptians, Greeks, ancient Chinese, and others down to the present is, of course, a mine of information on the opinions and attitudes of fictional men and women who were not "intellectuals" and who may often have been "typical" of their culture.

Finally, intellectual history has necessarily close relations with some of the social sciences, notably sociology and what is usually called cultural anthropology. The practitioners of cultural anthropology are now venturing increasingly into the study of developed societies with abundant recorded history. For these, and for some of the other social sciences, intellectual history—and, indeed, other kinds of history—can supplement observation and experimentation by providing materials essential for the understanding of development through time, materials comparable in no mere figure of speech to those that paleontology and historical geology contribute to the earth sciences.

CRANE BRINTON

[*See also* SCIENCE, *article on* THE HISTORY OF SCIENCE; *and the biographies of* CROCE; DILTHEY; FEBVRE; MANNHEIM; MARX; MEINECKE; ROBINSON; SARTON.]

BIBLIOGRAPHY

AMERICAN HISTORICAL ASSOCIATION 1961 *Guide to Historical Literature.* New York: Macmillan.

BARNES, HARRY E. (1937) 1961 *Intellectual and Cultural History of the Western World.* 3d rev. ed., 3 vols. New York: Reynal-Hitchcock. → A paperback edition was published by Dover in 1965.

BRINTON, CRANE (1958) 1963 *Ideas and Men: The Story of Western Thought.* 2d ed. Englewood Cliffs, N.J.: Prentice-Hall.

BRINTON, CRANE 1964 *European Intellectual History.* New York: Macmillan. → Contains a selective bibliography.

CHURCH, WILLIAM F. (editor) 1964 *The Influence of the Enlightenment on the French Revolution: Creative, Disastrous, or Non-existent.* Boston: Heath.

EKIRCH, ARTHUR A. JR. 1963 *American Intellectual History.* New York: Macmillan.

ERIKSON, ERIK H. 1964 *Insight and Responsibility: Lectures on the Ethical Implications of Psychoanalytic Insight.* New York: Norton.

HASKINS, CHARLES H. (1927) 1957 *The Renaissance of the Twelfth Century.* New York: Meridian.

HASKINS, CHARLES H. (1929) 1958 *Studies in Medieval Culture.* New York: Ungar.

*Ideas in Cultural Perspective.* Edited by Philip Wiener and Aaron Noland. 1962 New Brunswick, N.J.: Rutgers Univ. Press. → Essays from the *Journal of the History of Ideas* arranged to illustrate problems of method in intellectual history and its various fields.

LOVEJOY, ARTHUR O. (1936) 1961 *The Great Chain of Being: A Study of the History of an Idea.* Cambridge, Mass.: Harvard Univ. Press.

MANNHEIM, KARL (1928) 1952 The Problem of Generations. Pages 276–320 in Karl Mannheim, *Essays on the Sociology of Knowledge.* New York: Oxford Univ. Press. → First published in German.

ORTEGA Y GASSET, JOSÉ (1933) 1962 *Man and Crisis.* New York: Norton. → First published as *En torno a Galileo.*

RANDALL, JOHN H. JR. (1926) 1940 *The Making of the Modern Mind: A Survey of the Intellectual Background of the Present Age.* Rev. ed. Boston: Houghton Mifflin.

ROBINSON, JAMES HARVEY (1921) 1950 *The Mind in the Making: The Relation of Intelligence to Social Reform.* With an introduction by Stuart Chase. New York: Harper.

SMITH, PRESERVED (1930–1934) 1962 *A History of Modern Culture.* 2 vols. New York: Collier. → Volume 1: *Origins of Modern Culture, 1543–1687.* Volume 2: *The Enlightenment, 1687–1776.*

SOCIAL SCIENCE RESEARCH COUNCIL, COMMITTEE ON HIS-
TORIOGRAPHY 1946 *Theory and Practice in Historical Study.* Bulletin No. 54. New York: The Council.
SOCIAL SCIENCE RESEARCH COUNCIL, COMMITTEE ON HIS-
TORICAL ANALYSIS 1963 *Generalization in the Writing of History.* Edited by Louis R. Gottschalk. Univ.
of Chicago Press.

## VII
### ECONOMIC HISTORY

Economic history is broadly concerned with the performance of economies in the past. The issues that are relevant to an economic historian range as widely as an interest in the growth, stagnation, or decline of economies; the well-being of individual groups in the economy during the course of economic change; and the interrelationship between economic organization and performance. This last issue necessarily focuses on the institutional structure of the society. As a result, economic history frequently spills over into the allied fields of social and political history. However, the major issues of economic history fall into two rather broad categories—(1) the over-all growth of the economy over time and the determinants of that growth (or stagnation or decline) and (2) the distribution of income within that economy in the course of its growth or decline. The latter concern covers the whole range of issues of the well-being of diverse groups in the society during the course of economic change in the past.

The distinguishing feature of economic history as compared with the discipline of economics itself is its paramount concern with problems of the past rather than of the present. It is distinguishable from general historical inquiry not only by its specialized concern with economic aspects of past societies but also by its appeal to a systematic body of theory as a source of generalization and by the equally systematic use of quantitative methods of organizing evidence.

**Recent changes in the discipline.** The use of the above characteristics to separate economic history from general historical inquiry reflects a distinct change in the discipline in recent times. In the *Encyclopaedia of the Social Sciences,* John Clapham could describe the discipline as "a branch of general institutional history, a study of the economic aspects of the social institutions of the past" (1931, p. 327). In his article, Clapham made clear that economic theory had a minor role in economic history and "the relationship of economic history to social history is much closer" (1931, p. 329). Essentially, the field was a branch of historical inquiry employing the methods of the historian.

In the intervening years, the discipline has grad-

ually adopted more of the methodology of the social sciences. While this revolution in economic history is far from over, and while today much if not most economic history is still written by scholars trained as historians, the direction of change is unmistakable. The pioneering studies in this transformation include Clapham's emphasis on measurement (1926–1938); Eli Heckscher's plea for an increasing use of economic theory in economic history (Lane & Riemersma 1953); and the studies of the International Committee on Price History (Cole & Crandall 1964), including William Beveridge's work on England (1939), Earl Hamilton's on Spain (1934), N. W. Posthumus' on Holland (1943), and Arthur Cole's on the United States (1938). Occasional efforts to systematically apply principles of economic analysis to problems in economic history were highlighted by T. S. Ashton's work on the English industrial revolution (1948) and Walt W. Rostow's effort to analyze the British economy of the nineteenth century (1948).

In the period since World War II, and particularly since 1950, the professionally trained economist has led the new development of the field. In some instances, such as the work of the Entrepreneurial Center at Harvard, research was inspired by Joseph Schumpeter's emphasis on the creative role of the entrepreneur in economic development (1939). The direction of research under Arthur Cole's leadership of the center was an early (and perhaps premature) attempt to synthesize the social sciences in order to establish a more comprehensive theoretical framework for economic historians (Harvard University . . . 1949). [*See* HISTORY, *article on* BUSINESS HISTORY.]

Three developments have furnished the major stimuli to the redirection of economic history. First there has been the growing interest of economists in the study of economic growth. Since World War II economists have devoted a major share of their attention to attempting to understand the sources of economic development and to account for the widely divergent patterns of economic growth between the high-income countries of the Western world and the low-income countries of the underdeveloped parts of the world. The study of economic development has led economists to isolate important elements and determinants of economic development, even though they do not fit as yet into an over-all general theory. These elements include the problems of adapting and modifying technology from one economy to another having different factor endowments; the importance of investment in human capital; and the study of the development of efficient factor and product markets. The research of the economist on the sources of increased productivity, which underlies economic development, has revolutionary implications for re-examining the way in which economic historians have accounted for development in the past. [*See* AGRICULTURE, *article on* PRODUCTIVITY AND TECHNOLOGY; ECONOMIC GROWTH; PRODUCTIVITY.]

The second source of change has been the growing interest of economists in the more precise testing of their hypotheses. The development of operational propositions which can be tested has become a major concern of economists and is being extended to problems in economic history. This involves the sophisticated use of statistical techniques and methods as well, of course, as the careful use of economic theory. [*See* ECONOMETRICS.]

The third source of change has been the growing volume of quantitative information about the past. This concern with measurement of the performance of economies in the past has been largely the work of economists—or, in recent years, of economic historians trained in economics. The development of national income accounting has contributed significantly to the measurement of the performance of economies in the past. Simon Kuznets has played a pioneering role in both the development of national income accounts and their systematic application to the measurement of the past performance of economies (1956–1963). The pioneering studies in price history have been supplemented in many Western countries. The quantitative studies of the National Bureau of Economic Research in the United States have been paralleled in many other countries. The result is an enormous increase in quantitative information, which provides the economic historian with empirical data that he may put to systematic use in testing his propositions.

Taken together, these three developments have led to a growing reorientation of economic history toward the employment of scientific methodology and the systematic use of quantitative measurement. With these essential tools, the economic historian may be able to provide far greater understanding of the past than he has heretofore done. Therefore this article essentially offers a methodological prescription for the present and the future instead of surveying the past literature of the field. While the illustrations are drawn from American economic history, the underlying principles they illustrate are universally applicable.

**Explanation in economic history.** The primary objective of the economic historian is explanation. He seeks to understand the way economies have operated or the way the welfare of people in the society has been affected by economic phenomena. In this respect, explanation in economic history does not differ significantly from scientific explanation in the natural and physical sciences. It not only involves the careful unearthing of facts and evidence about the phenomenon to be explained but also requires the application of generalizations to reduce the shapeless mass of evidential information to an orderly explanation. Therefore, explanation in economic history, as in the sciences, involves the statement of the essential background conditions—that is, singular statements of facts which provide the setting for the particular pattern of events to be explained—followed by the application of general principles which will provide the explanation.

The economic historian, then, is concerned with determining the extent to which his explanation fits the empirical evidence he is able to obtain. Ideally, this empirical evidence is quantitative in nature; it may be, however, only a number of qualitative statements to which he assigns particular weights. To the extent that the empirical evidence runs contrary to his generalizations, the economic historian should re-explore the background conditions which he has assumed or modify and develop new generalizations which will be more consistent with the available empirical evidence. This process of give-and-take between the development of generalizations, the specification of background conditions, and the testing of the generalizations against systematic empirical evidence is the way by which the economic historian attempts to provide the explanation of historical phenomena.

The body of theory that the economic historian employs is that of economics. This theory rests upon a number of basic axioms and postulates from which are derived subsidiary propositions that express the general form of the functions used in constructing models. These models represent broad generalizations of economic behavior. [*See* ECONOMICS.] This body of economic theory has emerged in the past two centuries in the course of a continual interchange between the development of generalizations and their testing against empirical evidence. While economic theory provides certain basic models of economic behavior, application of these models to given historical situations requires the specification of the particular functional forms, parameters, or changes in parameters which may not be known to the economic historian. Therefore, the model that he constructs is one in which these forms and shifts of functions must be discovered and specified. The empirical verification of historical models requires the testing of the functional relationships implicitly or explicitly embodied in the explanation in order to see whether the parameters of these equations are consistent with available data.

For example, hypotheses that attribute the failure of the southern United States to industrialize before the Civil War to the small size of southern markets for manufactured goods rest upon assumed shapes of the supply functions of manufacturing industries at that time and can be tested, at least in part, by standard statistical procedures. Likewise, the contention that the discontent of farmers in western Massachusetts in the post-Revolutionary War period was due to the severe burden imposed upon them by a whiskey tax can be tested by measuring the elasticity of the demand for whiskey at that time. This information is needed to determine the incidence of the tax.

Causal explanations implicitly involve counterfactual propositions. That is, they imply that "had conditions been different" the causal sequence inferred in the proposition would not have taken place. A statement that the industrial revolution in Britain was induced by the expansion of population implies the counterfactual proposition that in the absence of this population increase the industrial revolution would not have occurred. A statement that the monopoly practices of the "robber barons" at the end of the nineteenth century significantly lowered the income of workers and farmers implies the counterfactual statement that in the absence of monopoly profits the incomes of farmers and workers would have been significantly higher.

*The testing of hypotheses.* The testing of explanations in economic history can take several forms. These include examination of (1) the empirical validity of the background conditions; (2) the logical consistency of the model; (3) the empirical validity of functions that relate the background conditions to the conclusions; (4) the empirical validity of the conclusions. The most appropriate point at which to test a given explanation depends on the issues under consideration and the availability of data. Thus, an explanation of the causes of farmer discontent in the late nineteenth century in the United States which asserts that the source of this discontent was the more rapid fall of farm prices than of prices of other goods can be refuted by empirical data showing that farm prices fell no more rapidly than other prices (North 1966). A hypothesis which maintains that slavery would have fallen under its own weight without a civil war rests upon the economic viability of slavery as an institution. It can be refuted by a sub-

sidiary hypothesis if, under testing, the latter shows that slavery was a profitable institution (Meyer & Conrad 1958). It should be noted that a confirmation of the profitability of slavery will refute the earlier hypothesis; but if slavery should prove to have been unprofitable, it still would not prove the institution was nonviable, since Southerners may have wanted to buy and hold slaves for noneconomic reasons.

The economic historian may also be able to test a given counterfactual proposition. Thus, an argument that the railroad was indispensable for U.S. economic development in the nineteenth century could be refuted by testing the counterfactual proposition on which it rests—that is, by showing that the cost of moving goods by the best alternative form of transportation would not have been substantially higher than the cost of moving goods by railroad. Such a test involves the determination of the supply function of rail and nonrail transport services (Fogel 1964). Similarly, the statement that the robber barons significantly lowered the income of farmers and workers by monopoly practices could be refuted if it were shown that the total amount of monopoly profit at that time, if redistributed among farmers and workers, would not have significantly raised their incomes (North 1966)—and under the further assumption that the misallocation of resources under monopoly conditions would not have significantly affected this.

**Methodological techniques illustrated.** An extended illustration can illuminate the whole process of research and testing and the problems involved. The hypothesis that British imperial policy significantly lowered the income of the American colonists in the period 1763–1775 will serve as the example. This hypothesis implies as a counterfactual statement that in the absence of specific British policies the income of the colonies would have been significantly higher. The information needed to obtain a precise answer to this question is the actual income of the colonists between 1763 and 1775 as against the hypothetical income the colonists would have received during this period in the absence of the British policies (i.e., as an independent country outside British regulation and protection). Since the actual income of the colonists is not known, the problem cannot be attacked directly, but it might be resolved indirectly by measuring the net difference in income that would have occurred had the specific policies been eliminated.

The researcher requires first an intimate knowledge of the structure and characteristics of the colonial economy and the specific aspects of the Navigation Acts and other British imperial policies that impinged upon the colonial economy. It should be noted that even the process of selection of facts as a part of the background conditions involves theorizing, since it is impossible to separate out relevant and important facts from irrelevant ones without a theory concerning the way an economy operates. Thus, when the economic historian discards as relatively unimportant the British restrictions on colonial manufacturing, he does so first because economic theory tells him that any economy characterized by a scarcity of labor and capital relative to land—the situation of the American colonies—will not typically engage in manufacturing because its costs will be higher than those of competing regions. He is furthermore supported in his initial assumption through examination of data on the economy of the United States after independence, which shows that manufacturing did not loom large even when the ex-colonists were free to engage in it. On the other hand, he will be impressed by the fact that tobacco and rice were enumerated (i.e., had to be shipped to England), and the requirement that imports move through Britain probably had a significant effect upon colonial income.

While the general shape of the relevant demand curves would stem from basic economic axioms (i.e., that the demand curves would be negatively sloped), it now becomes necessary to obtain a specific measure of the elasticity of demand and supply for tobacco in order to assess exactly the extent of the burden involved. By getting data on the spread between Virginia and Amsterdam prices of tobacco before and again after the revolution, the economic historian is able to show how the price spread narrowed. However, in order to be able to find out how much more tobacco would have been bought at the lower price that would have prevailed without British restriction, he must know the elasticity of demand. Since the data needed to compute that elasticity are not available, the historian may have recourse to other studies of commodities which appear to have similar characteristics and which give him the assumed elasticity of demand. He must also know how much more tobacco would have been supplied had a higher price prevailed (i.e., he must know the elasticity of supply). Here he may get a proxy by seeing how much the tobacco supply expanded after the revolution in response to a higher price. Alternatively, he might look at the conditions of supply in Virginia and Maryland to see to what extent the supply of inputs of land, labor, and capital was capable of providing more tobacco and whether at the same cost or at rising costs.

The economic historian must examine all other aspects of the colonial economy on which British policy impinged. The intimate knowledge of those facts of the period which theory attests to be relevant will lead him not only to assess individual burdens but also to recognize that there were benefits to being a part of the British imperial system which will have to be calculated in similar fashion. Thus, he will have to measure the extent to which income from shipping was increased by inclusion within the British imperial system. Similarly, he will have to measure the extent to which the colonists would have had to underwrite their own defense in the absence of British protection. He may find that a proxy for these counterfactual conditions can be found in the period from 1785 to 1793, after the colonies became independent. That is, he is assuming that the period 1785–1793 approximates in significant aspects the way the economy would have operated had it been free and independent in the years 1763–1775.

This illustration not only provides a capsule indication of the necessary and essential methods by which the economic historian may do meaningful research, but it also provides some indication of the problems and difficulties involved in his task. Has he really specified and taken into account all of the indispensable conditions? Was he correct in ignoring the Stamp Act as not imposing significant burdens upon the colonists? Are his assumed elasticities of supply and demand the correct ones, or can additional evidence be garnered which would indicate that they were different from those he specified? Were the conditions between 1785 and 1793 really a proxy for those from 1763 to 1775, thereby enabling him properly to employ this period as a proxy to the counterfactual situation? In fact, what he is doing is comparing a condition that existed—that is, income of the colonists between 1763 and 1775—with the hypothetical model of what would have occurred in the absence of British policies. This hypothetical model of a situation that did not in fact exist is essentially a general equilibrium model, and therefore it is essential to his argument and his conclusions that the repercussion effects of those things which he does not take into account or which he argues are of small magnitude are in fact immaterial and would not significantly alter the conclusions he reaches.

Advances in economic theory will lead to reappraisals of the economic past. Like the traditional historian, the present-day economic historian will frequently be guided by his ideological preconceptions in making a choice of issues to be examined; but his testing of the resultant hypotheses should be neutral with respect to current ideological biases and should result in a continuous narrowing of the range of disagreement and an increasing understanding of the past.

It can be seen from the above illustration that the limitations of inquiry in economic history are those imposed by the limitations of existing theory and of available evidence.

**The uses and limitations of theory.** While economic theory provides generalizations that can be applied to a broad range of issues in economic history, particularly to those dealing with the welfare of groups at particular times in the past, there is no general theory of economic growth to which the economic historian can turn in exploring this major aspect of economic history. While research in the study of economic growth of the past twenty or thirty years casts doubt upon many of the implicit or explicit hypotheses of economic historians, there is still no over-all framework which the economic historian can neatly apply. So, in this field, as in so many other aspects of economic history, the scholar must essentially develop his own theoretical framework. Similarly, where the economic historian wishes to explore the theoretical borderlines between economic and social history, he must rely on the other social science disciplines or develop a framework of his own to explore these relationships. There is no reason, of course, why the economic historian should be limited to received theory in economics. He is free to develop and apply theory of his own. However, caution in such an endeavor is obviously essential. The likelihood that the economic historian who is untrained in the principles of economics can derive theoretical propositions of any significance is very slim indeed. There is as wide a gap between common-sense observations in economics and economic generalizations as there is between common-sense observations in the physical sciences and the general laws of those physical sciences. We would not expect a layman to be able to derive from simple observation of physical properties the general laws of physics; nor can observations of economic phenomena lead an untrained economic historian to develop valid generalizations with respect to economic theory. Economic theory has evolved in the give-and-take between the development of generalizations and their testing over a long enough period of time, and it cannot and should not be ignored in the course of analysis. The economic historian trained in economic theory will be well aware of the pitfalls inherent in economic analysis. Therefore, if he wishes to develop his own theoretical framework, he will take careful account of the work that has gone on before and the degree to which previous generalizations are supported by available evidence.

**The limitations of empirical evidence.** Limitations of empirical evidence pose equally serious problems for the economic historian. He is faced with discrete, nonrepetitive, past performance: the artifacts and evidence that remain are his material. Therefore, it is essential that he attempt systematically to develop evidence about the past from this fragmentary information. As indicated above, that which comes closest to providing him with accurate tests is quantitative evidence which precisely defines and isolates the particular phenomena that he wants to measure. Quantitative information in such ideal form seldom exists, and the economic historian is forced to make use of the more fragmentary evidence which has typically survived from the past. Making the most of the evidence requires a knowledge of statistical theory so that he can use to the best effect whatever data are available.

The illustration used above indicates some of the ways the economic historian can employ bits and pieces of quantitative information when the ideal data are not available. In the above case, neither the actual national income of the colonists between 1763 and 1775 nor the hypothetical income in the absence of British policies is known. But the net difference in income can be derived even without the absolute figures. A complete series of prices and quantities for tobacco, rice, and other affected commodities is also not available, but proxies for these can be obtained that provide reasonably good measures for the unknowns with respect to the shape of the relevant demand and supply curves.

The further back in time the economic historian explores, the more inadequate the data are likely to be. However, the quantitative information may be far more abundant than economic historians have heretofore believed, since hypotheses dictate the search for data, and it is only in recent years that self-conscious employment of theory has characterized research in the field. The quantitative information available about the past has usually not been mined because its relevance has not been appreciated. In the absence of quantitative data, the economic historian is forced to fall back on the use of qualitative description embodied in other kinds of information; but it should be noted here that he does not thereby escape the essential rules of statistical inference. That is, it remains imperative that he demand that the qualitative information meet the same rules of statistical sampling and representativeness required in the use of quantitative knowledge. In this respect, Clapham's warning in the article on economic history in the *Encyclopaedia of the Social Sciences* is still timely.

Every economic historian should, however, have acquired what might be called the statistical sense, the habit of asking in relation to any institution, policy, group or movement the question: how large? how long? how often? how representative? The requirement seems obvious; but a good deal of the older politico–institutional economic history was less useful than it might have been through neglect of it. (1931, p. 328)

**The writing of economic history.** While explanation of the economic past is the ultimate objective of the economic historian, and an awareness of the principles of scientific method is an essential requirement in the pursuit of this objective, characterization of the discipline solely in these terms would give a distorted picture of the field. The traditional craft of the historian—the careful unearthing of evidence and the assessment of its reliability—is fully as important in economic history as it is in general history. The present-day scholar has inherited a rich store of descriptive material and data about the economic past which has been mined and assayed largely by historians. The present-day analytically oriented economic historian who ignores this treasure-trove from the past does so at the risk that he will be unaware of essential background conditions when he constructs his model. It is incumbent upon him not only to be thoroughly versed in the traditional literature in the field but also to be possessed of that fine sense of the detective, which has always been the trademark of the good historian.

Finally, the economic historian is attempting to provide a systematic and integrated explanation of the economic past, and this inevitably involves something more than the development and testing of a single hypothesis. It is a relatively easy task for any well-trained economic historian to test (and typically in recent research to destroy) a specific explanation about the past, but it is well for him to remember that the ultimate objective he seeks is far more difficult—to construct a unified explanation of the economic past. This involves the development of a set of consistent hypotheses together with the essential background conditions, both woven together in the fabric of a narrative. Such a story not only possesses the characteristics of good narrative but also makes clear the essential background conditions and states clearly the hypotheses involved, so that it is consistent with the principles of scientific explanation and so that its several parts can be tested by other economic historians.

DOUGLASS C. NORTH

[*Directly relevant are the biographies of* CLAPHAM; HECKSCHER; SCHUMPETER. *For discussion of the approaches of some other economic historians, see the biographies of* ASHLEY; BÜCHER; CUNNINGHAM; EHRENBERG; HAMMOND, J. L. AND BARBARA; LEVASSEUR; PIRENNE; POLANYI; ROGERS; SÉE; TAWNEY; UNWIN; USHER; WEBB, SIDNEY AND BEATRICE; WEBER, MAX.]

## BIBLIOGRAPHY

GENERAL

ASHTON, T. S. (1948) 1964 *The Industrial Revolution: 1760–1830*. Rev. ed. Oxford Univ. Press.

BEVERIDGE, WILLIAM H. 1939 *Prices and Wages in England From the Twelfth to the Nineteenth Century*. New York and London: Longmans.

CLAPHAM, JOHN H. (1926–1938) 1950–1952 *An Economic History of Modern Britain*. 3 vols. Cambridge Univ. Press. → Volume 1: *The Early Railway Age: 1820–1850*. Volume 2: *Free Trade and Steel: 1850–1886*. Volume 3: *Machines and National Rivalries (1887–1914)* with an epilogue (1914–1929).

CLAPHAM, JOHN H. 1931 "Survey of Development to the Twentieth Century" and "Economic History as a Discipline." Volume 5, pages 315–320 and 327–330 in *Encyclopaedia of the Social Sciences*. New York: Macmillan. → Definitive of earlier views of the discipline; includes a bibliography. These are two parts of the article "Economic History."

COLE, ARTHUR H. 1938 *Wholesale Commodity Prices in the United States: 1700–1861*. 2 vols. Cambridge, Mass.: Harvard Univ. Press.

COLE, ARTHUR H.; and CRANDALL, RUTH 1964 The International Scientific Committee on Price History. *Journal of Economic History* 24:381–388. → A review of the work of the committee and a bibliography.

FOGEL, ROBERT W. 1964 *Railroads and American Economic Growth: Essays in Econometric History*. Baltimore: Johns Hopkins Press.

HAMILTON, EARL J. (1934) 1965 *American Treasure and the Price Revolution in Spain: 1501–1650*. Harvard Economic Studies, Vol. 43. New York: Octagon. Cambridge, Mass.: Harvard Univ. Press.

HARVARD UNIVERSITY, RESEARCH CENTER IN ENTREPRENEURIAL HISTORY 1949 *Change and the Entrepreneur: Postulates and Patterns for Entrepreneurial History*. Edited by Arthur Cole. Cambridge, Mass.: Harvard Univ. Press.

HECKSCHER, ELI F. (1929) 1953 A Plea for Theory in Economic History. Pages 421–430 in Frederic C. Lane and Jelle C. Riemersma (editors), *Enterprise and Secular Change: Readings in Economic History*. Homewood, Ill.: Irwin. → First published in a supplement to the *Economic Journal*.

KUZNETS, SIMON 1956–1963 Quantitative Aspects of the Economic Growth of Nations. Parts 1–8. *Economic Development and Cultural Change* 5, no. 1:5–94, no. 4 (Supplement); 6, no. 4:part 2; 7, no. 3:part 2; 8, no. 4:part 2; 9, no. 4:part 2; 10, no. 2:part 2; 11, no. 2:part 2.

LANE, FREDERIC C.; and RIEMERSMA, JELLE C. (editors) 1953 *Enterprise and Secular Change: Readings in*

*Economic History.* Homewood, Ill.: Irwin. → Contains a number of useful articles on earlier views of methodology.

MEYER, JOHN R.; and CONRAD, ALFRED H. 1957 Economic Theory, Statistical Inference and Economic History. *Journal of Economic History* 17:524–544.

NORTH, DOUGLASS C. 1966 *Growth and Welfare in the American Past: A New Economic History.* Englewood Cliffs, N.J.: Prentice-Hall.

POSTHUMUS, NICOLAAS W. (1943) 1946 *Inquiry Into the History of Prices in Holland.* Volume 1: Wholesale Prices at the Exchange of Amsterdam, 1585–1914. Leiden (Netherlands): Brill. → First published in Dutch.

ROSTOW, WALT W. 1948 *British Economy of the Nineteenth Century: Essays.* Oxford: Clarendon. → A pioneering effort to apply Keynesian theory to analyzing the British economy in the nineteenth century.

SCHUMPETER, JOSEPH A. 1939 *Business Cycles: A Theoretical, Historical, and Statistical Analysis of the Capitalist Process.* 2 vols. New York and London: McGraw-Hill. → An abridged version was published in 1964.

PHILOSOPHY AND METHODOLOGY

*There is an extensive literature in the philosophy of science and the philosophy of history on the methodological problems of writing history. Two of the most lucid as they bear upon explanation in economic history are Hempel 1942 and 1962. See also Nagel 1952. For the application of these principles specifically to economic history, a pioneering article is Meyer & Conrad 1958.*

HEMPEL, CARL G. 1942 The Function of General Laws in History. *Journal of Philosophy* 39:35–48.

HEMPEL, CARL G. 1962 Explanation in Science and History. Pages 7–33 in Robert G. Colodny (editor), *Frontiers of Science and Philosophy.* Univ. of Pittsburgh Press.

MEYER, JOHN R.; and CONRAD, ALFRED H. 1958 The Economics of Slavery in the Ante Bellum South. *Journal of Political Economy* 66:95–130.

NAGEL, ERNEST 1952 Some Issues in the Logic of Historical Analysis. *Scientific Monthly* 74:162–169.

STATISTICAL SOURCES

*It is impossible to enumerate the large and ever-increasing body of statistical studies now appearing. The most convenient major sources are the statistical abstracts which so far have been done for three countries.*

MITCHELL, BRIAN R. 1962 *Abstract of British Historical Statistics.* Cambridge Univ. Press.

U.S. BUREAU OF THE CENSUS 1960 *Historical Statistics of the United States; Colonial Times to 1957: A Statistical Abstract Supplement.* Washington: Government Printing Office.

URQUHART, M. C.; and BUCKLEY, K. A. H. (editors) 1965 *Historical Statistics of Canada.* Cambridge Univ. Press.

## VIII
### BUSINESS HISTORY

Although business history in the broadest sense encompasses all the activities of businessmen in the past, the academic discipline, as developed by historians, has certain distinguishing characteristics. To date it has been primarily concerned with the written record of decision making by individuals seeking private profit through production of goods and services.

Business history in practice rests basically on one assumption and one derivative from it. The key assumption is that man enjoys a measure of freedom of will and, accordingly, that his individual decisions affect the course of historical events. From that is derived the conviction that human decisions, made with an eye to producing profit, have significantly shaped the stream of economic and social change over a long period of time and in many parts of the world.

In business history, change is regarded as continuous, interacting in character, variable in rate, and open-ended—but always initiated by man. Through a complex of interrelated decision-making processes, businessmen are seen to have contributed, together with other individuals and groups in society, to the generation of changes in their environment, both internal and external to their own institutions.

Certain methodological characteristics of business history follow from the foregoing assumptions and ideas. It emphasizes microeconomic elements in the past more than its parent discipline, economic history, and concentrates more on the process of change and the generation of change. To date, business historians have employed impersonal analysis of economic performance in the past less than those who have utilized the techniques of economists to evaluate trends in quantitative terms or to "fill in" gaps in historical knowledge. In fact, the tools of sociology, anthropology, and psychology are frequently as relevant to the questions business historians ask of data as is economic analysis, particularly with reference to motivation of men and their relation to the society in which they live. Concentration on businessmen as decision makers and as builders or destroyers of institutions, as well as on the ideas and accumulated knowledge affecting the place, timing, and conduct of business activities, has, of course, also differentiated business history from economic history.

The tools employed by the professional business historian depend on his objective and on the approach to the businessman that he selects. Each major approach involves a different context for viewing businessmen and business of the past. Concern with the businessman as an individual in society is the approach of the biographer of a businessman. Viewed in the framework of one or more organizations for the production of profit, with all that this implies for policy formulation and implementation, the businessman is the province of company histories and industry studies. Some students have chosen the functional areas of business development, such as finance, production, and marketing, as the subjects of historical research. Others have emphasized the implements and institutions of business. Still other scholars have concentrated their research on the interaction between businessmen and their environment in terms of its influence on developments both inside and outside the world of business.

These varied approaches indicate that business history embraces many diverse areas of study, accommodates many interests, and calls on numerous disciplines. It therefore attracts researchers from many areas of history, economics, and other scholarly disciplines, as well as those whose qualifications are based on other credentials. In the latter category are amateur historians with business experience and publicists employed to write business history for nonacademic purposes. Although a number of these contributions meet good scholarly standards and many contribute useful information, most significant works in business history are produced by scholars trained in one or more of the traditional disciplines. By no means all of this latter group, however, would claim to be professional business historians. In many instances their forays into the field are one-time expeditions, using the subject matter of business history to explore an area related to their primary interests.

Professional historians both benefit and suffer from the amorphous nature of their field. They have benefited most from outsiders' contributions to such areas as the theory of the firm and have suffered most from the popular identification of their field with histories of firms written by amateurs without scholarly standards. In part, this has been the price of progress, for business history has matured slowly as an academic discipline and until recently has concentrated on the study of business administration through the medium of company histories.

Since professional business historians have been located chiefly in schools of business administration, it is not surprising that the variety of their approaches to research and teaching has been governed in large measure by the applications that could be made of their work in such institutions. As the curricula of schools of business have broadened from functional specialties to such larger preoccupations as the responsibilities of businessmen in society and the challenge of undeveloped and underdeveloped areas to private enterprise, new applications of business history have been found. Some of these coincide with objectives of historians

concerned with all phases of social and economic change. In many business history courses, histories of firms have been supplemented by industry histories, by studies of the leadership styles and personal qualities of businessmen in the past, by analyses of government–business relations viewed in broad perspective, and by increasing concern with the historical problems and lessons of economic growth. Thus the field of business history has been in the process of change since it was first recognized as an academic discipline.

## Initial development by Gras at Harvard

Business history began as an area of academic research and teaching at the Graduate School of Business Administration of Harvard University. Dean Wallace B. Donham believed that scholarly histories of "specific situations as they came to businessmen in their communities in the past" were essential in order that those situations might be compared "understandably" with "current conditions" (Redlich 1962, pp. 61–62). Donham had in mind the use of business history for training prospective business administrators, the utilization of the case method, and the comparison of past techniques, decisions, and their implementation with those of the present.

To initiate such teaching, research, and writing, in 1927 Donham chose N. S. B. Gras, a scholar already manifesting an interest in the role of business and businessmen in history. In his classes at the University of Minnesota he had encouraged students to do research in this field and had embarked on assessing business activities in several areas. He was trained in economic theory as well as economic history, and he had read widely in the literature of sociology and social theory.

Given his training and experience, Gras at first visualized business history quite broadly. From his reading in social, political, and economic history he gathered data on the environments in which businessmen had operated, as well as information on the creation and evolution of business instruments and institutions. Gras accepted the concept of capitalism and made the study of the evolution of capitalism one of his major concerns. But neither in the publications of economic theorists and economic historians nor in the works of Marx, Engels, Sombart, and others did he find a satisfactory explanation of the changing character of capitalism over time. While recognizing that environmental factors influenced businessmen to some degree, he rejected economic determinism; he remained convinced that men have enjoyed some freedom of will and that, by choosing courses of action from a range of alternatives, they have changed the course of history.

Accordingly, to understand the process of change in the business sector of society, Gras believed scholars must study and analyze the decisions of men reflected in the policies and practices of firms, the basic units of business systems. In the studies of Richard Ehrenberg (1902–1905) he had examples of how meaningful histories of firms could be written. From such biographies of firms, written and to be written, Gras hoped to be able to learn how capitalism had evolved as a system.

With these ideas in mind, Gras embarked on an ambitious program for the development of business history at the Harvard Business School. With the aid of associates, notably Henrietta M. Larson, he started developing cases for the course he taught. That offering embraced discussion and analysis of activities of businessmen from the European Middle Ages to the twentieth-century United States; lectures on background materials alternated with class discussion of both specific and general situations. At the same time, to encourage publication of the current results of research, Edwin F. Gay, then a professor at Harvard, as editor, and Gras as managing editor, began issuing the *Journal of Economic and Business History* (*JEBH*) in November 1928. Some members of the group also undertook book-length biographies of businessmen and firms.

Soon after the beginning of this program, economic and other factors induced Gras to modify his approach to the new area of study. The financial crisis of 1929 and ensuing depression brought a drastic diminution in supporting funds. The *JEBH* ceased publication in 1932, a year after Gay and Gras disagreed on editorial policies and the latter became sole editor; not until 1938 did the business history group at the Harvard Business School assume responsibility for issuing the *Bulletin of the Business Historical Society*, known as *Business History Review* (*BHR*), a quarterly since 1954, and it was a much less ambitious periodical than the earlier one. Meanwhile, money to underwrite research in depth could be found only in limited amounts, often restricted to study of the families and firms providing the financial support. Simultaneously, the use of the case method in the course, as well as the lack of published information on the decision-making process and the policies of businessmen, fortified Gras's tendency to concentrate on biographies of businessmen and of firms.

In spite of serious difficulties during the 1930s, Gras and his group established the contours of the new field. They, as well as others, published their research findings in both the *JEBH* and the *Bulle-*

*tin.* In the Harvard Studies in Business History, under the editorship of Gras, appeared books dealing with merchants, an investment banking firm, a commercial bank, and an advertising agency. In 1939 Gras and Larson published the teaching materials assembled for the course—*Casebook in American Business History*—and Gras issued his preliminary synthesis of business history in *Business and Capitalism.*

In little more than ten years Gras had modified his concepts and had put a particular stamp on business history. Instead of realizing his early expectation of studying and writing the history of business within a broad political, social, and economic framework, he gradually came to visualize the field more narrowly. To him, business history became "primarily the study of the administration of business units in the past," administration being in two parts—policy formulation and management or execution of policy (Gras & Larson 1939, p. 3). From such statements, as well as the subject matter of the books published, many observers adopted the idea, unfortunately not yet fully abandoned, that to Gras business history was "company history" and nothing more.

Actually, *Business and Capitalism* indicated that Gras was seeking, through business history, an explanation of the changes in the character of private capitalism over a thousand years. Influenced by Karl Bücher and others, Gras related the evolution of stages in capitalism to changes in business systems, identifying each stage with dominant business types and groups—petty, mercantile, industrial (specializing), financial, and national. When he started writing the book, he did not think all the stages mentioned actually fitted the history of private enterprise in every national economy, but after its publication the idea became more than a tentative hypothesis in his mind. To supplement *Business and Capitalism*, he began writing a multivolume history of industries in the United States, a task never completed. However, Larson published her *Guide to Business History* in 1948, and the Business History Foundation, Inc., an organization chartered in New York by Gras and Larson in 1947 to forward research and writing on the history of business (chiefly on that of large-scale enterprise), is still active.

## Subsequent broadening of approaches

Starting with the *Casebook* and *Business and Capitalism* as the bases of courses in other institutions, historians soon began to utilize a variety of approaches to the history of business. Some accepted Gras's ideas generally, but increasingly used his stage theory for comparative purposes and not as a rigid framework for analyzing the history of businessmen and business institutions. Other scholars reacted more critically, explicitly and implicitly, to Grasian thought. Some regarded his stage theory as outmoded; they considered it too rigid and not sufficiently effective as an analytical tool. Others were convinced that his definition of the subject was too narrow; they thought the history of business and businessmen was more than the history of business administration and that Gras gave too little attention to the motivation and environment of businessmen. Many disagreed with the broad generalizations, especially those on the period since 1870, which Gras made on the basis of research by his group and by predecessors among economic and social historians. Still others sought a less positivistic and more theoretical base for analyzing the behavior and achievements of businessmen in history. Almost all were more interested in analyzing the activities of businessmen or in seeking explanations of changes in business than in the history of capitalism as such.

**Entrepreneurial studies.** One group of scholars, the most influential, sought understanding of change in the history of business through the concept of entrepreneurship. Arthur H. Cole reviewed the historical changes in that concept in his presidential address to the Economic History Association (1946). A year later, in a paper presented to the same body, Joseph A. Schumpeter built onto the idea of innovation that of the creative entrepreneur as the main force in generating change in business (1947). Jointly the two initiated the Research Center in Entrepreneurial History at Harvard in 1948. Led by Cole, and ably supported by Thomas C. Cochran, Leland H. Jenks, Fritz Redlich, and several others, the group brought together numerous scholars to enunciate their ideas and to discuss historical tools and techniques as well as concepts. Over a ten-year period the center helped to train a number of young historians and published many of the products of discussion and research in *Explorations in Entrepreneurial History.*

Cole has provided his personal interpretation of the significant findings of the center (1959). First, he assessed the relationship of the entrepreneur to his organization, to the process of social conditioning, and to elements important "for the proper functioning of an entrepreneurial flow." Then he turned to analysis of five categories of "entrepreneurial realities" drawn from historical data: the social order, underdeveloped areas, technological change, business organization, and the state. Each of these had three subsegments of illustrative material which not only summarized existing substantive knowledge about types of entrepreneurial activity but also presented other historians of business with examples which could be utilized in class, tested by research, and added to as the study of businessmen and their institutions continued.

Even before Cole's synthesis appeared, both older scholars and a new generation of historians of business began to fuse the center's products with those of the Grasian group. Some welcomed the center's analysis of business history in a broad sociological as well as economic context. Many noted with approval that Cole defined entrepreneurship as "the purposeful activity (including an integrated sequence of decisions) of an individual or group of associated individuals, undertaken to initiate, maintain or aggrandize a profit-oriented business unit for the production or distribution of goods and services" (1959, p. 7). That definition, business historians generally thought, embraced both policy formulation, which they now visualized as closely related to Schumpeterian creative entrepreneurship, and management (implementation of policy), which was seemingly included in an "integrated sequence of decisions."

In addition to concepts, ideas, and information adduced by the Gras and Cole groups, business historians have turned to other disciplines for tools and techniques. From writers on economic growth (Hirschman 1958) and on the theory of the firm (Boulding & Spivey 1960), as well as from anthropologists, sociologists, and social psychologists (Hagen 1962), scholars interested in the history of business have borrowed and tested concepts, theories, and research methods. They have been particularly interested in any study dealing with motivation of the businessman and his "need of achievement" (McClelland 1961).

In the 1950s and 1960s research continues to reflect the mixture of approaches noted early in this article. Some scholars focus on a businessman as an individual in society (see, for example, Nevins 1953). There have been numerous semipopular histories of firms (see, for example, Lief 1958; Blochman 1958). In some instances histories of firms written by insiders have been distinguished by thorough research and a comprehensive analysis (see, for example, Beaton 1957).

**Studies of firms and industries.** Since 1950 academicians have added significantly to the list of firms that have been studied in detail. Several large firms have submitted to detailed scholarly portraits. In large measure these works exhibit the increased sophistication arising from the fusion of ideas noted earlier. The most distinguished study of the much-examined late medieval period deals with the rise and decline of the Medici Bank (de Roover 1963). In their histories of large firms some students have focused their attention on the response and adjustment of businessmen to changing environment (Cochran 1948). One outstanding study is devoted to grand strategy on a global scale (Wilson 1954). Noteworthy have been the analyses of policy *and* its implementation on the part of firms in the petroleum industry, in particular those sponsored by the Business History Foundation (*History of Standard Oil . . .*, 1955–1956; Larson & Porter 1959). Recent histories of American railroad companies tend to present them broadly as common carriers operating for a profit within an environment experiencing rapid change (Overton 1965). Among studies of financial institutions, several life insurance companies have received detailed attention (Williamson & Smalley 1957). A midwestern historian has provided the best portrayal of a public utility (Miller 1957).

The history of small business has attracted fewer scholars than has that of large-scale enterprise. Only rarely has a small firm been appraised in detail (for one example, see Marburg 1956). More attention has been given to generalizations based on a study of a significant sample of firms within an industry, such as that of metal fabricators in New England (Soltow 1965).

Few historians have attempted histories of entire industries in recent years. Among the few examples are those on rubber (Woodruff 1958) and brewing (Mathias 1959), both within the British economy, and, outstanding in scope and economic analysis, that on the American petroleum industry —the authors having at hand at the inception of the research numerous histories of firms as well as special studies (Williamson & Daum 1959–1963).

**Recent trends.** A growing number of business historians have centered their interest on what has been labeled "business in history." They seek to understand the interaction between businessmen and business institutions on the one hand and pertinent, influential segments of the environment on the other. They are concerned with analyzing both the process and the results of the process. Most prominent in this area have been studies of government–business relationships, well exemplified by many articles found in the *BHR* (and elsewhere). For example, one author has focused on the roles of business institutions and values in relation to evolving political institutions in Africa, Asia, and Latin America (Robinson 1962). Another has evaluated the relationship of business to the emergence of

the Nazi dictatorship (Schweitzer 1964). A third has assessed the connection between a defensive national economic policy, coupled with a desire for political unity, and Canadian regulation of business (Aitken 1964). A similar but more specific approach to the history of government–business relations is exemplified in a study of the evolution of American petroleum pipelines and related public policy (Johnson 1956).

Comparative studies in business history have become more common in recent years, providing new and meaningful interpretations for business historians. Most noteworthy among studies dealing with early industrialization is the pioneer monograph on managerial techniques of British entrepreneurs (Pollard 1965). One author has analyzed causation and cycles in centralization and decentralization in administration of large-scale enterprise (Chandler 1956; 1959; 1962; 1965). Another has studied evolution of systematic methods for coordinating production flows (Litterer 1961*a*; 1961*b*; 1963). Still another can be cited for his evaluation of evolving financial reporting by American corporations within a changing environment (Hawkins 1963). One of the most significant books analyzes the attitudes and ideas of a broad group of railroad executives (Cochran 1953).

Most of these recent articles and books manifest more refined analysis than characterized the written history of business in earlier years, but conceptualization of thought in the field has grown slowly and theoretical works have been few. Fritz Redlich has written more in this area than has anyone else, and his essays dealing with the entrepreneur have now been collected (1964). His contributions range from an analysis of the "daimonic" in business history to categorizations of entrepreneurial types. To date, only one author has attempted to advance a theory of the growth of the firm (Penrose 1959).

No widely accepted synthesis of business history has yet been achieved, even for the United States, the country in which literature on the subject is most voluminous. To be sure, some narrations of national business achievement have been produced (Chamberlain 1963; Walker 1949), and some periods in the history of business have been objectively appraised (Cochran 1957).

In spite of vastly increased study of the history of business and of business in history, scholars still evince a marked lack of interest in numerous important topics. Business failures, labor–management relations, small business, and other likely subjects are receiving little, if any, attention. Moreover, although the preliminary moves mentioned above have been made, attempts to conceptualize and to theorize on the history of business have been few.

Formal courses in business history have been developed slowly but steadily. By the mid-1960s more than three-score universities, colleges, and schools of business in the United States listed courses in the field, but the focus on topics involving business history was their single common denominator; content and emphasis varied widely. Meanwhile, academicians in other countries, notably in the United Kingdom, Holland, West Germany, Australia, and Japan, have inaugurated research and/or teaching programs in business history, bringing the world total of institutions sponsoring such efforts to more than one hundred. Participants in such activities find continuous additions to their body of information in the *Business History Review, Tradition* (published in West Germany since 1956), *Business Archives and History* (published in Australia since 1956), *Business History* (published in the United Kingdom since 1958), and pertinent articles in many other periodicals.

The broadening of horizons noted in this article has destroyed the exclusiveness of the original small pioneering band of professional historians and to a degree has outmoded the original framework that once gave their study of the subject great unity. The results of this change are still far from clear, and the need for a new synthesis has become increasingly apparent. Nevertheless, the governing assumptions about the nature of economic change and the significance of the businessman in it still hold. The increasingly varied approaches and applications of business history are in the tradition of the evolutionary development that has characterized the field since it was first recognized as an academic discipline.

RALPH W. HIDY

[*See also* ENTREPRENEURSHIP; *and the biographies of* GRAS; SCHUMPETER.]

### BIBLIOGRAPHY

AITKEN, HUGH G. J. 1964 Government and Business in Canada: An Interpretation. *Business History Review* 38:4–21.

BEATON, KENDALL 1957 *Enterprise in Oil: A History of Shell in the United States.* New York: Appleton.

BLOCHMAN, LAWRENCE G. 1958 *Doctor Squibb: The Life and Times of a Rugged Idealist.* New York: Simon & Schuster.

BOULDING, KENNETH E.; and SPIVEY, W. ALLEN 1960 *Linear Programming and the Theory of the Firm.* New York: Macmillan.

BRUCHEY, STUART W. 1965 *The Roots of American Economic Growth, 1607–1861: An Essay in Social Causation.* New York: Harper.

CHAMBERLAIN, JOHN 1963 *The Enterprising Americans: A Business History of the United States.* New York: Harper.

CHANDLER, ALFRED D. JR. 1956 Management Decentralization: An Historical Analysis. *Business History Review* 30:111–174.

CHANDLER, ALFRED D. JR. 1959 The Beginnings of "Big Business" in American Industry. *Business History Review* 33:1–31.

CHANDLER, ALFRED D. JR. 1962 *Strategy and Structure: Chapters in the History of the Industrial Enterprise.* Cambridge, Mass.: M.I.T. Press.

CHANDLER, ALFRED D. JR. 1965 The Railroads: Pioneers in Modern Corporate Management. *Business History Review* 39:16–40.

COCHRAN, THOMAS C. 1948 *The Pabst Brewing Company: The History of an American Business.* New York Univ. Press.

COCHRAN, THOMAS C. (1953) 1966 *Railroad Leaders, 1845–1890: The Business Mind in Action.* Cambridge, Mass.: Harvard Univ. Press.

COCHRAN, THOMAS C. 1957 *The American Business System: A Historical Perspective, 1900–1955.* Cambridge, Mass.: Harvard Univ. Press.

COLE, ARTHUR H. 1946 An Approach to the Study of Entrepreneurship: A Tribute to Edwin F. Gay. *Journal of Economic History* 6 (Supplement):1–15.

COLE, ARTHUR H. 1959 *Business Enterprise in Its Social Setting.* Cambridge, Mass.: Harvard Univ. Press.

DE ROOVER, RAYMOND A. 1963 *The Rise and Decline of the Medici Bank, 1397–1494.* Harvard Studies in Business History, No. 21. Cambridge, Mass.: Harvard Univ. Press.

EHRENBERG, RICHARD (1902–1905) 1925 *Grosse Vermögen, ihre Entstehung und ihre Bedeutung.* 2d ed. Jena (Germany): Fischer.

GRAS, N. S. B. 1939 *Business and Capitalism: An Introduction to Business History.* New York: Crofts.

GRAS, N. S. B.; and LARSON, HENRIETTA M. 1939 *Casebook in American Business History.* New York: Crofts.

HAGEN, EVERETT E. (1962) 1964 *On the Theory of Social Change: How Economic Growth Begins.* London: Tavistock.

HAWKINS, DAVID F. 1963 The Development of Modern Financial Reporting Practices Among American Manufacturing Corporations. *Business History Review* 37:135–168.

HIRSCHMAN, ALBERT O. 1958 *The Strategy of Economic Development.* Yale Studies in Economics, No. 10. New Haven: Yale Univ. Press. → A paperback edition was published in 1962.

*History of Standard Oil Company (New Jersey).* 2 vols. 1955–1956. New York: Harper. → Volume 1: *Pioneering in Big Business, 1888–1911,* by Ralph W. Hidy and Muriel E. Hidy. Volume 2: *The Resurgent Years, 1912–1927,* by George S. Gibb and Evelyn H. Knowlton.

JOHNSON, ARTHUR M. 1956 *The Development of American Petroleum Pipelines: A Study in Private Enterprise and Public Policy, 1862–1906.* Ithaca, N.Y.: Cornell Univ. Press.

LARSON, HENRIETTA M. 1948 *Guide to Business History: Materials for the Study of American Business History and Suggestions for Their Use.* Harvard Studies in

Business History, No. 12. Cambridge, Mass.: Harvard Univ. Press.

LARSON, HENRIETTA M.; and PORTER, KENNETH W. 1959 *History of Humble Oil & Refining Company: A Study in Industrial Growth.* New York: Harper.

LIEF, ALFRED 1958 *It Floats: The Story of Procter & Gamble.* New York: Rinehart.

LITTERER, JOSEPH A. 1961*a* Alexander Hamilton Church and the Development of Modern Management. *Business History Review* 35:211–225.

LITTERER, JOSEPH A. 1961*b* Systematic Management: The Search for Order and Integration. *Business History Review* 35:461–476.

LITTERER, JOSEPH A. 1963 Systematic Management: Design for Organizational Recoupling in American Manufacturing Firms. *Business History Review* 37: 369–391.

McCLELLAND, DAVID C. 1961 *The Achieving Society.* Princeton, N.J.: Van Nostrand.

McDONALD, FORREST 1962 *Insull.* Univ. of Chicago Press.

MARBURG, THEODORE F. 1956 *Small Business in Brass Fabricating: The Smith & Griggs Manufacturing Co. of Waterbury.* New York Univ. Press.

MATHIAS, PETER 1959 *The Brewing Industry in England, 1700–1830.* Cambridge Univ. Press.

MILLER, RAYMOND C. 1957 *Kilowatts at Work: A History of the Detroit Edison Company.* Detroit, Mich.: Wayne State Univ. Press.

MILLER, WILLIAM (editor) 1952 *Men in Business: Essays in the History of Entrepreneurship.* Cambridge, Mass.: Harvard Univ. Press.

NEVINS, ALLAN 1953 *Study in Power: John D. Rockefeller, Industrialist and Philanthropist.* 2 vols. New York: Scribner.

OVERTON, RICHARD C. 1965 *Burlington Route: A History of the Burlington Lines.* New York: Knopf.

PENROSE, EDITH T. 1959 *The Theory of the Growth of the Firm.* New York: Wiley.

POLLARD, SIDNEY 1965 *The Genesis of Modern Management: A Study of the Industrial Revolution in Great Britain.* Cambridge, Mass.: Harvard Univ. Press.

REDLICH, FRITZ 1962 Approaches to Business History. *Business History Review* 36:61–70.

REDLICH, FRITZ 1964 *Der Unternehmer: Wirtschafts- und sozialgeschichtliche Studien.* Göttingen (Germany): Vandenhoeck & Ruprecht.

ROBINSON, RICHARD D. 1962 Interrelationship of Business Enterprise and Political Development. *Business History Review* 36:287–324.

SCHUMPETER, JOSEPH A. 1947 The Creative Response in Economic History. *Journal of Economic History* 7: 149–159.

SCHWEITZER, ARTHUR 1964 Business Policy in a Dictatorship. *Business History Review* 38:413–438.

SOLTOW, JAMES H. 1965 Origins of Small Business Metal Fabricators and Machinery Makers in New England, 1890–1957. *American Philosophical Society, Transactions* New Series 55, part 10.

WALKER, JAMES B. 1949 *The Epic of American Industry.* New York: Harper.

WILLIAMSON, HAROLD F.; and DAUM, ARNOLD R. 1959–1963 *The American Petroleum Industry.* 2 vols. Evanston, Ill.: Northwestern Univ. Press.

WILLIAMSON, HAROLD F.; and SMALLEY, ORANGE A. 1957 *Northwestern Mutual Life: A Century of Trusteeship.* Evanston, Ill.: Northwestern Univ. Press.

WILSON, CHARLES 1954 *The History of Unilever: A Study in Economic Growth and Social Change.* London: Cassell.

WOODRUFF, WILLIAM 1958 *The Rise of the British Rubber Industry During the Nineteenth Century.* Liverpool Univ. Press.

# HJÄRNE, HARALD

Harald Hjärne (1848–1922), Swedish historian and political writer, came from a family of the nobility. He studied at Uppsala University, where he became assistant professor of history in 1872 and professor of history in 1889. His historical works fall into three groups. Those written between 1872 and 1876 deal mainly with old Germanic and medieval law and social conditions; those of the 1880s deal with the history of Russia and connections between Russia and Sweden; and those from 1890 on deal with the Reformation and the seventeenth century in Sweden. His numerous political essays and articles exerted an important influence on conservative and right-wing liberal thinking, especially during the 1890s. Hjärne was a member of the second chamber of the Riksdag from 1903 to 1908 and a member of the first chamber from 1912 to 1918.

When Hjärne first emerged as a political writer, around 1875, Swedish politics was characterized by economic controversies about defense and taxation on the one hand and by a blurring of ideological positions on the other. The old conservative view of a society based on the estates had disappeared since the abolition of the four-estates Riksdag in 1865. The conservatives then tended to merge with the successful right-wing liberals, who in turn were becoming more conservative, intent on maintaining their conquests. This synthesis of conservatism and right-wing liberalism characterized most political argument and also colored the philosophical doctrine prevalent at the universities—the political idealism of Christoph Jacob Boström.

Hjärne cast off Boström's philosophy, with its idealization of the four-estate Riksdag and its liberal tendency to assert the rights of the individual and private interests. He also moved away from the national liberalism of his family, replacing this by a conservative philosophy of his own. According to this political philosophy, the functions of the state are purely juridical; on this point Hjärne agreed with classical liberalism and Boström's ideas, but private interests have no place in his system. The only object of the rights granted by the king, as representative of the state, to his subjects is to enable them to fulfill their obligations toward the state. The greater the personal contribution of the individual, the greater the rights to which he is entitled. Representation should be based on these principles and thus be regarded as a means of public administration, not as a tool for private interests. Hjärne himself maintained that his philosophy stemmed entirely from ancient Swedish law and the Swedish constitution under the Vasa kings (1875; 1876). Actually, however, all the essentials came from the German historian and right-wing liberal politician Rudolf von Gneist, whose works on English constitutional history Hjärne encountered early in the 1870s (Gneist 1857–1860). Gneist saw local self-government as the main way of fulfilling personal obligations toward the state, but Hjärne considered military service to be the most important form of such obligations. The great stress on duty in his philosophy reflects his contempt for the kind of haggling about defense and taxation carried on by the economic group interests in the Riksdag.

In the 1880s there arose a partly new, more extreme form of conservatism. Strongly nationalistic, protectionist, and decidedly antidemocratic in outlook, its adherents opposed the growing demands by Norway for equality and greater independence within the Union. At first, Hjärne's work reflected this outlook, but he rejected it after 1890, when its supporters threatened to become too powerful. It was then that he launched his own conservative reform program, "Defense and Reforms." In accordance with his early ideas about the connection between duties and rights he demanded the franchise for all citizens who had completed a year's military service, regardless of their income and property. He repudiated the Conservative party and its aggressive Union policy, calling himself a right-wing liberal. He retained his basic conservative antiparliamentary philosophy, however.

Hjärne's historical works helped to foster the patriotic trend in the cultural life of the 1890s, and at times he himself succumbed to the nationalist ethos. At the same time he sharply criticized the principles of nationalism and race prejudice and supported the stand of England and the United States against Germany (1903; 1908; 1932–1940).

Troubled by the growing threat of war and presumably also by his own lack of success in the Riksdag, around 1908 Hjärne began to develop a strongly antidemocratic outlook, maintaining that defense and foreign policy should take precedence over domestic reforms. As in the 1880s, he again considered Germany to be Sweden's potential ally against the hereditary enemy, Russia. In this belief he anticipated the reactionary trend that once more dominated conservative thought after the liberals came to power in 1911.

Unlike some other conservative thinkers, Hjärne avoided identifying himself with dogmatic policies and fatalistic conceptions about inevitable historical laws, and he was able to accept with equanimity the defeat of Germany and the victory of democracy. Primarily through his program "Defense and Reforms" he was a precursor of the moderate line, which was to inspire most conservative political activity during the following decades.

NILS ELVANDER

### WORKS BY HJÄRNE

1875  Våra ståndsriksdagar. Svensk tidskrift för literatur, politik och ekonomi [1875]:151–180, 550–569, 701–730.
1876  Skandinavisk laghistoria. Svensk tidskrift för literatur, politik och ekonomi [1876]:178–288.
1903  Blandade spörsmål. Stockholm: Bonnier.
1908  Svenskt och främmande. Stockholm: Geber.
1914  Från försvarsstriden 1914. Uppsala: Askerberg.
1932–1940  Samlade skrifter. Stockholm: Bonnier. → Volume 1: Karl XII, 1932. Volume 2: Gustaf II Adolf, 1932. Volume 3: Moskovitiska rikets uppväxt, 1933. Volume 4: Samfundsliv och tankevärld, 1940.

### SUPPLEMENTARY BIBLIOGRAPHY

ELVANDER, NILS 1961 Harald Hjärne och konservatismen: Konservativ idédebatt i Sverige, 1865–1922. Stockholm: Almqvist & Wiksell.
GNEIST, RUDOLF (1857–1860) 1871–1884 Das heutige englische Verfassungs- und Verwaltungsrecht. 3d ed., 2 vols. Berlin: Springer. → Volume 1: Das englische Verwaltungsrecht der Gegenwart in Vergleichung mit den deutschen Verwaltungssystemen, 1883–1884. Volume 2: Selfgovernment: Communalverfassung und Verwaltungsgerichte in England, 1871.

# HOBBES, THOMAS

Thomas Hobbes (1588–1679), English philosopher and political theorist, was one of the originators of the new mathematico–mechanical view of the world established in the seventeenth century through the interaction of philosophic reflection and natural science. While Descartes was the most influential thinker in the movement which gave rise to modern philosophy, Hobbes was equally representative of it and scarcely less important. During the 1630s Hobbes arrived, independently of Descartes, at the formulation of the mechanical conception of nature; he had also reached, independently not only of Descartes but also of Galileo, the notion of the subjectivity of sensible qualities such as light and color (Brandt 1921). Like

Descartes, Hobbes rejected scholasticism as a philosophy of sterile disputation and held that mathematical reasoning must provide the model of philosophic method. His thought differed from Cartesianism, however, in its thoroughgoing materialism. In Hobbes's view, bodies are the sole existents, and the sole cause of phenomena lies in the diversity of corporeal motions. Even more than corporeality, motion is the governing idea in Hobbes's materialist metaphysics, and he employed it with impressive ingenuity as the universal explanatory principle in his mechanistic account of the world.

Hobbes also made an important contribution to the establishment of psychology as a field of empirical inquiry. His interest in psychology derived from his preoccupation with sensation and imagery. Realizing that mental occurrences—i.e., the phenomena of experience itself—require explanation, he provided one which treated them as material movements in the brain. Thus, sense, according to him, "is but an apparition unto us of that motion, agitation, or alteration, which the object worketh in the brain, or spirits, or some internal substance in the head" ([1640] 1928, p. 4). He left unclear whether imaging is identical with certain minute motions in the brain or a concomitant of them. His analysis of mental phenomena has a reductionist tendency, in that it loses sight of what is distinctively psychological in its description of physical or physiological causes. His account did, nevertheless, adumbrate the possibility of a scientific psychology in which subjects such as sensation, dreaming, and imagery could be investigated by the same methods used in the sciences of nature.

Hobbes's most enduring intellectual achievement is his theory of politics. The first expression of his political interests, however, was historical and classical, rather than philosophical. The son of a Wiltshire clergyman, he began his classical education as a child and was sent to Oxford at 14. Following his departure from the university with the B.A. degree in 1608, he became tutor to the son of William Cavendish, Lord Hardwick, who was later created earl of Devonshire. This was the commencement of a lifelong connection with the Cavendish family, to whose friendship and patronage he owed the support that permitted him to pursue his career as philosopher. In 1629, after many years spent mainly, it would seem, in the study of classical literature, he published his first book, a translation of Thucydides' *History*. Hobbes conceived history's principal business to be the instruction of a governing class in political prudence. For this purpose he thought Thucydides' masterpiece unexcelled. It is highly suggestive that of all the an-

cient historians he should have preferred the writer who is the most naturalistic in his inquiry into the causes of events as well as the most profound analyst of the derangement of political life, and even of the meaning of words, which results from civil strife.

When the Thucydides translation appeared, Hobbes had already turned his attention permanently to philosophy. Until the age of 40 he knew nothing of geometry; but about 1629, according to the curious story related by Aubrey, his contemporary biographer, he came by chance on a copy of Euclid's *Elements*. From the study of Euclid he perceived the demonstrative certainty attainable through geometrical reasoning (Aubrey 1898). He held thenceforth that truth is a matter of the laying down of clear definitions and the correct deduction of all their consequences.

In the 1630s Hobbes visited the Continent several times, where he formed some important intellectual friendships and became *au courant* with the most recent philosophical and scientific developments. His earliest surviving philosophical composition (*A Short Tract on First Principles*), a work framed on strictly deductive lines, dates from this period.

This was the time also when the revolution against the government of Charles I was brewing. The beginning of rebellion in Scotland and England at the close of the 1630s evidently stimulated Hobbes to develop his political doctrines. Thereafter, wrote Aubrey, "for ten yeares together his thoughts were much, or almost altogether, unhinged from the Mathematiques" and intent chiefly on the philosophy of politics (Aubrey [1898] 1957, p. 151). The result was the composition of three works that contain the substance of his political theory: *The Elements of Law* (1640), *De cive* (1642a), and *Leviathan* (1651). In addition, Hobbes included observations of great importance in philosophical method and the nature of political philosophy in *Elementorum philosophiae sectio prima: De corpore* (1655). He also wrote two minor works expressive of his political views, both published posthumously: *Behemoth* (1679), an account of the English Civil War, and *A Dialogue . . . of the Common Laws of England* (1681a).

Hobbes's approach to political theory reflects the spirit of the contemporary scientific movement. In his view, the state forms one department in a tripartite division of philosophy, the whole of which centers on body. According to this classification, philosophy deals first with body under its simplest and most general aspects; next, with man as a natural body of a particular kind; finally, with the commonwealth as a type of artificial body contrived by reason.

Hobbes claimed to be the founder of politics as a science and boldly compared himself with such great inaugurators as Copernicus, Galileo, and Harvey. The meaning of this self-confident assertion is connected with his conception of method. The mode of proceeding in philosophy, he held, is exclusively by way of cause and effect; hence, to reason philosophically means either to demonstrate the effects of a phenomenon from its known causes or to demonstrate its causes from its known effects. He conceived of cause not as a necessary connection between occurrences verified experimentally but, in a purely intellectualistic–deductive sense, as a hypothetical explanation attained by correct reasoning and consistent with ordinary experience. In the study of natural phenomena, he believed man can attain only to a knowledge of *possible* causes; by contrast, in the study of the commonwealth, an artificial body contrived by human reason, man can establish causes with certainty. Indeed, he went so far as to compare civil philosophy with geometry in this respect. Just as geometry is demonstrable because men themselves define its figures, so "civil philosophy is demonstrable, because we make the commonwealth ourselves" ([1656] 1962, p. 184). More specifically, the definitions of just and unjust, law, covenant, etc., on which the political order rests, derive from human invention and agreement. To found politics as a science would therefore mean to propound definitions from which the generation of the commonwealth and the rules necessary to its being are strictly deducible. This is what Hobbes thought he had accomplished.

Hobbes began his political theory with an analysis of human nature. He portrayed man as a creature of incessant activity who can find no rest in any final end. Within this stream of activity man pursues specific ends. What man desires, he calls good; what causes him fear or aversion, he calls evil. Thus, good and evil possess diverse meanings according to men's purposes. In so describing how men form their notions of good and evil, Hobbes was not endorsing a relativistic conception of moral judgment; indeed, it was a cornerstone of his political theory that men must concur in certain common definitions if they are to achieve what they all evidently want, namely, self-preservation, the condition of any activity whatsoever. Nor did Hobbes blame man for or accuse him of being the self-centered creature he is. He held that political philosophy must take human nature as its datum if it is to show how peace and community can be-

come possible to creatures who necessarily refer all things to their own single selves. Hobbes's politics are therefore linked to his psychology. The task he assigned reason is not to conquer or extinguish passion—an impossibility anyway—but to instruct it. Reason will teach passion what it must refrain from and what rules it must accept in order to attain its ends of self-preservation and, beyond that, of well-being and the commodities of civilized life.

It was when Hobbes shifted from man in general and in the abstract to the state of nature, where allowance must be made for the coexistence of *many* men, that he confronted the political problem proper, namely, how to secure peace and order among a multitude. Whether a state of nature ever existed historically was of little importance to Hobbes. For him it represented the hypothetical alternative to the commonwealth and sovereignty and was therefore a condition in which men in the pursuit of their diverse ends are subject to no power other than that which they can casually impose on one another. Hobbes intended to think away civil society in order to picture life in the absence of a coercive political order. What he displayed was a state of endless and oppressive insecurity, a war of all against all, where nothing is anyone's with certainty, in which the notions of just and unjust can have no place, and where each literally has a right to everything.

Amid this very anarchy Hobbes discerned the basis of natural right in man's desire to live. As all men seek their own good, they also naturally shun death, the chief of evils. Reason accordingly dictates, said Hobbes, that men should attempt by all means to preserve themselves. Whatever is done according to reason is "done justly, and with right" ([1642a] 1949, pp. 8–9). Natural right was considered by Hobbes as antecedent to the political order: it is a moral claim logically derived from the premise of all human activity and passion, the wish to live. Thus, when reason teaches that to secure themselves men must renounce the liberty of the state of nature, the route from anarchy to the commonwealth and civilization has been pointed out. Moreover, only reason can demonstrate which means do in fact conduce to that which all men want, and such means alone will be real goods. They will be the norms that men as rational beings must maintain to make their right effective.

The precepts of reason that lead to self-preservation Hobbes called the law of nature. He listed a number of these precepts, of which the most important is that men should seek peace, and as a further deduction from this, that they should re-linquish their right to all things, each being content "... *with so much liberty against other men, as he would allow other men against himselfe*" ([1651] 1958, p. 100).

Yet in what sense are these precepts laws? Hobbes answered that they are such only if considered as the commands of God. Otherwise they are not properly laws, since they are merely advisive and not externally obligatory. A correct definition would be "Conclusions or Theoremes concerning what conduceth to ... conservation ..." (*ibid.*, pp. 122–123). Hence, to Hobbes the law of nature appears to signify little more than the means or conditions which the calculating intellect demonstrates to be necessary to preservation. This constituted a radical departure from the traditional view. In traditional political philosophy, the law of nature was held to be genuine law and to prescribe ethical rules originating in the divine order and binding upon earthly communities. Hobbes, however, was strongly skeptical of this conception and took a different line. He refused to derive the dicta of natural law from the supernatural realm, on the ground that neither God nor revelation can be a subject of knowledge and both are thus beyond the scope of philosophy. He held also that the dicta of natural law are vacuous until positive law defines their meaning. Accordingly, while natural law forbids theft, murder, and adultery, it remains for positive law to determine what actions are to be called by these names. Hobbes strove to remove the ambiguities in the concept of natural law in two ways: by denying that natural law is properly law at all and by deriving its precepts autonomously from the rationally instructed striving of men for self-preservation. In effect, therefore, he rejected the divine order as the basis of moral valuation. For him, values are neither divinely guaranteed nor cosmically underwritten; they are made by man.

The fundamental dictate of the law of nature, then, is that men should seek peace. This entails their renunciation of the right to all things, which is theirs in the state of nature. Yet while reason always obliges men to do this, the conditions have to be established in which they can do so with security. Agreement among themselves to lay down their right is insufficient unless there is also a power to ensure that they adhere to this rational resolution. Thence arises, as a further inference, the commonwealth in which a single will represents the wills of all and possesses the right to coerce those who violate the agreement to which reason compels them. Therefore the ultimate cause of the commonwealth, according to Hobbes, is the foresight of men who perceive that civil society is the sole means of self-preservation and a contented life. Proceeding from this view, Hobbes rejected the Aristotelian doctrine that man is a political animal. He did not deny that man is naturally sociable; but commonwealths, he insisted, are not mere meetings, but true unions to whose contrivance the making of compacts is necessary.

Hobbes explained with elaborate care how the consent of men to government is embodied in contracts or covenants. Like the state of nature, covenant for Hobbes is a necessary hypothesis: it is required to show that the commonwealth is unthinkable except as something to which men consent for the sake of life and civility. It also has the further function of justifying the coercion and punishment imposed by the state. If these are to be more than mere acts of power, they must be traced to a covenant whereby man himself, as a rational being, becomes the author of the punishment his transgressions incur in civil society.

In every commonwealth, Hobbes said, there must be a sovereign power to enforce the covenant to peace that men have made: "Covenants, without the Sword, are but Words, and of no strength to secure a man at all" ([1651] 1958, p. 128). So sovereignty is necessitated by the same sequence of deductions that accounts for civil society. The attributes of the sovereign are the same in any form of government—democracy, aristocracy, or monarchy—and are very comprehensive. The sovereign power is not removable or punishable by its subjects; it is the only judge of what conduces to peace and therefore of what doctrines and opinions may be taught; its will alone makes law and determines the rules of property, of good and evil, of lawful and unlawful actions; it rewards and punishes, commands the armed forces, decides on war and peace. (Hobbes, of course, recognized that in actual fact sovereigns neither exercise all these powers nor do subjects allow that they have the right to do so. This to him, however, was mere illogic: if the sovereign is to keep peace and order, subjects ought to acknowledge all its attributes as inescapable.)

With this rigorous reasoning Hobbes brought the modern doctrine of sovereignty into the world. That doctrine already had a long history when Hobbes wrote: an approach to it appeared both in the work of the sixteenth-century French thinker Jean Bodin and, much earlier, in the writings of the medieval canonists and publicists who upheld the most extreme claims of the papal monarchy. But Hobbes's conception was novel in that he allowed no *legal* limitation on the sovereign power. This was the consequence of his view of law, which was defined for him not by any moral content but solely by its character as the sovereign's command. The sovereign cannot be limited by positive law, because the origin of positive law is the sovereign's will; nor can it be limited by the law of nature, because the law of nature is, properly speaking, not a law.

Yet, since the right of nature—man's claim to self-preservation—is the root from which Hobbes's political doctrine grew, this right results in substantial qualifications upon the absolutist character of his thought. Although, for instance, obedience is a duty in civil society, Hobbes pointed out that the subject retains his liberty to do whatever he cannot be conceived to have renounced or transferred by any covenant. This liberty is, in fact, considerable. The subject is not obliged to obey a command to kill or wound himself and may also refuse to endanger his life by service in war; again, while rebellion is not justifiable, subjects have the right, once it is begun, to continue in their resistance in order to preserve themselves. Most important of all, Hobbes exempted the subject from the obligation to obey a command that ". . . frustrates the End for which the Soveraignty [sic] was ordained . . ." ([1651] 1958, p. 167). He thus left to subjects both a vital right of private judgment and a moral vantage point vis-à-vis the sovereign.

Hobbes also stressed that the sovereign has duties toward its subjects. It is obliged, he stated, to make the safety and well-being of the people the rule of its actions. While this is a moral rather than a legal obligation, it is nonetheless real, founded as it is on men's basic purpose in consenting to submit to the commonwealth and sovereignty. A sovereign which acts otherwise "will act against the reasons of peace, that is to say, against the law of nature" ([1642a] 1962, p. 167). And safety, Hobbes added, means not only bare preservation but happiness and living delightfully, so far as these are possible. His advice to sovereigns respecting taxation, equal justice, and other matters of government is unexceptionable in its care for the subject's interests. Nor did he fail to point out that the sovereign's disregard of its duty will lead to rebellion as a natural consequence.

It is evident, then, that alongside the absolutist element in Hobbes's thought is a strong tendency toward liberalism. This appeared not only in his account of the subject's rights and the sovereign's duties but also in his progressive theory of punishment, which anticipated Beccaria and Bentham, and in his dislike of religious intolerance and cleri-

cal pretensions. Hobbes's liberalism is intrinsic to his conception of natural right, the dominant theme of his politics. Hence there results the paradoxical fact that he established his absolutism on liberal presuppositions. For him the state is not an object of awe and reverence. No sacred mystique veils Leviathan, the "mortal God," created by human association, to which men owe their peace and defense. The commonwealth is the work of men; its utility is its sole justification. It makes men moral and educates them for civility, but does so by their own consent and to advance their own purposes. If Hobbes defended absolutism, it was because he assumed absolutism to be in the general interest. Without this premise, there would be no great difficulty in constructing a liberal system out of the materials provided by his own political philosophy.

Hobbes was one of the most famous thinkers of his time. His writings were widely read, and although he formed no school, he probably exercised a greater and more varied influence upon English political theory than did any contemporary. Of Continental philosophers, Pufendorf and Spinoza, to mention only the foremost, were strongly affected by his ideas. A royalist in sympathy, he emigrated in 1640 and spent the next 11 years in France. He returned to England after the defeat and execution of Charles I, justifying his return with the argument that a subject's obligation ceases when the sovereign can no longer protect him ([1651] 1958, see "Review and Conclusion"). Despite this conduct, Hobbes retained the favor and friendship of Charles II after the Stuart restoration of 1660.

Hobbes's materialism, determinism, and skeptical temper brought upon him a host of attackers. Clerical opponents accused him of heresy and atheism, and in 1683 the University of Oxford condemned a number of his works to the flames. Some of the controversies he waged, such as that with Bishop Bramhall over free will, belong to the great intellectual debates of the age. Even upon his critics Hobbes exerted a powerful influence. He obliged them to lay aside theological and moral conceptions, to meet him on his own ground of strict and severe reasoning, and to deal with issues on their intellectual merits. His remarkable prose style, perfectly expressive of the hard, confident, and probing character of his mind, also contributed not a little to the effect he had upon friend and foe alike. By virtue both of his positive doctrines and of the scope and rigor of his philosophical inquiries, Hobbes was one of the foremost agents in the dissemination of the rationalism that altered the moral and mental climate of Europe in the course of the seventeenth century.

PEREZ ZAGORIN

[*See also* CONSENSUS; CONSTITUTIONS AND CONSTITUTIONALISM; NATURAL LAW; POWER; SOCIAL CONTRACT; SOVEREIGNTY; UTILITARIANISM; *and the biographies of* AUSTIN; BACON; BODIN; DESCARTES; DURKHEIM; HARRINGTON; HEGEL; MACHIAVELLI; MANDEVILLE; VICO.]

### WORKS BY HOBBES

(1640) 1928  *The Elements of Law, Natural & Political.* Edited, with a preface and critical notes, by Ferdinand Tönnies, to which are subjoined selected extracts from unprinted mss. of Thomas Hobbes. Cambridge Univ. Press. → Written in 1640; first published in 1650.

(1642*a*) 1949  *De cive or The Citizen.* Edited and abridged by Sterling P. Lamprecht. New York: Appleton. → First published as *Elementa philosophica de cive.*

(1642*b*) 1962  Philosophical Rudiments Concerning Government and Society. Volume 2 of Thomas Hobbes, *The English Works of Thomas Hobbes of Malmesbury.* Aalen (Germany): Scientia. → First published as *Elementorum philosophiae sectio tertia: De cive.*

(1651) 1958  *Leviathan: Or, the Matter, Forme and Power of a Commonwealth, Ecclesiasticall and Civil.* With an essay by W. G. Pogson Smith. Oxford: Clarendon. → See also the introduction by Michael Oakeshott in the 1946 edition published by Clarendon, and the introduction by A. D. Lindsay in the 1950 edition published by Dutton.

(1655) 1951  Elementorum philosophiae sectio prima: De corpore. Volume 1, pages 1–431 in Thomas Hobbes, *. . . Opera philosophica quae Latine scripsit omnia.* Aalen (Germany): Scientia.

(1656) 1962  Six Lessons to the Professors of the Mathematics. Volume 7, pages 181–356 in Thomas Hobbes, *The English Works of Thomas Hobbes of Malmesbury.* Aalen (Germany): Scientia.

(1679) 1962  Behemoth. Volume 6, pages 161–418 in Thomas Hobbes, *The English Works of Thomas Hobbes of Malmesbury.* Aalen (Germany): Scientia.

(1681*a*) 1962  A Dialogue Between a Philosopher and a Student of the Common Laws of England. Volume 6, pages 1–160 in Thomas Hobbes, *The English Works of Thomas Hobbes of Malmesbury.* Aalen (Germany): Scientia. → First published posthumously.

(1681*b*) 1951  Vita. Volume 1, pages xiii–xxi in Thomas Hobbes, *. . . Opera philosophica quae Latine scripsit omnia.* Aalen (Germany): Scientia. → First published posthumously.

*The English Works of Thomas Hobbes of Malmesbury.* Edited by Sir William Molesworth. 11 vols. Aalen (Germany): Scientia, 1962. → A reprint of an 1839–1845 edition.

A Short Tract on First Principles. Appendix 1 in Thomas Hobbes, *The Elements of the Law, Natural & Political.* Cambridge Univ. Press, 1928. → Previously unpublished.

*Thomae Hobbes Malmesburiensis opera philosophica quae Latine scripsit omnia.* Edited by Sir William Molesworth. 5 vols. Aalen (Germany): Scientia, 1951. → A reprint of an 1839–1845 edition.

### SUPPLEMENTARY BIBLIOGRAPHY

AUBREY, JOHN  (1898) 1957  Thomas Hobbes. Pages 147–159 in John Aubrey, *Brief Lives.* Ann Arbor: Univ. of Michigan Press. → Written between 1669 and 1696.

BORING, EDWIN G.  1942  *Sensation and Perception in the History of Experimental Psychology.* New York: Appleton.

BOWLE, JOHN  1951  *Hobbes and His Critics: A Study in Seventeenth Century Constitutionalism.* London: Cape.

BRANDT, FRITHIOF  (1921) 1928  *Thomas Hobbes' Mechanical Conception of Nature.* Copenhagen: Levin & Munksgaard. → First published in Danish.

BROWN, J. M.  1953  A Note on Professor Oakeshott's Introduction to the *Leviathan. Political Studies* 1:53–64.

BROWN, KEITH C. (editor)  1965  *Hobbes Studies.* Oxford: Blackwell; Cambridge, Mass.: Harvard Univ. Press.

BROWN, STUART M.  (1959) 1965  The Taylor Thesis: Some Objections. Pages 57–71 in Keith C. Brown (editor), *Hobbes Studies.* Oxford: Blackwell; Cambridge, Mass.: Harvard Univ. Press. → First published in Volume 68 of the *Philosophical Review.*

GOLDSMITH, M. M.  1966  *The Political Philosophy of Hobbes: The Rationale of the Sovereign State.* New York: Columbia Univ. Press.

HOOD, FRANCIS C.  1964  *The Divine Politics of Thomas Hobbes.* Oxford Univ. Press.

KROOK, DOROTHEA  1953  Mr. Brown's Note Annotated. *Political Studies* 1:216–227.

LAIRD, JOHN  1934  *Hobbes.* London: Benn.

LEVI, ADOLFO  1929  *La filosofia di Tommaso Hobbes.* Milan: Società Editrice Dante Alighieri.

ŁUBIEŃSKI, ZBIGNIEW  1932  *Die Grundlagen des ethisch-politischen Systems von Hobbes.* Munich: Reinhardt.

MACDONALD, HUGH; and HARGREAVES, MARY  1952  *Thomas Hobbes: A Bibliography.* London: Bibliographical Society.

MACPHERSON, CRAWFORD B.  1962  *The Political Theory of Possessive Individualism: Hobbes to Locke.* Oxford: Clarendon.

MINTZ, SAMUEL I.  1962  *The Hunting of the Leviathan: Seventeenth-century Reactions to the Materialism and Moral Philosophy of Thomas Hobbes.* Cambridge Univ. Press. → Also available from University Microfilms.

NAGEL, THOMAS  1959  Hobbes's Concept of Obligation. *Philosophical Review* 68:68–83.

PETERS, RICHARD S.  1956  *Hobbes.* Harmondsworth (England): Penguin.

PLAMENATZ, JOHN P.  (1957) 1965  Mr. Warrender's Hobbes. Pages 73–87 in Keith C. Brown (editor), *Hobbes Studies.* Oxford: Blackwell; Cambridge, Mass.: Harvard Univ. Press. → First published in Volume 5 of *Political Studies.*

POLIN, RAYMOND  1952  *Politique et philosophie chez Thomas Hobbes.* Paris: Presses Universitaires de France.

ROBERTSON, GEORGE C.  (1886) 1901  *Hobbes.* Edinburgh: Blackwood.

SKINNER, QUENTIN  1966  Thomas Hobbes and His Disciples in France and England. *Comparative Studies in Society and History* 8:153–167.

STEPHEN, LESLIE  (1904) 1928  *Hobbes.* London: Macmillan.

STRAUSS, LEO (1936) 1961 *The Political Philosophy of Hobbes: Its Basis and Its Genesis.* Translated by E. M. Sinclair. Univ. of Chicago Press. → Written in German but first published in English.

TAYLOR, A. E. (1938) 1965 The Ethical Doctrine of Hobbes. Pages 35–55 in Keith C. Brown (editor), *Hobbes Studies.* Oxford: Blackwell; Cambridge, Mass.: Harvard Univ. Press. → First published in Volume 13 of *Philosophy.*

TÖNNIES, FERDINAND (1896) 1925 *Hobbes Leben und Lehre.* 3d ed. Stuttgart: Fromman.

WARRENDER, HOWARD (1960) 1965 A Reply to Mr. Plamenatz. Pages 89–100 in Keith C. Brown (editor), *Hobbes Studies.* Oxford: Blackwell; Cambridge, Mass.: Harvard Univ. Press. → First published in Volume 8 of *Political Studies.*

WATKINS, J. W. N. 1965 *Hobbes's System of Ideas: A Study in the Political Significance of Philosophical Theories.* London: Hutchinson.

ZAGORIN, PEREZ 1954 *A History of Political Thought in the English Revolution.* London: Routledge.

# HOBHOUSE, L. T.

Leonard Trelawny Hobhouse (1864–1929), British sociologist and philosopher, was educated at Oxford. He was appointed fellow of Merton College in 1887 and fellow of Corpus Christi in 1894. Early in his career he showed an active interest in social and political movements: he was secretary of the Free Trade Union from 1903 to 1905 and published several political works, notably *The Labour Movement* (1893), *Democracy and Reaction* (1904), and *Liberalism* (1911a). From 1897 to 1902 he served on the staff of the *Manchester Guardian,* and from 1905 to 1907 he was political editor of the *Tribune* in London.

The main lines of the social philosophy that he was to develop in his later studies can be clearly discerned in these early political writings. This philosophy is based on principles differing fundamentally both from laissez-faire liberalism and from the bureaucratic, or as Hobhouse called it, "official" socialism of the Fabians. It may best be described as social liberalism, and in working it out he presented a cogent and still vitally important analysis of the relations between individual freedom and responsibility and state control.

In 1907 Hobhouse was appointed the first Martin White professor in sociology at the University of London and thereafter devoted himself mainly to his scientific and philosophical pursuits; but he never abandoned his earlier passionate interest in the deeper issues of politics, internal and foreign, as can be seen in his important contributions to the *Manchester Guardian* during World War I and

in his work as chairman of trade boards and as arbitrator in various disputes.

The key to Hobhouse's work is to be found in his conception of development. He was profoundly dissatisfied both with Spencer's account of evolution as dependent on the struggle for existence and the survival of the fittest and with the idealist philosophers' metaphysical theory of an absolute mind reaching self-consciousness in the historical process. In his view, a theory of development has to be solidly based on empirical facts. In his early work on logic and epistemology, *The Theory of Knowledge* (1896), he had subjected the dominant idealist view of the nature of thought to a detailed critical analysis and worked out a realistic theory based on a synthesis of empiricism and rationalism. Subsequently he turned to the study of the growth of the mind in the animal world and of the transition to the mind of man. The results were embodied in *Mind in Evolution* (1901).

The publication of *Morals in Evolution* (1906) marked a new epoch in the development of sociology. Hobhouse revealed a grasp of anthropological data, of the history of law, morals, and religion, and of scientific and philosophical thought and laid the foundations of an impressive sociological system. A later work incorporated research on preliterate societies carried out in collaboration with G. C. Wheeler and the present writer and was published in 1915 under the title *The Material Culture and Social Institutions of the Simpler Peoples.*

From 1918 to 1922 Hobhouse published three works devoted to political and ethical theory, and in 1924 there appeared his *Social Development,* in which he presented a restatement of the whole of his sociological work. In this book he gave a fresh analysis of the nature of social development and of the factors making for progress, arrest, or decay. His treatment avoids both the mistakes inherent in the kind of crude evolutionism that has brought the theory of development into disrepute and those that result from the one-sided emphasis on economic factors implicit in many forms of historical materialism. Only the general lines of this methodology are indicated here:

(1) He worked out a social morphology, that is, a classification of types of society and of the forms of social institutions, based on a wide survey of the data of anthropology and history. He was well aware of the difficulties inherent in the comparative method but sought to meet them by penetrating beneath outward resemblances to basic functions.

(2) He attempted to correlate the various aspects of social change with their contribution to

the general advance of the community, as estimated by certain criteria deduced from the general nature of development. They are extension in the scale of organization, growing efficiency in control and direction, and increasing freedom and cooperation in the satisfaction of mutual needs. It should be noted that these criteria are, at this stage of the inquiry, to be taken as ethically neutral: scale and efficiency are clearly so, and even though freedom and mutuality might appear to be ethically tinged, they are defined by Hobhouse in a manner that does not involve any particular ethical theory. Thus, a society is said to be free internally if its component parts can operate with the least loss of energy, without interfering with or obstructing each other. Mutuality depends on the extent to which the parts not only do not obstruct each other but work together so as to maintain the system as a whole.

(3) He put forward a hypothesis that there is a broad correlation between mental development and social development as estimated in the light of the above criteria. To establish this correlation he undertook an elaborate analysis of mental development in (a) the growth of scientific thought, (b) the control of the forces of nature, including human nature, (c) the ethicoreligious sphere, and (d) more briefly, the history of art. It is not suggested that the movements in these various spheres are parallel or that their rate of advance is similar but that, making due allowance for conditions in different periods of time and different parts of the world, they may be taken as a general indication of the growth of the human mind.

(4) Hobhouse then tried to show that there is indeed a broad correlation between mental advance and the development of societies. Thus, in the earlier phases of thought and belief, societies grow in scale and efficiency and in control and direction, although at the cost of mutuality and freedom. Governments tend to be authoritarian in character, and social differentiation rests on subordination. In relatively higher phases this growth in scale and efficiency continues to increase as does subordination. But with the beginning of critical and systematic thought free forms of government arise, and, in theory at any rate, there emerge ideals of a unitary spiritual order. In the ancient world the embodiment of these ideals is still very restricted. In more recent times, in the stage of "experiential reconstruction," when conceptual analysis is combined with empirical verification, there is not only an increase in scale and efficiency but also the beginning of a concrete embodiment of the elements of mutuality and freedom on a world scale; and attempts are made at a genuine synthesis of personal and political freedom with moral universalism. A survey of history thus suggests that there has been, on the whole, correlated growth of mind and civilization.

(5) Hobhouse next argued that the process of development, so far examined by him independently of any ethical commitment, may be shown to be generally in the direction required by his theory of the rational good. This good consists in the harmonious fulfillment of human potentialities, and it is clear that it can be achieved only by the willing cooperation of all mankind. In theory, therefore, ethical and social development have a common end. But although they tend to converge, they do not in fact coincide. For this there are many reasons. Each different society develops, if not wholly independently, yet in its own way and in accord with its own peculiarities and distinguishable internal sources of change. Furthermore, they advance at different rates. As a result, inequalities in economic and political power arise that offer opportunities for exploitation and domination and have been among the root causes of war. Again, development in one direction may bring retrogression in another. Thus, the extension of the area of organization may reduce the chances of conflict but may make it more destructive when it does occur. The parts may develop at the expense of the whole or the changes that they undergo may not be duly balanced, with resulting structural strains and possible collapse. These causes of arrest or decay can easily be illustrated from the history of communities and are readily discerned in the contemporary world. It is in this connection that Hobhouse's analysis may be fruitfully extended in dealing with the problems of our own day. Progress is, in any case, not automatic or unilinear but depends on human thought and will: on the rationality of the mind and its capacity for forming an intelligible conception of a good in which all men can share and for securing an effective will directed to this good. Humanity has not yet reached the stage of self-direction; but reviewing the state of the world in the 1920s, Hobhouse felt justified in concluding, despite serious misgivings, that it contained many essentials of such self-direction and that these were sufficient to indicate the direction of future development.

Hobhouse further strengthened his argument by an examination of the conditions affecting social change: environmental, biological, psychological, and distinctively sociological. The great value of his contributions to sociology does not depend solely on the strength of his main hypothesis; it also lies in the light he threw on various phases in the history of knowledge, religion, and morals and their relation to social change, in the careful way in which he distinguished judgments of fact and of value, and in the skill with which he eventually brought facts and values together in a comprehensive synthesis.

Hobhouse will be remembered not only as a contributor to sociology and to comparative and social psychology but also as a philosopher of great distinction. The fullest exposition of his philosophical theories is to be found in his *Development and Purpose* (1913), which he himself regarded as completing a scheme that had occupied him for 26 years and that had been carried through successive stages in his previous major works. In this book he showed that development proceeds by the liberation of elements originally indifferent to or in conflict with one another and by the building up of structures of varying degrees of plasticity and coherence. The power behind development is mind, essentially a correlating activity, manifested in all orderly structures but most clearly in living organisms, in which mechanical and teleological factors are interwoven. Mind is, in this view, not coextensive with reality but is the principle of orderly growth within it. It is limited by the material it works upon, and its purposes themselves undergo development. His fundamental principle, which he entitled "conditional teleology," is examined both from the point of view of the logical requirements of explanation in dealing with systems undergoing change and from the point of view of its value as an instrument of investigation, especially in the fields of biology and sociology.

MORRIS GINSBERG

[*Directly related are the entries* EVOLUTION, *article on* CULTURAL EVOLUTION; LIBERALISM; SOCIAL DARWINISM; SOCIAL INSTITUTIONS. *Other relevant material may be found in* CONSTITUTIONAL LAW, *article on* CIVIL LIBERTIES; TRIBAL SOCIETY; WAR, *article on* PRIMITIVE WARFARE; *and in the biographies of* BOSANQUET; OGBURN; TOYNBEE.]

### WORKS BY HOBHOUSE

(1893) 1912  *The Labour Movement.* 3d ed. New York. Macmillan.
(1896) 1921  *The Theory of Knowledge: A Contribution to Some Problems of Logic and Metaphysics.* 3d ed. London: Methuen.
(1901) 1926  *Mind in Evolution.* 3d ed. London: Macmillan.
(1904) 1909  *Democracy and Reaction.* 2d ed., rev. & enl. London: Allen & Unwin.
(1906) 1951  *Morals in Evolution: A Study in Comparative Ethics.* With a new introduction by Morris Ginsberg. 7th ed. London: Chapman & Hall.
(1911a) 1945  *Liberalism.* Oxford Univ. Press. → A paperback edition was published in 1964.
1911b  *Social Evolution and Political Theory.* New York: Columbia Univ. Press.
(1913) 1927  *Development and Purpose: An Essay Towards a Philosophy of Evolution.* New ed., rev. & enl. London: Macmillan.
(1915) 1965  HOBHOUSE, LEONARD T.; WHEELER, GERALD C.; and GINSBERG, MORRIS *The Material Culture and Social Institutions of the Simpler Peoples: An Essay in Correlation.* London: Routledge.
(1918) 1951  *The Metaphysical Theory of the State: A Criticism.* London: Allen & Unwin; New York: Macmillan.
(1921) 1947  *The Rational Good: A Study in the Logic of Practice.* London: Watts.
(1922) 1958  *The Elements of Social Justice.* London: Allen & Unwin.
1924  *Social Development: Its Nature and Conditions.* London: Allen & Unwin.
*Sociology and Philosophy: A Centenary Collection of Essays and Articles.* Preface by Sir Sydney Caine. Introduction by Morris Ginsberg. Cambridge, Mass.: Harvard Univ. Press; London: Bell, 1966.

### SUPPLEMENTARY BIBLIOGRAPHY

BARKER, ERNEST  1929  Leonard Trelawny Hobhouse. British Academy, London, *Proceedings* 15:536–554.
HOBSON, J. A.; and GINSBERG, MORRIS  1931  *L. T. Hobhouse, His Life and Work: With Selected Essays and Articles.* London: Allen & Unwin.

## HOBSON, JOHN A.

John Atkinson Hobson (1858–1940) was a British economist. In his appealing autobiography, *Confessions of an Economic Heretic* (1938, p. 15), he described himself as "born and bred in the middle stratum of the middle class of a middle-sized industrial town of the Midlands." The town in question was Derby, and the family derived its income from the *Derbyshire Advertiser*, a Liberal newspaper. The family's resources sufficed to assure Hobson an adequate private income all his life and the chance to pursue a heterodox career free of financial strain. At Oxford he specialized in classics. He also made a close study of Marx, but *Capital* repelled him and he dismissed the dialectical method as frivolous. As a child he broke with formal religion because it failed "to satisfy my elementary sense of reason and of justice in the doctrines of the atonement and of everlasting punishment for unrepentant sinners" (1938, p. 20).

The intellectual influences that impinged on Hobson included Mill's *On Liberty* and *Utilitarianism* and Herbert Spencer's *Study of Sociology.* John Ruskin's message impressed him while he was teaching classics in two successive public schools. Even though Hobson recognized the speculative cast of much of Ruskin's thought, he was attracted by Ruskin's criticism of the conventional economists' tendency to identify economic value with the monetary costs of producing marketable commodities. Ruskin's slogan "there is no wealth but life" animated all of Hobson's writings, especially the two volumes that best express his humanistic conception of economics, *The Industrial System* (1909) and *Work and Wealth* (1914). Thorstein Veblen's criticisms of capitalist waste and capitalist standards of consumption also attracted Hobson. With American institutional economists of the period he shared a basic distrust of marginal economics and a disposition to interpret all aspects of economic activity within the broader framework of ethics and sociology.

Hobson's two enduring contributions to economic thought are connected with the doctrine of oversaving and the theory of imperialism. The possibility, even the probability, of oversaving is the central lesson of his first book, *The Physiology of Industry* (Mummery & Hobson 1889), which he wrote in collaboration with the businessman and mountain climber A. F. Mummery. Hobson directed this first attack at a central proposition of conventional economics—that a society can never save too large a proportion of its income— asserting that excess saving brings about the construction of unneeded capital equipment whose products lack consumer markets. In later works Hobson strengthened his argument with explicit emphasis upon the maldistribution of income, which causes the wealthy to save too large a share of their income and thus generates unemployment and economic depression. Hobson's conception of oversaving differs from contemporary theories in its assumption that saving is actually and necessarily converted into fixed investment. The Keynesian version maintains that an effort to save too much diminishes total spending rather than fixing itself in surplus machines.

Hobson's second major contribution is contained in *Imperialism* (1902). This was an extension of his oversaving theory, but its impetus and a great deal of its historical detail derived from Hobson's experience in South Africa as a correspondent of the *Manchester Guardian* just prior to the Boer War. He explained the revived drive for empire as the result of a search by English capitalists for savings outlets. Lenin borrowed freely of Hobson's doctrine.

Although trenchant as a critic, Hobson was less successful as an inventor of concepts and programs. He never put into acceptable theoretical style his human conception of value or his perception that the money costs of production inadequately measure the human pains of economic output. Nor did he find a completely satisfactory

political vehicle for his ideas. He began as a Liberal and then became a somewhat reluctant member of the Labour party. Never accepting class war as the proper route to a better society, always seeking to enlist portions of the middle class under his banner, Hobson was also skeptical of nationalization as the single remedy for a defective society. Although he was perfectly willing to nationalize industries which suffered from monopoly, inefficiency, or excessive routinization of their operations, he attached at least equal importance to less concentration within private industry, progressive taxation of income and wealth, and the social policies now embodied in the welfare state. Like R. H. Tawney and G. D. H. Cole, he emphasized the quality of consumption and the satisfactions of the worker as elements of a humane society. He took pride in what he called " 'the jumble' of politics, ethics, art, religion, which constitutes the setting of my thought" (1938, p. 164).

Orthodox economists admired Hobson little more than he admired them. F. Y. Edgeworth, in an influential review of *The Physiology of Industry*, denied Hobson and Mummery the "undoubted speculative genius" or the "extraordinarily wide learning" that alone might justify such paradoxical conclusions. As a direct consequence of the book, Hobson lost two extension lectureships and won a reputation for heresy that placed him on the fringes of the academic world for the rest of his career. As late as 1954, Schumpeter summed him up in this way: "In economics he was self-taught in a wilful way that made him both able to see aspects that trained economists refused to see and unable to see others that trained economists took for granted" (1954, p. 832, footnote).

Hobson felt himself vindicated, however, when Keynes in *The General Theory of Employment, Interest and Money* (1936) termed the publication of *The Physiology of Industry* "an epoch in economic thought" and credited Hobson with anticipating a good half of Keynes's own theory of underemployment equilibrium. As an anticipator of both Lenin and Keynes, Hobson seems to have a secure place in the history of economic doctrine.

ROBERT LEKACHMAN

[*For the historical context of Hobson's work, see the biographies of* MILL; SPENCER; VEBLEN; *for discussion of the subsequent development of Hobson's ideas, see* CONSUMPTION FUNCTION; IMPERIALISM; *and the biographies of* KEYNES, JOHN MAYNARD; LENIN.]

WORKS BY HOBSON

(1889) 1956 MUMMERY, ALBERT F.; and HOBSON, JOHN A. *The Physiology of Industry: Being an Ex-*

*posure of Certain Fallacies in Existing Theories of Economics.* New York: Kelley.

(1894) 1949 *The Evolution of Modern Capitalism: A Study of Machine Production.* Rev. ed. New York: Macmillan.

(1902) 1948 *Imperialism: A Study.* 3d ed. London: Allen & Unwin.

(1909) 1910 *The Industrial System: An Inquiry Into Earned and Unearned Income.* New ed., rev. London and New York: Longmans.

(1914) 1933 *Work and Wealth: A Human Valuation.* Rev. ed. London: Allen & Unwin.

1938 *Confessions of an Economic Heretic.* New York: Macmillan.

SUPPLEMENTARY BIBLIOGRAPHY

BRAILSFORD, HENRY N. 1948 *The Life-work of J. A. Hobson.* London: Oxford Univ. Press.

HOMAN, PAUL T. 1928 *Contemporary Economic Thought.* New York: Harper. → See especially pages 281–374 on "John A. Hobson."

HUTCHISON, TERENCE W. (1953) 1962 *A Review of Economic Doctrines: 1870–1929.* 2d ed. Oxford: Clarendon. → See especially pages 118–129 on "J. A. Hobson."

KEYNES, JOHN MAYNARD 1936 *The General Theory of Employment, Interest and Money.* London: Macmillan. → A paperback edition was published in 1965 by Harcourt.

SCHUMPETER, JOSEPH A. (1954) 1960 *History of Economic Analysis.* Edited by E. B. Schumpeter. New York: Oxford Univ. Press.

# HOLMES, OLIVER WENDELL

The career of Oliver Wendell Holmes, Jr., as a judge spanned half a century. Yet quite apart from this long and distinguished service on the highest courts of his state and nation, his pervasive influence as historian and philosopher of the law is bound to assure him a permanent place in American jurisprudence. It is his 30 notable years as an associate justice of the United States Supreme Court, however, that no doubt constitute his special claim to importance and fame as a jurist. In so many ways a true product of New England's intellectual aristocracy, in time he came to capture the popular imagination of the whole country.

His father was Dr. Oliver Wendell Holmes, whose work as poet, essayist, and physician was in itself a significant chapter in the flowering of America's cultural and scientific maturity. The future judge was born in Boston on March 8, 1841, and died in Washington, D.C., on March 6, 1935. In July 1861, shortly after graduating from Harvard College, he enlisted with the Twentieth Massachusetts Volunteers and was mustered out three years later with the rank of captain. Holmes was wounded three times—at Bull's Bluff, at Antietam, and at Marye's Hill, Fredericksburg. Both his philosophy and his rhetoric were destined to reflect his

Civil War experience. That experience may help explain "the inner resolution he felt bound to achieve . . . between skepticism and faith," as Paul A. Freund has phrased it (see the foreword in Frankfurter 1938).

Once out of uniform, Holmes resolved his doubts concerning the choice of a life's calling—philosophy versus law—by enrolling at the Harvard Law School, where he studied between 1864 and 1866. "A man may live greatly in the law as well as elsewhere," he was to say many years later in "The Profession of the Law" (1962, p. 29).

It is significant that almost from the start of his law practice, scholarly interests claimed Holmes's chief attention. As Mark DeWolfe Howe has noted, "the young lawyer's affiliations of mind and sympathy had early shown themselves to be more with the Brahmins than with the merchants of New England" (Howe 1957–1963, vol. 2, p. 2). He served as editor of the *American Law Review* from 1870 to 1873 and edited the twelfth edition of James Kent's *Commentaries on American Law.* But it was the publication of his book *The Common Law* in 1881 that doubtless established his reputation as a legal scholar, leading in the following year to his appointment as Feld professor of law at Harvard and shortly thereafter to his selection as an associate justice of the Massachusetts Supreme Judicial Court. The book is permeated by all of the major strains of thought that have come to be identified with Holmes's outlook and method both as scholar and judge: his deep sense of history, his rejection of the rigidities of legal logic, his aversion to the confusion between law and morals, and his awareness of the psychological roots of judicial decisions. Some of the sentences of the opening paragraph have become famous in themselves:

The life of the law has not been logic: it has been experience. The felt necessities of the time, the prevalent moral and political theories, intuitions of public policy, avowed or unconscious, even the prejudices which judges share with their fellow-men, have had a good deal more to do than the syllogism in determining the rules by which men should be governed. The law embodies the story of a nation's development through many centuries, and it cannot be dealt with as if it contained only the axioms and corollaries of a book of mathematics. ([1881] 1963, p. 7)

Holmes served on the Massachusetts bench for 20 years, 1882 to 1902, the last three as chief justice. Most of his opinions dealt with the traditional concerns of common law litigation—torts, contracts, and crimes—but there were cases in which he had the opportunity to discuss broader issues of public policy and constitutional law. When that happened he usually gave expression to ideas that can also be found in his legal essays; they foreshadowed the dominant themes of his philosophy as a Supreme Court justice. He insisted that the judiciary has but a limited role to play in the process of government and that the judge must allow ample scope to the provisions of constitutions and the discretion of legislators.

It was Holmes's dissenting opinions in labor cases, especially those in which he vindicated the rights to peaceful picketing and the closed shop, that made some circles think of him as a radical. Yet these seemingly pro-labor opinions were the result of his basically conservative slant—what he called "the battle of trade" or the "free struggle for life." If the pursuit of economic advantage was leading businessmen to combine, he saw no reason for keeping workers from cooperating with each other in promoting their interests.

Judging from the correspondence between Henry Cabot Lodge and Theodore Roosevelt, it may have been Holmes's views on the labor problem that induced Roosevelt to name him to the Supreme Court in 1902. Ironically, when Holmes, much to Roosevelt's displeasure, dissented only a year later from the Court's opinion upholding the dissolution of the Northern Securities Company, he invoked the same general economic beliefs implicit in his Massachusetts labor opinions.

Although the number of occasions on which Holmes differed from Supreme Court majorities was comparatively small, he came to be regarded as the "great dissenter" on the Court. It was largely these dissenting opinions that made the public think of him as a liberal judge, not realizing that in private he was opposed to many of the reforms that, as a judge, he was seeking to save (Biddle 1961, p. 68).

Holmes's reputation as a liberal no doubt originated with his celebrated 1905 dissent in *Locher* v. *New York*—an opinion which Roscoe Pound characterized as the "best exposition" of sociological jurisprudence. In eloquent and increasingly sharp language, the justice continued to protest against the tendency of many of his colleagues to annul labor and social welfare laws because they disapproved of the policies these laws embodied. He furnished one of the best clues to the reason why he often dissented on such questions in a case in which a majority of the Supreme Court had struck down an Arizona law forbidding the use of injunctions in labor disputes. "There is nothing I more deprecate," Holmes confessed in 1921, "than the use of the Fourteenth Amendment beyond the absolute compulsion of its words to prevent the making of social experiments that an important part of the community desires, in the insulated chambers afforded by the several States, even though the experiments may seem futile or even noxious to me and to those whose judgment I most respect" (*Truax* v. *Corrigan*, 257 U.S. 312, 344).

There is still another reason for the popular image of Holmes as a liberal dissenter. In a number of free speech cases he voted against the government and spoke out in defense of the individual's right of free expression. But he had also delivered the Court's opinions in several cases upholding convictions under the Espionage Act of 1917, including the conviction of Eugene V. Debs, the militant head of the Socialist party. It was in the first of these wartime cases—*Schenck* v. *United States*—that he set forth his celebrated formula of "clear and present danger." "The question in every case," he wrote, "is whether the words used are used in such circumstances and are of such a nature as to create a clear and present danger that they will bring about the substantive evils that Congress has a right to prevent" (249 U.S. 47, 52, 1919).

When Holmes became convinced—possibly through the influence of his frequent companion in dissent, Justice Louis D. Brandeis—that the objectionable speech or publication was not likely to bring about "a clear and present danger," he did not hesitate to register his disagreement. His opinions in *Abrams* v. *United States* and *Gitlow* v. *New York* (268 U.S. 652, 1925) are perhaps most notable. In the Abrams dissent, Holmes said:

But when men have realized that time has upset many fighting faiths, they may come to believe even more than they believe the very foundations of their own conduct that the ultimate good desired is better reached by free trade in ideas—that the best test of truth is the power of the thought to get itself accepted in the competition of the market, and that truth is the only ground upon which their wishes safely can be carried out. (*Abrams* v. *United States*, 250 U.S. 616, 630, 1919)

What Justice Frankfurter once said about these dissents is a good measure of Holmes's lasting contribution as a constitutional judge: ". . . some of his weightiest utterances are dissenting opinions—but they are dissents that record prophecy and shape history" (*Mr. Justice Holmes* [1916–1930] 1931, p. 116).

SAMUEL J. KONEFSKY

[*For the historical context of Holmes's work, see the biographies of* BRANDEIS; CARDOZO; POUND.]

## WORKS BY HOLMES

(1861–1864) 1946    *Touched With Fire: Civil War Letters and Diary of Oliver Wendell Holmes, Jr., 1861–1864.*

Edited by Mark DeWolfe Howe. Cambridge, Mass.: Harvard Univ. Press.

(1861–1932) 1954 *The Mind and Faith of Justice Holmes: His Speeches, Essays, Letters, and Judicial Opinions.* Selected and edited with introduction and commentary by Max Lerner. New York: Modern Library.

(1870–1935) 1936 *Justice Oliver Wendell Holmes: His Book Notices and Uncollected Letters and Papers.* Edited and annotated by Harry C. Shriver, with an introduction by Harlan Fiske Stone. New York: Central.

(1874–1932) 1961 HOLMES, OLIVER WENDELL; and POLLOCK, FREDERICK *Holmes–Pollock Letters: The Correspondence of Mr. Justice Holmes and Sir Frederick Pollock, 1874–1932.* 2d ed., 2 vols. Edited by Mark DeWolfe Howe. Cambridge, Mass.: Belknap Press.

(1881) 1963 *The Common Law.* Cambridge, Mass.: Harvard Univ. Press.

(1883–1902) 1940 *The Judicial Opinions of Oliver Wendell Holmes.* Edited by Harry C. Shriver. Buffalo, N.Y.: Dennis.

(1885–1918) 1952 *Collected Legal Papers.* Edited by Harold J. Laski. New York: Smith.

(1902–1928) 1929 *The Dissenting Opinions of Mr. Justice Holmes.* Edited by Alfred Lief. New York: Vanguard.

(1903–1930) 1931 *Representative Opinions of Mr. Justice Holmes.* Edited by Alfred Lief. New York: Vanguard.

(1903–1935) 1964 HOLMES, OLIVER WENDELL; and EINSTEIN, LEWIS *The Holmes–Einstein Letters: Correspondence of Mr. Justice Holmes and Lewis Einstein. 1903–1935.* Edited by James Bishop Peabody. New York: St. Martins.

(1916–1935) 1953 HOLMES, OLIVER WENDELL; and LASKI, HAROLD J. *Holmes–Laski Letters: The Correspondence of Mr. Justice Holmes and Harold J. Laski, 1916–1935.* Edited by Mark DeWolfe Howe, with a foreword by Felix Frankfurter. 2 vols. Cambridge, Mass.: Harvard Univ. Press.

1948 HOLMES, OLIVER WENDELL; and COHEN, MORRIS R. Holmes–Cohen Correspondence. *Journal of the History of Ideas* 9:3–52.

1962 *Occasional Speeches.* Compiled by Mark DeWolfe Howe. Cambridge, Mass.: Belknap Press.

### WORKS ABOUT HOLMES

BENT, SILAS 1932 *Justice Oliver Wendell Holmes: A Biography.* New York: Vanguard.

BIDDLE, FRANCIS B. 1942 *Mr. Justice Holmes.* New York: Scribner.

BIDDLE, FRANCIS B. 1961 *Justice Holmes, Natural Law and the Supreme Court.* New York: Macmillan.

BOWEN, CATHERINE DRINKER 1944 *Yankee From Olympus: Justice Holmes and His Family.* Boston: Little.

FRANKFURTER, FELIX (1938) 1961 *Mr. Justice Holmes and the Supreme Court.* 2d ed. Foreword by Paul A. Freund. Cambridge, Mass.: Belknap Press.

HOWE, MARK DEWOLFE 1957–1963 *Justice Oliver Wendell Holmes.* 2 vols. Cambridge, Mass.: Belknap Press. → Volume 1: *The Shaping Years, 1841–1870.* Volume 2: *The Proving Years, 1870–1882.*

KONEFSKY, SAMUEL J. 1956 *The Legacy of Holmes and Brandeis: A Study in the Influence of Ideas.* New York: Macmillan.

*Mr. Justice Holmes: Contributions by Benjamin N. Cardozo, Morris R. Cohen, John Dewey. . . .* (1916–1930) 1931 Edited by Felix Frankfurter. New York: Coward-McCann.

## HOLT, EDWIN B.

Edwin Bissell Holt (1873–1946) was an American psychologist-philosopher, an erudite scholar, a brilliant and graceful writer, a man of strong likes and dislikes in his opinions and social relations, and a thinker who had more influence than prestige, being more often followed than quoted.

Philosophically Holt was a radical empiricist, building enthusiastically on the foundation laid by his admired teacher William James. By 1908, when Holt had completed his *Concept of Consciousness* (although he did not publish it until 1914), he had accepted James's belief that the unit of nature is not an atom or a sensation, but a relation, and that consciousness is all those relations in which the nervous system makes possible responses of the living organism to particular objects in its environment. To such general views James gave the name "radical empiricism," and in 1910 Holt and five other philosophers laid down a program for what they called the New Realism; this became the title of a book that they published together in 1912. In it Holt's essay on illusion and error made his views clear. In 1915 he published *The Freudian Wish* (1915a), which became his most influential book, in part because it continued the fight against consciousness as Cartesian unextended substance, but chiefly because it fitted into the positivistic and physicalistic trend in psychology, which led from earlier materialistic and objective psychology to the behaviorism that was founded by John B. Watson in 1913. Holt gave behaviorism a philosophical sophistication which Watson was incapable of providing.

Holt's insight into the nature of consciousness connected him not only with behaviorism but also with the emergence of dynamic psychology. Holt took from Freud the word *wish* and employed it as the unit of his realistic monistic psychology, the relation of response that explains mind. To express this dynamic relation Holt in 1931 adopted the term *drive.* Dynamic psychology has now become the psychology of human nature, and its achievements, which are many, represent the success of the protest against the dualism of German introspective psychology, which initiated the experimental movement. Holt played a significant part in this development.

About 1920 Holt began to write *Animal Drive and the Learning Process,* intending it as a revision of William James's classic *Principles of Psychology,* but that task proved impossible even for Holt's brilliance. Instead, more than a decade later *Animal Drive* came out as a psychophysiological text that explicated the importance of radical empiricism for psychology.

Holt was born in Winchester, Massachusetts, went to school in Winchester, entered Amherst College for a year in 1892, and then transferred to Harvard, where he received the A.B. *magna cum laude* in 1896. After a year at Harvard graduate school, he volunteered for the army in the Spanish–American War, coming back to academic life with a virile and picturesque mode of speech that characterized him ever after. There followed a year abroad at the University of Freiburg, an A.M. from Columbia University, and then a PH.D. from Harvard in 1901. At Harvard, William James and Hugo Münsterberg stimulated him most; the latter made Holt first an instructor and then assistant professor, a position Holt held until his resignation in 1918. While Münsterberg lived—he died in 1916—Holt was his adjutant in the laboratory, helping the graduate students with the research that Münsterberg put them on, maintaining the apparatus in apple-pie order, and leading an experimentalist's life, not a philosopher's. However, he did not publish much experimental work of his own. On coming into a considerable inheritance in 1918 he decided to resign from Harvard, sticking to his decision in spite of the offer of a full professorship and the directorship of the psychological laboratory.

For the next eight years Holt lived in many places, reading, discovering that it was too late to revise James's *Principles*, starting to write the book that eventually became *Animal Drive*, and finally publishing it in 1931. Meanwhile, he had gone to Princeton in 1926 to spend ten years as visiting professor, where he taught a much-liked semester-course on social psychology and worked on a second volume of *Animal Drive*. He retired, however, without finishing the work.

EDWIN G. BORING

[*For the historical context of Holt's work, see the biographies of* JAMES *and* MÜNSTERBERG. *For discussion of the subsequent development of his ideas, see* DRIVES *and* MOTIVATION.]

WORKS BY HOLT

1912   The Place of Illusory Experience in a Realistic World. Pages 303–373 in Edwin B. Holt et al., *The New Realism: Cooperative Studies in Philosophy.* New York: Macmillan.
1914   *The Concept of Consciousness.* New York: Macmillan.
1915a   *The Freudian Wish and Its Place in Ethics.* New York: Holt.
1915b   Response and Cognition. *Journal of Philosophy, Psychology and Scientific Methods* 12:365–373; 393–409.
1931   *Animal Drive and the Learning Process.* Vol. 1. New York: Holt.

SUPPLEMENTARY BIBLIOGRAPHY

BORING, EDWIN G. (1929) 1950   *A History of Experimental Psychology.* 2d ed. New York: Appleton. → See especially pages 645 ff., 661 ff., and 718 ff. on Holt.
CARMICHAEL, LEONARD 1946   Edwin Bissell Holt: 1873–1946. *American Journal of Psychology* 59:478–480.
Edwin Bissell Holt. 1932   Volume 3, pages 238–239 in *Psychological Register.* Worcester, Mass.: Clark Univ. Press; Oxford Univ. Press. → A bibliography of 30 items.
LANGFELD, HERBERT S. 1946   Edwin Bissell Holt: 1873–1946. *Psychological Review* 53:251–258.

# HOME RULE
*See* LOCAL GOVERNMENT.

# HOMELESSNESS

Homelessness is a condition of detachment from society characterized by the absence or attenuation of the affiliative bonds that link settled persons to a network of interconnected social structures.

Homelessness takes many forms, depending on the type of detachment involved and the local circumstances. Homeless families and homeless men appear, so far as can be determined, in all large-scale societies. Homeless women and children are relatively rare. Their appearance denotes widespread disorder and instability, such as follow famines and civil wars.

**Degrees of homelessness.** Homeless families fall into three general types: permanent wanderers, such as gypsies and carnival performers; wanderers with a fixed base, especially migratory farm workers; and refugees, for whom homelessness is an accident and not a way of life. Homeless men fall into a variety of categories: single men in itinerant occupations, such as peddlers, tinkers, and sailors; migratory laborers; vagrants and beggars; religious mendicants; outlaws and other fugitives; and hoboes and derelicts.

These types suggest that homelessness is a matter of degree, ranging from temporary to permanent and from the loss of a single affiliation to the absence of all affiliations. In general, homelessness is less acute for families than for individuals. The homeless family may have no place in any community, but its members carry a web of roles and obligations with them wherever they go. Some, like the gypsies, develop something like a portable community independent of the surrounding social structure. Others, like the millions of families displaced toward the end of World War II, are rendered homeless without their consent and resume normal affiliations at the first opportunity.

There is even more variation in degree of homelessness among men without families. Some, like the itinerant worker, may preserve multiple affiliations: occupational, religious, political, and so on. They are only as homeless as their mobility forces them to be. Others, like religious mendicants, elect one overriding identification that supplants all of their former roles.

At the extreme point of the scale, the modern skid row man demonstrates the possibility of nearly total detachment from society. The present discussion is focused on this end of the homelessness scale and omits any consideration of the minor degrees of homelessness represented by Bohemians, "beatniks," troubadours, residents in alien societies, and other adventurers whose partial detachment from role obligations is arranged deliberately and with substitute goals in view.

**Homelessness as a syndrome.**    The common characteristics of homeless populations display a distinct and unmistakable pattern that is roughly applicable to any homeless population though fully descriptive of none. Homeless persons are poor, anomic, inert, and nonresponsible. They command no resources, enjoy no esteem, and assume no burden of reciprocal obligations. Social action, in the usual sense, is almost impossible for them. Lacking organizational statuses and roles, their sphere of activity extends no further than the provision of personal necessities on a meager scale. Their decisions have no implications for others. Only the simplest forms of concerted action are open to them, since homelessness is incompatible with sustained involvement in a complex division of labor.

The observable behavior of the homeless person consists largely of activities that furnish subsistence or enjoyment without incurring responsibilities: mendicancy, petty crime, scavenging, casual conversation, and an incurious attention at spectacles. This quality of social inertness renders him both innocuous and helpless. He is unlikely to engage in major crime or political movements or to protest his own condition forcefully. A certain apathy regarding self-preservation often develops in addition to the collective helplessness. The homeless in great cities and in refugee camps stand and watch their companions assaulted by strangers without offering to interfere and without taking any measures to protect themselves. The combined effect of poor nutrition, exposure of all kinds, neglect of injuries and illness, and insensitivity to emergencies leads to very high rates of morbidity and mortality among homeless persons as compared to the settled population around them.

**The homeless versus the settled.**    For reasons not entirely understood, the presence of homeless persons often arouses a degree of hostility in the settled population that seems entirely disproportionate. Ancient ballads preserve the image of the gypsy as rapist and kidnapper. Being homeless or vagrant became a felony in England in the fourteenth century and a capital crime under the Tudors; it is still treated as a criminal offense in most American and European cities. These external attitudes and the punitive measures to which they lead further separate the homeless man from his settled neighbor. Homeless populations often occupy an underworld with a special argot, secret signs, and a conventional refusal to communicate with outsiders. Such manifestations may lead romantic observers to imagine an entire clandestine social system, such as the "kingdom of beggars" or the "hobo republic," but on closer view, these fantasies disappear and reveal the homeless as an aggregate of unrelated individuals who share a common situation and some elements of a common culture.

**A theory of homelessness.**    The Germanic term "home," with its special connotations of warmth, safety, and emotional dependence, has no exact equivalent in other linguistic systems. Aside from its familiar overtones, it expresses the idea of a fixed place of residence shared with a limited number of other persons. In current usage, home does not imply a family (unrelated persons can "make a home" together), a household (a rest home may be much larger), more than moderate fixity (in any given year, more than one in five U.S. families moves to a new home), or exclusivity (a special body of tax law covers taxpayers with two or more homes). Living outside a family, with no permanent address, does not make a priest or a soldier homeless, but the man who occupies the same lodging on skid row for forty uninterrupted years is properly considered homeless. The essence of the concept goes beyond residential arrangements. Homelessness is best visualized as a relationship to society at large and best understood by examining the difference between the settled and the homeless.

A settled, active adult in any society participates simultaneously in several major types of organization. This participation anchors him in the social structure by linkages with near and distant kin, neighbors, compatriots, superiors and subordinates, co-workers, departed ancestors, sacred and supernatural personages, persons with the same special interests, and even those who like to play the same games. Each of these memberships involves duties and privileges, restraints and rights, status and roles. Each requires sustained interaction with particular other persons who enter into the subject's life history and become part of the audience for his socially meaningful acts.

The pattern of these affiliations varies in detail from one time and place to another, but the main outlines remain unchanged. In modernized countries of the twentieth century, the individual's attachment to society seems to be mediated through eight major types of organization: family, school, community, state, production group, occupational union, church, and recreational associations. Taken together, these memberships define who the settled person is, how he schedules his days and his years, and the benefits he may claim from, and the duties he owes to, the social order. Above all, they identify the others who are influenced by him and define the extent of that influence.

The fully homeless man is unaffiliated in all sectors. He is not an active member of any organization and therefore has no enforceable responsibilities toward fellow members, no audience of persons influenced by his actions, no claim on social rewards beyond whatever minimum has been set to avoid the scandal of his starvation, and no duties to fulfill except those imposed as a condition of remaining in the territory. Clearly, this condition will be uncomfortable and sometimes dangerous. On the other hand, it may be attractive to those who reject the cultural goals together with the means of achieving them.

**Homelessness as an ideal.** The age of modernization is singularly unsympathetic to the positive values of homelessness. However, in other times and places it has been regarded as a desirable, or at least admirable, way of life.

The exaltation of homelessness as an ideal is a central, recurrent theme of Christianity, reflecting such scriptural teachings as "lay not up for yourself treasures on earth." Poverty, detachment from previous affiliations, and the abandonment of worldly aspirations are the first principles of monasticism. The Christian ethos of vagrancy was most fully developed by St. Francis of Assisi and the several orders of wandering, mendicant friars who followed the Franciscan model.

A parallel theme runs through Muslim history. The "St. Francis of Islam" is Mulai 'Abd al-Qādir al-Jīlāni (1078–1166), the patron of the needy and suffering. From the Muslim viewpoint, the beggar performs a kind of social service by enabling others to attain merit by almsgiving: "As long as Islam flourishes," says one writer, "there will be beggars, for there will always be devout people who will give away all they have, and so become beggars themselves" (Edwards 1912, p. 931).

In addition to friars, hermits, and holy beggars,

Christianity and Islam recognize and honor the pilgrim, who becomes a homeless wanderer temporarily, partly for the spiritual benefit of visiting the sacred shrine and partly to withdraw from settled society. In the Middle Ages pilgrims played a vital part in integrating both the Christian and Muslim worlds. The pilgrim routes to Mecca and Medina, to Rome and Santiago de Compostela, are as crowded today as ever, but the modern pilgrim is more often a religious tourist than a holy vagrant.

The ethos of vagrancy is even more conspicuous in Buddhism. Buddha and his disciples were members of an already ancient order of wandering almsmen, and Buddha charged his disciples to "go forth and wander about for the good of the Many." The *bhikshu-sangha* was (and is) a community of homeless men entered by "going forth from a house to a houseless state." A *bhikshu* is an almsman. "He is differentiated from an ordinary beggar by the sacramental character of his begging. His beggary is not just a means of subsistence, but an outward token that he has renounced the world and all its goods and thrown himself for bare living on the chances of public charity" (Dutt 1962, p. 36).

Similar themes exalting homelessness and attaching a positive value to mendicancy may be discerned in Hinduism, the religion of Zoroaster, and a number of Hellenistic cults. Indeed, approval and abhorrence of religious mendicancy may occur together. One appeal of the world religions may lie precisely in their ability to combine doctrinal elements supporting the performance of status obligations with others that allow the believer to withdraw from the world without penalty.

## Modern forms of homelessness

Although the traditional types of homelessness may still be observed on the contemporary scene, they are overshadowed by new forms that arise directly from the dominant processes of the modern era: industrialization, urbanization, decolonization, and the redistribution of political power. The three types to be considered here are refugees, migratory workers, and skid row men.

**Refugees.** Involuntary migration has occurred throughout historic times, but the displacements of the twentieth century have been unprecedented in scale, scope, and duration. Refugees are persons who migrate to escape actual or threatened persecution because of their race, religion, political convictions, or for any reasons related to war (Proudfoot 1957, pp. 53, 446). A broader definition of refugees includes any persons compelled to abandon their homes because of events for which they cannot be held responsible (Vernant 1953, p. 3).

The involuntary migration of refugees contrasts sharply with voluntary migration in search of economic opportunities. Voluntary migrants are mostly young adults usually assured of a welcome in the host country and of continued ties with the country of origin. Involuntary migration often affects entire communities, including people of all ages and conditions, uprooted without their consent and set down in a place selected at random, where their numbers increase their helplessness.

The wars and revolutions of the twentieth century have created both temporary and permanent refugees. The temporary refugee may flee from his home in the face of an invading army to return at the first opportunity. The permanent refugee leaves a country where his enemies have come to power with no real hope of eventual return. Sometimes he is resettled after an interval of hardship in a new community among people of his own persuasion. But if no such place is available, he may linger indefinitely in refugee camps, living on a dole. One observer speaks of *Heimatlosenausländer* as "ultimate refugees" and describes their loss of affiliations:

Here you meet men whose environment has ceased to succour them. In their former normal life they had the solace of their homes in times of weariness or perplexity, perhaps even in times of unemployment. They had the consolation of their church in times of spiritual need and of family sadness. They had their trade union and political association in times when work and politics preoccupied them. They had their village inn and folk festivals on high days and holidays. All these props and cushions in life's pilgrimage are taken from them. . . .   (Rees 1960, p. 37)

The large-scale refugee movements of the twentieth century began with the Balkan wars of 1912–1914. World War I displaced several million civilians, most of whom were subsequently relocated. Almost every major disturbance of the interwar period generated a refugee problem, and World War II displaced between 20 and 50 million persons; the exact number is unknown and cannot be accurately estimated. In the postwar period, the displacement of populations continued unabated in Europe, Asia, Africa, the Near East, the islands of the Pacific, the Mediterranean, and the Caribbean. Not without reason has this been called the "century of the homeless man." Most refugees are ultimately resettled, but not without great cost in suffering and dislocation. Meanwhile, the making of refugees continues at a rate that reflects the peculiar and fanatical character of twentieth-century nationalism.

**Migratory farm laborers.**    Large-scale agriculture often requires large amounts of hand labor for brief seasonal periods. This situation frequently occurs during the transition from a plantation or family farm system with a fixed labor force to a fully mechanized system of cultivation. The transition may extend over several decades, during which the local labor force is incapable of planting and harvesting a crop without outside help. Arranging the appearance of the required number of workers at the right time and place is a perennial problem for the planters. Protecting the workers against exploitation and the natural hazards of migration is a major problem for whatever authorities assume the responsibility.

Seasonal migratory labor is required for such diverse products as coffee, cocoa, rubber, cotton, citrus fruits, wheat, apples, potatoes, and wild rice. The seasonal movement of migratory workers is significant throughout the world, often transmitting a modernizing influence from advanced to backward areas. The preliterate tribesmen brought to the coastal banana plantations of Central America, the Italian peasants cultivating sugar beets in France, the tribal Africans who migrate to cocoa plantations of Ghana, and the Mexican *braceros* picking peaches in Oregon all acquire new ideas and attitudes to carry back with them.

Movements of this kind are often internal as well as international. In the United States in the middle 1960s, for example, Mexicans were admitted annually on a temporary basis under a farm labor program jointly administered by the two countries, and sizable numbers were drawn under other programs from Canada, the British West Indies, Japan, and Puerto Rico. But the stream of migrants is also fed by many internal groups: Indians, mountain whites, Spanish Americans, and southern Negroes. The annual cycle begins in the South and moves steadily northward with the advancing season; some workers follow the wheat harvest all the way from southern Texas to Manitoba.

Migratory laborers vary in degree of homelessness. John Steinbeck's novel, *The Grapes of Wrath*, painted an unforgettable picture of migrant families displaced from their ancestral farms in Oklahoma during the depression and cut loose to drift helplessly from one temporary job to another. Even in times of prosperity, the United States has an estimated one million transients who have no fixed base (Shotwell 1961, p. 34); and there are many others who have home bases to which they return between seasons or when forced back by unemployment.

A migrant work force may be composed of single

men, entire families, or both. Their living and working conditions range from adequate to wretched. Like other homeless persons, migratory workers are prevented from forming or retaining normal affiliations and are subject to disproportionate hostility from their settled neighbors.

Migrancy engenders community resentment, puts in peril such practical aspects of normal family living as regular schooling for children, housing that is sanitary and convenient and conducive to whclesome family relationships, voting privileges, stable income, health and welfare services available to residents. Migrancy reduces to zero the chance to develop the feeling of belonging to a stable community. (Shotwell 1961, pp. 36–37)

The farm laborer occupies a place at the very bottom of the socioeconomic ladder, doing the most work for the lowest wages with less security and opportunity than any other segment of the population.

Solidary organizations among migrant laborers are rare. Attempts to unionize them, when not violently suppressed, have usually failed. However, a loose form of crew organization often develops, whereby a group of individuals or families is represented by a leader who negotiates with employers and arranges transportation and lodging.

The impact of this form of homelessness on individuals is mitigated by its temporary character. The available evidence suggests that most migratory workers return to a settled life at the first opportunity, often in an area they have discovered as migrants.

**The skid row man.** In proportion to their numbers, skid row men in the United States and comparable homeless men in western Europe have received disproportionate attention from both scientific and literary observers. In a study using 1950 census data, Bogue (1963) identified skid row areas in 41 American cities and estimated their combined homeless population at under 100,000. The individual settlements are correspondingly small. Careful enumerations in the New York Bowery, one of the most conspicuous skid row areas in the world, disclosed less than seven thousand homeless men in 1964 and 1965 (Baker 1965, p. 7).

The name "skid row" (or "skid road") apparently derives from the log skidways on which felled timber was transported in the forests of the Pacific northwest. It came to be applied to the Seattle area where lumbermen wintered and then to similar enclaves in other cities where single homeless men were housed in dormitories and lodging houses, surrounded by facilities that served their special needs.

Most of these enclaves, in their present locations, can be traced back about a century. In recent decades, their populations have been declining, although irregularly; and the migratory workers identified as the principal inhabitants of "hobohemia" after World War I (Anderson 1923) have given way to the practically immobile pensioners, alcoholics, and disadvantaged workers who make up the bulk of the population today.

The interest aroused by skid row may be explained partly by its unique institutions, partly by its high visibility, partly by the resistance of the skid row alcoholic to ameliorative programs, and partly by a life style that deviates dramatically from the success-oriented, family-centered ethos of the surrounding society. The visible facilities are cubicle lodging houses, cheap restaurants and bars, missions, barber colleges, secondhand stores and pawnshops, newspaper reading rooms, sidewalk gatherings, all-night movies and burlesque shows, tattoo parlors, "jungles" near railroad yards, and the "revolving door" of police court and workhouse. In several major cities the original area has been cleared in the course of urban redevelopment, but substitute skid rows have invariably appeared.

Ethnic and occupational characteristics vary somewhat from one skid row to another, but the population is almost exclusively male. Their average age is much higher than that of the general population; a large proportion are past the usual age of retirement (Bogue 1963, pp. 8–10). About a third of the men are heavy drinkers, frequently arrested for drunkenness and apparently addicted to alcohol, although there is some doubt about their being true alcoholics. The remainder are divided between social drinkers, whose need for liquor is apparently controllable, and moderate drinkers or abstainers (Bogue 1963, pp. 90–93). Most report themselves unmarried and without active family ties. Their histories show less than average involvement in family relationships from early childhood on (Pittman & Gordon 1958, pp. 10, 125–138). Their organizational affiliations have often been slight throughout adult life, reflecting a permanent state of social detachment. The typical skid row man has a background of intermittent unskilled or semi-skilled employment, with minimal involvement in political, religious, and recreational organizations (Bahr & Langfur 1966).

Morbidity and mortality rates are startlingly high. The risks of contagious disease, infection, exposure, injury, and malnutrition are greater on skid row than in any other urban environment (Bogue 1963, pp. 199–230). Most men live close to the margin of bare subsistence on sporadic earnings, pensions, relief payments, begging, or some combination of these. A few depend on savings or assistance from relatives; a few enjoy regular incomes and remain on skid row by preference (Bogue 1963, pp. 13–17; 46–77).

In addition to the core population, the skid row area provides temporary accommodation for migratory workers and work seekers, eccentrics, and fugitives of various kinds. Some of these men are not strictly homeless, and some homeless men have no contact with skid row. However, the predominant type is unmistakable.

The principal current trends in the status of skid row inhabitants are decreased mobility and a decline of relative income. There is, however, a rising provision of public assistance for them, and experimental programs are being undertaken in the rehabilitation of alcoholics.

THEODORE CAPLOW, HOWARD M. BAHR,
AND DAVID STERNBERG

[*Directly related is the entry* REFUGEES. *Other relevant material may be found in* DRINKING AND ALCOHOLISM, *article on* SOCIAL ASPECTS; MIGRATION.]

### BIBLIOGRAPHY

ANDERSON, NELS 1923 *The Hobo: The Sociology of the Homeless Man.* Univ. of Chicago Press.

BAHR, HOWARD M.; and LANGFUR, STEPHEN J. 1966 Social Attachment and Drinking in Skid-row Life Histories. Unpublished report, Columbia Univ., Bureau of Applied Social Research.

BAKER, MICHAEL A. 1965 An Estimate of the Population of Homeless Men in the Bowery Area, New York City, February 28, 1965. Unpublished manuscript, Columbia Univ., Bureau of Applied Social Research.

BOGUE, DONALD J. 1963 *Skid Row in American Cities.* Univ. of Chicago, Community and Family Study Center.

CAPLOW, THEODORE 1940 Transiency as a Cultural Pattern. *American Sociological Review* 5:731–739.

CIRTAUTAS, CLAUDIUS K. 1957 *The Refugee: A Psychological Study.* Boston: Meador.

DUTT, SUKUMAR 1962 *Buddhist Monks and Monasteries of India.* London: Allen & Unwin.

EDWARDS, ALBERT 1912 The Beggars of Mogador. *Outlook* 101:929–936.

GILMORE, HARLAN W. 1940 *The Beggar.* Chapel Hill: Univ. of North Carolina Press.

HOLBORN, LOUISE W. 1960 *The World's Refugees: Everyone's Concern.* Washington: American Association of University Women, Committee on International Relations.

INTERNATIONAL LABOUR REVIEW STAFF 1957 Interterritorial Migrations of Africans South of the Sahara. *International Labour Review* 76:292–310.

MARTIN, NORMAN F. 1957 *Los vagabundos en la Nueva España, siglo XVI.* Mexico City: Editorial Jus.

O'CONNOR, PHILIP 1963 *Vagrancy: Ethos and Actuality.* Baltimore: Penguin.

OREGON, BUREAU OF LABOR 1959 *... And Migrant Problems Demand Attention: The Final Report of the*

*1958–1959 Migrant Farm Labor Studies in Oregon.* Salem: The Bureau.

ORWELL, GEORGE (1933) 1950 *Down and Out in Paris and London.* New York: Harcourt. → Orwell is the pseudonym of Eric Blair.

PITTMAN, DAVID J.; and GORDON, C. WAYNE 1958 *Revolving Door: A Study of the Chronic Police Case Inebriate.* Glencoe, Ill.: Free Press.

POLLITT, DANIEL H.; and LEVINE, SELMA M. 1960 *The Migrant Farm Worker in America: Background Data on the Migrant Worker Situation in the United States Today.* Washington: Government Printing Office.

PROUDFOOT, MALCOLM J. 1957 *European Refugees, 1939–1952: A Study in Forced Population Movement.* London: Faber.

REES, ELFAN 1960 Common Psychological Factors in Refugee Problems Throughout the World. Pages 31–43 in World Federation for Mental Health, *Uprooting and Resettlement.* London: The Federation.

SHOTWELL, LOUISA R. 1961 *The Harvesters: The Story of the Migrant People.* Garden City, N.Y.: Doubleday.

SOLENBERGER, ALICE W. 1911 *One Thousand Homeless Men: A Study of Original Records.* New York: Russell Sage Foundation, Charities Publication Committee.

STOESSINGER, JOHN G. 1956 *The Refugee and the World Community.* Minneapolis: Univ. of Minnesota Press.

STRAUS, ROBERT 1946 Alcohol and the Homeless Man. *Quarterly Journal of Studies on Alcohol* 7:360–404.

SUTHERLAND, EDWIN H.; and LOCKE, HARVEY J. 1936 *Twenty Thousand Homeless Men: A Study of Unemployed Men in the Chicago Shelters.* Philadelphia: Lippincott.

VERNANT, JACQUES 1953 *The Refugee in the Post-war World.* New Haven: Yale Univ. Press.

VEXLIARD, ALEXANDRE 1956 *Introduction à la sociologie du vagabondage.* Paris: Rivière.

WALLACE, SAMUEL E. 1965 *Skid Row as a Way of Life.* Totowa, N.J.: Bedminster.

WOOD, MARGARET M. 1953 *Paths of Loneliness: The Individual Isolated in Modern Society.* New York: Columbia Univ. Press.

# HOMEOSTASIS

The concept of homeostasis is widely used, in physiology and psychology, to identify what seems to be a general attribute of living organisms: the tendency to maintain and restore certain steady states or conditions of the organism. An obvious example is that of body temperature, which in the human tends to fluctuate only in a narrow range about the value 98.6° F. When the temperature rises above the normal range, corrective reflexes (perspiration, reduced metabolism, etc.) go into action to restore the steady state. Persistent deviation may initiate other actions (moving into the shade, plunging into water, etc.). If body temperature drops, other corrective actions are observed.

Many bodily steady states follow this pattern. Blood glucose level, blood pH, and osmotic pressure are examples. The key concepts are: an observable steady state that persists over time with minor changes; thresholds above and below this normal range; a sensory input that reports changes in the steady state; and effector mechanisms for restoring the steady state.

When a deviation goes beyond either the upper or the lower threshold, energy is mobilized to restore the steady state to its optimal value. Physiologists have been concerned mainly with the reflexes triggered by such deviations, but psychologists have emphasized those homeostatic actions that are seen in learned behavior. Man will exert considerable energy to protect optimal states. He may take *restorative* action (building a fire when cold) or *forestalling* action (moving south before winter arrives). The simple reflex level and the complex learned response to homeostatic disturbance are often labeled differently: Stagner and Karwoski (1952) called the former "static homeostasis" and the latter "dynamic homeostasis"; Cofer and Appley (1964) used the terms "physiological homeostasis" and "behavioral homeostasis."

The biochemical and reflex defenses function adequately to protect some constancies; if blood osmotic pressure drops too low or vitamin concentration is too high, kidney mechanisms correct the situation. In other cases, the reflex machinery may fail, and learned behavior is activated. There are probably two thresholds in the system, one for reflexive response and another (further from optimum) that initiates voluntary action.

Damaging the biochemical mechanism forces increased reliance on the learned systems of defense. Thyroidectomized rats build nests to protect against heat loss; parathyroidectomy or adrenalectomy leads to increased drinking of solutions containing calcium or sodium. It seems reasonable, therefore, to consider the cerebral cortex as the highest level of a homeostatic protective mechanism.

**Heterostasis.** The concept of heterostasis must be introduced into any systematic discussion of homeostasis. Action to restore one steady state may disrupt another steady state (perspiration to cool the body upsets the osmotic equilibrium in the blood, triggering thirst). Heterostasis points to a hierarchy of steady states; deviation of an "important" value will initiate action that disrupts one lower in the scale, but the reverse is not true. Thirst dominates over hunger, and the need for oxygen is prepotent over either. Deviations from optimum dominate behavior as a function of their relevance to organismic survival. Oxygen lack can be tolerated for only a few minutes, water lack for a day or two, food lack for many days.

**Sensory controls.** Homeostasis depends upon a negative feedback loop; disturbance of a steady state initiates sensory cues that trigger responses tending to restore the previous state; and as the sensory input indicates that the optimal value is being approached, the intensity of corrective action diminishes. Each steady state must have built into its control system, in neural or biochemical form, some representation of the tolerable range of values and upper and lower thresholds. However, all such monitoring systems probably report to a central mechanism, giving rise to something like Morgan's (1957) "central motive state," a state of *tension* that elicits dynamic homeostatic responses. Tension is thus an important intervening variable in homeostatic theory.

Some types of stimuli have inherent equilibrium-disturbing or equilibrium-restoring properties. Sweet tastes not only signal reduction of hunger for infants; they also seem to have general tension-reducing value. Pain disturbs equilibrium and raises tension. Soft, warm contact may be a universal tension reducer for mammals (cf. Harlow 1958). This need not imply a one-to-one correspondence between pleasure or "subjective utility" and homeostatic value in a goal object. For example, the organism may make mistakes (saccharin is sought by the organism because it is misperceived as equilibrium restoring); and learning may cause the organism to value objects that are purely symbolic and not in themselves effective either to disturb or to restore steady states [see LEARNING, *article on* REINFORCEMENT].

*Imprinting.* Imprinting may be a determiner of cue value. When a gosling first hatches, it seems to fixate on the first moving object and endow this with positive valence; the gosling will follow this object and behave as if a steady state were disturbed when the object disappears [see IMPRINTING].

*Adaptation level.* Adaptation level modifies the sensory controls in homeostatic cycles. As Cannon (1932) pointed out, the "baseline" (herein referred to as optimal value) may shift as a result of experience. Infants learn to adapt to a two-hour, three-hour, or four-hour feeding schedule and become "hungry" at the proper time. If subjected to radio and television noises, they show distress at first but later may seem to enjoy the sound level (Chodorkoff 1960). Europeans find room temperatures comfortable that Americans experience as chilly and disturbing.

**Effector processes.** The effector mechanisms set off by homeostatic disturbances vary from simple biochemical buffering of the blood stream, through hormonal modifications and autonomic nervous system reflex changes, to complex and elaborate learned responses. As Bernard (1859) noted, homeostasis in its simplest form involves protection of constancies of body fluids. Life escaped from the sea when techniques evolved for carrying the sea (as cell environment) within the organism. He wrote that internal constancies are basic to the free life—free from the limitations of an oceanic environment, free to live on land and in the air.

The more complex activities described above expand this conception markedly. First, the organism may remove itself from disturbing stimuli (avoid heat, seek shade). Second, the organism may restore the constancy of the external environment (air conditioning, stores of food). There seems to be general agreement that these two kinds of responses, while remote from biochemical secretion or mechanical reflexes, qualify as homeostatic in nature. Third, the organism may seek to protect (or restore) symbolic conditions associated with homeostatic success—bank accounts, institutional systems, and the like. There is less agreement that these phenomena belong under the homeostatic rubric, yet it is difficult to find a logical rule by which to exclude them.

**Evaluation of homeostatic theory.** Critics have objected to homeostatic theory as being too conservative, as implying that motivation is conceived solely as operating to restore pre-existing conditions. In a very narrow sense this criticism is true: unless the essential steady states are restored to their normal range, the organism dies. (It is also true that most people are conservative unless deprived.) In a broader sense, homeostatic theory says that energy is mobilized to take action that will restore and protect these *steady states*, but that the *action* may be novel and inventive. Fire, clothing, and other inventions serve homeostatic uses. The individual, frustrated by inadequate habits, may acquire new ones which will reduce tensions.

The assertion that all energy mobilizations derive from disturbances of steady states does encounter problems. The phenomena of curiosity, manipulative motivation, and sensory deprivation, as well as the sex drive, offer difficulties. Some psychologists have preferred to treat homeostasis as one segment of the topic of motivation. Those who prefer to press for an inclusive view, in which all motivation obeys homeostatic principles, resort to assumptions such as efficient organismic func-

tioning "demanding" a certain level of sensory stimulation, just as it "demands" a certain level of glucose or vitamin B. "Sensory deprivation" may be motivating because the central nervous system has a normal activity level that is disrupted by either an excess or a deficit of external stimulation [*see* PERCEPTION, *article on* PERCEPTUAL DEPRIVATION; STIMULATION DRIVES; *see also* Hebb 1955; Miller 1960].

Aspiration level studies can also be incorporated into this schema. Motivation, in the sense of effort directed toward a specific goal, obeys aspiration principles. An incentive below present attainment levels is ignored; one that is too far above present achievement is perceived as impossible. Effective incentives, therefore, must fall within the "normal range" as a function of adaptation level. Repeated successes lead to a shift upward, failures to a shift downward, in aspiration level. Prior experience determines what will be anticipated [*see* ACHIEVEMENT MOTIVATION].

**Homeostatic conception of personality.** Personalities can be described by the hierarchy of steady states that are defended, by the cues that disturb these states, and by the techniques utilized to protect and restore equilibriums (Stagner 1961).

*Preferred steady states.* Some individuals value physical comfort; others, a quiet family life; others, a buzz of activity. Variations in adaptation or aspiration level may be involved. Objects that symbolize internal equilibrium, such as the mother, a house, or a bank account, become values protected in themselves. The self-image, the individual's percept of himself, becomes an object of value. Threats to the self-image (failure, social ridicule, loss of status) provoke blood pressure and glandular changes as well as vigorous action to restore the integrity of the ego.

*Sources of disturbance.* Some persons manifest phobias and other disturbances that are obviously not realistic. Neurotic aggressions and anxieties fit into this category. Others are disturbed only by realistic threats to physical constancies or to acquired values.

*Methods of restoring equilibriums.* The individual may rely chiefly upon overt muscular action to protect and restore valued constancies, or he may utilize symbols and fantasy. The whole range of coping and defensive reactions indicates individual differences in ways of maintaining steady states.

**Personality defense mechanisms.** Sigmund Freud has often been cited as a forerunner of homeostatic theory, although he never discussed negative feedback loops (Fletcher 1942; Walker 1956). His conception of repression, projection, dreams, rationalization, and other mechanisms as devices for protecting the individual against threatened disturbance, or devices for restoring equilibrium, places him in this category [see DEFENSE MECHANISMS].

When anxiety and tension are aroused, infantile ways of restoring equilibrium may be reinstated. Eating, drinking, and sexual contact are primitive devices for reducing tension. Unfortunately, if the steady state that has been disturbed involves a need for other substances, these defenses have only temporary effect; the tension returns promptly. Neurotic behavior, in homeostatic terms, is behavior that diminishes tension without correcting the basic imbalance (Menninger et al. 1963).

One must note that some psychologists take issue vigorously with attempts to conceptualize personality in homeostatic terms. Allport (1955) asserts that man can be understood more by what he is striving for in the future than by what he is seeking to restore of the past.

**Homeostasis as a social phenomenon.** Cannon (1932) noted that the concept of homeostasis seemed relevant also to social processes. One such implication derives from the process of mutual assistance (Dempsey 1951). There is some evidence (Chodorkoff 1960) that the mother–infant relationship is a true dyadic system, in which each organism can be a cue disturbing the other, and in which the behavior of one may be equilibrium restoring for the other. Most convincing is the fact that social conditions can trigger the same reflexive mechanisms involved in physiological homeostasis (cf. Denenberg et al. 1964; Hoagland 1964). Hoagland, for example, reported that rats reared in overcrowded cages develop glandular disorders and die at earlier ages than less crowded littermates. These animals show distinct evidences of tension and behavioral disturbance. Hoagland also commented that equilibrium develops at a given population density. Below this point, reproduction is usually accelerated; but above the equilibrium value, infertility and early death reduce the population. Thus he is disposed to favor the view that homeostatic functions are true group processes, not merely manifestations of individual disturbance. Allee et al. (1949) have pointed out that ecological balance often shows all the properties ascribed to homeostatic equilibrium.

To apply the concept of homeostasis to even more complex social phenomena, such as the market economy, one must identify the steady state, the factors disrupting this state, the cues indicating disturbance, and the restorative mechanisms. Equilibrium theory in economics seems to meet these requirements. In a specific economic market, for example, clothing, one finds a tendency for the price to stabilize. An increase in consumer demand will upset the existing steady state; information spreads by way of efforts to purchase; producers in the clothing industry scent possibilities for profit and increase output accordingly. Thus there is a feedback loop analogous to that observed in individuals.

**Failures of homeostasis.** One criticism of homeostatic theory is that humans often do things that disrupt, rather than restore, equilibrium. To some extent this is merely a function of errors in informational input or in guiding action. A young lion who charges his prey from too great a distance is not thereby proved to be disobeying homeostatic principles; he simply has not learned effective responses.

In some cases homeostasis operates inefficiently at the individual level because of inadequate sensory controls. Man is not endowed with receptors sensitive to gamma radiation, so, without warning, he may die of fall-out. If the species survives, mutation may provide such sense organs.

Group phenomena also show catastrophic effects of poor information input. War between nations has frequently come about because the leaders of one nation did not accurately perceive the situation (for example, in 1939 Hitler thought England would not fight over Poland). Disputes between a union and management can be settled more amicably if information flows freely between the two (Muench 1960).

These illustrations do not *prove* that the homeostatic model explains group action; no such logical proof exists at this time. Nevertheless, the homeostatic model has been a fruitful one in pointing to areas for research and in suggesting genotypic unities that cut across phenotypic discontinuities, just as the theory of gravitation cut across events from atoms to galaxies. Consequently, homeostasis has been a healthy influence in psychology and in the other social sciences.

ROSS STAGNER

[*Directly related are the entries* DRIVES; MOTIVATION. *Other relevant material may be found in* CYBERNETICS; STRESS; *and in the biography of* CANNON.]

### BIBLIOGRAPHY

*An extensive and scholarly discussion of homeostatic theories may be found in* Cofer & Appley 1964. *The homeostatic conception of personality is supported in* Stagner

*1961, and the opposing view is well stated in* Allport 1955. *Applications to social groups are proposed in* Cannon 1932 *and 1941 and to industry in* Stagner 1956.

ALLEE, W. C. et al. 1949 *Principles of Animal Ecology.* Philadelphia: Saunders.

ALLPORT, GORDON W. 1955 *Becoming: Basic Considerations for a Psychology of Personality.* New Haven: Yale Univ. Press.

BERNARD, CLAUDE 1859 *Leçons sur les propriétés physiologiques et les altérations pathologiques des liquides de l'organisme.* 2 vols. Paris: Baillière.

CANNON, WALTER B. (1932) 1963 *The Wisdom of the Body.* Rev. & enl. ed. New York: Norton.

CANNON, WALTER B. 1941 The Body Physiologic and the Body Politic. *Science* 93:1–10.

CHODORKOFF, JOAN R. 1960 Infant Development as a Function of Mother–Child Interaction. Ph.D. dissertation, Wayne State Univ.

COFER, C. N.; and APPLEY, M. H. 1964 Homeostatic Concepts and Motivation. Pages 302–365 in C. N. Cofer and M. H. Appley, *Motivation: Theory and Research.* New York: Wiley.

DEMPSEY, EDWARD W. 1951 Homeostasis. Pages 209–235 in S. S. Stevens (editor), *Handbook of Experimental Psychology.* New York: Wiley.

DENENBERG, W. H.; HUDGENS, G. A.; and ZARROW, M. X. 1964 Mice Reared With Rats: Modification of Behavior by Early Experience With Another Species. *Science* 143:380–381.

FLETCHER, JOHN M. 1942 Homeostasis as an Explanatory Principle in Psychology. *Psychological Review* 49:80–87.

HARLOW, HARRY F. 1958 The Nature of Love. *American Psychologist* 13:673–685.

HEBB, DONALD O. 1955 Drives and the C.N.S. (Conceptual Nervous System). *Psychological Review* 62:243–254.

HOAGLAND, HUDSON 1964 Cybernetics of Population Control. *Bulletin of the Atomic Scientists* 20, no. 2: 2–6.

MASLOW, A. H. 1937 The Influence of Familiarization on Preference. *Journal of Experimental Psychology* 21:162–180.

MENNINGER, KARL; MAYMAN, MARTIN; and PRUYSER, PAUL 1963 *The Vital Balance: The Life Processes in Mental Health and Illness.* New York: Viking.

MILLER, JAMES G. 1960 Information Input Overload and Psychopathology. *American Journal of Psychiatry* 116:695–704.

MORGAN, CLIFFORD T. 1957 Physiological Mechanisms of Motivation. Volume 5, pages 1–35 in *Nebraska Symposium on Motivation.* Edited by Marshall R. Jones. Lincoln: Univ. of Nebraska Press.

MUENCH, GEORGE A. 1960 A Clinical Psychologist's Treatment of Labor–Management Conflicts. *Personnel Psychology* 13:165–172.

SOUTHWICK, CHARLES H. 1964 Peromyscus Leucopus: An Interesting Subject for Studies of Socially Induced Stress Responses. *Science* 143:55–56.

STAGNER, ROSS 1956 *Psychology of Industrial Conflict.* New York: Wiley. → See especially pages 89–116, "Motivation: Principles," and pages 117–154, "Motivation: Some Applications."

STAGNER, ROSS 1961 The Nature of Personality Structure. Pages 69–86 in Ross Stagner, *Psychology of Personality.* 3d ed. New York: McGraw-Hill.

STAGNER, ROSS; and KARWOSKI, T. F. 1952 *Psychology.* New York: McGraw-Hill.

WALKER, NIGEL 1956 Freud and Homeostasis. *British Journal for the Philosophy of Science* 7:61–72.

## HOMICIDE
*See under* CRIME.

## HOMOSEXUALITY
*See under* SEXUAL BEHAVIOR.

## HONESTY
*See* MORAL DEVELOPMENT.

# HONOR

The notion of honor has several facets. It is a sentiment, a manifestation of this sentiment in conduct, and the evaluation of this conduct by others, that is to say, reputation. It is both internal to the individual and external to him—a matter of his feelings, his behavior, and the treatment that he receives. Many authors have stressed one of these facets at the expense of the others; however, from the point of view of the social sciences it is essential to bear in mind that honor is simultaneously all of these, for both its psychological and social functions relate to the fact that it stands as a mediator between individual aspirations and the judgment of society.

Like the other self-regarding sentiments, honor expresses an evaluation of self in the terms which are used to evaluate others—or as others might be imagined to judge one. It can, therefore, be seen to reflect the values of the group with which a person identifies himself. But honor as a fact, rather than as a sentiment, refers not merely to the judgment of others but to their behavior. The facets of honor may be viewed as related in the following way: honor felt becomes honor claimed, and honor claimed becomes honor paid. The payment of honor involves the expression of respect which is due to a person either by virtue of his role on a particular occasion, as when a guest is honored in accordance with the laws of hospitality, or by virtue of his status or rank, which entitles him to a permanent right to precedence marked by honorific insignia, expressed in modes of address and titles and demonstrated in deference. Honor is also exchanged in mutual recognition: in salutations and the return of invitations and favors.

The same principles that govern the transactions of honor are present in those of dishonor, though in reverse: the withdrawal of respect dishonors, since it implies a rejection of the claim to honor and this inspires the sentiment of shame. To be put to shame is to be denied honor, and it follows that this can only be done to those who have some pretension to it. He who makes no such claim has nothing to lose; he cannot be denied precedence if he prefers to go last. Those who aspire to no honor cannot be humiliated. Honor and dishonor, therefore, provide the currency in which people compete for reputation and the means whereby their appraisal of themselves can be validated and integrated into the social system —or rejected, thus obliging them to revise it. Hence, honor is not only the internalization of the values of society in the individual but the externalization of his self-image in the world.

The sentiment of honor seeks validation, but from what quarter? From God or from the conscience of the person himself? From friends or from kinsmen? From persons in authority or from the crowd? Public opinion, allegedly the arbiter of reputations, arbitrates with anything but a firm hand, since it varies according to the activity and the context. Consensus is not easily established in a complex society; individual views differ, and different groups have different standards. The significance of the acts of public honor and the granting of dignities is, therefore, this: they place the seal of public recognition on reputations that would otherwise stand in doubt and endow them with permanence. It is the function of authority to impose consensus, and it does this with regard to the worth of persons: it converts prestige into status.

Theories of honor have varied greatly as to the relative importance which they accord to different qualities, and this is due to the different social contexts and reference groups from which they derive.

**Honor as a moral concept.**    Honor is commonly considered by moral philosophers to be a state of the individual conscience and, as such, equivalent to the absence of self-reproach. It relates to intentions rather than to the objective consequences of action, and a man is therefore said to be the only judge of his own honor. If he knows his intentions to be "above reproach," then he is indifferent to the comments of others, who cannot evaluate the quality of his motives. He is committed by his honor to the fulfillment of duties that are recognized as attaching to social roles. The casuists recognized honor as a personal responsibility and admitted the defense of honor as a licit form of self-defense which could excuse actions that would otherwise be sinful. Neverthe-

less, the churches have always considered that, in the evaluation of his own motives, a man is bound to refer to their authority, which claims for itself the right to define honor in terms of religious virtue.

Somewhat different is the view of honor which derives it from civic virtue, for here it is ratified not by religious doctrine but by the market place. Popular acclaim comes in to qualify, if not to guide, the judgments of the individual conscience, and honor becomes the reputation for virtue. (This was Aristotle's view.) But once the notion of reputation is admitted as a constituent of honor, its value as a purely moral concept faces ambiguities: a potential conflict emerges between the dictates of conscience and the facts of recognition. This is brought to the forefront by those moralists (not by any means confined to churchmen) who have upbraided the code of honor of their day from the standpoint of morality. Public opinion cannot be trusted to confirm even the most modest man's claim to civic virtues or even to accord reputation on that basis at all. It is apt to give its applause to more spectacular qualities and to pay honor to other sorts of excellence. With regard to dishonor, it is yet more capricious, for here its great weapon is ridicule, which seldom employs a moral criterion at all, but destroys reputations on the grounds of a man's pretentiousness, foolishness, or misfortune, not his wickedness. As Molière observed, one would rather be Tartuffe than Orgon. Public opinion, in its sympathy for the successful, betrays the notion of honor as a purely moral concept.

**Honor as precedence.**    In contrast to the moral view of honor, which relates it to merit—whether religious, civic, or professional—other writers have insisted upon its factual aspect. For example, Hobbes (*Leviathan*, chapter 10) saw no more in honor than the achievement of precedence and the competition for worldly honors. Honor, in his view, is not a matter of sentiment and aspirations (since all men would like to be honored), but one of individual preferment, to the attainment of which virtue is quite irrelevant.

It is, moreover, from this aspect that the word honor derives etymologically: it first applied to grants of land or the privilege of levying taxes ceded by a sovereign to his eminent servants and supporters. Royal favor was, therefore, not only the "fountain of honor," as in the view of many later political theorists, but literally the origin of the word. As might be expected, honor was particularly to be earned through military prowess, and originally, it should be noted, it conceded not only social dignity but economic advantage as well.

Honor in this sense accorded precedence. This, however, is not only conferred by royal statute but derives from social interaction at every level in a society; the claim to honor depends always, in the last resort, upon the ability of the claimant to impose himself. Might is the basis of right to precedence, which goes to the man who is bold enough to enforce his claim, regardless of what may be thought of his merits.

Worldly honor validates itself by an appeal to the facts, submitting always to the reality of power, whether military, political, social, or economic and whether it rests upon the consensus of a community, the favor of superiors, or the control of sanctions. For this reason courage is the *sine qua non* of honor, and cowardice is always its converse. This fact is inherent in its nature and not merely the heritage of a class which once earned its status, or so it claimed, through feats of arms. The mottoes of the nobility (which may serve as a gloss upon their conception of honor) commonly emphasize not only the claim to prestige and status but, above all, the moral quality necessary to win and to retain them; when "all is lost save honor," this at least has been preserved, and while this is so, a return of fortune is always possible. Willingness to stand up to opposition is essential to the acquisition, as to the defense, of honor, regardless of the mode of action that is adopted. No amount of moral justification validates the honor of a coward, even where retaliation to an affront is ruled out on moral grounds; to turn the other cheek is not the same thing as to hide it. Indeed, in terms of the code of honor, turning the other cheek is simply a means of demonstrating contempt. Christian forgiveness cloaks a claim to superiority that cannot but irritate the sensitivities of the forgiven, for it not only implies disdain, it attempts to alter the rules whereby honor is achieved or lost.

However well courage may promote the claims of the courageous, the fact of triumph is ultimately what counts. The distribution of the spoils is the privilege of the victor; where claims to precedence conflict, the decision goes to the big battalions. It is the *fact* of precedence that establishes the *right* to command and the privilege of speaking first or last. In this sense, therefore, honor and leadership imply one another, for both are subject to the reality of power.

**Honor as a personal attribute.** Since honor is felt as well as demonstrated, it is allied to the conception of the self in the most intimate ways. It is a state of grace. It is liable to defilement. It is linked to the physical person in terms of the symbolic functions attached to the body: to the blood,

the heart, the hand, the head, and the genitalia. Honor is inherited through the "blood," and the shedding of blood has a specially honorific value in transactions of honor—the stains of honor, it was said, could be cleansed only by blood. The heart is the symbol of sincerity, since it is thought of—in the European tradition at least—as the seat of the intentions and therefore the home of the true self, which lies behind all worldly disguises. The right hand is the purveyor of honor: it touches; it shakes or is shaken; it is kissed or waved; it wins honor, for it wields the sword and pulls the trigger. The head is the representation of the self in social life, that by which a man is recognized, that which is placed in effigy on coins, and that which is touched in salute, crowned, covered or uncovered, bowed, or shorn. The private parts are the seat of shame, vulnerable to the public view and represented symbolically in the gestures and verbal expressions of desecration. In their association with the excretory function they are the source of pollution, yet as the means of procreation they are intimately connected with honor, for they signify the extension of the self in time. Sexual purity is, therefore, often regarded as the essence of honor in women, whose feminine status precludes their striving for it by might. The body as a whole is especially associated with honor, since physical contact implies intimacy and makes explicit the honorific relationship with another, whether to express attachment, obeisance, or contempt.

Because honor centers in the physical being, a person's presence bears a particular significance, as Simmel observed when he spoke of a sacred aura surrounding each individual. Whatever occurs in a person's presence obliges him to react in one way or another, positively or negatively, for he cannot hide his cognizance of it: he is inescapably a party to what he witnesses, and his will is thereby committed. This is important because the essence of the social person comprises his will and (as the moralists understood, though in a different context) his intentions. Hence, apologies for an affront normally take the form of denying the intention, thereby making the affront in a sense fortuitous because not willed. The true affront to honor must be intended as such. For the same reason oaths are binding only if freely sworn and, like the rites of the church, are invalid if devoid of good intention. The oath commits the honor of the swearer by guaranteeing his intentions, for it is not dishonoring to deceive another man, only to "break faith"— that is to say, to rescind an established commitment, for this implies cowardice. This is underlined by the mottoes of the aristocracy (so often devoted to the theme of steadfastness), the broken weapons which clutter up their arms, and the defiant invitations to fate to put them to the test.

This emphasis on intention or will marks an essential point: the essence of honor is personal autonomy. All men are bound by certain irrevocable ties, but the man of honor cannot otherwise *be* committed; he can only commit himself. To be forced by whatever circumstance to revoke his intentions once they are committed is to abnegate his personal autonomy. Thus, the concept of honor is tied to precedence, for to command over others enhances it, while obedience restricts it.

**Collective honor.**    The group possesses collective honor, in which the individual members participate. It affects their honor and is affected by their behavior. The honor of a collectivity is vested in its head and in symbolic representations; flags, crests, coats of arms, badges, uniforms, and all the insignia whereby members of the group are recognized are the objects of a greater or lesser degree of reverence and are treated as though they possess honor in themselves. In the anthropological language of an earlier generation, such objects have *mana*, a concept that also expresses the idea of honor when it is applied to individuals or to parts of their person.

While some types of groups are joined voluntarily and may be left in the same way (or may expel one of their number), membership in other groups is ascribed at birth. In the latter type of group, honor is bound up integrally, for the group defines a person's essential nature. The family (and in some societies the kin group) and the nation are the most fundamental of these collectivities, and thus traitors to their fathers or their sovereigns are the most execrable of all. (Parricide and regicide are sacrilegious but homicide is not.) The family is the repository of personal honor, for honor is hereditary, not merely in its aspect as social status but also with regard to the moral qualities which attach to it. Therefore, the dishonor cast on one member is felt by all.

Male and female honor are clearly differentiated with regard to conduct. A moral division of labor operates within the family, especially in the Latin countries: the aspect of honor as precedence becomes, according to this system of values, the prerogative of the male, while honor as sexual purity is restricted to the female. Hence, sexual conquest enhances the prestige of men; sexual liberty defiles the honor of women. (Congruently, a high value is attached to virginity in unmarried girls.) The defense of female purity, however, is a male responsibility, and men are therefore vulnerable to dishonor not through their own sexual misconduct but through that of their womenfolk—that is to say, members of the same nuclear family, including mother, wife, unmarried sister, and daughter. Hence, sexual insults that impugn the honor of men refer not to them but to their women.

The aspect of honor that is associated with social status descends preferentially in the male line —as hereditary titles, for example—but in its moral aspect a man's honor comes to him primarily from his mother, and further, his sister's honor reflects upon his through their mother. However, if a man inherits his honor in this way, he is, above all, actively responsible for the honor of his wife, and the cuckold (expressed in the Mediterranean by an analogy with the he-goat) is the paragon of dishonor, equal only, if in a different way, to the traitor. It should be noted that the cuckolder is exculpated: though he represents the cuckoo in the analogy on which the word is based, the title is reserved for the man whose marital right is usurped (and the same transposition is performed in the symbolism of the Mediterranean by endowing the wronged husband with the horns). Although the cuckolder may be thought immoral, he bears no stigma of dishonor. Once more dishonor goes to the defeated, and ridicule is visited on the defiled one rather than on the guilty. This code of honor is attenuated to the degree that women are regarded as independent of male authority.

**Honor and the sacred.**    The connection between honor and the sacred does not derive simply from the ambition of the church to stand as the arbiter of honor, a role that it has never entirely succeeded in achieving in the popular view, but rather from the sacred nature of honor itself, which, as the essence of the social personality and the personal destiny of the individual, stands in a preferential relation to the deity; a man's true self is known only to God, from whom nothing can be hidden and in whose eyes honor is ultimately vindicated. Honor is committed by invoking the sacred, whether in the form of a conditional curse witnessed by the spiritual powers or by implicating any other agency from which honor derives. The appeal to the sacred acts as a guarantee that the swearer will accept his shame under the prescribed circumstances. Hence, even in modern law courts oaths are required. The commitment of honor to the sovereign derives also from the fact that he stands, as divinely authorized ruler, in a preferential relationship to the Deity, a conception that has survived centuries of rebellion and even the passing of the monarchy altogether in many instances. Sacredness attaches to the notion of legitimate rule, regardless of the doctrine in which this is expressed. For this reason republics have tended to conserve the sanctifying rituals of the monarchies they superseded.

## Honor and social status

The distribution of honor in communities of equals, whether local groups or specialized institutions, tends to relate to eminence, recognized virtue, and age. However, in a stratified society it accords with social status, and as such, it is more often ascribed by birth than achieved. Thus, medieval society was ranked in terms of honor, from the aristocracy, who had the most—on account of their power, their valor, and their proximity to the king —to those who had none at all, the heretics and the outcasts, those who indulged in infamous occupations or had been convicted of infamy.

Honor is hereditary, as we have seen; the excellence that once brought honor to the forebears is credited to their offspring, even though it may no longer be discernible in their conduct. Titles and property, the honorific and effective forms of hereditary power, endow the social system with continuity in this regard; honor is ascribed. Yet, the supposition of excellence derived from birth is constantly betrayed, and a conflict therefore emerges between the criterion of prestige derived from personal worth and that which looks to social origins. This has provided one of the favorite themes of European literature from the twelfth-century *Poem of the Cid* onward, a theme which is matched in popularity only by its counterpart: the role of money rather than excellence in the acquisition of honor. The ideal unity of honor is apt to fragment when it strikes the facts, and the different bases for according it become opposed to one another.

Moreover, the criteria by which honor is bestowed have greatly varied in time: occupation and religious orthodoxy were once important, although they are no longer. With the evolution from a system of legal status to a class system, economic privileges ceased to be attached to status, and the contrary came to be true. In the modern world the criteria appear to be changing again: titles can no longer be purchased and wealth gives way to fame as the measure of reputation—a fact not unconnected with the development of the communications industry. The theater, which was once a dishonorable occupation, now presents candidates for the British sovereign's Honours List, which also finds a place for jockeys and football players.

The struggle for honor is palliated by a provision that saves society from anarchy. Indeed, this struggle is not only the basis upon which individuals compete but also that on which they cooperate.

Here the notion of steadfastness is crucial, whether it binds together those who recognize their mutual equality or those whose relationship is one of patron and client. The reciprocal demonstrations of favor, which might be called mutual honoring, establish relationships of solidarity. The notion of a community of honorable men replaces the competition for honor; reputation attaches to honesty, and the steadfastness that honor enjoins is seen in financial reliability and contractual faith—the "honoring" of a check or bond displays this sense. Honor then comes to be the guarantor of the credit system. This notion of honor was, in particular, the ideal of the Puritans, who attempted to suppress all its competitive and flamboyant aspects in favor of equating it to conscience (only to see them reemerge triumphant with the Restoration, whose literature pays more tribute to cuckoldry than that of any other period in the English language). The relation of the puritan ethic to capitalism, first stressed by Max Weber and R. H. Tawney, restricts competition to the field of wealth and, while giving financial probity a prime place in the notion of honor, makes financial success the arbiter of prestige. Under such conditions social status inevitably becomes increasingly an economic matter, to the exclusion of all other criteria.

Honor is always bound to wealth and possessions, for they provide an idiom in which to express relationships of relative inequality. Thus, hospitality, charity, and generosity are highly honorific; provided that they derive from free will, they gain honor as expressions of magnanimity. Beneficence transforms economic power into honor. However, honor is thus gained at the potential expense of the recipient. By doing someone a favor you humiliate him unless he may reciprocate. Hence comes the necessity for the return of hospitality and for accepting its return. The Northwest Coast Indians of America carried this principle to its limits in the potlatch, in which the demonstrations of largesse and the destruction of property were performed with the open intention of humiliating a rival. Through the challenge to reciprocate hospitality, they expressed their hostilities and, as they put it, "fought with property."

Honor is the backbone of the system of patronage. He who admits his inferiority and accepts patronage is not dishonored by attaching himself to a superior. On the contrary, his honor is enhanced by participating, through this attachment, in his patron's honor. The honor of a patron is equally enhanced by the possession of clients; he gains prestige in return for the protection that he affords to those who recognize his power. Honor accrues through being paid and is lost through being denied where it is due. By giving it away, you show that you have it; by striving for it, you imply that you need it. This is the meaning of magnanimity.

The struggle for honor takes place, therefore, only where precedence is both of value and in doubt. Competition for it has understandably been more acute in the higher reaches of society, where family pride and also the practical importance of precedence are greatest (this can be clearly seen, for example, in the descriptions of the French aristocracy in the memoirs of the duke of Saint-Simon). It must not, however, be thought that there is no competition for honor in plebeian communities. The agonistic quality of personal and kin-group relations in the villages of the Mediterranean is most striking, especially among pastoralists, whose unstable fortunes urge them to compete. This competition occurs, nonetheless, within a framework of moral values that public opinion upholds. The point of honor, whether among the aristocracies of former times or the modern Greek shepherds or Arab peasants, imposes a code for the distribution of honor that contains conflict within boundaries set by the ethical code of the community.

### The point of honor

In the courts of Renaissance Italy there arose a code of behavior which regulated the exchange of honor and the competition for it and whose ultimate sanction was the duel. This code spread, not without changes and adaptations, throughout Europe and America and persisted in many places into the twentieth century. A flow of published works four centuries long defined the modes and pretexts for taking offense, the formalities of challenge and the duel, and the circumstances in which honor could be judged to be lost or redeemed. A veritable jurisprudence of honor was elaborated, which makes explicit certain fundamental characteristics of the concept.

The point of honor, as this code of behavior was called, was confined to the upper class. The honor of a man could not be impugned by someone who was not a social equal—that is, someone with whom he could not compete without loss of dignity. The impudence or the infidelity of an inferior could be punished, but honor was not attained by reacting to the action of an inferior. Thus, honor was impregnable from below. Willingness to enter a duel depended upon the recognition of equality of class (but not of rank).

An affront depends upon being made public, for repute is lost only in the eyes of others. Hence, it was even sometimes maintained that no affront could be given in a purely private conversation. On the other hand, against public ridicule there is no recourse, since an affront must be performed individually to be resented by an individual. The act of resentment is always an individual responsibility; whether or not a man wishes to accept humiliation depends upon his own will. According to the code of honor, an insult could only be resented by the recipient himself, unless he were impeded from doing this because of age, sex, infirmity, or clerical status. Even then it could be resented only by a close kinsman—that is, one who participated in his honor. Briefly, the duel decided quarrels between individuals who competed for precedence and repute in the eyes of a public composed of their social equals. It was even at one time suggested that by destroying the honor of another man one might add to one's own, just as knights once added to their fame by their victories in single combat.

The affront placed honor in jeopardy, a state of threatened desecration from which it could only be saved by the demand for satisfaction. By showing his readiness to fight, a man restored his honor to a state of grace. Honor, however, was indifferent to the result of the duel, which demonstrated only the prowess of the victor and the choice of fate. The form of the act of resentment which constituted a challenge was the *mentita*, "giving the lie." Since deception was not in itself considered dishonorable behavior, it seems anomalous that the accusation of lying constituted the paramount indictment of honor. However, first of all, the accusation constituted a counterinsult and bound the man who delivered the original insult to issue the challenge, thereby permitting his antagonist to gain the choice of weapons. Yet, other than as a tactical device, this form of challenge relates to the obligation to tell the truth: one is under no obligation to tell it to an inferior; one owes it to a superior. (Children are required to tell the truth to adults, who feel no reciprocal duty.) To lie to an equal is an affront, since it represents an attempt to treat him as an inferior. On the other hand, lying could be interpreted as the subterfuge of one who lacked the courage to tell the truth or to act openly. The *mentita*, therefore, committed the response of the accused person, since failure to respond confirmed this implication of cowardice, while honorable response invalidated it at the cost of making manifest the intention to insult.

Failure to react to a slight was open to two conflicting interpretations. Either it implied cowardice and the acceptance of humiliation, which entailed the loss of honor, or it implied contempt, the denial that the author of the slight possessed sufficient honor to affront, that is, a denial of his equality. In the latter case the author, not the victim, of the slight was dishonored. Disregarding a slight could even be treated as magnanimity, on condition that the insulted person possessed the right to forgive or to overlook—that is to say, that he was indeed superior. On the other hand, to pick quarrels over nothing, to exploit the humiliation of others beyond the point that public opinion recognized as legitimate in order to establish precedence, was considered dishonorable, for it spelled lack of magnanimity. It was the court of public opinion that judicated between rival interpretations of the failure to react to a slight; in the last resort, a man was dishonored only at the point where he was forced to realize that he had been, where his shame was brought home to him. Those who possessed impregnable honor could afford not to compete for precedence, but to show those magnanimous qualities which are associated with it in the figurative senses of the words that denote high status: nobility, gentlemanliness, etc. Words which denote low status imply the contrary of magnanimity: meanness, villainy.

Although the point of honor was much criticized from the moral viewpoint, it provided a means of settling disputes. It did not permit the unbridled use of violence. Once satisfaction was accorded, the quarrel could not rightfully be taken up again. In this way it can be contrasted with the moral obligation to seek vengeance in order to redeem honor and with the state of feud that this commonly leads to. The point of honor was, therefore, a pseudolegal institution governing the sphere of social etiquette where the law was either not competent or not welcome.

### Honor and the law

The code of honor associated with the duel appeared in history at a time when the state was endeavoring to suppress private violence; dueling was made illegal, as well as condemned by the church, almost from its inception as a formalized mode of settling disputes. Yet, the duel was also, in some ways, a continuation of an earlier tradition. The right of knights to prove their worth in single combat was at one time inherent in the right to bear arms, and jousting provided a festive occasion on which to do so (though it finally developed into a sport). During the Middle Ages the private encounter was also recognized as a form of legal process. The judicial combat allowed for the settlement of disputes by remitting the decision to divine judgment; it was a form of ordeal.

With the development of the legal system and the increased centralization of power, sovereigns aspired to take the settlement of disputes out of the unpredictable hands of the Deity and submit it to the adjudication of courts. The courts, however, are ill-designed to fulfill the requirements of the man of honor, in that, first of all, they oblige him to place his jeopardized honor in the hands of others and thus prevent him from redeeming it for himself—the only way in which this can be done. The legal process involves delay (prejudicial to its state), expense (unwarranted for one who would settle accounts at once and for nothing), and publicity, which aggravates instead of mitigating the affront which is the cause of the dispute. Moreover, honor is not commutable into payment, so the compensation that courts impose offers no valid satisfaction. Finally, the settlement of a dispute in court excludes the possibility of demonstrating personal worth through the display of courage. The law has never, therefore, appealed to adherents to the code of honor, even where it has provided a means of redress against the kind of conduct that constitutes an affront. This it cannot easily do in any case, since it operates according to a different reasoning. Thus, although in all the countries of Europe legislation against dueling was passed repeatedly from the sixteenth century onward, the custom continued, with a large measure of connivance from the judicial authorities, until the twentieth century.

Although all the countries of Europe use the concept of honor in their ceremonial pronouncements, it is explicitly recognized only in the laws of the countries of southern Europe, where honor appears not only as a factor in the cultural background of court proceedings but also as a legal concept. In these countries the legal codes define the jural significance of honor. However, honor relates to conduct as a disculpating factor by making otherwise reprehensible behavior justifiable in terms of the legitimate motive which derives from the sense of honor. The right of a man to defend his honor is far more clearly recognized in the judicial procedures of southern European countries than in Anglo-Saxon law, which generally requires the demonstration of material damage for an affront to be actionable.

The constancy required by honor prefigures the law's demand for regularity; both establish a commitment upon the future. Nevertheless they differ in the way they commit the future, for honor demands fidelity to individuals, law to abstract principles. Therefore, where they exist together, they are liable to conflict, for one relates to persons and is centered in the will; the other aspires to reduce persons to legal categories, which involves attacking the fundamental principle of personal autonomy. The man of honor is a law, but a law unto himself. Wherever the authority of law is questioned or ignored, the code of honor re-emerges to allocate the right to precedence and dictate the principles of conduct: among aristocracies and criminal underworlds, schoolboy and street-corner societies, open frontiers and those closed communities where reigns "the Honorable Society," as the Mafia calls itself.

## Honor in literature

As we have seen, the different aspects of honor are liable to come into conflict with each other and to present individuals with an unenviable choice. This was the theme of the Spanish theater of the "Golden Century" in which concern for honor had become exacerbated. The dramatists presented this theme in the form of tragedy in an aristocratic setting while the novelists tended to treat it with comic satire in a plebeian context. Hence, the *teatro de honor* concerns such matters as marital honor, honor as precedence, honor as social status, civic virtue represented by plebeian honor, female purity, fidelity to the king, the duty to redeem honor by vengeance, the difficulty of hiding dishonor, and the power and perfidy of public opinion. The Spanish dramatists were, on the whole, critical of aristocratic honor and sometimes betrayed a reformatory intention, while the satires of the novelists frequently attacked the very notion of honor itself, contrasting it with the real power of money. The greatest and most savage satire on honor is assuredly the *Lazarillo de Tormes*, which antedates Falstaff's famous tirade by nearly half a century.

Every ruling power claims the right to distribute honor; to lay down the principles by which it is to be won is the essence of authority and the process of legitimation. Authority, like honor, is allied both to the sentiments and to the reality of social status and looks both to the possession of force and to popular consent, for authority is, as it were, the judicial aspect of honor, whose transactions and rituals set the seal of legitimacy upon the social order, making its commands appear necessary and right. The king can do no wrong. His word imposes consensus. Yet, if what is done in his name is unpopular, it does not escape criticism. His legitimacy is eventually brought into question. The frailty in authority qualifies its sacredness by exposing it to the danger that a counterconsensus will emerge to brand as infamous the fount of honor. The withdrawal of consent reveals the Achilles' heel of authority; the loss of respect foreshadows delegitimation.

Therefore, the polemics with regard to the nature of honor mirror the social conflicts of their age, for they reflect the interests of different groups and classes striving to impose their evaluations of behavior. The polemics both reflect and promote the struggle between these groups. The facts of power decide the moral arguments. Through its social function as a mediator, honor dictates the modes of allegiance that obtain throughout the social structure, and each particular notion of honor favors a certain faction. Hence, the aristocracy and the church adhered to quite different definitions of honor throughout the history of modern Europe. The new middle classes had a different notion of it, again, as Speier (1935) has pointed out. Different classes differ in their concepts of honor, and the concepts of rural communities differ from those of the city, though not always in accordance with that romanticized image of Arcadia which has stirred the literary imagination ever since Horace. A particular code of honor must be seen against its social background in order to be understood.

Modern urban society accords precedence largely on an economic basis. The independence of women has relieved men to some extent of their responsibility for them and, thus, of their vulnerability through them. The power of the law and the range of its competence have greatly increased, thus eliminating the possibility of winning honor through physical courage, save in certain sports and in war. The power of personal patronage has declined in favor of impersonal and institutional allegiances. The vocabulary of honor has acquired archaic overtones in modern English, yet the principles of honor remain, for they are not, like the particular conceptions in which they are manifested, the product of a given culture at a given time, but universal principles of social action that may be found clothed in the idiom of head-hunting, social refinement, financial acumen, religious purity, or civic merit. Whatever the form the principles of honor may take, they serve to relate the ideal values of a society to its social structure and to reconcile the world as its members would see it with the world as it is.

JULIAN PITT-RIVERS

### BIBLIOGRAPHY

ADKINS, ARTHUR W. H. 1960 "Honour" and "Punishment" in the Homeric Poems. London, University of, Institute of Classical Studies, *Bulletin* 7:23–32.

ASHLEY, ROBERT (c. 1600) 1947 *Of Honour.* Edited by Virgil B. Heltzel. San Marino, Calif.: Huntington Library.

BARBER, CHARLES L. 1957 *The Idea of Honour in the English Drama: 1591–1700.* Göteborg (Sweden): Elanders.

BRYSON, FREDERICK R.   1935   *The Point of Honor in Six-teenth-century Italy: An Aspect of the Life of the Gentleman.* New York: Columbia Univ.

CAMPBELL, JOHN K.   1964   *Honour, Family and Patron-age: A Study of Institutions and Moral Values in a Greek Mountain Community.* Oxford: Clarendon.

FARÈS, BISHR   1932   *L'honneur chez les Arabes avant l'Islam: Étude de sociologie.* Paris: Librairie d'Amé-rique et d'Orient.

HOOKER, TIMOTHY   1741   *An Essay on Honour: In Sev-eral Letters Lately Published in the* Miscellany. Lon-don: No publisher given.

JONES, G. F.   1959   *Honor in German Literature.* Chapel Hill: Univ. of North Carolina Press.

MENÉNDEZ PIDAL, RAMÓN   1957   Del honor en el teatro español. Volume 2, pages 357–371 in Ramón Menén-dez Pidal, *España y su historia.* Madrid: Ediciones Minotauro.

MONTESQUIEU   (1748) 1962   *The Spirit of the Laws.* 2 vols. New York: Hafner. → First published in French.

PERISTIANY, J. G.   1966   *Honour and Shame: The Values of Mediterranean Society.* Univ. of Chicago Press.

SPEIER, HANS   (1935) 1952   Honor and the Social Struc-ture. Pages 36–52 in Hans Speier, *Social Order and the Risks of War: Papers in Political Sociology.* New York: Stewart.

THIMM, CARL A.   1896   *A Complete Bibliography of Fenc-ing and Duelling, as Practiced by All European Na-tions From the Middle Ages to the Present Day.* London and New York: Lane.

WILSON, JOHN L.   (1838) 1858   *The Code of Honor: Or Rules for the Government of Principal and Seconds in Duelling.* Charleston, S.C.: Phinney.

# HOOTON, EARNEST A.

From 1913 until he died in 1954, Earnest Albert Hooton taught anthropology at Harvard. Born in Clemansville, Wisconsin, in 1887, he lived in a suc-cession of small towns in the state, moving from one to another as his father, a Methodist minister, received calls from various churches. His mother, of Scottish origin, remained in his memory as the decisive influence on his childhood.

An unathletic and bookish boy, young Hooton won distinction in school and was class valedic-torian at the age of 15, when he graduated from the Manitowoc High School. He was already an in-structor in anthropology at Harvard when he mar-ried Mary Camp in 1915.

Hooton was trained initially as a classicist at Lawrence College (B.A., 1907) and the University of Wisconsin (M.A., 1908; PH.D., 1911). While a graduate student he was awarded a Rhodes scholar-ship and spent three years at New College, Oxford. He was strongly influenced by the Oxford anthro-pologists, particularly R. R. Marett, whom he greatly admired; and it was probably an interlude of study with Sir Arthur Keith, the distinguished

British anatomist and student of human evolution, that bent his general interest in anthropology to a special concern with its physical or biological aspect.

Although Hooton never altogether lost his inter-est in cultural anthropology and for many years taught courses on European prehistory and African ethnology, he did become more and more involved with the problems presented by physical anthro-pology, the field with which his name is now prin-cipally associated.

He was perhaps the first in the United States to offer a systematic coverage of physical anthro-pology. During his lifetime Hooton's laboratory be-came the principal center in the United States for training specialists in physical anthropology, and as a result his students were established widely throughout the nation and even abroad. His suc-cess as a university lecturer, however, extended far beyond the corps of graduate students who worked closely with him. He possessed a witty, informal style that was extremely attractive and that drew large numbers of undergraduates and others to his courses.

Although it was Hooton's influence as a teacher that was especially noteworthy, it was his scientific and popular writing that made him known to a much wider circle than his professional activity alone could reach. His pungent and graceful style was notably successful in *Up From the Ape* (1931), in which he covered the traditional themes of physical anthropology: human evolution and the development of racial differentiation. In a similar vein he produced *Man's Poor Relations* (1942), which deals with the primate relatives of man; as well as *Apes, Men, and Morons* (1937), *Twilight of Man* (1939a), and *Why Men Behave Like Apes, and Vice Versa* (1940). In "Young Man, You Are Normal" (1945) he concerned himself with the dysgenic effects of modern society and the rela-tionship between body build and behavior. These books were written for the general reader and were widely distributed. They did much to introduce the subject matter of physical anthropology to a pub-lic unfamiliar with it. But because they were solidly written, several of them were quickly adopted as standard textbooks; *Up From the Ape*, for example, went into a number of editions.

Hooton's scientific writing embraced a wide variety of topics. He wrote on human evolution, developing among other ideas a concept of asym-metry in the morphological evolution of man. Origi-nally intended to account for the discrepancies in that now discredited fossil, the Piltdown skull, the principle of asymmetrical evolution has proven valid and useful. Instead of the widely held belief of that time that all segments of the body had evolved *pari passu*, Hooton envisioned an evolutionary process capable of producing apparent disharmonies by affecting one part more than another. This implied that the adaptive process is selective rather than necessarily general and total. He was a frequent contributor to discussions on the evolution of human dentition, a subject on which he also lectured at the Harvard Dental School.

The classification of human populations and their description was one of Hooton's abiding interests. Much of his work reveals a persistent concern with typology, exploring and refining the methods of analysis as well as the correlates of type. In his first major study, *The Ancient Inhabitants of the Canary Islands*, published in 1925, he had already come to grips with the problem. Influenced by Goring's applications of statistics to the analysis of a sampling of English convicts (1913) and by the voluminous contributions of Pearson to anthropometric data, he enthusiastically adapted these new mathematical tools to a relatively large series of prehistoric Guanche craniums and skeletons. By these statistical procedures he succeeded in identifying a number of coexistent physical types that he then attempted to derive from various related population groups in north Africa. On the basis of such type analyses and supported by archeological evidence he reconstructed a population history of the Canary Islands.

A similar orientation is clearly discernible in *The Indians of Pecos Pueblo* (1930) where, applying similar but more detailed methods of type analysis, he recognized a variety of distinct racial or subracial groups. Based on this typology, which was derived from the study of an Indian population in the Southwest, he reconstructed a tentative aboriginal history of the New World.

His interest in body build led him into the field of applied anthropology, in which he was a pioneer. He published studies on body build for use in designing furniture, and he carried out investigations for the government on other parameters of body build that were intended for guidance in selecting personnel for specialized functions. Later this interest was to involve him in problems of the association of body build with variations in behavior.

The attempt to isolate the various physical types in a random sample of a population was not original with Hooton. His colleague Dixon had embarked on a similar survey, and others had tried the same thing. But Hooton's distinction in this type of research was his far greater sophistication in statistical methods and his use of subjective sortings that were subsequently validated by mathematical tests. Type analysis, however, has not been very fruitful, since it assumes gene behavior that modern genetics does not support. In other words, type analysis implies that the various strains that compose a population somehow survive intact in the mixture of a breeding population; it does not take into account that some of the types defined may be artifacts of the mixture itself rather than survivals of original components.

For the remainder of his research career Hooton was primarily concerned with studies on living populations. During the 1930s he was mainly engaged in a very large-scale survey of the criminal population of the United States. In this study he sought to apply to a major social problem any insights to be derived from a racial and constitutional approach. But unlike the earlier researchers, he was primarily seeking to determine if relationships existed between body type and behavior, and, in this case, if criminal behavior or any of its varieties was linked with racial or physical criteria. His conclusion that such correlations did in fact exist recalled the work of Cesare Lombroso in the nineteenth century, which had long been repudiated. Hooton's investigations, however, were far more sophisticated and were free of the gross errors that had marred Lombroso's work. The reception of Hooton's results, published in *The American Criminal* (1939*b*) and in *Crime and the Man* (1939*c*), was negative on the whole. Some critics, in fact, were extremely harsh, attacking him primarily from the conviction that social behavior is determined more significantly by environmental factors than by biological ones. Nevertheless, when reexamined, his results cannot be summarily dismissed on such theoretical grounds. The questions raised by this monumental study have yet to be resolved, and Hooton's service in bringing them forward has not been fully appreciated.

His last researches were a natural outgrowth of the study of body build and crime, for he now turned to a broader application of these same theoretical principles. Using the principle of somatotype he investigated the association of varieties of temperament and behavior with body build in a carefully selected sample of Harvard students. He also followed the same procedures in analyzing large bodies of data derived from military sources. Much of this work has never been published.

Hooton was notable for his warmth and his ready responsiveness to people, his humor, and his acute perception. Among his other gifts he had a remarkable flair for light verse.

HARRY L. SHAPIRO

[For the historical context of Hooton's work, see PHYSI-
CAL ANTHROPOLOGY *and the biographies of* DIXON;
HRDLIČKA; MARETT.]

### WORKS BY HOOTON

1925    *The Ancient Inhabitants of the Canary Islands.* Harvard African Studies, Vol. 7. Cambridge, Mass.: Peabody Museum.

1930    *The Indians of Pecos Pueblo: A Study of Their
Skeletal Remains.* Phillips Academy, Andover, Mass.,
Papers of the Southwestern Expedition, No. 4. New
Haven: Yale Univ. Press.

(1931) 1947    *Up From the Ape.* Rev. ed. New York: Macmillan.

1937    *Apes, Men, and Morons.* New York: Putnam.

1939a    *Twilight of Man.* New York: Putnam.

1939b    *The American Criminal: An Anthropological
Study.* Volume 1: The Native White Criminal of Na-
tive Parentage. Cambridge, Mass.: Harvard Univ.
Press. → No other volumes were published.

1939c    *Crime and the Man.* Cambridge, Mass.: Harvard
Univ. Press.

1940    *Why Men Behave Like Apes, and Vice Versa: Or,
Body and Behavior.* Princeton Univ. Press.

1942    *Man's Poor Relations.* Garden City, N.Y.: Doubleday.

1945    *"Young Man, You Are Normal": Findings From a
Study of Students.* New York: Putnam.

### SUPPLEMENTARY BIBLIOGRAPHY

GORING, CHARLES B.    1913    *The English Convict: A Statistical Study.* London: H.M. Stationery Office.

# HORNEY, KAREN

The work of Karen Horney (1885–1952) influenced the course of development of psychoanalysis
decisively. Although her revisions of psychoanalytic
principles resemble those of Alfred Adler—which
has led some to label her as no more than an
updated Adlerian—she went well beyond his innovations to formulate a theory of psychopathology
that was at once more comprehensive in its scope
and more penetrating in its insights. Her ideas,
grounded in clinical experience, are almost totally
devoid of the dramatic speculation that frequently
marked the writings of the man she always acknowledged to be her indispensable forerunner,
Sigmund Freud.

Karl Abraham, Freud's student and close ad-
herent, supervised Horney's psychoanalytic training in Berlin. After completing her training in
1915, she spent five years in clinical and outpatient
work in Berlin hospitals and 12 years as instructor
at the Berlin Psychoanalytic Institute, supplementing her work with private practice. In 1932
Franz Alexander invited her to become associate
director of the Chicago Institute for Psychoanalysis; two years later she moved to New York to
pursue her own practice. Her dissatisfaction with
orthodox psychoanalytic theory is stated most ex-

plicitly in *New Ways in Psychoanalysis* (1939).
This was such a thoroughgoing critique of the
rigidities of Freudian doctrine that it placed her
in the forefront of that wing of psychoanalysis
which has since become known as the Neo-
Freudian movement.

**Critique of orthodox Freudianism.** Horney
took exception to several components of Freud's
system. The feature she found most objectionable
was the libido theory. She could not accept the
notion that an allegedly somatic, yet imperceptible, source of erotic instinctual energy called
libido could account not only for individual personality traits and individual behavior but also for
the character development of a lifetime. She
thought that this theory made most human relationships exclusively sexual relationships; that it
explained adult behavior as a mere repetition of
the experiences of infancy, to the virtual neglect
of the influence of later experiences; that it made
fixed and ineradicable instincts the controlling
forces of human destiny. Horney deplored the
psychic determinism Freud's libido theory inflicted
on psychology, as well as the excessive orientation
of that psychology toward biology and anatomy.
Thus, Freudian, or orthodox, psychoanalysis gave
the Oedipus complex a strictly sexual interpretation—that is, the child's relationships with his
parents, later transferred to others, are to be understood as symbolic of sexual desires and frustrations
—while Horney's clinical experience led her to
claim that this did not correspond to the facts of
psychopathology. Again, Horney disagreed with the
orthodox view that deprived the ego of its directive
and discretionary role, reducing it to a sentinel
eternally on guard against instinctual excesses and
dependent on the id (representing instincts) or
the superego (representing conscience) or objective reality for its activation and purpose. Finally,
orthodox psychoanalysis considered man to be
doomed by the "death instinct" to destructive impulses which must be turned against others if he
is to avoid self-destruction; Horney countered that
the prevalence of destructiveness or hostility did
not prove its instinctual nature and that hostility
might be an appropriate reaction to a provoking
social environment. These and other of Horney's
objections amounted to a revision of accepted
psychoanalytic principles and led, in 1941, to her
disqualification as training analyst by the New
York Psychoanalytic Institute and an abrupt severance from the New York Psychoanalytic Society.
Independence, however, brought the opportunity
to found the Association for the Advancement of
Psychoanalysis, whose very name indicates her

insistence on pushing forward the frontiers of the still young science.

**Anxiety.** Crucial to Horney's thought is the concept of anxiety. Conditions of life in infancy may generate a basic anxiety in which the child feels himself helpless and isolated in the face of a world conceived of as hostile and as jeopardizing his safety and security. The sources of all anxiety are to be found in interpersonal relations, chiefly those encountered in early family life, but at all events those resulting from the culture in which one lives. The unconsciously developed neurotic trends in personality—trends which enable the individual to cope with a demoralizing array of conflicting values presented to him by the patterns of his culture—assume a compulsory character, deflecting him from bringing his real self to maturity and substituting the vain pursuit of fantastic and unrealizable images of himself.

Contemporary Western society's contradictory demands of success (obtaining power) versus love (obtaining affection), of the arousal of desires versus their frustration, and of individual freedom versus the limitations imposed on freedom by reality, produce, as Horney described vividly in all her writings, an almost incredible variety of neurotic behavior patterns. The value given to individualistic achievement makes competition pervasive and leaves a heritage of isolation, fear, insecurity, hostility, and anxiety, which continually undermines self-esteem. The experience of the inadequacy and falsity of love is especially likely to turn healthy affection into neurotic defensive patterns. Clearly, the etiology of neuroses must be referred not to instincts and their vicissitudes, but to interpersonal relations and cultural exigencies. Psychoanalysis must become more a social than a medical science, Horney implied, and so make itself available as a basis for social and economic reform. The writings of her closest colleagues, Harry Stack Sullivan and Erich Fromm, point in the same direction; the three comprised the nucleus of the Neo-Freudian school of psychoanalysis, with Sullivan developing the concept of anxiety and its roots in interpersonal relations and Fromm exploring the deficiencies and incongruities in modern capitalist society that make it what he considers an insane society.

**Alienation.** The concept of anxiety enabled Horney to connect psychopathology with culture, thereby giving her work the dimension of a social philosophy. The concept of alienation, prominent in her later writings, coupled with that of conflict, strengthened the connection of psychopathology

with the inner dimension, the psyche, which some critics hold to be the true, if not the exclusive, concern of psychoanalytic psychology. Alienation refers to a condition in which the individual is divorced from his real self, a condition in which not only his standards and values but also his capacities for judgment, initiative, and self-direction, his very feelings and thoughts, are imputed to a false image of himself which he manufactures unconsciously to allay his basic anxiety. His psychic energies are diverted to the realization of this phantom ideal of himself, which is happily free of conflicting neurotic trends, while his real self comes to be regarded as an indwelling stranger who is to be hated and repressed. An internal numbness to genuine feelings, compounded into a loss of identity, supplants the vital dynamism of psychic development. Concealed from awareness are conflicts among neurotic trends, such as compliance, aggressiveness, and detachment, or the central inner conflict between the idealized image and the real self, whose healthy trend is to strive for its unfettered growth. As Horney's conception of neurosis matured, she saw neurosis not simply as a conflict among neurotic trends but as a process, culminating in alienation, in which these neurotic trends are pitted against healthy ones.

With her unusual insight into psychic malfunctioning, Horney saw that a neurosis, far from being a temporary maladjustment, has a dynamism of its own: it dominates the whole personality and becomes a way of life. The conditions of life in contemporary Western society, as often as not, compel the individual to relinquish his true identity if he is to survive and have any identity at all, to maintain an inferior type of psychic activity rather than undergo a total breakdown. Neurosis, in other words, has become virtually equivalent to "normality," by virtue of social conditions largely beyond individual control. But if mental illness has become a way of life, mental health may be attained not so much by sponsoring a crusade for social reform as by a reintegration of personality that enables each person to rely on his own inner capacities for psychic development. For therapeutic purposes, having satisfactory interpersonal relations in general takes second place to resolving intrapsychic conflicts by intensive self-analysis. Ultimately, psychoanalysis had for Horney more of a clinical than a political application, so that, surprisingly enough, this most outspoken of rebels against the conservatism of orthodox Freudian psychoanalysis in the end accepted its more conventional uses in psychotherapy.

**Psychic growth.**  Implicit in the foregoing is the idea of psychic growth, the postulate that under favorable circumstances—notably interpersonal relations featuring warmth and cordiality—the real self emerges, stabilizes, and develops; that is, the latent potentialities for constructive change in the personality are able to bring about a condition of inner freedom, unity, happiness, and self-direction that for want of a better term may be called normality. In a world where normality is an ambiguous standard, Horney believed that this tendency toward psychic growth provides the most nearly absolute criterion for human values. It is a morality of evolution, as she called it, an evolution of human personality whose *terminus ad quem*, however, can neither be prescribed uniformly for all people nor specified for any single individual. If, as critics charged, psychic growth provides a nebulous standard for ethics and if, as was also charged, it gives psychoanalysis an unwarranted—meaning unwonted—optimistic bias, Horney could retort to the first charge that a preconceived notion of what is good or bad presumes a universality of cultural norms that is contrary to fact, and to the second that clinical experience confirmed repeatedly the existence of a drive toward mental health making possible the liberation of developmental forces in the personality. Without it, psychoanalytic therapy itself could not proceed.

**Psychotherapy.**  Horney was led by both theory and practice to revise the principles of psychoanalytic therapy. A return to mental health involves more than bringing unconscious conflicts to the level of consciousness and more than the removal of overt symptoms, as Freud had thought. Since every neurosis is a disorder of personality, she held, therapy requires the reorganization of personality and the analysis of the entire structure of the neurosis and the current conditions necessitating it. While this idea also stems from the earlier work of Franz Alexander, Horney made it the linchpin of her innovations in therapy. Psychotherapy that proceeded by seeking a direct causal connection between infantile experiences and the present neurosis, on the assumption that the neurosis is an elaborate repetition of early instinctual life, tended to neglect the function performed by anxiety and neurotic trends in the current psychic situation, as well as the ramifications of the neurosis in all facets of the patient's daily life. Horney sought to return the individual to his own spontaneous self-direction and cognizance, free of the grip of neurotic trends and idealized illusions, by developing his emotional self-awareness as well as

by rational or intellectual introspection. The interaction between patient and analyst, known technically as transference, also received a significant modification in Horney's hands. Since it is but one type of interpersonal relation, and since all interpersonal relations involve feelings, the inevitable emotional confrontation of analyst and patient should not be avoided by constructing a façade of professional impersonality, as recommended by Freud, but should be used to obtain a more intimate understanding of the pervasive character of the neurosis. Love, hostility, defiance, pride, self-accusation, and so forth, permeate the analytic session; under the guidance of an alert and sensitive analyst they can be studied intensively and fruitfully. Horney accepted, without appreciable modification, free association and the interpretation of dreams and parapraxes, the other conventional tools of psychoanalysis.

**Feminine psychology.**  Not the least of Horney's contributions to a revised psychoanalysis was her reappraisal of feminine psychology. Unwilling to accept Freud's opinion of it as an offshoot of masculine psychology, an accidental, inferior, and necessarily warped by-product of women's genital differences from men, Horney argued that Freud had ignored the impact of cultural conditions on the psychic orientation of women. In a predominantly masculine culture women are deprived of considerable conjugal and maternal fulfillment by the undervaluing of love, and consequently they have neurotic problems peculiar to their sex. More than anything else, this protest against Freud's negative attitude toward women and their psychology seems to have been responsible for driving Horney from the Freudian fold and for giving her thought its characteristic turn. If women could and should have lives of their own, once the distorting pressures of culture were relaxed, by the same token other culture-produced neuroses might be eliminated, by reducing cultural pressures.

The goal of mental health and growth during a lifetime of psychic integrity and independence persisted in Horney's thought and received ever more resonant expression in her writings. To the blasé and world-weary generation of the 1920s her affirmation of positive and humanistic values was refreshing. The years of economic hardship and international tension that followed created an audience for her writings that responded to her sympathetic understanding of its plight. She gave a renewed impulse to the psychoanalytic movement and by her rebellion reaffirmed the principle of scientific inquiry free of the confines of dogma. The value of her work will be estimated in terms of the reduction of human suffering and the expansion of human living that it made possible.

MARTIN BIRNBACH

[*For the historical context of Horney's work, see* PSYCHOANALYSIS *and the biographies of* ABRAHAM; ADLER; ALEXANDER; FREUD. *Directly related are* ANXIETY; NEUROSIS; *and the biography of* SULLIVAN.]

WORKS BY HORNEY

1937  *The Neurotic Personality of Our Time.* New York: Norton.
1939  *New Ways in Psychoanalysis.* New York: Norton.
1942  *Self-analysis.* New York: Norton.
1945  *Our Inner Conflicts: A Constructive Theory of Neurosis.* New York: Norton.
1950  *Neurosis and Human Growth.* New York: Norton.

SUPPLEMENTARY BIBLIOGRAPHY

ALEXANDER, FRANZ  1940  Psychoanalysis Revised. *Psychoanalytic Quarterly* 9:1–36.
BIRNBACH, MARTIN  1961  *Neo-Freudian Social Philosophy.* Stanford (Calif.) Univ. Press.
Karen Horney Memorial Issue.  1954  *American Journal of Psychoanalysis* 14:5–133.
PORTNOY, ISIDORE  1951  [Review of] *Neurosis and Human Growth. American Journal of Psychoanalysis* 11:63–71.
ROBBINS, IRVING  1958  An Analysis of Horney's Concept of the Real Self. *Educational Theory* 8:162–168.
THOMPSON, CLARA  (1950) 1957  *Psychoanalysis: Evolution and Development.* New York: Grove.
WEISS, FREDERICK A.  1954  Karen Horney: Her Early Papers. *American Journal of Psychoanalysis* 14:55–64.

# HORTICULTURE

*See* AGRICULTURE.

# HOSPITALS

*See* ILLNESS; MEDICAL CARE; MEDICAL PERSONNEL; MENTAL DISORDERS, TREATMENT OF, *article on* THE THERAPEUTIC COMMUNITY.

# HOURS OF WORK

*See under* LABOR FORCE.

# HOUSING

I. SOCIAL ASPECTS            *John Madge*
II. ECONOMIC ASPECTS         *Sherman J. Maisel*

## I
### SOCIAL ASPECTS

Although it varies according to climatic differences, housing constitutes one of the most universal forms of material culture, being found in all except nomadic societies. Housing also represents an important element in all capital formation and the largest single component in the total building effort of any nation. From a sociological point of view, housing has a major part to play in ensuring continuity of community life.

There is also a close interrelationship between housing and family organization. In all cultures and at all times the type of housing has corresponded in some way to the organization of the family and has in turn sustained and reinforced existing forms of family organization. In many parts of the world, the extended family system is reflected in various clusters of rooms within which there are sections reserved for the basic units. The long house, for example, is found in a variety of cultures, from the Iroquois of North America to the peoples of southeast Asia; while the polygamous family structure still found in many parts of Africa requires a complex of huts, one for the husband and one for each wife and her children, arranged in order of rank.

The home is a ménage for production as well as for consumption and may therefore also reflect features of economic organization; for example, in the eighteenth-century wool centers in England many cottages included an upstairs room in which family members worked, and rural cottages everywhere tend to confuse the housing of humans and of livestock. The greater systematization of modern Western life has eliminated most of this form of provision, at least in urban communities; but new dwellings may still incorporate doctors' offices, artists' studios, or scholars' libraries, and new shops still often include living accommodations for owner or manager.

**Control of house building.**  Until the nineteenth century there were few specialist builders, and in most cases members of the family unit built their own houses. This is still the case in many parts of the world, with the result that there is a close correspondence between the dwellings built and the way of life of those who build them. However, in more industrialized societies this identity of aim is easily lost. Indeed there are typically three parties to the house-building operation: the builder and his workmen, the owner or entrepreneur who commissions the dwelling, and the family that will in due course occupy it. The situation is further complicated by the fact that in many cases the new development will be associated with the migration of families into towns, a move which in any case requires them to urbanize their way of life and may involve renouncing the extended family or tribal system to which they had previously been accustomed.

Where an entrepreneur or landlord places himself between the occupier and the designer and builder, it is inevitable that the housing type will to some extent be imposed on the occupier. The motives of a landlord can vary considerably; but whatever they may be, his control of the means and nature of house provision is very powerful.

Although public authority housing takes an important and increasing share in the total building effort of most industrialized countries, the share of the private landlord is declining even faster and is being largely replaced by a growth in owner occupancy. Even in the socialist countries of eastern Europe, an important proportion of new house building is being undertaken privately. But the number of custom-built houses in such cases is relatively small, and most owner-occupiers move into houses that were, for all practical purposes, designed without consulting them. If there is a greater correspondence in the private sector between design and family needs, it is because the unsuitable houses prove more difficult to sell and their design is therefore not repeated; such houses, however, will not be destroyed but will merely be passed down to a householder who is less able to pay for what he wants.

**Trends in housing standards.** In every industrialized and industrializing country in the world there is an acute shortage of urban dwellings, and a substantial proportion of the world's population is living in severely substandard housing: slums that have survived the uncontrolled building of the nineteenth century or shacks that reflect the uncontrolled urbanization of the twentieth century. But in spite of overcrowding and the physical decay of buildings, it is often difficult to demonstrate that bad housing is directly responsible for bad physical health; although bad health is often associated with bad housing, this is because both of these are generally secondary effects of poverty (Schorr 1964, pp. 6–7, 143–145).

*Space standards.* There is clearer evidence that inadequate space standards can disorganize family life. The current expert consensus in European countries is that the lower limit for mental health is 170 square feet of floor area per person (Chombart de Lauwe 1955; Musil 1962), and the desirable standards established by the American Public Health Association (1950) are twice the above figures. But these represent standards for new construction; and many European and North American families probably have a current space stand-ard of less than 80 square feet per person, while it is certain that families are to be found in Latin America, Africa, and Asia with less than 20 square feet of floor area per person.

There is also evidence that an equally important criterion is the number of rooms in the dwelling. A careful survey by Loring (1956), using paired groups of "well adapted" and "disorganized" families, showed that significant differences were associated with number of rooms available, floor area, and general surroundings, but not with other supposedly significant factors such as possession of a bath or the physical condition of the dwelling.

In spite of the gigantic backlog of substandard housing, it is expected that new construction will continue to improve its minimum standards of equipment and space. In Britain during the past sixty years, the recommended minimum space standard has increased by about 40 per cent (or 50 square feet per person), and it is believed that the increase may have been greater in most other industrialized societies, which started from a lower base. On the basis of a sustained 3.5 per cent annual growth in productivity, it seems very possible that the minimum standard of new housing will double in the next forty years; even if space standards increase at only half this rate, a standard for new construction of 250 square feet of floor area per person would then be commonplace by the early twenty-first century.

## The family and the home

In affluent countries, the rise of general space standards to the level previously reserved for middle-class homes has coincided with, and may have helped to stimulate, the growth of individuation in the home. Whereas in the traditional working-class home family life was lived collectively in the "living-kitchen," today there is more stress on individual privacy and a greater tendency for members of the family to follow their own pursuits. There is a consequent trend toward the use of study-bedrooms and a greater willingness to recognize the distinctive needs of children in the home.

At the same time, new dwellings continue to play a substantial part in bringing about changes in family organization. This is illustrated particularly vividly in the context of urbanization. In eastern Europe, for example, there is a traditional type of peasant cottage consisting essentially of two rooms: the white room, which contains all the most valued family possessions and also acts as a store for grain and other nonperishable food; and the black room, which is used for all normal household purposes and includes niches for sleeping. Comparable arrangements are found in most other rural economies in Europe. Obviously such a subdivision is not appropriate or even possible in a multistory apartment building; the application of urban behavior standards requires more individual privacy, for example, for sleeping, but also requires less space for food storage and for other functions around which the traditional rural home rotates.

The urban wife is increasingly employed outside the home, and the development of substitutes for household tasks—launderettes, partly prepared foods, ironing and mending services—is proceeding rapidly alongside industrialization. Meal-taking is unlikely to disappear from the home, but the habit of taking some meals in company cafeterias and in restaurants is likely to grow. The care of children will probably be increasingly shared between the family and the social and educational agencies, and there may even be an increase in the use of boarding schools (cf. Musil 1962, p. 555). This should not, however, be interpreted as indicating a reduction in the space requirements in the home. It is regarded as important for family cohesion that the child should feel a member of the household even when absent; few authorities anticipate a widespread adoption of the deliberate segregation of parents and children practiced in many Israeli kibbutzim.

It is anticipated that a decreasing proportion of households will contain three generations; if present trends continue, more separate accommodations will be provided for elderly couples and single or widowed old people. There will probably be a concurrent increase in the number of young people living alone or with their peers. The net result of these and other changes will probably be that the proportion of households consisting solely of parents and dependent children will further increase.

### The ecology of housing

In preindustrial countries, the majority still live in rural settlements, which have in most cases developed a close internal communication network commensurate with their internal social cohesion. With industrialization and the accompanying urbanization, the traditional close-knit integrated community is increasingly replaced by a pluralistic type of community comprising a number of subcultures, at once interlocking and independent of each other. To a considerable extent the ecology of the community will reflect these divisions among its population.

**Invasion and succession.** The ecological theories and studies of the early Chicago school were

to a large extent concerned with what classes of people occupied different zones of the city (for example, Zorbaugh 1929). Similarly the ecological principles of *invasion* and *succession* were applied by these authors to the successive waves of occupants that passed through old existing stocks of houses. That succession took place at all is a reflection of the durability of houses, which so regularly outlive their original purpose, so that mansions originally built for wealthy families and their servants survive in multiple family occupation or as small hotels and rooming houses.

As has been stated, the main tendency in industrialized countries in the past fifty years has been the convergence in space and other standards of middle- and lower-class houses. Particularly in town centers, the relatively small row houses built for lower-class families three or more generations ago are coming within the size range of the urban middle-class family; and if they survive the hazard of urban renewal they are liable to experience "succession in reverse," reappearing with brightly painted doors as bijou residences for those who can afford to buy out their less affluent lower-class occupants. Even in the United States, with its tendency to tear down and replace, succession is now sometimes a two-way process.

*Slums and ghettos.* One of the forms of succession that has been most documented and studied, particularly in the United States, has been the process by which immigrants or visible races such as Negroes have been forcibly segregated into slum-ghettos. This has come about because earlier inhabitants have typically first resisted invasion and then fled, leaving the newcomers in possession. Housing for nonwhites and for underprivileged immigrants is generally substandard in space, amenities, and repair; out-of-bounds for mortgage investment or other private financing; overpriced for what it is; and underprovided with public and social services (Abrams 1955, pp. 74–75).

Areas with the above characteristics are not inevitably turned into ghettos. Slums and substandard areas occur in almost all cities of any size, particularly if the population is growing. If obsolescent housing ripe for slum formation does not already exist, shacks are often built on the perimeter of the town to act as a substitute. This type of development is resisted by civic authorities with varying vigor and success.

**Urban renewal and relocation.** Unlike perimeter shack development, substandard areas are often well located near the city center, and some offer tempting possibilities for urban renewal. The extent to which this situation has been exploited for private gain has varied greatly, but there have been notorious examples in American cities and elsewhere in which whole neighborhoods of underprivileged families have been displaced in favor of luxury apartment buildings, creating even greater pressures on surviving slums. Until comparatively recently the net effect of urban renewal has probably been to increase the amount of segregation; and while, by the mid-1960s (except in countries such as the Republic of South Africa, which retained a philosophy of segregation) there appeared to be a tide toward integration and interracial housing, it seems probable that the general trend toward social stratification and class division is being accentuated.

Whether urban renewal reduces or increases the problem of the slums, it is commonly believed that its net effect is to harm the community spirit of the long-established neighborhoods. Young and Willmott (1957) and Gans (1962) have argued that relocation programs almost inevitably break up the cohesion provided by the kinship network, while Jacobs (1961) has stressed the inhumanity and monotony of many renewal projects. In discussing older neighborhoods, it is necessary to distinguish clearly between those sections containing a fluid, disorganized, and often no-family population, and those sections containing close-knit but poor families, often recent immigrants or otherwise underprivileged.

The success of relocation largely depends on how it is administered. The "melting-pot" theory, based on the idea that slum dwellers can be "reformed" by placing them in a project where they will be influenced by respectable neighbors, can produce a calamitous and quite unnecessary destruction of social cohesion and lead to loneliness, anxiety, and temporary neurosis. For all families that move there is a painful period of adjustment which is only bearable if the move was wanted and if established neighbors are welcoming. It has been shown (for example, by Festinger et al. 1950) that friendships can depend on physical layout and that satisfaction and morale in the neighborhood are maximized if the layout as well as the social climate encourage interaction. European research workers (for example, Kuper 1953) support this thesis but tend to set more store on the need for the individual to be able to select and regulate the extent of his interactions.

**Suburban development.** Whatever the density of redevelopment, a normal result of renewal is an increment of pressure on suburban housing. Even without these pressures, improvements in transport and communications are rapidly increasing the range and popularity of the commuter areas around cities [see TRANSPORTATION, *article on* COMMUTATION]. It is in the most urbanized and industrialized countries that the suburban belt is most clearly in evidence. The original "new towns," although planned as communities and occupationally more or less self-sufficient, have so far reflected in a more organized way the same demographic tendencies as have elsewhere led to peripheral suburban development. Their populations are generally to a large extent self-selected and consist mainly of upwardly mobile middle-class families. It has been claimed (for example, by Whyte 1956) that such families have developed a new interactive way of life that leaves little room for permanence or privacy, but more recent studies (Berger 1960; Dobriner 1963) have shown that new communities set up under different circumstances can develop along more traditional working-class lines.

Beyond the city suburbs and the "green belts" there is a still newer wave of community development. This may have started with the quest for exclusiveness of upper-class "exurbanites," but emancipation by automobile has brought whole counties into range, and the sprawl of an even looser suburbanism lacking either physical or social focus is extending every year. This type of development is occurring throughout the Western world in all regions of relatively high density, and it has so far overwhelmed the resistances of even the most assiduous planners. In the more industrialized counties it is becoming difficult to find a genuine rural village. The old types of social activity that generations of country dwellers have gradually built up are largely inappropriate, and the older rural institutions are unable, if not unwilling, to adapt to the new pattern of social demand.

### Status attributes of housing

In spite of the convergence of social class characteristics, there are distinctive class differences in ideology and behavior that transcend differences in wealth and can be readily detected by objective comparisons. The two main differences between middle-class and working-class ideologies that are reflected in their homes are the former's greater stress on individualism, which requires a home that gives some scope for privacy and self-expression to every member of the household, and the latter's greater stress on saving and repairing as opposed to spending and discarding, which requires greater provision for storage of possessions. The middle-class home is also used for more or less discreet displays of "conspicuous consumption." These early insights, including those of Veblen (1899) and the

Lynds (1929), were followed by the systematic attempts of Warner and Lunt (1941), Chapin (1947), Guttman (1942), and others to construct a scale of social status. In spite of various anomalies, it is clear that the importance of space and material possessions to the individual family, and the state of repair in which the home is kept, can quite properly be used as one component in the perennial search for an objective index of social class.

There is naturally a general correlation between the type of house and the neighborhood, both because of the tendency toward uniformity of standards in any particular section and also because of the physical fact that adjacent dwellings will often have about the same date of construction. As a general rule, the location of a home is likely to be even more revealing of the social status of a family than the type of house and its contents. In the United States a large number of ecological reports have been prepared since the early 1930s, with the help of the census tract data provided by the Bureau of the Census, showing social class and other related characteristics of cities and city neighborhoods all over the country. Similar information is becoming available in Britain and elsewhere and is being used for sophisticated forms of ecological analysis.

## Social policy

On a world view, very great variations are to be found in the extent to which different governments take responsibility for housing their populations. Some intervention is found necessary wherever urbanization is occurring, if only in order to prevent the outbreak of epidemics and other illnesses caused by unsanitary and overcrowded conditions. Furthermore, if the government is promoting industrial development, it will be under pressure to provide, or stimulate the building of, workers' housing within reach of the new plant; the incentive of good housing is an important lever in attracting suitable families into the towns from rural areas. In addition to these motives of enlightened self-interest, governments may also be impelled on grounds of social welfare to make provision for their less privileged citizens, for example, by producing houses for special groups such as old people, by creating new interracial neighborhoods, or by subsidizing the provision of new houses in order to raise housing standards.

Historically, the provision of housing for special groups in industrialized countries has been one of the responsibilities assumed by private charities. As still occasionally happens, the close-knit industrial and professional groups looked after the housing needs of the less privileged of their members' or ex-members' families. Other more general private charities in a great variety of countries have built almshouses and continue to build and maintain housing projects for low-cost rentals. In the nineteenth century money for these purposes was raised in Great Britain from so-called "five per cent philanthropists," who were willing to loan money for a return at less than the current rate of interest so that these projects could be financed.

**Subsidized housing.** It is only in the last fifty years that the burden of subsidizing the housing of the poor has been partly assumed by the state and the city authorities. Even today there are some industrialized countries in which the public provision of housing is negligible. The outstanding example is the United States, where new public housing represents only 3 or 4 per cent of new permanent starts (U.S. Bureau of the Census, as quoted in Van den Broek 1964), so that the total share of public housing is probably now only 1 or 2 per cent. Some states have even passed legislation containing clauses that effectively prevent any additional provision of public housing (in 1966 the constitutionality of such clauses was being tested in the courts).

In the United States and in other countries with similar policies, very substantial public funds are invested in the housing program; but they are used not as a form of social service but to help citizens to buy their own houses. This policy is intended to benefit those most able to help themselves; the assumption is that the houses thus vacated will become available for poorer families and that a general reshuffling will take place so that virtually all sections of the community may benefit.

In spite of the great divergence in philosophy between this kind of assisted self-help and the welfare-state policies now being implemented over much of the globe, the difference in *practice* has been far less striking. Governments have generally shied away from making direct provision by building new houses for the poorest families. This follows the experience of the private philanthropists that it is unattractively expensive to subsidize new housing to the point at which really poor families can afford the rents.

Even in countries with a relatively low economic growth rate, much of the current demand for housing at any date is from newly married couples and from upwardly (and, in the case of the urban population, outwardly) mobile families, and the provision of new housing is predominantly attuned to their needs. It is only in cities undertaking a vigorous urban renewal and slum-clearance program that a substantial number of really poor families are displaced and forced to seek new homes. Even with generous subsidies many of these underprivileged families find the new rents too high and tend to gravitate back to the remaining slums, thereby further overcrowding these areas.

There is by now a fair understanding in some countries of human needs in housing and also of the means by which these needs can be satisfied. This will have to be extended to other areas and also kept up to date as new housing forms are developed. What is now needed in addition is a fuller knowledge of what conditions are most favorable to satisfactory social organization and, in particular, what types of social planning should accompany the massive relocation and urban renewal programs that we shall have to undertake in the coming years. In other words, the balance of effort should swing from static to dynamic studies, from social investigation toward participation and social action.

JOHN MADGE

[*See also* PLANNING, SOCIAL, *articles on* REGIONAL AND URBAN PLANNING *and* WELFARE PLANNING; SEGREGATION.]

## BIBLIOGRAPHY

ABRAMS, CHARLES 1955 *Forbidden Neighbors: A Study of Prejudice in Housing.* New York: Harper.

AMERICAN PUBLIC HEALTH ASSOCIATION, COMMITTEE ON THE HYGIENE OF HOUSING 1950 *Planning the Home for Occupancy.* Chicago: Public Administration Service.

BERGER, BENNETT M. 1960 *Working-class Suburb: A Study of Auto Workers in Suburbia.* Berkeley: Univ. of California Press.

CHAPIN, FRANCIS S. (1947) 1955 *Experimental Designs in Sociological Research.* Rev. ed. New York: Harper.

CHOMBART DE LAUWE, P. H. 1955 Le logement, le ménage et l'espace familial. *Informations sociales* 9:956–980.

DOBRINER, WILLIAM M. 1963 *Class in Suburbia.* Englewood Cliffs, N.J.: Prentice-Hall.

FESTINGER, LEON; SCHACHTER, STANLEY; and BACK, KURT (1950) 1963 *Social Pressures in Informal Groups: A Study of Human Factors in Housing.* Stanford Univ. Press.

GANS, HERBERT J. 1962 *The Urban Villagers: Group and Class in the Life of Italian-Americans.* New York: Free Press.

GUTTMAN, LOUIS 1942 A Revision of Chapin's Social Status Scale. *American Sociological Review* 7:362–369.

JACOBS, JANE 1961 *The Death and Life of Great American Cities.* New York: Random House. → A paperback edition was published in 1962 by Random House and by Cape.

KUPER, LEO (editor) 1953 *Living in Towns.* London: Cresset.

LORING, WILLIAM C. JR. 1956 Housing Characteristics and Social Disorganization. *Social Problems* 3:160–168.

LYND, ROBERT S.; and LYND, HELEN M. (1929) 1930 *Middletown.* New York: Harcourt. → A paperback edition was published in 1959.

MUSIL, JIŘI 1962 The Sociological Approach in Planning Workers' Housing: The Experience of Czechoslovakia. *International Labour Review* 86:545–566.

SCHORR, ALVIN L. 1964 *Slums and Social Insecurity.* London: Nelson.

VAN DEN BROEK, J. H. (editor) 1964 *Habitation.* 3 vols. Amsterdam: Elsevier.

VEBLEN, THORSTEIN (1899) 1953 *The Theory of the Leisure Class: An Economic Study of Institutions.* Rev. ed. New York: New American Library. → A paperback edition was published in 1959.

WARNER, W. LLOYD; and LUNT, PAUL S. 1941 *The Social Life of a Modern Community.* New Haven: Yale Univ. Press.

WHYTE, WILLIAM H. JR. 1956 *The Organization Man.* New York: Simon & Schuster. → A paperback edition was published in 1957 by Doubleday.

YOUNG, MICHAEL; and WILLMOTT, PETER 1957 *Family and Kinship in East London.* Institute of Community Studies, Report No. 1. London: Routledge; Glencoe, Ill.: Free Press. → A paperback edition was published in 1963 by Penguin.

ZORBAUGH, HARVEY W. 1929 *The Gold Coast and the Slum.* Univ. of Chicago Press.

## II
### ECONOMIC ASPECTS

Economic problems, analyses, and policies concerning housing differ considerably between the various types of national economies. Dissimilar needs and suggested solutions appear among developed as compared to emerging economies. The market structure, whether planned, quasi-planned, or more laissez-faire, also strongly influences the manner in which problems arise.

Economists have approached the housing question from three rather disparate points of view: that of real investment, consumption, and technology. Most analysis has been concerned with construction and housing as investment problems. Major interest has focused on the fact that construction is a large, significant industry with one of the greatest year-to-year variances. This literature has dealt with fluctuations and possible cycles. However, other investment questions such as exploring optimum rates of construction in relation to a country's existing and planned expansion of capital and present and expected levels of consumption have received more attention in recent years.

For over one hundred years, housing has also played a prominent role in the theory of consumption and social reform. Housing takes a large share of consumption budgets. Individual standards of living are heavily influenced by the level of housing and the amount paid for it. Criticisms of the housing level achieved are common, and economists have sought the reasons why better standards of housing do not prevail.

Other economic problems arise with respect to the methods of production. Housing techniques have developed over thousands of years, but many feel that their rate of improvement has lagged behind other fields. Studies of production have attempted to find the economic rationale for existing techniques while searching for methods to improve the production process.

**New investment in housing.**    Table 1 shows the relative importance of construction and housing in different economies. Total construction expenditures range from 3.5 to about 15 per cent of the gross national product (GNP) and from 40 to 70 per cent of gross fixed investment. Depending on the economy, housing production varies from 2 to 5 per cent of the GNP. In each case, the magnitude of housing production is sufficiently large for its movements to cause related repercussions throughout the economy. The impact is heightened because construction in general, and particularly housing construction, is among the most volatile of all major industries. Housing fluctuations have had large amplitudes. In the United States, for example, the value of housing production in 1933 was less than 13 per cent of its value in 1929. In the post-World War II period, while economies experienced relative general stability, housing remained extremely unstable.

Economists have debated whether the fluctuation pattern of building differs basically from that of the rest of the economy. The evidence is not clear-cut, but most observers note that long swings or cycles of 18 to 20 years appear to mark the indexes of building construction in both the United States and the United Kingdom. Some of the literature on the subject attaches the name of "the building or construction cycle" to these observed movements. Abramovitz (1962) holds that since the Civil War there has been a succession of long swings in aggregate construction activity, consisting of upsurges followed by either protracted declines or pronounced retardations, in which all the major sectors of the industry have usually if not invariably participated.

*Causes of fluctuations.*    Many have attempted to describe the special factors which could make housing fluctuations differ from the rest of the economy. As in other areas of cycle theory, some have tried to derive simple, constant models for all past movements; the majority of theories, however, are eclectic. They hold that while housing fluctuations do take a unique form because of the nature of the industry, the proximate cause or causes of past movements differ.

The theories ascribe unique demand, supply, and market interactions to the housing market. Uniqueness arises from special demand factors, the size and durability of houses, the few times the average family enters the market and the family's relative ignorance, the importance of credit in facilitating construction and purchases, the entrepreneurs' small size and lack of capital, and the difficulties of market adjustment.

A high percentage of construction is that required to house or service net additions to households. An expanding population, either through natural growth as births exceed deaths or through migration, requires more dwellings. Another important demographic force is the splitting of extended families into separate households. Young couples may seek their own homes earlier in life rather than share units with their parents. The

### Table 1 — Patterns of investment, 1960

| | GNP (millions of dollars) | GROSS FIXED INVESTMENT (As per cent of GNP) | TOTAL CONSTRUCTION AS PER CENT OF: | | DWELLING CONSTRUCTION AS PER CENT OF: | |
|---|---|---|---|---|---|---|
| | | | GNP | Gross fixed investment | GNP | Gross fixed investment |
| Argentina | 9,444.1 | 20.9 | 7.8 | 37.6 | * | * |
| Canada | 37,046.6 | 22.7 | 14.9 | 65.6 | 4.0 | 17.7 |
| Chile | 4,892.2 | 8.7 | 3.6 | 41.2 | * | * |
| Germany (F.R.G.) | 67,708.2 | 24.0 | 12.0 | 50.2 | 5.4 | 22.4 |
| Japan | 38,845.0 | 31.4 | * | * | 2.3 | 7.4 |
| Kenya | 630.0 | 18.4 | 10.3 | 55.8 | 3.0 | 16.4 |
| South Africa | 7,433.5 | 20.7 | 11.8 | 57.2 | * | * |
| Sweden | 12,287.0 | 21.9 | 14.1 | 64.5 | 5.0 | 22.8 |
| United Kingdom | 71,068.8 | 16.1 | 7.9 | 48.7 | 3.0 | 18.6 |
| United States | 504,404.0 | 16.4 | 10.9 | 66.6 | 4.5 | 27.4 |

* Not available.

Source: Year Book of National Accounts Statistics: 1962. Copyright, United Nations (1963). Reproduced by permission.

number of single individuals, particularly widows, maintaining their own homes may rise.

In the past, waves of household additions appear to have resulted from variations in migration and from an uneven age distribution in the population. Even within given population structures the rate of family formation has varied significantly as a result of both social and economic forces.

The need to replace existing units is another demand factor. Net replacements have ranged from zero to a third or more of total demand. Several theories posit a replacement cycle. Required replacements could fluctuate as an echo of bunched dwelling construction in the past. However, replacement cycles are not evident in the data. Since the housing stock has been expanding rapidly, the percentage of the stock old enough to require replacement is minor. The useful life of dwellings is extremely long. Few buildings require replacement on merely physical grounds; most replacement takes place because the location is needed for other uses. Replacements appear more closely related to the size of the stock and to economic conditions than to the age and quality of existing units.

Over periods such as a decade, most of the demand for new construction is directly related to the number of net additions to the households in a locality, plus the net number of units demolished, replaced, or removed. Movements in unoccupied units (vacancies) are significant in short periods, but their importance diminishes the longer the time span examined.

The short-run movements in demand have causes similar to those of fluctuations in other spheres. Movements in employment, in assets (particularly equities of existing dwellings), in prices, costs, and in credit all change the demand for new units. Insofar as these variables move with business conditions, the resulting housing fluctuations resemble those of other spheres.

There are also logical reasons to expect that construction will at times fluctuate in a pattern differing from the remainder of the economy. Many authors place particular emphasis on credit. Because of size and cost of buildings, construction is highly dependent on the existence and terms of debt financing. Movements in credit availability, the required down payment, the period of amortization, and the interest rate can force individual owners and builders in and out of the market. Credit terms may move separately from other economic variables. The length of lag between the movements of credit terms and their impact in the construction market differs from that of other industries. Many writers believe that the post-World War II experience in both the United States and western Europe gave evidence that credit did cause special fluctuations.

Housing demand has two dimensions: one consists of the number of separate dwellings required; the second measures the amount spent per dwelling. This latter amount varies with the size, quality, and features included in a house. Economic variables appear to have a much larger impact on the amount spent per dwelling than they have on the number of dwellings demanded.

When the demand for the services of dwellings shifts, still larger fluctuations occur in required new investment. This creates greater amplitude in the movements of building. The acceleration principle is at work: a 2 per cent increase in the desire for housing may cause new construction demand to double, while in response to a similar decrease new construction might fall almost to zero. [See INVESTMENT, article on THE AGGREGATE INVESTMENT FUNCTION.]

Other reaction differences arise because of peculiar factors in the market and the real estate industry. Supply adjusts slowly. Because of lack of information much building, particularly of apartment houses, may occur even after an excess of supply exists. The "gestation period" for large structures is long. Apparent increases in demand can easily be multiplied through high expectations, easy credit, and the large number of small firms. Furthermore, builders or promoters who sell to others can often make a profit simply through the building process, even if the completed unit is unneeded.

When the new excess supply reaches the market, vacancies result. As these build up new construction is slowed down. If a demand drop occurs with vacancies already high, as happened after 1929, the disruption of the market is heightened. Since the number of units required has a low price elasticity, no fall in prices is sufficient to fill the vacant space.

*Stabilization policies.* Because the industry's structure makes large-scale fluctuations probable, interest has attached to governmental policies which might dampen some cycles. Suggested policies have included better market information, credit controls, varying subsidies, and direct governmental action either to remove old units from the stock or to purchase new ones.

Stabilization programs may attempt to increase the long-run basic demand or to concentrate more demand in particular periods. Attempts to offset short-run movements are difficult. Forecasting problems, the complicated lag situation, and a slow reaction time all make it extremely difficult to inject the stabilizing demand into the market at the necessary times.

*Other investment problems.* Developed countries have studied housing because of its fluctuations. In developing economies, housing investment has been looked at primarily as a major drain on limited funds. Industrialization and urbanization go hand in hand; individuals and families leave the farm village to work in the city, where they must be housed. Each industrial job requires additional investment in the urban infrastructure. Analysts cannot consider merely the direct investment requirements and the payoff for a transfer of employment from farm to factory. They must take into account many additional costs, of which housing is a major item. Investments in housing tend to be expensive and slow. In developing economies, slums and urban growth are virtually synonymous. Decisions as to how to meet these additional needs are difficult and complex. Significant social costs result when investment is channeled to housing rather than to seemingly more productive spheres. On the other hand, slums and housing shortages create social costs which may in turn reduce the productive effort.

Within developed economies, major debates have occurred as to the proper amount of investment to be allocated to housing when the economy is at full employment. Some feel that housing needs were given too low a priority as western Europe attempted to fight inflation in the post-World War II period. New housing space was rationed during a period when other parts of the economy were booming.

**Consumption of housing.** Housing standards vary greatly from country to country, and even wider ranges of consumption standards exist within countries. Almost everywhere some people live in shacks while others occupy mansions. Large numbers of families would occupy both more and higher-quality space if either their incomes were increased or the costs of housing lowered. The problem of why adequate housing is not made available to all income groups has received considerable analysis, but no generally accepted answers are available (Grigsby 1963).

Table 2 shows the percentage of expenditures going to rent. It shows large variations; the average spent on rent varies from 1 to nearly 15 per cent among the countries listed. Within individual countries the highest percentage spent is commonly double or triple the lowest.

Considerable effort has been expended on the analysis of these variations. The reasons for some

**Table 2 — Percentage of household consumption expenditures spent on rent**

| | | AVERAGE (MEAN) PER CENT SPENT ON RENT | RANGE OF PER CENT SPENT ON RENT |
|---|---|---|---|
| British Guiana | 1955–1956 | 2.9 | 0.6 to 5.9 |
| France | 1956–1957 | 5.2 | 4.3 to 6.4 |
| India | 1950–1951 | 1.1 | 0.5 to 1.7 |
| Nigeria | 1953–1955 | 10.0 | 9.5 to 10.6 |
| Philippines | 1956–1957 | 9.1 | 6.8 to 16.5 |
| South Africa | 1955 | 14.6 | 11.2 to 16.5 |
| Sweden | 1958 | 11.6 | 9.6 to 13.5 |
| United Arab Republic | 1958 | 12.4 | 10.5 to 17.0 |
| United Kingdom | 1959 | 10.3 | 5.9 to 15.6 |
| United States | 1950 | 11.9 | 9.5 to 17.9 |

Source: Compendium of Social Statistics: 1963.

differences are evident. One area's rents may appear to exceed others purely because of definitions—what is included in rent and the services furnished vary. The relative level of housing costs, frequently based on differences in climate and standards, will be important. Tastes in housing are also extremely broad, so that what is demanded and paid for will differ. Within a given country, factors influencing family expenditures are known to be numerous. Maisel and Winnick (1960) report results similar to those of many other studies. Tenure (rental or ownership) and the type of credit available for ownership cause significant expenditure variations. Among a given tenure group, income is the most important variable. The cross-section income elasticity of housing appears to fall around .5 and .6.

Family demographic features are also important. The type of head, the age of head, and race are all related to differences in tenure and in expenditures within tenure groups. Other factors which influence housing demanded and received include education, occupation, and the location of the family by size and type of community.

*Use of subsidies.* Many value judgments have been made that people underspend for housing. The level of housing purchased in a free market by many groups of the population is held to be below a desirable standard based on concepts of national health and welfare. It is argued that since housing of good quality is an expensive item, low-income families can purchase or rent sound dwellings only at the expense of other budget items. Since their income is inadequate for all wants, they tend to sacrifice the quality of housing. Compared to sacrifices of food, clothing, or other items, poorer housing can more easily be accepted.

In almost all countries the problem of inadequate housing has been met through subsidies. These tend to take the form of direct housing subsidies rather than general income subsidies which could be spent as the low-income family desired. Among existing types of subsidies are public ownership of dwellings with rents charged at less than costs, rent payments, government payment of part of the costs of construction, and government subsidies in the form of easier or cheaper credit.

The use of housing subsidies rather than income subsidies would appear to be based on the assumption that the housing market is special. It is feared that general income subsidies would be dissipated through higher rents with only minor improvements in the quality or quantity of housing. It is argued that unless the government uses its expenditures to assure an increased supply of adequate housing, the money will be wasted. Various reasons for such possible poor results are cited. Improper transmission of information in the housing market is one. The market structure may be such that unless the quality is controlled through the form of the subsidy most of the increased supply will be poor. Furthermore, if subsidies are general the recipients might choose to continue to live in housing deemed unsatisfactory by those favoring the subsidies.

Low-income housing programs have frequently been teamed with those for slum clearance. It is argued that the normal market cannot clear slums unless governmental powers are utilized. The external economies and diseconomies are such that a few property owners could frustrate the will of the majority by threatening or attempting to gather most of the joint values for themselves. Tying a housing subsidy program to slum clearance is not a necessary condition, but it simplifies the process. Joint programs make replacement units available for some of the displaced households.

*Effects of rent controls.* In many periods of housing shortages, rent controls have been adopted. Arguments for controls depend primarily on concepts of a fair distribution of income. Additional housing can be brought into the market only slowly, or, in periods of war or disaster, not at all. Since the price elasticity of household formation appears to be low, even rapidly rising rents would not have much impact on the number of dwellings demanded. Higher rents would have to be met from already inadequate budgets. These higher rents would increase the income of landlords, who are assumed to be among the wealthier classes. Rent controls are also used because they

are comparatively simple to administer. Potential capital gains on dwellings can be limited. Whether or not it is economically sound, the ability to contain one area of prices has obvious practical advantages.

Most arguments against rent controls consider difficulties that arise if controls are extended beyond immediate emergencies. It is claimed that controls halt market adjustments. They artifically raise demand because of lower prices, while they hold down supply since higher returns cannot be earned. Also over longer periods, the redistribution effects tend to alter. Instead of tenants being favored over landlords, old tenants are favored over new and some industries over others. The costs of operating in an artificial market rise with time, while the economic advantages fall.

**Production of housing.** The types of houses produced vary widely. The United States and England mix single-family units and larger apartments, with most emphasis given to single-family units. In Europe a higher percentage of apartments is produced. In many other areas small, simply constructed individual units predominate.

In most countries, however, the housing industry has roughly similar characteristics. Entry is simple, and the number of firms is large. The amount of overhead and of mechanical equipment required is low. The rate of technological innovation is slow, and labor tends to be skilled in specific crafts. Difficulties arise in training and in planning the progression of jobs. People compare housing to other industries and usually conclude that it is unprogressive or backward.

In many countries popular comment seems to attribute the difficulties of the industry to a "devil theory." Progress is thought to be blocked by some entrenched group, be it builders, labor, financial institutions, bureaucratic government, or others. The few economic studies of the housing industry (Maisel 1953; Kelly 1959) place much greater emphasis on its structure as a normal response to the unique problems of building dwellings.

Houses are primarily assembled and attached to individual plots of land. Land costs are significant, and each lot is unique. The joining of the land and building is complex and expensive. The buildings are large, heavy, bulky, and durable. A great deal of the expense in housing construction results simply from moving materials from point to point rather than from fabrication. In the assembly process, many different skills must be used because the variety of materials and finishes is great.

The industry produces a wide variety of custom-made products. Its demand is fickle and fluctuates widely; builders must be prepared to expand and contract production rapidly. Flexibility is possible through drawing on the labor and materials available in the much broader area of total construction; however, such flexibility tends to be at the expense of specialization and large-scale automated production.

Probably the rate of innovation has been somewhat greater than is commonly believed. On the other hand, it has certainly been slower than in most highly industrialized parts of the economy. It is virtually impossible to separate the structure of the industry and the uniqueness of the product and market from the rate of change. Many different types of control, of management, and of labor exist in various countries; nevertheless, no country or form of organization has developed a vastly different product or obviously more efficient techniques.

There is some indication that because of the industry's fragmented structure, research expenditures and results are less than elsewhere. Firms work on their own product but pay little attention to the process as a whole. No firm controls enough of the final product to make an over-all point of view worthwhile. While there appear to be potential external economies, governments have done small amounts of research; and their efforts and results thus far are minor.

Many observers conclude that any major changes in structure and technique will depend upon the discovery of new materials and vastly different methods of production. As long as houses continue to be built approximately as they were in the past, changes can only be gradual. No single part of the structure, or individual material, or task is important enough for a saving in its cost to be truly significant. More rapid progress appears to require the elimination of whole groups of materials and functions.

SHERMAN J. MAISEL

### BIBLIOGRAPHY

ABRAMOVITZ, MOSES 1962 Long Swings in Economic Growth in the United States. Pages 46–48 in National Bureau of Economic Research, *Annual Report, Forty-second.* New York: The Bureau.

BEYER, GLENN H. 1958 *Housing: A Factual Analysis.* New York: Macmillan. → Contains a bibliography.

BURNS, ARTHUR F. 1935 Long Cycles in Residential Construction. Pages 63–104 in *Economic Essays in Honor of Wesley Clair Mitchell.* New York: Columbia Univ. Press.

CALIFORNIA, UNIVERSITY OF, LOS ANGELES, REAL ESTATE RESEARCH PROGRAM 1966 *Essays in Urban Land Economics in Honor of the Sixty-fifth Birthday of Leo Grebler.* Los Angeles: The University.

COLUMBIA UNIVERSITY, INSTITUTE FOR URBAN LAND USE AND HOUSING STUDIES 1953 *Housing Market Analysis: A Study of Theory and Methods,* by Chester Rapkin, Louis Winnick, and David M. Blank. Washington: U.S. Housing and Home Finance Agency, Office of the Administration, Division of Housing Research.

Compendium of Social Statistics: 1963. 1963 United Nations, Statistical Office, *Statistical Papers,* Series K. No. 2. New York: United Nations.

GREBLER, LEO; BLANK, DAVID M.; and WINNICK, LOUIS 1956 *Capital Formation in Residential Real Estate.* Princeton Univ. Press.

GREBLER, LEO; and MAISEL, SHERMAN J. 1963 Determinants of Residential Construction: Research Study Four. Pages 475–620 in Commission on Money and Credit, *Impacts of Monetary Policy.* Englewood Cliffs, N.J.: Prentice-Hall. → Contains a bibliography on fluctuations.

GRIGSBY, WILLIAM G. 1963 *Housing Markets and Public Policy.* Philadelphia: Univ. of Pennsylvania Press. → Contains a bibliography.

KELLY, BURNHAM 1959 *Design and the Production of Houses.* New York: McGraw-Hill.

MAISEL, SHERMAN J. 1953 *Housebuilding in Transition.* Berkeley: Univ. of California Press.

MAISEL, SHERMAN J. 1963 A Theory of Fluctuations in Residential Construction Starts. *American Economic Review* 53:359–383.

MAISEL, SHERMAN J.; and WINNICK, LOUIS 1960 Family Housing Expenditures: Elusive Laws and Intrusive Variances. Volume 1, pages 359–435 in Conference on Consumption and Saving, University of Pennsylvania, 1959, *Proceedings.* Philadelphia: Univ. of Pennsylvania Press.

RATCLIFF, RICHARD U. 1949 *Urban Land Economics.* New York: McGraw-Hill.

TWENTIETH CENTURY FUND, HOUSING COMMITTEE 1944 *American Housing, Problems and Prospects: The Factual Findings,* by Miles L. Colean. New York: The Fund.

WINNICK, LOUIS 1958 *Rental Housing Opportunities for Private Investment.* New York: McGraw-Hill.

*Yearbook of National Accounts Statistics: 1962.* 1963 New York: United Nations Statistical Office, Department of Economic and Social Affairs.

## HOVLAND, CARL I.

Carl I. Hovland (1912–1961), American pioneer in communications research, began his career as an experimental psychologist working on classical problems of conditioning and human learning. By the age of 30, when he turned to the newly developing field of research on attitude change, he had already become one of the most eminent psychologists of his generation.

The most important of Hovland's early research studies were focused on the generalization of conditioned responses. During the 1930s, he also made significant discoveries concerning factors that influence reminiscence effects in human memory functioning, the efficiency of alternative methods of rote-learning, and the modes of resolution of motor conflicts. From 1942 until his untimely death from cancer in 1961, Hovland devoted the major part of his time to careful investigations of the effects of social communication, using research designs and analytic methods derived from the more highly developed fields of experimental psychology. It is primarily for his contributions in this area that he is regarded as one of the foremost social scientists of the twentieth century. Wilbur Schramm (1963, p. 5), in reviewing communications research in the United States, refers to the work that came out of Hovland's research program at Yale University between 1950 and 1961 as "the largest single contribution . . . [to this field] any man has made." The Distinguished Scientific Contribution Award was presented to Hovland by the American Psychological Association, in 1957, "for his original and provocative contributions to the scientific study of persuasive communications and the modification of beliefs and attitudes." The citation states further:

. . . Combining a sensitive use of controlled experimentation with penetrating logical analysis, he has done much to isolate the major factors at work when an individual is confronted with the complex informational input of a persuasive argument. By judicious use of psychological theory, he has been able to relate this area of social psychology to basic investigations of the higher mental processes. His work has been of central importance in advancing attitude research from the early stage of merely demonstrating that changes can be produced to the point of making predictions about when and where they will occur. His work has provided a convincing demonstration of the values of a sustained and integrated program of research.   (American Psychological Association 1958, p. 158)

**Formative years.**   A native of Chicago, Hovland attended nearby Northwestern University, where he devoted himself to acquiring as thorough a background as possible in mathematics, physics, and biology, as well as in experimental psychology. After obtaining his M.A. degree in 1933, he completed his graduate studies in psychology at Yale University. He remained affiliated with Yale throughout his entire academic career, starting as an instructor in 1936 (immediately after receiving his PH.D. degree), attaining the rank of professor of psychology in 1945 and the chair of Sterling professor two years later.

As a graduate student and junior faculty member during the prewar years at Yale, Hovland participated in the stimulating intellectual environment of the Yale Institute of Human Relations, which helped to shape his interests and approach to the study of human behavior. Of particular importance in Hovland's training was the influence of the great American psychologist Clark L. Hull. Using a rigorous empirical approach in conjunction with analytic theory construction, Hull was highly successful during the late 1930s in organizing and stimulating talented young psychologists at Yale to carry out research on significant problems of motivation and learning. After serving as Hull's research assistant for several years, Hovland became a coinvestigator in the series of studies on human learning, which led to his being a coauthor of the well-known book by Hull and his collaborators, *Mathematico–Deductive Theory of Rote Learning* (1940). Although not sharing Hull's predilection for far-reaching theoretical formulations, Hovland acquired an extraordinary degree of methodological sophistication, both from Hull himself and from other specialists whom Hull had recruited to participate in his research program. Of equal importance was the optimistic vision he acquired that led him to extend the analytic approach of experimental psychology to other research areas in the human sciences—particularly those suffering from a dearth of dependable generalizations in the midst of an abundance of vague theoretical speculations.

After he had received his PH.D. in 1936, Hovland's outlook and approach to social science research continued to be fostered by collaboration with the staff of Yale's Institute of Human Relations, which was at the height of its influence during the late 1930s and early 1940s. Outstanding social scientists from all over the world were brought together and given ample time and resources to pursue the inquiries of their choice. Hopes ran high that this would make for rapid cross-fertilization among traditionally isolated fields and lead to vital new breakthroughs, comparable to those emerging from interdisciplinary developments in the physical and biological sciences. Among the outstanding personalities with whom Hovland came in contact were Dusser de Barenne, Mark May, Walter Miles, Edward Sapir, and Robert Yerkes.

Although the senior members of the institute rarely achieved their high aspirations for interdisciplinary advances, the intellectual ferment created among the research assistants and junior staff members of Hovland's generation did produce unexpected gains. Coming from different social science disciplines, these well-trained young men began to influence each other as they examined the implications of generalizations that purported to account for complex aspects of human behavior. Among Hovland's contemporaries at the institute were John Dollard, Leonard Doob, Clellan S. Ford,

Neal Miller, O. Hobart Mowrer, George P. Murdock, Robert R. Sears, and John W. M. Whiting. With these men he formed bonds of personal friendship and often participated with them in lively seminars. One well-known product was the collaborative Yale volume *Frustration and Aggression* (Dollard et al. 1939). Several members of this group, together with Donald Marquis, Ernest R. Hilgard, and Kenneth W. Spence, who were also at Yale during the early 1940s, played an important role in the development of learning theory.

Following the lead of Hull, the Yale group attempted to formulate unambiguous behavioral laws concerning the conditions under which habits are strengthened and weakened. These laws were then used as a basis for explaining complex social phenomena, such as the displacement of hostility from the family to outsiders, observed by specialists in such diverse fields as anthropology, psychoanalysis, and social psychology. Hovland contributed to the work of this group not so much by suggesting comprehensive theoretical insights as by focusing on rigorous analysis of empirical evidence. His originality took the form of discovering new functional relationships by working closely with the available findings, noting inconsistencies and reversals that others might be inclined to overlook, and then proceeding to unravel the puzzles by ingeniously testing a series of alternative explanations with a new set of data. These qualities also characterized his later work on communication effects.

**Research on mass communication.**    In 1942 Hovland took a leave of absence from Yale in order to serve as a research expert on morale problems for the United States government. He became chief psychologist and director of experimental studies in the research branch of the information and education division of the War Department. In this role, he worked closely with two eminent sociologists, Samuel Stouffer, who was then the research director of the research branch, and Leonard C. Cottrell, senior social analyst in the same organization. For four years Hovland participated in the planning of a series of large-scale investigations on social psychological factors in military morale; the empirical findings from these studies were subsequently incorporated into the *American Soldier* volumes by Stouffer and his collaborators.

Hovland's main role in the military research organization, however, was to conduct psychological experiments on the effectiveness of training and information programs, including the series of "Why We Fight" films that were intended to influence the motivation of men in the American armed forces. In his own experimental section of the research

branch, Hovland assembled a group of six psychology graduate students, who worked with him on these studies for several years: John Finan, Irving L. Janis, Arthur A. Lumsdaine, Nathan Maccoby, Fred D. Sheffield, and M. Brewster Smith. Although partly oriented toward meeting the practical needs of the military services, the studies conducted by Hovland and his group embodied a research approach that led to major advances on many basic problems in social psychology.

Following the pattern of his earlier work at Yale, Hovland set up investigations designed to test hypotheses concerning the conditions under which mass communications are effective and to explore fully the implications of all the relevant data. But instead of confining the research to restricted laboratory settings, the mainstay of experimental social psychology up to that time, Hovland took advantage of the unique opportunities afforded by his military research mission. He and his group investigated the effects of different types of communication on "live" issues by conducting experimental studies with equated groups of soldiers at U.S. Army training centers. One of the most widely cited of these pioneering communications experiments involved testing the effects of a one-sided versus a two-sided presentation of a controversial issue. The results contradicted some of the well-publicized contentions of Nazi propaganda strategists who claimed that to be successful a communication should never mention the opposing side of an argument. Among men initially hostile to the point of view fostered by a communication (and particularly those familiar with cogent opposing arguments), it was found to be more effective to include mention of the opposing arguments than to give a strictly one-sided presentation.

Many of the investigations by Hovland and his group provide systematic data bearing on the sources of audience resistance to persuasive efforts and call attention to factors that help to overcome such resistance. These wartime studies formed the basis for a book entitled *Experiments on Mass Communication* by Hovland, Lumsdaine, and Sheffield (1949), which was published as part of the same series as the *American Soldier* volumes, jointly sponsored by the U.S. War Department and the Social Science Research Council.

**The Yale communication studies.**    After the war Hovland returned to Yale University as chairman of the department of psychology and was awarded a Sterling professorship. Having recruited for his department several members of his wartime research team, Hovland continued to devote his energies to systematic research on communication effects. With the support of the Rockefeller Foundation, he organized and directed the Yale studies in attitude and communication, which enabled a large number of junior faculty members and graduate students to participate in collaborative research on a variety of communication problems of their own choice.

The main purpose of the research project was to explore systematically the factors that influence the effectiveness of social communications. Hovland himself continued to take a leading role as an active research worker, and his own experiments set a high standard as models of analytic precision. Among his best-known studies are those elucidating the influence of the communicator's prestige and the ways that prestige effects disappear with the passage of time. Following a lead obtained from the wartime research reported in *Experiments on Mass Communication*, Hovland and his collaborators showed that when a persuasive message is presented by an untrustworthy source it tends to be discounted by the audience, so that immediately after exposure there is little or no attitude change; but then, after several weeks, the source is no longer associated with the issue in the minds of the audience and positive attitude changes appear (Hovland & Weiss 1951). This delayed or "sleeper" effect was shown to vanish, as predicted, when after several weeks the unacceptable communicator was "reinstated" by reminding the audience about who had presented the earlier persuasive material (Kelman & Hovland 1953).

For more than fifteen years Hovland systematically investigated factors that determine the effectiveness of persuasive communications, including studies of different sequential arrangements of arguments, the retention of arguments and conclusions, and judgmental processes that enter into attitude change. While pursuing his own research, Hovland continually encouraged his associates on the Yale project to select other variables in line with their own research interests, such as the influence of group affiliation, role playing, emotional appeals, and personality predispositions. The major research findings of the first five years of the communications research project, together with theoretical analyses of the problems under investigation, were summarized in a volume entitled *Communication and Persuasion* by Hovland, Janis, and Kelley (1953). This volume was followed during the next eight years by a series of four multi-authored monographs on more specific topics: *The Order of Presentation in Persuasion* (Hovland et al. 1957); *Personality and Persuasibility* (Janis, Hovland et al. 1959); *Attitude Organization and Change* (1960b); and *Social Judgment* (Sherif & Hovland 1961). The series of works by Hovland and his co-workers, according to Nathan Maccoby (1963), furnishes the empirical core of "the new scientific rhetoric," the body of psychological knowledge accumulated from objective description and analysis of the processes of persuasion.

**Research on thought processes.** In the last decade of his life Hovland's research on verbal concepts and judgment led him into an intensive analysis of symbolic processes. Once again he played a pioneering role in developing a new field of research—computer simulation of human thought processes. His first major contribution in this field was a "communication analysis" of concept learning (1952) which showed how a newly developed mathematical theory could be applied to computer simulation of the ways in which people form new concepts. His general method of analyzing concept learning and his notational system were soon adopted by many other research workers who were conducting experiments on human learning and cognitive processes.

Several years after Hovland's pioneering paper, there were some breakthroughs in the programming of digital computers, which Hovland immediately applied in constructing a computer simulation model of the steps a person goes through as he thinks out the solution of problems requiring the attainment of a new concept. Supported by generous research grants from the Ford Foundation and the Bell Telephone Laboratories, Hovland and his collaborators began devising a series of experiments in order to obtain some of the missing information needed for an adequate theory to account for human acquisition of complex concepts through experience. One of the main findings, reported in a paper by Hunt and Hovland (1960), was that most human learners readily make use of information about *conjunctive* concepts (for example, all members of the given class share two characteristics, A and B) but tend to ignore information pointing to *disjunctive* concepts (for example, all members of the given class possess either characteristic A or B). Accordingly, Hovland developed a computer model of concept formation in which a hierarchy of responses was programmed in such a way that the conjunctive concepts would be the first type tried out and disjunctive concepts would be scanned only after other approaches consistently failed. In a highly influential paper entitled "Computer Simulation of Thinking" (1960a), Hovland pointed out the potential advantages of making use of new developments in mathematics and computer technology for advancing the human sciences. Many research workers are now implementing the mixed research strategy he recommended, combining experimental studies of human thinking with the development of computer programs that simulate human psychological processes.

**Other contributions.** Hovland's influence on the methodology of social science research was consistently directed toward integrating seemingly divergent lines of research. One of his best-known papers deals with the problems of reconciling conflicting results derived from experimental and survey studies of attitude change (1959). He pointed out that one gets the impression from survey research that very few people are affected by mass communications, whereas experiments on opinion change show that from one-third to one-half of the audience is influenced by a single exposure to a persuasive message. This apparent divergence can be accounted for by a number of well-known factors that are often overlooked, such as the use of captive audiences and remote or unfamiliar issues in experimental studies, in contrast to the audience's self-selective exposure and high ego-involvement in the issues typically studied by survey research. Hovland's recommendation was that the two research approaches should be used conjointly, "combining their virtues so that we may develop a social psychology of communication with the conceptual breadth provided by correlational study of process and with the rigorous but more delimited methodology of the experiment" (1959, p. 17).

At a memorial session of the New England Psychological Association, held a year after Hovland's premature death, his former students and associates recalled his "uncanny ability to integrate and focus knowledge" and "to discern the central aspects of a problem" while at the same time fulfilling his leadership role in a "gentle and supportive" way. As Herbert Kelman put it, he was "the world's most non-authoritarian leader." Indeed, Hovland welcomed diverse theoretical viewpoints and encouraged those working with him to try out new research strategies. His incisive comments stimulated his co-workers and students to make their studies as rigorous as possible and to pursue fully the substantive inferences that could be drawn from the data. This type of direction, combined with the atmosphere of freedom of inquiry which he consistently fostered, nurtured the talents of the many younger psychologists whose names appear as coauthors of his books and articles, most of whom have subsequently become leading figures in American social psychology.

Not the least of Hovland's contributions was the public service he rendered in the role of a "statesman of the social sciences." As one of the few psy-

chologists of his generation elected to the National Academy of Sciences, Hovland was invited to be a committee member or consultant to the Rockefeller Foundation, the Ford Foundation, the Russell Sage Foundation, the Bell Telephone Laboratories, the Social Science Research Council, the National Research Council, the Research Development Board, the Fund for Adult Education, and a number of other private national research organizations, as well as to some of the social research agencies of the U.S. government. Hovland fulfilled his consultant role by consistently working to improve the standards and quality of research in psychology and related fields.

Perhaps the most comprehensive statement of the scope of Hovland's substantive contributions to social science research is contained in the citation of the Warren medal, awarded by the Society of Experimental Psychologists in the last year of his life: "For his systematic analyses . . . [in] four areas of research—verbal learning, conditioning, concept formation and attitude change."

Irving L. Janis

[*Directly related are the entries* Attitudes, *article on* attitude change; Persuasion; Social psychology; Suggestion. *Other relevant material may be found in* Communication, mass; *and in the biographies of* Hull; Sapir; Stouffer; Yerkes.]

### WORKS BY HOVLAND

1937a The Generalization of Conditioned Responses: 1. The Sensory Generalization of Conditioned Responses With Varying Frequencies of Tone. *Journal of General Psychology* 17:125–148.

1937b The Generalization of Conditioned Responses: 2. The Sensory Generalization of Conditioned Responses With Varying Intensities of Tone. *Journal of Genetic Psychology* 51:279–291.

1937c The Generalization of Conditioned Responses: 3. Extinction, Spontaneous Recovery, and Disinhibition of Conditioned and of Generalized Responses. *Journal of Experimental Psychology* 21:47–62.

1937d The Generalization of Conditioned Responses: 4. The Effects of Varying Amounts of Reinforcement Upon the Degree of Generalization of Conditioned Responses. *Journal of Experimental Psychology* 21:261–276.

1938 Hovland, Carl I.; and Sears, Robert R. Experiments on Motor Conflict: 1. Types of Conflict and Their Modes of Resolution. *Journal of Experimental Psychology* 23:477–493.

1940 Hovland, Carl I.; and Sears, Robert R. Minor Studies of Aggression: 6. Correlation of Lynchings With Economic Indices. *Journal of Psychology* 9:301–310.

1940 *Mathematico–Deductive Theory of Rote Learning.* New Haven: Yale Univ. Press. → By Carl I. Hovland, C. L. Hull, R. T. Ross, M. Hall, D. T. Perkins, and F. B. Fitch.

1940 Sears, Robert R.; Hovland, Carl I.; and Miller, Neal E. Minor Studies of Aggression: 1. Measurement of Aggressive Behavior. *Journal of Psychology* 9:275–295.

1949  HOVLAND, CARL I.; LUMSDAINE, ARTHUR A.; and SHEFFIELD, FREDERICK D. *Experiments on Mass Communication.* Studies in Social Psychology in World War II, Vol. 3. Princeton Univ. Press; Oxford Univ. Press.

1951  Human Learning and Retention. Pages 613–689 in S. S. Stevens (editor), *Handbook of Experimental Psychology.* New York: Wiley.

(1951) 1954  HOVLAND, CARL I.; and WEISS, WALTER The Influence of Source Credibility on Communication Effectiveness. Pages 337–347 in Society for the Psychological Study of Social Issues, *Public Opinion and Propaganda.* New York: Dryden. → First published in Volume 15 of *Public Opinion Quarterly.*

1952  A "Communication Analysis" of Concept Learning. *Psychological Review* 59:461–472.

1952  HOVLAND, CARL I.; and MANDELL, WALLACE An Experimental Comparison of Conclusion-drawing by the Communicator and by the Audience. *Journal of Abnormal and Social Psychology* 47:581–588.

1953  HOVLAND, CARL I.; JANIS, IRVING L.; and KELLEY, HAROLD H. *Communication and Persuasion: Psychological Studies of Opinion Change.* New Haven: Yale Univ. Press.

1953  HOVLAND, CARL I.; and WEISS, WALTER Transmission of Information Concerning Concepts Through Positive and Negative Instances. *Journal of Experimental Psychology* 45:175–182.

1953  KELMAN, HERBERT C.; and HOVLAND, CARL I. "Reinstatement" of the Communicator in Delayed Measurement of Opinion Change. *Journal of Abnormal and Social Psychology* 48:327–335.

1954  Effects of the Mass Media of Communication. Volume 2, pages 1062–1103 in Gardner Lindzey (editor), *Handbook of Social Psychology.* Cambridge, Mass.: Addison-Wesley.

1955  KELLEY, H. H.; HOVLAND, CARL I.; SCHWARTZ, M.; and ABELSON, R. P. The Influence of Judges' Attitudes in Three Methods of Attitude Scaling. *Journal of Social Psychology* 42:147–158.

1956  KURTZ, KENNETH H.; and HOVLAND, CARL I. Concept Learning With Differing Sequences of Instances. *Journal of Experimental Psychology* 51:239–243.

1957  HOVLAND, CARL I. et al. *The Order of Presentation in Persuasion.* New Haven: Yale Univ. Press. → Coauthors are W. Mandell, E. H. Campbell, T. Brock, A. S. Luchins, A. R. Cohen, W. J. McGuire, I. L. Janis, R. L. Feierabend, and N. H. Anderson.

1959  Reconciling Conflicting Results Derived From Experimental and Survey Studies of Attitude Change. *American Psychologist* 14:8–17.

1959  JANIS, IRVING L.; HOVLAND, CARL I. et al. *Personality and Persuasibility.* New Haven: Yale Univ. Press. → Coauthors are P. B. Field, H. Linton, E. Graham, A. R. Cohen, D. Rife, R. P. Abelson, G. S. Lesser, and B. T. King.

1959  MORRISETT, LLOYD N.; and HOVLAND, CARL I. A Comparison of Three Varieties of Training in Human Problem Solving. *Journal of Experimental Psychology* 58:52–55.

1960a  Computer Simulation of Thinking. *American Psychologist* 15:687–693.

1960  HOVLAND, CARL I.; and HUNT, EARL B. Computer Simulation of Concept Attainment. *Behavioral Science* 5:265–267.

1960b  *Attitude Organization and Change.* Yale Studies in Attitude and Communication, Vol. 3. New Haven: Yale Univ. Press. → By Carl I. Hovland, M. J. Rosenberg, W. J. McGuire, J. W. Brehm, and R. P. Abelson.

1960  HUNT, EARL B.; and HOVLAND, CARL I. Order of Consideration of Different Types of Concepts. *Journal of Experimental Psychology* 59:220–225.

1961  HUNT, EARL B.; and HOVLAND, CARL I. Programming a Model of Human Concept Formation. Pages 145–155 in Western Joint Computer Conference, Los Angeles, 1961, *Proceedings.* Los Angeles: The Conference.

1961  SHERIF, MUZAFER; and HOVLAND, CARL I. *Social Judgment: Assimilation and Contrast Effects in Communication and Attitude Change.* Yale Studies in Attitude and Communication, Vol. 4. New Haven: Yale Univ. Press.

SUPPLEMENTARY BIBLIOGRAPHY

AMERICAN PSYCHOLOGICAL ASSOCIATION 1958 Distinguished Scientific Contribution Awards, 1957. *American Psychologist* 13:155–168.

COHEN, ARTHUR R. 1964 *Attitude Change and Social Influence.* New York: Basic Books.

DOLLARD, JOHN et al. 1939 *Frustration and Aggression.* New Haven: Yale Univ. Press. → A paperback edition was published in 1961. Coauthors are L. W. Doob, N. E. Miller, O. H. Mowrer, and R. R. Sears.

JANIS, IRVING L.; and SMITH, M. BREWSTER 1965 Effects of Education and Persuasion on National and International Images. Pages 188–235 in H. C. Kelman (editor), *International Behavior.* New York: Holt.

MACCOBY, NATHAN 1963 The New "Scientific" Rhetoric. Pages 41–53 in Wilbur Schramm (editor), *The Science of Human Communication.* New York: Basic Books.

SCHRAMM, WILBUR 1963 Communication Research in the United States. Pages 1–16 in Wilbur Schramm (editor), *The Science of Human Communication.* New York: Basic Books.

# HRDLIČKA, ALEŠ

Aleš Hrdlička (1869–1943), a leading American physical anthropologist, was born in Humpolec, Bohemia (now Czechoslovakia), the oldest of seven children of Maximilian and Caroline Hrdlička. In 1882 he immigrated with his father to New York City where he first worked in a cigar factory while learning English in night schools. Later he attended the Eclectic Medical College in New York City, from which he graduated in 1892 at the head of his class. To improve his medical standing he then attended the New York Homeopathic Medical College and Hospital, also in New York City, graduating in 1894, and again topping his class. He immediately began interning in the State Homeopathic Hospital for the Insane at Middletown, New York. In 1896, after accepting a research position in the Pathological Institute of the New York State Hospitals, he went to Paris where, among other things, he studied anthropology under Léonce Manouvrier.

Hrdlička's program at the institute brought him

into contact with F. W. Putnam of the department of anthropology of the American Museum of Natural History. This connection led to an invitation to accompany the explorer and author Carl Lumholtz on a trip to Mexico in 1898. The resulting experience with American Indians was a turning point in Hrdlička's career; when the Pathological Institute closed in 1899, he turned his attention entirely to anthropology. From that time until the end of 1902, he participated in the Hyde expeditions of the American Museum to the Southwest and to Mexico.

In 1903 Hrdlička accepted an invitation from William H. Holmes to become assistant curator in charge of a new division of physical anthropology of the United States National Museum in Washington. In 1910 he was made curator, which position he held until his retirement in 1942.

One of Hrdlička's first acts as assistant curator was to arrange for the transfer to the National Museum of human skeletal material found at archeological sites which the Smithsonian Institution had deposited at the Army Medical Museum. He then devoted his energies to extending the geographical, chronological, and racial coverage of the collection. At the same time he continued his studies of living peoples. The extent of these activities can best be seen in the record of his travels: 1905—southern Arizona and New Mexico (Apache and Pima); 1906—Florida; 1909—Egypt and Europe; 1910—South America and Mexico; 1912—Europe, Siberia, and Mongolia; 1913—Peru; 1915—Minnesota and Missouri (Chippewa and Sioux); 1916—Florida; 1917—New England, Virginia, and Tennessee (Old Americans); 1918—Florida; 1920—Japan, Korea, China, and Hawaii; 1922—Brazil and Europe; 1923—Europe; 1925—Europe, India, southeast Asia, Australia, and South Africa; 1926–1938—Alaska and Commander Islands (Eskimo and Aleut); 1939—Europe and Siberia.

Ultimately Hrdlička accumulated for the museum one of the world's largest skeletal collections. By studying this material he was able to publish a large number of scientific reports, including catalogues of crania and monographs on the antiquity of man in America and on the most ancient skeletal remains from the Old World. He also published several reports on living American Indians, two books on the American white population (1925; 1931), and a book on anthropometry.

Hrdlička influenced anthropology through the *American Journal of Physical Anthropology*, which he founded in 1918 and edited until 1942, and through the American Association of Physical Anthropologists, which he founded in 1929, serving as president in 1930–1931. In these roles, unfortunately, he tried too much to control and dominate the thinking in the field.

Hrdlička also gave much of his time to general scientific organizations and international congresses. He was largely responsible for the organization of the 19th International Congress of Americanists held in Washington in 1919. He was elected a member of the American Philosophical Society in 1918 and of the National Academy of Sciences in 1921. In 1922 he received an honorary sc.d. from the University of Prague, in 1926 the same degree from the University of Brno, and in 1927 the Huxley Memorial Medal from the Royal Anthropological Institute of Great Britain and Ireland.

On his way to Europe in 1939 Hrdlička suffered a heart attack but, after a month in a hospital in England, continued on to Siberia. He died of a subsequent heart attack in Washington.

T. D. STEWART

[*For the historical context of Hrdlička's work, see* PHYSICAL ANTHROPOLOGY.]

### WORKS BY HRDLIČKA

(1920) 1952 *Practical Anthropometry*. Edited by T. D. Stewart. Philadelphia: Wistar Institute of Anatomy and Biology. → First published as *Anthropometry*.
1925 *The Old Americans*. Baltimore: Williams & Wilkins.
1931 *Children Who Run on All Fours, and Other Animallike Behaviors in the Human Child*. New York: McGraw-Hill.

### WORKS ABOUT HRDLIČKA

Dr. Aleš Hrdlička: Zivotopisný nástin. 1929 *Anthropologie* (Prague) 7:6–61.
SCHULTZ, ADOLPH H. 1945 Biographical Memoir of Aleš Hrdlička: 1869–1943. Volume 23, pages 305–338 in National Academy of Sciences, *Biographical Memoirs*. Washington: The Academy. → Contains a bibliography on pages 319–338.
STEWART, T. D. 1940 The Life and Writings of Dr. Aleš Hrdlička. *American Journal of Physical Anthropology* 26:3–40.
STEWART, T. D. 1964 Aleš Hrdlička: Pioneer American Physical Anthropologist. Pages 505–509 in Czechoslovak Society of Arts and Sciences in America, *The Czechoslovak Contribution to World Culture*. The Hague: Mouton.

# HUIZINGA, JOHAN

Johan Huizinga (1872–1945), the Dutch cultural historian, was born in Groningen and died at De Steeg, a village outside Arnhem. His family combined the deep piety of a long line of Baptist ministers with a scientific devotion to factual truth, exemplified by Huizinga's father, a doctor and professor of physiology at Groningen. Although in his mature years Huizinga subscribed to no religious confession, he was a lifelong believer; his nonconformist background was partly responsible for his toleration, his respect for the privacy of others, his strong ethical stoicism, and his moderation in political (even in historical) issues. His respect for factual integrity is everywhere apparent in his work and became the basis for his attack upon totalitarianism.

After studying Dutch language and literature at Groningen and taking his degree in 1896 in comparative philology (on a Sanskrit subject), Huizinga began teaching history to high school students in Haarlem. Here he did the research for his first— and only archival—historical work, a study of the rise of Haarlem (1905–1906). Through his mentor, the historian Petrus Johannes Blok, Huizinga was appointed professor of history at Groningen in 1905: his inaugural lecture, "Het aesthetische bestanddeel van geschiedkundige voorstellingen" (1905; "The Aesthetic Element in Historical Presentation"), gave promise of his use of literature and the visual arts to interpret history. Until his appointment as professor of history at Leiden, however, the harvest of this approach remained only a promise.

It was in his Leiden years, from 1915 until his death, that Huizinga's special talents were revealed. His youthful interest in *fin-de-siècle* literature (French, English, and Dutch) and his knowledge of Flemish "primitive" and modern painting provided him with a fresh view of the social significance of aesthetic forms. *The Waning of the Middle Ages* (1919), his masterpiece, is a study of the forms of life of fifteenth-century France and Burgundy, based upon his critical reading of aesthetic and philological sources normally overlooked by the working historian. Huizinga attempted to do for the late medieval North what his acknowledged master, Jacob Burckhardt, had done for the Italian Renaissance.

In 1918 Huizinga published "Mensch en menigte in Amerika" ("Man and Mass in America"), an extrapolation from American materials worked up to introduce his Leiden students to American history—itself an event of considerable cultural importance. After several studies of Renaissance history (1920; 1924), he published "De taak der cultuurgeschiedenis" ("The Task of Cultural History") in 1929. It was a description and prescription for his students and other historians, in which he plainly advocated subsuming to history other "philological" disciplines—the law, philosophy, histories of music, literature, and the fine arts—as

well as pillaging from the social sciences conceptualizations to facilitate both the setting of historical questions and the organization of historical answers.

Except for his study of Haarlem, Huizinga made no great contributions to political or economic history; unlike Burckhardt, he did not seem to regard even the state as a work of art. Huizinga was primarily interested in "intellectual" history, the history of the literate classes; but he was further interested in every aspect of "social" history, the forms through which men in the past conducted their lives. From texts normally regarded as nonhistorical, Huizinga produced evidence for forms of collective and private life of past periods and places. Like an archeologist, he excavated life "as it really was." His methodological writings from this period emphasize the usefulness to historians of the insights and methods of sociology and anthropology.

Although Huizinga never collected quantitative data for his own research, he nonetheless respected conclusions about social and cultural habits based on quantitative analysis. His own preference for the work of Max Weber and Ernst Troeltsch, among sociologists, and for Marcel Mauss, among anthropologists, was the result of his admiration of the hypotheses they framed and their use of hypotheses in the analysis of various data. His own comparable work is his study of seventeenth-century Dutch culture (1932), the best epitome of that complex period ever written; there he advanced the thesis that Dutch Calvinism was not of primary importance in the formation of Golden Age culture. *The Waning of the Middle Ages* and *Homo ludens* (1938) extrapolate cultural manifestations from surrounding historical data in order to draw up, more schematically than is usual in historical writing, the structure of, in the first instance, northern European society in the fifteenth century and, in the second, the functions and variations of play, playing, and games in human culture as a whole. Huizinga was much interested in the historical work of the group headed by Lucien Febvre and Marc Bloch, to be found in the periodical *Annales d'histoire économique et sociale*, with its self-conscious use of social materials and sociological method. However, despite this sociological emphasis, Huizinga reacted unfavorably to the work of Freud and seems to have made almost no use of Marxian ideas throughout his work.

From 1935 on, Huizinga's principal work was not historical, although it was certainly cultural, or moral–sociological. In that year, only two years after Hitler's *coup*, he published *In the Shadow of*

*Tomorrow: A Diagnosis of the Spiritual Distemper of Our Time*, a highly polemical study of contemporary mass culture. Although his critics attacked his disgust with the cheapness of the radio and of yellow journalism as reactionary, Huizinga regarded these as signs of a general loss of value far more seriously manifest in the political, social, and moral behavior of contemporary totalitarianism. Ten years later, his posthumous *Geschonden wereld: Een beschouwing over de kansen op herstel van onze beschaving* (1945; "World in Ruins: A Consideration of the Chances of Rebuilding Our Civilization") was published, both a sequel and a corrective to *In the Shadow of Tomorrow*. Like de Tocqueville (really, even more than Burckhardt, Huizinga's model) in *Democracy in America*, Huizinga was conservative in his insistence upon conscientious individual responsibility and optimistic in his conviction that by individual recommitment a collective responsible world could be reconstructed.

*Homo ludens*, Huizinga's most extraordinary and original book, is a study of the "play-element" in culture—occidental, oriental, primitive, ancient, and modern. He considered all sorts of playing, from children's games to the dialectic of philosophy and of the law courts. By no means a history book—its lesson is psychosociological or even metasocial rather than historical—*Homo ludens* is nonetheless the book of a historian who relates each specific form of such an activity as play to the temporal and local culture of which it is a part.

A generation earlier, Huizinga might have become a literary and artistic critic; a generation later, he might have become a sociologist. As it was, he practiced cultural history as if "high" culture and "sociological" or "anthropological" culture were mutually dependent. Although he preferred the man to the mass, the individual to the crowd, he saw the task of the cultural historian to be the interpretation of societies, or groups made up of individuals. Huizinga's work has made it difficult for historians to ignore the signs of nonpolitical social forms within which human beings have always lived their lives.

ROSALIE L. COLIE

[*For the historical context of Huizinga's work, see* HISTORY, *articles on* INTELLECTUAL HISTORY *and* SOCIAL HISTORY; *and the biographies of* BURCKHARDT; MAUSS; TOCQUEVILLE; TROELTSCH; WEBER, MAX.]

## WORKS BY HUIZINGA

(1905) 1952 Het aesthetische bestanddeel van geschiedkundige voorstellingen. Volume 7, pages 3–28 in Johan Huizinga, *Verzamelde werken*. Haarlem: Tjeenk Willink.

(1905–1906) 1948 De opkomst van Haarlem. Volume 1, pages 203–364 in Johan Huizinga, *Verzamelde werken*. Haarlem: Tjeenk Willink.

(1918) 1950 Mensch en menigte in Amerika: Vier essays over moderne beschavingsgeschiedenis. Volume 5, pages 249–417 in Johan Huizinga, *Verzamelde werken*. Haarlem: Tjeenk Willink.

(1919) 1924 *The Waning of the Middle Ages: A Study in the Forms of Life, Thought and Art in France and the Netherlands in the 14th and 15th Centuries.* London: Arnolds. → First published in Dutch. A paperback edition was published in 1954 by Doubleday.

(1920) 1949 Renaissancestudiën I: Het probleem. Volume 4, pages 231–275 in Johan Huizinga, *Verzamelde werken*. Haarlem: Tjeenk Willink.

(1924) 1952 *Erasmus of Rotterdam.* 3d ed. London: Phaidon. → First published in Dutch.

(1929) 1952 De taak der cultuurgeschiedenis. Volume 7, pages 35–94 in Johan Huizinga, *Verzamelde werken*. Haarlem: Tjeenk Willink.

1932 *Holländische Kultur des siebzehnten Jahrhunderts: Ihre sozialen Grundlagen und nationale Eigenart.* Jena (Germany): Diedrichs.

(1935) 1936 *In the Shadow of Tomorrow: A Diagnosis of the Spiritual Distemper of Our Time.* London: Heinemann; New York: Norton. → First published in Dutch.

(1938) 1949 *Homo ludens: A Study of the Play-element in Culture.* London: Routledge. → First published in Dutch. A paperback edition was published in 1955 by Beacon.

1942 *Im Bann der Geschichte: Betrachtungen und Darstellungen.* Basel and Amsterdam: Pantheon.

1945 *Geschonden wereld: Een beschouwing over de kansen op herstel van onze beschaving.* Haarlem: Tjeenk Willink.

1947 *Mein Weg zur Geschichte.* Basel: Benno Schwabe.

*Verzamelde werken.* 9 vols. Haarlem: Tjeenk Willink, 1948–1953. → Volume 1: *Oud-Indie; Nederland*, 1948. Volume 2: *Nederland*, 1948. Volumes 3–5: *Cultuurgeschiedenis*, 1949–1950. Volume 6: *Biografie*, 1951. Volume 7: *Geschiedwetenschap; Hedendaagsche cultuur*, 1952. Volume 8: *Universiteit: Wetenschap en kunst*, 1952. Volume 9: *Bibliographie en registers*, 1953.

## SUPPLEMENTARY BIBLIOGRAPHY

COLIE, R. L. 1964 Johan Huizinga and the Task of Cultural History. *American Historical Review* 63:607–630.

GEYL, PIETER (1946) 1962 De betekenis van Huizinga. Pages 122–127 in Pieter Geyl, *Nederlandse figuren I*. Amsterdam: Wereld-Bibliotheek.

GEYL, PIETER 1961 *Huizinga als aanklager van zijn tijd*. Amsterdam: North-Holland Publishing.

KAEGI, WERNER 1946 Johan Huizinga zum Gedächtnis. Volume 2, pages 7–42 in Werner Kaegi, *Historische Meditationen*. Zurich: Fretz & Wasmuth.

KAMERBEEK, J. 1954 Huizinga en de beweging van tachtig. *Tijdschrift voor geschiedenis* 67:145–164.

ROMEIN, JAN M. 1950 Huizinga als historicus. Pages 212–253 in Jan Romein, *Tussen vrees en vrijheid: vijftien historische verhandelingen*. Amsterdam: Querido.

VALKENBURG, CHRISTIAAN T. VAN 1946 *J. Huizinga: Zijn leven en zijn persoonlijkheid*. Amsterdam: Pantheon.

# HULL, CLARK L.

Clark L. Hull (1884–1952) was the most influential figure in the experimental psychology of learning during the decades immediately preceding and following World War II [see LEARNING; LEARNING THEORY]. This was not because his researches were unusually definitive or his theory universally accepted. If there was a single cause, it was that Hull presented his theoretical ideas with a degree of rigor and analytical detail then unfamiliar in psychology. A substantial proportion of the research in learning in this era was formulated in terms of Hull's theory, whether designed to sustain or to disprove it, and virtually all such research at least acknowledged a relationship to Hullian conceptions. Although Hull's theory contained some ambiguities and inconsistencies, it set a challenging level of explicitness that contributed in an important way to the developing image of psychology as a science.

Hull's ideas drew on many sources. Darwin had proposed the principle of natural selection that formed a rationale for much of Hull's theory. Many of the phenomena of conditioning that Hull described and some of the theoretical constructs that he espoused had been discussed by Pavlov. Freud had asserted the central role of motivation in behavior, a position Hull increasingly adopted. Watson had established the behavioristic departure from earlier introspectionism; Hull followed in the less radical, neobehavioristic tradition. Thorndike's law of effect, asserting the important role of reinforcement in learning, was central to Hull's major theorizing. Tolman had described the place of the intervening variable in behavior theory and had drawn the critical distinction between learning and performance, which Hull later formalized. Not only was Hull indebted to these predecessors, but he was unusually careful also to acknowledge the important contributions of his colleagues, notably Neal E. Miller and Kenneth W. Spence, in developing his approach.

To this potpourri of influences, Hull added integration and purpose. He made more explicit the ideas of these and other men and in so doing added a wealth of his own conceptual innovations. He believed that controlled studies of simple learning situations would reveal a core set of principles of behavior and that these could then be applied to the more complex conditions of individual and group behavior. If successful, this program, he felt, would have inestimable value for understanding, predicting, and, where appropriate, controlling behavior.

Hull was born in a log cabin on a farm in New York State in 1884. His education, which began in a rural school, was interrupted by a job as a mining engineer and an attack of poliomyelitis that made the use of a cane necessary thereafter. He was 34 when he received a PH.D. from the University of Wisconsin. Early in life, Hull began a series of personal notebooks in which he recorded a variety of facts, ideas, and reflections, hoping to preserve the thoughts of his youth for later, less creative years. These "idea books" show an early sense of destiny and a developing obsession with urgency. They also contain many detailed analyses of his theory-in-the-making which illustrate his conviction that the explicit, formal statement of an idea is most likely to reveal its weaknesses. As he said in *Principles of Behavior*, "It is believed that a clear formulation, even if later found incorrect, will ultimately lead more quickly and easily to a correct formulation than will a pussyfooting statement which might be more difficult to convict of falsity" (1943, p. 398). Hull was uncompromising in his expectation of speed, effort, and punctuality from his associates and intolerant of slipshod thinking by his students. He was generous both with personal attention and professional credit to all who worked with him. He consciously avoided vindictive arguments, to which some of the reviews of his work could easily have led, but accepted, indeed welcomed, considered criticism.

Hull's early scientific activities are noteworthy in themselves. Continuing at the University of Wisconsin after obtaining his degree, Hull worked in the area of the measurement and prediction of achievement. His first major work, *Aptitude Testing* (1928), reveals his principal concern—the problems of validation of tests. To reduce computational time and errors, Hull designed an automatic correlation machine, a beautifully complex unit that, as he said in his autobiography, "really worked," and that illustrates his unusual talent for gadgetry. He then became interested in hypnosis and conducted a series of experimental studies, published in his second major work, *Hypnosis and Suggestibility* (1933), that brought scientific rigor to this often quasi-scientific area. Hull moved to the Institute of Human Relations at Yale University in 1929 and there, at the age of 45, started to formalize a mechanistic theory of behavior. He was to make his major contribution to psychology in this area. [See ACHIEVEMENT TESTING; APTITUDE TESTING; HYPNOSIS; SUGGESTION.]

The institute housed a vigorous group of workers of varying ages, fields, and persuasions, all dedicated to the concept of a science of behavior.

Nevertheless, it was 11 years before Hull and several colleagues formalized a set of learning principles in *Mathematico–Deductive Theory of Rote Learning* (1940), a work less well known than it deserves to be, probably because of its use of the language of formal logic and mathematics. Three years later a more general and readable statement of the fundamental principles appeared in Hull's third and most influential major work, *Principles of Behavior* (1943). Another nine years passed before Hull's *A Behavior System* (1952a) described selected examples of more complex individual behavior in terms of his theoretical principles. This last work was published posthumously; the intended application to social and cultural problems remained to be written at the time of Hull's death in 1952.

**Reinforcement theory of learning.** Hull's theory can be characterized as a mechanistic stimulus–response conception of behavior. Learning, Hull believed, consists in the bonding together of some stimulus event (a light, a tone, a maze) with some response of the organism (salivating, running, turning). Behavior in general is describable in terms of hierarchies and constellations of such connections. Hull did not, however, deny the reality of ideas, knowledge, and purpose; indeed, he accepted these as obvious descriptive properties of molar behavior. He argued, rather, that these are not the basic units of behavior and that they are understandable in terms of more fundamental stimulus–response events. He introduced, therefore, the notion of the fractional, anticipatory goal response, which assumes that a portion of the reinforcing event at the end of a behavior chain can have an effect at the beginning of the chain. This response, or more properly, its response-produced stimulus, serves to guide overt behavior, as if purposefully, toward the goal. Whatever the complexity of behavior apparent to direct inspection, it could be reduced to simpler principles by the further discovery of response mechanisms, often hypothetical internal responses with no other function than to provide the organism with guiding stimuli.

*Principles of Behavior* provides the epitome of a reinforcement theory of learning: the formation of stimulus–response connections is assumed to depend on a subsequent reinforcing state of affairs, and the degree to which the connection is strengthened depends upon the quantitative properties of the reinforcement. That is to say, learning occurs only if the response is rewarded, and the larger and more immediate the reward, the better the learning. Recognizing the possible circularity of this theory in the absence of an independent definition of re-

inforcement, Hull proposed the drive reduction hypothesis [*see* DRIVES]. He assumed that a hungry rat learns to run through a maze because the turning responses at the choice-points are reinforced by the eventual reduction in hunger drive occasioned by eating in the goal box. Furthermore, since choice-points near the goal are followed most quickly by this reinforcement, Hull correctly inferred that errors would be eliminated in backward fashion, the appropriate responses at the beginning of the maze being learned last. These two explicit postulates—that learning occurs only if responses are reinforced and that reinforcement occurs only if a drive is reduced—generated a substantial proportion of the research of Hull and his colleagues.

**Habit and drive.** The stimulus–response connection, which Hull called habit strength and symbolized $_sH_R$, is itself not the sole determinant of behavior. In order to appear in overt performance, habits must be energized by drive. This latter construct, symbolized $D$, is related to presumed biological and survival needs of the organism and species (hunger, thirst, pain, sex) and is assumed to combine multiplicatively with habit to determine excitatory potential ($_sE_R$), which in turn determines performance. This equation—$_sE_R = _sH_R \times D$—formalizes the distinction between learning and performance and inextricably entangles learning with motivation. When elaborated and expanded, the formulation became a powerful source of hypotheses.

The proper use of this equation requires a sophisticated understanding of both habit and drive. Consider first $_sH_R$. The actual stimulus to which a response is attached is not the distal event as it occurs in the environment or even the proximal event as it occurs on the receptor. Rather, it is a trace of this latter event, which, according to Hull, decays over time. Moreover, because stimuli are never exactly identical, Hull further hypothesized that habit learned to one stimulus generalizes some habit strength to other similar stimuli. The postulates of the stimulus trace and habit generalization illustrate the way Hull derived behavioral phenomena.

Pavlov had shown that if the sound of a bell regularly occurs, say, ten seconds before food is delivered to a hungry dog, the salivation that had occurred only after the food was in the dog's mouth becomes anticipatory, i.e., begins to occur when the bell sounds and before the food arrives. Hull's theoretical interpretation is that the bell initiates a stimulus trace in the nervous system of the dog which immediately begins to decay, but which is present in some unique intensity ten seconds later when the food is delivered. Since the food elicits salivation as an unlearned reflex, and since it also provides reinforcement by reducing hunger, the appropriate conditions are present for the formation of a habit connection between the ten-second trace of the bell and salivation. Now, because earlier traces of a bell are similar to the ten-second trace of that same bell, the habit being formed to the latter will generalize to the former. Hence, the dog salivates anticipatorily as a result of generalization. By making explicit quantitative assumptions about the shape of the stimulus trace function and the degree of generalization between different traces, one can make detailed derivations about the expected latency of salivation at different stages of training and the importance of the time interval separating the ringing of the bell and the presentation of the food.

Hull also expanded the construct of drive. Perhaps his most important elaboration is the concept of the association of any particular intensity of any particular drive (e.g., a rat deprived of food for 24 hours) and a characteristic drive stimulus which differs to some extent from that produced by other drives (e.g., deprivation of water) or other intensities of the same drive (e.g., 12 hours of food deprivation). Hence, although Hull's conception of drive is that of a general energizer—hunger can as well motivate a response learned under thirst— drives do have a directing function, because each drive stimulus will tend to become selectively attached to those responses most likely to reduce it. Thus, a rat in a maze can learn to turn right when hungry and left when thirsty even though, as motivators, these drives act indiscriminately on all habits.

Given the fact that there is experimental extinction—the weakening and disappearance of responses when reinforcement is terminated—Hull was faced with two theoretical alternatives. One was the assumption that $_sH_R$ itself is weakened by nonreinforcement. However, there were a variety of reasons for believing that learning is a relatively permanent process, not the least of which is the dramatic evidence of memory Hull had obtained using hypnosis. Hence, Hull followed Pavlov in assuming that experimental extinction does not represent the loss of habit, but rather the accumulation of inhibition. Excitatory potential is reduced by inhibition resulting from nonreinforcement; the dog does not forget how to salivate to the bell; instead, learning is inhibited if food no longer follows the bell.

The system was completed by relating excitatory potential to performance. One common response

measure is the probability that a response will occur on any presentation of a stimulus. To adapt this measure to his theory, Hull borrowed the notion of a threshold from physiology and assumed that excitatory potential is subject to oscillation from moment to moment according to an essentially random distribution. A response will occur only if $_sE_R$ is above threshold at the moment and, if this is so, the speed and amplitude of response will depend directly upon the momentary value of excitatory potential.

One of the persistent problems that Hull faced in developing his theory was that the intervening variables such as habit and drive are inherently unobservable by direct inspection and hence cannot be measured. Since the theory is cast in quantitative terms, Hull's derivations typically consist of illustrative examples, with arbitrary values for the important variables. He foresaw the importance of quantifying these variables in units that might be applied to the wide range of situations to which the theory was intended to apply. Toward this end, Hull undertook a meticulous series of studies employing the Thurstone scaling technique to quantify habit and drive. Hull valued this work greatly, in keeping with his belief that mathematics is a fundamental tool of behavioral as well as physical science.

**Stimulus dynamism and incentive motivation.** Almost as soon as *Principles of Behavior* was published, major modifications of its theory began. One unsolved problem was the role of stimulus intensity; Hull became convinced that not only do drive stimuli have energizing and directing functions, but that all stimuli have dynamogenic as well as cue properties. Furthermore, the rapid changes in an animal's response after a change in the amount of reward suggested that reinforcement is a motivational variable as well as a learning variable. A new equation for excitatory potential therefore appeared. It included the concepts of stimulus dynamism based on the intensity of the eliciting stimulus, and of incentive motivation based on the amount and time of delay of reward as additional motivational factors multiplying habit. According to this new conception, a dog salivates more to a strong than a weak bell not because he has learned to salivate better, but because the stronger stimulus energizes a more vigorous response. A rat runs a maze faster for a larger reward than for a smaller not because he has learned the maze better, but because the larger reward provides more incentive to run. Motivational factors thus began to dominate Hull's learning theory, although he clung to the assumption that some reinforcement is required for the accretion of habit strength.

**Discrimination learning.** All these hypotheses were generated on the basis of data obtained in relatively simple learning situations. The logic of Hull's program, it will be recalled, is that these principles will be applicable, when properly interpreted and possibly expanded, to more complex situations as well.

In *A Behavior System*, Hull described the following case, among others: If an organism is confronted with two stimuli differing, let us say, in brightness, and is consistently rewarded if he chooses one of these, he will learn to behave adaptively; he will learn to discriminate between the stimuli and consistently to choose the rewarded alternative. In Hullian language, choice between responses is somehow based on excitatory potential. The simplest hypothesis is that if several responses are in competition the one that has the largest excitatory potential will occur. With the choice measure specified in this way, discrimination learning follows readily from the theory.

It is first noted that the excitatory potential of the positive stimulus will be increased by the reinforcement following responses to it. Although generalization will produce some excitatory potential for the nonreinforced stimulus, this will be reduced by the inhibition developed whenever response is made to it. Thus, continued training will lead to a gradual separation of the excitatory potentials of the two stimuli and hence a developing preference for the reinforced one. A number of additional and more detailed implications also follow. For example, the discrimination should be easier the more different the two stimuli are, since there will be less generalization between them and more rapid separation of their excitatory potentials. As is true of most useful theories, this analysis has more implications than appear at first glance, many of which have been derived by Spence (1960) from his related theory and tested with tolerably good results.

**Assessment of Hull's theory.** Hull correctly foresaw that the details of his theory were tentative and likely to require revision as relevant data were collected. His principal lasting contribution lies more in his extensive illustration of an approach to behavior theory than in the specific theory itself. This approach leans heavily upon the availability of empirical data, since it involves the postulation of intervening variables or empirical constructs which are intended to summarize the existing data and to generalize upon them for predicting new data. For example, it is known that rats run a maze to water faster the longer they have been previously deprived of water. The intervening variable approach assumes that deprivation of water affects the organism by producing thirst that potentiates the response. It is important to note the two essential criteria of an adequately formulated intervening variable: it must be anchored to some independent variable such as deprivation, and it must also be anchored to some dependent variable such as response speed.

Hull believed that intervening variables actually exist in the neurophysiological structure of the organism, and many of his postulates are couched in physiological-sounding terms. Some critics may therefore incorrectly assume that the usefulness of the theory is dependent upon the adequacy of such physiological speculations. But Hull intended only to stress the ultimate reducibility of molar behavioral events to more predictable molecular physiological events and to suggest possible rather than specific avenues toward such reduction. For example, he felt that his concept of drive might be related to endocrine and chemical mechanisms, and if this were true, an important link would be established between psychology and physiology. But such a result would be a bonus; the value of the approach is assessed by its ability to predict behavioral facts and not by its physiological validity.

The construct "thirst" integrates a wider set of findings than the single one that longer water deprivation leads to faster running. The same independent variable (deprivation of water) also affects behavior in a number of other ways—the amount the rat will drink, the vigor with which he will operate a manipulandum, the intensity of electric shock he will tolerate in order to obtain water, etc. Furthermore, a number of operations other than the withholding of water can be found to produce the same pattern of behavioral consequences (responses)—feeding dry or salty food, injecting drugs into the rat's brain, etc. All of these empirical relationships are tied together by the single notion of thirst. A quite similar constellation of findings appears with deprivation of food, and the construct "drive" integrates at a more abstract level the energizing and directing functions common to hunger, thirst, and other needs.

The postulation of the combination rule that drive multiplies habit permits novel predictions. For example, since the choice between two alternatives depends upon the difference between their excitatory potentials, rats will learn a maze faster under high than under low drive. This is because the developing differential in habit, resulting from the reinforcement of only one alternative, will be amplified in proportion to the prevailing level of drive. When such implications are tested and the results fail to conform to prediction, the theory necessarily is modified.

The extension of the simple principles to more complex situations follows a similar progression. For example, when it is observed that a previously neutral stimulus paired temporally with a noxious stimulus takes on some of the properties ascribed to drive, the richness of the theory can be drawn upon to develop the concept of learned drive. The principles of learning should describe the way drives are acquired, and the principles of performance should describe the way such acquired drives affect behavior. Dollard and Miller (1950) have carefully extended the application of the basic principles along these lines, and they have applied the resulting theory to psychotherapy.

Hull assumed further that these same principles could be applied to still more molar social and economic situations. This might require some additional principles not apparent in the simple situations from which the theory sprang. A boy and a girl on a date are reacting in accordance with their drives and habits just as much as a rat in a maze; the drives include a variety of social pressures toward conformity, approval, and morality, and the habits involve fine discriminations of the cues provided by the other person. Hull believed that the reduction of such situations to his theoretical conception was in principle possible, and certainly could not be proved impossible a priori.

Hull's program, even as far as he carried it, was certainly not flawless, and it led psychologists to overestimate the imminent attainment of a general behavior theory. Hull tended to oversell the program, to offer more than could be delivered, to be willing to guess at systematic behavioral facts in order to construct the framework of a theory. Partly as a reaction to this, subsequent workers have tended to have more modest goals, to build miniature models, or to delve in detail into circumscribed aspects of the larger problem. When and where behavior theory on the grand scale will again be promoted cannot be predicted. Hull, for one, was confident that it could be achieved, that it would be achieved, and that his work would provide a useful stepping stone to the goal. His last book concludes with this hope:

And finally, the crowning achievement of all will be the creation of a really quantitative system of social behavior. . . . It seems incredible that nature would create one set of primary sensory-motor laws for the mediation of individual behavior and another set for the mediation of group behavior. Presumably, then, the laws which are derived for social behavior will be based for the most part on the same postulates as those which form the basis of individual behavior. If this turns out to be true, we are even now an appreciable distance on our way toward the ultimate goal of integrating the individual-social sciences with the group-social sciences.   (1952*a*, pp. 355–356)

FRANK A. LOGAN

[*See also the biographies of* THORNDIKE *and* TOLMAN.]

### WORKS BY HULL

1928   *Aptitude Testing.* New York: World.

1933   *Hypnosis and Suggestibility: An Experimental Approach.* New York: Appleton.

1940   *Mathematico–Deductive Theory of Rote Learning: A Study in Scientific Methodology,* by Clark L. Hull et al. New Haven: Yale Univ. Press; Oxford Univ. Press.

1943   *Principles of Behavior: An Introduction to Behavior Theory.* New York: Appleton.

1952*a*   *A Behavior System: An Introduction to Behavior Theory Concerning the Individual Organism.* New Haven: Yale Univ. Press.

1952*b*   *Autobiography.* Volume 4, pages 143–162 in *A History of Psychology in Autobiography.* Worcester, Mass.: Clark Univ. Press.

1962   *Psychology of the Scientist: 4. Passages From the "Idea Books" of Clark L. Hull. Perceptual and Motor Skills* 15:807–882. → Published posthumously.

### SUPPLEMENTARY BIBLIOGRAPHY

BEACH, FRANK A. 1959   Clark Leonard Hull: May 24, 1884–May 10, 1952. Volume 33, pages 124–146 in National Academy of Sciences, *Biographical Memoirs.* Washington: Government Printing Office.

DOLLARD, JOHN; and MILLER, NEAL E. 1950   *Personality and Psychotherapy: An Analysis in Terms of Learning, Thinking and Culture.* New York: McGraw-Hill.

HILGARD, ERNEST R. (1948) 1956   *Theories of Learning.* 2d ed. New York: Appleton.

HOVLAND, CARL I. 1952   Clark Leonard Hull: 1884–1952. *Psychological Review* 59:347–350.

KOCH, SIGMUND 1954   Clark L. Hull. Pages 1–176 in *Modern Learning Theory: A Critical Analysis of Five Examples,* by William K. Estes et al. New York: Appleton.

LOGAN, FRANK 1959   The Hull–Spence Approach. Volume 2, pages 293–358 in Sigmund Koch (editor), *Psychology: A Study of a Science.* New York: McGraw-Hill.

SPENCE, KENNETH W. 1951   Theoretical Interpretations of Learning. Pages 690–729 in Stanley S. Stevens (editor), *Handbook of Experimental Psychology.* New York: Wiley.

SPENCE, KENNETH W. 1960   *Behavior Theory and Learning: Selected Papers.* Englewood Cliffs, N.J.: Prentice-Hall.

## HUMAN CAPITAL
*See* CAPITAL, HUMAN.

## HUMAN ECOLOGY
*See under* ECOLOGY.

## HUMAN FACTORS ENGINEERING
*See* ENGINEERING PSYCHOLOGY.

## HUMAN GEOGRAPHY
*See* GEOGRAPHY, *article on* SOCIAL GEOGRAPHY.

## HUMAN RELATIONS IN INDUSTRY
*See under* INDUSTRIAL RELATIONS; *see also the biography of* MAYO.

## HUMAN RIGHTS

The subject of this article is the international concern with human rights. The article cannot, however, concentrate exclusively on the activities of international organizations and on conferences which purport to promote respect for human rights. The instruments, institutions, and operations of the international organizations of our day have roots in the philosophical, constitutional, and legal developments of many nations spread over many centuries. The work on the international plane has in its turn had considerable influence on constitutional, legal, and political developments within nation-states, not least on the written law of many of the states of Asia, Africa, and the Caribbean which have recently acceded to independence.

### Origins and basic concepts

The expression "human rights," as a term of art, is of recent origin. Even in its French-inspired form "rights of man" (*droits de l'homme*), it goes back only to the last decades of the eighteenth century. The idea, however, of the law, or the lawgiver, defining and protecting the legal rights of men—mainly the mutual rights of the members of the community—is very old indeed. It would, perhaps, be somewhat farfetched to look for elements of the protection of human rights in the Code of the Babylonian king Hammurabi (about 2130 to 2088 B.C.), the most ancient code of law at present known. The sanctions which it provides in trying to protect worthy human-rights objectives (such as the administration of justice, marriage, and the family) are so disproportionately cruel that it is preferable to disregard this legislator in our context. However, as Rudolph von Jhering pointed out a century ago, the law of ancient republican Rome guaranteed to the Roman citizen (not to the foreigner or to the slave) the right to take part in the government of his country by participating in the exercise of the power of legislation, in the administration of criminal justice, in electing public officials, and even in having a share in the police power (Jhering 1852–1878).

An eminent American scholar has said (Yntema 1958) that the concepts of the Roman civil law, which were formulated by the Roman juridical genius in order to render justice in the mutual relations of individual men, are in essence a practical definition of the rights of man and a reasonable and authoritative criterion to which those who seek justice and protection of the inherent dignity of the human person can appeal. This holds true, in Yntema's view, of the Roman law as it was applied on the continent of Europe and of the common law of the Anglo-Saxon countries. The common law and the civil law, so different in their institutions and techniques and, at the same time, so similar in their criteria of what is fair, offer an objective yardstick for judging conduct in terms of individual rights and freedoms. These systems have, of course, also tolerated institutions and practices which are inconsistent with the modern conception of a public order protecting human dignity. Nevertheless, through many centuries communities have existed where at least part of what are now considered to be fundamental human rights were well protected by elaborate and refined bodies of law.

In England of the seventeenth century battles were fought against the nonobservance of the ancient rights of Englishmen. Out of these struggles there came two great documents: the Petition of Right of 1628 and the Bill of Rights of 1689. These did not purport to define the basic human rights of all mankind. They were intended to give relief for specific grievances by limiting the power of the king and by strengthening the power of Parliament and of the courts. Their ideas and even their texts are, however, reflected in the work of the American and French revolutionaries of the eighteenth century: in the immortal passages of the American Declaration of Independence, in the Virginia bill of rights of 1776, in the French Declaration of the Rights of Man and of the Citizen, and in the American bill of rights.

In the course of the nineteenth and twentieth centuries, the example set by the United States and France of adopting bills of rights or otherwise embodying such rights in their constitutions, was followed on the entire continent of Europe, and the movement spread to the Americas, Asia, and Africa, but until very recently Britain and the British dominions and possessions remained aloof from this movement.

The Russian Revolution of 1917, while following the American–French precedent in the form of its pronouncements, gave it a fundamentally different substance. The difference lies not in the emphasis on economic and social rights in addition to the traditional political and civil rights. Such provisions are also found in other constitutions, for example, in the Mexican constitution of 1917, in the Weimar constitution of Germany of 1919, and in the constitution of the Republic of Spain of 1931. The difference between the Soviet pronouncements and their Western predecessors lies in the complete transformation of the meaning of political and civil rights.

This basic difference in concepts becomes clear when one compares the provisions of the American bill of rights with the corresponding provisions of the first Soviet constitution. The first amendment to the American constitution provides, among other things, that Congress shall make no law abridging the freedom of speech or of the press; the Russian constitution of 1918 "for the purpose of securing freedom of expression to the toiling masses," abolishes all dependence of the press upon capital, and turns over to the working people and the poorest peasantry "all technical and material means for the publication of newspapers, pamphlets, books," etc. The American constitution prohibits abridgment of the right of the people peaceably to assemble, while the Lenin constitution, in order to ensure complete freedom of assembly to the working class and to the poorest peasantry, offers "all premises convenient for public gatherings together with lighting, heating, and furniture."

The Soviet constitution of 1936, while changing the wording, has, by and large, maintained this general approach. The Western constitutional ideas were designed to prevent interference with fundamental rights mainly, though not exclusively, by the public authorities. The Soviet concept does not treat of this aspect at all. It promises to make available technical facilities; it does not promise freedom in the choice of the purposes for which they will be used. In trying to draw conclusions from the existence in so many legal systems of catalogues of rights, one must keep in mind these differences in the basic concepts.

## Human rights and international law

Attempts to seek a foundation for the rights of the individual in the law of nations go back to an early stage in the history of international law. The work of the Spanish theologian–lawyer Francisco de Vitoria—born 1480, died 1546—is perhaps the first attempt to use legal reasoning, moral principle, and political courage in support of a cause which we might consider as involving human rights as well as international law. He lectured about "the Indians recently discovered" and pleaded for their rights vis-à-vis the Spanish conquerors. The greatest figures in the literature of international law in the seventeenth and eighteenth centuries exercised a powerful influence on the growth of the concept of the inalienable rights of man. In 1950 Sir Hersch Lauterpacht characterized the close connection between human rights and international law by saying that "the law of nations, in itself conceivable only as being above the legal order of sovereign States, is not only a law governing their mutual relations but is also, upon final analysis, the universal law of humanity in which the individual human being as the ultimate unit of all law rises sovereign over the limited province of the State" (p. 120).

In the field of action, as distinct from scholarship, the international concern with human rights has manifested itself in two different ways: by socalled "humanitarian intervention" and by the adoption of international treaties.

In traditional international law it was assumed that a state had the authority to treat its own nationals as it saw fit. When, however, the illtreatment by a state of its own population was of such an intensity that it shocked the conscience of mankind, other states, usually the great powers of the period, took it upon themselves to threaten, or even to use, force in order to come to the rescue of the oppressed population. While resort to this type of action was not infrequent, the doctrine underlying it has never become a generally recognized part of international law because of the abuse inherent in the concept of "humanitarian intervention."

The protection of oppressed or endangered groups by international treaty started in the seventeenth and eighteenth centuries in matters of religious liberty. In the course of the nineteenth century the international treaty was used also to protect ethnic and racial groups and to combat the slave trade and slavery; in the twentieth century it has been used to improve labor conditions, to arrange for the supervision of the administration of mandated territories, and to provide under the supervision of the League of Nations for certain rights of racial, religious, or linguistic minorities in a number of states, mainly in central and eastern Europe.

## The United Nations and human rights

Not until the world had passed through the tragic events of World War II and had witnessed the barbarous acts committed by the totalitarian regimes of that period was the universal organization of the international community, the United Nations, charged with some responsibilities in the matter of human rights, and its members pledged themselves to take action for the achievement of universal respect for and observance of human rights and fundamental freedoms for all.

The San Francisco Charter of 1945 through which the peoples of the United Nations reaffirmed their faith in "fundamental human rights" did not define these rights. The charter has made it abundantly clear, however, that one particular activity at least is repugnant to it: discrimination on the grounds of race, sex, language, or religion.

Nor has the charter established specific international machinery for the enforcement of its human-rights provisions, except for arrangements under the trusteeship system. But it has created organs of general and wide competence—the General Assembly, the Security Council, and the Economic and Social Council—and it has laid the foundations for the establishment of an unlimited number of subsidiary bodies, including commissions in the field of human rights.

The General Assembly, and to some extent also the Economic and Social Council, have not hesitated to use their general powers of investigation and recommendation to take action of varying character and intensity in such situations as violations of religious or political freedom in eastern Europe, race conflict in South Africa, forced labor in various parts of the world, infringement of trade union freedom, practices violating the human dignity of women in less developed communities, the status of Buddhists in South Vietnam, and many others. The fight against colonialism has been one of the characteristics of the international scene in the post-World War II world. Rightly or wrongly, the majority of governments have, to a large extent, identified the struggle against colonial domination with the struggle for human rights.

**International bill of rights.** Since the United Nations Charter had not defined human rights and had not created special international institutions for their enforcement, it was widely assumed in 1945 that this would soon be done in an "International bill of rights." In 1947–1948 it was decided that this "bill" would consist of two or more documents: a declaration, a covenant, and "measures of implementation." In 1948 the General Assembly proclaimed in a resolution the first part of this bill of rights as the Universal Declaration of Human Rights. The drafting of the other parts of the bill has not yet been completed; according to later decisions, they are to consist of two covenants, one on civil and political rights, the other on economic, social, and cultural rights, with provision for international supervision of their implementation. (By the end of 1963 all the general and substantive provisions of the two covenants had been approved

on the General Assembly level, while—as of 1965 —the international procedural arrangements have still to be agreed upon.)

The declaration of 1948 is the only world-wide official document where the human rights of which the charter speaks are set forth. Its range is very wide. It proclaims not only the traditional political and civil rights and freedoms of its national predecessors but also "economic, social and cultural rights." The declaration has, to some extent, filled the gap created by the delay in completing the covenants and acquired a status different from and more important than the one which was originally intended for it. It has been used by the United Nations, by other international organizations and conferences, and by governments as a yardstick to measure the compliance by governments with the obligations deriving from the charter in matters of human rights. It has penetrated into international conventions, national constitutions, and legislation, and even, in isolated cases, into court proceedings.

The technique of developing international standards by proclaiming instruments of the declaration type has been frequently used, the most potent post-1948 example being the Declaration on the Granting of Independence to Colonial Countries and Peoples, of 1960. Additional human-rights declarations were also adopted: the Declaration of the Rights of the Child, in 1959, and the United Nations Declaration on the Elimination of All Forms of Racial Discrimination, in 1963. In other fields examples are the declarations on Permanent Sovereignty Over Natural Resources, 1962, and on Legal Principles Governing the Activities of States in the Exploration and Use of Outer Space, 1963. Many more are in various stages of drafting and preparation.

**Conventions on specific human-rights subjects.** While the work of drafting the comprehensive covenants on human rights has been going on, the United Nations and its specialized agencies have produced a considerable body of treaty law on the subject of human rights by adopting and putting into force conventions on more limited subjects. Important examples are the Freedom of Association and Protection of the Right to Organize Convention, 1948; the Genocide Convention, 1948; the Convention on the Political Rights of Women, 1952; the Conventions on the Status of Refugees, 1951, and of Stateless Persons, 1954; the Conventions on the Reduction of Statelessness, 1961, and on the Nationality of Married Women, 1957; the Supplementary Convention on the Abolition of Slavery, 1956, and the Convention on the Abolition of Forced Labor, 1957; the Discrimination (Employment and Occupation) Convention, 1958, and the Convention against Discrimination in Education, 1960; the Convention on Consent to Marriage, Minimum Age for Marriage and Registration of Marriages, 1962; and the International Convention on the Elimination of All Forms of Racial Discrimination, 1965.

**Regional arrangements.** In the years during which the United Nations has been slowly working its way toward the completion of the world-wide covenants, much more rapid progress was achieved in western Europe. Under the auspices of the Council of Europe, the European Convention of Human Rights of 1950 came into being, supplemented by protocols of 1952 and 1963 and by the European Social Charter of 1961. By the convention, the 15 European states which are parties to it have undertaken to secure to everyone within their jurisdiction the rights which it defines—most of the traditional political and civil rights. The convention established two new organs to ensure the observance of the engagements undertaken by the parties: the European Commission on Human Rights and the European Court of Human Rights.

The existence of the court is significant primarily as a symbol. Its jurisdiction is very narrowly circumscribed. It was established in 1959, and by the beginning of 1965 only two cases had gone before it. The commission, however, has played an important and effective part. Ten of the European states (not including the United Kingdom and France, the latter not being a party to the convention at all) have accepted the right of individuals to petition the commission and to claim to be the victims of a violation of the convention by one of the parties. It has been the commission's examination of petitions, and especially the examination of their admissibility, which offered the commission the opportunity to build up an impressive body of case law. And although in the overwhelming majority of cases the commission has had to reject the petition, its work has transformed the abstract idea of the international protection of human rights into a concrete, tangible, day-to-day task. This operation has laid bare the formidable problems and pitfalls inherent in so novel an experiment.

For many years, the Organization of American States has tried to establish inter-American institutions for the promotion of respect for human rights. In 1948 the "American Declaration of the Rights and Duties of Man" was proclaimed at Bogotá; conventions on political and civil rights of women and on territorial and diplomatic asylum were signed in 1948 and 1954 respectively. An Inter-American Convention on Human Rights providing for the establishment of a commission and a court of human rights, on the European model, was drafted by the Inter-American Council of Jurists in 1959. At the beginning of 1965 final action on the draft had not yet been taken by the political organs.

**Program of practical action.** The effectiveness and desirability of the international treaty as an instrument for the promotion of human rights was challenged early in the history of the United Nations. The most weighty challenge came in 1953 when U.S. Secretary of State John Foster Dulles stated that the new Eisenhower administration did not believe in "treaty coercion" and did not favor "formal undertakings" as the proper and most effective way to achieve throughout the world the goals of human liberty. As a consequence the United States declared its intention not to become a party to any covenant on human rights or to sign human-rights conventions of a more limited scope. As we have seen, the majority of governments has continued to hold that multilateral conventions have their place among the endeavors to give effect to the human-rights provisions of the charter. Those governments consented, however, to a new program proposed by the United States, provided it was adopted in addition to treaties and not instead of them.

Thus, in 1955–1956 the United Nations started a series of new activities: (1) periodic (triennial) reporting by states on developments; (2) studies of specific rights or groups of rights; and (3) advisory services in the field of human rights. A great number of governments have participated in the reporting procedure in the first three triennial cycles; the Commission on Human Rights has, however, not yet arrived at a final policy about the use to be made of the reports. The first of the studies was a world-wide inquiry and investigation into the status of the right to be free from arbitrary arrest, detention, and exile. The most fruitful branch of the program of advisory services has been the convening of mostly regional conferences (called seminars) to exchange views and experiences on important and topical problems, such as the protection of human rights in criminal law and procedure, the role of the police in the protection of human rights, or the status of women in family law. It was a series of seminars on judicial and other remedies against the illegal exercise or abuse of administrative authority which made the institution of the "ombudsman" known outside the Scandinavian countries and led to its acceptance in at least two other countries (England and New Zealand) and to its consideration elsewhere (Canada and some United States jurisdictions). One such regional conference, held in Kabul, Afghanistan, in 1964, was devoted to "human rights in developing countries," a basic problem which deserves more detailed discussion (Seminar . . . 1964).

## Human rights in developing countries

Observance of human rights poses problems everywhere, and no country's record, be it highly industrialized or economically underdeveloped, is faultless. In most of the countries which have acceded to independence only recently the problems are aggravated. Many of these countries have implacable enemies: poverty, ignorance, disease, and inertia. Western commentators have tended to underestimate the importance of illiteracy and ignorance, particularly in unsophisticated rural societies (De Smith 1964, p. 237). At the Kabul conference it was agreed that there could be no meaningful exercise of many human rights in a country where economic resources were scarce and the bulk of the population lived on the margin of subsistence. It was argued that in such matters as the development of the whole economy and the improvement of health, education, and housing, the state needed the necessary powers to implement its plans even though, meanwhile, the rights of individuals or groups might be temporarily curtailed. Some speakers wondered, however, whether the governments of some developing countries did not show an excessive concern for the internal and external security of the state and apply unnecessary restrictions on human rights.

Developing countries experience difficulties not only in regard to economic and social rights, the enjoyment of which clearly presupposes a certain economic standard, but also in regard to the "classical" civil and political rights. A basic prerequisite of the right to a fair trial is the existence of an adequate number of well-trained lawyers, and "crash programs" for their training were recommended at the Kabul conference. The scarcity of competent and efficient public officials is also an obstacle to progress in the human-rights field. Another specific problem of the underdeveloped world arises in the very sensitive area of "labor mobilization." In some countries, it was alleged at the conference, it is not yet possible to rely exclusively upon systems of voluntary labor to satisfy the basic needs of the nation. Recourse has sometimes to be had to certain forms of labor mobilization involving the compulsory removal of people to areas other than those of their residences. It was claimed, however, that such national labor services should be distinguished from the practices of forced labor which were forbidden by international conventions (see also Cowen 1964).

Neither the human-rights provisions of the United Nations Charter and the Universal Declaration of Human Rights nor the other treaties and declarations mentioned above have brought about the millennium. It is therefore not the purpose of this article to convey the idea that the rights set forth in these instruments are, in fact, respected and observed throughout the world. In 1952, in 1957, and, again, in 1962 the General Assembly of the United Nations reiterated that notwithstanding the obligations arising from the charter and notwithstanding the Universal Declaration of Human Rights, violations of human rights continue to occur in various parts of the world, and that notwithstanding some progress the situation in many parts of the world was unsatisfactory.

The task of making the protection of human rights general, permanent, and effective still lies ahead. This should not lead us, however, to belittle the progress that has been achieved on the international and national levels since World War II. Whatever the technical position might be in particular instances, and however difficult it might often be to achieve redress through international or national remedies, the traditional concept, that the way a state treats those subject to its power and jurisdiction is within its unfettered discretion, is a thing of the past. A vast but asymmetrical structure of international obligations has been built, some vague, some precise; and injunctions and exhortations have been issued, some authoritative, others less so. The fate of the individual may still in fact be at the mercy of his state, but it is also a matter of continuing and increasing international concern.

EGON SCHWELB

[See also INTERNATIONAL CRIMES. Other relevant material may be found in CONSTITUTIONAL LAW, articles on CIVIL LIBERTIES and CIVIL RIGHTS; INTERNATIONAL LAW; INTERNATIONAL ORGANIZATION.]

### BIBLIOGRAPHY

BOUTMY, ÉMILE (1902) 1907 La déclaration des droits de l'homme et du citoyen et M. Jellinek. Pages 119–182 in Émile Boutmy, Études politiques. Paris: Colin. → First published in Volume 17 of the Annales des sciences politiques.

CASSIN, RENÉ 1952 La déclaration universelle et la mise en oeuvre des droits de l'homme. The Hague, Academy of International Law, Recueil des cours, 1951 79:237–367.

COWEN, DENIS V. 1964 Human Rights in Contemporary Africa. Natural Law Forum 9:1–24.

DE SMITH, STANLEY A. 1964 *The New Commonwealth and Its Constitutions.* London: Stevens.

FRIEDRICH, CARL J. 1963 Rights, Liberties, Freedoms: A Reappraisal. *American Political Science Review* 57: 841–854.

GANJI, MANOUCHEHR 1962 *International Protection of Human Rights.* Geneva: Droz.

GOLSONG, HERIBERT 1958 *Das Rechtsschutzsystem der europäischen Menschenrechtskonvention.* Karlsruhe (Germany): Müller.

GURADZE, HEINZ 1956 *Der Stand der Menschenrechte im Völkerrecht.* Göttingen (Germany): Schwartz.

HAMBURGER, ERNEST 1960 Droits de l'homme et relations internationales. The Hague, Academy of International Law, *Recueil des cours, 1959.* 97:293–429.

HOLCOMBE, ARTHUR N. 1948 *Human Rights in the Modern World.* New York Univ. Press; Oxford Univ. Press.

JELLINEK, GEORG (1898) 1901 *The Declaration of the Rights of Man and of Citizens: A Contribution to Modern Constitutional History.* New York: Holt. → First published in German. A third German edition was published in 1919 by Duncker and Humblot.

JHERING, RUDOLPH VON (1852–1878) 1906–1923 *Geist des römischen Rechts auf den verschiedenen Stufen seiner Entwicklung.* 6th ed., 3 vols. Leipzig: Breitkopf & Härtel.

LAUTERPACHT, HERSCH 1945 *An International Bill of the Rights of Man.* New York: Columbia Univ. Press.

LAUTERPACHT, HERSCH 1950 *International Law and Human Rights.* New York: Praeger.

LIN, MOU-SHÊNG 1963 The Human Rights Program. *Annual Review of United Nations Affairs* [1961/1962]: 102–136.

MCDOUGAL, MYRES S.; and BEBR, GERHARD 1964 Human Rights in the United Nations. *American Journal of International Law* 58:603–641.

ROBERTSON, ARTHUR H. 1963 *Human Rights in Europe.* Dobbs Ferry, N.Y.: Oceana; Manchester (England) Univ. Press.

SCHWELB, EGON 1960 International Conventions on Human Rights. *International and Comparative Law Quarterly* 9:654–675.

SCHWELB, EGON 1964 *Human Rights and the International Community: The Roots and Growth of the Universal Declaration of Human Rights, 1948–1963.* Chicago: Quadrangle Books.

SEMINAR ON HUMAN RIGHTS IN DEVELOPING COUNTRIES, KABUL 1964 *Seminar on Human Rights in Developing Countries, Kabul, Afghanistan.* New York: United Nations. → Organized by the United Nations in cooperation with the government of Afghanistan.

UNITED NATIONS, GENERAL ASSEMBLY *Official Records.* → Published since 1946. Contains resolutions adopted by the General Assembly, first to twentieth sessions.

U.S. CONGRESS, SENATE, COMMITTEE ON FOREIGN RELATIONS 1955 *Review of the United Nations Charter: A Collection of Documents.* 83rd Congress, 2d Session. Senate Document No. 87. Washington: Government Printing Office. → See especially pages 263 and 295.

VASAK, KAREL 1964 *La convention européenne des droits de l'homme.* Paris: Librairie Générale de Droit et de Jurisprudence.

*Yearbook on Human Rights.* → Published by the United Nations since 1946.

*Yearbook of the European Convention on Human Rights— The European Commission and European Court of Human Rights.* → Published since 1955. From 1955– 1957 published as *Documents and Decisions of the European Commission of Human Rights,* prepared by the Directorate of Human Rights of the Council of Europe.

YNTEMA, HESSEL E. 1958 Le droit comparé et l'humanisme. *Revue internationale de droit comparé* 10:693– 700.

# HUMBOLDT, ALEXANDER VON

Alexander von Humboldt (1769–1859), the most famous German of his time, was celebrated as a geographer, explorer, and naturalist; he was less well known for his valuable contributions to the development of the social sciences. He came from a Pomeranian family that had been lately ennobled. After the early death of his father, a major in the Prussian Army, his bourgeois mother ceased to keep up the family's connections with the court; instead, she employed excellent private tutors to set her two sons on the road traveled by the bourgeois elite—the sciences. Humboldt studied at Frankfurt on the Oder, Göttingen, Hamburg, and Freiberg (in Saxony). C. W. Dohm, Karl Ludwig Willdenow, and Georg Forster, his principal teachers, awakened his interest in political and botanical geography and in exploration. In his youth he also associated with Goethe, Schiller, and many other writers.

With this background he was exceedingly well prepared for his first voyage of exploration, which took place between 1799 and 1804. He was accompanied on this voyage by Aimé Bonpland, the French physician and botanist. Humboldt explored the territories of what are now Venezuela, Cuba, Colombia, Ecuador, Peru, and Mexico, sailed up the Casiquiare and determined its longitude and latitude, climbed Mount Chimborazo to the height of 17,900 feet, and suggested various improvements in mining technology and other aspects of the economy to the Spanish colonial authorities.

After a visit to the United States, where he met not only various scientists in Philadelphia but also President Thomas Jefferson, he returned to Europe. He then settled in Paris, where he proceeded to evaluate the results of his expedition and to prepare for a new project of exploration in Asia. This latter expedition did not take place until 1829, after he had spent two years in Berlin.

The preparation, execution, and evaluation of Humboldt's expeditions were exemplary and won him world fame. The 23 volumes of his travel descriptions (1805–1834) are the most comprehensive ever published by a private individual. He collaborated with German, French, and British scholars to produce the last major achievement of the republic of letters of the eighteenth century and so combined in characteristic fashion the *idée encyclopédique* with his belief in the division of labor among specialists.

Humboldt early rejected the purely utilitarian point of view in science, stressing instead the value of research for the sake of knowledge. This permitted him to give unbiased consideration to social scientific problems. In the field of anthropology, for example, he was able to appreciate without prejudice the culture of the Indian tribes of South America, since he did not believe in higher or lower races but rather in the unity of mankind and its destiny of liberty. In his celebrated *Political Essay on the Kingdom of New Spain* (1811–1812), he laid the foundations of modern regional geography on the basis of physical geography, using Mexico as his example. His portrait of colonial rule is based on statistical evidence, for Humboldt managed to gain access to the jealously guarded Spanish colonial archives. Both for the social sciences and for geography this early description of Mexico is still a useful source book.

Humboldt convincingly refuted Friedrich List's theory of economic stages. Whereas List conceived of the transition from hunters and gatherers to shepherds and peasants in terms of the development of material capital under Old World conditions, Humboldt demonstrated that in America agriculture must have evolved from gathering, without the intermediate stage of pastoral life, since no large domesticable animals had existed in the New World.

Political scientists should appreciate that Humboldt was one of the first Europeans to predict a great future for the United States. Publication of his travels also gave intellectual aid and moral support to the South American wars of independence.

Humboldt's efforts in the field of demography are of enduring value. He introduced the examination of the quotient of extremes into population statistics, thus making it possible to supplement the abstract figure of population density by citing the low quotient in countries uniformly densely (or sparsely) settled and the high quotient in countries unevenly settled. He also made allowance for population dynamics, furnishing birth and mortality rates for Mexico. These figures were long unavailable for such regions.

Humboldt's old age was devoted to completion of his *Cosmos: A Sketch of a Physical Description of the Universe* (1845–1858), in which he expanded his geographical thinking into a more general "description of the world in physical terms." His great prestige in Germany did much to shift attention from predominantly philological studies to the natural sciences.

HANNO BECK

[*See also* GEOGRAPHY *and* POPULATION, *article on* THE FIELD OF DEMOGRAPHY.]

WORKS BY HUMBOLDT

1805–1834 *Voyage de Humboldt et Bonpland.* 23 vols. Paris: Schoell. → Often cited by the title of Part 1: *Voyage aux régions équinoxiales du nouveau continent.* Complete sets are rare and vary in arrangement and collation.
(1811–1812) 1811–1822 *Political Essay on the Kingdom of New Spain.* 4 vols. London: Longmans. → First published in French.
1843 *Asie centrale: Recherches sur les chaînes de montagnes et la climatologie comparée.* 3 vols. Paris: Gide.
(1845–1858) 1850–1859 *Cosmos: A Sketch of a Physical Description of the Universe.* 5 vols. New York: Harper. → First published in German.
1959 *Gespräche.* Edited by Hanno Beck. Berlin: Akademie-Verlag.

SUPPLEMENTARY BIBLIOGRAPHY

AKADEMIE DER WISSENSCHAFTEN, BERLIN 1959 *Alexander von Humboldt, 14.9.1769–6.5.1859: Gedenkschrift zur 100. Wiederkehr seines Todestages.* Berlin: Akademie-Verlag.
BECK, HANNO 1959–1961 *Alexander von Humboldt.* 2 vols. Wiesbaden (Germany): Steiner. → Volume 1: *Von der Bildungsreise zur Forschungsreise: 1769–1804.* Volume 2: *Vom Reisewerk zum "Kosmos": 1804–1859.*
BRUHNS, KARL 1872 *Alexander von Humboldt: Eine wissenschaftliche Biographie.* 3 vols. Leipzig (Germany): Brockhaus.

# HUME, DAVID

David Hume was one of the most distinguished writers of the eighteenth century. Although he was only partly appreciated in his own period, with the passage of time his stature has grown, and his writings have attracted increasing attention from students in many disciplines.

Born in Scotland in 1711, Hume died in 1776, the year of the publication of Adam Smith's *Wealth of Nations*. His major work, *A Treatise of Human Nature* (1739–1740), lies in the field of philosophy. But the range of Hume's writings is vast. In a large number of essays (which in 1758 were incorporated into a volume entitled *Essays Moral, Political and Literary*) Hume dealt with the fields of economics, politics, and aesthetics, as well as with much that would now be regarded as sociological material. Hume was also a historian. His interest in history is reflected in many of his writings, and in the later years of his life he published (1754–1762), in serial volumes, a *History of England* that was a pioneering work in the area.

Owing to the subsequent compartmentalization of the fields that Hume explored, students of his thought have tended to treat his work in a compartmentalized fashion. This is difficult to avoid, since Hume dealt with a large variety of problems, and their analysis often requires specialized training. An unfortunate consequence of this, however, has been the tendency to overlook the important unifying elements in Hume's thought. Philosophers have argued that in turning to the essays, Hume was abandoning philosophy—allegedly because of the poor reception accorded his *Treatise*, and because of his passion for literary fame. Economists, on the other hand, have generally treated Hume's economic essays (which first appeared in 1752 under the title *Political Discourses*) as a substantially self-contained segment of his thought, bearing little or no relation to his philosophy.

Hume, however, made it clear that he intended his philosophy to serve as the "capital or center" of all the "moral" (i.e., psychological and social) sciences, or as the center of a general science of human experience ([1739–1740] 1958, p. xix). And as is evident from the prefatory "Advertisement" to the *Treatise*, he hoped, if the *Treatise* met with success, to incorporate a study of the various "moral sciences" into a subsequent edition of this work. Many of Hume's essays thus display relations to the substance of the *Treatise;* and this is clearly the case in his treatment of economics. Hume was pre-eminently, and notably more so than his close friend Adam Smith, the philosopher–economist of the eighteenth century.

A brief sketch of Hume's general system of thought will help clarify the relation between his philosophy and his economic thought. The "capital or center" of Hume's system consists of the "principles of human nature," those qualities and relations pertaining to the human understanding and human passions that Hume believed to be irreducible and common to all mankind. Discussed in Books I and II of the *Treatise*, these principles constitute the analytical phase of Hume's thought. The second and synthetic phase of Hume's thought consists of laws of human behavior in which Hume sought to show that various aspects of man's behavior are products of environmental forces operating on "human nature." The framing of these general uniformities is Hume's concern in his study of the various "moral sciences." An emphasis on psychology is thus a major distinctive characteristic of Hume's treatment of these sciences.

Hume's interest in history is likewise of major importance in his thought. This interest emerged early in Hume's life and was integral to his approach to experience. As a philosophical empiricist, Hume repeatedly stressed the importance of the study of history for achieving understanding of human experience, pointing out that history constitutes the exclusive source of our "experiments" concerning human nature and human behavior (*ibid.*, p. xxiii). Moreover, as both "moral scientist" and historian, Hume, by employing his principles of human nature, sought to frame historical laws of behavior, or laws that may explain basic transformations in human behavior. This approach he termed "natural history" (the word "natural" here denoting the "usual" or "probable"). Representing an attempt at "scientific history," this differs from conventional historiography, with its stress on unique particulars, which predominates in Hume's own *History of England*. Historical generalizations, reflecting the "natural history" approach, interlace much of Hume's work. And within the context of his economic writings the method of "natural history" is of central importance. Its role becomes fully apparent when Hume's economic thought is considered at three different levels of analysis: his economic psychology, political economy, and economic philosophy.

Before turning to this, however, it is well to consider one other aspect of Hume's thought: his treatment of the methodology of science, which, as one of the most important of Hume's contributions, is likewise relevant to his economic thought. Hume considered this question in Book I of the *Treatise*, where he was concerned with the basis of our "beliefs" concerning empirical events. His position represents an attack on the rationalist acceptance of a "necessary connection" between such events. As Hume argued, all beliefs concerning matters of fact are reducible to associations of ideas that are separable from each other. All causal relations take this form. We thus can "conceive any object to be non-existent this moment, and existent the next, without conjoining to it the distinct idea of a cause or productive principle." What is conceivable, moreover, is possible. And the demonstrability of a "necessary connection" requires that the opposite be shown to be impossible. Hence, "necessary connection" between matters of fact (unlike the logical relations between propositions, where validity depends wholly on the principle of noncontradiction) cannot be demonstrated (*ibid.*, pp. 79–80).

On what, then, are our beliefs in matters of fact based? All that Hume could find here was a psychological process. More specifically, we come to "believe," say, that a causal relation exists between two events because, as a result of our repeated observation of their contiguity and reoccurrence (their "constant conjunction"), the mind—simply through a nonrational associative mechanism—so firmly links the two that the occurrence of one leads us to expect its usual attendant (*ibid.*, p. 96). For Hume, "belief" is, in a word, a "habit." The implication of this for "science" is clear: since we have no a priori justification for beliefs in empirical events, the only way we can enlarge our understanding of experience is through further investigation with a view to establishing additional "constant conjunctions." It must be recognized, however, that the notion of the uniformity of nature itself, or the view that the future will resemble the past, is based on faith.

Hume's observations on the prospects for discovering uniformities in the "moral sciences" are also noteworthy. Although he believed that history had already provided an adequate basis for framing "principles of human nature" ([1739–1779] vol. 4, p. 69 in 1898 edition), he was acutely aware of the wide historical variability of human behavior and the difficulty, especially in view of the range and complexity of human passions, of specifying how man would respond to changing circumstance (*ibid.*, vol. 3, p. 163; [1739–1740] 1958, p. 131). With considerable caution, he sought to discriminate between different areas of human behavior in terms of their tractability to scientific treatment. It is very difficult, he pointed out, to discover uniformities in aspects of behavior which are peculiar to small numbers of individuals, since in such cases the passions involved are delicate and subtle and are often affected by imperceptible influences ([1739–1779] vol. 3, p. 175 in 1898 edition). It is difficult, also, to establish reliable generalizations in the field of "politics" (*ibid.*, vol. 3, pp. 156–157). Since mass behavior, on the other hand, is frequently governed by passions that are "gross" and "stubborn," reliable uniformities may be found here. Its dependence upon such "gross" passions as avarice, for example, would make it easier to account for the "rise and progress of commerce" than for the growth of "learning" (*ibid.*, vol. 3, p. 176). Significantly, it is with a justification of the use of generalization in economics (which he contrasted with the chance-ridden field of foreign diplomacy) that Hume introduced his economic essays ([1752–1758] 1955, pp. 3–4).

With a view to the central role of psychology and history, let us turn now to the substance of Hume's economic thought and consider first his economic psychology, which links his economic thought to the "capital or center" of all the "moral sciences,"

as developed in the *Treatise*. Here the analysis takes the form of a natural history of the "rise and progress of commerce" in which Hume sought to explain the economic growth of his own general period in terms of the impact of changing historical circumstance on human passions. In the economic essays these passions are regarded as "causes of labour." Because the analysis stems directly from Hume's general treatment of human nature, it is notably multidimensional and is considerably more complex than the economic psychology typical of Hume's own period. Beyond considering the importance of the desire for consumption pleasures as an incentive to economic activity, Hume called attention to the role played by the desire for "action" as well as a desire for "liveliness" (a state of lively passion that is common to the experience both of consumption pleasures and interesting activity). In turn, the desire for "gain," joined to the desire for action, is treated in large part as a desire for the trophies of success in the "economic game." All these motives are integral to the "rise and progress of commerce," the initial stimulus to which is found in the opening of foreign trade and whose self-perpetuating character is traced to the growth of new habits of industry (*ibid.*, chapter 2; Rotwein 1955).

Political economy, the second level of Hume's economic thought, comprises the main portion of his economic essays. Here, where Hume was concerned with specific aspects of market relations, he dealt with several of the principal controversial questions of his period: monetary theory, interest theory, the issue of free trade, the shifting and incidence of taxes, and fiscal policy. At this level the role of the natural history of the "rise and progress of commerce" is seen in Hume's critical evaluation of the doctrines of his period; for his analysis is predominantly concerned with one question: Are prevailing beliefs regarding market relations acceptable when considered in the light of economic growth and the psychological and other factors involved in the growth process?

A brief summary of several of the major aspects of Hume's political economy will serve to make clear the general importance of this perspective. One of the most frequently emphasized of Hume's contributions to later classical doctrine is his analysis of the quantity theory–specie flow mechanism. Here Hume sought to show that there is no ground for the mercantilist fear that without trade restrictions a nation will lose its money supply. The quantity theory–specie flow doctrine is thus introduced to show that it is ultimately a nation's level of economic development that determines the quantity of money it can attract and retain. "I should as soon dread, that all our springs and rivers should be exhausted, as that money should abandon a kingdom where there are people and industry" ([1752b] 1955, p. 61). Hume's interest theory—in its emphasis on the importance of real capital (as against the mercantilist stress on the quantity of money)—also anticipated the classical position. But, more fundamentally, Hume was concerned to show that the availability of real capital is itself determined by the impact of the growth of industry on economic motivation. And here he made use of all the "causes of labour" introduced in his economic psychology. In an industrially advancing economy, he argued, there is increasing opportunity for "action" in the form of "lucrative employment." This induces frugality both by providing an alternative to pleasure seeking (the preoccupation of the idle landowner in an agrarian economy) as a mode of gratifying the desire for liveliness, and by intensifying the desire for gain, or the desire to accumulate the tokens of economic success. As the income of the industrious class grows, along with its contribution to output, there is thus a substantial increase in the supply of real savings, and the interest rate inevitably falls ([1752–1758] 1955, pp. 53–54).

In his treatment of the issue of trade restrictions, Hume recognized that free trade increases real income (at any given level of economic development) by bringing about a more efficient allocation of resources (ibid., pp. 66, 75, 79)—the argument Adam Smith was later to elaborate more fully and systematically. Growth considerations, however, occupy the center of Hume's analysis: meeting the mercantilist argument for trade restrictions on its own ground, he sought to show that, far from inhibiting the economic growth of other countries, one nation's economic growth commonly contributes to the development of its neighbors. An expansion of industry abroad, he emphasized, yields new technology that the home country can emulate, and since such an expansion increases foreign income, it also increases the foreign demand for home exports. In his detailed treatment of the growth of foreign industry that competes directly with domestic output, Hume stressed the stimulating effects of foreign competition on the spirit of industry at home: he argued, for example, that such competitive pressure encourages a nation to divert unemployed resources to new uses and, further, that the resulting diversification will minimize the impact on employment of any subsequent fluctuations of demand in particular markets (ibid., pp. 78–81).

In some respects Hume's doctrine is a complex of classical elements and elements exhibiting an affinity to the mercantilist position (with inconsistencies between the two remaining unresolved). But this complex can itself be traced mainly to Hume's interest in stressing the importance of developmental considerations. For example, Hume generally employed the quantity theory of money to show that it is economic growth rather than the quantity of money that is of basic significance to a nation. But with a view to growth considerations he was also led to argue that gradual changes in the money supply (as against large absolute quantities of money as such) are desirable. By repeatedly stimulating employment in the short run, such changes, he contended, will in the long run enhance the spirit of industry itself (ibid., pp. 37–40). Similarly, although on quantity theory grounds Hume argued that money has no effect on interest rates, he also acknowledged that if it affects economic growth, a long-run increase in the money supply will lower interest rates (ibid., p. 59).

Hume's economic philosophy—the third level of his economic thought—is contained in his essay "Of Refinement in the Arts." Here, Hume presented a moral justification for a commercial and industrial society and, as a basis for judgment, invoked the utilitarian ethic, which he had earlier elaborated and extensively defended in Book III of the Treatise and in his Inquiry Concerning the Principles of Morals (1751). On this level of Hume's economic thought the perspective of "natural history" played an especially important role. In this context, where Hume considered the relation between economic growth and the happiness of the individual, the "causes of labour" (the desires for "pleasure," "action," and "liveliness") are treated as "ends" whose attainment is furthered by the development of industry ([1752–1758] 1955, pp. 21–22). His analysis here, both in its detail and in its adoption of a pluralistic position on human happiness, bears a direct relation to his earlier series of essays on the "good life" entitled "The Epicurean," "The Stoic," "The Platonist," and "The Sceptic." Among all ends, Hume placed the greatest emphasis on "action" (the response to challenge); and a reading of "The Stoic" makes clear that, when treating this end most broadly, Hume had in mind the value that is now generally stressed in justifying a free society—the striving for self-fulfillment (Rotwein 1955, pp. xcv–xcix).

Hume also considered the influence of economic development on the intellectual, cultural, moral, and political life of society; with regard to politics, he argued (in a passage Adam Smith was later to cite for its central importance and originality) that the growth of political liberty itself is traceable to the economic decentralization and individualism brought about by the development of commerce ([1752–1758] 1955, pp. 28–29). Making all allowances for gaps in Hume's knowledge of medieval society (with which he compared an industrial society) and for other shortcomings in his argument, his analysis—in its statement of the case for a liberal social order—deserves recognition as an early classic.

Compared to the *Wealth of Nations,* Hume's treatment of economics is brief. Hume, moreover, gave relatively little attention to the questions of value and distribution which absorbed much of Smith's analysis, and which were to become the dominant interest of the classical and neoclassical economists. In its theoretical treatment of psychological and historical influences, Hume's analysis, however, is both more comprehensive and more penetrating than Smith's, although Smith was more concerned with such influences than the generality of the later classical economists.

Since Hume's time, however, others have given these influences a prominent place in their work. The "historical" and "institutional" economists are cases in point. Other important themes that occur in Hume's work are to be found in contemporary economic literature. Most conspicuous is the revived interest in economic growth and in the cultural forces associated with this process, a product of the concern with underdeveloped economies. Also, interest in the question of full employment has led to a consideration of the psychology underlying aggregative behavior, while the shift in emphasis from impersonal markets to the role of individual units or collective entities (including business organizations and trade unions) and to the area of imperfect competition generally has likewise directed attention to a variety of psychological considerations not ordinarily stressed in "orthodox" economic analysis. In view of the rapidity of institutional change in recent decades, it is not surprising that the very question of the desirability of alternative institutional "systems" and the consequent normative and historical analysis of institutions should now be receiving increasing attention.

In various ways, these streams of thought differ from Hume's approach. Nonetheless, owing to Hume's remarkable capacity to treat important issues with a view to relevant psychological and historical factors, much of his economic thought still retains its freshness. In the standard literature it has long been the practice to give Hume relatively little attention (as one of a group of "predecessors" of Smith), although over the years several major technical aspects of his work have received general recognition. Hume's contribution can be fully appreciated, however, only when the body of his economic analysis as a whole is related to the context of broad and systematic social inquiry in which it was developed.

EUGENE ROTWEIN

[*Other relevant material may be found in* ECONOMIC GROWTH; HISTORY, *article on* THE PHILOSOPHY OF HISTORY; MONEY; UTILITARIANISM; *and in the biographies of* MANDEVILLE; RICARDO; SMITH, ADAM; TURGOT.]

### WORKS BY HUME

(1739–1740) 1958  *A Treatise of Human Nature.* Edited by L. A. Selby-Bigge. Oxford: Clarendon. → Reprinted from the original edition; contains an analytical index.

(1739–1779) 1964  *The Philosophical Works.* 4 vols. Aalen (Germany): Scientia Verlag. → Volumes 1 and 2 are reprints of the 1886 edition, Volumes 3 and 4 reprinted from the 1882 edition.

(1741–1742) 1912  *Essays Moral, Political and Literary.* 2 vols. Edited by T. H. Green and T. H. Grose. New York and London: Longmans. → First published as *Essays Moral and Political* and changed to the above title in the 1758 edition.

(1751) 1957  *An Inquiry Concerning the Principles of Morals.* New York: Liberal Arts Press.

1752a  *Political Discourses.* Edinburgh: Fleming.

(1752b) 1955  *Of the Balance of Trade.* Pages 60–77 in David Hume, *Writings on Economics.* Edited by Eugene Rotwein. London: Nelson; Madison: Univ. of Wisconsin Press.

(1752–1758) 1955  *Writings on Economics.* Edited by Eugene Rotwein. London: Nelson; Madison: Univ. of Wisconsin Press. → Also contains correspondence from 1749–1776.

(1754–1762) 1894  *The History of England.* 3 vols. London: Routledge.

### WORKS ABOUT HUME

JESSOP, THOMAS E. 1938  *A Bibliography of David Hume and of Scottish Philosophy From Francis Hutcheson to Lord Balfour.* London and Hull: Brown.

MOSSNER, ERNEST C. 1954  *The Life of David Hume.* Austin: Univ. of Texas Press.

ROTWEIN, EUGENE 1955  Introduction. In David Hume, *Writings on Economics.* London: Nelson; Madison: Univ. of Wisconsin Press.

SCHATZ, ALBERT 1902  *L'oeuvre économique de David Hume.* Paris: Rousseau.

SMITH, NORMAN K. 1949  *The Philosophy of David Hume: A Critical Study of Its Origins and Central Doctrines.* London: Macmillan.

STEWART, JOHN B. 1963  *The Moral and Political Philosophy of David Hume.* New York: Columbia Univ. Press.